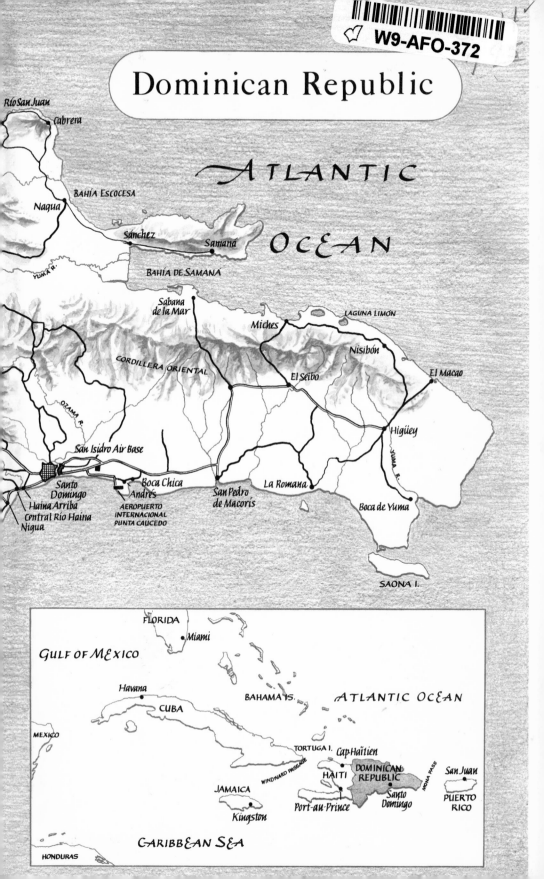

Dominican Republic

ATLANTIC

OCEAN

Río San Juan
Cabrera

BAHÍA ESCOCESA

Nagua

Sánchez

Samaná

BAHÍA DE SAMANÁ

YUMA R.

Sabana
de la Mar

Miches

LAGUNA LIMÓN

Nisibón

CORDILLERA ORIENTAL

El Seíbo

El Macao

OZAMA R.

Higüey

YUMA R.

San Isidro Air Base

Boca Chica

Santo
Domingo
Haina Arriba
Central Río Haina
Nigua

Andrés

AEROPUERTO
INTERNACIONAL
PUNTA CAUCEDO

San Pedro
de Macorís

La Romana

Boca de Yuma

SAONA I.

FLORIDA
Miami

GULF OF MEXICO

Havana

CUBA

BAHAMA IS.

ATLANTIC OCEAN

MEXICO

TORTUGA I. Cap Haïtien

WINDWARD PASSAGE

HAITI

DOMINICAN
REPUBLIC

MONA PASS

San Juan

PUERTO
RICO

JAMAICA

Kingston

Port-au-Prince

Santo
Domingo

CARIBBEAN SEA

HONDURAS

OVERTAKEN BY EVENTS

By John Bartlow Martin

THE PANE OF GLASS

THE DEEP SOUTH SAYS NEVER

BREAK DOWN THE WALLS

WHY DID THEY KILL?

ADLAI STEVENSON

MY LIFE IN CRIME

BUTCHER'S DOZEN

INDIANA

CALL IT NORTH COUNTRY

Overtaken by Events

THE DOMINICAN CRISIS FROM THE FALL OF TRUJILLO TO THE CIVIL WAR

John Bartlow Martin
FORMER AMBASSADOR TO THE DOMINICAN REPUBLIC

DOUBLEDAY & COMPANY, INC., GARDEN CITY, NEW YORK

1966

Excerpts from The Unfinished Experiment *by Juan Bosch are reprinted with the permission of the publisher, Frederick A. Praeger, Inc.*

To

THE DOMINICAN PEOPLE

It may be self-evident but perhaps should be stated explicitly that the views expressed in this book are mine alone.

FOREWORD

In the spring of 1965, violent events forced the Dominican Republic upon the attention of the American people. What ensued called into question our entire foreign policy.

This book, however, is not just about the Dominican Civil War of 1965. All commentators agree that behind that bloody episode lay deep-rooted conflicts that had wracked the Republic even before the time of the dictator Trujillo. This book is about those conflicts, as I saw them from inside the Embassy.

My purpose has been to *show*—not to *tell*—how it was. Necessarily, therefore, this book concerns itself with the day-to-day experience of living abroad as a representative of our country; with the sometimes effective, sometimes halting process by which over national will is expressed from people to President to State Department and Ambassador; with the exhilaration and despair which attend any attempt to translate policies into practice, ideals into reality. One of my intentions in writing this book has been to show the reader all I can about how things work—and don't work—in a U. S. Embassy in a difficult country. Another has been to help him see—as I saw—the pressures building that brought the Dominican people to disaster.

Part One relates briefly the history of the Republic, including Trujillo's tyranny and his assassination; and then it shows, in detail, how through 1962 we tried to help the Dominicans build a democratic society on the ruins of tyranny under a shaky provisional government.

Part Two shows the Presidency of Juan Bosch in 1963: What he did, what our policy was toward his regime, and how he fell.

Part Three describes our opposition under President Kennedy to the military *coup* that overthrew Bosch. It shows clearly, I hope, why our own power to influence events in other lands is severely limited.

Part Four relates how the Civil War of 1965 broke out and what I was called upon to do about it. It includes my views of our policy in the

Dominican Republic and Latin America and in the underdeveloped world at large.

I first went to the Dominican Republic in 1937 and lived there for several months. I resigned as Ambassador in February of 1964 to write *Overtaken by Events* from my notebooks and files. The manuscript was complete, except for final polishing, and the title chosen, when the Civil War broke out, on April 30, 1965—the Marines having already landed to let the bulk of the book stand as written.

I was able to update the book until April of 1966, when the printer took over. By the time it appears, new events may have overtaken it but they will flow from the events I saw; and I hope the book will help the reader understand them.

This book is, then, a picture of a complicated country in the grip of terrible forces. It is the story of what one Ambassador and Embassy staff did, tried to do, and failed to do in a small place of great importance to all of us.

April 1966.

JOHN BARTLOW MARTIN

CONTENTS

Foreword   ix

Part One THE SEVEN PRESIDENTS OF 1962

    1. A Fresh Start in Santo Domingo   3

    2. The Bloody Heritage   16

    3. The Era of Trujillo   33

    4. Presidential Mission: 1961   64

    5. Into the Jungle   84

    6. The Citadel of the Oligarchy   123

    7. The Great Sugar Crisis   145

    8. Whistlestopping   178

    9. The Cruise of the Angelita   202

    10. To the Summit   223

    11. Assassins and Generals   246

    12. The First Free Elections in Thirty-eight Years   282

    13. Waiting for Bosch   302

    14. Bosch Comes Home   321

Part Two THE SEVEN MONTHS OF PRESIDENT BOSCH

    15. Bosch Begins   343

    16. The Little Clinic of Higüey   372

    17. The Cruise of the Mella   387

    18. The "War" with Haiti   416

    19. The End of the Hundred Days   448

20. The View from the States   467

21. The Night of the Generals   479

22. Bosch at Bay   493

23. Between the Sword and the Wall   519

24. The Fall of Juan Bosch   547

Part Three THE SEVENTY-SEVEN DAYS IN WASHINGTON

25. Limits of American Power   593

26. Overtaken by Events   615

Part Four SEVENTEEN DAYS IN MAY—AND BEYOND

27. Presidential Mission: 1965   637

28. Each Must Act   704

APPENDIXES

The Principal Dominican Actors   747

The Political Parties   754

Acknowledgments   756

Bibliographical Note   757

Address to the Chamber of Commerce of the Americas, June 19, 1963 "Revolutionary Struggle in the Dominican Republic and its Lessons," by J. I. Quello and N. Isa Conde

INDEX   791

Illustrations

[*Following page 154*]

ARRIVAL IN TENSE TIMES

The new Ambassador and family are welcomed to the Dominican Republic

After the riot: The remains of Ambassador Martin's car

The car of the U.S. consul set afire by the same mob

Colonel Fritz Long, Chief of Protocol Logroño, and Ambassador Martin at the National Palace

Ceremony in the *Salón de Embajadores*

Ambassador Martin and President Rafael Bonnelly at the credentials presentation

With President Kennedy at the White House
   Photo by Abbie Rowe

[*Following page 274*]

DOMINICAN PEOPLE AND PLACES

In the interior with a Dominican farmer

Ambassador and Mrs. Martin visiting the *barrios*

Town meeting at San Juan de la Maguana

Viriato A. Fiallo

Donald Reid Cabral

Luís Amiama Tió

Commodore Julio Alberto Rib Santamaría

Juan Bosch whistlestopping on Sánchez

Colonel Elías Wessin y Wessin
   Arthur Schatz, Life *magazine,* © *Time Inc. All Rights Reserved*

A scene in the Dominican Campo

Fran, Fred, and Dan Martin, near Nisibón

[*Following page 538*]

THE LITTLE CLINIC OF HIGÜEY

The tent that was the clinic

Mrs. Juan Bosch, her sister, and a WHO representative make an inspection tour

Treatment of an old man at the mobile unit
Photo by Dan Perlmutter

The scene in a private house of a Santo Domingo *barrio*
Photo by Dan Perlmutter

One of those who brought their babies many miles

Dr. Pumarol inside the Little Clinic

Dominican woman and child
Photo by Dan Perlmutter

[*Following page 658*]

MISSION TO THE CIVIL WAR

General Antonio Imbert Barrera and Ambassador Martin face-to-face
Lynn Pelham, Life *magazine*, © *Time Inc. All Rights Reserved*

Negotiations with the rebels
Bill Eppridge, Life *magazine*, © *Time Inc. All Rights Reserved*

Rioting Dominicans surround a correspondent's car
Lynn Pelham, Life *magazine*, © *Time Inc. All Rights Reserved*

Children of the rebel cause
Bill Eppridge, Life *magazine*, © *Time Inc. All Rights Reserved*

The beginning of anarchy in the streets
Lynn Pelham, Life *magazine*, © *Time Inc. All Rights Reserved*

U.S. artillery emplacement near the Hotel Embajador
Bill Eppridge, Life *magazine*, © *Time Inc. All Rights Reserved*

Presentation of OAS flag by Lt. Gen. Bruce Palmer, Jr.
Wide World

U. S. Marines seek a sniper
Wide World

Harry Shlaudeman and McGeorge Bundy
Lynn Pelham, Life *magazine*, © *Time Inc. All Rights Reserved*

The Papal Nuncio and Ambassador Martin
Bill Eppridge, Life *magazine*, © *Time Inc. All Rights Reserved*

Undersecretary Mann and Ambassador Tapley Bennett
Lynn Pelham, Life *magazine*, © *Time Inc. All Rights Reserved*

ENDPAPER MAPS by Rafael Palacios

Front: The Dominican Republic

Back: Santo Domingo

PART ONE

The Seven Presidents of 1962

Chapter One

A FRESH START IN SANTO DOMINGO

On a bright Friday morning in 1962, black Cadillacs sent by the Dominican government drove slowly around the driveway that circles the clipped lawn of the United States Embassy Residence in Santo Domingo and, accompanied by ten members of the Embassy staff, I was taken to the National Palace to present my credentials as the first United States Ambassador to the Dominican Republic since the fall of the dictator Trujillo. We took back streets, we drove fast; our cars had no diplomatic license plates, and some contained armed guards. Yesterday anti-*Yanqui* rioters had burned my car. Ambassador Alvaro Logroño, the Dominican protocol chief, rode with me, on my left. I was learning—the ranking seat is on the right. We said little. My white linen suit, bought for the occasion and heavy with starch, felt like plywood armor. Already the day was hot, blazing hot.

The Palace, peach, squat, ugly, built by Trujillo, with massive columns and domes, stands on a hill on a bench of land rising up from the sea. The cars swept round the driveway up the hill and stopped at the bottom of the steps. The steps are broad, and there are twenty-eight of them. Ambassador Logroño walked up them at my left. The ten staff members followed, three of them military attachés. Our order was ragged; we had rehearsed but once. At the top of the steps we turned, the others scrambled behind Logroño and me, and we stood rigid at attention while down below on the blistered driveway the leader of the military band saluted, his sword flashing in the sun, then turned; and the band played full-throated the Dominican national anthem. It is one of the most stirring of all national anthems I know; it has never failed to move me. The steps were dazzling, a flag flapped loudly in the breeze, and beyond the scattered rooftops and trees of the ancient city lay the Caribbean.

The band finished, the leader saluted again, we turned around, Logroño and I got to the front, and we walked between the massive columns and arched open doorways into the Palace lobby, red carpet runners on polished marble floor. I slipped on the marble as we started up the broad interior stairs. All my life I had been retiring, had kept out of the limelight. I had lived close to great events, and a little had helped men make them, Adlai Stevenson, President Kennedy; but I myself had always stayed in the background, had made only a handful of public speeches, and once had said, in trying to explain, "I do not like to present myself." Now I had to. At the top of the stairs we turned and entered the *Salón de Embajadores*.

It was vast. It seemed a mile of rococo, all red and gold, plush and marble, with gigantic crystal chandeliers. Seated at its far end all in white were the seven members of the Consejo de Estado, Council of State, the "seven Presidents" who ruled the Republic after Trujillo. They rose as we entered, and we, as instructed by Ambassador Logroño, stopped and bowed, and they bowed; then we walked halfway across the room, paused and bowed again, they returning the bow, then approached almost to within arm's reach, paused, and bowed again. I stepped forward and shook hands with the President, Rafael Bonnelly, and, with my left hand giving him my credentials, said, "Mr. President, I have the honor to present my credentials as the Ambassador of the United States to the Dominican Republic." Then, as Logroño had told me to, I introduced each of my ten men to President Bonnelly; Logroño introduced me to each of the other six Presidents, and to the Foreign Minister, and I introduced each of my ten to each of them—some eighty introductions in all. It made a ragged ballet, and before it was over some of us, Dominicans and Americans, were half-smiling; yet though it was awkward, even foolish, it was touching too. After it ended, Logroño showed my people to their uncomfortable gilded high-backed chairs, and I sat on President Bonnelly's right.

We talked for about ten minutes, he and I, his bodyguard now and then peering out from behind a heavy red arras. I do not remember what we said; no doubt something about looking forward to working together to build Dominican democracy, sentences that in such circumstances become banalities no matter how deeply felt. I believe President Bonnelly, while not directly apologizing for the burning of my car, indicated his regret. (Later we protested formally, and the Dominican government paid for it.)

We arose together. We shook hands again. Nobody had told me what to do next, so I shook hands with each of the seven Presidents and the Foreign Minister, but my staff did not; we gathered again in ranks and bowed, the Dominicans bowed, and we left the room, stopping twice again en route to turn and bow and be bowed to; then walked downstairs and out.

At the top of the steps we stood again, and the band played "The Star-Spangled Banner," then we drove home. Indubitably the ornate rug in the *Salón de Embajadores* was a trifle frayed, the gilt on the mirrors cracked in places; to many watching, and to those of us who knew the staggering problems ahead, this seemed like nonsense. Yet when one is at the center of such an event, one cannot but be moved. Back at the Residence with my wife Fran, I read my copy of the credentials I had presented. I had not read it before. It was a form letter, its diplomatic usage evidently dating from another century; it was addressed to President Bonnelly and signed by President Kennedy, and it expressed President Kennedy's confidence in my ability to advance the interests of both the United States and the Dominican Republic. I said, "I hope he's right."

2

The date was March 9, 1962. I had known and loved the Dominican Republic since 1937. In September 1961, three months after Trujillo was assassinated, President Kennedy, whom I had known for several years and for whom I had written campaign speeches, had sent me to the Dominican Republic on a presidential fact-finding mission. Now he had appointed me our Ambassador. I was not a career foreign service officer; I had never worked for the government before. I was forty-six years old and had always been a self-employed private citizen, a writer.

The Alliance for Progress was new. President Kennedy was paying more attention to Latin America than any President since Franklin Roosevelt. He had a special interest in the Dominican Republic. He involved his personal prestige in making democracy work there. He trusted me and took my advice. When I had gone to say goodbye to him a week before in his oval office in the White House, we had talked about the Republic's problems. He said he intended to send Lyndon B. Johnson, then Vice President, down about mid-April "and we don't want any riots." He talked about some personal matters. Twice he said, "Let me know direct if there's anything you want." And he ended, sardonic, "If you blow this, you'd better not come home."

The Caribbean, deepest and biggest sea on earth and closest to us, was boiling. In the Dominican Republic a whole generation that had grown up knowing nothing but Trujillo now was free. Next door was Castro's Cuba, and the contrast was inescapable. There was talk—far too much talk—of creating a "showcase of democracy," combined with far too little understanding of the difficulties. The surviving Trujillos themselves had been driven from the Republic by our fleet but the political right still was strong. The left was preparing, and so were we.

An Embassy officer gave me a cable to sign and send, my first. It said, "Arrived. Took charge. Martin."

The Ambassador approves and signs all outgoing cables (just as the

Secretary of State approves and signs all cables leaving Washington). He may delegate approval or signature or both. But his name is on them. He is responsible.

President Bonnelly sent word he wanted to see me at the Palace on Sunday morning. I took with me Joe Fandino, a twenty-nine-year-old Foreign Service officer, short, round, quick, bilingual, dedicated, sometimes lazy; he became my constant companion, administrative aide, and interpreter, for while my Spanish is adequate for ordinary usage, I never transacted official business without an interpreter if I could avoid it— misunderstandings can be dangerous. We arrived at the Palace at 10 A.M. and were met halfway up the steps by a Palace functionary who led us inside to the first-floor office of the Consejo, the ruling Council. The way—I would walk it often, sometimes in success, sometimes in despair —the way led down a long narrow corridor, crowded with soldiers with submachine guns, some of them sprawling in chairs along the corridor, so we had to step over their legs and guns, some coming to attention as we approached. Offices of the Consejeros opened off the corridor. At its end was the presidential suite—a rather small corner room overlooking the sea with worn rug and frayed gold and red chairs, a smaller inner office used by President Bonnelly, and a large room with a long table used for meetings of the entire seven-man Consejo. All were there today. We shook hands and sat down, I beside President Bonnelly, Fandino beside me, the other six Consejeros and the Foreign Minister in a semicircle to right and left.

During the amenities I tried to sort them out:

—President Rafael F. Bonnelly, a rather tall, light-brown skinned, graying lawyer with big round soft brown eyes, a kind smile and a fast, skillful lawyer's mind. (The Consejo had both executive and legislative powers. Each Consejero cast one vote. Bonnelly was both President of the Consejo and President of the Republic);

—The First Vice President, Nicolás Pichardo, darker, handsome, well-dressed;

—The Second Vice President, Donald Reid Cabral, an aggressive young businessman and member of the oligarchy;

—José Fernández Caminero, a heart specialist like Pichardo, with horn-rimmed glasses and a shock of wavy brown hair;

—Monseñor Pérez Sánchez, fat, jolly, roly-poly, at least seventy years old, wearing the black and red robes of the Church;

—And the other two, the only survivors of the men who assassinated[1]

[1] "Assassin" in Spanish is a word of opprobrium. Trujillo's assassination never was called that. It was called the *"ajusticiamento."* The word denotes execution but connotes bringing to justice.

Trujillo—Antonio Imbert Barrera, short, paunchy, getting bald, wearing a wide heavy-buckled belt and a gold-plated .45-caliber Colt automatic with the hammer back; and Luís Amiama Tió, dapper, mustached, erect, reserved, impenetrable.

Now the seven had the Palace. Now, until a new President was elected on December 20 and inaugurated a year from now, February 27, they were the government. Theirs was the responsibility—a lawyer, a young businessman, two heart specialists, two assassins, and a priest.

They made clear at this first Sunday meeting that they looked to us for help. President Bonnelly led off.[2] He said the present situation was "dangerous," that unemployment was high, that Thursday's riots had clearly been organized by Castro/Communist subversive agents deliberately trying to create chaos and overthrow the government, that subversives had been burning the Republic's cane fields and pine forests, that citizens in the interior were arming themselves, that "we can't afford to get tied up in long-range programs" but that "we need solutions *now.*" Would U.S. help be slow, or fast enough to save the government and prevent chaos? He did not say so but I knew he was referring to the delay of our Agency for International Development (AID) in approving a twenty-five-million-dollar loan to the Republic.

The First Vice President, Pichardo, tall, in a white linen suit, spoke at length about the Republic's deplorable financial condition—it could not meet its present payroll let alone spend money on public works to reduce unemployment, AID demanded detailed plans on how the twenty-five-million-dollar loan was to be spent, "but we don't have experience to draw plans, and can't appoint a planning board until we get the money to pay them." The International Monetary Fund (IMF) had suggested new taxes, but the Consejo was too weak politically to impose them. The only solution was to get from the United States, immediately, twenty-two million dollars in sugar premiums which the U.S. had withheld from Trujillo and the Dominicans now considered due them. (This twenty-two million dollars would be a sore point for many months.)

The Foreign Minister, José Antonio Bonilla Atiles, an elderly, graying man of benign mein, with a fondness for democratic theory and eloquent speech, broke in with some mollifying remarks. But Bonnelly and Pichardo again emphasized the urgent need for the twenty-two million dollars in sugar money.

I responded to all this, explaining the reasons for restrictions on AID

2 The reader may wonder how I can recall who said what, or what happened when, in this passage and throughout the book. I carried a notebook virtually everywhere I went and made notes at the time. In addition, I sometimes dictated memoranda immediately after a conversation. I used these notes and memoranda in reporting to the State Department.

lending, promising to do everything possible to speed up U.S. assistance, urging the imposition of new taxes, inquiring into revenues from the industries formerly owned by Trujillo and now owned by the government, and touching gently on a question I knew would come up in a few months, the revision of the entire U.S. sugar quota system. Donny Reid exploded, "If we don't get the quota, we'll have to shut the sugar mills or face a revolution."

We talked about the burning of my car on Thursday. They almost took rioting for granted—and no wonder: All last fall and winter they had lived with rioting. Trujillo's fall had cut loose long pent-up tensions, and the streets were chaotic. President Bonnelly said that well-trained Castro/Communist agents were paying thieves and hoodlums to riot. I asked if we could help. Reid and Bonilla Atiles immediately said yes—they wanted technical help in training the police to control riots, in setting up a secret anti-subversive unit to deal with Castro/Communists, and in arranging deportations. Bonilla Atiles said deportations were essential—public trials created martyrs.

Pichardo now spoke. He disagreed. He said that in Europe civil liberties were respected. Men were granted fair trials, not deported arbitrarily; and Pichardo, educated in France, with the most cultivated mind on the Consejo, belonging to the Western European tradition of eighteenth-century liberalism, spoke quietly but eloquently about the natural rights of man. Bonilla Atiles, who believed with him in theory, nonetheless declared that the Dominican crisis demanded deeds, not theory. We were on treacherous ground—a month ago the Consejo had decreed the Emergency Law arbitrarily to deport or deny entry to anybody, and many had protested. Listening silent while the argument swirled through cigar smoke amid the faded elegance, the draperies drawn to shut out the sun, the electric lights feeble, a creaky air conditioner whirring, I thought about my own writing and politicizing in the United States on behalf of civil liberties.

Principles aside, a practical difficulty seemed apparent to me: Trujillo had trained his police only to shoot to kill when facing a mob, and since the Consejo forbade this in the name of freedom, the police knew nothing to do when facing a mob, and so did nothing. I spoke up. The entire question was difficult. Everyone would prefer to arrest rioters and try them fairly. But on the other hand, any government must protect itself. And since it was better that police handle mobs with nightsticks, not machine guns and tanks, perhaps training in riot control might be helpful.

All except Pichardo agreed, one adding that the real problem was not the police but the judges: The police might arrest a Castro/Communist but no judge would convict him because thugs filled the courtroom and

4

The next evening Donny Reid gave a farewell party for John Hill, who had been our *chargé d'affaires* until I arrived. Reid and his wife lived in her father's home not far from the Embassy, a high square commodious house, very old and very Dominican, with slatted doors, tiled floors, dark heavy cane-bottomed mahogany chairs.

In the Dominican Republic, a small and ingrown nation, family means a great deal. The oligarchy, based in Santiago but with ramifications in Santo Domingo, related by blood and marriage, has run the country for most of its history. Donald Reid Cabral belongs to the Cabral-Vicini-Bermúdez-Tavares family complex, one of the largest, richest, and most powerful of all. Its fortunes are based on sugar and rum and land; its other interests are manifold. The older generation stays in the background.

Donny—pronounced by Dominicans to rhyme with "pony"—Reid was thirty-nine, taut, thin, wiry, about five feet four and 130 pounds. He looked boyish. People seemed to feel sorry for him, to want to help him, to mother him. They underestimated his staying power. He could work sixteen or eighteen hours a day for days on end. He looked puny but could be stubborn and tenacious. He was mercurial, erratic, emotional, tense, and, above all, eager. Speaking good English, friendly and accessible, he was a key source for visiting United States newspapermen. He told me, "In the capital people are talking politics, but in the country they are talking hunger." Many things he said made good sense. But not all—at least twice in the next few weeks he told me he was going to kill some other member of the Consejo.

In theory each member of the Consejo had his own area of responsibility, with Cabinet ministers under him. Reid was in everything—commerce and industry, public works, the former Trujillo properties, police, everything. He saw between 150 and 300 people each day, mostly job seekers and favor seekers. They came to his house, to the Palace, everywhere he went. "When I go to the bathroom, they crawl through the window," he said.

As a boy, he had started with a bicycle shop; as a man, he had imported and sold automobiles. It was said he had made a million under Trujillo. Yet he deeply hated Trujillo. He left business to join the Consejo at financial sacrifice (which, of course, his family could afford). He professed to be a reluctant public servant, only doing his patriotic duty. His enemies thought he was protecting the family interests, and some politicians thought he aspired to the Presidency, though he denied it.

His wife Clara, young, pretty, funny, came to detest his involvement in public affairs. She and the children never saw him. "If this is up," she once said, "I want to be down." Clara too came from an old Dominican family. She was embarrassed at parties to see Ramón Cáceres Troncoso, a Cabinet minister, because her uncle had assassinated his grandfather, President Ramón Cáceres, in 1911. On that occasion a Cáceres body-guard cut her uncle's body to pieces in front of his mother, that is, Clara's grandmother. The Republic's society is inbred, its history bloody and inescapable.

Ten or a dozen couples came to that first party: President and Mrs. Bonnelly, Vice President and Mrs. Pichardo, Foreign Minister and Mrs. Bonilla Atiles, the assassins Amiama and Imbert and, I think, their wives, Imbert gun-belted. Others too—Lorenzo Berry, an American super-market operator universally called "Wimpy," after the name of his store; his flashy, high-strung Dominican wife; Andrés Freites, good-look-ing, forty, Dominican manager of Esso about to be appointed Dominican Ambassador to the United States; Luís Manuel Baquero, a psychiatrist and leader of the UCN (Unión Civica Nacional), then the dominant political party. We stood on the wide veranda overlooking the garden, drinking Scotch, talking volubly, Spanish and English, Amiama handsome and silent and alone in a white suit in the tropic night, Wimpy telling my wife about his life as a Caribbean flier and adventurer. It was widely believed in Santo Domingo, and published in the United States, that Wimpy had given guns furnished by the United States government to Trujillo's assassins. So far as I know this story is not true.

We dined at small tables on the veranda, and after dinner Donny led me into his library, took a gun from a rack and told me it was one used to kill Trujillo. After the assassination several of the killers had taken refuge in the home of Donny Reid's brother, Dr. Robert Reid Cabral, a pediatrician. They were captured or killed, and Dr. Reid committed suicide. Donny, once agitated by a quarrel within the Consejo, said to me, "I will not stand for it. I am a sentinel at my brother's tomb." He had suffered. So had so many. The Republic is a tragic place.

We went back to the porch to drink brandy and *cafecitos,* thick Do-minican coffee in demitasse cups. I talked to Antonia, the beautiful wife of Andrés Freites, about living in Washington after her husband became the Ambassador. A breeze rattled the palm fronds, suffused with a sweet odor from the peanut oil factory, once a Trujillo monopoly. The sound of music came from somewhere in the night, the most popular *merengue* in the Republic then, *"La Muerte del Chivo,"* "The Death of the Goat," celebrating the assassination of the goat, as Trujillo was called. Off to one side stood the assassins, Amiama and Imbert, talking in low tones, al-ways together, always whispering. Wimpy's explosive wife suddenly danced across the veranda, heels stamping, skirt billowing, fingers snap-ping.

There was an air of excitement and conspiracy in the night, of hope and mystery. And a little later an air of serious purpose too—President Bonnelly wanted to talk to me. I went to an inner room and found him with, as I recall it, Pichardo, Amiama, Imbert, Reid, and Bonilla Atiles. This was the government, Consejeros and Foreign Minister, talking to the new United States Ambassador. They spoke of money, the Castro/Communists, and plans for the future: A highway in the north from Santiago to Puerto Plata, a TVA-like development of the great Río Yaque del Norte. They talked of their difficulties but they also talked of the end of the Trujillo tyranny, of freedom, of the Alliance for Progress, and of their hopes. They were eager, serious, concerned. Above all, they said, the United States must help. I said we would. This was what I had come for.

5

So it began. So we spent our first week in the Republic during the first United States ambassadorship after Trujillo. I was there nineteen months. Nothing in my life, nor anything I was told before going, had specifically prepared me for the task; and yet in another sense all my life had been a preparation—everything I had done, knew how to do, everything I had learned and felt and believed in, went into my work in the Republic. Nineteen months can seem an eternity. José "Pepe" Figueres, the former President of Costa Rica, has named his plantation *La Lucha Sin Fin*— the fight without end. It is one. But it is a fight worth making.

I have chosen to be an historian of that time and that place because I felt I was living close to the central reality of our times. This book will raise questions of policy—non-intervention versus interdependence, the future of the OAS and the Alliance for Progress, and our own position in the Hemisphere. It will raise other questions often asked: "Why can't Latin Americans govern themselves? And, can democracy really work there? And, how far can we stretch our power around the world? And, do our interests in Latin America lie with the military and business classes who can provide stability and maintain the status quo (they say)? Or do they lie with the workers and *campesinos* and intellectuals and students who are making a revolution against the status quo?

For, whether we like it or not, a revolution is taking place in Latin America today. Indeed, it is only a part of a worldwide revolution that has been going forward for some time in a belt around the earth lying roughly between the Tropic of Cancer and the Tropic of Capricorn; and this revolution in my opinion will continue through our lifetime, and perhaps longer, and it vitally involves our nation's future. A not inconsiderable element in it is color, or race, even in the Dominican Republic, despite denials, and we see its reflection in the Negro question in the United States. The problem is not underdeveloped nations; it is underdeveloped people, here, in Africa, in Southeast Asia, and in Latin America. The struggle is principally political.

Communists hold that only bloody revolution can realize the legitimate aspirations of the Latin American masses. We believe them wrong, but we have not yet proved it. We are paying, and will continue to pay, for past errors in Latin America. Nationalism is rising there. It is ripe for Moscow and Peking. President Kennedy, for whom I proudly spoke, called Latin America "the most critical area in the world."

The Dominican Republic is an odd place, in many ways unlike any other, as each Latin nation is unique; and yet many of the problems of Latin America are to be found here—the gilded oligarchy, the miserable masses, nationalistic anti-American teen-agers, the real Communists trained in Moscow and Havana, a restless military, powerful upward-clawing business classes, scheming politicians, a few patriots, bombastic orators, and muddled intellectuals; the economic problems of tropical agriculture; the proud dreams of industrialization and tourism; a population explosion; and the classic power structure of military, money, Church, and masses.

Here too are the extravagant gestures and gaudy trappings of Latin power, the reckless adventures of gunmen in politics and politicians armed, the foolish dreams of poets in power. A saying goes, "What they make with their hands, they break with their feet." It is easy to dismiss the Dominican character as childlike, but it is far more complicated than that—proud, sensitive, friendly, devious, long-suffering, capable of bravery, sometimes foolish, time and again disappointing, and like the Republic itself, heartbreaking and tragic. We thought we had a chance, a great chance, after Trujillo fell. We tried to give the Dominican people an opportunity for representative constitutional democracy. And successes we did have, important ones, making choices, taking forks in the road, gripped by history, but in the end we failed, despite our great power. Why? What are the limits of American power? That is the question. It used to be said that all power corrupts, and absolute power corrupts absolutely. Today it might be said more trenchantly that all power has limits, and the greater the power the greater the limits. I saw it happen.

I hope this book will inform readers of the difficulties we face. We are a great nation, we can blow up the earth, but we lack the power to crack a nut. We simply cannot obliterate a little island when it displeases us.

And something more—that from power flows evil. Time and again, in person after person, I glimpsed the infinite capacity of men for evil and self-destruction as they maneuvered for power and as they used it. This book, then, is about power and evil, thrown against the background of tyranny and democracy and communism in the Caribbean. It raises not merely policy questions but moral ones, the big questions—justice,

means and ends, freedom and license, our own opulence and the wretch-
edness of most of humanity, and man's right to dignity and a better life.

Day after day, bogged down in the weary round of plots and abortive
coups, the dreary quarrels over political spoils, cheap Latin histrionics,
comic-opera derring-do, and hollow Washington speeches, I wondered
why we cared and why we strove so hard, and others working with me
must have wondered too. Yet we knew there was greatness in it. Free
man's fate was involved here. I, and many others, were totally committed. I took chances no Ambassador is supposed to take. Somebody in
the State Department refers to our 1962 effort as "the Lanny Budd
days." It was a somewhat unconventional effort. But then, so was President Kennedy's. Things we did we might not dare again. We knew the
immense difficulties. But there was hope. We were young beyond our
years.

This book is not omniscient. No Ambassador can know everything.
He cannot tell quite everything he knows. This is nearly everything I saw
in that place at that time.

Sometimes in those years when I came home to Washington for consultation, exhausted, disgusted by the stubborn, dangerous foolishness of
Dominican politicians, discouraged by our slow progress, I felt a great
surge of pride in my own country. I lost even this, for a time, after the
assassination of President Kennedy. Toward the end in the Dominican
Republic I had a feeling that the elected President, Juan Bosch, and his
political and military enemies were a group of men locked inextricably
together, stumbling in the dark along the edge of a windswept precipice,
and one night they fell over. It was senseless. So was the act of the kid in
Dallas from the Fair Play for Cuba Committee.

There is an element of personal failure in this book. For many years
I had cared deeply about the Republic and its people. The chance to do
something came in 1962, given me by President Kennedy. All our hopes
for the brave new world in Santo Domingo ended one night when President Bosch provoked a colonel. All the grandeur of President Kennedy's
designs ended in a sordid Dallas police station where bondsmen and owners of striptease joints congregate. I knew the United States at the summit
of its hopes and under its great men, and I knew the Dominican Republic
in the death throes of tyranny and the birth throes of liberty. And so
this book properly begins with the assassination of Generalissimo Trujillo
on May 30, 1961, and it might properly have ended with another
assassination, that of President Kennedy on November 22, 1963. But it
does not end there either—it encompasses the Dominican Civil War of
1965. For the struggle and our inescapable engagement in it never end.

Chapter Two

THE BLOODY HERITAGE

By chance, I lived in the Dominican Republic several months during the winter of 1937–38. I was a kid out of college, looking for a place to live cheaply and write. I had been working on a newspaper, the *Times,* in Indianapolis, Indiana, where I grew up, and I wanted to write magazine articles. I took a trip on a Caribbean freighter, stopped at several ports, and got off at Santo Domingo, then called Ciudad Trujillo. In those days nearly all travelers arrived by boat, their baggage hauled to hotels by horsedrawn carts. Men sipped rum in Parque Colón, affianced couples promenaded there of a Sunday evening, the streets were clean and the people well-dressed, and a room cost one dollar a day at a little thick-walled waterfront hotel. In 1962 the cost of living was higher than in Washington, D.C.

Behind this idyllic façade, however, lay the Trujillo terror. That year, 1937, was the year of the Haitian massacre, when Trujillo's troops butchered some twelve thousand Haitians. The massacre produced the first noteworthy international outcry against Trujillo. In power only seven years, Trujillo had already locked the Republic up tight.

When I traveled, I was stopped frequently by troops at checkpoints. My mail was opened. When I shopped in the capital, clerks, no doubt informers for the secret police, knew my name, perhaps because upon arriving I had listed my profession as journalist. The foreign press was censored. The local press was servile. Everybody feared Trujillo. Even Americans referred to him as "Mr. Jackson." One night I saw soldiers enter a bar, demand *cédulas*—identification cards—beat one man and, shooting, pursue others who fled; all over town that night troops were breaking up groups of three or more. I saw a soldier force a girl in mourning to dance with him. The troops were Trujillo's power base.

I had never before lived in a police state. Returning home in 1938, I wrote my first magazine article. Printed in *Ken,* a magazine then published by *Esquire,* it was, I believe, one of the first anti-Trujillo articles to appear in an American magazine. That year I quit my newspaper job and went to Chicago to freelance. I continued for twenty-four years, writing several books—and many articles for *Harper's, The Saturday Evening Post,* and other magazines—on America's problems, until I became our Ambassador to the Dominican Republic in 1962.

After 1938, I did not go back to the Republic until 1961, even while traveling in nearby Latin American countries, considering it unsafe. But for some reason the place had a hold on me, it was beautiful and the people seemed wonderful, perhaps because they had suffered so much; and during those intervening years I often thought what a marvelous place it could become, if it were free.

2

The island of Hispañola (formerly spelled Española) lies between Cuba and Puerto Rico, the second largest, after Cuba, in the Caribbean. The Dominican Republic occupies the eastern two-thirds of the island; Haiti occupies the western third. These islands and others, the Greater and the Lesser Antilles, separate the Caribbean from the Atlantic. To the south lies South America; to the north, the United States. This is the Caribbean Sea frontier, vital to our interests.

The Dominican Republic comprises some nineteen thousand square miles, about the size of New Hampshire and Vermont combined. Nobody knows how many people inhabit it. A story, probably apocryphal, goes that in 1960 Trujillo ordered a census, proclaiming beforehand that the Republic's population was 4.5 million, but the census-takers found fewer, so he had them shot. Today the population is conservatively estimated at 3.3 or 3.5 million. It is growing alarmingly, at a rate of 3.5 percent per year, far higher than that of either India or China, and one of the highest in the world. But unlike Haiti, its land is not staggeringly overpopulated. Not yet.

Other statistical yardsticks[1] place the Republic at about the average among Latin American countries. Many such statistics mean little. Thus the Republic's annual gross national product expressed in "per capita terms" of about $239 is derived by dividing the population into the total national income; but this is small comfort to a man in a hut with seven half-starved children who never sees fifty dollars a year. Thousands upon thousands live entirely outside the money economy, scratching the Dominican earth for enough to eat. Taken all in all, however, the Republic is no hopeless economic swamp. It contains minerals and merchantable timber. It is basically agricultural and, with technical help, could feed itself except for wheat. Sugar is the heart of its economy.

[1] All these figures are derived from the UN or the State Department and though not precise are those generally used.

To my mind, the Republic is the most beautiful of the Greater Antilles. Its variety is fantastic—the highest mountains in the Caribbean, verdant valleys and steep hillsides, tropical jungles, a vast desert, a strange southern peninsula where little lives but iguanas, rushing mountain streams and broad powerful coastal rivers, large areas still unmapped, and on every coast endless miles of glittering golden empty beaches— palms and coral reefs and breakers, sand and sun.

Towns in the interior have changed little in a hundred years, hamlets little in four hundred. Men still ride oxen or, lacking oxen, pull huge loads of logs on their bare backs, plodding and bent like the animals themselves. Men plow with a forked stick, some of them wearing but a single garment, a burlap covering the body diagonally, one shoulder bare, a belt of palm-lacing at the waist—while Soviet tankers and U.S. warships pass offshore.

In a provincial hotel at night one can hear native drums in the distance and a jukebox in the bar. One can find excellent swimming and hunting and fishing, and caves on whose cool rock walls are massive Indian carvings and under whose clay floors are buried the tools and relics of pre-Columbian tribes.

Despite the luxury hotels of Santo Domingo—gambling, drinking, lunch beside the pool—somehow the Republic never has been a major tourist center. Cuba was closer to the United States, Haiti more bizarre, Puerto Rico and Jamaica "safer." The Dominican Republic was always a backwater; and its turbulent politics and Trujillo's iron dictatorship kept it that way.

It is about 275 miles by road from Elías Piña, on the Haitian frontier, to the eastern tip of the Republic, near Higüey. It is about 140 miles from Santo Domingo on the south coast to Puerto Plata on the north. The Republic is crossed by two lesser mountain ranges and one great one, the Cordillera Central, running northwest to southeast, its craggy peaks beyond Constanza rising to the 10,300 feet of Pico Duarte (formerly Pico Trujillo), the highest point in the Caribbean. The high mountains are remote, cold, barren, and inhospitable. The population is concentrated in two areas—the capital and nearby towns, and the Cibao, the rich valley in the north whose capital is Santiago, seat of the oligarchy, birthplace of unnumbered revolutions in freedom's name throughout the Republic's history.

3

History—the history of the Dominican Republic is not auspicious. Let us glance at it briefly. For it illuminates the present, and to understand what seemed lunacy in our time one should know the lunacy that went before.

The history begins gloriously enough: One of Christopher Columbus' captains aboard the *Pinta* discovered the northeast coast of the island in 1492, on Columbus' first voyage. Columbus' brother Bartholomew founded Santo Domingo, and Christopher first saw it at the end of his third voyage, in 1498. Santo Domingo was the first permanent settlement in the New World. It has endured. Dominicans today call their nation "the land Columbus loved," and perhaps he did: He bestowed upon the island the honored name, Española, the Spanish Isle. But there, too, as Samuel Eliot Morison has pointed out, Columbus suffered his greatest humiliations—his flagship lost, wars with natives, imprisonment at the hands of a royal agent. It was a curiously apt augury of things to come—grandeur and humiliation.

The mark of the Spaniards is on the city yet—the oldest cathedral in the Western Hemisphere stands on Parque Colón, its dark weathered stone entombing Christopher Columbus' bones, seat of the primate of the Americas; old colonnaded government houses facing it; thick walls and tiled floors and mahogany beams; ancient churches and ruins. This was the seat, too, of the Spanish Captain-General. From here he governed the New World for Spain. From here set forth Cortés to conquer Mexico, Pizarro to conquer Peru, and Ponce de León to explore Puerto Rico and Florida. From here ruled Columbus' son, Diego, bringing his bride and building the Álcazar, all massive stone, high ceilings, arched doorways, dark private chapel. Sir Francis Drake sacked the city and stabled his horses in the cathedral.

The Indians, who were for the most part peaceable, lived on the coasts by fishing. They belonged to the Taino branch of the Arawak tribe and came, it is thought, from a fiercer tribe on the north coast of South America. The Spaniards enslaved a few and exterminated the rest. Relatively few Dominicans exhibit strong strains of Indian blood. Though officially a *mestizo* nation—mixed Spanish, Indian, and Negro— the Republic's people are mostly white or black or shades between. Nonetheless Dominicans have not entirely forgotten their Indian past. One chief, Enriquillo, who resisted the Spaniards, is a national hero. Before Columbus, the Indians called the country *Quisqueya,* and the word stirs patriotic feelings yet—orators use it, and the words of the national anthem begin, *"Quisqueyaños valientes."*

The Spaniards mined the gold then moved on to richer lands. Santo Domingo fell into neglect. Its peasants and ruling Spanish caste slumbered.

Upon this calm a storm broke at the end of the eighteenth century. As revolution convulsed France, half a million Haitian slaves revolted against their white French masters. Their battle cry was "cut and burn." They cut their French masters to pieces and burned their plantations, and out of this fiery furnace came Dessalines, Toussaint L'Ouverture, and the mad Christophe who built the Citadel. France declared war on Spain. Toussaint L'Ouverture betrayed the Dominicans. Napoleon sent an army, Spain regained control briefly with British help, Dominican plotters overthrew the Spanish regime and sought union with Simón Bolívar's Colombia.

From this shattering awakening at the end of the eighteenth century Santo Domingo never recovered. It was thrust onto the world stage, embroiled beyond its coasts, and so it is today.

4

Haiti conquered it in 1822, taking the historic invasion route through Azua. Haiti occupied it for twenty-two years, from 1822 to 1844, an occupation that to this day is more vivid and bitter in Dominican memory than the American Marine occupation of 1916–24. Haiti's rule was cruel despotism. Dominicans began to conspire and resist. Finally, after bloodshed and agony, they drove out the Haitians and won their independence in 1844. Their leaders were Juan Pablo Duarte, Francisco del Rosario Sánchez, and Ramón Mella—the Trinitaria honored at the national shrine which stands today in Parque Independencia at the head of Calle Conde. Here at the Conde Gate on February 27, 1844, Mella and Sánchez and other patriots—including Cayetano Abad Rodríguez— met to proclaim the Republic's new freedom, while General José María Imbert planned his victorious defense of Santiago. (One hundred and twenty-one years later, during the Civil War of 1965, General Antonio Imbert fought the rebels in Santo Domingo, and Cayetano Rodríguez was a central committee member of the Castro/Communist MPD.)

So began in 1844 the independent life of the Dominican Republic. One might have hoped that after so much suffering and sacrifice, a great free nation could be established. Unhappily, it was not so.

Scarcely had the last Haitian been driven from Dominican soil than the Dominican leaders quarreled. Duarte, Sánchez, and Mella stood firm for independence. Generals Buenaventura Baez and Pedro Santana argued that the Republic was too weak to stand alone and needed the "protection" of some foreign power. They chained and deported the three heroes of independence. President Duarte, who had stormed the Conde Gate for freedom on February 27, was sent to exile on September 10, a parallel precise almost to the day to the brief reign of President Juan Bosch 119 years later.

Generals Baez and Santana dominated the early years of independence, collaborators at first, later enemies. Baez lasted longer. Probably no more meretricious leader was ever visited on a hapless people. Greedy adventurer, liar, treacherous conspirator, he devoted his energies to throwing away his country's precious independence—to converting the independent republic into a protectorate of a foreign power, offering it first to the United States, then to France, then to Spain. His disastrous economic policies provoked revolt, and Santana, himself by then in exile, returned to lead the Cibaeños, citizens of the Cibao, the rich valley whose capital is Santiago. Full-scale civil war ensued. Santana laid siege to the capital, where famine and disease prevailed; death carts hauled the dead and dying through the streets, and the fortunate ate donkey meat. A U.S. warship brought food to starving Americans, and its commander mediated the war; Baez went into exile, and Santana became president. Immediately, he adopted Baez' policy, seeking to give his country away to a foreign power, this time Spain. Baez hastened to Curaçao to plan revolution against Santana. And so on—the dreary tale limps to a conclusion of sorts in 1861, when Santana actually succeeded in persuading Spain to reannex the Republic outright. So died after seventeen years the dreams of Duarte, Sánchez, and Mella.

No one protested, perhaps the result of sheer exhaustion, perhaps because the masses simply followed their local caciques—chieftains. Santana told a Spaniard: "I have made you an immensely valuable gift, for I have given you a people without journalists and devoid of lawyers."

The second Spanish occupation lasted only four years. At the outset, it was inept, indifferent, and corrupt. Soon it became cruel. Dominicans rebelled, at first in sporadic guerrilla bands, later openly. On August 16, 1863, at Capotillo, a town near the Haitian frontier, a small band of Dominicans overwhelmed the Spanish garrison and swept out of the mountains and down the Cibao, driving the Spaniards before them. The Spaniards retreated to the capital. Yellow fever broke out among them. Spanish reinforcements arrived from Havana. The Dominicans butchered them. In the west, San Juan, Neiba, and Azua rose. War engulfed the country, a cruel war with no quarter.

By the end of the summer of 1864, it was becoming clear the Spaniards could not win. That fall the Dominicans nearly defeated themselves. They proclaimed their own leader a traitor, tried to banish him to Haiti, discovered to their surprise that Haiti would not accept him, and, unable to think of anything better to do, assassinated him. Then they resumed the war. The last Spanish troops left July 20, 1865. The American Commercial Agent reported to Secretary of State Seward, "All is quiet under a Provisional Agreement," words with a chilling modern ring.

5

The last of the nineteenth-century history of the Republic is a repetition of the first—civil war, bloodshed, betrayal, corruption, government by assassination, coups and counter-coups, plots and counter-plots, chaos and anarchy. Indeed, throughout all but a dozen of its 122 years the Republic has been ruled by men who seemed determined to steal it, or ruin it, or destroy it, or sell it, or give it away.

Sumner Welles, in his excellent *Naboth's Vineyard,* the best history of the Republic, writes that the noble aspirations of the liberty-loving Dominican people were repeatedly thwarted by bad leaders. In public, as the Ambassador, I said the same thing. But I have often wondered whether political scientists are not nearer the truth when they say that people get the kind of government they deserve. It is a harsh judgment on the Dominicans. Perhaps it can be more fairly said that people, all people, in any time and any place, contain seeds of greatness and seeds of meanness; each, whether leader or follower, acts out the sometimes dreadful, sometimes heroic, role assigned by events, caught in his times and trapped by his temperament, shaped by history as well as shaping it. Welles seems to subscribe to what has been termed the "devil theory" of history. My own experience has led me to believe, rather, that infinitely complex man shapes events and is shaped by them; that a considerable charge of chance also goes into history's crucible; and that what may emerge is rarely predictable.

Amid the rebellions and counter-rebellions, European powers and the United States government and private plunderers intrigued ceaselessly. Their objectives were financial profit and the use of the strategic Peninsula of Samaná as a coaling station for ships, especially warships. British bankers loaned the beleaguered Republic a huge sum on outrageous terms. But we did worse. Misled by avaricious Yankee fortune-hunters and self-seeking representatives, bemused by visions of Manifest Destiny, and provoked by a Dominican general who ordered his creaky gunboat to fire on a U.S. steamship, President Grant committed himself not merely to the purchase of the Peninsula of Samaná, not merely to the "protection" of the Dominican Republic, but to outright annexation.

The Secretary of the Navy ordered full power used to capture the "pirate" gunboat. Grant's Commissioner, in the hands of unscrupulous U.S. adventurers, negotiated with the ineffable Baez, President once more. Baez sold the Republic to us for one hundred thousand dollars in cash and fifty thousand dollars in armaments. The U. S. Navy would place at Baez' disposal sufficient force for his purposes. All was to be kept secret "as long as possible."

Grant's Commissioner arrived aboard the U.S.S. *Albany.* On November 29, 1869, the treaty of annexation was signed. Grant's Commissioner planted the American flag on Samaná. The U.S.S. *Nantasket* was ordered to Puerto Plata to fire upon the town should resistance be offered. Baez proclaimed an immediate plebiscite on annexation. His official newspaper explained to the Dominican people that the United States was really nothing but a collection of free and independent republics, each with its own religion, language, and customs. The U.S. would save the Dominicans from the dread Haitians. Baez also let it be known that opposition to annexation would mean imprisonment, exile, or worse. Not surprisingly, on February 19, 1870, annexation was voted, about 16,000 to 11.

Did mutterings arise at Monte Cristi and Puerto Plata? U.S. warships paid them visits. Did the American Commercial Agent report fraud in the plebiscite? He was recalled.

But not everything could be fixed. The Treaty must go to the U. S. Senate for ratification. And there, after a bitter and protracted battle, it was defeated. Senator Charles Sumner of Massachusetts, Chairman of the Senate Committee on Foreign Relations, led the opposition. He said, in a speech foreshadowing the "Good Neighbor Policy" of more than half a century later: "Kindness, benevolence, assistance, aid, help, protection, all that is implied in good neighborhood, this we must give freely, bountifully; but [the Dominican people's] independence is as precious to them as is ours to us, and it is placed under the safeguard of natural laws which we cannot violate with impunity."

6

Annexation dead, the fever of revolt began again, as usual, in the Cibao, especially Santiago. More secret meetings and plots, armed uprising, death, betrayal, deportation—it went on and on. Now as before heroes arose, and villains fell, or the other way around, and their names echo in Dominican affairs today. Towns are named for them, and I knew their descendants in my own time—Luperón, Cabral, Espaillat, Hungría, Baez, Cáceres, Jimenes, Imbert. And sometimes the men I knew reenacted the roles their ancestors played in those long-ago days.

From this moiling mass of generals and politicians, two emerged worth remembering.

The first was Ulises Francisco Espaillat, neither an active politician nor a general, merely a patriot, one of the few good presidents the Republic has ever had, and elected, too. He took office May 29, 1876. A Santiaguero—his descendants are still prominent there—Espaillat believed in political freedom, an incorruptible judiciary, universal education, and fair taxation. He thought that a people indifferent to their own rights were inviting slavery. He once wrote, "our 'tomorrow' . . . never dawns, and it is always until tomorrow that we postpone our accomplishments."

The auguries were favorable. Espaillat had the support of a powerful general, Gregorio Luperón. He was widely admired. He named to his Cabinet the ablest men he could find, regardless of party. But the Republic proved unequal to the task of greatness he set it. He had time to launch but one project, monetary reform, and that was misunderstood. Within two months the plots of exiled, aging schemers had caused armed rebellions. Retreating, his Minister of War adopted energetic measures, to Espaillat's sorrow. Espaillat wrote to a friend:

"I, who made the immense sacrifice of accepting the Presidency because of the compelling argument that my acceptance of the office was absolutely essential if public order was to be preserved, have now to consent that the force of arms, civil war, be the means of maintaining me in power; power of which I never was enamored and which I am exercising with profound distaste. There is not a day that passes since I assumed the fatal Presidency which does not bring with it a bitter disillusion." He would gladly have offered "my name, . . . which is the sole legacy which I desired to bequeath to my children, upon the altar of the duty of a public man," if its sacrifice would have strengthened men of honor. But instead of honor, Espaillat encountered only betrayal and indifference; instead of lending him assistance to save the country, his colleagues behaved "as if the conflagration were only going to destroy me." He wrote: "What, after all, can I think or hope of such insanity, such madness?"

It is a very Dominican statement. I have heard others like it from two Dominican Presidents and numerous other public men.

Espaillat fell October 5, 1876. He went home to the Cibao and soon died brokenhearted. He had occupied "the fatal Presidency" a little more than four months. The Republic is a difficult country, and good intentions and high thoughts are not enough to run it.

Six years of almost constant turmoil ensued. They ended on September 1, 1882, when General Ulises Heureaux was inaugurated, the second time in the Republic's history when a President was elected and inaugurated in accordance with the Constitution.

7

Ulises Heureaux, called "Lilís," is the other man we must note, one of the most fascinating in Dominican history. More than any other, Ulises Heureaux set the pattern for Trujillo. He was a total dictator, and a successful one. For seventeen years he ruled the Republic, the longest dictatorship in its history save Trujillo's.

Of obscure and probably illegitimate birth, Heureaux had clawed his way up from the lower depths, once killing a man and almost losing his own arm in a quarrel over possession of a blanket. Then as now, apparently, a military career was one of the few routes open to an uneducated, ambitious, ruthless man. Heureaux rose rapidly in the War of Restoration and attracted the patronage of General Luperón. When he no longer needed Luperón, he cast him aside and took power when he was about thirty-seven. He was popular with the Army, which was crucial, and with the people, which helped. His first term was relatively uneventful. But he schemed to extend it, and did. Thereafter treachery and cruelty stamped his rule.

He bought off, deported, or assassinated his principal rivals. He executed his brother-in-law, telling him he would first feed and clothe him well so that he could face death bravely and not disgrace the family. As young men of promise arose, Heureaux' agents asked their support and offered them jobs; if they refused, they were imprisoned, deported, or killed. His spies were everywhere. (All these methods became Trujillo's.) Power secured, Heureaux bade Congress change the Constitution, lengthening the President's term and electing him not by popular suffrage but by a small, easily controlled electoral college. He successfully played off the great powers of Europe and the United States against each other. He played the old games but played them skillfully— he tried to lease Samaná to a foreign government or to private foreign investors, borrowed money in Europe, intrigued with a U.S. consul. The British loan, long since defaulted, was transferred to a private U.S. company. That company became the Republic's banker. It worked closely with Heureaux. He gave it the right to collect Dominican customs to secure its loans, a step which foreshadowed the U. S. Marine occupation.

Once, needing U.S. money to put down revolt, Heureaux became impatient at delay, and said, "I cannot ask insurgents to wait until I receive money from the United States with which to fight them." His last years were ones of almost total terror. He filled the prisons with political opponents. From the Fortaleza they were thrown to the sharks, attracted there by the city's garbage. He traveled ceaselessly throughout the Republic, moving fast, arriving without warning, and he maintained a mistress in each town, often herself his spy. (So did Trujillo.) His espionage apparatus reached far beyond the Republic's borders. (So did Trujillo's.) He sent his wife to Puerto Plata and brought women from abroad to his house, a seraglio. He took what women he wanted. (Thus, too, Trujillo.)

Inevitably clandestine opposition arose. When no one is safe, none has much to lose by desperation. Many plotted. Two persevered, Juan Isidro Jimenes[2] and General Horacio Vásquez, and those men, allies first, opponents later, and the parties they formed—the Jimenistas and Horacistas— dominated Dominican politics until Trujillo's time.

Juan Isidro Jimenes, the richest merchant in the Republic, had been exiled to Paris. In 1898 he bought a steamship, collected a few men, three thousand rifles, twelve cannon, and other equipment and landed at Monte Cristi. Jimenes evidently expected a great popular uprising to greet his return. (One thinks today of the Bay of Pigs.) Not at all— though he occupied the city easily, he was driven from it with equal ease by a few fresh troops.

General Horacio Vásquez was from Moca, a Cibao town known as

[2] Although Sumner Welles and other authorities spell it Jiménez, his grandson, Juan Isidro Jimenes Grullón, spells it Jimenes, and I have adopted that spelling. Dominican orthography, especially of proper names, is a briar patch.

the home of bravery and rebellion. Used then imprisoned, exiled then forgiven, always browbeaten by Heureaux, Vásquez formed an alliance in Moca with his cousin, General Ramón Cáceres.

Cáceres was determined to assassinate Heureaux; from childhood he had been taught that Heureaux was involved in the murder of his father. Vásquez considered open revolution more honorable. But Cáceres plotted with, among others, two men named De la Maza, a name prominent later in the assassination of Trujillo.

President Heureaux arrived in Moca on the night of July 25, 1899. Next day he would leave for Santiago. The Cáceres group would try to shoot him on the street in Moca, while the Vásquez group hid beyond Moca in case Cáceres failed. That afternoon Cáceres told his companions to stand back. But in the central square, where Cáceres' horse was hitched in front of a dry goods store, the storekeeper's teen-age son, one of the plotters, shot President Heureaux as he came out of the store. Cáceres fired, hitting Heureaux too. Heureaux shot back, killing a beggar. Cáceres shot him again, and Heureaux fell dead. They fired into his body, then turned and ran. One of Heureaux' followers buried his body hastily in Santiago. That night Vásquez rode into Moca with twenty-one men and proclaimed the revolution of July 26, 1899.

Now once more the Dominicans, thanks this time to the bravery of one man and a boy, were handed the priceless opportunity to make a fresh start. Again, they threw it away.

8

The followers of Vásquez and Jimenes fought a civil war, first against Heureaux' men, then against each other. In less than four years they destroyed their own hopes and ideals. It took less time after Trujillo fell.

New provisional governments were installed and, at the mercy of foreign creditors, homegrown generals, and the unremitting Horacista-Jimenista warfare, fell. Through 1903 and 1904, revolts flared, foreign warships returned; periodically leaders sought U.S.-protectorate status or raised cries of anti-Americanism and turned to Europe. Once the U.S.S. *Yankee* landed Marines. Amid complex quarrels over European debts and a 4.5-million-dollar debt owed the U.S. company, Belgium and France threatened to seize the customs house, whereupon the Dominican President threw himself wholly into the arms of the United States. President Theodore Roosevelt replied, "As for annexing the island, I have about the same desire to annex it as a gorged boa constrictor might have to swallow a porcupine wrong-end-to."

But Roosevelt thought the Monroe Doctrine needed strengthening. It merely warned European powers to keep hands off Latin America. Irresponsible governments in Latin America, secure behind it, went ahead borrowing money in Europe. The U.S. went ahead warning Europeans against intervening in Latin America. But Europeans were determined to collect their just debts. All this must inevitably lead the U.S. into defending irresponsible governments. It might lead to direct conflict with European powers. Moreover, Roosevelt was determined to check German expansionism. He devised the Roosevelt Corollary to the Monroe Doctrine—since we could not permit European powers to collect debts forcibly in the Hemisphere, the U.S. would undertake to collect Dominican customs revenues and distribute them equitably among the Republic and its creditors, both European and American. Roosevelt instructed the U. S. Minister in Santo Domingo to ascertain whether the government there "would be disposed to request" this. It would, and in 1905 the two governments signed the agreement.

Ramón Cáceres became President in 1906. Assassin of Heureaux, born in Moca, reared on the family plantations, vigorous and patriotic, a political realist, and a fearless man, he ruled wisely. The next five years was the longest unbroken period of orderly, stable, free government the Dominicans had enjoyed in all their history up to that date— or, as it has turned out, since.

Prosperity and progress prevailed. President Cáceres built schools and roads, reformed the public administration, put down sporadic revolts without repression. With the help of a U.S. financial adviser, he at last put the Republic's fiscal house in order.

But the old Dominican problem arose: A failure of politics. Time and again in the Republic, with affairs going well, the political machinery has broken down. It happened to Cáceres after 1908. Rivalries and intrigues split the Cabinet. Cáceres broke with Vásquez. Plotters in exile accomplished little, but one plot against Cáceres was serious.

Years earlier, Cáceres had rebuffed General Luís Tejera, the uncle of whom Clara Reid had told us. Tejera conceived the delusion that he might become President were Cáceres dead. He gathered a band of young thugs in the capital and plotted to capture Cáceres and force him to resign, a Dominican plot that has been tried since. Soon it became an assassination plot, which also usually happens. On November 19, 1911, a sultry, oppressive day, President Cáceres went for his customary evening drive (as did Trujillo later). Despite widespread reports that he would be assassinated, he was accompanied by only one aide (as was Trujillo on his own fatal drive). Out in the country a wagon, an automobile, and a band of men blocked the way. When Cáceres came near, the men fired. His bodyguard fired one shot, then ran behind a tree. Cáceres was already fatally wounded.

Troops soon captured the assassin Tejera, took him to the Fortaleza, and in its central court riddled his body with bullets. His deed brought on anarchy, and anarchy brought the United States Marines.

9

In a dozen years, from 1904 to 1916, the United States moved from the Roosevelt Corollary to full-scale Marine occupation of the Dominican Republic. First we collected customs, then we forbade insurrection in order to maintain stability, then we held elections with warships in the harbor and sailors or Marines at the polls, then we demanded full control over internal revenues and expenditures as well as over customs, then we demanded the disbanding of the Army and establishment of a Guardia Nacional (Constabulary); then we sent the Marines.

U.S. historians dispute our motives in occupying the Republic. Were we simply trying to "collect debts" for U.S. bankers (as many Latin Americans maintain)? Or were we protecting our national security— safeguarding the new Panama Canal, preventing European designs on Dominican sovereignty, and, as we moved closer to war with Germany, opposing pro-Germanism in the Republic? Or did we drift and merely blunder into the occupation? The evidence is contradictory. This is not the place to discuss it in detail. What mattered to the Dominicans was not our motives but the Marines' presence.

What apparently triggered the occupation was the Dominican President's call for elections to fill Congressional vacancies. We feared the Congress would be dominated by a pro-German leader. (Today one thinks of "pro-Castro." One wonders whether the real pro-Germanism of some Dominicans at that time was not magnified by our own almost phobic fear of the Kaiser, just as in my time with pro-Castroism; whether some "pro-Germanism" was not really anti-Americanism, as some "pro-Castroism" is today; and whether we did not permit our fear of the Kaiser to control our Dominican policy.) At any rate, eight days after the Dominican President called for elections, Secretary of State Lansing asked President Wilson for a decision. Wilson approved military occupation "with the deepest reluctance." On November 29, 1916, Captain H. S. Knapp, aboard his flagship, the U.S.S. *Olympia,* in the ancient harbor of Santo Domingo, proclaimed the U.S. military occupation of the Dominican Republic. So died for eight years the Republic's hard-won and ill-used independence.

10

Although for a few weeks at the outset we attempted to maintain the fiction that Dominicans still governed, we failed, and as soon as the United States entered the war in Europe, it lost interest in the Dominican Republic and the Military Governor reigned supreme.

Fortunately, Captain Knapp was by all accounts a judicious man who intended to enforce the occupation but without harsh repression and at the same time to promote progress in the Republic. His successor, Rear Admiral Thomas Snowden aroused bitter Dominican resentment.

Captain Knapp considered his first task to pacify the Republic, so he disarmed it: He confiscated all guns and ammunition, by force when necessary. He disbanded the Army and established a Guardia Nacional. He built schools and highways, raised teachers' pay, brought in experts to increase agricultural production, improved sanitation, improved harbors and the telephone and telegraph systems, reformed the country's fiscal methods.

The Marines did their worst in two eastern provinces, Seibo and San Pedro de Macorís. There, resisting disarmament, Dominicans took to the hills and conducted guerrilla warfare. The Marines, terming them bandits, hunted them down mercilessly. Soon the Marines were perpetrating atrocities. In a subsequent Senate investigation, a citizen of Hato Mayor said: "A rope was put around my neck, my hands tied, and I was taken to the country about four or five kilometers from town on foot and had to keep up with a horse trotting. . . . and when in the country I was tied by the feet, placed on my back with my face to the sun, and with a funnel, water was poured into my mouth from a demijohn. I was in that state about three or four days." The police chief in Hato Mayor said that Marines took a man prisoner, tied him up, took him out of town, brought him back three days later, formed a firing squad, and shot him dead, then an officer plunged a dagger into his throat and slashed his body open from neck to belly.

The Military Governor tried to stop such atrocities with court-martial. The officer held chiefly responsible killed himself before trial. But retribution solves little. In those eastern provinces years later, anti-Americanism remained. I sensed a sullen hostility in Hato Mayor— averted or hostile gazes, *los tigres,* young men given to violence hanging around on street corners. Castro/Communists captured trade unions at the U.S. sugar company at La Romana. One of the first Communist cells in the Republic was formed in San Pedro de Macorís.

Even without atrocities, resentment was no doubt inevitable. No people enjoys a foreign military occupation. The Marines unquestionably sowed the seed of anti-Americanism throughout the Republic. In our own time, I found that in some towns the anniversary of their departure is celebrated as a holiday. Some political leaders I dealt with had begun their public careers by opposing the Marines, and said so proudly. And the Castro/ Communists sought assiduously to make capital of the occupation.

It is, however, one measure of the occupation that the Castro/Communists accomplished surprisingly little by this tactic. I found a few people who praised the occupation, some who even wished it had continued or led to annexation, an idea I strongly resist.

In sum, it is probably fair to say that our occupation of the Republic was neither so bad as Dominican nationalists picture it nor so good as our own apologists used to picture it and that, coupled with the Marine occupations of Nicaragua and Haiti, it damaged our position in the Hemisphere more than in the Dominican Republic itself.

The trouble with most military occupations is that they build nothing but material things. They do not build a free society or free political institutions. "Only liberty," Gladstone said, "fits men for liberty." Thus when the time comes for the occupiers to get out, they cannot, for they dare not leave a vacuum. It is always far easier to get the Marines in than to get them out.

The time came to get the Marines out of the Dominican Republic after the war in Europe ended. But it took years of quarreling among rival Dominican politicians and years of negotiation by the U.S. In 1922 the task was entrusted to Sumner Welles, Commissioner to the Republic with the rank of Envoy Extraordinary and Minister Plenipotentiary.

His task foreshadowed mine forty years later—to keep the provisional government in office, help it hold elections, and help get the winner into the Palace alive. He succeeded and so did I. But before he succeeded, he encountered nearly every obstacle I encountered.

After much difficulty with the Horacistas and Jimenistas and other parties, a provisional government was installed, headed by Juan Bautista Vicini Burgos, a wealthy non-political sugar planter. Immediately his government was beset by hordes of office-seekers and plagued by inexperience. Quarrels broke out among Cabinet ministers and subordinates. Rumors of thievery spread. And Francisco J. Peynado, theretofore non-political, announced his candidacy for the Presidency and received Jimenista support. Other men scrambled to campaign too.

But much had to be done—an electoral law implemented, voters registered, polling places set up, and so on. By mid-1923 everyone was discouraged, the ordinary people seemed apathetic, burning with no zeal to free their nation from the odious occupation, and their leaders, instead of working to make free elections possible, sought only personal advantage. By November the whole process had broken down.

Welles called a meeting of political leaders in his own office. He made it plain that their selfish maneuvering was jeopardizing the entire project; finally, after many days of pressure, he got what was needed—postponement of the elections, amendment of the electoral law, reconstitution of the Electoral Board, changes in local officials and the Cabinet, and a temporary political cease-fire. It succeeded. (I held an almost identical meeting in 1962.)

As campaigning began, old General Horacio Vásquez seized a commanding lead. His opponents were unable to agree on a coalition to stop him. They considered boycotting the elections, a step which would have made it impossible for Vásquez, though elected, to govern. But Peynado went to the election on March 15, 1924, and was beaten decisively by Vásquez. For the first time in Dominican history, the loser congratulated the winner.

Vásquez, after a trip to the United States, was inaugurated President of the Republic on July 12, 1924. The last Marine left the Republic on September 18. Welles wrote, "A new era of liberty and independence had commenced."

What did Welles conclude from his study of Dominican history and his own experience there? He believed that the Haitian occupation and the Spanish restoration had stunted the growth of the Republic. To escape anarchy, Dominicans had accepted dictatorship. Thus the Republic came to know only two kinds of governments—the "strong" ones, such as Heureaux', which lasted long but hurt much, and the "well-intentioned" ones, such as Espaillat's, which never lasted long or accomplished much. Welles wrote:

"It is therefore not surprising that the chief menace today to a continuation of orderly democratic government in the Dominican Republic lies in an utter disregard for the sanctity of the Constitution. Instead of being regarded as the sacred charter of the people's liberties, the Constitution has been considered a legitimate source of advantage to the party or to the person in control, and has consequently been modified at frequent intervals solely to satisfy the desires or requirements of those enabled thus to advance them.

"Until the time arrives when the present system whereby the Dominican Constitution can be amended or replaced merely at the instance of the Dominican Congress, with the subsequent approval of a Constitutional Convention elected ad hoc, is abolished, there can exist no positive assurance that the instability of the past will not persist in the future."

Prescient words—less than six years after they were written Trujillo set the Constitution aside. And two years after Trujillo fell, other military men set it aside again. Constitutionalism was the fundamental principle for which we fought throughout my tenure.

Perhaps I have sketched enough of Dominican history to suggest the difficulties we faced after Trujillo. Not only did we have no democratic traditions or institutions to build on, worse, we confronted deep-rooted traditions of authoritarianism and anarchy. Down its history, before Trujillo, the Republic had no fewer than 123 rulers—Spanish governors and Captains-General, French Governors, a Colombian Governor and President, Haitian Presidents, Dominican Presidents and Provisional Presidents. In modern times, two were archbishops, two were civilians, the rest military men. The history of the Republic is really non-history. It shows no development of social or political institutions. It shows no growth of a nation. We ourselves seldom realize how much we owe our past. Dominican history, unfortunately, despite all the bravery and bloodshed and sacrifice, comes to nothing. The Dominicans have ended where they began.

Perhaps too, I have said enough to indicate the striking—and disheartening—parallels between the Republic's nineteenth-century history and the events of 1961–65. Most of the disasters of my years, and some of the successes, had been acted out a hundred years ago.

And finally, perhaps this historical account has shown that Trujillo was no accident. For nearly a century scores of Dominican leaders had sought the total dictatorial power only he achieved. Generalissimo Rafael Leonidas Trujillo y Molina, to give him his full name, has no parallel in the history of the Republic—and perhaps nowhere else. Yet he was the inevitable end result of the historical process we have witnessed. In a sense, all Dominican history prepared the Dominican people for this tyrant.

Chapter Three

THE ERA OF TRUJILLO

Trujillo was no old-fashioned comic-opera Latin American *caudillo*.[1] Except that it lacked an ideology, his was a true modern totalitarian state, complete with racism, espionage apparatus, torture chambers, and murder factories. Trujillo's spies, or informers, were everywhere. And fear was everywhere, a sickness on the land.

Trujillo's instruments of control were the Army and the secret police. (Over the years, the secret police had various titles. The last, and the one hated today, was the SIM—Servicio de Inteligencia Militar, Military Intelligence Service.)

Trujillo took power through the military. He used it to keep power, although in the end its leaders betrayed him. He made the military the privileged class of the Republic. He gave its officers fiefdoms, and they grew rich. He saw to it that the non-commissioned officers and privates were the best-paid, best-fed, best-housed men in the nation. If a soldier wanted a horse, or a cow, or a house, he took it. If he wanted a girl, he took her. To understand what it meant, one must remember that the Republic, long isolated, maintained the customs of Spain longer than most Caribbean lands. Respectable young unmarried women did not go out with boy friends without *dueñas*.

The soldiers swaggered and drank, plundered and bullied. Every few miles on each highway was a checkpoint—two bumps built into the road, a soldier's sentry post between them—and every car must stop and its driver must give his name, *cédula* (identification card) number, destination, intended time of return, and, if the soldier wished, must submit to a search of his car and his person. I have been obliged to do it.

Arrests were arbitrary and capricious. A man could never be sure whether he was arrested on orders from on high or simply at the whim of

[1] Strong man, chief.

a soldier or an agent of the secret police. When a serious—i.e., political —crime was involved, an arrest order did not name merely one man. It named him "and family," and the police arrested him and all his relatives up to and including first cousins.

Trujillo's informers and thugs were called in later years calié.[2] By no means all became calié willingly. Trujillo was expert at forcing people to work for him. His agents forced British West Indies bartenders, waiters and hotel chambermaids to become calié on pain of deportation.

I. subtle means at higher social levels—blackmail, threats, economic pressure. Before it was over, he had forced virtually every man of ability in the Republic to serve him. A promising young man would receive a call from a political leader offering him a public job. He would refuse. Another call, offering a better job. Another refusal. A third call and then a fourth, more ominous: Did he perhaps aspire to the caller's job? Or even to the Generalissimo's job? That last threat brought, ordinarily, capitulation. I know dozens of men, decent men of character and ideals, who were pressed into Trujillo's service. The only escape was to leave the Republic, and that in itself was not easy—a passport might cost a thousand dollars or be unobtainable. The alternative was secret flight, which might mean death. Trujillo did not want Dominicans to leave. Nor did he want people to enter. The Republic was a vast prison.

Nothing pleased Trujillo more than to force a former enemy to serve him, thus humiliating him publicly. He elevated men to places of his highest confidence, then broke them mercilessly. He seemed capricious. Men never knew where they stood with him.

Rafael Estrella Ureña, Trujillo's first Vice President, left the Republic and denounced Trujillo. Congress declared him a traitor. Returning in 1939, he seemed on the road to rehabilitation, but was suddenly arrested for a 1930 political murder probably perpetrated on Trujillo's own orders. He was held without trial more than a year, then abruptly freed. He sent a telegram of lavish thanks to Trujillo, as have scores of others. Soon the police accused him of being a former Fascist; five months later Trujillo had him elected a Justice of the Supreme Court. Then Trujillo invited him to form an opposition party. He accepted. The kept press immediately attacked him viciously. He died a few days later. Trujillo went to the funeral.

Germán Ornes, once a close Trujillo collaborator, later an exiled enemy, today publisher of El Caribe, the Republic's leading newspaper, in 1946 wrote a letter to Trujillo, stating that he had been incarcerated in Fortaleza Ozama for anti-Trujillo activities, that he had been suddenly

[2] This is the common Dominican spelling; the word, however, is probably of Haitian origin and may, properly, be spelled caliae.

set free on order of Trujillo himself, and that he wished to offer his
"sincere gratitude." He went on to confess that as a high school boy
his studies had "caused me to gravitate towards the sphere of Marxist
ideas." Indeed, he said, he remained a Marxist. (I know few more unlikely Marxists. Ornes is bourgeois through and through, if anyone is.)
Ornes' letter dilates at length on "what is a revolutionary" and concludes
that Trujillo himself was "eminently revolutionary," going on to say
that the advances won by Trujillo's suppression of political democracy
could best be guaranteed by political democracy. But, he hastened to
say, this did not mean he and his associates were not grateful for what
Trujillo had done. And so on—it is all just tortured doubletalk. Thus did
fear distort the thought of so many men of my time. The letter was published. Ornes received his reward: Trujillo gave him the newspaper *El
Caribe.*

Telephones were tapped, hotel rooms were wired with microphones.
Mail was opened, cables scrutinized. Worst of all, as the dictator's secret informers seeped throughout the land, no man could know whether
his neighbor, or his lifelong friends, or even his brother or son or wife,
might inform against him. To "talk politics"—there was no politics,
really—was dangerous, even with your closest friends or family. Everyone whispered. Everyone feared. No one trusted anyone.

Trujillo's internal espionage apparatus was almost surely the tightest in
the Hemisphere, perhaps the tightest anywhere. Moreover, it spread far
beyond the Dominican Republic. It reached into virtually every Latin
American capital. It reached into high places in Washington. Nobody
knows how many hundreds of thousands of dollars Trujillo spent in the
United States, trying to influence votes in Congress, policy in the Executive Branch, and public opinion through the press. United States journalists were on his payroll. He used other means. Sometimes, when dignitaries from the United States visited the Republic, his agents provided
them with women and then secretly photographed them. His blackmail
photographic library was extensive. Everything he touched he corrupted.

He put down opposition with utter ruthlessness. Did underground opposition attempt to form? Its leader was run over by a truck, or shot
from a speeding car, gangland style, or waylaid on the highway, killed,
his car wrecked, to make it appear an accident. Or he simply disappeared. Sometimes he was tortured in prison, killed, and thrown to the
sharks. Sometimes he was picked up by the secret police and sent to work
at bayonet point in a slave-labor camp, a Trujillo plantation. If there he
dropped from exhaustion, he was shipped to some remote place and
killed. One man was shot down in the great Cathedral.

Toward the end, the most notorious torture chambers were La Cuarenta—The Forty—and Kilometer 9. Here tortures to obtain confessions

or satisfy sadism became bestial—naked prisoners were shocked in an electric chair; an electric prodder—an electrified metal rod used to prod cattle in stockyards—was applied to their genitals, and a dwarf bit off their testicles.

Trujillo appears to have had a strange contempt for the military. He kept its leaders divided; having climbed to the top of the heap himself, he feared another might do the same. But more than that, he went out of his way to denigrate them. He made his son Ramfis a colonel at the age of three, and a general at nine. Later Trujillo reorganized the Air Force and gave it to Ramfis. The reorganization was thorough. With the advice of a former Luftwaffe officer, the Trujillos created their own little Luftwaffe at San Isidro Air Base outside the capital. The Air Force had not only planes; it had its own infantry and all the military's tanks. Under Ramfis it became the elite striking force of the entire military establishment. In the Republic the military is the key to power; and within the military, Ramfis' Air Force became the key.

Ramfis was handsome, dashing, mustached, with polished riding boots and leather crop. He was a playboy and, visiting the United States aboard his father's yacht, the *Angelita,* entertained movie girls on board. He attended the U. S. Army's Command and General Staff School at Fort Leavenworth, did poorly, and departed, somewhat scandalously. At home most of his cronies were young Air Force officers, some related by blood or marriage to the Trujillo family. They abused their power, treated older officers with contempt, and behaved without restraint in private and public life. They gave orgiastic parties at Ramfis' villa at Boca Chica. After Trujillo was assassinated, their torture of prisoners shocked even the jailers of Kilometer 9.

Almost from the beginning of his rule, Trujillo commanded adulation and even veneration for himself and his family. The name of the capital city, Santo Domingo, bestowed by Columbus and his brother, was changed to Ciudad Trujillo. Provinces and cities throughout the Republic were renamed for members of his family. Maps were redrawn, history rewritten. His photograph was everywhere. So were statues of him. Streets were renamed for him and his relatives. His mother, Doña Julia Molina, was virtually canonized. So was his third wife, María Martínez. She had been his mistress, had had the laundry concession for the military, and he had altered the divorce law to marry her.

His sycophants vied in inventing new titles to bestow upon him in the name of a grateful nation: Generalissimo, Doctor, Benefactor of the Fatherland, Father of the New Fatherland, and many more. Books were written and his name signed as author. An official history of the Republic in twenty volumes was prepared, his history. He was declared an authority on all subjects. License plates and newspaper mastheads bore, in addition to the date as ordinary calendars reckon it, "25th year of the era of Trujillo." Signs everywhere read: *"Dios y Trujillo."* Late in his reign Trujillo wanted the order reversed: *"Trujillo y Dios,"* and got in trouble with the Church by seeking the title, "Benefactor of the Church." It was one of the few battles he lost.

Soon after he took power newspapers became servile or were suppressed. Germán Ornes fled the Republic, he has said, because a typographical error in his paper, *El Caribe,* read that children had laid flowers on the "tomb," not on a "bust," of Trujillo. Trujillo used a newspaper columnist to warn people of his imminent displeasure or tell them he knew what they were doing; people read the column daily with dread.

Press and radio became simply propaganda organs of the government. Nor were the few foreign correspondents who dropped in permitted to cable the truth about the Republic.

Trujillo was the only five-star general, the only *Generalísimo.* Because he liked superlatives so well, after his death he was called the *Difuntísimo,* the Most Defunct. In his lifetime his five stars were everywhere. He had a house and an office in nearly every provincial capital; the five-star emblem adorned each. Like Hermann Göring, he doted on uniforms and is said to have designed them himself. He favored hats with long white plumes. For civilian dress, he favored formal attire. Old-time diplomats recall suffocating in tail coats at official functions. (Official legend said that Trujillo did not perspire.) Diplomats' wives recall shivering in evening gowns at nighttime horse shows or cattle shows he arranged. (His horses and cows always won.) He indulged his tastes— drank Carlos Tercero brandy brought from Spain, canned spring water brought from France. After his death, the new government found an entire shipload of canned water in the Palace.

When his daughter, Angelita, was crowned Queen of his World's Fair in 1955 there was talk of crowning him king in fact. Angelita was deemed as gifted as her father. His wife was acclaimed as a writer and philosopher.

Trujillo lived in an enormous house next door to the U. S. Embassy, guarded by a high stone fence. (The Embassy was there first; it was Trujillo's desire to be close to us, not the other way around.) In his birthplace, San Cristóbal, which became little short of a national shrine, he caused to be built an enormous palace high on a mountain, though it was announced that the money was raised by the grateful people of San Cristóbal. The story goes he never used it. On the day of its grand opening, he asked a European Ambassador what he thought of it, and the Ambassador replied, "What awful taste!" Trujillo never went back to it.

Sometimes Trujillo seemed as much the victim of his own megalomania as was his nation. His sycophants used him. Some stole enormous sums of public money. Some, through sheer ineptitude, embarrassed him by failing at his grandiose projects—built roads that went nowhere, designed uneconomic monopolies, engineered canals that ran backward. He commanded an irrigation system to be built in the arid southwest near Neiba, intended to catch the rainfall in the mountains, spread it over the dry land, and empty it into Lago Enriquillo, a salt lake below sea level; but it was engineered wrong, and, instead of sweet water flowing into salt, salt water flowed onto the land, probably ruining it forever. Other mortifications befell him, and the people snickered.

Despite all the pomp and foolish grandeur, the palaces and uniforms, Trujillo was no fool. He could not have been—without ability no man could control, even with terror, for thirty-one years the powerful forces which wrack that nation. He worked hard, harder than most of his sycophants—from 5 A.M. till late at night. And, as nearly as any man has anywhere, he harnessed the nation's entire economy to his own and his family's bank accounts.

He, or his relatives and cronies, held monopoly or near-monopoly on the production of salt, peanut oil, shoes, matches, cement, soap, paint, glass, beer, meat, chocolate, cigarettes, flour, and more. Their avarice virtually ruined the Republic's coffee and cocoa export business. The Trujillos controlled gambling and prostitution. They took much of the best farmland in the Republic from private owners. Trujillo paid for such lands, but only a fraction of their true value. He owned vast *fincas* (farms) and *haciendas* (estates or plantations) around the Republic. He imported agricultural experts. He also imported armaments experts from Eastern Europe and built at San Cristóbal an excellent arsenal. The famous San Cristóbal carbine was a rapid-fire weapon considered better than the U. S. Army's.

Toward the end, Trujillo appeared to be reaching for a sugar monopoly. At Haina (properly Jaina), a town some seven miles west of the capital, Trujillo built what some say is the biggest and best sugar refinery in the world. Acquiring control of other *centrales*—sugar mills—and their lands, he tied them to the Haina complex. The Dominican Republic produces slightly less than one million tons of sugar a year. Sixty percent of this comes from the Haina complex. Thus, at six cents a pound, its annual production was worth $72,000,000. Yet Haina is inherently uneconomic. For Trujillo it was economic. He worked some of its land with slave labor, paying no wages, and other with Haitian labor, paying low wages. Moreover, Trujillo hauled sugar cane to Haina from the far north side of the island in Army trucks. After he was assassinated, it was considered that all the Trujillo properties belonged to the Dominican people and that they were of great value. Actually, few were—and the biggest white elephant of all was vast Haina. For without Army trucks and slave labor, Haina could not earn a profit.

Nobody knows how much money Trujillo sent out of the country in his lifetime, nor how much his family took out or sent out after his death. Most of it went into numbered accounts in Swiss banks. One careful estimate published in Europe in 1962 put the total at 800 million dollars. My own guess is far less—on the order of 150 million dollars or 250 million, though it is quite possible that by 1962 such a sum could have been used to gain control of assets worth 800 million.

This, we must remember, is cash outside the Republic. It does not include Haina, nor the farmlands, nor the factories inside the Republic. Trujillo, like many Dominicans, had an old-fashioned way of investing in real estate, and of paying cash if possible. No estimate of the total value of his holdings means much anyway. It is enough to say that for thirty-one years Trujillo plundered the Republic.

His private life was tangled. It is generally accepted that he had three wives and at least two mistresses and that he fathered at least nine children.

He had six brothers and four sisters. He made one brother, Héctor, President for two terms. Héctor, called Negro, probably because of his negroid features, appears to have been equable and unimportant. A second brother, Arisméndi, called Petán, was different. People feared Petán and called him crazy. He carried a submachine gun and always seemed to be about to use it. Perhaps even Trujillo feared Petán. Petán wanted to be President but Trujillo would not let him. Instead, he gave him, as a sort of feudal fief, the town of Bonao and the area around it running back into the high Cordillera Central. Here Petán had a private army, *Los Cocuyos de las Cordilleras*, the Fireflies of the Mountains. Here Petán ruled supreme. Bonao was the cleanest, most silent, most fearful town in the entire Republic.

Trujillo's other noteworthy relatives were his son, Ramfis, who was his apparent heir; his younger son Rhadamés; and his daughter, Angelita, married to Colonel Luís José León Estévez, a playboy crony of Ramfis. Other brothers and relatives were Army generals. Another seems to have been an unfortunate ne'er-do-well—when, after the assassination, he and the rest were obliged to leave, he boarded the airplane wailing, "I never got to do anything I wanted."

What did the Dominican people think of Trujillo? Who knows?

Almost certainly the upper class, including the oligarchy, despised him as a parvenu and a danger.

The middle-class businessmen, except those who worked closely with him and profited by it, probably disliked him, though after his death, some said, "After all, he did keep order."

As for the ordinary people, the *campesinos* and the city poor, who knows? His monopolies hurt them most of all—peanut oil, in a land abounding with coconuts, was the only cooking oil available, and extremely expensive. But the poor did not understand. His reign of terror bothered them least—they had neither property nor talents he needed.

The intellectuals—that curious Latin American classless class, educated for professions that do not exist, turning to politics for want of other occupation—probably felt his lash the most, and hated him the most.

But taking the nation as a whole, and thinking particularly of the poor, it would seem impossible that, after thirty-one years of constant propaganda, Trujillo did not command the allegiance of hundreds of thousands of the people. In villages all over the country, women to this day walk to a bubbling well, and over it is a sign: "Trujillo gives us our water." Well, he did have the well drilled. Before his death, in the humblest thatched huts around the countryside, the dwellers had scrawled, *"Dios y Trujillo."* Dominican *campesinos* are a little like the Negro sharecroppers of South Carolina: They are intelligent, they recognize danger and power instantly, and they have learned to conceal their true feelings. Who can say how many who erased *"Dios y Trujillo"* did so gladly, how many because the winds of power had shifted?

Trujillo was elected President of the Republic four times—in 1930, 1934, 1942, and 1947. Three times he chose not to run—in 1938 his handpicked candidate, Jacinto B. Peynado, was elected; Peynado died and his Vice President, Manuel de Jesús Troncoso de la Concha, succeeded him; in 1952 Trujillo's brother Héctor was elected; in 1960 Joaquín Balaguer, Vice President under Héctor, a wispy, pretended intellectual and poet who had served as a Trujillo front man for many years, became President when Héctor resigned. Nobody was fooled. None of these men ruled; Trujillo ruled. Neither they nor he had meaningful political opposition.

Now and then toward the end, when Trujillo wanted to bait the United States and promote the idea of "de-Trujilloization," he would bring in from exile a hired Communist, Máximo López Molina. Once Trujillo even gave López Molina control of a radio station. Then when Trujillo tired of him, or no longer needed him, the police would "discover" López Molina's "secret headquarters," smash it, and throw him in jail—then release him when Trujillo needed him next. I believe it happened thirteen times.

Although at various times when it suited his need for "de-Trujilloization" Trujillo made show of permitting political opposition, his basic method of political control was as simple and direct as his method of police control: Through the one party that was always legal, his party, the Partido Dominicano. Trujillo was the President of the Partido. That was the heart of his political power. (Just so, Party control is crucial in Soviet Russia.) Only the Partido could nominate candidates for election.

Trujillo handpicked them. On the day they took office they had to submit to him signed but undated resignations.

The Partido took 10 percent from all government employees' salaries. It used the money to pay its party workers, to profit its leaders, and to operate a national relief program for the poor. Membership in the Partido was automatic. Upon becoming eighteen every person had to have a *cédula.* This entitled him to vote, and by law, voting was compulsory. On election day, the Partido's precinct captains throughout the nation simply went around from house to house, collected everybody's *cédula,* took the *cédulas* to the voting place, cast the votes for Trujillo, had the *cédulas* stamped *Votado,* and returned them to their owners. Woe to him who later was caught with a *cédula* not stamped *Votado.* If he had not voted he was obviously a suspicious person.

During his time, Trujillo built two short concrete four-lane super-highways from the capital to Haina and the airport, and a highway, unfinished, to Santiago. He is usually credited with building other roads, but he inherited the basic road network from the U. S. Marines. He built housing and hospitals in the capital and the interior, though not much housing and ill-equipped hospitals. He is usually credited with having built schools. But the schools were few, and trained teachers scarce. He balanced the budget and increased national production. He paid off fully the internal and foreign debts. He liquidated the U.S. customs receivership and maintained the currency at par. He reorganized the banking system. He constructed many public buildings. By his decree, no man appeared on El Conde, the capital's main street, without a coat. The garbage was collected on time.

After his death some people complained that ragamuffins were everywhere, robberies increased, streets were dirty, garbage lay in the gutters, and men in T-shirts roamed El Conde. All true. Trujillo kept the peace— the peace of Trujillo. That was the trouble. The price of order was liberty, too high a price.

No good biography of Trujillo exists, nothing but books by sycophants or exiled enemies. It is a terrible story, the story of a people destroyed, a generation lost, a nation's character undermined. It is a dreadful story never written and never, perhaps, to be written. For the history of Trujillo's regime really lies in the files of his secret police, and those files, or most of them, were burned immediately after his assassination. What follows is not a history of his regime, but merely a few landmarks we may wish to remember as we move along in the 1960s.

2

He was not a big man, though official photographs in full regalia make him seem big. He was only five feet seven inches tall. In later years he was inclined to corpulence. Most of his later photographs have been so heavily retouched that it is hard to tell what he looked like. One taken in 1927 shows him oval-faced, with a brushy mustache, heavy-lidded eyes, a thin nose, a cleft chin, eyebrows that look plucked and, being raised a trifle, gave him a rather superior expression. His first inauguration photo, 1930, emphasizes that quality even more; he looks calm, superior, but not haughty, and almost compassionate, an odd word to apply to him. In most pictures his face is heavy and without expression; in some it is stern, forbidding, sometimes resigned at a ceremonial state occasion, occasionally hostile or suspicious. I do not remember a picture of him looking directly into a camera lens; his eyes are always averted and, so, masked.

He was born in San Cristóbal on October 24, 1891, the second of seven sons. His paternal grandfather had been an officer of the Spanish secret police during the Spanish restoration. Perhaps in childhood he acquired the curious nickname, *Chapita,* which never left him.[3] His first known job was as a telegraph operator, at sixteen. About that time he married his first wife, the mother of their daughter Flor de Oro.

It has often been said that the U. S. Marines, or the U.S. government during the Marine occupation, put Trujillo in power. That is not true. It is true that he rose from obscurity during the occupation. In 1918 he applied for a commission in the *Guardia Nacional,* the national police force, or constabulary, that the Marines had organized to replace the Army. Trujillo's official military biographer says he did so because of "the things he saw—our flag trampled, the army destroyed, and the country becoming more and more entangled in economic commitments." However dubious this proposition, the official statement is of interest since it contradicts the charge of U.S. support.

Trujillo was appointed a second lieutenant in the *Guardia* on January 11, 1919. In 1922 he was transferred to the Northern Department; two years later the commandant there "died tragically," according to Trujillo's biographer, and Trujillo replaced him, with the rank of major.

At that time, as we have seen, General Horacio Vásquez became the freely elected President, and the Marines withdrew. Sumner Welles' "new era" had begun.

Vásquez began well, and indeed ruled well. But, aging and ill, he made the fatal mistake of trying to extend his term beyond its constitutional limit. The ensuing political turmoil opened the door to Trujillo.

Early in his regime, Vásquez had transferred Trujillo to the capital and promoted him to lieutenant colonel, Chief of Staff, and Assistant

---

[3] *Chapita* is usually translated in the Dominican Republic as "scrap iron." Some say Trujillo as a child picked up pieces of scrap metal, or bottle caps, or coins, on the streets. *Chapita* is also a diminutive form of *chapa,* whose dictionary translation is "sheet [of metal], plate; veneer; flush (on cheek); rouge; (colloquial) judgment, good sense; (Latin American) lock." The plural, *chapas,* means the game of tossing coins.

Commandant of the *Policía Nacional*.[4] Numerous biographers, both sycophants and enemies, have said that Trujillo quickly caught Vásquez'
eye. Only eleven days after being appointed Chief of Staff, Trujillo suggested a "reorganization plan." On August 18, 1925, the Secretary of
Interior, Police, War, and Navy appointed Trujillo Commandant of the
National Police, closing his letter, "It is their duty to follow you on the
road to glory." At thirty-three, Trujillo was launched. Before long, the
public park next to Fortaleza Duarte in San Francisco de Macorís was
renamed Parque Coronel Trujillo—the first monument.

On August 13, 1927, Trujillo was promoted to brigadier general. *La
Revista*, official military and police publication, said: "It is essential that
this force [the National Police] become a true army. It is evident that
General Trujillo is the true creator of this corps. . . . The organization
of an army is always the personal work of a man. Caesar, Alexander the
Great, and Napoleon are but the creators of armies."

No public proclamation converting the Police into the Army appears
in Trujillo's military biography; but by January 16, 1929, the Dominican
Secretary of Interior was addressing Trujillo as "General Rafael L. Trujillo, Commander in Chief of the Army"—the occasion was a decoration
bestowed by the Mussolini government—and, replying, Trujillo identified
himself as Command in Chief of the Army. The official history of the regime, *La Era de Trujillo*, says that on May 17, 1928, "On his [Trujillo's]
initiative the National Police was converted into the National Army."
He had already created a Secret Police attached to the National Police.
Thus by mid-1928 or early 1929, the Republic had an Army and a Secret
Police, and Trujillo was the undisputed chief of both. Already a writer
in *La Opinión* had mentioned him for President. President Vásquez, who
had made him Army chief, was the first man he betrayed.

In February 1930, during the political turmoil over Vásquez' effort
to extend his term unconstitutionally, insurrection began in Santiago. Its
leader was Rafael Estrella Ureña. The rebels marched on the capital.
Trujillo kept his troops in barracks in the capital and offered no resistance. The U. S. Minister later reported, "There is no doubt whatsoever that [Trujillo] had been conspiring with the revolutionaries from
the beginning."

Once more the Dominican politicians met in the U. S. Legation. They
reached agreement—Horacio Vásquez resigned and Estrella Ureña became Provisional President. An election would be held May 16. Trujillo
would not be a candidate. (Trujillo was not a party to the agreement.)

---

[4] By this time, Dominicans were speaking of the *Policía Nacional*—that is, National
Police—not of the *Guardia Nacional*, the National Guard or Constabulary established by the Marines.

Soon President Estrella Ureña complained to the U. S. Minister that Trujillo would run for President using force and asked that the U.S. declare publicly it would refuse to recognize Trujillo's government if he were elected. The U.S. declined—the State Department instructed the Minister to advise Trujillo to abstain from politics and remain head of the Army, but not to offend him in case he disregarded the advice and won election. In retrospect, this may appear mistaken or even wicked. But at the time, in view of the Republic's past history, Trujillo may well have seemed just one more ambitious Dominican *cacique*. And why should the U.S. government publicly oppose a candidate in a foreign election in these circumstances?

Unable to beat Trujillo, Estrella Ureña joined him—he ran for Vice President on Trujillo's presidential ticket. The opposition slogan, *"no puede ser"*—it cannot be—was chalked on walls, and sometimes these words were added: *"por ladrón de caballos"*—"for [the] horse thief," a reference to the story that Trujillo's father had been arrested for stealing horses. Against the opposition, Trujillo unleashed terror. La 42, his gang of thugs, broke up political meetings, wrecked a union headquarters, and, when the opposition party went to court to contest Trujillo's packing of the Electoral Board, stormed the courtroom. I have been told that scores of Trujillo's opponents died or disappeared during that campaign. On May 14 the opposition candidates withdrew from the campaign. In the election two days later, Trujillo received 223,731 votes and his opponent 1883. The U. S. Minister reported that the total vote "far exceeds" the number of voters in the country.

The official Trujillo version, of course, differs. His military biographer wrote:

"Seven parties were ready to participate in the election of a Constitutional Government. . . . None of the parties was strong enough to defeat the others. Furthermore, none of them believed in political freedom or was interested in the progress of the country. The men who led the parties were selfish, petty politicians of the old school, incapable of mending their ways for the good of the country which had suffered for such a long time."

This reveals the Dominican military mind, seeking order, then and now mistrustful of politicians.

3

President Trujillo was sworn in on August 16, 1930. He consolidated power quickly. He smashed political opposition. He built his own party, the Partido Dominicano. Only two weeks after his inauguration a hurricane devastated Santo Domingo. Trujillo suspended constitutional guarantees, piled the bodies up, added, many claim, the bodies of his murdered enemies, and burned them to avoid a plague. He rebuilt the city and before long renamed it.

By 1932 nepotism had begun. Trujillo made his older brother, Virgilio, Secretary of Interior, Police, War, and Navy. He made his father a Deputy. He appointed his brothers, Héctor and Anibal military attachés abroad. And so on—his family, his relatives, and his favorites had the government. His daughter, Flor de Oro—Flower of Gold—married Porfirio Rubirosa, launching that man's flamboyant career.

Veneration began too. In 1932, a postage stamp commemorated Trujillo's birthday. A province was renamed for him. Congress passed an "urgent" resolution naming him Benefactor of the Fatherland. Former opponents eulogized him. Two men were nearly ruined because they neglected to mention Trujillo's name in public speeches. Even the respected newspaper *Listin Diario* began to use the new system of dating things according to the year of "the Era of Trujillo."

By the time I arrived in 1937, it was clear that Trujillo was firmly in power. He had, however, committed his first serious blunder: The Haitian massacre.

In the first few days of October 1937, Dominican troops slaughtered some twelve thousand Haitians inside the Dominican Republic.[5] (Haitians, crowded and starving at home, spill over the border constantly, seeking space to live and a job cutting cane.) After investigation by an international commission, Trujillo paid an indemnity of $750,000 to Haiti, about $62.50 per Haitian if twelve thousand were killed. He also announced the imprisonment of sixteen men who were "responsible."

Why Trujillo perpetrated the massacre has never been clear. His enemies said he did it to avoid paying Haitian cane-cutters the wages due them. His apologists said he was "purifying" the Dominican "race" or protecting the Republic from its ancient enemy, Haiti. (Haitian currency was circulating in the Republic at the time.) No doubt ancient hostility played a part. So did racism—Trujillo insisted the Republic was a "white nation." The massacre is all the more puzzling inasmuch as before the massacre Trujillo had taken pains to improve relations with Haiti.

The massacre rallied world opinion against Trujillo. And it forced him to abandon election to a third term in 1938. In his stead, Jacinto B. Peynado was elected. But Trujillo was re-elected in 1942, announcing, "I will continue riding my horse."

World War II gave Trujillo a splendid opportunity to rehabilitate himself. He had always followed the United States line. Already he had

[5] Estimates of the number massacred range from five thousand to twenty-five thousand. The truth is probably about twelve thousand or fifteen thousand, though nobody knows. The Haitians were killed in scattered *bateys*—settlements—in small towns and on sugar lands throughout the Republic, though the heaviest slaughter evidently occurred in the west, near the border.

signed, with Secretary Cordell Hull, a treaty finally freeing Dominican customs. Trujillo traded heavily on this, naming a principal street in the capital for Cordell Hull and erecting a statue in his honor. Now at war, the United States wanted stability in the Caribbean; Trujillo could provide it. He used the "Good Neighbor Policy" to tighten his grip at home. For this reason, the "Good Neighbor Policy" became odius in the Republic, and after Trujillo fell, Hull's statue was one of the first to be pulled down. Trujillo declared war on the Axis. He invited Jews who escaped Hitler to find haven in the Republic, and they came and established a colony on the north coast at Sosua.

4

The end of World War II set new tides in motion. Trujillo needed to permit the appearances of democracy, but he had to be careful, lest he lose control. During 1945 and 1946 he played a dangerous game. He decided to establish diplomatic relations with Soviet Russia. He maneuvered deviously with Dominican Communists, first encouraging them, then jailing them. He invited other political parties, long banned, to become openly active. He encouraged a labor movement to begin. He sent an emissary to a leading newspaper to urge it to criticize his regime. Real clandestine opposition began among university students. Finally, military officers plotted against his life.

Things had gone too far. He executed the plotters, smashed the clandestine opposition, and clamped down iron rule.

World events played into his hands: Soviet Russia became the adversary, not the ally, of the West. Trujillo sought to become the leading anti-Communist in Latin America. He issued anti-Communist declarations and rounded up "Communists" in the Republic. And the Cayo Confites expedition played into his hands, too.

The Cayo Confites expedition was launched by the Caribbean Legion. Although sometimes called a Communist movement, the Legion was apparently principally composed of exiles from various dictator-ridden nations of the Caribbean and Central America, plus the usual number of Caribbean political adventurers. Their avowed purpose was the military overthrow of dictators. Trujillo was their first target. They hoped to prevent his inauguration on August 16, 1947. Indeed exile action was by then the only hope. For Trujillo had smashed all internal opposition.

The Caribbean Legion, after training in Cuba, gathered on Cayo Confites, a tiny, deserted key off the Cuban coast. Present were many men we shall meet in the Republic during my ambassadorship—Juan Bosch, General Miguel Ángel Ramírez Alcántara, Diego Bordas, Horacio Julio Ornes, Juan Isidro Jimenes Grullón, many more. If everyone who later claimed he was at Cayo Confites had actually been there, the invaders could have overwhelmed Trujillo by sheer numbers. The leader or financial backer was Juan Rodríguez García, called "Juancito," a wealthy landowner of La Vega who had fallen into Trujillo's disfavor. The invaders had collected three ships, guns, ammunition, and probably several light bombers, all purchased in the U.S.

The plan was supposed to be secret but the leaders were little better at keeping their secrets than the Cuban exiles of the 1960s. Finally, neither the U.S. nor the Cuban government could ignore it any longer—the U.S. shut off arms purchases, and the Cubans told the invaders to disband.

They decided to sally forth anyway. The Cuban fleet seized them the next day. So ended the first attempt to overthrow Trujillo by invasion from exile.

Next year the Caribbean Legion successfully invaded Costa Rica, installing as President "Pepe" Figueres, leader of the Caribbean non-Communist left. Two Dominicans played key roles—General Ramírez (he was a general of the Costa Rican Army), and Horacio Julio Ornes, Dominican politician and brother of the editor of *El Caribe*. Of General Ramírez and Ornes we shall hear more.

In 1949, "Juancito" Rodríguez and General Ramírez led the second anti-Trujillo invasion from exile, the invasion of Luperón. Luperón is a hamlet on the north coast of the Republic near Puerto Plata. Several airplanes took off from Guatemala on June 19. All but one stopped on the Mexican island of Cozumel. A seaplane commanded by Horacio Julio Ornes, carrying fourteen other men, landed on the sea before Luperón. The invaders hoped to move on to Puerto Plata, where they expected to find revolutionaries ready to rise. But in Luperón a Dominican soldier shut off the electric power. In the darkness Ornes' invaders commenced shooting at each other, killing one and wounding one. Government troops arrived. The invaders returned to their seaplane, but in the darkness took off in the wrong direction and ran aground on the beach. Trujillo's coast guard arrived. Four invaders fled; later, they were reported killed in battle. Three burned to death when coast guard fire destroyed the plane. The remaining seven took to the hills. Two escaped and later were announced dead. Ornes and four others were taken prisoner. Originally sentenced to thirty years' imprisonment—the maximum sentence in the Republic, which has no death penalty—at least two of them were subsequently released. The two were Horacio Julio Ornes and Tulio Arvelo. (Arvelo became in time a leading Castro/Communist.)

These threats disposed of, Trujillo installed his brother Héctor as President in 1952 and ascended to the international scene. Appointed Dominican Representative to the United Nations with the rank of Ambassador, he traveled to New York and Washington and, according to his official history, was received by both President Truman and President Eisenhower—he arrived during the interregnum and stayed beyond the inaugural—had interviews with both Secretary of State Acheson and Secretary Dulles, attended or gave luncheons and dinners and receptions at which he met numerous senators and generals and State Department officials, signed a treaty of mutual defense, and everywhere played the role of the arch enemy of communism in the Caribbean. He traveled to Spain and was received in state by Franco. Back home, he was visited by Vice President Richard Nixon. He began maneuvers to establish his son Ramfis as his heir.

Many people say the United States "supported" Trujillo. At times we smiled on him, at times we frowned, usually depending on our current position in the world (though sometimes appearing to depend on our Ambassadors' personal inclinations). During World War II we were friendly, for we needed stability in the Caribbean. In the 1950s we turned against him, as Latin America did. One measure of our "support" is this: During the fifteen years between 1946, when our foreign aid program began, and 1961, when Trujillo died, we loaned or gave him some five million dollars. In 1962–63 we loaned or gave his democratic successors some seventy million dollars.

In 1955, the anniversary of the first quarter century of his rule, Trujillo held a World's Fair. It was to run for two years. He built its grand structures on the seafront, at the edge of the capital where Avenida Jorge Washington sweeps curving along the sea toward San Cristóbal. He spent at least fifty million dollars and publicized it lavishly in the United States. But few tourists came, and the Fair was a disaster.

Thereafter, the scene darkens. Some people say that in these later years Trujillo lost his mind, crazed with power. He was in fact sixty-four years old. Some think he had kept the lid on so tightly for so long that the pressures simply exploded. He seemed to lose the skill of years, to revert to the terror with which he had begun. In any case, from the ill-omened Fair onward, it was all downhill for Trujillo.

5

In 1956 Dr. Jesús María de Galíndez disappeared. Galíndez had been teaching in exile in New York at Columbia University and had written a book about Trujillo. The full truth about what happened to him never has become known. Throughout my time in the Republic the case was under investigation by Dominican and American authorities. After Galíndez disappeared, the story was published that he had been kidnaped in New York, drugged, put aboard a private plane piloted by a young American flyer, Gerald Murphy, flown to the north coast of the Dominican Republic, then flown to the capital by a Dominican pilot, Octavio de las Maza. There, it was said, on Trujillo's order, Galíndez was executed. The motive advanced was the book and, more particularly, its supposed slighting references to Trujillo's mother and its statement that Ramfis was an illegitimate child, born to Trujillo's mistress before he divorced his second wife and made her his third.

I have never considered the book a sufficient reason for murder. It is a scholarly doctoral dissertation, not a sensational exposé. While it says that Trujillo was a megalomaniacal tyrant seeking personal power and wealth, it also says, "The Trujillo regime is not a bloody one when compared to some other Latin American tyrannies. It also has to its credit a very considerable record of economic improvement." As for the story that Ramfis was an illegitimate child, I had printed it myself in 1938, and it had been a joke throughout the Caribbean for many years. Nor did Galíndez write slightingly of Trujillo's mother.

The Trujillo regime, of course, always denied it had anything to do with Galíndez' disappearance.

Numerous alternative theories have been advanced—that Galíndez was killed over funds he had collected for the Basque government-in-exile, that he had been a CIA agent or a double agent, that the killing had been private, that he had disappeared voluntarily.

To this day the case is open. Galíndez' body has never been found. My own opinion is that Galíndez was killed in the Republic on Trujillo's orders and his body thrown in the sea. (He may have been choked to death by Trujillo himself.) This is not an official view—I encouraged the investigation, and did everything possible to assist it but never asked the results, feeling they might impede my own work.

The American flyer Murphy disappeared, too, and his body has never been found either.

The Trujillo regime said Murphy had been murdered by Octavio de la Maza, the Dominican pilot. Octavio de la Maza, according to the Trujillo version, was arrested for the murder of Murphy and hanged himself in his cell, leaving a suicide note confessing the murder of Murphy and saying he had killed him because Murphy had made homosexual advances to him.

It has since been rather well established that Octavio de la Maza's suicide was a fake. The hook, or pipe, from which he was supposed to have hanged himself was apparently not strong or high enough to support his body, and the "suicide note" was forged.

My own opinion is that Gerald Murphy was murdered in Santo Domingo, and his body thrown to the sharks; and that Octavio de la Maza was murdered in his cell in Fortaleza Ozama. Murphy probably was killed because he knew too much about Galíndez' disappearance. Octavio de la Maza may have been killed for the same reason, though he is said to have turned on Trujillo and to have been plotting to assassinate him.

In any case, the death of Octavio de la Maza was an important event in the tangled chain of events that led, five years later, to the assassination of Trujillo himself. A prime mover in the assassination plot was Antonio de la Maza, seeking revenge for his brother's murder.

No single event, not even the Haitian massacre, had hurt Trujillo's international reputation as much as the disappearance of Galíndez. And now another force manifested itself in the Caribbean: Communism—for Fidel Castro took Cuba and marched into Havana on New Year's Day, 1959. Trujillo had aided the Cuban dictator Batista; his arms factory at San Cristóbal had worked "day and night" manufacturing arms for Batista, according to a Trujillista. On the morning of that New Year's Day in 1959 when Castro entered Havana, Batista arrived in Ciudad Trujillo.

One of Castro's principal aides in the Sierra Maestra had been a Dominican and, after Castro won, he persuaded Castro to bring a Dominican exile group from Venezuela, give it a training camp in Cuba, and train its men in guerrilla warfare.

At dusk on the 14th of June, 1959, the Dominicans, some fifty-five strong, made the first of three landings in the Dominican Republic: In a DC-3 airplane, piloted by a Venezuelan, at Constanza in the middle of the Republic's central mountain range; six days later two landings by boat brought another 180 men to Estero Hondo and Maimón, towns on the north coast. They came from Cuba, eighteen or twenty Venezuelans, ten Cubans, two Americans, the rest Dominicans, including sixteen Communists; and it was widely considered the first attempt by Castro to extend his revolution "from the Sierra Maestra to the Andes." Since then, however, people involved have said bitterly that Castro double-crossed the invaders.

In any case, they failed. Trujillo's troops quickly caught and killed them. "It was a rabbit hunt," one officer recalls. A half-dozen were killed in fire fights in the hills. Most surrendered and were taken to San Isidro Air Base and butchered. Some were killed in the electric chair at La Cuarenta, a torture chamber. Trujillo's son, Ramfis, was in charge.

In the Republic, a slang word for homosexual is *pájaro,* bird. One invader was thought to be a homosexual, and he was put aboard a plane at San Isidro, taken aloft, and dropped out, "to see if the bird can fly," as Ramfis is said to have put it. Young Air Force officers were ordered to stab the prisoners repeatedly with their daggers, "to toughen them up."

Only three Dominican—and two Cuban—invaders survived. Some who perished belonged to leading families of the Republic. Hatred of Trujillo deepened, and among influential people. Ever since, "Constanza, Maimón, and Estero Hondo" have become a Dominican slogan for heroism and martyrdom, and the 14th of June, the date of the landing, is a powerful symbol in the Republic's politics.

During December of that year, 1959, and in the early weeks of 1960, the SIM suddenly arrested more than three hundred men inside the Republic whom it accused of plotting against the regime. This huge roundup involved many prominent citizens, including, for example, a leading heart specialist, Dr. José Fernández Caminero, later a Consejero, and many young intellectuals and students, including Manuel Tavárez Justo. Today some say the entire incident was trumped up by agents provocateur of the SIM. But it seems likely that at least some of those arrested were indeed involved in plots against Trujillo. Apparently a number of underground cells were scattered through the Republic, each small, few connected, so that the arrest of one man could endanger only a few.

Some of the prisoners were tortured severely. About sixty were killed, some in the electric chair at La Cuarenta. Some bore torture heroically. Some who survived recall that they were held for many months, and their relatives had no idea where they were; they had simply disappeared. A few were Communists when arrested. Others became Communists during their imprisonment.

It was in Trujillo's prisons that the 14th of June movement was born. The men imprisoned had not actually been involved in the invasion at Constanza, Maimón, and Estero Hondo on June 14, 1959. But in prison, and later when freed, they came to be known as "the 14th of June group." This later became the leading Castro/Communist political movement in the Republic.

Meanwhile, Trujillo made another disastrous move. He tried to have President Rómulo Betancourt of Venezuela murdered, and almost succeeded. They had been enemies for a long time. Trujillo apparently believed Betancourt had aided the 14th of June invaders. Exiled Dominicans such as Juan Bosch had found congenial asylum in Venezuela. In the United States John F. Kennedy was running for President, and after he was elected he espoused the cause of the non-Communist democratic left, which offered a democratic alternative to both Castro's communism and Trujillo's tyranny, and of which Betancourt was the pre-eminent leader. On June 24, 1960, while Betancourt was riding in a parade, a device detonated explosives concealed in a parked car along the parade route. Betancourt's hands were badly burned and he was fortunate to escape alive, but the man sitting next to him was killed. The SIM, under the direction of the odious Johnny Abbes, had bungled.

Betancourt promptly asked the Organization of American States to move against Trujillo. While the United States supported Betancourt's position, we were also interested in obtaining action against Fidel Castro. In August 1960 the OAS meeting of Foreign Ministers in Costa Rica reasserted that "any form of totalitarianism" is incompatible with the inter-American system and rejected "the attempt of the Sino-Soviet powers to make use of" the situation in any Hemisphere state. The OAS found that "high officials" of the Dominican government had aided the attempt on Betancourt's life. The OAS at its meeting in San José declared the Dominican Republic an aggressor nation and imposed diplomatic and economic sanctions. It required its member states to withdraw their ambassadors from the Dominican Republic and forbade them to export to the Republic, first, arms and, subsequently, on January 4, 1961 by vote of the Council of the OAS, trucks and truck parts, petroleum and petroleum products. The sanctions hurt. Without trucks or repair parts or gasoline, the Republic's wheels would in time stop turning, and so would its economy.

By law, the United States had been paying a premium price for Dominican sugar above the world market price. The Eisenhower administration, acting in the spirit of the OAS sanctions, imposed a special tax on Dominican sugar equal to the U.S. premium. In a little more than a year this amounted to some $22,750,000—money which Trujillo would have received. Before many months passed, the sanctions, plus Trujillo's own plundering, brought the Republic's economy near ruin. Finally, the moral effect of the OAS sanctions, making the Republic a pariah, hurt Trujillo badly.

But the Generalissimo careened on. To a diplomat's suggestion that he retire, he replied, *"Señor Embajador,* I will retire when I am killed." That November 1960, while the prisons still were filled with political prisoners, three pretty young sisters were murdered, the Mirabal girls. One of them was married to Manuel Tavárez Justo, then in prison. He later became the leader of the 14th of June movement, and his wife's death gave the 14th its martyr. Another was married to Leandro Guzmán, also then in prison and later Tavárez Justo's closest associate. The brief newspaper story published at the time said that the three sisters were killed accidentally when the Jeep in which they were riding plunged over a cliff between Puerto Plata and Salcedo. The truth was that they had been murdered by SIM agents.

The girls had been arrested before, and had made no secret of being enemies of the regime. According to a subsequent indictment, Trujillo himself had said on November 2 that he had only two political problems left—the Catholic Church and the Mirabal family. The Mirabal sisters visited their husbands regularly in prison in Puerto Plata. On November 25, 1960, five SIM agents in a truck waylaid them on a mountain road, took them and their driver away, probably to a nearby *finca* belonging to Trujillo, and strangled and beat them to death. They then put the four bodies in the jeep and pushed it over the cliff.

Two years later, Trujillo himself having been assassinated, the accused SIM agents were convicted. Five were convicted of the actual murders, three being sentenced to thirty years' imprisonment and two to twenty years. Their two superiors were convicted of complicity and sentenced to twenty years. The defense was in part the Nuremberg defense—they had no choice but to carry out orders. They served notice of appeal. The indictment declared that the "intellectual author" of the murder was Trujillo himself.

6

On the night of May 30, 1961, Generalissimo Trujillo was assassinated.

I have heard it said that more than a hundred plots against his life existed at that time. That is not impossible. The leaders of the one that succeeded were Juan Tomás Díaz and Antonio de la Maza. Antonio de la Maza, as we have seen, was a brother of Octavio de la Maza, murdered in the Galíndez case; he once had been a captain in Trujillo's Corps of Military Adjutants. Juan Tomás Díaz had been a general in Trujillo's army. Díaz' sister, apparently fearing she had fallen under suspicion of opposing Trujillo, had taken asylum in the Argentine embassy. Trujillo sent Díaz to persuade her to leave. Díaz failed. Trujillo publicly humiliated him, hit him across the face with his riding crop, and stripped him of his rank. No Dominican can endure public humiliation; it strikes at his most precious possession, *macho*—that is, manhood. Juan Tomás Díaz began, early in 1961, to plot against Trujillo.

The full story of the 30th of May plot has never been told and probably never can be told, for all but two of the plotters are dead and most of the documentation was burned by the SIM. From various conflicting sources I have reconstructed it as best I could—the contradictions among the sources cannot be reconciled—along the following lines:

About twenty people were directly involved beforehand. Others knew of the plot then, still others were drawn in later. The plot was in three parts. One group of eight men, the actual gunmen, would kill Trujillo. They would deliver his body to the second group at the home of Juan Tomás Díaz. This group would present the body to General José René Román Fernández, Secretary of State for the Armed Forces. General Román would take over the government. General Román was married to a niece of Trujillo. Shortly before the assassination, Trujillo gave Román $130,000 (paid a $400,000 debt he owed, by one account). He was almost a member of the family, although later he told one of his inquisitors that Trujillo constantly called him stupid, imbecilic, and idiotic, apparently for no other reason than to humiliate him. Seeking power, and resenting Trujillo's unconcealed scorn, Román joined the plot. He was drawn into it by Luís Amiama Tió.

As we have seen, Luís Amiama Tió turned out to be one of the two survivors of the plot and later became a Consejero. Formerly he had been a businessman who had operated a string of filling stations and had been well connected in high political and military circles. Amiama Tió and General Román had been close friends for many years and were the godfathers of each other's children. In February 1961, Amiama Tió, attending a birthday party for General Román at the General's valuable country estate, told him that he, Juan Tomás Díaz, and Antonio de la Maza, were plotting to kill Trujillo, and invited General Román to join them. Román, interested, said he thought it unnecessary to murder Trujillo—they need only kidnap him and force him and his family to leave the country. Amiama Tió said this was naïve. General Román told him to return with a detailed plot. He did—Trujillo himself would be killed; all other Trujillos would be arrested and deported; President Balaguer would be arrested; Ramfis Trujillo, who was in Europe, would be arrested if he returned; a military junta would be installed with General Román as its head; Juan Tomás Díaz would be restored to the rank of general and made a member of the junta; and three months later elections would be held.

General Román agreed, though he had no intention of holding elections. He would use the troops to seize the government only if the assassins would actually show him Trujillo's body. Thereafter, Amiama Tió addressed General Román as the future strong man of the Republic. But weeks passed, and months, and nothing happened. And General Román, incredibly, decided the whole thing was a game. It slipped his mind. He forgot it.

Not only did the plotters fail to keep General Román informed of their progress that spring, they did not prepare a plan for their own escape if the plot failed. They did not even maintain close liaison between their own two key groups—the gunmen and the Díaz group. The whole affair was rather haphazard—all but the assassination itself.

The plotters had little in common. Several were military men in Trujillo's service. Nearly all were in one way or another involved with him, and some were close to him. Their motives varied. To be charitable, some were undoubtedly pure patriots. In some, patriotism mingled with self-defense. And some may have been merely adventurous young men.

Several had a personal reason—revenge. Juan Tomás Díaz had been publicly humiliated by Trujillo. Antonio de la Maza had sworn to avenge the death of his brother, Octavio. Trujillo evidently had feared the De la Maza family for a long time. It was a large family and is said to have maintained something approaching an armed encampment at its farm. After Octavio's death, Trujillo sent a general to see to it that they lacked for nothing. He especially charged the general to visit Antonio de la Maza himself frequently and, if he ever had a problem, to report immediately to Trujillo, who would take care of it. Once Trujillo sent Antonio de la Maza twenty thousand dollars and a fancy revolver. Several times he visited him personally. During this period, De la Maza became involved in several scrapes involving land and women; Trujillo knew but did nothing.

Antonio Imbert Barrera, one of the two survivors and later a Consejero, had been governor of Puerto Plata province under Trujillo. His brother, Segundo Imbert, had been the most powerful—and some say the cruelest—military man in that province, but he had fallen into Trujillo's disfavor and, suspected of being connected with the Luperón invasion, had been sentenced to thirty years' imprisonment.

Luís Amiama Tió once told me the story of his own involvement, saying, in the end, simply, "I had to do it. It was him"—Trujillo—"or me."

Modesto Díaz, a cousin of Juan Tomás Díaz, had once been close to Trujillo but had fallen into disfavor—had appropriated property, ordered people arrested or killed and run off with their wives, all in Trujillo's name but without his knowledge, according to a Trujillista—and finally Trujillo had sent word that their former friendship was ended and Modesto must stop bothering him. Now Modesto joined the plot.

An investigator once provided this background on Miguel Angel Baez Díaz, another cousin of Juan Tomás Díaz: Miguel Angel Baez Díaz said that long ago a close Trujillo adviser had told Trujillo in Díaz' presence that Díaz had no interest in affairs of state but only in drinking and girls. Trujillo had laughed and asked Díaz to introduce him to some girls. Díaz had introduced him to one he had been keeping; Trujillo liked her and kept her himself. Díaz resented it. Years later, Trujillo criticized Díaz harshly in front of his friends, saying he was tired of fathers complaining that Díaz had taken up with their daughters and then abandoned them. Later Díaz' own daughter had become Trujillo's mistress; when Trujillo tired of her, he ordered an Air Force lieutenant to marry her, and she died brokenhearted. The lieutenant, for revenge, paid court to Trujillo's favorite daughter, Angelita, married to Colonel Luís José León Estévez, and also to Colonel Estévez' own girl friends. Before long the lieutenant died in "an accident," actually murdered for his sexual adventures. At the time of Trujillo's assassination, Miguel Díaz still was close to Trujillo. Visiting his cousin Juan Tomás Díaz one day that spring, he found him talking conspiratorially to several men and asked what was going on. Juan Tomás Díaz told him. Miguel Díaz joined the plot, observing that if it failed, Trujillo would kill half the population of the Republic.

And so on—each for his own reason joined the plot. One, Huascar Tejeda Pimentel, an unemployed architect who was drawn in when he went to Juan Tomás Díaz to borrow money, said he didn't know how to handle a gun. Juan Tomás Díaz replied, "All you have to do is pull the trigger." The list of people who knew about the plot is astonishingly long. Some thought to warn Trujillo, but did not because they feared he would laugh at them, humiliate them, or even punish them.

For weeks during the spring of 1961, the gunmen laid their plans and awaited a propitious time. Every night just before dusk Trujillo was accustomed to walk from his home to a broad residential street, Avenida Máximo Gómez, and downhill on that street to Avenida Jorge Washington by the sea, where he would sit on the seawall and talk with his cronies; then his car would pick him up and take him home. The assassins had absolutely no chance of killing him during this period. His gunmen lurked behind every well-trimmed hedge and nobody was allowed on the street. But on some nights, as mood moved him, he would don his dress uniform and, after returning home, be driven to San Cristóbal. On that occasion, and only on that one, was he without bodyguard—accompanied only by his driver who, though armed, was unskilled in gunplay.

Juan Tomás Díaz provided three cars. A Spanish mechanic rebuilt their engines so they would go more than 125 miles per hour. At the garage De la Maza ordered a hanger-on to transfer two burlap bags from one car to another. They were filled with guns. Night after night the gunmen deployed the three cars along the route Trujillo would take. Two who were engineers tried to estimate auto, wind, and bullet velocity. They kept rehearsing. And awaiting word that Trujillo was going to San Cristóbal. It came late in May, and they deployed, ready; but Trujillo was sick and did not go. A week later, on May 30, he went.

At 8:30 P.M. one of the plotters, Lieutenant Amado García Guerrero,[6] of Trujillo's Corps of Military Adjutants, telephoned the officer on duty at Trujillo's house and asked if Trujillo was leaving. The officer said

[6] Juan Bosch appears to consider Amado García Guerrero the most admirable of the assassins. In his book, *Crisis de la Democracia de América en la República Dominicana,* written in exile after his overthrow and published in November 1964 in Mexico (all quotations refer to the English translation, *The Unfinished Experiment: Democracy in the Dominican Republic,* New York: Frederick A. Praeger, 1965), Bosch writes, "Lieutenant García Guerrero, a man of humble origin, had that integrity and moral fiber that are found in the common people of the Dominican Republic, but not in the middle class, except under rare circumstances." As a member of Trujillo's Corps of Adjutants, Bosch says, García Guerrero learned to hate the vulgarity and rapacity of Trujillo and resolved to free his people. Once, a month or two after he joined the plot, Bosch writes, García Guerrero was summoned in the middle of the night to La Cuarenta by the SIM and there ordered to kill a prisoner. It was a test, Bosch writes, and García knew it—if he refused, they would torture him to learn the names of his fellow conspirators. He took the pistol from the chief of the SIM and shot the prisoner dead. Thenceforward, Bosch writes, García Guerrero lived only to kill Trujillo.

Trujillo had already donned his uniform. This meant he was going to San Cristóbal. Lieutenant García Guerrero notified Juan Tomás Díaz. He alerted the assassins in the cars, parked near his house. Trujillo went for his nightly walk with, among others, General Román. He was picked up as usual in his bulletproof Chrysler Imperial. Unexpectedly Trujillo first took General Román to San Isidro Air Base for a surprise inspection—he had found "irregularities" there earlier that day. (By one account a guard had failed to call "Attention" when he arrived.) Trujillo then went home, changed cars to a 1957 or 1958—the authorities differ on this and other details—Chevrolet, and about 9:25 P.M. left for San Cristóbal.

As he turned from Avenida Máximo Gómez onto Avenida Jorge Washington, the first carload of gunmen fell in behind him—Salvador Estrella Sadhala and Pedro Livio Cedeño.

As he passed the Fairgrounds, the second car of gunmen fell in behind—four men, Antonio Imbert driving and Antonio de la Maza sitting beside him; in the back seat, probably, Lieutenant García Guerrero and Bienvenido García.

The third—Roberto Pastoriza and Huascar Tejeda Pimentel—waited up ahead, parked across the double-lane highway, a roadblock just beyond the end of the string of fluorescent street lights, at the edge of darkness. Dominican nights in the countryside are black.

As Trujillo's car approached the roadblock, the second car following his drew alongside. Antonio de la Maza had a double-barreled 12-gauge shotgun. He fired through the rear window of Trujillo's car. By most accounts, that first shot tore Trujillo's side away and probably would have been fatal. De la Maza fired the second barrel through the side window of Trujillo's car, and his companions fired on the car with .38s and .45s. They speeded up, passed Trujillo's car, and at the third-car roadblock whirled their own car around and stopped, their headlights aimed at Trujillo's oncoming but rapidly slowing car. The first assassination car, still behind Trujillo's car, made a sudden U-turn and headed back to town, perhaps in confusion, perhaps in last-minute panic, and one of the two men in it, Pedro Livio Cedeño, fell out on the parkway separating the traffic lanes and was shot in the fire fight that now began.

According to Trujillo's chauffeur, when the first shot was fired, Trujillo said, "Stop the car. We will fight. I have been wounded." The chauffeur saw the rear window was blown out and Trujillo was leaning on the right door, bleeding. He suggested turning around and fleeing. Trujillo said it was too late; they must get out and fight. The chauffeur stopped, bright headlights of the two cars facing him blinded him, and, inexperienced, he didn't think to shoot the lights out. The assassins were shooting and Trujillo got out the right rear door. The chauffeur, still behind the wheel, smashed the windshield and began firing with a San

Cristóbal automatic carbine. He was hit once, then again, then several more times. He emptied the thirty-shot San Cristóbal, picked up another, emptied it, picked up a 9-millimeter Luger, emptied it, staggered out, saw Trujillo lying on the pavement, dropped his gun, walked to a low concrete wall, sat down blinded by blood, and fell over the wall unconscious. (Miraculously, he survived, and is today in Puerto Rico.)

The assassins, who had been firing crouched behind their two cars, advanced. They found Trujillo lying on the road. De la Maza said he was dead. Pastoriza, who had not yet fired, now fired a *coup de grâce* bullet into Trujillo's head, then jumped on his face and head. De la Maza said, "This son of a bitch will not kill any more people," and dragged the body by one foot to one of the assassination cars. They put it in the trunk of the car. They moved Trujillo's car, partially concealing it in shrubbery. From it they took his briefcase containing three hundred thousand dollars. Four of the assassins were wounded, Pedro Livio Cedeño the most seriously. All went to the home of Juan Tomás Díaz and reported. Díaz and Amiama Tió viewed the body. The gunmen had done their part—assassinated Generalissimo Trujillo.

Thereafter the plot collapsed.

Confusion prevailed. Unaccountably, the plotters did not immediately take the body to General Román; they left it in the trunk of the car parked at Juan Tomás Díaz' house. They scattered, some to go into hiding, some to seek medical attention for the wounded gunmen, some to try to see General Román.

But a SIM agent got to General Román first.

By coincidence almost too strange to be coincidence, Arturo Espaillat, Trujillo's intelligence aide, had been following Trujillo's car when the two assassins' cars passed him and fell in behind Trujillo. (A variant version is that Espaillat was at The Pony, a restaurant at the Fairgrounds favored by young Trujillistas.) Hearing the shooting, he hurried to the home of General Román. Román telephoned SIM headquarters. SIM agents sped to the scene. So did General Román. Only then, Román later declared, did he recall Amiama Tió's plot.

Román and a SIM man went to Román's house, and Román telephoned the Army, Navy, and Air Force chiefs and ordered them to mobilize all troops and take orders from him alone. He was surprised they were already at their posts—the SIM had already notified them. General Román telephoned SIM headquarters and told the officer in charge to tell Johnny Abbes, head of the SIM, to report to military headquarters. This would set the *coup d'état* in motion. But the SIM men were suspicious. The weapons at the scene had led them to conclude quickly that the plotters had been military men. The plotters' next logical move would be to seize control of the SIM. So they telephoned Abbes, and he, agreeing, came to SIM, not military, headquarters; and they barricaded it and stationed three men with machine guns at each window, ordered to fire on any Army troops who approached.

Juan Tomás Díaz and Luís Amiama Tió made one or two attempts to see General Román at his house and to telephone him at the Palace that night. They were too late. Román made one half-hearted effort to carry out the *coup*—he ordered soldiers to President Balaguer's house. But again the SIM was ahead of him. That was the end of the plot to take over the government. The plotters could do nothing now but hide.

That night the Dominican Republic was entirely in the hands of the SIM. By 3 A.M. they had filled the jails and prisons and fortresses of the Republic with enemies of the regime. SIM agents found Pedro Livio Cedeño at a hospital; delirious, he kept repeating "Juan Tomás" and "De la Maza."

At about 1 A.M. the SIM arrested the only De la Maza they knew in the capital, Ernesto de la Maza. He was taken to the SIM's torture chamber, La Cuarenta, and the man in charge was ordered to make him talk. Other SIM men, meanwhile, had accounted for the whereabouts of most high-ranking military officers and so concluded that the plotters were former military men, not ones on active duty. When Pedro Livio Cedeño mentioned "Juan Tomás," they remembered Juan Tomás Díaz. Before they acted, however, Ernesto de la Maza, fearfully beaten, talked—he said his brother Antonio, Juan Tomás Díaz, and others had plotted to kill Trujillo.

SIM men went to Juan Tomás Díaz' house. In the house they found Trujillo's briefcase, containing $230,000—several plotters before scattering had taken $70,000 from it—and, outside, the assassins' car with Trujillo's body in the trunk. An investigator[7] who was present recalls the sad scene when they found the body: "Among those present, Colonels Abbes and Figueroa Carrión and their retinue, was produced a sepulchral silence. And instantly all broke into tears. It was evident that they loved Trujillo like a father." They took the body to the Palace and laid it on Trujillo's bed in his upstairs apartment.

At La Cuarenta, SIM agents were beating and questioning Ernesto de la Maza. He furnished nine or ten more names. Then he collapsed. A doctor said he was dying. The SIM men carried him outdoors and laid him under a tree, and he died.

The SIM began hunting those he named, found some that night and forced them to talk. The family had notified Ramfis in Paris, and he chartered a jet and arrived, one hand bandaged because of a polo injury, with his entourage the next day. The SIM was holding the Re-

[7] Teodoro Tejeda. Tejeda was prosecuting attorney in Ciudad Trujillo at the time. In his book, *Yo investigué la muerte de trujillo* (Barcelona: Plaza & Janes, S.A., 1963), he claims that Ramfis put him in charge of the investigation. Others have made the same claim.

public for him. He took charge. He ordered the investigation moved from La Cuarenta to Kilometer 9, the torture chamber of the SIM branch attached to his Air Force. By then—it was less than twenty-four hours after Trujillo was shot—it took fifteen trucks to move the prisoners.

Sheer nightmare ensued. All the hate, all the fury, all the contempt for the people and the feelings toward the *Jefe,* Trujillo, all the sadism and techniques of torture were vented now upon the assassins and their relatives. How many were killed is unknown. How many were tortured is unknown. How many were simply arrested, questioned, and then released is unknown. The death agony of the Trujillo regime perhaps has no parallel. Men, women, and children were arrested. Of all those arrested around the nation, at least one hundred received the personal attention of high SIM officials at La Cuarenta and Kilometer 9. Throughout this entire period, the President of the Republic was Joaquín Balaguer.

7

With a few exceptions, the women—wives and daughters of suspects or of people related to suspects, including the wives of Imbert and Amiama and Amiama's young daughter—appear not to have been mistreated physically, though some were held for weeks. But the men were stripped naked and beaten mercilessly with clubs and fists and pistols, shocked in the electric chair, and choked. If one refused to talk, his son was seized and in front of him threatened with torture. A homosexual was brought in, and two prisoners forcibly photographed compromisingly with him. One prisoner was taken out of his cell and strangled by two soldiers; his body was taken out the Boca Chica road to a grove of palms and thrown into *La Piscina,* "the swimming pool," the deep, shark-infested place in the sea. Another man died in the electric chair simply because a bungling inquisitor gave him a heavier shock than he intended, angering his superiors. A key figure, Lieutenant García Guerrero, was killed by SIM agents who went to arrest him. A brother of General Román, questioned at great length and then released, committed suicide when agents arrived to rearrest him. A son, an aide, the adjutant, and the driver of General Román all were arrested, along with a sergeant who happened to be at Román's house, and killed forthwith in the electric chair at La Cuarenta. So was a son of Juan Tomás Díaz. Segundo Imbert, serving his prison sentence in La Victoria, was killed, according to the prosecutor Tejeda, by order of General Román. So was another prisoner there. Two common criminals hoping to curry favor tried to tell Ramfis that high SIM officers were in the plot; they were murdered. The father of one suspect requested permission to kill him. Another De la Maza brother was strangled to death in his home.

There had been, I believe, seven De la Maza brothers in all. Today only one is alive. (In 1964, attached to the Dominican Embassy in Bonn, he was involved in a killing, according to press reports.)

Ordered to search every house in the city for the last two plotters, Luís Amiama Tió and Tony Imbert, SIM agents looted heavily. The price on Imbert's head was ten thousand dollars dead or alive; on Amiama's, twenty thousand dollars alive, nothing dead. Throughout, old rivalries among the various intelligence services hampered the investigation. None trusted the other. One night several Air Force officers showed up at Kilometer 9 and said everyone else was torturing the prisoners, why not they? Every now and then Rhadamés Trujillo and his young cronies would stop by from a party, call for the prisoners one by one, put them in the electric chair, give them shocks, beat them with riding whips and fists, kick them, apply electric prodders to their genitals, and throw red ants and itching powder on them, laughing the while. Ramfis himself, determined to root out the conspiracy fully, tried to restrain senseless sadism and killings, at least until he was certain the prisoners had told all they knew. He gave much appearance of being courteous to women. And when SIM agents proposed to torture General Román after he was taken prisoner, Ramfis told them imperiously, "He is a general," and forbade it.

The places where some of the plotters hid had better be kept secret, even now. It is public knowledge, however, that one hid in the rectory of a church and that two slept one night in a tile factory owned by Manuel Tavares, a wealthy and intelligent young member of the oligarchy. Tavares was imprisoned.

The two chief plotters, Juan Tomás Díaz and Antonio de la Maza, together with Salvador Estrella, hid in the home of Dr. Robert Reid. They originally had gone to him to get first aid for Estrella. They stayed several days. Apparently the pressure crazed one or two of them; bestiality ensued, and when, to escape the horror inside, Estrella bolted for the dangerous outside, he was caught almost instantly and forced to tell where he had been hiding.

As the SIM closed in on the Reid home, Juan Tomás Díaz and Antonio de la Maza fled. They stole a car, had dinner at a public restaurant, were recognized by a general who notified the SIM, slipped away again, and were seen a few minutes later near Parque Independencia. All SIM cars—all Volkswagens (and even today the hum of a Volkswagen sounds sinister in the Republic)—closed in on them at Parque Independencia, and one hundred agents killed them in front of the hardware store on the corner. When the SIM came for Dr. Robert Reid, he committed suicide.

The main "investigation" went on for about three weeks. The last to break was General Román. Although not tortured like the others,

Román was kept sleepless for many days and nights in a small room absolutely bare of furniture, bright lights on his eyes, and if he tried to lie down, or sit down, or if he fell asleep standing up, he was wakened. It was a trick borrowed from the Soviets. Once a stupid jailer allowed him to go to sleep; the painful process had to begin all over. Finally he confessed.

He was tried by court-martial—curiously, only he and Manuel Tavares were tried at all, so far as I know—and sentenced to thirty years' imprisonment. Subsequently General Román was given "truth serum," something new to the SIM, and under it confessed that had the plot succeeded he had intended to shoot or deport all members of the Trujillo family as well as the Estévez brothers and Johnny Abbes and other SIM leaders.

After his court-martial, Román was mistreated and tortured almost continuously by Ramfis, Rhadamés, and others. Finally, according to one authority, Ramfis ordered General Román taken in the trunk of a car to Ramfis' *finca;* Ramfis took him to the firing range, showed him his father's famous big revolver, a .357 magnum on a .44 frame, and shot him fifty-three times, reloading eight times, commencing with the feet and slowly working up to the face and head. He then ordered the body put in a burlap bag and, with a caravan of more than a dozen cars, took it by night to *La Piscina*. There in a palm grove by the sea a colonel ordered every officer present to plunge his knife into the body. All did, then threw it to the sharks.

Early in July, the SIM began moving from place to place the important prisoners still alive—OAS investigators were coming. One, Miguel Ángel Baez Díaz, apparently was murdered at this time. Months later, after many events had intervened, the SIM still held six—Pedro Livio Cedeño, Modesto Díaz, Salvador Estrella, Huascar Tejeda Pimentel, Roberto Pastoriza, and Luís Manuel Cáceres Troncoso. On November 18 Ramfis Trujillo was forced to leave the country, but before departing he ordered those six taken to Nigua, near San Cristóbal and Haina, and there he and several close associates killed them. So ended the bloodbath in which the Trujillo regime had been born and drowned.

Trujillo had entangled many men in his murderous schemes. He had despised them and ruled them by fear. Fear breeds hate, as does indebtedness, and in the end it was all the collective hate in the Republic that brought Trujillo down. Like so many in Dominican history, he had carried within himself the infinite capacity for evil, and self-destructive evil, for by creating the military machine that gave him power, Trujillo ultimately destroyed himself.

The only two survivors of the 30th of May plot, Luís Amiama Tió and

Tony Imbert, did not come to the surface until after all the Trujillos had departed in November.

Memorial tablets have been placed at the locations where some of the 30th of May group died. At the scene of the actual assassination a modest monument was erected, inscribed with this line:

Gloria a la Gesta Liberatadora del 30 de Mayo.

Tony Imbert's Christmas card in 1962 displayed a picture of the scene. It is just a spot on the four-lane road, not far beyond where the city dumps garbage and the SIM dumped bodies to the sharks, the sea on one side, scrubby trees and a fence and a few palms on the other. My wife and I used to drive at dusk out to this place, to drive by slowly. I do not yet quite understand why we did it. We never saw other sightseers there; Dominicans sped by heedless. Now, living in the United States, it seems a little macabre. It did not then, and there.

Chapter Four

PRESIDENTIAL MISSION: 1961

After the 1960 election campaign I had returned to writing, declining the proposal of an ambassadorial post. In February 1961, before Trujillo's death, my wife and I had gone to the Caribbean and had stopped briefly in the Dominican Republic, taking the precaution of sending our itinerary to friends in the White House, and leaving carbons in my briefcase in the hotel. Back home, I had sent a memo to Arthur M. Schlesinger, Jr., in the White House, reporting some things I had learned about Trujillo and Castro.

After Trujillo was assassinated, I told Schlesinger and others that if we sent an Ambassador to the Republic, I would like to be considered.

One day at the end of that summer, in remote Upper Michigan, I came out of the woods in a Jeep to be told that President Kennedy had been telephoning me. By the time I got my call through, the President had left Washington; I talked with his brother-in-law, Steve Smith. He said the President wanted me to come to Washington at once about the Dominican Republic. I arrived in Washington on Labor Day 1961.

There I was told that at a meeting on August 28 the State Department had asked President Kennedy for some policy decisions on the Dominican Republic. The main question was: Should we urge the OAS to lift its sanctions against the Republic? This, in effect, would mean that we regarded the sanctions as directed against the Generalissimo personally and that, with him gone, we now accepted his heirs as rulers of the Republic. President Kennedy felt he lacked sufficient facts to base policy on. He wanted me to go to the Republic, investigate, and report to him.

I spent a week reading the cables and getting my bearings in the State Department. The Department, vast and new and blocky, seemed sterile. I got lost in its endless corridors down which, occasionally, anonymous people moved on unknown missions, silent men with papers, girls carrying coffee, all sound muffled and subdued. The building seemed like an abandoned hospital from which all the patients had fled. Desks were nearly always empty. No papers lay atop them, the drawers were empty. The reason, of course, was security: When a man left his office, his secretary locked his classified papers in padlocked steel filing cabinets. It was an eerie place, somehow Kafkaesque. High on the seventh story were offices of the Secretary and the Undersecretaries, richly carpeted in blue, paneled in brown wood, a world power center, outwardly quiet and orderly, inwardly seething.

The Department's basic organization is geographic. Below the Secretary and the Undersecretaries sit the Assistant Secretaries for regions of the earth—Latin America, Southeast Asia, and so on. Under each Assistant Secretary sit the directors of various offices—under Assistant Secretary Ed Martin were the regional directors for the offices of Caribbean-Mexican Affairs, Central American Affairs, West Coast of South American Affairs, and East Coast of South American Affairs. And under them sit the country desk men, one for each country—Dominican desk, Haitian desk, Bolivian desk, etc.

In addition, the Department is cross-hatched horizontally—administration, economic affairs, public information, visas, cultural affairs, protocol, international organizations (UN, OAS), and so on. It also contains numerous other sections, including the message and operations centers to which upwards of half a million words in cables come each day from our embassies around the world.

Everybody knew that what we did in the Dominican Republic that summer had extraordinary importance throughout the Hemisphere. In his inaugural address, President Kennedy had proposed the Alliance for Progress; in March he had made his proposals more specific; in April the Bay of Pigs had occurred; and on August 17, in the very midst of the Dominican crisis, the Charter of Punta del Este had actually established the *Alianza*. But what mattered immediately was that several million Dominicans had suddenly been set free. What were we going to do to help them?

I arrived in Ciudad Trujillo, as Santo Domingo still was called, on my presidential fact-finding mission September 10. I was there a little less than a month. Joe Fandino, the student affairs officer at the U. S. Consulate, assisted me. (John Hill was *chargé d'affaires;* we had had no Ambassador since OAS sanctions had been imposed the preceding August.)

Ramfis Trujillo, behind his puppet President Balaguer, was making great show of "democratizing" the Republic. He wanted the OAS sanctions lifted, which would help him keep power.

The opposition declared his "democratization" a sham. It wanted the OAS sanctions kept on. I talked to leaders on both sides, to ordinary

Americans and Dominicans, to workingmen, businessmen, and professional men—to everyone I could.

The capital was a silent city. As soon as the swift tropic dark fell, the city went dead. Restaurants were deserted; so were hotels, barrooms, and the streets. There was such a stillness in the city those nights it was almost tangible. It was the breakup of the old order.

Exiles were bravely addressing mail to fearful friends "Santo Domingo," and Castro's Radio Havana was blaring, "Don't trust the OAS and the *Yanquís*—we have twenty-four thousand machine guns for you," but Dominicans were silent, waiting. For what?

People were leaving, sending their families to the United States, and everywhere Joe Fandino and I went, people pleaded for visas. Army troops, armed with San Cristóbal carbines, controlled the capital streets. Ramfis had changed the name of the SIM and sent the notorious Johnny Abbes out of the country; but the SIM was the same. We saw SIM men, wearing sport shirts outside their pants to conceal their pistols, in restaurants, on the street, entering a house to search it, driving about in their Volkswagens. They were still hunting Amiama and Imbert. One man I interviewed seemed inordinately nervous; later I learned Amiama had been hiding in his house while we were there.

Calié were everywhere. The radio in my room at the Hotel Embajador contained a microphone. Phones were tapped, rooms bugged. The SIM hired gangs of alley thugs, called *paleros*—clubbers—to terrorize the anti-Trujillo opposition; they roamed the streets of Ciudad Trujillo by night, carrying clubs and rocks and nail-studded baseball bats. In Santiago, the opposition hired bands of thugs of their own, and the two met in nightly street battles.

In the interior at least two private Trujillista armies stood waiting: *Los Jinetes del Este* (The Riders of the East), about forty-five hundred cowboys, controlled three remote eastern provinces for Senator Felix Bernardino, once Dominican Consul General in New York and a notorious Trujillo henchman; and *Los Cocuvos de la Cordillera,* six thousand mountaineers, controlled Bonao for the Generalissimo's dangerous brother Petán. Fandino and I expected to be stopped only at checkpoints en route to Santiago, but once two soldiers with San Cristobáls stepped out of a thicket, made us get out, opened the trunk, and searched the car.

Most people we talked to were afraid. "A shattered country," my notebook reads. Time and again they said if the United States didn't help them there would be a bloodbath, or they would go Communist—asking us to save them from themselves. They seemed disoriented. Dominicans in those days were like moles blinded by sudden sunlight. A lawyer who aspired to political leadership asked me for copies of the U.S. and Uruguayan constitutions and of political party platforms—soon he might have to draft a Dominican platform and constitution. I suggested he go to the library. He stared at me as if I were insane: Trujillo had permitted no such subversive literature.

Two days after I arrived, an OAS mission came to study the sanction question, and a crowd gathered at the traffic circle at the Río Ozama bridge to demonstrate. While they were waiting, the chauffeur of the brother of Luís José León Estévez, the cruel young man who was married to Trujillo's daughter Angelita, tried to drive León Estévez' Mercedes through. The crowd, evidently recognizing it, stopped it. The chauffeur stepped out shooting, spraying the crowd with an automatic rifle. Two men fell dead, many were wounded, and the crowd scattered.

That afternoon I went downtown with two or three U. S. Consulate attachés. Calle Conde was jammed curb to curb, indeed wall to wall, with people, young and old, men and women and boys, shirt-sleeved, sweating. Cars crawled through the crowd a few feet at a time, four or five policemen at each corner doing nothing. The crowd booed the police, clapping their hands and chanting rhythmically, *"Da-da, li-ber-tad; da-da, li-ber-tad,"* over and over, beating out the rhythm on the stalled automobiles. Those shouting were mostly young. Older men stood silent. The sun blazed on the white and yellow storefronts. Stores were closed and steel-shuttered, their owners peering out through slits. Somewhere a bell was tolling. Loudspeakers boomed from the second-story headquarters of two of the new political groups that had sprung up.

That night I went downtown with Fred Somerford, the shirt-sleeved U.S. labor attaché. Parque Independencia, shrine of Dominican liberty, was still jammed, cars loaded with young men circled the Parque in slow procession, honking their horns in the five-beat chant, *"Da-da, li-ber-tad"* over and over and over, and the crowd took it up, chanting. Vendors moved about selling cigarettes—a penny each—Chiclets and *galletitas* (crackers) and children walked around holding up signs, *"Libertad."* Police watched from balconies, waiting; and on shadowy sidestreets, in dark doorways stood little restless groups of men, waiting, too.

Walking through the Parque near the bandstand, we stopped to talk to two boys in their twenties, and one, a dark thin lad with gleaming white teeth, wearing khaki pants and a *guayabera,* a white sport shirt, said tensely, spreading his tendon-tautened arms wide and low, "Everywhere we gather, the police club us down." In a moment there were thirty more around us, then fifty, all talking at once—"We should be allowed to speak," "We are hungry," and "They wrecked the FNR headquarters," and, over and over, "The Trujillos must go."

Somerford offered one a cigarette; the others clawed at the pack, tearing it apart, emptying it. One, realizing Somerford was a U.S. official, asked for a visa. Somerford gave him his card, and instantly all closed in, yelling for visas, clutching at his cards, crying *"Consulado Norteamericano,"* though one said to me, "If you don't help us, we're going to ask

Russia," and another, "You may be an agent." Somerford, short, fat, affable, and out of cigarettes and cards, moved smiling to the street, I with him, and the crowd followed, cheering, slapping us on the back, shaking hands, blocking traffic, bicycles and automobiles, a policeman helpless, until finally we found a taxicab. Riding along Jorge Washington by the sea, the moon behind the palms, passing a fashionable seafront restaurant, Somerford said, "Even Vesuvio's is closed. Those boys would risk anything anywhere. They could burn the city. They'd as soon go up against the troops as not. They'd tear down the statues, set fire to the homes. They are hungry. They've done without a hell of a long time."

A little later, sitting in the bar of the Hotel Paz, I heard a strange sound on Avenida Independencia. It was like a huge machine used to sweep streets. But too loud and metallic—I went to look. The tanks were coming. There were nine or ten of them, a soldier in the turret of each with a San Cristóbal carbine. They were Ramfis' tanks. A crowd gathered in front of the hotel to watch silently. The tanks turned the corner, crossed Avenida Cordell Hull, drove through the turreted gate, and disappeared into the Fortaleza across the street from the hotel.

A hotel maid murmured, tentatively, *"Tanques de guerra."*

I said in Spanish to a young Dominican in a white shirt next to me, "Tanks against the people."

He looked up at me, his brown eyes wide, but said nothing and turned away.

Another man said flatly, without expression, "For protection."

Nobody said anything more.

Next morning I found their treads: They had left the Fortaleza later and headed back toward the center of town on Jorge Washington.

At 10 A.M., a mass was scheduled at ancient Columbus Cathedral for the two men whom the chauffeur had killed at the bridge, and I went downtown to watch from a second-story window across the street. By nine, scattered knots of people had gathered in the shaded Parque Colón, near the statue of Columbus, in front of the great Cathedral. Squads of khaki-clad soldiers were arriving in Jeeps and armored trucks. Armored cars were parked in sidestreets. The Cathedral was already filled. More people came to the park. The troops formed a skirmish line under the balcony of a massive Spanish government house. At a few minutes past ten, they stepped out of the shadows of the balcony and, guns unslung and carried slantwise at port arms, crossed the street in a ragged line. The crowd in the park broke and ran, flowing like running water through the palms across the park. The great doors of the Cathedral swung open, and hundreds of people came out, women wearing black dresses and black lace mantillas, men in black or in white with black sleevebands, a priest in his robes leading them, all moving slowly across the Parque past Columbus' statue and starting up Calle Conde, hundreds more pouring out of the great cavernous Cathedral behind them. They were going to walk to the homes of the dead men to get the bodies and bear them to burial.

Now from other streets came more people, hundreds of them, then thousands of them, all walking slowly up Calle Conde, choking it wall to wall, black suits against white walls in the morning sun, all moving silently. Long after the first had disappeared thousands kept coming. They walked all the way to the cemetery, miles away, beyond the Upper Town. Busloads and truckloads of police were there, waiting. And thousands of automobiles and thousands of people, all silent. This was no mob of street ruffians. Some belonged to the leading families in the Republic. At the cemetery gates, the police refused to let them in; they had no permit. They stood quietly, waiting before the iron gate. The police said they must get the permit forty-eight hours in advance.

One of the mourners said, "If you want us to get a permit in advance, you will have to give us forty-eight hours' notice of the next murder so we can comply with the law." It was past noon when they buried the bodies.

2

I interviewed opposition leaders at length, some of them several times. Scenes remain, and men.

The leader of the UCN—Unión Civica Nacional (National Civic Union) was Dr. Viriato Fiallo, a big, elderly, graying, friendly man, politically naïve, brave, once a foe of the Marine occupation, later a foe of Trujillo. He received me first rather formally in his doctor's office in his house in the old Spanish part of town. The second time he unbent and took me to the patio for a glass of *guanábana* juice, a Dominican fruit drink.

The UCN represented the middle and upper class. Born in Santiago about a week after Trujillo had been shot, it was spreading now throughout the country. It forswore politics, insisting it was not a party but a civic movement. Dr. Fiallo was rapidly becoming a national hero, symbol of the respectable resistance. The night before I saw him, a gang of *paleros* had attacked his home.

Dr. José Fernández Caminero, later a Consejero, a heart specialist, belonged to both the UCN and the 14th of June, the young people's movement that the Castro/Communists hoped to capture. The 14th was split; Fernández Caminero hoped to fuse its moderate elements with the UCN. Like many of the 14th's members, he had been imprisoned in 1960 after the invasion of June 14, 1959, and released only after Trujillo's death. Recalling his months in prison, he said, "One thing gave me hope. Someone smuggled in a translation of President Kennedy's speech about the *Alianza*. From then on we came to think that at last and finally the

United States was going to pay some attention to Latin America. It would be a fantastic hurt if those hopes were ever cast down."

One Sunday the UCN held an outdoor meeting on Jorge Washington, and I watched from a second-story balcony. Down below, the crowd was gathering. Delegations began pouring in from the sidestreets, bearing banners naming the towns they came from; and as each arrived a man's strident voice roared from a loudspeaker, "Moca is here," "Azua is here," "Monte Cristi" is here, and the crowd on the street took up the cry.

The UCN's purpose was to put pressure on the OAS to keep the sanctions on and thus force the Trujillos out. Each delegation bore signs, *"Libertad"* and *"Viva Democracia"* but also "OAS—Now or Never" and "OAS—Open Your Eyes." A holiday atmosphere prevailed, the sign-bearers snake-dancing through the crowded street. This was *libertad,* forbidden for thirty-one years.

The speaking began, speakers talking endlessly; but the crowd paid little heed. A group would start a chant, set to the hand-clapped five-beat rhythm, *"Da-da, li-ber-tad," "Tiranía no, Democracia sí,"* and the whole crowd would take it up, the speaker falling silent or joining in. Then they set up a new chant, this one more ominous—"Boo boo Balaguer."

Until then the speakers had been careful to avoid the names of either Trujillo or President Balaguer. But now the roaring "Boo boo Balaguer" rolled across the square, echoing from the old Spanish buildings, out to sea. The speaker nervously tried to break in.

The main speaker, Fiallo, began. He spoke of the two men killed at the bridge, "killed for doing nothing but claiming liberty," and the crowd broke loose, chanting and clapping powerfully, *"Qué se vayan los Trujillos"*—the Trujillos must go. Squads of police watched from the mouths of the sidestreets. Fiallo went on: *"El noble sufrido pueblo Do-minicano"*—the noble suffering Dominican people.

Out of the brilliant sky over the sea appeared an airplane, diving steeply down at the crowd, down, down, then at treetop height leveling suddenly and flying flat along the seawall behind the palms, its roaring engine drowning out the speaker's voice. It was gone in a moment; silence ensued. Uncertainly, Fiallo began again. But the crowd was watching the plane. It banked sharply out to sea, turned tightly into the sun, and dived again, this time flattening out so low it was beneath the palms, almost skimming the heaving sea.

It had come from Ramfis' airbase, San Isidro, and its purpose was to harass the meeting. It kept it up. At first, the crowd watched with interest, as a crowd might at a county fair, but its mood changed swiftly to hatred. Fiallo called on Balaguer to stop the plane; and the crowd broke loose again with its five-beat handclap chant, "Boo boo Balaguer," and then another, *"Asesino,"* assassin, a chilling word coming from twelve thousand throats. The sun on the balcony where I stood became scorching; a woman beside me held a parasol over my head. It attracted the attention of the people below. I told Fandino the parasol was conspicuous. Too late: Rumor swept the crowd, and in a moment everyone had turned to face me, and in another moment the speaker announced: "There is a representative of the OAS on the balcony." The crowd cheered loudly and pressed toward me, thrusting signs up, "Washington— Don't Repeat the Stupidities of Cuba," "Santo Domingo is the Berlin of the Americas," and "OAS—Libertad." Then suddenly everyone in the crowd began to wave a white handkerchief. Looking out, all you could see in the heat and blinding sun was the sea of white handkerchiefs; all you could hear was the roar "Boo boo Balaguer," and *"Qué se vayan los Trujillos."*

I told Fandino, "We'd better get out of here, we're breaking up the meeting." I waved to the crowd then slipped out the back door.

Those were the Dominican people, and they looked to us.

One day I climbed three or four flights of narrow stairs on Calle Conde, meeting at each landing men armed with long sticks and iron pipe, emerged onto a flat rooftop, and crossed it to a little wooden shed, where Ángel Miolán, leader of the opposition PRD—Partido Revolucionario Dominicano—was at work on a radio broadcast. The PRD was an exile party. It had been founded in Cuba in 1939. Its maximum leader, Juan Bosch, had not yet returned to the Dominican Republic. The PRD was generally considered to be left of the UCN, to represent the lower classes, and to be the most professional of all the political parties. No wonder. Miolán, a short, square-built powerful man with an Indian's copper skin, high cheekbones, and straight black hair, had learned his politics from Lombardo Toledano, the Mexican Communist, politician, and labor leader, though many of his ideas seem to have come from Haya de la Torre's non-Communist APRA in Peru. Miolán talked little and gave an air of knowing exactly what he was about.

I found the leader of the 14th of June in the little out-of-the-way home of a relative—Manuel Tavárez Justo, called "Manolo." Many U.S. officials already considered the 14th of June Communist-dominated. I was far less sure. It exerted a powerful pull on young people, especially students—it had originated in a clandestine plot to assassinate Trujillo, whereas the UCN was a post-Trujillo civic movement with respectable middle-aged leaders. But that certainly didn't make it Communist-dominated.

Manolo Tavárez Justo was thirty-six, tall, slender, handsome, olive-skinned, with luminous tragic dark brown eyes, a soft sad voice, a subdued manner, and delicate hands. There was a messianic quality about him. In Trujillo's prison, he was said to have borne torture bravely. That, and the murder of his wife, one of the Mirabal sisters, had given the 14th of June a mystique, martyrs, and a heroic leader—assets no other Dominican political group had.

He told me the story of his wife's death. He told it often, in public speeches. He told me, too, the story of his party, "born out of desperation." I asked about its program, and, like nearly every political leader I talked to, he was first vague, then pompous and empty. But how, really, could he, or others, be expected to be otherwise only three months after Trujillo died?

In two or three conversations with me, Manolo Tavárez Justo did not use the Communist jargon or follow the Communist line. I put him down as a Dominican nationalist. He would, however, be a real asset to the Communists if they could capture him.

Everybody knew the 14th of June was deeply split. A struggle was going on to capture Tavárez Justo—a struggle between such "moderates" as Fernández Caminero and such extremists as Alfredo Manzano, some of them Communists trained in Havana or Moscow. I talked to Alfredo Manzano. He was a rather short young man, hard, intelligent, disciplined. For an hour, Manzano evaded every question I asked. A few times he used the language of Communist dialectics. But mostly he evaded, and seemed to enjoy it. There was no way, really, to talk to him. I left, convinced I had finally met one of the new breed of Moscow-directed Dominicans.

I thought we should help the moderates in the 14th of June against the Manzanos. For I felt that the 14th of June might well turn out to be the party of the future—its appeal was to the young, the fervent, the intellectual or pseudo-intellectual, and in a revolutionary time those are the people who will win, not the moderates nor the oligarchy nor the old-fashioned hack politicians. If we turned our back on Tavárez Justo, he would move leftward, toward Fidel Castro. But at the same time I did not feel we could support him wholeheartedly. He was a liar; he told me his party was not split; he shrugged off Manzano as inconsequential, though from other inquiries I knew better. There were good people in the 14th; but unless we were prepared to plunge into the struggle for control of it, we dared not support its leader.

That weekend the 14th held its first rally in Parque Colón, and I attended. It was a hot Saturday afternoon, raining off and on, and the crowd in front of Columbus Cathedral was small but enthusiastic. It cooled off after two hours of speeches and toward dusk drifted away, though the speeches, in Dominican style, went on late into the evening. But I shall never forget one thing. Before the speaking started, a group of girls and women standing in the rain beside the speaker's platform, in front of the ancient Cathedral, sang *a capella* the Dominican national anthem, and the crowd stood, and fell silent, bareheaded, a vast silence in the city with only the thin voices rising:

I

Quisqueyanos valientes, alcemos
Nuestro canto con viva emoción
Y el mundo á la faz ostentemos
Nuestro invicto glorioso pendón.
¡Salve! el pueblo que intrépido y fuerte
A la guerra á morir se lanzó
Cuando en bélico reto de muerte
Sus cadenas de esclavo rompió.

Ningún pueblo ser libre merece
Si es escavo indolente y servil;
Si en su pecho la llama no crece
Que templó el heroismo viril.
Más Quisqueya la indómita y brava
Simpre altiva la frente alzará;
Que si fuere mil veces esclava
Otras tantas ser libre sabrá.

Bold Quisqueyans, let us raise
Our song, with all emotion vibrant;
It plainly to the world displays
Our glorious, unconquered pennant.
Hail that people, fierce and proud,
Which casts in battle life aside,
In warlike challenge of death's shroud
Breaks the chains that held them tied.

No nation has its freedom earned
If it in servile slavery kneels,
If in its breast the flame n'er burned
Which manly heroism steels.
Quisqueya still, untamed and brave,
Will always raise on high its brow;
If yet a thousand times made slave,
That many times will freedom know.

The author, Emilio Prud'homme, had been a Dominican teacher, lawyer, and poet who inflamed the Republic's youth against the dictator Ulises Heureaux—and later was honored by the dictator Trujillo.

Máximo López Molina was head of the MPD, Movimiento Popular Dominicano. Although he had been Trujillo's paid Communist, his MPD became the terrorist wing of the Communist movement. I found López Molina in a tenement in the old Spanish quarter near the waterfront—a high, yellow, thick-walled building on a narrow clamorous street, the interior dark, a patio rising like a well open to the sky, stairs climbing steeply, tiny bedrooms off balconies above, López Molina in one of them. Poor, dark-complexioned, soft-faced, he described himself as a "professional revolutionary." Born in the Dominican Republic, law student there, he was jailed by Trujillo in 1946, went to Cuba, was jailed there by Batista, and worked with Castro.

López Molina spoke forcefully. But when I asked if he had been with Castro in the Sierra Maestra, he said, surprised, "Oh no—I'm not a shooting man." I could believe him—he acted anything but dangerous. But he had terrorists with him. López Molina may have started out as a genuine Communist revolutionary, returned to the Republic attempting to turn Trujillo's predicament to his advantage, been caught in the shifting political tides, and ended as "Trujillo's Communist," of little use to anybody. I thought he was playing the same game in 1961: Alone among opposition leaders, he did not say that Ramfis Trujillo must go. I think he was working for Ramfis as he had worked for his father, possibly even taking money from both Castro and Ramfis.

3

I talked with dozens of other people—university students, some of them considered Communists, though I didn't think they were; businessmen who, convinced that all the Trujillos must go, wanted the sanctions kept on even though it would hurt business; a frightened Negro dock worker who hoped to organize a union; a wizened little Communist, flesh shrunk so his skin hung loose, "Twenty-three years fighting," he said, a defeated man now, one of twenty-five brothers whose father, hating Trujillo, had given them all the same first name to plague the secret police.

But I think the people I remember most vividly were two women. One night in the capital I was picked up by a friend and driven all around the city, twisting and turning, until I was hopelessly confused, then taken to a house and into a bedroom and told to wait. After a time, a stranger brought a woman in, young, slender, dressed in black, with high cheekbones and dark hollow eyes. She looked disheveled.

She apologized—they had brought her here on foot across vacant lots and wire fences. Her husband was Manuel Tavares, member of the oligarchy, businessman, educated at Yale, owner of the tile factory where two of the assassins had hidden. He was still in prison.

His wife had gone to the police, to "the security people," to the Ministry of Justice, to the Palace—through her family connections, she even had gotten to see President Balaguer himself. But the security people told her the case was in the hands of the Minister of Justice, Justice said the reverse, and the police said the Procurador General—Attorney General—was handling it. His office said he was unavailable, but she went back six times, and finally he gave her permission to go to La Victoria prison. But when she got there, they told her her husband wasn't there. Finally, she learned her husband was, in fact, at La Victoria, and she took food and clothes once a week, standing in line with other women.

She had been there today. She never could see her husband. She wanted help. And she wanted the United States to know what was going on. "Nothing is changed. A different boss; junior, not senior. All this talk of democracy is a big show. He [Ramfis] can't be good if he was born bad. Since he was a child, all he saw was murder. There's been thirty-one years of murder. People now don't want any more Trujillos," and she clenched her fist and leaned forward tensely. "If it doesn't happen now, it will happen later and be worse." She meant a bloodbath, and many said the same.

Had she gone to see the OAS mission, now here?

"No, I'm afraid to go alone. I have no confidence the OAS would protect him. If those sanctions are lifted and Ramfis gets a little stronger, then we'll have it." She was speaking rapidly and tensely. "People say the United States has a debt with the Dominican people after the occupation for eight years and the Trujillo regime supported for thirty-one years. President Roosevelt used to say he is an SOB but he's our SOB. There is a feeling that if you won't help us, we will let anyone else do it. But we don't want to. We go to vacations in the United States, we send our children there to school, not to Czechoslovakia. Those sanctions—please don't lift them."

One day in Santiago while I was having lunch outdoors by the empty swimming pool—the Hotel Matúm itself was almost entirely deserted—a waiter in a dirty jacket brought me an engraved card: "Ana Idalia B. [Bermúdez] de Batlle."

She was waiting, well-dressed, handsome, an *oligarquista*, sitting stiffly upright on the edge of a broken-down chair near the dirty bar, staring straight ahead. When I told the waiter to ask her to join us, she walked toward us, almost trance-like, very tall, very pale, dressed all in black—the whole Republic was in mourning in those days. She sat stiffly erect at our table, and tried to speak calmly about Trujillo and the sanctions, but it poured out: Her brother had recently been killed by Ramfis' troops; mail was still being opened, the press censored, there were shootings nightly in the streets, and beatings; the regime was putting on a show of democracy for the OAS but nothing had changed.

She had read in the press that the Americans feared chaos, and perhaps a Communist takeover, if Ramfis left. She said the OAS mission had flown to Santiago for one day. "We went to the airport," she said. "The OAS men had one hundred guards with machine guns. The officer in charge—we know him but they don't. He is one of the worst, a hyena. Mrs. Cabral"—a sweet, kind, educated woman who later became our friend—"Mrs. Cabral and I went together, and the officer pushed us with a machine gun and told us to leave. We walked, we didn't run. He was furious. He told the OAS that 'all those Santiago whores were here.' That's the way things run around here. My sister-in-law and I went up to make a crowd, the townspeople applauded, they cried out, 'Here are Erasmus' widow and his sister. Open up and tell them they are here; they speak English,' and I tried to tell them but I was very nervous and excited. I was well impressed, though." Then suddenly, sitting in the shade at our table, upright in a wire-backed chair, she began to weep, and, fumbling, unknotted her balled handkerchief and took out two bullets: "This is what they used on my brother. This is the democracy we have."

4

The Hotel Matúm stands on a high hill overlooking Santiago. And in front of it, dominating Santiago, the city he never had really controlled, Generalissimo Trujillo had erected a statue of himself, ugly, massive, powerful. Stonecutters prospered under Trujillo—monuments and tombstones. The statue sat on a great mound of earth hauled up the hill by hand. Men must have built pyramids this way. Even now the work had not quite stopped. Tiny figures toiled, aided by a huge steamroller built in the 1920s, a ponderous machine with heavy flywheels, chugging, grinding away. It made no sense—if the regime fell, so would the statue. But the work went on anyway, unable to stop. And it seemed to symbolize the regime: Ponderous, clumsy, repeating the old slogans, chugging away senselessly, but in low gear, unable to stop, an anachronism but still powerful.

One Saturday afternoon in Santiago I went to a Partido Dominicano rally held in the concrete baseball stadium, below a cliffside of slums. Hundreds of trucks brought thousands of workers and *campesinos* to it, filling it—fifteen thousand people. The Partido paid each one dollar to attend. All seemed to be enjoying it—a happy crowd, jostling, waving pennants, drinking beer and pop, cheering and yelling, boys moving around yelling the old PD, Trujillo party, slogans, "The Party of the Poor, of the Worker, of the *Campesino.*"

An oligarch told me, "The people in the country, they follow a leader. I told them to sign up with the UCN. They did. The Rurales beat them, stole their hogs and chickens, and told them if they didn't go back to the Partido they'd kill them. So they did."

How would they vote in a free election? No one knew.

That night, driving back to the capital in a hard rain on a muddy detour, we pulled off into the ditch to let pass a long procession of oncoming trucks. They were Haina sugar trucks, filled tonight with people—men and women packed in and standing in the rain, coming from a huge Partido Dominicano rally in the capital, and one truckload was chanting defiantly, "The Trujillos are still here." The Partido had given its answer to the UCN rally.

The Partido's boss, Luís Mercado, told me the Partido had lost some members, the opposition might poll half the urban vote, but, "There are country districts where they haven't even entered." (They hadn't dared.) Unquestionably, the Partido was still the biggest, best-organized, best-financed, most powerful party in the Republic. It supported President Balaguer.

I saw President Balaguer in his office in the Palace, at the end of the long corridor clogged with machine gunners. (Once, when an OAS mission called, the machine gunners disappeared.) Balaguer was a frail man, slight, so short his feet kept reaching for the floor and not quite touching it. Past middle age, he was self-effacing, apologetic, with a weak handclasp, an air of deep melancholy, an odd, soft, monotonous voice —but shrewd. He wore a cheap suit and white socks. He looked fatigued and, sometimes, frightened. Yet I am told that before a microphone, Balaguer has a resonant, compelling voice.

His posture before me was that of a poet, writer, intellectual, who favored liberty and democracy, had reluctantly occupied the Palace in the hope of moderating Trujillo's excesses; and now wanted only to retire from public life and end his days with his books. "Books have been my life," he said, "and if I could return to that, it would be perfect." The trouble with that was that the books that had been his life had been, for the most part, hymns of praise to Trujillo. (He compiled the first volume of the official twenty-volume history, *La Era de Trujillo.*)

Balaguer's long service to Trujillo had begun, according to the official history of the regime, in October of 1937 when, as Secretary of State for Foreign Affairs (interim), he sought to patch up an accord with Haiti to cover the Haitian massacre. Now, after holding many other posts, he had ended as Trujillo's last puppet President.

With me, Balaguer took the official line—he and Ramfis were trying to democratize the Republic; the opposition was provoking the soldiers; the regime was in grave danger from either a military *coup* or a Communist revolution; the nation was nearly bankrupt; ultimately Ramfis and the other Trujillos would depart. For now, however, Ramfis was essential to prevent chaos, and even he might not succeed unless the sanctions were lifted. Balaguer played heavily on the Communist danger.

Of all the men I met on this trip, Balaguer remained the most enigmatic. I could not understand why he was playing this role, pressed by the military and the opposition, booed in the streets by his fellow citizens, presiding over a bankrupt government facing chaos. For love of country? For money? For the trappings of power? In fear? I never knew.

I saw Ramfis Trujillo twice. His financial adviser, Marco Gómez, took me to Ramfis' office at San Isidro Air Base. Who holds San Isidro holds the Republic.

The Air Force pilots were good. They had to be—some of their planes were falling apart. The pilots swaggered around, dirks at belt, silk scarves flying. Once they mistakenly pursued a U.S. courier plane, waggled their wings dangerously close, fired across its bow, and forced it to turn back and land; then, climbing out of their cockpits, approached the American pilot and said with a flourish, "And now we will have a drink at the Officers' Club."

Marco Gómez told me that Ramfis disliked politics, wanted neither power nor money, wanted only to solve the present impasse. Ramfis' enemies, however, said he had been transformed from polo-playing playboy to bloody power-seeker.

His office was paneled in dark wood, the shades drawn, the furniture all massive carved Spanish mahogany and red leather. Despite the gloom, Ramfis was wearing, as nearly always, large dark sunglasses. He was young, handsome, and, beneath all the uniform and braid, surprisingly short and slender. He seemed a dandy, with plucked eyebrows, a little mustache, manicured nails, and polished riding boots. His manner was cold, distant, and very correct.

At that first interview he talked a long time without saying much—about the imperative necessity to lift the sanctions to avoid bankruptcy, about communism. The only solution lay in keeping Balaguer in power. His and Balaguer's efforts to "democratize" the Republic were threatened by the left and suspected by the military.

Balaguer, Ramfis said, would offer coalition to the opposition. If the opposition refused, Balaguer would run for President next May. As for himself, Ramfis would "retire from military life" after the elections. He saw his future as one of coming and going from the Republic. As for the rest of the Trujillo family, Héctor would gladly go abroad but could not leave his aged mother; Ramfis had "advised" Petán to travel abroad and "hoped he would go." Ramfis wanted to sell the Haina sugar complex and other Trujillo properties.

A good deal of this was nonsense, and when I saw Ramfis a second time, he was more frank.

It was at dinner in his villa at Boca Chica. Ramfis was in a sports jacket and slacks. He introduced his companion as "Señorita Hildegarde," a pretty though not beautiful blond girl who looked about twenty. (He kept bringing in girls from Europe that fall.) Ramfis, relaxed and affable, drinking anisette all evening, made small talk through cocktails and dinner, displaying a deep contempt for the Dominican people, particularly the upper class. With my encouragement, he talked about his father, the Generalissimo. He described his father's death graphically—his false teeth had been found on the floor of the car. He thought the assassins had intended to capture his father alive. If so, they didn't know his father—he feared nothing. Ramfis was glad he "went that way," and compared him to Heureaux. Throughout all this, Ramfis seemed affable yet somehow incapable of emotion, as though the interior of his character were blank, void.

Once during dinner he fell into a long conversation with Marco Gómez and Fandino about Paris, and the absence of art, literature, or drama in the Dominican Republic. They were speaking rapidly in Spanish. With effort I followed the conversation a while, then, since they were only small talking, quit listening. Señorita Hildegarde, seated across the table from me on Ramfis' right, spoke no Spanish. Without thinking, I smiled at her, as one does to a dinner companion left out of a conversation, and she smiled back.

Ramfis saw it. He stopped talking in midsentence; his face grew dark. She quickly looked down at her plate. For several minutes total and uncomfortable silence prevailed. Then he started talking again, though more distantly. She did not say another word. Dinner finished, he rose immediately, offered her his arm, and led her upstairs.

He returned to the table at once. I am glad I had not yet heard a story told by a young man who was once Ramfis' friend. He said that after a similar dinner, Ramfis had announced, "And now gentlemen, for the dessert," and led his guests to the kitchen and opened a deep freeze door to display the bodies of several murdered men.

We took our coffee to the patio and finally began talking seriously. (Dominicans almost never talk business in front of women.) Ramfis said he wanted to see things through to stability, leave Balaguer in control of the government and, probably, General Fernando A. Sánchez, Jr., in charge of the military. Ramfis said he would like to join his family, but had no intention of going into exile. He would keep his home here and come and go as he wished—and as needed, "to maintain stability" (the magic phrase).

The conversation was drifting. It was my last night in the Republic. I urged him to speak frankly, for he had little time, so did his country, and so did mine. I said I thought I detected a good deal of unrealistic thinking on all sides. He was talking about resigning and coming and going as he pleased but, in fact, if he came back the opposition would try to kill him, and if he tried to leave, his own officers—who needed his protection—would try to kill him. He was a prisoner here. Balaguer was talking coalition, which would be political suicide for the opposition leaders. The OAS was talking about legalisms and economics, but the real importance of the OAS sanctions was not economic but moral and symbolic. The opposition was talking about throwing the Trujillos out, but Ramfis had the guns. His government and mine were talking about the Communist menace, but there weren't many Communists here except the puppets his father had imported. Everybody was talking about free elections, but they were impossible so long as the Partido continued to vote its members' *cédulas*. After thirty-one years, we were not going to get democracy this way—the Dominican people knew nothing about it, the Republic had no democratic traditions, and his father had made democracy impossible. This was a destroyed society.

Ramfis had listened carefully. When I finished he said, "I see the situation the same as you do," and during the rest of the evening he spoke so frankly he dismayed Marco Gómez.

Ramfis said there was no one and nothing of importance in the country but the Armed Forces, and only he could control them. As for the Communists, or the opposition parties, he could get rid of them whenever he wished, and he snapped the fingers of his right hand together sharply, a Dominican gesture, chilling when a Trujillo makes it. His big problems were to build up confidence in Balaguer among the officers and to make the opposition leaders understand how dangerous a game they were playing.

"They say they want to eliminate me. We can kill them. They ask us to leave. We're supposed to make sure they can get rid of us. I don't understand that kind of democracy."

He seemed genuinely surprised that the opposition was not pleased with the "democratization" to date, and seemed to think they should be content if allowed to hold meetings and talk against the government. "It shows a lack of appreciation," he said, appearing hurt.

I said I thought the screws were tightening, and a bloodbath might come yet.

"If it does," he said, "they'll get the worst of it." And then, "I see the future as very, very dark."

I never saw him again.

I took one other memory home with me. One evening when Fandino and I were downtown near Parque Independencia, we heard horses' hoofs and saw a crowd gather in front of Mario's Restaurant. We approached. It was General Sánchez of the Air Force, Ramfis' crony. He and about thirty or forty of his henchmen had ridden to the center of the city on horseback, shepherded by several carloads of SIM machine gunners. They had stopped in front of Mario's and, surrounded by soldiers and civilians with submachine guns, called for drinks. Waiters brought drinks to the sidewalk, and they drank in the saddle, talking and laughing boisterously, while a few curious townsmen watched in silence. Sánchez was wearing a cowboy hat and boots. Two six-guns were tied to his thighs with thongs. He seemed simply to be defying the populace. He gazed over their heads contemptuously, finished his drink, and then, with his friends, galloped away.

5

Back in Washington, I wrote a long report to President Kennedy and the State Department. I said the Republic was a sick, destroyed nation, to be viewed as one ravaged by a thirty-years war, even one to be occupied and reconstituted. I thought Ramfis was beginning to like the feeling of power, of usurping his father's place, and that his proposed "retirement" might well become a sham, as his father's periodic "retirements" from power were. I thought General Sánchez at least as dangerous as Ramfis. Balaguer's "democratization" was window dressing to fool the OAS. If we supported Ramfis and favored lifting sanctions now, we might gain "stability" for a time but we would lose what mattered, the people. The Trujillo right, not the Communists, was the danger to Dominican democracy.

We should encourage and support the opposition. But it was divided, its leaders childlike and politically naïve, patriotic but of doubtful ability to govern. They looked to us, not to themselves, to solve their problems. UCN was clearly the strongest party, upper-class led, but its leaders were reluctant to "get mixed up in politics" and wanted to remain a "civic movement." The PRD was just getting started. The 14th of June was unreliable. I saw no opposition party or leader we could support wholeheartedly.

Until now, we had merely praised Balaguer's "democratization," deplored violent "incidents," and urged everyone to be "moderate," hoping a "moderate and responsible" government would emerge. I thought that no longer possible—soon we must face the critical decision on sanctions. Not even the Dominicans themselves appreciated the cataclysmic nature of what was going on. We must adopt a policy.

Several choices were open, all bad.

We could simply do nothing. Dominicans kept saying, "If you don't help, we'll kill each other," and one might be tempted to reply, "Go ahead." But we could not.

Or we could support the Balaguer-Ramfis regime—recognize it, vote to lift the sanctions, and send an Ambassador. That would, in my opinion, be wrong; we would be turning our backs on the people.

Or we could help establish a broad-based provisional government until free elections could be held with OAS help; negotiate Ramfis out of his economic power at once and later negotiate him out of the country; force Héctor and Petán to leave the Republic immediately; arrange for the other Trujillos and General Sánchez to leave soon; disband the SIM, end the terror; establish political freedom, break the Partido's power; help the Republic borrow money to get the economy moving; send in numerous missions, both civil and military; and lift sanctions gradually. It amounted to negotiating the Trujillos out if possible and, if not, throwing them out. I recommended sending a high-level negotiator immediately and sending the fleet to the horizon to back him up.

That course was, with some modification, the course President Kennedy adopted when Department officials and I met with him in the Cabinet room in the White House on October 5, 1961. The President read my report fully, though it was more than a hundred pages long. He said, greeting me and grinning, "I've been reading your novel," and said he'd enjoyed it. He sent Undersecretary George McGhee direct from our meeting to the airport to put the policy into operation. The policy meant, of course, that we would not send me or anyone else as Ambassador soon, maybe not for a long time.

The negotiation began well. McGhee and Ramfis reached agreement in principle at their first meeting, and Petán and Héctor Trujillo left the country. But, just as in the nineteenth century, the political leaders could not get together. Sporadic riots began. Troops shot students on rooftops on Calle Espaillat. Ramfis' relatives teased him about being taken in by the Yankees. He seemed desperate. On November 15 Héctor and Petán returned.

Our *chargé,* John Hill, told Balaguer flatly we would not recognize the regime nor vote to lift sanctions in these circumstances. Plotting began inside the Armed Forces, and General Pedro Rafael Rodríguez Echavarría soon emerged as the strongman. Balaguer feared a *coup.*

On November 19 we sent the fleet to the horizon. On Rodríguez Echavarría's orders, Dominican Air Force planes from Santiago bombed San Isidro. Our military adviser, Lieutenant Colonel Ed Simmons, was there, talking to General Sánchez. Petán Trujillo came in, demanded to know what Simmons was doing there, pulled back the bolt on his submachine gun, and aimed it at Simmons' stomach. Simmons told him our fleet was on the horizon. Petán lowered his gun. General Rodríguez Echavarría declared for Balaguer and ordered Héctor and Petán Trujillo and General Sánchez to leave the country. Hill supported him. They left, Ramfis himself having left the day before on the yacht *Angelita,* first killing the six surviving imprisoned assassins, and taking his father's body with him. The *Angelita* was stopped at Guadeloupe and returned. Ramfis flew on to Paris, followed by the body of the dead dictator.

We were considering recognizing a seven-man Consejo headed by Balaguer and asking the OAS to lift sanctions. Negotiations limped on between Balaguer and the opposition. A general strike of businessmen, UCN-led, began. The people rioted against Balaguer. Violence ensued. So did looting. Plotting began anew inside the Armed Forces. Balaguer made concessions. A seven-man Consejo was patched together. But the anti-Balaguer riots continued. General Rodríguez Echavarría sent his tanks against the people. He seemed to be taking over. In January Balaguer caved in under pressure—he took asylum in the Papal Nunciatura. General Rodríguez Echavarría locked up the remaining Consejeros. But we refused to recognize him, and so after only two days, other military officers perpetrated a counter-*coup*—they put guns on Rodríguez Echavarría while he was inspecting the imprisoned Consejeros, disarmed him, unlocked them, and locked him up.

Rafael Bonnelly succeeded Balaguer as President. We recognized the Consejo, so did Latin American nations, the OAS lifted sanctions, President Kennedy nominated me Ambassador, and the Senate confirmed it.

President Kennedy said, "The Dominican people and their leaders confront a great and seldom given opportunity: The construction of a democratic society on the ruins of tyranny. It is a noble task, but it is not an easy one. We wish them well, and we assure them of our desire to assist them in their efforts."

Chapter Five

INTO THE JUNGLE

So we return to my ambassadorship. I was sworn in in Washington on March 2, and flew to Santo Domingo with Fran and our sons two days later—on Sunday, March 4, 1962.

On the plane, headed for this strange assignment, I thought of other trips I had made as a young man, traveling the United States and writing about it, finding so much wrong, wishing it were better, never for an instant doubting it was possible to make it better, young then and eager, and loving the United States; and so into politics with zest and hope and dreams, traveling America with Adlai Stevenson and John F. Kennedy. From all this, from the United States, from writing and politics—in a sense I was going to the Dominican Republic to test the dream, going with the same zest and zeal, the same hope. President Kennedy, I thought, must dream and hope for the world what I dream now for the Dominican Republic. This was the link—the shared hope and dream.

In Santo Domingo we faced Dominican reality—the difficulties scarcely imagined, the "stark reality of responsibility" Adlai Stevenson had sought.

General Rodríguez Echavarría was still locked up and ex-President Balaguer was still in asylum. And discontent was still widespread. Rodríguez Echavarría's two-day *coup* had occurred only six weeks before. Political leaders were demanding that he and Balaguer be tried for crimes against the people.

On Wednesday, an Embassy officer told me that the Consejo was permitting Balaguer to leave the country. It would give him safe conduct and secretly send him to Spain, where most of the Trujillos lived. John Hill mentioned Balaguer's departure casually.

But on Thursday morning *El Caribe,* the leading newspaper, carried a banner headline: Not only Balaguer but Rodríguez Echavarría as well had left Wednesday night, had left openly, and, worst of all, had gone to the United States.

That meant trouble. It would enrage the Dominican people. For it appeared that we were welcoming to the United States the last two men who represented in the popular mind the Trujillo tyranny and helping them escape trial in the Republic—and at the very time I had arrived as our new Ambassador; I was scheduled to present my credentials that same day.

The Department had told me that to present credentials I would need a morning suit—striped pants and cutaway—and so I had bought one. But now I discovered that such formal attire had been greatly favored by Trujillo and was therefore unacceptable. Instead a white linen suit was required. I had ordered one from a Spanish tailor on a narrow street just off Calle Conde. That morning at ten o'clock I was scheduled to pick it up, but appointments kept me busy, so I sent our driver Bailey down to get it. Near the tailor shop, just off Calle Conde, he ran into a mob. They surrounded him, pulled him out, then smashed and burned the car. They burned our consul's car and a USIS mobile unit and other cars. They surged up and down Calle Conde from Parque Colón to Parque Independencia. They smashed windows and wrecked storefronts. They looted, they littered the streets with broken glass. They stoned our Consulate. They came down from the Upper Town and up from the Old Town, old thick-walled Spanish houses. They demonstrated on narrow Calle Espaillat off Conde, where the previous fall students had been shot off the rooftops by troops. The loudspeakers of the political parties spurred them on, blaring from balconies over Conde and palm-shaded Parque Independencia, blaring from cars racing around the park. The mob marched on the National Palace; troops barred the spiked iron fence. The Consejo, led by President Bonnelly and aged Monseñor Pérez Sánchez in flowing robes, finally went on foot unarmed into Calle Conde, and marching steadfast on the splintered glass down the narrow street, bade the angry young men on the curbs go home.

I was at the Embassy, a dozen blocks from downtown, ignorant of all this. The rioting must have started about 10 A.M. About noon someone told me a mob had tried to break into the school where my sons, Dan and Fred, were. Lorenzo Berry—"Wimpy"—brought the boys home. They said the mob, armed with chains and manhole covers, had attacked the school, torn down the American flag, wrecked the first floor, and finally been driven away by two truckloads of soldiers with machine guns. Dan and Fred had watched from their upstairs classroom window.

John Hill told me that John Crimmins, the Caribbean-Mexican Area director in the State Department in Washington, had telephoned. Hill had reassured Crimmins, saying the crowd was small and the incident not serious.

But it was serious. I said little—Hill was being transferred—but I was angry. "Unflappability," a quality much admired by some in the Department, is sometimes hard to distinguish from fatuity.

That night the Consejo imposed an after-dark curfew. And, as we have seen, next day I presented my credentials.

2

The Embassy Residence is a large white oblong concrete building, two-storied, the exterior rough-textured, the porch roofs red tiled. It stands on spacious grounds, as wide as a city block and deep as two, surrounded by a low stone wall. Royal palms, gently curved and plumed on high, line the circular driveway in front. On one side are lush mango trees. We used to pick the mangoes and set them out on the sidewalk for anyone to take. Behind the house is a beautiful garden—an enormous tree like a banyan tree sending trunks and roots down like posts from great spreading limbs, a swimming pool shaded by an even more magnificent tree, an acacia which rises to the sky, festooned with split-leaf philodendron vines thick as a man's leg.

Inside the front door is a circular foyer tiled black and white and, beyond, a big rectangular living room, sunporch, state dining room, breakfast porch, study, a guest wing, a servants' wing, five family bedrooms upstairs, twenty-five rooms in all. The house is unadorned and bleak and cold, though excellently designed for an official Residence. Next door was the gaudy, splendid mansion of Trujillo. In a closet in our bedroom was a canister of tear gas and an emergency walkie-talkie. I kept my shotgun beside them throughout my tenure.

I spent the first days talking alone for an hour or more with each senior and several junior members of the Embassy staff, getting to know them, asking each what he did, learning where things were and how things worked. My office was in the little Chancellery (State Department usage is Chancery), the Embassy office building at the rear of the Embassy Residence grounds. The office of the Deputy Chief of Mission (DCM) was tiny, and the political officers worked in partitioned-off cubicles. The rest of the building was filled with cable and code equipment. The military attachés, economic officers, and administrative officers of the Embassy worked in rented buildings across the street. The Consulate was downtown. Our other missions were scattered all over town— Agency for International Development (AID), Peace Corps, U. S. Information Service (USIS), Military Assistance and Advisory Group (MAAG). Hill took me to visit them. I was responsible for all—eventually nearly 350 people, including 160 Peace Corps volunteers.

The Dominican Republic was small, but it was a testing ground. The success of U.S. policy in the Caribbean swung on the Dominican hinge.

We had three policy objectives there that year—to help keep the Consejo in office, to help hold free elections, and to help get the winner into the Palace alive on schedule.

By and large, the history of provisional governments in Latin America is that they fall, or that they try to extend their term. Our task was to prevent either from happening.

The omens were not good. The riot that burned my car was only a symptom. More riots quickly followed. Even before I could locate all the Embassy offices, I found myself deep in Dominican chaos.

The first U.S. warship arrived on a friendly visit amid rumors that Castro/Communist agitators would attack the sailors on shore liberty. To protect them I asked the help of Amiama and Imbert, and they paid off a leader of the taxi drivers, and while the sailors were in town, each taxicab driver had a tire chain or heavy wrench on the cab floor beneath his feet. The liberty passed quietly. President Bonnelly thought it would be safe to have Vice President Johnson visit the Republic in April. (But his visit was postponed, for other reasons.)

Pressure was rising on the twenty-two million dollars in sugar fees. Every time I went to the Palace reporters asked about it, and I kept taking refuge in a pat answer, "It is under urgent and active consideration," then hurrying back to the Chancellery to cable or call John Crimmins in the Department.

The CIA station chief told me that Haitian exiles opposed to President Duvalier of Haiti had turned up in Santo Domingo. Petán Trujillo was reported planning to go to Haiti. The Haitians closed a Dominican consulate in Haiti; the Dominicans retaliated.

During the third week, a chain of events began—political maneuvers behind the scenes and riots in the streets—that swiftly built into an obscure, swirling crisis.

By now, Trujillo's old Partido Dominicano had ceased to exist. New parties were springing up. The towering figure in Dominican politics at that time was Viriato Fiallo, leader of the UCN. Hero of the struggle against Balaguer and Ramfis Trujillo, Fiallo overshadowed even President Bonnelly and the Consejo. Fiallo's UCN, originally a civic movement, was rapidly becoming a political party. Everyone assumed Fiallo would run for President. Meanwhile, his UCN was the chief base of support of the Consejo. Suddenly now Harry Shlaudeman, the political section chief, told me that the UCN was threatening to pull its members out of the government. It felt that the Consejo was moving too slowly, unemployment remained high and business stagnant, the Consejo refused to purge the military of Trujillistas—and the UCN would be blamed.

If the UCN pulled out of the government, the Consejo might fall. I invited Fiallo to lunch at the Embassy Residence. Big and amiable, Fiallo did not seem to realize how serious a UCN pullout might be. We discussed it at length. He said he had no intention of bringing down the Consejo. But the Consejo must act.

Both the UCN and PRD split. An important UCN leader in Santiago, Juan Isidro Jimenes Grullón, deserted the UCN and announced his own presidential candidacy. Fiallo minimized it. In Juan Bosch's PRD, Ángel Miolán banished Nicolás Silfa. I saw Miolán, and he told me that the PRD was now the biggest party and the best organized, with its greatest strength among the workers and *campesinos*. He had filed an electoral petition containing three hundred thousand names. That was a real shocker; it meant the PRD was almost even with UCN.

Everybody said the Consejo too was split. But everybody had a different version of the split.

Rioting resumed in Calle Conde. The city was filled with rumors of plots and counter-plots. One said that Imbert, Amiama, and Donny Reid were plotting with rightists in the military to provoke leftist disturbances, intending to use the disturbances as a pretext for a *golpe de estado*,[1] *a coup d'état.* Another said that the Castro/Communists intended to assassinate President Bonnelly; another that Trujillistas would kill Bonnelly, make it appear that the Communists had done it, and seize power.

Little was clear except that the splits within the Consejo, the splits inside PRD and UCN, and UCN's drawing away from the Consejo meant political trouble. And so did the rioting.

Thus the Consejeros who had been picked because they were not notably party men, now found themselves deeply enmeshed in politics. The parties for their own advantage were beginning to attack the Consejo. But that endangered the very government that was to give the parties a chance to win an election. To ask the parties not to attack the do-nothing Consejo was to ask them to commit suicide. Yet by attacking it they kept it off balance, and it could do nothing. And so long as the Consejo did nothing, it kept losing the people's support. If it fell, they would lose their chance for a free election.

I called President Bonnelly. He suggested I come to his home at night, not to the Palace. He lived in an attractive, modest house down the street from the Embassy, just beyond the former mansion of Trujillo. Ordinarily, an Ambassador requests an appointment with a Chief of State formally, through the Foreign Office, but Bonnelly and I called each other directly and saw each other at least once a week and, in time of trouble, several times a day. He gave Fandino his private telephone number, and told me, "Our fate is linked. We will stand or fall together."

Bonnelly was then fifty-eight years old, an educated man, a lawyer.

---

[1] Literally, "blow of State," though the phrase calls up a not inappropriate image of gulping down the government.

He often talked about his childhood in Santiago. He had been the youngest of nine children, "the baby," he said, "raised on everybody's lap." Bonnelly was gray-haired and light-brown skinned, with soft kind brown eyes, long fingers, a sensitive face. Usually he wore gray suits. Because of his dignified bearing, he looked taller than he was. He was connected, by marriage and friendship, with the Santiago oligarchy.

Many times Bonnelly told me that when Trujillo sought his services he at first had resisted, "but he finally put me between the sword and the wall." ("Between the sword and the wall"—it is an excellent Dominican phrase.)

The question of guilt by association with Trujillo lay heavily over the Republic. Obviously, all who had served Trujillo could not be treated as pariahs—almost no able man had been able to avoid serving him. On the other hand, his torturers, killers, SIM leaders, and generals who had operated his slave-labor camps could not be forgiven. It was the same problem faced after World War II in countries whose leaders had collaborated with the conquering Germans. An Italian journalist once wrote, "After the storm, all the corpses float to the surface."

Bonnelly was not in principle a Trujillista. He had the contempt for Trujillo's blunders, crudities, and cruelties that so many Santiago oligarchs feel. Nevertheless, beginning in 1944, Bonnelly had served Trujillo in various important Cabinet posts, including the powerful and feared position of Secretary of State of Interior and Police; Trujillo had attended the burial of Bonnelly's mother in Santiago, and Trujillo and his wife had acted as "sponsors"—roles similar to those of best man and matron of honor in the U.S.—at the wedding of Bonnelly's daughter; Bonnelly had been Trujillo's Ambassador to Venezuela at the time the Venezuelan dictator Pérez Jiménez was in power, and when Pérez Jiménez fell, Juan Perón, the exiled dictator of Argentina, took asylum in the Dominican Embassy in Caracas and subsequently went briefly to the Dominican Republic.

Despite all this, immediately after Trujillo's fall, Bonnelly secretly helped establish the UCN in Santiago in opposition to the Balaguer-Ramfis regime—he told me UCN was founded in his home—and certainly he was not so tainted by Trujillismo that he was unacceptable as the President of the Consejo.

I liked Bonnelly from the outset—I thought him a decent, sensible, patriotic, upright, intelligent man. He often told me he would never leave the Palace before his term expired, February 27, 1963, unless he was killed. He also told me he would not seek to extend his term. I believed him, though many did not. He was brave. He had gone afoot into Parque Independencia when Rodríguez Echavarría turned his tanks on the people, and when a soldier had trained a machine gun on Bonnelly, an Army officer named Miller had stepped in front of him. From that day onward, Captain Miller, a silent man with a pockmarked, mask-like face, was Bonnelly's bodyguard. (The Dominican phrase is, characteristically, *guarda de espalda*—literally, guard of the back—the implication being that a man who is a man can guard his own front.)

Bonnelly was always conscious of his place in history. More than anything else, I think, he wanted history to remember him as having carried his country through the difficult transition from Trujillo tyranny to democracy. Something else moved him, too—his memory of his father. He often said, "I can never surpass my father." He gathered around him men whom he regarded as his sons. Donny Reid was one; Ramón Tapia, a volatile young lawyer, Secretary of State for the Presidency, was another. Sometimes, while we were drinking together as the year wore on, it was not clear whether Bonnelly regarded himself as my father or my son. As both, at different times, perhaps.

Bonnelly was a sentimental man, extraordinarily fond of his grandchildren. My own two sons passed his house every day walking to and from school, and he sometimes stopped to talk to them or give them Indian arrowheads. He said he had "a heart condition" and joked that he was in good hands—those two fellow Consejeros that were heart specialists. Bonnelly could be moody, and toward the end of the year when it often seemed doubtful that his government could survive, he seemed obsessed with death. He often referred to "my star," saying it would not fail to guide him; there were times when, discouraged, I would tell Fandino wryly, "I think his star's about to go out—and ours too."

Increasingly Bonnelly worked and lived at home, staying in his little book-lined room. Some considered him an intellectual, but now and then he lapsed disconcertingly into discussions of the occult and even seemed to put some faith in astrology.

Bonnelly was no leftist, no revolutionary—the oligarchy ran too deep in him for that. His instincts were humanitarian but paternalistic. If he lacked a burning desire to reform, he was politician enough to recognize the necessity of reform. Once, shortly before I arrived, when somebody—Castro/Communists and Trujillistas, the Consejo said—was burning cane fields, Bonnelly led citizens in trucks out into the fields to cut cane. But he seldom exerted such popular leadership. His basic method of running the government was to postpone decisions as long as possible, maneuver within the Consejo, and hope for the best. He preferred to operate quietly behind the scenes. In Palace intrigue, amid the intricate rivalries and friendships of the seven-headed Presidency, Bonnelly was a master. Only his great skill held the split Consejo together.

As an administrator, Bonnelly left much to be desired. He tried to do too much, and gained the reputation of putting papers in his desk and forgetting them. But his good sense and judgment saved him and saved the Republic. Above all, he never once forgot that the real power in the Republic resided with the Armed Forces. Bonnelly often told me, "The same soldiers who salute me now arrested me in January."

When I went to see him, on Monday, March 26, during that first political trouble, he seemed remarkably calm. We talked, as always, in his tiny study crowded with desk and chairs, cluttered with documents, books, newspapers, and tape recorders.

Bonnelly thought the political situation "very confused—the 14th of June is always split, but now the PRD and the UCN are split, too." He seemed confident, even to be enjoying the parties' difficulties; partly, I thought, because he was contemptuous of most of the party leaders. He said big political meetings in the capital meant nothing—70 percent of the vote was in the *campo,* the countryside, and there the people, uneducated, turned to their local leader, the lawyer, businessman, druggist, doctor, landowner, priest. So far, no party had captured that vote.

Bonnelly denied that the UCN and the Consejo had broken. But he was angry at the UCN—he said that it had promised privately to support the Consejo when it decreed the Emergency Law, then publicly denounced deportations under it. He said, "The Consejo only wants to provide an interim government for the transition. Everybody should support it. But they don't."

I didn't understand the crisis fully. He didn't either, yet. (And in retrospect, it really wasn't clear, everybody was still confused by Trujillo's fall; the government, the parties, and the American presence all were new.)

I said, "I've never been an Ambassador before."

Bonnelly said, "That's all right—I've never been a President before."

Things got worse during the ensuing weekend. Soldiers shot a man in Puerto Plata (though apparently accidentally). In Santiago, a mob swept through the central plaza, wrecked storefronts and the USIS center, while the police stood around doing nothing. And in Santo Domingo, a policeman standing on a street corner was shot dead by men in a passing car. The killers apparently were members of the MPD, López Molina's Communist party that advocated terror. This was the MPD's first direct challenge to authority. If unpunished, it could destroy what little police morale remained and lead to terror in the streets that might topple the government.

On Monday morning, April 2, trouble broke out downtown. A mob surged by our Consulate chasing a *calié;* the students went on strike; a crowd, Castro/Communist inspired, gathered on Padre Billini Street to denounce Fiallo. Lieutenant Colonel William Richardson, our air attaché, came in from San Isidro Air Base. He said the Base was tense, the junior officers were plotting. The CIA chief said Imbert was reported plotting a *golpe de estado* with Fernández Caminero, his fellow Consejero; General Miguel Atila Luna, Air Force Commander; and General Belisario Peguero, Commander of the National Police.

I called in Al Hemba, the DCM; Harry Shlaudeman of the political section; the CIA chief, and the three military attachés. We thought matters had not yet reached the flashpoint. But the tensions were building. To deflect them, the Consejo must act. It was in danger of falling—a "do-nothing" government. It could not stand still in the post-Trujillo turbulence.

We worked out a program it might follow:

To maintain order, arrest the MPD members who killed the policeman, appoint courageous judges, and train the police to handle mobs.

To placate the impatient people and promote the *Alianza* ideals, get on with tax reform, agrarian reform, and public works.

To let off steam, bring to trial a few *calié* for crimes committed under Trujillo and remove notorious Trujillistas from government.

To reassure the military, decree that military men could be tried in military courts only.

I would try to sell it to the Consejeros, one by one.

The police arrested a Communist, Andrés Ramos Peguero, and charged him and others with the murder of the policeman. The CIA agreed that Ramos Peguero was a Communist. He had come to the Republic several years earlier with the MPD's leader, López Molina. The police began a search for López Molina.

I went back to President Bonnelly. He was far less confident. He saw in the incidents of the last weekend an organized chain of events well planned on Fidel Castro's instructions.

It had started with the shooting in Puerto Plata on Friday. On Saturday, the UCN had publicly attacked the military for that shooting. That night Ramos Peguero had killed the policeman in the capital, using, Bonnelly said, a .45-caliber pistol brought in from Cuba two months ago. On Sunday, a mob paid by a Trujillo henchman had gathered in San Cristóbal, where Trujillo sentiment still lingered, and burned a bank. The Santiago riot had been organized by Castro/Communists. On Monday the students had gone on strike and demonstrated in the capital. And more trouble was planned.

All this was a plot by the Castro/Communists, Bonnelly said. Their pretext was the "do-nothing Consejo." But their real purpose was to seize control of the capital streets, the first step in the classic Marxist revolutionary pattern. And the political parties were playing into their hands.

Bonnelly was sending Donny Reid and others to tell the political parties they were facing not public impatience with the Consejo but a Castro/Communist conspiracy to overthrow it; that the Consejo wanted only to maintain order and create an atmosphere in which elections could be held so that it could leave office on schedule; that it needed the parties' support; and that it would distribute lesser jobs, and even Cabinet posts, if necessary, among them.

Bonnelly said this would not succeed. The parties were interested in maneuvering for their own advantage, not in saving democracy. Instead of campaigning against each other, the parties were attacking the Consejo. If the Consejo cracked down on the Castro/Communists, the parties would denounce it as a dictatorship. In the end, the Consejo would probably have to go ahead on its own, arresting leftists and at the same time prosecuting Trujillista *calié*, taking its chances.

I asked about the military. Bonnelly thought it loyal—*"hasta ahora,"* till now, as he always added, with a little smile. It was rumored that Balaguer and General Rodríguez Echavarría were in Puerto Rico. Bonnelly said Rodríguez Echavarría was brave, ambitious, and popular with the enlisted men, whose pay he had raised before leaving; "so it doesn't make us happy to see him so near." Balaguer, he thought, was, at least for now, too compromised as a Trujillista to be dangerous.

I asked if he thought the Consejo would survive. (And I had been here only a few weeks!)

He said, "We will leave only feet first. It is very difficult. The military learned a lesson when it put us in jail. And they are aware that a leftist victory would be their death. The UCN is not smart enough to let them alone. Therefore, the Armed Forces only feel safe with the Consejo. So long as this is true, we dominate. The only thing that might give the left control is a general strike. That is not possible now—it costs too much." Amid all these pressures, Bonnelly saw the Consejo's only salvation in close identification with the United States.

I told him we would support him fully and publicly if he wished. A soldier had been wounded in the last few days' disorders; we would fly him, with full publicity, to the United States for treatment. I would ask for increased naval visits and would ostentatiously take Bonnelly to lunch aboard a U.S. warship. Lieutenant General Andrew P. O'Meara wanted to visit from Panama, and I would take him to the Palace to call on the President and give a dinner for him and the President. More importantly, I would press hard to get a U.S. public-safety mission sent down immediately to train the Dominican police to handle mobs. For if the Consejo could maintain public order in the streets without harsh repression, it could protect itself against both Castro/Communist disorders and criticism from the parties all too ready to cry "dictatorship." In the meanwhile, I urged Bonnelly to appoint braver judges and speed up the vigorous but fair prosecution of *calié,* Trujillistas, and Castro/Communist rioters.

What of the other Consejeros?

I found Donny Reid in a rare euphoric mood. He had been talking to the UCN, and it would support a government crackdown on the Castro/Communists. So would all the other parties, except the 14th of June. Indeed, the UCN and other parties, again except the 14th of June, would even come into the Cabinet. (They never did—how could they? This was the old discarded and doomed idea of coalition. No party would jeopardize its chance of winning the December presidential election by joining now a tottering, unpopular, do-nothing government that was preparing to use force against people in the streets.) Reid said the Consejo could count on the police "100 percent." He, Imbert, and Amiama were agreed the police must "get tough" with the leftists in the streets. Pichardo opposed, he said, while Fernández Caminero was wobbling.

Pichardo told me he reluctantly considered a crackdown necessary to preserve public order, but would insist that the police arrest only the guilty, not everybody, and try them fairly.

Fernández Caminero said the parties were really to blame for the disorders—by refusing to support the Consejo, they had invited disorder.

I went to see the two assassins, Amiama and Imbert. Almost always I saw them together, never at the Palace, usually late at night in Imbert's house or Amiama's, sometimes at a more secret place. Since May 30, 1961, Imbert and Amiama have lived in fear that the Trujillos will have them killed. No wonder—few men in history have killed a chief of state and survived. In a sense, their lives ended the night Trujillo's did. They often told me "We are living on borrowed time."

Each traveled in a fast-moving car loaded with machine gunners, followed by a second car loaded with machine gunners. Their homes and offices were closely guarded. They never left the Republic. They were always armed. I saw Imbert without his .45 just once, swimming (but then he unbuckled his gun and laid it on a rock on the beach nearby). Amiama trusted no one. One hot, tense night, arriving at his house, I tossed my coat onto a bed adjoining his study. Leaving, I went after it, and he followed me. Only when I picked it up did I realize I had thrown it atop his machine gun. Amiama watched while I put my coat on, one hand on his hip near his pistol. He opened the door to let me out and stepped back, so it was I, not he, who first stepped into the open doorway, silhouetted in the light.

Imbert lived in a nice but not ostentatious house on a little hill on the edge of town near the Hotel Embajador. Fandino and I drove to its gate, stopped, identified ourselves to the soldiers on guard, then mounted the curving driveway and walked in through the open door to the living room, tiled and glassed and open-louvered, and sat talking to Imbert's wife, waiting. He was always late.

Presently, cars roared outside, and in a moment Imbert, short, nearly bald, pot-bellied, came in through the back door and tossed his grease gun—a small rapid-fire submachine gun—clattering onto a glass-topped table. Home from a hard day at the Palace. Then he led us outside and downstairs to "my talking room," a basement room with solid concrete walls, heavy solid sliding glass doors, soundproof and bulletproof, bare of any ornamentation. Amiama joined us, white-suited, black-eyed, mustached, silent, his face pale, almost waxy and without expression. Imbert shouted on an intercom system for drinks.

I asked if they thought the Consejo could survive the UCN's threatened pullout and the rioting in the streets.

Amiama always stood erect, and he sat that way, too, his torso slanted stiffly back. I thought he must wear a bulletproof vest. Characteristically, he kept his gun concealed, while Imbert wore his .45 on his belt. Now Amiama leaned forward stiffly and said, "Before I answer, I want to say this: We need help with equipment for the Armed Forces. In the Air Force alone we have three thousand men we want to keep busy— so they won't think of other things. The best thing is training and maneuvers. But they have no shoes and no olive-green uniforms. We have troops sleeping on the floor in barracks or on bare bedsprings. Your military attachés have promised us these things. But where are they? I realize you have good intentions. Your attachés say the clothes are scheduled but we need shoes, not schedules."

Imbert spoke placatingly, told Amiama not to be so harsh, explained the U.S. rules and regulations. But then he made the same piteous plea: "They need to go to the field, to train, Mr. Martin," his voice rising, "but they have no shoes," and he spread his hands eloquently, his liquid face agonized.

I realized what they were doing—the trick of a Chicago detective team questioning a suspect, one threatening, the other friendly.

I promised to look into it. (It turned out we had indeed promised the shoes, but we had only black shoes—the Dominicans wanted brown. I told Amiama and Imbert this; that ended the shoe question.)

Amiama said, again leaning forward uncomfortably, "I want to make it clear. Things have to be done, right now, if we are to avoid another Cuba. The United States won't tolerate another Cuba. We agree. We are on your side. But you have to do things now. If López Molina needs money, he gets it. Three hundred thousand dollars."

I asked if he really thought Castro had sent López Molina and the MPD three hundred thousand dollars.

Imbert said it didn't matter; for two or three thousand he could buy off the 14th of June's Manolo Tavárez Justo.

Amiama said, "I want to make it clear. What we need now is a program to take care of the problem in the Republic. Not us, necessarily. Anyone. We," nodding at Imbert, "are only interested in the country."

He was lapsing into an oblique language I learned later to understand better. "For example," he went on, "López Molina. If we could suborn the people we know we can suborn, we could deliver López Molina here in the hands of his followers tomorrow. Buy the men."

He seemed to be suggesting two things: That the U.S. provide money to buy off the Castro/Communist left, and/or that he and Imbert could keep the Republic safe from communism if we gave the word. I did not want to confront either question head-on. I asked how they saw the present political situation.

Amiama sniffed contemptuously and leaned back in his chair, put his pale fingertips together, stared up at the ceiling, and hummed softly and tunelessly. He despised all politicians.

Imbert replied that the UCN, ostensibly non-political, now was deep in politics, was Communist infiltrated, and was demanding a purge of Trujillistas in the Armed Forces, a step that would surely provoke a military *golpe* against the Consejo.

I suggested the Consejo bring some *calié* to trial. Imbert agreed, but said Attorney General García Vásquez had told him it would take four months. He thought it more important that Ramos Peguero had been arrested for killing the policeman, and said with satisfaction, "He is saying he only intended to wound him. But we are squeezing him. We are hunting for López Molina," and he told me how dangerous López Molina was.

In subsequent meetings he and Amiama emphasized López Molina so much that I became suspicious. Apparently, my predecessors had considered López Molina an extremely dangerous man. I did not, since, having talked with him, I considered him a coward and hopelessly compromised. In these early days, Amiama and Imbert tried to get concessions from me by mentioning his name, until finally I told them bluntly that I cared little what he was doing and that I thought they probably knew where he was and had him on their private payroll. They laughed and desisted.

At the time of this meeting in early April, however, we were less frank. I asked again if the Consejo would survive the current disorders.

"*Sí, Señor,*" Amiama said, his face expressionless, "but don't resent tough measures. We will survive, at whatever cost. We will enforce all the laws. The parties—ah," and he shrugged and looked at the ceiling, humming.

Imbert attacked the parties at length.

Amiama observed, still looking at the ceiling, "It would be better if there were one President. I like democracy but it won't work. We are trying to go from dictatorship to democracy too fast. We should go gradually. The people cannot digest freedom. They are not ready."

I suggested that a little dictatorship was like a little pregnancy. Amiama gestured impatiently. He said, "I told the President to go away for three days and everything will be all right." The meaning was clear enough.

Pending the arrival of our permanent AID director, President Kennedy had appointed Rafael Picó, an able Puerto Rican banker, to handle our economic aid to the Republic. Working directly with the Consejo, Picó accomplished a great deal—he used part of our twenty-five-million-dollar loan to augment the Consejo's work relief program, rearranged the banking system, helped the Agricultural Bank make small loans to farmers, set up a national Planning Board, presented a program for agrarian reform, tried (unsuccessfully) to persuade the Consejo to put the Haina sugar complex into an autonomous corporation and (successfully) to put the other former Trujillo industries into another autonomous corporation. Probably Picó's greatest single accomplishment was in showing the Consejo how to use part of the twenty-five-million-dollar loan to get the economy moving immediately.

When Picó encountered roadblocks, he came to me, and I urged his programs on President Bonnelly and the other Consejeros. He wanted me to press them for agrarian reform, an income tax, property tax (there was none), taxes on cacao and coffee, and for a Court of Claims—Picó feared that without judicial safeguards the Consejo might cave in under political pressure and give away our loan money to people who claimed Trujillo had wronged them.

But during those first few weeks, trouble smothered such sensible projects. Rioting continued. Once more, as during my 1961 presidential mission, Calle Conde's pavement was littered with broken glass, storefronts were steel-shuttered, and gangs roved the city. A United States journalist called the Republic "nightmare island," and wrote of burning cars, looting mobs, and turmoil everywhere. The Consejo lost control of the capital streets.

By this time it was clear from the reports of Embassy political officers, the Embassy labor attaché, and the CIA, as well as the Dominican authorities, that the organized mobs were composed mostly of teen-agers and young men in their twenties and that they were hired near the market by the Castro/Communists. An ordinary *turba*—riot—cost $150, but if one wanted cars burned and store windows smashed, the cost went up to $500. Day after day, night after night you could hear the clapping and horn-honking from the Embassy—the rhythmic five-beat sound, *"Da-da li-ber-tad,"* the sound which in September 1961, with Ramfis still here, had sounded thrilling but which now was directed against the Palace or the Embassy. Sometimes it changed to, *"Da-da pa-re-dón"*—to the wall, the Castro cry.

The organized *turbas,* even the spontaneous *calié* hunts, were dangerous. Once afoot downtown I saw a *turba* coming, hurried toward my car, could not find the driver, and finally found him on the corner, getting his shoes shined. My secretary, driving on Avenida Bolívar, usually safe, suddenly found her car stopped by a mob; someone hurled a chunk of a broken manhole cover through the windshield and others smashed the windows before she escaped, covered with broken glass. By May most of the manholes in town were open—the mobs had used their lids.

Our Consulate was far from the Embassy, in the center of the city. Dominicans by the thousands were still trying to get U.S. visas. Trujillo fallen, they were free to go. Some, fearing the riots foretold chaos, were fleeing now. Others simply wanted a visa as an escape hatch in case of chaos. The Consulate had a backlog of thousands of applications for visas, a waiting period of months. Every morning by 10 A.M. applicants formed a line four abreast from the sidewalk around the corner into the building and upstairs to the office, jamming the stairway, standing in the fetid heat pressed tightly together. Police could not keep order.

Every time a *turba* erupted, it hit the Consulate, for the Consulate was on the line of march from the old Spanish quarter near the waterfront up to the Palace on the hill. Rioters found ready recruits among hundreds of disgruntled people waiting in line. So day after day *turbas* turned into full-fledged anti-American riots at the Consulate, and on some days it almost seemed to me that the young vice consuls spent more time throwing tear gas out the windows than issuing visas. I cabled and telephoned the Department repeatedly, trying to move the Consulate and get more vice consuls.

A few in the mobs were leftists and knew exactly what they were doing. Some were thugs, working for pay, hoping to loot stores after they had smashed the windows. And some were simply the disoriented teen-agers of the Republic who had grown up under Trujillo and now confused liberty with license. One told my wife he liked the *Americanos* all right—it was the *Yanquis* he hated. Our daughter, home from college on vacation, taught English to Dominicans at the Bi-National Center. One of her brightest students, a boy of about seventeen, told her that he had worked hard and saved his money to pay for the lessons in order to go to the United States to better his lot. She praised him and asked what work he had been doing. Working in the *turbas,* he said, for fifty cents or a dollar a day.

Watching the students riot, I remembered wryly that in Washington I had dreamed of inviting Adlai Stevenson and others down to lecture at the University. We in the United States, more concerned with our children's marks or morals than their politics, are often puzzled by student riots abroad. Latin American university traditions are wholly different from ours. Like most Latin American universities, the University of Santo Domingo, oldest in the Hemisphere, is supported financially by the government but is wholly autonomous. Not even the police can enter its precincts. The students tend to terrorize its administrators. No student is expelled for failing his courses. Courses need not be completed, or even attended. Some "students" are scarcely students at all, but rather permanent political agitators enjoying immunity. Some began as bona fide students, then realized they were preparing themselves for unneeded vocations.

Santo Domingo has thousands of engineers, architects, artists, writers, poets, and philosophers who cannot earn a living. It has few plumbers or electricians. But university graduates haughtily reject such "menial" jobs. Thus arises the class—and a class of vital importance throughout Latin America and the other underdeveloped continents—of alienated intellectuals: Young men who feel themselves cut off from their own societies. Not unnaturally, they turn to politics. Their views sometimes have little contact with reality. Communists seduce them.

During my time, the Embassy, private foundations, and international bodies tried to rebuild the University. We accomplished little. So the University struggled on, not really an institution of learning but a political battleground. Sometimes Communist students and Social Christian students shot it out. Guns were buried all over the campus. When campus rioting started, soldiers and police could only ring the fence to contain the trouble.

Now, in April, secondary school students too, emulating University students, began forming pro-Communist, or anti-Communist, or anti-American, groups; and so the mobs in the downtown streets were filled with youngsters in school uniforms, white socks and loafers, in dubious battle.

The riots mounted. Cautiously, the Consejo began to deport agitators under the Emergency Law. The Castro/Communists denounced it in the name of freedom. So did the political parties, seeking the votes of deportees' relatives. And we became involved—we had to issue U.S. visas for people that the Consejo deported to the United States. So the Castro/Communists denounced us too.

Sometimes Amiama or Imbert would simply send a man's passport to our Consulate for a visa. I told them they must give us forty-eight hours' notice so we could check the man. I took personal charge of all such visa requests. Increasingly I authorized transit visas, permitting deportees to enter the U.S. only long enough to catch a plane somewhere else.

Some of the deportees bounced back to Santo Domingo—if they had money from Havana or Moscow, they no sooner landed in Paris or Curaçao than they booked passage back to Santo Domingo. Some, not Communists, simply paid their own way back. And some were sent to countries that would not accept them. One bounced to and fro more than half a dozen times. The Consejo forbade airlines and steamships to sell them returning tickets. It had already asked us to impose departure controls on people deported to the United States—that is, to keep them there. By the end of the year, we had some 125 deportees in the United States, most sent before I arrived.

Deportations were no real solution to the riots. The Consejo, fearing the parties' wrath, did not deport many. Furthermore, lacking an effective anti-subversive police unit, it was not catching the important Castro/Communist leaders.

Once again I urged Bonnelly to arrest rioters on the spot and prosecute them vigorously. But the Consejo did not crack down; and so I found myself urging other measures—methods once used by the police in Chicago.

There, if a policeman saw an ex-convict or a known hoodlum on the street, he picked him up "on suspicion," took him to the station, held him the legal limit, then released him—only to raid his flat that night, rout him out of bed, and start all over; time after time harassing him, hoping finally to drive him out of town. It was illegal detention, and often worse—prisoners were sometimes beaten. It is one of the gravest abuses of a citizen's constitutional rights. Frequently as a writer I had inveighed against it, and my wife had been a member of the Illinois board of the American Civil Liberties Union.

Now, trying to support a faltering Caribbean government that the Castro/Communists sought to overthrow, I favored such methods. The alternatives simply seemed unacceptable—a leftist takeover, a military takeover in reaction, or slaughter in the streets. Just the same, I knew that bad means tend to corrupt good ends. And I remembered Adlai Stevenson's denouncing Senator McCarthy's methods of attacking communism: "We begin to resemble the thing we hate."

The Dominican police never really learned how to harass rioters, despite my good advice and my bad conscience. Indeed, that spring they did little at all. Nor did the Consejo act decisively. But somehow the March and early April crisis receded. It did not stop. It simply sputtered out. And that was the way of so many crises in the Dominican Republic—nothing came of them. The trouble was, you never could be sure when something might. You could ignore none, for fear of ignoring the one that would topple the government. So throughout my time, the Crisis Crowd met night after night, usually on weekends, when crises seemed to come. The Consejeros and the military leaders and the politicians met separately on those same nights. All of us caught—watching, waiting, scheming, listening to the winds of chance and history.

That spring a thin, aged, haggard man with the tremulous hands and the mottled, cadaverous face of a drinker, Eduardo Sánchez Cabral, the Dominican Ambassador to the OAS, went on television in the Republic and spoke eloquently for hours, sipping a clear liquid the while; and he said, *"Estámos en plena selva"*—"We are right in the middle of a jungle." We were indeed.

3

Sometimes I felt that I was imprisoned in the air-conditioned Embassy Residence, an impenetrable wall between me and the people. On my presidential mission, I had been able to move about freely among the crowds in Parque Independencia, or among party leaders, or in slums. Now, as Ambassador, it was impossible—tours of slums become official tours. It is one of the gravest limits imposed on power.

I did manage on occasion to mingle with the people. I took Fran and the boys down to Parque Colón of a Sunday evening to sit on a stone bench with Dominicans and listen to the band concert, went quietly to dinner at Vesuvio's or Lina's or other restaurants, went shopping downtown and to the market. Invariably we were well received by ordinary Dominicans; some, who seemed to feel that we were taking part in their national life, as at a band concert, appeared proud and grateful. But the opportunities for fact-finding were better in the interior than in the capital, where I was too well known. I had resolved to spend all the time possible in the interior. I was the Ambassador to all the Republic, not just problems, and at first hand. In the course of doing this, I visited many places where no Ambassador had been and some that few Dominicans had visited. One must understand that no passenger railroad exists in the Republic; that, apparently for security reasons, Trujillo had deliberately wrecked airstrips throughout the country; and that in the dictator's time travel inside the Republic was severely restricted. It is therefore not surprising that many Dominicans are ignorant of regions of the Republic other than their own.

After more than a month in the capital jungle, we were ready to go. The logical choice was to the north—Santiago, in the rich Cibao, the second city of the Republic. But it was too obvious. We decided to make our first official trip instead to the poorest, most neglected region: The Southwest. On Friday, April 6, we set forth.

The road headed west along the sea, past the Fairgrounds, past the place where Trujillo was killed, and on to Haina; there the four-lane pavement ended abruptly. We passed through the sugar mill town, slatted tin-roofed shacks, naked black babies, and followed a crooked blacktop road over low tumbled hills to San Cristóbal, Trujillo's home town.

The monument to him had been smashed; so had his Partido building. High far off on a hilltop overlooking the city stood his deserted palace. Beyond San Cristóbal the road soon flattened out on a hot plain planted in sugar cane, green, tall, and thick, stretching all the way to the distant sea and, on the north, to the Cordillera Central, the great central mountain range. Clouds threw dark purple patches on its steep slopes; the highest peaks were lost in clouds far beyond. The cane thinned out, the land grew drier, and west of Baní the desert began: Crops ended, green ended, the land turned gray and stony and dusty, nothing but cactus and mesquite grew; and the desert stretched all the way to the Haitian border. It was unbearably hot; the air shimmered. A spur of the Cordillera Central closed in, came down in ragged peaks, and we rose, climbed steep and high and slow to the top—the historic Haitian invasion route. Then down we came, to Azua.

Ten thousand people lived here. They lived, nearly all, in small square houses built of split palm trunks, chinked with mud or lime, and painted red and pink and green and yellow, the roof thatched with dry palm fronds. The dirt streets were strewn with huge boulders and lined with high crumbling sidewalks, and the streets straggled out to the desert below the dry ragged mountains. Everywhere were heat and dust.

At the edge of town a Jeep loaded with soldiers met us to escort us to the Governor, delighting our boys, Dan and Fred. The Governor, a tall thin elderly man, took us into his office, called in the Mayor and the Army and Police commanders, and we sat in stiff-backed cane-bottomed shiny dark mahogany chairs. President Bonnelly had told him we were coming; he was at our service. I said that on the contrary we were at his service—I had come to meet his people, to talk to whomever he wished, to see whatever he thought I should see. Moments of uncertainty while the Governor conferred with the others, then we got into several cars and drove fast through the city, a military escort following. I was uncomfortable with a military escort. The Governor explained that although the recent riots in the capital had not thus far spread to Azua, he was taking no chances.

We crossed the dead, dry plain to the port. Like so many things Trujillo built, it was deserted and unfinished—there were reefs no one had thought of, a breakwater was needed.

A few miles away was a vast sisal plantation. Sisal, a fibrous, cactus-like plant, grows with little rainfall in hot climates. The mill was excellent. But it was uneconomic: Instead of being made into rope here and shipped direct to the States, the raw sisal fiber had to be trucked all the way to the capital to the rope-making factory. Why? Trujillo had so arranged it to the greater glory of his capital, Ciudad Trujillo. For him, of course, the enterprise had paid—he had hauled the sisal in Army trucks, had used slave labor in the fields. Throughout the Republic we came upon the same thing.

We drove on, and suddenly on the dry plain came upon a lush forest of banana trees. The reason was water; the company had put down wells and found sweet water and irrigated the land. It gushed from the earth and glowed in the irrigation ditches through the cool dark forest, smelling sweet and thick. This desert land would grow anything if you put water on it. And the Governor began talking about water, a subject I heard ceaselessly during this entire trip through the Southwest.

Driving on, we paused at a collection of huts in the cactus jungle, and, walking through a thorny thicket, came upon a brick ruin: Old Azua, destroyed by an earthquake in Spanish times. Cortés had been a notary public here before he set out to conquer Mexico. Today only a handful of hungry naked people dwell here, trying to live by burning wood to sell for charcoal.

We drove to the sea, a long crescent beach deep with dark gray sand and shaded by palm trees, and boys shinnied up the trees to knock down coconuts, knocked their tops off with machetes, and we drank the coconut water, always cool in the hottest midday sun. Our leaders made long speeches about the beauty of the beach, the magnificent prospects for tourist trade. I soon learned that this too was a pattern: The Republic was beautiful; and always by the sea the people hoped tourists would come, not realizing that natural beauty is almost the last thing rich Americans seek. Tourism means flashly hotels, golf courses, gambling, drinking, dancing, and, above all, other tourists; tourism costs millions for roads, airports, hotels. But I seldom tried to disabuse these people of their dreams, except Presidents or Cabinet ministers that seemed about to waste money on them.

It was long past noon; we drove back to the Governor's home, a small frame house, and had lunch: Fried pork, beef, plantains, potatoes, rice, chicken, and the Governor, a friendly and almost courtly man, served Scotch whisky hot in little glasses. I with an ulcer did the best I could. After lunch, we sat in rocking chairs on the tiled living room floor, the Army and Police commanders and their aids sleepy and sweaty in uniforms, all, I suspect, sensibly wishing I would disappear so they could take a siesta, something I learned later to do; but now, new on the job, I was eager to press on, see more, learn more.

What were the Governor's problems? Water, he said. And jobs—the emergency work-relief program, instituted by the Consejo with part of our twenty-five-million-dollar loan, was providing only five hundred or six hundred jobs in Azua. Unemployment was terrible, and discontent was growing.

Was there anything else the Governor wanted me to see? Once more we piled into cars and drove to an arid hilltop to inspect the waterworks. It needed repair. Was there more? We drove to a capped and abandoned oil well. A boy drew a bottle of oily liquid from it. I had lived in Azua twenty-five years before, and had arrived on the same boat with the first oil drillers. Finding oil had been Trujillo's fondest dream. But they never found it in commercial quantities. Yet the story persists that they really did, but for mysterious political reasons had lied. Azua still dreamed.

We left Azua toward dusk. It had changed little since I had been there in 1937. And probably not much in the hundred years before that.

We followed the curving, tortured road around an enormous mountain, and by the time we reached Barahona it was dark, and we were exhausted. The Governor of Barahona, however, and the Mayor and Police and Army commanders, and several politicians, were waiting for us. While hotel boys carried load after load of our baggage—suitcases, hampers of food and bottled water (outside the capital, roadside restaurants are rare and unsafe)—and while Fran put the boys to bed, I talked to the Barahona officials about their problems. The same problems—jobs and water. But here civic leaders had drawn up elaborate plans for diverting rivers for irrigation, and gave them to me. I told them I was not competent to give an opinion of their plans but the plans should be submitted to the Consejo, and they were acting precisely in the spirit of the *Alianza*—we could best help those who helped themselves. Near midnight, I went to bed under mosquito netting, the window open to the jukebox and the sea.

Early in the morning, several Barahona men drove us out into the country. We left the highway and turned onto a road so deep in dust we were in danger of getting stuck. But these men wanted to show us something. We were passing through the same stony cactus desert of yesterday. Suddenly on our left appeared a thick, lush grove of banana trees. Irrigation. The water had come from the Yaque del Sur. We crossed it and came to the village of Vicente Noble: Mud huts set stark on a dusty plain, women in black lined up with cans at a trickle of water from a rusty pipe; nothing green, nothing growing, the whole place a gray, baked plain, gray earth, gray dust, gray and silent people. They scarcely gazed up at us, somehow imprisoned by the heat, the grayness, the dust, the hunger, like patients in a locked ward in a mental hospital, inert, dull-eyed, staring at space. I never forgot it. Here was, to me, our opportunity: To change this place. I resolved to do it. We shall see what happened to that resolve.

Driving back, one of the men told me expansively, "You are our safe-deposit vault," and chuckled, "because we know you won't go Communist." He expalined: Like many wealthy Latin Americans, he sent his profits to U.S. banks. I told him he could do nothing for his country and little for himself or his children that way, and he could scarcely expect the United States to develop the Río Yaque del Sur and help his country if he himself and others like him refused. He was more surprised, I think, than hurt or angered—it was simply what one had always done if one had money. And that, of course, is the heart of the matter in Latin America: The feudal structure, the few who send riches abroad and at home ignore the many.

All unwitting, he did it again: Blandly took us in his Cadillac for a rapid drive over rutted stony streets in the Barahona slums, while dull-eyed women stared at us from the dark doorways of huts. Once a gaunt man said rapidly, almost dispassionately, "What are you looking at us for? Why don't you look at yourselves?" Our host glanced at him contemptuously.

That afternoon we left Barahona and headed south for Cabo Rojo, where the Aluminum Company of America (Alcoa) mines bauxite. We were moving down the long wedge-shaped peninsula of Pedernales, the rugged isolated land mass that juts deep into the Caribbean from the Dominican-Haitian frontier. Here for miles the mountains—the Baoruco range—come right down to the sea, and the road swoops and dives over ridges and ravines, hugging cliffsides, dark vine-clotted jungle on one side, on the other the sea, waterfalls tumbling into the sea, rock walls rising sheer out of the water, and each cove is a golden beach with booming surf and flying spray and yellow sand. It is one of the most beautiful places in the Caribbean.

Seeing a few huts and fishermen's nets, we wondered why the poor and hungry from the baked Azua plain did not come here and become fishermen; but the odd truth is that Dominicans, though island people, are not notably fisherfolk or seafaring men (but the Indians had been).

Beyond Enriquillo, a squalid little town, we turned inland. The land grew stony again, houses and people disappeared, cactus rose. Soon we entered one of the strangest pieces of terrain I have ever seen. The earth was jagged rock, not soil. The rock was coral limestone, gray and brown. It lay every which way, crisscrossed, striated, filled with crevasses, undermined with caves, ragged and razor-sharp on top. To walk was agony. Nothing grew here but cactus and thorny trees, so closely intertwined they cut your clothes and skin to ribbons. It was dry—no water anywhere. It was hot—burning hot. Nothing stirred. The road was a twisted wagon-track, mostly naked rock. Suddenly rounding a turn we saw a strange beast scrabbling in the cactus, saw him slither over the rock and disappear into a cavern, gray-green himself, huge, with sawtoothed serrated back, hooded eyes, and armor-plated side and long whiplash tail: A giant iguana. We saw two more that day, only flashing glimpses. They look evil. Only they inhabit this desolation.

Near dark we reached the sea and the Alcoa installation—wire-fenced property, company guard in pith helmet, airstrip, huge loading dock, mountains of blood-red bauxite ore from which aluminum is made, and on a high cliff above the sea, the guesthouse complex: Swimming pool, glassed-in dining room, gleaming kitchen. So I crossed another bridge:

Having all my sheltered life deplored the habit of U. S. Ambassadors barricading themselves behind a fence in a U.S. corporation compound, I now without a murmur took a shower, put on fresh clothes, had a long cool drink, and dined on food imported from the States with the Alcoa manager, Pat Hughson.

Hughson, a short, heavy, red-haired, friendly man, was head of Alcoa in the Republic, and one of the best members of the U.S. community there. Married to a handsome Dominican woman, speaking Spanish, he understood the Dominican people. I wish we could be as proud of all our businessmen in Latin America.

I had planned to pay an official visit to nearby Pedernales, a tiny provincial capital on the Haitian border. But I suddenly fell ill with a high fever, and Fran and the boys represented me. A band greeted her, and she met with the Governor and leading citizens in the government house. Then she walked, followed by men and women and scores of children, through the *barrios,* the slums, going into huts to talk to the women who, she later said, were voluble and demonstrative, embracing her, showing her a naked sick baby wrapped in a torn bath towel, the bedroom with a single bare bedspring supported by blocks of wood for wife and husband and eight children, the kitchen a separate lean-to with a well of charcoal sunk in the middle of a bare wooden table.

A young woman pushed through the crowd and asked if the *Alianza* would give her four palm-tree posts to build a house for her mother. Once Fran turned to locate our own boys in the sea of children and spotted Fred, who was nine, blond, round-faced, and sweating in the wool suit he insisted on wearing on official trips, walking with a dark-skinned naked boy about his own age, talking animatedly, scuffing the thick dust, one arm thrown across the other's bare shoulders. Pedernales is poor, one of the poorest areas of the Republic, for little grows there, no decent road connects it with the outside, people merely exist, starving beside a sea filled with fish. Fran was told a child dies of hunger in Pedernales every day.

One night that weekend at Alcoa—it may have been our first—while we were having after-dinner coffee under the stars and listening to the surf on the cliff below, several big cars whirled up, and out stepped José Fernández Caminero, the Consejero, and several high-ranking Dominican government and military men. They had been inspecting Beata, a nearby island used as a concentration camp by Trujillo. They were considering exiling Castro/Communists there. Fernández Caminero took me aside.

He told me, in effect, that he planned to run for President with the support of Imbert and Amiama. That, of course, is not what he said. What he said was that the political situation was improving and the Consejo would survive if he could assert leadership and push through certain reforms. But Imbert and Amiama were blocking reform—they saw no future for themselves, felt hurt because they were disliked instead of admired as heroes, feared for their lives if one of the present political parties won the election, and—finally—told him they would feel safe only if he, Fernández Caminero, became President.

That, if he did it, would be dangerous. The seven Consejeros had agreed that none would be a candidate for President in the December election and that all would leave the Palace on schedule, February 27, 1963. Were Fernández Caminero to breach the agreement, he might set off a ruinous power struggle inside the Consejo. I suspected that Amiama and Imbert were simply using him to advance their own purposes.

We left Alcoa, heading up a Jeep road in the mountains on the Haitian border. The Pedernales Governor insisted on sending a Jeepload of six soldiers with us carrying submachine guns and San Cristóbal carbines. In case our car broke down, he said; I suspected he feared Haitians or bandits. The road climbed steadily, and high on a cliff we stopped and beheld a medieval fortress: A blockhouse of concrete and stone, built in a hollow square, its high wall crenelated, and commanding a field of fire across the boundary river far below. Through binoculars we watched Haitian women toiling up the mountainside with buckets of water from the river, and saw one or two ragged Haitian soldiers. The Dominicans were contemptuous of them but feared them almost superstitiously, an officer saying, "You only see two, but don't worry, others are hiding. They hide like animals."

Farther on we stopped to inspect some scrawny olive trees: Trujillo had ordered them planted here experimentally. Perhaps they would have flourished if tended, but they had not. It was another caprice of his, never carried to fruition. One might have thought the pine here would encourage a lumber industry, but it had not. This frontier was desolate, empty, and impossible to patrol: Guerrillas, Haitians, smugglers, anybody could cross without detection.

As we climbed higher, our car gave out. The Dominicans said there was clearly nothing to do but abandon it. I got a screwdriver and fixed it (and I am by no means a mechanic). I do not know how many times, traveling in the Republic, I stopped to ask directions and was told with a shrug that the place I wanted to go was too far, the road was too bad, getting there was impossible. It never was; and I somehow instinctively refuse to believe that any road is too far to travel, while they believe the contrary. But then, I did not grow up under Trujillo.

We topped the mountains and started down, the road switchbacking steeply, Lake Enriquillo spread out below, a salt lake, below sea level, named for the Indian chief who surrendered last to the Spaniards.

Jimaní, one of three chief border towns, has no reason to exist. We had expected a helter-skelter collection of palm-thatched huts. Instead, we found a modern city neatly laid out, concrete streets, concrete houses spaced among palm trees, government buildings big enough for a good-sized city. The whole place looked unreal, a mirage. Trujillo had built it to "Dominicanize" the frontier. Probably he had intended to do the same the length of the frontier. But, again, he had not; and now some of Jimaní's houses were deserted, the hotel empty, and its swimming pool filed with stagnant water.

We drank a beer and tried to talk with the dozen men who had met us at the hotel. But the UCN leader and PRD leader would not talk in front of each other, and abruptly the local military commander, Colonel Ney Garrido, a big dark powerful man, arose and said, "Let's go," and leaving the others with scarcely the amenities, took us to his own house close to the frontier gate. He told us we would sleep here, he would take care of us; he spoke contemptuously of the hotel, the town, the townsmen, the politicians, the parties, the civil authorities. Expansive at dinner, he opened his refrigerator, kept proudly—like those of many Dominicans— in the dining room, and drew forth cold German beer, French wine, imported cheeses and tinned chickens and tinned ham, saying, "I like to live like an American." The Dominican contempt for Dominicans: Few Americans I met were as anti-Dominican as the Dominicans themselves.

After dinner the Colonel turned his office over to me, and only when he sat me down at a massive mahogany desk did I notice it had been Trujillo's; it bore his five stars. The Governor and other officials, the local politicians and businessmen, came in one by one, and though I told each I would have preferred to call on him, they thought this was the proper way. Trujillo's hand lay heavy here. We slept that night in a small house beside the Colonel's, and all night sentries tramped around it.

Early next morning we left for the capital, stopping at another pro-vincial capital, Neiba. Again the road ran through stony, gray, burning cactus desert, the towns were little but hamlets, thatched huts on boulder-strewn streets, naked black children with bloated bellies playing in gray dust. Again we heard but one request: Water.

Despite the odds, had the people really tried everything? Splendid grapes grew profusely at an oasis near Neiba, and I asked why nobody canned jelly or made wines. Nobody knew. Lake Enriquillo is full of caimanes, alligators, and I asked why there was no leather industry, adding that I had seen one in Nicaragua. The man I was talking to paused, was nonplused; obviously this never had occurred to him. Then he brightened, he had thought of an answer: It was dangerous, the caimanes were very fierce. So, I said, were they in Nicaragua. But, he asked, with a cunning half-smile, were those fresh-water or salt-water caimanes? Fresh-water, I said. Ah, that was it—as everybody knew, salt-water *caimanes* were far fiercer than fresh-water *caimanes*. Such an industry was clearly impossible here.

We had planned to spend a day at Neiba, but had telegraphed ahead that because of my illness we could stay only a couple of hours. The telegram had not been delivered; the Governor and Mayor had called a meeting of townspeople and they had waited patiently all morning in the town hall. I could do nothing but apologize. (We had invited President Bonnelly to dinner in Santo Domingo that night.) For an hour or two we sat in the town hall at Neiba, the Governor, Mayor, and members of the Ayuntamiento (Town Council), Fandino and I, ranged in wooden chairs at the front of the room, Fran and the boys with the people in front of us, anyone who wanted to come. I spoke briefly— the United States admired the Dominican people's struggle and that of the Consejo to emerge from Trujillo tyranny to democracy; we were here to help, I was traveling to learn. I invited questions. Various people spoke. Once more, it came down to jobs and water. Plus politics: A young 14th of June leader wanted to know why the twenty-two million dollars in sugar money had not been returned and who had pocketed it. I answered him rather sharply, and left with a feeling that while I had convinced the older people that he didn't know what he was talking about, I might well have been less sharp.

4

We had been gone seven days. I intended to visit all twenty-five provincial capitals that year, if possible. But I knew now we must allow more time for each stop, avoid identification with any one host, talk politics only in private, hold more and bigger public meeetings, spend more time afoot, and see and be seen more.

As to the Southwest, five things stood out in my mind.

The emergency work-relief program was helping little in the provinces. The people's lot had hardly improved at all since Trujillo fell. And something must be done for the jobless displaced *campesinos* who lived in the Barahona slums.

Second, civilian control in the provinces was extremely tenuous; the military still was the real power. Governors and other officials appointed by the Consejo deferred to it. The provinces looked to the capital for help.

Third, the PRD was rapidly catching up with the UCN and perhaps had already passed it. Most UCN leaders I had met were elderly, respected gentlemen, physicians, ranchers, with no political experience, offering only personal local prestige which could evaporate in an instant in this revolutionary time. On the other hand, the PRD leaders seemed young and aggressive; they came, by and large, from the lower classes, and many were experienced politicians—they had worked for Trujillo's Partido Dominicano. Indeed, I had met one who was telling the *campesinos* that the PRD was really the old Trujillo PD with another initial added, that the Trujillos would return soon, and that the *campesinos* had better be on the right side—the PD, or PRD, side.

Fourth, José Fernández Caminero wanted to be President—and thought he could be, with the help of Amiama and Imbert.

Finally, I had seen a great opportunity for the United States to help change the face of the Southwest permanently: Put water on the land. We ought to do it because it was politic but more because it was right. Nobody ought to live as the people at Vicente Noble lived. If we didn't help them, no one would. I talked at once to our AID people. Damming the Río Yaque del Sur was a huge project, expensive, slow, requiring years. Something was needed now. I talked to Andy Hernandez, the Peace Corps director. He suggested I get the Dominican government to request the Peace Corps for well drillers. Meanwhile, he himself would help. I proposed to President Bonnelly that I appoint Hernandez, he appoint a Dominican, and we send them together to the Southwest immediately to start drilling wells and developing communities. AID would put up some money.

Bonnelly was enthusiastic. We would announce nothing until we had water flowing, ditches dug, and land under irrigation. Trujillo had raised too many false hopes. Bonnelly named his man, I talked to him and Hernandez, and they set forth in a Jeep with high hopes.

Thereafter, every now and then, between political crises, I inquired how the project was going. Slow, the report always said. Once they dug, or rebuilt, one small well, and women lined up for hours with cans to fill. Bonnelly and I rejoiced—there was plenty of water under the ground. Months later, some thirty Peace Corps well drillers arrived. But progress languished, Hernandez' Dominican counterpart could hardly get an appointment with the man in the Palace who was administering the money, Hernandez' own duties at the rapidly expanding Peace Corps took all his time, the drillers couldn't get rigs from the Dominican ministries. The local people would not work without pay; we ran out of money. Why drill, they wondered—their wives had always carried water from the river in pails on their heads. Bonnelly and I tried to spur the work on. But as elections drew near and political pressures mounted, we had no time for it. The subject became painful to us both; we did not mention it any more. "Community self-help"—the idea sounds great in Washington. But who will do it?

The project was a failure, lost in the jungle of political pressures. I could name a dozen projects like it. But, as we shall see, until the very end we did not stop trying to bring water to the poor Southwest.

5

I plunged back into the jungle. On Monday the blow fell—the UCN ordered all its members to pull out of the government within ten days.

Shlaudeman said that only last week Fiallo had publicly renewed his pledge to support the Consejo. But leftist extremists in the UCN had overridden him. Now it was not impossible they might overthrow the government.

We decided to launch a two-pronged political offensive.

We would first urge the UCN Consejeros not to resign—that was crucial. We would try to persuade the party leaders not to destroy the Consejo, their best hope for elections. We would watch the military closely—they might seize this opportunity to move.

If all that succeeded, we would urge the Consejo to take the initiative, stop being a do-nothing Consejo and enact reforms immediately, and immediately and publicly invite the OAS to send a mission to help prepare for elections.

As we separated to go to work, John Crimmins called. Could I come to Washington for consultation in ten days, on April 26? I would. But it would be a busy ten days.

I invited Fernández Caminero, the most avowedly UCN Consejero, to the house for coffee and asked if he intended to follow the UCN directive and resign. He did not.

Next I saw Pichardo. He seemed calm, said the UCN had to leave the government in order to lead an independent political life. The UCNers in the Consejo itself would not resign, though lower-level government officials would. In the long run, he thought, the move was healthy —the UCN, which he considered the "real hope for the future of the country," would no longer be held responsible for the Consejo's failures; and the Consejo would be able to stand on its own feet.

President Bonnelly shared Pichardo's views. I told him people in the interior were calling it a do-nothing Consejo. He said he would soon speak to the people on radio-TV, recounting the Consejo's accomplishments. I urged our program on him—agrarian reform, tax reform, trial of *calié* and military, and OAS election help. He liked it but he was not sure the Consejo was yet strong enough to attempt it all. He did not have the votes inside the Consejo for agrarian reform. I told him I had to go to Washington, and he looked shocked—he didn't want me to leave. I was thinking of making a speech reaffirming our support for him before I left. Bonnelly thought it an excellent idea.

I turned next to the major parties themselves. Fiallo assured me the UCN had no intention of pulling the government down. So did Luís

Manuel Baquero, his number two man. I believed them and urged them to moderate their public attacks on the Consejo.

I met Juan Bosch of the PRD for the first time—I invited him to the Residence for a drink. He did not drink, but took a Coke. He was a tall, erect man with curly snow-white hair, high cheekbones, high broad forehead, and striking bright blue eyes—his gaze was always darting about suspiciously. His features looked chiseled. Bosch bore himself with great dignity and, at that first meeting, with considerable formality. He had the air of one fit to lead. I asked about his party and its growth. He took a piece of paper and drew a pyramid, something like this:

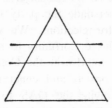

He said, "We are strong here," pointing to the bottom, the masses, "and a little here," pointing to the middle, the middle class.[2] "We are strong

[2] Class stratification was of crucial importance to Bosch's political thought. In his book Bosch stresses it again and again. He says the high-middle class was composed of the more successful business and professional men, with an added mixture of landowners, some public officials, and industrialists. "Somewhere above these people" was the "'first' caste" people socially but not economically superior to the middle-middle class. The high-middle class contained no more than fifteen thousand adults, Bosch thought. It was a secure class, economically and socially. The much larger middle-middle class was insecure. It contained most professional men, small business-men, most public officials—perhaps 150,000 or 200,000 adults. The lower-middle class was smaller and contained another 150,000 adults. The entire middle class, Bosch wrote, was "like a cloud which changes shape every five minutes." It had no faith in its destiny. It had no "scale of moral values," was loyal to no one—"not to a friend nor to a party nor to a principle nor to an ideal nor to a government. Their only important value is money." Its moral fiber had been destroyed by civil wars, the U.S. occupation, and Trujillo. But "the great popular masses" of workers and campesinos are "an entirely different matter." Bosch wrote, "Here, intact, are the national virtues: love of their compatriots, their land, their music, their food; loyalty to friends and party, and to certain simple but generous ideas." After Trujillo's fall, Bosch wrote, the social classes polarized. On the one hand stood the upper-middle class and part of the middle-middle class; on the other, part of the middle-middle class, the lower-middle class, and the masses of workers, campesinos, and unem-ployed. Bosch's construct of Dominican society was highly theoretical and abstract. He used it constantly in his work as well as in his book. He planned his campaign strategy, he wrote his speeches, to fit the pattern he envisioned. He said his votes came entirely from "the poorest masses"—all three sectors of the middle class voted for other parties. Even so, he said, and rightly, the masses had no power to act. "They were simply spectators at a Dominican drama."

in the *barrios* of the cities, among the poor. We are growing in the university and the new middle class. We have 70 percent of the *campesinos* and the workers and the urban poor. I talk economics to them. They did not know their rights." Bosch spoke English with a curious sharp angular accent, unlike the usual Dominican accent. He had been in exile for twenty-five years—the United States; Chile; Cuba under Prio Socarrás; Caracas; and Costa Rica, where he had taught at the Institute of Political Education while José "Pepe" Figueres was President.

"The middle and upper classes talk politics, not economics. The UCN is men of prestige but not real power. It is an anachronistic class. The lower class and middle class want power. The Consejo de Estado has made no reforms. It has refused our proposals. The present crisis," speaking calmly, "is a crisis of the UCN, not of the government. We would win the election now. But I do not know about later—there will be guerrillas in the hills in two or three months."

Why did he think so? "Fidel Castro has chosen the 14th of June, not the MPD, and is giving them guns. Last night two generals and three colonels told me about them and said some Army units might join them." He delivered this prediction—which, if true, meant bloody disaster—with absolute equanimity. "There is no danger from the right. The real danger is the 14th of June."

Juan Bosch always underestimated the military right, overestimated the Castro/Communist left.

He went on, "The Consejo de Estado won't take our program. So we will not give them our men. The Consejo will not move because the Americans said it should only be a caretaker government for order and elections and it must not lose money. But there is a revolution going on, the Consejo must act, it cannot last nine more months without action. I do not think," he said calmly, "it will last."

Bosch talked about his campaign plans—he would organize a *campesino* school to train *campesino* leaders, send Jeeps throughout the country, and himself speak over the radio. Ángel Miolán was his principal organizer. Sacha Volman, Bosch's confidant, would run the *campesino* school, as he had in Costa Rica.

I said I thought the Consejo knew it must cease being a caretaker and must act, and I hoped that the parties would moderate their attacks on it. Bosch said, "Help us to convince the Consejo to act. We want it to survive." He gave me no commitment not to attack it.

Bosch left the Residence about 6 P.M. that day, Tuesday, April 17. While I was having dinner with my family, Donny Reid bounded into the Residence unannounced and said excitedly that the Consejo had just smashed a military *golpe.* A general and two colonels had led it.

"They went to jail a few minutes ago. We are investigating now." The general was a UCNer. The two colonels had told several other officers that Amiama and Imbert were plotting a *golpe,* and they wanted to beat them to it. One of the officers to whom they talked had been Colonel Elías Wessin y Wessin, the tank commander. That afternoon Wessin had gone to General Elby Viñas Román, the Secretary of State for Defense, and together they had reported to President Bonnelly.

The plot—if plot there was, you never could be sure—may have been a reaction to Castro/Communist disorders in the streets. Military men, thinking the Consejo unable to maintain control, may have decided to take matters into their own hands. Or to use the disorders as a pretext to seize power for themselves. We never knew.

In any case, the plot, coming as it did on the heels of the UCN pullout, sharply changed the course of events, and in a surprising direction. It unified the Consejo—Reid said he was proud of the Consejo and would never resign; Amiama and Imbert abandoned their schemes. And a feeling quickly arose that the people did not want the Consejo overthrown.

I impressed on Donny Reid the Consejo's need to seize the initiative now—to act, to enact reforms for the people. He was adamant against agrarian reform. He said, "I will fight it in the Consejo and if it passes anyway, I will fight it outside." It was the oligarch in him. Bonnelly had told me he didn't have the votes for agrarian reform. So Reid was the problem.

Pierre Salinger, an old friend and then President Kennedy's press secretary, arrived. He was on vacation, island-hopping with his wife and another couple in a private plane. I gave a party for them, inviting Reid and other Dominican officials. I asked Salinger to take Reid aside and tell him President Kennedy was very much interested in the Consejo's progress, particularly in agrarian reform. Salinger did it. In a few days the bill passed. Thus agrarian reform came to the Dominican Republic.

At noon on Saturday Reid came again to the Residence greatly agitated. He had met with President Bonnelly, Amiama, and Imbert that morning, and they had agreed to go ahead with several parts of our program— agrarian reform, the trials of *calié,* the appointment of new judges. But they also had decided to call a meeting the next day of the Armed Forces leaders to assert the President's supremacy as Commander in Chief and to notify them that the Consejo intended to proceed with the trials of several military men accused of killing civilians under Trujillo and since.

That was, in my opinion, quite probably the most dangerous thing the Consejo could do—provoke the military.

Reid said he knew it. He said, "It might provoke a reaction. We want you to know—if there is a reaction, we will count on you for help."

I asked what he meant by help.

"It doesn't mean Marines landing. But we would want you to tell the

Armed Forces we are against foul play. You would have to decide in a matter of hours," and he rushed on, naming a dozen or so high-ranking military men he wanted to purge, calling one a "monster," another a "butcher," and relating their crimes. Reid ended with a flourish: "The die is cast. No one knows what is going to happen." And rushed out.

I called in Hemba, Shlaudeman, the CIA chief, and the military attachés at once that Saturday afternoon. We did not want to discourage the Consejo from acting, but neither did we want it to huff and puff and blow itself over.

We relied heavily, as usual, on the three attachés—Lieutenant Colonel Bevan Cass, a six-foot-five crewcut Marine who was sentimental, a likable man who could lead a bumbling Ambassador through the protocol of a military reception and could also talk diplomatically but firmly to Dominican officers; Lieutenant Colonel Luther F. Long, called Fritz, a short, wiry Army man who talked bluntly to the Dominican military but defended them vigorously against all attack, and who, though he once had been a small-town mayor, had rather less political feel than Cass; and Lieutenant Colonel William Richardson, a bilingual Air Force man who probably had more friends among the Dominican officers and enlisted men than anybody else, who probably understood them better than anyone, who heard everything and reported everything but, no politician, sometimes did not grasp its political significance. I never knew three men who worked harder, or with more devotion to their duties.

The attachés picked out a few military men the Consejo might safely try. But we decided I should tell President Bonnelly that while we were in complete sympathy with his desire to purge the Armed Forces of Trujillistas, he could not count on United States help at this time in this matter. Instead, we favored strong Consejo action in other fields directly affecting the people—agrarian reform, tax reform, and arrangements for the elections.

I could not reach President Bonnelly. The attachés scattered. That night they reported that Bonnelly, Amiama, and Imbert had met with General Viñas Román. The outcome was unknown; they would meet on Monday.

Should I try to see Bonnelly? If the purge process was already started, my intervention might make matters worse. Knowing Bonnelly, I thought he would move cautiously. I decided to wait till Monday.

Monday I was occupied with economic affairs. Rafael Picó, our economic adviser, feared inflation. Before fleeing, former President Balaguer, trying to save himself, had given away taxicabs and bicycles and farms and cows to ordinary people and put hundreds of people to work on government projects. *Campesinos* had flocked to the cities where the jobs were, and as wages rose but production stayed low, prices began to rise. In the view of Picó and the IMF, if the Consejo did not quickly enact new taxes, get its budget under control, increase production, and commence development projects, inflation might get out of control. I promised Picó to press the Consejo as soon as possible.

I had another economic problem that Monday. George Walker, an executive of the Koppers Company, had come to the Republic on behalf of the Businessmen's Council on International Understanding, a private U.S. group, and had brought in high-level U.S. industrialists to study the former Trujillo properties and advise the Consejo what to do with them. Walker now gave me a preliminary report, industry by industry.

But Walker differed fundamentally from Picó. Picó wanted all the non-sugar industries put into a Fomento, a development corporation whose profits would finance industrial expansion, as in Puerto Rico. Walker, on the other hand, thought that if the government continued to own and operate them, it would use them as patronage grab bags and, moreover, private capital would not invest. He, therefore, favored gradually selling or leasing the properties to private investors, Americans or Dominicans or both.

I told Walker our basic policy objective was, first, to conserve the properties as the patrimony of the Dominican people and, second, to prevent Americans from buying them. If Americans bought them, we would be accused of having sent the fleet to throw the Trujillos out in order to get our hands on their properties. Moreover, the properties did and ought to belong to the Dominican people. Their ultimate disposition was a Dominican matter. In my opinion the caretaker Consejo would decide nothing—final disposition would have to await an elected government.

That Monday night, Imbert called. He wanted to see me at once. I went to his house, and found General Luna, the Air Force Commander in Chief, with him. Imbert said that every day that passed weakened the Consejo. UCN's withdrawal had hurt. Now UCN was proposing a military purge, and a police purge too.

Luna complained bitterly about our Military Assistance and Advisory Group, MAAG. It had promised much *matériel* but delivered nothing. "The boys are scared to fly. The planes are old, they are afraid. We have no nose tires for the B-26's."

Imbert took it up: "You could do it right away."

And Luna, "Cuba could fly rings around us with their MIG's."

And Imbert, "It is essential that the pilots see United States backing."

And Luna, "Our pilots live well. But they hear the Russians have given the Cubans seventy-five MIG's, and what has the U.S. given them? Nothing."

And so on, for an hour and a half. General Luna was a tall, muscular, swarthy, mustached young man. He had a superior attitude and dressed almost foppishly; his appearance always reminded me of Ramfis Trujillo's. During cruises on the presidential yacht, he used to read my sons' comic books, seeming to favor "Batman."

I reminded them gently that the Armed Forces' purpose was not to fight MIG's—we would do that if necessary—but to maintain internal security against guerrilla action. I also deplored delay, and told them I would look into it personally in Washington.

Leaving, I wondered if Imbert, about to embark on the Consejo's military purge, had staged the show for Luna.

The Dominican military—what a problem!

My attachés, of course, saw them daily. They made friends among them. Assiduously they worked at convincing them that democracy was here, and in a democracy the military is subordinate to the civilian power. They came to think the Dominican military believed it. Time and again they told me, "The Armed Forces will remain loyal to the President." And time and again I replied, "Don't forget, it's still Trujillo's military."

Trujillo had won power by taking illiterate peasants, putting them in the Army, and elevating them to high rank. The result, by and large, was an Army of *campesinos*—uneducated or ill-educated officers, loyal to the man who elevated them, until they see a chance to do better.

After Trujillo fell, the worst of his military butchers had fled, been imprisoned, or been shunted aside to obscure posts in the interior. Three young new service chiefs—Army, Navy, Air—had been elected by their officers. Over them stood the Minister of Defense, General Victor Elby Viñas Román, also elected by the military, a career military officer himself but with Cabinet rank and wearing two stars. General Viñas was short and square and young, his face unlined, almost soft. He never talked unless asked a direct question; then he answered yes or no. He was very, very careful. I considered him a decent man. I never thought Viñas a strong leader but, rather, a compromiser and pacificator among quarreling factions, chosen for that very reason. He was a key figure throughout my time.

The military did not want to govern. They knew nothing about it. They only knew they hated and feared the Communists. Batista and his officers, fleeing Castro, had told the Dominican officers how Castro had shot their confreres at the wall; they never forgot. But though the military formally acknowledged the supremacy of the civilian government, they never, I was and am convinced, surrendered the view that they and they alone were the true guardians of stability and constitutionality, as they understood it. They not only wanted to stay out of politics, as they declared;

they despised political parties and politicians, considering themselves serving the higher national interest: The national motto, *"Dios Patria Libertad."* But their God, their country, and their kind of liberty.

The officers' natural interests lay with the ruling classes, not with the masses. They had escaped from the masses; they feared their vengeance now. And some hoped to become rich and were becoming so as they rotated the lucrative graft posts.

As for the troops themselves, they were the usual Latin American garrison army—lounging around scattered *fortalezas,* providing for their wives and many children, ill-trained, ill-equipped, idle. There were ten thousand in the Army, six thousand in the Navy, and four thousand in the Air Force—twenty thousand in all, plus another ten thousand that Imbert poured into the police. That was an Armed Forces ridiculously bigger than needed to "defend the Republic." And, except for the Air Force, useless as well. Both we and the Consejo wanted to reduce the Armed Forces. But we couldn't. It was, really, a relief program. To cut it drastically would simply increase the unemployed.

In our efforts to contain the military leaders in 1962, we had several advantages. Fresh in their memory was the appearance of the U.S. fleet on the horizon in November 1961. Fresh, too, was General Rodríguez Echavarría's unsuccessful two-day *coup* in January 1962. And we persuaded them that the civilian Consejo protected them from the people's vengeance.

Even so, throughout the year, scarcely a week passed that a rumor did not race through the city that the military was plotting a *golpe.* Sometimes we heard about it from a Consejero, as from Reid that week. More often *we* heard it first, usually on Thursday or Friday. Through the weekend the attachés and political officers would meet at the Residence and chase around the city to talk to military men and politicians, while I hurried to the Consejeros or the President. Sometimes the entire rumor proved false. I will never know for sure how many times we were chasing shadows—or how many times we saved the government. Often I thought of "Dover Beach":

> *And we are here as on a darkling plain,*
> *Swept with confused alarms of struggle and flight,*
> *Where ignorant armies clash by night.*

That, then, was the Dominican military the Consejo now proposed to purge.

On Tuesday morning I met President Bonnelly at Donny Reid's house. We sat on the veranda, overlooking the lush and lovely patio, and I asked about the purge. Bonnelly agreed it was difficult and dangerous. Gone were Donny Reid's excited pronouncements. Bonnelly said,

"It is my project"—he had taken it away from Reid, taken it away, too, from Amiama and Imbert. He would move slowly and carefully. Bonnelly seemed to have his program so clearly in mind that I did not presume to offer him the list we had prepared.

We discussed at length the problem of helping him establish an anti-subversive unit. This time we got down to details—who would set it up, how it would work, how much it would cost, and, most important, to whom it would be responsible: Himself. Various Consejeros had been maneuvering to establish intelligence services of their own, and had repeatedly asked me for help. I wanted to be sure it was responsible only to Bonnelly.

I asked Bonnelly how he saw the present political situation. He thought the danger from the UCN pullout had passed—only two of fourteen Cabinet ministers had resigned, and only four or five governors.

Bonnelly had finished drafting a decree encouraging, though regulating, foreign investment. He would implement agrarian reform immediately. He was "putting the finishing touches" on a Court of Claims decree. The new election law was drafted. In his forthcoming nationwide speech to the people he would stress elections and agrarian reform. I suggested he write out his speech in advance, recounting my work on speeches for President Kennedy and Adlai Stevenson.

I told him what I proposed to say in my own speech the next day to the American Chamber of Commerce—that the Consejo had accomplished much despite great difficulties, that the times demanded responsible politics, a steadfast government, a loyal military, and a responsible citizenry. I would review the *Alianza's* progress and explain the United States' purpose—we wanted a Dominican government run not from Havana or Moscow or Washington but from Santo Domingo. The United States government firmly supported this transition from tyranny to democracy and any usurpation of power by force or violence would be a betrayal of the hopes of the Dominican people.

In many Latin American countries, a public speech so interventionist would have been unthinkable. But Bonnelly agreed that it would strengthen the Consejo's hand against the parties and the military.

The State Department cleared the speech with a few changes and I delivered it on Wednesday and left the next day, April 26, for New York and Washington. Just before I boarded the plane, a CIA man came hurrying to the airport: He had a list of the Armed Forces officers that would be purged. It went far beyond what Bonnelly had indicated. I hesitated—had Bonnelly lost control of the other Consejeros? Then I boarded the plane. While I was in Washington, the purge took place, but many on the list were not included. It was not opposed. Once more a crisis sputtered out.

6

Airborne, I went over my long agenda for Washington—the visa mess, the twenty-two million dollars, Trujillo properties, anti-subversive unit, the Armed Forces purge, MAAG and AID speedups, the University, the growing budget deficit, and much more. When the jet began to descend, and the shining towers of Manhattan rose out of the haze, and later in the day as the plane sailed over the Washington Monument and the dome of the Capitol, I felt a sudden surge of pride: This was a real country, a great nation. But what could we do for the gray people at Vicente Noble?

I was in Washington six days. I had lunch the first day atop the Department with Secretary Rusk, Undersecretaries Ball and McGhee, and Assistant Secretary for Latin America Edwin Martin. All happened to be in town and unengaged, though their inviting me to lunch did indicate the Administration's concern about the Republic.

I raised four major questions with them.

It was a fact of political life, right or wrong, I said, that Dominicans regarded the twenty-two million dollars as theirs. Secretary Rusk replied there were facts of political life here, too, and getting the twenty-two million dollars out of either AID or Congress would not be easy.

On the Trujillo properties, he appeared to agree with our present policy.

On the sugar quota, the Administration would soon ask Congress to switch from a country quota system to a world quota system, with serious consequences to the Republic. It probably would not pass, though no one could say what Congress would do.

I described the visa mess—incredibly, I had to ask the Secretary himself to resolve it. He was wholly sympathetic, and said we should send a planeload of young visa officers to the Republic immediately. But as so often happens, that vast juggernaut, the State Department, overruled the Secretary (just as the Department by sheer inertia sometimes overrules the President, and as my staff overruled me). Several months later, however, we finally got what we needed—a new Consulate building out at the Fairgrounds, far from downtown Santo Domingo, three extra vice consuls, and a new consul, Pancho Withey. By fall the visa uproar had ended.

I saw a host of other people in the Department, in CIA, in AID; and out of the endless meetings emerged, after many drafts, a paper laying out our policy on the Dominican Republic through next February 27, when the Consejo was due to leave office; and we took it to President Kennedy.

We went into the White House through the West Basement entrance as always, not the ceremonial or public entrances, and upstairs to the

Cabinet room. We were, as I recall it, Undersecretary Ball, Assistant Secretary Ed Martin, and John Crimmins from the Department; Teodoro Moscoso, coordinator of the Alliance for Progress; plus a CIA man, a military man, Picó, and myself. We waited in the Cabinet room, some sitting at the long gleaming oval Cabinet table. It was a beautiful late-April afternoon, the greening garden shadowed now. An usher opened a door, and said, "Gentlemen, the President." He strode in rapidly, saying, "It's all right," to those of us who had quickly gotten to our feet as he entered, and, sitting in the center chair at the long table, immediately picked up his copy of the policy paper and began going through it, pencil in hand.

He knew the material intimately. Reading, he looked up quickly to ask us questions.

Wasn't there a danger that so many political parties and so complicated an electoral law might produce a splintering election, with no party able to govern? Couldn't the Trujillo claims be paid out of the profits of the Trujillo properties? If it proved necessary to postpone elections, shouldn't the OAS do it? How clearly could Radio Havana be heard in the Republic? Should we jam it?

As for the twenty-two million dollars, we didn't have it, but maybe it would be better if someone in Washington, not I in Santo Domingo, said so. We couldn't go to Congress for it—Congress would say we didn't owe it and would fear the sugar companies would get most of it. So it had to come out of AID, but until the foreign aid bill was passed, AID didn't have it. In any event, we hadn't yet agreed with the Dominicans on which projects to spend it.

I explained the Dominicans' view of the twenty-two million and its political importance. Moscoso supported me. The President said, "There's no sense arguing about it—we haven't got it. We have to go to Congress," and he ticked off the Congressional reaction precisely; then, to me, "We'll try to work out some kind of an agreement to save everybody's face, but it won't be easy."

He went on—was the MAAG any good? How could it be improved? Did I want more military? What about coastal patrol? What about counter-insurgency training? What about the Social Christians—was there any hope there? What was the chance of Bosch's PRD winning?

I answered as rapidly and directly as I could; he was always impatient with long-winded replies. I told him the MAAG was too slow but starting to move; it was big enough. I favored counter-insurgency training and coastal patrol because guerrilla action was a real possibility. The Social Christians couldn't win this year, but we should stay close to them for the future. Bosch's PRD was now even, or almost even, with the UCN, but the election wasn't till December.

I said the military was getting restless and asked how far I could go in stopping a military *golpe*.

The President glanced around the table, and said, "Why don't we give him the Loeb formula?"

Jim Loeb was our Ambassador in Peru. With elections there nearing and the chances of the non-Communist leftist candidate improving, the Peruvian military was growing restless, and so Loeb had been authorized to tell the military that "the United States would find it extremely difficult to recognize and almost impossible to assist any regime which took power by force or threats of force."

President Kennedy now told me I could say the same thing in the Dominican Republic in private conversations.

I said we had omitted something vital. The Consejo had lost control of the streets to the mobs. I had thus far been unable to get any help to teach the Dominican police riot control, and I didn't see why we couldn't get a couple of cops from Chief Parker's Mexican squad— W. H. Parker was Chief of Police in Los Angeles.

The President turned to Ralph Dungan, his staff member who handled Latin American affairs, who always sat in on such meetings, spoke seldom but with great cogency, and said, "Ask Bobby if he can get him some help." Bobby was, of course, the President's brother, the Attorney General.

A week or two later two excellent Spanish-speaking Los Angeles detectives arrived in Santo Domingo. They trained the Dominican police in riot control, gave them nightsticks, tear gas, and gas masks, and white helmets—they became known as the Cascos Blancos, white helmets— and in a few weeks the Consejo rewon the streets, thanks almost entirely to those two detectives.

In retrospect, it seems incredible that we had to go all the way to the President of the United States to stop teen-age *turbas* in Santo Domingo. But we did.

As the meeting broke up and he headed across the Cabinet room and back toward his oval office, he stopped for a moment with me, and said, "I saw you last night," and then, "Good luck—and let me know if you need anything."

The night before I had attended the annual White House correspondents' dinner, and President Kennedy, in top form, had done a take-off on himself that was one of the funniest I ever heard. That week, too, staying at Arthur Schlesinger's, I had helped Schlesinger work on a speech the President gave to a gathering of Nobel Prize winners at the White House, and we wrote a line which said, "I think this is the most extraordinary collection of talent, of human knowledge, that has ever been gathered together at the White House." Delivering it, the President added, "with the possible exception of when Thomas Jefferson dined alone." It was the Kennedy touch.

Chapter Six

THE CITADEL OF THE OLIGARCHY

On May 3, I went back to Santo Domingo, three hours and a half by jet and a century and a world away, feeling renewed and immensely buoyed up. It was a feeling with many sources—seeing Washington and New York in the spring, seeing the President, seeing friends from the political campaigns—Bob Kennedy, George Ball, Dick Goodwin, Newt Minow, others. So was their interest in the Dominican Republic—one night when I was introduced to a Department official as our Ambassador there, he cried in mock alarm, "What are you doing here? Go back, go back." Everyone in the Department—from the Secretary down—seemed eager to help. The Department itself seemed, if not friendly, at least no longer a vast bulky obscure antagonist. Sometimes an Ambassador feels all alone, and Washington far away. I did not feel that way now.

That year, 1962, was a good year for President Kennedy. Nineteen sixty-one, with Laos and the Congo, the Bay of Pigs and the Berlin Wall, had been a bad year, but 1962 was a time of hope, and the President seemed ebullient, confident, and funny again. I always saw him when I went home. In 1962 our world was still dangerous, and we knew it, but when President Kennedy walked into the Cabinet room, moving fast and erect, always surprisingly tall, always young and vigorous, blue eyes questioning and sometimes mocking, his mind restless—when he came in, even the worst problems somehow seemed at least manageable.

That Sunday Fran and the boys and I went with Manuel Tavares and his wife and children to a secluded beach he owned near Haina. As we have seen, when I had met his wife secretly on my presidential mission the year before, he had been in Trujillo's prison because some of the assassins had hidden in his tile factory. Now he was a Cabinet member, Secretary of State for Finance. The beach was gravelly, the bottom stony, and the swimming not very good, but we had a fine time. They were young and attractive, he had been educated at Yale, and I told them about President Kennedy's speech to the Nobel Prize winners. A Haitian woman who spoke neither English nor Spanish came down to the beach to bathe naked. We put a bottle of wine to cool in the sand at the water's edge, and lay half in, half out of the sea, leaning against a driftwood log, watching the children hunt for shells, and talked about America's purpose here. We watched Tavares' burro train hauling gravel, each burro plodding down the path alone, reaching the water's edge, waiting while a man loaded the grass baskets slung across the burro's back, first one side, then the other, and the burro, knowing when his load was balanced and completed, turned without command and plodded back up the path to the top of the hill where he stood to wait for the man to come up and unload him. It was a long, peaceful afternoon when nothing happened; a rare day.

Later I learned that Tavares' attractive wife was a cousin of General Sánchez, Ramfis' friend on horseback. Dominican relationships are bewildering. Much later, Manuel Tavares came to oppose the elected Dominican President, Juan Bosch, and went to the United States, withholding his education and talents from his country's first democratic government in modern times. Many Dominican events took curious turns, many Dominicans were disappointing.

Next day I called on President Bonnelly at the Palace—we wanted publicity this time—and told him about my trip to Washington. Bonnelly had spoken to the people on radio and television, one of his best speeches, stressing agrarian reform. I gave him a speech notebook I had bought for him in Washington.

He was eager to get a Palace press officer—I had told him that people who complained about the "do-nothing" Consejo didn't realize how much it had accomplished. But whom could he hire? Dominicans were either hopelessly compromised by Trujillo or hopelessly inexperienced. Puerto Ricans under Governor Muñoz Marín had gained much experience in democracy, but were attacked as Yankee lackeys, and we were in danger of bringing too many of them here to help. Nevertheless, I suggested several Puerto Ricans. He couldn't have a North American.

President Bonnelly hoped to have an OAS mission by June 1 to help prepare for elections. He said decrees were drafted for the Fomento, the Río Yaque del Norte development study, an income tax, and a public housing authority. He asked when the police training would commence, and the training of an anti-subversive unit, and whether I could get technicians to help the Agrarian Reform Institute begin soil classification at the first two agrarian reform projects, near Bonao. For once, I could promise him fast action on all three.

Bonnelly said that Castro/Communists had incited riots on May Day, the Latin American Labor Day, and police had killed three men.

University students had made trouble, too—Marcio Mejía Ricart, deported, had slipped back into the country, gained sanctuary at the University, and delivered a pro-Communist speech, precipitating a riot. Marcio Mejía's father was in the process of being appointed Ambassador to Spain. He had called on President Bonnelly, apologized for his son's behavior, and asked clemency for him. Bonnelly had agreed that if Marcio Mejía would leave the country the next day, he would not be prosecuted. The father had promised but failed to produce the boy.

Bonnelly did not say so, but it appeared that he was holding the father's ambassadorial appointment as hostage for the deportation of the son, another Dominican private tragedy. But there were so many, we could scarcely afford the luxury of human concern. A few months later, Marcio Mejía's father having been duly appointed Ambassador to Spain, he unwisely praised Franco on arrival, was immediately attacked in the Dominican press, and died. He was given a state funeral, and I, who had been involved in his son's deportation, had to stand as honor guard beside the casket. Foreign Minister Bonilla gravely read a eulogy, then, during the rest of the service, whispered comically to me, "These are very bad times for diplomats."[1]

2

I decided to visit Santiago and the Cibao and sent Fandino ahead to advance it, as we say in U.S. politics.

The week was busy. A U.S. warship arrived. I talked at length to Attorney General García Vásquez, ostensibly about extraditions, actually to try to gauge him better, for I had seen him often at Imbert's house.

Rexford Tugwell, the old New Dealer now at the University of Puerto Rico, came to visit, and so did our Ambassador to Haiti, Raymond

[1] Much later, an Embassy officer had a long talk with Marcio Mejía Ricart. Mejía was about thirty-five. His parents were well-to-do. He said his brother had been shot by a firing squad at San Isidro after the Constanza invasion in 1959. He said he himself had been jailed five times by Trujillo but beaten only in a U.S. deportees' camp—he'd refused to get off the deportation plane, demanded a copy of the Bill of Rights and the Immigration Law, demanded a doctor, and gone on a hunger strike. He was an economist and, we thought, brilliant but erratic. He was certainly anti-American but not necessarily under Communist Party discipline—we detected in his conversation many deviations from Communist orthodoxy. Mejía said he had been expelled from the 14th of June. He saw everything in black and white, could not believe we were not imperialists, and also found fault with the Russian and Chinese Communists. He seemed to think our imperialism in Latin America inevitable and "too bad." He likened our behavior to that of a man left alone in a room with a woman—even if she were ugly, he'd have intercourse with her. He thought we should create a small institution to lend money to small shops for artisans and craftsmen, hardly a Marxist idea. He was, our people thought, one of those alienated Latin American intellectuals with a closed mind, educated, intelligent, but by now, unfortunately, probably lost to us forever.

Thurston, with his wife. Thurston was approaching a crisis: The anniversary of the "reelection" of President Duvalier of Haiti, a "reelection" that was illegal, in our view.

Rumors spread that week that Amiama and Imbert were plotting. I went to see them and used the Loeb formula, making it clear I had just returned from Washington. They did not like it, but I thought they would heed it.

There was labor trouble. After Trujillo's fall, ORIT, the international arm of the AFL-CIO, had sent organizers to the Republic, and our labor attaché, Fred Somerford, had helped them. They followed the traditional Sam Gompers line: Unions should not be affiliated with political parties, should pursue their own economic interests. This had thrown them into direct conflict with the UCN, the PRD, and the Social Christians, each of which, like most Latin American political parties, had its own labor union. Time and again for a year and a half I tried to work for labor unity—talked repeatedly to Somerford, to visiting ORIT representatives, and to Dominican labor leaders; talked repeatedly to UCNers, who publicly demanded that Somerford be thrown out of the Republic, and to Ángel Miolán, who was organizing workers for the PRD. All to no avail Somerford and ORIT insisted on non-partisan unions; each political party insisted on having its own union. As a consequence, the Dominican labor movement was hopelessly splintered. This made Castro/Communist infiltration easy. Labor is a prime Communist target. Already, Fred Somerford said, Castro/Communists had captured certain small key unions in the sugar mills and FENEPIA, the union of government employees. These unions now were threatening to strike. That could be dangerous, especially FENEPIA's strike against the government.

Manolo Tavárez Justo declared on radio from Santiago that our failure to return the twenty-two million dollars was a political maneuver to force the Republic to borrow money and mortgage its future to *Yanqui* imperialism, denounced "secret conditions" on the twenty-five-million-dollar loan (there were none), declared the 14th of June would not go to elections without "de-Trujilloization" of the Armed Forces and government, said that Marxism-Leninism was not correct for the Dominican Republic, and denied that Fidel Castro was using "Marxist-Communist" methods in Cuba. A little later, on the anniversary of the June 14, 1959 landings, Tavárez Justo said that if "peaceful struggle of the people proves impossible—listen well, gentlemen of the reaction—the 14th of June knows very well where the craggy mountains of Quisqueya are—and we will go to them—because no other alternative will remain to us except liberty or death."

At a party for the Dominican military given by Colonel Long, I first met Colonel Elías Wessin y Wessin, the tank commander at San Isidro.

He was a short, stocky, powerful, youngish man. I had heard that he had led the officers who arrested Rodríguez Echavarría, ending his two-day *golpe*. I had heard he was brave, dollar honest, and "sincere." But nobody seemed to know much more—unlike other Dominican military leaders, he kept to himself, had few friends, spent his time with his family and his tanks, not at parties—and I was curious, for, since he commanded the tanks, he held the key to power in the Republic.

I talked to Wessin only about twenty minutes that night, but he impressed me greatly. He said what they all did—he had opposed Trujillo, he favored democracy, he supported the Consejo as the constitutional government. But what Wessin emphasized, and what I never forgot, was what he said about Communists. He hated them. He considered them the embodiment of evil. He would give them no quarter. If they ever became a serious threat to his country, he would not hesitate to do anything necessary to defeat them. He had small burning eyes; they burned when he said this.

All Dominican military men hated Communists, of course. But not like Colonel Wessin y Wessin. His hate was "sincere," all right—the sincerity of a fanatic. You could almost feel its force in this small, compact man. And anti-communism was his whole politics—he knew nothing else whatever about politics and did not want to know. Indeed, he did not even regard communism as a political matter, but, rather, as a moral or religious question. I used the Loeb formula, not as a warning but to congratulate him on his support for the Consejo. He did not care; I felt sure he would brush it aside if I ever used it to deter him from what he considered his duty. For you could feel something else about Wessin, or so I thought that night: He was a man.

A day or two later, talking politics with Shlaudeman, I mentioned Wessin. Shlaudeman had talked to him briefly, too, that night and had received precisely the same impression. I pressed it on the attachés, who knew Wessin only slightly. Looking back now, I count it probably my most serious single error that I did not take on Wessin as my own special project. It has been said that war is too important to be left to generals. It could be said that Wessin y Wessin was too important to be left to military attachés.

The lines of conflict were drawing tighter, or at least becoming clearer. On the far left, Manolo Tavárez Justo had come into the open with his anti-American speech, threatening guerrilla warfare. On the far right, such military men as Wessin y Wessin were prepared to take a stand. And these were the two extremist hammers that would beat ceaselessly upon the government, and upon us, throughout my time in the Republic. These were the dangers to our policy objectives, and to infant Dominican democracy.

3

The Castro/Communists—I call them by that somewhat ambiguous term deliberately. Some Dominicans considered anybody to the left of the oligarchy or the Consejo, or anybody who advocated social justice, or anybody who was simply anti-American, a Communist. But the Social Christians, for example, were always far left of the Consejo, always demanded social justice, sometimes demanded death for the oligarchy, and sometimes were deeply anti-American—yet the Social Christians were the bitterest, most belligerent opponents the Castro/Communists had. No, under the term Castro/Communist I mean to include people who took money and instructions from Communist parties outside the Republic, submitted to their discipline, and acted as their agents; and people who joined the groups those agents formed and did their work actively in the Republic. (I include the word "Castro" in "Castro/Communist" because so many of the latter group were attracted far more to Fidel Castro than to Marx or Lenin.)

Real Communists we had in the Dominican Republic. One attended the worldwide congress of Communist parties in Moscow as the official Dominican representative. Another went to the Congress of the International Union of Students in Leningrad. One, a poet and friend of Castro, acted as a courier between Havana and Santo Domingo. A good many traveled frequently to the U.S.S.R., Czechoslovakia, and Cuba; at least one visited Hungary and one East Germany. Later a few went to Red China. A good many received guerrilla warfare training in Cuba. Some received training of other kinds in the U.S.S.R., Soviet bloc countries, and Cuba. In various countries, such as Argentina and Chile and Mexico, some of them met with local Communist Party leaders. In some countries, such as Cuba, they were in touch with the Soviet Embassy.[2] They were under Communist Party discipline. Their ceaseless travel was paid for by foreign funds. They brought money to the Republic from Cuba and Europe to finance their parties. Their purpose was to subvert, infiltrate, or forcibly overthrow the Dominican government and convert the Republic into a Communist state. How they did it mattered not at all so long as it succeeded—murder, civil war, rural uprisings or city street fights, education, indoctrination, infiltration, and elections were all the same to them, mere means to the end. They tried them all. Nearly all were native Dominicans. Most were young, urban, educated, of middle-class or upper-class origin. They had learned their lessons well; their minds were closed; it was impossible to get through to them. They were gone. They believed deeply, each according to his own

[2] There was, of course, no Soviet Embassy in the Dominican Republic.

dedication, in Soviet statements made during the Cold War of implacable enmity toward capitalism, in Castro's promise to extend his revolution from the Sierra Maestra to the Andes, and in Chairman Mao's explicitly stated purpose of defeating the democracies by guerrilla warfare. These Dominicans' basic loyalty lay not to the Dominican Republic but to Moscow or Cuba or, later, Peking. How numerous were they? I would estimate that communism could count on not more than one hundred well-trained, fully committed, and fully disciplined Dominicans.

Ranged alongside and behind them were a much larger number of young men and women who followed them, were taught by them, sympathized with them, joined their parties, and did their work, but were much less dependable, from the Communist point of view. Most of these belonged to the 14th of June. They were not under Communist Party discipline. They were Dominican nationalists (as the true Communists were not). They were anti-American and anti-Trujillo. Most were enthralled with Castro. Some were mere rebellious teen-agers—rebels who had found a cause they imperfectly understood. Some were the sons of oligarchs—rebellion against parental authority may have moved them more than devotion to Marxism-Leninism. It was extremely difficult to talk to them but sometimes not impossible. It was still possible to talk to Marcio Mejía Ricart, if not to convince him, as we have just seen, and in 1961 I had talked to Manolo Tavárez Justo himself. But it had taken only a brief interview in 1961 to convince me that meaningful conversation with Alfredo Manzano, a true Communist, was impossible. He inhabited a different world than I.

In my time, there were four Castro/Communist parties in the Republic, as follows:

—The PSP, Partido Socialista Popular, was the orthodox Communist party, probably tied to Havana by Blas Roca, head of the "old Communists" in Cuba, himself acting on Moscow's orders. The PSP was a small party, a leadership cadre, and it believed the correct revolutionary tactics at that time were infiltration of the government and parties, indoctrination and education of the people, and establishment of a "popular front" of as many political elements as possible. In 1961 it had had some success in infiltrating the amorphous UCN, but had no real future there (and indeed, in the fall of 1962 it was purged from the UCN). At this time it seemed to show little interest in Bosch's PRD (though after the election, of course, it did). So it turned to the 14th of June. Its leader had been Pericles Franco but by 1962 probably was Juan Ducoudray Mansfield. One expert called the PSP members "mink coat" Communists. He was wrong.

—The MPD, Movimiento Popular Dominicano, was, as noted, a small group headed by Máximo López Molina, probably receiving guns and money from Havana but under less rigid international Communist Party discipline than the PSP. It considered terror and violence the tactics appropriate to the time. As the Sino-Soviet split widened, the MPD's views seemed to correspond to Peking's, the PSP's to Moscow's. In my time as Ambassador, however, Peking had little or no direct influence in the Republic, so far as we knew, though we were not unaware of the danger.

—The PNR, Partido Nacionalista Revolucionario, was the smallest of all four parties and, indeed, consisted principally of two men, Pedro Pérez Cabral, called "Corpito" Pérez, and Dato Pagán. Some said these two had formerly belonged to the PSP but had been expelled as Trotskyites or because of personal disagreement with Juan Ducoudray and his brother Felix; others said they were still secretly allied. "Corpito" Pérez and Dato Pagán were often accused of teaching young men to make Molotov cocktails, but most of their work seemed to be education and indoctrination. They were probably the closest thing the Republic had to an intellectual Communist elite.

—The 14th of June, as we have seen, was by far the biggest Castro/ Communist party, the only one with a charismatic leader, Manolo Tavárez Justo, was a mystique and heroes and martyrs, and the only one with any mass following. The other three parties,[3] especially the PSP, constantly tried to infiltrate the 14th of June, for they saw in its youthful following their own road to power and they saw in its leader, Tavárez Justo, their instrument. But others in the 14th, who were really just Dominican nationalists, contested with them for possession of Tavárez Justo. And Tavárez Justo himself never seemed comfortable with the Havana-directed PSP; once in a public speech, he reeled off a list of heroes who had opposed Trujillo tyranny and Yankee imperialism, and a PSP claque kept shouting, "Y Fidel, y Fidel," but Tavárez Justo stubbornly refused to mention his name.

Nevertheless, the CIA was certain the 14th of June received money and probably guns from Castro. Indeed, some thought they could determine, by watching the riotous streets of Santo Domingo, who was on top in the power struggle inside Cuba between Fidel Castro's "new Communists" and Blas Roca's "old Communists"—if the 14th of June had the money to hire rioters, Castro was on top; but if the PSP or MPD had it, Blas Roca was on top. Some Cuban experts doubt this.

Each party published a "clandestine" newspaper, sold openly on the streets, and if one missed several issues, some thought its money had been shut off. The only entertaining paper, however, was *Claridad*, the personal vehicle of Alfredo Manzano and Ramón Alberto "Chino" Ferreras, both expelled from the 14th of June as too far left. In a reply to my April speech, *Claridad* expressed surprise at finding a U. S. Am-

[3] The 14th of June insisted it was not a *partido*, a party, but an *agrupación*, group. So did other new political groups that were springing up. To avoid confusion, however, I shall refer to all as parties.

bassador with ideas, but said I knew better than to advocate social justice —the United States was living in an eighteenth-century political system devoid of ideas, given to persecution of intellectuals, governed by the rich and well-born, and overrun by "the Mafia, the Ku Klux Klan, and *gangsterismo*." *Claridad* proposed to help us with a revolution of our own—"For a Yankeeized Santo Domingo, *no!* For a Fidelized United States, *sí!*"

I wanted to talk to Manolo Tavárez Justo now—why should we abandon him by default to the Communists? But Hemba, Shlaudeman, and others strongly advised against it, saying it would increase his stature, and reluctantly I took their advice. I wish I hadn't.

The 14th of June was the only Castro/Communist party that during the spring looked as though it might go to elections. How many votes Tavárez Justo could get was wholly uncertain—perhaps fifty thousand?— but I felt sure he could not come close to winning. And I did not think he was bright enough to subvert a government or brave enough to go to the hills—he seemed to prefer driving a white Thunderbird and sipping *cafecitos* at fashionable Vesuvio's by the sea.

None of the Castro/Communist parties seemed to me prepared to try to overthrow the government by force. Communists at that time rarely made revolutions; they let others make them, then took over. Anyway, I believed that Moscow and Havana had been as unprepared for Trujillo's downfall as we.

Nevertheless, the Communists in the Dominican Republic made a great deal of trouble—they stirred up anti-American feeling, infiltrated the government, incited student groups to riot and labor unions to strike, set up front organizations which demonstrated against us and the Consejo, incited and paid for general riots in the streets, and sometimes resorted to naked terror. All this was dangerous—dangerous directly, and dangerous indirectly because it might provoke, or excuse, a rightist military *golpe*. It was this last, I believe, that was the real objective of the Communists—a rightist military *golpe*. For, in the long run, communism flourishes best not under democracy but under repression. After all, much of the best Castro/Communist leadership had become dedicated men under Trujillo's torture. What saved us, probably, was that the four Castro/ Communist parties never united in their cherished *frente*.

4

I had refused a Cadillac as an official car and chosen a Checker—less ostentatious and, built high, better for the rough Dominican roads—and we used it now. The road to Santiago runs ninety-five miles northwest from the capital. Below massive foothills, the valley unrolls lush and green, planted to sugar cane impenetrably thick, higher than a man's head; oxen draw big-wheeled lumbering sugar carts across the road. The highway crosses flooded rice fields, a barefoot boy with pants rolled up washes an ox in a rice canal, groves of palms are everywhere—the berries make hog food, the trunks make huts, the fronds thatch them. Here, near Bonao, would be our first agrarian reform project.

A detour led into Bonao, stronghold of Petán Trujillo, the Generalis-simo's explosive brother. When Petán finally fled his fief here, *campesinos* overran it, dragged his purebred cattle on chains through the rocky streets, tortured them, and ate them. But vestiges of his rule remained. Bonao was always quiet.

Out of Bonao, the concrete highway continued briefly—it has since reached Santiago—then reverted to the old road, rough crooked blacktop twisting around foothills and ravines, climbing, the narrow central valley closing in, thatch-roofed huts scattered on the hillsides, women doing their laundry in a stony river and a barefoot black girl in a shapeless shift walking stately up from a stream, a five-gallon tin of water balanced on her head. The tin originally held cooking oil that women buy at the little store, a nickel's worth at a time, carrying their own bottle to the *colmado* to be filled. After the storekeeper has sold the whole five gallons, he sells the empty can.

Long loops of sausage hung, gray with dust, from hooks at a roadside store. You could buy it by the yard, sixty cents a yard then. Cars dodged burros, dogs, bicycles, and jerry-built carts. Children walked a deep-trod path beside the road. Every now and then a *público* piled full of people, its trunk roped shut to hold in baggage and chickens, stopped abruptly to take on or let out a passenger. Everybody was friendly. Down the road came a clutch of oxen, and a man occasionally waved a switch at them—not an ordinary switch, but a spray of blood-red flowers: *campe-sinos* have a streak of the antic in them.

The road, climbing through red clay hills, now suddenly broke out over their rim, and we beheld the Cibao, the long, broad valley which angles across the Republic from the head of the Bay of Samaná all the way west to the Haitian frontier. It is the richest land in the Republic, deep topsoil so rich, the story goes (as it does elsewhere in the Antilles), that if you toss a seed into the dirt, you must stand back to get out of the way. It is the agricultural heartland of the Republic. The Cibao is con-sidered by its people the best, the proudest, the most cultured and most freedom-loving section of the Republic, breeder of revolutions, strong-hold of the oligarchy, cradle of liberty, dwelling place of courage.

We passed through La Vega, big, busy, jammed, and went on to Moca, a quieter, smaller place and, one sensed, sterner. In the center of town near the pure beautiful church is the place where Ulises Heureaux was shot dead in the street. Near one edge of town is the home of the tragic

De la Maza family; near the other is the Fortaleza—the Republic's bloody past, its fatal present.

On a hill overlooking Santiago stands the gigantic statue, La Paz de Trujillo, never finished before half-wrecked. Calle Sol runs into the heart of the city, the most Spanish city in the Republic and possibly in the Antilles—a twin-spired church on a rising hill, narrow streets and narrower sidewalks, streets like tunnels, walled in with flat-faced buildings yellow and pink, high arched doorways, massive wooden doors, grilled iron balconies, a teeming market, a shaded central plaza fronting the Governor's building and the ancient club, the private club which denied Trujillo admittance long ago, aroused his wrath, and led him to try to ruin Santiago.

The ancient battle cry of Spain is "*¡Santiago, y cierre España!*" —"Santiago, and close [upon them], Spain!" This city is properly called Santiago de los Caballeros, Santiago of the Gentlemen. It was traditional in Santiago for fathers to give their sons revolvers at puberty. The taxicabs are horse-drawn carriages, old, battered, but still used by fairskinned ladies with parasols. People here are white. They are busy: This is the second city of the Republic, and contains industry—rum, cigars, cigarettes, textiles, leather, many more. They are proud. They are ruled by the oligarchy.

The oligarchy—to Castro/Communists, to vote-hungry politicians, to liberals like myself, to many who favor change in Latin America, the oligarchy has become a dirty word. In the Dominican Republic, if you know it well, matters are not so simple. The oligarchy here consists of perhaps a score of families related by blood and marriage. They bear such names as Tavares, Cabral, Vicini, Cáceres, Bermúdez. They have ruled the Republic—furnished its Presidents and generals, dominated its finance and business—for more than a hundred years. Their fortunes were based on land, sugar, tobacco, rum; on cattle and rice and coffee and cacao; on trade and finance.

So intertwined are they by blood and marriage that only they can explain their relationships. Their ramifications reach everywhere—President Bonnelly, for example, was close to them because his wife was one of them—but the core of the oligarchy is a few families, and within each family, or family complex, is one man, usually not a public figure at all, to whom, when things are truly serious, the others turn for decision. Thus young Juan Vicini ran the sugar mills, and young Donald Reid Cabral sat on the Consejo, and his uncle Marco Cabral was probably Santiago's leading lawyer, and young Manuel Tavares was a Cabinet officer; but the real head of the family complex was a quiet, handsome, courteous man seldom seen in public, José María Cabral.

The people of the oligarchy live exceedingly well, though usually without ostentation. Their homes are old and well-preserved; you feel that every time a screw comes loose in a doorknob, it is instantly repaired. They travel often to the United States. They send their children to the best preparatory schools and universities there. They have small retreats in the mountains or at the sea. They own *fincas,* sometimes vast ones, in the rich valleys.

They are humanitarian and paternalistic. They are likely to despise the military as *campesinos* with guns, and politicians as untrustworthy power-seekers. They hated Trujillo—an uncouth butcher, and one who had sworn to break their power, though he never could. They are beyond any question the ablest, best educated people in the Republic.

A few resist any change. Most encourage it, to varying degrees and in different ways. Put at its worst, they are realistic: They know if they do not give up something to the poor they will lose everything, possibly even their lives, and so, having much, are practical enough to give up a little. Put at its best, they favor justice. It may seem odd that a liberal Democrat like myself should come to consider the Dominican oligarchy as one of the really hopeful groups in the Republic.

Nevertheless, the oligarchy is, clearly, an anachronistic institution. One of its members had a carpenter on his personal payroll at all times. He was, simply, his carpenter—to build his cupboards, remodel his houses, design trinkets. Only an oligarchical, low-wage society could afford such luxury or command such loyalty. The relationship between *patrón* and *campesino* in the Cibao was in some respects not unlike that between master and slave in colonial Virginia. Once we stayed at the summer cottage of an *oligarquista,* and the maid made a great fuss over our sons, fluttering about helplessly and excitedly, urging sweets on the boys, seeming about to swoon—Uncle Tomism at its worst. The time lag in the Republic was nearly two centuries, not one.

Plainly, if the revolution really came here—for Trujillo's overthrow was not a revolution—it would be quite a wrench if it encompassed only such things as a steeply graduated income tax, inheritance tax, and property tax. Once we spent a weekend at an *oligarquista's finca.* He rode horseback, attended by a horseman; leaving in the twilight, he stopped at each hut on his property where families had lived for generations and handed out a few dollars to each, all gratefully received, the *campesinos* calling him "Don ———."

One family took its maid to the seashore. She was from the mountains, not many miles away, but never before had seen the sea. The first day she sat all day on the porch and looked at the sea. Finally she asked her question—did the sea really go on forever without any end? No, her mistress said, and explained that if one took a boat and went far enough, one would come to land on the other side. She took a bottle of seawater back to her village.

The UCN, which began with the oligarchy's support, was counting heavily on this paternalism politically, certain that the *campesinos* would vote the way Don Juan, or Don Eduardo, told them to. I was far less sure they would. The *oligarquistas* gave the UCN its peculiarly Dominican flavor—nationalistic, patriotic, paternalistic, old-fashioned, and civic-minded. And they urged on UCN a liberal line. How liberal they would be when the time came for actual reform remained to be seen.

The leader of Santiago society was Doña María Grieser Viuda Tavares.[4] Doña María lived in a beautiful house on a landscaped hillside, next door to a walled and guarded estate once occupied by Angelita, daughter of Trujillo. Doña María's house was low and rambling and airy, built of wood, narrow boards dating to the 1920s, with well-trimmed trees and bushes, orchids, and a tennis court. When ladies came to call, Doña María showed them around the patio and gave them an orchid, then served tea or a drink. She was the *grande dame* of Santiago.

She was magnificent. Far from the wispy little old lady we had expected, Doña María was forthright, vigorous, intelligent, educated, opinionated, a woman of great character. She and her husband had owned much land behind the house and had kept cows there, but now people were stealing the cows, and she thought she would get rid of them. She was sixty-four years old. Speaking casually of Puerto Plata, she said, "Oh yes, we spent a revolution there once." One day two men came to her door, one with a gun, and threatened to rob her. She bade them begone, saying, "I'm not afraid of you, I'm from Moca."

Her father, born in eastern Germany, had gone to Scotland and, thence, to the Dominican Republic to build a railroad, and she had married a member of the Tavares family. One of her uncles had been Horacio Vásquez, elected President of the Republic in Sumner Welles' time, and when in 1928 he said he felt duty called him to extend his term, Doña María told him, "Uncle Horacio, you just like the job." Extend it he did, and gave Trujillo the pretext he needed.

Once Doña María was Trujillo's dinner partner. Every plate set before him he gave to her. She asked, "Are you trying it out on the dog?" A woman she knew played canasta with three friends and next day received a phone call from one of Trujillo's men—he knew she had spoken against Trujillo.

Once the teen-aged Ramfis Trujillo gave a birthday party for her young daughter, Ana. Ana sat at the Generalissimo's table. Doña María

[4] When Spanish-speaking women marry, they keep their maiden name and add "of——," their husband's name. After he dies, *Viuda*, "widow," is inserted. Thus Doña María's maiden name had been María Grieser. When she had married Gustavo Tavares, her name had become María Grieser de Tavares; after he died it became María Grieser *Viuda* de Tavares. Dominican custom, however, is to drop the "de"—"of"—upon adopting *"Viuda."*

sent word when she thought it time for Ana to leave. The terror-stricken waiter refused to carry the message. Doña María herself took her firmly home, despite the frantic pleas of her friends, an unheard-of affront to the Generalissimo.

Once when one of her *oligarquista* friends had fallen into Trujillo's disfavor and been ousted from his job, and then, after many devious maneuvers, had been rehabilitated, Doña María approached Trujillo at a party after dinner to thank him for his generosity. Trujillo turned to his aide, Manuel de Moya, and said, "Manuel, what time tomorrow did I tell the Captain to shoot him?" Doña María said, "I see you still have your sense of humor, Generalissimo." Doña María told me that President Kennedy reminded her of the young Lindbergh, a startling idea I never heard from anyone else but somehow, in the Republic, very apt.

Her two daughters were married to Eduardo León and Tomás (Jimmy) Pastoriza. León and Pastoriza, together with Doña María's son Gustavo and Marco Cabral's son Manuel José, and perhaps a half-dozen other young men in Santiago, such as Alejandro Grullón and Victor Espaillat, represented an element unique in the Republic—young businessmen, eager, smart, volatile, but checked by the balance wheel of family from the excesses and disorientation of less fortunate eager young men. While other eager young men drew up great plans which made little sense, these men conceived and built, with AID and private foundation help, an agricultural college in Santiago, the first in the Republic. Sometimes, finding both Dominican and U.S. governments too slow, they carried out their projects alone.

5

When we arrived in Santiago, Fandino and I called on the Governor and other officials then toured the city with them. We saw a new factory; Trujillo's gigantic baseball stadium, where I once had attended a Partido Dominicano meeting; new housing; but what we saw that mattered most were the *barrios,* the slums: Thousands upon thousands of people packed into shacks under the bridge on the muddy banks of the Yaque, packed into shacks in a deep hole not far from the center of town, packed into shacks they threw up overnight on anybody's land.

Governor Virgilio Mainardi had no idea how many there were—probably twenty thousand under the bridge alone. They were *campesinos* come to the city, drawn by the worldwide urban trend and by Balaguer's jobs, hoping for a better life, now squatting in squalor without jobs or decent homes or hopes. Here was the social dynamite in the Republic, in Santiago, in Barahona, in the capital, in every city. At first, the police had tried to keep them off people's land. Owners had put up fences. The *campesinos* had torn them down, built their fetid shacks, and sat.

And still more came. One day a starving woman jumped naked off the Yaque bridge. Housing—this was what Governor Mainardi wanted. But what good would it do? Would it not only increase the rush to the city?

We stayed at the Hotel Matúm, another of Trujillo's architectural monstrosities, empty, overlooking the hideous great statue. Ours was the "Trujillo suite," the only suite in the hotel. Every hotel had one, fancy, faded, sleazy. At a press conference there, a reporter asked about Manolo Tavárez Justo's recent radio declaration that we were withholding the twenty-two million dollars in order to tie the Republic to our imperialistic schemes. I said it was "ridiculous and irresponsible." This ended any chance of rapprochement with him. Probably it was too late anyway.

For two or three days, I met privately in my room with labor leaders and the leaders of all the political parties. One was a huge black man much feared locally as a dangerous Communist; he turned out to be a poet and presented me with a volume of his verses, written in a Trujillo prison. Another was Juan Isidro Jimenes Grullón, related to oligarchs but said to have leftist connections, a shaggy orator with a winning way who had recently deserted the UCN and formed his own party, Alianza Social Democrática (ASD).

I visited our USIS office, frequently smashed and once burned by *turbas*. Now children scrawled Castro/Communist slogans on the plywood that had replaced its windows. The director wanted to put a policeman on guard. I suggested that instead he install crayons on strings, and had to explain that I was serious (but I don't think he ever did it).

Jimmy Pastoriza took me for a drive down the Río Yaque del Norte Valley. People had been talking about developing it for many years. Balaguer had promised it. Teodoro Moscoso, Coordinator of the Alliance for Progress, had sent David Lilienthal to see it. The Consejo and AID had underwritten studies, then studies of the studies. The river seemed to have great potential—power, irrigation, flood control. But now the project was mired in political controversy and local jealousies. Pastoriza urged, "The United States has to get into it. If it flops, the United States will be blamed anyway." I tried, time and again, during that year, but accomplished virtually nothing—just more papers, studies, surveys, and reports, enough to choke the Yaque.

6

Early one morning we crossed the mountains, the Septentrional range, a two-hour drive, to Puerto Plata.

Puerto Plata looked dead. It was like an architectural museum—a jumble of old Spanish colonial stone, frame houses with mansard roofs similar to our own post-Civil War houses, new ranch houses, vulgar square frame houses on stilts probably built during the American occupation. Over all brooded a mountain, Isabela de Torres.[5] Years ago Puerto Plata had had an elegant club, several banks, string quartets, a railroad, a busy port, and French, Dutch, Italian, Cuban, and U.S. residents. It had resisted Trujillo, and he had killed it. Now the warehouse at the port and the dock itself were sagging, industries were run down, stores empty, streets almost deserted, and an air of sullen suffering hung over the city.

We called on the Governor and other officials and held a town meeting, perhaps fifty or seventy-five men, businessmen, farmers, labor leaders, doctors, politicians, others. They told us their problems—jobs, a port, a decent road over the mountains—and their ideas for improvement, some good—farm-to-market roads to get the coffee and cacao down to the highway from the mountains, agricultural technicians and Peace Corpsmen and free medicines to vaccinate cattle; some foolish—send a jazz combo here, build a sports arena, start heavy industry. It was a good meeting. Thereafter, I labored to help, as everywhere, with mixed success—we built farm-to-market roads, improved the highway, helped with the livestock, spent enough money to get business started, brought in Navy experts to survey the port.

On another day, still working out of Santiago, we went to Moca. The Governor was only twenty-three, his name was Mario Cáceres, the grandson of President Cáceres, who had assassinated Ulises Heureaux here. Governor Cáceres spent most of his time talking to men looking for jobs. He had eight or nine hundred applicants for white-collar jobs, no such jobs to offer, and only eighty or ninety jobs for manual laborers on emergency road maintenance. "We are waiting on the capital," he said. Meanwhile, thousands had moved to Moca from the country, and more were coming, already filling up ground set aside for public housing, spilling over into private property, building new slums. A doctor said, "Children are dying of malnutrition but not only because of lack of food —also because of ignorance." They died because their mothers simply did not know the rudiments of nutrition and hygiene. Could we not teach nutrition and hygiene to the women of Moca, then send the women to the *campo* to educate the *campesinos*? I thought it a good idea. But it

[5] Here I have adopted the Spanish spelling used by the historian Samuel Eliot Morison and others, although Dominicans call the mountain variously Isabel de Torre or Isabel la Torre. Christopher Columbus, who saw it early, apparently called it Monte de Plata—Silver Mountain—before naming it to honor his queen. Dominican Spanish usage, especially of proper names, frequently varies from both Castilian and dictionary Latin American Spanish. In most instances, unlike this one, I have tried to reproduce Dominican Spanish.

died—AID would not get into health. Later I encouraged the Peace Corps to step in.

We walked into the slums of Moca, fetid, hot, squalid, hideous—pigs, children, and nursing mothers penned up in six-by-six dirt-floored huts jammed almost wall to wall, only narrow urine-muddied dirt pathways between them. I asked the Governor what would become of these people. He shrugged. What could be done for them? Jobs, perhaps housing. He seemed not deeply troubled. And I must confess that some of my own ideas changed during my time in the Republic.

In the beginning, horrified, I had wanted to plunge in with massive work-relief programs and massive housing programs—a New Deal. But were these the solutions? Would not better housing simply lure thousands more to the cities? True, we could not stop the worldwide trend to the cities; but ought we accelerate it? And did they need concrete houses? In this climate, what was wrong with palm-bark and palm-thatch? Trujillo had built concrete houses. We built some, too, in 1962—the Consejo *must* build houses at least as grand as Trujillo's. Ours cost more and were less useful than Trujillo's. Some were so expensive that workers couldn't afford them, so they stood empty. We learned, and stopped it.

Beyond that, however, lay larger questions. Our foreign aid is limited; obviously we cannot build a house and create a job for every impoverished *campesino* on earth; so ought we not spend our loan money on infrastructure—electric power, ports, dams, highways—which in the long run will develop the country? But that takes years—a shaky Consejo cannot wait. Moreover, we talked a lot about private foreign investment, but little would come in while Dominicans sent their profits abroad. First the political situation must stabilize. But the political situation would not stabilize until people found jobs. And so on—the hopeless circle seemed unbreakable.

And always behind these policy questions were the drawn faces of mothers, the pinched faces of babies, waiting in the dark and dirt-floored huts—for what? I kept going back to them. They were, after all, what mattered. When, troubled by such a trip, I asked my economic adviser back at the air-conditioned Embassy, "But what are these people going to do?" he replied, "What have they done for four hundred years?" I never thought it a sufficient answer. But I had none better—at least none I had time to think through in the political hurricanes of 1962–63.

I have often thought that were I doing it over, I would loan the Republic money to experiment with housing—buy ground, build sewer and water lines, and make small loans to men who wanted to build their own houses on lots big enough to ensure some privacy. Such housing would be scattered throughout the Republic to arrest the urban rush. But people want to live where jobs are, so before you can successfully decentralize housing you must first decentralize industry, and that means you must establish small industries based on agriculture throughout the Republic. Who will do it? Not Dominican capitalists, nor American. The government can't—it is graft-ridden and patronage-ridden, and its direct entry into small business would bar private business. It could offer tax and other incentives to private businessmen. But all this takes time —and time is what we never had.

Perhaps I have said enough to indicate that there is no easy solution even to what appears so simple a problem as decent housing; not in the Dominican Republic, not in Latin America, not anywhere in the underdeveloped world.

7

In the midst of our trip Hemba telephoned from the Embassy: Rioting had broken out in the capital, an Embassy car had been wrecked, and President Bonnelly had told the press that the proposed new United States sugar legislation, now coming before Congress, would seriously affect the Republic.

We spent that weekend with Marco Cabral and his wife in their old timbered house at San José de las Matas, an hour's drive up the steep foothills of the Cordillera Central above Santiago.

Marco Cabral, a middle-aged man going gray, his face getting leathery, was quick, alert, inquisitive, intelligent; he was always asking questions eagerly, talking and moving constantly. His wife, Rosita, said, "Poor Marco, he had to keep silent so long under Trujillo he can't stop talking now." She spoke perfect English; he none. She was a handsome woman in her fifties, calm and sensible and strong; no doubt one day she would replace her aunt, Doña María, as the *grande dame* of Santiago society. But more than most, she knew that their way of life was gone. She told us almost with disbelief how her own mother, taken ill in this same house not many years ago, had been carried in a rocking chair slung on two poles down the mountain to Santiago by human bearers. Marco, too, more than most oligarchs, favored change.

We had gone to Las Matas to rest but, as at Cabo Rojo where Fernández Caminero revealed his ambitions, we worked. Foreign Minister Bonilla Atiles and his wife were there. He was a kindly man passing middle age, given to elocution and sweeping theories about the democratic process, a somewhat old-fashioned liberal. He had lived in exile in the United States for many years. Once he told me his son was the fifth generation in his family born in exile.

In 1961, when we sent the fleet to throw the Trujillos out, Castro's Cuba had complained to the United Nations about U.S. military intervention, and Bonilla Atiles had told the UN Security Council: "A country is not merely a soil. A homeland is the people that live in it. They are our brothers, they are our children, our friends with whom we grew up. A homeland is our tradition. What good is it to exterminate us? What does count is the country itself. The extermination of the Dominican people has been ghastly. But today that extermination ceases, and the American Fleet helped to stop it. Then that being the case, I say blessed be the moment when the American Fleet came to Dominican waters."

Now at Las Matas I took him aside for a serious talk. In Washington, President Kennedy and Secretary Rusk and others had suggested that we send a U. S. Special Forces counter-insurgency team into the Republic to train the best Dominican troops in anti-guerrilla warfare, and that we send a U.S. battalion of engineers to train other Dominican troops in civic action programs—construction of side roads, bridges, and fire breaks in the forests and mountains.

President Kennedy himself, seeking alternatives to the Eisenhower-Dulles policy of "massive retaliation," hoping to prevent a jungle skirmish from escalating into nuclear war, had created the Special Forces, and we trained thousands of them.

In the Republic we wanted Dominican troops trained in counter-insurgency in case Castro/Communist guerrilla activity began (although we wanted them carefully selected—they would become the crack troops of the Republic, and we didn't want them shooting the wrong direction). We wanted civic action in order to teach troops trades, enabling them to find jobs if we could cut the size of the Armed Forces.

Both projects were delicate. The Castro/Communists would denounce our counter-insurgency troops. Military officers would say that civic action would take jobs away from civilians (and would think their troops would not want to do pick-and-shovel work).

I tried the ideas out first on Bonilla Atiles. He was enthusiastic about both, though he anticipated the same difficulties I did. I decided to go ahead and discuss it with President Bonnelly.

Just before dinner, Donny Reid arrived from the capital—Marco Cabral was his uncle—and, sitting down at the table, he said abruptly to me, "If you don't get your visa mess straightened out this week, I'm going to spread it all over *La Nación*," the government newspaper. He went on attacking, voice shrill, eyes flashing, while Marco Cabral and Bonilla sat silent, embarrassed.

Doña María once recalled taking Donny to the United States when he was a little boy, and one day finding him perched atop one of the lifeboats, hanging out over the open ocean. He's done it all his life.

Now at Las Matas I let him go on—by then I knew enough to let him talk it out—then explained patiently what we were doing about the visa mess. He subsided reluctantly. Later Bonilla apologized for him, but need not have. Reid was exhausted.

It rained that night, the mountain air was cool, we slept under blankets, the best night's sleep in a week. Sunday our boys went horseback riding, and various Cabral relatives arrived. We organized a Jeep trip into the mountains, three Jeeps sliding on mud roads up through pine forests and rain and fog and mist. Foreign Minister Bonilla was cold, and I gave him my jacket; and we stopped briefly for a glimpse of the cabin the Bonillas had honeymooned in years ago, and I thought: We can do more for Dominican-American relations this way than at the Chancellery. Far in the distance loomed mist-shrouded Pico Duarte, the highest peak in the Republic. I resolved that one day I would climb it.

In the morning we rose early and drove through Santiago and on to La Vega, our last official call at a provincial capital before returning to Santo Domingo. Hot again. We spent the morning in the government house, talking to the Governor and others—slums, housing, jobs. All morning I heard the sound of a crowd outdoors—"Yankees go home" and "Twenty-two million" (which, in Spanish, fits the hand-clapping five-beat rhythm) and "Down with the Yankees." Our two little boys, Dan and Fred, stood at a window and called back, *"Viva los Dominicanos,"* and the crowd, many of them primary and high school kids, laughed. It all seemed rather good-natured, though the Governor was nervous.

Past noon, we had finished with our interviews. An official, glancing out the window, suggested we wait, the crowd would get hungry and go home. We kept talking. The crowd grew. It began chanting, "We're not hungry." It was no longer only kids. It had been organized in advance —they carried handbills and signs. One sign read, "Give us our $22 million," and the little boy holding it was naked.

I suggested inviting a delegation inside. Nobody agreed. I considered going down to the doorway myself and inviting a few in but that might embarrass the Governor. About one o'clock I decided we would leave.

Fran, Dan and Fred, Fandino, and I went downstairs, the Governor and other officials hanging back uncertainly. I shook hands with them, then we went out into the blazing sunlight.

The instant we appeared, the crowd changed: Not friendly, hateful. And it moved: Surged forward through the police line to the car. We walked fast toward the car but did not run and told Dan and Fred not to. I waved to the crowd, but it was too late—now at best we could only escape.

Above the crowd's roar, I yelled to Fran and the boys and Fandino to get in on my side, the sidewalk side. Fran and the boys did, but Fandino went round to get in on the street side, and our driver Bailey, always correct, tried to open the door for him. Fandino reached it about the time the crowd did. He scrambled in. Bailey, still trying to maintain dignity, shut the door and got in behind the wheel. But the crowd surged against the car, shoved on it, beating on it with their hands, and throwing things. Two stones whizzed into the front seat where our boys were, and someone heaved a heavy object into the back seat at my feet. It landed with a crash and Fran thought it was a bomb, but it was only a heavy bundle of leaflets.

Bailey was starting the car. A student shoved his fist into the car and shook it and screamed over and over in our face, "Yankee go home," the whites of his eyes enormous, his mouth gaping wide, the cords of his neck taut. Bailey got started, we moved slowly away from the curb, the crowd ran after, banging on the car, until, gathering speed, we pulled away.

I felt defeated and wished we had not run. One of the stones in front that had fallen at our boys' feet turned out to be only a mango pit. But I never again, I am afraid, try as I might, felt quite the same about the Dominican people after they had threatened our children.

We spent that afternoon and evening at a hotel in the foothills, and by prearrangement leaders of all the political parties came to see me separately, including the 14th of June. I felt sure the 14th had organized the demonstration. The printed handbills, headed "Communiqué," were signed by the National Association of Secondary Students, a group largely taken over by the 14th of June. The ink on the handbills was dry. Like the signs, they had been prepared in advance. They declared that the sugar bill pending in the U. S. Congress would give us domination over the Dominican Republic's economy and disregard its misery. They declared that *"el imperialismo Yanqui"* had long oppressed and subjugated the people of Latin America "to satisfy the voracious appetites of the rapacious capitalists." My visit to La Vega was "undesirable and inopportune and of an interventionist character."

That was the straight Castro/Communist line; no secondary students thought it up unaided.

When two young local leaders of the 14th came to see me at the hotel, they blandly asked for U.S. financial help to carry out social reform in the Republic, but "it must come without interference—we are very nationalistic." What kind of help, I asked. "Economic aid in the form of developing ways of eliminating unemployment," one said. I asked for specifics. They had none. I tried to talk to them, but it was no use. They seemed young, brainless, posing as intellectuals but only mouthing canned slogans and speeches.

I accused them of organizing the demonstration, and told them that anyone who was teaching teen-age children to go into the streets and throw rocks at other children was doing his country no service. They were untroubled by this.

I do know, however, that progress of any kind is difficult without public order. I refuse to believe that public order means repression. I believe it possible to distinguish in law between peaceful picketing and inciting a riot, as in La Vega; between an orderly demonstration and burning cars, as in Santo Domingo. The Republic had laws prohibiting riots and inciting riots. Time and again, under two governments, I urged the government to enforce them. Not much, really, ever was done; though, with the help of the two Los Angeles policemen, the Consejo did regain control of the capital streets.

Until the Dominicans—and others in Latin America—find legal ways to preserve public order and at the same time permit individual liberty, they can hope for little of either. Further, I should think the OAS might usefully address itself to this problem—establish an inter-American police academy, and work through inter-American bar associations to teach the prosecution and defense of the accused. The problem is, of course, political. But at the least the techniques can be taught.

Next morning we drove to Santo Domingo. A few days later a delegation of citizens from La Vega called on me to apologize for the incident. They said the city was ashamed; "a few agitators" not representative of the people at large had caused the trouble; its better citizens were taking steps to rid themselves of agitators, though it would be painful to certain local families. I thanked them, told them I regretted having been the cause of a community problem, and assured them of continued American friendship toward the people of La Vega and all Dominicans.

Chapter Seven

THE GREAT SUGAR CRISIS

I felt I had never really gotten hold of the Embassy and other missions. MAAG and AID were growing rapidly. The MAAG chief, Colonel David C. Wolfe, a big tall Marine flier, had about forty-five officers and men under him. His job was to help train the ragtag Dominican military and to deliver to it some three million dollars' worth of training and equipment—a control tower for San Isidro, a hospital plane, trucks, Jeeps, radio equipment, replacement parts for the Navy (but no weapons or munitions). Wolfe also selected Dominican military men to send to various specialized schools in the United States and Panama.

Perhaps MAAG's most successful program was counter-insurgency training. (President Bonnelly approved it but not the battalion of engineers.) By the end of the year, despite Castro/Communist outcry, we had trained three companies of counter-insurgency troops, one at Constanza, the others at the 27th of February Army camp in the capital.

Our AID—Agency for International Development—mission was headed by Newell Williams, formerly a businessman, bespectacled, kind, and friendly, a capable administrator, bilingual, with years of experience in Latin America, but forever frustrated by the swampy AID bureaucracy in Washington. Williams, and the economic counselor in the Embassy, Harlan Bramble, took over the tasks Rafael Picó had performed temporarily.

Some Americans seem to think we simply sign blank checks for aid to foreign governments. Nothing could be more wrong. The Dominican government could not spend our loan money as it wished without our approval—to pay its employees' salaries, for example. It could spend it only on projects that we approved. Each project had to be covered by a separate agreement negotiated between Williams and a Dominican Cabinet minister, then approved by the Consejo, me, and AID in Washington. Moreover, each project was hedged about with many restrictions.

Anything used on a project that had to be bought abroad had to be bought in the United States. At least half of such purchases had to be sent to the Republic in United States ships. I have been told that AID bureaucrats in Washington must check each loan agreement against a list of more than a hundred restrictions enacted by Congress alone. And AID has its own restrictions. All these restrictions make good sense in the U.S. But they caused delay, and the Consejo could not wait.

AID's principal programs were housing, farm-to-market roads, agrarian reform, agricultural production, and education. In all, during my time, from March 1962 until September 1963, we made available to the Dominicans a total of about eighty-four million dollars. Few Latin American countries received more per capita.[1]

The main difficulties with AID were that both the U.S. and Dominican governments were slow in working out project agreements; that Washington sometimes delayed things unconsciously, and that technical experts blew in and out rapidly, leaving behind only surveys and hopes.

In addition to the U.S. government missions, several important international bodies sent technicians in and out of the Republic—the International Monetary Fund, the Inter-American Development Bank, the OAS, and various United Nations agencies. So did the Ford Foundation and other private foundations. "Technician" became a magic word. In fact, at times, there seemed more technicians than Dominicans.

Besides all this, CARITAS, a Catholic welfare service, was feeding as many as 350,000 Dominican people. CARE and the Church World Services, a Protestant welfare service, were active too.

By the time I left, we had some 160 Peace Corps volunteers. I invited each arriving group to the Residence and explained the Dominican situation and our purposes. The volunteers were scattered all over the Republic, living in pairs out in the *campo,* working with ordinary people, raising chickens and hogs, teaching English, and above all attempting all the numerous and potentially revolutionary tasks called community development. Two Peace Corps boys would settle down in a town, talk to local citizens, explain they were there to help them, and ask what needed doing. If a school was needed, they might scrounge around for a machine to make cement blocks or adobe bricks and help the people

[1] By mid-September, 1962, in the Dominican Republic we had signed nineteen agreements for AID projects that would cost almost twenty million dollars (of the twenty-five-million-dollar loan). The biggest were for schools (five million dollars), agricultural credit (two million), reconstruction of the Santiago–Puerto Plata road (one million), agrarian institute (1.7 million), emergency housing (two million), plus five million for budgetary support. Other projects costing less than one million each included the national planning board, agricultural extension service, re-forestation, the Fomento, community development, the agricultural school at Santiago, cattle and poultry improvement, and farm-to-market roads. We had enough money to put several thousand men to work, if necessary during the election campaign.

build a school. If that succeeded, they might next tackle a log bridge, a mountain trail, a recreation center, a baseball field, a cooperative, anything.

I call this community development "potentially revolutionary" because under Trujillo, Dominicans had always looked to the National Palace for help. If they ever learn what they can do for themselves, they will be a different people. This is one reason why people both in the United States and abroad intuitively feel that the Peace Corps, or something like it, just may possess the power to change the world. The volunteers were, of course, non-political but, being young, they naturally congregated with young Dominicans, who are strongly inclined against the Yankees and cannot be reached by older men in high official positions.

By and large, I consider the Peace Corps our best program. It was not an unqualified success. A few volunteers went home. Some were miscast, such as a New York philosophy major who was dumped into a village where hungry children were dying from eating dirt. Peace Corps kids, being young, sometimes attempted too much. One became so enamored of adobe bricks that I feared he would transform the Republic into an adobe wasteland. So many raised chickens that they broke the market price. Projects went awry, dreams soured. The Dominican government often failed them.

Our Peace Corps director, Andres Hernandez, a sentimental, dedicated man in khakis, was an inspiring leader, in the field. But as the Peace Corps grew, he simply was not able to administer it, and time and again one of the kids would come to the capital and sit around for a couple of days, waiting for someone to get him a drill bit he needed for a well. When it got to the point where the kids would come to the Residence and persuade my wife to haul a sack of cement out to the interior in my official car, I took steps. On a trip to Washington I told Sarge Shriver he would either have to get Hernandez an administrative number two man or else get me a new wife and car. We got the number two man.

2

In all, by the time I left, the Embassy and collateral missions contained more than three hundred people. That is a small mission—in 1950 our mission in London contained some 1950 civilians. Santo Domingo was a Class IV post, the lowest class, the Ambassador being paid $20,000 a year, though it was raised to Class III—and I to $22,500. (London is a Class I post; the Ambassador gets the magnificent sum of $27,500.)

Small though it was, I couldn't know what every member of a three-hundred-man mission was doing. But I was responsible.

I relied heavily on Al Hemba, the Deputy Chief of Mission (DCM), to keep me informed. Hemba, a good detail man, was the number two man in the Embassy; when I was out of the country, Hemba was in charge.

I asked Harlan Bramble to keep track of AID and the international missions and to try to keep watch on the innumerable carpetbaggers— fly-by-night U.S. businessmen.

I asked Hemba to keep track of AID, MAAG, USIS, and Peace Corps. But he was chained to his desk with paperwork. He held a staff meeting for Embassy section chiefs every day. I rarely attended, relying on him to keep me informed.

I left the mechanics of running the Embassy to the administrative section chief under the DCM. He had to pay everybody, maintain security, remodel the building, run the commissary, arrange transportation to and from the airport for official visitors, hire and fire local employees.

I reserved the CIA chief for myself. His functions were basically two— collecting information; and conducting operations, such as penetrating Castro/Communist groups with agents. Some Ambassadors, I understand, take the position they do not want to know what the CIA is doing. I always insisted on knowing. Sometimes its information-collecting developed into a rivalry with Shlaudeman, head of the Embassy political section. I did nothing to discourage this—competition would produce more information.

To try to pull everything together, I held a Country Team meeting once a week—met in my study at the Residence with the DCM, the military attachés, and the chiefs of all collateral missions. I have never thought big meetings produce much, but they did help make sure we were all heading in the same general direction.

In time of trouble, I found myself calling in half a dozen men— Hemba (and Spencer King who succeeded him as DCM in a few months); Harry Shlaudeman, the Embassy's chief political officer; the CIA station chief, and the three military attachés. These men formed the policy core of the Embassy. As explosion followed explosion, I came to call them the Crisis Crowd.

Because the Ambassador is the chief of mission, everything that matters, and a good deal that doesn't, winds up in his lap. I spent hours dissuading our people from renting ostentatious Trujillo dwellings. I forbade them to abuse their diplomatic immunity by parking their cars in no-parking zones. I forbade them to carry guns. I refused to expand our commissary, which sold only liquor and cigarettes (though this was difficult, particularly when MAAG members flew the MAAG plane regularly to Puerto Rico and did their shopping in the PX there).

The demands on an Ambassador's time are limitless. Every visiting fireman wants to "pay a courtesy call." Group after group wants a speech. (I gave only three prepared policy speeches in my entire time.) But there are many things an Ambassador must—and should want to— do. I wrote most, and saw all, policy cables and dispatches, a ceaseless flow.[2] Only I could make major policy decisions; not only for the Embassy, but for AID, MAAG, and the other collateral missions.

Sometimes I had to resolve a relatively minor dispute—e.g., whether the first-grade readers that we were providing free to all Dominican first-grade school children would be hardbound or paperbound. (Reading the textbooks, I noted that the illustrations portrayed smiling mothers in gleaming kitchens in comfortable suburban ranch houses—and all the faces were white. I ordered changes.)

I probably spent less time with the resident American business community than many Ambassadors, and some of them resented it; but I felt my first duty was to my government and the Dominican government. I never failed to see an American businessman who had an important problem. I received all visiting Senators and Congressmen (only a handful) and Admirals and Generals, representatives of innumerable private groups such as the American Legion, and such distinguished private citizens as the late Henry Wallace, former Vice President.

Wallace came several times to the Republic, always bringing a new variety of corn or other crop; once, despite his age, he arrived in the afternoon at Aeropuerto Punta Caucedo and took a taxicab all the way to Constanza to plant some perishable strawberry plants before dark. In the swamp of Dominican politics he seemed somehow a splendid gentleman, dedicated to helping men grow better things in the earth's soil.

We gave a great many large "receptions," or cocktail parties, for the Dominican government, the diplomatic corps, the American business community, the Dominican military, and so on, 250 or 300 people at each one, arriving promptly (Trujillo made prompt arrival obligatory, and the habit stuck) at 6:30 P.M. and departing promptly at 8:30 P.M. We always invited several staff members. We were there to work, not to enjoy ourselves.

[2] In describing crises, I sometimes mention cables to Washington. I wrote and sent them all the time, almost daily, though have mentioned it only occasionally in this book. In addition, I wrote a long interpretive summary of the situation about every six weeks and sent it by airmail diplomatic pouch to the State Department and the White House. All these were policy cables and dispatches. Other Embassy officers cabled and airmailed a heavy volume of routine economic and political reports, plus occasional special papers, sometimes requested by the Department, on Castro communism, youth groups and so on. Keeping Washington informed is a large part of an Ambassador's duty, and as a lifelong journalist it came naturally to me.

Big receptions seemed to me largely a waste of time, though necessary. More important were a series of small dinner parties for Consejeros and influential private Dominicans. Most important of all were the lunches I gave for one Consejero, or one politician, or one private citizen, each alone. I developed a luncheon routine for a lone Dominican guest: A drink in the study with small talk, turning to substance just as the house-boy announced lunch, and continuing it through lunch in the state dining room, listening mostly; then, over brandy in the living room, hammering the point I wanted to make.

Each of the foreign embassies gave a reception on its national day; I went when I could, and if I couldn't, Fran went. The other Ambassadors gave frequent dinner parties for each other; I went to only a few. The other Ambassadors understood that I was busier than most of them, and forgave my rudeness. In such a country some Ambassadors are nearing retirement, have only a small staff, spend their mornings attending to their countrymen's commercial interests, their afternoons playing golf or swimming, and their evenings at dinner parties.

Fran and the wives of other diplomats met every Tuesday morning to sew for orphanages. She paid and received countless official calls. With the help of USIS, she sought out Dominican artists and hung their work on the Residence walls (and sold a few paintings for the artists). She worked with Dominican government officials and their wives on char-itable and cultural activities. An elaborate "Afternoon of Dominican Arts" at the Residence, involving the National Chorus and students and teachers from the Palace of Beautiful Arts, nearly collapsed because a young male ballet dancer who had rehearsed in leotards became in-volved in one of the sporadic gun battles at the University.

Once a month the diplomatic corps met at the Papal Nunciatura. I attended when I could. The monthly meetings were a trial—once the Ambassadors spent nearly two hours discussing whether to rent a beach house at Boca Chica. Yet many were extremely able men, particularly the Papal Nuncio, Emanuele Clarizio. In this country, which had a Con-cordat with the Vatican, the Nuncio was the highest-ranking member, the dean, of the diplomatic corps. Monseñor Clarizio was, I thought, a deeply spiritual man. At the same time he worked ceaselessly to improve the lot of the ordinary Dominicans in their daily lives, and he possessed an acute understanding of politics. I came to know and like him immensely and to work with him very closely.

An Ambassador's life is a lonely one. The reason is simple: He never can open his mouth without speaking for the President. That meant I never could relax and speak freely with Dominicans, and with only a few Embassy men. Friendship, in the easy way one knows it in private life, could not exist. I really could talk to no one freely except Fran, and there were some things I could not tell even her.

At the end of May and first of June, disorders in the streets broke out anew. This time they were clearly anti-American: The Castro/Communists were exploiting the sugar problem and the visa mess.

I felt sure they would do everything possible in the fall to disrupt the elections. By then, too, the Armed Forces, recovered from the shock of Trujillo's fall, might once more become a political force. I thought we dared not go into the fall with massive unemployment, and misery in the *campo*. President Bonnelly agreed. I therefore asked Williams and Bramble to speed up agrarian reform and prepare for emergency public works.

Oddly, despite all these problems, U.S. newspapers were at this time saying that the Republic, next door to Castro's Cuba, was rapidly becoming a "showcase of democracy," a phrase I had long since learned to detest, considering it not only falsely hopeful but also invidious.

Amiama gave a party for his daughter on her sixteenth birthday. It was, I think, the most lavish party I ever saw. Spotlights and floodlights lit trees and garden, waiters moved among scores of tables, two orchestras played for dancing outdoors, and truckloads of flowers brought down from Constanza adorned the stone and concrete walls. The guests ran into the hundreds; the cost, I should guess, into the thousands; and I spent most of the evening splitting a bottle of Scotch with President Bonnelly, while bodyguards hovered dimly among trees behind us. His daughter deserved this party, Amiama explained: Last year, at the time of the assassination, she had spent her birthday in jail.

Suffering was everywhere a dark thread through Dominican life. And there were others—family blood feuds inextricably bound up with old assassinations and new elections. And dependence, and discouragement and deprivation—once, driving down a road along the coast, we passed a young man afoot, and he cried out, *"Llévame allí"*—"take me there," not knowing where we were going, just wanting to go, too. Wherever it was, it could be no worse than where he was.

Driving in the interior, Donny Reid and I came upon some workmen repairing the road, and one of them threw down his shovel, flung wide his arms, and cried out to us as though in agony, *"Dáme algo,"* "give me something." But he had a job. What did he want? Who knows?

"Tírame cinco," the urchins in front of Vesuvio's restaurant used to say, a slangy, "Toss me a nickel." The children were heartbreaking. And cruel as well—I have seen them at the zoo dropping rocks on the crocodile's head, putting a Coke bottle in the elephant's trunk, while elders laughed.

It is a strange society. If you sent candy to a children's hospital, the doctors and nurses took theirs first before passing it out to the patients. Everyone said habitually, *"Si Dios quiere,"* "If God wishes," it is more than a farewell, it is self-absolution: Who needs assume responsibility, if it is in God's hands anyway? No one will assume responsibility: Some doctors urge patients to hurry abroad for treatment.

Sometimes Dominicans seemed disoriented, especially the young. Leftist high-school students adopted, for their newspaper's masthead, the slogan "Culture or Death." A sign scrawled on a wall, and signed MPD, read "Away with Yankee communism, long live socialism." One was tempted to dismiss all that as nonsense—until one recalled that Mao Tse-tung began as a student leader and, disoriented in an underdeveloped nation under the impact of the 1917 Russian Revolution, became in rapid succession a monarchist, idealist, liberal, democratic reformer, utopian socialist, anti-militarist, autonomist of Hunan, anarchist, and, finally, Communist.

When the Consejo announced it would grant a concession to a company to build a refinery in the capital, two whole cities, San Cristóbal and San Pedro de Macorís, went on strike, and the people, enraged, marched on the main highway to the capital, tearing up—of all things—trees on the way. A policeman whom I met while walking along a remote trail wrote down directions for me on a police report he was taking to headquarters —another unreported crime. Worst of all was what I have heard more than one Dominican say about his fellow countrymen: *"Son salvajes, son brutos"*—"They are savages, brutes." And, always with contempt, yet a certain fondness, too, "I know my people."

Many Dominican men of the upper class keep mistresses. Sometimes they import them from abroad. Several high-ranking officials asked us for U.S. visas for Cuban girl friends of whom they had tired. Numerous expensive prostitutes lived in the big hotels. High-ranking officers swaggered through the lobby of the Hotel Embajador, a girl on each arm, the Ramfis tradition. Some high officials maintained their mistresses in villas in the suburbs; more than once we had to seek them out there during crises. Sometimes the government paid the bills for the girls. Now and then we heard that the girls were deeply involved in political intrigue or arms smuggling. I used to wonder where these men got the energy to work, plot, maintain families, and keep mistresses. I concluded they could do it because they were not really serious men. Dominican boys are doted on; many Dominican men are still little boys, seldom serious, *siempre jugando,* always playing.

Despite their protestations, Dominicans are not free of race prejudice. It does not exist in law, but it exists in fact. An article in *El Caribe* said that "it is very difficult to find a Negro girl employed in the big stores of the country, or in commercial banks." White-skinned Dominican women at bathing beaches wade into the water carrying parasols; white skin is a caste mark. A skilled Negro physician had little practice. Most of the people high in government, the oligarchy, and even the military, are rather light-skinned, while the poor in the *barrios* are mostly black. Since, however, "light-skinned" includes many shadings, prejudice singles out other Negroid features—thick lips, flattened noses, kinky hair. Few so marked rise high. One of our Peace Corps boys, a Negro, went home, saying, "I can be called a nigger at home."

Dominicans, trying to explain the national character, have told me that from the Spaniards they derive cruelty, from the Indians duplicity, and from the Negroes stupid kindliness. Cruelty and kindness—our houseboy taught our boys how to saddle their burro, touching them lightly and lovingly on the shoulder the while; but this same houseboy once caught a rat and buried it alive to its head, then poured gasoline on the head and lit it. Duplicity—many Dominican families made sure to have one member in each of the political parties so that no matter which won the family would be safe. Many prominent Dominicans were called *insumergibles*—unsinkables—men who could leap lightly from Trujillista to democrat to leftist to rightist, always landing on their feet; one said to me, "I always have to be up, never down. Whoever is up, I am with him."

The conversation of many high-ranking Dominicans is strikingly barren. On social occasions, they turn the phonograph up loud and dance and drink and gossip. (*"Chisma,"* rumors, "is our country's principal product," more than one Dominican has told me.) Is this emptiness why they plot? They seemed to enjoy talking about Trujillo. He interested them. In one sense, they resemble Chicagoans—talk of gangsterism, crooked politics, and "the fix" is dear to the hearts of Chicagoans. This is their baseball. Just so is plotting the Dominicans' baseball. Perhaps if Trujillo had not existed, the Republic would have had to invent him.

Often at parties, or aboard the presidential yacht *Angelita,* watching Dominicans drinking and dancing the *merengue,* I thought that Trujillo's guests must have behaved just that way. Yet, so thinking, I have never forgotten the great days of 1961 after he fell, when the people faced Ramfis' tanks in the streets of the capital, a nation reborn. As I have said, what Trujillo did to them, and the worst thing he did, was to destroy their character, their trust in each other and in themselves. It is a bitter joke that Amiama, plotting the assassination, used to throw the cat out of the house so it would not overhear. To this day, nobody trusts anybody. Yet trust is the glue that holds civilization together. Even Hitler won no such triumph over man's spirit—after all, he had only twelve years, while Trujillo had thirty-one. This is a sick and shattered people.

It is, however, still a kind people. Nearly always, whether talking with the poor in the interior or with the oligarchy in Santiago, we felt we were among friends. More importantly, watching Dominicans' everyday life, one feels that these people like each other. They seem affectionate, sympathetic. Perhaps it is because they have suffered so much together.

This is, too, a religious people. I hesitate to generalize, but I gained the impression that the poor were inclined to be more devout than the rich, and that among high government and military officials the women were more inclined to be devout than their husbands. I also have the impression that the Church was more influential in the *campo* than in the cities. Certainly, it was a force in secular affairs, including political affairs. Two archbishops have been President of the Republic, neither notably successful. And in my time Monseñor Pérez Sánchez was a Consejero.

Monseñor was an old man, at least seventy, white-haired, fat, jolly, warm-hearted, widely respected, filled with good will, in love with the people, all heart. When Rodríguez Echavarría had imprisoned the other Consejeros but, out of respect to the Church, not him, Monseñor had gone to San Isidro and demanded that he too be locked up; he loved to tell that story, leaping up from the sofa in my study to bang on the closed door as he had banged on the jail door at San Isidro. In Council, he usually voted with what he thought would be the majority. Amiama and Imbert used to play tricks on him. Amiama, expressionless, would lay on the Council table a decree, and ask all to sign, and all would sign, but when it got to the Monseñor, Imbert would say perhaps he should read it, since it affected his interests, and he would read it and explode wildly: It decreed all churches closed and all Church property confiscated. Nonetheless, Monseñor Pérez Sánchez was a moral force, and a symbol of stability, and the Council needed both.

On a Sunday at the end of May, I took a weekend off—took my family up to Constanza alone in our Jeep; no driver, no Fandino, no plans, nothing, not even, I fear, much good sense: We did not start until 11 A.M. and thought to be back by dark, but took the longest way—west to Baní, then north to San José de Ocoa and then on north straight into the heart of the Cordillera Central. (I understand that since then a storm destroyed this road.) Beyond San José de Ocoa the road turns gravel and climbs switchback after switchback, straight up the face of sheer rock walls, and the cliffside drops a thousand feet or more to the rushing river below, the air grows chill, and high up above the pine, the clouds close in suddenly and, above them, gray mist—a desolation and emptiness found only in the highest places. Here the road runs across a narrow saddle little wider than the road itself, cliffs dropping sheer away on both sides, nothing below but clouds and fog and the lost tops of trees.

Beyond, the road descends a bit, once more into pine, pine burned after Trujillo's death, mile upon mile of it destroyed, some say by Castro/Communist saboteurs. At La Nevera—the Ice Box—ice forms at night. We were wearing only cotton clothes in an open Jeep. Far to the west rose the highest peak of all, Pico Duarte; but even from here we could not quite see it, for fog shrouded it. It was late afternoon, raining and getting dark, and we were nearly out of gas. Starting down, I shut off the

ARRIVAL IN TENSE TIMES

The new Ambassador; Chargé d'Affaires John Calvin Hill; Fred, one of the Martin sons; Fran Martin; Dominican Chief of Protocol Logroño

After the riot: The remains of Ambassador Martin's car

"On Thursday morning *El Caribe*...carried a banner headline: Not only [former President] Balaguer but [General] Rodríguez Echavarría...had gone to the United States. That meant trouble. It would enrage the Dominican people. For it appeared that we were welcoming to the United States the last two men who represented in the popular mind the Trujillo tyranny."

The car of the U.S. consul set afire by the same mob

"Near the tailor shop, just off Calle Conde, he ran into a mob. They surrounded him, pulled [the driver] out, then smashed and burned the car. They burned our consul's car and a USIS mobile unit and other cars.... They smashed windows and wrecked storefronts. They looted, they littered the streets with broken glass. They stoned our Consulate...."

Colonel Fritz Long, Chief of Protocol Logroño, and Ambassador Martin at the National Palace

"At the top of the steps we turned...and we stood rigid at attention while down below on the blistered driveway the leader of the military band saluted, his sword flashing in the sun, then turned, and the band played full-throated the Dominican national anthem."

"The *Salón de Embajadores*...was vast. It seemed a mile of rococo, all red and gold, plush and marble, with gigantic crystal chandeliers. Seated at its far end all in white were the seven members of the Consejo de Estado, Council of State, the 'seven Presidents' who ruled the Republic after Trujillo...."

Ceremony in the Salón de Embajadores, embassy personnel at the left, four of the "seven Presidents" visible at the rear

Ambassador Martin and President Rafael Bonnelly during the presentation of credentials

"We talked for about ten minutes, he and I, his bodyguard now and then peering out from behind a heavy red arras. I do not remember what he said; no doubt something about looking forward to working together to build Dominican democracy, sentences that in such circumstances became banalities no matter how deeply felt."

Ambassador Martin and President Kennedy at the White House, March 1962

"President Kennedy...had a special interest in the Dominican Republic....When I had gone to say goodbye to him a week before in his oval office in the White House, we had talked about the Republic's problems....Twice he said, 'Let me know direct if there's anything you want.' And he ended, sardonic, 'If you blow this, you'd better not come home.'"

engine on the downhill runs to save gas; and then we topped a range and saw below, as in a well, Constanza, lights and houses far far down a tiny valley amid the mountains. This was the scene of the invasion of June 14, 1959.

We thought to push on; but a filling station man advised against it. We gave up, spent the night at the almost-empty hotel built by Trujillo for tourists, and, I was told, designed by Trujillo's sister, whose talent had been thought to lie in the field of architecture. She had set this hotel down in this high valley, surrounded by peaks lost in clouds, one of the most magnificent sites in the Caribbean; and she had designed the hotel so that not a single room faced outdoors; all looked inward on dirty corridors and concrete patios.

We rose at 3:30 A.M. and started out in the dark, bumping across the valley and starting the climb up, for I had early appointments in the capital. As the sun came up, we were on a one-track mountain road, hugging rocky shelves, inching our way around landslides that went almost to the edge of the cliff and would have stopped anything but a Jeep. Below us lay clouds. Soon the sun burned them off, and they trailed wispy white vapors across the deep-cut valleys, lush with plantains and beans and corn and coffee and cacao, huts hidden among the trees, the sun blood-red slashing on the green cliffs and rock walls. So we wound our way, warming as the sun warmed, following ridges, climbing still higher, and at length descending into Jarabacoa and so to La Vega, the central highway, and home. A foolish trip, but one of the best we made. And the first day since I had come to the Republic that I had managed to spend entirely alone with Fran and the boys. I began laying plans for an assault on Pico Duarte. And when we told the Bonnellys and Bonillas and Reids about it, they said we must all explore the Enchanted Valley where dwelt the *ciguapa*, a mythical creature somewhat like the Abominable Snowman, and said to be a giant woman who walked with her feet turned backward. We would seek her on the weekend of July 1.

3

Playtime was over. Two problems were approaching: One over elections, the other over the sugar quota. By now, the Consejo had strengthened its position considerably. It was not yet a solid power, but neither was it a shaky freak. It had adopted some popular reforms, and was beginning to feel strong enough to arrest *calié* and crack down on rioters. President Bonnelly's confidence had risen and so had his popularity. Increasingly, the other Consejeros deferred to him. The budget was in better shape than anyone had had a right to expect.

The Consejo was even feeling strong enough to bait the Republic's ancient enemy, Haiti. Foreign Minister Bonilla Atiles told me that

Dominican relations with Haiti were deteriorating; President Duvalier was an odious tyrant; Duvalier had closed Dominican consulates; and now two Dominicans, probably drunk, had wandered across the border and disappeared. Bonilla intended to ask the OAS Human Rights Commission to investigate. I told him we, too, were concerned about Duvalier, but that the Dominicans had enough problems at home without taking on problems abroad, and that we hoped he would maintain "cool and correct relations."

Our own position in the Republic had changed, too—but for the worse. By now the Dominicans, in March so grateful to us for having sent the fleet to throw out the Trujillos, had forgotten. Nationalism was rising. The twenty-two million dollars, the sugar quota, and the visa mess had hurt us badly, but worst of all we had failed to produce. AID had laid much groundwork, but had made no visible impact on the daily life of the ordinary Dominican. Dominicans felt we had let them down. Obviously, in so vast an undertaking, time is needed. I do not know how often I told Dominicans, "We know it is slow. But we are trying to repair the damage of thirty-one years. I hope it won't take thirty-one years to repair it. But it will take more than thirty-one days—much more." Nevertheless, the Dominicans were impatient. And no wonder. Daily I saw signs of rising anti-Americanism. Amiama warned that he and I must meet very secretly—he was being accused of being pro-Yankee. When a newspaper said that our counter-insurgency team had arrived to train Dominicans and help teach them how to behave in a democratic society, General Viñas Román said publicly that the Dominican Armed Forces needed no foreigner to teach them civics. These men were not anti-American. They were simply protecting themselves.

The first problem of June, the problem of elections, could become a constitutional crisis.

The Consejo was governing under the old Trujillo constitution—not a bad constitution, in form—as amended by the Trujillo Congress in December 1961, to set up the Consejo.

Under this constitution, an election for delegates to a Constituent Assembly was scheduled for August 15, 1962—now just two months away. This Constituent Assembly would meet the next day—traditional day for the Assembly to convene—and write a new constitution. General elections for President, Vice President, and Congress would be held on or before December 20. The new government would take office and the Consejo depart on February 27, 1963.

The first step to elections was a new election law. OAS experts had drafted one. Pichardo had redrafted it. But instead of simply promulgating it, the Consejo had called in the political parties to discuss and rewrite it, perhaps in an access of zeal for democracy, perhaps to escape responsibility. Pichardo had spent all spring at this terrible task. For by then some twenty-six political parties or groups had arisen. The smaller parties, knowing they could not win, wanted to stall and delay elections. The meetings had gone on for weeks. Now at long last the law was promulgated. I invited Pichardo to lunch to find out how things were going.

Pichardo, as I have said, possessed probably the most cultivated mind on the Consejo. Tall, handsome, polite, always immaculate in white linen suit, brown-skinned with soft brown eyes, he graced any drawing room. It was hard to believe that for months after Trujillo's assassination he had carried a suicide pill hidden in his lapel, for he had been in the underground opposition.

The Consejo had given him charge of economic affairs. He knew little about them. At first, Rafael Picó and Newell Williams of AID considered Pichardo obstructionist, anti-American, and leftist. I agreed he had a streak of nationalism, but I thought he moved slowly on AID projects we suggested because he refused to sign documents he did not fully understand. Intelligent and tenacious, he would not be stampeded, least of all by *Yanquís*—he read the fine print. And he wanted to protect the Republic's interest. Picó and Williams came to agree.

The election law was terribly complicated—Pichardo, at lunch that day, said, laughing, that even he couldn't answer some of my questions about it—and it would be extraordinarily difficult to administer mechanically. The Consejo, still avoiding responsibility and having let the parties write the electoral law, now proposed to let the three-man Electoral Board arrange the election. But the Electoral Board didn't know where to start —no such thing as a free election had happened here since 1924. So the Board and the Consejo had asked the OAS to come in. But the OAS was reluctant—would this not be intervening deeply in the Republic's internal affairs?

It appeared to me that much of the talk now was not about how to hold elections, but how to postpone them. Pichardo said if the OAS and Electoral Board so recommended, the Consejo must postpone them. But did it possess the constitutional power to do so? He thought so, though was not sure. If it postponed them, would it thereafter possess the power to govern? Pichardo thought so, others thought not.

What it came down to was this: The August election was only two months away, no one was ready, and a constitutional crisis could result.

Legalities aside, whether the elections would be postponed was pre-eminently a political question. I decided to see what the political situation was.

I asked Viriato Fiallo to come to the Residence. Big and friendly and lumbering, he said only his UCN wanted elections on schedule. It was drafting a constitution.

Horacio Julio Ornes, brother of the publisher of *El Caribe,* one-time leader of the Cayo Confites and Luperón invasions, now leader of the Vanguardia party, came to the Residence. A pale, black-haired, mustached man, smart, young, and ruthless, with something reptilian about him, Horacio Julio Ornes told me that the elections must be postponed —no one party if elected could govern alone. A coalition of Vanguardia, PRD, and the Social Christians—"the parties of the revolutionary left" —was essential. He would arrange it but needed more time. If elections were held on schedule, the 14th of June would smash them. I took all this to mean that he didn't think his Vanguardia could win at this time, so wanted to postpone elections, and was raising the Communist bogeyman.

Shlaudeman, who kept in close touch with the parties while I worked with the government, reported that Juan Bosch was ambivalent about August elections. Certainly the PRD would be stronger by December. Bosch was determined against coalition.

I gave a party for members of the Armed Forces, about two hundred of them. Moving among them, I found none who would say he thought elections should be postponed but none who was enthusiastic about them either.

What of the Consejo?

President Bonnelly doubted that the August election for a Constituent Assembly could be held on schedule—all the minor parties opposed, so would PRD, the Consejo would not intervene, the Electoral Board and OAS must decide.

Reid was certain the elections must be postponed until September or October: The election machinery simply could not be set up in time. This meant the December election must be postponed until February (unless the Constituent Assembly election could be put forward till next year.)

Imbert and Amiama thought that all elections were impossible until public order had been established for several months. Anyway, the Armed Forces would overthrow either Fiallo or Bosch if elected. They were talking of a new party or coalition of parties. We had heard their candidate might be Julio Peynado, a distinguished elderly lawyer for the biggest American sugar company, son of an unsuccessful presidential candidate in 1924, nephew of one of Trujillo's "presidents." (They apparently had all but given up on Fernández Caminero. So had I, but for a different reason—he had told me he had been reading an "excellent" book, *The Protocols of the Elders of Zion!*)

Of the entire Consejo, only Monseñor Pérez Sánchez wholeheartedly favored elections on schedule, probably because he had not thought about it lately. The other Consejeros had omitted him from their discussions.

The Consejeros wanted postponement for various reasons. Some may have hoped to perpetuate themselves. Some may have wanted to stop Fiallo or Bosch. Some simply feared elections—they represented a big step, and what might result no one knew. Amiama and Imbert would not willingly leave power until their futures were assured. Fernández Caminero was a candidate without a party. Reid said he would run for Vice President if Bonnelly ran for President. Bonnelly said he might consider running four years later but not now. And some said the Republic was "not ready for elections"—the phrase politicians used to conceal their real reasons for wanting postponement.

In a literal sense the Republic was not ready—the parties had not begun campaigning, and the sheer mechanical difficulties were staggering. The Electoral Board must appoint eight departmental boards, twenty-six provincial boards, ninety-six municipal boards, and set up about forty-four hundred polling places. That meant hiring nearly twenty-five thousand poll watchers, judges, and the like. The ballot of each party must be printed on paper of the color of its choice. Voters must be registered. And the Electoral Board had not even begun.

But when most people said that "the Dominican people are not ready for elections," they really meant that the people were not ready for democracy. And here we come to the crux of the matter. I must confess that often, driving through the countryside or walking through a *barrio*, seeing a women staring into space from the doorway of a thatched hut, I wondered. I wondered, too, when I reflected upon the Republic's history and the sheer lack of education of the Dominican people. A generation had grown up knowing nothing but Trujillo. Were we foolish to hope for representative democracy in such a country?

Yet, in the United States, walking through a black ghetto in a northern city, seeing the young men out of school and out of work, the uneducated and illiterate, the hopeless and almost mindless faces buried in the slums, I had misgivings. And I had misgivings too in many of our middle-class and upper-class suburbs.

Democracy is, after all, first an act of faith—faith in the people. Perhaps Lincoln was a romantic when he said, "Why should there not be a patient confidence in the ultimate justice of the people?" But democracy is more than an act of faith; it is also a political belief. And if we believe, as we say we do, that people ought to have the right freely to choose their rulers, then I know of no way we can help them exercise that right except by helping them hold free elections.

To be sure, it is late in history to start—late in the Dominican Republic, late in Latin America. But if we don't start now, when do we? What will make the people better prepared for democracy? More tyranny? Education, perhaps; but education for democracy does not descend on a people from heaven. It can come only from practicing democracy. The 1960s may be too dangerous to attempt learning democracy by trial and error. But if we so decide, we had better say so and be prepared to conduct our affairs in a world far different from today's— different because we will have switched to empire (or to total self-isolation).

In any case, in the Dominican Republic in mid-June of 1962 we were committed to elections. And we stood alone, except for UCN. Elections on schedule heavily favored UCN. It alone could nominate outstanding men in almost every province for delegates to the Constituent Assembly, could thus probably sweep the August election, and could thus probably create a bandwagon that would carry Tiallo to presidential victory in December. The August election was, quite simply, UCN's road to power. And Bosch and the PRD knew it.

What, then, should be our policy? For here, now, we did confront a fork in the road—we had a choice.

If mechanical difficulties truly presented insurmountable obstacles, then the August election could not be held. And that seemed likely. If it were held, all parties except UCN might boycott it, and some might create disorders. On the other hand, if the election were postponed over UCN objections, a constitutional crisis might result: The Consejo's legal power to continue might be called into question. Moreover, postponement to September or October would shorten the time until the December election, leaving the Constituent Assembly too little time to write a constitution, and so the December election might have to be postponed, and so the Consejo's departure in February might have to be postponed—and that might wreck the whole democratic structure.

The hard facts were that no party that expected to lose would ever be "ready for" an election; that it would be many years before all the Dominican people would be ready to make a truly intelligent choice in a free election; that indefinite postponement would merely give the right and left new opportunities to destroy what "readiness" the parties and the people might summon up if faced with an inescapable deadline. One was tempted to teach the child to swim by throwing him into the water.

On the other hand, the hard facts were that the Consejo was not determined to hold the August election come what might; that all but UCN felt the same way; that UCN was so confident it probably would consent to postponement on the ground of "mechanical difficulty"; and that mechanical difficulties were very real.

And the final hard fact was that the Consejo itself had no popular support and could not survive for long. Nor could it be reconstituted. An elected government was indispensable. There simply was no alternative.

I reluctantly recommended to the State Department that we change our policy. What would really establish Dominican democracy would be the

December election, not the August election. It was in December that the people would elect a President and Congress to govern them. And they —and we—badly needed an elected government. So long as the Consejo remained in power, it would remain in danger, for it had no popular base, and we would have to nurse it—and be blamed for its mistakes. The December election must be saved. Merely postponing the August election would imperil the December election. I, therefore, favored abolishing the August election.

But I did not think we should work to do so, at least not yet. Instead, we should take the position that we assumed both elections would be held on schedule unless mechanical difficulties proved insurmountable, urge the Electoral Board to begin registration quickly, watch the drift of opinion for the next two weeks, and await the recommendations of an OAS commission.

The auguries were not auspicious. On June 9 Peru held elections. The voters split almost evenly three ways. Haya de la Torre, the non-Communist leftist who most closely resembled Juan Bosch, seemed to have won narrowly. The Peruvian military refused to allow him to take office. In Santo Domingo, we felt the shock waves. The Dominican Armed Forces noted Peru well. So did Juan Bosch. But now the election problem was suddenly swallowed up in the most dangerous crisis yet—the great sugar crisis.

4

For many years the United States has bought sugar abroad at a premium price—a price above the world market price. Originally it did so to ensure the U.S. of a sufficient supply of sugar. It distributed quotas—portions of our needs—among various countries. Thus did the quota system acquire important foreign policy implications. Nations with one-crop sugar economies became virtually dependent on the U.S. sugar quota. Trujillo and others had spent millions lobbying to get a big quota.

In 1962, the Kennedy Administration decided to abandon the country quota system and to adopt instead a world quota system—we would immediately purchase the huge former Cuban quota on the world market without paying a premium, instead of purchasing it from several countries, including the Dominican Republic, at a premium; and, except in the Philippines, we would gradually eliminate in five years all quotas and all premiums. Many factors lay behind this decision—economy, pressure from our own beet sugar producers, our balance of payments deficit, encouragement to Cuba to return to the fold, and concern about what would happen to our other sugar-producing friends, such as the Dominican Republic, if Castro fell and Cuba could once more sell us sugar; for they had increased their sugar production to grab the Cuban windfall.

And many experts believed that the country quota system gave large sub-
sidies to both foreign and domestic producers, thus artificially raising the
price of sugar and imposing an unjust burden on U.S. consumers—Senator Paul H. Douglas of Illinois once said, "If bananas were grown on
Pike's Peak, and if the American Government subsidized the domestic
producers in order to make it profitable and if we then, in turn, paid the
producers of bananas in the Caribbean this same price, we would have
almost an identical analogy to the sugar program."

Before I became Ambassador, I had scarcely known a sugar quota
existed. I learned fast that June. And despite my high respect for Senator Douglas, whose constituents do not grow sugar, I found myself opposing him on behalf of my own "constitutents," the Dominicans, who do.

It was the Kennedy Administration's announcement that it would ask
Congress to abandon the country quota system and go to the world
quota system that had first triggered outcry in the Dominican Republic.
The Republic produced nearly a million tons of sugar a year; its U.S.
quota in the first three months of 1962 had led it to believe it could
sell about nine hundred thousand tons at the U.S. premium price in the
year as a whole. Then came the bombshell—the world quota bill. Dominicans felt betrayed. I could not even get most Dominicans to understand that "a bill" in the U. S. Congress is far from law.

I must say they had reason to be alarmed. Sugar brings about 50 percent of all the foreign currency the Dominican Republic receives—the
hard cash it needs to buy things abroad. But the Dominican Republic
simply could not produce sugar at the world market price. It must have a
U.S. quota premium price. To make matters worse, about 60 percent
of all Dominican sugar, as we have seen, was produced by Haina, that is,
the Dominican government. And Haina was the most inefficient producer
of all. It was inherently inefficient; moreover, the Consejo could not
withstand political pressure to put on the Haina payroll thousands of
people who did no work at all. Thus, the government was caught in a
dilemma not uncommon in Latin America. It owned a major share of the
nation's biggest industry, but was forced by political pressures to run it at
a loss. To put it bluntly, the Dominican Republic might go broke if it lost
its U.S. sugar quota. Not immediately, not certainly—but that is the way
it would look.

To make matters still worse, the world quota bill came after months
of agitation over the twenty-two million dollars.

The present sugar bill would expire June 30. Toward the end of May,
Congressman Harold Cooley's House Agricultural Committee announced
it would reject the Kennedy world quota bill, revert to a country quota
system, and write its own bill in committee. Jubilation swept the Republic
—all too prematurely. For on June 15, the Cooley Committee came out
with its own bill—and it gave the Dominican Republic a basic quota of

only 200,000 tons, plus 150,000 tons of the Cuban windfall—a total of 350,000 tons, compared to the present 900,000 tons. It did provide for payment of the twenty-two million dollars.

That Sunday, Donny Reid came to see me. He looked like a little boy, worried and heartsick. Leaning forward on the edge of the deep sofa in my study and looking up, he said, "Can you help us? I mean, the sugar. It all came so sudden. We never thought it was going to happen. It is quite unfair to us."

I tried to reassure him. It was no use.

Reid said, "We will have to close the sugar mills. We are losing the fight on communism. We are in a very difficult situation. The next sixty days are crucial."

I asked what he wanted.

He wanted a high fixed quota for five years to give the Republic time to diversify out of sugar. I told him it was in Congress' hands, though I would do what I could.

He shook his head. "I will recommend that we stop spending the AID twenty-five million dollars. You can't just be friendly. You have to act as a friend."

He said he would lead a delegation of sixteen Dominicans to Washington to press the Dominican case. "But I can't go without an appointment with President Kennedy."

I tried to talk him out of it. As a Consejero, he could scarcely appear as a lobbyist for the sugar interests. President Kennedy, I was sure, would not receive a lobbyist. Pressure now might jeopardize the twenty-two million dollars.

Finally Reid said, "That you won't get an appointment for me?"

I said no, not at this time, and suggested that a Palace spokesman announce that a delegation of businessmen, labor leaders, and sugar experts was going to Washington.

Next day Bramble, running down a rumor that Pichardo had ordered a small AID program stopped, sought him out. Pichardo said that he, Reid, and others in the Consejo had decided to stop spending any more of the twenty-five-million-dollar loan. If the Cooley bill became law they would cancel all their AID agreements under the twenty-five million dollars and use part of the twenty-two million to repay the nine million already spent. If they did not get the twenty-two million, they would do the best they could. In the past, foreign loans had plunged the Republic into disaster. Pichardo said, "We would rather do what we can with machetes than go in debt."

What all that amounted to was this: The Consejo had gone on strike against the Alliance for Progress.

On Tuesday, the House passed the Cooley bill and sent it to the

Senate. There the Administration would fight for its world quota bill. In Santo Domingo, Reid declared publicly that the Consejo should stop using *Alianza* money.

Until now I had done nothing. I was at the Residence alone, trying to think it through. We could lose the Consejo on this issue. The Consejo felt betrayed. The U. S. Executive—White House, State, AID, and Embassy—had promised to help the Consejo. Now Congress, all unknowing, was revoking the promises. Empty promises, they must seem.

The sugar crisis gave the Castro/Communists a perfect issue. The Consejo had to veer far left, to pre-empt the ground of the left, to become almost anti-American, in order to save itself. There may also have been an element of blackmail in the Consejo's reaction. But behind all the politics lay the harsh economic realities.

I was against my own Administration's sugar bill. And against the Cooley bill, too, though no doubt the Congressmen had good reasons for writing it. Either bill might be enough to overthrow the Dominican government.

I thought Congress must be uninformed. If this bill passed, our whole effort to build a democratic bastion in the Caribbean next door to Castro would almost surely come crashing down. We must, we simply must, move. Ambassador George Kennan had just cabled Washington from Belgrade to protest Congress' denial of aid and trade benefits to Yugoslavia—"the greatest windfall Soviet diplomacy could encounter in this area." I determined I would not let Congress unknowingly wreck our policy here.

I sent a long and strong cable to the Department. I telephoned John Crimmins in the Department and asked him to pass the cable to Ralph Dungan at the White House, and offered to come home to explain the situation to Congress.

Then I called the senior Embassy staff and Williams together, told them what I was doing, and told them we must slow down the Dominican reaction before it got completely out of control. We must immediately talk to all important Dominicans—explain the situation, urge everyone to await developments, and reaffirm our determination not to abandon the Republic. We divided up the people we would see—Consejeros, political party leaders, government men, sugar men.

Fandino and I spent nearly four hours that night alone with President Bonnelly in the little study at his house. He said, "I think this is our great crisis. So I am pondering it with great calm." He agreed with me: They would send a delegation to Washington tomorrow, but not headed by Reid. Expenditure of the twenty-five million dollars had indeed stopped. "But everything brings effervescence, wait until the waves break on shore. There was no formal vote in the Consejo to withdraw from the *Alianza*. I'm working on it, exchanging ideas, I have no answer yet but a final solution is not opportune or necessary yet. The problem is political, sensitive. It is very dangerous."

Bonnelly was himself writing a note that his Ambassador in Washington, Andrés Freites, would deliver to the Department. Going behind his cluttered desk and picking up some papers, he began reading, calmly, clearly, and with dignity, making an excellent lawyer-like case for the Dominicans.

He was impressive, peering closely at his notes through thick glasses, all the more impressive because he spoke so quietly. He put his notes aside, took off his glasses, raised his eyebrows, and threw up his hands. I said I could not quarrel with his logic.

He knew—as most did not—that even with the Cooley bill the Republic could survive this year economically. But the political effect would be disastrous. What, then, to do? An austerity program would worsen unemployment. European loans were impossibly expensive. More U.S. loans—"We'd be overthrown, everyone would say we had sold out to the *Yanquís*." A U.S. grant—the U.S. would probably not make one. "So I have no fixed position. So?" and he raised both hands. I stood up, and he did. We always had trouble, he and Fandino and I, maneuvering in the tiny office to get the door open. "We have to let the violent reaction take place," he said. "I have faith in my star." I told him I hoped it would produce quickly. He grinned, we embraced, and as always he saw us to the outside door.

Next day we kept sending cables—what our sources said, what the press said, the talk on the streets, over-all wrapups, everything. We simply kept piling the cables in, marking them for immediate action and transmittal to the White House. I telephoned Dick Goodwin, then deputy to Assistant Secretary Ed Martin, and Ralph Dungan, in the White House.

We thought our best hope lay in a stalemate in Congress and extension of the present law. Therefore, we kept urging the White House to fight hard in the Senate for the world quota bill. I sent Bramble to Washington.

We won our first victory: A small Dominican delegation went to Washington without Reid. We began winning a few others—calming people down, persuading them to think twice about officially leaving the *Alianza*. Tad Szulc of the New York *Times* and other U.S. reporters came to the Republic, sensing crisis. Szulc wrote that the next six months in the Dominican Republic might decide the fate of the *Alianza,* and that the key to that fate was the sugar bill. Assistant Secretary Ed Martin called —he expected the Senate Finance Committee to report the Administration's world quota bill out favorably and unanimously on Friday. The

Administration would fight for it. Such a fight would probably produce stalemate—make enactment of any new bill impossible by June 30.

I went to the Palace and saw President Bonnelly and, without going into details, indicated that I thought we could work something out in Washington if he could keep things quiet here. He would try—he would ask Fernández Caminero to postpone a nationwide radio-TV speech relating how President Kennedy had raised his hopes while he was in Trujillo's prison but now had let the Republic down.

As I left the Palace, newspapermen stopped me. I said that President Bonnelly and I had discussed the sugar question, and I wanted to once more assure the Dominican people that the Republic's sugar problem was receiving the sympathetic consideration of my government.

One crisis always seemed to breed another. Colonel Cass told me he had seen a group of the worst elements in the Air Force huddling secretly in a back room. Colonel Richardson heard at San Isidro that "something was brewing." One of Cass' sources warned him not to bring a ship in. Amiama said publicly that a plot had been discovered in the Navy. The Navy commander, Commodore Francisco Rivera Caminero, went to Amiama and accused him of framing him. Imbert was transferring men rapidly from the Armed Forces to the National Police. The Sub-Secretary of State for Defense for Air told Richardson he was being forced out. Other officers reported receiving phone calls at 3 A.M. from officers close to Imbert or Amiama. Richardson believed the long-discussed military purge was starting anew—but perhaps without General Viñas' knowledge.

I sent Richardson to San Isidro, and sent Cass and Long out to see the Navy and Army. Richardson reported back late that night, Friday: Everything was quiet, no tanks or troops were moving; the ranking officers had met with General Luna and worked out transfers satisfactory to all. Nonetheless, to be safe, on Saturday I went to see Amiama and Imbert.

We talked for hours. They began by saying of the sugar crisis, "If you don't get it fixed, you'd better find us homes somewhere." Imbert then launched a bitter attack: "When is the United States going to make up its mind? Does the United States want a crisis to come?"

Amiama broke in, calm and cynical—the U. S. Congress was simply thinking of its own fall elections.

But Imbert plunged on: "Why do you delay everything so long? Why so slow? No wonder Latin America is sympathetic to Russia. We dominate here through the stomach. We are not scared of the Communists, those little Negroes. They only want a television and a car, and if they get that, communism can't be a danger. We get hundreds of pleas for jobs, people are dying of hunger, and if this country is not thrown into civil war because of hunger, misery—"

Amiama made a spitting sound.

Imbert said, "Not one school started. One AID man in education. A construction company was trying to get a road built but now it has to wait —why do there have to be foreign technicians to go over the plans?" (I had always thought Imbert was inordinately interested in that road.) "The Consejo is still here because of us," pointing to Amiama, who was staring at the ceiling and humming to himself. "We are sentenced to death and we know it. We will die with our boots on."

I asked about the military purge. They said it was all right. General Luna had met with his Air Force officers and straightened things out. In a few days the Navy would be straightened out too. They were deporting the editor of *Claridad,* the leftist extremist newspaper.

I asked why, instead of deporting him, they didn't buy him off? Why didn't they stop printing plants from printing the Castro/Communist clandestine newspapers? And why not tighten up law enforcement in general? They seemed surprised.

Imbert said slowly that they had talked about buying off *Claridad* many times, and the print shops, too.

Amiama said, "But we can't put any more on the line. We're spending too much." And Imbert, "We only get paid two thousand dollars a month. We do need some money to keep people quiet. A special fund." And Amiama quickly, "But not us—don't give it to us."

Imbert said, "We can't go on this way. We're risking our position, the respect of the Dominican people. In the long run, Luís and I are the ones that are going to pay the tab."

Amiama said, "Manolo can be bought"—Manolo Tavárez Justo.

"The other five on the Consejo have nothing to lose," Imbert said. "But after February 27, what about us"—himself and Amiama. "All the political parties are scared of us. We know *we* are the only ones we can trust. We don't want to get mixed up in politics. But we have to. If we depend on the party that gets elected, that party can get rid of us. We don't want power and money ourselves. Just our lives."

I was sympathetic. We talked on. And before long they had slid into a strange proposal. They never quite said it in so many words but they made it clear enough: If I would tell them whom I wanted for President, they would form a party and put him into the Palace. Via elections, of course. Legitimately. We talked late. I made no commitments.

5

On Monday we entered the second week of the sugar crisis. That night, I gave a reception for the diplomatic corps and invited the Consejo. Only Reid showed up, and he briefly. Sugar was infecting everything. We dropped our plans to go to the Enchanted Valley with the Reids,

Bonnellys, and Bonillas. We were still planning our Fourth of July party. I had thought that the customary "National Day" champagne party at the Embassy for the American colony made no sense in that revolutionary time and so had invited instead about 15 Dominican underprivileged children for a Fourth of July picnic—swimming, baseball, running races, prizes, a magician, a band, hot dogs, and ice cream. President Bonnelly had promised to provide Army buses to haul the kids to the Residence and to appear himself to distribute prizes. But now the heart had gone out of our planning.

That Monday, June 25, the Senate Finance Committee approved a bill that was basically a world quota bill but contained special quotas for nine countries, including the Dominican Republic. We waited. Tension rose. Rumors swept the city—the sugar bill was a Wall Street plot, the Consejo had made a secret deal with the United States, the Consejo had fallen, someone had been assassinated, the sugar bill had passed.

All of a sudden on Wednesday, the long-awaited trial began of the men charged with murdering the Mirabal sisters, and for days Dominicans listened to radios and television sets. Next day, the Senate passed its bill, but gave the Republic far less than the hated Cooley bill's 350,000 tons. On Friday, the New York *Times,* while agreeing in principle with Senator J. W. Fulbright's view that we should put our sugar trade on a firm business basis, argued that the Dominican case was special.

So did I—and poured the cables in. In the midst of this, Shlaudeman came hurrying in and said, "Bonilla Aybar's been shot." He was editor of *La Nación,* the government-owned newspaper, an ambitious scandalmonger who soon turned rabblerouser. Later, it turned out, Bonilla Aybar hadn't been shot—a citizen who resented something he had written had gone to Bonilla's office with a case of pistols to challenge him to a duel, Bonilla had called for help, *La Nación* employees had fallen upon the citizen with iron bars and thrown him out, and, on the street, he had pulled a gun and begun firing wildly, hitting two men. Thereafter a *turba* had been broken up by the police, but not before a woman had been wounded.

That Friday night, John Crimmins and I exchanged phone calls and cables. He had new sugar proposals but none solid or good enough. (All such phone conversations were long and difficult, for, assuming the line was monitored, we spoke an Aesopian language. Sometimes we used a prearranged system of code words, changed frequently. Sometimes we picked out paragraphs or sentences or words from previous cables to construct the sentences we spoke to each other.)

The next day was Saturday, June 30; the existing sugar act expired. The local press carried a UPI story from Washington saying a House and Senate conference committee had worked out a compromise bill. Dominicans considered it the worst bill yet—said it gave the Republic a basic quota of only 190,000 tons and eliminated the twenty-two million dollars.

I called the Crisis Crowd and Newell Williams of AID to the Residence. Donny Reid came in out of breath. The Consejo had been meeting all morning and was going to issue a statement on sugar. I asked if I could see President Bonnelly. Reid, by now frightened, too, drove me there fast. We went in a Palace back door to avoid the press, and up to a third-floor bedroom apartment. President Bonnelly was waiting, tired.

I said I hoped the Consejo's statement wouldn't close the door on the *Alianza,* for despite the press reports, I still felt that if I had a few more days, I might be able to straighten things out. Bonnelly said the statement was already issued.

Back at the Residence, we listened to it. It said that despite "official assurances," the sugar problem had not been resolved satisfactorily. The U.S. now threatened to frustrate the basic and legitimate aspirations of the Republic. The Consejo had no intention of saddling future governments with hopeless debts. The U.S. government was "thwarting" the purposes of the *Alianza.* Therefore, the Consejo had suspended use of our twenty-five-million-dollar loan and was now "studying" the need "of thoroughly reviewing, or a new basis," its basic policies, both foreign and domestic.

It did not quite close the door—the Consejo was "studying" the situation—but it was bad.

I called Crimmins and Dungan, and said this crisis was really dangerous. They knew it, were working on it, and hoped to have something tomorrow or Monday. President Kennedy was out of town that night, Saturday.

Crimmins called me at ten-fifteen Sunday night: He was cabling a proposal and wanted my comments quickly. It came in at 5 A.M., and the duty officer wakened me. It said in substance that the conference bill's quota, plus the Cuban windfall, was worth at current prices about thirty-one million dollars less in profits than the Republic would have received this year under the present law. President Kennedy, recognizing the special case of the Republic, would undertake to make up the difference—to establish a special economic readjustment fund over three years, with up to thirty million dollars the first year and lesser amounts in the next two years, provided the Consejo would use this special "Kennedy Fund" to gradually diversify out of sugar. As for the twenty-two million dollars, it would be paid as a grant, probably out of AID funds. If the Consejo accepted the proposal, President Kennedy would receive Ambassador Freites in the White House on Wednesday, and they would announce it though at present neither the Secretary nor the President had approved it.

It looked good to me. I thought the Consejo would accept it.

I called Crimmins at 6:45 A.M. Monday and asked if I could take it to the Consejo immediately. Crimmins said he'd call me back. Waiting, I spoke to the head of La Romana, the big U.S. sugar company, and arranged to meet with leading U.S. businessmen in the Republic at 10 A.M. But Al Hemba had to meet with them, for Crimmins called at ten, told me to take our proposal to the Consejo immediately, and to report to him by 1 P.M., at which time the Senate would take up the conference bill. He warned me, however, to be as "nonspecific" as possible about the twenty-two million dollars—Senators preferred to look on it, if at all, not as a debt we owed the Republic but as an "act of grace" on our part.

At the Palace, the full Consejo was waiting in the big, high-ceilinged room with its faded carpet and wine-red draperies, seated in a semicircle, two chairs empty on the President's right. We all shook hands, then sat, and the President nodded to me.

I said I had just received new word from Washington, but first wanted briefly to review matters, speaking frankly, not as the Ambassador, but unofficially. I said I recognized that this was our worst crisis. I also realized—and so did they—that they might well represent the last chance for Dominican democracy. Working together, we had accomplished much. Now they would go down any of three roads. They could head into a dictatorship of either right or left—but the Republic had had enough of that. They could turn their back on the *Alianza* and the U.S. and go it alone—but in the 1960s no nation could live alone; the earth had shrunk. Finally, they could stick with the *Alianza* and the U.S.

Then, speaking officially, I set forth the new proposal—a quota worth nineteen million dollars less than that of the present law, a special "Kennedy Fund" of up to twenty million dollars this year to make up the difference and promote diversification, and the twenty-two million dollars.

When I had finished, the big room was dead quiet except for the air conditioner.

Pichardo spoke first: "We will have to consider it. This morning the Consejo approved creation of a commission for diversification."

Bonnelly said, "I'm interested in Vice President Pichardo's position. The Consejo announced it was studying the question and leaving the doors open. Now our new policy will be the result of that study."

Pichardo said, "Speaking as a friend, this is dynamite."

Fernández Caminero said, "Dynamite. There is a fourth road— Europe. We know the United States has supported us. But the people think the United States supported Trujillo. The position of the Consejo de Estado is not one of politics—it is one of dignity in front of the people."

There was a pause. Amiama asked, "How much of this is a grant and how much is a loan?" I said this had to be worked out carefully in Washington—we had certain problems, too. But I thought I could say safely—though unofficially—that the twenty-two million dollars would be a grant, and that the special "Kennedy Fund" might be partially grants, though more likely long-term low-interest loans.

Bonnelly had left the room, Donny Reid with him. Pichardo said, in a tone less formal than previously, "Since this is a new proposal, it merits consideration, and probably would change some decisions taken."

I knew then we were all right—they would accept.

The others talked a bit. Bonnelly and Reid returned, listened to the drift of the conversation, and heard Pichardo say, "Since it's all up in the air, we can only say that our impression is better than formerly. Also, tell Washington that the *return* of the twenty-two million will have a greater impact than a *grant* of twenty-two million."

Bonnelly said, "Speaking as a lawyer, I can see the United States objection to saying it is 'returning' the twenty-two million. It might be open to many other claims. You might save the U.S. legal position by saying you recognize no legal obligation with respect to the twenty-two million but a moral obligation."

I agreed that the language must be worked out carefully.

I wanted something a little more concrete to report to Washington by 1 P.M. It was past noon. Pichardo said, glancing about, "I view the new proposal with sympathy." Fernández Caminero said, "I view it with a big smile, but the bureaucracy is in the way—would it be as slow as everything else?"

President Bonnelly, with an air of summing up, said, "I think you can say that in principle the Consejo de Estado views with sympathy the form in which the United States is considering the grave problems that the Dominican Republic faces."

Leaving the Palace, I told the reporters I had met with the Consejo and was confident we would find a satisfactory solution.

I called Crimmins. He said, "Sympathetic, are they? That's damned nice of them." I agreed, but that's how it was. Much later I heard that a military *coup* had been afoot that day and that only my opening "unofficial" remarks to the Consejo had stopped it.

That same night the Senate passed the conference bill and sent it to the President. It gave the Dominican Republic a basic quota of 190,000 tons plus a Cuban windfall of about 215,000 tons—a total of 405,000 tons. Over the weekend, Administration and Senate leaders hit upon yet another device for increasing the Dominican quota: Adding an amendment to a wholly different bill, giving the President discretionary power to distribute a quota of 225,000 tons over the next two years among the Dominican Republic and two other Latin American countries. Crimmins thought we might get 120,000 tons for the Republic. (The "Kennedy Fund" would be reduced accordingly.)

The sugar controversy began to explode all over Washington. On Tuesday, Tad Szulc wrote in the New York *Times* that documents "from the Trujillo archives" showed that Congressman Cooley and others had in the past defended Dominican sugar interests and consulted with Trujillo's agents, though the *Times* was careful to point out that no evidence supported any charge of "specific wrongdoing." Cooley promptly rejected any implication of improper conduct. Soon Senator Fulbright, comparing the sugar lobbyists who filled the Senate corridors to flies around a sugar bowl, announced a full-scale investigation of foreign agents.

On Tuesday, too, Secretary Rusk said publicly that the United States viewed "with sympathy" the Dominican Republic's desire to obtain a large quota. AID officials were said to feel that the Dominican Republic was "a special case needing especial help."

I saw President Bonnelly that afternoon. Everything we were doing was most helpful, he thought, since it satisfied Dominicans' feeling that they deserved special attention. "Once we know the detailed conditions, the Consejo de Estado won't find it inconvenient to say we do accept."

The next day, Wednesday, was the Fourth of July. In the morning Fran, the boys, and several Embassy officers began setting things up for the party in the garden and around the pool. The Dominican children were to arrive at 2 P.M. I worked in the Residence, now and then walking out to the garden—reading cables, making notes, waiting for authority to act. It came around midday—Crimmins told me to go ahead and talk to the Consejo. I thought it best to see Bonnelly alone; the Consejo probably did not want to listen to another speech by me.

In the Palace, I told the President that the "Kennedy Fund" would be a three-year program of outright grants, not loans. It would not exceed twenty million dollars this year and would be less during the next two years. We would attach no strings except for U.S. procurement. We would make an immediate advance of one million dollars. In return, the Consejo would diversify out of sugar and issue a conciliatory statement, returning to full participation in the *Alianza*. We also would return the twenty-two million dollars as an outright grant, though I did not know when, and we would not in our own statement use the word "return." Bonnelly would have liked more details, but thought he could sell it to the Consejo.

Back at the Residence the hot dog stand and ice cream stand were set up, lifeguards were at the swimming pool, bases had been laid out for ball games, and a magician was on hand. The first busload of children arrived, and Fran and I greeted them. They were from six to ten years old, all dressed neatly in their best clothes, solemn and quiet, shepherded by teachers and priests. More came, bus after bus. We had had swimming suits made for them, and soon half of them were splashing and yelling in the pool. A CIA man was playing left field, Marines and visa officers and a code clerk were guarding the pool, the wives were dishing out ice cream. (But the kids didn't like the hot dogs, only the bun with mustard.) The Police band arrived.

At 4 P.M., Bonilla Atiles came to the house, and, over the muffled noises of the band and children, reading from a lengthy paper, said formally that the Consejo accepted our proposal.

Outside, the party was breaking up. I went out. As prearranged, the band got up and walked across the beautiful garden under the great tree, teachers and staff leading the children after them. It was 5 P.M. Out in front our Marine guard, in dress uniform, marched to the flagpole. The band played the Dominican national anthem then "The Star-Spangled Banner." The band had not known our anthem, so Colonel Cass had taught it to them by ear, and the Marines lowered the flag at the wrong time. Nonetheless it was a stirring scene, everyone, children and all, standing at attention (but one could not help remembering Trujillo had taught them that). The music ended, the sun was sinking red behind palms and mango trees, the children made a last rush for party favors, then walked to the buses, and Fran and I shook hands with as many as we could. One little boy from an orphanage called her "mother," and another asked, "Can I come back tomorrow?"

That evening, I invited all the mission members who had helped at the party to the Residence for food and drinks. My mother and aunt were visiting us at the time. The front doorbell rang: It was President Bonnelly and Foreign Minister Bonilla, come unannounced to pay their respects on our national day, and I introduced them to the staff and my mother and aunt. They could not have been nicer. The American business community had resented the children's party since it deprived them of the traditional Fourth of July reception at the Embassy they had come to think their due. So had some of the Embassy staff. Later all came to think of the children's party as a great success. Even the leftist newspaper *Claridad* applauded. It had been a strange day.

6

The sugar crisis was not quite over. On Thursday Crimmins called. Nothing at all would be said publicly about the twenty-two million dollars at this time. Freites would see President Kennedy tomorrow. The White House would then issue a statement, timed tentatively for 3 P.M. Santo Domingo time. I could issue a statement simultaneously, and so could the Consejo. Crimmins would confirm the time.

In the morning, I went over the MAAG program for the next three years with Colonel Wolfe. A CIA man came in; he had it from good sources that a man had left San Juan, Puerto Rico, for Santo Domingo on June 26 with instructions from Castro to help the MPD and 14th of June prepare for armed insurrection. Arms were being smuggled in through Haiti under Raul Castro's direction. Four uprisings were planned: The 14th of June in Santiago, Salcedo, and San Juan de la Maguana; the MPD in Puerto Plata. Since Juan Ducoudray of the PSP did not appear to be involved, it appeared that not Blas Roca but Castro's own "new Communists" were in charge. I told the CIA man to check airplane manifests and see if the agent had been on the plane. He had. The CIA man did not know the agent's whereabouts, but thought he was a tailor.

At noon Crimmins called: Freites' appointment was confirmed; the press release could be made at three-fifteen.

The CIA station chief came in: Castro/Communists planned to demonstrate at the Chancellery tomorrow, Saturday, July 7. Obviously, the Castro/Communists, having lost the sugar issue, seeing the Consejo moving back to our side, would resume attacking us together.

We made plans—warned staffers and wives to say home, decided to arm our eight Marine guards with .38s and station them in the Chancellery and at the attachés' building across the street, made sure we had tear gas grenades and guns, gas masks, a loudspeaker, and explosives. (In any such situation, if a mob actually storms an Embassy, one's first duty is to blow up the code machinery.) Jacob Jackson, the AID public safety adviser in charge of the police training program, said General Belisario Peguero would send police to guard the Chancellery tomorrow. Jackson had heard of a shakeup in the Army high command. I asked the attachés to check it.

I felt nervous. I wondered if the Armed Forces were thinking of a *golpe*. Tomorrow's demonstration, coming on top of the sugar crisis, would provide an excuse. I called in the Crisis Crowd and asked them to make their rounds. During the evening, reports came in that tomorrow's demonstration might be serious. I decided to send Fran and the boys to the Hotel Embajador.

Next morning's papers carried full coverage of the solution of the sugar crisis and said President Bonnelly would speak to the nation.

On Saturdays the Chancellery is always closed, the windows are covered with heavy wooden shutters, and the front door is barred by a locked iron gate. A uniformed Marine let me in. I talked to the Crisis Crowd and Gunnery Sergeant Samuel Trizza, in charge of the Marine security guard, the only persons we had permitted to come to work. Trizza said everything was ready. I gave instructions that nobody should do anything—throw gas, shoot, or blow up the code equipment—except on my order.

I went into my office alone and made a few notes. If the demonstrators wished, I would receive a delegation of three. I resented the demonstration at the end of the three-week sugar crisis, now resolved so favorably to their country.

Newspapermen and photographers arrived. The police arrived in trucks, scores of them, Cascos Blancos, with tear gas and long nightsticks.

At 10 A.M. Colonel Cass came: Commodore Rivera of the Navy was being replaced today by a relative of Amiama. Yesterday President Bonnelly and Amiama and Imbert had met for six hours aboard the *Angelita,* the Trujillo yacht. The Army Commander in Chief, General Jorge Moreno, also was apparently out.

At ten-fifteen a man called me from downtown. A crowd of about four hundred had gathered in Parque Colón, getting ready to march, and a riot squad had come out of the Fortaleza Ozama into the street. Many in the crowd wore red or green shirts, symbols of the MPD and 14th of June. He called back in fifteen minutes to say the crowd had suddenly swelled to two thousand and had started up Calle Conde, headed toward the Chancellery, some of its members wearing white armbands to indicate they would keep order.

One of the Crisis Crowd came in at ten-fifty. He had seen Reid, and Reid had said Amiama and Imbert had forced Bonnelly to replace Commodore Rivera. It was very serious; the Navy officers might not accept it. General Moreno was out, too, Reid said. Reid appeared to be on the edge of a breakdown, highly excited, saying, "If they try this, I'll be the first to shoot," and "Don't be surprised if half the Consejo is dead before today is over." And he sent word that I must see President Bonnelly immediately.

I said that right now I was busy. I was—at that moment, ten fifty-five, the crowd arrived in front of the Chancellery. The blacktop driveway slopes down a short hill and enters a street intersection. At first, the crowd stayed on the opposite side of the intersection. Quickly others behind them forced them into the intersection. The lone traffic policeman retired. The Cascos Blancos formed a skirmish line on the sidewalk alongside the Chancellery grounds. The crowd was chanting, singing the national anthem, yelling—*"Quisqueya sí, Yanqui no";* then, to the rhythmic five-beat handclap: *"Da-da pa-re-dón,"* "to the wall."

I went to the door to see better. The crowd started pushing against the police. The police held. Some of the reserves closed in behind them; others took up a second position on the Chancellery grounds in front of the flagpole, not far from the door. Confusion ensued, the line became blurred, people milling and yelling louder, and I heard the officer in charge of the reserves say something to them sharply, and they loosened their gas mask bags and grenade containers.

I glanced around. At the rear of the little round lobby, Sergeant Trizza was bent over a big oil drum, busy. In a moment, he told me, "I've got the thermite in the can." He was ready to blow the code equipment.

We watched the crowd, shoving against the police. A time might come to receive a delegation; not now. The crowd was chanting louder, their voices hostile and strident.

A little car came down the hill to the intersection and, in one of those strangely Dominican incidents, the crowd parted to let it pass, then resumed its solid front, never pausing in its chant. But I thought it was going to be all right. It was. The police pushed a little, the crowd gave way, then retired across the intersection, stood chanting a few minutes more, then turned and headed for the Palace. I told Fandino to tell President Bonnelly the crowd was on its way to visit him next. They had finished with us.

It was eleven-thirty. I called Fran, had some lunch sent down from the Residence, then told Fandino to call Bonnelly again. Bonnelly said the mob had been and gone, and Fandino asked if we could visit him.

We found him in Trujillo's third-floor apartment and sat down to drink with him by an open door overlooking the sea.

I asked about the shakeup in the military.

He said, "I changed the Navy chief—Julio Alberto Rib Santamaría will replace him." It would not be Amiama's relative; it would be Rib. Bonnelly insisted he had acted alone with General Viñas' advice—not under pressure from Imbert and Amiama. Rivera was going to Washington as naval attaché. (Latin American rulers often get rid of bothersome people by making them ambassadors or military attachés abroad. The Dominican Republic must have one of the largest foreign services on earth.) Several naval officers had come to Bonnelly to protest Rivera's removal. He had told them he was "supreme," and they had backed down. A week earlier he had quietly sent General Jorge Moreno to the United States, on Viñas' recommendation, and was replacing him temporarily with Colonel Rivera Cuesta. He had done it all quietly, but it was part of the long-talked-of purge. Bonnelly, Pichardo, and Reid would speak to the nation on sugar, the *Alianza,* and Consejo reforms on radio and TV Monday.

"After that I'm going to tighten up," he said, starting to make another drink—Fandino made it for him, translating skillfully without a break as he did so. "Submit a law," Bonnelly went on, "forbidding communism and possibly Communist demonstrations."

I told him about the agent who, we had heard, had come from Puerto Rico to help the 14th of June and the MPD.

Bonnelly knew him, had been a co-revolutionary with his father thirty-two years ago, had seen his father today, and was keeping the boy under surveillance. The father, who had lost another son at Constanza and now was under jail sentence himself for not paying his social security tax, "is helping me keep him under control," smiling. (The poor country!)

I asked if on Monday he would talk about the *Alianza* and the "Kennedy Fund." Bonnelly did not answer directly; his speech would be "strong." I asked again about his mentioning U.S.-Dominican relations and the *Alianza*. Again he replied indirectly, veering off: "Today everybody is attacking me. But when this is over, I'll pass into history, and I am cautious and deliberately interested in passing into history," and he recalled the long-ago President, Ulises Espaillat, from Santiago like Bonnelly, who was reviled and overthrown in his own time, but was now revered.

I decided I had pushed him enough on his speech—it would be all right. (It was.) We talked about other things, ending, as usual, with Santiago and his father. We even mentioned a subject long since become embarrassing: Wells in the Southwest desert.

So the great sugar crisis ended.

Chapter Eight

WHISTLESTOPPING

Foreign Minister Bonilla came to the house and said that the parties were "playing the Communist game"—using every pretext to make trouble for the Consejo. And the Consejo was not defending itself, had not yet even hired a press secretary. "After the President's speech, *Radio Caribe* attacked him," Bonilla said. "Its director is a hero. We have too many heroes. *Radio Caribe* is owned by the government. So it attacks the government. Reid wants to fire the director; Imbert defends him. Strikes can paralyze the government. Now we have the show trial, the Mirabal trial. Nobody knows who started it. I saw pictures of the crowd that picketed your Embassy. I recognized three—one works for the Foreign Office, one in Public Works, one in Labor. Picketing the United States Embassy with the Communists. For six months the parties have been criticizing the Consejo. The Army is restless because the Consejo is not imposing its authority. I told Bonnelly, 'I came here to fight communism, not commit suicide.'"

As I have said, no fewer than twenty-six political parties had arisen. Almost daily they issued communiqués and manifestos. The Consejo had spent so much time patiently drafting the Electoral Law with the parties, and so much time in the sugar crisis, that now, July 10, only five weeks before the August election, it had done nothing to prepare for it. The Consejo considered it the Electoral Board's problem; the Electoral Board was reluctant to move alone; the OAS mission had made recommendations about registration—but nothing had been done. All was adrift.

Clearly it was now mechanically impossible to hold the August election for a Constituent Assembly to write a new constitution. That election must be postponed or abolished, and since no one else would take the initiative, we must. We would work actively for abolition.

The two key men were Bosch of PRD and Fiallo of UCN. If we could get those two to agree, the smaller parties, which had no chance of winning now, probably would fall in line.

The Department approved this new policy. We had picked a fork in the road, for better or worse.

I invited Fiallo to the house and, as usual, found him reasonable though not closely informed. He was convinced the August election was mechanically impossible. Even though the UCN was probably at peak strength and stood a good chance of sweeping the August election and, thereby, the December presidential election, Fiallo was either patriotic enough or confident enough to consent to abolishing the August election. But he did not know how to go about it.

So Fiallo was no problem. But Juan Bosch was. The newspaper quoted Bosch as saying if elections were not held on schedule, the Consejo was illegal. He said it was not the job of the parties to be for or against elections. And he said this was a government that did not know how to govern.

Until then I had talked to Bosch only a few times. He was often out of town, traveling the interior quietly, his activities unreported in the press. I knew and liked Ángel Miolán, Bosch's stocky, swarthy, Indian-featured party boss. Shlaudeman and other of our people had been keeping in touch with Bosch. Shlaudeman considered Bosch a master at political tactics. Alone among the many parties' ceaseless manifestos, his were drafted with great skill. Bosch could write, and used his talent to cut his chief opponent, the good lumbering Fiallo, to pieces. Alone, really, among the politicians, he knew precisely where he was going and how to get there.

Bosch was also, it appeared, emotionally unstable, given to wild emotional swings from highest elation to deepest despair. Several times he had told Shlaudeman he was going to withdraw from the campaign and leave the country. He was furtive, secretive, suspicious, given to unreasoning fears. More than once during crises he went into hiding or took to his bed, pulled the sheet up to his neck, said Imbert or someone else was coming to kill him, and declared over his wife's protestations he must abandon the country.

Although Bosch knew elections could not be held in August, he was insisting on them to gain another pretext to attack the Consejo and so advance his own campaign. I thought this reckless and irresponsible politics. What he was saying publicly could lead only to a military *coup,* not to an election. The day he made his statement, I sent word I wanted to see him at the Residence.

He came at once, tall and straight in his white linen suit, white-haired with bright blue eyes. I asked Bosch how he saw the elections. He said, "If elections are not held before August 16, the Consejo de Estado will be an illegal government. It cannot amend the constitution. I could convoke the Congress. It could do many things, but it does nothing," and he launched a long, bitter attack, ending, "The Consejo feels it is strong

enough, with North American help, to ignore the parties and the elections."

I told him his position could lead only to a military *coup;* if indeed the
government were unconstitutional after August 16, it must fall, and
nothing could replace it but the military.

With some satisfaction, Bosch agreed. He said, "This government is
no good. No one wants this government."[1]

I said, "We do." I said it quietly and coldly.

Bosch glanced at me sharply and hesitated. Then he went on, "The
Electoral Board wants the names of our members. They say they want
to register the voters, but to do this would violate the secrecy of the
election. Why cannot the people vote by *cédula,* not by registration?
We want to establish respect for law. So we want the August election. Why
does the Consejo sabotage the August election? The only explanation is
the lack of unity in the Consejo. Some of them want to stay in power.
If they cancel the August election, they will surely cancel the December
election." Then he launched a long attack on the OAS electoral mission.

When he had finished and leaned back, looking as though he had
proved his case, I said, "I want to tell you something. The Consejo
may not be a perfect government, but it's the only government you've
got, and we want it to stay in power through its term. We also want it
to hold elections, but the August election is impossible because there
isn't time. And you know it. I want to tell you something else. The statement you made in today's paper, and the road you are heading down,
can only lead to a military takeover. Well, we are not going to have a
military takeover. We are going to have elections."

I was angry. I got up and started pacing the floor, continuing, "The
Consejo would be a better government if the parties would give it a
chance—stop tearing it to pieces and start writing platforms and campaigning. There are too many people here who are thinking only of themselves, not of their country. And this may be your last chance at democracy."

Bosch's face was dark-red with anger. Perhaps I should not have
spoken to him so. Later, I would fight as hard to save him as I was fighting

[1] At the time, I did not fully appreciate the depth of his feelings. In his book he
repeatedly displays a deep underdog feeling, real contempt and hatred for the UCN,
the middle class, and the Consejo, which he considered Trujillista, upper-middle-class,
and UCN-dominated—its cabinet "swarmed with personages from the incredible
Dominican aristocracy." He also believes, wrongly, that the State Department, and
probably I, thought the UCN would win the election, and were pleased. He writes
that the UCN had been the dominant force in the Republic in December 1961. "But
in June 1962, and even much later, the State Department did not know the true
picture, because its officials had not gone out into the countryside or visited the
urban slums, and therefore were not accurately informed on the change that was
being wrought in the nation." On this last point, Bosch is misinformed.

now to stop him. We said little more, then he left. Neither he nor I ever in the future mentioned this interview. But I feel sure he never forgot it, and probably never forgave it. And, from his point of view, I must say I don't blame him.

I sent a cable, ate lunch, took a nap, then with Fandino secretly went to see President Bonnelly at five o'clock aboard the Trujillo yacht, the *Angelita*,[2] long, white, trim, beautiful. She was tied up at the mouth of the Ozama River, and to reach her we had to pass through the 27th of February military reservation, stopped several times by soldiers with fixed bayonets.

White-uniformed naval officers took Fandino and me aboard. Bonnelly met us on deck and showed us around the yacht, getting lost once or twice—spacious bedrooms below, spacious saloons above, dark rich wood-paneled walls, massive carved furniture. (Why was so much that had been Trujillo's massive?)

Bonnelly said, "It's crazy. Completely crazy."

The Consejo was trying to sell the *Angelita*. It was asking, I believe, two million dollars, but probably would have taken whatever it could get. Who could afford to buy, let alone maintain, such a vessel?

A waiter brought drinks. We sat in the dark dining room, and I asked Bonnelly how plans were coming for the election. "Very bad," he said. "The parties did not do what the OAS recommended. They spent three months arguing over the Electoral Law, and now an important leader of the UCN tells me he knows nothing about the law." He shrugged. What of Bosch's statement? "I do not think there will be a *coup*. But a strange fear has taken hold." He said he would see the Electoral Board tomorrow and quietly prod them. We discussed the OAS recommendations and the mechanics of elections. I urged abolition, not postponement. He would, as usual, delay decision.

We discussed AID projects he and Williams had planned to avoid heavy unemployment and unrest during the presidential election campaign. I told him what Foreign Minister Bonilla had said about the leftist extremists. He said he would tighten up on them once employment programs were launched. He had found a publicity man and tomorrow would start a propaganda campaign about the Consejo's accomplishments. (But it never really succeeded.)

I asked about the military. En route here tonight, Bonnelly said, he had stopped at the 27th of February camp and "suppressed" three generalships and four hundred other jobs in the name of economy and gotten away with it—at least for now. Did he expect trouble later? He said, "No, I've told them I would resign if they do. They all said no." We

2 The Consejo had renamed the *Angelita* the *Patria,* but everybody still called her the *Angelita.*

feared, however, that he might get into deeper trouble as the August 15 election date approached. I suggested we bring in the *Boxer*, a U.S. aircraft carrier, and take him aboard for lunch to impress the military, and he agreed. I told him I wanted to make another official trip to the provinces. Did he think it all right for me to leave? He did.

Outside, darkness had fallen, and through the portholes we could see the lights of the old city rising up across the water. We went on talking. Suddenly a heavy explosion shook the yacht. We felt the concussion, and heard men running outside. I think we might both have wanted to hurry out, but we finished our conversation, then strolled, with some pretense of leisureliness, to the deck.

Soldiers with machine guns were running around in the dark, on deck and on shore. An officer spoke briefly to Bonnelly.

Fandino told me, "He thinks it was a grenade. They want us to get out of here."

Bonnelly turned, we shook hands, then he walked down the slanting gangplank as a cavalcade of long black cars drew up with lights on bright. They roared away, and we got into my car and followed, rushing through thick clouds of dust, trying to keep up, falling behind, finally crossing the high steel bridge into the city. Much later Bonnelly said he thought a "battery" below decks had exploded. We never really knew.

2

Next day Bailey drove us east from the capital along the coastal plain, planted with cane waving high over the heads of the sweating machete-wielding cutters, then north through rolling cattle country, swiftly through sullen Hato Mayor. We climbed through rolling hills, crossed a jungle stream on a log bridge, and descended to a broad flat plain and Sabana de la Mar.

Fandino had been ill that morning, so Fran and I had Dave Shaw with us, a rather shy, tall young political officer in the Embassy. We had our daughter Cindy, too, home from college on vacation, as well as our two sons. After lunch at a small U.S. base formerly used to track missiles downrange from Cape Canaveral, but soon to be abandoned, we drove to the dock in Sabana de la Mar. The wooden timbers of the wharf were rotting and sagging, great holes in it where planks had disappeared. A Dominican Coast Guard ship was tied up at it, and Lieutenant Bolívar de León, a quick, quiet, youngish Dominican, led us up to the bridge, covered with an awning, where four small chairs stood in a neat row. He took his place at the big, spoked wooden wheel and skillfully backed the ship out into the Bay of Samaná. She was a coastal patrol boat, about ninety-five feet long; she had been freshly painted gray; she was old and creaky, and I doubt if she could have caught many gunrunners. Samaná Bay was considered a likely place for arms smuggling.

Across the Bay, we could see the long jutting peninsula of Samaná, green high hills rising out of the sea. To the east was the open ocean: Mona Passage, seventy miles of sea separating the Republic from Puerto Rico. We headed west to cruise the Bay.

Lieutenant de León had lived here all his life, and knew every trail and cave. Up the Bay he nosed the boat in toward shore, passing between two high rock islands so near you could almost touch them, then yet farther in, the jagged coral bottom visible in the shallow, clear water, giving orders quietly, working calmly, no excited flourishes. A man at the bow heaved a lead on a string and called out depths until finally we stopped, incredibly close to shore, in 2½ fathoms of water, and dropped anchor.

The sailors lowered a lifeboat and we all got in, badly overloading it, and a sailor sculled us ashore, using a single long sweep in the deep-worn groove at the stern. Ashore, we suddenly entered the black mouth of a cave. Daylight dimmed, and we made our way among stalactites and stalagmites in echoing silent darkness, water dripping all around us, and, just before the black closed in, came to a place lighted as if by a spotlight on stage: The roof opened up fifty or sixty feet overhead, and great trees, encircled with thick vines, grew rooted where we stood, aspiring to the sun.

Fran and the boys and Cindy picked up stones, looking for Indian relics. De León led us down a passageway and into a huge arched room where the sea lapped under a low rock ledge, and fishermen's boats were pulled up and hidden inside the cave. Fishermen had built fires and stayed here for generations. A small army could have hidden here. De León said he checked it now and then and found no arms.

Back on the ship, heading out into the Bay, we dined on *sancocho*, the Dominican national dish. *Sancocho* is really a stew, containing potatoes and yucca and plantains and other vegetables and, if possible, three kinds of meat—always goat, sometimes pork, beef, chicken, whatever is available—the whole cooked for many hours in a big iron pot. That day's *sancocho* contained birds de León had shot, doves or pigeons. (I have eaten *sancocho* containing parrots and egrets.)

We headed for the town of Samaná, a cluster of pink and red and white houses clinging to steep hillsides on the north shore. It was dark when we arrived. Nearly the whole town, it appeared, had come down to greet us. The Governor, Mayor, members of the City Council, Army and Police commanders, shook hands with us; and the crowd pressed close, friendly, calling out to us, and we shook more hands; then the police opened a lane and the officials led us afoot up the cobbled street.

It was a beautiful, soft, moonlit night, the sea smelled sweet and so did the air coming down from the dark green hills.

On a narrow street beneath a towering hill, we came to the square frame house that had been loaned to us. A crowd of officials came in and we all sat down. A row of children stood silent, watching through the open door, where a policeman lounged with a gun. The house looked as if it might have been empty until that afternoon, when townspeople had hurriedly furnished it for us. Dominicans are kind, hospitable, friendly people. Fran and several ladies of the town went to make up beds in a big barrack-like room, lacing the room with white mosquito nets strung on cords from screws in the bare walls.

Dave Shaw opened a bottle of whiskey, and we men sat in a little ring of rocking chairs and straight chairs, a single small electric bulb hanging from a cord, putting our glasses on the floor, drinking and rocking and talking for hours—the problems of the province and the town, plans for our stay. A little dog wandered in and defecated on the floor, and we went on talking until the whiskey ran out and the hour grew late, then all departed, shaking hands twice, the Dominican style, once when they say goodbye, again at the door. It must have been near midnight when I crawled under the mosquito net and went to bed, at long last in Samaná, the peninsula that the United States had once tried to buy or lease or steal from the Dominican people.

We had left the Checker and Bailey at Sabana de la Mar; another driver had brought my own Jeep here from the capital. In Michigan, I relax by driving my Jeep in the woods. I had had the Jeep box, which in Michigan carried fishing tackle and camping equipment, filled now with canned food, beer and mineral water, Coke and ginger ale; a first-aid kit with dysentery pills; tools and a spare can of oil; whiskey and cigarettes for gifts to soldiers; my shotgun for hunting; bundles of *Alianza* comic books and boxes of candy bars for Dan and Fred to give to Dominican children.

Early in the morning the Governor and other officials arrived in a military Land-Rover, and we started out in a rain. The road spiraled steeply up, then dipped and swooped and climbed and dropped among the high, rough hills. The sun came out, the thick-growing palms steamed, and the beaches and sea and a beach-rimmed islet emerged from the mist, green and blue and gold in the Bay far below. A young soldier drove the Land-Rover and I drove my Jeep, and we stopped several times to exchange passengers, so I could have the Governor or other officials or plain citizens beside me. A man who seemed intelligent but oddly silent, followed us to the next town, took me aside, told me I had spoken with Trujillistas, warned me against them in other towns, and told me how after the assassination, because a relative of his was thought to have been involved, the SIM had arrested him and in La Cuarenta applied an electric prod to his genitals.

Nowhere else did so many people wave friendly greetings from their huts as we passed by—or so many people ask me to arrange for the United States to annex the Republic, or failing that, the Peninsula. Some people in Samaná are descended from U.S. slaves, and bear such names as Williams and Green and Jones.

We looped north and descended steeply on a gravel road that men were patching with slabs of beautiful marble. On a Jeep trail on the Atlantic coast, the earth was red with bauxite. We passed an abandoned marble quarry, machinery rusting, and came, at length, to an Army outpost. There the road ended.

An Army officer hurried to a row of small wooden houses. We waited, parked in a shaded grove of coco palms beside the sea, massive Atlantic combers breaking on the shore. The beach stretched golden farther than we could see. The officer returned, followed by the outpost troops, six or eight of them, and drew them to attention before us, bayonets fixed. Behind them were their women and children, one tiny naked baby peeking shyly from behind a palm tree.

I thanked them for the welcome and proposed we rest awhile. The officer said we would have lunch, and soon we did, *sancocho*.

Two men came along in a boat, each rowing with one oar, and pulled up at the Army outpost and went to work, carrying heavy sacks of charcoal from boat to shore. The boat was a dugout, carved with dull tools out of a great log. The men wore nothing except shifts made from sugar sacks, reaching from shoulder almost to knee, tattered and patched many times. They had made the charcoal—thousands of Dominicans have no other way to earn money than by making charcoal—and now were bringing it to market, selling what the Army would buy, sending the rest to town. They worked silently and steadily, barefoot, from beach to shore, piling the bags, paying us no heed, and, when they had finished, got in their dugout and rowed away.

The soldiers ate with us. Little boys, naked except for a shirt, little girls, naked except for underpants, hovered near. Women carrying babies carried food to us out of a thatch-roofed kitchen. One soldier asked me to come with him, he wanted to show me something. He showed me his infant child, held by its mother. The child had no eyes.

We got back to Samaná near dark, worn out, and went to a meeting in the club. Nearly every town has a club, a place where people drink, dance, transact official business, and hold political meetings and ceremonial functions. Increasingly, we used these, asking the Governor to invite everybody in town, instead of holding small meetings in the Governor's official hall.

The Governor spoke briefly, saying I was here to learn about the Province's problems, and mentioned several—the highway to the capital, farm-to-market roads, squatters, development of marble, coal, graphite, and bauxite—then I invited the audience, some two hundred, plus others outside, to speak. In rapid order, they did. Agrarian reform was slow. The Banco Agrícola was not making loans to the most needy small farmers because it required security, and if a man owned five cows, he didn't need a loan. The United States must put people to work, stop unemployment, develop tourism, loan money to establish industries. The coco industry should be developed, the wharf rebuilt. This was "the long-forgotten Province"—nearly every Province said it was, and most were right.

More important than all that, one man said, was education. A young man spoke with passion: University graduates here had nothing to do, needed scholarships, needed financial help for more study, and couldn't we help by sending students to the U.S. or Puerto Rico? The crowd applauded him. Another said: The people were grateful for my visit, but we must make haste, the people were in misery and the Communists were coming. Another: Why not start a fishing industry? Why couldn't a U.S. warship visit Samaná once in a while? Once this had been a busy harbor, with foreign consulates here and in Sánchez up the Bay, but now it was dying—could we not revive it? And so on for nearly two hours. This was an audience where everybody had ideas.

I responded. Many of their problems were the legacy of Trujillo—I had seen it in the sisal fields of Azua and the port of Puerto Plata. Many of their problems were for the Consejo to solve. We were helping, with money and technicians, through the *Alianza*. It was true that unemployment breeds communism, but there was a better reason to end it— people living on rich land are entitled to a good living. As to specifics, the new Agrarian Reform Institute should be functioning well soon. So should the Agricultural Bank. I would look into the loan problem. We would send a ship to Samaná. We did have a scholarship program, and the young man should see the Embassy's cultural attaché. As to new industry, if anyone here wanted to invest or to explore U.S. markets, he could come to the Embassy and talk to the economic counselor. I ended by praising their Province, thanking them for talking with me, and saying we had not solved any problems tonight but I knew of no better way to start than in a democratic town meeting.

3

I had heard it was possible to traverse the entire remote north coast, from Samaná to Sosua, by Jeep. In the morning, we left early while it still was cool. Of all the areas of the Republic, this was, I thought, the most lush. Coconut trees grew everywhere, the jungle was impenetrable, green, wet. At the head of the Bay was a vast swamp, the mouth of the great Yuma River which rose in the Cordillera Central. We crossed the throat of the Peninsula and drove along the coast, all palms and beach, to Nagua, formerly named Julia Molina in honor of Trujillo's mother, now called by its old name. The Province, too, had been named Julia Molina; now it was María Trinidad Sánchez, after a martyred heroine of the 1840s.

Nagua was a dusty, hot, little low-roofed town by the sea, with dirt streets, a huge Fortaleza, and a collection of splendid government buildings. The military commander and Governor and other officials met us and took us to see the rice mill several miles inland. That sounded unpromising, but I had learned years ago as a reporter to see whatever local people thought important: Usually they were right. They were this time.

Trujillo had dispossessed hundreds, perhaps thousands, of *campesinos* of their rice land—simply sent troops to drive them away—and built a rice mill and worked the vast plantation with slave labor. An infamous general had run it for him. He used political prisoners to do the work, at bayonet-point. They lived in barrack-like buildings near the mill. When one wore out, or tried to escape, he was taken away and murdered. People in Nagua told me that more men were killed in the Fortaleza here in this remote town than anywhere else in the Republic, and that every day their bodies were washed up on the beach, to be eaten by dogs.

Now the rice mill was empty, its machinery rusting, and squatters had moved onto the rice fields and were living all over them, living in thatched huts, living in the barracks, the factory, the tool shed, living everywhere, under any roof. The Agricultural Bank was trying to help. I talked to its local man, and he threw up his hands. Before you could divide the land for agrarian reform, you had to find out who owned it; before you could cultivate it properly, you had to drive the squatters off; when you drive squatters away, the police get involved, and if they couldn't handle it, the troops; if you were not careful, you would have the Agricultural Bank, the Agrarian Reform Institute, and the U.S. AID program using the Dominican military to drive starving Dominicans off the land. It was another of those tangled grandiose Trujillo disasters we kept running into everywhere. Who in the United States imagines such problems behind the phrase "foreign aid"?

At the crowded town meeting that night, nearly every man had a gun. Dan and Fred said later it reminded them of an American television Western. The place felt tense, the people spoke bitter words—murder, misery, thirty-one years, hunger, no jobs or hope. The UCN leader, young, crewcut, bespectacled, and bright, said, "President Kennedy should not put the Dominican Republic in the same class as the others. This country had a mortal illness. It needs special consideration." The hospital director said: "Help us combat diseases, dysentery, syphilis, malnutrition. The people cannot work. They are sick. Do as the Russians do—teach. Send technicians. The Dominican Republic is a friend of the United States. But sometimes the United States doesn't help us much. If we are against you, we end as Cuba." Another: "Since North Americans know so much, see if they can send technicians to study a way to stop the sea—this town has nearly disappeared." And another: "Why cannot the Yankees even give us a visa?"

I spoke to them in similar tone. We were here to help, the *Alianza* wanted to help, so did the Consejo, but nobody could do everything at once; and while there were many things wrong with Nagua, Castro couldn't fix them. Perhaps we couldn't either, but we were trying, and as for special consideration, the Republic had received more from President Kennedy and the U. S. Congress than any other Latin American country. I told them what we were doing. But I said there was no magic in the word "technician," a new society could not be built overnight, and the road ahead was long.

Some liked it; several teen-agers sneered openly. We left the club and walked, with the Governor and other officials, through the dusty streets to a Chinese restaurant hanging over the sea and sat at a long table on a thatch-roofed dimly lit dance floor. Behind the thin cane wall soldiers stood on guard. The place filled and some danced to the jukebox, dancing the spirited though monotonous Dominican *merengue*. Several young men of the 14th of June were sitting in a far corner; the officials with us were watching them. Cindy, then a Sarah Lawrence sophomore, went over and sat down and drank Cokes with them. Later she reported they could not have been nicer. So much could not be said for the respectables. The Governor, a tireless politician, moved around the room shaking hands. The place was getting noisy, the hour late. We got up to leave.

The Governor, the local PRD leader, was standing by the jukebox, talking to the UCN leader. To say good night, I got between them. As I did so, the UCNer, immaculate in white linen, set his horn-rimmed glasses atop the jukebox and drew back to punch the Governor. Instantly the big military commander stepped in, took me by the elbow, and, police following with Fran and Cindy and the boys, pushed through the crowd and walked with us up the street to the hotel—a rickety old two-story frame building right on the main intersection, a noisy, dirty firetrap with no toilet or sink or bath upstairs, the beds hard as stone slabs, covered with mosquito netting. Exhausted, we slept.

We were wakened about 4 A.M. by a raucous voice in the street outside: "Down with the Yankees" and "Yankees go home." Dressing, I heard a crowd gathering, and looked out: The street was filling with people. No policeman was in sight. The man was yelling louder. I told Fran and the boys to get dressed but to stay in the bedroom. I went downstairs. The little lobby opened to both streets; the crowd by now filled both.

I went back upstairs, wakened Dave Shaw, and began collecting baggage. We had brought my shotgun, thinking we might do some hunting, and I found it and some shells. I also found an upstairs back porch; it might be possible to escape over rooftops should this turn into a mob that might burn the hotel. But it was odd—though the crowd was big, I could still hear only one voice clearly, the same one. Looking out the front window, I realized what was going on. A drunk left over from last night had stopped by the hotel to yell "Down with the Yankees," and the crowd, simply people going to work or market, had stopped to watch. He was staggering around, yelling, and they were baiting him. In a few minutes a policeman came and led him away.

4

The Governor, white-suited, arrived in a Jeep and insisted on accompanying us, taking the Army commander and a couple of policemen and one or two others with him, and we left town early, I driving my own Jeep, the Governor in his, heading west along the coast for Sosua, ninety miles away. We had gone only a few miles, however, when the Governor stopped in a hamlet and took us into a house and introduced us to a group of people gathered there. We had coffee, talked awhile, then went on— only to stop again, this time at a roadside bar.

I realized what the Governor was doing: Whistlestop campaigning, using me to get votes for himself and the PRD. As we got back in the Jeep I told Shaw to tell him we were in a hurry and hoped we wouldn't make more stops. But we did—at a town square where men and boys were sitting on benches in the shade; at a beach resort in a hidden cove; out on a cape at a hamlet around a lighthouse; and in a town where a group was gathered in the Mayor's house. We walked down the street to a crowd receiving food from CARITAS under our Food for Peace program, and an old man, seeing us, set up a cry, "¡Viva los Norteamericanos!" A truckload of teen-agers roared by, yelling, "Down with the Yankees." We waved to them. Two young women came out on a porch and called, "¡Viva los Norteamericanos!" We waved to them, too.

When, at 1 P.M. with two-thirds of the distance yet to go, we stopped again, this time at a house in the hills where a score of people were cooking a *sancocho* and roasting a whole goat on a spit (which meant that if we stopped we would spend the rest of the afternoon), I said flatly no —telling the Governor and the hostess that it was impossible. He was embarrassed, she disappointed, I regretful.

Inland, we suddenly came upon a cluster of tiny square concrete cubicles, children playing in the dirt: The Spanish colony. Trujillo had imported Spaniards, Japanese, and German and Austrian Jews to plant colonies in the Republic, just why I am not sure, though I have heard various reasons advanced: That he hoped to "improve the breed" and "whiten" the population, or to teach skills to Dominicans, or to make friends abroad, or to get cheap labor to replace Haitians. By now most of the colonies had failed. The Spanish colonists here appeared to have sunk to the level of the Dominican poor. We were once again driving through a land of fat cattle and thin people.

Most of our way onward lay along the sea, mile after mile of sandy beach, some sheltered, some open to the booming Atlantic surf, sea grapes and palm trees growing out of sand, scattered clusters of fishermen's huts, nets drying in the sun. We came to Sosua.

5

Sosua is one of the most beautiful beaches I have ever seen. It is small, less than a mile long, and at either end honeycombed rock walls rise up and long rocky peninsulas jut out into the Atlantic. The beach itself is almost all sand, not pure white, not dark, but golden yellow. Offshore is a coral reef, covered at high tide, and from a boat you can gaze down into huge underwater caverns filled with fish and sea urchins and waving coral fronds, blue and yellow and black and green.

At certain times of day, the sun hits the sea so dazzlingly that it is impossible to see the sea at all. One sees only a great blinding light. At night, in the dim distance far across the bay, one can see the lights of Puerto Plata. Sosua is about two hours' drive across the Septentrional range from Santiago. Sosua is to Santiagueros what Boca Chica is to the capital, though, till now, less crowded.

On the western peninsula that forms one arm of Sosua Bay stands Charamicos, a little native town of dirt streets and huts, bars and prostitutes. On the eastern arm is the Jewish colony.

About 1940, when Jewish organizations all over the world were trying to save Jews from Hitler's gas chambers, Trujillo offered them a haven. He sold (the impression abroad was that he gave) the colonists a large tract of farmland at Sosua. The Dominican version is that he had bought it cheap, under pressure, from United Fruit and sold it to the Jews at a large profit in cash and stock in DORSA, the name of the colony, which was financed from New York by a subsidiary of the American Jewish Joint Distribution Committee. Some 350 Jewish families, mostly from Germany and Austria, settled here.

At first they had a terrible time. Most were from the cities of Europe; they knew nothing of farming, let alone the tropics or the Spanish language. One said, "I had never touched an animal till I came here." They tried raising vegetables, failed because they had no market. They tried several other things; all failed. But at least they were alive.

They finally hit on a solution: Raising cattle and hogs, making milk and cheese and sausage. Their task was enormous. The land was arid; they irrigated it. They built a slaughterhouse, a sausage factory, a cheese factory, planned a milk pasteurizing plant. They established markets and trucking systems, first locally, then in Santiago, then in the capital. In the end, they succeeded.

Now all their effort was endangered. Although, over the years, more than a thousand Jews have passed through here, only about two hundred of the original settlers remain. Nearly all the colonists are elderly. Their children born here left, going to the United States. Moreover, the Consejo took over Trujillo's one hundred thousand shares of DORSA stock and for a time considered expropriating the property, as it did other Trujillo property. Worst, Dominican *campesinos* resented the colonists as Trujillo collaborators, moved in, overran their grazing lands, built squatters' shacks, cut down splendid timber, and planted corn on hillsides so steep that after a single season rain washed the topsoil away. Then they abandoned the land they had ruined and moved deeper into the colony's lands.

That spring of 1962 an ominous note of anti-Semitism cropped up in the Republic—a childish scrawl on a wall, "Down with the Jews" or "Jews go home." The colonists were afraid of the squatters. They had appealed to the police and to the local Army commander. They had received no help. Authority had nearly broken down even in the capital; it could hardly be expected to operate here. I asked the colonists what they thought might happen to them. One said, "We might be murdered." Some carried guns.

We stayed in one of the DORSA houses out on the peninsula, and visited the factories and farmlands. Every day at noon Dominican children jogged past the beach on burros on the dusty road from squalid Charamicos, taking lunch in tin cans to their Dominican fathers who worked for the Jews; every evening they came back once more, empty milk cans banging rhythmically against the grass saddle, then homeward once more, their fathers riding now, the children walking, the milk cans filled and silent.

One night the handful of remaining colonists gave a reception for us, serving cookies and cakes they had baked, some speaking neither English nor Spanish after all these years, only German, offering a glass of champagne for a toast rather tentatively made, a toast to democracy and freedom. These people who, pilloried about the dangerous world during the Hitler madness; these poeple who, having made a pact with one devil to escape a worse, now found themselves hated by other of the devil's victims, were toasting Dominican democracy and freedom. "To

Dominican democracy." We stood and drank. And "To the DORSA colony; may it prosper."

It was not really a U.S. problem, few of them had American citizenship; most were German, a few married to Dominicans; but later on I spoke about their plight to Tony Imbert. He understood at once, and I think their troubles eased thereafter.

6

Harry Shlaudeman reported that the Electoral Board was calling in the parties to tell them that it was administratively impossible to hold the August election on schedule. All indications were that the parties would protest. The next move was up to the Consejo, but would the Consejo meet its responsibility?

Once more the city was filled with rumors—that Imbert and Fernández Caminero were plotting to reconstitute the Consejo and extend its term for two years; that the U.S. was financing Bosch and his PRD. (The proof advanced for this was that an Embassy officer called "Mac"—there was none—had met secretly with Bosch in Santiago at the home of Antonio Guzmán, brother-in-law of General Viñas, and "a lot of money had changed hands." It was true that an Embassy officer had met Bosch at Guzmán's—but that is all that was true.)

Shlaudeman went on: In recent days all the parties had shown signs of uniting against the PRD. The Social Christians and UCN were accusing the PRD of working hand-in-glove with Foupsa Libre, the non-political labor federation that was advised by the AFL-CIO's ORIT and my labor officer, Fred Somerford. That was absurd: The truth was that Miolán of PRD hated Foupsa Libre—he wanted his own labor movement. But UCN and the Social Christians each had its own labor movement too, and Foupsa Libre obstructed them, so they accused it, and Fred Somerford, of helping PRD. This, coupled with the story that we were giving money to PRD, was dangerous to us.

I told Somerford to take a couple of weeks off, play golf, stay out of sight, while I tried to straighten it out. We would stay away from Bosch for a while, too.

After the Peru military *golpe,* the United States suspended diplomatic relations and stopped economic, military, and technical aid and tried to influence the military back to constitutionalism. It was a tough position. Like other hemisphere Ambassadors, I was instructed to make it clear. I gladly did so, hoping to restrain the Dominican military.

On Wednesday, I had President Bonnelly to lunch. He was worried. FENEPIA, the Castro/Communist-dominated union of government employees, was set to strike the next day against the withholding provision of the new income tax law. The strike could turn into a general strike and topple the government. I urged him to stand firm against FENEPIA's demands. He feared to. The political parties, continuing to make capital of the election postponement, were attacking the Consejo heavily. I urged him to take the initiative and solve the election problem quickly. And I offered our support: The *Boxer* would be here during the weekend, and I would follow it next week with a speech supporting him.

In the afternoon, we heard that General Peguero had ordered his police to fire on the FENEPIA strikers tomorrow, but to shoot low, at their legs. I went to see Imbert alone that night, and told him the Consejo should stand firm against FENEPIA but without gunplay, told him about the *Boxer,* our position on elections here and on the Peruvian *coup,* and asked him point-blank if he and Fernández Caminero were thinking of keeping power. He reassured me about everything.

The next day, Thursday, July 26, the anniversary of Castro's 1956 assault on the Moncada Barracks, FENEPIA struck. By midmorning our people reported that the strike was only partly successful, that more than half the government agencies seemed to be working. The city was filled with police. Stores were closed, some banks were open, the airport was closed, traffic was light, several bands of young thugs were roaming Calle Conde and Parque Colón; the Cascos Blancos moved out and troops with guns moved in.

FENEPIA was trying to pull other labor unions out—to make it a general strike. Bonnelly met with the Consejo in the Palace and let it be known that it would stop the strike but was at the same time disposed to "study" the income tax law which FENEPIA opposed; it was a weasel statement. The strike did not gain wide support during the day. Vital public services—electricity, water, transport—operated normally.

By Saturday the strike seemed to be over. But later the Consejo quietly gave in to some of the union's demands.

On Saturday, the *Boxer,* too big to get in the harbor, arrived and anchored offshore, a majestic aircraft carrier looking as big as an island, as powerful as the nation that sent it. Throughout my tenure I, who had never been an admirer of the military, found our military visitors unfailingly understanding and eager to be helpful.

The *Boxer's* show began on Sunday morning. Its helicopters flew a circling shuttle between the ship and the Palace, first on trial runs, then ferrying the Dominican military commanders and the Consejeros and the wives of both. They flew low, passing over the Embassy Residence and the city. Crowds came out to watch. When told to, Fran and I drove to the Palace and met President Bonnelly and his wife. A helicopter slanted in, seesawing gently to rest on the Palace lawn, and, with the Dominican Palace guard at attention, we climbed abroad.

Fran and Mrs. Bonnelly dislike flying, particularly in helicopters, and tried to look any way but down, but Bonnelly and I leaned out the open side as the helicopter rose above the Palace and on high up above the city, the old Spanish houses and the palm-lined boulevard, the sea and the breaking surf spread out below. I had not realized how green the city was. Then we were over the *Boxer,* its small boats coveying beneath us, white-uniformed sailors standing at attention around the rim of the entire flight deck, and as we circled the ship, her guns fired the twenty-one-gun presidential salute, to us puffs of smoke first, then distant booms through the helicopter's rattle. We made a complete circle around the rim of the deck, then descended gently.

Bonnelly got out first, we following. We stood on the deck—officers and men in dazzling white drawn up at attention in the sun, the Consejeros and Dominican military commanders, my attachés and MAAG commanders behind them—while the band played the Dominican national anthem and the "Star-Spangled Banner." ("Manning the rail," as naval tradition requires for a chief of state, is a tricky business on a carrier with no rail, for the helicopter's rotor could blow a man overboard.)

We shook hands with Vice Admiral Ward and the other ship's officers. Bonnelly inspected the honor guard; we all inspected various pieces of equipment, then we went in to a buffet lunch. Already we had done what we wanted to do: Made it clear to the Dominican Armed Forces and the other Consejeros and, indeed, to the city at large that Bonnelly was the President and Commander in Chief, and that we supported him.

Back at the Palace, we drove to a little orphanage on the edge of town, Casa Providencia, Bonnelly's favorite charity. Marines off the *Boxer* were rebuilding it. They had brought lumber, wire, pipe, tiles, cement, everything with them. They climbed all over the house, tearing out walls, putting up new ones, installing new plumbing and drainpipes, wiring and screen, painting inside and out, rebuilding the kitchen—constructing, really, a new house. The midday sun was blazing down; they were laboring and sweating in the dirt, and we walked among them, and I said to one sweaty gang, "I'm the U. S. Ambassador—come here and meet the President," and one said, in the accent of Chicago's West Side, "Ah, knock it off," and went on working, thinking I was kidding. Fandino translated for Bonnelly, he laughed, then all shook hands.

Fran asked one Marine how he felt about the anti-American catcalls in town. He said, with a southern drawl, "Ma'am, I been yellin' 'Yankee go home' all my life."

Off to one side under a mango tree, a Marine was playing a harmonica for a knot of little Dominican orphans squatting on the ground. I told Bonnelly, "This is a different kind of Marine occupation."

"Sí, señor," he said.

The Marines had volunteered for this work.

Leaving, Bonnelly said little, but he was visibly moved. We dropped him and his wife at their house, then went on down the block to our house. En route we passed a red-shirted Dominican teen-ager who, seeing our car, yelled, "Down with the Yankees."

The *Boxer* did our policy as much good as anything that happened all year. When she left, the sailors and Marines donated what Dominican money they had to Dominican charity. I was proud, proud of my country and my countrymen. But baffled too: How do you reach the red-shirted Dominican teen-ager? What about him?

7

I finished the speech I was to deliver, discussed it with Bonnelly and cleared it with the Department, and on Wednesday, August 1, delivered it on an occasion we had manufactured for the purpose. A group of U.S. newspaper editors was visiting the Republic, and I arranged for them to give a dinner at the Hotel Embajador for Dominican journalists and leading citizens, and to invite me to address them. I had drafted the speech with care. I used the pretext of describing the Republic and its problems to the editors to say some things about the election crisis that might otherwise be unacceptably interventionist.

I praised President Bonnelly and the Consejo and recounted their progress. I said flatly, "We support this government." To handle the electoral-constitutional crisis without seeming interventionist, I used an historical parallel: The deadly parallel between what had happened in Sumner Welles' time and was happening today. In 1923, the provisional government had promulgated a new Electoral Law but it was complicated and difficult to administer. The parties had maneuvered for selfish advantage. The whole electoral machinery appeared to have broken down. But the party leaders were persuaded to put patriotism above partisanship, the provisional government moved forcefully, and the Electoral Board took up its duties with dispatch.

Today as then, I said, delays and difficulties abounded. But the Dominican people had overcome those difficulties once and would again, with firm leadership by the government, responsible behavior by the political parties, and confidence of the people in their government. Castro/Communists might try to create terror in the streets, topple the government, and strangle Dominican democracy. They would fail. "For the Dominican people and their government now recognize the imperative necessity of the immediate tasks ahead, to:

"—hold elections;

"—maintain both personal liberty and public order;

"—employ the people;

"—pay taxes;

"—and support the government.

"And they are prepared to do them."

It was a risky speech. It struck directly at the most sensitive of internal affairs—an election. But I thought we must take the chance, did, and got away with it.

The speech made our position clear—we favored abolition of the August election but insisted on the December election—but it did not turn the tide. Faced with the constitutional crisis, the Consejo showed signs of disintegrating. Fernández Caminero told me, "I can't go on. The Consejo can't go on. I have not wanted to resign but I see no solution. The UCN calls me a Communist and the 14th of June calls me a Trujillista. We can never last until December."

Private sources—by now I had several—told me that certain government leaders were stealing public funds and trying to frame each other, that Reid planned to announce publicly he would not be a candidate and challenge the other Consejeros to do likewise. Rumors flew wildly— that Imbert had offered the Presidency to Fiallo, that Pichardo was plotting, that the Consejo was paralyzed and the military plotting a *golpe*.

The parties were jockeying for position, demanding elections. The Consejo was doing nothing. Several influential private citizens came to see me to say they were disgusted with the Consejo, and that the only solution was a military takeover.

For the first time, I began to have serious doubts that the Consejo would survive the year. We had foreseen this crisis for weeks, had told the Consejeros there would be no elections unless they exerted leadership. And in this crisis, unlike the sugar crisis, we could help them little.

Months ago when we began, we had deluded ourselves. The opportunity had seemed so glittering and so close within our grasp that we had thought we could straighten it all out—win over the students and start an intellectual ferment, bring Adlai Stevenson and others down to help, educate the people for democracy, and hold free elections with OAS help. The reality was quite different. There simply had been nothing here to build on—no government, no labor unions, no free civic associations, no men experienced in government (they were dead, in jail, or in exile), no money, no work, no going economy, no civil service, no democratic traditions, nothing. The Consejo had learned to walk, but it would never run, and we would be lucky to keep it alive.

Peru had given me pause. Ambassador Loeb's warnings to the Peruvian military had failed there. Would mine fail here? I was convinced, privately, that we absolutely would not permit a Castro/Communist takeover in the Dominican Republic, even if we had to use force. I was almost as certain that we would throw the Trujillos out again should they return. But I was far less certain we would move against a rightist *golpe*. I was certain that Washington had been badly shaken by the

Peru *golpe,* especially by the Peruvian people's apparent acceptance of it. In Washington one tended to idealize Latin Americans—to conceive them as suffering under dictatorship, eager for democracy if only given a chance. On the scene they seemed far less eager for freedom, which entailed responsibility and uncertainty.

Dostoyevsky once wrote, "Man was created a rebel; and how can rebels be happy? . . . For nothing has ever been more insupportable for a man and a human society than freedom. . . . In the end they will lay their freedom at our feet, and say to us: 'Make us your slaves, but feed us.' . . . Nothing is more seductive for man than his freedom of conscience, but nothing is a greater curse of suffering . . . the fearful burden of free choice."

In the Dominican Republic, people seemed to be pro-government— to support whoever occupied the Palace. I even entertained the heretical thought that perhaps the people who had suffered under Trujillo and who had known they were gaining freedom were but a tiny minority, that the vast mass neither knew it was suffering nor cared if it was freed.

Though the situation was in truth bad, part of my malaise probably was due to an ulcer attack. I had had an ulcer for seven or eight years; dormant for some time, now in early August it became painful.

Shlaudeman brought in a new rumor about Imbert and Fernández Caminero, my favorite so far. The scenario called for a *turba* to invade the courtroom where the Mirabal killers were still on trial and to murder them. General disorder would ensue; President Bonnelly, powerless amid chaos, would step down, and Imbert and Fernández Caminero would reconstitute the Consejo.

Donny Reid pleaded with us to take care of his wife and children if anything happened to him. He also asked for a U. S. Navy show of force and, if necessary, a landing by U. S. Marines. Imbert summoned a CIA man and a Dominican security man to a secret meeting. Imbert's and Amiama's wives were leaving the country, ostensibly on a vacation. Police Chief Belisario Peguero's family was reported gone. President Bonnelly was said to be staying at home, sick.

When I had first arrived we had stayed up long past midnight several times a week, chasing down such plots and rumors. Now, however, we decided to ignore them and bear down on the real problem at hand—the electoral-constitutional crisis.

Harry Shlaudeman was only 36, tall, getting bald, contained, with a disconcerting practiced habit of smiling while saying unpleasant things. (Perhaps he had learned it in Bulgaria, where he had served two years.) His mind was fast, imaginative, analytical, precise. I suspect when younger he may have been inclined to rashness because he cared passionately about his work. He had become more judicious and deliberate,

but he had lost none of his imaginativeness or passion; the dead hand of
caution that the State Department lays on so many bright young men
had not smothered Shlaudeman.

Shlaudeman had served three and a half years in Colombia and spoke
Spanish well. He was an activist. Creative, determined, he was so dedicated to his work he sometimes neglected his family. He was a student
of Marxism-Leninism and of Dominican history. He wrote well and admired good writing, though I knew him for some time before he told
me he once had wanted to be a writer. Shlaudeman had a fingertip
sensitivity to politics. All spring he had kept track of the twisted maneuvers of the 26-odd Dominican political parties. His knowledge of the
ways of Balkan politicians had helped him in the Dominican Republic.
Now, with elections approaching, he put to use what he had learned.

On August 8, Shlaudeman told me the Consejo would meet that
night to discuss the electoral-constitutional question. We could try to influence the Consejo or the parties, but I decided not yet—we had intervened enough lately. Let the Consejo start facing this one alone. We
would watch closely, and move in if we had to.

So far as we could discover, the Consejo decided only that Pichardo
would meet with the party leaders on Friday, August 10. I told Shlaudeman to find out before that meeting where the parties stood and gently
to remind three of them—the Social Christians, Ramón Castillo's PPDC,
and General Ramírez' PNRD—where we stood.

Shlaudeman came to the Residence on Monday and said that the Friday meeting of Pichardo and the party leaders had made the lineup fairly
clear. The left was maneuvering to wreck the elections—insisting on
holding the August election, now only two days away, knowing very well
it was impossible or, alternatively, trying to postpone the August election,
thus postponing the December election. Fiallo of UCN was arguing for
abolition—only one election this year, in December, with the Constituent
Assembly question left till later. That was the only formula that would
guarantee an elected President this year. And the Republic badly needed
an elected President. The Consejo simply could not survive much longer.

Shlaudeman said the parties were meeting again with Pichardo today.
He was afraid the left would win. Although some twenty-six parties had
been formed, only thirteen were participating in the meeting—the rest
chose to abstain or were not registered with the Electoral Board. It
appeared that our policy of abolition would lose. Incredibly, each party,
big or small, would have one vote—Ramón Castillo's vest-pocket party
and the massive PRD were equal. (Ramón Castillo had been pushed out
of the PRD by Bosch and Miolán. Though Dominican, he had acquired
U.S. citizenship. He had asked me if his political activity would endanger
his U.S. citizenship. I had told him it might, had told him what the limits
were, but had not told him to desist; he was often helpful to us.)

Next day Shlaudeman reported that the parties, meeting with Pichardo, had, as we had feared, voted to hold the Constituent Assembly election. With typical irresponsibility, they had set no date but had simply voted to hold the election, thus putting the Consejo squarely on the spot. For under the Constitution the election had to be held tomorrow, an absolute impossibility. The Consejo did not seem disposed to act. Thus, the parties had finally precipitated the crisis we had feared, opening the door to the Consejo's resignation, leftist disorders, or a military takeover.

Two of the thirteen parties had been absent. The vote, Shlaudeman said, had been six to five.[3] Juan Bosch's PRD, together with four small parties which considered themselves "revolutionary," (two of them Castro/Communist parties), had lined up with the Castro/Communist 14th of June, which had no intention of participating in elections anyway and wanted only to disrupt them; while Viriato Fiallo's UCN had held with it the Social Christians plus three small parties of conservative bent.

The whole situation was absurd. The Electoral Board had done virtually nothing to prepare for elections. Neither had the Consejo. Neither had the parties. Nor had the OAS helped much. Each blamed the other. And now disaster had occurred.

Shlaudeman said that Ramón Castillo had left yesterday's deliberations to try to find two other vest-pocket parties to vote for abolition. But he couldn't find one party leader, the other was asleep and wouldn't get up, so Castillo had gone back alone. Pichardo had not wanted to bring the question to a vote, and had recognized Castillo, who had talked endlessly, filibustering, hoping the other two would show up. But another party representative in favor of abolition had misunderstood the situation and, against their own interests, brought the question to a vote. And lost, six to five.

So tomorrow the Consejo's constitutional powers would expire, and nothing existed to take its place. Bosch, the 14th of June, and the rest of the wrecking crew had succeeded. Bosch was playing the leftists' game. At the time we thought he was doing so because he knew he could not win an election now against the UCN. Later we discovered that what he really wanted, not unreasonably, was removal of a constitutional requirement that a President must have lived in the Republic during the preced-

---

[3] The five voting for abolition had been UCN, PRDA (Nicolás Silfa's vest-pocket splinter off the PRD), PNRD (General Ramírez' party, strong in only one western province), PPDC (Ramón Castillo's tiny splinter off the PRD), and PRSC (the Social Christians, not a big party but the only one that competed with the 14th of June for the loyalty of students). The six voting for the August election were Juan Bosch's PRD; FNR, probably a Castro/Communist front, though we knew little about it; ASD (Juan Isidro Jimenes Gullón's splinter off UCN); PNR, the Castro/Communist party led by "Corpito" Pérez Cabral and Dato Pagán; Vanguardia, the vest-pocket party of Horacio Julio Ornes; and the 14th of June.

ing five years and that one of his parents be Dominican born—requirement that would have barred Bosch's candidacy, since he himself had been in exile in recent years and his father was Spanish and his mother Puerto Rican. This was surely not unreasonable, but Bosch had gone to unreasonable lengths to get it.

The Crisis Crowd and I decided to try to save the situation. We considered several possibilities—putting pressure on Bosch (but several of our indirect channels to him were out of the country, and Shlaudeman felt sure he would not yield to direct pressure); persuading the UCN bloc to denounce the vote and walk out; trying to get a new meeting and a new vote with the two absent vest-pocket parties participating; and trying to persuade the Consejo to act. We decided on the last two courses. Shlaudeman went out to talk to the parties. I called President Bonnelly, and he came to the Residence. I had been in bed and was wearing pajamas and robe. We talked in my study, the lamps turned low. I was not drinking, but Bonnelly was.

Bonnelly said the party leaders were all fools, personally ambitious, caring nothing for the country. He did not seem concerned about anything—the election, rumors of a *golpe,* anything. He kept telling me not to worry, to take care of my ulcer; we would get through. He kept saying, "I may look like a fool but I'm not." He said last night's vote was binding on no one, had merely been the parties' recommendations. The Consejo need not accept them. The Consejo was now determined to govern.

I gathered the Consejo would simply ignore both the legal requirement of—and the parties' vote for—an election tomorrow. But Bonnelly did not say so directly. Instead, he told one of his oblique stories; he said that, to settle the dispute over development of the Yaque del Norte he had announced that the first meeting would be held in Santiago but it wouldn't be (waggling a finger slyly), it would be held privately, here, and it would be small; then his people would control the big meeting in Santiago. He would do the same within the Consejo when the parties' recommendations reached the Consejo.

I suggested that little time remained and it might be well to reconvene a meeting of the parties tomorrow, for we had heard that some might want to reconsider their votes, and perhaps Pichardo could entertain a motion to reconsider. "*Sí, como no,*" Bonnelly said—"Yes, of course" —and then went calmly on: Speaking of Santiago had reminded him of a sentimental speech he had made to the Cibao delegation and he went on talking about his father, his mother, and me. His father had been "a great man." He still reread the letters his father wrote him after he went off to college. His family had taken him to the mountains, and there he had taken a burro, then a *público,* and so reached the capital, all alone for the first time. (It seems to have been a watershed in his life. He mentioned it many times.) He said he never had heard his parents quarrel. He had tried to re-create the same life. He could never equal his father.

As President, he wanted only to be well remembered by his grandchildren. He did not want to stay in office. He adhered to certain fixed principles, especially honesty, and was deeply troubled by stories that men in government, including some close to him, were dishonest. He wanted to meet me in the U.S. later, "as friends, not as Ambassador and President," when "this is all over." Waggling a long finger, the President said, "¡Embajador! You and I think and feel alike."

That Sunday, Bonnelly said, the Armed Forces, "a little intranquil," had called on him to say they were loyal to him, and he had "taken the liberty" of telling them he had my support. (So, I thought, the *golpe* rumors had not all been false.) Before he left, I pressed him again: Pichardo should reconvene the parties tomorrow.

Pichardo did reconvene the meeting and, over the vehement protests of Bosch and his leftist allies, did entertain a motion to "impugn" the previous vote. This time Ramón Castillo had made sure that the UCN's vest-pocket allies were awake and present. The parties wrangled bitterly nearly all day, a stormy session of shouting men. Pichardo put it to a vote. The abolitionists won, seven to six. The 14th of June, PNR, and Jimenes Grullón's ASD walked out, and Bosch denounced the meeting. There would be no election for a Constituent Assembly. The Consejo would simply stay on in power and would hold a presidential election December 20.

Subsequently Bosch, Fiallo's brother, and Social Christian leaders met privately. The UCN agreed that the constitutional bar to Bosch's candidacy would be removed; in return, Bosch agreed that a single election would be held on December 20 and the congress elected at that time would write a new constitution.

I thought one more thing had become clear: We could not trust Juan Bosch. For President he would not do. It was not that he had fought us now on this issue. It was, rather, that he was a reckless political plunger, willing to risk everything, including the democratic system itself, to gain a personal political objective.

Not surprisingly, my ulcer did not respond to treatment. My doctor recommended surgery at Bethesda Naval Hospital. Assistant Secretary Ed Martin arrived on Sunday, August 19, on a previously scheduled trip. President Bonnelly came to the house for a long talk with him. Next day I left for Washington and Bethesda Naval Hospital.

Chapter Nine

THE CRUISE OF THE *ANGELITA*

A hospital in the United States afforded a fresh vantage point from which to view the Dominican predicament. Outwardly, my own country seemed wonderful. Emerging from the Dominican darkness into the light of Washington, I felt, "Now *here* is a great nation." It seemed big, beautiful, powerful. Everything worked—the hospital plumbing, doctors giving pain-killers to patients, competent nurses making the rounds by night.

But outside this hospital haven, I knew, the nation was uneasy. Uneasy in its power and greatness. As the most powerful nation, we must lead, but without imperialism. We did not want to rule the Dominican Republic, nor any other nation. What we wanted to do was create a situation where nobody but Dominicans could rule it. The trouble was that the Dominicans didn't seem very capable of ruling. People were always saying, "They must help themselves, we can't do it for them." But could they? And if not, what then? If our purpose was, as President Kennedy said, to defend freedom around the world, we could not turn our backs on unable governments and hapless people. Neither could we impose our will. Thus was our great power limited.

How could we explain the United States to Dominicans? Our presence there had no ideological content. The student bookstores were full of Communist books, and all but empty of ours. Time and again I had tried to get USIS to do something. Little was done. Moreover, the book we needed did not exist. So in the hospital I wrote one—a pamphlet history of the United States and its meaning, aimed directly at young Dominicans. Later we published it anonymously in Spanish and distributed it, somewhat inadequately, throughout the Republic.

Foreign Minister Bonilla came to the hospital, worried about the December election. The Dominican desk officer in the Department brought news out regularly. It was all bad. I quit reading and writing.

I had to get back. By the time I did it was worse, much worse. Tony Imbert had quietly moved for power. Whether my absence gave him his chance I do not know. But now he became our Number One problem.

2

Amiama and Imbert, caught by destiny in the assassination, stayed close together. But they were very different men.

Imbert was only forty-one when I first met him but looked older. (No wonder.) He was short and heavy and looked powerful, but his arms and calves were surprisingly thin. He had blue eyes, and an old scar beside one eye that made him seem to squint. He was a sentimental man, emotional, even kind; fond of children, hard outside, soft inside. His eyes had a humorous glint. But when he was angered they went suddenly dead flat. He was an intelligent man, shrewd and devious. He could not easily conceal his emotions, and it was never difficult to tell when he was lying. Many thought Imbert nothing but a blunt power-grabber. He was far more complicated than that—was, indeed, one of the most complex and interesting men in the Republic. In public, he was a poor speaker, nervous, unsure of himself, but in private conversation most eloquent. He was bilingual, had learned English as a child near Sosua, where his stepfather had managed the United Fruit plantation that later was sold to the Jewish colony.

He came from an old family—General José María Imbert had led the campaign against the Haitians in 1844, and a town near Puerto Plata is named Imbert. When as a child Tony Imbert went swimming at Sosua, his mother hired a band to wade out ahead of him and stand in the water and play music to frighten sharks away. While I was in the Republic, Imbert returned frequently to Sosua, and when offal was thrown from a slaughterhouse into the bay and the sharks gathered, Imbert used to shoot them. So poor were the people from a neighboring village that they, too, gathered and they would jump into the water alongside the sharks to contest with them for the discarded offal.

General Segundo Imbert had been Vice President under Ulises Heureaux. Tony's brother, Segundo, had been a much-feared Army officer at Puerto Plata under Trujillo, and Tony himself had been Trujillo's Governor of Puerto Plata province, head of the national *cédula* office, and head of the national lottery.

Imbert always professed—and I believe he felt to some extent—sympathy for the underdog. To me he constantly pleaded their cause. He treated the poor as a feudal lord might have. Traveling the country, he carried large rolls of ten-dollar bills and distributed them to crowds. Often he would give fifty or a hundred dollars to a man who came to him at the Palace or at home; often, too, he gave them jobs on the police force or at the sugar mill at Haina. Sometimes they turned out to be Castro/ Communists. It was not all humanitarianism. Imbert was playing with the left, as Trujillo had. He believed anyone could be bought. It was Trujillo's way.

Tony Imbert had no real conception of the depth and sweep of the revolution going on all around us. Imbert, for all his intelligence, was a political primitive. He did not understand ideas. It is significant that it was he, not Amiama, who was out on the highway with a gun the night of May 30, while Amiama was waiting back in town with other plotters. I think he enjoyed power more than he admitted to himself. Once in 1962, he designed a special hat for himself (Trujillo used to do the same).

Luís Amiama Tió was quite different. He was handsome, mustached, very Spanish, all steel. He wore white linen suits, and enjoyed dressing well. Women liked him. He was immaculately clean, too clean, almost as if he scrubbed himself to scrub away guilt. Neither he nor Imbert drank much. Amiama was much less explosive than Imbert, much more calculating, an odds player, never a plunger. Where Imbert might be soft and sentimental, Amiama would sniff and turn away.

Amiama seldom smiled. He had a deep contempt for the politicians, the military, everyone. He used to relate how he would call in high-ranking military officers, curse them, and tell them they had groveled at Trujillo's feet "until a real man with balls came along and killed him." Once Amiama said he would start a political party called the PPP— "Plata para los amigos, palos para los indiferentes, y plomo para los enemigos," that is, "Money for friends, clubs for the indifferent, and lead for enemies."

Amiama liked money more than Imbert did. They both made a good deal of it. Amiama lived rather lavishly. Somehow he acquired banana lands in the Northwest. According to the former prosecutor, Tejeda, Amiama "enjoyed" the cattle and the celebrated finca confiscated by the Consejo from General Román, Amiama's co-conspirator in the Trujillo assassination. "Things of Latin American politics," Tejeda writes.

I was told by staff members that some four million dollars disappeared from Haina during 1962 and 1.5 million dollars from the Foreign Office petty cash fund. Imbert was deeply involved in Haina, in the cement factory, in the sale of the Republic's entire molasses production. Amiama had a brother at the Foreign Office. During the political campaign, he sent agents around to collect funds, though not a candidate himself. We would have liked to have stopped graft, but it was more important that we stop political power plays, and our energies were limited.

All that spring Imbert and Amiama had been quietly collecting power. They got up at 4 A.M. and drove around the city and countryside, talking to their network of private informers, visiting Army and Navy barracks. They assumed the role of protecting the Armed Forces from the people's wrath, hoping to gain its support. Repeatedly they resisted politicians' demands to purge it of Trujillistas. They kept pushing their relatives and friends deeper and deeper into the Government's power centers. They tried to put a relative of Amiama in command of the Navy. General Luna, then close to Imbert, was Air Commander. They never stopped trying to get their own man in as Army Commander, but never quite succeeded. They did get control of the police, maneuvering the appointment of General Belisario Peguero, a big tough cop. Imbert also was believed to control the Attorney General, García Vásquez; the chief of the Immigration Service; and the head of the police security service, "Pupito" Sánchez, a soft man in a straw hat.

It was odd, the case of Imbert and Amiama. One would have thought they would have been national heroes—they had rid the Republic of the dictator. Somehow during that spring their heroism became tarnished. Instead of being admired, they were suspected and feared, and they resented it bitterly. Almost without exception, the leaders of the major political parties dreaded them. So did other Consejeros. So did some people in the U. S. Embassy and in Washington. Most people seemed to fear they would become a new two-headed Trujillo.

I probably spent more time in 1962 on them and their plots than on any other single problem. Yet although I shared everyone's misgivings, I saw something else in them: Manhood, for one. The longer you worked with Dominicans, the more you respected the strength of the women and disliked the weakness of the men, and, searching for explanations, you noticed how pampered are the infant males in Dominican families, how undisciplined the schoolboy males, how feckless the teenage males, and how vain and proud and sometimes absurd the adult males. They were not men, many of them, only spoiled brats grown up. Amiama and Imbert were men. And I saw other things in them. They could laugh, even at themselves. They did not botch things, as did so many Dominicans in government. It may be unpleasant but it is a fact that when I wanted to be sure a deportation would work smoothly, I turned to them. They were reasonable men, realistic men, not hotheaded patriots or melodramatic *poseurs* ready to fling themselves over the cliff. They would listen to me, at least up to a point, and they respected the power of the United States.

Amiama lived in a sprawling, ornate, expensive house set on several walled and closely guarded acres, resembling a Trujillo estate. His small air-conditioned study contained expensive furniture, ornate silver trays and coffeepots, elaborate intercom and microphone systems. Over the door was a crucifix and on the walls were the photographs of men who had been in the assassination, all dead now. Once Amiama, brooding, pointed to one, Modesto Díaz, and said, "He was the best of all." On the wall, too, was a motto, framed as Americans once framed such homilies as "Home Is Where the Heart Is." This motto of Amiama's was from a Dominican poem, written at the time of the assassination of Ulises Heureaux, and it said:

> *¡Benditos los que matan,*
> *si es un monstruo de sangre el que se hunde,*
> *y un pueblo el que se salva!*

> *Blessed are those who kill,*
> *if it is a bloody monster who is drowned,*
> *and a people who is saved!*

A commentator who reprinted the poem in 1962 wrote, " 'Blessed are those who kill!' says the poet. It is the consecration of tyrannicide in the Republic." It is.

3

A riot was scheduled at the Embassy for 11 A.M. the day I returned from Bethesda. (The Castro/Communists usually advertised them in the press in advance.) It did not take place. But there were enough other problems waiting.

The pre-campaign maneuvering of the numerous political parties was becoming furious. All made a great deal of noise. But polls, my conversations and those of Shlaudeman and others, CIA reports, every sign we could read, showed indisputably that only two parties had a chance of winning—Fiallo's UCN and Bosch's PRD. We had no desire to influence the outcome. We could live with either. Neither was Castro/Communist-dominated. Neither was hopelessly rightist.

Neither was ideal. The UCN was too upper-middle-class, too heterogeneous, too politically naïve, and lacking in real understanding of the people's needs. Fiallo was, however, a man of courage and integrity.

The PRD leadership, though politically expert, was too doctrinaire, too ideological, too theory-ridden, alienated from the Dominican scene, for it was an exile party. Moreover, its lower ranks were filled with some of the worst elements in Dominican political life, the remnants of the old PD. Bosch himself, as I have noted, I considered somewhat unreliable and unstable.

Whichever won, I thought, the country would need a constructive opposition; it was therefore important that the winner not smash the loser.

The UCN, if it failed to enact reforms, might inadvertently play into Castro's hands. The PRD, committed to reform, might be unacceptable to the military. In short, if the UCN won, the danger to it would come from the left; if the PRD won, the danger to it would come from the right.

I thought we should espouse the cause of neither but should continue to maintain close ties with both and, for the future, with the Social Christians. For the present, we should prop up the Consejo.

All very neat. Hah!

I saw President Bonnelly, the Consejeros, and the party leaders. How were things going?

Donny Reid was discouraged. He feared Amiama and Imbert, said they had no place to go after the Consejo's term ended, and were becoming desperate. He felt sure that either they or the Castro/Communists would wreck the election, and he said, "Please help us."

Amiama and Imbert seemed calm—business was good, the military was quiet, the far left was under control.

Fernández Caminero sounded very different—things were "the worst ever," elections were the only hope but probably could not be held; one time he and Imbert had thought to take over the government but now the time had passed; he himself intended to resign. As always, I urged him not to.

Pichardo thought everything was fine, the Consejo would bequeath to the new government a solvent treasury, the technical electoral problems could be solved—and he could hardly wait to get out of government.

Shlaudeman reported that Amiama and Imbert were maneuvering to form a party but so far had no candidate. Both Bosch's PRD and Fiallo's UCN claimed to be ahead. Shlaudeman thought they were about even, with the UCN probably having a slight edge. The decisive and unknown factor was the *campesino* vote.

Bosch's aide, Sacha Volman, had started a worker and *campesino* school. Miolán was organizing the PRD party workers. Bosch was traveling the country, talking to the *campesinos*. But he was short of money, Jeeps, and trucks.

Fiallo's UCN had more of all three, had outstanding civic leaders in most provincial capitals, was relying on them to deliver the *campesino* vote, was presenting Fiallo as "the father figure" (as Luís Manuel Baquero, Fiallo's campaign manager and a psychiatrist, put it), and had mapped out an expensive publicity campaign of newspaper ads, radio spot announcements, and so on.

Nobody knew whom the *campesinos* would vote for. I thought they cared little for politics, simply wanted jobs, enough to eat, a house, perhaps land, a way to care for their children. They wanted help—and had received little from either the Consejo or the United States. The next government had better move fast or be prepared to lose them quickly, perhaps to Castro. Civil government hardly existed in the provincial towns and hamlets; out there I always felt that this was hardly a nation at all, just a collection of people who happened to inhabit the same island and were trying to scratch out a living from it.

We were not sure of the Castro/Communists' plans. The 14th of June had announced it would abstain from the election. It said the election was illegal; we believed it did not want to reveal its weakness. The other three Castro/Communist parties were trying to form a common front with it. The stumbling block was Manolo Tavárez Justo. We heard the far left had rewritten Che Guevara's handbook on guerrilla fighting, substituting terror in the streets for fighting in the hills.

Everybody was nervous. Nasty reports came in from the provinces. Stones were thrown at Fiallo, his meetings were broken up, sporadic street fights were starting. Bosch accused the UCN of breaking up *his* meetings. The campaign would be bitter and might even be bloody. I made a quick trip to see our new consulate at Santiago, and the consul, Francis Withey, called Pancho, said business in Santiago was good but it was not expanding, everybody was waiting to see what would happen. Everybody was armed. Incendiaries were setting new forest fires in the hills. An aura of fear seemed to be settling in over the Republic. Fear of the unknown. Few people had really thought we would have an election. Now suddenly the election was only ten weeks away. Nobody knew what it might bring.

On October 3, Ambassador Freites, home "on consultation" from Washington, came to see me: President Bonnelly had passed through a crisis last weekend and had emerged badly shaken. The Armed Forces had called on the President. "I thought they were all going to shoot each other," Freites said. "I've never seen him so mad. He offered to resign."

This sounded serious—a confrontation between the President and his own military.

I went to see Bonnelly, found him discouraged, nervous, worried. When he was worried, his eyes had an almost hunted look. They had it now. Fiallo, he said, was stupid—had said in a radio speech that high officials of the Armed Forces would guarantee free elections. And Fiallo had been meeting with the military. So Bonnelly had called the military in, told them to stay out of politics, and told them the Consejo, not they, would guarantee elections. He had written out his resignation. The military had backed down, and issued a public statement taking themselves out of politics.

This seemed to me an example of Bonnelly's ability to hold the military in check—no small accomplishment. I told him so.

I also told him I thought we somehow had to get agreement among the major parties, particularly the UCN and PRD, that the loser would support the winner, that the winner would let the loser survive, and that the winner would guarantee the future of Amiama and Imbert. Both needed, and deserved, protection at the very least. Neither could leave the country—the Trujillos would surely have them killed. Bonnelly thought it a good idea but thought it hopeless and obviously would not attempt it himself. He said the UCN was split, and Bosch of the PRD was only a demagogue. Castro/Communist unions were making impossible demands on Haina. Bosch had encouraged *campesinos* to overrun the Spanish colony. The Social Christians had inspired a strike at *El Caribe*. The UCN had incited a strike at the big American sugar mill, La Romana. Troublemakers were everywhere, and only the Castro/Communists were benefiting. "And if we give them four hits in the head, they all jump on us. For the first time, I feel indecisive. And as the elections get closer the Armed Forces get more restless."

Never before had I heard Bonnelly talk this way. His indecision at this juncture might create a dangerous vacuum. I decided we ourselves must move. And this decision changed the course of events.

4

On October 3 I told the Crisis Crowd the steps I thought we should take. After the August election crisis, we had tried to bring the PRD, UCN, and Social Christians together in an arrangement to ensure some degree of party responsibility during the campaign and an orderly transfer of power. We had urged the Social Christians to act as a bridge between the PRD and UCN. I proposed now that we try to build on that foundation. We worked out what we wanted—agreement now among those parties, later among all who wished, that after the election the losers would support the winner, the winner would let the losers survive as parties and offer them posts in his Government, all parties would let the labor movement alone, the parties would now agree on what they would give Amiama and Imbert. Once this arrangement had been made, we would seek guarantees from the Armed Forces to support the winner.

Too ambitious? We began to explore the possibilities.

I saw Fiallo that afternoon. He was feeling good, his party was gaining, he felt confident of victory.

I asked Fiallo what he thought should be done about the central problem, Amiama and Imbert. My attachés had told me that Imbert and Amiama were increasingly nervous—they had discovered they had less support inside the Armed Forces than they'd thought.

Fiallo said Imbert wanted control of the Armed Forces. He had sent an emissary to Fiallo asking for it. Fiallo had sent back word: No; the most the UCN would do was promise to enact a law guaranteeing his safety and giving him a pension. Imbert had sent word he wanted to see Fiallo tonight. Fiallo would go. "He feels abandoned," Fiallo said; "I may make him a better offer, but not Secretary of State for Defense. He might become a dictator. I might talk about a Senatorship." I asked what he thought Imbert wanted. Power, Fiallo said. Not honor? Perhaps; they would make him a hero. What if all three parties, or even all parties, were to nominate him for Senator? Sure, Fiallo said—he, at least, would agree. What about a pension for all the Consejeros? Fiallo was not unwilling—perhaps all Consejeros should be given life pensions and all the prerogatives and protections of a former President, including the right to sit at the elected President's right hand. What if the election winner persecuted the losers? He must not, Fiallo said—that would be dictatorship. I asked if he thought the losers should agree to support the winner and the winner should give the losers places in his Cabinet—it would mitigate campaign bitterness. He liked the idea. So I took the plunge— said I was willing to undertake to arrange agreements along these lines at some appropriate time. He said he would cooperate fully. It was a hopeful start.

Next day I invited Guido d'Alessandro to the house, a leader of the Social Christians, Partido Revolucionario Social Cristiano (PRSC). After World War II Christian Democratic parties had come to prominence in Germany, Italy, and other Western European countries as an answer of progressive Catholicism to communism. Now they were emerging in Latin America. In Venezuela they were an important part of the coalition of President Rómulo Betancourt. In the Caribbean they had come to stand for the militant non-Communist democratic Christian left. And throughout Latin America they had stamped *Latino* on their politics and strongly opposed any suggestion of U.S. domination or intervention. In the Dominican Republic they were not always easy to work with. Their leaders were young and educated but some were ideologues, rigid in thought and violent in their proposals—during the campaign their party symbol was the machete and one of their slogans, "machete to the oligarchy." Their party was small but we wanted to encourage them, for almost alone they offered young people an alternative to Castro communism and they were committed to the *Alianza*'s revolutionary changes. Shlaudeman had been keeping in touch with Guido d'Alessandro; I had not.

D'Alessandro was a slender, earnest young man with haunted, almost pleading eyes. Once he had been on good terms with Ramfis Trujillo. His grandmother had been one of Trujillo's closest cronies. He had narrowly escaped arrest in the big roundup by the SIM of purported conspirators in January of 1960 in the wake of the Constanza landing; one of his brothers, less fortunate, had been arrested and killed in the electric chair at Kilometer 9.

When I met Guido d'Alessandro he had just been released from La Victoria prison; the previous Sunday, September 30, he had been involved in a confused political *turba* in La Vega, and a man had been killed. The charges against d'Alessandro, still pending, were complicity in involuntary manslaughter and using a gun, but could become murder. Imbert had arranged his release, called him in, and given him back his gun.

Now d'Alessandro told me he had been framed at La Vega. He and other Social Christians had gone there armed to hold a meeting, and, when a *turba* attacked them after the meeting, had started shooting and accidentally had hit a bystander. Since then, he said, he had been continually harassed—enemies tried to burn his house and car, and attacked him and his student friends. The police had done nothing. "So we are arming ourselves," he declared. "We do not care if it is against the law. We obey the law of God."

The police, he said, were putting on plain clothes and joining roving bands of thugs. Workers were arming themselves at La Romana, Haina, and elsewhere. La Victoria still contained four or five hundred SIM agents who had been there for months without charge; they were being indoctrinated by Communists. Communists, d'Alessandro said, had infiltrated the Planning Board, the Agrarian Reform Institute, the Air Force, the Civil Aviation authority. The Social Christians were trying to stay close to the Air Force. D'Alessandro feared that Castro/Communist disorders would give the Consejo a pretext to extend its own term or give the military a pretext to overthrow the Consejo. D'Alessandro said, "The key is Imbert"—if Imbert encouraged Castro/Communist disorders, they were inevitable, for Imbert controlled the police.

Yesterday an emissary had come to him from Amiama and Imbert, asking the Social Christians to make them an offer so they could support their party. "We'd like to help Imbert," d'Alessandro said, "to offer him a guarantee or something."

I encouraged the discussion—could UCN, PRD, and PRSC (Social Christians) agree on a common offer to Imbert and Amiama? The best d'Alessandro came up with was "an honorary post or Senator for lifetime as an ex-President," plus "security and money recognizing their heroism."

I explored the chance of a UCN-PRD-PRSC accord. It did not look promising. Bosch had denounced the Social Christians as "killers" after the incident at La Vega, d'Alessandro said, and the UCN was so split it could enter into no agreements.

When d'Alessandro left, I thought there was little chance of getting him into any constructive agreement with Fiallo and Bosch at this time.

I invited Germán Ornes, publisher of *El Caribe,* to lunch. I had first met him before Trujillo's death, exiled in Puerto Rico. After the assassination, Ornes had returned to the Republic and, supported by the Inter-American Press Association, had regained control of *El Caribe.* Ornes' constant fear was that somebody would take it away from him again. *El Caribe* was the best and most influential newspaper in the country. Its campaign coverage attempted impartiality, though it gave ridiculous prominence to Vanguardia, the vest-pocket party of Ornes' ambitious adventurer brother, Horacio Julio Ornes. Lately *El Caribe* had seemed to oppose the election.

Ornes, a big, shambling man, was disillusioned with both UCN and PRD. Pressed, he agreed on the need for elections. He understood the Imbert-Amiama problem but had no solution to offer. I said I was disturbed because lately he had been printing inaccurate pieces by two notorious Yankee baiters and several pieces on anti-Semitism and on the terrorist Puerto Rican independence movement. We reached a reasonable accord.

The next day our daughter Cindy was married in the Embassy garden to an engineer for the Shell Oil Company she had met in Santo Domingo, Anthony V. M. Campbell, and the Consejo, the diplomatic corps, the politicians, the military, and many others came. Dominicans are affectionate, and they responded that afternoon to the family scene in the Embassy garden—the bride's young brothers in the procession down the flagstone walk to the arch banked with palm boughs and white gladioli, the organ music played by Newell Williams, the soprano voice of an officer's wife, the absence, unheard-of in fashionable Dominican circles, of television cameras during the ceremony. After the ceremony, while guests sipped champagne and Cindy was cutting the cake and her husband proposing a toast and Fran and I talking to President Bonnelly, a photographer's flashbulb exploded loudly. Bonnelly's bodyguard, the faceless Miller, reached for his gun, and Imbert's eyes narrowed to slits.

5

Back to the wars—on Monday I was told that Horacio Julio Ornes was trying to put together a coalition of four or five parties around Imbert—his own Vanguardia, Social Christians, Ramón Castillo's party, the PN of "General" Virgilio Vilomar, and "General" Ramírez' party. Except for the Social Christians, they were all vest-pocket parties. ("General" Vilomar's PN, Partido Nacional, was a handful of old men left over from the Horacista party. "General" Vilomar, an old man whose military title was of obscure origin, had come to see me soon after I arrived, and when I asked him how big his party was, had drawn himself up and said, "My party, sir, is a colossus." I doubted the colossus could have polled a thousand votes, but I always treated him respectfully.)

What of Juan Bosch? His strength was growing. PRD now claimed 372,000 names on its rolls. This, if true, would probably mean he would poll at least 50 percent of the vote. But Bosch was worried about Amiama and Imbert and willing to discuss their future with the UCN and Social Christians. Some outsider, however, would have to take the initiative in bringing them together.

On October 10, I saw Bonnelly. He looked worried again. He was drafting Imbert's speech for tomorrow. He considered the Imbert-Amiama problem serious. Bonnelly would support my proposal to bring the PRD and UCN together but he simply had no faith in the UCN or the PRD. He had asked Imbert what he wanted. Imbert had said another party. Bonnelly thought it too late. What he really feared was an error in judgment by Amiama or Imbert. He was taking them on a trip to Samaná. He invited me to go along.

What was happening was perfectly clear. As elections drew near, Amiama and Imbert were determined either to arrange for their own protection after leaving power, or to keep power. The parties had offered them nothing worthwhile. And anyway, Amiama and Imbert did not trust the parties. So they were trying to put together a third-party coalition of their own, hoping, no doubt, to use gangs of thugs, leftists, and police to win or steal the election.

I could understand Imbert's and Amiama's motives. They, who had killed the tyrant, were unappreciated and unprotected. But their maneuvers endangered a free election.

We believed the Armed Forces supported a free election. But Imbert controlled the National Police. A showdown was not impossible—the Army Fortaleza, kitty-corner from the Embassy Residence, had mortars in place aimed at the Police headquarters across the street. The Army would no doubt win, but civil war would hardly help democratic elections. I did not think it would come to this. But it had before when the Dominican political system broke down. It was up to us to save the political system, since no one else seemed able to.

Amiama and Imbert should find it easy to put together their small-party coalition—they could use heavy pressure, such as the murder charge hanging over d'Alessandro's head, blackmail, bribery, threats of force, all their powers as Consejeros. And they were dealing with weak parties.

By contrast, it would be extremely difficult for us to bring the major parties together. It was difficult for the very reason that the parties were strong—both UCN and PRD thought they could win alone. The Social Christians could no longer make a bridge between them. Bosch was going around the country accusing the UCN-Consejo axis of "terrorizing" his local leaders. In reply, the UCN was renewing old charges that Bosch had worked with Ramfis Trujillo and Balaguer.

It was in this atmosphere that we made our cruise to Samaná. It was a strange trip, and a major turning point in our work and in the Republic's progress—if that is the word—toward representative democracy.

6

The day we left the capital, Thursday, October 11, the news was bad. The municipal employees in Santo Domingo announced a strike. A report came in from Puerto Plata: Fiallo's meeting there had been stoned, and his photographer, a talented, promising young man, had been shot dead.

We watched Tony Imbert speak on TV. Flanked by Bonnelly and Amiama, looking solemn, he read his speech, seeming nervous and hurried, his voice curiously high and strained. He announced that the Electoral Law had been promulgated. The Consejo had given him the task of expressing to the people the firmness and disinterested convictions of the Consejeros about the election. He had accepted because, "modesty aside, I believe I possess credentials more impressive than words." He distributed credit generously among all who had opposed Trujillo, praising especially the clandestine 14th of June, the Catholic Church, and his own companions, especially the Nigua martyrs. Now, he said, the people wanted liberty and work. But the Consejo was deeply concerned by "the agitation which at times has put in danger public order." He denounced "professional agitators" who obeyed narrow party interests or "demagogic directives outlined from Communist centers of the hemisphere."

Imbert said, "I feel obliged to express emphatically that I did not participate in the dangerous, decisive, and patriotic event of the 30th of May that annihilated an opprobrious tyranny in order to perpetuate its dangerous derivatives." The Trujillo dictatorship had brought hunger and misery to the people. But the people ought to understand that overnight transformation was impossible. Under the Consejo, he claimed, the Dominican people had enjoyed "the most liberties, the most democracy, the best wages, the greatest capacity of consumption, and one of the highest indices of social assistance" in their history. The Consejo had confronted serious adversity and had endured patiently "the most unjust and absurd criticisms." Only fools persisted in criticizing it. Now "we have arrived at a crucial crossroads." The only road to liberty, democracy, and social justice required putting a stop to agitation, ensuring order, and holding elections.

"I assert with firmness that the Consejo de Estado . . . will take all measures that may be necessary to guarantee that the general elections of the 20th of December will not only be carried out cleanly but also that the result of them will be a genuine expression of the popular will. If to attain that noble end the Consejo de Estado has to act with strong hands, it will do it without vacillation. For it will not be sparing of its measures and it will make use of all the resources that the governmental machinery puts at its disposal."

Fran, Fandino, and I and our two boys drove to President Bonnelly's house. Mrs. Bonnelly, a sweet, motherly woman, greeted us and Bonnelly arrived soon. And we waited, waited an hour and a half for Imbert to arrive.

We then started out in seven cars, a motorcade led by two motorcycle outriders. I rode with Bonnelly and Imbert, a machine gunner in front beside the driver. A gun car followed us. The women rode in another car, also with an armed escort car. Our Checker carried the baggage, and two other gun cars were spread among us. We whirled east through the city, passed the airport, and hit the gravel and the narrow blacktop beyond, eighty miles an hour, two motorcycle outriders a bare car-length in front of us scattering cows and burros. It had been raining all evening, the night was black, the road narrow, twisting up through Hato Mayor toward Sabana de la Mar. Around a sharp bend on a hill we stopped short: Cars and a dozen men with guns were waiting, a roadblock, it appeared. But it turned out to be the military high command, waiting. They fell in behind us.

Bonnelly, Imbert, and I talked hardly at all. I complimented Imbert on his speech. He only nodded. He seemed restless. Now and then he picked up the radio-telephone and called people in the capital. Bonnelly, settled in a corner, said almost nothing.

In Sabana de la Mar, we drew up at the rotting wharf, and from a bayside saloon a crowd came out, yelling, "Viva Bonnelly" and "Viva UCN," confusing the government with the party. While Imbert and the gunmen hung back, Bonnelly walked up the muddy street, surrounded by the crowd, to the local club, and the people crowded in, cheering and pushing and yelling. Bonnelly climbed onto the bandstand, the trumpet played a flourish, and Bonnelly made a short speech, praising the beautiful ladies of the town, the people's friendly and civic spirit, and adverting to the democratic process. Everybody cheered, and the band blared a *merengue,* everybody began to dance, Bonnelly danced one dance with a pretty girl, then we all walked back down to the rotting dock through the dark in the mud. He remarked to me that the dock reminded him of the Consejo—about to topple, but not quite falling.

The coastal patrol boat took us across Samaná Bay and there, anchored in front of Samaná, the *Angelita* loomed up, long and white and graceful, with swooping bow and lights on masts sky-high. With white-uniformed officers standing at attention, we went up the gently swaying gangplank and into the main saloon. It was crowded—President Bonnelly, Imbert, General Luna, Commodore Rib, Attorney General García Vásquez, the President's daughter and son-in-law, a friend, and most of their wives. It must have been near 2 A.M., but we all sat at a long massive carved table, Trujillo's table, and were served drinks, *sancocho,* salad, soup, dessert. The glasses were five-starred and initialed RLT.

At last the President and his wife led Fran and me downstairs to a bedroom across the corridor from theirs. Ours was a large bedroom richly carpeted, a canopied bed, an electric fireplace. The huge bathroom had gold faucets and an Oriental rug and a toilet which leaked all over the rug.

In the morning we were wakened by shooting. On deck, Imbert and the military men were shooting at bottles, tin cans, and debris in the water, using .45s, submachine guns, and machine pistols, while President Bonnelly watched and officers reloaded the guns. Tony Imbert would run a clip out, hand the empty gun to someone behind him without taking his gaze off the target, then receive the reloaded gun and fire again. He was a crack shot. With a .45, he could hit the neck of a whiskey bottle bobbing on the water as far as you could throw the bottle.

Donny Reid and Ambassador Freites had arrived by helicopter from Washington. During the day Colonel Cass, our AID officials Newell Williams and Norm Ward, and their wives joined us, as well as several Dominicans. It was a glorious day, bright hot sun, shimmering bay, and the pink and blue town of Samaná clinging to the cliffside. Around the *Angelita,* with her gold eagle on the bowsprit, skipped little boats, clumsy sailboats and rowboats from town, and a fast motorboat General Luna owned, said to have belonged to one of Trujillo's sons. A fishing boat tied up alongside and barefoot fishermen tugged aboard two mammoth turtles—giant animals weighing perhaps a hundred pounds each— and all the rest of the day they lay, alive, on their backs in the hot sun on deck, helpless against the teasing prodding of every passing cabin boy.

Luna and others went off in a small boat fishing. Bonnelly and I and several others—Newell Williams, Norm Ward, Manuel de Jesús Viñas Cáceres of the Agrarian Reform Institute—got into a small local wooden boat and chugged up the muddy Río Yuma. The Consejo and AID were considering a project to change its channel, drain its swamps, and reclaim the land.

It was hot and still on the river. Once we stopped at a shack on shore, and two *campesinos* who lived there scurried to bring Bonnelly a chair so he could sit in the shade beneath a palm, then climbed the palms to knock down coconuts. They owned no land here. The owner lived far away. They harvested the coconuts and took them out by boat. They could earn between fifty and a hundred dollars in a good year. Every year the river flooded and washed away all the houses. As we talked, other boats passed up and down—the river was the only highway here.

Bonnelly, Williams, and I thought the swamp project worthwhile but too big to undertake now. We went back to the *Angelita* and had lunch and a short nap. The President was called to the telephone. It was Amiama, in the capital. He said that the municipal workers of Santo

Domingo were going on strike today or tomorrow but Bonnelly should not worry, he and General Viñas would control the situation. Amiama would speak to the people on national radio and television tonight.

In the Coast Guard boat Bonnelly and I went to Sabana de la Mar to the U.S. missile tracking station. We were giving it to the Dominicans. Since it had sleeping and eating facilities and well-equipped shops, I suggested they convert it into a vocational school. The President agreed.

Once again, however, he seemed preoccupied. As we went back aboard the Coast Guard boat, dark rainclouds were lowering over the Bay. The boat pulled out and headed across the Bay. He said nothing. Darkness swiftly fell, the lights came on dimly far across the Bay, and fog crept in. I began to understand what was going on. The night before, Imbert had spoken to the nation about maintaining order. Now a relatively minor strike had occurred—and Amiama would speak to the nation. They were, quite simply, usurping the Presidency.

Or was I wrong? To find out, I asked the President when the decision had been taken to have Amiama speak. He said, without looking at me, "He told me this afternoon."

So there it was. Imbert and Amiama were running the country. I realized it fully for the first time, and I think Bonnelly did too.

Last spring, maintaining tranquillity among the discordant Consejeros, Bonnelly had kept hold of all the levers of power. But he could do so no longer—his term was nearing its end, his passive detachment had let power slip away from his fingers.

Imbert and Amiama already controlled the machinery of criminal justice—police, secret police, immigration, and Attorney General. They were maneuvering to get hold of the Army—ballooning a petty strike into a national crisis. They were putting themselves forward publicly as the guarantors of elections and law and order, the strong men in the Consejo. The strikes, the shooting of Fiallo's photographer, the shooting at La Vega—everything was playing into their hands. And they were maneuvering to form a third-force political coalition to win the election. They were far ahead of us and the President, and now we both knew it.

It even occurred to me that they might intend this weekend trip to show that their political coalition had the blessing of the United States government—I was here, and Freites and Reid had joined us direct from Washington. And sure enough, when I returned to the capital, I found this rumor spreading.

It began to rain as we reached the *Angelita;* in another moment, the downpour came. We hurried into the saloon. The phone rang. It was Amiama, Fernández Caminero was with him, he had spoken with Tábare Álvarez, Secretary of State for Interior and Police, and the situation was in hand. Imbert, toying with a spoon, watched and looked pleased.

Bonnelly sighed. He had to go to Samaná that night, the townsfolk insisted. He looked exhausted as well as depressed. He changed his clothes, and went off with a few others. But not Imbert. Imbert stayed aboard, and talked to Amiama by telephone almost constantly. Amiama, in the capital, was giving orders. He told one government official to join us at Samaná at 6 A.M. He made no apologies for inconveniencing him. He was a hard man who simply did not care. Amiama never went on these trips. He knew they were only window dressing.

In the morning some of the young people aboard started a big *merengue*—they brought the ship's band onto the afterdeck and danced and drank while it loudly played, eating lunch at 4 P.M. But underneath the gaiety a darker stream was running. Men were going off together in pairs and talking quietly, were watching others pairing off. The phone kept ringing; it was always for Imbert. Sometimes he would tell the President who had called, sometimes not.

I talked privately to Donny Reid. He said Attorney General García Vásquez was making trouble over d'Alessandro, whose gun was not even fired at La Vega. The stupid political parties were playing into the hands of Amiama and Imbert. Reid saw no hope.

Freites took me aside and asked how things were going. Not very well, I said. I was usually cheerful around Freites. He was close to Imbert and Amiama. He said Washington thought everything was all right. I said nothing. He asked what was wrong. I said I was concerned about the rising political tensions—Dominicans were shooting each other for the first time—and I thought the role of Amiama and Imbert not clear. Freites said the President should call a meeting to discuss it, he would go to work on it and, puffing thoughtfully on a cigar, walked away.

In the evening I took Fran for a walk around the deck, and told her I was worried. I told Fandino to talk to the Attorney General. I decided to have a talk myself with Imbert.

The President retired to the lounge with his daughter, son-in-law, and Fran. The ship got busy with sailors weighing anchor, and soon we were moving. Nearly everybody went to bed. I suggested to Imbert that we go up on the bridge.

We made our way forward through passageways and up ladders, in pitch dark finally reaching the bridge. We stood in the open in front of the pilothouse, leaning on a rail, looking ahead at the black sea and white combers split by the ship's bow, the ship rolling ever so gently, the high headland of Samaná Peninsula rising high on the left.

As usual, I asked Imbert how things were going. Fine, he said, everything was all right. The strikes were settled, then? Not yet, but they would be. "We are determined, Mr. Martin," he said. "We will have peace, we will have order, we will have elections." I asked who he thought would

win—UCN, PRD, who? He sneered. "Those little parties, they don'
mean nosing. Nosing," and he spat. "You cannot trust them, Mr. Martin.
You know I told you that." I said I knew, but they were all we had. He
grunted, and we stood awhile, the ship heaving a little more now as it
neared the open sea. I asked why Luís—Amiama—hadn't come with us.
Imbert laughed. "Luís never come. He gets seasick. Besides, we need
him in the capital just now." I said I had noticed he and Amiama never
left the capital at the same time. It was true, he said; they were brothers.
I asked him to tell me how they had killed Trujillo and, standing in the
dark on the bridge, he did.

He said, "We were four months making plans. One month before we
got the guns. I had a .45 and an M-1 machine pistol. Antonio de la
Maza had a 12-gauge sawed-off shotgun. Every night four of us went out
there. We were waiting for one night he would go to the farm."

Imbert went on, "That night, May 30, we were at Estrella's house.
García Guerrero, one of Trujillo's bodyguards, got word to us that he
was going to the farm." Some versions say that Imbert was in the Number
Three car with one other man, parked up ahead as a roadblock. Imbert
said he had been driving the Number Two car, with Antonio de la Maza
beside him. He said, "We were parked by the Fairgrounds when we got
the word. He came along, and we followed him. We were not going fast,
about sixty kilometers. I was driving. We passed him, and De la Maza
shot his shotgun. I said, 'You missed him—shoot again,' and he shot
again, the second barrel, but missed again." (Most versions say De la
Maza's first shot probably was fatal, though not immediately.) "I passed
him, turned around, and faced him with our headlights, and he stopped
and got out. We got out. We were about thirty meters apart, we were
flat on the ground, and we fought about four minutes. Ten or twenty
cars passed while it was going on. Trujillo was hiding behind his car, not
shooting. De la Maza went up along his car and got behind it and shot him
with the shotgun. He sat down. I came up with my .45 and shot him. He
did not shoot back. I found his gun on the back seat. I said, 'Put the body
in my car.' They did. The other two cars were up ahead. It was all
over when they got there. We went to Juan Tomás' house"—Juan
Tomás Díaz.

Amiama was there. "Juan Tomás and General Román and the
others"—this included Amiama, though Imbert did not say so—"they
didn't do nosing. Nosing at all," bitterly. "We did our first part. Correctly.
They didn't do nosing. It was a shame. Luís said he looked all over for
Román and can't find him. Román and Juan Tomás did not know that
this was the night. Nobody had told them. We were all supposed to go
to the Palace and call the rest in and seize the government."

Imbert went on, "I was shot in the shoulder and hand and I was all
scratched and bloody. I went to a doctor at 1 A.M. and stayed there till

four. My wife came. I wanted to go see what was happening. They wouldn't let me. Later I went into hiding," and he told me where.

I asked Imbert how he had happened to get mixed up in the plot. "I had no personal reason to kill him," he insisted. "I had no personal reason. I just did it because somebody had to do it. For my country, Mr. Martin. For my country." I was skeptical but said nothing. Imbert went on, "He was shrewd. He was mean, very mean," shaking his head. "I don't see how he lasted so long, Mr. Martin. He didn't think he needed anybody. He didn't care nosing for nobody." Then, "My wife and little boy were in jail two months. Finally the United States and the OAS helped get them to Puerto Rico and helped them there. Luís' family, too." He shook his head. "It was all too bad."

Sometimes alone with Tony I could gently swing him to my side. I tried now. I said it certainly was all too bad. And it would be even worse if now, after all the blood and bravery, Dominican freedom were to be lost. He agreed—the Communists must be stopped. I said I was concerned not only about the Communists. He knew what I meant. He paused.

Then he went on talking about the Communists, declaring that Castro was the danger; Castro must be killed; Che Guevara, an Argentine, never could run Cuba.

I tried to draw him back, taking another tack. What the Republic needed now was a freely elected President, its first since 1924, a new chance at democracy, a President elected without pressure. He agreed, of course. I said that many people made the mistake Trujillo had made— thinking they needed no one, caring nothing for anybody, seizing absolute power only to find that absolute power, in the end, brought their own downfall. He agreed calmly but said, "These little parties, Mr. Martin, they are no good, you cannot trust them, the United States cannot trust them. You must have somebody you can trust, really trust."

I said we had to trust the people.

He looked away, toward the dark shape of the Samaná headland, now slipping behind us. We plunged into the open sea. He said, "Not one single party is supporting us against the strike. They are for themselves, not for nothing else."

I said I'd heard that Bosch had approached him. He said it was true but he had not replied and did not intend to. "They are all alike, you cannot trust them."

We fell silent, gazing at the sea heaving dark and vast beyond the whitecaps in the running lights. The wind blew strong in our faces then, as the ship turned southward, slackened. I felt we both were waiting, each waiting for the other to speak. I decided not to. It was too soon; right now he was set too tight. The best I could do now was not let him know precisely where we stood. We waited a long time. Finally Tony turned toward me, said, "You want to go to bed, Mr. Martin?" I said I guessed so and we slowly left; both, I think, a little reluctant.

Everything was going their way. I wondered whether the President, seeing the inevitable, might not throw in with them. With elections nine weeks away, the storm was gathering, and soon would break upon us.

7

When I wakened Sunday morning we were anchored off Saona Island. We breakfasted on deck almost alone. The others had gone swimming or fishing or boating. Fran and Fandino and I watched them, their boats racing through the water in the bright sun. The scene was gorgeous—deep green sea, island of palms and golden curving beaches, birds circling low over the water, on the beach men and women moving among boats and visitors, puffy white clouds sailing overhead against the deep blue sky. It was spectacularly beautiful; but Trujillo had kept political prisoners on this island. Now the men who had killed him to give their people freedom were about to kill freedom. So doing, they might destroy themselves. Like Trujillo, they carried the seeds of their own destruction. And perhaps the destruction of the nation they had rescued. Last night, standing with Imbert watching the bowsprit of the beautiful *Angelita* lifting and plunging over the dark night sea, I had thought of Moby Dick, of Captain Ahab's pursuit of the great beast, evil, around the oceans of the world. Viewing on deck this morning the Caribbean isle over the green shimmering sea, I could not shake last night's dark vision, and the sun and beach and palms and sky sharpened it; Trujillo's bloody tyranny, his assassins' mixed purpose, and the evil and good in all men.

8

In the hard midday light the others came back for lunch, first drinking, and dancing the *merengue,* then sitting and talking; lunch was gay, filled with chatter. They made jokes about the politicians. They mentioned Fiallo often, Bosch almost never. Their tone was one of derision and contempt.

All watched Imbert, walking about, short and stocky, a scar beside his left eye, his eyes flat and cold, wearing a tight T-shirt and military-style khakis, .45 on hip. When he spoke, the others paid heed; when he moved, they watched. President Bonnelly seemed alone, subdued, depressed. He was rapidly being reduced to an honorific position—President Emeritus of a sinking government.

We spent all Sunday anchored off Saona, and in the afternoon I took Dan and Fred fishing for barracuda. At 6:30 P.M. the President called a meeting, at Freites' suggestion, and we all sat down at the long dining table, Bonnelly at the head, Freites and the Consejeros and Cabinet ministers and I, a foreigner, ranged down the table.

Bonnelly said he had wanted to let us have his thoughts on the new political situation which was developing. He said that strikes were occurring, more could be expected, and the political parties would do nothing helpful. That was all—an incredibly vacuous performance, I thought, by a Chief of State. He then invited the views of others.

Reid said, "I agree with the President."

Imbert said, "I agree with the President."

Freites said, "I agree with the President."

And so on, all saying the same, until they came to me. I said I was rather hesitant to speak, Bonnelly invited me to, and I said two questions troubled me: Why did the full power and majesty of the national government have to be thrown against a strike of some zookeepers and garbage collectors? And why wasn't the present labor law being enforced to prosecute illegal strikes?

Nobody replied directly, though all agreed the strikes were illegal under Dominican law.

The conversation turned to the election campaign, and someone said of course the losers would claim fraud.

I took this opportunity to say I thought it desirable that all the parties agree in advance on three points—that the losers would support the winner, that—

But at this point all broke out in loud laughter—it was absurd to think the parties would make such agreement.

I said I was not so sure, and went on with the other two points.

More laughter; it was not worth talking about.

I said doggedly that a similar agreement had been made once before, in 1924, when the candidates were patriotic men, and we should not assume the candidates of today were not patriotic until they had proved otherwise.

President Bonnelly thought it would be nice but was impossible.

Imbert said, "What good would that do us?" He seemed to mean the Consejo but he really meant himself and Amiama. I said such an agreement might cause the parties to stop creating the difficulties the President had described and might work toward an accord that would take into account everybody's future, including Imbert's.

Imbert grunted, a silence ensued, and the others changed the subject. Presently Imbert, bored, simply got up and left.

We steamed back past the capital and on to the harbor at Haina, arriving about 11 P.M., and were met by virtually the entire government and military, led by Luís Amiama Tió.

Chapter Ten

TO THE SUMMIT

Monday we set to work. It was late—October 15. The presidential election was scheduled for December 20.

The city workers' strike was broken. Haina was standing firm—offering not a cent. But other strikes were spreading—at San Pedro de Macorís, at La Romana, at Cabo Rojo. Sabotage was reported in the Vicini sugar mills. *El Caribe*'s workers' demands were exorbitant. A pattern was emerging—the regular trade union leadership had lost control, the leftist extremists were moving in, the PRD and Social Christians and probably other parties were busy too.

Colonel Cass said Imbert was planning to transfer several colonels; the military high command feared him; young Army and Navy officers had been meeting nights, trying to rally others against him, to no avail. Imbert was ready to move against General Rivera Cuesta, the Army Commander. The attachés feared the high command would not stand up to Imbert. The military was not sure where we stood. I sent the attachés to tell them.

Shlaudeman had visited Imbert in his office and seen him shuffling stacks of telegrams and stacks of money, handing out jobs, ordering people arrested, firing policemen, hiring others. Running the country, I thought.

Imbert had several options open—to put together a coalition of small parties, to support Juan Isidro Jimenes Grullón, to wait till after election and demand power, to attempt a *golpe* either before or after elections, to create terror and derail the election.

Our options were fewer—to support Imbert, to threaten him, or try to bring the UCN, PRD, and Social Christians together in common front against him.

The Venezuelan Ambassador, Alejandro Izaguirre, came to see me. He thought a *golpe* imminent. He wanted to stop Imbert. The trip on the

Angelita was causing trouble: People thought I was behind Imbert. If something were not done quickly all the democratic governments in the Caribbean, including his own, Betancourt's, would be in grave danger. He said, "I am at your disposition. Let me do your dirty work."

I decided the time had come to make our move.

I told all my people to spread the word that we favored free and open elections, that we did not support the Imbert maneuver, that aboard the *Angelita* I had been the guest of the President and the trip had no other significance.

Early on Wednesday Ramón Castillo came to see me, bringing with him a big man I never had met—"my cousin, Mr. Brouwer." Imbert and Amiama had sent them to me as their emissaries.

Castillo said several politicians felt they were being shut out of the elections and so intended to wreck them—Horacio Julio Ornes of Van-guardia, "General" Ramírez, and "General" Vilomar, the proprietor of the colossus. He described a complicated series of meetings with Luís Amiama Tió. It was leading to an Amiama-Imbert small-party coalition. Soon a hundred "political independents" would call for the candidacy of Imbert. General Rivera Cuesta, Army commander in chief, favored the coalition. Amiama and Imbert now wanted to know what our view was; and Castillo stopped, an eager little man wanting to be liked, sitting on the edge of his chair, waiting.

I said, "I think I should make our position very clear. We support the Consejo as a transitional government, and we mean it: The Consejo is going to finish out its term. We support free elections for everybody, and free of force or the threat of force. Whoever wins, we support the orderly transfer of power to him on February 27. Now then, in my own judgment, and that of others, the political situation has developed to a point where only the UCN or PRD has a chance to win. It is too late for a new coalition. No new coalition could win without force. And we are against force. We are not supporting Amiama and Imbert."

Castillo looked somewhat crestfallen but pressed his case—the UCN lacked the common touch, the Army feared "the Communist danger" in Bosch's PRD, and General Rivera Cuesta and other Army officers seemed to favor the return of former President Joaquín Balaguer. Rivera Cuesta's wife, I knew, was strongly pro-Balaguer.

I said this was all very interesting, but I thought the last thing we needed now was Balaguer, the tool of Trujillo. I told him, "Have faith in the people. I understand why everybody is looking for a third party—these are the first free elections in thirty-eight years. Everybody is afraid. But they should have faith in the people and in the elections."

They left. I knew they would go straight to Imbert. This was the last sparring match.

2

Wednesday night I called the Crisis Crowd to the Residence. We had to move fast. We would try to bring Bosch and Fiallo together at a "summit" meeting tomorrow night. If that succeeded, I would then talk to President Bonnelly and to Amiama and Imbert.

We saw Castillo and pulled him out of Imbert's coalition. Castillo said he could pull Vilomar out too. The attachés set out to see the military, particularly Rivera Cuesta. For the present, we would omit the Social Christians—it was too complicated, and Bosch opposed them vigorously. Shlaudeman would try to bring Juan Bosch to the summit. I would try to get Fiallo.

Fiallo came to the Residence in the morning. I described the situation as we saw it and asked if he would meet with Bosch and me that night and make a four-point agreement: The loser would publicly support the winner, the winner would permit the loser to operate politically, the winner would offer the loser's party seats in his Cabinet, and the loser would conduct a constructive opposition. I also proposed that they make an offer to Imbert and Amiama.

Fiallo hesitated. His brow furrowed, he said the PRD had no men of Cabinet caliber; Bosch was untrustworthy; and as for Imbert and Amiama, President Bonnelly had told him they were of secondary importance. Fiallo was, as often, out of touch. I pressed him, emphasizing that Imbert and Amiama were on the move, and unless he exerted patriotic leadership now, putting country above party, the Republic might lose this last chance for a free and democratic election. He agreed: He would meet with us tonight at 9 P.M.

Ambassador Freites came to see me urgently. He brought alarming reports about Communist activities, said that all Communists must be deported, that Bonnelly was weakening, and that the only men who could save the situation were Amiama and Imbert. This seemed to me a transparent fraud. Imbert or Amiama, having received a report from Castillo and Brouwer, had now sent Freites to pressure me. I told him I had always thought the Consejo should act firmly against the Castro/ Communists and I saw no reason why the Consejo, using its ordinary police powers, could not do the job without unusual efforts by Imbert and Amiama. Freites left.

Ambassador Izaguirre of Venezuela came to see me. We had only a few minutes. I asked if he could hold the "summit" meeting at his home tonight—neither Bosch nor Fiallo would go to the other's home and my Residence was too exposed. He agreed at once. He would give a cocktail party at 9 P.M. The guests would be Fiallo, Bosch, and the aides of each, Shlaudeman, Fandino, and me. We worked out a brief scenario.

Fandino called Fiallo to notify him of the time. He would be there. Shlaudeman came in; Bosch would be there. Shlaudeman had found him in a little house near the airport, wearing swimming trunks and a robe. Shlaudeman had told him of our position on elections. He had listened very intently, then sat silent a moment, then said, "So at last there will be elections. And to think I should receive this great news in my bare feet."

Bosch had said now he saw things clearly. Now there would really be elections. He never had believed it before. Now he even believed there would be no *golpe*—we would not permit one.

He had gone on, more thoughtfully. Now he must convince Amiama and Imbert that the PRD would not abandon them. Of course, they would not believe it. He was grateful for our intervention. This was not odious intervention, Bosch said. "There comes a time when your interests are at stake, and ours too, and they coincide. I had misunderstood. This is a great day for the country. And for the party." Of course there must be no leak before the PRD convention—his whole posture was one of intransigent opposition to the UCN, and it must not become known he had sat down to treat with Fiallo.

We planned further moves. We must close off Juan Isidro Jimenes Grullón, deny him to Amiama and Imbert. I would undertake it, but it could wait till Sunday. If we got through tonight successfully, tomorrow I would talk to President Bonnelly and the Consejeros. Shlaudeman and others would talk to the minor parties; the attachés would talk to the military.

After dinner Shlaudeman and Fandino came to the house, and we went to Ambassador Izaguirre's home at 9 P.M. Bosch, accompanied by Miolán, arrived about a half hour before Fiallo came in with four aides. Izaguirre himself served drinks, having dismissed his servants for the evening, and we tried to chat. It was, after all, billed as a *"coctel,"* a cocktail party, offered by the Ambassador; but everybody knew what we were there for, no women were present, the talk was strained, the laughter loud and nervous, and after twenty minutes, Izaguirre, as planned, suggested to Bosch, Fiallo, and me that we go in another room "for a talk," and, with Fandino, we went to the dining room. Bosch's gaze swiftly surveyed the windows and doors.

The house was Spanish style, tile-floored, low white ceilings, louvered wooden slats for windows, heavy furniture. Izaguirre sat at the head of the table. Fandino and I sat on one side of the table; Bosch and Fiallo sat side by side on the other, facing us, a little distance apart. Izaguirre, a rather short, swarthy man with a bristly mustache, youngish, bright-eyed, spoke briefly, saying he was honored by the presence of his distinguished guests; he appreciated fully the delicacy of the situation, but had decided the extraordinary times demanded extraordinary measures; and he deemed it an honor, as the representative of another great Caribbean power, Venezuela, to assist the great Dominican nation through its own crisis. He nodded to me.

I said that in my judgment the next President of the Dominican Republic was in this room tonight. The future of Dominican democracy was in their hands. My Venezuelan colleague and I were not here to intervene but to succor democracy, now under attack around the world. Defending democracy was the responsibility of all. We all knew that campaigns for high office were hard fought, even fiercely fought. I recalled that 1952 was a bitter year in the United States, the year of McCarthy and the Korean war. I described election night in the Governor's mansion in Springfield, Illinois, when Adlai Stevenson, having lost, went alone to his study and wrote out a concession speech; and I read part of it to them:

"The people have rendered their verdict and I gladly accept it. . . .

"That which unites us as American citizens is far greater than that which divides us as political parties.

"I urge you all to give General Eisenhower the support he will need to carry out the great tasks that lie before him.

"I pledge him mine."

I said, "In my opinion, those words exemplify the sense of responsibility that a great statesman exhibits in his hour of defeat. I am confident that you gentlemen represent the same great tradition of statesmanship. What the Republic will need on December 21 will be not a good winner but several good losers, especially one, one of you gentlemen. We, the United States—and I am sure my Venezuelan colleague joins me in this—support free elections. By that we mean free of force or the threat of force, free of pressure or coercion. We intend to exert our influence to see that such elections are held. We intend to see that the winner is able to take office. We intend to use our influence to see that his government is not dominated by the military or by the police, or by elements controlling them. Tonight, I hope you gentlemen can take an all-important first step in this process," and I passed out copies, in English and Spanish, of a four-point agreement Shlaudeman and I had drafted.

It read:

1. The loser in the forthcoming election will, as soon as the election result is known, publicly congratulate the winner, publicly recognize him as the President of all the Dominican people, and publicly call upon his own supporters to so recognize him.

2. During his tenure, the winner will not suppress or persecute the opposition party or its leader and will permit it to continue to operate as a political entity.

3. Before taking office, the winner will offer Cabinet seats to members of the loser's party. (They may decline.)

4. After the winner takes office, the loser and his party will perform as a "loyal opposition" in a constructive manner:

   a. They will not oppose, within the legislature or public opinion, merely for the sake of opposing.

   b. On main issues where the national interest is clearly involved, especially in matters of international character, the government will consult the opposition, though it will not be bound by the opposition's views.[1]

They read it in utter silence. I could hear only the voices from the living room at the *coctel*. They finished, and I said, "What do you think?"

Bosch lifted one hand, raised his eyebrows, turned down his mouth, and said, "Any believer in democracy would accept that."

Fiallo said, "I think one, two, and four are all right. But on number three, I've said that if the PRD has capable men, I would use them, but I can't promise myself to that, because at the moment either of us is elected, we are no longer party leaders, we are the President of all the Dominican people, and I would think of the best people, not of the parties."

Bosch, treating Fiallo with elaborate courtesy, said, "I must diverge from that. I can say that the PRD has always had the unspoken intention to offer to the UCN, and the other parties as well, positions in the Cabinet, this offer to be made to the parties, not to individuals."

Ambassador Izaguirre agreed. "From our experience in Venezuela, party discipline is needed. Patronage is important."

They discussed it further, Bosch always deferring to Fiallo, as though Fiallo were years older. They were fascinating to watch—Fiallo, slowly laboring over the draft, marking changes, crossing them out, absorbed in his work, almost oblivious of us; Bosch thinking fast, acting intuitively, quickly agreeing, at pains to disagree with Fiallo only reluctantly and with elaborate courtesy, and always watching the effect he was having on Izaguirre and me.

In a short time Fiallo and Bosch reached agreement on an amended text, leaving the basic points intact, particularly the one I then thought the most important, the first; only once in Dominican history, in 1924 during Summer Welles' time, had the loser of a Dominican presidential election publicly congratulated the winner and pledged his support and that of his followers. Tonight Bosch and Fiallo agreed to do so.

They finished at 10:55 P.M., and we all made short speeches of gratification. Then I suggested we take up the question of Amiama and Imbert.

Fiallo said the UCN was prepared to offer them bodyguards, pensions, and all the honors due ex-Presidents for life. Bosch said it wasn't enough and advanced his own proposal—that both parties agree to

---

[1] Since only Bosch and Fiallo were present tonight, "loser" was singular. Later, if other parties wished to join, it would, of course, be made plural.

make Amiama and Imbert Secretaries of State without Portfolio, with salaries and bodyguards for life, plus pensions for their wives and university educations for their children.

Fiallo agreed to everything but taking them into the Cabinet without portfolio.

I said I doubted they would accept. I asked if both parties would nominate them for the Senate.

Fiallo would not. Bosch said those two votes in the Senate could be crucial. Izaguirre told him it was the least of the risks he ran. He didn't think they'd accept, so why not offer anyway?

Bosch said coldly, "We want this to come to crisis."

With some difficulty, I kept still.

Izaguirre didn't: "We diplomats are up to here with the ingenuity of you two. The situation is desperate, but you offer no solutions. The 30th of May did not cleanse the country. Amiama and Imbert must be removed. You can't govern with them behind you."

Fiallo said, "If a crisis comes, let it be now."

They talked more, and got nowhere. I said, "It appears you," nodding to Fiallo and Bosch, "cannot reach agreement on this problem tonight. I suggest you both think it over, then let me know by tomorrow. If you come up with a good offer, I will undertake to transmit it to them and persuade them to accept it. These men will not just go away. You have to make a deal of some kind with them. This is just about your last chance."

Bosch and Fiallo agreed to give me their proposals by 5 P.M. tomorrow. We went out into the living room. The men there had long since given up the pretense that they were at a cocktail party. It was past midnight. We all shook hands and left.

I saw Donny Reid early the next morning, Friday, and told him what had happened. He was delighted. "You have done a great thing for this country," he said. "Some day people will know."

Shlaudeman came in. He had been to the Palace. "Imbert is imposing order, period." The struck sugar mills were back at work. Imbert had a list of from twelve to twenty leftists he intended to deport, and he wanted no difficulty from us on visas. He had fired Bonilla Aybar, editor of *La Nación*. Monseñor Pérez Sánchez had come in shouting, "There's a *turba* outside." Tony had laughed and said, "Remember I told you the way to handle them was to give them a few *palos* [blows]. What do you think now?" Two Cabinet ministers had come in, and Imbert had told them to bring their sub-secretaries, he had news for them. Betimes, he had spoken eloquently to Shlaudeman for forty-five minutes—no party could govern alone, Fiallo was well-meaning but surrounded by crooks, Bosch was a devil surrounded by angels, we should bring everybody together in one room, pick a man, and "take him to the Presidency." Democracy would never work. What would happen in the Armed Forces when he and Amiama left the Palace? Nobody was taking into account a powerful force in the Republic—the Trujillistas. Dominicans were all cowards. Nobody went to the streets after he killed Trujillo. They would not stand up now. He was being shoved aside. He would not give up the country now. We had underestimated him. He and Amiama had put their people in key positions. They could not be thrown out. The Consejo had talked about communism but only he was acting. He would clean things up or resign.

I told Fandino I wanted to see President Bonnelly right away, Fernández Caminero for lunch, and Amiama and Imbert that night. Shlaudeman left to talk to the leaders of the small political parties.

We found President Bonnelly in his house, depressed and hurt. Reid had told him what I had done. He told me, "I am in accord fundamentally with your objectives. But I am not in accord with what you have done because I feel downgraded. I feel it was an act of intervention. Put yourself in my place. When you tell me of the new United States policy, that there will be elections and only the PRD or UCN can win, my principles tell me it could be someone else. No one has confidence in those two candidates." And then, "I am thinking of the 1916 resignation." The Dominican Provisional President had resigned when the U. S. Marines landed. "You make me feel I am no longer President."

I told him this was the last thing I intended, that I had the utmost respect for him and no other wish than to strengthen his own position, that our policy was not a new one, and I spelled it out. It was not that we WANTED a UCN or PRD victory; rather, in our judgment, no other party or coalition of parties now had a chance of winning without using coercion or force. The "summit" meeting had simply been a means of helping to guarantee the free elections Bonnelly wanted and stopping an Amiama-Imbert power play.

Bonnelly shook his head. The formation of a third force could upset all these plans. Amiama and Imbert did not trust either Bosch or Fiallo. And so on—I had heard it all before. Bonnelly said, "If you insist on seeing Imbert and Amiama, do not tell them you have told the President of the new American policy. The President of the Republic must ignore what you have told me. I may not be able to control the situation. But they must not know I think I can't."

Leaving, I felt sorry for him. No matter how he put it, I thought, what really troubled him was that last week he had seen Amiama and Imbert taking power from his faltering hands; now he thought he saw me doing it. We had no choice but to keep moving.

Fernández Caminero came to lunch. Last week he had considered resigning, he said. "But now I have had an offer, and I am considering it, considering it very carefully." Tomorrow, Saturday, was the announced deadline for the resignation of any Consejero who wanted to run for President. (The Consejeros had altered their original renunciation of candidacy.) Vanguardia had made the offer; so had Amiama and Imbert. Fernández Caminero meant so well, knew so little of politics, and was being used by everyone. I told him about the summit meeting. He took it very well. Perhaps he did not fully understand it meant that we would oppose any such coalition as the one he was being lured into.

At five forty-five I received the Bosch and Fiallo offers to Amiama and Imbert. The PRD offered them pensions, bodyguards, and the rank of Secretary of State without Portfolio. The UCN offered pensions, bodyguards, and membership on a five-man Advisory Council with two men chosen from each of the parties that came in second and third in the election—one of those complicated, absurd devices so common and disruptive in Dominican politics. I wasn't sure the offers were worth transmitting. Fandino and I left for Imbert's house.

He and Amiama were in the basement room, bare walls, fluorescent lights, guards outside. Imbert immediately took the offensive: "You have to understand that we have no desires for political position. We only want to guarantee our personal position," and, his voice rising and eyes flashing, hands chipping the air, "We who gave this country its liberty, who gave all this, we are mortified and irritated and let down. The Department of State and the Dominican people say we are empty husks that can't fill posts in government. We are to be guaranteed and given pensions. We are supposed to have confidence in Bosch and Fiallo," and he said loudly, "Huh," leaning back on the sofa, hitching up his gun belt, then going on. "Posts in government or the military, no, we cannot have them. We would feel secure in the military. People like us should not be feared and thought capable of betraying what we have done in the past. We should be respected. Whenever there is a harsh decision, if we were not there it would not be made. You know that, Mr. Martin," lifting his hands palm up, widening his eyes. "Or hitting people in the streets, or sending the Communists to be abroad—*we* are the ones. So we have gained the antipathy of the people—by saving them. So that those two can sit back and become President. *No, Señor. No, Señor.* We have been throwing on ourselves a lot of shit. We won't do it any more. Let someone else do it. Let it go to pot. We'll retire from the Consejo de Estado. They can't have elections without us," and he leaned back, thin arms folded.

I said, "I want you to understand—we are going to have elections. I'm speaking now for the United States government."

Amiama, who had been sitting silent, looking at the ceiling, now leaned forward and said to me directly, "Does your government regard us as two men beyond suspicion?"

I said, "I cannot answer that."

"I thought so. The United States would not want us in those key positions."

"None of this is the point. The point is free elections—free of force."

Amiama ignored me. "We are supposed to make common cause with Bosch and Fiallo. That we might betray—this is what you are afraid of."

I said, "The parties won't give you Secretary of Defense or Police."

Amiama said, "I don't want it. I don't want anything."

I said, "You must. What is it? What do you want?"

"I want nothing. Tony deserves to be Secretary of Defense. He has done more and given more than anybody else."

Imbert said, "Do they want an Armed Force for politics? We don't. We are not politicians. We are patriots."

I said, "I know you are. I think you should stay that way—stay out of politics. You will only get dirtied up."

Imbert said, "I think I will resign."

I said, "You won't."

He said, "It's not the people, it's the leaders. If we resign, the President will, too."

"You won't resign. Your country needs you. Bosch and Fiallo will need you, too."

Imbert said, "Hah," and then, intensely, leaning close to me, tapping my knee, "What bothers us in that Bosch, that exile shit, should be able to convince you that we are a menace. Democracy will not last here unless in the Armed Forces there are people to back it up with power. In Latin America, you need it. I know my people, *si Señor,* I know my people." And he leaned back on the sofa, moving away from me, looking at the far side of the room.

Amiama said, "If you can't guarantee our safety, we'll have to do it ourselves."

I said, "We'll guarantee that the parties will keep any promise they make to you."

Imbert said, "They think they have to be baby-sitters. If they take our guard away, there'll be a revolution."

"They won't take your guard away. I'll guarantee that part of it myself. What else do you want?" They said nothing. I said, "Look. You are friends of the United States beyond any doubt. We know that. But you can't have it all. Nobody can. Now what do you want?"

Imbert said quietly, "Maybe we can pass into the Army. We would feel secure there. They should know we'd guarantee the Armed Forces against a *coup* against them."

Amiama said, "If the problem is the two of us, I'd feel secure without anything—if Tony has the job, I'm all right."

Imbert said, "They want power, not us. They have to get confidence

in us. I could pick up the phone and Fiallo and the whole bunch would
be in jail in five minutes."

I said laughing, "Sure you could. That's the trouble."

He grinned in spite of himself. But then he said, "We do the dirty
work—deport the Communists—and they throw shit on us to get votes."

"I know it, it's true."

Amiama said, "It's us that has to convince the Consejo de Estado to do
something."

"I know it. You're the strong men in the Consejo."

Amiama said, "Why does not the U.S. influence the parties?"

"We can't. They won't give you power, that's all."

Imbert said, "I'll go to the Army, and Luís can go to the Cabinet
without portfolio."

Amiama said, "I don't care. I don't want Tony in politics, though."

Imbert said, "Baquero [of UCN] wishes we were dead," and he went
on, and I let him, then I said, "They won't give you Secretary of Defense.
What do you want specifically?"

Imbert said, "I want to be a general."

"Where?"

"Here, any place, what I care?"

"Not Commander in Chief?"

"General."

"All right. I'll see if I can get it for you."

Imbert said, "Their agreements mean nothing."

I said, "I told you I'd guarantee any offer they make. I don't know if
they'll make this offer. But if they do, I'll guarantee it."

3

Trouble started the next day, Saturday, October 20.

Shlaudeman came to the Residence and said that the military had
heard that Bonnelly was going to make Imbert a general. The military
would meet at noon. President Bonnelly had held a meeting last night,
with whom no one was sure. I told Shlaudeman to sound out the UCN
and PRD on this idea of making Imbert a general.

Donny Reid came to see me, agitated. The President and Consejo
were meeting now in secret at Amiama's *finca* in the country. Last night
Vice President Pichardo, having heard about the summit meeting, had
demanded that the entire Consejo resign *en masse* in protest at my intervention, and had calmed down only when Bonnelly promised to call today's meeting. Reid had found the President very upset last night. Imbert had joined them, then Amiama and Fernández Caminero. And
"Pupito" Sánchez of the security police. At first all had been calm, then
increasingly excited, first over my intervention, then over what posts Im-

bert and Amiama deserved. Imbert finally had said he would accept Sub-
Secretary of the Armed Forces and a generalship. Reid said he was
pressing the PRD and UCN to offer him Secretary of State without Portfolio. I told Reid that Imbert wouldn't take it, he should try to persuade
them quickly to make Imbert a general.

We were in some danger now. Our maneuver might boomerang.

I told Fandino to ask for an appointment with Pichardo. He couldn't
find him. We ate lunch in my study, Fandino telephoning incessantly,
nervously. Shlaudeman and the attachés came in at three-thirty. We heard
that Amiama had called Bosch to the Palace at 11:30 A.M., told him he
knew about the summit agreement, called it U.S. intervention, and said
he would resign. Pichardo had said he too would resign. Amiama was
trying to find "General" Ramírez to have him go on the radio, presumably
to denounce my intervention. And, we heard that since the secret had
leaked, Bosch was threatening to take an anti-American position.

The attachés reported that the Armed Forces chiefs, sub-chiefs, and
sub-secretaries had met, together with Inspector General Rodríguez
Reyes, General Félix Hermida, Jr., and Colonel Wessin y Wessin, the
ascetic tank commander. All had favored our position. They thought it
strengthened the Consejo's hand and their own against the irresponsible
parties. This made me nervous, and I wondered if the military might use
our maneuver as a pretext for a takeover. Viñas and the three service
chiefs intended to give Bonnelly their views today. But they wanted advice from us. What should they do on December 20 if there were no
elections? Why did we not force the President to deport all Communists?
—this came from Wessin y Wessin. Most important, they would accept
Amiama and Imbert as one-star generals without power. They were seeing
Bonnelly at 4 P.M.

I gave the attachés the answers. As they left at 4 P.M., Reid came in.
Things were better, he said. Nobody had resigned. All would meet again
at 7 P.M. Imbert was happy. Pichardo, however, insisted that the Consejo
protest our intervention. This didn't sound like things were much better.

Foreign Minister Bonilla joined us, looking solemn. He said our policy
coincided with the President's but we had made a serious error—had
said that only the UCN or PRD could win. He wished to remind me
that months ago he had asked my help in "resolving the problem of the
electoral quotient." I presumed he referred to a system he had devised
of proportionate representation, though I really had forgotten it. He said,
"If at that moment you had paid attention to what I said, there would be
no problem."

I said it was a most interesting proposal, I spoke in generalities of the
advantages and disadvantages of proportionate representation, striving
desperately to remember my college textbooks and hoping he hadn't read

the same texts. He seemed pleased with my thoughtful response—we would meet at 9:30 A.M. on Monday to discuss it further.

Throughout the day I kept getting reports that the Consejo was meeting at Amiama's *finca* or Bonnelly's house. Shlaudeman was extremely concerned—they might protest my "intervention" officially. What they seemed to resent most was my saying that only the UCN or PRD was able to win the election.

Bonnelly called. Fandino and I walked along the block-long stone wall of the Trujillo estate which separated Bonnelly's house and mine. Bonnelly was alone and smiling. He said, "The reaction was tremendous. Really tremendous. The military was here, and the Consejo was here, Pichardo was volcanic, Amiama and Imbert were here," and he defended Amiama and Imbert saying, "They have done nothing. They never tried a *golpe*." After long and stormy meetings, he had, he said, succeeded in calming everybody down. He advised me to see Pichardo and Monseñor Pérez Sánchez. We thanked him and left.

Fandino finally got Pichardo, and he came to the Residence at seven forty-five and stayed two hours. I explained our position and maneuvers. He listened carefully, then said, "As a friend, not as an Ambassador, and entirely off the record—is that really all you did?" I said it was. He sighed and shook his head. "Then there has been a misunderstanding. What I had been told was a wholly different version," and he described it: The United States had decided arbitrarily that only the PRD and UCN would be allowed to take part in the election, no other parties or candidates would be allowed to run, if another won we would not recognize it and would shut down AID. Nothing, of course, could be farther from the truth, and I said so. He believed me.

But this did not solve the problem. Juan Isidro Jimenes Grullón was going on the radio tomorrow night to denounce us and the Consejo. So would the leaders of other small parties. Pichardo suggested I see them all.

Early next morning I learned from a private source that Pichardo and the President and probably one other Consejero had sat up until 2:30 A.M., discussing an official protest of my "intervention." Fernández Caminero's plan to run with Amiama-Imbert backing was being revived. Imbert's wife was telling him he was selling his honor for a generalship. A big meeting was to take place at the Palace at 10 A.M.

A little before noon the top-secret control officer from the Chancellery came to the Residence. He had a top-priority, top-secret cable, marked "Eyes Only Ambassador." The Cuban missile crisis had begun.

The cable said what only a few knew then but what all the world knows now—that we had discovered indisputable evidence of Soviet offensive missiles in Cuba and President Kennedy would speak to the nation today or tomorrow.

On a coded signal I was to tell the Foreign Minister that we possessed intelligence which indicated that in the next few days local violent Communist uprisings might begin, directed against U.S. property, citizens, the Dominican government, and public order; that we possessed stockpiles of anti-riot material in the Canal Zone that would be available on request; and that I would have more information in a few hours.

The cable continued: I would receive an advance text of President Kennedy's speech and a letter from him to the Chief of State, Bonnelly. I should deliver both to the Foreign Minister and Chief of State. We intended to ask for an emergency meeting of the Consultative Organ of the OAS at 10 A.M. tomorrow to ask the OAS to invoke Article 8 of the Rio Treaty, which provides for diplomatic, economic, and military sanctions against an aggressor nation. I should ask the Dominicans to support us in the OAS. I should tell them that this was only the first step, that the Soviet missile presence in the Western Hemisphere created an entirely new situation endangering the free world, that no one could foresee the future, and that we therefore wanted to keep the Consultative Organ in continual session; and I should ask the Dominicans' support. I should offer consultation by representatives of the American Joint Chiefs of Staff for possible military collaboration. (All other U. S. Ambassadors in the Hemisphere received identical instructions.)

I thought: This may be World War III. And then: Maybe this will make all of us here understand how little our own affairs really matter.

Now I had a truly serious problem. I would have to ask the cooperation of the Dominican government in the Cuban crisis—yet that same government seemed to be discussing protesting my "intervention." Thus can an Ambassador trap himself.

I was still rereading the cable when Shlaudeman called from the Chancellery. A functionary of the Dominican Foreign Office had telephoned and insisted on delivering a diplomatic note immediately. I told Shlaudeman to tell him he didn't know where I was and he himself was not authorized to receive formal diplomatic communications.

Juan Isidro Jimenes Grullón arrived for lunch. An elderly disarming shaggy-haired old-time politician with an old-fashioned oratorical style, Jimenes Grullón talked through lunch about his party, the ASD. Over brandy and coffee, my turn came. Many inaccurate rumors were spreading about our supposed "intervention," I said, and I wanted him to know the truth. So far as we were concerned, anybody could run for President or anything else. He said he never had believed the rumors but was greatly relieved. What I really wanted was assurance he wouldn't denounce us on the radio tonight. I finally got it.

I sat down alone a minute in my study to think. I could say nothing to anybody—not even my own staff, not even Fran—about the Cuban missile crisis. If I wanted the Dominican Government's cooperation on it tomorrow, I somehow had to get straightened out with it tonight. And I couldn't use the Cuban missiles to do it.

I called the Crisis Crowd to the Residence. Shlaudeman said a man from the Foreign Office had delivered the note. Bramble had told him that he wasn't authorized to receive it officially, that he could leave it on a desk, that it could cause a serious misunderstanding, that he, Bramble, must tell the Ambassador and could only hope everything would be all right. A little later President Bonnelly had telephoned Fandino at home, told him the note was not the one he had authorized and he wanted it back. Fandino had picked up the note and taken it to Bonnelly.

Fandino came to the Residence at 2:35 P.M. Bonnelly had explained he had sent the note only to appease Horacio Julio Ornes and Fernández Caminero. Fandino had the note. It said that while the Dominican Government did not doubt that the U. S. Government's position on the Dominican election was intended only as a friendly suggestion, it wished to make it plain "with emphasis" that it defended the OAS's principles, including non-intervention, and wished also to state that all political groups could participate in the election under the Electoral Law.

The language was mild. But if it became public, it could make the United States an issue in the Dominican electoral campaign, a serious matter. The note had never been officially delivered. We decided to try to get it withdrawn. Then if anyone made it public, we could deny it. I told Fandino to call the President and said to the others, "I'll go put on my white suit. You figure out what I ought to say to him." Dressing alone, I thought, "All this foolishness—and with missiles in Cuba."

President Bonnelly would see us at once. Shlaudeman said that since the note was a *note verbale,* if delivered officially, it would have to be answered officially by the U.S. Government. He suggested the Dominicans substitute an *aide mémoire,* which required no answer. He thought I should be stiff and formal.

Bonnelly was in his shirtsleeves in his little room alone, drinking a Scotch. Half-empty glasses were in sight. Bonnelly looked exhausted, his large round eyes sad and questioning and fearful. I shook hands with him rather formally, waited for him to sit, and affected more reluctance than usual at sitting in his own reclining chair. I had the note in my hand. He offered us drinks, but I declined. He immediately began explaining how difficult the situation was, how he had spent all night trying to soften the note so it would do me no harm.

I did not much like the role of injured dignity but played it. "Mr. President, I am shocked and deeply hurt by the note. My personal feelings do not matter. But the relations between our governments do matter. This is a very serious step that has been taken, and the timing is most unfortunate." (How unfortunate he had no way of knowing.) "In any case, now that the note has actually been delivered, I have no choice but to forward it to the Secretary of State, who will reply to it."

Bonnelly protested, "No, no, I don't want it answered."

I said, "It will be answered nevertheless. According to the diplomatic usage of the United States Government, a *note verbale* must be answered."

"Take it back, change it, anything," he said, pouring another drink. "Find a solution."

I said I simply had no choice but to transmit it, so long as it remained in this form. Of course, if it were an *aide mémoire,* not a *note verbale,* things would be different.

He said, "Give it to me," and took it and laid it on the cocktail table. "We will pretend it never has been delivered. Don't you want a drink?" I said I would take one, and Bonnelly went on talking; the entire incident had been a misunderstanding; we must let nothing come between us or our governments; and he recalled other crises we had been through together, becoming sentimental. I felt a little ashamed of myself. Several times I tried to leave but he insisted we stay. He spilled a drink on the note. Small wonder—the pressures he had been under were enormous. Finally, we left.

An urgent cable came in from Washington, saying that Ambassador Freites had made a copy of the Dominican note available to the Department.

I was furious. I thought I'd been double-crossed. While President Bonnelly was pretending to withdraw the note, his Ambassador in Washington had delivered the note to the Department.

Foreign Minister Bonilla and Donny Reid came to the Residence, they with whom we had spent the weekend at Las Matas.

I said stiffly, "Your Ambassador in Washington has made this note available to the Department of State in spite of your President's assurances."

Bonilla said, "That is not so."

"Mr. Secretary, it is so."

Donny said, "But it can't be—we told him."

I said to Reid, "Mr. Vice President,"—how odd it sounded!—"it is so. We have the note in Washington. My government will have a reply in due course," and turned away.

They sat a moment. Then Bonilla, adopting the funereal tone he reserved for ceremonial occasions, said, his own dignity now wounded, "This note was the product of the decisions that neither the President, nor the Vice President, nor I could hold. As you see, the note has been detained until Tuesday," and he held out a paper but I ignored it. "I hope that if there are no complications before Tuesday we may be, perhaps be, able to get the note withdrawn. This is naturally a personal opinion on my part."

He stopped and waited. I said nothing.

He went on, "In any case the President told you this afternoon his personal regard for you and his desire that this note not influence in any way the relations that have existed on your part. My opinion as Foreign Minister is the same."

I said nothing. Bonilla said, "In any case, the note will be withdrawn."

"Very well. Now gentlemen, if you will excuse me, I have some work to do," I said, and stood up. They walked out, Bonilla bowing slightly, and, at a little distance, I followed them to the door and shut it. I went back to the living room. Fran, recalling her affection for Dora Bonilla and the shopping trip with Clara Reid to buy her dress for Cindy's wedding, shed her first tears for Dominican friends.

It was absurd. On Friday morning Reid had been at the house thanking me for saving the country; now by Sunday evening I had practically ordered him out of the house. (He did not come back until New Year's Day.) Later I heard that Bonilla had indeed telephoned Freites in Washington, telling him not to deliver the note, but that Freites, close to Imbert, had delivered it anyway. This may be so.

And anyway—Cuba. I sat at my desk in the study. Cables kept coming in all night. I went to bed late, got up early, put on a fresh white suit—I would soon run out of white suits if this kept up—and went to the office. More cables, and then the text of President Kennedy's speech. I was assembling my instructions. I would have to be able to reach President Bonnelly, the full Consejo, and Foreign Minister Bonilla quickly. I told Fandino to call Bonilla and tell him that something of extreme urgency was coming up—something new—and I wanted to know where he and the President would be during the rest of the day. Then I called in the Crisis Crowd and told them about Cuba. President Kennedy would speak at 6 P.M. Release time for his text was four o'clock. The coded signal came at 2:30 P.M.

Fandino called Bonilla, and he came to the Residence, with good grace indeed. Apologizing for not going to him and explaining that highly important cables were coming in and I dared not leave, I told him what I had been instructed to tell him and said I expected more information shortly, and at 4 P.M. I would want to see him and the President, and, if the President wished, the full Consejo. We shook hands cordially, though gravely, and Bonilla left.

I called the office, told Bramble and Shlaudeman to have a radio set up in my office, to invite leaders of the American community there to hear President Kennedy's speech at 6 P.M., and to tell Sergeant Trizza to have his Marines stand by. I collected my notes, told Fandino to make sure my car and driver were ready, and, at a few minutes before four, we

went to the President's house. Bonilla was with him. I gave him a
cabled copy of President Kennedy's letter, explaining the original would
arrive later by mail, and summarized briefly what was going on.

We drove fast to the Palace, entering by a rear gate, and went into
the long room of the Consejo and sat as we had the first time we had
met. The President said he had called them together in extraordinary session at my request, and invited me to speak.

I said that at six o'clock President Kennedy would speak to the world,
and I read his speech, Fandino translating, announcing, in this faded
room, amid seven men now foes, now friends, the first head-to-head
thermonuclear confrontation in history.

The Consejo listened carefully. Imbert was smiling with satisfaction.
I said that with their permission I would outline the next steps we would
take, steps which my Government hoped they would support—OAS sanctions tomorrow morning against Cuba, and a naval quarantine against
further shipment of Soviet missiles to Cuba. Should local Communists
rise here, I offered military advice and riot control equipment from the
Canal Zone. I asked protection for United States property and citizens.

Finished, I waited. Imbert said, "I want more." I asked what he
meant. He meant war—we ought to go into Cuba, kill Castro, and end
the problem, once and for all. He was not arguing it—only expressing a
boisterous, almost boyish, enthusiasm. I said I could understand how he
felt but the result might well be a nuclear exchange between the United
States and the Soviet Union, and Castro wasn't worth it. He agreed, and
said, "Anyway, at last we're doing something."

I said we certainly were.

Pichardo said, "You've said you'll be getting more information during
the night. Tell us as fast as possible—we'll be in continuous session
throughout the night. Off the record, unofficially, though we haven't decided officially," glancing around the room, "I think I can tell you in
general that we agree with everything." The others murmured or nodded.
Bonnelly said, "We're going to talk. We'll let you know. I can tell you
now we'll support the first step in the OAS—to convoke the Organ of
Consultation. Then we will want to see the resolution."

I said I was pleased and would notify my Government. We shook
hands all around with great cordiality and Bonilla walked with me to
the door, his arm around my shoulders.

4

My office was filling with U.S. citizens; a communications man was
tinkering with the radio, set against a wall. I shook hands with several
men near me, the Voice of America came in loud, the room fell quiet,
I waved to Fran and Dan and Fred, sitting on the sofa, and sat down

near the back of the room, and we heard from far away President Kennedy's high, flat voice, edged with strain: "Good evening, my fellow citizens." Everybody listened in absolute silence. He detailed the evidence of Soviet missiles in Cuba. He described the steps we had taken and were about to take. He declared, "It shall be the policy of this nation to regard any nuclear missile launched from Cuba against any nation in the Western Hemisphere as an attack by the Soviet Union on the United States, requiring a full retaliatory response upon the Soviet Union." He said, "I call upon Chairman Khrushchev to halt and eliminate this clandestine, reckless, and provocative threat to world peace." He closed:

"The path we have chosen for the present is full of hazards, as all paths are—but is the one most consistent with our character and courage as a nation and our commitments around the world. The cost of freedom is always high—but Americans have always paid it. And one path we shall never choose, and that is the path of surrender or submission. . . .

"Thank you and good night."

The Marine turned the radio off. I got up and went to my desk and stood behind it, between the American flag and the blue Chief of Mission flag. The people looked up, some, I knew, vigorously opposed to President Kennedy's policy in Latin America and mine here, some friendly and sympathetic, but all now united. I told them this was a solemn hour in our nation's history, we were at the world's first nuclear confrontation, nobody could predict the future, but we would support our President. I had just come from the Palace and the Consejo was with us. It was not impossible that the Castro/Communists might make trouble here, and the Consejo had assured me of full protection for American lives and property. If anybody felt endangered, he should notify me immediately. They departed, some stopping to shake hands and say good luck. Fran and the boys wanted me to go to the house for dinner, but I had to send a cable first, and more cables were coming in.

The text of our resolution invoking the Rio Treaty came in, and Fandino and I took it to the Palace. Bonnelly said instructions were already going out to the Dominican Ambassador to the OAS.

Back at the office, I received a cable instructing me to tell the Dominican government that we considered it essential that OAS action be completed tomorrow and that the issue should not get into the UN Security Council (where Russia had a veto).

Back to the Palace I went with this message. President Bonnelly agreed. He said he and the Consejo were discussing other steps—a roundup of Castro/Communists, a speech to the nation. I said both were excellent ideas and suggested his speech might say that the Republic's first democratic government in a generation would stand with the forces of freedom all the way. At one point I asked the Consejo whom I should notify if American lives or property were threatened. Pichardo said that in an emergency I should call the police, and if there was time I should also call any Consejero. Reid added, laughing, "If we are not available, call Wimpy," the U.S. supermarket operator always active in Dominican politics.

During the next few days I went back and forth from Embassy to Palace. We worked late every night. The duty officers slept on the couch in my office. We doubled up the Marine guards. We gave American citizens telephone numbers of the police, the Consejo, and the Embassy. The MAAG and attachés met repeatedly with the Dominican military on coastal patrol and counter-insurgency. The Navy needed help with refueling, the police needed trucks, Luna wanted more planes, Peguero wanted more tear gas. The rumor on the streets on Monday said that my car had been burned, I had been assassinated, and a *coup* in Washington had toppled President Kennedy. Amiama said, laughing at the *coup* story, "You caught it from us." A heavy Dominican police guard surrounded the Embassy grounds, and guards with submachine guns and grenades manned a little gatehouse pillbox at the driveway to the Residence; soon we found our kitchen filled with a chow line, our cook ladling out rice and beans.

Two Dominican ships became the first to join the U.S. on the quarantine line, cheered wildly on departure. (They soon developed trouble, and limped into Puerto Rico, where we spent about a hundred thousand dollars repairing them and paying the crews—Dominican officers had pocketed the subsistence money sent by the Dominican government. We installed some three hundred light bulbs in the ships; the crew promptly stole them. And, returning to Santo Domingo, the quarantiners smuggled in eighty-two refrigerators duty free. Despite all this, I thought a show of Hemispheric solidarity worth the price.)

General Belisario Peguero furnished his list of riot control equipment, outrageously long, but I transmitted it. A day or two passed. We had no huge stockpiles in the Canal Zone. I protested vigorously—probably other Ambassadors did too—and by the end of the week the State and Defense Departments got together, and a Dominican plane picked up some gas masks and tear gas grenades in the Canal Zone. Amiama asked where the trucks and radios were. I said it would take three weeks. He said, "I'll give you two." At their own expense, the Dominicans moved a leaky old oil tanker all the way to Puerto Plata to supply their own— and our—quarantine ships. No government in Latin America cooperated more wholeheartedly.

The expected violent leftist reaction did not come. Toward the end of the week, several hundred students gathered at the University and marched toward the Embassy, and General Belisario Peguero called out the Cascos Blancos. The students passed us by, however. One night a Dominican Air Force lieutenant was stabbed in a bar, and police who responded were attacked by a mob yelling Castro slogans. Teen-agers burned an empty Dominican school with Molotov cocktails. Police broke up a political meeting. But that was all.

The CIA chief received reports that the reaction would come later, after the Soviets and Castro got their lines straightened out, and that it likely would be terror in the streets—shooting at American and Dominican government cars, possibly assassination attempts. I thought privately it might never come: The missile crisis, if we passed through it successfully, might keep Castro too busy to undertake Dominican adventures.

5

During those early days of the crisis, I felt that the Consejo almost welcomed it. Bonnelly appeared to reassert his authority. Amiama and Imbert were pleased—it gave them a chance to again become the great friends of the United States, the great enemies of communism. One night while Imbert and I were talking at his house, in bounded Fernández Caminero, the little heart specialist, all decked out in a new uniform, khaki pants and shirt, carrying a huge machine gun, it might even have been a BAR, and so weighed down with machine gun clips and field equipment, all new, that though he tried to strut he could hardly walk. Seeing me, he paused, a little embarrassed—his conversations with me always had been quiet, carried on in his physician's consulting room—but then he recovered and played his awkward, unfamiliar role, swaggering about the room in front of Tony Imbert, who told him with a straight face he looked ready for anything. He was, he said—they were going to search cars entering and leaving the city. When he left, Imbert looked at me, his hands raised palm upwards, eyebrows arched.

As everyone knows now, the danger of a Soviet-U.S. missile exchange increased as the week passed. But in the Dominican Republic, a feeling of letdown set in—no Communists rose up, no arms caches were found, searched cars were empty. I believe few Dominicans realized fully the awful import of the thermonuclear confrontation. Soon, I thought, we would go back to the same old political problems. Well, at least protest at my "intervention" had been swallowed up by the missile crisis—been overtaken by events, as they say in the State Department.

During that week, I suspected Amiama and Imbert might try to seize the missile crisis as their road to power. They barred the radio to the 14th of June and another Castro/Communist party. They demanded to know why we didn't "make a final solution"—the phrase chilled me—of the Castro problem. They were as impatient with diplomacy in the OAS and UN as with politics here. They made lists of agitators and told me they had sent the police to scour the city and nation for them.

I tried to calm a rising warhawk feeling in the city. The government began broadcasting an hourly communiqué warning the people that Communists would create disorder in the streets, that citizens should stay away from places where trouble started, and that the National Police had orders to act firmly.

The attachés reported that the military high command, plus General Belisario Peguero, had decided to offer Imbert and Amiama generalships provided they did not support anyone for the Presidency.

On Sunday afternoon, while I was resting, Imbert called: "Can you come to my house? I have something to show you."

Imbert was in the living room. So were Belisario Peguero, Attorney General García Vásquez, several soldiers and policemen, Imbert's wife, and several other people. They were standing around in a circle, smiling broadly and gazing down at the floor. On the floor were heaped Springfield rifles, boxes of ammunition, a tape recorder, radio equipment, rifle clips. Imbert kicked a burlap sack, and a soldier sprang to dump its contents clattering to the tile floor—more guns and ammunition. Mrs. Imbert said, "Ah." Outside the patio the sun was shining peacefully on flowers and an empty wading pool. I said, "Where'd you get it?"

Imbert said, "We got López Molina."

"¡No me diga!" I said—"Don't tell me!"

"Sure," he said, drawing it out, smiling broadly. "We caught him and three others. One was a Cuban. We also got that man who was along when they killed the policeman."

"And they had all this stuff."

"Sure," drawing it out. "Sure they had."

"Where were they?"

"Some house out there," and waved vaguely northward. Someone else supplied the address. It was a bourgeois house in a suburb. When they had captured the dread terrorist, López Molina; he had been relaxing in his swimming pool. I didn't ask why they hadn't caught him sooner. I felt sure they had known where he was for a long time and now, at the appropriate moment, had produced him.

President Bonnelly arrived, and widened his eyes when he saw the haul. I asked where the prisoners were. In jail. Imbert wanted U.S. visas for them, and for others he had rounded up. I asked him for the list and went back to the office.

Shlaudeman was waiting. He had just come from Bosch. Bosch was leaving the country. "He thinks it is obvious Imbert is going to be a candidate. He knows you are against it but 'Washington's policy' is to put Fiallo in and use Imbert to make it look good. He thinks 'they' are going to kill him." I asked who "they" were. "I don't know," he said. "People from the secret police, Imbert, somebody—he thinks they are plotting to kill him and hang it on the Communists so the government can smash the Communists and Imbert can take over. Besides, he hasn't got any money, so it's useless to campaign. He's sick, he has colitis, and he's in a state of depression."

So ended the reaction in one small volatile country to the first thermonuclear confrontation in human history.

Chapter Eleven

ASSASSINS AND GENERALS

September's steamy heat and rain had died. Now there was a quickening in the night November air. Less than two months remained to the election—the first free election in the Dominican Republic in thirty-eight years. Two months is the duration of a U.S. presidential campaign; two months can be a lifetime in Dominican politics.

Five problems would beset us until election day—Amiama and Imbert, the threatened return of ex-President Joaquín Balaguer, Castro/Communist agitation, the mechanical problems of the Electoral Board, and the party struggle. These were the things that might disrupt the election.

2

We still had some Cuban fallout. A representative of the Joint Chiefs of Staff thanked the Consejo for its cooperation and consulted with the Dominican military. The Republic continued to support us in the OAS. President Kennedy had been dissatisfied with U.S. communications, and so a "hot line" telephone was installed in my office and bedroom, in President Bonnelly's office and bedroom, and in Foreign Minister Bonilla's office and bedroom. That was done in every country in Latin America except Cuba, making it possible to pick up the phone and get a call through directly, interrupting other calls if necessary, to any President, Foreign Minister, or certain other officials of any government in the Hemisphere. The "red phone" made problems. Once a Dominican used it to make personal calls to the States, and we got the bill. In my office it rang several times in the early weeks, almost giving me heart failure—the telephone company was testing it. Once I saw the maid in my bedroom dusting near it. I said, "You don't dust that phone, do you?" She said, *"O, sí señor,"* and brightly picked it up off its cradle, thereby flashing lights in high places all over the Hemisphere. The first time I tried to use it during a real emergency, it didn't work.

The most dangerous Cuban fallout was the continuing drive for power of Amiama and Imbert. Cuba had given them an opening; they were determined not to yield it. They were busy seeing officers of the Armed Forces and deporting Castro/Communists. The deportations took an uglier turn—not only Castro/Communists themselves but also their lawyers. Then Spaniards. Then others.

I talked to Imbert alone one night, our conversation long and relaxed. I told him how much we appreciated his efforts and how much his country needed him. He said he sometimes felt bitter at the way he was treated; no matter, he would continue. He intended to make a speech renouncing any political ambition. This was final, he said. I told him I hoped so. "Politics isn't for you, Tony. You're not made for it. It would ruin you. I'll tell you something else—there are people around here that are trying to use you, to use your reputation. They don't care about you. They care about themselves." He said he knew it. I went on, "Anyway, whoever is elected President here, the next four years are not going to be any bed of roses. You can do more for your country in some other role." He said he agreed, and repeated with finality that he would not seek political power.

The next night Fernández Caminero went on national radio and television and, in a bitter speech, perhaps the most devastatingly self-destructive speech I have ever heard, declared he would not be a candidate for the Presidency. Watching him on television that night, I remembered when first I had met him in September 1961, young, fresh-faced, earnest, hopeful, telling me how in Trujillo's prison he had taken heart when President Kennedy announced the Alliance for Progress, and had emerged from the underground after the assassination filled with ideals and hopes for his country; he had tried to lead the 14th of June toward liberal democracy and helped Fiallo and Baquero with the UCN, even had risen to sit on the Consejo as one of the seven Presidents—but then had yielded to ambition and week by week, month by month found himself entangled more and more in the jungle of Dominican politics, compromising, hedging, trying to please everyone, and now, self-betrayed and self-destroyed, ending thus.

The political significance of his speech was that Imbert was no longer backing him for President. Soon we decided Imbert was not backing Horacio Julio Ornes either. Maybe he had indeed renounced politics.

3

It is the habit of Dominican politicians to talk, and of Dominican writers to write, at great length. Daily the newspapers printed articles on their editorial pages many columns long. Usually the writers began by declaring they would examine the political panorama; soon they took off on philosophical, economic, historical, ethnological, or literary diversions and ended nowhere—but if they were good they managed to end with a flourish. (I connected them somehow with the young pilots at San Isidro, dirks at belts, scarves flying.) Dominican literature is likely to be polemics, scrappy essays, *belles lettres*, bits of history, snatches of poetry intermingled with paragraphs clipped from the patriotic speeches of long-ago heroes. Solid formal histories and biographies are virtually unknown; I know of only one Dominican novel. Just so, Dominican politicians and government leaders tended to ramble. A conversation almost never lasted less than an hour and usually two or three, and if I were not careful I would completely miss the single hard political point. In charity, I ascribed it to the old-fashioned flowery and rather likable Dominican way; in irritation, to pretentiousness and fake intellectualism. In any case, it was the Dominican way, and I have thus far spared the reader examples. I now will offer one.

Imbert's trio came to see me—eager Ramón Castillo, old "General" Vilomar, and the big stranger in the white suit, Pompilio Brouwer. They sat in my study, I slouched on the striped sofa under pictures of President Kennedy and President Bonnelly and Adlai Stevenson, Vilomar sinking uncomfortably in a big soft armchair on my left, Brouwer in a high upright chair on my right, and Castillo in a straight chair facing me across a coffee table. And they talked.

Vilomar opened with a shocker: "There will be a third force in the elections with Washington's backing," he announced. "The CIA man is coming tomorrow. The Partido Nacional," his "colossus," really a miniscule Horacista party, "will remain in continuous session until November 5," the deadline for candidates' filings.

Some Dominican or Puerto Rican was always telling me that "Washington," or "the CIA," or "the Pentagon" was sending a special emissary who would bring "the word." Dominicans delighted in being the first to inform me. Now I said, as usual, "Really? I hadn't heard about it. Frankly, I find it hard to believe. Who is Washington's candidate going to be?"

Brouwer answered, taking a somewhat different tack. "It was going to be a third force. At one time Tony put forward José Fernández Caminero." (I always listened, rarely indicating whether what was being said was new to me. This was part of the game.) Brouwer went on, "But now I don't know. The parties are fighting for themselves. The masses are still waiting for someone to come along. The people are like a tribe. They need a father who has a strong hand and will give them a whipping if they need it. There is not such a one now. Today there is an abuse of liberty."

Old Vilomar put in a lengthy digression, beginning, "In the old days, they sent out an arrest order for so-and-so and all of the same stripe, meaning all of his family, but today it is confusing, people in the same family are of a different stripe," but Brouwer cut him short, saying, "One cannot lead tribes by ideas, only by well-intentioned dictatorships. This pains me very much," and he described the pain; then, "If we do not get this, we will see things clearly, we will see them moving inexorably to civil war."

Brouwer recalled at length events of the past, saying he had been at the Luperón landing with Horacio Julio Ornes, describing how he had been jailed after the assassination of Trujillo and narrowly escaped the Nigua massacre. "There are not the same men now. Fernández Caminero was my teacher. I take my hat off to him. He took part in the student strikes. But he has no definite character, he cannot give orders. General Ramírez is a good man but he is a soldier, he has not the culture of civilian government. My wife is a first cousin of Manuel Tavárez Justo; I was their mentor, but now they are Communists, the 14th of June. *Sí, Señor*—I put Quisqueya in their flag. So I am a man without a party," smiling sadly. "I was in the 30th of May. I was twice a Secretary of State for Trujillo. Ramón," gesturing to Ramón Castillo, "and General Vilomar," gesturing, "are my cousins. I suffer for my country. I have to see how we can go together in good will and form a union to do the best thing for the country I love so well."

Vilomar spoke then: "I have made a trip around the country. I am going to campaign without a presidential candidate. My party will win in San Pedro, Altagracia, La Romana, and El Seibo and Neiba. So I have six Senators, for sure. Ornes will get Puerto Plata, and La Vega, probably. General Ramírez is sure to win San Juan and maybe Azua and Elías Piña. Juan Isidro will probably win in the Northwest and will make a good fight in Santiago. Juan Bosch will carry four provinces, Fiallo will carry five or six. So we will repeat what we had under Monseñor Nouel," the archbishop who was President briefly long ago. "He could not govern. He had to flee to Rome. One cannot govern without a Congress. It is a carnival."

And Brouwer again: "I roam the Palace," confidentially, "as an old adviser to the Consejo de Estado. I tell them they are all gelded. They should have hit the left six months ago. But there is no election machinery now. One does not even know who belongs to which parties. If there are elections, the results will not be good. We are not like the United States. You lose the election and wait four years. We are like the Mexicans—like Jaliscos. If we lose, we have to fight. So—," spreading his hands, "if the elections do not give a clear result so that there is no doubt, there is going to be a fight. We should wait a while, see things clearer. Elections are premature now; they should be postponed five or six months or even a year. But that raises the question and creates doubt about the intention of those in government to stay in government. Perhaps we should get an elected provisional government for one year," musing.

Vilomar, forever recalling the past, remembered now the term of Horacio Vásquez, elected in 1924, and dilated on it at length. Brouwer listened courteously, then returned to the present situation, saying, "Antonio Imbert does not have the—what shall I say—the culture, the understanding, to govern. An educated person has an equilibrium that prevents certain things," and he paused to indicate what things. "But Don Antonio is not educated. Yet we see in him the myth, the only survivor. Moreover, he has something else, and he knows it—a group that supplies him with what he lacks. When Trujillo came to power, he was illiterate. But he used the brains of others to do what he ended up doing. Naturally, he had one fault—he came from a family of thieves. Why do I say family? It was not even a family, it was just roamers, they could not maintain a home, they had no decency, that one gets from the mother's breast. Don Antonio comes from a good family. His grandfather was General Imbert, the liberator."

Vilomar put in, "His great-great-grandfather was one of Napoleon's lieutenants who ruled here."

And Brouwer, "We think Don Antonio could be a useful instrument." (So here it was—the point.) "He won't be the one who would rule over us. So—," spreading his hands, "he is an element we could use because of his background and his future."

He leaned back in his chair. Vilomar said, "Don Antonio is an unconditional friend of the United States."

Castillo: "Imbert and Amiama have told me they are pro-American. They said they will not act outside the policy lines of the United States even though they thought it was wrong."

Vilomar said eagerly, "And he told me there would be no force or violence."

Brouwer said calmly, "I was one of the brains behind the 30th of May plot. I know what forces we command. We dominate the Armed Forces. Naturally I don't think it good to use the Armed Forces. But if we wanted to, we could use the Armed Forces and no one could stop us." Castillo looked a little alarmed. Brouwer said, "I am not thinking of myself. If only we could unite. Juan Bosch and Fiallo are like brothers to me. I'll always be around them. They need me."

Vilomar said, "But we are heading to chaos now. Fiallo is inconsistent. Look at what he has said about the sugar question—to sell it to Germany! For me there is no matter. Trujillo threw me out and I made a million in the United States. I live like a king."

Brouwer said, "I created all the anti-Communist fronts."

Vilomar, not to be stopped, said, "My grandfather returned here and overthrew the government, and when they came to congratulate him and make him President, he said, 'Oh no, you'd knock me over in ten days.'"

Castillo said, "If one doesn't smell of gunpowder, one doesn't count for much here. Look at Imbert. He knows the Dominican Republic has to go with the United States."

This reminded Vilomar of the U.S. occupation, and he described it at great length. They had been there about two hours. Castillo said to Brouwer, "You should make a definite statement, with total frankness. You are here to represent Amiama and Imbert. We are not. If Imbert wants to run, say so. We need frankness. But Imbert is shy in front of the Ambassador and the people."

Brouwer said judiciously, "His problem is that he wants to be a candidate. But he feels sure he has no capacity. That is why he planned to use José Fernández Caminero." Vilomar began to interrupt—he feared the Castro/Communists might influence Fernández Caminero—but Brouwer held up his hand and went on. "I disagree about Fernández Caminero. But the United States refused to accept Fernández Caminero, so you knocked down the house of cards. But Don Antonio has a certain fear of not being acceptable to the United States. Not me—I do not have that fear. I go ahead regardless. So if we can show him by popular clamor, he would accept. But he is afraid this will not be the case and we are not telling the truth to him because he does not trust politicians. If he could count on support, or if his candidacy could be seen with, ah, complacency, by the United States, he would go into it. I think you would get a better result than if it is a fight between the other two. We need the United States more than the United States needs us. If there is a nucleus of anti-Americanism here, it is bad for the United States. And we think the United States will not give us orders."

They seemed to have talked themselves out. Now they fell silent, waiting. I roused myself and spoke. I agreed the political situation was cloudy, that Imbert was a good friend of the United States. In my personal opinion, it was unlikely that he could put together a coalition of parties that would win a free election, but if he could, well and good. The United States would have nothing to do with influencing the outcome. But we would oppose postponement. And we would support the winner. The United States would find it extremely difficult to recognize and next to impossible to support any government that came to power by force or violence. This included a regime imposed forcibly, not through free election, by Imbert or Amiama.

They left, Castillo looking a bit crestfallen. I don't think they really had expected any other answer. They had just been making a try.

4

A last try, it turned out. The next day, Friday, November 2, talk stopped, action started.

I discounted the morning's first alarm. Castillo came hurrying in, saying, "These people are going to bring Balaguer here—Amiama, Imbert, and Vilomar." Last night an unnamed Balaguer emissary had ordered Vilomar to Washington to confer with "President Kennedy's brother," presumably Attorney General Robert F. Kennedy, and, though Vilomar had not gone, another emissary had. Today I would get a cable confirming it "from the Department of State or the Pentagon." Balaguer would arrive in a U. S. Air Force plane.

While I was attending Newell Williams' biweekly meeting of international agencies—the only such meeting, incidentally, I ever was able to attend—I received a message that President Bonnelly wanted to see me at the Palace right away. Fandino and I hurried there. Bonnelly and the full Consejo were waiting. Spread out on the table were the maps and battle plans of López Molina.

Several were crudely drawn maps of the interior; I thought them astonishingly poor and impractical. They dispersed forces widely on various "fronts," one, for example, in the barren wasteland near Cabo Rojo where it could easily be sealed off and starved out. On a map of Santo Domingo someone, presumably López Molina, had marked various locations. The Consejeros thought these his strategic objectives. I thought they were more likely places where he had cells organized inside labor unions—they appeared to be factories, not strategic objectives such as the waterworks, telephone company, radio stations, electric plant. I congratulated them on finding the maps, expressed my views, and left.

At 4 P.M. Shlaudeman and Colonel Fritz Long reported a rumor that Amiama and Imbert had been made four-star generals. At 5:15 P.M. they confirmed it. The decree would be published tomorrow. They had a copy of the decree. Not only did it make both Amiama and Imbert four-star Generals of the Army, thus outranking all military men in the Republic, it also made them *supervisores* of all the Armed Forces. We looked up *supervisores*. No such word appeared in any Spanish dictionary we could find. But the purport was clear enough. Moreover, they could assume their new duties as soon as their functions as Consejeros ceased—presumably immediately, if they chose to resign. Finally it gave them a permanent bodyguard of no fewer than six officers. (What if they wanted six hundred? Or six thousand?)

This was serious. Under the Consejo, all generals were one-star brigadiers except the Secretary of Defense, Viñas, who wore the two stars of a major general. (General Felix Hermida also wore two stars but held no power position.) Since Trujillo's time no one had had four stars. Now Amiama and Imbert had. This gave them control of the Armed Forces as well as of the National Police and the administration of criminal justice. It ensured their continuing domination of the present government and probably of the next one.

I called the Crisis Crowd together. With us was the new DCM, Spencer M. King, just arrived from Washington—Hemba was being transferred to Ecuador. King was a bald bachelor with glasses, about my age. He was not prepossessing in appearance but was solid, knew his business, and became a strong key man in the Embassy. I told the Crisis Crowd to find out quickly what the decree meant and what the chances were that Amiama and Imbert could make it stick. Colonel Cass asked me for instructions. The same, I said—free elections, difficult to recognize a *golpista* government—and they should put it firmly. If pressed, they might say that the four-star generalships created a new and obviously serious situation. It looked like a long night. I went to the Residence to get something to eat, asking Fandino to stay with me.

I was angry. The decree was dated yesterday, and this morning the President had called me to the Palace to fiddle around with López Molina's battle plans but had said nothing at all about this. Yet this move from the right was clearly far more dangerous to the Consejo, the election, and constitutional representative government than any López Molina battle plans.

How it happened was clear. I myself had unwittingly started it—closed all the political avenues to Amiama and Imbert but opened the military door. I had intended that they be made one-star generals. The Armed Forces had tentatively agreed. Imbert and Amiama probably would have accepted this. But the UCN and PRD, maneuvering for their own advantage, had not made up their minds until it was too late. So Imbert and Amiama, riding the Cuban crisis as strongmen fighting Castro, had tried to seize full power. In a sense, President Bonnelly too was responsible. This fall when Amiama and Imbert had begun to move, he had collapsed.

Eating off a tray on a cocktail table with Fandino in my study, I said that this was probably one of the few times in history that a government had perpetrated a *coup* against itself.

What should we do? See the President, or the other Consejeros? What good would that do? Imbert and Amiama had them.

At eight-thirty my troops began returning. Colonel Bev Cass said he couldn't find General Viñas but had found Commodore Rib, the Navy Commander. Rib had heard the news from Cass—his own government hadn't told him. "He was dumfounded. He kept trying to call Viñas. He said, 'Four stars—why not five and get it over with?' He says he'll talk to the President tomorrow." Cass left. Shlaudeman came in. D'Alessandro of the Social Christians wasn't interested or excited—he thought it a gesture. Miolán of the PRD thought it meant a *golpe,* and said it was our problem. All left, came back later.

Bev Cass and Fritz Long had now found General Viñas and General Rivera Cuesta, the Army Commander. Neither would accept the decree. Nor would General Luna of the Air Force, Colonel Pagán, and several other colonels. Luna wanted to bomb the Palace. Rivera Cuesta wanted to temporize—to wait till March 1, when a new government would be in office and politics adjourned. (Naïve dream!) What angered them most, perhaps, was that none had known about it until we told them. They were furious at the President. They said he had broken faith. They were meeting now.

Shlaudeman said nobody in UCN had known anything about it; all felt angry and double-crossed. According to Luís Manuel Baquero, Fiallo had met with President Bonnelly tonight and had asked twice if the military agreed to making Imbert and Amiama one-star generals, and Bonnelly had said yes and had said nothing at all about the four-star decree. Baquero would try to quiet things down. I wasn't sure we wanted things quieted down—not yet, anyway.

The word was spreading around town. More reports came in. The Venezuelan Ambassador was getting his family out. Bosch, near collapse all week, was reported in hiding. He was deathly afraid of Imbert.

The evening wore on, the Crisis Crowd coming and going and telephoning. Always on such nights the study looked like a candidate's hotel room during a political campaign, not at all like an Embassy Residence. Juancito, the houseboy, counting his fingers when nervous, kept bringing in drinks and coffee and Coke, cheese and crackers and sandwiches. Automatically, we stopped talking when he appeared, though so far as we knew he spoke no English. The study got smokier and smokier, the ashtrays full, pieces of crumpled paper lay about.

I asked where Wessin y Wessin was. At San Isidro with his tanks. Nobody had talked to him, but everybody felt sure he would stand firm with the other military leaders. At eleven-fifty Cass and Long returned. The meeting of the high command had broken up. All, even Rivera Cuesta and Pagán, the most cautious, agreed they would not stand for the four-star generalships. They would decide at 8 A.M. tomorrow how to protest to the President.

All evening we had been discussing what we ought to do. Several alternatives were open. We could encourage the Dominican military to refuse to accept Imbert and Amiama as four-star generals and thus precipitate a *golpe,* bringing down the government. But we did not know what we might get in its place. My notes of November 4, 1962, show, "It seems likely we might get Col. Wessin y Wessin, the strongman in

San Isidro, a man who seems to be a McCarthy type. I am not sure at all that I prefer him to Imbert."

Second, I could tell Bonnelly and the Consejeros bluntly we didn't like it. But that, coming after the affair of the Bosch-Fiallo summit meeting, might be viewed as serious intervention. Moreover, since the Consejo had already acted, the chance of getting it to reverse itself looked slight.

Third, I could tell Imbert and Amiama flatly we would not stand for it. How much backing could I get for the bluff? It was one thing to send the fleet to throw out the Trujillos, quite another to send it against Trujillo's assassins.

We decided to make it our objective to reduce them to one-star generals and to get the word *supervisores* removed from the decree. But we must be very careful. Much would depend on what the Armed Forces did tomorrow. Perhaps our initial moves tonight had generated enough pressure to do the job. I sent a cable and went to bed at 4 A.M.

Early next morning Colonels Cass and Long got me out of bed: The military high command had met with Amiama and Imbert, told them they would welcome them as one-star generals but not as four-stars, Amiama and Imbert had agreed, then all had called on President Bonnelly and he had agreed. Tonight Imbert would speak to the nation on radio and television, announcing that he and Amiama would be just one-star brigadiers among the boys. A new decree would be issued later.

Colonel Bill Richardson came in. Things were not quite so simple—the officers had had a difficult time persuading Amiama and Imbert; and President Bonnelly had suggested, under pressure from Amiama and Imbert, that Generals Viñas and Hermida also take one-star rank, not the two-star rank they now held. The organic military law was now being revised, limiting everybody to one-star. Military and Consejo would meet tonight at the Palace.

John Crimmins called. The Department wanted us to temporize, avoid pressure, and continue probing.

At 7 P.M. we gathered to hear Imbert on radio-TV. He renounced political ambition, said he would support the winner of the December election; said he and Amiama would not accept appointment as four-star generals, which had been offered, but only as one-star generals, the highest rank anyone should have.

The attachés scattered. Soon Cass telephoned: Viñas had issued an innocuous statement. Richardson called: The reduction to one-star status would take effect only after February 27. What were they now? Four-stars? One-stars? Or civilians? And were they still *supervisores*? The whole thing seemed to me as ambiguous as ever. The military, however, appeared to regard the question as settled. Cass called back: The military was at Imbert's house, celebrating, welcoming Imbert and Amiama into the Armed Forces. Thus Luna, who on Friday night wanted to bomb the Palace, was by Saturday night congratulating Imbert. Soon Amiama and Imbert turned up at a military function wearing their one-star generals' uniforms. We heard they had had them made months ago.

5

Whether or not Imbert and Amiama were formally subordinate to higher commanders, I thought that in fact they probably could dominate them. Imbert had indicated in his speech that he intended to maintain the military subordinate to the civilian government. But it is the history of such men that they are not moderate or subordinate. It is history that when men assassinate a dictator and survive, they tend to become dictators themselves, sometimes almost against their wills. We had been trying to maintain some separation of power among the military, the civil authority, and the police and criminal justice. Amiama and Imbert now might control all three, the entire power apparatus of the State. It seemed almost inevitable they would use their power.

Imbert and Amiama probably would see to it that good clean elections were held and the winner installed in the Palace. Why not? They could dominate him anyway.

What none of them realized—not Imbert, not Amiama, not even President Bonnelly—was that the situation today was not what it had been one hundred years ago or even fifteen. Until the end of World War II, it was possible for a local *caudillo* to cow the people and do as he pleased. Now, however, a new factor had been introduced—the confrontation between two great powers, the Soviet Union and the United States. Even if the United States were to stand aside, the Soviets would not. If Amiama and Imbert did embark on a Trujilloesque dictatorship, the final result was easy to predict—a true proletarian revolution, Marxist-led and Marxist-oriented. All the brave young men—14th of June, Social Christians, PRD, non-aligned—would have no choice but to go underground against the new dictatorship. This would inevitably throw them into the arms of the Communists—and their country into Moscow's hands.

If I were a Castro/Communist leader this weekend, I would be delighted. I would tell my young pupils that things were turning out just as I had predicted: The bourgeois Consejo had arrested López Molina and his friends and with the help of the *Yanqui* imperialists deported them; now the bourgeois Consejo and military, with *Yanqui* agreement, had installed Amiama and Imbert firmly as military dictators.

In short, I felt on that Sunday night as though we had just about lost our last chance in the Dominican Republic. Absolute power once collected must be used. Already the signs could be seen—dubious deportations, a self-censored press and radio-TV afraid of Imbert and Amiama.

Some of this had begun during the Cuban crisis, and, I fear, we had applauded some of it—e.g., deportations—for it had been in our interest. What Amiama and Imbert were doing now was distinctly not in our interest; but what could we do? Weren't they anti-Communist? Weren't we? We were in danger of getting caught in a trap we had helped build.

Amiama and Imbert need not hold elections. Their choices were endless. Suppose, for example, they loosed their five hundred *calié* from La Victoria prison, put them in the streets to create terror, and ordered their police to stand aside. We and President Bonnelly would beseech them to stop disorder—and having done so would be at their mercy. Or they might send their men to the hills to commence guerrilla activity. We would have to ask them to put down the rebellion. Not inconceivably, we might have to help with "military advisers." It would not be the first time, or the first place, where the U.S. had gotten trapped. Last week they had seized López Molina. Who would be next? Miolán? Many Dominicans considered him a Communist. (But now he thought this our problem!) Imbert and Amiama could imprison or deport anybody who stood in their way. Would they take the further steps Trujillo took —torture and murder? They had never seemed Trujillos to me. But perhaps Trujillo hadn't either, before he began. The danger was there. For power was their, too much power.

Responsibility for what had happened, I thought, belonged to all of us—President Bonnelly, the Consejo, the military, the political parties, ourselves. It had all happened before here, many times. The Republic's nineteenth-century history was replete with similar power grabs, petty partisanship, wasted opportunities. Were the people themselves to blame? Obviously it was too much to expect the uneducated, inert Dominican masses to understand and resist. Was it, however, too much to ask that the educated men of the Republic, the professional men and businessmen and oligarchs, speak up? They had not. Perhaps it was not in their tradition. This populace was still bound together by only the most slender of threads, the thread of family. It was almost a tribal society, where a man's responsibility reached only to the limit of his own family, not to the wider national community.

I could not find it in my heart to blame any of these people locked in struggle—not Imbert and Amiama, not the politicians, not the President or the Consejeros, not the military, not the Dominican people, not myself. We were simply people caught, trapped. People do what they have to do. Each of us, feeling the relentless pressures of life, had done what he had to do, or thought he ought to do. Bonnelly and the Consejeros had found themselves suddenly thrust by history into the Palace, and had done what they could. So had the young men plucked up almost by chance to lead the hated military. So had old Fiallo, proud civic leader, suddenly cast in the preposterous role of politician. So had

Bosch—after making a career of twenty-five years of exile, how could
he not come here, though crippled by fancies woven in exile? So had I,
following a long road that had begun by chance twenty-five years ago
because a freighter had dropped me on this island I never knew, leaving
it to pursue a wholly different course but never quite forgetting the
twenty-five-year-old dream, and suddenly, after the shots in the night,
leaving the Middle West and coming here. All of us had helped to
build our prison, most of all Amiama and Imbert. I did not know in
full what tortured course their lives had followed to set Imbert on the
highway with a gun that night, and Amiama waiting for the corpse at
the house of Juan Tomás Díaz; but I knew that if ever a man constructed a deadly trap to catch himself, Imbert had done it. All of us
were both shaping events and being shaped by them, but he most of
all. Killing the tyrant, he had pronounced his own death sentence. Without power he could not protect himself from the Trujillos' vengeance.
None of us was wicked, all were caught, Imbert most of all, pushed and
pulled by powerful political forces and even more by the great force of
life itself.

I had the feeling that we were dealing here with something far deeper
than mere politics. I dimly felt that somewhere on this tragic island
adrift in limitless, meaningless seas, beyond the air-conditioned Embassy
walls, on this tumbled land of city slums and desert dirt, of torture chambers and palm-lined beaches, these people, looking back to Trujillo's
butchers and ahead to the dark unknown, had come unhinged, that they
were cut adrift from creation itself, that they were not only disoriented
but also alienated from a world where things had meaning, and, that
being so, men's boundless capacity for good and evil had somehow become unloosed and was lashing around like a live wire in the dark. The
connection between man and the universe had snapped, what he did no
longer mattered or need have meaning, and one act was like another—
not good, not bad, not anything; the dam had burst, the flood was near.

6

For the moment, there was nothing to be done. I took my family out
of town for the weekend to visit the largest U.S. company in the Republic, La Romana, owned by the South Puerto Rican Sugar Company,
and to get some rest, the last before the election. The company's offices
and executives' houses were inside a fenced and guarded compound by
the sea. The buildings were the sort built by American companies and
occupation troops throughout this part of the world—square frame, standing on posts several feet off the ground, with overhanging eaves and
broad screened verandas. J. W. Tatem, Jr., a company official from New
York, and I sat up late, talking.

Tatem was here on a painful mission—to retire or reassign older men, Americans who knew sugar but were accustomed to "the old way of doing things," as Tatem put it. Times were changing, "we know that"; things "will be different from now on"; the company "has to readjust." The workers' company-owned houses, filthy shacks in a roadside slum, would have to come down, they were a red flag to agitators. Cane cutters who a year ago had earned a dollar a day were getting $3.25 and ready to strike for more, the company found itself making contracts with more than a dozen labor unions, it had hired an expert to negotiate with them, and suddenly he, not the mill boss or the field boss, was the most important man here.

The slime the company must have walked through here in the Trujillo years and in Washington among the sugar lobbyists was not hard to imagine. We did not discuss that, nor what might be in the minds of the Haitian cane cutters, working while the white American field bosses rode by on horseback wearing pith helmets. The question was: How could the company find its new place here in the Republic now, when a new world was being born? Sitting in the old-fashioned living room, watching Tatem, seeing him deeply concerned about things he had never needed be concerned about before, knowing he understood the broad shape of the problem but was perplexed and troubled by how to do what must be done, I saw one small side effect of the enormous shock waves running round the world in revolution.

La Romana had a guest house at Nisibón, far up the northeast hump of the island, and we drove there next day through miles of company land, flat cane fields and deep-grassed cattle land rolling eastward. It was always hot in the cane, and from the highway you could see the *bateys,* clusters of houses and barracks put up by the company: Haitian cane cutters lived there, shunning the towns, living alone together in the cane, speaking little Spanish and no English; they sweated and swung the machete all day, ate and went to bed with their women at night, walked barefoot in thick red mud, dwelt in filth, almost subhuman. Many times when we came this way we saw a funeral on the road: A score or two score Haitians, trotting very slowly down the road, men in the center bearing on their shoulders a child's tiny casket, slapping it gently as they trotted, and chanting a strange tuneless dirge in patois as they went, then turning into a muddy road to the burial ground. We pulled off to the side of the road, though other cars passed them; they seemed, trancelike, to notice nothing, a people and world apart (but more alienated than we or others?).

Far beyond the cane, past Seibo, past Higüey, through the rolling cattle country and in the rising foothills, was Nisibón. There was a river Nisibón, and on the map a hamlet Nisibón, but to us the word meant only the guest house we used. Nisibón—of all places in the Republic where we went to rest, it was the best. No one ever came here; we were alone. The guest house was a plain little concrete oblong, long and narrow, three bedrooms, a dining room, all small, a kitchen, plain furnishings. It stood on a high, grassy, breeze-swept knoll. On another knoll stood a windmill and several houses where cowhands lived. Behind rose purple mountains, steep and jungle-clad. In front, the grass was clipped to the fence, then sloped steeply in pasture over rolling ridges down to a swamp and so to the sea, dimly seen in the distance.

An aged woman cooked for us, and at night we used kerosene lamps and went to bed early and arose at 3:30 or 4 A.M., had breakfast, then got in the Jeep and drove at dawn down through the pastures, opening and closing wooden gates, heading for the sea. All my life I had hunted and fished, in recent years had taught my sons to, and in the States when written out had gone to the Michigan woods; here, when exhausted by politics, I went to Nisibón, nothing else really helped. I never felt so good as in the morning, in khaki pants and shirt and leather boots, driving the Jeep in four-wheel drive, low range, through swamp or heavy sand, one foot slung outside the Jeep, the sun coming up blood red over the sea, the boys and I with shotguns, Fran along for the ride, looking in this first dawn for guinea or pigeons or doves as we went through the pasture, then following a Jeep trail through a swamp to the coast, turning there, and driving along the beach.

Somehow there was more to it than merely feeling good. In the capital's vortex of power and politics, I, we, the Dominicans, all of us, had somehow lost touch with reality. Here, on the beach, in the sea, in the swamp, in the pasture, cows and horses and white birds flying, was reality again, the creation, and only touching it, smelling it, breathing it, restored and renewed and even saved sanity. The beach ran farther than you could see, ran the whole coast of the island, it seemed, curved and lonely and quiet but for the surf, the sand deep and gold. A few yards back from the water's edge a sand ridge rose, and coconut palms grew thick, and we wound our way along this ridge through the palms, their fronds rattling in the breeze; on the other side the land dropped into a swamp, dark, deep, impenetrable.

The Jeep crawled through sand for miles, then came to the river, the mouth of the Nisibón, broad, almost blocked by a sandbar, running deep in narrow current to the sea, surf pounding on the bar, white birds standing on one leg, sandpipers hopping about. A lighthouse stood at the point, and the lighthouse keeper lived there, but we seldom saw him. Sometimes an old man rode up on a burro, a coastwatcher, one of those employed by the Armed Forces to Guard the island's coast: An ancient, gray and ragged, silent and slow as his burro, smoking a pipe with a little tin lid when it rained, sitting his burro under the palms and watching us launch our boat and pile our casting rods in and push off and row upstream. The water was dark and brackish. It flowed sluggish through a mangrove swamp, widening broad and shallow and then, far across this muddy lake, the river itself came in, sweet water running thin and fast into the fetid muck. All the shore was mangrove swamp, mangrove trees rooted in the water, their limbs matting above and sending down shoots to grow into new trees in the water, a densely packed, impenetrable black wall: I never could understand how guerrillas could land on a mangrove coast.

We came several times to Nisibón; each visit was different. One day we drove farther north toward the Bay of Samaná. The wooden bridges were rotted out, and jungle covered their foundations. Up there was a lake, Lago Limón, and we drove the Jeep through wheel-deep mud, getting stuck in the rain, past scattered shacks, and talked to soldiers at a sentry post by the lake and, receiving at length permission from the *cabo* —corporal—fished the lake, and as we put out on it two great brown ducks rose, and Fred and I shot both. We got no fish, but we found the outlet to the sea, a channel so narrow that the mangrove trees and lush vegetation overarched entirely, and the sunlight was yellow-green, and the current ran swift, and we came to a series of bamboo gates, fishtraps, we thought at first, for most Dominican rivers are crisscrossed with fences made by poor people trying to catch fish to eat, but these were so strong we thought they might be barricades against guerrilla incursions; we turned back before reaching the sea.

On other days we drove back south, turned east near Higüey, and bounced over a rocky road to the most magnificent beach in the Republic: Macao, on the easternmost tip of the island. It stretched for miles in an enormous crescent between two rocky horns; so far as I know, though I never walked it all, it was all sand, deep yellow golden sand. There was no proper reef, only a few jagged rocks far out; and the surf boomed in powerfully from Mona Passage, and the swimming was excellent: To dive into the breakers, to struggle against them and win or lose, get knocked around by the sea's inexorable force, pounding, pounding, pounding endlessly.

On Sundays now and then three or four cars might come here, but no more. On one rocky horn stood two native huts. Back of them the rocky land rose steep to a ridge; here Fran would dig and find Indian relics, fragments of pottery, little carved faces, one inexplicable since it was a monkey's face, though monkeys are unrecorded here. While she dug, the boys and I and José, our driver who'd replaced Bailey, hunted guinea in the thickets. These birds always flew into the deepest, thorniest tangles; I do not remember ever killing one. But I do remember sitting with the boys on the tip of the cliff overlooking the beach and Bay of Macao, the surf booming far below.

And some days we simply drove the roads in the rolling country

around Nisibón, the blacktop roads, the muddy trails. It was cattle country, horse country, the only cowboy country left in the Republic, and on
Sundays the *finca* owners rode to town to a political meeting wearing
boots and starched white suits and broad-brimmed hats, a dozen horsemen galloping around a bend in the road, fine horses, expert horsemen.
At certain seasons flocks of pigeons and doves darkened the sky, and
hunters from the capital simply parked on the road at dawn, waited
by their car for the birds to come over, then shot, and kept shooting,
till their shoulders ached, and sent boys out to pick up the birds and
stuff them into hundred-pound sugar sacks. We sometimes saw great
piles of feathers by the roadside.

Once only did we find the tarpon feeding in the brackish mangrove
swamp of the Nisibón—that first time. High up where the sweet water
meets the salt, the water was boiling with them. We were casting bass
spoons and plugs; they hit them all. We could not hold them on our
light tackle, they broke lines and straightened hooks with a single powerful lunge, a silver streak knifing high in the air almost to the leafy arch
over the water, then splashing down and racing into the mangrove roots,
gone. We landed one, a small one about two feet long. Other days we
found them here, the water again churning with them, but we never
again found them striking. Nisibón, whether bright or rainy, fish or
no fish, guinea or no guinea, was the place, the best place, for us, the
most like the Michigan woods, the most alone. Toward dark, returned
from fishing or hunting or swimming or jeeping in the hills, we could
shower and make a drink and sit outdoors on the breast of the grassy
knoll and watch the horsemen herding the fat cattle slowly up the hills,
the windmill turning gently in the dying wind, white birds in great flocks
winging in from the far mountains and flying over the rounded hills
sailing in the air currents to alight in a tree, whitening it in the dusk—
cows and peace and white birds flying, sailing in the hills. Dusk dropped
black; we went indoors. Nisibón was the best.

7

Back in the capital on Tuesday, November 13, I read in *El Caribe*
that the previous night police had shot up the 14th of June headquarters
on Calle Conde. The 14th had been badly split again, this time by
the prospect of elections—Félix Germán, a popular non-Communist 14th
leader, had published an attack on the leadership, and it had called
him a deviationist. Shlaudeman heard that Amiama and Imbert were trying to take over the 14th of June. I went to see Imbert. He said he
was indeed trying to take the 14th of June away from Manolo Tavárez
Justo. But he said nothing about why the police had shot up the 14th's
headquarters. I thought he had gone too far, though I said nothing now.

Imbert had another list of deportees, mostly MPD and 14th of June men already under arrest, plus Havana-controlled PSP men still being sought. "I want to catch little Juan," Imbert said, smiling a little, savoring it already, Juan Ducoudray, maximum leader of the PSP. For deportees, Imbert needed U.S. visas to transit Puerto Rico. He was taking personal charge of anti-leftist activity. He said, "The newspapers are angry at me because I deport everybody. What can I do? No one else wants to take responsibility. We have to get ready for elections."

But how ready?

Suddenly Nicolás Silfa, purged from the PRD long ago by Bosch and Miolán, nominated ex-President Joaquín Balaguer for President on the ticket of his tiny PRDA—Authentic PRD. The Consejo adopted a decree heavily fining any airline or steamship company and canceling its landing rights if it sold a ticket to Balaguer. President Bonnelly told me he considered Balaguer a dangerous demagogue, with a following in the Army because he had raised their pay just before departing. Nicolás Silfa's party had asked the Electoral Board to certify Balaguer as a candidate. Bonnelly hoped it would refuse but said the Consejo probably would not intervene.

Soon Spence King, the DCM, reported that Foreign Minister Bonilla wanted us to keep Balaguer out of the Republic—if the Electoral Board did it, the Consejo would be accused of interfering with free elections. It struck me forcibly that the same Dominican government that recently had objected to my far milder intervention was now asking us to prevent a former Dominican President from participating in his own country's election.

Imbert told me that Nicolás Silfa's wife had told the police that President Kennedy was backing Balaguer personally. I denied it. Colonel Wessin y Wessin thought Balaguer's return would split the Armed Forces. I told the attachés to tell the military we were against Balaguer's return. A Dominican commander told me a few days later: "Balaguer is the elected President. He has every right to return. If he charters a plane and lands at San Isidro, we will give him all the honors due the President of the Republic—a twenty-one-gun salute. Right between the eyes."

The Department called: Héctor Trujillo wanted to leave Miami, where he had been living, and go to Panama. Panama was a crossroads of Caribbean intrigue. Reluctantly, I approved. I wondered if it was connected with Balaguer's moves. Coincidentally, Imbert received information from the States—he and Amiama had an intelligence system, of doubtful worth, spread around the Caribbean—that Héctor Trujillo had been talking to Balaguer.

The Department cabled that Balaguer's attorney had protested that the United States was preventing him from returning to the Dominican

Republic although the Dominican government never had officially notified him he could not return. The Department instructed me to ask what the Consejo proposed to do about it. I went to see President Bonnelly.

He said the Electoral Board had not decided yet whether to accept Balaguer's candidacy. The Consejo had kept out of it. If Balaguer returned, the Consejo could not guarantee his safety. I said the Consejo should tell him so. We could not keep him in the United States unless the Consejo officially notified him he could not return. Bonnelly refused to do it now: He would await the Electoral Board's decision.

Bonnelly and I discussed the mechanical problems of the election. The Electoral Board had at last pulled itself together and was making preparations. These were its plans (though some were changed later): Two ballots for each party would be printed, one for President and Vice President, one for other offices. At each polling place, the ballots of the different parties would be placed on a table in separate stacks in full view of the judges. Each voter would take two ballots from each stack, go into the curtained voting booth, choose two ballots, put them in an envelope, deposit it in the "urn" (ballot box), and throw the rest into a wastebasket. People would have to vote by *cédula;* it would be impossible to register them or bring their addresses up to date on their *cédulas.* Each polling place would be manned by representatives of the parties and the Board. To avoid repeat voting, I suggested each voter be required to dip his finger in indelible ink after voting. Bonnelly had already thought of it. The Armed Forces would keep order on election day under direction of the Electoral Board. The Electoral Board was sending mobile units we had provided for the Education ministry around the country, urging everybody to vote and explaining the procedure.

The filing deadline passed. We would have seven presidential tickets (eight if the Electoral Board accepted Balaguer). They were UCN (Fiallo), PRD (Bosch), PRSC, i.e., Social Christians (Moreno), VRD, i.e., Vanguardia (Ornes), ASD (Juan Isidro Jimenes Grullón), PN (Carbuccia), and PNRD (Mainardi, the governor of Santiago—the party belonged to "General" Ramírez but he was wise enough to run only for Senator from San Juan, thus ensuring his own election, and giving the presidential slot to Mainardi). We expected coalitions to reduce the number by one or two.

8

As I have said, the military high command had at first appeared satisfied with giving Amiama and Imbert one-star generalships. General Viñas himself, a square, short man with a clipped mustache, had told me, "It is the best solution for now, at least." Was Wessin y Wessin satisfied? *"Sí, señor,"* Viñas had said. "He has the armor. He is responsible to me." And the three service commanders? *"Sí, señor."* And all were behind the Consejo? *"Sí, señor."* I tried to draw him out but, as always, failed. I never could decide whether General Viñas thought silence prudent, whether he enjoyed being Sphinx-like, or whether he had nothing in his head. I could not believe the last, largely because his wife was quick and bright. Viñas had not even been disturbed by the proposal that he himself be reduced to one-star rank: Armed Forces regulations said that the Secretary of Defense must have ten years of active service, a qualification he had but neither Amiama nor Imbert did. As for *supervisores,* Viñas would tell Amiama and Imbert what to supervise.

But ominous signs appeared. Reid said that Amiama and Imbert themselves were not satisfied with one-star rank. The Consejo would rewrite the organic military law, providing that no higher rank could exist, but this would not help: Amiama and Imbert were frightened, for they now knew they were not really acceptable to the Armed Forces. This, I thought, was dangerous. Sure enough, the military, sensing trouble, began to harden its attitude against them. In revising the organic law, the military sought to insert a clause that could deprive them of their generalships. But they had friends inside the Armed Forces who opposed. I told the attachés to work to avoid a split in the Armed Forces. If a move was made, I wanted to be sure we made it.

But Amiama and Imbert moved first.

At 10:30 A.M. on November 15, Foreign Minister Bonilla told me we have "a grave problem." The Consejo was about to adopt a new decree giving Amiama and Imbert the rank of one-star general but also making them *supervisores* of the National Police as well as of the Armed Forces. Thus far President Bonnelly, Monseñor Pérez Sánchez, and Fernández Caminero had signed it. One more signature was needed.

At one forty-five Donny Reid came to see me, greatly agitated. Sitting on the edge of the couch, pounding his fist slowly into his palm, his face tense and drawn, he said, "I am not going to sign the decree. Pichardo is not going to sign." Would Reid resign? "No. I am going to stay and fight." This was good. What was the next step? "President Bonnelly will call a meeting to discuss the decree and the organic law. The Armed Forces will stand up to them. Why can't we, in the Consejo?" Was he sure the Armed Forces would stand up to them? He was. When had this happened? Yesterday—"the decree came to me at 4 P.M. with three signatures. I read it and asked about the Police part. They said they didn't notice, they thought it was only changing it to one star. I said no to the President." I wanted to understand as precisely as possible. Would Reid sign a one-star decree without the police? Yes. A one-star decree making them *inspectores instead* of *supervisores?* Yes. A one-star decree simply omitting the paragraph on their duties. Yes. Reid seemed depressed but determined. For once, I thought, Reid would not budge.

I sent out the Crisis Crowd. That night the Consejo met. So did the Armed Forces. So did the political parties. Word came in late that General Luna said the military didn't care what decree was promulgated —the military had an agreement with the parties to annul the decree anyway, February 27, when the elected government took power. If this story reached Imbert and Amiama, it might trigger a real showdown.

I decided to stay out of it for now. I hoped we could contain Amiama and Imbert without a showdown. The problem was to recognize our Munich—the point at which we would have to say, "Enough." But Munichs, though clear enough to historians, are less easy for participants to identify.

9

The UCN, to avoid an open factional struggle in Santiago, nominated for Vice President a man from Puerto Plata who was virtually unknown in the country at large. Bosch had even worse trouble with the PRD. It disregarded his advice by a single vote and nominated a bespectacled, routine politician from the Southwest, Buenaventura Sánchez, for Vice President over Juan Casasnovas, a younger man from San Pedro de Macorís. Bosch was furious—Buenaventura Sánchez was challenging his leadership. Sánchez had long ago told me he was better qualified for the Presidency than Bosch and must have said similar things to other people. Moreover, the story now went, Bosch was deathly afraid of Sánchez, a startling idea, for Goodluck, as we call him, seemed a mild enough fellow and looked like a schoolmaster. But Bosch, it seemed, lived in dread of him because once, while they were sipping *cafecitos* in Barahona, or some such place, several teen-agers had gathered to taunt them, and Goodluck, seizing a chair, had charged them, terrifying Bosch. And now Bosch, from his hiding place, was sending forth emissaries to treat with his running mate Goodluck, and, at the same time, sending other secret emissaries to try to reconvene the PRD convention. Lo and behold, he succeeded, and this time the convention nominated Segundo Armando González Tamayo, a young man little known to anyone. I learned later that Bosch failed in a more devious and important maneuver. Anticipating attack as a leftist, he had tried to persuade a priest or bishop to be his running mate. Had this succeeded, history might be different.

In any case, now at last the campaign proper had begun. A television commentator declared that if Bosch won, he would "let Fidel in" to the Republic. Bosch was gaining strength daily among the poor. Luís Manuel Baquero of UCN was talking about shooting Bosch—Bosch had introduced the "race issue" and the "class issue" into the campaign, calling UCN the white man's party and the party of the *tu-tum-potes. Tu-tum-*

pote[1] was, so far as I could discover, a made-up word, invented by Bosch and used tauntingly by him to mean the rich and well-born. It swept the country and passed into the language. It was marvelously effective with the poor. And so was his use of *compañero,* which means "companion," though UCNers reminded people that Fidel Castro used *compañero* to mean "comrade." Another word new to the Republic became part of the campaign vocabulary, *burgués,* bourgeois.[2] Some took it as evidence of Bosch's "leftist tendencies." I thought it simply represented the spread of an idea, a century late, to the Republic.

Until very recently, the UCN had complacently assumed an easy victory. Now it had suddenly wakened to the truth. It had emphasized Fiallo's nobility, the people's nobility, freedom's nobility. This was wearing thin. A favorite Fiallo phrase from the summer of 1961 had been *"El noble sufrido pueblo Dominicano,"* "the noble suffering Dominican people." The only glimmering of humor I ever detected in Fiallo came now: He told me, with a half-smile, that he did not think he would talk much more about "my noble suffering Dominican people." Fiallo was, as ever, patriotic, brave, well-intentioned, filled with integrity, but a bumbling politician. UCN could draw on men of ability around the country to form a government; Bosch had almost nobody. Fiallo was still the closest thing to a national hero the Republic had; Bosch had to fight uphill. But heroism too wears thin; and of what use is it to be able to form a government if you can't get elected? And all this while, Bosch was out in the provinces or on the radio, cutting Fiallo to ribbons and pounding away at the gut issues—jobs, food, land. Everybody said he promised the people the moon. He has often denied it, said he promised the *campesinos* nothing but land. He has also denied fomenting class antagonism—it always existed—or race hatred. Bosch spoke to the *campesinos* with simple, powerful eloquence.

Shlaudeman said the UCNers, knowing their campaign was somehow going wrong, were sitting around wringing their hands. The oligarchy was depressed about UCN's chances. Fiallo had made a trip around the Caribbean, intended to enhance his international prestige, but it had not gone well. His reception in the democratic nations with ties to Bosch had been poor.

[1]Bosch has said that *tu-tum-pote* had been current in the Cibao when he was a child there but had fallen into disuse. He says its origin is obscure—perhaps it comes from Latin "because it seems to sound in that language very much like what it meant to the Dominicans in the Cibao around 1912—'Señor todopoderoso,' an all-powerful gentleman with an abundance of money." On the other hand, he says, it could have arisen during the Haitian occupation, since the Haitian language contains many words with the sound of "tuntun" or "tutun."

[2] Bosch writes that *burgués* was current, with all its Marxist overtones, in the Republic when he returned from exile in the fall of 1961. According to Bosch's structure of Dominican society, no native bourgeoisie exists in the Republic.

The UCN made dreadful mistakes. Fiallo, completing his Caribbean tour, said in Puerto Rico that some points of the Vatican concordat might need reform, thereby disturbing the Church, which might have been expected to favor him. Bosch, who expected Church attack, said he felt sure Fiallo had been misquoted—he could not believe Fiallo opposed the Vatican concordat. Infuriated, Luís Manuel Baquero launched a bitter personal attack on Bosch. Bosch immediately ascended to a lofty moral position and said that all candidates should respect one another. Upon Fiallo's triumphal return, the UCN took him straight from the airport to the poorest *barrio* in Santo Domingo, Güaley, a PRD stronghold, without advance preparation; he was booed and stoned. Bosch immediately issued a statement decrying stone-throwing and repeating his respect for his patriotic friend, Fiallo—then went himself into the same *barrio* and was wildly applauded. Apparently hearing that Bosch was making headway with the race issue, Fiallo went into a *barrio* and referred to "my little Negritos," a patronizing phrase that could scarcely have been better calculated to cost him their votes. Bosch quickly dropped the race issue and tirelessly accused Fiallo, more in sorrow than in anger, of having raised it.

Fiallo's managers, Baquero and Alfredo Lebrón, a devoted young Trujillo fighter, really knew nothing about politics. Bosch's campaign, on the other hand, was thoroughly professional, organized by tough, professional Ángel Miolán. Bosch never attacked the Castro/Communists, the military, or the Trujillistas. Why alienate voters? UCN attacked all three. Bosch went into the countryside in a Jeep. UCNers went in cavalcades of big cars, wearing business suits.

UCN accused Bosch of owning five hundred thousand acres in Costa Rica and having two million dollars in Venezuelan banks—a *tu-tum-pote* himself. Bosch scornfully offered to sell his land for twelve cents an acre and his money for a nickel on the dollar. Fiallo defined *tu-tum-pote* as anyone with a fine house, many cars, and a large bank account amassed in exile—Bosch, obviously—while Fiallo had stayed home to fight Trujillo and owned no large house, cars, or bank accounts. He declared triumphantly that some who called others *tu-tum-potes* were themselves *tu-tum-potes*. Most of the campaign was carried on at about this level.

Fiallo's managers fought for the places where Fiallo was weak, such as San Pedro de Macorís, instead of getting out his maximum vote where he was strong.

The UCN was beating itself. Day after day the UCN radio program attacked Bosch by name on a nationwide hookup, free advertising Bosch could not have afforded. This upper-class party had a leftist ensconced in an air-conditioned suite in the fanciest hotel in town, the Embajador, writing a lofty platform and program of government for the party. When it was finished, Fiallo handed it over to some priests so they could remove any taint of socialism from it, as he put it. Next Fiallo would give it to some leftist economists who would put the socialism back in. After this they would prepare a digest of it. Then they would get it printed. Half the populace is illiterate. By the time the platform finally did come out, shortly before the election, it was an interminably long screed, more tract than platform, that few people read and fewer understood. Meanwhile Bosch was going around the country promising the *campesinos* land. Fiallo's worried advisers told Fiallo to outpromise Bosch. This was obviously hopeless. UCN grew shriller; Bosch stayed on the lofty plane Fiallo should have occupied. The Fiallo campaign was about the worst I had ever seen.

Obviously Bosch was a much better candidate than Fiallo. Fiallo probably would make a more reliable President but I doubted he would get a chance to prove it. I did not think Bosch would double-cross us on foreign policy. I told the Department that, assuming Bosch had been checked meticulously by our intelligence agencies, he would probably handle the Communists' attempts to infiltrate his government more skillfully than Fiallo, since, in exile politics, he had had more experience with them. Bosch would join the growing list of non-Communist leftist Presidents in the Caribbean, another leader who was enthusiastically in sympathy with the progressive goals of the Alliance for Progress. But Bosch looked much better from afar than from close up. What worried me was the man himself, his character—arrogant, vain, erratic. I thought it not impossible he might resign within a year if elected. I feared that if he won he would have more difficulty getting into the Palace alive than Fiallo, and, once in, would face formidable opposition: The *civicos* had money and power, and they were for Fiallo, and, in opposition, could make serious trouble for Bosch, whereas Bosch's own followers, in opposition, could do little to a victorious Fiallo, for they lacked power and money; they were simply the people. And I feared too that the demagogic candidate might become a charlatan President. I feared, in short, that while Bosch might win, he would have great difficulty governing.

Shlaudeman began making some preliminary computations. It wasn't easy—we didn't even know how many people lived in the Republic. But we wanted something. The Electoral Board expected nine hundred thousand votes, the top serious estimate was one million. Shlaudeman was guessing as of now that no one party would get a clear majority. He guessed as of now, a month before the election, that UCN would poll 38 percent (a fifteen-thousand-vote plurality), PRD 36 percent, Social Christians 11 percent, and the remainder scattered. But PRD was pulling ahead fast.

The UCN was strong, Shlaudeman thought, in the capital and Santiago, the central Cibao, and a few scattered provinces. The PRD was strong in the Southwest, the lower Cibao, the cities near the capital, along the frontier, and parts of the East. To put it another way, the PRD was strong on the fringes, the UCN at the center. The other parties were nowhere, except that General Ramírez was strong in his home province in the West, San Juan de la Maguana.

We still heard grumbling that "the people are not ready for elections." But as each day passed, nothing, I thought, except widespread disorder, could stop the election now.

10

A cable came in Sunday night, November 18: Balaguer was thought to be planning to come to the Republic and would land at San Isidro Monday night at eleven o'clock. I went to Bonnelly's house at 7 A.M. on Monday and warned him.

At 8:30 A.M. Fran and I went to the beautiful Cathedral for a memorial mass for the Nigua martyrs, the six men murdered a year ago when Ramfis Trujillo had left. In front pews sat the entire diplomatic corps and the government. In front of us on straight-backed benches sat the widows and mothers of the martyrs, all in black with black mantillas against a massive white column. Behind us the beautiful and awesome cathedral was filled to overflowing, white vaulted ceilings high as the sky, gold and splendor at the candlelit altar, the benches and railing dark mahogany worn by ancient guilt and grief. The Mass began. Fran and I watched an old man by the altar rail who signaled the diplomatic corps and government to rise or sit at the proper times.

I was trying to sort out the problems we had, the moves we must make, the cables to send, the people to see. The majestic Mass moved on, the Papal Nuncio, Monseñor Clarizio, celebrating it, resplendent in scarlet robes, with bishops and priests and altar boys assisting; the Latin rolled out over the silent people to the catafalque of Columbus; the widows and mothers and sisters of the dead sat in silence, some weeping quietly in black, comforted by a white hand on a shoulder, while outside a bicycle bell jingled once. Throughout, the wives of Amiama and Imbert wept; their husbands alone had been saved from death. Could the purity of the white ceiling, the purity of faith, expunge so much evil that had gone before and that almost surely lay ahead? The women in black sat, and Mass ended. President Bonnelly rose and gravely walked to the altar rail and shook hands with each widow and mourner, the Consejeros following, followed by several other Ambassadors and I, and I shook the hand of each, mumbling, blind to them, they blind to me, then found Fran and dropped money in the alms box and went outside into the blazing light. The city streets still smelled fresh and wet from the night, though the sun was burning.

At the office, a CIA man said Balaguer would arrive at Punta

Caucedo airport, not San Isidro. I told Fandino to telephone Bonnelly.

A strange telegram came in from the Department. Fabio Herrera, the Republic's only permanent civil servant, the only indispensable man in the Palace, had turned up in Washington on an urgent mission. Bonnelly had sent him secretly to tell the Department he needed a show of U.S. support immediately—Imbert was insisting on immediate promulgation of the generalship decree and on permitting his cousin, Moncho, to keep control of Haina; a long-brewing scandal concerning four million dollars missing from Haina might wreck the Consejo; the attack on the 14th of June headquarters had been an Imbert plot; Amiama was encouraging Balaguer to return so Imbert could arrest him personally and restore himself as hero. Herrera suggested a ship visit so I could take Bonnelly and the military high command—but not Imbert—aboard for lunch. I must not mention Herrera's trip to anyone in Santo Domingo, not even to Bonnelly himself.

The Department said that, if I wished, it would try to get a ship into the harbor in twenty-four hours. The excuse would be that it was off the Cuban quarantine line. The Department asked me to telephone immediately. I did. The ship would arrive Wednesday.

The Electoral Board rejected the Balaguer candidacy on a technicality. Nicolás Silfa announced he would appeal. The CIA chief reported both San Isidro and Punta Caucedo airports heavily guarded.

I went to see Bonnelly and gravely invited him and his military high command to lunch aboard the ship. Gravely he accepted. (I never learned why I could not mention to him Herrera's visit to the U.S.) Bonnelly said that Pan American had sold a ticket to Balaguer on Flight 229 to Santo Domingo from New York on Thursday. The President asked me to stop him from departing if possible.

Washington called Wednesday: It was absolutely essential that the Dominican government this afternoon order its consul in New York to inform Balaguer formally that he could not return to the Dominican Republic; the U.S. could not hold Balaguer unless the Dominican government formally exluded him. Our warship arrived, the U.S.S. *Davis,* and I took the President, General Viñas, and the three service commanders aboard for lunch, and during lunch told Bonnelly flatly he had to notify Balaguer this afternoon. Bonnelly promised to do it immediately and to call me by 4 P.M. By six I had not heard from him and called him. He said the Consejo had decided not to do it; they feared to give Balaguer a weapon he could use against them. This annoyed me. I would be glad when we got a government willing to govern.

The next day, Balaguer declared in New York that Pan American had told him it could not take him to Santo Domingo because Dominican authorities had threatened to confiscate any aircraft that took him there.

Pan American said it had done so on instructions of the U. S. Immigration Service. A Balaguer representative told the press that Balaguer would go to the Republic in any airplane that would carry him.

Bosch announced publicly that he would withdraw from the election campaign if each party did not have a ballot of a distinctive color. The Social Christians said the same. Vanguardia and ASD were meeting to decide their own position. The Electoral Board declared all ballots would be white, and would not discuss the matter with the parties. Bosch denounced its "trickery."

Though it seemed absurd, the issue was important. Illiterate voters could not distinguish readily among the parties. So each party's ballot must have a distinctive color. Furthermore, the parties had counted on this and used it: Bosch had chosen white as the color of his party's ballot and had urged his voters to "vote white." The Social Christians' campaign slogan was *"Vota verde"*—"vote green." I told Shlaudeman and Serban Vallimarescu, USIS head, to find out whether enough colored paper existed in the Republic, and, if not, where we could get it quickly.

I dictated letters to journalist friends in the States, inviting them to cover the Dominican election. I wanted as much press coverage as possible, hoping that *golpistas* would hesitate if the eyes of the world were on them.

11

At 6 P.M. on Friday, November 23, I went to a reception at the Foreign Office. At eight I hurried over to a labor rally. President Bonnelly spoke, and spoke well, and was cheered. I left with him and went to his home, where he was giving a party in honor of his daughter's birthday. The little house was filled. I had scarcely greeted the President's wife and daughter when Tony Imbert saw me, abruptly left some people he was talking to, and came to me. We stood in the center of the living room and talked. We talked for about two hours. Now and then other guests would drift near; we would ignore them. Once or twice Fran came by, bringing coffee or a plate from the buffet. She told me later everybody had watched us talking loudly and gesturing violently. They were afraid we were arguing. Indeed we were.

Imbert said he was fed up. He said that if the question of his generalship was not resolved next week he would resign from the Consejo and from the Army. So would Amiama. He was hurt, deeply hurt, by the way people were treating him. He had done so much for his country and now everyone despised and distrusted him. He had had enough. He wished that he had gone the political route and backed the coalition. On my advice he had not. Now he only wanted to be a general, but even that was opposed. He would retire and go home and sit in his house and be a simple citizen.

I said, "Bull shit. You can't be a 'simple citizen,' not ever, and you know it."

Imbert said, "*Sí, señor.*"

"*No, señor.* Look. You have two problems right now. You went too far in the deportations and in sending the police to shoot up the 14th of June headquarters ten days ago. And you went too far in collecting power for yourself."

He frowned. "*No, señor.* The problem is Donny"—Donny Reid, who had refused to sign the generalship decree.

"You're wrong. The problem is you and Luís. You have tried to collect too damn much power. You want to be a general. You want to be the supervisor of all three branches of the Armed Forces and the police too. And so the military, the parties, the man in the street, and everyone else is afraid that you want to be another Trujillo, another dictator."

"But I don't."

"I know you don't. But everyone else thinks you do. Look, Tony. It is an axiom of politics that power gained must be used. History, all history, shows that too much power leads to dictatorship whether it is intended to or not. I personally don't think you intend to be a dictator. But you have collected so much power that you may go down that road whether you want to or not."

Imbert shrugged, unimpressed.

I said, "Let me tell you something else. You can't get away with it. Not in the 1960s. It is too late in history. Listen to me. Thirty years ago these little countries could do as they pleased. Anyone with power could set himself up as a dictator. But not now. You know why?" He was listening now, for the first time. "Because even if the Dominican people would allow it, and even if we, the United States would keep hands off, Soviet Russia would not. Look at what happened to Fidel Castro. He seized all power—the Army, the police, the economy, everything. And the Russians moved in, in a few weeks, and they took him over, and now that they no longer need him they sent Mikoyan in—and Mikoyan stuck a knife in his heart and cut his heart out. They would do the same thing to you, or anyone else, who tries it here."

For once, Tony Imbert seemed impressed with an idea. He had stopped talking, was listening intently. I do not think this had occurred to him before. Then we returned to the generalship decree. It had been hanging fire now for about two weeks. Imbert said he was going to bring it to a head. I asked if he was willing to remove the phrase "*y policía*" from the decree. He said he was. I said *supervisores* is not in any Spanish dictionary and asked him what it meant. He said it simply meant that he could go around and supervise things and see what was going on in the

Armed Forces. Did this mean he would be an inspector? He said yes. I proposed then the word be changed to *inspectores*. He indicated he would agree.

I asked if he intended to back a political party. He said no. He said he thought the PRD was sure to win. I asked what this would mean for him. He said, "We can get along with Bosch." But the interregnum between the election and inauguration would be highly dangerous. The losers would make trouble. "You still do not understand my people, Mr. Martin," he said. "You cannot trust any of them." Bosch's and Fiallo's agreement with me that they would accept the result of the election meant nothing. "Nobody can trust any Dominicans. Least of all Dominican politicians."

Agitated again, he said once more he would retire to his home and become a simple citizen. I told him again this was nonsense—what would he do at home? He said he would just sit and maybe travel around the country. Doing what? Resting, he said. "Baloney," I said, "I know you better than that." I told him he was trying to "do a De Gaulle"—go into seclusion and wait for his country to call him back to save it. He admitted something like this was on his mind—but it might be only a couple of weeks before he would be needed.

Imbert went on. He could not live anywhere except in the Dominican Republic. I agreed. In Chicago, New York, Paris, anywhere, he risked assassination by Trujillo agents. Nowhere else could he be so well-guarded as here. I told Imbert I sympathized fully with him but he must understand how other people feared the power he possessed. He said that had it not been for him and Amiama the Consejo would long since have fallen. I said President Bonnelly's skill in political maneuvering had helped it survive. He said he did not wish to comment on this.

Imbert said he could make a lot of trouble. I told him I could make trouble too—any jerk could make trouble—but it took a man to make peace and do constructive things. I recalled to him that some time back everyone had agreed that he and Amiama could be simply one-star generals. Why didn't everybody return to this position? He wasn't happy about it. But when we finally parted, I believed that if Reid held firm, and if the military did, Imbert would back down.

12

Vice President Pichardo's bodyguard, a young Army lieutenant, was getting married next evening and had asked me to be a witness. The bride's parents lived in a little house out on the edge of town. As the big cars drew up—Bonnelly's, Reid's, Pichardo's—a crowd gathered. Inside, the house was jammed, all was confusion; as always Fran and I simply waited and smiled until told what to do. Soon we drove in procession a

DOMINICAN PEOPLE AND PLACES

Ambassador Martin and a Dominican farmer, in the interior

Going into the barrios, interpreter Joe Fandino at right

"Sometimes I felt that I was imprisoned in the air-conditioned Embassy Residence, an impenetrable wall between me and the people...tours of slums became official tours. ...I had resolved to spend all the time possible in the interior. I was the Ambassador to all the Republic, not just the capital. I wanted to learn everything possible about the Republic's problems, and at first hand...."

5

Addressing the town meeting at San Juan de Maguana, with the local officials

"For an hour or two we sat in the town...with the people in front of us anyone who wanted to come. I spoke briefly—the United States admired the Dominican people's struggle and that of the Consejo to emerge from Trujillo tyranny to democracy; we were here to help, I was traveling to learn. I invited questions. Various people spoke. Once more, it came down to jobs and water...."

"The Second Vice President Donald Reid Cabral, an aggressive young businessman."

Viriato A. Fiallo, physician and unsuccessful candidate for President

Commodore Julio Alberto Rib Santamaría, Navy Chief of Staff

"Luís Amiama Tió…dapper, mustached, erect, reserved, impenetrable."

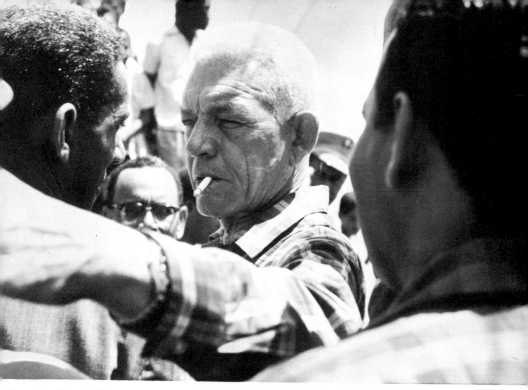

Juan Bosch, whistlestopping at Sánchez

"...as Bosch walked slowly through the palm grove beside the row of tin-roofed houses, a crowd gathered, scores of people pressing on him, asking him for jobs, and he stopped and made a speech to them....He was very good, whistlestopping. He shook hands, embraced anyone who offered, smiled often, asked people precise questions about prices, crops, wages, his gaze darting quickly over the crowd, spotting someone he knew....He was friendly and expert."

Colonel Elías Wessin y Wessin

"He was a short, stocky, powerful, youngish man ...kept to himself, had few friends...was brave, dollar-honest, and sincere. He hated [the Communists]. He considered them the embodiment of evil. He would give them no quarter."

Dominican poverty is never far away: on the road to Nisibón

"Nisibón—of all places in the Republic where we went to rest, it was the best. No one ever came here; we were alone. The guest house was a plain little concrete oblong...on a high, grassy, breeze-swept knoll....Behind rose purple mountains, steep and jungle-clad. In front the grass was clipped to the fence, then sloped steeply in pasture over rolling ridges down to a swamp and so to the sea, dimly seen in the distance....Nisibón was the best."

Fran, Fred, and Dan Martin near Nisibón

few blocks to the church, and, prompted by Donny Reid, I went to stand behind the bride and groom at the altar, flanked by President Bonnelly, First Vice President Pichardo, Second Vice President Reid, and Foreign Minister Bonilla, then signed the witness book. Then we all went back to the house and in the little walled patio drank champagne in the soft tropic night. Pichardo told me the entire Electoral Board was going to resign.

It would resign because the Social Christians had complained that only one ballot instead of two would be used and because Bosch had complained that all the ballots would be white. All this, the Electoral Board members felt, impugned their honor. So they would resign.

"So?" I asked.

"So," Pichardo said, "no elections," and shrugged.

From the bride's house we went to a ball at the Armed Forces Club. While the band blared and the officers and their wives ate and drank and danced, and the flashbulbs popped and the floodlights glared, I took Pichardo aside, said we could not let this happen, and told him that if the problem was finding colored paper for the ballots, we would supply it. He thought this might help. Suddenly Pichardo left with the President and Imbert. Obviously something important was up.

I went home, called Shlaudeman, and he came to the house and I told him what had happened. The OAS advisory mission to the Electoral Board was here. I told Shlaudeman to go see its head, Victor Goytía of Panama, waking him if necessary. He did, and Goytía confirmed it: Despite his urging, the Board had reached an irrevocable decision to resign. This, if it happened, would mean the death of Dominican democracy.

On Monday, Shlaudeman reported that the Electoral Board said it would be extremely difficult to find seven distinct colors of paper; in any case it had no colored paper at all. It must use single ballots because the voters simply would not have time to handle double ballots—the polls were open only for about 720 minutes, each polling place had five hundred voters, and they could not vote fast enough to get finished if they were handed fourteen separate ballots to choose among.

I saw President Bonnelly. He said he could handle things. The Armed Forces leaders had called on him Sunday to assure him of their support. This had bucked him up considerably. He told me he would not permit the Electoral Board to resign, and if they did he and the Army would run the elections themselves. I told him we would get colored paper. Shlaudeman scurried around, trying to find out just what the problem was. Confusion increased. Finally, either the President or Pichardo called the parties and the Electoral Board together. After long speeches and deliberations, they worked out a series of private and public declarations that saved everybody's face—the parties recognized the disinterest of the Electoral Board, accepted a perforated single ballot instead of two ballots so that a voter could quite literally split his ticket by tearing the ballot in half, and reached agreement on the question of colored ballots. As a standby, I told Vallimarescu to order colored paper from the USIA. By Tuesday this crisis was over.

13

The Consejo caved in to a new FENEPIA demand—it agreed to pay the traditional 100 percent Christmas bonus. *El Caribe* said editorially the country was confused about elections, blamed all the parties, and called for an end to bickering.

A strange calm appeared to have set in. The government appeared simply to be waiting for the election. Bosch was certainly going to win. He was talking about getting six hundred thousand votes, about Fiallo's getting only two hundred thousand. Bosch and his wife came to lunch with Fran and me. I had never seen him so calm and confident. I told him, as I told all the others, that if he won we looked forward to working with him. His wife, Carmen, a Cuban, was small and soft-faced and seemed sweet.

General Viñas came to lunch. We discussed military matters and the MAAG program, then I turned to the elections. I told him we were neutral and asked how he felt. He said he agreed. I asked him specifically if he, and if the Armed Forces, would accept a Bosch victory. He said they would. It was a flat commitment, unmistakable, and we both knew it.

Three weeks to go. Journalists and OAS observers were arriving. Everyone was saying that everything would be all right. The left was quiet. So was everybody else. Too quiet. I had the feeling that beneath the surface a good deal was going on that we didn't know anything about.

Amiama broke a date with me on Tuesday night, November 27. I had not seen Imbert since our long talk at Bonnelly's party. On Thursday an emissary brought me word that Imbert wanted to see me immediately—he proposed to reconstitute the Consejo and wanted to know whom I wanted him to put in power for the next two years or so.

He and Amiama were hiding out in a little police building on Avenida Independencia. They wanted me to bring with me Colonel Cass, Colonel Wolfe of the MAAG, and Jackson, our police adviser. I sent word back I would see them alone. They finally agreed to see me Saturday at Imbert's house.

What had they been up to? I sent out the attachés. They reported that Amiama and Imbert had been telephoning Army headquarters, pretending to be at various military camps around the country and giving orders. They had ordered troops stationed along the Punta Caucedo runway to watch for Balaguer, ordered Air Force jets into the air to shoot down unidentified aircraft, and finally summoned Colonel Wessin y Wessin and several Air Force colonels and accused them of mixing in politics.

The colonels denied it and reported to General Luna. The military high command met *en masse* with Viñas on Friday afternoon. They were united—they would not accept Amiama and Imbert as generals under any circumstances. Furthermore they were determined to hold the elections, come what might. Luna demanded that the military force Bonnelly to defy Amiama and Imbert.

Saturday I went to my appointment with them at Imbert's house. They seemed rested, cheerful, jovial; we spent nearly an hour kidding each other. I gave them some information we had received about the activities of the Trujillo family in Spain and Paris, indicating they were plotting to assassinate Imbert and Amiama. Finally Imbert got to the point. "Mr. Martin," he said, "I don' see clear." It was a favorite expression. "I don' see clear," shaking his head. "Luís and I have been talking and thinking about our position in front of the Dominican people, in front of history, in front of the world." Then, gesturing eloquently, he went into the story I had heard so many times—they, who had done so much for their country, were misunderstood and unappreciated. "So you see, Mr. Martin—it is impossible, it cannot be." He waited. Amiama was looking at the ceiling, humming tunelessly. "So Mr. Martin, what do you think?"

I said, "I understand. But what do you want? I can't presume to tell you what to do."

Imbert said, "But what is your position?"

I repeated that I would not presume to tell them what to do, but since he had asked I would give them my views. I then repeated, Fandino translating for Amiama, what I had told Imbert the other night. But when I said they had gone too far in shooting up the 14th of June headquarters, Amiama suddenly sat up straight and asked what I meant. I said I thought that whoever had ordered the shooting of the headquarters had made a serious political mistake.

Amiama said, "Do you think we gave that order?"

I said I didn't know but that's what the talk in the streets was.

Amiama said, "Listen to me. I will tell you the truth about that." He said that on that night he had been sitting at home with his wife listening to phonograph music when the telephone rang. It was a girl he knew. She had run over a policeman with her car and wanted him to straighten it out. He went to the garage, got into his car, which was equipped with a two-way police radio, and called police headquarters. While so engaged he heard an emergency call that a policeman had been killed on Calle Conde at the 14th of June headquarters. He grabbed his machine gun and immediately raced down there.

He found police converging on the scene. They were going in after

the 14th of June men and invited him to come along. He said he
would not because he was not a policeman. He waited. Presently they
brought three men out. He told them not to mistreat the men but to take
them to police headquarters and lock them up. By this time at least sixty
policemen had arrived, all nervous and heavily armed. He started to
walk back to his car. Suddenly he heard a powerful explosion and heavy
firing. He whirled with his machine gun ready. The policemen were
shooting. He saw there was nothing to shoot at and screamed at them to
stop, to find out what they were shooting at and stop acting like damn
fools. They finally did, then went away. "So that is all there is to it," he
said leaning back and smiling. "Nothing. Later I had to buy a new
bicycle for the policeman the girl ran over."

I said—truthfully—that I believed this story, it was just another crazy
mess, but it didn't change his problem and Imbert's. They simply had
been collecting unto themselves too much power and for that reason
everybody feared they wanted to become dictators; and I repeated at
length what I had told Imbert previously—even if we and the Dominican people let them seize power, the Soviets would not let them keep it.

Amiama, who had listened thoughtfully, asked, "Do you think I intend
to be a dicatator?"

I said, "I told you in the first place I didn't think so—but a lot of other
people do. And no matter what you intend, if you collect too much
power, you'll go that way whether you intend to or not. History will push
you into it."

Amiama said bitterly, "What do you think we ought to do—get ourselves put in a glass jar and put in some museum?"

I said, "No. And I don't think you can become just 'simple citizens'
either, as Tony said."

"Then what," scornfully, "do you think we ought to do?"

I said that, if they wished, speaking unofficially and as a friend, I
would tell them what I would do in their situation. They wished. I said it
seemed to me inevitable that they would be people of importance in this
country for a long time to come. I said I thought they now possessed,
or were seeking, all power—civil power, political power, power of public
opinion, military power, and police power. I said if I were they I would
strip myself of some of these powers.

Amiama said, "Which ones?"

There was a silence in the bare, fluorescent-lit room. Then I said that
their civil-political power would automatically end on February 27 when
they would depart from the government, so that was settled. The question of public admiration or hostility would depend entirely on their own
future conduct. If I were they I would drop the police power because it
meant nothing but trouble.

Imbert exploded, "But we don't have it."

I said, "The talk on the streets is that you do."

"*No, señor.*"

"All right—but if you haven't, you're trying to get it."

Amiama said, "We are not."

I said, "It's in the decree."

Imbert said, "*No, señor.*"

"Tony, I've seen a copy of the decree. It's in there. Look, what do you want the police for? If what you really want is what you say you want—protection and honor, and to serve your country—then the best place for you is inside the Army."

Amiama grunted. I went on. I recommended that they accept one-star generalships without any definition of their duties—not supervisors, or inspectors, or anything else, but simply one-star generals, and that they place themselves at the disposition of the Commander of the Army, who in turn was under the Secretary of Defense, who in turn was under the President.

They were silent. They glanced at each other. Then Imbert said, "I would accept this. But no one else would have a higher rank, except the President."

I said I thought the Secretary of Defense or Chairman of the Combined Chiefs should have temporary two-star rank. He disagreed. I told him he would have to work that out with the Army.

Amiama said, "I am willing to accept this for Tony but for myself I want nothing at all if Tony gets this."

I said, "Fine."

The phone rang. It was General Viñas summoning them to the Palace to a meeting of all the military.

Belisario Peguero, their man, also called.

They let Viñas wait about fifteen or twenty minutes and then we all left.

Fandino recalled that once before I had used the truth about power the same way: When I had talked to Ramfis Trujillo long ago. Fandino also said that during these confrontations with Amiama and Imbert he was extremely nervous—"it's you who's telling them where to get off but the words are coming out of *my* mouth!"

I quickly called the Crisis Crowd to the Residence and told the attachés to find out what was happening at the Palace. King handed me a message: Balaguer had slipped his surveillance in New York, gone to Florida, and was planning to enter the Dominican Republic secretly this weekend. Rodríguez Echavarría was said to be behind the plans. I went immediately to see President Bonnelly.

I found him surrounded with his friends—Bonilla, Reid, Ramón Cáceres, Tapia, his son, his son-in-law. They left. He was drinking. It was noon. I told him first about Balaguer, then about my conversation with Amiama and Imbert, making it clear I had gone to them at their request and had spoken unofficially.

The President was feeling cocky and confident. He said several times that nobody fooled him because he was fifty-eight years old and knew his way around in politics. The important thing, however, was to appear to be a fool. He applauded what I had told Amiama and Imbert. He said he had repeatedly postponed decision on the generalships. Finally yesterday he had told General Viñas to handle it. He hoped Viñas would tell them what I had now already told them.

It was his way—arranging things so that Viñas and I would do his work for him. He went on. If necessary, he would assume his role as actual Commander in Chief in order to hold the election. He had been warned of a plot to kidnap him. He never left the house day or night without his full bodyguard.

After February 27 he was going to the United States. He had a farm which he thought he could sell for nine thousand dollars; could he and his wife live in the U.S. for a year on nine thousand dollars? I offered him my home there. I told him I envied him and reminded him that my work would only begin February 27. This came as a new thought to him—he and the other Consejeros seemed to feel that I was one of them.

That evening Cass and Long reported that at the Palace meeting, Amiama and Imbert had agreed to accept one-star generalships without any designation of duties and without inclusion of the police. The military was now reporting to the President at his house.

It appeared that once more a solution, at least a temporary one, to the Imbert-Amiama problem had been achieved.

14

During the first week in December the campaign heated up. Severo Cabral of UCN predicted widespread election fraud. A UCN meeting at Baní ran into a hail of stones. Baquero demanded an investigation. A man was caught smuggling four revolvers through the airport. The electric company struck; the Consejo gave the workers what they wanted. Bosch said the UCN was buying *cédulas,* and told his crowds, "Take their money but give us your vote." The police found guns and ammunition in two houses in a suburb of Santo Domingo and arrested four members of the 14th of June. Haina demanded complete autonomy and gave the Consejo five days to grant it. Parties maneuvered for coalition. The 14th of June, in one of the flood of "manifestos," "communiqués," and full-page political ads, declared that the Yankees, the police, and the oligarchs were behind the plot to discredit the 14th by "finding" a "fake" arms dump. Lieutenant General O'Meara came in from Panama, and I took him to the Palace to call publicly on Bonnelly.

The parties' charges grew sharper and more ominous. Baquero insinuated publicly that the PRD was supported by Communists. Bosch replied that a plot was afoot to defame his party and that certain persons had adopted the Trujillo tactic of first accusing someone, then killing him. Bosch told one of our people that *El Caribe* intended to publish everything about the summit agreement in the last days of the campaign, that Imbert was plotting to kill him or break up his meetings as an excuse for a *golpe*, that the four Castro/Communist parties had sent an emissary offering their support in return for being given free reign if Bosch was elected, that he never would make such a deal and suspected the other parties had sent the emissary in order to trap him, that Miolán was convinced the UCN would steal the election—"the PRD masses contain many of the bravest people in the Republic, and if they are cheated, they will rise."

The Department called: Information from Madrid and Paris said that Johnny Abbes, Trujillo's SIM chief, last reported in Tokyo, had reached Paris by journeying overland across Asia and had met the exiled Trujillos there or in Madrid. Petán Trujillo had told Abbes that everything was ready for Petán's return to the Republic on December 20, election day, with Ramfis' support. He would fly to Guadeloupe, go thence to Haiti, and would take command of some seven thousand troops who would mass on the border. Héctor Trujillo refused to participate. Fantastic? What wasn't? I warned Bonnelly. A day or so later the CIA confirmed at least a part of it—airplane tickets had indeed been bought, Haitian visas would be issued. Another Trujillo, called Néne, widely feared in the Republic, would go, too.

And at long last, on December 7, some nine months after I had been promised it, we got the twenty-two million dollars. Bonnelly and the Consejeros, Williams and Bramble and I, carefully worked out a public statement, preserving the U.S. position that the money was a grant yet recognizing the Dominican view that the money was due them. The Consejo agreed to sequester it for the next government.

Chapter Twelve

THE FIRST FREE ELECTIONS IN THIRTY-EIGHT YEARS

Now it was a straight downhill run to the election, only ten days away. The Castro/Communists seemed to have given up hope of disrupting things. The 14th of June was painting on walls, *"Ni Khrushchev, ni Kennedy, ni Kastro, solo Kisqueya."*

The campaign had been incredible. The party of the oligarchs, UCN, had succeeded in mainly irritating the oligarchs, while the party of the people, the PRD, had taken care not to offend the oligarchs, the military, or the Trujillistas. Neither PRD nor UCN had proposed any solutions to the staggering problems inherited from Trujillo. Fiallo regarded *"libertad"* the best issue, forgetting that that issue was more than a year old and memories are short. Bosch one day announced solemnly that he would probably not have to raise taxes, for the mountain streams near Constanza were filled with gold. (My family and I looked for some; he was wrong.) All the parties had spent most of their energy attacking the Consejo and the Electoral Board, the single effective organ in the entire exercise.

None of this was really surprising—after thirty-one years of Trujillo, little more could be expected. Nevertheless, it seemed a shame.

We felt sure the PRD would win, perhaps win big. The shift had come in the last two weeks. Bosch, in a campaign lacking issues, had managed to make the UCN itself the issue. He was a virtuoso. The only thing that could beat him now was a bad mistake, or a sudden UCN surge in the cities. Ten days is a long time in any campaign. But Shlaudeman's checking showed a real surprise: PRD now was strong in the cities.

Everything we had done had been aimed at two policy objectives: To help keep the provisional government in power and to help hold elections. It looked as if we would achieve both, despite the powerful forces cut loose by Trujillo's fall. The task that remained was to create an atmosphere in which the winner could take office peaceably and the loser could accept defeat gracefully. What we needed now was not only a good winner, but six good losers. Building on the Bosch-Fiallo summit agreement, and on General Viñas' direct commitment to me, I now began talking privately to all presidential candidates, party leaders, the military, the press, and others with power. After the election we would quickly demonstrate our support for the winner.

It all seemed so neat, so sensible, when I wrote it out and sent it off to the Department on Sunday, December 9. Two days later the worst crisis of the year exploded.

2

Monday was quiet—I even went shopping (and was surprised and immensely pleased to see long lines of people patiently queued up at *cédula* offices. After all these years, the Dominican people really *wanted* to vote).

Tuesday, too, was an ordinary day. I saw Bonnelly to give him intelligence reports on the Trujillos' movements. Bonnelly, warned he might be assassinated on Saturday, was starting an around-the-clock guard of the Palace, his house, and vital installations. We had a ship coming to port Sunday; I invited him and the Consejo aboard for lunch, and he accepted with alacrity. The new Amiama-Imbert generalship decree was signed at last.

Shlaudeman telephoned at midnight, got me out of bed, and asked if he could come to the Residence. He had just come from Juan Bosch. Bosch was quitting the campaign.

The Catholic Church, Bosch said, had prepared a pastoral letter denouncing him as a Communist, and it would be read in every pulpit in the country on Sunday. Bosch had sent a committee to the Papal Nuncio, and if by 7:30 A.M. he did not receive assurances that the pastoral letter would be withdrawn, or that the Church would issue a declaration of neutrality, he would publicly withdraw.

We had heard rumors for several days that some priests were opposed to Bosch. The UCN had been accusing Bosch of Communist sympathies or worse. We had decided we could not get involved. I could not imagine anything more risky than for an American Ambassador, appointed by a Catholic President, to become involved in a quarrel between a leading presidential candidate and the Church in a Catholic country at the height of an election campaign.

I told Shlaudeman to check early in the morning.

He did—Bosch had not received his reply and intended to quit. He had brushed aside Shlaudeman's remonstrances. But a friend of his had wired Betancourt in Venezuela and someone in Costa Rica, asking for endorsement by a Church official. I thought this a good sign—perhaps he would stay and fight.

At 11:15 A.M. Shlaudeman came back. From a private source, he had obtained a copy of an unsigned communication intended for distribution by hand to priests. It called Bosch's ideas "Marxist-Leninist."

I closed the doors and started walking around in my office, a habit I had. What would happen if Bosch withdrew? Fiallo probably would be elected. Could he govern? Probably not. And in the long run, the Castro/ Communists alone would profit. They would say, and people would believe, that the Church, the Yankees, the UCN, the oligarchs, the *tu-tumpotes,* and the would-be dictator Imbert had conspired to drive out the people's champion, Bosch. This was the Castro/Communists' golden opportunity. The priests were all unwittingly handing it to them.

But what could we do? Any other force we could fight. But the Church? Hardly. Perhaps we could persuade Bosch to stand and fight. Perhaps his wife Carmen could. We got in touch with her.

Luís Manuel Baquero of UCN came to see me, an appointment made some time earlier. He was no longer optimistic about Fiallo's chances. And what if Bosch were elected? He seemed not to know that Bosch was withdrawing. He said hesitantly, "We want to be as democratic as possible. If Bosch wins, we'll give him a chance—three, four, five months. But if he goes wrong, as he is now, and ruins the country, we'll cancel him."

I didn't like this and told him so.

Baquero still had high hopes for the Cibao. Furthermore, he said, "We are going to use some psychological tricks." I asked what he meant. He said, "The Church priests are saying quietly, Bosch is bad." I told him carefully I thought this tactic might boomerang—make an underdog of Bosch, to the UCN's disadvantage. And what if Bosch withdrew? An election without him would be meaningless. Baquero seemed given pause.

That evening I met with King, Shlaudeman, and the CIA chief. Carmen Bosch doubted she could persuade her husband to stay in the campaign, thought she might persuade him to see me tomorrow.

The election was a week from Thursday. Even though the Bosch-Church problem might derail it, we had to plan as if it would not. The OAS observers would arrive on Saturday. Bonilla planned a symposium on democracy with them. We hoped the OAS observers would immediately inspect the Electoral Board's work and pronounce it good; this might undercut any subsequent charge of fraud. I would ask the Department to issue a statement for Wednesday morning papers, calling attention to the historic event in the Dominican Republic.

While we were meeting, *La Nación,* the government-owned newspaper, came out. It contained an article entitled "Juan Bosch—Marxist-Leninist," by Father Láutico García, a Jesuit priest.

Father Láutico García accused Bosch of being a Marxist-Leninist and offered as evidence articles that Bosch had originally published in Caracas in 1959 or 1960 and that had been reprinted in a Dominican publication, *Renovación*, in 1962. According to Father Láutico García, Bosch had written that the first phase of a revolution was not simply a leftist movement but rather violent action. Once in power, the revolutionary party must convert its principles into laws of the state and norms for people's lives. All this, Father Láutico García wrote, was contained in Lenin's *State and Revolution*. Once successful, power must pass from the masses to the leaders of the revolution. Revolutionary leaders fell into two categories—those who after taking power can keep it only by continuing to agitate, and those who know how to govern. Of all revolutionary leaders, Bosch wrote, Lenin was the archetype of the revolutionary leader who knew how to govern. The power to order people's lives was the only end of a revolutionary government. Its weapon was coercion by the state.[1]

So now the controversy was public. This made it possible for me to get into it. Thursday morning—election day was just one week away—*El Caribe* carried a speech by Bosch saying he had predicted that "false documents" would be circulated in the capital in an effort to smear the PRD as communistic. A political officer brought in a clandestine flysheet distributed during the night, supporting Bosch and purportedly signed by the Communist PSP, a classic "black operation" probably perpetrated by the UCN. UCN was hammering a new slogan: "The ballot is white but the party is red." Rumors spread that Bosch's wife was a Castro agent. Would Bosch withdraw? "He says so," Shlaudeman said. "He says the Church is campaigning against him all over the country. He says it has two radio stations, at La Vega and Higüey, and the priests are telling the people that if they vote for Bosch they will be excommunicated."

At eleven-fifteen Carmen Bosch called me. Bosch was meeting now with his party committee; he would withdraw at 1 P.M. The only thing that would stop him would be a call from the Papal Nuncio. I asked if she and her husband would come to see me. She said they would, at 3 P.M.

I told my secretary to get the Nuncio on the phone. She did, and I asked him if I could see him immediately on a matter of great urgency. He said of course, but it would have to be later in the afternoon; he was on his way to the airport, and was leaving now. I asked if I could ride to the airport with him. He said yes, if I could get to the Nunciatura right away. I hurried out alone, trying to think what to say.

I had seen Monseñor Clarizio only at diplomatic functions. He looked to be in his fifties, graying, erect, vigorous, with glasses and quick bright eyes. His face was habitually grave, his manner reserved, his bearing

[1] I am told that Bosch felt his articles were an attack on Castro, a mere agitator in power.

dignified. I had been impressed by the breadth of his knowledge, by his professional diplomat's touch, and by his progressive views, in accord with Pope John's great encyclicals, *Mater et Magistra* and *Pacem in Terris*. As I came to know him better, I saw that he was deeply compassionate, highly intelligent, and very funny.

At the Nunciatura we got into my car—it had a glass partition separating us from the driver, and Monseñor Clarizio didn't trust his driver's skill on a fast trip—and he told his to follow.

As we drove through the Upper Town, I told him I was deeply concerned about a recent development in the political campaign as exemplified by the article about Bosch in last night's *La Nación* attributed to Father Láutico García. I said I wanted to talk to him urgently, not as emissary from anyone—the United States government was absolutely neutral in the election—but only doing what I thought my duty. I apologized for forcing myself on him at an inconvenient time, but felt I must because Bosch had indicated he would withdraw from the campaign at 1 P.M. today, and this might endanger the entire electoral process. I came to the point. I said I wanted to give him one piece of information and ask him for one. As to the first, I thought he should know that we, the United States government, had been checking on Bosch for some twenty-five years through our various intelligence agencies, and that—although anything was possible—so far as we could determine, Juan Bosch was not a Communist. This, I thought, was something he and the other churchmen might want to take into consideration. Then I asked him for information: Had the Church taken, or did it intend to take, an official position on Bosch?

The Nuncio said the Church had taken no official position. In fact, right now he was on his way to the airport to meet the Archbishop of Santo Domingo, who was coming in by plane. The Republic's four bishops would be there too. They would meet immediately to discuss this very question. Monseñor Clarizio said that some time back the Church had drafted a pastoral letter simply saying that every citizen should vote according to the dictates of his conscience. Bosch had been pleased and had asked if he could publish the letter. They had thought not. Bosch had persisted, trying to work through the bishops, as, earlier, he had tried to nominate a priest or bishop for Vice President. Nothing had come of this.

During the last few days things had changed. Bosch had sent emissaries to the Nuncio to complain that priests would attack the PRD from the pulpit next Sunday. They had given him a list of priests who opposed Bosch, said the Social Christians had been egging the priests on, and declared that if the Church opposed Bosch, he would withdraw. The Nuncio had told them he would check on it—if it was true, it was not the Church itself, but only a few individual priests. The Nuncio was disturbed by Bosch's articles. A Bosch emissary had assured him that Bosch, if elected, would not govern in accordance with those ideas. The Nuncio had replied that Bosch should say so publicly. The emissary had asked for a meeting of bishops and an announcement by them giving Bosch a clean bill of health.

Some priests, the Nuncio went on, believed Bosch was a Communist. But, he said, no anti-Bosch pastoral letter was in existence, in preparation, or contemplated. He would consult with the bishops today, taking into account what I had told him, for which he was grateful, and he would let me know later today what resulted. He thought he could safely say now that the Church would take no official position.

We were not far from the airport. The Nuncio said perhaps it would be best if we did not arrive together. We stopped near the little palm grove where Trujillo's SIM had dropped the bodies of their victims to the sharks. The Nuncio waved to his driver, his own car pulled up alongside mine, we shook hands, he opened the door and, pulling up his long white robe, skipped nimbly around, got in his own car, and, waving, drove off, while I told José to make a U-turn and drive back to the Chancellery fast.

I had time only to tell King what had happened; Pichardo was coming to lunch by prearrangement. King said a hot cable was in: Petán Trujillo was reported on his way from Madrid to Port-au-Prince.

I went to the Residence and lunched with Pichardo. We were interrupted several times by the telephone. Bosch had told us privately that his decision was firm, he would withdraw. The PRD would issue a statement at 7 P.M. calling the bishops' attention to the priests' campaign. And now Bosch was on the radio, threatening to withdraw. Pichardo and I did not discuss the problem, as I recall. But he said the Consejo might resign before February 27, or bring in the newly elected President to sit with it, for troubles were mounting, and a lame-duck government could not deal with them. Pichardo left.

King called: Colonel Fritz Long said the military was talking about nothing but the Church problem. The Nuncio called me. He had spoken with all the bishops. There would be no pastoral letter, no communication of any kind, from the Church. It was for Bosch, not the Church, to make a declaration—to renounce the views he had held in 1959 or 1960.

Bosch and his wife arrived at the Residence promptly at 3 P.M. We sat in my study, she looking anxious, he pleasant. I told him I was deeply concerned about recent developments. I said I could assure him that the Church had not taken any official position and would not take one.

He was leaning back in the sofa, white-haired, smiling, looking relaxed or resigned. He shook his head. "I shall withdraw. You do not understand, Mr. Martin. The priest at Altagracia is on the radio. The Spanish priests at San Cristóbal told Delegate Peña Gómez that they would not accept any other President than Fiallo. One of my men's children were told by the nuns at school that Bosch is the godfather to Fidel's children. My own daughter was told by the nuns that anyone who votes for Juan Bosch will go to hell. The priests at a school told the students to tell their friends and families that anyone who voted for Bosch would be excommunicated. No, it is a national campaign. The radio at Higüey and La Vega are saying the same thing. It is a national campaign. I shall withdraw."

I said I thought this would be most unfortunate. The Dominican people had waited thirty-eight years for a chance to vote in a free election. This election was important far beyond the Republic. It was important to the Hemisphere. The cause of democracy was involved.

Bosch kept shaking his head, kept smiling, a little sadly. He had the air of a man composed to die. (I would see it often.) His wife was sitting on the edge of her chair, tense; she spoke rapidly to him in Spanish, telling him that he should heed me. He just kept shaking his head and smiling wanly. I told him that some individual priests might attack him, but not the Church, there was no nationwide conspiracy. He kept shaking his head.

I said, "Does everything have to be a plot? This isn't a plot. It's a confusion. And you could clear it up."

"How?" he asked.

"By going to see the Nuncio. Or by making a public statement."

He said, his voice soft and deep, "No. It is not for me to go to them or to make statements. It is for them. I shall withdraw," and he sighed wearily, waited a moment, straightened, then put his hands on his knees and stood up. Carmen said, "But Juan—" He held up his hand sharply, she fell silent, we shook hands, and I saw them to the door.

I was not sure what he was doing. I suspected he might be bluffing, trying to reverse the issue, trying to develop an underdog position, leading the masses against the Church, the rich, the white, the powerful, the *tu-tum-potes*. He had shown himself a plunger and a skillful enough politician to attempt it. Or he might be doing exactly what he said he was doing: Quitting. He had threatened it several times. And I had often wondered if he really wanted to be President—if he did not fear power. Or he might be doing neither, just waiting to see how things developed.

We had a choice—to do nothing, or to strive to keep him in the election. We had reached another fork in the road.

We would try to keep him in. The only way to do it at the moment was to try to moderate further the position of both the clergy and Bosch.

3

That night Shlaudeman came to the Residence. A PRD delegation had sent to the Nuncio, to all five bishops, and to the press a statement threatening to withdraw from the election, denouncing clerical interference, reciting the democratic history of the PRD, attacking the UCN, and saying that "a Dominican *campesino* is more afraid of excommunication than a bullet in the head." The Archbishop of Santo Domingo, Octavio A. Beras, had received the delegation at five-thirty; the meeting was thought to have been cordial. The Nuncio had told the delegation that no pastoral letter would be read Sunday.

The PRD tactic, Shlaudeman said, was to threaten to withdraw, making it clear that this would throw the masses into the hands of the Castro/Communists, unless the Church declared its neutrality. The UCN radio program denounced Bosch's threat to withdraw as the last desperate act of a loser, and pointed out it was the third time Bosch had threatened to quit.

Friday morning John Crimmins called from Washington. The Department, concerned, supported my policy fully and offered to help. I said I didn't think we needed help, at least not yet. The Nuncio telephoned. The situation was greatly improved; the PRD delegation had called on him at ten o'clock and left "quite happy. So unless something else happens it's all over, practically. He will stay in the race." I was less optimistic.

As a precaution against the Trujillos' maneuvers, Imbert was sending three generals to the Haitian frontier. The PRD came on the air, its announcer crying excitedly. "*¡Atención! ¡Atención!*" and saying a transcendental announcement was expected momentarily. At one o'clock President Bonnelly called. Fandino and I hurried to him.

Bonnelly was furious. Bosch, he said, was unloosing a "ferocious attack" on the Consejo, tying it to "attacks" by the Church and the UCN. The Consejo must answer and defend itself. I tried to calm him. It was useless. The Consejo could not endure it. Bosch's attack might even drag the Consejo down, particularly if Balaguer were to return now, and "I would rather leave than go down trying to keep order." I asked what I could do. "Nothing. You can go to the Nuncio but it will do no good. Everything is unpredictable now. Events have outrun us."

I went back to the house and called King and Shlaudeman. Bosch went on the air at one-thirty. He mounted his main attack against the UCN, the Consejo, and the oligarchy. He did not attack the military; indeed, he praised it. And he was careful with the Church. He said the PRD had been faced with unfounded and false accusations of communism, and "with this we cannot go to elections," the closest he came to an outright withdrawal.

Saturday morning's *Caribe* said editorially that the Republic was in the throes of a grave crisis, declared it could not believe that the Church had taken an official position, and hoped that a way out could be found. Two bishops said they did not favor priests' involvement in politics.

Today, Saturday, was the day President Bonnelly was supposed to be assassinated.

The Nuncio telephoned me. "The situation is confused," he said. "They want more. Bosch should not press too much. Personal opinions are a little too hard—to interfere so strongly. Now they want an official document. It is a little too much at the moment." I asked what kind of document Bosch wanted from the Church. A clean bill of health, he supposed, or perhaps a declaration of neutrality. I suggested that since the Church was indeed neutral, as we were, perhaps it could say so publicly. He wasn't sure; the bishops were scattered, and there were other problems, presumably with various priests or orders. "I told him to be satisfied with what he has."

I felt nothing but sympathy for the Nuncio. He was being forced into an almost impossible position, first by pressures from inside the Church, now by pressure from Bosch. I told him I had tried to soften Bosch's position without success, but would try again. He said he too would do what he could.

King and Shlaudeman and I considered trying to take the military away from Bosch, thus weakening his resolution to press the Church, but decided it was too dangerous, particularly if he became President. We considered other possibilities, but got nowhere. In the end I sent word indirectly to Bosch that he should be careful lest he overplay his hand. I doubted it would help.

It was now perfectly clear what he was doing. He knew that by threatening to withdraw he would frighten everybody who wanted elections, and they would all work to persuade him not to withdraw. Doing so, they would inevitably moderate all attacks on him. If he played it right, he would soon have everybody, even the UCN, campaigning for him. In the end, he could either actually withdraw or he could stay in the race, depending on whether he thought he could win. He would pursue this course to the finish.

4

That afternoon the Nuncio called again, and I went to see him. He was coldly angry at Bosch. The PRD was still saying that the radio station at La Vega was broadcasting anti-Bosch propaganda. It was not true. They were saying that other priests were working against Bosch.

That was not true either. "This is their way of making an attack. They should be careful." The bishops, he said, would issue a statement to the press today. It would reply to yesterday's letter from the PRD and would declare neutrality. They would go no further. Some felt they had gone too far already. Now Bosch should stop entirely. "His people are talking of getting what they want or else provoking revolution. This is not the way democrats talk. They are still accusing us. It is not fair. Some of them are ex-Communists. If they want peace, they will have it. If they want trouble, they will have it."

I said I understood perfectly, agreed Bosch now should desist, said the Nuncio had gone very far indeed in accommodating Bosch, and if now the election proceeded successfully, it would be due largely to his efforts, which in fact it would.

That Sunday morning *El Caribe* carried the bishops' statement: The Church was neutral. It also carried the PRD's reply: The bishops' statement was not enough.

Now *I* was angry. Bosch was going to squeeze this tube dry. He was going to keep the pressure on right down to election day. Thus he would monopolize the news and make the overriding question his own decision: Will he quit or won't he?

I called Shlaudeman in at eleven and said we must slow Bosch down. He agreed. But there was more. Bosch had challenged Father Láutico García to a television debate, and he had accepted. The PRD had announced it was suspending all political campaigning. The Consejo had challenged the PRD to prove its accusations against it.

Shlaudeman also warned me that the Consejo had announced publicly it would not permit foreign interference in the elections. He thought this might be aimed at the Venezuelans—a man from COPEI, Venezuela's Social Christian party, had been here, advising the Social Christians—but we must be careful. It was almost too late to be careful.

At noon I took the President and Consejo to lunch aboard the U.S.S. *Roberts*.

At 4:30 P.M. U.S. newspapermen came to the Residence for a press conference—AP, UPI, the New York *Times, Time, Newsweek, Reader's Digest,* NBC, CBS, others. No American publication could afford to keep a full-time staff man in a small place like Santo Domingo. Major newspapers, radio-TV networks, wire services, and magazines sent men in, usually in the midst of trouble. This meant they ran into a complex political situation, and if they were new to the Republic, or even if they had been absent several months, they lacked background, and so, working against a deadline, were in danger of getting the story slightly out of focus, though technically accurate on the hard news. It was part of my job to give them background. They respected the ground rules—I would talk for background only, not for attribution; on a few questions I might go off the record entirely and they could not use what I told them; I would not lie; to them; I might refuse to answer some questions entirely.

Today, however, I had one thing to say on the record, attributable to me by name if they wished. I read it: The United States government would support whoever won the election. Then I went ahead with non-attributable background.

I made the "support" statement for Bosch's benefit alone. I wanted him to know that we intended to go ahead and support the election winner whether Bosch withdrew or not. And I wanted to say it publicly, since private persuasion had had no effect. It succeeded, I learned later: He was angry and thought I had undermined his position. That was what I had intended to do. Moreover, I sent word privately that if he pulled out now he had no future with us.

Crimmins telephoned from Washington to caution me to say "assist" rather than "support" next time. I can recall no other time when the Department rebuked me.

5

That evening Fran and I went to an elegant reception for the OAS observers in the Penthouse at the Hotel Embajador. Everybody was there—Goytía and the other OAS observers; the Nuncio; almost the entire diplomatic corps; President Bonnelly, Imbert, the other Consejeros; and, I believe, all the presidential candidates but one—Bosch. Juan Isidro Jimenes Grullón seized my hand, beckoned to a photographer, and told me, while our picture was being taken, that with Bosch out he expected to win big. I told him to go get 'em—and quickly moved through the crowded room, making sure to be photographed with every other candidate present.

From the reception Fran and I went to dinner at Dr. Aulio Brea's. Dr. Brea had been a contact man for Amiama and Imbert while they were hiding after Trujillo's assassination. It was a beautiful party, with drinks on the terrace and dinner at tables in the garden. Imbert and I stood talking a long time by the terrace wall, the city's lights spread out below and the sea beyond. Imbert was drinking straight gin. He rarely drank much; like Amiama and other Dominicans and myself, he had an ulcer, but tonight he drank. He was talking about the elections. He kept saying, "I'm afraid, Mr. Martin, I'm afraid, I'm afraid." He was not drunk. He was thoroughly frightened. He feared that if Bosch withdrew, the masses would rise in the streets, and Imbert would have to put them down with force. With all the world watching.

Monday morning's *Caribe* had a large headline on my statement that we would support the winner whatever happened. Its editorial said that the Church had made its position clear and it hoped that now the priests would stop attacking Bosch and Bosch would accept this as enough.

But the same paper carried a new statement by Bosch: He demanded a postponement of the election until January 21.

At 10:30 A.M. the Nuncio called and said, "Something can be done," and I went to see him.

He said Bosch had complained that the Archbishop of Santo Domingo was withholding his blessing from Bosch. The Nuncio had told him, "Why don't you go see him?" They were meeting now. The Nuncio had suggested to the Archbishop that he celebrate a public Mass. All candidates could be invited. Perhaps this would succeed. He added contemptuously, "They are behaving like little children."

"They always have," I said.

6

At the office, Shlaudeman told me other parties were threatening to withdraw—Silfa's PRDA, Horacio Ornes' Vanguardia, possibly others. We had to stop them.

I hurried to the Palace and asked Bonnelly what the Consejo intended to do about Bosch's request that the election be postponed.

Bonnelly, by now both frightened and angry, said, "We will not postpone. If there is a crisis, let it come now."

Donny Reid was pressing the Consejo to deny Bosch's request for postponement and to slap Bosch hard. This might drive Bosch really to withdraw. I suggested that Bonnelly stall for another twenty-four hours —after all, this was Monday, the election was Thursday; if we could get through each day, we might survive yet. Bonnelly, angry, refused. I had to be careful lest he think I was working for Bosch.

Back at the office, Shlaudeman said that, in order to withdraw from the election, any candidate must notify the Electoral Board. So far, none had. We must quiet the little parties, not let Bosch stampede them.

I called Imbert, told him I needed his help, and asked him to tell Horacio Julio Ornes not to withdraw Vanguardia. He said he would. I told him I'd heard the Consejo might issue a statement today flatly refusing to postpone elections. I hoped he could hold the line, try to gain twenty-four hours, get me a little time to work things out. He said he'd try. (Later Reid complained that he couldn't get the Consejo to take a firm stand against postponement that day; even Bonnelly and Imbert were against it. I never told him why.)

King called our new consul in Santiago, Ben Ruyle, and told him to tell Governor Mainardi for me that he must not withdraw. Shlaudeman got hold of the Social Christians; they would stay in. He told Ramón Castillo to persuade another small party not to withdraw.

At 1:30 P.M. Bosch went on the radio. He said he had withdrawn but would debate with Father Láutico García tonight. He demanded the election be postponed but on new grounds: 120,000 *campesinos,* he said, would be disfranchised because the voting address on their *cédulas* was outdated and they would not be allowed to vote at a polling place distant from their homes.

The Nuncio told me Bosch's meeting with the Archbishop had been satisfactory. I said I thought we were on the verge of success and hoped that in tonight's television debate Father Láutico García would be gentle. The Nuncio assured me he would.

At 3 P.M., Shlaudeman checked with the Electoral Board. Bosch had not officially withdrawn. Neither had any other candidate. I began to feel sure they would not. That evening, with the Crisis Crowd, I watched television—the great debate between Bosch and Father Láutico García. Father Láutico García was very quiet, very calm, almost expressionless. Bosch, in a white suit, obviously enjoying himself hugely, was the embodiment of courtesy, respectful to the priest, sometimes firm, looking up thoughtfully, frowning as though in deep concentration, leaning forward to make a point, leaning back gravely, grimacing and posing in front of the camera. When, after about two hours, they were still defining the ground rules for their debate, I went to bed. Tuesday morning Shlaudeman told me that neither Father Láutico García nor Bosch seemed to know much about Marxism and Leninism. He said the priest, an intelligent man, had obviously been told to behave with restraint, perhaps even to let Bosch win. This succeeded: *El Caribe* said Father Lautico García had withdrawn his accusation against Bosch. It was the face-saver Bosch needed.

Nevertheless, in that newspaper Bosch called on his followers not to vote, not to riot, but simply to stay home on election day. The Consejo promised to answer today his request for an election postponement. *El Caribe* said postponing was all but impossible. It set a bad precedent, and added that the people were prepared to vote and ought not be disappointed. I called Germán Ornes to congratulate him.

Shlaudeman said Bosch next would declare he would stay in the election only on the following conditions: That campaigning could continue tomorrow, Wednesday, contrary to the previously announced rule and that on election day buses or trucks would not be permitted to carry people from town to town but within a town people could vote near their present homes regardless of their *cédula* addresses. I thought this might be the last straw—President Bonnelly hadn't appeared able to stomach much more from Bosch.

I went to see Bonnelly and told him we understood Bosch might switch his position again, adding even new conditions; I suggested the President might simply want to announce that the election would be

held on Thursday in accordance with the Constitution. As to the Trujillos, I assured him that an Embassy staffer in Madrid had seen Petán
and we were watching closely all around the Caribbean. At least he
needn't worry about that. He was grateful.

The Nuncio came to see me. He was on his way to see the Bishop
of La Vega. He had talked to Bosch; he thought, but could not be sure,
that everything would be all right.

Shlaudeman said Vanguardia would coalesce with the PRD. The PRD
executive committee had been assured its *cédula* problem would be
solved. It was meeting now. At 1:30 P.M. Vallimarescu telephoned: The
radio was announcing that the PRD would stay in. Campaigning could
continue till 6 P.M. tomorrow, as Bosch wished, and voters could vote
from any street address but could not travel in and out of cities, also as
Bosch wished.

At three-thirty Bosch announced publicly that one of his conditions
had not been met, that rural voters could vote from any address. That
was really too much.

And now rumors ran through town that the UCN would quit. Shlaudeman started checking. The Voice of America said that the Dominican
elections would test the vitality of democracy after a period of tyranny.
(I thought: They have already tested my vitality.) President Bonnelly
spoke on national radio and television. He began by saying he might
sound bitter but that was inevitable, in view of the systematic and in-
comprehensibly stubborn obstruction the Consejo had faced. He related
the Consejo's progress during this transitional year—press freedom, human rights, freedom for labor unions, tax reforms, agrarian reform, independent judiciary, educational reform, general prosperity. The Consejo
had only marked out the path to a solution of all problems; the next
government must do much more. The Consejo had maintained order without repression. The Consejeros had renounced personal ambition, and as
they returned to private life were convinced they would receive the respect of their fellow citizens. Bonnelly welcomed the OAS observers who
had come to the Republic, pointing out that the Consejo had pursued a
foreign policy of "continental fraternization," at the same time maintaining the national sovereignty and dignity. Finally, the Consejo had overcome all obstacles and brought the country to elections. *Cédula* offices
would remain open till midnight tomorrow to put voters' documents in
order. Bonnelly declared the election would be held on schedule the day
after tomorrow. The Government had taken measures to see to it that the
elections would be free and orderly. Bonnelly concluded, "It only remains
to me now to exhort all citizens to comply with their constitutional duty
to vote, and to remind each Dominican that his vote is secret and that
at the hour of casting it he ought to do so guided only by the dictates of
his own conscience."

When he finished, I went to his house and congratulated him, not without emotion.

Wednesday's *El Caribe* announced that the electoral crisis was over and called on all to vote. In Puerto Rico, Governor Muñoz Marín issued a belated statement that Bosch was not a Communist. (Muñoz was always very careful.) Radio Havana denounced the elections and me. Secretary of Interior and Police Tábare Álvarez said the police were ready to maintain order. They might have to: Two PRD men had been shot after a meeting last night in Parque Enriquillo.

At the office, King gave me a report that Petán and Héctor Trujillo were in Miami, that a private Beechcraft plane from Miami had been cleared in Puerto Rico for landing in the Dominican Republic. I told him to notify General Viñas at once. Shlaudeman telephoned from the Hotel Embajador. He had planned to accompany an OAS observer to a remote polling place in the interior. But now, when the OAS observers trooped out of the hotel to leave, they found that the taxi drivers refused to haul them. They were PRD members, and if they made this trip they would lose their votes. So now that the great day had come, now that the statesmen had gathered from throughout the Hemisphere, now that they were prepared to scatter throughout the reborn Republic to observe democracy in action, they couldn't get a cab. We spent hours helping straighten it out.

During the day I kept hearing of plots and scandals. At two-thirty Bosch went on the radio to tell his voters that if they did not have a *cédula* containing their current address, they were being cheated out of their vote. They should not create disturbances or behave violently. Over and over he repeated such words as violence, extremism, disturbances. He said the Armed Forces would protect the voters. Voters should return to the polling places after 6 P.M. to observe the tally. He seemed to be laying the groundwork for a charge of fraud, courting the military, and repeatedly suggesting violence though taking care not to advocate it, a dangerous tactic that, months later, would be used effectively against him.

Fran, returning from Santiago, said that the director of the children's hospital there had told her that half of his patients had been taken home by their parents for safekeeping until after the election. Late that night Imbert telephoned. Johnny Abbes had arrived in Puerto Rico. I telephoned Bill Sowash, the Dominican desk man in Washington. He called back at 1 A.M. He could not confirm it. Balaguer had been seen in New York at 4:30 P.M. I went back to bed. I couldn't sleep. And we had no sleeping pills. I had sent the driver for some earlier in the day. He reported there was not a sleeping pill left in town. No wonder.

7

Election day, December 20, 1962—what we had been working for all year. The weather was perfect. All was quiet. I took a ride around the city. Long lines stood at some polling places, all orderly. They had arrived early, were standing patiently. They seemed in a holiday mood, laughing, talking. I thought: Everyone is exhausted but the people. I had noticed recently that the people seemed to be having a good time. They had never seen anything like this. The vote would be big. And very likely peaceable.

President Bonnelly voted next door to the Residence, in Trujillo's mansion, now used for Agrarian Reform and, today, as a polling place. A maid insisted on splitting her ticket—PRD for President, Social Christians for Congress. (I know many educated Americans who are afraid of spoiling their ballot by ticket-splitting.) In midmorning the PRD began shrieking on the radio that the election was being stolen, its announcer crying, "¡Atención! ¡Atención! Señor Soandso, go to polling place number such and such; there are no PRD ballots there"; "¡Atención! ¡Atención! The vote-buyers are out. All PRD lawyers and students come immediately to headquarters"; "¡Atención! ¡Atención! Electoral Board, what's going on?" And so on.

I had twice suggested to Bonnelly that he shut the stations down on election day. Now, at last, he did it.

I stayed home or at the office, dreading phone calls. We had made elaborate arrangements to keep in close touch with Army and Police headquarters.

But nothing happened. The election was absolutely quiet, quieter than most elections in Chicago. During the afternoon it became apparent that the vote was heavy everywhere. Shortly after the polls closed we knew Fiallo was being swamped in the capital.

The Crisis Crowd came to the Residence, and we watched television and listened to radio. As early returns came in, it was clear that Bosch was winning by a landslide. The total vote was huge. The trend was never reversed. And we heard of not a single incident of violence or disorder.

At 10:20 P.M. Fandino and I went down the street to President Bonnelly's house. He was in shirt-sleeves in his study, watching television. We embraced, and he said, "We have passed into history." He was smiling broadly. He looked like a man who had miraculously recovered from a fatal illness. He said, "A triumph. It is incredible," and he watched television in silence a few minutes as the announcer, wearing a plaid jacket, read more returns. I put my hand on Bonnelly's shoulder and said, "You did it. Your place in history is secure. You should be very proud, of yourself and your country." We embraced again, and Fandino and I walked back to the Residence.

8

The days that followed were bittersweet, filled with feelings of relief and foreboding.

The day after the election, Shlaudeman came in laughing—Bosch had telephoned him to ask if he could see me, and to ask if we could help get his wife a U.S. visa. The President-elect! I sent word I would call on him, and, of course, we would get the visa. Shlaudeman reported back: No, Bosch insisted on paying a courtesy call on me. He wanted to go to the States Sunday; could I see him tomorrow, Saturday? Of course.

Shlaudeman said Bosch wanted to visit his son Patricio, in school in South Bend, Indiana. He might make a private visit to Washington but feared publicity because he did not want to be too closely identified with the United States. (As a matter of fact, the Department didn't want any publicity either, for Bosch had not yet been declared officially elected.) How did he seem? Friendly, Shlaudeman said, and calm. Not at all surprised by his victory.

News of a different sort came from a newspaperman. Luís Manuel Baquero of UCN had received an offer of a *coup* last night from a high-ranking military man. He had refused—for now.

That evening Bonilla gave a reception at the Foreign Office, and in the crowded room I heard many people say, "I am proud to be a Dominican today." Well might they be. The election had been a triumph for the Dominican people and for the cause of democracy.

After the reception Shlaudeman and his wife, Carol, and King and a couple of others went with Fran and me to Vesuvio's and we dined outdoors with drinks and wine and brandy and *cafecitos,* white tables full, waiters scurrying, and sat till late under the palms and stars, watching the cars whiz by on Jorge Washington and listening to the sea; we sat talking, remembering the other nights we'd sat and talked, tense, plotting and planning, working for elections, the first time in more than a generation that the Dominican people had been allowed to choose their rulers. We had no illusions about the difficulties ahead, but we were proud of this year, and of the Dominican people, tonight.

9

Bosch and his wife came to the Residence on Saturday. She was smiling, he calm. I congratulated him and told him that my government and I looked forward to cooperating fully with him and his government.

He said his party had swept both houses of Congress; indeed it had: Twenty-two of twenty-seven Senators, just short of a two-thirds majority in the House of Deputies. He said that now full responsibility was his.

How long would they be gone? He wasn't sure—perhaps they would go to Europe and not return until shortly before inauguration time. I said in the interim we would prepare AID plans for his consideration. Could we help with their travel arrangements? He had given it little thought—and would be traveling during the Christmas rush. (With considerable difficulty, we got reservations for them from New York to South Bend.) I suggested they might want to meet some friends of mine in Washington privately—Attorney General Kennedy, Adlai Stevenson, Undersecretary Ball, John Crimmins; Senators Humphrey, Douglas, Dirksen; Newton Minow, Sargent Shriver, Judge David Bazelon, Arthur Schlesinger, Ralph Dungan. In New York, would they like to meet some publishers and editors I knew?

They would indeed—Bosch had a new book coming out, a "biography" of King David, and hoped it and his other books could be translated and published in English.

That afternoon Bosch on the radio announced he was leaving tomorrow. There would be rumors that he was sick or wouldn't return. They would be lies. There would be rumors of a *golpe*. More lies—the Armed Forces had behaved in exemplary fashion. He had not wanted to be President. (He said this twice after the election, and said it again at inauguration time: "I would rather be a citizen than a President." I thought it no mere gesture. Unconsciously he shrank from power. It worried me. People who fear the power they possess may use it erratically.) While he was away, he said, the people must watch for "tricks," especially in the economic field. He attacked the Consejo—he related in detail how much sugar Haina was producing, said the Consejo was converting sugar into molasses, declared this would result in a loss to the government, and said this was "a mystery that ought to be explained." He went further: Anything the Consejo did from now until February 27, especially in the economic field, would not be binding on his own government.

He had won but he was still campaigning. Not a word about the election's being a triumph for democracy and the Dominican people. He seemed totally out of phase with all other Dominicans, a stranger in a foreign land.

I spent the afternoon and evening writing letters and cables to forty or fifty friends in New York and Washington, people interested in books and ideas. I thought Bosch had been too long submerged in the conspiratorial underworld of Caribbean exile politics. He needed to get out in the fresh air among people who were not afraid to discuss ideas in public.

By next morning, Sunday, the Electoral Board's unofficial tally showed that Bosch had received 623,205 votes to Fiallo's 337,697. I wanted Fiallo to recognize Bosch's victory. Fandino and I went to Fiallo's house down in the old Spanish quarter, the thick-walled doctor's office where I first met him long ago. He looked tired, sad. He was sixty-seven. A joke had circulated that he had been so confident of victory that he had tried on the presidential *banda,* the splendrous sash of office. At the end of the campaign he had been appearing on television like a voice from the past, talking about the *noble sufrido pueblo Dominicano* again just as he had more than a year before. He was a brave and patriotic man, but events had outrun him. Today, as we sat in straight-backed mahogany chairs, I felt very sorry for him. I said it appeared that Bosch had won and I had come to tell him that he need have no regrets; he had campaigned honorably and by his patriotic example had taught the Dominican people much about the democratic process.

He said bitterly that Bosch had won by fraud—by buying votes and convincing wealthy contributors in the Cibao that the U. S. Embassy favored him. He himself refused to believe we had favored anyone, and I assured him we had not. Then, with some difficulty, he referred to our "summit" agreement. He said that although he considered Bosch's victory fraudulent, he would not contest it but would recognize it publicly as soon as the official tally was announced. I said I had known he would; he had always been a patriot. He thanked me, and we left. The same sun blazed in the narrow street that had blazed in Ramfis Trujillo's time, when Fiallo faced the Trujillo tanks, the people's hero. A year and a half ago. It seemed an age. It was.

From Fiallo's we went to the airport to see Bosch off. He was bareheaded, wearing the crepe-soled shoes and sport shirt and corduroy pants he had campaigned in, crushed by people. All around stood bodyguards, young men in civilian clothes cradling submachine guns. We managed to get near him and his wife and to give him a paper with the names and addresses of people in the States, wish him and his wife *bon voyage,* shake hands with Miolán, armed and beaming. We left. The bodyguards troubled me deeply. I had never seen them before, did not know whether they were "Pupito" Sánchez' men or Bosch's own PRD gunmen. One haunted me. He was in his twenties, of medium height, thin; he wore a brown suit, its jacket buttoned tight, a black shirt, and a white necktie. His face was absolutely without expression. It was marked, perhaps by some childhood disease, perhaps by terrible burns. It did not look like a human face at all but like a cardboard mask.

10

Next day was Christmas Eve, and Fran and I gave a party at the Residence for the Embassy children, then went to a party at President Bonnelly's house. He and Foreign Minister Bonilla and I were sitting on the sofa, talking quietly about the election, when Horacio Julio Ornes planted himself in front of us and, teeth bared, said to Bonnelly and Bonilla, "You see now—we smashed your oligarchy. The revolutionary parties smashed your oligarchy forever," and he went on, taunting them. At first President Bonnelly tried to smile and placate him. It did no good, he drove ahead, baiting the President and the Foreign Minister mercilessly. I got up, turned my back on him, asked the President and Foreign Minister to excuse me, and walked away. A little later, Fran and I went downtown to midnight Mass at the great Cathedral. It was filled with peace and beauty. This was the Misa del Gallo—the Mass of the Cock—traditional on Christmas Eve and probably the most beautiful Mass of the year; so many people we knew were there that we felt a little the spirit of Christmas at home.

We had some Peace Corps kids in for Christmas dinner. Afterward we slept, rested, and read the papers. Dominican and American, the papers commented on the triumph of democracy in the Republic. That night, on the spur of the moment, Fran and I drove unannounced to Imbert's house—not really a safe thing to do, to arrive unannounced— and sat and talked awhile with him and his wife and mother, and his sister and her husband, all in their bathrobes, just family talk, not politics; then drove, again unannounced, to Amiama's house, even more dangerous, and, admitted after considerable delay by the surprised guards, talked to him and his wife. He had sent us a roast pig for Christmas dinner, a red apple in its mouth, a bow tie around its neck, and a straw hat on its head.

His wife showed Fran around her house and woke her daughter to greet her; Amiama and I sat in his concrete study, and he talked about the assassination of Trujillo and showed me pictures on the wall of many of his companions, all dead now. Two had left widows pregnant. We all had a drink together, to the last year and the new, then Fran and I went home. Our calls had flabbergasted Imbert and Amiama at first, then touched them. I am not sure myself why we did it. A human gesture, I suppose, a sort of truce; even, perhaps, a reunion after a civil war, brothers, once enemies, now friends again.

Next day, Fran and the boys and I piled our fishing and hunting equipment in the car and set out for a holiday of our own at Alcoa's guest house at Cabo Rojo, the southwesternmost tip of the Republic, where we had made our first visit nearly a year earlier. This time we saw no iguanas on the way, but the terrain was as strange and mysterious as ever, and the sea as blue and the wind as fresh.

Chapter Thirteen

WAITING FOR BOSCH

We had planned to stay at Cabo Rojo five or six days. At daylight the third day, a company official wakened us. There had been an uprising in the hills near San Juan de la Maguana, the government had sent troops and a general had been killed, and the Embassy had chartered a plane to take us back to the capital. We had been warned many times that Castro/Communist guerrillas would rise near San Juan. Furthermore, San Juan is not far from the Haitian border—could this have been a Trujillo incursion? No one knew.

Fran, who fears flying, wanted to take the boys back by car. But guerrillas might cut the road. They would have to come with me. I told José to start driving to the capital but, if stopped by mobs, to abandon the car and save himself. Fran and the boys and I squeezed into the two-engine plane and took off.

The pilot had heard that six hundred men had been killed. He couldn't remember the general's name, but thought it was Rodríguez something. I said, "Not Rodríguez Reyes?" That was it.

I was shocked. I knew him well. Rodríguez Reyes was an older man, gray-haired, intelligent, giving an impression of strength and decency. I had had my eye on him against the day when a shuffle of the high command might take place. We had invited him and his wife to an open house on Tuesday, New Year's Day.

The little plane sailed around the Baoruco range, then followed the seacoast past Barahona. Somewhere up there in the desert and dun hills below the Cordillera Central, the battle had occurred. Soon the tower at Aeropuerto Punta Caucedo told us to watch for a Pan Am jet that had just taken off for Kingston and a Pan Am plane from Port-au-Prince that would land ahead of us. We headed straight across the sea for the airport. The plane shuddered suddenly. We had lost the right engine. The pilot succeeded in feathering the propeller, declared an emergency, and got clearance to land immediately. Freddy pointed at the immobile propeller: "Hey Mom, what's—" then stopped, put his hand over his mouth, and didn't say another word. The pilot kept saying loudly there was nothing to worry about. We crossed the long bay in front of the capital and landed perfectly.

Colonels Bev Cass and Fritz Long had gone to San Juan de la Maguana. Pending their return, this was what King and Shlaudeman knew:

During the U. S. Marine occupation, a man named Liborio had founded a religious cult, apparently opposed the occupation, and, the story goes, been killed by the Marines. Early in 1962 several brothers named Ventura had deified Liborio, revived the religious cult, and built a town in the foothills northwest of San Juan de la Maguana called Palma Sola. Palma Sola was accessible only by foot. Thousands of *campesinos* made pilgrimages there and participated in religious rites. Some stayed; nearly all brought contributions. Palma Sola became a permanent settlement. Other villages were built, the cult was spreading fast. The cultists were called *mellizos,* twins, because two of the Ventura brothers were twins.

Citizens of San Juan and Las Matas de Farfán had said the rites were orgiastic and voodooistic and had complained that thousands of pilgrims returning from Palma Sola were spellbound, hallucinated, and dangerous. Landowners complained that their *campesinos* left them, attorney General García Vásquez had scouted Palma Sola and recommended it be destroyed—the cultists were carrying on paramilitary training and might be Communist guerrillas or Trujillo mercenaries.

The Saturday after the election, local police had tried to stop a group of pilgrims. The pilgrims had killed a policeman. Thursday García Vásquez, Imbert, and General Belisario Peguero had flown over Palma Sola in a helicopter equipped with a loudspeaker and ordered the cultists to disperse. They had not. Yesterday a small detachment had moved in, led by García Vásquez and General Rodríguez Reyes, who, having come from that area, thought he might be able to reason with the people.

According to the official story, upon reaching Palma Sola General Rodríguez Reyes had gone alone into the compound to talk to the Ventura brothers. Apparently Palma Sola was enclosed by a stick stockade, and inside the stockade were huts, a prayer platform, and pathways and prayer circles outlined in whitewashed stones. It had looked deserted. But suddenly hundreds of men had rushed out of the huts and beaten Rodríguez Reyes to death with clubs. The police had moved in with tear gas and guns, and a fire fight had ensued. Three officers of the police had been wounded. The police had killed twenty or twenty-five of the cultists, including two Ventura brothers, captured 673 prisoners, rounded up three rice bags full of guns, and burned Palma Sola to the ground. About five hundred pilgrims had fled to the hills. Two counter-insurgency companies were pursuing them and P-51s were strafing them. Last night our MAAG chief, Colonel Wolfe, had been summoned to the Palace and asked for four helicopters to airlift troops into the hills, five hundred 2.7-inch rockets, and sixty napalm tanks for the P-51s. He had stalled and notified King and Shlaudeman.

King and Shlaudeman were, quite rightly, somewhat skeptical of the government story. Shlaudeman himself had visited one of the cultists' settlements near Palma Sola on election day with OAS observers and had seen much that was strange but nothing subversive. The theory of a Communist rising seemed unlikely: So many *campesinos* concentrated in one place? So did the Trujillo theory: The Trujillos would more likely move by assassination or Palace revolution. Yet we could not be sure; the whole affair was bizarre.

The Armed Forces were eager to retaliate. We certainly did not want United States napalm dropped on religious pilgrims. We noticed something else too—with the P-51s and the two counter-insurgency companies gone, San Isidro was left to Wessin y Wessin and his tanks.

I took King with me to see President Bonnelly. We found him saddened and subdued. "It is terrible. He was one of the best"—meaning Rodríguez Reyes. He told me substantially what King and Shlaudeman had, adding that García Vásquez had saved himself by throwing himself into a ditch. Bonnelly was convinced the *mellizos* had had guns. He said the Dominican military would destroy other *mellizo* encampments nearby and disperse the prisoners around the country. He agreed it best that we stay out of it. I expressed condolences and the hope that reprisals would not occur.

Cass and Long came to the Residence about 6 P.M., worn out, dirty, wearing dusty field uniforms. They had walked into Palma Sola with the troops. They put together this story:

Rodríguez Reyes had gone into the Palma Sola compound alone and was talking to a *mellizo,* trying to persuade him that the pilgrims should disperse, when a policeman, seeing a man with a dagger, had tried to take it away from him. They had wrestled, Rodríguez Reyes had ordered them to stop, a *mellizo* with a machete had run toward them, the policeman had shot him, eighty or ninety cultists had emerged from their houses, the police detachment had run up, throwing tear gas into the wind, which blew it back in their faces, and a thousand *mellizos* had streamed out of the huts. A general melee had ensued in a swirl of gas and dust, and Rodríguez Reyes had been beaten to death with clubs.

What had happened after that was not a battle but a massacre. Cass and Long had counted forty-four cultists' bodies. Some had been killed inside their huts. Some lay alongside the trail on the way out—taken prisoner, then shot in vengeance. Many of the dead were old men, two were women, one was a child. Cass and Long felt certain that many more had been hunted down and killed in the hills. The huts had been burned to the ground, bodies incinerated. Troops were mopping up now. Worst of all, Cass and Long were absolutely certain the *mellizos* had had no guns. No fire fight had occurred. Cass said flatly, "It was wanton killing."

I asked if it were possible that Rodríguez Reyes had been shot from behind by one of his own men. They could not say. King didn't know whether there had been an autopsy; probably not. Rodríguez Reyes' body was already buried.

At 7:15 P.M. President Bonnelly called me to his house. Bonnelly was angry. "Your attachés are proving embarrassing," he said. I asked why. "Because this is an internal political matter." I thought that a peculiar comment—what was political about it?—but said nothing. He went on, "García Vásquez has been to see me about it."

I said I would not have sent the attachés had I known it would displease or embarrass him. They had simply been doing their duty—to report to me on military matters. I was fully responsible. I felt reasonably sure they had obtained permission from the Dominican commanders. I did not apologize for their having gone but said that if the President requested, I would instruct them not to go to Palma Sola again. He did, and I left.

I checked with Long and Cass. Long had told General Viñas last night they were going; Colonel Pagán had welcomed them, but Attorney General García Vásquez had not. I saw what had happened: García Vásquez had persuaded the President to complain to me. I wondered again just what his role had been, and Imbert's—he was, after all, an Imbert man. Why had only Rodríguez Reyes been killed? How? Why was this a "political matter"? I went to see Imbert.

He repeated the official story. He called the *mellizos* "poor starving people" and wanted to take me to see them at police headquarters, wearing rags and stinking. I probed for political implications but got nothing.

We never learned the full truth about Palma Sola. The Red Chinese called it a massacre of *campesinos* by those who had forced "antidemocratic" elections on them. Probably it was nothing more than a bungled police action. The cultists, having defied authority and created a state within a state, did represent a threat to the state. This hardly justified massacre. Nor did the official explanations satisfy. Palma Sola remained, like so much in the Dominican Republic, shrouded forever. Throughout the entire year we had predicted every imaginable disaster— but not the blood on the stones and dust of Palma Sola. Because it was so totally unexpected, it was deeply disturbing, as any insane act disturbs in an understood universe. And frightening. It was a reminder that violent death was never far below the surface in this terrible land.

2

On January 3 President Bonnelly invited Fran and the boys and me, Cass and his wife, and Fandino to accompany him on a trip on the yacht *Mella*. We set sail at midnight. Aboard too were the British Ambassador, Stephen A. Lockhart; the Colombian Ambassador, Jesús Zárate; Imbert; Commodore Rib; and their wives. Of all such trips we took, this turned out to be the most pleasant.

We were gone six days. We headed east that night and next day steamed through Mona Passage, far out from the beach at Macao and the mouth of the Nisibón, the water deep, deep blue and flying fish playing all around. We passed the mouth of Samaná Bay and rounded the shoulder of Hispañola, then turned westward in the Atlantic. Tony Imbert and I stood once more on the bridge over the curling sea, watched the navigator raise a sextant to the stars and, inside his chartroom, put precise calipers on the universe.

Far at the northwest corner of the Republic, near Monte Cristi, we tied up at the dock whence La Grenada, a United Fruit subsidiary, shipped bananas. Across the bay the mountains of Haiti rose steep and bare. We got into a long string of cars and roared away to Dajabón, the frontier-outpost town. We walked to the precise middle of the bridge over the Río Massacre, where a mark denoted the border. Bonnelly put one toe across it, laughing. Imbert said darkly, pointing to the thick under-brush along the riverbank on the other side, "You don't see them," that is, the Haitians, "but they are there. Like animals." I had heard it before.

Back in the cars, we drove on, climbing up from the flat banana plain into the mountains, the Cordillera Central, up and up and still on up, a twisting, circling mountain road. At a frontier town, Restauración, we stopped in a muddy street and, followed by a crowd of children, walked to the club, a dismal tiny bar. As we entered, a band in the dim interior suddenly blared the Dominican national anthem, and we stopped in our tracks on the worn wood threshold and stood at attention, stiffly erect. Back in the car, I said to Bonnelly, "You must feel very proud. The past year, I mean." He understood, and touched my knee lightly with his hand.

That night we went to a party at La Grenada and danced and drank till late. Poor Fran had to get up at daybreak and drive all the way to the capital. This was January 6, the Day of the Three Kings, and we were giving a Christmas party for three hundred Dominican orphans at the Embassy. I stayed here, and Imbert took Dan and Fred and me guinea hunting, a bizarre trip, for we climbed aboard a motor scooter on the banana company's narrow-gauge railroad and rode and rode, bouncing, crowded onto the little car, Imbert in front, the two boys and I clinging to one side, a local hunter clinging to the other, the driver in the middle. Suddenly, far down a rusty section of the track, in a shadowy patch of ground where banana trees and silky guinea grass grew thick, we saw them—a flock of gray guineas, almost hidden. Imbert snapped, "Faster, faster," and the little car went full speed, rocking and swaying and banging ahead, and Imbert raised his gun and so did I, and just as we came within range the guinea flushed. We both fired, two birds dropped, the flock wheeled full circle and came back toward us at the edge of the trees, and we each fired again, and two more dropped. Imbert kept firing his automatic 12-gauge as they went into the brush; my gun, a 20-gauge over-and-under, was empty. I was glad it was—I'd already made a double, on the wing, from a motor scooter moving thirty miles an hour. I told him that now I'd stop shooting. He chuckled. He liked to hunt, Tony Imbert. He taught Dan and Fred to shoot.

That night at sea Imbert baited François Duvalier, called Papa Doc, the voodooist President of Haiti: He steered the *Mella* well within Haitian territorial waters, and next day, as we were sailing southward down the Windward Passage between Haiti and Cuba, took down our flag. President Bonnelly, laughing by the rail, said, "We are pirates." Later I was told that our unexplained presence had touched off an alarm in Port-au-Prince, as Imbert had hoped it might.

So we passed on through the Caribbean, picking out Cabo Rojo and Isla Beata, then Barahona, where the waters of the heaving sea were rough, our last night out. President Bonnelly, chatting idly, said that the people had ceaselessly criticized the Consejo throughout last year but the day would come when they would look back on it as the best government they'd had in many years, very likely better than the one they'd get from Bosch. Was he right?

Beyond politics, we had been through a great deal with these people, Fran and I—with Imbert, Bonnelly, the rest. We were friends as only people who have struggled together, sometimes against each other, sometimes side by side, can be friends. Nostalgia settled on us. Whatever lay ahead, this was finished.

3

What prospects now lay ahead?

Bosch's electoral sweep had been tremendous. The official vote showed that he had received 619,491 votes out of a total of 1,054,944 cast— 58.72 percent. Fiallo had received 317,327—30.08 percent—only a little more than half of Bosch's vote. The Social Christians had come in third, and they had polled only 5.18 percent of the total. The other six parties had polled only a few thousand each—for example Juan Isidro Jimenes Grullón's ASD had polled only 17,898, General Horacio Julio Ornes'

Vanguardia only 6886, and "General" Vilomar's colossus 1667. In the capital, Bosch had swamped Fiallo, 152,404 to 35,376. Fiallo had carried only four provinces—Santiago, Puerto Plata, Duarte (San Francisco de Macorís), and Espaillat (Moca). General Ramírez had held his home province, San Juan. Bosch had carried every other province.

Clearly, Bosch's mandate was overwhelming. He had won the votes of the *campesinos*, of the displaced *campesinos* in the cities, of old PD men and Trujillistas, of Castro/Communists, and of the relatives of soldiers and police—of nearly everyone. Some said the PRD did not win the election—the UCN lost it. But at bottom, in my opinion, the vote showed the existence in this Republic of a deep and powerful revolutionary current. These people wanted a better life. Bosch somehow convinced them he would give it to them. In September 1961, I had felt I was in the presence of a revolution. But fervor had died—during 1962 the people were patient and docile. The Consejo did little for them. It resembled somewhat the Trujillo regime—white, oligarchical, and remote. The people waited. Finally their time came to speak, and they spoke, unmistakably. A Communist, Dato Pagán, said that among all the new Senators and Deputies, not one bore a familiar name. All the old names that had ruled the Republic for a hundred years were gone— Cáceres, Tavares, Cabral, Santana, Baez, Bermúdez, Vicini. Could Bosch deliver?

4

The fragmentary reports on Bosch's sojourn in the United States and Europe were not reassuring. With the vote official, he saw everybody— President Kennedy[1] himself received him and put an airplane at his disposal. Members of the United States Supreme Court received him. So did Secretary Rusk and Attorney General Robert F. Kennedy. George Ball and Ted Moscoso and Ed Martin met with him, as did various Senators and Congressmen and officers of international agencies. He was virtually lionized at first. One night he dined at Arthur Schlesinger's home in Georgetown and talked late with Schlesinger and Adlai Stevenson. He said in an interview that his election had dealt communism a heavy blow in the Caribbean. Radio Havana called him a Yankee puppet.

But some of his talk baffled people in Washington. He talked of gold mining and fisheries, of turning the giant Haina over to the workers. He was ignorant of his own country's finances and our loans, which he had thought carried high interest rates. He announced that he would invite

[1] Bosch seems to have thought that President Kennedy dressed plainly in a business suit to receive him "as if in an effort to avoid offending Dominican poverty with an exhibition of American wealth." He recalls that when he told President Kennedy that Dominicans suffered hunger, "he moved as if he had been wounded."

Juan José Arévalo, the anti-American former President of Guatemala, to the Republic. Bosch refused to attend an elaborate official OAS function in his honor because the OAS President planned to praise the Consejo in his speech. In New York, Bosch simply canceled at the last moment a private luncheon arranged by editors, publishers, and diplomats I knew.

When Bosch left Washington, Assistant Secretary Ed Martin called me: "I think we have our problems, but it was a good visit." "Our problems"—Martin was never one to overstate.

Suddenly Bosch denounced a contract the Consejo had made with Esso to build a refinery in Santo Domingo. The refinery, though not in itself of vital importance, was the only new investment by a big U.S. corporation since Trujillo's fall. Thus Bosch virtually threw away any chance of large reputable foreign investment, at least for some time. He then went off to Europe, where, I believe, he was received by President de Gaulle and Chancellor Adenauer, among others, and whence reports trickled back of his adventures with the French police, through whom he seemed to be trying to trace Trujillo loot. He kept sending cables to the Consejo, asking for details on the budget, and making mysterious telephone calls to PRD leaders about the proposed new Constitution. Somehow it all had a quality of make-believe.

The Bosch fallout began to descend from Washington—requests for plans of action, proposals Bosch had advanced, the view of those proposals held by the White House, the Department, and AID. A two-way flow of planning papers commenced between the Embassy and the Department. They too sounded like make-believe.

Presently the Department told me that, since Bosch did not want to appear a U.S. puppet, my AID people should work with the PRD experts on planning. This was somewhat mystifying—the PRD had no experts on planning. Miolán told us that Bosch's confidant Sacha Volman was in charge of planning. Volman knew nothing of planning, we would have to do it. But if it went wrong, we would be the goat. I told the Department so. After a good deal of pulling and hauling, Washington decided that Bosch, instead of working directly with AID or with the Consejo's leftist-infiltrated planning board, would set up a shadow planning board in a new agency called CIDES, organized by Sacha Volman. The CIDES planners would be drawn from throughout the Hemisphere, financed by the Dominican government, the U.S. government, and private U.S. foundations. Alvin Mayne, an expert planner with long experience in Puerto Rico, would advise the planners. But what its relation would be to AID or the Embassy, or to Bosch, was not entirely clear.

Sacha Volman was thirty-eight years old, a rather small man, tightly knit, sharp-featured intense. He spoke both English and Spanish with a Russian accent and in a voice so soft one could scarcely hear. Born in Bessarabia, he had, he said, "run away from home at the age of eleven to become a revolutionary." When he said it, women swooned. Wandering the earth at his trade of revolutionary, he was imprisoned by Hitler's troops and persecuted by Stalin's; escaping, he turned up in Costa Rica and established an institute for political education to train democratic leaders. Bosch met him there in 1957.

Volman was probably the only confidant Bosch had. In those first days after the election, Volman was riding high, shuttling by jet between Santo Domingo and Washington, his briefcase full of plans and his head full of plots. His mind was quick and devious; he could be charming and ingratiating or murderously tough; his basic instinct was conspiratorial, and his manner, like that of a wild creature, was always feral.

One evening, just back from Washington, he came to see me. Harlan Bramble, the Embassy economic counselor, had said the Bosch government would need a financial expert—Volman had several. And he had more: Men to plan sugar reconstruction, agrarian reform, co-ops, electrification, taxes, cattle and agricultural development; most of all, men to plan planning itself. Cubans, Venezuelans, Brazilians, Chinese; men from Harvard and other universities; men from the United Nations, the Pan American Health Bureau—Volman had them all. He set forth the views of Bosch and of men Bosch had seen—Juan Trippe of Pan American Airways, Senator Hubert Humphrey, Secretary of Agriculture Orville Freeman, Laurance Rockefeller, Mayor Wagner of New York, many others. Bosch, he said, planned not merely an oil refinery, which Esso had contracted to build, but a "petrochemical complex." Volman had drawn up a budget for CIDES, including the cost of typewriters and filing cabinets. I told him he was a bureaucrat at heart.

I asked what Bosch was going to do fast to help the people who elected him. Build roads, Volman said, and public eating places where the poor could eat cheap. Then he came to the point: Imbert must go. I demurred—why? Because with Imbert here, Bosch would feel "insecure."

I asked about Cabinet appointments. Volman unreeled a complicated series of maneuvers. Juan Isidro Jimenes Grullón would be appointed Secretary of State for Foreign Affairs, then fired for incompetence. Horacio Julio Ornes wanted to be Secretary of State for Interior and Police; Bosch would instead appoint him Secretary of State for Public Works, where graft was easy, then fire him after a few months. Bosch would honor his summit agreement to use UCNers. He would get rid of General Belisario Peguero of the police immediately. We must help set up a security police unit at once. I agreed, but I envisaged it as primarily an anti-subversive force, while Volman thought its primary duty that of guarding Bosch's life. For many weeks and months, the apparatus remained one of our most difficult and important problems: Who would staff it, who would pay for it, to whom would it report, and what precisely would it do? The problem never was satisfactorily resolved.

5

Volman disappeared into plans; Ángel Miolán now emerged as Bosch's man. A sudden wave of strikes brought him to the fore, for neither the Consejo nor we had anyone else to turn to.

Workers abruptly struck Haina, the Grenada Company, and other companies. The Grenada strike sounded nasty. Imbert called me at 10 P.M. on January 10, the night after we returned from our trip, to say the strikers had shut off the lights and water at Monte Cristi. He had sent forty policemen and the Secretary of Labor there, and tomorrow would send Attorney General García Vásquez. Next morning I called our consul in Santiago, Ben Ruyle, and told him to go to Monte Cristi, taking another man with him. At two-thirty Imbert called. The electricity and water were turned back on, there was no danger to American lives or property. To make sure, I asked President Bonnelly. He said there was no danger. He said the strike had been instigated by a leftist PRD leader. But how to settle it?

Shlaudeman saw Miolán, and Miolán said the Consejo had lost control of labor. He himself would go to Monte Cristi tomorrow to try to stop the strike. I saw Bonnelly again. He had sent word to Miolán that the strikes must stop or Bosch could take office now—the Consejo would resign. I asked Miolán to come to see me.

I told Miolán I knew nothing about the merits of the Grenada strike but was concerned about the possibility of violence, and I pointed out that if the strike was not settled peaceably the effect on foreign investors might be disastrous. He said he would go there immediately. But later that night he canceled his trip.

I called Ben Ruyle again and told him to check with the company, the Governor, and the military commander. Harlan Bramble, just back from a trip to that area, said everything had seemed peaceful to him. Ruyle called back late that night. The military commander said all was quiet, he had been there himself and had sent troops to guard the company's property. Fred Somerford checked with his labor people; all was quiet.

But at the Hotel Embajador Fran ran into a group of women from the Grenada Company who said they had been "evacuated."

Ruyle called back next morning and said everything was peaceful but the strikers expected the company to answer their demands by tomorrow.

That day, January 18, a Grenada official named Von Wald called on me. He gave me a copy of a letter that the president of United Fruit,

T. E. Sunderland, had written to Secretary Rusk, complaining that American lives and property were gravely endangered and I had done little or nothing about it. I was angered. I told Von Wald, using my notes, what we had done and told him Sunderland's letter was erroneous and unjustified. He said the letter wasn't important, but I told him it was. He apologized. I said I wanted Sunderland to write a letter to the Secretary apologizing and telling him the truth.

Von Wald said he intended to go to President Bonnelly and warn him there might be bloodshed. I told him he could do anything he pleased, but in my opinion he was grossly overstating the problem, and I thought it my duty to tell him that the Republic was in a difficult political situation, our national interest was involved, and he might give some thought to his country's interests as well as his company's. I told him we would do everything possible to protect his people and his property, but we could do far more if he would keep us informed instead of the Secretary of State, who was too far away to be much help. I asked twice if he wanted me to do anything now. He didn't. He left.

After negotiations arranged by Bonnelly failed, I talked to Miolán privately. Miolán arranged a truce till March 18, when Bosch would be in office, and arranged it at considerable cost to himself—the workers, who had voted for Bosch, didn't like the settlement.

During the entire time I was in the Dominican Republic this was the only time that any U.S. company attempted to put on such pressure. Perhaps I was unduly incensed by Von Wald. I had some reason— while I was talking to him, a demonstration began outside the Chancellery—the U.S. had permitted Héctor Trujillo to go to Panama. and Dominican leftists, unable to locate the Panamanian Embassy, demonstrated at ours. The Cascos Blancos protected us.

6

Shlaudeman reported that Miolán was beside himself. Bosch, talking vaguely about a "total economic survey of the island," had left Miolán in charge of everything—inauguration, the writing of a new Constitution, economic problems, strikes, party problems, and patronage.

Moreover, Miolán had to arrange Bosch's triumphal return from Europe. Bosch insisted that no military greet him at the airport—only the people. But how could Miolán guarantee his safety? Miolán, by nature suspicious, did not trust the National Police or "Pupito" Sánchez' secret police, so he was arranging his own private guard. I knew that as soon as word of this reached the military, they would explode—one of the first things Castro did when he came to power was to establish a "people's militia." Had the black-shirted, pockmarked man at the airport been only the first of many?

Some of the PRD were enjoying life hugely—one day one of them, passing a Trujillo house with a swimming pool, grandly offered it to two *campesinos* riding with him. But not poor Miolán—squatters moved in on the rice fields at Nagua, reserved for agrarian reform, Bonnelly refused to act, and Miolán had to persuade them to leave.

But Miolán could not forever reject the voters' demands. And the Consejo had come virtually to a standstill. Bosch had made it clear that he would not consider himself bound by its actions. It, on the other hand, would do nothing unless he shared responsibility. I feared a real vacuum. Bonnelly was nervous, worried. We brought in a big cruiser, the U.S.S. *Newport News,* and once more in a stream of helicopters Bonnelly and Pichardo and Reid and I and our wives went out to lunch aboard, a lovely day, a good political move. I wondered whether Bosch would welcome such support. Not at first. Maybe never.

7

The Consejo replaced the Army commander, Rivera Cuesta, with General Renato Hungría. We watched the Armed Forces shift carefully—lately they had been showing signs of increasing restlessness over Bosch. But Rivera Cuesta was satisfied to become Undersecretary of State for Army. A little later a new police general staff was announced, and lo, who was on it but Imbert.

I felt like saying, "Honestly, now, Tony—when are you going to quit?" I knew the answer: Never. He was almost like a wayward schoolboy.

Going to see Imbert, I found his house being remodeled. He said he was adding a two-story wing—he needed a place to talk and work, the basement talking room was no good. A long corridor led to the stairs far at the rear—a perfect shooting gallery. At the top, the stairs were blocked by a solid door.

I said it looked very secure.

"Sure," he said, drawing it out slowly with a rising inflection, a way he had, his eyebrows raised, his face blank.

He seemed glad to see me. I asked why he had so many policemen—close to ten thousand. He said, almost boyishly, that Jackson, our police adviser, had recommended it. Laughing, I said I didn't believe it. He grinned; he hadn't expected me to. What was he going to do after February 27?

He laughed. "Go to my army camp. Stay up there," pointing upstairs to the new second-story wing.

"Are you all right with Bosch?"

"Yes. He came to me and Luís before he left and asked us to keep things quiet for him. I saw Miolán yesterday for two hours. I told him to fix the Grenada strike. He did it. He's a good man. They say he is a

Communist but I don't believe it. He worked for Toledano but he's no Communist. He talks straight."

At this time Betancourt and the Castro/Communists were battling openly in the streets of Caracas. We had heard that the FALN, a Caracas terrorist movement, was planning to send men to Santo Domingo to assassinate Betancourt during the Bosch inaugural. Imbert showed me a letter he had just written, taking, he said, great pains with it. On plain paper, it was addressed to Betancourt. It's first page was a flowery paean to liberty and against tyranny. It ended by inviting Betancourt to stay in *"mi hogar,"* my humble house. This, then, was the real reason he was building the new addition: For Betancourt.

I asked if it were so. He shrugged, as though it didn't matter. "He'll be safe here, you can be sure." It mattered a very great deal indeed. Once again I was deeply touched. There was a heartbreaking quality about these people. Imbert's shy invitation to Betancourt—after all, Imbert had killed the man who had almost killed Betancourt—a UCN leader's asking me in 1961 for a copy of the U. S. Constitution—these people, these Dominicans, beneath all their pride and *macho* pretense, had a heartbreaking innocence about them, even the strongest and bravest. As I tried to leave that night, Tony kept talking, and I knew he had something he found it hard to say. Finally he said it. His wife, and Amiama's, were going to Miami tomorrow. Could we help keep them safe? Of course we could. I sent an urgent cable, asking that they be given all courtesies on arrival and that the Miami police or FBI call on them and offer full-time guard or other assistance. And, even while writing the cable, I could not help wondering why they were going, what they might be carrying. Cash? As I went to bed that night, I thought what a queer, wrenching country this was.

8

People we never had heard of began to turn up in all sorts of connections—security police, government contacts, American carpetbagger businessmen. We checked them. Some were Cuban, some Venezuelan, some from central Europe. All seemed to be friends of Bosch's and, we suspected, influence peddlers and fixers (though some people thought them Communist agents). All sorts of plots began to swirl around. And, as they would henceforward under Bosch, the plots took on an international character. Haitian exiles suddenly arrived.

The Department was pressing for inauguration plans. Plans! Everybody in town was talking about Bosch's crazy plans, or lack of plans. Bosch refused to receive power from the Consejo. He wanted the Consejo to resign in front of the National Assembly, then be sworn in himself in front of the Assembly. Bonnelly refused—the PRD-dominated

Assembly might boo him. Miolán had tried in vain to dissuade Bosch. Moreover, Bosch wanted to invite no official delegations to the inauguration, only "personal friends," including Vice President Lyndon Johnson. Foreign Minister Bonilla and the protocol chief, Ambassador Logroño, said it was impossible. Miolán would try to telephone Bosch in Naples.

Bosch was adamant. He insisted on no official delegations, no receptions, no decorations, no soldiers—now we would have the people's government. Once more Miolán was caught between Bosch and reality.

I told Vice President Pichardo that if Bosch did not make suitable preparations for security, neither Vice President Johnson nor any other high U.S. official would attend. Bosch might find himself all alone at his own inaugural and he might not survive it.

Pichardo suggested Bosch might be making inauguration impossible, and mentioned Jânio Quadros, the Brazilian President who resigned. Now Bosch had another idea: He would send his invited guests out around the country to great fiestas. Where they would sleep and how they would travel he apparently had no idea. The whole thing was rather funny. Pichardo said he had seen Bosch only twice in his life—once as a patient, and once when Bosch summoned him to discuss affairs of state. On the second occasion, he found Bosch in bed. Bosch said: "What are you going to do about the rootless masses who are roaming the country and are ready to rise?" Pichardo explained patiently that the Consejo had put some of them to work on emergency relief programs and would like to put more to work, but had a problem—it had no money. Bosch said immediately, "Money, I will take care of that," and reached for the telephone and said, "Get me Muñoz Marín." At that point an earthquake occurred, the telephone line went dead, Bosch pulled the covers over his head, and Pichardo ran home to see if his wife was all right. What happened to the rootless masses nobody knows; they never came up again.

The Consejo had made the mistake of sending Foreign Minister Bonilla Atiles to New York to discuss the inaugural with Bosch. Bosch despised Bonilla. Bonilla got off on the wrong foot by telling him there were two ways to hold the inaugural. Bosch cut him off immediately and said, "There is only one way—mine."

I decided Bosch, given to historionics, was behaving this way deliberately. He knew he would confuse and irritate the Consejo, just as he had mystified official Washington. It was part of Bosch's play-acting. He and Imbert had much in common. Both liked to agitate people, to stir things up, to play games, to take risks and dramatize themselves. Bosch had a real flare for capturing the center of the stage. During the last ten days before the election he had done it with the Church issue. Now he was doing it again. He had not invited Muñoz Marín to the inaugural. I thought he was determined to take the leadership of the democratic left in the Caribbean away from Muñoz, Betancourt, Figueres, and all others. His way of doing it was to dramatize himself—an eccentric intellectual and idealist, but a man of the people.

Of course, in doing it, he was creating serious problems. As in the past he was counting on others to solve them—Miolán, the Consejo, or the U.S. government. But, as always, there was danger in his course. He was becoming the laughing stock of the capital. Some of the jokes were more menacing than funny—"Where the goat is, there is room for the sheep"; that is, if Trujillo could be killed and stuffed into an auto trunk, so could Bosch.

Moreover, all problems were being postponed until he returned. Where would he get the people to run his government? Where was his program? His first three months in office would be critical. There is no magic in a hundred days. But if Bosch had not made good on his promises to the people in his first hundred days, they might not wait much longer.

9

On January 25 the first free Assembly in the Republic in thirty-three years met to write a new Constitution, and, sentimentally, I watched. At a party a few days later, President Bonnelly, Donny Reid, and Tony Imbert took me aside into a little room and demanded indignantly to know what I thought of the new draft Constitution. It had been published, prematurely, the PRD claimed, to arouse opposition to Bosch. It certainly had aroused opposition. President Bonnelly, leaning forward and tapping my knee, declared it was "a Communist Constitution" and would ruin the Republic. As a lawyer, he said the Constitution was loosely drawn. It would frighten away investment. It did not protect any property right except the right to "enjoy" private property. It authorized expropriation of property without compensation. It forbade foreign persons and all corporations from owning property. It said property must serve the needs of the masses. It prohibited *latifundio* but left it to Congress to define *latifundio*. It legalized concubinage and made divorce easy, "rudely" infringed the Dominican tradition that the man was the head of the family by declaring the sexes equal, did not guarantee civil liberties, and did not consecrate the Vatican Concordat.

Imbert joined in vociferously. So did Reid. The country was a keg of dynamite with a very short, burning fuse. Throughout the conversation flowed venom against the new regime. Reid showed Bonnelly a letter he had received from the new mayor of San Cristóbal, requesting a thousand dollars to pay for the visit of inaugural dignitaries to San Cristóbal. Reid said with contempt that the new mayor was the garbage-truck driver in San Cristóbal; Reid would throw this letter into the garbage where it belonged. President Bonnelly agreed—the people were ignorant and needed to be educated to own land and participate in business and in government.

This was the first outcry of the propertied class against the revolution.

Reid said, "We should leave government now. Let Bosch have it." Bonnelly did not demur. Reid continued, "If this Constitution passes, the bloodshed will begin, for the people will rise." I asked who would do the shooting. They said everybody. I said I couldn't imagine the masses rising to defend rights of the propertied class. Then I tried to placate them. I said that first of all I did not think Bosch and the PRD intended to turn this country into a Communist state. Imbert interrupted hotly, "There is already one Communist state in the Americas because the United States did not believe Castro would go Communist."

We were determined, I said, there would not be another Fidel in the Caribbean.

He said, "I understand this, you will not permit it—but you had better be careful this time."

I said we were discussing a mere draft of the Constitution that had appeared in *El Caribe*. No one was certain that this draft would actually be introduced into the Assembly, let alone be adopted. I suggested we give the new Assembly a chance.

They didn't like this. They had set their faces against this proposed Constitution. They made it absolutely clear they did not intend to sit idly by and—as they saw it—let the new government hand their country over to the Communists.

I thought this protest serious. It was a glimmer of just how hard Bosch's way would be. These men were not making idle talk. This meant real trouble. Unless handled carefully, it could mean Bosch's doom.

I asked Shlaudeman to go through the draft Constitution carefully, identify the problem sections, and discuss them with the PRD. I would talk to Bonnelly alone and try to moderate his views. Shlaudeman and Bramble would talk to Reid. All this might help some. But the venom against Bosch was real.

10

I had long wanted to visit Ambassador Raymond Thurston in Port-au-Prince. The time seemed now—once Bosch returned, I could not leave. On February 1 Fran and Dan and Fred and I drove to Port-au-Prince, ten hours via Jimaní. We spent four or five days in Haiti, sightseeing in Port-au-Prince, driving to Cap Haitien and riding horses up a mountain to mad Christophe's fantastic Citadel, learning about Haiti. I told Ambassador Thurston that I might come here often: When discouraged in the Dominican Republic, I could always come here and feel better. Haiti seemed totally hopeless.

Haiti has at least as large a population as the Dominican Republic but only half the area—and much of its land is arid, bare, and mountainous. This basic arithmetic smothers Haitian hope. The people are packed into a few valleys and cities, living in abysmal poverty, the average per capita income about sixty-five dollars per year, half the population unemployed, 90 percent illiterate. The main crop is coffee, which is grown wild and picked sporadically. The next crop is sugar—eighty thousand tons per year, compared to nearly a million in the Dominican Republic. The economy was going downhill. In 1788 Haiti exported forty-one million dollars' worth of produce; in 1962, less than forty million dollars.

The tyranny of Duvalier was dreadful. He had smashed the Army and built up a private police force and a Palace guard. He had a band of thugs and informers called the Ton-Ton-Macoutes—not uniformed, armed, present in every village. Checkpoints, murder, and torture were common.

Whether Duvalier would survive was uncertain. Plotters talked openly everywhere. Our own policy was one of disengagement—maintaining "cool but correct" relations. Ambassador Thurston had seen Duvalier only once in the last three months. Duvalier had been legally elected for a six-year term in 1957 and, in our view, under his own Constitution his term would expire this May. He claimed he had been re-elected two years before. We considered that re-election illegal. What would happen between now and May was anybody's guess.

I left Haiti February 5 by helicopter with Colonel Robert Heinl, commander of the U. S. Marine Mission in Port-au-Prince. That morning Duvalier had declared Colonel Heinl *persona non grata*. Heinl loved the Haitian people but hated Duvalier and sometimes went out of his way to show it. Duvalier retaliated: Once his thugs had arrested Heinl's twelve-year-old son and thrown him into the Palace dungeon. Now Heinl must go home. As our helicopter skimmed the mountains, Heinl started dropping something from a paper bag out the open helicopter door onto the barren land. Mahogany seeds. "Every time I make a trip like this, I drop them," he said. "Some day the people will have a mahogany forest here."

The Dominican frontier town, Elías Piña, resembles Jimaní—an artificial town created by Trujillo during his "Dominicanization" of the frontier. The hospital administrator said he needed fifty thousand dollars for rehabilitation and a new building. What he really needed was nurses and doctors—and janitors to keep the building clean.

We drove to Las Matas de Farfán, near Palma Sola, visited several Peace Corps farming projects, then went on to San Juan de la Maguana. There we were in the hands of "General" Ramírez, the burly veteran of assorted Caribbean adventures and now political boss of the province, its

Senator-elect. We sat up late one night while he told stories. At Cayo Confites, he said, Juan Bosch had promised large quantities of arms, ships, munitions, and supplies but arrived with nothing. The other leaders of the revolution decided to court-martial and shoot him. Ramírez took him under his protection, dug a hole in the sand on the key, put Bosch in it, told him to stay there all night, and slept beside it, saving his life—or so Ramírez said. Later Ramírez had joined Castro in the Sierra Maestra, opened the second front in the Escambray Mountains, been jailed by Castro, and been released in 1960. Ramírez was sixty-two and had spent most of his adult life in exile, fighting in the Caribbean. His brother had been murdered by Trujillo; the husband of his niece had died in the Estero Hondo landing. Many could tell similar stories.

In San Juan we held a big town meeting, and the people asked for help with water and employment, and Ramírez made a speech which discomfited me—he presented a plan for the development of the valley of the San Juan River, a tributary of the Yaque del Sur, implying that it already had been approved by AID and me. Vallimarescu, our USIS man, killed the story in *El Caribe.*

We walked through a *barrio,* surrounded by hundreds of men and women and naked children. The *barrio* was beside the muddy river; every September it flooded. The squalor and stench and misery were unbelievable, two men and their wives and all their children living in a hut six feet square, taking turns sleeping on the bed and floor; no lights, no sanitation, nothing but dirt. There was not a latrine in the *barrio.* Nobody knew how many people lived there. We were told that at that time about a thousand had typhus. Some, Ramírez' precinct captains, got jobs on the road. In one house I asked if things had improved for them since Trujillo's death. They had not.

We toured the *campo,* beautiful farms, and were told that Spaniards, Syrians, and a few Dominican politicians controlled all the good land and all the water. Once again, seeing the misery in the *barrio* and the arid plains, seeing the lush fields where the river had been harnessed, I left the Southwest determined to develop the Yaque del Sur.

11

Bosch decided to invite official delegations to his inaugural after all. We would send a distinguished one, headed by Vice President Johnson. His staff and the Secret Service arrived in advance. With King and the Embassy staff, they worked out a minute-by-minute schedule for the Vice President. I talked to President Bonnelly about security, told the CIA chief to check immigration constantly, and went over several alternative routes for the Vice President's motorcade from airport to hotel. He wanted to bring his Cadillac convertible. I demurred—it was unsafe.

I asked for the aircraft carrier *Boxer,* ostensibly to render honors to Bosch, actually to provide helicopter air cover for Vice President Johnson. And I asked the Secret Service men one final question: Who was responsible in case of serious trouble—who would declare the emergency and ask the *Boxer* for help? I would, on the Secret Service men's advice if possible; if not, on my own. History would hold me responsible in any case.

During this period before Bosch's return, I gave thought to resigning: 1963 would be totally unlike 1962. Any Ambassador would have trouble with Bosch—he was a difficult man—but I might have more than some, for I had had a serious collision with him once and when necessary had sided with the Consejo against him. True, he was a writer and so was I; he was a liberal and so was I. But he had shown character traits I did not like. And no doubt I had shown some he didn't like. Finally, Bosch would face formidable difficulties, and from a purely selfish point of view, I would be better off to leave, for we had achieved a real triumph in 1962, and if Bosch failed, I would fail with him.

At that time, foreign aid and the Alliance for Progress were being questioned even by their friends. In his State of the Union message, President Kennedy defended them. The New York *Times* said that tremendous social, political, and economic changes must precede private investment, and this in turn raised "the most burning of all questions in Latin America: can the necessary drastic transformations be made peacefully, or must there be revolutions either of the Castro or of the military-fascist type? The Cubans said: revolution. We say: Alliance for Progress."

But criticism mounted. In mid-February, James Reston wrote in the New York *Times,* "A strange kind of malaise now pervades Washington. The exuberant optimism of the first few months of the Kennedy Administration has vanished. There is a feeling that events are controlling men rather than the other way around. Both at home and abroad, the President is in trouble. . . . He is depressed. For he thought, even at the beginning [of 1963], that he was gaining on history, and now, after only a few tumultuous weeks, history seems to be gaining on him."

Sometimes the Dominican Republic was singled out as the testing ground. The Washington *Post* said, "If the *Alianza* fails in this critical country, it is difficult to see how it could succeed in any other place." I remember talking to Shlaudeman about it late one night at Vesuvio's, under the stars by the sea. Everybody was discussing economic development. But here at least the basic struggle was political. Could Bosch make his revolution? Could we help? Would he let us?

Well, we could try. We would make it work if it was possible. We would hold this place for the President, our President.

Chapter Fourteen

BOSCH COMES HOME

Juan Bosch came home on Sunday afternoon, February 17.

I did not go to the airport—Bosch, sensitive about Yankee domination, might resent it. This was his day, the crowd his people. Fran and Shlaudeman and I watched on television.

The homecoming was a shambles. It started beautifully—the enormous crowd, excited announcers, the Pan Am silver jet sailing in, and then Bosch at a railing on the airport platform, white-crowned, saluting the crowd. But the screaming crowd, his sycophants, his security guard, crushed him, crushed his wife; the microphone tottered, almost fell, Bosch frowned, stood waiting; the crowd kept screaming, a police line broke, the crowd surged in; he tried to speak, but the public-address system did not work; the crowd seemed about to engulf him, his face darkened with anger, then all at once he disappeared in a swirl of humanity, leaving the toppling microphones behind.

A few minutes later, the announcer said he had not been able to speak and a helicopter was taking him away, and we watched it rise, flapping, against the sky. Shlaudeman shook his head and said, "The poor people. The poor country. They blew it again." I thought incongruously of an old cartoon: An unhappy husband hangs himself and somehow manages to get his arm as well as his neck through the noose, and his wife, on finding him, says pettishly, "Can't you ever do anything right?"

About eight-thirty that night Shlaudeman telephoned—Bosch wanted to see me at once.

Bosch was staying in a little house beyond the Fairgrounds. Guards were numerous, and highly suspicious, but the house could not be made safe. Tonight it was filled with people talking noisily, and a radio was blaring. Bosch and Sacha Volman took Fandino and me into a tiny room alone. Bosch, talking above the uproar, insisted on speaking English. He was angry and tense and bitter—indeed, he seemed near the breaking point. He declared indignantly, "I was mistreated. Badly. The crowd. Mishandled. Mrs. Bosch too, she was afraid. I could not speak." I sympathized, said I had watched on television. He shook his head impatiently. "You do not understand. It was a plot. I was taken in a helicopter to the Fairgrounds. When I got there, who was waiting? Imbert. He put me in his car. I was his captive. His police are here now," lowering his voice, leaning forward, his gaze darting rapidly to indicate the guards outside. "Those police are *his* police. They know who comes here. They report to *him*. It is either him or me. Now," bobbing his head violently. "We will have a showdown. I prefer it now, not later. He cannot stay." He looked like a trapped animal. Volman put in quietly, "We believe that Imbert made the crowd happen, you know? And arranged to capture him at the Fairgrounds with his gunmen."

I asked what Imbert had done while he had him "captive." Brought him here, Bosch said. Home. What did he think Imbert had intended to do? To kill him, or at least kidnap him. But he hadn't? Not this time— next time he would. His spies were everywhere. He had planned the whole disaster today. Bosch had prepared a fine speech for the airport but been unable to deliver it because of Imbert's near-riot. Once home, Bosch had thrown away his prepared speech, a conciliatory one, and taped a three-hour speech extemporaneously.[1] "That's it now," Volman said, nodding toward the sound from a radio in the other room. Bosch said, "There are only three solutions—to kill him, put him in jail, or deport him."

I said, slowly and carefully, that I hoped he could find a fourth solution. He said flatly, "No," and turned his head away, chin up. I said carefully, "Mr. President, as you know, we support you fully, and we will see to it that your government is not dominated by the police or military or elements that may control them. This is central to our policy here. We want you to be free to govern as you wish. I hope a fourth solution can be found. Imbert will never leave the country voluntarily. He thinks his life would be endangered, and I must say I agree. You will have to use force, perhaps kill him. I know what you think of him, and we share some of your feelings. But if I may say so, killing him would not be a good start for your Administration."

Bosch shook his head hard. I went on, knowing it was risky. "I'm afraid I think it would be dangerous to your government. I dislike offering unsolicited advice, but I should like to take the liberty of saying I hope you will move carefully. For example, you must first be sure of the support of the Armed Forces."

[1] I have since been told that Bosch, in London, had become alarmed by reports from home, that he had taped at least some of the speech in London, and that he had never intended to deliver a more conciliatory speech. At the time, however, our understanding was as I have described it.

He said, a little more thoughtfully, "I am going to see the Armed Forces tomorrow."

Had he chosen a Minister of Defense? He said, "No. Let them choose one," meaning the three service chiefs. We began discussing the high command, man by man. I told him we thought rather well of some of them and could sometimes influence them. I said they didn't like Imbert and told him how one night Luna had wanted to bomb the Palace because Imbert and Amiama had made themselves generals. Bosch seemed interested, and I told him more, including that before the election Viñas had specifically assured me of the Armed Forces' loyalty to Bosch if he won. "They come to us for advice. If you want us to, we'll tell them again tomorrow to support you." He nodded, then asked about each. Some he knew but slightly. He thought, for example, that General Hungría, a hulking man whom I rather liked but never had suspected of harboring an idea, was "too intellectual."

But Volman egged him on—he said Imbert had told the colonels and majors they should run the country, not Bosch, for Bosch had been elected by an ignorant rabble.

I said that, after all, Imbert was a general, and if Bosch moved against him, the other generals, though they disliked Imbert, might wonder which general Bosch would move against next. Bosch had begun to listen. Soon he was talking about deporting Imbert instead of killing him, then about appointing him Ambassador to Canada. Imbert wouldn't go to Canada, I said, then steered the conversation back to the military high command. I feared that, quite apart from Imbert, in his present mood Bosch might do something ill-considered about the high command, and there might be no inaugural. I had no illusions about the high command, but thought Bosch would be unwise now to disturb its precarious balance.

"Mr. President," I said, "what we want is for you to succeed. Nothing more. We will not presume to tell you what to do or how to run your government. I have only one recommendation I would like to make, if you would like to hear it."

He said he would.

"My only suggestion—and it is a personal one, not an official one— is that, at least for the time being, you leave the military high command alone. I am not talking now about Imbert or the police. I mean the Armed Forces—Secretary of Defense Viñas, and the three service commanders, Hungría, Rib, and Luna. This is, in my opinion, the single most dangerous—potentially dangerous—area. They are quiet now. They know we support you. They listen to us. Some day they may not, things may be different, who knows what will come. But for now, I would leave it alone."

It was the only advice I offered on his cabinet. It was not the advice of the U.S. government; it was mine alone. As it turned out, he took it.

We talked awhile longer. The conversation became somewhat more relaxed, although it never became really cordial. But, leaving, I thought we had made a start.

Much later Imbert told me that he simply had been driving near the Fairgrounds that day when he saw a helicopter descending. He went to it. Bosch and his wife stepped out, Imbert asked what had happened, they told him, and Imbert offered them a ride home. That, he said, was all there was to it. Perhaps it was.

Whatever the truth, the incident got Bosch off to a bad start from which he really never recovered. Once again malevolent fate, ill luck, call it what you will, had intervened; an unruly crowd too hot in the sun, a balky public-address system, had changed history's course. Bosch's three-hour extemporaneous speech, coming as it did amid violent opposition to the draft Constitution and on top of his denunciation of the Esso refinery contract, began Bosch's ruin.

In that homecoming speech of February 17, Bosch attacked the Consejo bitterly, hinting darkly that there was something mysterious about its having spent $180 million in 1962. Sarcastically he demanded why it permitted the import of whiskey when no poor *campesino* drank it, only the *tu-tum-potes* at "their nightly celebrations at the Embajador."

He discoursed in rambling fashion on vast plans—a free port at Puerto Plata, a huge cement factory, reclamation of the Yuma River swamp, rehabilitation of the Sánchez port, a tourist zone at Samaná complete with hotels and motels and roads and an international airport, a tourist zone near Higüey, a petrochemical complex, oil exploration ("I have conviction that we have petroleum in our country," a view often expressed by Trujillo), cleaning irrigation ditches on the northwest frontier, banana plantations in the southwest, the Nagua road, three hundred tent hospitals and fifty ambulances and five hundred small buses, cattle-raising, veterinary school expansion, schools, housing.

Little of it was new. Much of it was sound. A Dominican said he sounded as if he had but to utter the words and the dream would come true.

He had arranged for all this, he said in his speech, in Europe. The Dutch, Germans, French, and British were going to help. His only mention of the United States was in connection with a private foundation and a request for wheat under the Food for Peace law (PL 480). Denouncing sugar speculators, he declared his Administration would not honor sugar future sales made under the Consejo. And he denounced the Esso contract again—though careful to say only that it must be "re-

2 In his book, Bosch has written that if he had made a single change in the high command on taking office, his government would have lasted only a few weeks or days.

viewed," he called it a secret contract entered into by the Consejo and hinted at scandal.

He called for austerity—fewer imports, harder work, more production: "We must increase our production this year even if we are forced to work like slaves." He proposed "public denunciation" for anyone who stole public money—"the moral firing squad," a public ceremony complete with army and flags "and muffled drums and trumpets," which would degrade the culprit's "children, grandchildren, great-grandchildren, and great-great-grandchildren." He announced prizes for painters, musicians, writers, poets, actors, dramatists, for "we must make of the Dominican people a people capable of understanding and admiring works of art" and "a creative artist is much like God."

Saying he had "something spectacular" to announce, he described at length his efforts in Zurich and Paris to locate and recover "the Trujillo family boxes"; but it had all come to naught—"even now we do not know what the boxes contain." A moment later he was discussing the huge Tavera and Valdesa dams, saying, "We did not want to dwell on little things. We wanted something big whether it works or not. We want to negotiate big things. We preferred to fail negotiating big things rather than succeed negotiating small things."

He scornfully taunted *tu-tum-potes* who had not believed his party was the country's strongest. Defending the draft Constitution, he declared that "intense propaganda" had confused the people about it. Those who had lost the election now wanted to win the constitutional battle. "This we cannot permit. They lost the elections because they had backward ideas. We won the elections because we had revolutionary ideas. The people voted for a democratic revolution. . . . This revolution cannot be given to them if we do not have a revolutionary Constitution. . . .

He had made his point and made it well. But then he continued:

"The Dominican Republic is forging a new image, like young girls who, when they become about fifteen years old, begin to make themselves pretty. We are changing our image—the moral, political, economic image of the country. We are changing it into a revolutionary democracy, a democracy which will maintain public freedoms, but which at the same time will give our people the progress, the social justice, the economic democracy they have never had. This national image, this new image of the Dominican people, must be engraved now in their Constitution. It is sad that the young people should allow themselves to be confused. It is sad that the people who voted for us, these unknown people, these ignored people, these people of the city districts and the hills, these people of the highways who brought a white ballot to the polls in order to win on December 20 should have to permit those who voted against the people . . . to impose [their] views. . . . A revolutionary constitution is indispensable if we want a revolution in this country."

He concluded eloquently:

"While I was traveling in Europe and the United States, across white landscapes, the snow falling in some places day and night, filling land and sky, I thought of the many men and women here struggling, struggling to defend the people. . . . I thought of the men of the party, of the leaders from the smallest committees to the national executive committee, of my colleague Ángel Miolán, made of bronze, made of quiet love for this suffering country, working day and night . . . to face the thousand rumors with which the people were being confused.

"The people are like a child and are deceived with lies like a child. To all these *compañeros* fighting here against an overly malicious enemy, too much the master of the unsound knowledge of how to deceive the people, to all of them, my sincerest thanks. . . .

"Never abroad did we receive an honor which we considered ours. Rather we considered it the people's. We are nothing but the representative of the people. When at the Paris Arch of Triumph the troops presented the flag and the martial bands played the Dominican national anthem before the French anthem as a homage seldom paid to anyone, I was thinking . . . for the people the honors, for them the advantages. For me there is only one satisfaction . . . the satisfaction and the honor to see that over the hotels the flag of the white cross was raised, the blue and red flag, the flag of Duarte. . . . Everywhere I conduct myself with the dignity of a man who owes allegiance only to the land over which that flag flies. . . .

"Good night, Dominicans."

2

This speech was a good sample of pure Bosch. Whether or not he knew it, he was incarnate "the agitator in power" that he himself deplored. How different from a U. S. President! Where President Kennedy asked for unity, Bosch attacked. How different from Bonnelly! Where Bonnelly would have maneuvered quietly behind the scenes, Bosch aimed over the heads of the powerful at the ordinary people.

The reaction of the power structure was almost instantaneous.

Important Dominican and U.S. citizens considered the speech anti-American. Businessmen were particularly incensed at the renewed denunciation of the Esso contract. The Dominican press and politicians increased their attacks on the Constitution. Churchmen thought their worst fears confirmed. And the military showed signs of growing restless or worse.

Commodore Rib called Cass to his headquarters and, with a machine gun on his desk, locked all the doors and declared that a plot was afoot among several naval officers to kill Bosch. Rib blamed Imbert. Imbert sent for Cass and requested that we get word to Bosch that he would not leave the country, wanted to keep his generalship, would accept any job under Viñas, and would not object if Bosch fired Belisario Peguero.

Colonel Fritz Long said Rivera Cuesta's house was full of officers ominously unwilling to talk in front of Long. Shlaudeman said that Donny Reid considered Bosch a Communist and said, "They are going to kill me, but at least I will die on my own soil. And my country will become another Cuba." John Perkey, our commercial attaché, who knew people all over town, told me he was getting phone calls every five minutes from businessmen. For some reason, business had come to a standstill. King took a call from the Operations Center in the Department at Washington: Ed Martin wanted to know if everything was all right in Santo Domingo; he had heard alarming rumors. I went to see President Bonnelly.

He was bitter and angry at Bosch's speech. The Consejo would answer it. Bosch was creating a dangerous situation unnecessarily. Business had stopped, the Cibao was "paralyzed," everybody was afraid. Bosch had refused to invite inaugural delegations from Haiti, Paraguay, Nicaragua, and Guatemala because he considered them governed by dictators. He was about to recall his invitations to Spain and Argentina. The result might be a break in relations—how could the Dominicans keep track of the Trujillos in Spain if they had no diplomats there? In his speech Bosch had not mentioned the Alliance for Progress or U.S. assistance, had said instead that he had obtained two hundred million dollars' worth of help in Europe, which nobody believed. Bonnelly said, "Who will help us now? He has made a lot of promises he can't fulfill. He has stirred up the lower classes too much. 'Tu-tum-potes,'" he said, with disgust. "He just creates class hate. That hate will keep on growing. And there will come a moment when it all will explode."

I said we could live with Bosch's nationalistic refusal to mention the United States and asked if Bonnelly thought anybody would try to impede the inaugural. He didn't. Was the military quiet? For now. Then what were the military rumors all about? He didn't know—just general fear. He thought the crisis would come after Bosch had been in power two or three months. "If he gains international sympathy," i.e., U.S. support, "and if he takes the necessary measures in the country, it will be all right. But if he continues attacking—" and he broke off and shrugged, said, "Interests are interests, and they are powerful."

No real plot seemed afoot, just a general unease.

Shlaudeman had discussed several Controversial provisions in the Constitution with Molina Ureña, the PRD speaker of the House whom we both thought well of. Shlaudeman said the PRD was trying, without success, to amplify satisfactorily the right merely to "enjoy" pri-

vate property. But it would not budge on the crucial sections—it would
not remove the provision prohibiting but not defining *latifundio,* would
not remove other provisions on property objectionable to the propertied
classes, would not consecrate the Vatican Concordat, would not remove
the provisions on concubinage and divorce nor that putting all education under the Minister of Education (thus, in the Church's view, severely
undermining its role in education). So far it had done nothing to appease
the Armed Forces, which wanted the Constitution to provide for the trial
of military men by military tribunals only, or the political parties, which
complained that political parties should be represented on the Electoral
Board.

3

Julio Postigo, a publisher and bookstore owner downtown, gave an
autographing party for Bosch's new book, *David.* Behind the bookshop
was a garden surrounded by the ruins of an ancient thick vine-covered
Spanish wall, now shaded over, cool and green and quiet, and Bosch
and I talked to Postigo, a gentle, quiet man, and a handful of guests.
We had sent word indirectly to Bosch recommending that he get an
Army, not a PRD, bodyguards, and today he had one, Colonel Juan
Calderón, a big, rangy man with an honest face, whom I had known last
year in Bonnelly's corps of bodyguards. Once at a glittering Embassy
reception, Colonel Calderón, stationed as customary in full uniform and
with submachine gun in the Embassy foyer, had dealt quietly and kindly
with our son Fred, who had had a bad dream and had come down the
long marble stairway in his pajamas and bare feet, crying. Unlike most
Dominicans, Calderón left the stock on his Thompson submachine gun.
Most removed it to make the gun lighter—and made it far less
accurate. Today at the bookshop Calderón seemed unsure of himself; as
we were leaving, Bosch stepped through the doorway first, Calderón
hung back to let me pass, but I pushed him ahead, saying, "No—from
now on, you stay with *him,*" and he grinned, half-saluted, and hurried
after Bosch. At the time I saw nothing at all incongruous in a machine
gunner at a literary party; in fact it had not occurred to me till now, as I
write far away. I never read Bosch's *David.* Some who have tell me
they think Bosch saw himself as David facing Goliath. But who was
Goliath?

4

Bosch retreated a bit—he told *El Caribe* there was no cause for alarm
in his proposed social reforms or his Constitution. In a three-hour talk,
he won the enthusiastic support of Newell Williams, our AID chief. Wil-

liams told me, "I got the impression Juan Bosch is not a Communist. Quite the contrary. He is fomenting private enterprise. He wants to pass an incentive law to encourage foreign investment. I asked him if he wanted 50 percent Dominican partnership and you know what he said," leaning forward with his cigar. "He said, 'No.' How do you like that?" And so on. Williams' conversion was complete. But what was significant was his casual assumption that already a question existed whether Bosch was a Communist.

Williams said the peso was dropping fast—men on the street were offering a peso and a quarter for a U.S. dollar, with no dollars available. This reflected the general unease. Bosch liked the program presented by Al Mayne's CIDES group—a "crash program" to set aside land for home-building in a "planned slum" pattern, promote public health with tent clinics, build farm-to-market roads and people's restaurants, establish a commission to study government offices, train schoolteachers; a "mid-term" program to speed up agrarian reform, reorganize the government machinery, and increase chicken and hog production; and a "long-term" program for cattle, highways, ports, and development of the two Ríos Yaque and the Rio Yuma. Nothing was new except the "planned slums" and the health program. But Bosch liked it because he thought it was all new and all his—Mayne had presented it.

Cass came in. General Luna of the Air Force had summoned him and demanded, "What is the U.S. policy about Juan Bosch? It's easier now than later." Luna had said Miolán was a Communist and Bosch was at least beholden to Communists. Who did Bosch think had kept things quiet for the election? The military, of course. "Don't think we won't act when needed. We'll give him three months."

My notes, made on Saturday, February 23, only four days before Bosch's inaugural, read:

You can only be a virgin once. I'll never again feel the eagerness, enthusiasm, eagerness to help, hopefulness for a better day, willingness to take risks, vigor, almost naïve belief in opportunity here, confidence of cooperation of the Consejo, goodwill, boundless goodwill—that I felt a year ago, on arriving here.

All is different now. When Bosch returned from Europe, all he wanted to talk about was Imbert. Not the *Alianza*, not the trip to Washington or New York which I helped to arrange, not Europe, not his writings, not his plans for his Administration, or his inaugural speech, or program, or the planning we've been doing secretly for him—only Imbert, in a suspicious, tense, hateful tone.

What a start!

Bosch is a divider, a splitter, a schemer, a destroyer. Can he build? I doubt it. Not unless he gets good advice. And he won't take advice.

He is more a De Gaulle than a Castro.

A year ago, while recognizing problems, I felt optimistic, for I never doubted my own or the Consejo's goodwill. Nor the people's. Nor the capacity of any of those three, except maybe the people.

Now I doubt them all.

I am frankly heartsick. That after thirty-one years the people got stuck with him. I said last summer, Bosch won't do. He won't either.

And the alternatives were probably as bad or worse.

The opportunity here one year ago was so great. Now look.

Maybe he can do it. Maybe there will emerge from those around him, whom his revolutionary election has brought to the surface of national life for the first time, sufficient men of talent and goodwill to really make something of his place. Maybe. The beginning is not encouraging.

I wish I could be more charitable. Until we hear his inaugural and see what programs he sends to Congress, I really should follow the advice I give everyone else—let's wait and see. But it's hard to.

The rumors in the streets are all bad.

Even an orange seller has misgivings: After Bosch's three-hour speech, he said he was afraid Bosch would think *him* a *tu-tum-pote*, for he liked Scotch; now he'd have to hide in his room or drink rum.

5

I was awakened at seven o'clock Sunday morning by a cable. U.S. immigration authorities had stopped two Communist terrorists from leaving New York for Santo Domingo. They would hold them as long as legally possible but they might reach the Dominican Republic via Canada. We knew them. They were terrorists all right, trained in Cuba or Prague. I warned President Bonnelly.

King came to the house. The Communist López Molina was reported in Colombia, heading for Panama and, presumably, here. The Venezuelan Ambassador had misgivings about Betancourt's coming. Colonel Richardson said Wimpy, the supermarket operator, had demanded to know what our attitude would be if a *golpe* against Bosch were to take place. He said businessmen were "highly disturbed" at Bosch's speech, at the Constitution, at the "known Communists" close to Bosch. They were convinced that "something had to be done" before the inauguration. I told Richardson to tell Wimpy and his friends that we supported the constitutional, elected government. I told Richardson to try to get the names of the *golpistas*.

Should we, really, bring Vice President Johnson into this mess?

The Crisis Crowd assembled at the Residence. For once, most of the news was good.

Bosch had summoned Shlaudeman. Shlaudeman had rarely seen Bosch so calm and self-possessed. Bosch wanted me to know he had offered the UCN two cabinet posts. They had refused. This, Bosch felt, fulfilled his commitment to Fiallo and me made at the October summit.

Bosch, I was told, had told a friend, "In the Dominican Republic, the way to beat Fidel is to make a democratic revolution. And here I had the great good fortune to start out with Standard Oil." He meant that by denouncing the Esso contract, he had by a single stroke established his reputation as a revolutionary. Now he was free to do as he pleased, even adopt conservative measures. I heard that Bosch, believing the state ought not administer anything, intended to sell the Trujillo industries, turn Haina into a cooperative, get the government out of business completely. It was astonishing. Did he mean it? If so, why didn't he announce it quickly to allay rightists' fears? He never did.

King had completed Vice President Johnson's schedule. I asked all hands whether he should come. It was about our last chance to reconsider. We decided to go ahead, always reserving the possibility of last-minute cancellation.

6

The festivities started Monday.

At noon I put on my white suit and went to the Foreign Office and, on behalf of Vice President Johnson, the other members of the U.S. delegation, and myself, formally presented our credentials to the Foreign Minister.

At one-thirty, with the rest of the diplomatic corps, I went to the airport to meet President Villeda Morales of Honduras.

Back at the office, King and the CIA chief had news—the two Communist terrorists were still being held in New York but eight of their associates were probably already in the Dominican Republic, including Islander Selig Delmonte, Tomás Parmenio Erickson Álvarez, Máximo López Molina, Juan José Matos Rivera, and Gustavo Federico Ricart-Ricart. CIA checking showed that they had been in Prague, passed through Ireland on December 14, and gone on to Cuba via Czech airline.

At four-fifteen I went to the airport to meet President Francisco Orlich of Costa Rica. He would not arrive until seven-fifteen. I left, and, riding back, noticed that traffic was normal. There should have been no traffic on the route.

I went to President Bonnelly, gave him the names of the eight Communist associates supposed to be in the Republic, and told him the police were not keeping traffic off the route from the airport. He said they would tomorrow, when Vice President Johnson and President Betancourt would arrive. Like us, Bonnelly had heard rumors that the FALN would try to assassinate Betancourt. Vice President Johnson might be killed, too, inadvertently. Bonnelly was worried. So was I. Human considerations aside, it was not inconceivable that should Vice President Johnson be assassinated here, events might escalate rapidly into World War III—

Castro would be blamed, pressure on President Kennedy to retaliate against Cuba would be enormous. Khrushchev must know this, must have warned Castro. But if so, why had the two terrorists turned up in New York?

I went to the airport again at seven-fifteen to meet President Orlich. Back at the office, Shlaudeman showed me a leaflet signed by the PSP attacking Betancourt.

I went to the airport to meet Prime Minister Bustamante of Jamaica at nine-thirty. The security was better along the route.

Back home in the study, I checked lists of things to do, worrying about Vice President Johnson. In the notebook I always carried, I wrote out a statement to be used if anything happened to him tomorrow.

At 11 A.M. on Tuesday I went white-suited to the Palace and, in the Salón de Embajadores where I first had presented my own credentials, formally presented the U.S. delegation's credentials to President Bonnelly. Betancourt was due at 1 P.M., Johnson at two-thirty. I went home, had lunch quickly, got Fran, and went to the airport. Beyond the bridge, soldiers were shunting other traffic aside. Our cars carried flags and special markers. Along the highway naval frogmen stood guard, looking formidable in their black uniforms and polished boots. Nearly all were facing the highway, not the brush, whence any attack would come. Somebody had painted *"Betancourt Asesino"* in huge letters on a wall along the road. The *Boxer* stood offshore, majestic at anchor on the deep-blue Caribbean. Fandino had his own contingency plan: He figured that if trouble started, two *Boxer* helicopters would swoop down and rescue the Johnsons and the Martins but abandon him; he, being bilingual and looking Latin, would simply yank off his necktie, rumple his hair, and jump out of the car to join the rioters, yelling, *"¡Abajo Yanqui!"*

The day was beautiful. At the airport our motorcade and Embassy officers and Secret Service were on the apron. So were the Dominican band and honor guard. Other Ambassadors began to arrive, and the Nuncio, and President Bonnelly and the rest of the Consejo. Word came that Johnson's plane and Betancourt's would arrive at the same time, two-thirty. The control tower decided that Johnson would land first, while Betancourt's plane slowed and, if necessary, circled. That would give Johnson Betancourt's crowd. It might also give him Betancourt's assassin, if there was one. How can you cope with such chance?

High in the sky the plane appeared and sailed down onto the runway. At the last minute, somebody remembered to tell the band leader this was Johnson, not Betancourt—the band must play the U.S. anthem, not the Venezuelan. Then the silver jet rolled to a stop, emblazoned with the emblems of American power, and men pushed stairs to the door; it opened, and Vice President and Mrs. Johnson stepped out and waved, and came down, the other delegates following, we shaking their hands at the bottom of the steps, a small crowd cheering, the Consejo and Foreign Minister and Armed Forces forming a receiving line on the sun-dazzled concrete, Secret Service men guiding the tall Vice President to inspect the honor guard alone, then to a speaker's lectern and microphones, the rest of us behind him, photographers everywhere; and in the sunlight guns boomed out a salute and the band struck up "The Star-Spangled Banner," then the Dominican national anthem. I have seldom been so stirred as on that day.

The Vice President spoke briefly and well, then, guided by Secret Service men and aides, we got into our cars, First Vice President Pichardo riding with Vice President Johnson, Mrs. Pichardo in the second car with Mrs. Johnson, Assistant Secretary Ed Martin riding with me, the rest of the delegation, including U.S. Senators and other high officials, following, security cars interspersed. We started off fast, small fender flags flying, the highway absolutely empty except for the spaced-out soldiers and frogmen. Approaching the capital, where the highway begins to slope down to the bridge, stood a crowd. The cars ahead of us stopped; Vice President Johnson got out and moved into the crowd, shaking hands.

I said to the Secret Service man in my car, "He shouldn't do that." He said, "If you want him to stop, you'll have to tell him yourself." I said, "He can't do it at the bridge or the traffic circle or the park— it isn't safe."

I got out and pushed through the crowd. He was moving, tall and straight, an unshakable smile on his face, through the crowd shaking hands, jammed in tight. I finally reached him. I said, as I recall it, "Mr. Vice President, this is all right here but don't do it again until you get to George Washington Avenue." Without pausing or stopping his work he nodded. I fell back a little. A Dominican helicopter dropped down from overhead, so low its rotor threw swirling, slashing sand and dust over us, and I ducked behind a car to escape it. The Vice President got back into his car, and we started off once more.

The crowd was thicker now, a friendly holiday crowd. It was waving and calling to us, calling *"¡Viva los Yanquís!"* and *"¡Viva el vice-presidente!"* and some, evidently recognizing me, called my name. Johnson was waving back, and I did too, and so did Ed Martin.

We crossed the bridge, rounded the circle bottleneck, and started down steep, narrow Avenida Mella to Parque Independencia. Here the crowds were huge, close-pressed against the police lines at the curb, and suddenly dozens of men on bicycles appeared, riding tight against our cars, Miolán's men, I thought, honking horns and cheering, ostensibly welcoming Johnson but in fact guarding him with their bodies. Once they and the crowd pressed in so close we almost came to a stop, and the police tried to get them away, but they would not go, they stayed with us as we

turned, barely moving, around Parque Independencia; and here too Miolán's men were in the front row solid at the curbs. Still the crowd was
friendly; in all the trip I heard only one yell, *"¡Afuera los Yanquís!"*
Then we had passed the park and turned onto Avenida Jorge Washington by the sea, and Vice President Johnson stopped and got out and
began handshaking again. It was safe here. So we passed on, till the
crowd dribbled out to nothing, then went fast to the Hotel Embajador,
entering by a rear door and going straight up to the penthouse. We had a
drink or a Coke, and Vice President Johnson took his coat off. I explained
why I had stopped the handshaking, told him that I had been surprised
at the size and friendliness of the crowds, and told him he had done the
United States a great deal of good here today.

Shlaudeman sent a message in to me: Miolán was here and asked if
Vice President Johnson would receive him. I advised him to, and he
assented, and Miolán came in, short and stocky, looking only two feet
high before the tall Vice President, and uncomfortable in a heavy dark
suit and tie. It was not a very satisfactory interview; Miolán seemed ill-
at-ease, really had little to say, and I think he was intimidated by the
Vice President's high office. Fran told me later that Miolán's wife had
told her and Mrs. Johnson that the ladies would not wear hats at the
inaugural reception; since the Bosch government proposed to raise the
masses and lower the rich, they would wear "simple sports dresses."

Inasmuch as the two governments, Bosch's and Bonnelly's, were not
speaking to each other, each had decided to hold its own reception. The
Consejo's was that night. While Fran and I were dressing at the Residence, our son Dan's burro threw him, and he broke his arm. The doctor
took him away to put it in a cast. I wanted it X-rayed by a U.S. doctor
too, and Colonel Cass arranged to have it done aboard the *Boxer* in the
morning.

King had checked the cables and our security sources; nothing was
going on. We went back to the hotel, met the Johnsons upstairs, and,
together with the other official delegates and their wives, drove to the
Palace. The reception was a shambles. The huge room was jammed to the
walls with people. Photographers and television men were everywhere.
A receiving line had been set up but people kept crowding in, disrupting
it. Once or twice in political campaigns I have been caught in such a
crowd. It can be dangerous. Vice President Johnson had shaken hands
with Bonnelly and several Consejeros but now was totally boxed in. Now
and then I caught a glimpse of Imbert, hidden behind an arras. I think
he wanted to come out and meet the guests but was embarrassed—the
reception was a mess and he had so badly wanted it to go well.

Somehow the Secret Service men extricated the Vice President, and
we moved to the center of the room where the crowd seemed thinner. I

found a few people I wanted the Vice President to meet and be photographed with, and avoided others. I made sure he met every Consejero except Imbert, who by then I could not find. We had intended to stay until all the Chiefs of State had departed, since they outranked Vice President Johnson, but so confused was the scene that I thought we could slip out now.

Riding back to the hotel, the Vice President said his schedule was too full. I went over it with him, told him what I thought he could omit—a concert tonight, a Mass early tomorrow, an appearance tomorrow morning at the Residence before the U.S. mission and the U.S. community, one or two lesser affairs—and what he couldn't—Bosch's swearing-in, the parade, and Bosch's reception. He took my recommendations. I also suggested he talk privately with Bosch, and he agreed. Before he had arrived, I had heard that he was difficult, and that other ambassadors dreaded his visits. I did not find him so. Fran had been scheduled to accompany Mrs. Johnson to the Dominican School for the Blind next morning. I explained she couldn't go because Dan had just broken his arm and she had to take him out to the *Boxer;* Shlaudeman's wife would go instead. The Vice President said, "Why don't you let me take the boy, and his mother, too, up to Washington with me Thursday? They can take better care of him at Bethesda than here." He said it spontaneously. As I say, I had heard Vice President Johnson criticized, but from that moment I could not but feel deep gratitude toward him. As it turned out, he saved Dan's arm. The break had been near the growth center at the elbow.

7

At ten the next morning our entire mission, our Dominican employees, and the leaders of the American community gathered in the shady garden of the Residence. I expressed the Vice President's regrets, then introduced Senator Jacob Javits, Congressman John Brademas, Ambassador Moscoso, and Assistant Secretary Martin, and each of them spoke, and spoke well indeed, and Senator Hubert Humphrey arrived, shaking hands in the crowd. At the end, I thanked the people and said that during the year our national purpose had been to assist the Dominican people in their efforts to make a successful transition from tyranny to democracy. Our reward had come yesterday, when thousands of Dominicans who understood our purpose had lined the streets of Santo Domingo and cheered our Vice President and our delegation.

If there was going to be trouble, it would come today. Bosch was to be sworn in at noon, outdoors at the Palace of the Congress in the Fairgrounds. We left our wives home. I rode with Vice President Johnson.

As we approached, Secret Service men up ahead kept reporting on what was going on.

This ceremony, too, was a shambles, an uncontrolled crowd without any security—ordinary people, dignitaries, troops, policemen all mixed up together in the heat, with bands blaring and colors flying. The crowd pressed in so close on Bosch while he was taking the oath that he was almost knocked over. Vice President Johnson and the visiting Presidents could scarcely get near him. His speech was almost completely inaudible to me. I read it later, an excellent speech, asserting his own and his nation's independence, but not doing so belligerently, and asking for unity. He said he intended to establish a government that would work constantly "to give the Dominicans a place in the sun among the advanced countries of America." All America was "observing us with interest and love." Never before had such illustrious elected officials gathered in the Dominican Republic for such an occasion. The Dominican nation would requite that interest and love by acting together with its brother nations "in defense of their democratic liberties" but at the same time would maintain its "living feeling of pride in the legacy of sovereignty which it had received from its founders."

He said, "As an American country we find ourselves in the center of the great revolutionary current that is shaking the New World." That current was most potent in countries stunted by tyrannies; the Dominican Republic must advance as rapidly as possible "without departing for a moment from democratic norms." Bosch wanted political peace, he said, and therefore had offered Cabinet posts to five parties. Four had declined. Nevertheless, they deserved respect; and he named them—UCN, PNRD, Vanguardia, and ASD (Juan Isidro Jimenes Grullón's party). He wanted the country to know that he had not wished to base his government solely on his own party, the PRD. "We had wished those who fought yesterday were reunited today giving, each one, the best of its forces to the people which is ours and is theirs. We do not desire the power to govern as friends against enemies, but to govern as Dominicans for the good of Dominicans. . . . Nobody should expect the use of hate while we are governing. We are here with the decision to work, not to hate; disposed to create, not to destroy; to defend and protect, not to persecute. Let us all join our soul together in the task of ending hatred among Dominicans as weeds are ended in the seeded ground; let us all join our soul together in the task of building a regime that gives protection to those who never had it, that gives work to those who looked for it without finding it, that gives land to the *campesinos* who need it, that gives security to those born here and to all those who wander the world in pursuit of shelter against misery and persecution." The world was full of arrogance and hatred; millions worked in silence for a better tomorrow. "We Dominicans must be united with that legion of men and women who march toward the future, because if the creature of God is not given the faculty of remaking its past, it is given in exchange the power to build its future. . . . The good work of the dead, like their bad work, is the property of history; but the good work of the future is the fruit of good intentions and of the capacity to convert them into deeds." Although during thirty-one years of tyranny Dominicans were obliged to ask the democratic world for help, they ought not grow accustomed to living on it; though grateful, they must build their future "with Dominican hands." They could do it with work, persistence, and faith. They had done it before—faith and persistence had sustained those who rewon the Republic's freedom in 1924 (when the Marine occupation ended, though Bosch did not say so), and in 1961, when Trujillo was killed. Without the persistence and faith, the courage and martyrdom of those who had won those struggles, today's events would be impossible.

Nothing was won without struggle. "We have to fight and we will fight against the obstacles that stand in the way of the Republic." The coming months would be a bridle for many—runaway inflation must be avoided. The nation, however, possessed "great riches" and sold more than it bought. If Dominicans collaborated with the government in halting "unnecessary" spending, "in a short time" foreign exchange controls could be ended. If Congress worked with tenacity to enact agrarian reform and measures to increase agricultural productivity, inflation could be avoided.

"Our country is rich and our people intelligent. We have a fertile earth and people who want to work it. In other countries of America, most *latifundio* is found in private hands, but here the largest farms belong to the state. We are going to join the man with the soil, the intelligent Dominican man with the rich Dominican earth, and we should be clear that this will be done or there will be no democracy in this country.

"We Dominicans commence today to be actors in our drama and all America is here, around the continent, like an eager spectator. We must work for our people and for America. We must work with tenacity and with humility. This day of Juan Pablo Duarte, of Francisco del Rosario Sánchez, of Ramón Matías Mella, to whose memory we offer this ceremony, is also, by destiny's chance, Ash Wednesday; and on Ash Wednesday, at the time that the cross was being prepared, the faithful heard the eternal words: 'Remember, man, that dust thou art and to dust thou shalt return.'

"All of us will be dust some day; and our memory will remain only if we give to the people and to America what the Dominican people and America expect of us."

He told the visiting dignitaries that all Dominicans, military and civilian alike, soldier and worker and *campesino* and middle-class man, looked on them with affection. All had voted according to their conscience. Thus they had provided this occasion "under this bit of American sky"; and he closed:

"Don Rómulo Betancourt, Don Ramón Villeda Morales, Don Francisco Orlich, Don Lyndon Johnson, Don Alexander Bustamante, Don Luis Muñoz Marín; most excellent diplomatic representatives of friendly nations; professors, writers, poets, journalists, political leaders who visit us; friends who have come from afar to be with us in this solemn hour; to all of you, to those who govern peoples, to those who represent them and guide them, to those who enhance them with their works; to all we give a most cordial welcome and to all we ask that when they return to their native soil they carry with them and disseminate the words with which we end this address:

"While we govern, in the Dominican Republic liberty shall not perish."

Close, hostile, and sophisticated listeners might question his intention to grant security to foreigners "who wander the world in pursuit of shelter against misery and persecution"; his praise of the heroes and martyrs who fought Trujillo (which could be interpreted as sympathy for either the 30th of May plotters or the 14th of June); his vague reference to the "bridle." But all this was overridden by his plea for unity, abjuration of hatred, and dedication to freedom. Unfortunately, good as it was, his inaugural speech could not erase the impression made by his February 17 homecoming speech. As a matter of fact, Bosch's inaugural address was little remarked, at least by other Dominican politicians.

After lunch came the parade. Grandstands had been erected on Avenida Jorge Washington, and Vice President Johnson and the visiting Presidents sat with Bosch to review it. I sat some distance away, where I could watch the crowd across the street and behind the grandstand. This time the crowd seemed less friendly, a tension was in the air. The parade began, soldiers marching, bands marching, tanks rumbling by, airplanes swooping low overhead, naval vessels circling offshore. As the parade neared its end, across the street from Bosch and his guests I saw a sign go up: FALN, the Venezuelan Castro terrorist group. Suddenly the crowd there surged forward, Dominican police and soldiers with fixed bayonets met them, the police line bulged. I hurried down toward Vice President Johnson, found one of the Secret Service men, told him to get the car, it drove up and the Vice President and I got in, and while the troops thrust the crowd back, and more troops ran up, we drove away, our Secret Service trotting alongside the front fenders. A couple of blocks away we heard on the two-way radio that the troops had regained control, though two men had been shot.

I left the Vice President at the hotel and went to the Residence to talk at length with Senator Javits. He wanted to know what Bosch's prospects were, and I told him that it was all uphill; that the opposition was formidable and might prove irreconcilable; that we would give him all the help we could. Senator Javits was concerned lest Bosch irrevocably cancel the Esso contract and thus virtually foreclose the possibility of other U.S. investments in the Republic. He offered to talk to Esso officials in the States to see if they could reach some accommodation with Bosch. I welcomed his help.

The Bosch reception at the Palace was worse than the previous night's. There seemed to be no door check, no security, no scrutinizing of invitations—nothing. The people simply came in. No doubt Bosch had wanted the ordinary people there, and who didn't; but it made security impossible. The people simply overran the Palace. I suppose Andrew Jackson's inaugural must have been like this. We tried to go down the receiving line, but the crowd pressed in, the line broke up, and suddenly I felt we were being crushed. I told a Secret Service man, "We'd better get out of here." He asked which way. I pointed to a door that I thought (correctly, it turned out) led to a private office. Secret Service men moved in to Vice President Johnson, formed themselves around him and his wife, and headed for the door, knocking people aside. Betancourt followed, his own generals closing around him; I grabbed Fran with one hand and Betancourt with the other, his generals formed a flying wedge, and we drove through the crowd behind Vice President Johnson, finally reaching the door.

The visiting Presidents soon found their way there, and so did Bosch. I talked a bit to President Betancourt, his hands still terribly scarred by fire from Trujillo's attempt to murder him. President Bosch agreed to receive Vice President Johnson privately tomorrow at 7:30 A.M. Imbert came in, I introduced him to Vice President Johnson, and they talked a bit. Through it all, the Vice President seemed absolutely imperturbable. Fandino bribed a guard and got in—this indicated how good the security was—and I sent him to try to rescue Senator Humphrey and the rest of our delegates. At length we left.

At home, King and the Shlaudemans came over, and so did Senator Humphrey and his wife and we sat up late talking. I had known Humphrey for several years, considered him one of the ablest men in the United States, as well as one of the best companions, and I told him now about our problems here, about Bosch, about our policy and hopes and fears. Listening, he said, "I think from now on I'll only go to over-developed countries."

8

Early next morning we met the Johnsons at the hotel, took them to the Palace, and waited while the Vice President talked alone to President Bosch. When they emerged, the Johnsons presented the Bosches with gifts and presented an ambulance as a gift from the American people to the Dominican people. (I had tried in vain to persuade the Department to send several Jeep-style ambulances instead of this one twenty-thousand dollar ambulance.)

We had expected that Vice President González Tamayo would accompany Vice President Johnson to the airport, but at the last minute President Bosch decided to go himself, and the next thing I knew the motorcade was flying off. Vice President González Tamayo and Fran and I scrambled into the nearest car and chased the motorcade out to the airport.

Dan was already there, Congressman Brademas having taken him. Fran and Dan watched from the plane's ramp while once more the honor guard drew up, the Vice President inspected it, and the band played "The Star-Spangled Banner" and the Dominican anthem. The Vice President made a short speech, and Bosch and I shook hands with him and said goodbye. At the top of the stairs he waved, ducked inside, then came back out and motioned to me. Bosch, he said, had told him he needed one million dollars for an IBM system, intended to use twelve million of the twenty-two-million-dollar sugar money for agrarian reform, expected to make no new requests for money, intended to adopt a nationalistic position, considered Imbert a serious problem, and thought well of me. We said goodbye, and I went back to the ramp and stood alone, watching while the plane climbed eagerly north for Washington.

Now I was alone. Alone with Bosch. So ended the year of the Consejo. So began the term of Juan Bosch, the first freely elected president of the Dominican Republic in nearly four decades. So began what might well be the Dominican people's last chance at free and democratic representative government.

PART TWO

The Seven Months of President Bosch

Chapter Fifteen

BOSCH BEGINS

Few men in our time have come to presidential power with a more splendid opportunity, or been confronted by more formidable difficulties, than Juan Bosch. He himself once said, "My country is one of hope and hunger."

Plainly, the overwhelming majority of the Dominican people expected him to make a revolution. He had a powerful political machine and, in Miolán, a good man to run it. He had enormous international goodwill —the support of the United States and of democratic Latin American statesmen who were striving to lead their nations out of feudalism. He had personal ties to many of them—Betancourt was the godfather of his daughter—and might well succeed them as the maximum leader of the Hemisphere's progressive forces in a time of cataclysmic change and enormous hope, a hope his own election quickened. The New York *Times* said editorially, "If he gets the chance and the support he requires, he can prove that what Latin American countries need is democracy, not Marxism-Leninism." Just as 1933 was a revolutionary year in the United States, so could Bosch make 1963 a revolutionary year in the Dominican Republic—and set a democratic pattern for all Latin America.

Lovers of liberty who had despised Trujillo rejoiced in the free election of a man who declared in his inaugural, "While we govern, in the Dominican Republic liberty shall not perish." They now flocked to the Republic, scores of them, all eager to help. No wonder they were drawn here. Bosch followed Trujillo, shared an island with Duvalier, and Castro had called him a Yankee puppet and confiscated his Cuban wife's property.

He was fifty-three years old, born in La Vega June 30, 1909, son of a Catalonian builder and a Puerto Rican mother. He had a high, bulging forehead, prominent facial bone structure, snow white hair and startling blue eyes, an actor's voice and mannerisms. He had a swift, winning smile, and a habit of leaning back in his chair, looking pensive, wan, thoughtful, helpless, enlisting instant sympathy. He made people want to help him. He was seldom still, gestured constantly, got up suddenly and stalked stiffly across a room, a commanding presence. An apostle of the poor, he had a sense of messianic mission. Author of several books, he tended to intellectualize, almost dehumanize, everything. His thought was highly abstract; he was a theoretician. Unlike most politicians, a gregarious lot, Bosch operated politically from a lonely theoretical base.

As a young man, Bosch, like most Dominicans, had apparently made some effort to come to terms with Trujillo. His enemies say that he once wrote a letter of lavish praise to Trujillo, saying that it was not the Generalissimo but the capital itself that was honored when its name was changed to Ciudad Trujillo. But he had gone into exile in 1937 and thereafter had opposed the dictator from exile. He had barely supported himself by writing and teaching in Costa Rica, Venezuela, Puerto Rico, and the United States, observed closely presidential power in Prío Socarrás' Cuba, founded the PRD in Cuba in 1939, taken part in Cayo Confites in 1947, and helped plan Luperón in 1949. During his twenty-five years in exile, he had had time enough and more to plan what he might do if ever he became President. Now President he was. As a young man he had belonged to a literary group called *La Cueva,* "The Cave," because it met in the home of a poet who seldom went outdoors. Bosch had emerged from the cave into the light.

Or had he? Throughout his tenure Bosch feared plots dark as the inside of a cave. His was a dark and conspiratorial mind, a quality essential to a man trying to survive the murderous plots of Caribbean exile politics and useful to a campaigner, but not necessarily helpful to a President. As President, he must live in the harsh glare of reality and responsibility. He was brilliant, but he was unstable and reckless. He was a complicated and a concealed man, with few friends. He was moody and unpredictable, arrogant and vain, and streaked with martyrdom.

Largely self-educated, he was not well-informed on many subjects he must deal with as President. His basic political tactics were never to offend any voters, to blackmail everyone by threatening to quit, and, like Lenin, always to split, never to unite, all tactics useful in a campaign but not in the Palace. From a purely political point of view, his tremendous landslide was unfortunate. It left no workable political party opposition. This election had destroyed, not created, political parties. Therefore, opposition to Bosch was likely to seek not a political channel but a more sinister one, the military channel. And Bosch would have great difficulty in finding, within the PRD, men of ability and experience to help run his government.

Often I felt I was judging him too harshly, perhaps, even unconsciously—and unfairly—comparing him to President Kennedy. As a political leader, Bosch, the wandering writer and teacher, had virtually been invented—invented by the non-Communist Caribbean leftist leaders and their friends in Washington. Or Bonnelly—how compare Bosch fairly with Bonnelly, whose roots were comfortably deep in the Santiago oligarchy? Bosch, for virtually all his adult life, had been buffeted by the Caribbean storms. What was he, and who? Dominican, Cuban? Writer, teacher, politician? Small wonder that when he finally was thrust to the center of the stage by over six hundred thousand voters he said he would rather be a citizen than a President. Small wonder he felt himself forever a persecuted underdog. And if being lionized in Washington and Europe went to his head, small wonder.

In his book Bosch speaks well of Newell Williams and me, saying we proposed and helped implement programs under the *Alianza* with surprising speed. He writes, "And to deal with me was not easy—I am conscious of it—because I had a very lively sensitivity for everything that could affect Dominican sovereignty. My poor country—from its first day of life as a republic, it had a multitude of political leaders who dedicated their capacity and strength to looking for a mother country to which to surrender our independence. . . . I suffered in my living flesh. . . . In my infancy I had seen lowered from public buildings the Dominican flag in order to hoist in its place the flag of North America, and no one could ever imagine what that meant to my little soul of seven years. Surely it would be difficult for me to say by what route arrived at La Vega—the little town where I had been born and where I grew up—the Mexican songs which related how Pancho Villa had confronted the North American troops who entered Mexico, but I can say without fear of contradiction that Pancho Villa became my idol. . . . In the nights I prayed for the appearance of a Dominican Pancho Villa, who would do what he did in Mexico, and what Martí, Gómez, and Maceo had done in Cuba. The man of today comes prefigured in the child of yesterday. Perhaps I could hope so passionately for my little country of the Antilles because when I became conscious of it, it was because it was still not a country but a dominion, and that produced in me a living pain, almost indescribable, which many times kept me awake a long time when they told me to sleep, and to be awake at night is hard for a child. I can be sure that at the age of ten I felt ashamed that Santana, who annexed the Republic to Spain in 1863, and Baez, who wanted to surrender Samaná to the United States, were Dominicans. As I passed through those years, that pain and that shame were converted into Dominican passion; and when I began to write I did it with that passion, and when I was called to be the leader of a political party and the President of my country, I took good care to always conduct myself as a Dominican who had pride in his nationality."

It is a revealing passage.

Often I felt deep sympathy for Bosch. Both his mother and his father died shortly after he took office. When his father died, I went impulsively to his house and told him I wanted to offer my sympathy. His face showed surprise, then set tight. He motioned me to a chair, and we sat down, and I told him my own father had died less than three years before, I thought I knew something of how Bosch must feel, and it might help him if he remembered that his father had lived to see him elected President, and so had his mother—he had made them very proud, and that was all a son could do. He said nothing for a moment, nothing at all. Then, looking away, he said yes, his father had been proud, and he was glad. His mother too. He fell silent again. Then he asked, "How is Mrs. Martin?" I said fine. "And the boys?" They were fine, too. He smiled. "They are wonderful boys." We sat another moment, then I got up and said I did not want to bother him longer. Standing, he said, "May I embrace you?" He was a strange man. He wanted no ceremonial funeral for his father and discouraged other proffers of sympathy. He plunged deeper into his work. Being really close to anyone was almost impossible for him.

Personality aside, President Bosch faced on March 1 problems that would have given any President pause. He faced the terrible legacy of Trujillo and all the problems the Consejo had postponed. He faced the inherent economic problem—in the short run meaningful economic betterment was almost impossible, and austerity, not bold spending, might be necessary but politically impossible. He faced the entire terrible history of the Republic—nothing to build on. And he was caught between the left and the right. He owed political debts to the far left—it had voted for him. He was unalterably opposed by the right—by remnants of the political parties he had defeated, by much of the oligarchy, and by nearly all of the rising business middle class. And he was viewed with grave suspicion by segments of the military and the Church. All these elements comprised the real power structure of the Republic.

As Bosch took his place on the stage of the Dominican drama, men of goodwill abroad applauded but some who knew the Republic and its new President well might have remembered what skeptical Edmund Burke had said: "I should therefore suspend my congratulations on the new liberty of France until I am informed how it has been combined with government, with public force, with the disciplines and obedience of armies; with the collection of effective and well-distributed revenue; with morality and religion; with the solidity of property; with peace and order. . . . Liberty, when men act in bodies, is power. Considerate people, before they declare themselves, will observe the use which is made of power." This was the essential question. To what use would Bosch put his power? To what extent was it limited? And to what use would we put our own power in his support? To what extent were we limited? For we were involved too, deeply involved, in his fate.

2

We had our own problems with Bosch. Bosch had made it very clear he intended to pursue a nationalistic course, independent of the United States. Rightly proud of his electoral majority, he was extremely sensitive about being dominated by anyone, especially the United States. Nor in fact had we any desire to run his government. Propping up a one-year provisional government was one thing. Presuming to give advice to an elected President starting a four-year term was quite another. Moreover, I had felt all along that, essential as our open support of the Consejo had been, it had also exposed its weakness. Bosch would have to govern, grow strong, and consolidate his victory, himself.

We would do everything possible to help him. But only if he asked our help. The difficulty was that he might come to us too late.

In our own interest, we could not ignore several possibilities—that Bosch himself was a deep-cover Communist (I did not and do not believe it); that he would lose control of his PRD to the Castro/Communists (but I thought he and Miolán could prevent that); that if he failed to meet the people's expectations he might be overthrown.

I recommended that we help him make his revolution in every way possible but avoid smothering him with kindness; and above all that we avoid last year's mistake of overoptimism, for just as Trujillo's fall did not solve all the Republic's problems, neither did Bosch's election.

3

In these circumstances, it was unfortunate that I was obliged to go to him several times in his first two weeks in office on disagreeable business.

The first time, indeed, was on his second day in office, March 1. The Department instructed me to inform Bosch that we were lifting all departure controls on Dominicans immediately.

As we have seen, the Consejo, under the Emergency Law, had deported to the United States and forbidden to return some 125 Trujillistas and Castro/Communists. Few Dominicans had known that the United States had cooperated, at the Consejo's request, by refusing to permit the deportees to leave the United States—that is, those who had been sent there; many had been sent elsewhere. During the campaign, all candidates, including Bosch, had favored the repeal of the Emergency Law. Recently Bosch's enemies had been predicting he would repeal it and thus permit Castro/Communists to flood the country. Indeed, this very day, UCN delegates had demanded the law's repeal, no doubt to embarrass him. At the same time, the deportees were embarrassing us—Balaguer had criticized us and so had *El Mundo* of Puerto Rico; a deportee in the United States was suing us; and we at the Embassy had heard that Dominican Senators soon would investigate.

We had imposed departure controls to help maintain stability so elections could be held. Now the Department felt the elected Bosch government should handle the problem. But by so deciding, it was inadvertently handing Bosch's opponents a weapon—the return of deportees to the Republic almost immediately after he took office.

Fandino telephoned for an appointment, and Bosch suggested we come to his house that night at eight. From the beginning I saw him, as I had Bonnelly, at his house or somewhere else, and usually at night, never at the Palace unless we wanted to make news.

Bosch had a new house. Soon a cement-block wall was built around it, and as the months passed we used to gauge Bosch's mood by noting whether he was building the wall higher. The house itself was one-storied, designed in the Dominican style—tile floors, wide open doorways, few interior walls, so that any breeze could flow through freely. Beyond a small patio off the living room you could see not far away the giant screen of a drive-in movie. Living room and dining room were one. The furniture was new and modern, low chairs and benches. Books and paintings and statuary stood about. Bosch showed us around proudly, and joked that this was "a *tu-tum-pote* house." Once, fretting about not having sent a gift to Vice President Johnson, guiding me around the room to examine objects of art that might be appropriate, he seized on one, a big carved wooden abstract David, and said, drawing suddenly back and ducking his head in one of his gestures, "Ah-hah! This we will send." But it turned out to be cracked. So much did.

On this night I told him that I had come on instructions to say that as of March 1, that is, that day, we would take off all controls on Dominican deportees in the United States.

Bosch looked shocked. I am convinced he had not expected this or wanted it. He said, "No, no. We are not prepared. Can't you do it little by little? Three or four at a time. Don't let the whole 125 come in at one time. The group that went to Puerto Rico from Paris—only one is really a Communist but everybody thinks they are all Communists, and they will say Bosch let them in."

I suggested he invalidate their Dominican passports, or simply order the airlines and steamship companies not to bring them here on pain of penalty.

As though he had not heard, Bosch went on. He was not prepared to cope with a Castro/Communist influx. He still had no trustworthy security apparatus.

I told him we would help him establish one, provided it reported directly to him and no one else.

He went on, "I am not really afraid of the Communists if I can play with them face to face. The danger is in Imbert's playing with them," and, leaning forward on the edge of his chair, a butterfly chair of black wrought iron and black canvas, he said, "I am taking control of the police step by step. But Imbert is a madman and can make a conspiracy with the left. The left is divided. I have to keep it divided. Manolo," Manolo Tavárez Justo of the 14th of June, "said he was supporting my government," as indeed he had, that day. "He has a split in the executive committee, two or three are convincing him he has ruined the party by going with Fidel, and here the only road to revolution is that of the PRD. Without getting into a fight with the Communists I can nullify them. But anti-Americanism is harder. It takes time to explain to children that the United States is not responsible for Trujillo. The middle class of the cities is nationalistic. They are the most potentially dangerous. I cannot be pro-American. We need concerts, artists, actors, painters, from the United States, Vice President Johnson, to create an atmosphere."

I told him Sargent Shriver, head of the Peace Corps, was coming in a few days—would he receive him? He would. Bosch liked the Peace Corps. Later, traveling with him in the interior, I saw him pick a Peace Corps boy out of a crowd and shake his hand, saying, "I knew you were Peace Corps—you have a Peace Corps face."

He went back to talking about departure controls, asking if I could not at least persuade the U.S. government to delay a little while. I promised to try and asked what he would do about the Emergency Law. He said he probably would have to repeal it, though the draft Constitution, if adopted, would invalidate it.

I suggested he substitute other methods to protect his government from subversion. I told him, as I had told the Consejo so many times, that I did not favor shooting people in the streets but that on the other hand every government had the right, indeed the duty, to protect itself from being overthrown, a right inherent in the concept of sovereignty, and I hoped that now his elected government, stronger than the provisional Consejo, would protect itself against subversion by using the ordinary processes of the law—an anti-subversive force; a law similar to our own Smith Act, which makes it a crime to conspire to advocate the overthrow of the government by force or violence; riot control training; vigorous prosecution; courageous judges; and an effective director of immigration. He said this was what he intended to do.

He talked on and, talking, relaxed a bit, as he always did. He fell to theorizing about the Presidency. "Do you know why leaders in Latin America fail? No? Leaders in Latin America lose when they drink too much, or they keep mistresses, or they are lazy, or they do business," rubbing thumb and forefinger together, that Dominican gesture indicating graft, "with the Army or the Cabinet," and he leaned back in his chair, bobbing his head, puffing on his pipe. Bosch had a highly mobile face. Its expression changed constantly.

"But now I am angry," he said, and indeed he looked it. "Very angry.

There is a forty-three-million-dollar deficit. I have found hundreds of salaries over one thousand dollars a month in the government," and he slapped a thick stack of documents piled on the floor. "I am going to work tomorrow and Sunday to make drastic cuts. Everybody above four hundred dollars must go. The old government in the last few days took money from the Banco de Reservas. We are without one cent. Our capital is nothing. Nothing," and he slapped the papers.

I told him I had had the impression his finances were in good shape.

He scoffed. "It is worse than one year ago. Much worse. The twenty-two million dollars," the sugar money, "now I am trying to get approval from Washington to use fifteen million of it to pay United States exporters their money." He asked my help. He also asked me to speed up the MAAG's delivery of equipment to the military. I said I would try and asked if he would like a briefing by the MAAG on our program of military assistance for the year. He would.

He walked out to our car with us. Beside the porte cochere was a pool of water filled with lily pads and fish, carp, I think, and while we waited for my car, we stood looking at the fish.

I thought the interview had gone well. Bosch had been very sensible about the Castro/Communists, and I wished we hadn't had to put him on the spot by allowing them to return to the Republic. I told the Department so, and it agreed to maintain departure controls in the continental United States until March 10. I notified Bosch.

4

A representative of Esso arrived from the States, reasonable man. Explaining our basic policy, I told him Bosch had announced he would send a message to Congress, asking it to cancel the Esso contract, which could get nasty, but that so far he had not actually done so, and I hoped things could be straightened out.

The Esso representative saw Diego Bordas, Bosch's powerful new Minister of Commerce and Industry. Bordas said the contract was null and void, had been illegal from the start, since, before Esso took it over, it had been negotiated by someone else with Ramfis Trujillo. Bordas had suggested that the government put the refinery up for bids. Esso's man said he would have to present the idea to his board of directors. He did, and returned, and saw Bosch himself, but was unable to reach agreement; and in the end the Esso contract was quietly canceled.

5

Sarge Shriver came down and one evening ate hamburgers in the Residence garden with Peace Corps volunteers, then went off to tour the country. His observations confirmed mine—the best Peace Corps pro-

grams were in community development and agriculture, they needed
more support from the Dominican government, the English teachers were
wasting their time. We had about 140 volunteers here now. We should go
up to three hundred or four hundred during the year, a very large program for so small a country. But we would have to tighten it up administratively and insist that the Dominican ministries support it. We
would speak to President Bosch.

At the Palace, however, instead of talking to Shriver about the Peace
Corps, Bosch immediately launched a furious attack on foreign sugar and
molasses buyers, going into detail about a "dirty contract" the Consejo
had made.

I managed to steer the conversation to the Peace Corps. Shriver made
our recommendations. Bosch agreed to them. He asked if Shriver could
not send some fishermen—he was convinced the seas around were filled
with fishes, and that Peace Corps volunteers could teach Dominicans how
to set up commercial fishing cooperatives at such places as Samaná, creating a whole new industry. Shriver did, but they caught few fish, at least in
my time, and also ran into trouble preserving what they did catch long
enough to get them to market.

6

Time and again during these first weeks when I went to see Bosch,
I found him bending over stacks of papers and figures, line-cutting his
budget himself with a pencil. Almost every time Fandino and I arrived
he greeted us with an announcement of how much cash the government
had in the till that day. He was running the government like an old
lady saving string in a country store. I heard that he ordered that smaller
scratch pads be used in the Palace to save money. Money became an obsession; I could scarcely get his attention for anything else, nor could his
own Ministers. He simply immersed himself in financial problems for
three or four weeks, to the neglect of party and people.

Fiscal responsibility was, of course, laudable. But not at the expense
of everything else. I thought the times demanded, his voters demanded,
a government that would spend money, redistribute income, put people
to work, and give them an opportunity to create a better life—in short,
a New Deal. Inflation might result but he must take that chance.

Bosch, however, refused, tried to balance the budget, and adopted
a deflationary policy. He was, he once told me, "a classical economist."
He was the only revolutionary I know of who enshrined Adam Smith.

I began holding a series of meetings with Williams and Bramble on the
Republic's financial problems. I could not understand why they were so
pressing.

Shortly before Bosch's inauguration, a heavy flight of capital had occurred, worsening his foreign exchange position. Commercial arrearages had mounted, causing stagnation in the Dominican economy. That is, Dominican businessmen, lacking dollars, could not pay their bills in the United States, so had stopped importing. Business was slowing down. And the peso was slipping. Rumor said it was selling at a discount of thirty cents or even fifty cents on the dollar in the black market.

In a similar situation last year, AID had released 7.5 million dollars of its original twenty-five-million-dollar loan to the Consejo to pay off a backlog of commercial arrearages. But now AID would not release any of the twenty-two-million-dollar sugar money, still to come, for the same purpose. Bosch had asked that twelve million dollars of it be freed immediately to pay arrearages (thus freeing the twelve million pesos generated for credits to farmers.) I understood that Moscoso had promised to do it but now refused.

Therefore, to pay off these commercial arrearages, Bosch had been forced to borrow against his sugar at commercial interest rates. Williams and Bramble said if he wanted to he could borrow similarly against the twenty-two million dollars from commercial banks. I thought this outrageous. Why should Bosch be forced to pay commercial interest to get the use of the twenty-two million dollars which Bosch and I believed he had been promised would be available to him when he took office? We had been told repeatedly that the twenty-two million dollars would come with no strings attached. Now it appeared that it would have to go through the "restricted account," with United States dollars spent on United States goods in the United States, because of our balance of payments problem. Due to these cumbersome procedures of ours, the peso equivalent of the twenty-two million dollars would not start becoming available at all until the end of May, and it would not become a steady flow, Williams said, for three or four months more. Our restrictions, necessary though they might be, were working against our policy. They were driving our friend Bosch away.[1] What it all came down to was this: Bosch had no cash now and would have none for several months. And to a considerable extent it was our fault. We were being far less generous and helpful to Bosch than we had been to the Consejo.

Bosch's solution was austerity. AID had no cash for new programs.

[1] Bosch, with Williams' concurrence, had earmarked the twenty-two million as follows: Twelve million dollars for small agricultural credits, five million dollars for large agricultural credits, three million for farm-to-market roads, two million scattered. This left nothing for agrarian reform, housing, education, health, or other projects. Agrarian reform was standing still. By mid-April, about twenty-two hundred families had been put on the land, at an almost prohibitive cost of two million dollars in our money and two million dollars in Dominican money—and nearly all had been put there by the Consejo. The Dominican budget was expected to be out of balance by twenty-two million dollars this year, unless the IMF agreed to postpone collection of the twelve million dollars due it.

The World Bank and several private investors were talking about big projects—port and river valley development—but such projects were years away, awaiting surveys of studies, feasibility surveys, and so on and so on, endlessly, mountains of paper bigger than the mountains they proposed to move.

Meanwhile, where was the revolution? During the first few weeks when I saw Bosch line-cutting his budget, I said nothing. But soon I began asking his advisers, and then Bosch himself, what had happened to the revolution. When would he launch programs for the poor? What about unemployment, high as ever? I was not in a very good position to ask it—we were not being much help. But I asked anyway. I felt I had to. It was all very well for economists to say that all Bosch had to do if he really needed money was to borrow against the twenty-two million dollars or ask me for a new loan. But it left out of account the political realities—that Bosch was too independent to ask us for a new loan, and that the people who elected him to make a revolution would not go on forever doing the same thing they had done for four hundred years—starving in huts.

7

The Department instructed me to find out why Bosch would not honor sugar and molasses contracts that the Consejo had made the year before with American sugar dealers. During the months since the Consejo had sold sugar for future delivery, the market price had risen greatly; if Bosch now made delivery at the contract price, he stood to receive between three and four million dollars less than he would receive if he could sell at today's market price. Bosch was balking—had refused to load a boat sent to pick up the sugar. Minister Bordas was trying to pressure the U.S. sugar dealers into letting Bosch cancel last year's contracts. But a contract was a contract, in the Department's view. And rightly, of course. I stalled as long as I dared, then once again went trotting out to Bosch's house on a disagreeable errand.

As always, I took Fandino, but again Bosch insisted on speaking English. He did not speak English as well as he thought, and understood it even less; it was an effort for him, and, when tired, he simply quit listening.

That night began, as usual, with a long lecture on how much money he had saved by cutting salaries. When he had finished, I told him I had several things to talk to him about. The man had arrived to help set up his counter-subversive force; when could he see him? Tomorrow, at 7:30 A.M. (I believe the meeting was postponed.) Our investigators working on the Galíndez case wanted to see him to regularize their status. He asked Fandino to call him Monday at 9 A.M. (Fandino did, but could not reach him.) When did he want the MAAG briefing? Soon; he would let Fandino know. (He didn't. He kept postponing the MAAG briefing for months, until a misunderstanding made it imperative.) What about the Dominican liaison man to the Peace Corps? He was considering two candidates, soon would choose one.

Then he told me a long, complicated story about the mysterious "Trujillo family boxes" in Paris, and he went on to say that Trujillo agents had taken suitcases "full of big bills" to New York after his own election. He thought Imbert might be involved. I said I didn't see how Imbert could be involved with the Trujillos. He said there might be two separate plots—one by Imbert, one by the Trujillos. In any case, during the first eighteen days of February, one million dollars had disappeared from the Republic, and he asked me to try to trace it in the States. I said I would, and did subsequently, without success. Bosch went on, "So I am fighting corruption as far as I can. Including in Agrarian reform and in AID."

I asked what he meant about AID.

He had no specific information but had "been told" that there "was a scandal" in AID. I said we would take this very seriously and asked for details. He had none, and went on talking, really paying little heed to what I had said. "So we are going to cut the Armed Forces," he said. "I have talked to the Secretary of Armed Forces. We have removed Colonel Fernández Smester." My attachés already had reported this—Colonel Smester, complaining about Air Force salary cuts, had said the only solution was a *golpe*. I was worried—Smester had been close to Colonel Wessin y Wessin, the tank commander; I asked about it but Bosch brushed it aside, and went on, "We cannot close the advance against our sugar with the banks because of the opinion of Peynado," apparently a reference to a lawyer, Julio Peynado, which mystified me. "Williams gave me today the documents implementing the twenty-two million dollars. Williams is very cooperative. It is extraordinary." These documents were mere formalities, but I suggested he and Williams make a ceremony of signing them, and they did, Bosch taking the occasion to praise the Alliance for Progress.

Bosch began talking about the University: "The problem is autonomy —for people who cannot handle it. I shall try to get Congress—" as though it might be difficult—"to pass a law to let me appoint seven men to reorganize the University. What is his name, Domínguez, came to me about it. I said that Article 35 makes me supreme at the University. I ordered the Director of the Budget not to give one cent till they fix up that mess. Now the University council is starting to accuse me. The Social Christians want autonomy. If they keep on, the only solution will be a new university. In four years. If," smiling engagingly, "I last four years."

I said I would like to get to know his Cabinet members. He said,

"You should. I am greatly impressed with my Cabinet members. They are working eighteen hours a day. We are all working eighteen hours a day. I am seeing at least 150 people a day. We have stopped sixteen strikes a few hours before they started."

Riding home, Fandino said that at least we had learned one thing: Imbert and the CIA had, independently, been right—both had told us that Asdrúbal Domínguez had visited Bosch. Asdrúbal Domínguez was a PSP man who led a Communist-penetrated student group, FED, and in 1962 had been a delegate to the Congress of the International Union of Students in Leningrad. I had first met him, a dark, forceful man who looked to be in his late twenties, on Fandino's porch during my mission for President Kennedy in 1961.

Bosch's mood tonight had puzzled me. Why had he been so euphoric, with things going as they were? I had mistrusted him tonight, and so had not brought up the thing I really had been under instructions to take up with him: The sugar contracts.

Over the weekend, Fran and Dan came home from Washington, Dan's arm in a sling. We rested, and Dan and Fred began building a shack in the Embassy garden, a shack which turned into a miniature fortress, with a concrete floor, walls built of wood, and roof thatched with palms, where they and their friends played guerrilla warfare. In the swimming pool they played Cuban quarantine.

The Department instructed me to inform the Dominican government that its failure to honor legitimate contracts with U.S. sugar firms would certainly have most serious repercussions for the Bosch government and might even lead to invocation of the Hickenlooper amendment, which would end AID to the Republic.

This was a hard line. But the law is the law. Yet I did wish they'd give Bosch a little time to get his feet on the ground.

We found Bosch angry and nervous, talking about the Tavera dam and the Puerto Plata harbor. I told him we'd made a thorough study of the Puerto Plata harbor. "Nobody told me about it," he said. He went on, "There is no land for agrarian reform. And they are spending two hundred thousand dollars a month on salaries alone at the Agrarian Reform Institute." This was shocking. And what had happened to the Trujillo lands? "The Secretary of Recuperación says they were given back, or leased, or sold by the Consejo. We will use hard methods," his voice harsh, his face red, "to get it back." He pulled a slip of paper out of his pocket, and read off the figures: January budget deficit $246,000, February $270,000, March worse. "Tomorrow I am meeting with the business people to collect the taxes on time. We are cutting our salaries at Haina. We gave orders to the military to guard the cane fields. The irrigation to the agricultural sugar lands is poor. I want to put the Haina sugar lands in the hands of the cane cutters. I can't sell the Haina to private industry—there would be a revolution. But the state can't manage them properly either. Especially here, where people have no conscience," and he rocked rapidly in a high-backed rocking chair, his jaw tight.

I said I wanted to talk to him about the sugar contracts. Without looking at me, he said, "I told Bordas to get as much as he could. Before I took power I gave instructions that I wanted no more contract with Lobo," one of the sugar dealers. "In spite of that the Consejo went ahead. Now Lobo is trying to get United States influence to get completion on a dirty business. When I was in the New York sugar market, I said I would not deliver the sugar. Then he made fun of me," scowling, his red face deeply furrowed.

I said I knew nothing about Lobo but understood he had a valid contract and considered it wise for Bosch to honor it.

Still not looking at me, still rocking, Bosch said, "Lobo will get his sugar. But he'll be squeezed first for all he's worth. We will make him sweat. And then he can't come back here. Bordas has warned me about all this. Bordas knows sugar. Lobo means wolf in Spanish, and that's what he is. Cubans and Japanese and United States sugar men will take six and a half millions out of here in profits."

I said again I did not know the background of the contracts but I thought him wise to honor them to protect his government's reputation. He relented a little, and stopped rocking. "I know. It is not you." He looked at his watch. "I beg your pardon, I am late, I have to go and meet with twenty senators at my old house."

He did honor the sugar contracts. Riding home, Fandino said, "I wish you could go to him sometime when you've got something nice to tell him." So did I.

8

Bosch had been in office a little less than two weeks, and already something approaching a crisis of confidence existed. He had buried himself in the budget, presented no program to Congress, so nobody knew what he proposed to do. We heard on every hand that Bosch had not forthrightly spoken out against communism, that one or more of his Cabinet ministers was a Communist, that Bosch had lost touch with the people. And, talking about Lobo, he had seemed tense and near exhaustion, almost cornered, ready to lash out at someone.

During this uneasy period, both left and right began to move.

Shlaudeman said the PSP, the Communist party directed from Moscow via Blas Rocas in Cuba, had several men here again—Juan Ducoudray Mansfield, who probably was its Dominican maximum leader and had gone as the official Dominican delegate to the worldwide Communist Party Congress in Moscow in 1960; José Espaillat Rodríguez and Tulio Arvelo. The PSP was following the Moscow line of coexistence, though moving slightly toward the MPD, which still took the Peking line of terrorism. The PSP was trying to infiltrate the 14th of June at high levels, the MPD was trying to infiltrate it at low levels. All really saw their future through the 14th of June. The 14th of June, for now, was trying to align itself with Bosch. Seriously eroded by the October missile crisis, the 14th now had moved right—was regrouping under a purely nationalistic banner. Manolo Tavárez Justo was openly supporting Bosch. He said so in the newspapers almost daily. Once he announced that "reactionaries" were trying to foil the PRD's revolution, that the PRD's "solutions" were the only way to correct the Republic's "colonial" status, and that "everything that the PRD offers the people has only one name: the anti-feudal, anti-imperialist, democratic, national liberation revolution." Dato Pagán, head of the PNR, the two-man Communist splinter party, announced publicly that he would establish an Institute of Political Science and Economic Planning. Shlaudeman said Dato Pagán was giving Bosch all-out support. We did not think Pagán had lines to Castro or Moscow but he was getting money somewhere, possibly from Venezuelan Communists.

Even before the election we had suspected that Bosch had some sort of understanding with elements of the extreme left. Now we became daily more sure of it. The PRD and a Castro/Communist student group at the university, Fragua, were jointly demanding temporary measures tantamount to giving them control of the University. Manolo Tavárez Justo went on a speaking tour around the country and, in Hato Mayor, the old center of anti-Americanism, blamed the Yankee imperialists and Dominican oligarchs for all the Republic's problems. At Pedernales, he denounced Alcoa for denying him admittance to its fenced "concentration camp" and declared Alcoa was getting six hundred dollars a ton for bauxite and paying the Dominican Republic only twenty-five cents. Alcoa's manager, Pat Hughson, told me the 14th of June was infiltrating the Alcoa workers' union.

The CIA chief independently confirmed the drift of things. A reliable source had seen Juan Ducoudray in the Republic. His brother Félix would come this month. They intended to cooperate with Bosch for the time being. They had penetrated Fragua, the student group, and its leaders had met with Bosch and reached an agreement—Bosch would help Fragua break the Social Christian movement at the University, then build up FURR, the Bosch group there.

We did not think Bosch was a Communist. We did not think he was the Communists' creature. But we felt sure they were trying to capture him. The real test, we thought, might come on some foreign policy issue. And if, to hold the left, Bosch drifted toward anti-Americanism, he would expose himself to grave danger from the right, out to get him for its own reasons.

Imbert told Colonel Cass that the PSP leader José Espaillat Rodríguez was the house guest of Miguel Ángel Domínguez Guerra, Bosch's new Minister of Interior and Police. We had heard Domínguez Guerra had two PSP house guests—José Espaillat Rodríguez and Juan Ducoudray himself. This was disturbing, to say the least, since Domínguez Guerra, as Minister of Interior and Police, controlled internal security, public order, and immigration.

Several members of the U.S. press began picking up the story. Jules Dubois wrote in the Chicago *Tribune* that conditions in the Republic favored a Communist takeover and that leading non-Communist leftists were dismayed at Miolán's influence, suspecting Miolán was under Communist Party discipline. UPI reported that Bosch, in a statement made to an Argentine radio station, declared that Latin America must work out its own problems and not rely on the *Alianza*. Henry Raymont, then of UPI, later with the New York *Times,* wrote that after only twelve days in office Bosch was in trouble.

The old parties seemed to be breaking up. A UCN deputy resigned. Seven members of UCN's central committee resigned. Donny Reid announced he was quitting public life. Several Vanguardia leaders announced they would support the PRD rather than their own party.

The CIA chief told me several former UCNers were meeting regularly with several military leaders and Amiama and Imbert. They hoped to form a new unified group to oppose Bosch. If they opposed Bosch on everything, they would, of course, unwittingly drive him into the hands of the Communists. And a new group, not a political party, but simply a group, was indeed formed. It called itself *Acción Dominicana Independiente* (ADI)—Dominican Independent Action. It published an ad attacking Bosch in *El Caribe*. It was composed mostly of businessmen, members of the rising middle class, former UCNers—the group in the Republic loosely called *civicos*. At the time we paid it little heed. Groups were always turning up. We were wrong.

Colonel Wolfe of the MAAG said he had several projects ready training an engineering battalion, rebuilding the shipyard at Haina, extending the naval study of the port at Puerto Plata, rebuilding three coastal patrol boats and building a new one. But the entire MAAG program had come to a standstill.

So had the police training program—Jacob Jackson, our public safety man, said Bosch had shut off all funds to the police. Nobody knew why.

High police officials were saying in front of their men that what was needed was a strong man.

Donny Reid came to see me, visibly upset. He said Diego Bordas had four jobs—Secretary of Commerce and Industry, head of the Committee for the Defense of Sugar, head of Haina, and head of the *Fomento*. He was the economic czar of the Republic. And people didn't trust him. Business was virtually at a standstill. Businessmen feared Bordas. And they feared that Bosch was handing the country over to the Castro/Communists. Moreover, obscure young leftists, probably acting as a front for others, had gone to the Attorney General with complaints against President Bonnelly, Reid, and Pichardo, charging them with murder, torture, and misappropriation of public funds.

I said I couldn't believe it. Reid said it was true. What murder? The killings at Palma Sola, he said. But surely no formal charges would be filed? He said they would. And they were.

But none of this, he said, was really what was bothering him. It was that the Bosch government was no good. His appointed judges were lawyers of no standing—one had been an assistant to a local prosecutor, another was a kidnapper, another had been a Trujillo *calié*. A Cabinet Minister once had sold visas. ("Minister" was a Cabinet officer's title under Bosch, not "Secretary of State" as formerly.) Another had been raised from obscurity by Marco Gómez, Ramfis Trujillo's financial adviser. Another had fled the country to escape prosecution for writing bad checks. Bosch was having trouble borrowing money against his future sugar harvest; bankers felt that as things stood the sugar never would be produced. Fires had started in the cane fields again. (I always questioned whether Communist saboteurs were setting the fires, as Reid assumed, or whether cane cutters were doing it because they could earn more money cutting burned cane than green cane.) Reid said the Emergency Law was ended, in fact if not by law, and Communists were flocking back. "Everyone is scared," he said. "It can end only in a leftist or rightist dictatorship. Everyone expected Bosch to have a program ready. Where is it?"

I tried to calm Reid, told him that, after all, Bosch had been in office only a few days, surely no one could expect miracles; it was not surprising that Bosch was obliged to rely on inexperienced people; they would need time. And I made it clear that we were supporting Bosch just as we had the Consejo.

How much time was there, Reid asked, with business stopped and the left on the move? "These are hectic days for my country. It could lead to what Figueres wanted after Trujillo fell—an OAS occupation force for four years." (This was, incidentally, the first I had heard of that proposal. In retrospect, it might not have been a bad idea, but there wouldn't have been a chance in the world that the OAS would have done it at that time.)

Bosch announced the appointment of Andrés Freites, the Consejo's Ambassador to the United States, as Foreign Minister. This should have reassured the *civicos*. But *El Caribe* pointed out that Freites was a cousin of Imbert. Bosch, inordinately sensitive to press criticism, declared the President would choose his Cabinet freely and alone.

Trouble began inside Bosch's party, the PRD. Miolán told an Embassy officer, "Bosch is going to have to choose between me and Diego Bordas." This was unlike Miolán. Miolán was a plotter, but he was also a professional politician, not given to burning bridges behind him. Now, however, Bosch was ignoring Miolán and the PRD itself. Bosch had given the PRD patronage jobs. Its local leaders, who had been paid twenty-five dollars a week before the election, now were receiving nothing. If the PRD disintegrated, Bosch would be left all alone, without the support even of his own party, and, alone, might fall. Not yet, however—we thought Miolán would fight back. We would watch it closely.

Sacha Volman came to see me. He confirmed our suspicion that Diego Bordas was trying to destroy Miolán and seize PRD leadership. He might succeed—Bosch had said, "Let the party die." Volman said Bosch needed Bordas. "Bosch is worn out," Volman said. "So Bordas has undue influence. If we can get a good planning board going and make him less dependent on Bordas, he'll get rid of Bordas. But until then he needs him."

Volman said, "But what he really sent me to talk to you about is Imbert. He feels his authority is going down and Imbert is defying him. Meetings are going on all the time between the four chiefs—" Viñas and the service commanders, Hungría, Rib, and Luna "—and Fiallo and Bonnelly and Imbert." Bosch, he said, had made a mistake. He was not in touch with the military. "I advised him to get rid of Belisario Peguero, or to have Peguero and Amiama and Imbert arrested and deported to Puerto Rico. He first said no. But he wants to do something with all three. He asked me to talk to Molina Ureña and some of the old contacts and make a list and get one hundred loyal soldiers to use for the arrest."

I said, "You mean the arrest of Belisario Peguero, Imbert, and Amiama?"

"Yes. We won't act till we have checked with you. He wants your suggestions. It is urgent, a day or two. He also wants you to tell your attachés to say the United States supports the Bosch government." I said they already were saying this. Volman smiled. "He hopes you can make them more enthusiastic."

I said I thought there were some steps that Bosch himself might take to restore confidence. Volman said quickly, "He is waiting a little, that's all."

9

Bosch did take five steps to meet the rising pressures.

He ordered work stopped temporarily on the Constitution.

He honored the sugar contracts.

He agreed to address the American Chamber of Commerce.

He publicly praised President Kennedy, the Alliance for Progress, and the generosity of the United States.

He declared in a graduation speech at the Armed Forces artillery school that "Communism means death, war, destruction, and the loss of all our possessions."

But the sense of unease persisted. Most of the criticism was aimed at the men around Bosch. The *civicos* derided and feared what we would call, I suppose, his staff, as we spoke of President Kennedy's "White House staff," though it is difficult to think in that context about the crowd of fixers and gunmen and influence peddlers who flocked to the Palace with Bosch. Some were Puerto Ricans, some Cubans, some Dominicans, some Europeans. Some seemed to be close to Bosch. His house was always full of people; nearly every evening I went there, more than one Cabinet minister would be there, and a hanger-on or two, and Bosch's niece, Milagros, and Mrs. Bosch's sister, and other people I did not know.

Actually the Bosch hangers-on probably made off with less money than other men had under the Consejo. But they went at it blatantly. In a well-established society, where everybody understands the ground rules, thievery is quiet, unnoticed, even decorous. But Bosch's people were new to government, and his election had broken the Dominican establishment and its ground rules. Once a PRD politician threatened to demand publicly an investigation of a U.S. company, saying it was exploitative but hinting that of course such things could always be straightened out. A U.S. businessman who unwittingly poached on an influence peddler's preserve found himself served with a summons by the security police. Slot machines spread to remote areas of the Republic, as they had under Trujillo but not under the Consejo. At one point known racketeers from Chicago and Las Vegas tried to move in.

Nevertheless, I am convinced that in its lifetime the Bosch government was one of the most dollar-honest governments in the Republic's history, and would compare favorably with many Latin American and United States governments. If Bosch caught a man stealing or otherwise abusing his authority, he got rid of him almost instantly. Moreover, although a few of the hangers-on possessed considerable power—one was briefly entrusted with secret police matters—most were mere flunkies. Quite naturally the *civicos* could not distinguish among them, they were strangers, aliens, even, and the *civicos* thought them all alike, and despised and feared them, feeling that they were foreigners overrunning the country.

The hangers-on created endless confusion, for none had ever worked in a Palace, and some must never have worked in an office—they would answer the phone then, going in search of the person wanted, hang it up. Or they simply would let it ring. Or take it off the hook and leave it off for hours. Ceremonies were disastrous. Other ambassadors became disgusted. So did distinguished visitors. Not Communist infiltration, not thievery, but sheer incompetence seemed at times the bane of living under Bosch's government.

The hangers-on wasted Bosch's time fearfully. For Bosch loved to talk, and to listen, and though he regularly arose before dawn and got to the Palace at 5 A.M., worked till 1 or 2 P.M., went home for lunch and a brief *siesta,* then worked again till midnight, sleeping in all no more than six hours in twenty-four and often less, he accomplished very little. Hundreds of callers beset him, and instead of fending them off, his aides assisted them in wasting his time. No wonder he was exhausted. The Consejo had been confused, but the Bosch government, especially in the beginning, was chaotic.

And to treat with these dubious characters came equally scabrous men from the United States, from Latin American countries, and from Europe. I could no more control the carpetbaggers than Bosch could control his hangers-on. One weekend a man telephoned me and got me out of bed, gave me his name, said he was an American and had come to the Republic to present a scroll to President Bosch from a governor in the States. He said Diego Bordas had suggested he call me and invite me to participate in the ceremony. I said it was impossible that day, to call Monday, we'd see. King, Bramble, and my secretary could not find out what it was all about. Bosch's office called and set an appointment for 7 P.M. Monday. I went, alone.

Bosch had changed offices. The big room the Consejo had used was now the anteroom. It looked like a Chicago ward headquarters, dim-lit, smoky, filled with cigar-smoking men whispering to one another. Two men guarded the door to the little corner office that Balaguer, and now Bosch, used as his own. The men in the anteroom appeared to be Americans, Dominicans, Cubans, Puerto Ricans, others. I finally located the American, surrounded by several other Americans, and asked him if they were all together. He said, after some hesitation, that he was alone, the others were just there. I suspected they were his business associates and the scroll from the governor only an opening wedge. I asked if he was on private business. He said, yes. I said I could not get involved; if I sponsored one private businessman I would have to sponsor all. I would permit a photograph of him, Bosch, and myself in the presentation of the Governor's scroll and nothing more.

I went in to President Bosch. The others followed, including photographers. Privately, I explained to Bosch. His eyes crinkling, he said, "You are like the *campesino,* always careful." He called the American and told the photographers to go ahead. They did. President Bosch suggested we three sit down. The others left, but then came back, with more photographers who said they had missed the pictures, but Bosch said no more—lights bothered his eyes, he had a headache, fever. One of them, a Cuban, I believe, began explaining to Bosch that the American represented large industrial interests prepared to make huge investments in the Republic. I excused myself and departed.

As time passed, President Bosch got rid of people, stopped seeing so many visitors, reorganized his workload. The administrative functioning of his government improved somewhat. But from first to last, Bosch's single greatest handicap was a lack of experienced and able people to help him run his government. True, Bosch would not delegate power. But considering the people around him, perhaps it was fortunate he did not. He really was all alone. Most Dominicans with ability and with experience in government were either dead, or in prison, or in exile—Trujillo had ruined them. Many who had escaped those fates had served the Consejo; Bosch, having campaigned against the Consejo, could not use them. He was a prisoner of his own politics. Moreover, the enlightened young members of the Santiago oligarchy, who had held themselves aloof from the Consejo, now held themselves even more aloof from Bosch. He simply could not draw on the best men in the Republic to help him. Would not at first; could not, ever: They would not serve him.

The crucial fact was that Bosch's election had brought to power a whole class of people who never before had had a place in the mainstream of Dominican national life. Bosch's votes had come from the *campesino,* the displaced *campesino* in the cities, the small shopkeeper in the roadside store, the workingman, the poor. I happened to think that it was long past time for the ordinary people to take their rightful place in the national life. But they lacked any experience at government. And many were uneducated. How could they not be, after Trujillo? I knew a governor swept into power with Bosch who could not sign his name, a mayor who never before had worn shoes. No doubt many of these people possessed a great deal of latent talent. But meanwhile, who would run the government? Under our cultural exchange program, we tried to send some of Bosch's people to the United States for training in government. But any worth sending could not be spared. We offered to help him set up a school in government and business administration in the Republic. It never got started.

The greatest danger any public man faces in high office is sycophancy. It is absolutely indispensable to his success and even his survival that he have a "no" man, not all "yes" men. Bosch had nothing but "yes" men.

And of all high officeholders I have known, none was more vain than Bosch—and, so, vulnerable to flattery. Night after night, time after time, he and I were interrupted by one of his hangers-on or Cabinet ministers who insisted on bringing him good news or on praising him. Bosch loved it.

Of the men Bosch did manage to secure for his Cabinet two are of particular interest—Diego Bordas, Minister of Commerce and Industry, and Domínguez Guerra, Minister of Interior and Police.

Bordas was big, dark, handsome, mustached; he was smooth, careful, intelligent. He was by all odds the most controversial, the strongest, and the most capable man in the Bosch cabinet. He was about forty. Originally from Puerto Plata, he had operated an export-import business. He spent fourteen years in exile, most of it in New York and Puerto Rico. He was thought to be well-to-do. He had connections everywhere with persons as diverse as Ramfis Trujillo and the 14th of June leaders. He said he had been at Cayo Confites and had been a delegate from Puerto Rico to the Democratic National Convention in 1960. He had returned to the Republic after Trujillo's fall, and had been deported to the United States by the Consejo and spent time in Opa-locka, a United States detention center near Miami. He told me, laughing, "I was deported because I was supposed to be a Communist." Speaking of the "so-called Constitution," he showed the same contempt for law as Trujillo. He talked a good deal about honesty in government. He was convinced Imbert and Belisario Peguero intended to kill him. He denied he was the strong man in the Cabinet, but seemed to realize he had become a focal point for Bosch's opponents. They considered him a Communist or a crook or both. I considered him an opportunist, a buccaneer; and I thought he had a strong streak of anti-Americanism.

Domínguez Guerra, Minister of Interior and Police, was youngish, stocky, pale, cocky. Born in Puerto Plata, he said he had attended the University of Santo Domingo, gone to San José de Ocoa to visit a sister, and stayed twenty years, running a drugstore. He said he had always been a fighter against Trujillo, first jailed at the age of thirteen. He claimed he had worked with "three of the seven groups" that had tried to kill Trujillo and that he had been in the 30th of May plot as a "collaborator of Severo Cabral and López Molina." This seemed most unlikely—Severo Cabral was a far-right reactionary, López Molina was head of the MPD, and so far as I knew neither had been in the 30th of May plot. Domínguez said he used to distribute López Molina's clandestine newspaper. He said he had grown up with Tony Imbert and considered him "always an assassin."

Domínguez Guerra had been head of the first PRD committee to come into the open right after Trujillo was shot. He had been in the party's rooftop headquarters when Ramfis' troops slaughtered the students. In the election campaign, he had worked with the PRD organization under Miolán. He told me he had organized San Cristóbal, Baní, the entire south, Santo Domingo, and the Cibao—most of the country (some of this was demonstrably untrue). He said Bosch used him now as a "troubleshooter," sending him on missions not really related to his own ministry. (I asked for examples. No answer.) He certainly knew little about the police, which one would have expected to be his prime concern. Bosch probably intended to handle the police himself.

Domínguez characterized himself as a "revolutionary and a nationalist" and said, "I am not against foreign countries except as they exploit us." He seemed to think the United States was exploiting the Republic. He complained bitterly that AID and the *Alianza* were slow and behaved "like bankers, not revolutionaries." He opposed the Emergency Law, favored free speech for all, including Communists, and said this was the "pure" PRD position.

Domínguez Guerra acted as though he were close to Bosch. I saw him often at Bosch's home. But I doubted that he influenced Bosch much —he did not seem intelligent enough. Many people considered him a Communist. The Ocoa crowd, his hometown crowd, was certainly Castro/ Communist infested. Dominguez was related by marriage to Tulio Arvelo Delgado, the PSP leader. And, as we have seen, the talk now was that José Espaillat Rodríguez and Juan Ducoudray, PSP leaders, were living in Domínguez' house.

Although to me Domínguez spoke well of his experiences in visiting the United States, I put him down as a small-town braggart, a loudmouth with an empty head, a strong nationalist, a naïve man with leftist tendencies who would collaborate with anybody, including Communists— in short, a man whom a capable Communist could rather easily convert into a enemy of the United States.

Bordas and Domínguez Guerra were the two Bosch Cabinet ministers I was most concerned about.

The others were quite different.

Three we had known a long time—Goodluck Sánchez, now Minister of Education; Andy Freites, now Foreign Minister; General Viñas, still Minister of Defense.

The rest were new, Boschistas. Samuel Mendoza Moya was a tall, thin physician who had grown up with Bosch in La Vega, spent the last eighteen years in Puerto Rico, worked, he said, in Muñoz Marín's Health Department, acquired U.S. citizenship, and now risked losing it by yielding to Bosch's entreaties to return and become Minister of Health. An admirer of the United States, he was developing a ten-year health plan in accordance with the *Alianza*. He was appalled at the incompetents in his ministry, the indifferent doctors in the hospitals, and the endless politics. He seemed to be one of the few Cabinet ministers appointed for sheer knowledge of his job. Like many Boschistas, he felt himself almost a stranger here. He told me, "Puerto Rico and the United States gave me the chance that my own country denied me. I have lost touch with my own people. I feel confused, don't know what to do, whom to listen to." His wife was here but his children were in Puerto Rico, and she wanted him to go back.

The Minister for the Presidency, Abraham Jaar, also felt himself a stranger in the Republic—had been in exile in Venezuela too long. His wife and one of his sons still were there. He was about forty-five, thin, ulcer-ridden, a passionate believer in Bosch's cause, with the look of a man who has suffered. I came to know him well, and went hunting and fishing with him. His grandfather had been born in Palestine under the British protectorate; his father was a Santo Domingo merchant. He himself was a surgeon, he said. In the election campaign Jaar had been a Bosch fund-raiser, especially in Venezuela. He wished Bosch would settle down and get his program moving. Most people thought he was mesmerized by Bosch, but I got the impression that Jaar maintained a certain perspective, and he told me things he kept from Bosch. Jaar was Bosch's buffer and made most of his appointments. He was very close to Bosch, and Bosch trusted him, though I doubted that in a crisis Jaar's influence would count for much. He sought anonymity. He was friendly to the United States and to me, and told me more than once, "We need you."

Jaar's own closest associate seemed to be the Minister without Portfolio, Humbertilio Váldez Sánchez, an elderly, smiling elfin dentist who later, after the overthrow of the Bosch government, was able to joke that he was the "Minister without Government." Humbertilio, as we came to call him, had been Bosch's chief fund raiser in the Republic during the campaign. He had done his job with a toughness astonishing in one who seemed so gentle. Once he said to a Santiago merchant who was reluctant to contribute, "You give to the 14th of June, don't you?" Yes, but only because the 14th of June might throw rocks through his windows. Humbertilio responded, "What's the matter, don't you think we can throw rocks?" Humbertilio and Jaar proved to be good channels for me to Bosch.

The Minister of Labor, Silvestre Alba de Moya, was a middle-aged lawyer, able, smart, accustomed to good living, experienced in government, a Trujillista. He intended to force the unions to obey the law. (Of hundreds of strikes in 1962 under the Consejo, not one had been legal.) He probably cared little about labor's aspirations but would probably run a pretty good ministry if let alone. He was one of those attractive Dominican *insumergibles*—unsinkables—a minor professional politician who served Trujillo and always landed on his feet.

The Minister of Public Works, Luís del Rosario Ceballos, was a handsome, inexperienced, arrogant young man of twenty-seven who was engaged to Bosch's niece and was close to him in a personal, but probably not in a policy, way. His brother Enriquillo became Ambassador to the United States and impressed President Kennedy favorably.

The Minister of Justice, Luís E. Lembert Peguero, was reputed a former visa-pusher and altogether a disaster. I scarcely knew him.

I did, however, come to know and think well of two other Bosch Ministers—the Minister of Agriculture, Antonio Guzmán, and the Minister of Finance, Jacobo Majluta. Both were very close to Bosch.

Guzmán, a rather slight, retiring man who looked to be in his forties, was married to the sister of General Viñas' wife. He was friendly to the United States. Politically naïve, able enough in business but lost in both the jungle of politics and the spaces of policy, Guzmán was one of the Cibao independents, men who had abstained from public life. He was no revolutionary, simply a devoted friend of Bosch, with whom he had grown up. Guzmán had friends in the oligarchy, though he did not quite belong to it, and was a large landowner himself. He never seemed quite at home in the Bosch entourage.

Minister of Finance Jacobo Majluta was an obese young PRDista of twenty-eight from Puerto Plata, a PRD organizer, a man who, though inexperienced, was friendly, hard-working, and eager to do his best. *Civicos* considered him a leftist. His wife was a strong and striking raw-boned woman with Indian features and a tragic face and long black uncombed hair, really the only person in the entire Bosch entourage who looked like a revolutionary, for one could imagine her at the barricades before the Bastille.

The *civicos,* of course, made sport of the Bosch Cabinet, and held them in contempt. In his book Bosch says that he was frequently accused of having assembled a government of "garbage," men who did not belong to the *altura,* the upper crust. Of course, he writes scornfully the PRD leaders were not "gente de primera," "first class citizens."

All in all, I suppose, the fairest evaluation of Bosch's Cabinet was that it was extremely uneven and quite undistinguished. For months Bosch kept telling me—telling me too often—how good it was. The more it became the laughing stock of the *civicos,* the more he insisted on its excellence. At first I accepted what he said; as I came to know them, I expressed reservations or fell silent. Soon he fell silent too. Then, during the summer, he admitted the Cabinet was inferior, said he wanted to replace several members, and complained bitterly that the "best people" in the Republic would not join his government. All true, too true.

Vice President González Tamayo was very young, only thirty-four, a doctor. He had been chosen almost by accident during the bitter struggle in the PRD convention. The *civicos* suspected he belonged to the Communist PSP but we thought him too confused for the PSP's taste. He drank, and seemed rather frivolous, and not long after he had taken office became involved in a reckless driving incident that had to be hushed up.

The Speaker of the House and President of the Senate were quite different.

Senator Juan Casasnovas Garrido, in line to succeed to the Presidency behind Bosch and the Vice President, was a short, heavy physician of forty-five from San Pedro de Macorís, a man who used joviality to conceal the fast mind of a professional politician. Jailed and briefly exiled by Trujillo, Casasnovas had returned to the Republic in 1961, become an active organizer for the PRD, risen rapidly to the party's inner circle, and contested for the vice presidential nomination with Goodluck Sánchez. Their deadlock had produced González Tamayo. Casasnovas ran the Senate well.

I came to consider the President of the Chamber of Deputies (Speaker of the House), José Rafael Molina Ureña, the best man washed up on the Dominican beach by the Bosch tidal wave. Molina Ureña was forty-two but looked younger. He came from San Francisco de Macorís, born to poor *campesino* parents. He was slender and not very tall, with big sad eyes and a gentle manner. He was reserved, a little shy. He had worked his way through the University and its law school. He had joined the clandestine 14th of June in Trujillo's time, had visited Venezuela and the Volman school in Costa Rica, and had joined the PRD in 1961. He had risen rapidly in the PRD and been active in organizing the *campesinos*. Ineffective at the outset in handling the Constitution, as he grew in experience Molina Ureña became increasingly impressive, for he was intelligent, sensible, serious, interested in ideas, educated. Of all the men in the Bosch government, including Bosch himself, Molina Ureña embodied, I thought, the very best of that wholehearted dedication to the ideals of democracy and peaceful revolution and betterment of the masses which all the PRD professed but many did not fight for.

In the party itself, though not in public office, was another like him—José Francisco Peña Gómez. Black, young, buoyant, dedicated, and determined, he was a worker and *campesino* leader, one of the few who had been trained at the Costa Rica political institute and risen from the masses by sheer latent strength. Later on Bosch dedicated his book to Peña Gómez "and in him to the youth of the country, seed of hope in the Dominican earth."

10

In the early weeks it was plain to anybody that Bosch's administration had not got off the ground. What surprised me was that Bosch himself had done nothing dramatic. There was none of the lightning of revolutionary change flashing around the Palace as it had flashed around the White House in 1933. Where were the bold new programs everyone had been led to expect? In the Palace, he served ice water and fruit juice, not champagne. Was this revolution? Where were the jobs? Where was the land for the people? The food, the houses, the medicine, the money? Privately Bosch complained that U.S. journalists wanted him to denounce Castro and praise the *Alianza,* but the *Alianza* was too slow, and Betancourt had got in trouble by provoking Castro/Communists. I agreed we didn't need anti-Castro statements from him. What we did need was democratic action. Drama, change, new life. Who were the revolutionaries? Bordas, the adventurer? Worried Jaar? Old Goodluck Sánchez? Why was the presidential anteroom full of bums and crooks, not revolutionaries? Even Bonnelly had gone into Parque Independencia afoot with the people against Rodríguez Echavarría's tanks. And what did we now behold? What but plots, jealous place-seeking among hangers-on, and a sordid struggle inside the PRD.

True, the people were quiet, the left no longer rioting. Peace reigned. Businessmen were uneasy and afraid, the military slept with one eye open, as they said; but there was none of the tension of a year ago, when, day to day, it was not certain that either right or left might not bring down the government.

But the atmosphere inside the government was wrong. The whole-souled dedication was missing. The fervor.

Whom did you see? Young men, teens, early twenties, with machine guns and frozen faces. Stupid soldiers. Confused young PRDistas—one told Fandino that one could not yet judge Castro objectively, and all Latin America must thank him for freeing Latin America from the *Yanquí* imperialism.

And more—these men of the revolutionary government were too young to have suffered at Trujillo's hands, or, if older, had been in exile. While Bosch was safe in exile, Imbert was out on the highway with a .45, killing Trujillo, and Fernández Caminero was in Trujillo's prison, and Pichardo carried a suicide pellet.

I knew this was not fair. I knew we must forget the past. But just which was the revolutionary government? Last year's? Or Bosch's?

While everyone else was nervous because they thought Bosch was moving too far left, I was worried because he was not moving at all. And we were not helping him. And it was in truth hard to help someone who didn't ask for help.

Was he up to the task? I didn't know. You never know what kind of a President a man will make until he becomes President.

He was losing his momentum and had better regain it quickly—and not necessarily in a conciliatory way. He had simply better move and give the impression that something was happening.

He did.

When Bosch had returned from his trip abroad he had said he had received offers of financial assistance in Europe of two hundred million dollars, far more than he had received in the United States. At the time, few people had taken him seriously. Now suddenly on March 14 he announced that he had borrowed 150 million dollars from a European consortium to build the Tavera Dam on the Río Yaque del Norte, a power plant at Puerto Plata, a waterworks at the capital, and another dam. This deal became known as the British Overseas contract. When we scrutinized it closely, we discovered it was not really a 150-million-dollar loan but merely a 150-million-dollar line of credit—an agreement in principle that made available to Bosch 150 million dollars for mutually agreed projects. Bosch was firmly obligated to use only fifteen million dollars in the next two years, and he told me privately he expected to use only seventy million dollars in his entire four-year term. The interest rate would be high—the rate current on the London money market at the time he actually borrowed the money.

The deal eroded Bosch's political position seriously. It increased the rapidly spreading suspicion among Dominicans that Bosch was turning his back on the United States and the Alliance for Progress. Juan Isidro Jimenes Grullón and other politicians attacked it immediately, hinting at graft. It astounded businessmen, who thought Bosch had saddled the Republic with a debt it never could repay. It revived memories of the foolish high-interest European loans of the last century which in the end had led to the U. S. Marine occupation.

Bosch told me he had turned to Europe because AID was slow and because its funds were dollars which must be spent in the United States, whereas what he needed was pesos here and now. He said it without rancor, assuring me he understood our balance of payments problem. He may also have felt he had to do something spectacular fast and have wanted to show his independence of the U.S.

I didn't blame him, but the deal worried me. I was afraid in the end it might lead him to disaster. To help him repay his high-interest loan we might have to come in with virtually no-interest loans which would not help us economically and might not save him politically. I again asked that the cumbersome AID restrictions be waived. But they were not.

The official United States position was that we welcomed European aid in Latin America, though in this instance we were somewhat concerned about the interest rate and repayment schedule. But at the same time the Overseas deal meant that the generators and everything else needed for the dams would be bought in Europe—sales which should have been ours. So our rigid policy had hurt us—and hurt Bosch.

In the British Overseas deal, the individual contracts on projects were what would really matter. Although outward appearances indicated that

Bosch was plunging ahead under the contract, he actually was proceeding cautiously. He arranged to have the individual contracts scrutinized by a highly reputable and skillful Washington attorney, Lloyd Cutler. Cutler represented, among others, the Edgar Kaiser interests. Bosch, no fool, quietly set Kaiser Engineering up as a sort of watchdog over the contracts.

At about this time I received a cable from Secretary Rusk informing me that, in view of the changeover from the Consejo to the Bosch administration, I would be replaced. The telegram was cordial and expressed President Kennedy's gratitude for my service.

I had mixed feelings about it. I did not want to leave—I still felt, as I do today, an abiding affection for the Dominican people. I did not want to leave when the task of building a democratic society was really only beginning. On the other hand, I knew that from a purely selfish point of view I should leave now and I also knew the difficulties ahead. Moreover, this job was never finished. When you have written a book or magazine piece and made it as good as you know how, you can publish it and say, "There, that's done." If I stayed here as Ambassador ten years or a hundred I still could not leave with that satisfaction.

I cabled my resignation. But soon Secretary Rusk rescinded his decision and asked me to stay. I do not know the whole story of what happened. Later I was told that Bosch, while in Washington after his election, had indicated he would prefer another Ambassador, since he felt I had been too close to the Consejo, but later had changed his mind and sent messages asking that I stay. But other influences must have been at work in Washington. I never discussed it with anybody in the White House or the Department, nor of course with Bosch. Government is not only cruel; it is also mysterious, and few people in it, even at high levels, know all the facts about what decides their fate. It is a strange world to inhabit. Nor do those who think they are making the decisions, not excluding the President of the United States, always know how the decisions finally get made, for even presidential directives get lost in the labyrinthine corridors, the files and out-boxes and in-boxes. In a sense, government is the perfect reflection of life itself, vast, sometimes fumbling, often capricious, sometimes benign, more often malevolent, always and finally as inscrutable as creation.

Chapter Sixteen

THE LITTLE CLINIC OF HIGÜEY

In the *barrio* at San Juan, in the dust of Vicente Noble, in other slums and other towns, I had seen people living so wretchedly that it made me ashamed to be a human being. Who was helping them? No one. Not Bosch, not me, not the *Alianza,* no one. The local politicians treated them the way a Congressman from Chicago's slums treated his constituents—resisted slum-clearance, which would destroy his grip on them. Moscoso of the Alliance came down for the inaugural, had his picture taken ploughing the agrarian reform rice fields near Bonao—our own Potemkin Village—then flew back to Washington. I had my picture taken in a tobacco field near San Juan, then went away. Bosch pored over the budget. A CBS crew made a documentary about the showcase of democracy. Dignitaries came and went, inspecting, dictating reports. The people stayed, stayed the same, filthy, hungry, wretched. Who could help, who cared? No one, Castro and Khrushchev perhaps least of all. It was all Madison Avenue press agentry and politics, cold war and policy—nothing more.

Frustrated by the AID bureaucracy, disappointed by Bosch's beginning, I wanted to go over the head of governments, his and mine, directly to the people; to get out of the capital; to get something done, somehow.

Often, driving past the huts in the mountains and the deserts in the interior, I had thought that four things could change these people's lives—water, electricity, medical care, and education.

Water in the Southwest could transform the desert. Now with the Yaque del Norte gone to the Overseas consortium, the United States must develop the Yaque del Sur. I sent cables and dispatches saying so. But that was a long-term project.

Cheap electricity could lighten the burdens and brighten the lives of the people in the huts everywhere. It might even slow down the astounding birth rate—when the sun went down there was nothing to do but go to bed, whereas with electricity the *campesinos* could sit up later and read or listen to the radio or television. But rural electrification too was a long-term project.

Medical care, or at least education in health and nutrition, could be done now, in the sacked and empty Partido buildings in every town, in tents if need be.

Education was usually considered a long-term project—building schoolhouses, training teachers. But our AID program was too slow, we could never build schools and train teachers fast enough to fill the Trujillo void and keep up with the exploding population. Why could we not find shortcuts—educate the people by radio and television, use audio-visual aids, do our teaching not in new schoolhouses but almost anywhere? Last fall we had sent sound trucks out to teach the people to vote. Television might have done in hours what it took the clumsy sound trucks weeks to do. Television, I thought, was the answer—television and radio. The Dominican people, repressed for so long by Trujillo, needed to learn so much. And in the long run only education, both vocational and academic, could bring economic development, for the problem was not really an underdeveloped economy, the problem was underdeveloped people. Even political development would ultimately depend upon education. The Dominican people were intelligent, and many of them, suddenly freed, were like sponges, soaking up any knowledge. By TV and radio you could teach them anything—hygiene, nutrition, carpentry, plumbing, auto mechanics, how to vote, build a house, plant crops, raise chickens, care for babies, anything. You could even teach them to read.

Almost everybody in the Republic had access to a radio. Relatively few had access to television—there were only some seventeen thousand sets in the country, most of them in Santo Domingo and Santiago. I had not wanted to get into this during the election campaign, fearing a demagogue might use television to catapult himself to power. But now we could move.

I wanted to put a television set in every town hall or Partido building. The government station could furnish the time. We could help prepare the programs. They would have to be non-political, purely educational. Additionally, someday, inevitably, commercial television would come to the Republic, and we would be prudent to encourage U.S. and Dominican private capital to get a channel. For now, however, educational TV would let us help the people directly as nothing else could.

I had put all this into a dispatch to the Department in October of 1962. Now suddenly I had a chance to revive it—Supreme Court Justice William O. Douglas came to town.

2

Justice Douglas, I suppose, like many liberals from the United States and other countries, was drawn by the magnet of Bosch's reputation, by his matchless opportunity to build a democracy, and by the desire to help. Justice Douglas was one of those rare men whom I had admired for many years from afar and, upon meeting, found even better than I had thought—not only highly intelligent and courageous and dedicated to liberal ideals but also a warm, sensitive, acute, and very funny human being. He had first come down to the Republic right after the inauguration with his friend, Albert Parvin. Douglas was president of the Parvin Foundation.

Now Douglas returned, full of ideas. I had been breathing the dreary fog of the Bosch administration for what seemed years, and talking to Douglas seemed like breathing fresh air. I had not realized how ingrown the Dominican world is, how one's horizons contract if one stays too long.

Douglas, believing we must promote education in democracy after Trujillo, thought perhaps he could start an institute and bring in such speakers as Robert Oppenheimer and Rexford Tugwell and Jaime Benítez, rector of the University of Puerto Rico. (How similar an idea I had abandoned long ago!) He thought he might send promising young members of the Bosch government to Princeton for a few weeks' intensive training in government. The Parvin Foundation had decided to commit its resources to the Dominican Republic this year, and he was open to suggestions.

I told him first about the problems of the Dominican Constitution. The Assembly had now resumed its work, making Bosch's opposition more nervous. Douglas might be able to advise the Constitution drafters, particularly on an independent judiciary and civil liberties. I suggested to Bosch that he ask the Assembly leaders to invite Douglas to assist. He went to work, I believe, that afternoon. (I have the impression that not many of his suggestions were adopted, though I did not inquire closely.)

But I had another scheme—educational television. I thought Douglas' idea of importing eminent lecturers on democracy was too sophisticated here. What we needed was to reach the people directly and simply by television. He was enthusiastic. Similar programs had been tried in at least two other Latin American countries. Douglas might be able to get American television set manufacturers to contribute the sets. He would see LeRoy Collins former governor of Florida and then president of the National Association of Broadcasters, whom I knew. He would talk to

Harry Ashmore, formerly executive editor of the *Arkansas Gazette,* later editor-in-chief of the *Encyclopaedia Britannica* and chairman of the executive committee of the center for the Study of Democratic Institutions. I knew Collins and Ashmore and would write them too. I would try to persuade Bosch to give us time on the government station and permit us to put a television set in every town hall or Partido building.

Bosch gave a lunch for Douglas and government leaders, civilian and military, a bright, sunshiny day, with good toasts (drunk in water). Then Justice Douglas and Fran and Dan and Fred and I headed for the mountains. By car and Jeep, we arrived at Constanza as dark dropped fast over the high valley. We had a drink in the hotel's small, deserted bar, and the bartender whispered to me that the local 14th of June was plotting guerrilla activity, they had been here last week, whispering together, and after they had left he had picked up bits of paper they had scribbled on and found they contained battle plans. Later that night at dinner Justice Douglas and I amused ourselves briefly by whispering conspiratorially and scribbling on scraps of paper and napkins, drawing crude hills, marking X's to designate machine gun nests and minefields, writing instructions in Spanish, Justice Douglas adding a few words in Persian. It was a lighthearted moment. Early next day, we arose before first light and started out at dawn to cross the backbone of the Cordillera Central, highest in the Republic, I driving the Jeep, Douglas sitting beside me, the wind cold, talking little, then descending through clouds the bleak peaks to San José de Ocoa. There we switched to the car for the long hot ride to the capital through Baní, and made plans for the television enterprise, and I told him what a wonderful place this country could be if only we could make things work.

During the ensuing months, he sent people down, Harry Ashmore, television engineers, a writer, others. Sacha Volman helped. They searched endless files for television tapes in Spanish but found none suitable so made their own. They got help from educators in Philadelphia, wrote scripts, found a Dominican teacher, took him to the States, began taping a hundred programs to teach the Dominican people to read and write. Unnumbered snarls occurred, and sometimes I could help unravel them. Once AID provided some money. The Peace Corps helped. Local teachers in the villages would have to be found, workbooks written and printed to be used by people watching the programs. Electricians had to be found to hook up the sets. And how would we service them? It was a formidable enterprise. But by late summer the first tapes began to arrive, and we began pressing to get the television sets. And always we knew what we could do if we succeeded: Transform the Republic, recapture the generation Trujillo had wasted, and give the children of this generation a chance no other here had ever had.

3

During the entire past year, Fran had worked at a baby clinic in the poor Upper Town in the capital. Traveling through the interior with me, she had seen how badly such help was needed there. Though without any previous training, she had thought she might start a clinic in the remote Southwest but Bishop Reilly at San Juan had discouraged her, saying that belief in voodoo was strong there and intimately tied up with medicine. So she had decided to go to the East, also remote, as we knew from our trips to Nisibón and Macao and Higüey. Higüey, the provincial capital, had no functioning public medical facilities—its moribund Public Health office contained a medical cupboard bare except for a bottle of furniture polish. A friend of ours from Chicago, visiting the Republic, gave Fran five hundred dollars to get started. I checked the politics of Higüey and found that the PRD had carried it; an important consideration, since inevitably she would become involved with the Bosch government.

She went to Higüey, called on Bishop Pepén, one of the ablest of the Dominican clergy, called on the newly elected governor, mayor, and city councilmen, called on the local police and military commanders, talked with the doctors and the wives of leading citizens. What she wanted, she told them all, was to help them set up a clinic that they themselves could run. Not an American charity but a Dominican clinic.

The idea had been germinating nearly a year, ever since a doctor in Moca had told us that many babies died of malnutrition, not because food was scarce but because their mothers were ignorant, and had suggested that American women teach Dominican women in small towns basic nutrition and hygiene and let them go into the *campo* and teach less educated mothers there.

Fran picked a site in Higüey where the poor would not hesitate to come—a muddy square behind the market. Two Peace Corps boys poured a fifteen- by twenty-foot slab of concrete. Sacha Volman found a military tent. People in town gave lumber to make tables and chairs. Fran bought, at cost, through a local druggist, gallons of medicine for diarrhea, worms, and colds. The wife of a CARE staff member made illustrated signs, in Spanish and brightly colored, to pin to a bulletin board—"Wash your hands before eating" and "Brush your teeth after eating"—and Fran affixed illustrative soaps and tooth brushes. Five local doctors agreed to donate one afternoon a week of their time apiece. Ten or twelve housewives of Higüey volunteered to do the same. Fran taught them to keep a card index to list each baby length, weight, condition, treatment. Since this was a "well-baby" clinic, it would treat only children with minor ailments. The key was the weight chart—it would weigh babies regularly to see that they were gaining at the proper rate, and give dietary counsel to the mothers of those who weren't.

When the clinic opened, the Papal Nuncio came from the capital to bless the tent. The German Ambassador and his wife came, too— she had a similar project in the *campo* near the capital. The tent was christened "La Pequeña Clinica de Higüey"—the Little Clinic of Higüey. Thirty or forty mothers came the first day. Soon, as word spread through the *campo*, over sixty were coming each day, mothers and often fathers bringing their babies on horseback or carrying them miles afoot, waiting patiently for hours. Medicine ran short, doctors didn't show up, neither did volunteers, and when it rained the clinic flooded. Once the tent blew down. And once, early, it was almost knocked down by an inadvertent near-riot—Fran had planned a mass inoculation against whooping cough, diphtheria, and tetanus; she had been given 350 shots by an American church agency in Santo Domingo but had made the mistake of announcing the inoculation program in advance, using a sound truck in the *campo,* and two thousand mothers with babies showed up—for 350 shots.

Negotiations were endless—with the Bishop, the police, the soldiers, the citizens. Fran persevered. The clinic became a passion of her life. In a sense she found herself there. It was something she, something any American, could do to help. She went to Higüey weekly, or twice a week. She bedeviled CARE, the Peace Corps, Minister of Health Mendoza, the sub-minister of Health, and Bosch's friends and fund-raisers. One night two Cabinet ministers, Jaar and Humbertilio Váldez, went to Higüey with her and squeezed the townspeople for contributions which they banked locally. Other friends of ours in the States made contributions. She set up a tax-exempt foundation in the States.[1] She wrote to drug companies in the States; they donated medicines, sometimes so many medicines they filled the Residence. I teased Fran, told her she was working against us—saving babies' lives, while we were struggling to develop the economy faster than the population grew.

The Higüey clinic expanded—why not build a community center? The old Partido building in Higüey had been sacked by the people after Trujillo's death and now stood empty and gutted. Fran held a town meeting, and nearly the whole town came. Her Spanish has some of the appeal of a TV quiz game. She speaks a kind of audience-participation Spanish—her listeners often conjugate verbs for her, supply missing vocabulary, and interrupt with spontaneous applause when she gets the subjunctive right. That night the people immediately decided they wanted

[1] The foundation still exists and functions. It is called "D. R. Fund for Children's Clinics," and its address is the First National Bank of Highland Park, Illinois; anyone who wishes can send contributions there.

a community center. But what would it do? What, really, was a community center? It would be whatever they wanted, she explained—sewing classes, vocational school, library, recreation center. They made donations on the spot. The street vendors who sell lottery tickets agreed to scrub the Partido building. The carpenter's union offered to rebuild doors and windows. Fran wangled lumber and paint from merchants in Higüey and in the distant capital.

After the meeting, sitting with some teen-agers in the bar, I asked what they thought ought to be in the center. They had no idea. Vocational schools? What were they? A library? Yes. What books? A long pause; then a thin quiet one in a white shirt, with large brown eyes, said, "Books about Trujillo. So we can find out what happened to us."

Carmen Bosch went to Higüey to see the clinic. She wanted to start one in the capital, and did, and disaster ensued: She started it in one of the poorest *barrios* without careful advance preparation, and an unmanageable horde of women descended on it, seeking free flour and powdered milk. They came close to riot, and when the tent's collapse seemed imminent, Fran grabbed the swaying tentpole and shouted, "Hey, don't trample *me* to death—I'm not even a Dominican." The women laughed, trouble stopped, and an old dark-skinned woman came up to her and said, "You have come here to work with us from your white heaven. God bless you."

Driving to and from Higüey, living in the miserable hotel there and in the Peace Corps house, Fran learned, I think, more about ordinary life in the Republic than any of us. Sometimes she would leave the capital at daybreak and stop along the road between Hato Mayor and Seibo to breakfast at a country store, squeezing the juice from two large sweet grapefruit she bought for 2½ cents each, eating a round flat dry biscuit for two cents, drinking black Dominican coffee for a nickel, a total of twelve cents. People in the *campo* eat regular meals only once or twice a week but constantly nibble—a stick of sugar cane, a piece of local white cheese, a cracker, an orange, *salchichón*—Dominican hard sausage; or what the Peace Corps kids called a "grease ball"—a soft round mass of hot fried pork fat, big as a baseball, sold on the streets and served on a square of paper. In the beautiful Spanish colonial church at Seibo she found blue and white tile mosaic, its Moorish origin clear in the Arabic inscriptions translatable by an erudite Peace Corps boy but presumably untranslatable by the good Catholic father—"Allah is the only God, and Mohammed is his prophet."

And sometimes driving back in the evening dusk to reach the capital for an official function, driving through the soft night of the Dominican countryside, she would hear the high thin voices of children calling out as her car passed; not hostile, just childish greetings floating on the night air—*"Civico-o-o,"* or *"tu-tum-pote,"* or *"carrito,"* "little car," or *"cuarenta-uno-cuarenta-uno,"* our license number.

Most of all, Fran learned the difficulties. They were enormous, and they came from every direction—from poor Dominicans who saw her as simply that nice American lady with the big basket of goodies; from provincial officials who thought their cooperation with the Ambassador's wife might advance their political fortunes; from local doctors who were eager to please yet saw both their medical practice and their siesta hour threatened; from some of our own Embassy staff who looked upon this as the foolish pet charity of the Ambassador's wife in which, God save them, they must indulge her. It was hard to make it clear that she was attempting that most difficult venture of all—a cooperative enterprise between North Americans and Dominicans, a sort of *Alianza*-in-miniature, with all its promise and problems.

But she had steadfast allies—in the capital, Ministers Jaar and Humbertilio Váldez, Peace Corps director Andy Hernandez, and the CARE directors; in Higüey, Bishop Pepén and the lone Peace Corps volunteer, Keith Olson, a blond twenty-year-old college boy from Albert Lea, Minnesota, with an ardor for his work, a sunny disposition, and a Boy Scout face. CARE contributed sewing machines for a sewing co-op, gave vocational tools and educational booklets to the Community Center, and loaned a splendid mobile health unit for extension of the clinic's services to the *campo*. Bishop Pepén loaned a parish sewing machine and shared his monthly ration of CARITAS powdered milk with the little clinic.

Among the citizens of Higüey, Fran's hardest task was to make clear the idea of self-help. Dominicans understand well charitable works and governmental largesse. Trujillo taught them. But he did not teach them community projects, in which the citizens themselves participate. Indeed, why should he?—it is, potentially, a revolutionary weapon. Fran also learned quickly that Dominicans are generous but cautious: Leading citizens were eager to contribute money but reluctant to head a committee. They encouraged the establishment of vocational classes in carpentry and plumbing and electrical skills for youths in the Community Center but none volunteered to conduct the classes. They encouraged a radio program to solicit support for the Community Center but none wanted his name used. Privately, almost surreptitiously, many helped—the hardware store owner gave time, materials, his pick-up truck; the local druggist contributed hundreds of dollars' worth of medicines and a hundred dollars in cash; the banker's family gave money and counsel but declined to lend their names. And even the poor—the carpenter worked wholeheartedly yet asked that his name not be used. "Acceptance of responsibility" was the stumbling block. Was it reluctance to become identified with the Yankees? With other Dominicans? Or simply the ancient tribal feeling that restricts responsibility to one's family? Once again we saw not a community, but simply a collection of people.

For weeks Fran worked to train the young women volunteers in the simple routine of keeping a card-index file on each baby. They were attractive, intelligent, voluble, eager, proud of their new white uniforms made by the sewing co-op. But somehow the card-index file languished and so did the educational work. Finally it was clear—the mimeographed instructions in hygiene, written in simple Spanish, the diet lists, the pamphlets on boiling water and killing flies and washing your hands—all were useless, for the attractive white-clad volunteers were as illiterate as their clients. They couldn't keep a card file because they didn't know the alphabet. Fran suggested they come to the capital to observe the clinic's routine there; but they were afraid, it was too far, they would learn as the babies' mothers did, by rote, listening to Fran read and memorizing the instructions.

Fran opposed the dispensation of any antibiotic or other powerful drug except by a Dominican doctor. The girl volunteers should give only cold remedies, anti-parasite medicine, vitamins, powdered milk, and advice. But that was almost impossible to explain: Most Dominicans in the country buy antibiotics complete with syringe at any drugstore without a prescription and administer them to themselves. Once Fran stepped bodily between a baby and a girl volunteer with a needle, then explained to the doctor that he, and only he, was to prescribe and administer shots. Fran explained the responsibility of the U.S. government, the welfare of the child, and the need for qualified personnel. Reluctantly, they complied.

Even in hospitals, few doctors wore masks or surgical gloves, or sterilized needles. Doctors laid down syringes on desks cluttered with overflowing ashtrays. Nurses covered open abdominal incisions with the same sheet used on other patients. During a mass inoculation at the Little Clinic, a doctor injected half a syringe of serum into one baby's arm, then withdrew the needle and plunged it into the arm of the baby next in line. In a deprived country, nothing is wasted. Once Fran took eighty or ninety boxes of antitoxin deep into a jungle and destroyed it—it had expired and was dangerous and she knew no other way to make sure it would not be used.

Among the middle-class volunteers and professional men, the siren song was modernity. Doctors demanded the newest thing out of the test tube in the U.S. laboratories. Everyone wanted to give shots, none was interested in the fundamentals of sanitation. Doctors complained that the tent-clinic was far too modest for Higüey. Higüey needed a hospital, they said, and when Fran pointed out that Higüey had little prospect of getting one and meanwhile, wasn't it better to have a tent-clinic than no clinic at all, they shrugged and continued their learned discourses on modern hospitals. The trouble was that no one wanted to learn first-aid, everybody wanted to be a brain surgeon.

Often in the evenings, after they had closed up the tent and locked the baby scale and bottles of medicines in cabinets, Fran and the Peace Corps boy, Keith Olson, would go to his little house to review the day's progress, make plans for tomorrow, split a bottle of cold Dominican beer, play records on the music box, and open the doors and windows so that the town kids could hear the music. The living room and porch were always filled with passersby, kids and adults, some stopping just to pass the time, others to seek help—mothers with feverish babies, mothers with starving, dull-eyed babies, boys who wanted to organize a Boy Scout troop, a man with a cut hand, a man badly hurt. Fran squeezed orange juice in the kitchen for hungry babies with arms and legs like toothpicks; Keith supplied Band-Aids or, if an accident was serious, ran up the street to the doctor. All who came watched the films they projected over and over on the whitewashed wall, using a machine Fran had wangled from Bell & Howell in Chicago—Walt Disney's educational color cartoons, an *Alianza* low-cost housing project in Colombia, Mrs. Kennedy's tour of the White House, films on irrigation, a United Nations kindergarten in New York. It made no difference, these people watched them all, absorbed, starved in mind as well as in body.

Somebody was pilfering medicines from the tent, despite its police guard. One night Keith happened to return to the tent after locking up and found the pilferer at work—the policeman on guard. Next day Fran called on the captain at the local police headquarters and, without mentioning the offending officer, asked sweetly if the guard could keep a "sharper eye" on the Clinic at night. The pilfering stopped.

Fran and Keith wondered whether the volunteers and doctors would ever be able to run the Clinic themselves. They had thought at the outset that the Clinic would become self-sustaining in six months. But their girl volunteers dwindled from ten or twelve to five or six. And of the five original volunteer doctors, one left Higüey to practice in the capital. His partner could give even less time to the Clinic. And others might defect. Should they try to recruit another doctor? One existed, young, ambitious, with a flourishing practice. But everyone suspected he was a leader in the 14th of June and advised against using him. Fran called on him anyway and asked his help. There ensued one of those stonewall dialogues with a half-educated young Dominican leftist. *Non sequiturs* abound, political ignorance is shrouded in slogan, passion smothers ideas. He refused to work at the Clinic—he "didn't believe in it."

Why not?

"Three days later they are the same," meaning, apparently, that giving medicine to sick babies of the poor was hopeless because, back in their palm-thatched huts, their illnesses returned, their condition of life remained unchanged. Fran heartily agreed—this was precisely why this small program of educating mothers was so important, and his role was to teach as well as heal. She said she was not interested in his politics, this was not a political problem but a human one. This was his community, not hers; these were his poor, his uneducated, his suffering people, not hers; she and the Peace Corps and the United States government might all go away but he and Higüey and the *campo* around it, filled with starving men and women and diseased children, would remain —and in the long run, he and the other good people of Higüey would have to do something about it. The little tent-clinic was only a way to help them get started.

He refused. She never saw him again. Many months later, a band of guerrillas went into the hills nearby, and after the fighting ceased, the Army brought down four bodies to the *Fortaleza* in Higüey. Several families refused to identify the bodies as their sons'. One was the family of this young doctor.

4

That spring and summer, Fran and Keith held meeting after meeting, raised funds among the local people, and tried to organize a women's group designed to take over both the Clinic and all the planned activities in the Community Center. One afternoon thirty or forty women gathered to hear Fran's plea for a sewing committee, a library committee, a cooking class committee. They responded with vigor, drew up long lists of committee members, levied a two-dollar tax on each woman present, talked excitedly about their plans, screeched, laughed, giggled, proclaimed loudly the future success of the project, planned an inaugural, and went off in glee, never to meet again.

Fran was told that they had been too numerous and diverse, drawn from disparate economic and social groups. They might work better in smaller, more homogeneous groups. Undaunted, and perhaps unwise, she and Keith Olson held other meetings, some big, some small.

Beneath it all ran a deadly serious thread. This great unfortunate mass of underprivileged people would not hold still forever. Someone, the rich Dominicans, the Yankees, someone, must help alleviate their misery or live with the consequences. And Fran learned something too about anti-Americanism. As the Clinic and Community Center prospered, the Castro/Communists began to attack her. As she left a meeting where she announced a five-hundred-dollar drug contribution from Smith Kline & French, a boy on a bicycle in the little park called her *"Exploitadora."* The MPD newspaper in the capital demanded she be banished from Higüey because she was planning a Community Center in which to expound her imperialistic propaganda. She was amazed, had thought Castro/Communists sought more important targets. A week or so later, she and Keith were sitting one evening in his house, discussing the storage of twenty one-gallon jugs of worm medicine she had brought out from the capital—refrigeration in a town with little electricity was always a problem—when in drifted two young town boys. One was a tall, gangly seventeen-year-old, the other a somewhat undernourished sixteen-year-old. Fran was about to essay a pleasantry when the younger of the two launched a stormy attack on the jugs of worm medicine. How did the Yankees happen to bring them to Higüey? Why didn't the Russians contribute medicines too? Fran answered, pleasantly enough, that she didn't know anything about the Russians' interest in medicine. The boy persisted, haranguing her as though she were somehow accountable for what the Soviets did or did not do. She tried to shut off the argument, said this wasn't Yankee medicine; she had merely brought it here from the Dominican government's Department of Health—*your* government—to be dispensed to Dominican children—*your* children—here in this province —*your* province. After demanding cigarettes, and making another half-witted reference to Soviet largesse in the field of health, the two young men departed. Keith asked Fran if she remembered the attack on her in the MPD paper. She did. He said, "Those are the two boys who wrote it."

5

Fran saw everything—babies with swollen bellies and copper-colored hair and skin shredding off of tiny legs, all signs of malnutrition; babies with acute, contagious, and often fatal diarrhea; babies so tiny that when she unwrapped the scrap of torn bath towel in which they were swaddled she found little sticks of hands and feet that resembled more a bag of chicken bones than a human life; babies with umbilici so distended as to seem to be a third leg growing out of small stomachs swollen with parasites. Almost without exception the children's maladies resulted from faulty nutrition or hygiene. There was little evidence of such contagious childhood diseases as measles and chicken pox. It was disease resulting from the mothers' ignorance, not contagion, not neglect, not lack of concern, but simple ignorance.

Indeed, concern was strong in the mothers, and in the fathers, too. Once Fran weighed a baby that had gained two ounces in the week since it had been there; the mother watched tensely during the weighing and then, in a burst of emotion, snatched up the baby off the scale and smothered Fran in her embrace. Once a beautiful young mother riding sidesaddle on a thin horse, holding her baby in front of her in the grass saddle, brought two grapefruit to the tent in gratitude. The young bartender in the hotel in Higüey, one of the bitter youths who denounced the rich and was widely believed to be heading for Communism, typed lists of medicines available at the Clinic, making carbons for the doctors, then, finished typing, asked Fran if she could set up facilities for teen-agers to combat juvenile delinquency. Once, reporting to a group of lead-ing citizens on contributions, Fran said a Washington cabdriver, hearing of the Clinic from a friend of ours, sent a dollar because of his first-born, "a healthy, perfectly beautiful five-week-old girl." The Dominicans cheered.

As word spread, help came from all directions. A committee from the PRD Juventud, the party's youth group, called on Fran at the Resi-dence, bringing 162 pounds of dry-goods remnants for the sewing co-op and presenting her with an eloquent letter thanking her for dropping a "grain of sand" in a sea of Dominican misery. A Dominican soap sales-man, driving through Higüey, stopped to admire the little tent and left three hundred bars of laundry soap. Secretaries at the Embassy saved whiskey bottles for liquid medicines and cigarette boxes for aspirin, and Embassy wives saved their baby food jars, for women from the *campo* often had not even an empty bottle of their own to carry medicine home in. Fran caught one enterprising little Dominican boy outside the Clinic tent selling empty bottles to mothers; she persuaded him to give away his bottles in exchange for a Polaroid snapshot of himself. Once when a little girl responded well to the vitamins she'd been given at the Clinic, the mother, in rags and carrying the child, too big to be carried but too undernourished to walk, came to Keith's house and offered to buy two chickens at the market to repay Keith and Fran for their help. Fran thanked her but suggested she get a chicken, some green vege-tables, and some oranges in the market and give them regularly to the little girl. Always, in spite of disappointment, it was this responsiveness from the *campesinos* that kept Fran and Keith going.

They had other successes. Bishop Pepén loaned them a registered nurse from the States whom the Church had sent him. Bilingual, she was on a month's vacation from her American hospital job. She started working at the Clinic, extended her stay another month, and soon had a little group of teen-aged girls from Bishop Pepén's parish trained in clinic work. This increased the volunteer staff by five or six, thereby mak-ing it possible for the Clinic to operate in the tent three afternoons a week and on the other two to take the mobile unit out into the *campo*.

Shortly after Bishop Pepén's nurse returned to the States, the Peace Corps director came up with the one thing Keith and Fran had wanted— a newly arrived Peace Corps volunteer who was a U. S. Public Health nurse and who wanted to work in the provinces, Sue Feldman. She was good at her profession but more importantly, she cared about the people, and she understood that you can't just give handouts, you must teach. And so each afternoon, whether in the hot, airless tent in Higüey, or in the big white-and-blue CARE mobile unit, with its stainless steel equipment, parked beside the pounding sea at the hamlet of Boca de Yuma, Sue doled out medicine to kill parasites, and explained tirelessly about the germs in the dirt on the floor of the palm hut and the germs in the polluted water from the river, explained that the baby would continue to be sick, would have these same parasites next week if the mother didn't wash everything the baby touched and didn't boil the water she used to cook and wash and drink.

6

Superstition surrounded every area of health; in child care it flowered fully. Mothers tied narrow strips of ribbon, soaked in camphor, tightly around the baby's upper arm to ward off illness and there the ribbon stayed for months, dirty, frayed, tightening as the child's arm grew. In childbirth in a palm-thatched hut, a neighbor assisted, buckling a leather belt tight around the mother's waist during labor and pulling it gradually, inch by inch, downward over the abdomen to the knees, slowly and painfully forcing the baby downward until it was finally born, then cut the baby's umbilicus and heaped on the open cord a mound of fresh cow manure to promote healing. Nearly all the babies wore voodoo charms— an animal's polished tooth on a string around the neck to ensure proper teeth, two halves of a dried fruit seed on a chain around the neck to ward off chest infections. If a child had a respiratory illness the mother sought out a man who was a stranger to the baby's father, and if that man would breathe in the baby's mouth it would cure him. In the afternoon, Fran would watch the miracle drugs dispensed from the gleaming mobile unit at Boca de Yuma, but at night there she could hear the voodoo drums only a few yards away.

Despite all difficulties, during the first eight months of 1963 the little Clinic treated more than six thousand children. Some might otherwise have died; who knew what one might become? Moreover, Fran felt in the end that the community was well on the way toward supporting the Clinic. Perhaps most important of all, these people had gotten a taste of what they could do for themselves. And this seed took root, though the Clinic itself was swept away by other events.

When the mobile unit wasn't in use, the Dominican driver saw no reason not to take it anywhere it could go, including to the beach with his wife on Sunday afternoons. Because he was industrious and willing and kind, Fran did not reprimand him. But she had to when one day he loaded two goats into it. She told him it was a magnificent and costly piece of professional equipment, and he was abusing it. Oh, he hadn't meant to, he said quickly. And furthermore, she said, it was irreplaceable, there was no other in the entire Republic. Yes, he said eagerly, and it was too bad, why didn't she write to the United States and ask for four or five more units to help the poor people in the *campo?* That wasn't the point, she said; this was the only one and they must take care of it. And that meant he must stop going to the beach in it and stop transporting goats in it. Only when she threatened to fire him did he promise to desist. But he really couldn't see why anything big enough to carry goats in shouldn't be used to carry goats in.

Once Fran saw an elaborate Red Cross ambulance picking up passengers on the highway, used as a *público,* jammed with Dominicans and fighting cocks and produce. The tape recorder Mrs. Lyndon Johnson had given to the School for the Blind lay in disuse after the Peace Corps volunteer who knew how to run it was reassigned. The four "isolettes"— expensive incubators for premature babies which CARE had contributed to the Maternity Hospital in Santo Domingo—fell into disuse because three of the four nurses we trained to use them quit to take better jobs, and the fourth refused to "accept the responsibility" of running the isolettes. So the premature babies went back to the cardboard boxes lined with flannel in which they died.

All this disturbed Fran greatly. She said over and over, "We don't need money down here, we don't need equipment down here, what we need is people. People to teach. We can't just give handouts, we've got to teach." She was convinced these people wanted to learn. They were not lazy, they were industrious; they were not lethargic, they were responsive; they were not stupid, they were intelligent. "They can learn anything. But there's no one to teach them." A priest in Higüey told her no one had volunteered to teach young men plumbing, even though the Community Center would provide the place and CARE the equipment, because in that provincial capital of twelve thousand people there was not one man who knew how to be a plumber himself, let alone how to teach anyone else to be.

This was our problem, in Higüey, everywhere. The tent Clinic was a pathetically small drop in an enormous bucket. The plan for educational television was a far bigger one. So was AID's. Could we, in the Dominican Republic or in any other of the emerging nations, move fast enough? Could we recover the wasted years, the lost generations, the wasted people, in time?

Chapter Seventeen

THE CRUISE OF THE *MELLA*

Bosch was still bogged down. Nothing immediate could result from the British Overseas deal. And the pressures against him were rising. Luís Amiama Tió called me to his house, the first I had heard from him since Bosch took office less than a month ago. Imbert was there too. They were blunt. Imbert, as usual, spoke first. The situation of the Republic was "very dangerous." "Everybody is afraid."

Who, I asked?

"Everybody," Amiama said. "All the businessmen, everybody."

Why?

Because of the rise of Communist influence. Bosch himself was not a Communist. But he was "playing with the Communists." He had offered the ministry of Education to "Corpito" Pérez Cabral.

Why was Bosch playing with the Communists?

Amiama said, "Because he has no balls." The Communists were more organized and intelligent than the democratic forces. "We simply cannot permit it. Here we are, stupidly sitting around, watching him win their battles for them. Everyone knows it. If he gives them six months more, a year, four years, it will be all over."

Imbert said, "Do you think, with the agrarian reform program going very slowly, and with the very slow creation of jobs and the means of production, because of the slow investment of capital, because Bosch has not defined his position on communism—do you think this will stop communism?" The Consejo had stopped the 14th of June radio broadcasts. Why didn't Bosch? Dato Pagán was running a school for Communists in a public school building. Why did Bosch permit it? Pagán's partner, "Corpito" Pérez Cabral, was now "the Number One Communist" in the Republic. Where was he getting his money?

I told them that Bosch was not in our opinion a Communist, that he believed the way to defeat communism was to make a peaceful revolution, that he disliked violence and wanted to avoid bloody conflict in the streets like that in Caracas. I said that everybody was demanding that he "define himself" on communism but that already he had done so when he had said in a speech that communism meant death, war, and destruction.

Amiama said, "I'd prefer he said nothing and deported Dato Pagán."

Imbert said the government was infiltrated with Communists. I asked for names. He mentioned—they all did—Domínguez Guerra.

I asked what they thought should be done.

Imbert said, his voice rising, "They should declare war on communism. Kill them if necessary, put them on planes, get them out of here. We should make an anti-Communist revolution. All the world eyes are on Santo Domingo."

And Amiama, "You either fight the Communists or sympathize with them. There is no third way."

And Imbert, "Everybody is ready to fight. It is a great opportunity. Now there is a united front. The ASD, the PNRD, the UCN, the Social Democrats of Read Vittini—" a splinter off the Social Christian party "—everybody. They will publish a document tomorrow. They will unify in opposition against the totalitarian forces of the left and right."

It was their old dream—a coalition of small political parties. And it might be their old game—using "soft-on-communism" as a pretext to seize power.

Imbert hitched his gun around and sat up straight on the sofa. "The Department of State should know that Bosch did not win because the people thought he would be the best man. It was really an anti-UCN vote."

I said Bosch won because the people thought he would give them a better life.

Imbert paid no heed. "People are saying the United States is indifferent."

I said, "They're wrong—indifferent is the last thing we are. Who says we're indifferent?"

Amiama said, "Marino Auffant," a well-to-do merchant and business leader, "was here and he said it. All the people who really count think it."

We talked on awhile. I kept looking at the motto framed on the wall along with the photographs of men who had helped kill Trujillo: "Blessed are those who kill, if it is a bloody monster who is drowned, and a people who is saved."

2

In a day or two the new united front did publish its manifesto, signed by UCN and the parties of Juan Isidro Jimenes Grullón, "General"

Ramírez, and Mario Read Vittini. We were not impressed. Bosch had beaten these parties, most of their leaders were largely discredited.

We were more impressed by a line of unemployed that began showing up every morning at the Palace gates. And with a report from Ben Ruyle, our consul in Santiago, that a big meeting of the unemployed had been held there. The speakers had attacked Bosch and the United States violently. Ruyle did not know who had organized it.

Several U.S. businessmen who had come down seeking investment possibilities had run into the Bosch influence peddlers, felt they had been misled, and were going home. Fandino spent a day with several young PRDistas and found them defensive about communism and dissatisfied with the way things were going.

Even optimistic Newell Williams of AID was beginning to worry. He had heard that Bonilla Atiles, Foreign Minister under the Consejo, was lobbying in Washington against Bosch. Williams said, "We feel a stiffening toward the Dominican Republic in Washington."

I asked for examples.

He could not get thirty thousand tons of wheat under PL-480, the Food For Peace law. He had been turned down again on the twenty-two million dollars. He said, "Ever since Bosch has been in, we've been turned down. The fact is, we're just no longer the fair-haired boys up there." This was highly disturbing. If Washington was really cooling off on Bosch, he had no chance.

I kept hearing that people in AID and MAAG were talking at cocktail parties about the danger of communism in the Republic. This was most serious. At the weekly country team meeting I told all our mission chiefs that while I didn't like to clamp down on free expression, such talk tended to undermine confidence in Bosch and therefore ran counter to our basic policy, and that they were responsible for seeing to it that the people under them were discreet.

I was using any tie I could to build bridges to Bosch. I suppose any Ambassador uses whatever assets he possesses. I had been a writer, so had Bosch, and he wanted to get his work published in the United States. I got him a New York literary agent, my own, Harold Ober Associates, and Shlaudeman translated a short story, "The Indelible Spot," and the agent sold it to *The Saturday Evening Post*. It was a fantasy, describing how the protagonist had gone, on instructions, into a chamber where an unseen voice commanded him to take off his head and put it on the shelf "as all the others have," how he had escaped and run to a cafe, how there two men had watched him closely, how, nervous, he had spilled his coffee on his shirt, how now he could not remove the stain nor get another shirt, and wondered whether the two men had been members or enemies of "the Party."

3

Bosch went back to the people: He spoke to them weekly on radio and television.

During the campaign, his speeches had been extremely skillful and carefully thought out. But now they were long and rambling and usually extemporaneous. He would read off long lists of companies and private individuals who had "donated" land to the agrarian reform. Nothing could be more boring, but he ploughed through it with great seriousness. (Humbertilio Váldez, his old arm-twisting fund-raiser, was persuading people to "donate" land.) Frequently Bosch's speeches contained sentences that further alarmed the propertied class, sentences that seemed capricious—an offhand declaration that sugar cane burning must stop since all cane, including that privately owned, belonged to the people. He reeled off long strings of figures—his eternal budget. Often half of his speech was a pedantic lecture on economics, usually ending with an attack on the Consejo—still campaigning, "the agitator in power."

But his speeches set no hearts aflame, proclaimed no revolution. They were simply pedestrian monologues. On TV he looked worn out. He always referred to himself in the royal "we." Yet, he made it known that he preferred to be called "Citizen President." I wondered to how many minds the phrase recalled the tumbrils in the streets of Paris during the Terror.

He did make several conciliatory gestures—invited leading businessmen to a series of breakfasts in the Palace, made a conciliatory speech to the American Chamber of Commerce. Perhaps more significant, when, as instructed, after President Kennedy's agreement in Costa Rica with Central American chiefs of state to reduce travel to and from Cuba, I asked Bosch if he wanted additional U.S. training and other assistance to improve coastal and border patrols, he said immediately, "Yes. We're interested in little Coast Guard patrol boats, at least a dozen, and as soon as possible. Some amphibious planes, perhaps three. And some helicopters." I cabled his requests.

This move, made throughout the Hemisphere, was a part of our general policy of tightening the noose on Castro. I thought it particularly interesting that Bosch, accused of being soft on communism. had so readily accepted our offer of help. He had said emphatically, "We want to avoid having Dominicans going to Cuba." It was too bad he did not say it publicly. But he didn't—he did not want to provoke the local Castro/ Communists.

More often Bosch seemed unreasonable. One day he sent word in a roundabout way that he wanted to come to my house urgently that night. I waited. About 10 P.M. he telephoned Shlaudeman, and said he wanted instead to see me at 8 A.M. tomorrow at his house—he had discovered a dangerous plot against him.

The plot, he said, was a vast conspiracy involving not only the Social Christians and Imbert but also the Venezuelans, the Communists, some military chaplains, a Miami newspaper, pro-Imbert elements of the Dominican Navy, Ramón Castillo, Bonilla Aybar, and the Papal Nuncio. He was sending Volman to Puerto Rico to ask Muñoz Marín if he would accept "six or seven people" as deportees—Imbert, Belisario Peguero, García Vásquez, and others.

Moreover, Bosch said, a man in the U. S. Embassy was in close contact with Guido d'Alessandro and Alfonso Moreno, the Social Christian leaders, and had said that in four months Moreno would be in the Palace, put there with U.S. support. The Embassy officer was, in short, arranging a coup against Bosch.

Astonished, I said, "Mr. President, I can't believe it. We support you. You know that. No Embassy officer said this. I would bet anything on it. What's his name?"

Bosch said he didn't know, but understood he was not a high-ranking officer.

I said I wouldn't ask who had given him this false information but I urged him strongly to go back to that person, obtain the name of the Embassy officer, and inform me, so that I could investigate.

Then I returned to the plot. I suggested that instead of deporting Imbert and others, he simply fire Belisario Peguero. He said he couldn't— Imbert was on the police general staff. I suggested he pass a law abolishing the police general staff. He said it would precipitate a crisis. I said fine, let it come now, anyone opposing him would be in open rebellion against his government, and we would support his government. He shook his head, and said Imbert would assassinate him. In any case, he said, the decision had already been taken.

I didn't think he'd deport Imbert. I thought he was simply trying to use his almost pathological fear of Imbert in order to explain away his government's failure to get started. But next day the consulate reported to King that it had received a note from the Foreign Office, enclosing a new diplomatic passport for Imbert—but not signed by Imbert—and asking for a U.S. visa.

King said we could stall awhile. I suspected Imbert didn't know anything about it. But I couldn't ask him—I might precipitate a *coup* against Bosch. We waited. A week later Imbert called Fandino and demanded to know why we hadn't given him a visa—"Do you think I'm a Communist?" He said he simply wanted to make a trip to Puerto Rico. We gave him the visa. I still do not understand this—Imbert never left the Republic.

4

Andy Freites, returned from Washington and taking up his duties as Foreign Minister, came to see me one Sunday morning to ask about our policy on Haiti: "Is it ripe? Are you ready? Who is your candidate?"

I said, "Ripe for what?" He said he did not mean ripe for invasion by the Dominicans but perhaps for "harassment"—troop movements on the border, air overflights, ejecting the Haitian consul. President Duvalier of Haiti had declared the Dominican *chargé d'affaires* in Port-au-Prince *persona non grata.*

The CIA chief had told me the day before that Bosch was talking about Haiti. The new Bosch fantasy, we had decided. We'd been wrong.

I told Freites what I had told Bonilla Atiles the previous year—that while we shared some of the Dominicans' feelings toward the Duvalier regime at that time, we maintained cool and correct relations with it and recommended that the Dominicans do likewise, since they had their hands full here. Freites, however, went on to talk about various Haitian exiles who, as everybody in the Caribbean knew, aspired to overthrow Duvalier—Rigaud, Fignole, Dejoie, and several others. I knew none of them personally, and, for that matter, don't know them to this day.

I turned the conversation to Bosch. Freites said the people close to Bosch who disturbed the *civicos* would be gone in six months. By then, too, he hoped Bosch would feel strong enough to face the inevitable confrontation with the Communists. Freites himself had been appointed to "calm people down"—he had been Esso's representative here for years, was related to Imbert, had ties to Donny Reid, Bonnelly, and the oligarchy. Freites feared that if all "the good people" deserted Bosch, they would drive him into the arms of the left. We would try to devise means of bringing Bosch and his enemies together.

I told Freites that any overt Dominican act against Duvalier would lead to Haitian complaint to the OAS and might rally the Haitian people around Duvalier against the ancient Dominican enemy.

Apparently Ambassador Thurston in Port-au-Prince got wind of the Dominican plans; he sent a cable saying that Dominican incursions would be unwise. At the same time, we heard that Betancourt of Venezuela seemed to be encouraging Bosch to help the Haitian exiles. Colonel Cass made a weekend trip to Haiti and was stopped at the border when trying to return. Shlaudeman went there too and reported that Duvalier's position, usually represented abroad as shaky, was actually strong, and if he survived May 15, the day when we and others claimed his term would expire, he probably would emerge stronger than ever. If Duvalier did start to slide, there was always the nightmare that he might make a deal with Castro.

5

Suddenly the former editor, Bonilla Aybar publicly attacked Sacha Volman virulently. Bonilla Aybar, a onetime gossip columnist, probably had the biggest radio-TV audience in the Republic. He had a strident rabble-rouser's voice, he excited his listeners, and he dealt in scandal, sensational exposés, and inflammatory political polemics. Attacking Volman, he also said that the U. S. Embassy was putting pressure on Miolán to get rid of the leftist Washington de Peña.

By chance I ran into Bonilla Aybar that night at Vesuvio's, where Fran and I had gone for dinner alone. Black-haired and mustached, he looked something like Horacio Julio Ornes, except heavier. The year before we had sent him to the United States on a cultural exchange grant, since he had been one of the few promising Dominican journalists left after Trujillo. Standing at Vesuvio's tonight under the stars, I told him that he was one of the most influential journalists in the Republic, that as a former journalist myself I admired his ability to attract so large an audience, and I reminded him that such power entailed heavy responsibility. I said his story about the Embassy and Washington de Peña, as a matter of simple fact, wasn't true.[1] I didn't attach any great significance to the incident but would be grateful if in the future he would check anything involving the Embassy with Vallimarescu, or with me directly, to make sure it was true. He offered to retract what he had said, but I thought this would simply emphasize it. I suggested we have lunch some day. He'd be delighted. But we never got around to it. I made a mistake in not cultivating him more, for later on he became extremely important.

6

A rumor flew through the city that six ships were loading arms and ammunition and a thousand troops, Venezuelan, Colombian, and Dominican, to invade Cuba; Colombia had put its entire navy to sea and was sending B-26s aloft; Venezuela was ready to do the same. I sent the attachés scurrying around. Nothing.

But Argentina was in crisis. And in Guatemala the Ydígoras government fell. *U.S. News & World Report* said that the military in Latin America was curbing leftists, and Honduras and the Dominican Republic might be next. Anti-Bosch Dominicans cheered. I went, on instructions, to ascertain Bosch's attitude toward the new Guatemalan government. I found him relaxed and talkative. Ydígoras had been overthrown by

[1] Washington de Peña did soon resign as Secretary-General of the PRD, purged by Miolán; we had nothing to do with it.

the military because Juan José Arévalo, the former Guatemalan President who was strongly anti-American, had returned to the country briefly. Bosch saw only one danger in the present Guatemalan situation. If the new regime were to kill Arévalo, it would make him a martyred, almost mythological hero to the *campesinos*.

Bosch began talking about his financial problems, "very bad." Still he did not ask me directly for help, so I did not offer. He brought up a paragraph in the *Wall Street Journal* saying that business confidence in the Republic was waning. I agreed it was unfortunate but feared it was true. Frowning, he changed the subject. He had appointed a new man to run Haina and another to run the Electricidad. He gave me a legal document which appeared to be a copy of one filed in a Miami court and asked me to check on what he suspected was a complicated Air Force gun-running plot involving General Luna.

Bosch said he would get agrarian reform moving in fifteen days. He needed new taxes to run the government—taxes on rum, sugar, and income. I suggested he tax gambling, imported liquor, and cigarettes heavily.

He said that yesterday the MPD and PSP had encouraged squatters to move onto public lands in the Northwest. He was also worried about the demonstration of the unemployed in the Cibao. I suggested he begin public works immediately. He said one of the Overseas projects would start this month.

Bosch went on to talk about Haiti. He said that Duvalier had appointed a *chargé d'affaires* in Santo Domingo for the express purpose of arranging to have Bosch assassinated even before he was inaugurated. In January a foreign diplomat in Port-au-Prince had warned the Dominican government. The Consejo had not granted credentials to the *chargé*-to-be, and so he had not come. When Bosch took power, he found the file. It showed that the *chargé*-to-be once had been Haitian consul in Camagüey, Cuba, and also had once been a SIM agent for Trujillo in Cuba.

Now Haiti had again asked the Dominican Foreign Office for credentials for him. Bosch had refused credentials and ordered a further investigation. He had discovered that a former sub-chief of police under Trujillo and intimate of Petán Trujillo, the dictator's dangerous brother, was now in Port-au-Prince as a leader of the Ton Ton Macoute. Bosch said, "So I have laid on strong diplomatic measures to see if Duvalier reacts. If he does, we will move troops to the frontier and make overflights. To tell the Haitian military that we are anti-Duvalier. It might produce a reaction in his military." Bosch also had smuggled a Dominican girl into Haiti, appointed a new *chargé* there, and soon would send three military men in civilian clothes to the Dominican embassy in Port-au-Prince, disguised as chauffeurs, cooks, gardeners. He had instructed his *chargé* there to ask other diplomats to help protect Dominican exiles who lived there. If Duvalier reacted, Bosch would start a violent radio campaign against him and would publicly receive anti-Duvalier Haitian exiles in the Palace. "By the 15th of May there will be trouble, violence. We want to give hope to the Haitian people, to show them we don't like Duvalier. Short, of course, of crossing the frontier ourselves or plotting inside Haiti or showing partiality to any Haitian exiles."

I thought I had best speak out. I told him what I had told Freites.

Bosch dismissed the OAS impatiently—he did not like Gonzalo Facio, the Costa Rican President of the OAS Council. I said I thought he could not disregard the OAS, however he felt. I added that I was deeply shocked at Duvalier's attempt to assassinate Bosch. (At the time, I was somewhat skeptical. But later we were able to confirm it—Bosch was entirely right.)

Bosch appeared to agree with me, said he wanted no trouble. But he went on to ask me about the Haitian military. I told him they had no guns; Duvalier had virtually destroyed the regular army, given real military power to his private army, and kept all the guns and ammunition in the basement of his Palace and in the Dessalines Barracks.

This shook Bosch badly; he had thought the Haitian army powerful and had hoped to split it off from Duvalier. He asked about a battalion he had heard was near Cap Haitien. I said there was none. He said several Dominican high commanders wanted him to move against Duvalier. "The Haitians want me for their President." He was leaning back in his rocker, in his shirt-sleeves, one arm thrown up over his head. "Many Haitians want me for their President. I have great sympathy for the Haitian people. My two brothers were born there."

I told him we too had a deep sympathy for the Haitian people but we did not believe that the way to help them was to incite them to rebel against Duvalier, for rebellion could only result in slaughter.

Leaving him late that night, I thought I had detected more than a hint that Bosch actually aspired to rule the entire island. I wondered also if he was toying with the idea of a foreign adventure to bail himself out of his difficulties at home. As always, throughout the interview he had become most animated and confident when discussing Caribbean politics, Haitian, Guatemalan, anything but the hard and real Dominican problems he must face every day. I have always wondered if his principal interest did not lie so much in the Dominican Republic as in the Caribbean.

We had heard that Bosch's teen-age son, in school in the United States, had injured his knee and might need an operation. Without saying anything to Bosch, I had asked the Department to try to get the boy into Bethesda or Walter Reed Hospital. It was difficult, but the Secretary of the Army approved it. I went back to Bosch's house and arrived just as Carmen Bosch finished talking to the boy by telephone. He had arranged an operation on his own, and they were frightened, and she looked terribly troubled. I told them what I had done. They were very grateful. (On the way home, Fandino said, "We'd better pray for that one—if the operation turns out badly, we're in trouble." Politically, I suppose it was indeed risky. But it had seemed the human thing to do. The operation turned out well.)

7

Bosch said that an officer in my Embassy was spreading rumors against him. I asked who the Embassy officer was. Bosch could not remember the name, thought it was "Hungarian" or thought the man had a Hungarian wife, and thought the name began with a K. We had nobody of Hungarian descent on the staff, so far as I could recall, but Vallimarescu, the USIS chief, was from Rumania—was it he? No, Bosch said—the name began with a K, he was positive of that. And he thought he held high rank. K—I could think of no one except King. I told Bosch so. That must be it, Bosch said—King.

I told him forcefully that King was my second-in-command, was an excellent foreign service officer, completely loyal to our policy of supporting Bosch, experienced and discreet. Besides, King had no wife, Hungarian or otherwise—he was a bachelor. In fact, this whole tale was so ridiculous, I said, that it confirmed my suspicion that someone close to Bosch was deliberately trying to make trouble between him and me, and therefore between his country and mine. I urged him to find out who it was. I also proposed bringing King around to talk to Bosch (and later did).

Bosch apparently had no real conception of how serious this charge was—he went blithely on to discuss other things. That disturbed me more than anything else, the assumption, so widespread in the Republic, that everyone is perfidious, personal honor absent. As I have said, Trujillo left a shattered nation and a shattered people. Such a charge, so dangerous both to an individual and to policy, was incapable of refutation—here was no Bill of Rights, guaranteeing the accused the right to face his accusers. Try as we would, we never found out for sure who was poisoning Bosch against us.

Bosch described more plots against him, plots involving the CIA, Cuban exiles in Miami, and a State Department officer there, and asked me to check. I said, without enthusiasm, I would. Privately, I thought he ought to get on with his work. (Checkups proved his suspicions groundless.)

I asked how the agrarian reform was going. Great, he said—the Grenada

Company had just donated fifty-three thousand *tareas* of land and a tractor; and pulling out a list of more "donations," he began reading it to me. This had a revivifying effect on him, though a soporific one on me.

Finished, he said he would welcome a visit by Dick Goodwin, formerly in the White House, then at the Peace Corps. He said he had appointed a splendid young man as liaison man with the Peace Corps and he was out in the country now, "organizing the committees." I didn't know why we needed committees out there—the Peace Corps needed the young men in the Palace to nudge the Ministers.

Bosch went on. What a pity it was that the rich Dominican heritage of folklore had been lost. He intended to use Radio Caribe and Radio Santo Domingo to revive it. He said, "The Dominican people have forgotten how to be amused. They only know how to drink, dance, and play pool. I want to educate the people." Bosch himself once had told me that every great leader needs a mystique—Castro's, for example, was that of the bearded guerrilla fighter. Now I suddenly realized that Bosch had conceived his own role as the Great Teacher. He might have been happy and perhaps successful had he been able to play that role.

He said he had learned that Radio Santo Domingo was giving a half hour's time nightly to the 14th of June, owing to a UCN program director; Bosch had ordered it stopped. Bosch said he had put the Director of Sports into the office of the Presidency because the Olympic Committee, with three hundred thousand dollars to spend, had been in the hands of the 14th of June, which hoped to use it to gain control of the Republic's youth. I applauded both moves. (Soon the 14th of June publicly denounced the "anti-popular" and "reactionary" position of the government, blaming it on a plot by unnamed "superreactionaries." It did not attack Bosch himself. This was the first sign of a break between them.)

Bosch had another idea. He would put an open air movie in the poorest *barrios,* send an entertainment film and an educational film to each. Could we help? I would ask USIS.

8

At the end of March, Bosch counterattacked his enemies.

He publicly ridiculed accusations that he was a Communist. He said they originated with Cuban exiles who were angry because he wouldn't get rid of Castro for them. If the United States with all its power couldn't get rid of Castro, why should anyone think he could? It was a carefully prepared and skillful statement—too clever. The people who were saying he was a Communist were not Cubans; they were Dominicans.

In a radio speech on March 28 Bosch abandoned his usual subjects and took up the criticisms being leveled against him, replying to them one by one. He took action defying his critics—rammed through controversial sections of the Constitution on *latifundio,* on agrarian reform, on marriage. He publicly congratulated the United States-trained counter-guerrilla troops on their showing during maneuvers. He went to Santiago and promised that land distribution would begin in mid-April. When he returned, Jaar denied a rumor that someone had tried to assassinate him.

El Caribe published an ad announcing the curriculum and list of "professors" at Dato Pagán's night school, and among the "professors" were "Corpito" Pérez Cabral, Alfredo Manzano, José Estrella Jacobo, and Dato Pagán himself, all considered Castro/Communists. They would hold classes "temporarily" nights in a state-owned secondary school building. Tuition would be ten dollars per semester, plus ten dollars a month per course for a maximum of forty students. Registration would take place on March 30.

On the last day of March, Máximo López Molina and another MPD leader returned to Santo Domingo from Paris, and several hundred people, according to *El Caribe,* went to the airport to meet them, crying *"Patria o Muerte"* and *"Fuera los yanquís."*

The newly formed rightist ADI published ads listing the names of men who were joining it. The political pot was boiling.

And now the right renewed its attack on Sacha Volman. The broadcaster Bonilla Aybar said that "Pepe" Figueres had accused Volman of absconding with funds in Costa Rica—actually, their differences had been personal—and demanded he be expelled from the Dominican Republic. The PRD issued a communiqué defending him. On April 4 Bonilla Aybar demanded over and over in strident voice Volman's deportation. Next night, at 8:15 P.M. on April 5, a Friday—why did everything happen on Friday?—King and Shlaudeman came to the Residence, both excited, and quickly turned on the television set in my study. Station Rahintel was showing a program which seemed to be live, the cameras kept tilting as though being jostled, dozens of people seemed to be milling around, a camera would focus for a minute on Alfonso Moreno of the Social Christians shouting into the microphones, then would abruptly shift to Viriato Fiallo, then to another politician, then to another, then to a man with what seemed to be blood dripping down his shirtfront, then to policemen. It looked as though a riot were going on in the studio. I asked what had happened.

I had missed one of the greatest live television programs of all time. Bonilla Aybar, in the midst of delivering his nightly diatribe, had been arrested by the heavy arm of General Belisario Peguero, on camera, and hauled off to jail. The police had stopped a riot, and at least two people had been shot.

Shlaudeman and Vallimarescu began checking fast.

It appeared that during the afternoon Bonilla Aybar had telephoned Germán Ornes, publisher of *El Caribe,* from hiding in a friend's house and said the police had surrounded his own house. He had slipped out of his hideout and into the TV studio and, on his regular 7 P.M. news broadcast, had declared that "they" were after him and that he had asked political leaders and students and labor leaders to come to the studio to help him defend freedom. He had appealed on TV to the diplomatic corps to protect him from persecution, had begun putting anti-Bosch politicians on TV in behalf of free speech. During all this, a crowd of people had gone to the street in front of the studio, first several leftists with two submachine guns and five sidearms, then several *civicos.* Secret police cars had arrived, then the police, and a scuffle had begun, rapidly turning into a riot, and Horacio Álvarez, a businessman, had been shot in the arm and his son shot in the shoulder. Meanwhile, inside the studio, Bonilla Aybar was hammering away, until suddenly the large arm and then the large back of Belisario Peguero had come on the screen, blotting out Bonilla, and when arm and back were gone, so was Bonilla. A moment later the studio was full of politicians, denouncing the police and Bosch, and a man who soon became Bonilla's lawyer, Bienvenido Mejía y Mejía, screamed into the microphone, "Antonio, we need you, only you can save us, otherwise the people will have to take up arms." Antonio was Tony Imbert: Mejía y Mejía said he had been with Imbert when the Bonilla show began and had gone to the studio to help "save freedom."

At 9:10 P.M. the police announced on television that Bonilla was merely being held in protective custody. We had sent a young political officer out; he reported all quiet at the studio and at Bonilla's house but said the crowd had moved to police headquarters. Sure enough—we went out the front door of the Residence and saw, across the street, scores of automobiles in front of the Police Palace, and extra policemen all around.

Our police adviser, Jackson, came in at ten and said the police had taken Bonilla before a prosecutor and announced he was being held in protective custody pending investigation. The police said it had been "Pupito" Sánchez' men who had done the shooting; Ramón Tapia was telling a crowd at the hospital that the secret police of a Bosch hanger-on had done it.

At ten-twenty Vallimarescu, who had gone out scouting, called. Bonilla had been charged with "malversation of funds," the authorities claiming they had discovered financial irregularities at *La Nación,* which he had edited last year. Now he was in La Victoria Prison. He denied the charge.

At 11 P.M. John Perkey, our faithful commercial attaché, called. The wife of an AID man said that the wife of a defeated politician said that the *golpe* was on tonight.

I called King, who had by then gone home, and told him to send Cass and Long out quickly. Cass got to the Residence at eleven-fifteen, and said the city was flooded with rumors. Earlier Williams had called him from the Hotel Embajador—people there were saying that troops were "storming the Palace." Cass had checked at the Palace; nothing was going on. He had driven past Imbert's house; it had been quiet. But now, Cass said, half a dozen carloads of men had arrived at Imbert's house, Cass didn't know who they were, and at the hotel, Dominicans and Americans alike were excitedly denouncing Bosch and telephoning their friends all over town.

Shlaudeman came in five minutes later with the same report. He called Germán Ornes. Ornes said Bosch was furious, convinced that Ornes was conspiring with Bonilla Aybar to overthrow him.

Minister of Police and Interior Domínguez Guerra went on television and declared the men who had done the shooting were agents of "Pupito" Sánchez, sent to take Bonilla into protective custody.

The attachés reported that the military leaders, homes and headquarters were quiet. By midnight, everybody had left even Imbert's house. Fritz Long had followed one car from near General Rivera Cuesta's house to Bosch's house. He had the license number. I sent everybody home, waited up awhile to see if Bosch would call, then went to bed.

9

It had been a wild night. And the consequences made Bonilla Aybar a national figure, much more than a mere commentator and gossip columnist—a rallying point for the rightist forces opposed to Bosch. Freedom of the press gave them an issue. The whole outlandish episode was one of those totally unexpected events, those sudden shattering flashes of lightning in a nighttime sky.

At the time, it seemed only another of those worrisome, foolish incidents that plagued us. But it triggered a series of other events.

Horacio Álvarez, the wounded man, was president of the Association of Industries. King told me Sunday morning that the Association had met, condemned repressive methods, asked Bosch to punish those responsible, and expressed concern at organizations of armed civilians. Ministers Domínguez Guerra and Diego Bordas had appeared before the Association and expressed rather stiff regrets, then called on the wounded Álvarez. He told them if they didn't take steps against the man who shot him, he would.

The PRD counterattacked Miolán said that a conspiracy against the government could not be permitted, that the government had been heavily criticized ever since the elections, and that while possibly the police had made "small errors," the government intended to continue to "apply the law." In an effort to "prove" Bonilla Aybar's "malversation" of funds, Domínguez Guerra on television displayed a check for 150 dollars from the Reid and Pellerano Company made out to *La Nación* and declared Bonilla had spent it himself. Reid was Donny Reid; a member of the Pellerano family was associated with him in his auto business. (The family was backing the newly reopened newspaper, *Listin Diario.*) Reid and Pellerano replied that the canceled check had been stolen from their files by a man who said he was a tax inspector. The association of Dominican newspapermen called on Bosch to protest violent interference with freedom of speech and press. I went to see Bosch that Sunday night.

He was inclined to make light of the whole affair. He said they had the evidence against Bonilla Aybar. Then he went on to describe a new plot, or, rather, to add more about an old one—he had received information that a friend of General Luna was in Miami buying airplane and gun parts in the name of the Dominican Air Force but that they really would end up in Cuba. He said that absolutely no one in the Republic but I must know of this. He did not dare ask Dominicans to investigate, but wanted me to do it. (We did investigate, using several agencies of the U.S. government, and in the end decided that what was going on had nothing to do with arms—that, rather, certain Dominicans were buying such household appliances as refrigerators and television sets in the United States and flying them into the air base at San Isidro duty free. Rather than Caribbean gun-running, this appeared to be a cheap smuggling ring.

Bosch said that because of the way the Bonilla Aybar affair unfolded, he suspected someone close to him of leaking information. When he added the new "arms plot," I wondered whether he suspected I was the leak—whether in giving me this new plot and insisting so strongly that not a soul in the Republic could know about it, he was testing me. Or had I simply been here too long, was I succumbing to the Dominican conspiracy view of history?

On Monday the Bonilla case started snowballing. The Santiago Association of Businessmen and Industrialists condemned the affair. The newspapermen's association called a meeting for Wednesday. *Caribe* editorially criticized Miolán and the tax inspector who supposedly had filched the Reid and Pellerano check. An association of former political prisoners demanded the government fire all public officials involved in the affair. Imbert told Cass that Bosch was letting the Communists take over the government and that Mejía y Mejía's televised outcry for him proved that "the people are turning to me."

Bonilla Aybar himself was riding high. He received reporters and friends and relatives in La Victoria Prison and said his cell was comfortable and his treatment excellent—the photographs made La Victoria look like a resort.

Horacio Julio Ornes delivered a violent radio-TV speech. He declared that "a crisis of liberty" existed in the Republic and denounced "administrative corruption" in the Bosch government, accused the government of unduly censuring critics and making "an aggression of power" against them, defended Bonilla Aybar against Diego Bordas' and Domínguez Guerra's attacks (though saying he did not necessarily agree with what Bonilla Aybar had said); and, waving documents which he said could be published as proof "if anything happens to me," documents apparently relating to the management of the former Trujillo cement factory, long the subject of controversy over thievery, he charged specifically that Diego Bordas had improperly taken from the government twenty thousand dollars he recently had donated to agrarian reform. This was the first public attack on the Bosch administration by Horacio Julio Ornes.

Diego Bordas resigned as Minister of Commerce and Industry in order to sue Horacio Julio Ornes and his brother's newspaper, El Caribe, for libel. A little later Bordas and Horacio Julio Ornes met in a fashionable restaurant and one challenged the other to a duel. Shlaudeman picked up an "inside" rumor—Bordas was to leave the government, sue El Caribe, bankrupt Ornes, get the newspaper cheap, and re-enter the government more powerful than ever.

On Tuesday we heard that Alfredo Manzano, the Castro/Communist, would be appointed manager of the cement plant and that Marcio Mejía Ricart, the intelligent young leftist often deported last year, would get a job in the Palace. Vice President González Tamayo publicly denied rumors he would resign. Jimenes Grullón again attacked the Bosch government. So did UCN. El Mundo of San Juan, Puerto Rico, expressed hope Bosch would be able to stop "in time" the regrettable course events were taking.

Shlaudeman said the rightist opposition parties were determined to bring Bosch down now. They thought if they kept the pressure on, he would flee the country. It wouldn't work if Bosch stood firm—and if we did.

Things began to look serious at 3 P.M. that Tuesday. The military was getting involved. Cass said that Commodore Rib had come to him to ask what the U.S. attitude was toward the Bosch government. Cass had given him our regular line: We support Bosch. Rib had said, "That's not what I meant. What is your attitude?" Cass had said the same thing. Rib had said, "But what do you think?" Cass had told him he had some "personal questions" about some things but had reminded him Bosch had been in office only a little more than a month. Rib had said he was very worried because Bosch was appointing people to important jobs who were considered Communists. He asked if Cass would check a list of government employees whom the military considered Communists, since our intelligence service was better than theirs. (I told Cass that Rib and others like him were really acting rather foolishly, were saying, in effect, "We don't like all these Communists in government. Tell me, who *are* these Communists in government?" But I told him to accept any list Rib offered.) Then Rib had said that the opposition party leaders wanted the military to overthrow the government. Rib thought they only wanted the military to do their dirty work. Cass was certain he had received a direct approach from politicians. Cass was sure Rib had discussed the matter previously with General Viñas. Fritz Long had had a similar conversation with Colonel Rivera Cuesta at breakfast.

Luís Manuel Baquero was leaving the UCN. He was "fed up"— Fiallo had sold out to the conservatives, who thought that if they could bring down Bosch, Fiallo would become President. Baquero thought they were wrong—if Bosch fell, "a group," or coalition, not one man, would replace him.

Volman came to see me. He was chiefly interested in Al Mayne's planning group and in getting Edgar Kaiser to come down soon. I was more interested in whether we would get through the next few days.

I told Volman that I didn't think it was going well at all, that Bosch was not effective, that we had intended to let him alone until he came to us for help, but how much longer could we let it drift before he got in so much trouble we couldn't get him out?

Volman was encouraged by Bordas' resignation, said Bosch was very worried about unemployment, and needed money from the U.S. Bosch believed that Imbert was behind the Bonilla Aybar mess but felt he had waited too long to get rid of Imbert. For now, Bosch wanted to let things cool down. I said I was for that, but would they? Volman thought so.

I was less confident. Before going to bed that night—it was April 9, just six weeks after Juan Bosch's inauguration—I made the following notes: "Are powerful forces beneath surface. Pop up now and then— Bonilla Aybar and Bordas incidents. Pres. not leading. Forces contending. He slipping. Forces not yet out of control of him, or us. Could get out. Serious trouble ahead. I here for 1 purpose—help him make it work. Hard to help someone who doesn't ask for help. You don't offer unsolicited advice to a Chief of State, esp. a sensitive one."

In retrospect, that seems correct. It was indeed the start of the breakup of the delicately balanced political structure into which Bosch had fit himself. The UCN collapse and consequent rise of the ADI, the pointed inquiries by the military, the conversion of Bonilla Aybar into a national hero, the attacks of Horacio Julio Ornes, his brother's fears about his newspaper, the ugly arm of the police, the deadly aim of the right at Bordas and Sacha Volman and the "foreigners," the restlessness of the people—these forces were now unleashed.

10

Next morning Miolán called early and asked to see me urgently, and when he arrived at the Residence he asked for guns and the U.S. fleet. Short, squat, straight-haired, wearing a dark heavy suit, hitching his gun around to be more comfortable as he sat down but too troubled to apologize to me as usual for wearing it, he said, "We are getting in a corner more. Every day. Imbert has gathered all the opposition. He does not enjoy the support of the people. But the government is not able to put the people to work. So he moves them to seek solutions. Imbert has the police, the key jobs. He also has friends in the Army, with guns. The government needs the Army. But the Army says wait and see. If we do not take energetic action, we will lose." He sipped coffee. "We find the *golpe* will be the 15th," next Sunday, Easter weekend. "Sunday or Monday morning. It could be earlier. I am going to the Palace to see President Bosch in one hour," glancing at his watch. "I am going to ask him for energetic action. To destroy them first. I ask your help urgently. If Bosch fell, it would be very bad for President Kennedy."

I asked what he wanted. He said, "I am going to ask the President for permission to mobilize the PRD and the people to protect the government. We will need help. In two forms. We will need a naval visit by your ships. And we will need enough equipment to give arms to the party. We want to form a commando group of two hundred men with automatic weapons. Such a group could decide." He leaned back in his chair, sipping coffee, waiting.

I said that of course we supported President Bosch and would do anything we could. I asked whether his information on Imbert's Easter *golpe* was trustworthy. He had received it from independent sources in Puerto Rico and La Romana. Was he sure Bosch could not count on the Army? He was. I told him we were keeping close track of Imbert, he had been quiet lately. Miolán disagreed. I said that if Bosch asked me for a ship we probably could bring one in and take him to lunch aboard, making our support visible, but we would not bring the fleet in these circumstances. We could not supply weapons indiscriminately to civilians; anyway, this would only inflame the Armed Forces. But if the President himself asked me for weapons to arm a security force which we helped build, I would recommend it. I asked what, precisely, Miolán planned to say to Bosch. He said he would ask him to declare a state of emergency, dismiss Belisario Peguero, and deport Imbert. Did he think the President would do it? He did not know—but the party was for it. He hurried off to the Palace.

I called the Crisis Crowd to the Residence. Shlaudeman said Miolán came up with a new plot every sixty days. Colonel Wolfe said that only last night General Hungría, the Army chief, had said that every day diminished the chance of a *golpe*. What if Bosch declared martial law, fired Peguero, and deported Imbert? The Army would back him, Wolfe thought. Long said the Army was "concerned" but was being patient. Nobody seemed to think a *golpe* imminent. They left, the CIA chief staying to say that the PRD security police was continuing its work on telephone taps. Its primary targets were Amiama and Imbert and "Pupito" Sánchez. After that, it would start on well-known rightists. It was doing nothing whatsoever about Castro/Communists. And the CIA chief had confirmed that Juan Ducoudray and José Espaillat Rodríguez were living with Minister Domínguez Guerra.

I decided to wait and see what happened—I had an appointment with Bosch anyway at 2 P.M.

He seemed relaxed, at ease. I gave him the results of our checking in Miami, on bank accounts in New York and Puerto Rico, on the Miami smuggling ring. (This was all a rather dirty business and I thought, *Everybody is keeping files on everybody else. Some day the world will be one big filing cabinet.*)

Then I waited, waited to see if Bosch would tell me about Miolán and Imbert's Easter plot. He did not mention it. Instead he asked if I would accompany him tomorrow on an Easter weekend cruise aboard the *Mella*.

I was flabbergasted. Why was he doing this, in the midst of crisis? He gave no clue, except to say casually he might take some military men along.

That night, packing, I decided he intended to throw Miolán's plot into the teeth of the plotters, to use me to consolidate his position with the military, and to let things cool down. Shlaudeman came over. The 14th of June was demanding on the radio that I leave the country within twenty-four hours because I was plotting with the "ultra-reactionaries" to overthrow the government. Shlaudeman said Fiallo thought a *golpe* was coming and wanted to see me.

Next morning at six Fran and Dan and Fred and I met the President and his party at Haina, went aboard the *Mella,* and as we had done before stood by the rail while the ship moved through greasy water past the drydocks and the vast hulking sugar mill, then out into the bright and heaving open sea.

11

We were gone four days. It was a strange trip. The company aboard was predominantly military—Commodore Rib, Colonels Rivera Cuesta and Pagán, and Bosch's Army bodyguard, Colonel Calderón. At

Samaná, Generals Viñas, Luna, and Imbert met us. Our civilian companions were the sad-faced surgeon Jaar, Minister for the Presidency; Bosch's black-haired, explosive niece, Milagros; her fiancé, the arrogant tall young Minister of Public Works, Luís del Rosario; Bosch's male secretary; and a PRD gunman.

Bosch was in fine form. He worked at his desk an hour or two each day; went through the motions of swimming or fishing; and at meals held forth at length to the military. Colonel Pagán and Colonel Rivera Cuesta a few days earlier had declared they intended to catechize him on communism. They never got a chance. Bosch lectured them, bedazzled and overwhelmed them. He talked about ports and tourism, millions of dollars' worth of new hotels and an airport at Samaná, a hotel on Saona Island; about sugar sales and *golpes;* about being aboard this ship "a prisoner of the Army and Police and the United States Ambassador."

Endlessly he talked about communism. He told of a priest who had said, "If Juan Bosch is a Communist, then I am a Communist." He explained Betancourt's "errors" in forcing the Communists to fight, deplored the killings then going on in the streets of Caracas, described his own devious approach, said that Betancourt had succeeded because the military supported him—and the military supported him because it knew if it didn't the people would rise against it.

He spoke at length about honesty in government, denouncing graft under the Consejo, all, I thought, for the military's benefit.

He discoursed on Latin American history. Latin America was closer in traditions to the Orient than to the West, especially to Syria, where a bloody *coup d'état* had just occurred. Like Syria, Latin America lacked the Western traditions of peaceable political change, an apolitical military, civil service, and independent judiciary.

He lectured on the Dominican Republic. It was really two countries, the cities and the rural areas, thirty or forty years apart. I remarked it reminded me of the United States in 1930, before Roosevelt had transformed the nation's farms with rural electrification, TVA, soil conservation, cheap agricultural credit, AAA, and so on. Bosch quickly agreed, and asked if I had seen the photographs taken for the Farm Security Administration in the Museum of Modern Art in New York, and the conversation drifted to photography and art, then to literature. Skillfully he brought it back, saying, "But here there is no art," then, sadly, "No wonder, the people must work, they are hungry," and he launched a description of Dominican society: It possessed a cultural middle class but not an economic middle class, hence the frustration of the alienated intellectual who had no place, hence *chisma,* the political rumor factory; and so back to communism: "I was pretty radical myself in my youth. But I was never anti-American. And you know why?" leaning forward, white eyebrows raised and forehead wrinkled and throat cords taut: "Because I read Mark Twain. I read Sherwood Anderson too, and Sinclair Lewis, and Upton Sinclair, and *The Scarlet Letter,* Dos Passos, Mencken, but especially Mark Twain. I do not see how anybody could be anti-American who read *Huckleberry Finn.*"

Then in a moment he would dart off on another subject—pre-Columbian Indian civilization, Surgeon General Gorgas' conquest of mosquitoes and malaria during the building of the Panama Canal, Dominican folk dancing, a conversation with Betancourt, the history of the Dominican Indian chieftain Enriquillo, various species of fish. And his Cabinet —what an excellent Cabinet it was! He extolled the virtues of each. (But he did not mention Domínguez Guerra.)

He wore corduroy pants, a plaid shirt, loafers. And long underwear. So animated was his face that he looked young. His age showed most in the loose flesh on his throat below the sunburned area, exposed now by his sports shirt as it was not when he wore a necktie. His bright eyes shifted constantly, his gaze flicking rapidly about the table from face to face. He gestured, grimaced, reared back then close to peer at his food, and revealed what seemed to me unusual preferences in food, as for the head of a fish. He made a point of saying at almost every meal, "Without protocol," but nevertheless always insisted I sit on his left and Fran on his right. Sometimes he would discuss literature and writing with me in English and in Spanish, then would interrupt to say loudly to Colonel Calderón, his husky sweaty good-hearted bodyguard far down the long table, "*¡Coronel!* How are you enjoying your trip?" (Great, *Señor Presidente.*)

Always he returned to communism. He said Pérez Cabral was not a Communist, merely anti-American. During World War II Pérez Cabral had been a Nazi, now he was a "Communist," all simply because he was anti-American. Why was he? Because he was raised during the Marine occupation in La Romana, where the occupation was harshest. Dato Pagán, he declared, was originally a PSP member, was expelled as a Trotskyite, now was neither for nor against communism, was simply anti-American.

We considered both Pagán and "Corpito" Pérez Cabral to be Communists, but I did not contradict President Bosch in front of his military (though I did privately).

I once heard how Dato Pagán and Pérez Cabral became Communists. One early Sunday evening in the 1930s, they were strolling around the plaza in San Pedro de Macorís, as everyone did, there being little else to do in those towns in those days and Trujillo's having prohibited more than two or three people to forgather. On that evening, two young strangers fell into step behind Pérez Cabral and Dato Pagán and, while still walking, and without quite joining them, struck up a conversation with them—what did they plan to do that evening, go to the movie? Pérez and Pagán said they had no money. The strangers would pay their way. They accepted. Nothing more happened. The next Sunday Pérez and Pagán were strolling again; the same two young men appeared, again invited them to the movie. Pagán and Pérez declined, embarrassed to accept more hospitality, but the strangers persuaded them. The third Sunday, however, Pérez and Pagán declined firmly; their honor had somehow become involved. So the young men invited them to a house to talk. Pagán and Pérez were afraid—such meetings were prohibited—but, curious, went. The strangers talked about books, literature, poetry, things Pagán and Pérez were interested in. That was all. The next Sunday the same thing, and the next. Presently they were discussing Marxism. It interested young Pagán and Pérez greatly. They never had had an opportunity to learn about it under Trujillo. The strangers even had a few books on the subject, unheard of in the Republic. The strangers were Spaniards, Communists, refugees from the Spanish Civil War. So communism came to the Dominican Republic. It is a nice romantic story with a legendary quality, though it probably isn't true.

Bosch's was a dazzling performance, and it lasted throughout the trip, all intellectual fireworks, designed, I thought, to overwhelm the military and show them how close he was to me. Rib looked noncommittal and a little nervous; this was, after all, President Bosch's first voyage, and, as naval chief, Rib hoped it would go well. Colonel Rivera Cuesta looked sleepy. Colonel Pagán became a sycophant, currying favor. Imbert sat silent and glowering, sometimes visibly angry. Jaar, who almost always seemed wholly dedicated to Bosch, sat silent. Only young Minister del Rosario talked. He even occasionally overtalked Bosch, which Bosch did not like. Del Rosario was highly opinionated though frequently mistaken. His fiancée, Milagros, a slender but full-figured girl of twenty-six who wore tight dresses, as do so many Dominican girls, seemed by turns almost stuporous and almost maniacal. Sometimes Bosch's political stories —how a woman had told him she had borne a child on the day he was elected and named it "Democracia"—seemed to set Milagros off into loud, exuberant gaiety. Sitting at the table she would burst into the PRD song, del Rosario, who had a beautiful voice, joining her. Sometimes Bosch would try to quiet her by saying gently, *"No, mi hija, no, mi hija,"* "No, my daughter, no, my daughter." One evening while we were drinking coffee after dinner she suddenly leaped upon a chair, made a long, impassioned, and almost unintelligible speech at the top of her voice, leaped onto the dining table, twirled, then leaped across it to the piano and began to play wildly, singing at the top of her voice. The piano was out of tune.

We anchored at lovely Saona Island, darkened with memories of torture, and went near shore in a sporty launch the *Mella* carried, then transferred at the coral reef to wooden rowboats, and when the rowboat bearing Bosch and Calderón touched bottom an old man fully clad waded out and carried Bosch ashore piggyback. I declined similar assistance. A handful of children, naked from the waist down, greeted us on shore, as always, and as Bosch walked slowly through the palm grove beside the row of tin-roofed houses, a crowd gathered, scores of people pressing on him, asking him for jobs, and he stopped and made a speech to them, lecturing an insistent one, severe as a schoolmaster is severe, explaining that he could promise nothing, he never made promises— perhaps for my benefit—it would not be fair to give him alone a job when so many needed jobs, but there was land enough in the Republic for all, and all would share. Then, raising his voice, Bosch spoke to the crowd, repeating what he had said, promising to send a commission to investigate the water supply on Saona, since now fresh water had to be brought here by boat, to investigate the land, the fishing, the farming, everything that might enrich Saona. He was very good, whistlestopping. He shook hands, embraced anyone who offered, smiled often, asked people precise questions about prices, crops, wages, his gaze darting quickly over the crowd, spotting someone he knew, embracing him wholeheartedly; and, speaking, he stood erect, even leaned back a little, speaking very directly and simply, almost pedagogical. He was friendly and expert. Yet somehow I felt something missing. Warmth, genuine warmth, perhaps? A reserve, something within not freely shared or given? I always felt it. Bonnelly had moved through crowds with far more dignity and far heavier bodyguards yet somehow had managed to convey more warmth; and though his speeches in the clubs, with a band and drinks, had said nothing at all, mere foolish hymns to the beauty of the local ladies and the warmth of the sunny reception, he had drawn a better crowd response than Bosch.

Walking, Bosch told me he had campaigned here, and he remembered the vote precisely: He had beaten UCN 89 to 53, as I recall. He paused at a store to ask sharp and knowledgeable questions of the owner, to stoop and pat a small child's head, to smile into the face of an infant in its mother's arms; and, saying farewell, made a point of saying again that, just as he had during the campaign, he would make no promises. I was now sure it was for my benefit, and the military's.

Back aboard, he lectured us all on this, and said one man had shown him a PRD card, hoping it would get him a job, but it wouldn't—no favoritism, absolutely no favoritism. He looked very stern.

One morning anchored in the Bay of Samaná we went swimming at 7 A.M.—"bathing," Bosch called it, not inaccurately: He would wade into the water waist deep, dip under quickly, then straighten and stand, arms folded tight across chest, looking cold, gazing at the mountains and sky and sea and remarking upon their beauty. Once in a while he would splash a bit, or wade about. I do not believe I ever saw him swim. Most of the time he stood, and sometimes he talked to his companions there in the sea about affairs of state. His skin was very white. He always "bathed" early in the morning or late in the afternoon, when the sun was low.

We went ashore at a village, and a crowd met us on the rotting wharf, and we walked with them to shore, Bosch dressed in swimming trunks and a bathrobe and slippers. I had not known we were coming ashore and was wearing nothing but swimming trunks, scuffling through the hot and dirty dust barefoot in the crowd, my feet trampled by barefoot townsmen and booted bodyguards, and under a coconut tree Bosch spoke to the crowd. His subject was economics and austerity and U.S. aid, and he developed it this way: The United States was sending men to study their problems, perhaps to loan them a burro or a horse or whatever they might need. The country's money problems were serious. Becoming President was like coming home to your little house and finding it had been robbed, somebody had broken in and taken all the food, and the chairs and tables and stove as well, and so you had to start all over. And so on—it was a model of whistlestop economics to a first-grade audience. "Democracy in shirt-sleeves," he told me. After it, we drank coconut juice in the shade, walked around the rusted marble works, and went back to the wharf, Bosch working the crowd like any politician, telling me the while by how many votes he had beaten Fiallo here. Yet not wholly professional either: He also said, "You see? To them, I am not the President, I am Juan Bosch," and he told again the story about the newborn baby named Democracia. As we shoved off, the crowd on the wharf began singing the PRD song, and Bosch, standing in the boat, sang, too. He did not know all the words.

Back aboard the *Mella*, we had breakfast at eleven, and moved up the bay to anchor off the lovely high-perched town of Samaná. A flotilla of small boats hovered round, a half-dozen motorboats, a half-dozen native rowboats, some with sails, and a high white fishing boat with a flying bridge owned by the Navy which had followed us from the capital. Bosch could joke about being a *tu-tum-pote* himself, with that beautiful fishing boat at his disposal, but the huge cost of the boat, bought, I was told, by the Trujillos seemed to disturb him. How different this cruise was from last year's with the Consejo. The Consejeros had taken their surroundings for granted. This crowd did not. Some were curious as children, examining the ship's rich fittings; some sneered. This crowd did not drink, either, except for wine with meals.

We went whistlestopping in Samaná, walking up and down streets, Bosch shaking hands, going into the house of the new governor, meeting a Peace Corps boy who was working on a fishing co-op. Then we climbed into a motorcade and roared off through the coconut groves to Sánchez and on to Nagua. Bosch made a point of having Imbert and me ride with him. But once inside the car we lost him. For sizable crowds stood along the route, at intersections, in front of houses, by the side of the road, and they waved, and Bosch waved back, putting not merely his arm and shoulder but his head out the window, calling to them, *"Adios compañero"* and *"adios mis hijos,"* "Hello my children," and at times like that he was gone, you could not get through to him at all, he was totally absorbed. It could not be dismissed as mere vanity. Buffeted in the maelstrom of capital politics, beset and besieged on every hand, frustrated, plotted against, threatened, now here he had come back to the people, the people who had elected him and given him his power, and, seeing them, he felt he drew power from them once more, a power denied him by his enemies in the capital; he might be castrated in the capital but out here he was a man, almost a white-haired god.

In Sánchez he spoke to a big crowd from the porch of a house, drinking a Coke, speaking of his love for the people and for Sánchez, promising to send a dredge to deepen the harbor (it was hopelessly silted in, and Imbert said to me sourly, "The Navy dredge will only make it five feet deep"). Entering Nagua, Bosch was met by a crowd of PRDistas on bicycles, all blowing their horns, and he called out the window to them to desist, explaining to me Trujillo's local men always had done this. He made the same speech in Nagua—the government was poor, he would help all alike. The crowd filled half the plaza—burning sun, dust, heat, bodies packed tight in the dusty street, the reserved professor under the shade of a tree lecturing his children. No bands, no music, only Bosch. Afterward, we walked around the town and, as always, the house he chose to enter was not on the best side of town, nor a government building: It was a modest house in a rather poor section, and the people crowded in, and when the bodyguards moved to stop them Bosch said to let them come on, and received them in a dirt patio, while I stood off to one side with Jaar, watching.

Driving back to the ship, Bosch saw a *público* pulled up on the wrong side of the road to let a passenger off and ordered his own driver to stop, and, as the whole motorcade came to a screeching halt, Bosch leaned out the window and lectured the *público* driver on safe driving: It was dangerous to park on the wrong side of a narrow road.

Throughout the whistlestop tour, the people called him "Juan Bo," as though it were one word, spelled "Hwanbo." But, to his embarrassment, one called him *"Jefe,"* and an old woman embracing him called him "Bonnelly." Nobody, I think, called him *"Presidente."* He kept telling Imbert and me, "To them I am not the President, I am Juan Bosch." It was true.

We ran into a huge crowd at Sánchez and Bosch plunged into it, embracing everyone, his bodyguards hopelessly engulfed with him, and I thought how easy it would be to assassinate him. On the edge of the crowd, while Bosch embraced, Imbert was peeling ten-dollar bills off a roll and handing them out to people. Then we got into the speedboat and raced back to the *Mella,* spray flying, palms and pink and white buildings and thatched roofs on the hills sinking back, white clouds and blue sky overhead, Rib standing solid and mustached and gun-belted at the stern between Bosch and Imbert, both looking grim, Bosch's eyes squinting and almost closed and mouth turned down, Imbert's jaw set.

Aboard, Bosch talked about his crowds. Pagán said eagerly how impressed he had been. The others said little. Imbert said nothing at all. They had seen crowds before. In the Dominican Republic, the people are not against the government. *Any* government. They cheer it. *Any* government. In Nagua, while he was speaking, I had moved around the edges of the crowd, listening, talking to people. And what I remember most was a man who said, when I asked how things were going, nodding toward Bosch, "We are waiting."

12

There was no question about it: He was an expert campaigner. Yet I sensed a jarring note. Was it an almost feral wariness? It infected his every thought and move. And other things bothered me—his inattention to the welcoming bouquet of flowers, his puritanism, his pedagogy, his paternalistic *"mis hijos"*—once he even blessed a woman. Did these things bother others?

Homeward bound, the talk aboard turned serious. Bosch said the Haitian Army had attempted a *coup* against Duvalier this morning. It had been smashed. The Haitian Army had no arms. If Duvalier fell, the *ton-ton-macoute* would vanish. Chaos would follow. A Communist government might emerge. There were more Communists in Haiti than here. He had confidential information that Haiti was Castro's next target. There were many plots afoot to give arms to Haitian exiles. He was being very cautious. I said Duvalier looked stronger now than two months ago. Bosch did not answer. He returned to the subject of communism in the Dominican Republic.

This, clearly, had been the main purpose of his voyage. And now he had Imbert here too. He said that since his own election the 14th of June had declined in strength until now it was nothing. Manolo Tavárez

Justo was speaking to audiences of thirty or sixty. The 14th was a *"grupito,"* a little group. All the 14th had gone into the PRD. I did not agree—the 14th of June was actually growing stronger—but again I did not say so at the table.

Imbert took me aside, said he didn't agree with what the President had said, and said he wanted to talk to him alone. I encouraged him to.

Later Imbert told me, "I told him he should trust me, should use good men, should change the Cabinet. I suggested he make Marino Auffant the Minister of Commerce and Industry, in place of Bordas. I said I wanted nothing except respect, confidence, and to help my country. I said what the hell I want to be President for. I said I have a position. I killed Trujillo. I gave Bosch his chance."

"What did he say?"

"He said he knew this, he appreciate it, he said I should stay where I am so if there is trouble I can stop it. This is what he wants me to do. To help the country."

I asked how he felt about all this. Imbert seemed depressed. He said, "I don' know, I don' see clear. He don' talk about communism, all this freedom for Manolo, and this Domínguez Guerra, what a hell, and Bordas and López Molina."

I said, "I know how you feel, Tony. I think he's wrong about the 14th of June. And other things. But everybody says he's got to 'define his position' on communism. What the hell good is that? What he does is what counts, not what he says. He's a good politician. He thinks that right now it's best not to attack the Communists or praise the *Alianza.* That's all right with me—provided he goes ahead with programs to help the people. I wouldn't push him right now on communism."

Looking downcast, leaning against the rail in the half dark, the sea black below, Imbert grudgingly agreed. But he added, "He won't get investment that way."

I said I knew it but that wasn't his main problem right now. His main problem was to get some programs moving, put people to work— Imbert's own favorite phrase the year before.

Jaar took me aside. He was worried. Things did not look bad on the surface but underneath it was not going well at all. I agreed completely, Bosch had been elected to make a revolution. Why didn't he at least put some people to work?

Jaar threw up his hands. "That's what I keep telling him. You know what he says? 'Not one cent. We have not one cent.'"

I said I thought Bosch wrong—this was a time to spend money, not save it. I didn't think Bosch's financial position was as bad as he said and if he didn't move within the next three months he would be in serious trouble, for he was losing the people.

Jaar said, "I don't think he's got three months. I think he's got three weeks," and he told me of the thousands of people who were asking him, Jaar, for jobs, of the squatters who had moved onto the land in the northwest, of the demonstration of the unemployed.

I said, "What is he going to do about it?"

Jaar said Bosch would like to borrow money from the United States.

I said Bosch had never told me that—and, in fact, complained that the United States was too slow so he had turned to Europe.

Jaar said, "He needs you and he knows it, but he is too proud."

I said I was here to help him but he had not come to me, and until he did I hardly saw how I could force our money on him—and I didn't know whether I could get the money anyway.

"He wants to talk to you, I know. I will arrange it," and he went off.

I sat alone on the afterdeck, watching the sea slide past. Bosch, I knew, was in his little office amidships. I waited. Presently Bosch came out, saw me alone, walked round the afterdeck once, said he had finished his work, and sat down near me.

I asked if he'd got much work done. He said yes but there was always more than he could do, it was terrible, and we talked awhile about how restful the sea was, then I said I had been doing some thinking and talking to my people at the Embassy and had wondered what Bosch considered his priorities.

Instantly he told me. For immediate impact he wanted agrarian reform, small agricultural credits, a health program, farm-to-market roads, and a hundred waterworks for villages. Housing would have to wait, the port at Puerto Plata was long-range, he could do no more in electrification in his four-year term than the two dams and thermal plant envisaged under the Overseas deal. For political reasons he needed three things fast—agricultural credits and agrarian reform for the *campesinos,* farm-to-market roads to employ the restless masses in Santiago, and street repair to employ the restless masses in Santo Domingo.

How much time did he think he had?

Three months at most, he said. And then Bosch said, "The cry I hear in the *barrios* is, first, jobs, and second, the high prices of food." Price rises, especially in rice, had hit the poor hard. Bosch said, "For the *campesinos,* land and credit. But I do not have the money."

I asked how much money he needed. He did some calculations, program by program. He did not say so, but it added up to this: If he could get a ten-million-dollar advance against the twenty-two million dollars in sugar money, he would be all right, and even five million dollars would help. But he did not ask directly.

I listened sympathetically, then told him I could promise nothing but I would do my best. He thanked me. It was the first time he had turned to us.

13

Home, the attachés said that if the purpose of the *Mella* trip had been to reassure the military leaders, it had failed. They were as suspicious as ever.

López Molina of MPD held a public meeting in Santiago. He publicly supported Bosch's PRD. But the 14th of June attacked Bosch and me jointly, me for running the country, Bosch for not pushing agrarian reform. Increasingly the *civicos* blamed us for foisting Bosch upon the Republic, while the Castro/Communists increasingly attacked us as imperialists.

If Bosch ever became truly isolated from all but the masses he would be in danger, and if he then lost them he would fall—and things were drifting in that direction. Moreover, he had tended to isolate himself in the Hemisphere from the United States, the OAS, and the *Alianza*.

We were heavily committed to Bosch, and if we seemed to hedge that commitment we would bring him down fast. I thought we must support him firmly and at the same time try to drive wedges between him and the left. To do it, I needed standby authority to give him ten million of the twenty-two million dollars on short notice, or, if that was impossible, then a new loan or grant. And we would also insist that Bosch maintain close control of Castro/Communist activity, and we would step up our own intelligence operation. I wrote a long message for the Department and White House.

Chapter Eighteen

THE "WAR" WITH HAITI

On the evening of April 26—a Friday, of course—I went to President Bosch's house to discuss several matters with him. In the course of the long conversation, he mentioned rather casually that the Dominican Embassy in Port-au-Prince had been "assaulted" by Haitian police that day. He said, "We are waiting for more reports on it. Our military is indignant. Very probably if the word is bad, we will send three or four Dominican airplanes to fly over Haiti. Because if we do not show strength, they may assault all the peoples in asylum." He also said that at 5:30 P.M. today the Haitian *chargé* in Santo Domingo had announced precipitously he was leaving.

I said that I hoped nothing serious would come of the incident, that we were attempting to trace the movements of several members of the Trujillo family reported headed for Haiti, and that I would keep in close touch with him. He gave me a night telephone number, a phone that rang beside his bed.

When I left him a little before 10 P.M., I had the impression that he did not attach much importance to the Haitian incident. Nonetheless, I went back to the office and sent a brief cable on it. Over the weekend the incident mushroomed into a major crisis that set Santo Domingo and Port-au-Prince and Washington to boiling, called the OAS into emergency session, and, before it was finished, threatened war in the Caribbean.

Moreover, the Haitian crisis is of special significance to us. For it became inextricably intertwined with Bosch's fate, and therefore with the fate of Dominican democracy.

2

The Dominican-Haitian problem was, at bottom, quite simple. While Trujillo lived, Duvalier was comfortable. After Trujillo fell, Duvalier became uneasy.

As we have seen, from 1822 to 1844 Haiti occupied the Dominican Republic. Dominicans, high and low, hate, disdain, and fear Haitians. In view of the Dominicans' obviously superior strength, their continuing fear of Haitians is irrational. For that very reason, it is all the stronger—the nameless fear of the unknowable.

Dominicans consider themselves white, Catholic, Spanish. They consider Haitians black, voodooistic, African. Few sizable islands in the world are inhabited by two peoples so disparate. From time to time over the last hundred-odd years, Haitian-Dominican incidents have occurred, and in 1937, as we have seen, Trujillo slaughtered twelve or fifteen thousand Haitians. Clearly, with that background, any dispute between these two governments was potentially dangerous.

Although racial discrimination exists in the Dominican Republic, Dominican society is not nearly so tightly stratified along color lines, so caste-like, as Haiti's. There a tiny minority of mulatto elite, French-speaking, educated in France or the United States, comprises the professional and wealthy class; the masses are black. Bosch, recalling the slave revolt of colonial times, has written it was a "perpetual social struggle—which had its origin in black against white," and it goes on yet. Race is the hinge of Haitian politics. On it, President Duvalier had swung to power.

During Duvalier's corrupt and bloody six-year rule, scores of opponents died or disappeared, and hundreds fled into exile. Duvalier himself was widely believed to practice voodoo. Legends of his cruelty abounded. One said that he had a trap door beneath his desk in the Palace which he could open to observe the torture of prisoners in dungeons below. He rarely left the Palace himself, and when he did he went unannounced and heavily guarded. He was openly anti-American and anti-white. This spring, while tensions rose as the May 15 deadline of his term approached, his henchmen made speeches that revived the ancient chilling slogan of Haiti's slave revolt, "Cut and burn," that is, put the whites to the sword and their homes to the torch, and one warned that if Duvalier were attacked, Haiti would become "a Himalaya of corpses."

In 1962, several Haitian-Dominican incidents had occurred, as we have seen, and the Consejo had somewhat reluctantly accepted our counsel of restraint. But Bosch was different. Bosch was the spearhead of democracy in the Caribbean; Duvalier was the last of its old-fashioned dictators. Bosch meant to set his stamp on Caribbean politics; Duvalier could not let him. Bosch had trouble at home; a foreign adventure was, in one sense, not unwelcome (though Bosch did not start it—Duvalier did). Finally, Bosch could scarcely fail to oppose Duvalier after Duvalier, as Bosch had told me, had in fact sent an agent to have him killed. Crisis was inevitable. It came on that day, April 26, 1963.

The Trujillo family was deeply involved. Foreign Minister Freites had told King on April 12, while I was aboard the *Mella,* that he had firm evidence that Petán Trujillo, the erratic brother of the dictator, and two other Trujillos had obtained Spanish passports and Haitian visas. We had immediately asked our agencies to put them under surveillance.

During that same time, I had heard that Bosch was in contact with several Haitian exiles in the Dominican Republic. He had known them while he himself, as well as they, had been in exile, and they had promised to help each other. Now at least six different Haitian groups had formed in exile, and five underground groups inside Haiti, all anti-Duvalier.

On April 18 Ambassador Thurston reported there was shooting at Duvalier's Palace. The airport was closed, and the *ton-ton-macoute* was cruising Port-au-Prince with rifles. Four 75-millimeter cannon and one tank had been placed at the Palace. This turned out to have been an abortive military *coup* against Duvalier by the Haitian military, quickly crushed.

It was quiet for a week. Then on the morning of April 26, a cable came in from Madrid saying that several Trujillos were ticketed aboard KLM Flight 775, scheduled to leave Madrid at 5:45 A.M. for Curaçao and to go onward to Port-au-Prince, probably via Kingston—Luís Reynoso Mateo, a son of Petán; Teresa Oviedo de Reynoso, probably the wife of Luís; José Rafael Trujillo Lora, son of Virgilio Trujillo; Francisco José Reynoso Mateo, probably a false name for Francisco Trujillo Reynoso, another son of Petán. That is, three nephews of Generalissimo Trujillo, and the wife of one of them.

I went to Bosch that morning and recommended he notify the OAS as soon as we could confirm that the Trujillos were actually on the plane. Peace in the Caribbean certainly would not be served by having the Trujillos here. Bosch said he would do it. I also told him, as instructed by the Department, that on May 15 when Duvalier would celebrate his "reinaugural," Ambassador Thurston would not be present. Bosch would instruct his own Embassy in Port-au-Prince to do likewise.

3

But I had other matters to discuss with Bosch that morning of April 26. I had decided, after the *Mella* trip, that the time had come to draw Bosch closer to us publicly and to tackle him on his handling of the Castro/Communists. For with Bosch ignoring his own PRD, the 14th of June was the only really active political party in the Republic, and Bosch might soon find that he had only Castro/Communist support. We must drive wedges between them. I had loaded up for that morning's interview with no fewer than eleven separate items.

As usual, I started with the easy ones. Would he give me permission to bring Louis Armstrong and his band to Santo Domingo to play for a street dance in Parque Independencia on our national day, the Fourth of July—I hoped to attract young people, who admired not only Castro and Manolo Tavárez Justo but also Louis Armstrong; and Parque Independencia, the shrine of Dominican independence, with its recent history of student resistance to Trujillo's tanks, was a perfect place to celebrate the birthday of our own revolutionary independence (and Armstrong's own birthday as well). Bosch gave permission enthusiastically.[1] Would Bosch send a representative to a meeting of Hemisphere presidential press secretaries arranged by Pierre Salinger? He would. Was he still interested in the coastal patrol boats? He was, "very anxious." Would he like to go to lunch aboard the flagship of Vice Admiral Horacio Rivero, Jr., Commander of Amphibious Forces of the Atlantic Fleet, on May 6, taking his military high command along? He would, very much.

All this was fine—it would tie him to us and loosen his ties to the Castro/Communists.

I moved to more difficult matters. Tension seemed to be increasing between him and Germán Ornes, publisher of *El Caribe*. Ornes suspected that Bosch was trying to take *El Caribe* away from him. With some heat, Bosch denied it and said Ornes was goading him daily almost beyond endurance, exceeding the bounds of respect due the Presidency. I saw an opening—if "the Presidency," not Bosch, could become the issue, I might be able to bring about a rapprochement between Ornes and Bosch. Might I try? Bosch said he would be grateful.

Then I moved to the Castro/Communists.

I said we had learned that Castro planned to invite people from all over the Hemisphere to celebrate May Day in Havana. We hoped Bosch would take steps to discourage Dominicans from going. Bosch said he would instruct Foreign Minister Freites immediately not to issue any new passports until after May 1. I suggested making all passports invalid for travel to Cuba. He said this would be difficult since the constitution guaranteed freedom to travel, but he would try.

I went on: Dato Pagán's Communist political school was hurting him. Bosch's opponents were saying it proved he was "soft on communism." Dato Pagán was a Communist; there could be no doubt. (As we have seen, on the *Mella*, Bosch had said he was not, at least not now.) On the influential radio-TV program *"Ante La Prensa,"* "Meet the Press," Pagán had talked four hours and had not once strayed from the Moscow line

---

[1] Armstrong agreed to come for expenses and minimum union wages, a total cost of about six thousand dollars. The State Department would not pay it. Nor could I raise it in the American business community in Santo Domingo. Armstrong did not come. We gave another children's party at the Residence instead. This, and similar frustrations, suggest that ambassadors should have contingency funds for projects that fall outside the bureaucratic bailiwick.

—the major problem facing the Republic was "Yankee imperialism," the problem of communism was "academic" because the "objective conditions" did not exist here for the creation of a socialist state, all "progressive" forces should unite in a "national liberation front," the Berlin Wall had been built to keep spies and saboteurs out of the glorious people's republic of East Germany. We had known Dato Pagán a long time, I said, and I recited his history. We understood Bosch's devotion to civil liberties, and his view that it was best to fight Communists by permitting them to operate openly while making social and economic progress of his own. I myself had spent a good part of my life working for civil liberties. But the purpose of this school of Dato Pagán's was to subvert and overthrow the democratic Bosch government. Communism would destroy civil liberties, as Bosch well knew. Bosch's security forces were not yet capable of coping with well-trained Communist agents—and Dato Pagán was training them. And in any case, Pagán's school would almost surely be misunderstood by the U.S. press, Congress, and public. Having said all this, I went on, we recognized of course his sovereign right to manage his own internal affairs. I was speaking so frankly only because we wanted so much to see him succeed. For that reason, I strongly urged him to close the school.

Bosch had listened calmly to all this. When I finished he said slowly that he knew about the school—but did I know that not he but the Consejo had authorized Dato Pagán to run it?

Yes, I said, I knew that. The problem, was, however, that the school was actually operating now, and in a building owned by the government, Bosch's government.

Three weeks ago, Bosch said, he had ordered an investigation. He had been asked to give financial aid to the school and had refused. Now he was considering two ways to solve the problem. He could wait until June, when all schools closed automatically for the summer, and close this one of Dato Pagán's. Or he could find out where Dato Pagán was getting his money and shut it off. I asked whether the school would reopen in the fall. He said no—it would be closed in June at the latest, and it would not reopen.

I told him I was grateful, and I was sure my government would be pleased, for his decision indicated his awareness of the Communist danger. He said of course.

4

As I have said, this meeting took place on the morning of April 26. I hurried back to the Residence and invited Germán Ornes to lunch. We could still talk as fellow journalists who had known each other a long while. Ornes said he had cabled SIP, as the InterAmerican Press

Association was known here, that Bosch had accused him of trying to overthrow his government.

I said, "Are you?"

Ornes said, "No. The whole thing started because I reprinted articles from two papers that said he wouldn't define himself on communism. I won't conspire. Bosch has to learn to live with a free press. He is too sensitive."

I thought this my opening. As we moved into the living room for coffee and brandy, I agreed that Bosch was too sensitive but at the same time, recently Ornes really had been goading him almost beyond endurance; and I cited several recent stories and editorials, telling him I had been a journalist long enough to know when a paper was "riding" a public official and when it was simply reporting the news. He conceded the point. I said, "I may be wrong but I have a hunch I know what you're doing. You figure that as long as you stay on the offensive against Bosch, he won't dare take your paper away from you, because if he does, you can scream bloody murder to SIP and bring the whole international press down on him. This sounds like a good theory. But he's so sensitive that he may take your paper regardless of the consequences. This would probably hurt him badly in international opinion. But it wouldn't get your newspaper back for you."

I went on. Whatever he or anyone else thought of Bosch, the fact remained that Bosch *was* the elected President. The United States wanted him to succeed. We also believed the Republic needed a free press. Ornes was becoming a symbol of the free press, as Bosch was the symbol of elective democracy. I wouldn't lecture either on their responsibilities, and I didn't want to get in the position of mediating, but I did have some reason to believe that if he'd quit goading Bosch, Bosch would let him alone. "What it really comes down to is this. You and he are on a collision course. You can stay on the offensive, and he may grab your paper, and in the end somebody may knock him over. But that won't help you—you'll be back where I first met you, working for *El Mundo* in San Juan, Puerto Rico. And it won't help him. The question is: Do you want to be an editor here or a martyr in Puerto Rico?"

He thought only a moment then said, "I want to be an editor. Of *El Caribe*. The country needs a free newspaper."

"I know it does."

"I have no interest in goading him. Or 'tumbling' him," the word Bosch had used. "I will support him when I think he's right and oppose him when I think he's wrong. I will not make systematic opposition to him. I want independence. But I will use restraint and responsibility."

I told him this was fine, he was doing a great service to his country, and I hoped the President would meet him halfway. Seeing him to the door, I thought I might succeed.

Fandino made an appointment with Bosch for that night.

At six-thirty Vallimarescu called and said he had a report from Port-au-Prince that Duvalier's car had been fired on and his chauffeur and bodyguard had been killed, but he and his two children had escaped. Actually, Duvalier himself had not been in the car. The car had been taking his twelve-year-old son and fourteen-year-old daughter to school. Gunmen had fired on it, killing their three escorts, but the children had escaped into the school. It was this shooting which triggered the entire Haitian crisis. Duvalier's own gunmen immediately cordoned off the Palace area, set up roadblocks, and started rounding up opponents of the regime. Opponents took asylum in various Latin American embassies, including the Dominican Embassy. By nightfall at least six men had been killed. I ate a little dinner and went to see President Bosch.

I told him about Ornes. Bosch said he was grateful but then he began telling me the full history of his quarrel with Ornes, and recalling it made him angry all over again: "I can't forgive him. It is lack of respect for the President. I was elected to govern. Not he. He is mentally sick. I am going to let him keep going until I bring psychiatrists in to prove he's crazy," and he went on and on, red-faced. I listened in silence then patiently went over the ground again, as I had with Ornes: Neither would profit, both would get badly hurt, by a head-on collision. In the end a somewhat uneasy cease-fire had been achieved.

5

As I have said, it was during this evening conversation that Bosch mentioned that Haitian police had "assaulted" the Dominican Embassy in Port-au-Prince that day. I went to the office to send the brief cable.

At 10:05 P.M., while I was writing it, Foreign Minister Freites came to my office. He was usually neat and well dressed, but tonight he was unshaven, with loosened tie and dirty shirt, and at times his eyes looked wild. He showed me a document indicating that Duvalier had signed a secret agreement with Czechoslovakia for economic aid, that Czech and Polish missions were reported advising Duvalier, and that Duvalier was purging all career military officers. Freites asked if I could get in touch with Frank Bobadilla, the Dominican *chargé d'affaires* in Haiti, via our own Embassy in Port-au-Prince, ask him exactly what had happened that morning, and instruct Bobadilla to send another Dominican diplomat, Mejía Saufront, overland to the frontier that night so that Freites could send someone to meet him at Jimaní at 8 A.M. the next day.

We sent the cable to Port-au-Prince. Freites left. At 11:50 P.M. he called to say that the Trujillos were ticketed on KLM Flight 975 from Curaçao to Kingston and thence on Pan Am Flight 431A to Port-au-Prince the next day. We confirmed it.

6

Early the next morning, Saturday, I heard that Bosch said if the Haitians "jump on" the Dominican Embassy in Port-au-Prince, he intended to bomb Port-au-Prince.

From Port-au-Prince, the Dominican diplomat Mejía Saufront reported that he had reached the frontier that morning but Haitian guards had turned him back. He would try to fly to Santo Domingo in the afternoon. He said that the previous day's assault on the Dominican Embassy had occurred after the attack on Duvalier's children's car. About 10 A.M. two Haitian policemen with rifles had entered the Embassy office—not the Residence—despite the protests of a girl secretary. They had made threatening gestures but had disturbed nothing. The *chargé*, Bobadilla, had ordered them out. They had obeyed but had stayed on the grounds. Soon they were joined by nine or ten soldiers. Their purpose seemed to be to prevent about sixteen Haitians who had taken asylum in the Dominican Embassy from leaving. (Later the number of asylees rose to twenty-two, then finally to twenty-three.) Among them was Lieutenant François Benoit. Benoit had taken asylum, the Dominicans said, on Thursday night, the night before the attack on Duvalier's children's car. *Chargé* Bobadilla said that Lieutenant Benoit had been in asylum at the time of the attack on the children's car, but the Haitians said the attacker's car had belonged to Benoit and hinted that he had left asylum, made the attack, then returned. The Dominicans said this was ridiculous. It was, however, apparently the reason for the assault on the Dominican Embassy, which also housed as asylees other military enemies of Duvalier. In further reprisal against Benoit, Duvalier's militiamen had murdered members of Benoit's family and burned their house.

At 3 P.M., I went to see President Bosch. Freites was with him. We sat in a triangle beside his open patio, and I told him what Mejía had reported. Bosch listened in silence, then sat awhile frowning, very still. Suddenly sitting upright, face taut, brow creased, he said to Freites, "Mr. Chancellor, send this message: 'Duvalier: If your police are not gone from our territory by 4 P.M., my air and ground forces will invade. Signed Bosch.'"

Freites looked stricken. He said nothing. It was dead quiet for several minutes. This was an ultimatum that could only lead to war.

When it appeared that nobody else would say anything, I asked the President's permission to speak. I pointed out that it was now past three o'clock and he was giving Duvalier less than an hour to perform. I also said I had understood he intended to bring this matter to the attention of the OAS, which seemed to me a good idea. I pointed out that up to now

Duvalier had been the aggressor and that Bosch would best keep him in that role in world opinion, not permit himself to be cast in it.

Freites supported me somewhat timidly. After considerable thought, Bosch ordered Freites to modify the ultimatum. It gave the government of Haiti twenty-four hours to remove its police from the Dominican Embassy in Port-au-Prince and to "render honors to the Dominican flag"—Bosch never explained what that meant—said that if the Haitians failed to comply the Dominican government would take all measures necessary (I suggested this vague language rather than a flat threat to invade), and informed the Haitians that the Dominicans were notifying the OAS. I urged that the ultimatum be drafted with extreme care to make clear that Bosch's quarrel was with Duvalier, not the Haitian people. Bosch agreed. Tomorrow, Sunday, he would speak to the people on radio-TV and order a military alert. "By Monday," he said, "we can act." He seized the telephone, and ordered the government-owned radio station to begin at once announcing every half hour that he would make a speech "of transcendental importance" on Sunday.

I asked what he had meant by "acting" on Monday. He said he would send military aircraft to overfly Port-au-Prince.

"Will they drop anything?"

"Perhaps some leaflets," he said.

"You don't intend to bomb it?"

"No."

"Do you intend to invade by land?"

He did not answer directly but indicated he would not act precipitously. Again I cautioned him to keep Duvalier in the aggressor's role and told him I thought he had an excellent case—Duvalier's repressive regime, his plot to have Bosch assassinated, his bringing the Trujillos to Haiti, his "invasion" of the Dominican Embassy, his murder of a Haitian officer's family, his reported dealings with the Czech mission, and so on. Bosch agreed, and said he intended to discuss these things in his speech. He did not want us to impede the Trujillos' travel to Haiti, thinking their arrival there would strengthen his case. I left him. Soon Bosch telephoned: He had asked for an extraordinary meeting of the Council of the OAS for Sunday night, tomorrow night, and been assured it would be held.

Fifteen minutes later, Freites telephoned—the Trujillos had arrived at Jamaica, missed their plane for Port-au-Prince, and would take another tomorrow. Therefore Freites would postpone the ultimatum. The countdown on the twenty-four-hour ultimatum would begin running as of tomorrow.

Freites called again—the Haitians now said they would not consider military personnel entitled to asylum and had notified the Dominican, Mejía Saufront, that they would take all necessary steps to see that Lieutenant Benoit fell into Duvalier's hands. Bosch would delay his speech until the Trujillos left Kingston. We ascertained that the only flight the Trujillos could use was Pan Am 431A leaving Kingston at 2:45 P.M. Sunday and arriving at Port-au-Prince at 5:05 P.M.

Ambassador Thurston reported from Port-au-Prince that the *ton-ton-macoute* had killed at least a dozen people, stores were closed, tanks and troops surrounded the Palace, militiamen were searching cars at roadblocks and had apparently shot two motorists capriciously, and a foreign newspaperman had been arrested.

Freites told us that Haitian police now had entered the Dominican Embassy Residence and were in the garage under the *charge*'s office, apparently searching for the automobile used in the attack on Duvalier's children.

The Commander in Chief of the U. S. Atlantic Fleet ordered the aircraft carrier *Boxer,* two destroyers, and two other vessels to stand by in the Gulf of Gonaïves in front of, but out of sight of, Port-au-Prince, prepared to evacuate Thurston's Embassy if necessary.

Freites was working with functionaries of the Dominican Foreign Office—*pontificios,* Bosch called them contemptuously—trying to draft the ultimatum to Haiti. The drafting was going slowly. A couple of times Shlaudeman went to Freites' house to help out. The functionaries finally finished a draft about 1 A.M., took it to President Bosch, and Bosch nearly threw it at them, then wrote out the ultimatum himself and ordered it sent. We thought if Bosch played his cards right he had a good chance of getting OAS action against Duvalier or putting so much pressure on him he would flee the country.

7

Sunday morning we worked on the cable traffic and talked to Freites. The ultimatum had been a strong one. President Bosch had given it to *El Caribe.* He had alerted his military high command. His Ambassador to the OAS in Washington, Arturo Calventi, would appear today before the Council of the OAS. The Dominicans had instructed their consul in Jamaica to go through the motions of trying to stop the Trujillos' departure but doing it too late. Bosch's speech was postponed until 7 P.M. to give the Trujillos time to land in Port-au-Prince.

I sent the attachés out to locate the Dominican high command. General Luna of the Air Force was in Boca Chica, with his boat. General Hungría of the Army was at his *finca* in the country. Commodore Rib had gone fishing for a little while early in the morning—I had gone with him—and now was resting. No troop or aircraft movements were reported.

Freites told me that Gonzalo Facio, President of the OAS Council, thought the Dominicans had a good case.

Fritz Long relayed a report that Duvalier had signed a secret military assistance agreement with Castro.

At about 5 P.M. Assistant Secretary Ed Martin telephoned me from Washington. The Council of the OAS was in session and Martin thought it might invoke the Río Treaty against Haiti and condemn or at least investigate Haiti's threat to hemispheric peace; but, he said, Bosch was undermining his own position by threatening to act militarily before the OAS had time to act. President Facio had telephoned Freites but received no assurances. Could I get assurances from Bosch?

I went immediately to Bosch's house. He said sternly, "I have received a message from the OAS asking me to wait. I cannot wait forever. The excitement in the Dominican people is great. I fear for the Haitian Embassy here—a group of young people is getting together. There is an internal political problem too."

I made the case for restraint. Finally Bosch said, "Tomorrow the Constitution will be promulgated." Then I saw—he wanted to keep the Haitian crisis boiling so his controversial Constitution could be promulgated without much notice.

I told him that if the debate in the OAS turned against him, it would be a serious political blow.

He frowned, thinking. Finally he said, "If the OAS could send me a message tomorrow publicly asking me to wait, I might not find it inconvenient to wait."

I pressed him further. Reluctantly, he gave me his personal assurance that he would not invade tomorrow—that he would wait "until twenty-four hours from tonight, and that will really be Tuesday morning." Would he say this in his speech tonight? He did not reply directly.

It was almost time for him to leave for the Palace to deliver the speech. I hurried back to the Residence and telephoned Ed Martin in Washington and reported, adding that at this point I did not believe Bosch really intended to invade at all, though I could be wrong. Martin expected the Council of the OAS to act by 10 P.M. tonight.

Freites called: Haiti had officially broken relations with the Dominican government. We recommended that he ask the Haitians for safe-conducts for the asylees in the Dominican Embassy there and their transfer to another Embassy.

At 6:50 P.M. a private source told me that the Trujillos had actually landed in Port-au-Prince. Shlaudeman immediately telephoned President Bosch at the Palace and told him so. Ten minutes later Bosch came on television, flanked by his military high command. We watched, then I telephoned Ed Martin. Bosch had said Dominican sovereignty and dignity had been insulted and must be defended at all costs. Duvalier was conspiring against the Republic "in alliance with the Trujillos." Dominican diplomats would not leave Haiti until they had received safe-conducts for the twenty-two asylees then in their Embassy in Port-au-Prince. The OAS was "studying" the matter, but "with study or without it, the situation is grave." He said, "We have suffered with great patience the outrages of the Haitian government. But those outrages must stop now. If they do not stop in a period of twenty-four hours, we will put a final point to them with the measures that may be found in our capability."

At 9:30 P.M., Cass told me that the Dominican Navy had a frigate on the north coast ready to put to sea and that three thousand ground troops had begun to move to the border at Dajabón, Elías Piña, and Jimaní. Colonel Long, however, said all Army troops were confined to their barracks—none were being moved to the border. I told the attachés to recheck. Long finally reached General Viñas, and he said that the troops were being rounded up all over the country and this process would probably take most of Monday. They were getting into a position to "do something" Tuesday morning. Viñas understood, as I did, the twenty-four-hour ultimatum would run out on Monday night.

Our Embassy in Port-au-Prince ordered all Americans to stand by for evacuation.

Late that evening the Council of the OAS voted 16 to 0 with two abstentions to invoke the Río Treaty and convoke itself as a ministerial-level Organ of Consultation to make peace between Haiti and the Dominican Republic. It authorized President Facio to appoint a five-man commission to fly to Haiti immediately. It urged both governments to refrain from any actions that might disrupt its peace-keeping efforts.

8

On Monday morning Colonel Cass reported that Commodore Rib was talking irresponsibly about bombing the Palace in Port-au-Prince. A private source told me the Navy had asked for two hundred thousand gallons of diesel fuel oil and the Air Force three hundred thousand gallons of gasoline for the tanks.

Kennedy Crockett, who had replaced Crimmins as Caribbean area director in the State Department, called King—several OAS ambassadors were saying that Bosch was the problem, not Duvalier. And Duvalier, or his Foreign Minister, René Chalmers, had made a clever move. The Haitian government had notified the OAS that it had withdrawn its troops from the Dominican Embassy and would guarantee the safety of Dominican diplomats until they left the country and the safety of twenty-one persons who had taken asylum in the Dominican Embassy. We had understood there were now twenty-two asylees. The figure twenty-one sounded ominous—did Duvalier intend to guarantee safety for all but

Lieutenant Benoit, whom he blamed for the attack on his children? Would the OAS understand this?

Long reported that the high command was scheduled to meet at the Palace at 10 A.M. Bosch had the Armed Forces excited. And the people too—a crowd rioted at the Haitian Embassy, the radio was filled with announcements—a druggist was offering free drugs and a man his truck to the troops—and the streets were filled with talk of war. Bosch had support as never before.

At 12:30 P.M. Freites told King that Bosch had received a message yesterday from the OAS but had not yet replied. Betancourt had called Bosch today and told him that Venezuela was "100 percent for him"; Bosch took this to mean that the Venezuelan Navy and Air Force were at his disposal. Freites had vainly warned Bosch to be careful. Freites said that if the OAS Commission did not at least prepare to leave Washington today, Bosch might do anything.

At 12:45 P.M., Long said that General Viñas planned to begin at once reinforcing three frontier battalions with four companies, including the crack troops trained in counter-insurgency. The Navy was moving four units along the south coast and three along the north coast toward Haiti. The Air Force would patrol the frontier but stay on the Dominican side. Tanks were going to San Juan de la Maguana. Long had told Viñas they'd be wise to keep the quarrel in the OAS, pointing out that thus far no Dominican lives had been lost but some might if the troops crossed the border. He had made little impression—the Dominican military was talking about their patriotic duty to die for their country. The ultimatum would expire at 7 P.M. No Dominican military man knew what would happen after that.

Kennedy Crockett called me that afternoon. Bosch had not replied to a personal appeal from Facio. The OAS had selected only four of the five members of the Commission—Ambassadors of Chile, El Salvador, Ecuador, and Colombia. (Bolivia later was added.) It was not even certain the Commission could get into Port-au-Prince, for Duvalier had not replied to two telegrams from Facio. It was absolutely impossible for the Commission to get to Port-au-Prince by seven o'clock that night, but the Dominicans in Washington insisted it must. Crockett said, "We feel this is inconsistent with what President Bosch promised you." Port-au-Prince was quiet—but Santo Domingo was mobilizing. Crockett asked me to go to Bosch again. And so at 2:30 P.M. I did.

Bosch was taking a shower. Servants were setting his luncheon table. I waited, talking desultorily with members of his household. Sunlight streamed into the room, and a gentle breeze blew. Bosch appeared, wearing a dressing gown, apologizing for his attire, explaining he was dressing to attend the ceremony promulgating the Constitution. Sitting with him while he ate his lunch, I asked if he considered that the OAS action, plus the Haitian note and the withdrawal of police from the Dominican Embassy, met the requirements of his 7 P.M. deadline.

Frowning, Bosch said, "In the note, Duvalier assured that Haitian public order forces never had gone into the Dominican Embassy. And last night they were there on the street outside when he wrote the note, so his guarantee is not worth anything. He did not offer any satisfactions. Now he has broken relations with us. So our situation is worse. I do not comprehend how it is possible that the OAS with so many personnel has not enough to send a mission just in a moment. We are going to give Duvalier a fright. We are not going to kill Haitians. We are going to move troops inside our own territory."

He was winning; as always, he intended to push his victory too hard. I tried to dissuade him, pointing out that he had won his original objectives —withdrawal of Haitian police from Dominican property, guarantees to the asylees and Dominican diplomats. Bosch kept talking about moving troops. Finally when I again pointed out that the Haitian guard had been removed from the Embassy property, he said, "This is the first time I had known of that." (This seems doubtful.) He paused, leaned back, sat rigid and silent a few minutes, then ordered his secretary, "Get the editor of *La Nación*."

I didn't know what he was going to do. When the editor came on, Bosch said, "I wish to dictate a headline. For this afternoon. The headline is: 'Dominican Victory, Duvalier Retreats.' Put it in the biggest type that you have." Then he called Freites and told him to reply to the OAS, assuring it that the Dominicans would await OAS action. I went back to the Residence, telephoned Ed Martin, then changed clothes and hurried to the Assembly Hall for the promulgation of the Constitution.

It began at 4 P.M. President Bosch sat on the dais with the Vice President, the President of the Senate, the Speaker of the House, and others. The Cabinet and military chiefs sat in the front rows. So did the diplomatic corps—but the Nuncio was pointedly absent, his vacant chair objecting to the Constitution. Behind us sat the Senators and Deputies, and at the rear stood the general public. Miolán was in the crowded balcony. Outside, a heavy gun began booming 101 times, its sound reverberating through the chamber, and below the dais clerks began reading the Constitution.

Bosch looked grim, his face set. Television men scrambled around, cables strung out. The reading droned on and on. I noticed that the Deputies had only seats, not desks, as in a theater—the chamber had been built by Trujillo, when Congress' duty was to listen, not to work or think. Freites kept going in and out. So did the military high command. Bosch had deliberately whipped up a war atmosphere. He had told me that he was engaged in a great democratic experiment here in the Dominican Republic and that if he failed, it would be bad not only for the Republic but for the cause of democracy in Latin America. This was the leverage he had on us, and he knew it. He had behaved similarly on the Church issue during the campaign—dug himself into a hole then let everyone else help dig him out.

The clerk was reading Article 168. He had eight more to go. I was getting fidgety. It was only fifty-five minutes to the 7 P.M. deadline. Bosch had said he would ignore it—but would he? Watching Bosch, I thought: He'd better not forget that Trujillo's end began when he tried to kill Betancourt. He'd better not go too far with Duvalier.

Finally at six-fifteen the reading finished. Bosch stood, and nearly all stood; Bosch applauded, and nearly all applauded; and so did I, though several of the diplomatic corps remained seated and did not applaud. Speaker Molina Ureña declared the promulgation done. A ceremonial signing of the Constitution began. Thelma Frías presented Speaker Molina Ureña with a big bouquet "on behalf of the Dominican women." Bosch, white-suited, grim and erect, strode out rapidly. I started to follow. It was 6:30 P.M. Another Ambassador said to me, "We should all not applaud, I think." And another, "Or else we should all applaud. We should be together." I said, "I'm sorry, I disagree, and I'd like to discuss it with you, but I'll have to ask you to excuse me now," and hurried away through the crowd, found my car, and told the driver to get to the Chancellery fast. Driving, he said, "Every people must have a Constitution, Mr. Ambassador." As we turned off Avenida Jorge Washington by the sea, a loudspeaker was blaring the headline from La Nación, "Dominican Victory, Duvalier Retreats."

Back at the Chancellery, King reported that the OAS Commission would arrive the next morning at 7:50 A.M., stop for ten minutes, and continue on to Port-au-Prince.

It did. The military appeared more relaxed. The capital was quiet. The trouble seemed to be flattening out. The New York Times said editorially that both sides must accept OAS mediation. The next day, Wednesday, was May Day, but nothing happened, perhaps because everyone was exhausted.

9

On Thursday, May 2, I sent a cable asking that the visit of Vice Admiral Rivero be canceled. I did so with great reluctance—we had intended this as an impressive public demonstration of our support for Juan Bosch. But we could not do it now, because of Haiti.

The OAS Commission was returning from Port-au-Prince at six-fifteen. I wondered why it had stayed so briefly. Several ambassadors there had urged it to stay longer. The Times estimated that at least a hundred persons had been killed since last Friday's attack on Duvalier's children.

Bosch held a press conference at 6 P.M. I got a report on it quickly. He said he would ask the OAS to impose diplomatic sanctions on Haiti. Asked if he had the votes, he didn't know and didn't seem to care. Asked what he would do if the OAS refused sanctions, he said, "We must do what we think is right." Off the record he added, "When you live with a person in the same bed who has tuberculosis, you have to do something about it. This is that situation." He seemed firm and determined. I went to see him alone at eight.

His wife, Carmen, sat with us in the living room. Bosch said, "If one Dominican is hurt in the street in Port-au-Prince, I will send planes to bomb the Palace. If Haitian police or troops enter the Embassy, I will send the Navy and the ground forces and I will inform the OAS from the road."

His wife said it was "nice" that the Venezuelans were going to send the Navy because "then we can send our ground forces," and she picked up an oil company map and began showing how Dominican ground troops could be pushed across the border at Elías Piña and Jimaní, how the Venezuelan Navy could come up from the south, how Port-au-Prince could be encircled, surely as bizarre a military strategy conference as anyone ever attended. Often a rather wan person, she seemed happy that night, animated. She said, "It's nice to have these military things for a while—to give us time, you know." Bosch didn't like that—it implied, of course, that he was using the whole incident to cover political difficulties here at home.

Bosch told me one thing more that night. He had ordered Minister Domínguez Guerra to forbid political meetings in town halls such as those Manolo Tavárez Justo had been holding. Bosch thought the measure unconstitutional but necessary. I agreed.

10

Later that evening, and next morning, Vallimarescu reported that the American press was saying that the OAS Commission's audience with Duvalier had been a "farce" and its report would whitewash him. Obviously Duvalier or Foreign Minister Chalmers had put his house in order. The Commission had spent only fifty-six hours in Haiti. It would spend sixty-seven hours in the Dominican Republic. Reporters felt that the Commission was uninterested in the Trujillos or the plot against Bosch, but did seem concerned about the right of asylum and the violation of Dominican sovereignty.

All this was disturbing. If the OAS did in fact give Duvalier a clean bill of health, Bosch would look foolish in world opinion and therefore would be in deep trouble here at home—and he would blame us for having pushed him into the OAS.

That day, Friday, May 3, Duvalier declared martial law in Haiti and a nighttime curfew. Bosch told the press this brought "new tensions" He met with the OAS Commission. A Latin American diplomat in Port-au-Prince said that Latin American embassies there could not guarantee protection of asylees and proposed that the OAS assume the task, sending if necessary a small U.S. or multinational force to do the job.

In Santo Domingo I detected a letdown. The military no longer seemed bellicose. The people were quiet. A joke went round: "After we invade Haiti, we can send our technicians to help them build democracy." Jokes are fatal to crises. If Bosch, fearing an OAS rebuff, intended to try to heat up the situation again by himself, he might run into trouble.

11

Saturday morning I went to the Palace to see President Bosch and ask how the situation was. "Bad," he said. "Very bad." He had made his charges against Haiti to the OAS Commission and said that "if something happens" in Haiti he would order his troops to cross the border to protect Dominicans in Haiti and defend hemispheric democracy. The Commission had not replied—"they did not answer me one word." He took their silence for assent. He spoke again about joint military action with the Venezuelan Navy and U. S. Marines. "This could be a Congo," he said. A dozen Haitian refugees had crossed the border today. Then, musing, he said, "Early in January I received news in Europe, and in February here, that the Haitian common people looked to me and to democracy for help."

At this point Foreign Minister Freites arrived, and so, as I remember, did General Viñas and Commodore Rib, and we all studied a map of Haiti, the oil company map, discussing the question of violation of national territory at sea, and I explained that, as I understood it, most countries recognized the three-mile limit, but Haiti insisted on a six-mile limit, another strange high strategy conference. I left.

In Washington, Facio said the OAS was "very alarmed" by the situation in Haiti. Back at the Chancellery, Commander Engelman, our Naval MAAG Chief, reported Commodore Rib was considering trying to put a ship at the very edge of the six-mile limit off Port-au-Prince. Colonel Richardson, our air attaché, reported that the Dominican Air Force was getting a C-46 ready, presumably to transport paratroops. I went back to the Palace.

Bosch said he was going to send the counter-insurgency troops to Jimaní—three companies plus some armor. He was sending troops to Elías Piña. He was sending five planes to Barahona. He would have a ship ready to sail tomorrow. He had ordered Freites to get the Dominican diplomats, Bobadilla and Mejía, out of Haiti tonight. Troop movements would start at dawn.

This sounded—and Bosch looked—serious.

I sent all our military people out to get a firm fix on just what troops and equipment were being moved. And I met with King and Shlaudeman, whom I had sent to talk to Freites, the OAS Commission members, and the Colombian Ambassador here.

They reported that Bosch had declared he would not order his diplomats, Bobadilla and Mejía Saufront, home until he had received safe-conducts for all the asylees. Thereupon the Colombians had told Freites that they would not, as planned, protect Dominican interest in Port-au-Prince. So Bosch had ordered his diplomats home. But Freites now feared Duvalier would double-cross them or the asylees—give them safe-conducts, then have them killed en route to the airport, an old Trujillo trick. The OAS Commission seemed personally sympathetic to Bosch, or at least unsympathetic to Duvalier, but did not seem to see any legal basis for recommending action against Duvalier. So Freites was urging us to unleash Bosch with token support of forces from the United States and Venezuela.

The attachés began returning to the Residence with detailed reports on plans for troop movements. The commanders were encountering difficulties—Air Force ground troops would move to Jimaní this afternoon if they could locate enough trucks, Wessin y Wessin would send tanks there if he could find ships or flat-bed trailers, some military headquarters "seemed more like a big bull session" than a strategy meeting, and the tank commanders were worried about the road from Jimaní to Port-au-Prince, for beyond Jimaní the road goes through a narrow defile between a mountain and a lake, and Haitians might stop the tanks simply by rolling rocks down from the hills.

Was it all just talk? Alone, I drove down to Avenida Jorge Washington to see for myself. The sun was setting, the sky magenta, with towering black thunderclouds over the western mountains. Presently I saw eleven trucks and a dozen Jeeps and ambulances and other small vehicles, all loaded with troops, headed west. People on the sidewalks paid little attention. Vesuvio's was getting crowded.

Back at the Residence, Freites called. The diplomats Bobadilla and Mejía had arrived safely. The attachés confirmed actual tank and troop movements that earlier had been mere talk. The Army was sending its best. So was the Air Force infantry. So was the artillery. So was Wessin y Wessin. I asked our Colonel Long if the equipment and men the Dominicans had moved were those he would move if he seriously intended to invade Haiti and kill Duvalier. He said yes. The capital was stripped as bare as was safe—perhaps too bare.

The New York *Times* reported from Washington that although the

Boxer's task force contained about two thousand Marines, the Kennedy administration was "extremely reluctant" to land them in Haiti. No wonder. It is always easy to get them in but hard to get them out.

Newspapermen kept asking us whether Bosch really intended to invade or was "playing a game." We said truthfully we didn't know. Our private opinion was that Bosch himself had not yet decided. He was doing precisely what he had done during the Church crisis in the electoral campaign—getting himself into a position from which he could jump whichever way he thought best for him at the time of decision. The difficulty, however, was that this tactic is easier in a purely domestic situation than in an international one, because while the UCN would try to help him get back into the election, Duvalier wouldn't help him do anything.

12

The next day, Sunday, May 5, events took a wholly new turn. The Dominican military high command began to show disenchantment with the entire Haitian venture.

Cass came to the Residence. Commodore Rib had examined maps carefully. Rib said that landing from sea was absolutely impossible for the Dominicans—they did not have either the knowledge or the equipment. Moreover, General Hungría was worried about the overland route —tanks and infantry could be stopped and chopped to pieces in the mountain defile.

Colonel Richardson said that the Air Force, which formerly had been eager to attack Haiti alone, now wanted to go in behind the United States. High-ranking officers at San Isidro that morning had reverted to talking about Bosch and communism, not about invasion. Perhaps, they said, Bosch was using the Haitian adventure to distract everybody from communism. That sounded ominous.

Fritz Long said "Viñas is getting fed up with this jazz. He says he doesn't even know what he is being expected to do." Long said that last night Wessin y Wessin and other officers had been asking themselves "what kind of spot the Dominican Republic would be in if we go in." They wanted U.S. military support or at least OAS moral support.

I ate some lunch and took a nap; it looked like a long night. A call from Chicago wakened me—a man wanted me to ascertain the whereabouts of his daughter inside Haiti. Newspapermen came to see me, some of them now excited about the troop movements we had known of the day before. They thought war imminent. Not suspecting that the Dominican military was weak, they were cabling stories that the Dominicans could take Haiti in two days. They believed the myth that Trujillo had built a powerful army. It never had been anything but a repressive force.

The Crisis Crowd gathered. Richardson had just learned that yesterday the military high command and their staffs had met at the Palace and Wessin y Wessin, pointing his finger at the others, had told them that their forces were inadequate and incapable of invading Haiti. The chiefs had received his words well. Everybody had asked, "Why are we being mobilized?" Several officers had again suggested Bosch was using the Haitian adventure to distract attention from communism and the Constitution. Some even had suggested that Bosch might be deliberately sending the Armed Forces into a suicidal Haitian venture to destroy them. They had wanted President Bosch to meet with them but he had not. General Viñas and the three service chiefs intended to ask Bosch tomorrow why they were being mobilized.

Cass came in and said, "We need guidance. The military disaffection has blossomed. They are asking us what they should do."

I asked Cass if from a strictly military viewpoint he agreed with the Dominican military—that they did not have the capability to invade Haiti. Presumably the primary objective would not be simply to cross the border but to drive to Port-au-Prince, attack it, and kill Duvalier. Probably some sort of an occupation would have to follow.

Cass said that he certainly agreed, if Bosch had all this in mind. Indeed, he did not believe the Dominicans even capable of invading successfully if the Haitian people rallied around Duvalier, took to the hills with machetes, and then fell upon the Dominicans. He was not at all sure the Dominicans could get to Port-au-Prince and kill Duvalier. They had no way to support themselves—they lacked trucks, gasoline, food, communications. As for an occupation, it was out of the question. The other attachés agreed.

I told the three attachés that if the Dominican military commanders asked their opinion, they should give it honestly and strictly on a military basis. I instructed them not to discuss any political matters. If the Dominicans concluded they were indeed incapable of doing what Bosch asked of them, then it was the Dominicans' duty to tell Bosch so.

This was a crucial—and inescapable—decision, and I knew it when I made it. Our attachés' opinions would weigh heavily in the Dominican military's decisions. If the attachés did not respond when asked their military opinion, the Dominican military would lose confidence in them. On the other hand, if they did as I instructed them, Bosch might conclude I was conspiring against him with his own military. I made the decision on the military merits—the Dominican commanders couldn't invade and ought to tell Bosch so. I think Bosch subsequently suspected I had discouraged his military, just as I had urged him to cooperate with

the OAS. But it was in fact the Dominican military commanders themselves who first felt misgivings.[2]

Late that evening the newspapermen Tad Szulc and Henry Raymont
came to see me in some agitation. They had just come from Bosch. He
had told them flatly that he would invade at 4:30 A.M. on Tuesday, the
day after next. They could accompany him. He would be in Port-au-
Prince by ten in the morning. He would meet with the Cabinet and the
military at 8 A.M. in the Palace. At that time he would give Szulc and
Raymont credentials that would permit them to accompany his invading
troops. They were convinced that Bosch was serious. Minister Jaar had
cheered Bosch on, saying, "If we had Haiti this would really be the jewel
of the Caribbean."

At 1:15 A.M. I telephoned the Operations Center in the Department.
and said that Bosch had told two reliable American newspapermen that
he would invade at 4:30 A.M. Tuesday, that I was still not convinced,
that he had scheduled an important meeting for 8 A.M., that I was sending a cable now and would like to have it considered at high levels before 8 A.M.

13

We had one principal concern on Monday, May 6—that Bosch would
override his own military's advice, order the military to invade, and thus
force them to obey or rebel.

---

[2] In his own book, Bosch writes that at the start of the Haitian crisis he had conceived a plan to get rid of Duvalier which was simple and "would not cost a drop
of blood." He would mobilize troops on the frontier, and his Air Force would
fly over Port-au-Prince and drop leaflets "in French" telling the people to evacuate
the environs of the Palace because Dominican warplanes would bomb it in a few
hours. "I was sure that . . . Duvalier would flee before a single bullet need be
fired," Bosch writes. Bosch would actually send Dominican troops across the border
"to advance onto Haitian territory at least a few miles, enough to give the impression
of a genuine attack." He was sure the Haitian population near the frontier would
not resist. If it did, "the Air Force could drop two or three bombs where they would
cause no casualties." But at this point, Bosch writes, "a mystery arose"—his generals told him "that their trucks had no spare tires and were in no condition to
transport troops. Who had told them to use that alibi? Until the previous night,
all of them had enthusiastically supported the mobilization plan. . . . Ambassador
Martin came to see me. He was quite alarmed. It was the first time I had ever
seen him alarmed. The possibility of a Dominican-Haitian war had greatly upset
him, undoubtedly because it had upset the State Department. And at that moment,
Moscow, Peking, Havana, and the MPD in Santo Domingo were all charging that
if I attacked Haiti, I would be acting as a puppet of 'Yankee imperialism.' The
situation was sadly comic. It was precisely 'Yankee imperialism' that was impeding
the Dominican decision to settle the Haitian problem."

The attachés began checking early. I had a line open to a source inside the Palace. Cass saw Commodore Rib at eight-ten. He said Rib knew nothing about a meeting at eight, was not prepared to invade, neither were the other service commanders, and they might see Bosch that afternoon. He received a phone call, appeared distraught, and excused himself. Long and Richardson said nothing was going on.

I called President Bosch direct. He received me at 10 A.M. As I entered his Palace office, his military commanders were leaving. So there had been a meeting after all. They looked grim. So did Bosch. They left. I asked Bosch directly if it was true, as I had heard, that he intended to invade at 4:30 A.M. tomorrow.

He said, "No. It is not true. We are moving our troops to organize for anything that could happen. Many Haitians are crossing the border."

How many, I asked.

"Yesterday nine civilians and one corporal with a gun and bullets crossed. The mayor of Hinche, a soldier with a rifle and sixty-seven bullets. Twelve in one day. There is a Haitian Army detachment ready to cross," that is, ready to defect to the Dominicans. "The military chief at Cap Haitien says he will not rise by himself, with his 300 or 350 people, but he would join. But there is no leadership. The Army is waiting for leadership." Then, musing a bit, "If we could get to Colonel Biambi or Benoit or Major Álvarez," all Haitian asylees. "There are twenty Haitian military men here already." For the first time, he seemed to be turning from thoughts of invading with his own Armed Forces to thoughts of sending Haitians to subvert or invade. He said, "If their force is too weak, we will not let them go. It is clear to us and to everyone that Duvalier is crazy but we can't go in and get him."

"What do you mean?"

He leaned back on the sofa. "We have not the capability. We cannot. We have no ways. We need transportation and radios. The Navy is impossible. Frankly, we cannot do it. It would take seventy-two hours to get the troops there in trucks from Haina. And if they could get to the frontier, they couldn't get to Port-au-Prince. They would have to walk. The Navy is no good," he said again. "Its boilers are worn out. Three Vampire jets almost fell down. We grounded them. The only air capability we have is the P-51s."

He said all this in a sad voice, regretful but resigned. He had talked to Facio by telephone. But the OAS would meet only to receive the Commission's report. He would move more troops around, "but don't worry —we will do nothing. And *you*," the United States, "can't land troops either."

I sympathized with his difficulties and urged him to keep pushing the OAS for action. I left, feeling sorry for him and wondering what the reaction would be if all this became known. It would not become known through me—I refused to talk to the press on leaving the Palace.

This was the turning point. Bosch's commanders had at last told him the truth. The man who had done the telling, I understood, was Colonel Wessin y Wessin.

14

Haiti asked the United Nations Security Council to consider the threat of Dominican aggression. The Department instructed me to tell Bosch that he should do nothing further outside the OAS—and there was little or no chance that the OAS would approve an OAS military action against Haiti. It instructed Ambassador Thurston that his highest priority was to safeguard American lives and asked if it was not time to evacuate all dependents of official U.S. personnel from Haiti.

I went to see Bosch and informed him that Duvalier was taking the question to the UN Security Council, that if the question reached the UN General Assembly the Soviets and the African nations might espouse the Haitian cause, that we would try to get it sent back to the OAS,[3] that we probably would succeed, that Bosch could then try to get the OAS' standing Commission on Human Rights sent to Haiti, and that until then we hoped he would take no hostile action.

Bosch replied he would await tomorrow, when the OAS Commission was due to report. The New York Times said that "real responsibility" lay with the OAS and quoted El Tiempo of Bogotá which criticized "the indifference or, what is worse, the tacit complicity of the hemisphere."

That night, reviewing events in my mind, I wondered whether our policy had served us well. Events had taken a strange turn. At the outset, Bosch, our friend, had clearly been the aggrieved party. Now, eleven days later, the OAS had refused to succor him, he stood accused in the UN as an aggressor although he was in fact incapable of being one, and he had lost whatever confidence his own military might have had in him. At the same time, Duvalier, of whom we disapproved, appeared to be as strong at home as ever—and to be winning the diplomatic war. So long as Duvalier and Bosch remained, there would be trouble on this island. Human rights would be denied in Haiti, Bosch could use Haiti as diversion from troubles at home, and progress in either country would be difficult or impossible. We unwittingly had helped bring all this about. And so had Bosch. Always a gambler, this time he had overplayed his hand.

[3] The UN Charter is ambiguous, setting forth at one point that primary responsibility for keeping the peace rests with the UN but at another point that primary responsibility rests with regional international bodies. It is standing U.S. policy to keep inter-American affairs in the OAS.

15

On Tuesday, May 7, the Department instructed Ambassador Thurston to evacuate the dependents of U.S. officials by commercial planes and to urge private U.S. nationals to leave Haiti. The *Boxer* would move in closer. We would also assist Dominicans in leaving Haiti. Bosch was pleased. In Santo Domingo, FENEPIA struck, and during a demonstration at Juan Pablo Duarte School police threw tear gas. Bosch said, "This gives me a chance to get the Reds out of FENEPIA, to kill FENEPIA and fire the Reds out of government jobs." The 14th of June attacked him publicly.

Freites said Haiti was on the brink of joining the Soviet bloc. He proposed five solutions—fast OAS action, UN intervention, U.S. military intervention, "police action" by the Dominican Republic, Costa Rica, and others, or unilateral invasion by the Dominican Republic. This sounded desperate. Where was the proof that Haiti was going Communist?

At 4:35 P.M. a private source called to tell me that a DC-3 was on the runway at the airport in Port-au-Prince ready to take off. Duvalier had sent a request that it be allowed to land at Curaçao. The implication was that Duvalier was getting ready the flee the country. We began trying to confirm it.

Cass reported that a Haitian captain, cashiered with sixty other officers, had gone to Port-au-Prince in secret, seized a Jeep and, with a sergeant and four enlisted men, fled to the Dominican Republic. One of the Trujillos had been consorting with Haitian government officials. Clement Barbot, who once had led Duvalier's *ton-ton-macoute* but now had gone underground in Haiti against Duvalier, had led a band of partisans in shooting up a truck containing militiamen with rifles, machine guns, and grenades, and had killed about thirty. A half hour later three high-ranking *ton-ton-macoutes* led an attack on Barbot's hideout. Several men had been killed, and Barbot had escaped but had left behind his grenades and machine guns.

The asylees in Port-au-Prince had been offered ordinary, not diplomatic, passports. These would not guarantee them diplomatic immunity. Haitians feared a bloodbath. The first targets would be Barbot and his partisans, but the terror would spread, quickly engulfing the mulatto upper class and all white foreigners.

At 7 P.M. that night President Bosch spoke to the nation. He said, "Haiti is a powder keg and we are a lake of gasoline." He indicated that the Republic would rely on the OAS but that his military was ready, that he was faced with an insane dictator and the possibility of a catastrophic bloodbath, and that he proposed to adopt an attitude of great care and vigilance. He insisted on safe-conducts for all asylees and re-ferred specifically to Benoit. The speech was curiously clouded with ex-traneous matters—donations to agrarian reform, the Republic's economic situation, an attack on FENEPIA.

16

On Wednesday, May 8, the OAS voted 18 to 0 to send its Commission back to Haiti with broader authority. Originally limited to fact-finding on the situation, the Commission now could inquire into the causes of the conflict. Well, this was something. But not much. By going to the UN, Duvalier had forced the OAS to act fast, and there had been no time to rally support in the OAS for a stronger resolution. In the UN Security Council, Haitian Foreign Minister Chalmers said he was defending the cause of the black peoples everywhere. President Kennedy said at his press conference that we must "proceed in company with the OAS." That day's paper carried stories by Tad Szulc and Henry Raymont saying I had stopped Bosch from invading.

I went to see Bosch at 4:30 P.M. at home. He seemed to feel betrayed and alone. He had hoped for OAS sanctions against Duvalier. "I am going to fight the OAS," he said. "This is a serious political defeat for me. I cannot stand it." He was courteous to me, as always, but I felt sure he blamed me for forcing him into the OAS. He said bitterly, "The OAS is always trying to get out of doing anything. Duvalier looked fierce, spoke of a massacre, and so they jump me. Now we go to war against the OAS. Against Gonzalo Facio's army. If they come here—" the OAS Com-mission "—they will be received by very bitter speech. The bitterest they have ever heard from a President. The left will hit me hard now. I have to hit them first. There will be no Red FENEPista in the government by Saturday morning. This is the turning point. I must get a victory. I will throw everything I have into it. Perhaps some are plotting my overthrow. If I am going down I am going to fight them until I fall."

It had been raining for two or three days in Jimaní and the troops there were getting restless.

17

On Thursday I was told that the OAS Commission had asked Foreign Minister Chalmers for safe-conducts for the asylees but Chalmers had received them coldly. Freites wanted to cooperate with the OAS. But Bosch said he would have nothing to do with the OAS.

On Friday morning we received word from Ambassador Adlai Steven-son that the UN Security Council had refused to act on the dispute, thus in effect sending it back to the OAS. We learned that Betancourt had advised Bosch not to invade. Vallimarescu reported that Bosch had held a press conference, had seemed relaxed, confident that Duvalier would fall, and had said that the matter was in the hands of the OAS, and he would welcome its return. We were puzzled. That afternoon I found him bitter, angry, and cornered. He said, "Duvalier has insulted me. I cannot sustain that. It would be better if I were to fall." He spoke of committing suicide.

He said, "The Haitians killed a Dominican woman. They tried to kill me. I am a good friend, but a bad enemy. I will not forgive. I have my ways. There are many Haitians here. I am Duvalier's implacable enemy. The OAS has hurt me, not helped me. I will not tell Calventi to demand a faster report and sanctions. It would take the OAS six months to do anything. There is no point in any of this."

Patiently I spoke to him about Ambassador Stevenson's efforts in the UN. I recalled Bosch's own trip to Washington, where he had met Stevenson, and reminisced about my own relationship with Stevenson. Bosch relaxed a little and talked about what a beautiful city Washington was and how many friends like Stevenson he had in the United States. He was pleased by Stevenson's help in the UN. He began musing a bit—he did not have the worldwide responsibilities of Kennedy and therefore was freer to act.

His wife joined the conversation and said she thought it would be better to send the Army than to let Duvalier kill all the Haitians. Bosch disagreed with her, saying if he did send his Army, Dominicans would kill Haitians, and this he could not face—he was a man of peace. Then he swung back to another bitter tirade against Duvalier.

La Nación arrived. It said Duvalier had told Facio that he would not give safe-conducts to seven of the asylees. Face blackening, Bosch said, "This is the final defeat for me."

I tried to argue that, instead, it was a club he could use against Duvalier—now at last, rebuffed by Duvalier, the OAS might be willing to act against him.

Bosch said, "The OAS acted against Trujillo only after he made an actual assassination attempt against Betancourt." He was convinced the OAS would do nothing for him. I continued to urge him to stay with it. But during the conversation it became obvious that he was thinking of subverting Duvalier.

18

On Monday and Tuesday, May 13 and 14, we heard that Dejoie and Fignole were asking Bosch for recognition as co-heads of a Haitian provisional government-in-exile. Other Haitian exiles were maneuvering for position in Santo Domingo, Puerto Rico, and the States. Undersecretary Ball briefed the U. S. Senate Foreign Relations Committee on Haiti. Its chairman, Senator Fulbright, accused most Latin American countries of indifference to conditions in Haiti.

Bev Cass reported that Duvalier was distributing machetes and Czech rifles to his militia. Pistols were being handed out to *ton-ton-macoutes* near Barbot's former hideout. Barbot was reported in the hills. Ambassador Thurston had heard that the *ton-ton-macoutes* had orders to massacre Americans first and then mulattoes. The *ton-ton-macoutes'* automobiles had machine guns, grenades, and flame throwers.

The Haitian government was accusing the United States government and the Dominican government of conspiring against Duvalier. The OAS Commission arrived back in Santo Domingo. Newsmen said the Dominican military had set up training sites for Haitian exiles. Venezuela and Costa Rica broke diplomatic relations with Haiti.

The next day, May 15, was D-day for Duvalier, the anniversary of his "re-election." Tension was increasing inside Haiti. Everyone seemed to think something would happen the next day, but no one knew what.

Now at 4 P.M. on the 14th I went to see Bosch. I found him in a rage. He said, "The OAS is here. I will not talk to them. I will not receive them. There are rumors that the day after tomorrow Duvalier is going to declare Haiti a socialist state. If he does, in a half-hour it will become a world problem. So the only possibility is for the United States to do something there. Because we are not going to do anything else about the Haitian problem. Maybe the United States Ambassador can see Duvalier. Maybe he can tell him that if he declared Haiti a socialist state, the United States will invade Haiti. Maybe you can get the Marines ready. I have retired my troops from the border since last Thursday, little by little. I implore you—do something before this happens."

He was making it absolutely clear that he was handing the problem to us. He himself had had his fill of jousting with Duvalier.

I asked him where he had heard that Duvalier would declare Haiti a socialist state. From a man who knew Haiti and formerly had worked for Castro, Bosch said, and from his own secret agents who last week had been keeping several Communists under surveillance in a house in Santo Domingo. One of the Communists had said Haiti was going Communist that week; now he had disappeared, traveling on a false passport, and turned up in Haiti.

I was inclined to discount the story but dared not, entirely. Back at the Embassy, uneasy, I asked King and Shlaudeman to stay, and my own secretary too, and asked the CIA man to see what he could find out about the story.

He came back at five-thirty with a wholly new story. Reservations had been made for tomorrow on a KLM flight leaving Haiti at eight o'clock for Duvalier, his wife, his four children, and two others. They would go to Curaçao. They would leave Curaçao at 10:40 A.M. on KLM Flight 991 and arrive at Idlewild at 3:10 P.M. They would stay overnight at Idlewild. They would leave New York on Pan Am Flight 114, arrive at Paris at eight twenty-five Friday morning, and connect with Air France to Algiers where they would find asylum with Ben Bella. (A variant version said they would not stay overnight in New York but would go on immediately to Paris and Algiers.) The CIA chief also said that the Haitians were expecting trouble tonight.

I hurried back to President Bosch's house. He said, "I don't believe it. Why would they use their own names if they were really going? It strengthens my own suspicions that he is going to do something very strange tomorrow."

Back at the Embassy Shlaudeman told me that Tad Szulc had picked up the same story.

I sent urgent cables to the Department, went to the Residence, and had some dinner. At nine-fifteen Shlaudeman called and asked if he could come up. Arriving, he said, "This is the craziest telegram that I've seen in this whole crazy mess. See if you can guess who's involved now." I couldn't. It was De Gaulle.

The Haitian Foreign Office had told Ambassador Thurston that they had received a special message from De Gaulle implying that De Gaulle pledged his support to Haiti.

We guessed that at most Duvalier had invited De Gaulle to visit him routinely and the French Foreign Office had replied routinely. Cables were flying all around the Caribbean and across the Atlantic.

At 10:02 P.M. the duty officer brought a cable to the Residence. It confirmed the plans of Duvalier and his party, with slight variations (Pan American, not KLM, would carry them). We would be notified as soon as he was airborne.

The UPI reported that Latin American diplomats said that two Haitian columns had marched into Haiti from the Dominican Republic.

The Colombian Ambassador in Port-au-Prince requested us to notify the Dominican government that twenty of the asylees would reach Kingston aboard Pan American Flight 432A from Port-au-Prince at eleven o'clock tomorrow.

At ten-fifteen the Department cabled its views of the situation. There might be trouble in Haiti starting tomorrow. Although the United States held that Duvalier would no longer be President after tomorrow, we would not close our Embassy—we wanted to know what was going on. The Department would not recognize the "exile government" of Dejoie and Fignole. There was no evidence to support stories that French-speaking Africans from Cuba were entering Haiti, but the possibility could not be ruled out that Communists would seize power in Haiti, create a socialist state, and quickly seek recognition from Russia and Cuba; that would have serious repercussions in Latin America and require close consultation among the American republics. We were, however, mainly concerned at new reports of arrests and murders inside Haiti and plans to take vengeance against foreigners and mulattoes. Joint action might be required to prevent a bloodbath. The U.S. military was there if needed. Duvalier might flee, confronting the OAS with an important and difficult problem. I was to report reaction.

I went immediately to see Bosch. As I recall it Fran had taken the Checker to Higüey, so I drove to President Bosch's house in my Jeep myself, taking Fandino with me.

President Bosch seemed calm. It was our problem now. He wondered, "Could Duvalier make a bloodbath tonight before leaving Haiti? It could be a curtain for his departure." I asked about the report that two Haitian columns had crossed into Haiti from the Dominican side. Bosch picked up La Nación and showed me a story saying that one group of Haitian exiles had disappeared from the capital and said he had "heard" that "a group" had tried to cross in the north two or three days ago but had "dissolved in the jungle" and nothing had happened. He said no more, and I did not press him. He could not believe the story about De Gaulle —"My friend, President de Gaulle, would not do this without letting me know."

Back at the Residence, King said that Freites believed Duvalier meant to kill the remaining asylees and demanded to know what we were going to do about it.

At midnight Thurston called to say that the French Ambassador in Port-au-Prince had merely delivered to Duvalier a letter from De Gaulle replying to Duvalier's request last March for French economic assistance. It bore no connection with the present crisis.

Shlaudeman went to see the British Ambassador, told him that tomorrow was D-day for Duvalier, and elucidated our policy.

And now past midnight a long cable began coming in from the Department. The code clerk brought it up to the Residence as it came in, a long scroll that stretched across the room. It said that if Duvalier actually left tomorrow, chaos might ensue; the Boxer would move in by morning, though it would stay in international waters. As soon as Thurston knew that Duvalier had left, he and the Latin American diplomats should help set up a temporary governing council of Haitians in Port-au-Prince, rejecting any efforts by Duvalier's henchmen to seize power. Later, returning exiles could establish a broadly based provisional government. The governing council should seek provisional recognition from other governments, ask the OAS nations for help temporarily in maintaining law and order, and quickly announce its intentions to ask OAS and UN for help. We would not land any forces unless asked, and then only to protect the lives of Americans and others, including the asylees.

A separate long cable to all embassies in the Hemisphere said that if Duvalier left and chaos ensued, the Ambassador should ask the government to support us in the OAS. We were to consult our host governments a few hours from the time this cable stopped coming in.

I went to bed at 3:30 A.M., couldn't sleep, and got up at four-thirty. Fandino had dozed on a couch downstairs. At 5 A.M., first light, we went in the Jeep to see President Bosch. We met him just as he was leaving for the Palace. I told him about the cable. He simply smiled a little and shook his head and said, "Duvalier will not leave."

I asked why.

"He would not make his reservations in his own name."

I asked what forces might be available to help maintain order and protect lives and property. He said obviously the United States forces were nearest and could move immediately.

19

Bosch was right: Duvalier did not leave.

Bosch serenely invited Newell Williams to breakfast at seven-thirty and talked about AID. He did not mention Haiti.

All day long Thurston kept sending cables replying to the Department's suggestions about a temporary governing council. As the day wore on, they sounded hollow.

I heard that a Haitian expeditionary force which had been training for fifteen days in a forest near Dajabón had jumped off for Cap Haitien at 1 A.M. By now I was convinced that something had happened in the North during the night and that Bosch knew about it.

At 3:30 P.M. Cass received naval intelligence that some twenty-five truckloads of Haitian militiamen, three-fourths of them armed, all nervous, were at the Palace gate in Port-au-Prince—shooting appeared to be imminent.

At four-ten the office of the newspaper, La Nación, blew its siren four times, as it did to signal great events. We called La Nación. A man there said Duvalier had fled.

At four-fifteen Vallimarescu said La Nación reported that all twenty-three asylees had left Port-au-Prince.

King came in from talking with Freites—only twenty asylees had left. The three left behind were Lieutenant Benoit and two others.

UPI checked with Pan American. Its New York office was still holding four seats from New York to Paris.

At four thirty-five Dominican radio stations were broadcasting the word that Duvalier had fled Haiti, and Haitian exiles were "preparing themselves."

On my instructions, the CIA had been trying all day to check the story about Duvalier's flight. The station chief now reported that Ben Bella of Algeria denied any knowledge of the affair.

At 5:15 P.M. Vallimarescu said *La Nación* had blown its siren because UPI had filed a story from Port-au-Prince saying Duvalier had fled. Immediately thereafter UPI had filed a "kill" order on the story. One small radio station was still broadcasting intermittently from Port-au-Prince; otherwise all was silent.

That evening we went to a party at the Colombian Embassy in honor of the OAS Commission. I talked to the Commission members briefly and came away with the impression that they were divided among themselves and that they would probably write an innocuous report which would not help Bosch. Worn out, I went to bed early, telling the duty officer not to wake me except for urgent messages. I also told King to arrange relief for the duty officer tomorrow—he had been up all last night too.

The last message I took before going to bed said that at his press conference today Duvalier had said, "I am still here," and the country was calm and peaceful. The Dominican Republic under Trujillo had been calm and peaceful too.

20

So ended the Haitian crisis. It kept sputtering throughout the spring and summer, indeed, throughout the rest of my time in the Dominican Republic. But it sputtered in secret, by night, behind a veil. Bosch and I avoided the subject. Exiles were busy plotting against Duvalier and each other, Haiti was wracked by gun battles and bombings and executions, uprisings and small invasions occurred and were put down, rumors thickened like clouds of smoke, and occasionally a flash of lightning appeared—Clement Barbot and his brother were hunted down and murdered. But other than that, night descended on Haiti.

The United States suspended diplomatic relations with Haiti and called Thurston home. He did not return. Later we resumed relations and sent a new Ambassador.

President Bosch never forgot or forgave Duvalier or the OAS. Probably he always blamed me and the United States too. But the fact that his old tactic of digging himself into a hole so deep that everyone would help pull him out had failed; far from helping pull him out, Duvalier had almost buried him. And us too—Duvalier still sat there in the Palace in Port-au-Prince, reportedly ready to be crowned Emperor for Life, no doubt laughing at us, the greatest power on earth. Bosch believed he had suffered a grievous defeat at Duvalier's hands. He was right. He never recovered from it. And he had squandered valuable time during it.

Worst of all, the Haitian crisis fertilized the seed of mutual suspicion between Bosch and his own military. He had always thought they might destroy him. During the Haitian crisis, they began to suspect he intended to destroy them. Henceforward he and the military so deeply suspected each other of wishing the other's downfall that, in the end, it happened.

Often, in retrospect, I have wondered whether our policy during the Dominican-Haitian crisis was not wrong. Things could scarcely have turned out worse—Bosch was gone, Duvalier stronger than ever. Several months after the crisis ended, President Kennedy asked me, during a relaxed private conversation, "Wouldn't it have been better if we'd let him go?" that is, permitted Bosch to invade. I said I didn't think so—he almost surely would have been branded an aggressor in the OAS or the UN, or both, and this would have done him, and us, no good. Indeed, the OAS might have imposed sanctions on him, as it had on Trujillo. Moreover, it had not been us alone but his own military which restrained him —they might have lost.

Of course, if he had struck quickly at the outset, sent planes to bomb the Palace and kill Duvalier, he might have gotten away with it. If—but there is no good in speculating. One never knows what course history might have taken if, at any fork in the road, a leader had chosen differently.

Chapter Nineteen

THE END OF THE HUNDRED DAYS

One day during a lull in the Haitian crisis I had asked President Bosch if he would like to have me try to build a bridge between him and the Dominican professional and business men—the *civicos*. He had eagerly said yes.

I feared an isolated Bosch. He had entered office separated from the Republic's power centers: the *civicos,* the oligarchy, the Church, and the military. By his actions since, he had further alienated them. All he had was his own voters, the poor. They had nothing but their votes. Only about fifty people in the Republic possessed real power. If Bosch became permanently isolated from them, he would be in grave danger. They were afraid of Bosch; he was out of touch with them. If I could even bring them together physically, I might at least start a dialogue.

With the greatest care, we planned a dinner party. We worked out an elaborate minute-by-minute scenario, and chose each guest only after the most careful study. The date, set well in advance, was May 16, and it turned out to be the day after Duvalier celebrated his victory; and when President Bosch arrived at the Residence, I felt sorry for him. Since his inauguration, he had shunned the endless round of receptions at embassies or the Hotel Embajador. This, really, was his first.

And what a first! Fran and I stood by the piano in the doorway to the living room just beyond the oval foyer, with its black-and-white tiled floor, and shook hands with the guests as they arrived—Donny Reid, who had been the Consejo's Second Vice President and whom Bosch's administration apparently would prosecute for murder; José María Cabral, the quiet behind-the-scenes leader of the Cabral-Tavares-Vicini-Bermúdez oligarchy complex; Marino Auffant, leading businessman, a member of the ADI which had been criticizing Bosch vigorously; Gustavo Tavares Espaillat, leader of the Tavares clan in the capital. Bosch's only friends were Minister Freites, Minister Jaar, and Amadeo Barletta, a wealthy businessman. We had two buffers, the German Ambassador and

Dr. Jordi Brossa, a well-known physician. As the guests mingled, I thought how striking the contrast to the Consejo days. Then everybody had known everybody else, and the comfortable air of a clan drawing together had prevailed. Not tonight. The guests stood about nearly silent.

Bosch was magnificent. He moved among them, taller than most, his white hair always visible, making sure he missed no one, shaking hands and greeting each as though each were an old friend.

Bosch did not drink, but the others did. I did not want conversation to start too soon, before the guests had loosened up a bit, and so announced a film, *Eyewitness to History,* a CBS documentary on the Bosch inauguration, and the lights went down, and there on the screen was the sight and sound of Juan Bosch's inauguration as President—pictures of Trujillo, the post-Trujillo riots, then the parade in front of Bosch, the swearing-in, his inaugural speech, the dignitaries congratulating him, Betancourt, Villeda Morales, Muñoz Marín, Vice President Johnson. Then Peace Corps and AID projects, an engaging closeup of Bosch, and an interview with me declaring our support for him, saying that we wanted a government run not from Havana or Moscow or Washington, but from Santo Domingo. The film may have seemed rather bland in, say, Chicago, but here, in this room, with this audience, it had a cutting edge; Juan Bosch, who sat among us, was the first freely elected President of all the Dominican people in our time, and some of those present didn't like it, but we, the United States government, supported him.

The lights went up, and we dined at once at small scattered tables, Fran leading President Bosch to a table on the porch with Donny Reid and Mrs. Shlaudeman, while I took Mrs. Bosch to a table in the living room with Barletta and Clara Reid. Shlaudeman and King skillfully guided the others to the right tables. My task, and King's and Shlaudeman's, throughout the evening, was to see to it that Bosch had a chance to talk to Donny Reid, José María Cabral, and Marino Auffant.

After dinner I had planned to take the men out to the garden for brandy and coffee, but the houseboys began bringing coffee and brandy to the tables. I glanced at Fran's table. Bosch looked restless. I excused myself, wandered about a moment, managing to tell King and Shlaudeman I thought Bosch would leave soon, then went to Bosch's table. Fran, having seen me coming, had gotten up, and I sat down in her chair, and Mrs. Shlaudeman had left, and in a moment King and Shlaudeman brought Cabral and Auffant over. They talked, they seemed affable, Bosch was at his best, but very little of substance was said. And in a few minutes Bosch announced he must go: He must be at the Palace next morning at five o'clock.

After the guests left, King and the Shlaudemans and we conducted a post-mortem. Mrs. Bosch had not gotten on with Mrs. Reid during dinner. Reid and Bosch had talked constantly, but mostly small talk. This was the one thing we had not expected. We had hoped for a triumph, feared a disaster. Instead, we had gotten mostly small talk. Well, that in itself was a gain. The next time I saw him, President Bosch was unusually lavish in his gratitude, saying it had been the first time he had been able to talk to these people as one human being to others, and he hoped we would do it again.

2

Bosch had lost strength with the poor in the cities. They had no jobs. Jaar, still pleading with Bosch to spend money and put people to work, was almost in despair. One day a committee came to the Palace from Güaley, one of the poorest *barrios* in the capital, where Bosch had gotten almost every vote. They had demanded jobs. Jaar had begun, "Gentlemen, I promise you—" Their spokesman had held up his hand, said, "That's enough," and they had walked out. They wanted jobs, not promises. They would wait no longer.

The PRD, Shlaudeman said, was losing ground everywhere. Jaar was highly unpopular within it. Miolán had only thirteen hundred patronage jobs—the government employed about forty-two thousand, not counting Haina—and was hard put to it to fill them with competent people. Bosch seemed to be shunning the PRD, perhaps fearing a rival power source. The old PRD hands—Molina Ureña, Casasnovas, and others—said privately that Bosch was not making his revolution.

Bosch was behaving far more like an old-fashioned Latin American personal chieftain than a Communist. In the very first days of the Russian Revolution, Lenin and Trotsky began to identify the Party with the state, a policy which led to Stalin's betrayal of the Revolution. But Bosch, in his very first days, shut the Palace door on his party. Never after he won did he give the PRD its due, let alone use it to transform Dominican society.

As early as April, I had heard servants say, *"Juan Bo no sirve nada,"* "Juan Bosch is good for nothing." Now I heard it from the poor wherever I went. So did King, so did Shlaudeman, so did the visa section. And the people who were saying it had been Bosch's voters. Bosch was, quite simply, losing his people. They were too impatient, of course. But why wouldn't they be? If he really lost them, he would have lost the last brake on his political opponents.

The government's finances were improving. Bosch was pleased. His current operating budget would be balanced by June. He would repay nine million dollars the Republic owed the IMF.

Newell Williams of AID now proposed to ask Washington for a new loan of fifteen million dollars for eight new agricultural projects. I was somewhat dubious. This would not create employment. Nor would it reassert the U.S. presence. I thought we must capture the valley of the Río Yaque del Sur for U.S. development. I suggested Williams inquire into that and go over the list of programs Bosch had given me aboard the *Mella*.

Williams said, rather casually, "Moscoso and Betancourt and Harriman have agreed that Bosch is gone and so hands off."

I asked what he meant.

He said he understood that "Washington" had decided Bosch would fail, or fall, and did not intend to put more money into the Republic.

Obviously, if this was true, it was crucial. Williams had said it before. I had no way of knowing whether it was true, especially his specifically naming Moscoso, Betancourt, and Harriman. But the mere fact that Williams believed it was important.

Upon reflection, I realized that I too had thought I detected a certain reserve, or skepticism, in Washington about Bosch. It was not surprising. I myself, by my detailed reporting, had probably disabused Washington of any notion that Bosch was an ideal President. And the CIA's reporting on the Castro/Communists had hurt him. It is the CIA's duty to collect information—facts, rumors, everything. It also must evaluate the information. Several times recently I had noticed routine CIA reports on the Castro/Communists that gave rumors a credibility far higher than I would have, and I had talked to the CIA station chief about it. (In reporting a Castro/Communist plot, however wildly implausible, it is obviously safer to evaluate it as "could be true" than as nonsense.)

Moveover, such Dominicans as last year's Foreign Minister Bonilla Atiles were convinced Bosch was handing the government over to the Communists; they preferred not to stay here and help but to poison Washington against Bosch. It showed up in little things—the casual way the Department informed me that Juan Isidro Jimenes Grullón had made a trip to Washington to propose a *coup* against Bosch, which I thought clearly treasonable. It showed up in big things—we had committed something over fifty million dollars to last year's Consejo but not a cent to Bosch.

In sum, reserve and doubt in Washington appeared to have replaced last year's enthusiastic determination to create a "showcase of democracy." At the very least, Washington had decided against loaning or giving money to a government too ineffective to make good use of it!

And this had a tremendous effect on Dominicans. During the Trujillo years they had learned to distinguish between what the U. S. Embassy in Santo Domingo thought and what the U.S. government in Washington thought. For they had seen times when the Ambassador was personally friendly with Trujillo while Washington frowned at him, and times when it was the other way around.

I decided to go to Washington. I wanted to try to get an AID loan and to capture the valley of the Yaque del Sur, tangible evidence of our confidence in Bosch. And I wanted to discuss the crisis of confidence. I wanted, in short, to demand that Washington "define itself" on Juan Bosch.

But I was not ready. So absorbed had I been in the Haitian crisis that I had lost touch somewhat with the Dominican political situation. I wanted, before I went, to do my own legwork—not to rely on the staff, but to travel and talk again to people in every sector of Dominican life.

3

As usual, of those opposed to Bosch, former President Bonnelly made the most sense. He came to my house of an evening, and he looked good, an old friend.

I asked how he thought things were going. Leaning forward, fiddling with a drink, looking down at the coffee table, Bonnelly shook his head, and said, "Very bad. Very bad." I asked why, and he drew up a lawyer-like indictment of Bosch's errors, failures, and transgressions. He began calmly, but after a time his voice became edged, now with contempt, now with indignation. "He has no good people. He is following a wrong economic policy. He has stopped the flow of *divisas*," foreign exchange, "and he counts his money. People don't care about money. They think with their stomach." How odd to hear an oligarch saying, and rightly, what a revolutionary should have known. "Business is at a standstill. There is no development. Instead, we are going backward. He has made promises he cannot fulfill. The Tavera Dam," first project on the Yaque del Norte under the British Overseas contract. "Impossible. There is no road to it, no studies, no townsite. And it will employ only two thousand people anyway. A cement plant at Monte Cristi," scornfully. "It will cost eight million dollars to take electric power up there to run. And we have no power anyway. Industries for twenty-five thousand people at Puerto Plata—where will he even find twenty-five thousand people at Puerto Plata? The tourist site at Samaná—there are nothing but trails there, no beaches. These are the dreams of a novelist. These are not facts. Where is the revolution? He has done nothing for the people."

I asked why people lacked confidence. "Because of the Constitution," he said, and detailed again its provisions on private property. "In the year of the elections and the *turbas*, we produced progress, with your technicians. We just told the Secretary of Agriculture to work with the technicians. And took a chance. Bosch won't delegate authority. I don't see why it is so hard. Where are all the difficulties—except those he is creating."

And now Bosch's administration was allowing charges of murder and thievery to go forward against Bonnelly, Reid, Pichardo, and Fernández Caminero. Bonnelly was, understandably, bitter. I thought Bosch would be well advised not to press the charges. Bonnelly had kept public silence till now.

Bonnelly reserved his heaviest scorn for this: Bosch had demeaned the Presidency by confusing democratic behavior with undignified behavior and by using the language of the street. Most interesting of all, Bonnelly said nothing at all about communism. I brought it up: Did he consider the Communists a danger? "No," he said. "At least not now. The trouble is, Bosch is afraid of them, he overestimates them. They would not be important if he would start his own programs. Of course, if Bosch fails, the Communists would gain."

I said I wished he would tell his friends he didn't think communism was an immediate danger. Then I went on to say that Bosch was, after all, the constitutional, elected President and needed all the support he could get, difficult though it was. Bonnelly said he would have no part of a *golpe*, and he would do anything he could to help.

I talked to many others in the capital—to Viriato Fiallo and Donny Reid and Amiama and Imbert, to Jaar and Humbertilio Váldez and Goodluck Sánchez and Molina Ureña and Casasnovas. I talked to the military. They seemed quiet but watchful. I talked to the Papal Nuncio. He would help support Bosch, though he would not abandon the ecclesiastical principles on which he had opposed some provisions of the Constitution. I made a trip to the eastern provinces and talked to *campesinos* and ranchers and PRD young people and kids in the 14th of June. I went north to Santiago and, surprisingly enough, found more support for Bosch among the oligarchy than anywhere else. The reason was not hard to discover: Business was good in Santiago. I publicly reaffirmed our support for Bosch. And I found, oddly, that the oligarchs, too, favored big-spending, leaf-raking projects to put people to work, while the revolutionary President was an economic conservative. They recommended several sensible Cabinet changes.

Returning, I told Bosch I had been in the Cibao, preaching the Bosch gospel to the oligarchs, and had found ready listeners: Those people were not his enemies.

I did not tell him, however, that once, touring a *barrio* in Santiago, I had heard a slum-dweller, mistaking me for Bosch, say sneering, "Look —he says he never rides in a *tu-tum-pote* car." Nor that I had heard poor people calling him *"Juan Bocina"*—Juan the Horn—and making jokes about his speeches on "donations" to agrarian reform.

Our task, I thought, was to split the businessmen off from the rightist politicians and tie Bosch to the businessmen; and to split Bosch off from the left.

4

But Bosch made more of his interminable speeches about economics, "donations" to agrarian reform, morality. In one he said, "As you know, ever since February 27, coconut milk, cane juice, and coffee have been drunk at the National Palace, or perhaps a little bottle of Coca-Cola by those who like it. Therefore, we have absolutely no use for the following liquor which we found in the Palace: Seventy cases of champagne, four cases of martini, rye, a case each of cognac, rum, and martini, a case of Lepanto cognac, a case of Cinzano vermouth, a case of rosé wine, a case of Barsac rosé wine, two cases of white wine, two cases of sherry, two cases of white wine, a case of Dutch gin, three bottles of manzanilla, a bottle of crème de menthe, and eight bottles of cocktail mix."

In one speech he said that "we" must give the workers culture, newspapers, magazines, folk-dancing, plays, for "otherwise, what do the workers do when they have money—drink rum, play cards, run around all night, play pool and dice, and, when they get drunk, start burning cane fields." He declared he would not tolerate dishonesty in government— "the President does find out and the President will send for the police and will have his most useful friend or his closest collaborator arrested." He was referring to one of the hangers-on, whom he had just dismissed, having caught him in what he considered a "dirty business" with foreign businessmen. (Charges against the man were subsequently dismissed.) This allayed somewhat the fears of those who had mistrusted the men around Bosch. But then Bosch went on virtually to accuse two U.S. newspapermen and the South Puerto Rico Sugar Company of trying to overthrow his government. Why South Puerto Rico Sugar, I never knew for sure. But the reason for his attack on one of the newspapermen (though not the other) was clear enough—Hal Hendrix of the Miami *News* had just published a series of articles attacking Bosch hard, and me, too.

5

Bosch handled the U.S. press badly. He played a few favorites, thereby antagonizing all others. He quickly forgot his friendly early press and fumed at criticism. Some newspapermen considered him a "starry-eyed idealist professor" so dedicated to civil liberties that he permitted Castro/Communists free rein. The fact is that not once to me did he defend freedom of speech for Castro/Communists on civil libertarian grounds but always on pragmatic political grounds. And indeed I, as a friend of press freedom, was disturbed by his contemptuous manipulation of the news in *La Nación,* his quarrels with Germán Ornes, his public denunciation of Hal Hendrix and another reporter, and the arrest of Bonilla Aybar on television.

The Hendrix articles, and others, presented us with a new and serious problem: Open hostility to Bosch in the United States on the ground that he was dangerously tolerant of Communists. Some of the stories were inspired by Bosch's political enemies in the Republic. The stories were printed first in the United States, then reprinted in the Dominican Republic, where Bosch's enemies—who had inspired them in the first place —displayed them to the military as proof that "even the impartial United States press" considered Bosch dangerously "soft on communism."

No doubt most of the U.S. journalists believed what they wrote. Possibly some of them, who had been friendly to Castro early in his career, were playing it safe on Bosch.[1] I considered the Hendrix articles a vicious hatchet job, and later told Hendrix so. But whatever the correspondents' motives, they fed the fires both in Washington and Santo Domingo.

The Hendrix articles produced a quick reaction in Washington. On May 31 Congressman Armistead Selden of Alabama, Chairman of the House Subcommittee on Inter-American Affairs, made a speech on the floor of the House—"the advancing Communist offensive of subversive penetration in the Dominican Republic apparently is not being effectively countered by the new Dominican government"; since Bosch's inauguration, "more than 150 Communists" deported by the Consejo had been allowed to return[2] and were now teaching in "a Communist-front school" and had made gains in civic organizations, the police, labor unions, schools, and student groups. President Bosch accused Congressman Selden of trying to "dictate" to the Republic. Selden denied it on June 4. He inserted into the Congressional Record one of the Hendrix pieces, "Red Tide Rising in Dominican Republic," warned that Bosch was mistaken if he thought he could permit uncontrolled Communist activity without endangering freedom, and said that the State department had "misjudged" Castro disastrously, must not repeat its miscalculation, and ought not discount the reports of Hendrix and Jules Du Bois of the Chicago *Tribune*. The State Department disavowed Congressman Selden's remarks.

On June 10 Senator Hubert Humphrey spoke on the Senate floor in indirect reply to Congressman Selden. Describing Bosch as a member of "the reform-minded, non-Communist democratic element in the Carib-

[1] There is an old story about a father's parting advice to his son appointed to a U.S. embassy in a Latin American country: "As soon as you arrive, predict a revolution. One is almost certain to happen sometime, and you will have called the turn. If it does not happen, you will get credit for having prevented it."

[2] As we have seen, the U.S. government had lifted departure controls on deportees and so was in part responsible for their return under Bosch. I feel sure Congressman Selden did not know that when he spoke.

bean," Senator Humphrey said Bosch had "drafted a program of reform within a democratic framework which he regards as a clear-cut alternative to communism." He said that many deportees had returned before Bosch took office and that Bosch had broken two illegal Communist-led strikes, including that of FENEPIA. He said he was "disturbed" by "prejudicial" news stories. He inserted into the Record a Washington *Post* editorial criticizing the recent "press campaign seemingly designed to prove" that Bosch was a Communist.

The columnist, Max Freedman, visited the Republic and reported favorably on Bosch, contrasting him with Castro. Hal Hendrix had written that I had failed to keep the Department and the White House informed; Freedman denied it and praised me. Tad Szulc wrote that Dominican right-wing groups and politicians who lost the election, hoping to overthrow Bosch, were telling visiting foreigners that Bosch was tolerating communism.

A small paper called the Washington *World* said that "the advance of the communist apparatus in the Dominican Republic had assumed alarming proportions." The *Kiplinger Letter* said the Bosch government was moving left, was wobbly, might fall, and U.S. policy was drifting.

The lines were hardening. In his book, Bosch wrote later that few enemies of Latin American democracy "cause such immediate damage as irresponsible U.S. newspapermen."

6

In preparation for my trip to Washington, I had asked Shlaudeman's political section to make a careful report on communism. They tried to trace out every rumor of a Castro/Communist in the entire Bosch government. They said that most opposition attacks centered on two Cabinet ministers, Diego Bordas and Domínguez Guerra; the Vice President; five lower ranking PRDistas; Ángel Miolán and Sacha Volman; and several men whom not Bosch but the Consejo had put into the Agrarian Reform Institute, the National Planning Board, and various government-owned companies.

The political section had examined all these and more. Some they concluded were dishonest schemers but not Communists. One or two were strongly nationalistic and had formerly been pro-Castro but now showed no leftist leanings, nor did the government agencies they ran. Bordas they considered an opportunist and adventurer. Miolán in the Dominican Republic had always led the center, not the radical wing, of the PRD. Volman we knew was not a Communist. The Vice President, as I have said, we considered too confused to belong to anything so disciplined as the PSP. Domínguez Guerra seemed to have little or no power over the National Police. Senator Thelma Frías, usually called a "fellow traveler," carried no real weight. When Bosch had taken office he had told me the Agrarian Reform, Planning Board, and FENEPIA had been Castro/Communist infiltrated. He had destroyed FENEPIA. Several men still in Agrarian Reform were at least Castro/Communist sympathizers, and one was reported to have been trained in Cuba; he had been hired by the Consejo, and retained by Bosch. Another was said to be a member of the 14th of June. Much the same situation existed in the National Planning Board, and Bosch was bypassing it with Al Mayne and CIDES. Radio Santo Domingo recently had added two questionable people to its staff—a former editor of the 14th of June's newspaper, and a known associate of various Communist-front groups. These appointments probably were balanced out by the new rightist editor of the government-owned *La Nación*. The *Electri cidad* and the National Institute of Potable Water each contained two men whom the political section considered questionable. It was impossible to determine how many Castro/Communists worked for Haina, due to its disorder, but the CIA and Embassy political officers agreed they were not significant. Rumor said that Castro/Communists were working on lower levels in the post office and the cement plant; we confirmed one at the cement plant, appointed by the Consejo through the influence of Viriato Fiallo. At the University there appeared to have been no significant changes under Bosch. The political section was concerned about one important man in the Ministry of Agriculture. Three traditional Communist targets, the ministries of Labor, Education, and Justice, seemed unscarred. Widespread earlier rumors that Bosch would put in high places such known Castro/Communists as Rafael Miguel Faxas Canto had simply proved not true. The political section concluded on balance that the total number of Castro/Communists in all branches of government was surprisingly small.

As for the Castro/Communist parties, the political section thought the MPD was softening its line and moving toward the PSP. Both hoped to make common cause with the 14th of June, but Manolo Tavárez Justo's *personalismo* still blocked them. He was struggling to reconcile nationalism with the straight Communist line, and finding it hard going. His leadership was still split. The political officers guessed Manolo might be getting ready to run for President. The real danger was that someone more manageable by Castro or Moscow would take Manolo's organization away from him. The organization had made headway since Bosch took office.

We were watching closely several real Communists, not in government, that Bosch's rightist opposition didn't even know about. They were holding secret meetings in a house in Santo Domingo. One had lived in Moscow for three years, spoke Russian, and had been Fidel Castro's interpreter; he had arrived from Havana under the Consejo. Another had been deported twice from the Dominican Republic, once by the Consejo, and once by Bosch, and had spent time in Prague and Cuba and possibly in Moscow. Another had lived in Russia two years. And, we now understood, Juan and Félix Ducoudray never had been deported by the Consejo but had been in the Dominican Republic since early 1962.

The political officers were also concerned about the lack of non-Communist opposition. The old parties were virtually wrecked. The two-party system had failed. Should we let matters drift? Or should we try to help create a leftist opposition party to Bosch, perhaps building around the Social Christians? Moreover, the Republic needed a party to replace Fiallo's UCN. For the rightist opposition, if deprived of a normal political channel by the UCN's dissolution, might turn to non-political means.

I had always thought the danger from the far right greater than from the far left. And I had always regretted that we spent so much time and effort on Castro/Communists. But we had to—a Castro/Communist takeover was the one thing the U.S. government, and the American people, would not tolerate. Now, with the political section's detailed and precise report, I felt I would be well armed in Washington.

7

About June 10, when Bosch's first hundred days were over, I wrote a long dispatch, setting forth what I had learned by my recent legwork, relating Bosch's failings but nevertheless urging strong support for him both in Washington and Santo Domingo.

The hundred days—in the United States in 1933, Franklin Roosevelt had used his first hundred days to make a revolution. What had Bosch done with his? Not much. He had devoted March and April to line-cutting his budget with a pencil, organizing his government, and lashing out at critics. He had spent May in the Haitian crisis. Thus he had almost wholly squandered his hundred days.

I had spent two hours with President Bosch at his house the night of June 6. He seemed relaxed and calm. He said he was ready to get some programs moving and wanted our help—farm-to-market roads, housing, and rural waterworks immediately and, for the long run, electric power, housing, and harbor, highway, and valley development. It was a sensible program, though I was interested to note a curious streak of puritanism when he declared that "for moral reasons" all housing must have three rooms—one for the parents, one for male children, and one for female children.

Bosch urged me to help quickly with the anti-subversive force, and asked me, surprisingly, to put it under "Pupito" Sánchez, the old head of the secret police under the Consejo, and Imbert's friend. Moreover, for the first time he said he wanted to use it to keep Castro/Communists, not merely rightists, under surveillance. And he said he did not want it under Minister Domínguez Guerra. "I will hit the Communists hard if they try to subvert my government," he said. "Then the others will pull back, just as they did after I hit FENEPIA."

Bosch considered the violent MPD the most dangerous of the Castro/Communist parties—the PSP was an old-fashioned intellectual Communist party that wanted co-existence and a slow road to socialism; the 14th of June was wracked with division, and Manolo Tavárez Justo was too "soft" to go to the hills; Pérez Cabral's and Dato Pagán's party (PNR) was impotent; but the MPD was attracting the sons of lower-middle-class shopkeepers and minor bureaucrats, plus criminals, adventurers, and Yankee-haters, and as soon as López Molina could build his cadres he would go to the hills. He would never get the poor masses—"the lumpen proletariat are mine," Bosch said, smiling.

He thought the Castro/Communists would continue indoctrinating and organizing while Bosch started his own programs. It was a race between them. Coexistence might end in six months. He would hold the ground of nationalism in order to deny it to the left. Bosch made a speech which played back my own earlier speech—that we wanted a Dominican Republic governed not from Havana, or Washington, or Moscow, but from Santo Domingo. He said: "When they ask that I define myself ideologically, they believe that I am going to get on my knees before one of these two capitals [Washington and Moscow]. On my knees before no one. I was elected by this people because I am a Dominican—in order to govern the Dominicans for the benefit of the Dominicans—I am covered by the Dominican flag and no other flag will cover me, alive or dead."

Bosch told me that to prevent the Castro/Communists from seizing the initiative he needed to enact two laws—a *plus valía* law, giving land to the government when it made public improvements that increased the value of the land, and a law defining *latifundio*. But these were not merely political moves—he actually needed them for agrarian reform: He did not have enough land to distribute to *campesinos*.

I said I had thought the former Trujillo lands were ample. He said he'd thought so too, but it wasn't so. Much Trujillo land was timberland and sugar land, unsuitable for farming. Subsequently I had a study made, and Bosch was right: If he was to make a meaningful agrarian reform, he did need to expropriate private land.

Right now his problems were two. He must pacify the "dangerous middle-class right," the *civicos,* in case business declined. He was at last convinced he must put the poor in the slums to work, and had begun. With these two done, and agrarian reform moving ahead, "then we can march." He said, "I am a gambler in a crisis, but I plant my feet on the ground."

Edgar Kaiser, the U.S. industrialist, was coming down soon; I suggested taking the occasion to give another party, this time bringing Bosch together with leaders of the American business community. "Especially bankers," Bosch said, smiling.

I talked to him about the Hendrix articles, warned him about the danger in adverse U.S. public opinion, and emphasized, as I had before, the need to close Dato Pagán's school, curb travel to Cuba, and stop Manolo Tavárez Justo from using public buildings as a platform. He repeated that he would close the school this month, said he had ordered passports invalidated for travel to Cuba, and had again ordered local authorities to forbid political meetings in public buildings. We checked. He had forbidden political meetings in public buildings. Passports were stamped not valid for travel to Russia or Russian satellites, which might or might not include Cuba. Dato Pagán's school did not close.

8

On June 11 Muñoz Marín arrived, bringing Pablo Casals, the cellist, together with the Casals festival group. That night, in the Palace of Beautiful Arts, Fran and I joined President and Mrs. Bosch, Governor and Mrs. Muñoz, and the diplomatic corps to hear the Beethoven Ninth. I have spent few evenings as inspiring as that one, hearing the great man, who had refused to visit the Republic under Trujillo, and the great music, both now glowing despite all sordid Dominican politics as a shimmering tribute to Dominican democracy.

Next evening we sailed out into the Caribbean aboard the *Mella*. This time our companions were more numerous and even more varied than before—President Bosch and his daughter, Barbarita, who was a playmate of Dan and Fred; Commodore Rib and his wife and young son; Luís Moreno, the Palace lawyer, called Luisito, a little man with an ashen face who seemed to sleep a good deal and drink whiskey in the morning; fat Minister Majluta and his handsome wife; Minister of Agriculture Guzmán and his wife; the omnipresent Milagros, Bosch's niece, with her disagreeable swain, Minister del Rosario. By now Fandino was about to be transferred, a loss to me, and a new young man, Marc Cantolla, replaced him and accompanied us on this trip. We anchored off Saona Island and there, by prearrangement, Edgar Kaiser, the U.S. industrialist, joined us, together with his lawyer, Lloyd Cutler, and two of his associates. Sacha Volman brought them to the boat. An odd company, surely.

Sometimes Kaiser, a friendly, quick U.S. business leader, seemed a bit bewildered. Milagros played the piano *fortissimo* in the midst of after-lunch conversations and between times carried on her love affair openly. Barbarita and my boys fished from the lower deck. Bosch by turns retired to his room to work and emerged to sit on the afterdeck, arms stretched along the back of the curved blue sofa, talking expansively about plans for tourism. Groups were constantly leaving the *Mella* or coming back to it from swimming or motorboating—humanity in swimming trunks, sand and sun. Sometimes to escape the din Fran and I would go up to the top deck and sit under an awning with Mrs. Guzmán, the sister of General Viñas' wife, a pixyish, bright woman whom we always had liked.

Native fishermen at Saona brought enormous sea turtles aboard. Many times Bosch had asked me what he should give Vice President Johnson for a gift; I now suggested he have a shield-like turtle shell lacquered and appropriately inscribed, and he thought it a splendid idea, and bade it be done, only to discover the shell had warts or ulcers or something— it was hideous. One day he led us ashore to swim at beautiful Saona, having described the beach glowingly to Kaiser, but someone erred and put us ashore not on a sandy beach but on one strewn with razor-sharp coral, so that to wade or swim was impossible, while ashore we confronted miserable native huts and the smell of pigs and garbage and stinking fish offal. I said to Cutler, the Washington lawyer, "It's a hard luck country, I'm afraid, and maybe he's a hard luck President." Luisito, the Palace lawyer, sat down on a driftwood log and began aiming his gun at various targets, including some of us. Just practicing aiming. Fran, who had observed his interest in guns and liquor all morning, shielded Dan and Fred. A few days later, Kaiser and his associates, taking Bosch's son and daughter along, went in a small private plane to inspect the valley of the Yaque del Sur; fly-boys from the Dominican Air Force rose swiftly to the sky and forced their plane down. But not always hard luck either—near evening one day Fran and I and Rib and his family went fishing near Saona, and of a sudden while we trolled, fishless as usual, the sky turned dark, a storm rolled up, the pale green sea turned black, a flight of white birds swirled in low, and the sea came alive with fish, foaming all around, and we hauled them in as fast as we could and filled the boat with threshing three-foot barracuda, while the wind roared up, the sea boiled suddenly black and white, and, soaked in spray, we made for the *Mella*. Luck was not gone.

I had let Bosch and Kaiser alone. As always, I thought it best not to push Bosch. But talking with Volman and Cutler, I discovered that Kaiser was nonplused and Bosch disappointed. Somehow, as so often seemed to happen, Bosch and this man new to him, though sharing common interests and objectives, had been talking in skew lines, superficially in agreement but somehow never quite meeting. Volman and Cutler thought I ought to intervene.

I took Kaiser to the top deck and tried to identify the problem. It was, basically, this: Bosch knew little about business and concealed it by dominating the conversation, thus forcing Kaiser to speak bluntly whenever he got a chance to speak at all, which in turn irritated Bosch. And there were other problems. For example, Bosch kept talking about tourism, but secretly knew it was impossible without electric power. Perhaps the way into power, Kaiser's interest, was via tourism. And so on— Kaiser and I went over the scenario in advance, as you always had to do with Bosch.

In the end, Kaiser Engineering did act as watchdog on contracts under the Overseas deal, as has been said. Kaiser would submit a proposal to Bosch on building electric power plants and doing the engineering on the Yaque del Sur. He considered building a wallboard plant that would use Dominican gypsum, the only fresh money of his own that Kaiser would consider investing—an illustration of the difficulty of attracting U.S. venture capital, however enlightened, into a political situation so volatile. In the end, he didn't do it.

I had brought along the text of President Kennedy's speech of June 11 on civil rights. It was, I thought, the greatest utterance on civil rights by an American President in the White House after Lincoln. And somehow reading it on the deck of the *Mella* in the Caribbean, surrounded by these people, it seemed not only clear and courageous but almost piercingly sane. I was never, I think, more proud of my country and my President. I showed the speech to Bosch. To my surprise, he only said politely he thought it an excellent speech. I wondered, as I so often had before, if we ever could bridge the gap. I had with me, too, President Kennedy's speech at American University on peace and the limited nuclear test ban treaty, probably his greatest presidential speech on foreign affairs, and I had thought to show it to Bosch but now did not. Many times in many ways Bosch was disappointing.

This trip was the last: After we returned, *El Caribe* published a brief item about it, and soon street gossip made fun of Bosch for cruising about on a *tu-tum-pote* yacht, and, with what seemed to be his increasing lack of political judgment, he publicly defended himself, declaring angrily that he had been working aboard the *Mella*. He never went aboard it again—except into exile.

9

We returned on Sunday night, June 16. Next day the Chamber of Commerce of the Americas met at the Hotel Embajador, and Bosch made a good speech. He said the Alliance for Progress was not a U.S. handout, but rather, a doctrine under which the United States made long-term, low-interest loans to Latin American nations and they, in return, undertook "profound" and "revolutionary" reforms of their societies in accord with the revolutionary current of our times. Of these, he said, the most important was agrarian reform. Undertaking agrarian reform, he said, he had been accused of being a Communist. He said, "We are not Communists. We have arrived in power by free elections and we maintain a regime of democratic liberty. . . . We will prove it that this regime will end as the democracy that could make a revolutionary agrarian reform."

During the day, a crowd of teen-agers appeared at the Chancellery. They wanted jobs. Joe Quintanilla, the administrative officer, talked to them. They said, "Arrest us." He asked what for. They said, "We are invading your soil, your territory. Call the police and arrest us." He said that would be ridiculous and asked what they wanted. Jobs, they said. He said he had none right now, but might later on. That night we gave the second of our series of dinners for Bosch, this time with Kaiser and leaders of the American community, plus the British Ambassador and the English representative of the Overseas deal. The evening went very well indeed.

On Wednesday, I spoke to the Chamber of Commerce of the Americas, the most important speech I made in the Republic.[3] I reaffirmed the United States' close ties to President Bosch. I said that we were in the midst of a revolution in Latin America, wrenching change was inevitable, and the only question was whether it could be peaceful and maintain liberty, as we believed, or must be bloody and destroy freedom, as Communists declared. We had peaceably made profound changes in the United States in the 1930s and since. The same must be done in Latin America today. The people in the *barrios* deserved a better life.

But we could not do it if we lacked confidence. And too many Latin Americans and North Americans did lack confidence because they feared that this country or that would "go Castro." Castro was no military threat to the United States, I said, except as an extension of Soviet military power, but he was a "clear and present danger" to Latin American nations. And his best weapon was the fear we felt of him. Fear made men of good will seek refuge with the discredited political right. Fear made us allow leftist extremists to take over nationalism, the most powerful force at work in the Hemisphere today. Fear made us dissipate our energies looking under the bed for Communists. And fear made responsible men mistrust the leaders of the democratic left.

"Let us never close our eyes to the very real danger of Castro/Communist subversion. But let us not permit that danger to blind us to our might or deflect us from our goal, to tie our hands or paralyze our will or mesmerize our minds."

A better life for the ordinary man was not merely the bar to Castro but the only acceptable road to national independence and individual human dignity. Change was long overdue and inevitable. We should welcome it—as Franklin Roosevelt said, "The only thing we have to fear is fear itself."

[3] The text will be found in the Appendix.

The audience reaction to the speech was highly favorable, and Bosch called me to praise it with unusual warmth. In the United States the reaction was mixed. Al Burt, in the Chicago *Daily News,* suggested that critics would make familiar charges against "fuzzy-minded liberals." Senator Humphrey inserted the speech into the Record, and the Department circulated it widely.

But it did not make a dent on those who stood in intransigent opposition to Juan Bosch.

10

Preparing to leave next day for Washington, I went to see President Bosch. He was angry at the man we had sent to help "Pupito" Sánchez set up his counter-subversive force—and no wonder: He had established an office openly in the Palace and had sent out applications for jobs with the force which asked, among other things, whether the applicant was or ever had been a member of the Communist Party. (Later the CIA station chief told me the application had been "Pupito" Sánchez' own idea, but our man had indeed worked openly in the Palace. I said we'd have to replace him and start over.)

I told Bosch I would return July 9 or 10. General O'Meara was due here from Panama on the 10th; would Bosch come to dinner that night, together with his military high command? He would. Would he like me to give a third dinner party for him, one with the Santiago oligarchs, a few nights later? He would.

Bosch asked me to make known to President Kennedy and the Department his concern that the Venezuelan military was plotting a *coup* against Betancourt, that Haiti might be taken by Castro, and that the United States might misunderstand when he seized land from big land-owners without paying them. He planned to ask Congress to impose a tax on land declared *latifundio,* to be paid over a period of five years, and amounting to 20 percent of the value of the land each year. Payment would be made in land, not cash. This was of course confiscation of private property by the state without compensation. He did not intend to do it immediately. I said that, with his permission, I'd like to make some inquiries in Washington to see how the problem had been handled in other countries. Bosch would be most grateful. He complained that the U.S. government had declared the sale of Dominican cement in the United States "dumping." This, he said, ruined his idea of building a cement plant at Monte Cristi. And Monte Cristi was "a dangerous place," a 14th of June stronghold. He spoke at length about the Castro/Communist parties. He asked me to take up several trivial items with President Kennedy.

Leaving him, I wondered if he was really concerned about the Castro/

Communists. Or did he think this the way to arouse my interest? What a commentary on the view foreigners had of us!

I have concluded that Bosch was genuinely afraid of the Communists, and that he also was convinced that the way to get things out of Yankees was to raise the Communist cry. I believe, as I have said, that during the campaign, before he was sure of victory, Bosch had reached an understanding with certain Communists, almost surely including Dato Pagán; that, as President, he overestimated their strength and so feared them unreasonably; and that, possibly, he lived quite literally in terror that one or another of the Castro/Communists would kill him if he double-crossed them. I am also convinced that Bosch meant it when he said that the way to defeat communism was to make social reforms better than they, and that he wanted at almost any cost to avoid blood in the streets. Only all these theories, and they can be only theories, can account for the tortured line he followed, his highly selective attacks on the left and tolerance of it—breaking FENEPIA but never closing Dato Pagán's school nor effectively curbing travel to Cuba. He seemed to know precisely what he could and could not safely do to the Communists. Unfortunately, he never understood with equal precision how far he could and could not go before the rightists would overthrow him. Perhaps his exile years had equipped him less to understand them.

11

Next morning during my final talks with King, Shlaudeman, and the CIA chief, a demonstration began at the Embassy, teen-agers again. I told King to invite two or three of them in. They came, three ragged boys about seventeen, and sat down at my desk. One, appearing a little afraid, stared down at the floor throughout the interview. Another gazed about the room. The third spoke for all, and spoke well. They had no jobs, they had no money, their clothes were rags, they had no shoes, their mothers and fathers and sisters and brothers were starving, they wanted work, work, work.

I asked if they had gone to the Palace—President Bosch had announced that people wanting work would be enrolled on a list there.

The boy said contemptuously, "He has no jobs. He will not see us. *Juan Bo no sirve nada,*" Bosch was worthless. "And we are the Juventud," the Young People's group of the PRD. "We helped him."

I asked if they had gone to PRD headquarters. Yes; there was nobody there nowadays, just boys like themselves, jobless. Had they gone to Public Works? Yes; it had no jobs. I said I knew it was a difficult time in the Republic. When I had been their age during the great depression in the United States, I had stood in lines at factory gates looking for work. Things would get better here soon, President Bosch could not see each person singly, and they could be sure we were helping in every way we could. I realized this did not help them now, and had inquired whether we had any jobs open at the Embassy; we did not, but they could leave their names if they wished. Then I said, "The other night, I was talking to a man from La Romana and he told me he couldn't find enough men to cut sugar cane. I'm sure you could get a job there." They said nothing, looked down. I said, "It wouldn't cost much to go there in a *público*. In fact, I'll pay your way."

Finally, embarrassed first, then defiant, the spokesman spoke: "It is not convenient for Dominicans to cut cane."

"It is not convenient"—this was the final Dominican no, and made further discussion impossible, since honor was involved. I always had heard sugar owners say Dominicans wouldn't cut cane, considering it work fit only for black Haitians. I had suspected it was a myth perpetuated by the sugar owners to keep wages down. Now I had heard it from these boys.

I said I was sorry that was so but since it was, I was afraid I had no other suggestions. I wished them luck, and we shook hands, and they left, appearing pleased with their interview. Watching from the window, I saw them telling the others. Soon all departed. What do you do about them? The question keeps at me—*what do you do about them?*

Chapter Twenty

THE VIEW FROM THE STATES

It was Thursday night, June 20, in New York. I had the weekend free. I went on to Chicago, and our neighbors in Highland Park, Jerry Goldwach and his wife, met me at O'Hare Field, and I spent the weekend with them, next door to our own high narrow white frame Victorian house. I saw dozens of people, then went to Indianapolis for a day's visit with my mother.

It was the first time I had been in my native Midwest since going to the Dominican Republic. Riding down to Indianapolis on a train named the *James Whitcomb Riley,* the conductor, taking a ticket from a woman wearing a flowered dress, straw hat, and thin-rimmed glasses, said, "Greensburg, Indiany—when you git there, don't forget the tree in the courthouse roof." It was a local marvel, a tree growing out of the courthouse roof. I used to see it as a boy hunting rabbits down that way with my father, now dead nearly three years, and the woman said, "Yes, I live there," and the conductor, "I've lived there all my life. Be there tonight," and she, "It's a garden spot, Greensburg," and he, "Pret' nice little town." He passed on, taking tickets in his blue serge suit. Neither had smiled, their faces had shown nothing at all, it had been human contact, that was all, but enough, it had reaffirmed their faith; they seemed smug, calm, confident, settled in a world where nothing ever changed, not even the tree on the courthouse roof. Had they never heard of Latin American revolution? Perhaps. But they were absolutely imperturbable, unshakable, absolutely invulnerable. Their world was as expectable as sunrise. The sun slanted in over the flat rich earth, the farmhouses stood neat and wide-spaced in the rich corn country, black dirt country, best there is, best on earth.

2

Coming into Idlewild (now Kennedy) Airport at dusk the other night, New York had been breathtaking. It was so big. It seemed so organized. The taxi driver had been irritated because I was only transferring from

Pan American to American, not going to Manhattan, but he was angry, not defeated. The businessmen in the Idlewild bar were young and crew-cut, wearing tight pants that did not touch their shoes, carrying dispatch cases, moving fast, talking fast, their faces already showing strain, though they were only in their thirties, advertising men, perhaps, and a woman going alone to Hawaii was having a drink with a salesman going home for the weekend. All seemed capable, determined; all seemed to know exactly where they were going and how to get there.

The plane had arched up over southern Canada and Detroit and crossed the lake and come up on the unbelievable, shimmering beauty of Chicago's shore at night, and I had thought, "Chicago. My city. My beautiful great ugly city. Which I love." Fran had said in Santo Domingo on the way to the airport that day, "You miss Chicago and Highland Park and the United States more than I do." She was right. Then O'Hare, big and solid; and the Goldwachs, driving me home, had threaded with unbelievable skill the maze of expressways, many new to me. Chicago was flinging up bridges and towers and roadways overnight, like play-things, soon to be torn down as obsolete, and new ones to rise—new expressways, new factories, a nation in danger of being paved whole.

When I had wakened in Highland Park on a bright June morning the trees and shrubbery had shocked me—it seemed at once so lush and yet so strange. Then I realized why: There were no palm trees or banana trees. And it was a different kind of lushness than the Dominican—softer, and richer. Especially richer. The train to Chicago ran through a string of North Shore suburbs so opulent they were disquieting, almost shameful, children rushed from school to dancing lesson to bowling alley to tutor, hurried always, mothers tense in station wagons driving them. And Chicago, huge and new, with crowds everywhere, on trains, express-ways, sidewalks of the Loop.

3

The *Riley* leaving Chicago ran past the cars flowing smoothly on the Outer Drive, then on past steel mills, boxcars, coal cars, oil cars, flatbeds, endless houses, hundreds, thousands of houses, crossing the ship canal, a thin trickle leading to the St. Lawrence and the far-off sea, the sea so very far away, and trouble outside and beyond. Then finally after slashing the miles of flat prairie the train reached Kankakee and went on to Indiana, where the Battle of Tippecanoe was fought, now forgotten.

In the Dominican Republic, American power seemed political. Here, you could see what it rested on—industry, wealth, and, above all, people, people educated and trained to do things, taught and believing they could do anything. Perhaps they could. This was a great nation, ever rebuilding. To go to work in rush hour, to claw all day, home again in rush hour, fast and skilled in traffic, millions doing it, and doing it well—this was power. People. People diverse, each pressing relentlessly his own interests, yet concerting themselves in history's vise: This was power.

Yet singly, face to face, they did not seem so impressive. When I talked about the Dominican Republic's problems, my friends were eager to help. And they had ideas about what the Republic ought to do. But since the ideas had to come from their own experience, and since they had no experience of the Republic, the ideas wouldn't work. And if you explained Dominican pride, or Dominican politics, they were bewildered, uncomprehending. Theirs was a world away. So they went back to small talk— a child's birthday party, what camp their son was going to this summer, theater tickets, the race track, the musical season at Ravinia, golf and tennis, bridge and travel plans, who died, who was sick, whose daughter got into what college, whose son was getting married. Visiting our house was like revisiting one's childhood, the rooms and yard seemed small, I had laid each stone in the front walk, had moved the porch steps with my father. I asked the tenant if he could get someone to pull the wild grapevine out of the shrubbery, it was strangling everything.

On one subject, though, people did not small talk. Race. They feared the Negroes. They feared trouble in Chicago, in the United States, even, unbelievably, in Highland Park. These people were well-to-do Jewish liberals; they had strongly favored civil rights. But now all at once they were afraid. It was the summer of 1963, and President Kennedy had sent the civil rights bill to Congress, and there was trouble in the land, and they knew it and were afraid.

Some were trying to do something about it. They were engaged with the race problem, and wanted to be with foreign affairs. But even to those who were engaged, the issues seemed marginal, not really touching the core of their lives, which was rooted on personal relationships, the people they loved, the people they worked with, the people among whom they had carved out their place. Well, why not? Each found rewards in his own work beyond money. They would like to have done more; many wished they could do what I was doing. But they were helpless. They simply did not have anything to do with policy. They couldn't, in private life, and knew it, and probably preferred to leave it at that, though stirring restlessly now and then. At first to me, remembering the riot at La Vega, the plots against Bosch, the struggles with Imbert, their lives seemed empty. But were they really? Living was nothing but personal relationship, private relationship. I went to a hospital with a friend whose wife had just had a cancerous breast removed, and learned another friend's father had died, a beloved man. What else, really, did matter? The Dominican teen-agers who wouldn't cut sugar cane? There had been a time in my life when I had thought improving America was what mattered, and I had written books and articles about prisons, mental hospitals, segregation, slums, the problems of a society that did not always work as well as it should. Then had come a time when I had thought all this mattered less than personal life, inner life. Now I was involved with large public issues and thought they were what mattered. Did they? It was an unsettling trip.

I wondered whether it was not a mistake to send Dominicans to the United States. What could they see here, in our powerful cities, our great structures, our fast and rich and complex life, with which they could connect? Our opulent "way of life" could never prove to poorer peoples our success. It was more likely to arouse envy than admiration and to prove the Communists right: We must be exploiters, else we could not be so rich. And we took it all for granted.

The gap was too wide. We were too big, the Republic too small; we were too rich and powerful, they too poor and weak; we were too organized, they scarcely a nation at all. A few weeks later we sent several Dominican Senators to the United States, and, as always, I insisted they be shown not only Washington and New York but the Midwest, small towns, farming country, and they were taken up to the smiling dairy land of Minnesota, with its sleek cattle and green pastures and solid Scandinavians; and one of the Senators, observing this good fortune, sighed and said, "If only all the Haitians were Swedes."

4

On the plane to Washington, I prepared my shopping list and arguments for the Department and the White House. In spite of all Bosch's shortcomings and the heavy criticism he had run into, I was determined to make a strenuous effort to rally U.S. support for him and try somehow to pull him through. We would not permit another Castro in the Caribbean. The best way to prevent it was to help Bosch succeed.

The United States had loaned or given the Republic under the Consejo nearly fifty million dollars, but had loaned or given Bosch virtually nothing except the lagging twenty-two million dollars in sugar money—and that had been arranged under the Consejo anyway. True, until now Bosch had not asked for help. But the bald figures seemed to prove our support lukewarm.

At last Bosch had said he was ready to launch reform programs with our help. In his race with the Castro/Communists, time was of the essence —young unemployed Bosch voters were drifting to the 14th of June. Very soon Bosch would be forced to make political speeches moving left. This would sound like neutralism or worse in the United States. And it would not be enough to hold his people. By September, he would likely be in serious trouble and have to do something spectacular and revolutionary. My best guess was that it would be agrarian reform begun by expropriation of *latifundio* without compensation. This would alarm the United States.

To make this unnecessary, or, failing that, to discount it in advance, I wanted a new fifteen-million dollar AID loan and a commitment to develop the valley of the Yaque del Sur; to explain Bosch to the Congress and the press; to try to encourage U.S. private investment; and to see President Kennedy, be photographed with him, have the photograph published in the Republic, and return there myself with a public statement reiterating our support for Bosch and announcing the new fifteen-million-dollar loan and the Yaque commitment.

However, I was unwilling to put my President out on a limb unless I could be sure that the Castro/Communists would be controlled. I therefore intended to ask for help in training an effective anti-subversive force for Bosch. And, as a double check on that force, I wanted a greatly stepped-up intelligence service of our own—one capable, if necessary, of keeping several people inside and outside the Bosch government under close surveillance. The more I thought about it, the more convinced I became that the only real solution to the "soft-on-communism" problem was tight counter-intelligence work.

In short, I would make one more try to save Bosch. For I thought if we did not, he would run into serious trouble, probably in September. September is a month of high seasonal unemployment, a traditional time of troubles, and Bosch had indicated he would propose radical legislation in September. If he got through September, I thought, he might get through October. If he did that, he might make it the rest of the year. And if he did that, he might serve out his four years. But from now through September, he would be in real danger.

5

In Washington, I told all this to the Department, the Congress, the press, and the President. Sometimes in meetings, sometimes alone, sometimes in their offices and sometimes at lunch or dinner, I talked with George Ball, William Crockett, Ed Martin, Bob Manning, Arturo Morales Carrión, Allen Robbins, John Crimmins, Kennedy Crockett, Bill Sowash in the Department; with Dave Bell and Ted Moscoso and others in AID; with Ralph Dungan and Arthur Schlesinger in the White House; with Sargent Shriver and Dick Goodwin and others in the Peace Corps; with several CIA men; with Senator Humphrey and Congressmen Selden, Fascell, and Brademas; with Justice Douglas; with Edgar Kaiser and Lloyd Cutler; with Ambassador del Rosario. Newell Williams and Al Mayne attended the economic and AID meetings. I went over to the Pentagon, trying to get Bosch's patrol boats; went to the CIA and asked for help; went to lunch with Kaiser's lawyer; saw several businessmen; had lunch with Justice Douglas to discuss moving the educational television idea faster; had dinner with fifteen or twenty leading bureau chiefs, columnists, and editors from the newspapers, magazines, and wire services; asked Abram Chayes, the Department's legal adviser, to work out an acceptable method of land expropriation; talked to Bob Kennedy, the Attorney General, about the same question and about deportations and setting up an anti-subversive force for Bosch and one for me; and appeared, eager to explain Dominican problems, in executive session before Senator Morse's Latin American subcommittee of the Senate Foreign Relations Committee and Congressman Selden's subcommittee of the House Foreign Affairs Committee.

At lunch with Senator Humphrey in his office I asked what he thought the U.S. reaction would be to Bosch's proposals to expropriate land. He said the average Congressman thought there hadn't been enough land reform in Latin America, though it would be better if Bosch gave the landowners fifty-year bonds or some other compensation, and he couldn't expropriate United States-owned land. And his reforms would have to be genuine—not just political window dressing. Bosch's fiscal responsibility already had made a good impression in the United States, he thought. But he had better get moving in the Dominican Republic. Humphrey was afraid we would only go part way in helping Bosch. "If we do, there'll be hell to pay—he'll go so far left we can't support him, or he'll get knocked over, and then, O my God."

Congressman Selden received me courteously and sympathetically, and I tried to disabuse him of some of Hal Hendrix' notions and to explain the Dominican situation as I saw it. He said Bosch's nationalism was acceptable but he should throw in a sop of gratitude to the United States. Nobody here wanted to run Bosch's affairs, everybody recognized his political problems, but Congressmen had their own political problems, so Bosch shouldn't make statements that made it impossible for them to support him. Congressman Selden said he was as anxious as anyone for Bosch's government to succeed. As for land expropriation without compensation, he felt certain the reaction in the United States would be bad. It would help some if Bosch gave the landowners bonds in return. He said Bosch had invited him to visit the Republic, and I urged him to do it.

I bought several copies of David Lilienthal's book on the TVA to give to Bosch and my own people. I was dreaming too, as people said Bosch did. Dreams die hard. This one had begun a long time ago, at parched Azua and Vicente Noble. Now I pressed the Yaque del Sur project everywhere in Washington. I hit a stone wall. Ed Martin refused to go into the Yaque until we were certain the French, who had made a preliminary survey, would not. I understood—Martin and Moscoso had to face Congressional appropriations committees, and Congress was always arguing that our NATO allies should help shoulder our burdens. I agreed, in principle. But the trouble was that the Europeans usually grabbed off the cream—the high-interest, hard-currency loans for projects that were self-liquidating and safe—leaving us to pick up the tab later with low-interest, soft loans. I kept trying, arguing that at least we could make some preliminary surveys and perhaps start building an access road to a Yaque damsite. In the end, I got cables sent to our Embassy in Paris, inquiring about the French interest. And I got a firm grant of three hundred thousand dollars, with likelihood of two hundred thousand dollars more if needed, for engineering studies of the Valley. Moscoso said he could get people from the TVA to go to the Republic at once, if the French bowed out. As of now nobody even knew how much water the Yaque contained; we'd pay three hundred thousand dollars to find out; I should ask Bosch if he wanted AID, Kaiser, or the TVA to do it.

Moscoso thought Williams had not made out a case for his fifteen-million-dollar agricultural loan. He favored instead such projects as the Yaque del Sur. So did Ed Martin. I wanted the fifteen million dollars for political purposes.

Ed Martin denied there had been a change in Washington's attitude toward the Republic. He said the Department was as ready to help as ever. Somewhat irritably, he asked if I was willing to give Bosch a blank check. I said I wasn't but if we didn't help Bosch fast, we might lose him. Help him with what? Martin asked. The Yaque, such AID projects as farm-to-market roads and housing, patrol boats, and other tangible evidence of our support, plus a statement reiterating President Kennedy's support. Martin said that if Bosch wanted financial help he'd have to come up with sensible projects. Bosch's idea of expropriating land without compensation would almost surely be calamitous, Martin thought—the U.S. press, already deeply suspicious, would scream that it was Cuba all over again. Furthermore, how could Bosch dare expropriate only Dominican-owned land, not U.S.—the Dominican political reaction would be terrible. And if he expropriated U.S. land, he would run into the Hickenlooper amendment, be denied all U.S. aid.

At that time Congress was slashing the foreign aid bill heavily, and even some of the *Alianza*'s best friends were beginning to have misgivings. Three governments it had tried to help had fallen, and soon a fourth would fall. Obstacles seemed insurmountable. President Kennedy's "soaring dream," as Tad Szulc called it, was, some thought, incapable of fulfillment. No wonder Martin and Moscoso were less than generous to Bosch. It had been a bad year for them.

By the middle of the second week, with the Fourth of July weekend coming up, I left Washington for the Midwest. I was still not convinced that Washington was as enthusiastic as it had been last year; I'd had a better reception from the press and Congress. I intended to try again when President Kennedy returned after the Fourth.

In Chicago I talked to editors and editorial writers, explaining Bosch and the Dominican situation, trying to make it clear that I was no apologist for him but hoped to provide some background for an explosion that might come later. Then I went up to our camp in the Upper Peninsula of Michigan for the holiday weekend.

6

This was where I had been when President Kennedy called two years ago—only two years?—and asked me to go down to the Republic and find out what was going on. Now this weekend, as soon as I saw it, the pine and lakes and rocky bluffs and deep blue sky, I knew it still held me. Washington no longer had the same attraction as before, nor New York, nor Chicago, nor Highland Park. Upper Michigan did—the people we knew, and the woods. Maurice Ball, a roadhouse keeper and some-time miner, met my train and took me out to our camp at Three Lakes. I went trout fishing one day with John Voelker, who under a pseudonym had written *Anatomy of a Murder,* and as always we caught no fish but had a fine time talking and riding through the woods in a Jeep. Another day I went bass fishing with Gwen and Joe Heikkinen, who run a garage and filling station and lunchroom, she French, he Finnish. The third day I walked into the woods to locate a lake where I thought I might buy property with Earl Numinen, born in Finland, risen to proj-ect engineer for the Michigan highway department. These were our friends, the best, I thought, we had, and evenings having dinner with them, or sitting alone in camp in front of the fireplace, I thought again the long thoughts, the night thoughts, that always seemed to come in Michigan. It is the most healing place on earth for me.

Often I thought of a passage from Archibald MacLeish's *J.B.:*

> *If God is God He is not good,*
> *If God is good He is not God;*
> *Take the even, take the odd.*
> *I would not sleep here if I could*
> *Except for the little green leaves in the wood*
> *And the wind on the water.*

Years ago I had first come here to Michigan to fish, or thought I had, but as years passed I was less interested in fishing, more in merely being in the woods, driving the Jeep or walking, watching for deer and coyote and partridge and bear. Once I had seen a timber wolf. They are scarce now, but one day in the mysterious Burnt Plains, a great sand plain burned years ago by the Indians driving deer, now grown up in jackpine, a full-grown wolf had trotted right up to the Jeep. They are so powerful they are not afraid, and they are curious. Hence they are nearly extinct. And maybe we are too.

When I had first started coming here in 1940, traffic had been thin, tourists few, and our camp, years ago a schoolhouse at a gold mine, had been one of only about a dozen on our lake, even though it was just off the highway. Nowadays the highway was thick with traffic, and a real estate developer was cutting up sixty-foot lots on a lake in the woods I used to walk miles to. But even yet there are places, many places, where tourists never go, and that is where I like to go, and where I hoped to buy land. Most tourists do not venture far off the highway. This is not yet resort country, roads off the highway soon peter out into logging roads, and the woods are big, and strange, and filled with wild animals; tourists fear it, and stay close together. The truth is, however, as I have always taught my sons, that in the woods your enemy is not animals, not the woods, but only yourself. It is always so, really, and not only in the woods. The great ills of mankind are ones he makes. President Kennedy said in his speech at American University that the problems man made, he can solve. I'm afraid I don't believe it. And I doubt that President Kennedy, who knew, better than most Presidents, the limits of American power and, better than most men, the limits of human perfectability, believed it either. Yet, rallying his countrymen, he pretended not to know, and acted *as if* those limits did not exist. This is, really, the heart of leadership, and of human courage. Man needs the grand illusions which alone sustain faith in hopeless struggle. We lose all when, like Athens, we come really to believe in our illusions, believe in our own perfectability, or invincibility, when we forget that we are only acting *as if* we could overcome our enemies completely. Those that forget tend to seek "final solutions," even in foreign affairs. This is dangerous. For, since the great ills of man are without solution, and the power of men and nations is hedged about in narrow limits, people who seek "final solutions" are doomed to frustration and rage. Americans, eternally hopeful because of our unique history, expect happy and final solutions. We would fare better, and stand a better chance of surviving, if we recognized that final solutions are rarely, if ever, possible. And we would succeed more often if we acted *as if* we thought that not to be true, and so moved forward with courage and resolution, yet accepting as our lot on earth the Spanish phrase, *La lucha sin fin,* the fight without end.

7

Acting *as if,* I went back to Washington on July 8 to fight for Juan Bosch. Ed Martin and Kennedy Crockett and I walked over to the White House in the morning, and on the way Martin asked if I knew anything about a story that I was being replaced by a certain Puerto Rican. I said I didn't, though from time to time the same story, more or less, had appeared in a San Juan, Puerto Rico newspaper. Martin said he'd been asked over the weekend and had denied it. In the White House we asked Dungan. He said no. Then Martin, Dungan, Crockett, a high CIA official, and I talked for nearly an hour, going over all the ground, and finally clearing a statement, including the use of President Kennedy's name, that I would issue on returning to the Republic. All week I had been drafting and redrafting it and trying to get it cleared in the Department and AID. No outsider can imagine how much effort goes into the clearing of a single paragraph. I was dealing only with the State Department, AID, and the White House. Those who have done it tell me that if a paper must also be cleared by other governmental departments, such as Agriculture or Defense or Treasury, it may take days or weeks or months of effort. The negotiations with the various departments resemble negotiations among foreign powers.

After our meeting, while Dungan and Ed Martin were talking alone about another country's problems, I talked to the CIA man, with Kennedy Crockett present. I asked if I understood correctly that the CIA had been checking Bosch since about 1940, that so far as the CIA knew he was not a deep-cover Communist or under Communist Party discipline, that he owed his basic loyalties to the Dominican Republic, not Moscow or Havana. The CIA man replied affirmatively, reserving the point that no one can ever be absolutely certain of anything. Crockett added that Bosch's record in exile indicated the Communists always had appeared to think they could work with him if he ever attained power.

I explained my intention to publicly reaffirm our support of Bosch, using President Kennedy's name, and the imperative necessity therefore of continuing and strengthening our intelligence operations in the Republic. This meant two things: First, helping Bosch establish a security service; and, second, establishing a security service of our own. The CIA man promised help.

I raised the question of the evaluation of CIA information, saying that it inevitably spreads through the U.S. government and might reach the U.S. press, thereby undermining our basic policy of helping Bosch succeed. The CIA man said that perhaps some evaluations should be lowered, as I proposed.

Dungan and I had lunch together. He suggested that Bosch make a strong case for the need for land and give the landowners thirty-year bonds. Dungan thought AID should do more impact work—schools, health clinics, and so on—and, except for the Yaque del Sur, place less emphasis on long-range development. I agreed completely. Dungan understood better than most Bosch's need to move left. And he understood fully the risks involved, and our need to protect ourselves with an increased CIA effort.

I saw Secretary Rusk briefly that afternoon. When I asked about land expropriation, the Secretary said he thought it would raise serious questions. At the end he said, shaking his head, "I'm afraid there's going to be trouble on that little island for a long time." He neither approved nor disapproved my proposal to issue a statement reiterating our support for Bosch, saying nothing at all.

At 5 P.M. I went back to the White House and saw President Kennedy. Ed Martin and Ralph Dungan were there too, and we sat in the President's beautiful oval office. I reminded the President of what he had said when I went down to the Republic, "If you blow this, you'd better not come home," and said we hadn't quite blown it yet, had achieved our goals last year, but now we had Juan Bosch. I intended to see it through, but I wanted to warn him it would get worse before it got better. I told him what the problems were—Bosch had squandered his first three months, now the left was moving and the PRD slipping, Bosch's and our programs were not enough, and by September he was likely to be in serious trouble. If he survived September, he might make it, but it was going to be uphill, and I told him why—Bosch's way of dealing with the left put him in danger from the right. He had lost support both in the Dominican Republic and the United States; Washington, I thought, lacked last year's sense of urgency; and I told him what I had tried to do about it. We were gambling. But the alternatives were worse—a rightist *coup* that would put us back where we started, or a leftist takeover, another Cuba.

President Kennedy listened carefully and asked hard questions. Why hadn't he been informed that we were lifting departure controls on deportees? Dungan would find out. Couldn't the FBI do better than the CIA on intelligence? Ed Martin said no, the CIA would handle it well. The President thought it impossible to predict the reaction to land expropriation without compensation; it would create problems no matter how Bosch did it. He approved getting some AID projects ready to go if needed in September. He liked my talking to Congress and the press. Ed Martin told him about the Puerto Rican's effort to get my job. The President laughed. Once he got up from his rocking chair and, walking to look at a blue green naval painting on the wall, asked if I was coming back to help him in the campaign next year, that is, 1964. I told him I was at his disposition. He though a minute, said, "Maybe you can do more for us holding that place together. Well, we'll see." He read the statement I proposed to issue, asked Martin and Dungan if it had been cleared, and said it was all right with him. The photographers came in and made the picture, Martin and Dungan slipping out.

Leaving, I asked the President if he had any message for Bosch. He stood in the doorway, thinking a moment, and, as always, I was surprised at how tall he was. He said, "I'm wondering if the day might not

come when he'd like to get rid of some of the left. Tell him we respect
his judgment, we're all for him, but the time may come when he'll want
to deport thirty or fifty people, when it'd be better to deport them than
to let them go, I suppose he'd have to catch them in something—well,
tell him if it does, we'll help him out, we'll take 'em." I said I would
and he shook hands and opened the door. As I walked out past the
desk of Kenny O'Donnell, his appointments secretary, the President,
pointing his finger at me, said loudly so O'Donnell and the others in the
room could hear, "There he goes—the Earl E. T. Smith of this Administration." They roared—Smith had been Eisenhower's Ambassador to
Cuba when Castro came to power. I was so startled I could only say to
him, "What a thing to say," and he grinned and waved, and I left.

Next day I caught a late afternoon plane to New York, took another
to San Juan, Puerto Rico, stayed overnight at the airport hotel, and got on
an early plane to Santo Domingo.

8

It had not been an easy trip. They never were. Some of the meetings
in the Department had been extremely difficult. I have often thought
that those senior people in Embassies, the Department, and the White
House, who routinely put in fourteen- or sixteen-hour days and often
longer ones, seven days a week, give the taxpayers far more than they
realize.

My trip had not all been grim. I had stayed with Arthur Schlesinger
and attended a meeting of the "Hickory Hill Group," informal gatherings
of Cabinet members and other high officials to hear lectures by visiting
intellectuals, originally conceived by Bob Kennedy (and named after
his Virginia estate) and largely run by Schlesinger. The people seemed
so bright and able, and so sensible, and, since they were all in the U.S.
Government, I could talk freely to them, something I never could do in
the Dominican Republic, and I fear that on some evenings I scarcely
stopped talking at all. Returning to Santo Domingo, I once more felt
renewed. And again it was President Kennedy who was mainly responsible for this sense of renewal, he and his intelligence, his confidence that
made almost anything seem possible, even Bosch's success.

Chapter Twenty-one

THE NIGHT OF THE GENERALS

We launched our counterattack to rescue President Bosch the day I arrived in Santo Domingo, Wednesday, July 10.

I went to Bosch's house at 2:30 P.M. He greeted me warmly, and then, and at a subsequent longer meeting, I reported to him fully on the views held by the White House, State Department, Congress, and press—eagerness to help, grave concern at Castro/Communist growth, and so on. He did not dissent when I said true neutralism was impossible in the Caribbean. He was not surprised by the unfavorable reaction to land expropriation without compensation and grateful for Bob Kennedy's and Abe Chayes' help in solving the problem. (Both had promised memos by September 1.) He wanted TVA to make engineering studies of the valley of the Yaque del Sur and wanted simultaneously to start actual construction of dams on two tributaries of the Yaque. He was glad Dick Goodwin was coming down the next week to talk about a Dominican Peace Corps, that the Parvin Foundation would have the first educational television programs ready by mid-July, and that Kaiser would announce in the *Wall Street Journal* a proposal to build electric power. He was disappointed that Treasury was adamant on cement "dumping." He was grateful for Senator Javits' efforts to get large quantities of polio vaccine flown into the Republic—experts predicted an epidemic—for prices and specifications on surplus Army diesel power plants; for the Navy's offer to resume work on Puerto Plata if asked; for everything else I reported. He would welcome Congressman Selden and Senator Paul Douglas. He did not seem unduly disappointed that AID had turned down Newell Williams' fifteen-million-dollar proposal for an agricultural loan; he wanted to work up other AID programs before September.

Bosch had some new problems. He desperately needed ten thousand tons of rice under PL-480—the Food For Peace law—by the end of July or the first of August; rice was scarce, and the price had gone up to eighteen or twenty cents a pound, more than the poor could pay. The electric power shortage was critical; two nights ago one plant had broken down and nearly the entire eastern and southern regions of the Republic had gone dark.

He wanted me to thank President Kennedy for his support. And, walking to the door, he laughed and, referring to President Kennedy's offer to admit the Communists if he wanted to deport them, he said, "You are not afraid of the infection." I said no, we could handle it.

I held a press conference at four and issued my statement—said that in the United States I had traveled rather extensively and had found among businessmen, journalists, intellectuals, and many others a deep admiration for the Dominicans' emergence from a generation of tyranny, their conduct of a free election, and "their continuing struggle under a democratic and constitutionally elected government, against both leftist and rightist totalitarianism." In Washington I had conferred at length with President Kennedy and many others. "I wish at this time to reaffirm the support of my government for the Dominican people in their efforts to maintain and strengthen their own free democratic society and to build a better life for themselves. And I wish to reaffirm the intention of my government to cooperate fully with President Juan Bosch and the Dominican government in their programs to advance those purposes."

The statement announced the Río Yaque del Sur study and said we were seeking other projects, particularly in agriculture.

Only at the last minute did someone notice that USIS, in translating the statement into Spanish, had omitted the key words, "President Kennedy." It was corrected.

That night we entertained President Bosch, General O'Meara, the Dominican military high command, and our own MAAG leaders and attachés at dinner at the Residence, and after dinner O'Meara and I talked privately with Bosch. Bosch complained that our MAAG and his military were pushing civic action programs without informing him. O'Meara and I agreed this was improper; I would investigate. O'Meara discussed the whole question of external security fully; he had brought officers with him to survey the Republic's coastal patrol needs.

2

I had a long talk with Colonel Wolfe, the MAAG chief. Bosch had been misinformed. The four major civic action programs had been started only after program agreements had been signed by MAAG, AID, and the Bosch government. The reforestation projects had been proposed by Minister of Agriculture Guzmán, the school construction by Minister of Education Sánchez, the water exploration by another Dominican, and the farm-to-market roads, of which Bosch had complained most, by the Minister of Public Works, young del Rosario. The planning was done by

Dominican Cabinet ministers, with AID advice. Wolfe and Williams implemented it with General Viñas. The Dominican Armed Forces supplied the labor. MAAG furnished materials and advice. I told Wolfe to collect a complete set of the program agreements, with signatures, and we'd talk to Bosch about them. If he had accepted the MAAG briefing when I first had offered it, he would not have been so misinformed.

I asked Wolfe about reports that his men were criticizing Bosch. He thought some of them might feel that way but didn't think they'd say so. He himself had reservations about Bosch, but he was fully aware that our policy was to support Bosch and that any talk to the contrary could seriously undermine our position. King told me that to everyone's surprise Bosch had appointed a new Minister of Commerce and Industry to succeed Diego Bordas, and a good one, Ramón Vila Piola. Right now, however, the big problem was rice. Several months ago our economic counselor, Harlan Bramble, had warned the Dominicans they would need rice but they hadn't believed it. Now suddenly rice was scarce, and they needed help. We had cabled for fifty-five thousand tons, and despite difficulties, King and Bramble were pushing for it.

Late Friday afternoon Bosch telephoned me and said stiffly, "Discontinue the rice negotiation." He said Bramble had offered the Dominicans rice on unacceptable terms—not under PL-480, the Food for Peace law, but on straight commercial terms. I told him I'd call him back, there must be some mistake. There had been—again Bosch was misinformed.

Irritated, I tried to call Bosch back but couldn't get him.

Why I didn't get him became clear soon enough.

At 6 P.M.—it was a Friday, of course—Sacha Volman came to the house unannounced, nervous and tense. The military chiefs had asked Bosch to join them at San Isidro at 4 or 5 P.M. They intended to press him for a stronger anti-Communist policy. Bosch had told Volman that either he or the military would run the country.

This, it turned out, was no ordinary rumormonger's invention. Instead, it was the beginning of the most serious confrontation to date between Bosch and his military.

That night we went to a dance at the Armed Forces Club. Everything seemed normal. The confrontation apparently had not occurred. Next morning El Caribe said nothing. Its editorial called the military golpe in Ecuador a "backward step." It was the fourth since the Alliance for Progress began. Each one made us more nervous.

At nine-thirty Saturday morning, Bev Cass came to the Residence. Imbert had called him in. President Bosch wanted Imbert at the Palace at 10 A.M. Imbert would go but was upset. He said the service commanders would meet at San Isidro at 11 A.M. to demand that the President take strong action against the Communists. The meeting had been called by Colonel Wessin y Wessin. Imbert feared that if Bosch refused, they would imprison Bosch at San Isidro. Cass had urged Imbert to support the President.

I asked where the other Dominican military leaders stood. Cass thought General Hungría of the Army would support the President fully. Commodore Rib would straddle, Defense Minister Viñas had almost lost control, and as for General Luna of the Air Force, who knew? The other day, a high-ranking officer had told Cass that General Viñas should be replaced as Minister of Defense by the former naval commander, Francisco Javier Rivera Caminero, now naval attaché in Washington. I asked if a real move was afoot to get rid of Viñas. Cass didn't know but wouldn't be surprised. Was Rivera Caminero tough enough to run the Armed Forces? Cass thought so. (I didn't, though Cass knew him better.) Cass said the commanders wanted Miolán "removed," presumably deported, and wanted "all the Communists" deported. I told Cass to hurry back to Imbert and tell him I hoped he could prevent the other generals from putting the President between the sword and the wall. Cass left.

So here it was again. Instead of developing the country, we were once more back in a weekend military crisis. Sometimes I came near despair. What good did it do to fight for the Río Yaque, work with Justice Douglas, chase all over Washington trying to get money and support for Bosch, when the machine gunners at San Isidro kept yammering about deporting Communists or suspected Communists? And this move looked serious—Wessin was its leader. He was tough. And he had the tanks.

Colonel Richardson, the air attaché, telephoned at eleven-twenty. The meeting was in progress at San Isidro. Everyone was there, including Bosch. San Isidro seemed normal, although a helicopter was hovering. I asked why. Richardson didn't know.

King came to the Residence. Imbert, he said, had not gone to the meeting. He had met the President and Viñas at the Palace, but they had left for San Isidro without him.

Throughout Saturday the trouble sputtered on. We could learn nothing definite. The attachés were working but couldn't find out what had happened, a bad sign. Was the military acting, not talking? Finally the attachés did learn that the meeting had ended, and Bosch had left San Isidro. Well, that was something—he wasn't a prisoner.

On Sunday, Cass said the best he could make out of it was that the military, faced with Bosch, had lost their nerve. They seemed smoldering, not satisfied.

3

Sunday was Bastille Day, Fran and I went to the usual big reception at the French Embassy, and I got Viñas aside and asked about the meeting. As usual, he volunteered nothing but answered my questions.

Yes, the military and Bosch had exchanged views. The impetus for the meeting had come from the young pilots. Not from Wessin? Yes, from him, too. No, Amiama and Imbert had not attended. Yes, Belisario Peguero had. Yes, communism had been the subject. Yes, all were satisfied. Had his own personal position been damaged? No, smiling a little.

I also ran into Ramón Baez, a young descendant of the nineteenth-century President, Buenaventura Baez, who was South Puerto Rico Sugar's manager in the capital. A strike by a few factory workers had shut down La Romana entirely, throwing seventeen thousand men out of work. The Communist PSP, using the 14th of June as a front, was running the strike. The workers wanted a 41 percent pay increase, and the 14th of June publicly demanded the expropriation of La Romana. Baez said the company was considering selling out. Bosch had told him the strike was illegal and he would support the company. But Miolán was supporting the strike. Miolán's objective was to break *Conatral* (formerly *Foupsa Libre*), the labor federation supported by the AFL-CIO's ORIT which had consistently, if not obstinately, refused to merge with Miolán's federation. And this objective happened to coincide with the PSP's and 14th of June's. So Miolán was, in effect, fighting Bosch alongside the Castro/Communists. And it all went back to last year's quarrels among the rival labor federations which we had tried, and failed, to stop. In the end, Bosch broke the strike. Thus he held firm against the left at La Romana, as the Consejo had not.

We left the French party about 11 P.M. At 3 A.M. I was wakened by the phone: Volman wanted to come to the Residence. I went downstairs in my pajamas and let him in.

He said that Bosch suspected that the San Isidro meeting really had resulted from a vast plot involving an American newspaperman, un-identified agents from Miami, our MAAG and attachés, and "the CIA in Puerto Rico." The CIA was the moving force, not Imbert, as Bosch had first thought. President Kennedy and I were for Bosch, he believed, but we could not control the U.S. military and the CIA. The economy was in bad shape, unemployment was high, Bosch could not fire Belisario Peguero, he dared not move directly against Wessin y Wessin, the most he could do was move against the military chaplains. Bosch intended to resign. He would present his resignation to the Assembly and put the responsibility on the military.

Earlier, near midnight, Volman had found fifty or sixty soldiers surrounding Bosch's house. Inside, Bosch was talking to Minister Majluta, Minister José Brea, and Majluta's wife. They said the *Cascos Blancos,* the police riot squads, had surrounded Santo Domingo. Bosch had telephoned Belisario Peguero, been unable to reach him, and been told by a police captain on duty that the city was not surrounded, he had merely reinforced key installations because he had information that "the Communists" were about to attack them. Brea and Majluta declared Wessin y Wessin was the spearhead of a move to overthrow Bosch. They wanted to send him to France. Calderón said the police caused all the trouble. Mrs. Bosch asked if that was so, why was Belisario Peguero home in bed? Calderón had verified that he was indeed in bed. So all had concluded the leader was Wessin y Wessin. The military had met secretly earlier that night at Wessin y Wessin's house. Calderón would bring two tanks into the front yard of the President's house. Most of the 19th Battalion was already there, or coming, the troops assigned to guard the President and Amiama and Imbert. The San Isidro meeting had been triggered by Bosch's intention to arrest Luna for thievery. Now Bosch couldn't do it.

None of this made much sense (except Mrs. Bosch's remark that Belisario was home in bed, where I thought they all ought to be). And some of it—suspicion of the CIA—was downright dangerous fantasy. Moreover, why attack the chaplain?—this might pull the Church in on the side of the military. And, if Wessin was the menace, why bring Wessin's tanks into Bosch's front yard? I told Volman this, said I'd see Bosch tomorrow, and went back to bed.

4

Wessin y Wessin seemed to be emerging as the dominant figure. He was a stocky man just under forty, tight-lipped, heavy-browed, his face getting full. He habitually wore field uniforms, not dress uniforms. His eyes were deep-set. He was a deeply religious man. He was under the influence of an adventurer close to Bonilla Aybar, the anti-Bosch TV commentator, and of the Air Force chaplain, Father Marcial Silva, who had been giving courses in Christianity to Wessin's officers and men. The Social Christians thought Wessin fanatic; some military men thought him ambitious, but none said he was dishonest. Born of middle-class Lebanese parents, he had graduated from high school, entered the Army as a private, and attended the Dominican Armed Forces Training Center; had never visited the United States; he had known no other life than the Dominican military's. He lived modestly, drank little, smoked constantly, had no social life, and often visited his mother and his military friends. He talked ceaselessly, to the point of obsession, about communism. He never talked about women, as so many Dominican officers did. He distrusted all politicians. The only one he admired was long dead, President Ulises Espaillat. He was naïve, inarticulate, blunt. In the Armed Forces Training Center which he commanded he held his subordinates' loyalty by seeing to it that they were the best-fed, best-clothed, best-equipped, and best-trained men in the Armed Forces. He seemed to feel that many high officers lacked intelligence, ability, integrity, and moral stature. He wanted to remove them and promote younger, abler, more professional soldiers. He was politically naïve, unable to distinguish between the non-Communist revolutionary left and communism. He saw only black and white. Recently he had published an article in an Armed Forces magazine addressed "To all My Brothers in Arms," calling for unity among the Armed Forces to safeguard the Republic. He was only a colonel but he had the tanks, and more: Conviction and courage.

In the morning, I made an appointment with Bosch for twelve-thirty, then talked with the Crisis Crowd. The new police adviser, Tony Ruíz, said he'd heard of no unusual police activity during the night. Cass said that three middle-level officers had told him they had lost faith in the high command. King said thievery in the Armed Forces was dividing them—quarrels over the spoils. Cass said that an officer at San Isidro had alerted senior sergeants to stand by for a possible clash between the President and the military over the Communist question. The sergeants had been fully in accord—the price of rice was high, Bosch had not made good on his promises. Cass said rumors were flying around that Bosch had threatened to resign. Viñas, Rib, and, especially, Hungría, still supported Bosch, but that was about all. The CIA man said Bosch wasn't yet convinced Wessin was the leader of the forces against him. Shlaudeman reminded us that the PRD once had thought well of Wessin. I asked where the tanks were. At San Isidro, Richardson said.

At ten thirty-five our MAAG Chief, Colonel Wolfe, called to say something was going on right now in the military. The attachés hurried out.

They returned at ten-fifty. The high command was meeting in the Palace. Luna seemed to be the leader, presumably insisting again that the military require Bosch to "define himself" on communism. Bosch was going on national radio-TV to denounce "reactionary elements" in the Armed Forces. The Communist PSP was saying we were urging deportations. Bosch and we were getting caught between left and right.

I asked what Bosch ought to do to improve his relationship with the Armed Forces. The Crisis Crowd thought he ought to get rid of Belisario Peguero and Commodore Rib and do something about the Castro/Communists that would make the military happy, something not necessarily important but spectacular, such as deporting López Molina. I asked if a Dominican version of our Smith Act, making it a crime to conspire to advocate the overthrow of the government by force or violence, would please the military. The attachés thought it would, provided Bosch made clear it was aimed at the left, not at the military. What would the military think if he pushed agrarian reform? They'd be for it. Even if it meant expropriation of land? No, they'd be against it. (Some owned a good deal of land, and nearly all wanted to.) What if he repealed the old de-Trujilloization law? Fine, if he also made it clear that crimes committed by military men could only be tried in military courts. What if he fired Belisario Peguero? They weren't sure.

I ate lunch on a tray—from then on I seldom ate any other way—making notes for my meeting with Bosch, then went to his house at twelve-thirty. I began gently, to test his mood—asked if I could give a party for Bosch and the Santiagueros Thursday night, told him I hoped to propose an AID program to him next week. He was pleased with all this and did not seem unusually tense. So I went ahead.

I reminded him that before his inauguration I had made only one recommendation: That he leave the military high command alone. I now wanted to withdraw that recommendation.

Bosch asked what our assessment of the high command was. I had thought he might ask this, and had worked it out with the Crisis Crowd. I said we considered Hungría of the Army capable and loyal to Bosch. Bosch agreed. If he wanted to make a change, José Antonio de León Grullón, now in Washington, was equally capable professionally. Luna we considered dishonest and perhaps disloyal to Bosch. Bosch agreed. Should Bosch want to replace him, we thought Colonel Juan de los Santos Céspedes capable but too simple-mindedly opposed to everything he considered "Communist," and Colonel Juan N. Folch Pérez able but not popular with the men; the best bet was probably Colonel Cruzado Pena, already Sub-Secretary for Air—he was loyal to Bosch, and elevating him would look like the old Dominican game of musical chairs. In the Navy, we considered Commodore Rib a fence-straddler—Bosch agreed—and dishonest—Bosch disagreed. If Bosch decided to shift him, two capable men were Captain Amiama Castillo and Francisco Rivera Caminero.

I recommended he fire Belisario Peguero to assert his authority. He said all right, but the Communists feared him, and who should replace him? I agreed he was a tough cop whom the Communists feared but was expendable; to replace him, Bosch might consider Imbert. He liked this.

As Minister of Defense, we considered General Viñas both loyal and capable—Bosch agreed—but we thought he might be slipping. If Bosch wanted to replace him, I could only recommend one man: Wessin y Wessin. Bosch looked surprised but said nothing. I said Wessin was strong, brave, patriotic, and, so far as we knew, honest. He was almost fanatically anti-Communist. Full responsibility probably would moderate his fanaticism. Appointing him undoubtedly would blunt the politicians' attacks on the Communist issue.

I recommended Bosch couple any changes with other measures—repeal of the old de-Trujilloization law and enactment of a law providing for the trial of military personnel only by military tribunals. He already had, he said. I said we didn't know it and neither did the Dominican military. I recommended that Congress adopt a resolution declaring it the sense of the Congress that communism was incompatible with the inter-American system, as set forth in the Declaration of Punta del Este, and that it enact a Dominican version of the Smith Act. Bosch first said he already had such a law, then said such a law would be unconstitutional. I said he should go ahead anyway and let the courts rule on its constitutionality. I recommended he deport López Molina, who wasn't dangerous but was a symbol, and make mass deportations if the left reacted strongly to the Smith Act. He said the UCN would scream that he was resorting to illegal, arbitrary, and unconstitutional deportations. I said the UCN would scream no matter what he did. I recommended he hold back on agrarian reform if it entailed confiscation laws. He said he had decided to wait till next February.

In any case, I concluded, there was trouble ahead because the revolution had not been made, there was grave danger of a vacuum, the left might try to fill it, and then the right would knock him over.

I had finished, and waited for Bosch. He said, "There is a crisis in the Armed Forces. Today I ordered General Viñas to cancel Father Marcial Silva, the chaplain of the Air Force. He is the motor. He organized twenty-five or fifty young men around Wessin y Wessin. Later he went to Severo Cabral," an extreme rightist UCN leader, "and Jimenes Grullón and Mario Read Vittini [another politician]. The young officers at San Isidro wrote the conditions for Saturday morning's meeting. The high officers stopped them. I told them they were under the influence of political groups, I didn't want the officers to divide and cause a civil war, so I was ready to deliver power," that is, to resign. "They became afraid, said they did not want this," and he seemed rather satisfied with this. "Today I asked them to cancel Major Hache from the Air Force too and to investigate the others and cancel them too. I am preparing a list. There are many officers ready to support me. This means civil war."

I said I hoped not and didn't think it had to if only he would assert his authority and make his revolution. He shook his head sadly. "There can be no revolution—there is no money. The Armed Forces is divided. Some of the low command are for us and some against us. It is worst in the Air Force. Molina Ureña is going to introduce a law tomorrow to repeal the de-Trujilloization law. I submitted it forty-five days ago. I am going to change the Attorney General. We cannot have military trial courts. I am going to send Wessin y Wessin abroad."

He said he agreed with my analysis in general. "But there is no vacuum of power, only a vacuum of movement. I had intended to make the currency convertible but I cannot do it," and he spoke at length about his finances. I asked about unemployment. He declared he had two thousand men working on the Santo Domingo aqueduct and would start today building sewers and water mains in Santiago. I said rather forcibly that this wasn't nearly enough.

He went on, "I have a plan. At Baní, they are building houses with just a ceiling and posts. Three rooms," he added, explaining again, "one for the father and mother, one for the girl babies, one for the boy babies. The people did it, and the house costs only four hundred dollars. I told the Minister of Public Works we must build ten thousand of them in the capital. It will cost four and a half million dollars. I would like to borrow it from the United States."

It was the first time he had said that.

Bosch had more plans. "CIDES is making a survey, we need to classify lands, a sociological and economic survey of land and people. Agrarian reform must be done right. Yes," emphatically.

He was not talking about anything relevant to the present military problem. Did he know it? He leaned back in his chair and sailed on. "I am ready to take help from the United States. A study has been done on a dam by the Grenada company and the Minister of Agriculture on a river near the Yaque del Norte, you know, coming in from the South," and he looked around for a map but could not find one. Sitting down again, he went on talking about various public works projects, and called loudly, "Luís," and young del Rosario, Minister of Public Works, appeared and Bosch asked him how many millions altogether for public works, and he said ten. Del Rosario was usually at the house in the daytime, with Milagros, Bosch's niece. But one night I saw her in a shadowy place in the house with another man, not del Rosario, and I felt encouraged—until I was told that her new boy friend once had been deported from Mexico as a Communist, not an easy distinction to acquire. Ultimately, she jilted del Rosario and married this man. By then, it didn't matter.

Bosch talked about rice, and I told him he had been misinformed. He waved it off. I said I understood he believed members of the MAAG were talking against him; what were their names? He didn't know. What about the CIA? He did not seem greatly concerned. I left and hurried home to change clothes—I had to meet him at 4 P.M. to dedicate a school in diesel mechanics we had established in the Fairgrounds. There, Bosch was all but rude to Rear Admiral Henry H. Caldwell, who had come from Puerto Rico for the dedication ceremonies.

5

Next morning's *El Caribe* finally mentioned the San Isidro crisis—it editorially deplored *golpes* in general and said that all political parties should put aside their differences and support the democratic regime elected by the people. It was a remarkably friendly editorial.

A government spokesman announced that Bosch would make a "transcendental" speech to the people tonight. Ads supporting the government against the rumored *golpe* were published by a University faculty group; an engineers' and architects' association; and the employees of the National Institute for Potable Water, an agency we suspected was leftist-infiltrated. Several Santiagueros, including Marco Cabral, published an ad declaring themselves apolitical and calling on "all honest men in public life" to close ranks in defense of the Constitution. The MPD said in an ad that General O'Meara's visit undoubtedly accounted for the rumored San Isidro *golpe*—high-ranking U.S. military officers had visited Ecuador just before the *golpe* there.

Dick Goodwin arrived from Washington and, with King and Shlaudeman, we watched Bosch's speech on television. Bosch looked grim, and delivered a grim speech.

He denounced his political enemies—they were telling the people "lies" on radio, press, and television. Buried in a long passage about price controls on rice and medicines and help "from the Massachusetts dam" (presumably TVA) was a brief statement that he had sent to Congress the *plus valía* bill—the highly controversial land bill which some Dominicans considered outright expropriation without compensation.

At last he said:

"I am sure everyone is waiting for me to mention what happened in San Isidro last Saturday." He said the military leaders had told him they were "very worried about the activities of certain political segments" and would support him in any measures he took against those segments. "I told the officers the following: A government cannot be democratic toward some groups and dictatorial toward others. . . . If the Armed Forces persist, they must look for someone else to rule because I am not willing to lead a dictatorship—total or partial—in the Dominican Republic." Bosch's Cabinet, standing behind him, applauded.

He went on:

"The officers . . . started to protest, saying that under no circumstances could they accept my resignation from the Presidency." He had replied that they had urged a political line on him and, as the constitutional President, he could not accept it. "I told them that, 'You have ceased, as of this moment, to be apolitical officers and have become political officers and since you have at this moment ceased to be military men in order to be politicians, I cannot continue to rule the country, because I fear that what happened here will be repeated in another form, no longer with these friendly words and discussion but with deeds. I fear that some group of officers, led on by politicians, . . . may appear at the presidential Palace to attack me. When that occurs, there must also be Army officers who will defend the constitutional government. Then, there will be a fight among the Armed Forces. And there will be bloodshed. I did not return here to shed blood. I do not want blood to be shed on my account.' They requested that I reconsider my position. I promised to think about it."

Today, Bosch said, he had discharged Major Hache and "a political priest," Father Marcial Silva. (Applause.) "The military people do not conspire, unless civilian politicians urge them to do so. A conspiracy has been under way, but the military personnel are not responsible for it. Those who want power at any cost in this country wanted to use military officers as a stepping-stone to seize it. No one has a magic crystal ball in his hands to be able to read the future. I do not know what may happen to me as an individual or as President of this Republic. I do think, though, that a *golpe de estado* in this country will last less than a *cucaracha* in a chicken house, because I know that there are military forces ready to defend the Constitution at any cost. . . .

"I repeat that I do not know what is going to happen. However, if something should happen to me, I wish to say the following to the democratic soldiers, the people, and the youths of this country: No matter what may happen, do not allow this country to become involved in contracts with oil refining companies, Dominican land to fall into the hands of foreigners, and the *latifundistas* to live on your shoulders and force the landless peasants to travel about, starve, and come to the towns to beg for a piece of bread. Fight for the independence of the Dominican Republic; fight for the maintenance of public freedoms.

"If something happens to me, I adjure you to use these words—words that I want to repeat tonight and with which I ended my inauguration speech on February 27, 1963: 'Dominicans! freedom will not perish in this country while we are in power.'"

Prolonged applause, then the program ended.

I thought he had spoken truthfully but unwisely. Afraid to strike at Wessin y Wessin or other dangerous opponents, he had hit Major Rolando Hache and Father Marcial Silva. Thus he had risked bringing the Church and military together in opposition. He had promised more public works. But he had said nothing about moves against the Castro/ Communists. And he had raised the dangerous issue of the *plus valía* law. With this morning's surprisingly favorable editorial in *El Caribe,* he could have risen above the petty plots and called for national unity. But that was not Bosch's way. He was, as ever, a splitter.

6

We got the fallout fast.

At 11 P.M. Colonel Richardson reported General Luna had said, "He's won the first round. He better not try the second."

Next day various unions declared in full-page ads they would call a general strike if a *golpe* occurred. The 14th of June supported Bosch's call to defend political freedom and constitutionalism. The MPD called for unity against a *golpe,* thus moving right, toward the PSP "common front" with the bourgeoisie. The Social Christians denounced *golpismo,* and most of the other non-Communist parties, even the UCN and Juan Isidro Jimenes Grullón's party, issued statements supporting constitutionalism and civil supremacy over the military. Several American businessmen came to ask me what was going on.

At 2:25 P.M. that day Bosch sent word to me that Viñas and the high command were meeting at San Isidro about the discharge of Major Hache and Father Marcial Silva. Miolán and Minister Brea thought their real intention was to mount a *golpe* now.

At four-ten Shlaudeman got a phone call: The military was at the Palace now, presenting Bosch with an ultimatum. Minister Jaar had disappeared.

At four-twenty Volman came to the Residence. Everything was all right—President Bosch was home now and General Viñas was with him. There had been a brief flurry of excitement. Luna had given Viñas a document cashiering Major Hache and Father Marcial Silva; with Bosch's permission, Viñas had called a meeting of the military at San Isidro to get formal concurrence; Viñas had then approved the document, and Bosch had signed it. But a cousin of Vice President González Tamayo, hearing of the meeting at San Isidro, had jumped to the conclusion that a *golpe* was afoot and had told a friend in the 14th of June, and the 14th of June had started mobilizing, and rumors had started flying around town, and by early afternoon half the Cabinet was at Bosch's house.

Viñas was there now, reassuring them. And Bosch, upon learning that a cousin of his own Vice President had touched off a 14th of June mobilization, had lashed out. He told Volman that the Minister of Justice was through, for he had not prosecuted groups who were inciting riots, and so was the editor of the government paper, *La Nación.* There would be other Cabinet changes. Tomorrow morning the military would send five tanks to the Palace. I asked why. To guard it. Against whom? Against what? Volman didn't know.

The attachés reported that Wessin y Wessin had seen the President, and the President had assured him that so long as he was in the Palace, communism would not take over the Republic. Wessin had appeared pleased. The Armed Forces were going to make an announcement about the San Isidro incident. I asked if there wasn't any way we could stop all these announcements—what we needed around here was a good epidemic of sleeping sickness or lockjaw.

At six I took Dick Goodwin to see Bosch. Bosch talked rather vaguely to Goodwin about a Dominican Peace Corps—a few days before he had been highly enthusiastic—then told us at considerable length how he constructed a speech, drawing a triangular diagram like the one he had drawn for me before last year's election and explaining he aimed a segment of each speech at each segment of Dominican society. Goodwin, who had written speeches for President Kennedy and later wrote them for President Johnson, left the Republic somewhat dispirited.

Next day's *Caribe* carried a communiqué signed by all the military commanders saying that complete normalcy reigned. In a few days the San Isidro crisis died out, publicly at least.

But now we knew we no longer possessed the influence over the military that we had had last year. And Wessin y Wessin was the emerging power. Perhaps I should have sought him out. It would have been dangerous—Bosch would have suspected me, and so might Viñas. I did not. I regret it.

The San Isidro crisis—an abortive *golpe*—had derailed our political and economic counterattack. Well, now we would try again.[1]

[1] I suggest that this 1963 speech of Bosch's—especially his references to bloodshed, constitutionalism, and a potential split in the Armed Forces—and the rapid mobilization of the 14th of June in his defense, are of special significance to the Civil War of 1965, covered in Chapter Twenty-seven.

Chapter Twenty-two

BOSCH AT BAY

On July 18, we gave our third dinner party for Bosch, this time with people from Santiago. The first had been held when Bosch was suffering defeat by Duvalier; this one found him in uneasy stalemate with his own military. Eyed by everyone, he handled himself magnificently.

The Santiagueros arrived in festive air. Self-assured, they always did. Bosch had suggested that I rearrange the seating to have eight at each table, so he could talk to more than one man through dinner. At his table were Jimmy Pastoriza and Eduardo León, and he heard plenty of talk. Afterward, all the men had brandy and coffee in the garden, and I showed Bosch the ducks in the swimming pool—Marco Cabral had given my boys four ducks, and we had bestowed on each one of the four names of Juan Isidro Jimenes Grullón, the politician, but somebody had stolen and no doubt eaten two, and one had jumped into the deep end of the swimming pool when there was no water in it, and in the end only Grullón remained, and I now gave it to President Bosch for his daughter Barbarita; then Bosch and the men from Santiago sat under one of the big beautiful trees festooned with great philodendron vines, blue and white spotlights in the trees. Unlike others, these men were not afraid to ask hard questions. They were respectful, as befit his office, but forthright, and they would not let him deliver monologues, they spoke up. Weeks later I learned that before arriving they had planned their conversational attack—who was to lead off, who would take up which subject, and so on—but Bosch handled them so skillfully they had no wish to attack. He stayed much later than previously; it was a highly successful party.

2

Results of my trip to the States began to appear. The Department sent a circular to all U.S. embassies and U.S. military headquarters in Latin America, carrying its own and Senator Humphrey's replies to Hal

Hendrix' accusations and Congressman Selden's warnings. Editorials and news stories favorable to Bosch began appearing in the U.S. press—the Washington *Post,* referring to the abortive San Isidro *golpe,* said editorially, "It is not the job of military officers to tutor their constitutional chief on political theory"—and *El Caribe* reprinted some of them.

I pushed Newell Williams and Harlan Bramble hard to prepare a program, present it to Bosch, then ask for a new AID loan. Bramble thought Bosch did need a loan of seventeen million dollars for public works to create employment. But in the long run unemployment probably could not be ended in such a country, and certainly underemployment couldn't. We would have to justify the loan on purely political grounds, no easy task. Well, we'd try.

Fran and I ran into Donny Reid and his wife at dinner at Vesuvio's, they came back to the Residence with us, and Reid said the pressures on Bosch were building up dangerously and rapidly. Horacio Julio Ornes said publicly that political forces were preparing for "the beginning of a struggle which may be bloody," and added that some parties were arming themselves. Juan Isidro Jimenes Grullón declared in a speech that civil war was inevitable. Severo Cabral, the UCN right-winger, said the Republic faced either a *golpe* or a Communist takeover. Bonilla Aybar, editing a new tabloid, *Prensa Libre,* kept up a steady attack on Bosch.

One of his more scurrilous cohorts signed himself "J. Mejía" and wrote in poor English. In one column he attacked Sacha Volman as "probably a despised Jew." In another he compared the Bosch government to Al Capone's gang and wrote, "Frankly speaking, we in a hell of a situation in this Country." Bosch, "the Professor," was a "prisoner" of the Communists. Miolán, "the Premier," was putting together a Trujilloesque power apparatus. The U. S. Ambassador must "stop that nonsense of publicly backing President Bosch with words, which only prolongs our agony still further." And "Cuban history is being repeated in Santo Domingo." And, "The Professor and the Premier are they NUTS?" It was all semiliterate, shrill, and ignorant.

A private source told an Embassy officer that he was one of thirty Dominicans invited by Castro to attend a celebration in Havana on July 26, honoring Castro's revolution. From the CIA, the attachés, the Embassy political section, and other sources, I began getting other names. Some had already gone. Some were traveling by roundabout routes— Alfredo Manzano, for example, was said to have gone from Santo Domingo to New York to Paris to Prague to Havana—and some more directly—Cayetano Rodríguez of the terrorist MPD was said to be going to Jamaica to Mexico City to Havana, and then on to Peking. As I have said, Dominican passports were now stamped not valid for travel to Russia or Russian satellites. That might or might not cover Cuba, but it certainly covered Czechoslovakia, and anyone who went by way of

Prague ought to be subject to legal action. I cabled for close checks on airports—I wanted a solid case to take to Bosch.

On July 22 the Palace suddenly announced President Bosch would make another "transcendental" speech that night. We watched television. Bosch sat erect at a round table covered with microphones and papers, his Cabinet behind him. He followed his script with one finger. The prose was pudgy. He stumbled, lost his place. He did not seem to care.

The speech began with a long, complicated—and dull—account of a purported plot by the Trujillos to recapture their properties, confiscated by the Consejo. We kept wondering why all this. Then we found out: He was sending to Congress a new Confiscation Law. He said: "The Dominican people are in danger of seeing all the confiscated properties returned." The present law was inadequate. The threat was urgent—"I want to warn you that events are moving fast and will be upon us in just a few days." This could "provoke an uprising." Some former Trujillo properties had already been returned. "Tonight I am asking the Dominican people" to press for the new Confiscation Law.

It made Congress the supreme tribunal in cases alleging that property had been acquired illicitly, through favoritism, or other means declared illegal. Introducing this law was one of the most ill-advised, or ill-timed, moves Bosch ever made. It hit a nerve—the money nerve. Coming as it did after the controversial Constitution and the *plus valía* law, it galvanized the bitter enmity of the propertied classes of the nation. And it handed to the political right "proof" that Bosch was heading down the Castro road—confiscation of private property by the state.

El Caribe went all-out against the Confiscation Law. After I mediated between Bosch and Germán Ornes, *Caribe* had been neutral and sometimes friendly toward Bosch. But now Ornes switched back to the attack. And thereafter he never abandoned it. Whether he feared the Confiscation Law would take his newspaper away from him or his motives were loftier did not matter. What mattered was that he attacked. So did the political parties—Fiallo's UCN, Horacio Julio Ornes' Vanguardia, Juan Isidro Jimenes Grullón's ASD. So did associations of property owners, agriculturalists, and businessmen. An Associated Press reporter wrote that Bosch's Confiscation Law was supported by "Castroites." Bishop Polanco of Santiago said from the pulpit that Dominican youth was being infected with Communist ideas.

The Papal Nuncio, seated in his high-backed gilt chair with portraits of the Popes looking down, told me, "When I suggest to the Bishops that they make contributions to the agrarian reform, they say I'm stupid, telling them to contribute to the Communists. Every day I am all the more alone." So was I. The U.S. business community could scarcely think me wise to support the author of the Confiscation Law.

Last fall we had avoided disaster. Could we now, with Bosch?

3

The day after Bosch's speech, I took Bramble and Williams to present their program to him. Sitting in rocking chairs pulled out onto the patio, we discussed for two hours programs he might launch, some his ideas, some ours—waterworks, low-cost housing, farm-to-market roads, schools, community development, health clinics, sports parks, reforestation, reconstruction of irrigation ditches, vocational training. Bosch kept rambling on. Young Minister del Rosario kept joining us, then wandering off. Finally I said, "There are two important things we have to decide now, Mr. President. Do you want to move ahead immediately with these programs? And do you want a loan from the United States to do it?"

Bosch said he did. In the end we agreed on projects that would cost about 15.5 million dollars (*not* including sports parks). Bramble discussed, in his precise way, the nation's economy. Bosch appeared impressed with him (and later I urged him to use Bramble often). Then I said I wanted to talk to the President alone. The others left.

I gave Bosch a list of Dominicans traveling to Cuba and recommended he prosecute any who violated passport restrictions, and take another step—ask the Mexican government to refuse them visas. (At that time, there were only two air routes to Cuba. One was via Mexico, a single scheduled flight a week. The other was a fantastic non-stop flight from Murmansk to Havana, an eleven-hour flight aboard a Russian jet that usually arrived with only a half-hour's fuel to spare.)

Bosch doubted Mexico would cooperate but said he would ask. He said he would invalidate all passports specifically for Cuba. He agreed that several Castro/Communists were dangerous—the Isa Conde brothers, Islander Selig, Fidelio Despradel, Cayetano Rodríguez, Alfredo Manzano, and "Bebe" Mejía. He said Dato Pagán's school would close at the end of this month, July. (Previously he had said June.)

I gave him another list of twenty Castro/Communists who had chartered a Dominican plane last Saturday for Panama. At least one taught at Dato Pagán's school. I told Bosch firmly that in the present circumstances, with rightist opposition crystallizing around his Confiscation Law, free movement by the left was more dangerous to him than ever before. Furthermore, my own government would find it difficult to understand why he did not stop travel to Cuba.

I left him. Now we would see.

4

Fran had been badgering me to take a week off—we never had had more than three days in a row. Next morning, Wednesday, July 24, despite my misgivings—I could always return in five hours—we and the boys left for Sosua's healing sun and sand and sea, taking along fishing tackle, shotguns, a homemade glass-bottomed box to use in looking at the underwater coral caverns on the reef, and books. We stayed in the lovely little house of Gustavo Tavares, overlooking the shimmering bay. In the garden grew papaya, sweet lemons, plantains and bananas, mangoes, oranges, limes, peppers, vegetables, fruits of all kinds. By day the breeze blew from the land, at night from the sea, making chimes tinkle in a tree. Much imagination and thought had gone into the house, but nothing Dominican except paintings. Most of the furnishings had been bought in New York—a hammock from Abercrombie & Fitch, Jensen flatware, Italian glassware, a bowl of glass balls blown in Italy or the States.

Gustavo Tavares was the son of Doña María Tavares, the *grande dame* of the obligarchy. Saturday night she was giving a dance for her granddaughter home from school in the States, a sort of coming-out party, she had invited two hundred guests, and at her home in Santiago carpenters were building a bandstand and dance pavilion in the garden, and she had let it be known that while *etiqueta tropical*—white dinner jacket, black pants—would be acceptable, she would prefer black dinner jackets. This, I thought, might very well be the last such function ever given in the Republic—Marie Antoinette while the tumbrils were in the streets.

This was the twilight of the old order. The Republic's political leaders did not seem to realize that this was their last chance at constitutional democracy. If they threw this one away, they were finished. The next revolution would be proletarian and Communist-led, and the present politicians would be among the first to go to the wall.

If they overthrew Bosch they could not succeed him—only the military could. A military junta probably would promise elections. A long period of strife would ensue, followed in the end by a Communist takeover. If only the politicians could learn to live with Bosch and then defeat him at the polls. Indeed if only they understood politics as well as Bosch did. But they didn't.

The second night we were at Sosua, King telephoned. The Chamber of Deputies had passed the Confiscation Law that day, while more than two thousand people, rounded up by Miolán and hauled in Haina trucks, demonstrated outside, crying, according to press reports, "Down with the Yankees" and "Down with *El Caribe*" and "We have to take it away from Ornes."

In the middle of that night, Fran became very sick, with a high fever and severe abdominal pain, and I went at 4:30 A.M. to Puerto Plata, finally found a doctor and a Jeep ambulance, returned to Sosua, put Fran in the ambulance, and bounced her over the terrible roads to a clinic in Puerto Plata. For several days she was too weak to move. Finally on August 1 we took her by car to Santo Domingo, next day flew her to the U. S. Army hospital in San Juan, Puerto Rico, and surgeons at once removed her appendix and a cyst. As soon as she regained consciousness, I flew back to Santo Domingo in the MAAG plane, urged by King's alarm.

5

The day the Confiscation Law had passed the Chamber of Deputies, the city had been filled with rumors that the government would fall. *El Caribe* and various groups denounced both the Confiscation Law and the *plus valía* law, exhorting Congress not to permit the Republic to become another Cuba.

Soon Bosch, faced with so much opposition, apparently decided to pull back. He closed *La Nación,* the government newspaper, for printing an MPD ad. He wrote a reassuring open letter to Fiallo of UCN. He invited the lawyers' association to submit a new Confiscation Law. He ordered Haina not to permit the PRD or any political party to use its trucks for political purposes, thus rebuking Miolán.

The Chamber of Deputies sent its Confiscation Law to a committee. Nonetheless, *El Caribe* renewed its attack. Bonilla Aybar appeared on *"Ante la Prensa"* to denounce communism; several men tried to attack him as he left the studio. Father Láutico García reappeared on the scene. The annual assembly of bishops expressed profound concern at the current uncertainty, said that recent political events had failed to "establish a reign of peace," and said that no Dominican home enjoyed tranquillity. Bosch met with several churchmen.

On August 2, Friday, *El Caribe* had printed the first advertisement of a "Committee for Manifestation of Christian Affirmation." It invited the public to attend the demonstration at the national shrine at the head of Calle Conde on Sunday, August 4, at 9 A.M. The Committee's president was Enrique J. Alfau, a right-wing UCN engineer.

On Saturday, I arrived back in Santo Domingo and met with the Crisis Crowd. The Confiscation Law had solidified Bosch's opposition. The opposition thought it had Bosch on the run. Its new weapon was the next day's Christian Manifestation. "Christian Manifestation" was purportedly a meeting in favor of Christianity and opposed to communism, but actually a political demonstration against Bosch. Bonilla Aybar was pushing it. So were various priests and rightist politicians, although the Church had disassociated itself officially from it.

Shlaudeman reported the Social Christians had heard there would be a *golpe* tomorrow—the United States Embassy was supporting it, and the U. S. Fleet would arrive at dawn. The Social Christian leaders didn't believe it but their student group did and, together with a Communist-dominated University group, was denouncing *golpistas* and imperialists. They seemed convinced they would all be shot tomorrow.

The PRD and the Castro/Communists believed that the Pentagon was opposed to me, the Department, and the White House, and intended to overthrow Bosch with the help of the Dominican military and the Church.

The Social Christians had proposed mediation between Bosch and the opposition parties. Ángel Liz, who had been Secretary of State for Justice under the Consejo, was to be the chief mediator. Two Social Christian leaders announced to the press that Bosch had accepted the Liz mediation. I didn't see how anything could come of it if it was conducted publicly in the newspapers.

I went to see President Bosch that evening, and he and Volman and I talked till midnight in Bosch's study, filled with books and objects of art, at the back of the house. Bosch had the air of a man who had done everything possible and now awaited the inevitable. He seemed lonely. He said, a little sadly, "It is not easy in this country. The Constitution, the twisted, tortured Constitution, stops the revolution. The housing law is not going to pass Congress. I cannot put people to work—I have no money. I am ready to build the first little Villa de Libertad," workers' villages in the cane fields, a project long cherished. "But it is bad. I have only seven good Cabinet ministers." He spoke of several plots. "Imbert," darkly, "is deeply involved in all this. But the inevitable result will be a military *golpe*. Nothing can be done. I am not alarmed. It is simply inevitable."

I tried to cheer him. It was no use. I congratulated him on various conciliatory moves he had made and suggested he could make another on August 16, the hundredth anniversary of the *Restauración,* when the Dominicans drove out the second Spanish occupation; Bosch had planned a great celebration at Santiago, where he would address a special session of Congress; I suggested he make a conciliatory speech. He did not respond. He seemed to feel backed into a corner. Bosch was a successful exile politician and could always go back to being one if he turned out to be a failure as a President. In such a mood one day, he might resign or provoke the military.

I asked him if the Dominican Republic wanted to adhere to the Limited Nuclear Test Ban Treaty. No, he said—Russia had signed it, and "people would think I am a Communist." I suggested that on the contrary Dominicans would think he was tying himself tighter to the U.S. and certainly his signing would be very favorably received in the U.S. He then said, "Yes, I want to sign. In forty-eight hours. You arrange the details. I want to be the first in Latin America." He had turned around 180° in a few minutes.

6

Bosch seemed to be stuck tight on dead center—he dared not move to either right or left. It was hard to tell these days what pleased him and what didn't, hard to get him to focus on anything. He seemed more distracted than ever. And no wonder—the pressures were building up inexorably.

The rumors that flew through the streets were unbelievable. One said that U. S. Secretary of Defense Robert McNamara had decided to overthrow Bosch. Almost every day we heard of new plots, new military alignments, new names of people who would constitute the junta after the *golpe*. Bonilla Aybar's attacks became hysterical. The 14th of June was almost alone in supporting Bosch, saying now it was neither pronor anti-Communist but pro-constitutionality and against a *golpe*. The *civicos* seemed to no longer fear Bosch's mass support—and no wonder, with the PRD disintegrating. Rumor said that Santiagueros would close their businesses, the old UCN tactic of a general strike of employers. In 1961 businessmen had gone on strike in protest against the heirs of Trujillo; now their enemy was Bosch, whose Constitution and Confiscation Law threatened their property, whose fiscal policies hurt their purse, and whose politics they suspected was communistic. *El Caribe* was daily carrying large advertisements listing the names of people who opposed communism. A leftist radio commentator warned that low-level officers and noncoms might rise in the barracks at San Isidro to support constitutionality and stop a *golpe,* and declared the Christian demonstrations were "using Christ as a banner" for a *golpe.*

El Caribe kept reporting on "the present political crisis" and the efforts of the mediator, Ángel Liz, to solve it. Fiallo was reported "pessimistic" about Liz's mediation. During a confused riot at Public Works, Minister del Rosario appeared swinging a machine gun. Incredibly, six Dominican Castro/Communists returned from Cuba aboard a commercial plane, including Alfredo Manzano and José Estrella Jacobo, and declared publicly that one must see Cuba at first hand to appreciate the accomplishments of Castro. Juan Isidro Jimenes Grullón kept blasting away, now saying Bosch was flirting with fascism, not communism. The Palace announced that due to the press of work, President Bosch would make no appointments for a week—not till after the August 16 *Restauración* celebration at Santiago. He had invited the Diplomatic Corps to attend, and I had discussed with him what he and I would do there.

The first two Christian Manifestations had been only moderate successes, but the third, held in La Vega, lasted nearly three hours, the crowd was big and well organized, and it was addressed by seven speakers, including José Aybar Castellanos and Bonilla Aybar, the guiding spirits of the ADI, the new organization to which we at first had paid little heed. People in the crowd cried, *"¡Cristianismo sí, comunismo no!"* and *"¡Cristo sí, Yanquís no!"* and *"¡Iglesia sí, comunismo no!"* and *"¡Juan Bosch, a la reja!"* Bonilla Aybar received a great ovation. He proclaimed a "fight to the death against international communism which wants to convert our country into a new Cuba." The crowd responded, *"¡Bonilla, seguro, a los rusos dale duro!"* "Bonilla, for sure, give it to the Russians good!" a curious switch, for an old Fidel Castro battle cry in Cuba had been, *"¡Fidel, seguro, a los Yanquís dale duro!"* and that in turn had been used in the Dominican Republic by the 14th of June when Manolo Tavárez Justo spoke: *"¡Manolo, seguro, a los Yanquís dale duro!"*

The newspapers and radio, the talk in the streets, were full of the Christian Manifestations. The opposition had found a lever. And it moved segments of the U.S. press again—Jules Du Bois of the Chicago *Tribune* wrote, in a story datelined Miami: "A Communist takeover of the Dominican Republic is nearing hard reality with extraordinary speed. President Juan Bosch . . . appears to be neatly laying out the carpet for the Reds." Clearly my effort to win support for Bosch had failed, at least in some newspapers. Now our influence was almost wholly negative—we could do little but keep telling everybody we supported the constitutionally elected President.

7

We probed for a political solution.

Shlaudeman reported that Donny Reid and his friends did not want a *golpe* but thought one imminent. Reid considered the Liz mediation among the political parties doomed. The real struggle was not between Bosch and the political parties; it was, rather, between Bosch and the *civicos,* that large amorphous group of middle-class business and professional men who had no political party allegiance and hated Bosch. The charge of communism was only a symptom of the underlying problem and, for most of the *golpistas,* a pretext. Reid thought the only solution was for Bosch to take several *civicos* into his government. Reid was willing to mediate. Reid said ex-President Bonnelly was bitter; perhaps if Bosch would call on him and Fiallo, it would help. Reid said if such a rapprochement could be achieved, Bonilla Aybar would vanish from the radio. (We had been wondering where Bonilla Aybar was getting his money.)

I would see Fiallo, Bonnelly, and Johnny Vicini, on the one side and, on the other, Bosch. We would try to create a climate in which Reid or someone else could mediate successfully if Liz failed. I considered going to Washington to make sure we wanted to continue our present policy, but feared to leave and decided to send King quietly instead.

On Friday, August 9, I began the talks.

In quick succession I saw Fiallo, Bonnelly, Vicini, and Imbert. All denounced the Confiscation Law and *plus valía* law. All talked about Cabinet changes. All complained of Castro/Communist infiltration of the Bosch government; all furnished the same old names. Imbert said the Castro/Communists were urging the troops of the Armed Forces to oppose the *golpe* being prepared by their commanding officers, and said the troops were selling San Cristóbal rifles for $250 each to the Castro/Communists.

Fiallo said, "He should define the Communists as illegal." I pointed out that no Communist Party by that name existed here and asked if Communists should be deported. Fiallo hesitated, smiling—he himself during the campaign had denounced the Emergency Law. Bonnelly acknowledged that Bosch probably was not strong enough to deport the Castro/Communists; every political party would attack him for it. Imbert disagreed. "It would be easier now than six months later; there might be two or three killed now, but later there would be a bloodbath," and said the country was headed for civil war.

I appealed to all for support for constitutionality. Fiallo shook his head, deeply troubled. "The left is against a *golpe*—what should we do, be with them? No. We cannot. But there is no future in a rightist *golpe*, a military *golpe*. We are on the edge of a volcano. It will explode before December. I don't know, I want to avoid bloodshed." Imbert cared little for constitutionality and said people were blaming the United States and me personally for continuing to support Bosch. (Clearly, little was standing in Imbert's way, except me.) Pressed, Bonnelly said he was "being urged" to act, presumably by *golpistas*, but would refuse—"you can count on me." I left him far from sure I could. He meant it, but if his friends convinced him he must join a *golpe* to save the Republic, he might yield. And this time he had spoken of the Communist danger, as he had not previously.

Shlaudeman, King, and I talked Sunday morning, August 11. In order to step in with a new mediation immediately if Liz failed, we sent word to Bosch indirectly that we hoped he would invite two of Fiallo's men to visit him. We might suggest to those two concessions we thought Bosch might be able to make. The key was Cabinet posts—patronage jobs— not communism or anything else. We were trying to help broaden the government and promote harmony. If all else failed, I myself might try to persuade Bosch and Fiallo to meet face to face, difficult or impossible as that would be.

Shlaudeman said the Christian Manifestations would continue, although some of the more moderate founders of ADI, its sponsor, such as Marino

Auffant, were withdrawing, alarmed at its extremist turn. Miolán had gone to Bosch and offered to leave the country. Bosch had said he might as well—he wasn't effective. The PRD really would stop political activity. Probably Majluta, Molina Ureña, José Francisco Peña Gómez, and Sacha Volman would lead what remained of it.

I cabled all this to the Department and told King to discuss it in Washington, as well as the proposed new loan, the TVA mission to the Yaque del Sur, and the step-up in our intelligence efforts. I also told him to discuss contingencies—we intended to continue to try to save Bosch but what ought we do if we failed? What were the Department's views? King left for Washington.

8

I saw the Papal Nuncio on Monday and asked what he thought Bosch ought to do. He should stop making speeches and introducing inflammatory legislation, the Nuncio said, and amend the Constitution to reassure propertied people. Working through the bishops, he should establish lay schools in Christianity; the Nuncio was under constant pressure from priests who complained that Communist schools were operating openly. "But most of all, he should do something, not talk," Monseñor Clarizio said, his bright eyes flashing behind his glasses. "Inaugurate a highway, houses, anything, just do something, accomplish something. He should work for the people, give them jobs, give them bread."

I saw President Bosch that night in his study. He seemed tense. I asked about the *Restauración* arrangements.

He intended to go on Thursday morning to Capotillo, near Dajabón on the Haitian frontier. A hundred years ago, Dominican patriots had risen there and driven out the Spaniards in a series of battles that spread throughout the Cibao and the nation. Bosch would drive to Santiago Thursday afternoon. We decided it best, in view of the tense Haitian situation, that I not accompany him to Capotillo but meet him in Santiago.

I asked about the Liz mediation. His face darkening, Bosch said, "Liz told me the first thing I had to do was to persecute the Communists. I told him the first thing the *civicos* had to do was recognize me as the legal government," acidly. He went on attacking the UCN and Social Christians. I knew now the Liz mediation would fail and our own would be very difficult. Bosch said that a sign at the Christian Manifestation at La Vega had read, *"Bosch a paredón."* He said, "There is a crisis." He had not admitted it before. "I am going to make from four to six Cabinet changes in the last week of this month. Important ones."

Somewhat hesitantly, I told him Shlaudeman and I had been thinking about his important speech at Santiago. He expressed interest, so I told him we thought its purpose should be to unify the nation and assert leadership and its tone should be lofty, above the partisan battle, conciliatory, historical, sober, stressing difficulties and making no promises, asserting that he was the President of all the people and asking the help of all. Above all, it should not be an attack speech. He said he agreed and would welcome written notes from me.

On Thursday morning Harlan Bramble, who was replacing King while King was in the United States, brought good news: We had received a firm commitment for fifty thousand tons of rice under PL-480, enough to meet the Republic's needs through December and amounting to a loan of from eight to ten million pesos. In addition, we could make available ten thousand tons of corn under PL-480, worth 450,000 pesos more. (The peso and the dollar were nominally at par.) An outright cash loan or grant was in dollars; a crop loan generated pesos. Thus crop loans did not provide the Dominican government with foreign exchange but did provide it with pesos it badly needed. The terms were extremely lenient. This was very good news indeed; I would take it to Bosch in Santiago.

The Department felt that Bosch's primary need was to improve the quality of his administration. New Cabinet ministers should come from the PRD or be apolitical—to bring them in from UCN or other parties might simply be disruptive. It was not useful to press him to outlaw Castro/Communist parties but he must do something—control travel, close Dato Pagán's school. The Department was considering a new loan but could not assure it; Bosch would receive the twenty-two-million-dollar sugar money and more than eight million pesos from the new rice and corn loans. In announcing this, he could say that other loan applications were being urgently considered by AID under the *Alianza*. The Department hoped to have something from TVA on the Yaque del Sur by tomorrow. But the Department felt there was little point in further help to Bosch unless he carried out his development program and ran an effective administration.

9

I told Bramble to telephone me the minute any cable came in on TVA, then I left for Santiago. Just as I left, the CIA chief told me that fighting had broken out that morning in Haiti across the border from Dajabón. I was glad I hadn't gone with Bosch to Capotillo.

I invited Bev Cass to ride with me and my aide, Marc Cantolla, to Santiago. Cass was having problems of conscience about Bosch. As our naval attaché, he was obliged to urge Dominican military officers to support Bosch, but he himself had misgivings about Bosch's attitude toward the Castro/Communists, was not altogether sure Bosch's critics were wrong, and didn't know "how much longer I can go on supporting him

like this." I invited him to voice his criticisms of Bosch to me and tried
to counter each. I told him that if a time ever came when in all good
conscience he could not maintain our policy line firmly, he must tell me
at once. Any slightest sign of hesitancy on his part could bring Bosch
down; he was probably our most influential attaché. He said he would. I
knew he would carry out instructions faithfully. But I wondered if he
could keep a straight face while doing it. Cass was, in a sense, too honest.

We arrived at the Hotel Matúm in Santiago at 4 P.M. Fritz Long and
Vallimarescu met us, having driven up ahead, and so did our consul in
Santiago, Ben Ruyle, together with the head of the USIS branch office in
Santiago. We walked to our rooms along the open second-story balcony,
overlooking the enormous, almost obscene statue I had first seen long
ago, *La Paz de Trujillo,* now about to be renamed the *Restauración*
statue, standing on the empty dirt hilltop, the fields graded but not landscaped, a breeze blowing dust clouds, mountains in the distance.

Ben Ruyle, the consul, a hard-working, earnest man with thinning hair,
said he had attended a big Christian Manifestation that morning at San
Francisco de Macorís. It looked spontaneous, but somebody had been
sending sound trucks out all morning, and the public address system
had been well set up. A taped speech of Father Marcial Silva had been
played. Bonilla Aybar, the principal speaker, had attacked the Bosch
government directly, all but advocating its overthrow, crying, "It is not
I who am shouting *'abajo el gobierno';* it is you," then pausing, and the
crowd had roared back dutifully, *"abajo el gobierno,"* "down with the
government." Though no churchman had been present, the crowd probably felt the Church had sponsored the meeting. "It was a rough one,"
Ruyle said. Another was scheduled for Azua today. It didn't sound good.

Minister of Agriculture Antonio Guzmán called—Bosch had arrived,
was staying at Guzmán's house, and wanted to see me at seven-thirty.
I slept forty-five minutes, ate in a hurry, and left.

In front of Guzmán's house below the statue stood a long string of
cars. Soldiers and policemen with submachine guns guarded the entrances. A brightly lit basement room was jammed with double-decker
bunks for guards and guests. Guzmán's house was modest but tasteful,
built on a hillside, with wide open doorways and louvered windows, all
tile and glass and airiness. Off the living room was a patio. It was surrounded by a low wall with a cement top and it jutted out over the hillside like a promontory over the sea in the night. Below grew palm trees,
their topmost branches rustling in the wind against the wall. White helmets showed in the shadows below. The night was black but the stars
were out, and a cool breeze blew.

President Bosch was sitting on the patio in his shirt-sleeves, talking
to Marco Cabral, Jimmy Pastoriza, Luís A. Franco (editor of *La In-
formación* of Santiago), and one or two others. Greeting him, I asked how

the day had gone. Well, he said. I moved away, wanting the Santiagueros to talk with him. He was scowling darkly. They seemed not to notice— they talked about business (pretty good), unemployment (still high), the climate, the Agricultural College. Bosch said little. I stayed in the background at the low wall. Minister Jaar, hovering in the background too, told me they had skipped a stop at a town en route and Governor Mainardi was pained, the day had not gone well at all.

Presently the Santiagueros left. Came then Governor Mainardi and a few others, including Foreign Minister Freites, young Minister del Rosario, and Bosch's wife Carmen. These were Bosch's own people. And now, instead of glowering in silence as he had before the Santiagueros, he unleashed a tirade at his own. There was no water in the house, there was no water in the town, why was this, had he not given Governor Mainardi the money to build the waterworks in July and ordered it done immediately? Why was it not done? Mainardi blamed the *civico* mayor. Bosch would not have it. Mainardi, starting to sweat, tried to explain pumps that wouldn't work, equipment that did not arrive. Bosch would not listen. Someone, hoping to change the subject but doing so ill-advisedly, asked about the access road to the Tavera Dam, and Bosch declared it was not finished because the *civicos* owned the land and refused to give it to the government. "More sabotage," he declared. All agreed quickly, muttering.

I was tempted to leave; I could accomplish nothing tonight, with him in this mood. Yet I dared not leave—he might speak extemporaneously tomorrow and in this mood might lash out at anyone.

An historian in a white suit came to call on the President, and Bosch listened to his lengthy disquisition, then told him he would make an historical speech tomorrow to the Congress. I hoped so.

The historian left; Bosch resumed his tantrum. Today's Manifestation at San Francisco had been an outrage. "I will not tolerate any more," he said, his face black, forehead deeply creased. He was sitting in a chair at the center of the porch, legs crossed, arms folded, the others around him. "No. Enough. We will fight. At Azua, the first truck will be shot up. The party will do it. I cannot trust the military. I will go down fighting. An explosion is inevitable. Bloodshed is inevitable. Let it come now, the head-on collision with the right." His people looked around nervously. Colonel Calderón could hear this. So could General Viñas, near the doorway. But Bosch went on, "The *civicos* are in league with the military to make a *golpe*. We will go down fighting."

Somebody tried to change the subject, talk about the great celebration of the *Restauración,* and this brought up the President's various appearances, including one in a *barrio* where he was to hand out keys to newly built houses for the poor. He asked if all was in readiness. Governor Mainardi squirmed. *"Sí, Señor Presidente,"* he said. "There is one small difficulty—there is no water in the houses, so—"

Bosch exploded. "No water! And all this time you have had the money for the *aqueducto.*"

Mainardi explained uselessly, Bosch fumed, Mainardi said eagerly, "It doesn't matter, *Señor Presidente.* You can present them with a symbolic key."

Bosch said, "I am not going to present anything symbolic," and folded his arms, staring straight ahead.

Awkward silence; then Mainardi asked timidly if the President intended to go to the midnight Mass tonight. Bosch blew up. "No. Absolutely no. Bishop Polanco's statement said the Army should guard democracy. But the President should. It is an insult to the Presidency. I will not go to his Mass."

Panicky, Mainardi tried to protest—the Mass would be held in the baseball stadium, thousands would be there, it had been announced in the press.

Bosch waved him aside, declared categorically he would not go, the military and Church and *civicos* were bound to overthrow him, he would not go.

The others, horror-stricken, drifted away. I moved close to him and said I thought he might want to reconsider. He said he was afraid Bishop Polanco might say something at the Mass that would force him to leave. I said I doubted it—Bishop Polanco's statement of the other day had been conciliatory, not antagonistic. He said stiffly, "I beg your pardon, Mr. Martin, I am not wrong." I gestured to Marc Cantolla—did he have the newspaper with the statement that I had asked him to bring? No. Bosch called Guzmán—did he have it? No. A great search for the newspaper began. I sat beside Bosch, both silent. Guzmán found the newspaper. Bosch showed me the paragraph that offended him. I said I could understand his feelings but pointed out that the rest of the statement was conciliatory. He wouldn't look at it, and sat with arms folded.

Guzmán announced that now we would see some movies, and guards and children and waiters brought in a screen and a projector and there was a general shifting of chairs, then the movies began; but the wind blew the screen over, a waiter tried to hold it but got in the way of the picture, the expensive new projector wouldn't work, and what snatches of the movies we saw were mostly out of focus and panned too fast—they showed our trip aboard the *Mella* but they seldom showed Bosch, mostly Ministers del Rosario and Guzmán and Majluta and their wives.

This concluded, Bosch summoned General Viñas and Colonels Pagán and Rivera Cuesta and took them inside the house, taking the newspaper with him.

Instantly hand-wringing began. What to do? Mainardi was aghast—

if the President didn't go to the Mass, it would be disastrous. Others agreed. I kept out of it, sitting on the wall. Cantolla asked what I thought. I said he'd go to the Mass and he wouldn't shoot anybody at Azua either. Freites came to me and said, "It would be fine if you'd all arrive at the Mass together—you, the President, the military." I said it would but apparently he wasn't going. Freites drifted away. Carmen Bosch came to me and said tentatively, "It might be misunderstood if he doesn't go." I said it probably would be—or, rather, wouldn't be. She said, "We must find a way to fix it up. You can think of something." I said I'd try. But though I didn't say so, I was by now tired of Bosch's familiar tactic: Digging himself into a hole then forcing everybody to pull him out. Suddenly in our midst a terrible dogfight started, a big police dog of Guzmán's and a smaller strange black dog. Uproar ensued—women screamed, men yelled, dogs growled, chairs and tables flew, Guzmán and del Rosario seized chairs and, like lion tamers, moved in on the dogs. They accomplished nothing—they just kept poking the chair legs at the snarling, fighting animals. A soldier rushed in with a machine gun. I thought: Good God, what a way to die! Bosch came hurrying out, followed by Viñas, then went back inside, and the dogfight went on, uproar mounting. Finally Mrs. Guzmán, a rather slight woman, ran straight in and grabbed her dog, the big one, by the collar, and, though her husband cried out, "No, he is dangerous," she hauled on his collar with all her strength, got him disentangled from the other dog, started dragging him to the doorway, and though he lunged, throwing her, she held on, got to her feet, and dragged him to the steps and outside.

Everybody resumed worrying about affairs of state, i.e., the Mass. By now it must have been 10:30 or 11 P.M. Mass was at 12:05. With some feeling of resignation, I decided to try to get it straightened out. I asked Carmen Bosch whether Bishop Polanco had officially invited Bosch to the Mass. She didn't know. The others joined us. They said the Bishop had not invited Bosch officially. I said in that case we could send Governor Mainardi to get Bishop Polanco to come here at once and invite the President officially, provided either Carmen or Guzmán could first persuade Bosch to receive him. Guzmán went inside to Bosch, returned, and said Bosch had agreed but on one condition: That it be announced in the newspaper tomorrow that Bishop Polanco had called him to pay his respects and extend a personal invitation to the Mass. (Always Bosch squeezed out one final concession.) Mainardi hurried away.

I told Cantolla I wanted to talk to Bosch alone and was determined to do it through Cantolla acting as interpreter, speaking English so fast Bosch couldn't catch it. I didn't want any misunderstanding and I wanted to control the conversation. Bosch and the others came out. The silence was heavy. I asked Bosch for a few minutes and, taking Cantolla, we went to a far corner of the patio.

Speaking rapidly, Cantolla translating rapidly, I said I had a piece of news for him—we could get him fifty thousand tons of PL-480 rice, told him the generous terms, and said it would help him hold the price line, feed the people, and see him through December. He said, "You don't know how good news this is."

I said, "Yes I do, Mr. President. I've been working on it for a week." Then I went on. I had some other things to say. This was a bad time to say them, perhaps, but I had too much respect for him to try to maneuver for a propitious time. I hoped he would take what I said in the spirit it was offered—not as the Ambassador but as a friend who wanted to help him. I told him I quite agreed that the extreme right was going too far, especially with the Christian Manifestations. But the fact remained that he was in trouble, and its political root was his handling of the Communist problem. This had made him two sets of enemies: Those who sincerely feared Communists, and politicians who hoped to use the issue for their own advantage. Meanwhile, he was losing his own support, was immobilized, could not govern. He must regain the initiative. But the Liz mediation appeared likely to fail.

He murmured, "It is finished."

I said, "I suggest you use it anyway as a smoke screen for your own political moves—change your Cabinet, seek a real understanding with the opposition. But to start, you have to do something about communism, and fast. Two things—first, close that damned school of Dato Pagán's."

Frowning, he said, "It is closed."

"I'm sorry, Mr. President, but it is not—we had a man there Monday. It was open Monday, though most of the faculty wasn't back from Cuba yet."

He said, "The letter ordering it closed is on the Minister's desk."

"All right—but the school still isn't closed. Now, second. In my opinion, if I may say so, you've got to punish the Cuban travelers."

He said, "The Constitution prohibits it."

"Let the courts decide that—do it anyway."

"I have put new limits on passports forbidding travel to Cuba but there is no law to enforce it."

"Then pass one."

"It would be unconstitutional."

"Let the courts decide. Look—you have to either pass an illegal law against travel or illegally harass and detain them after they return. Alfredo Manzano undoubtedly got instructions in Havana. We understand one or two others were in Moscow. They're dangerous. Some of them undoubtedly violated your passport restrictions. Yet they passed through your immigration at the airport freely. You've got to stop it for three reasons. First, this is the first really good issue the extreme right has had. Second, it is getting harder and harder for us to defend you on this one, because you are running counter to President Kennedy's policy. And finally, Hal Hendrix is here and knows this story and will publish it in about a week, and it would be better for you to take the initiative now than to wait and do it under his pressure."

He hadn't known Hendrix was here. It angered him. But he saw the point.

I said, "May I continue, Mr. President?"

"*Sí*, of course."

"Forgive me, but time is running out. I want to get you a loan but I'm getting pressure from Washington. Your government is no good, it doesn't function, it lacks good people, and you must improve it. I know all the reasons why it's hard. Just the same, you've *got* to find good people. You told me you intended to make changes in your Cabinet. You can use that as an opportunity to improve the quality of your government."

He said he agreed. I went on. "You can use the classic tactics of Lenin —splitting, and taking two steps forward and one step back. You can split the right by bringing the one who's screaming loudest about communism into the Cabinet and making him responsible for handling communism. You can postpone the revolution, since you can't make it anyway now, dig in, move right, hold on, improve your government, and make the revolution in the future. The thing to do now is to try to unite the country."

He was listening but saying nothing. I went on, "Tomorrow you have a chance to rise above the partisan battle, make a lofty speech, and lay the groundwork for behind-the-scenes maneuvering for Cabinet changes. I've written out some speech notes," and I took them out of my pocket— I'd had them translated into Spanish and typed on plain paper—and gave them to him, saying, "I've written speeches for other writers and it's an unrewarding job, but here it is."

Bosch read it. It was designed to unify the nation, assert leadership, and deal with four fears which, justifiably or not, haunted Dominicans and created Bosch's political crisis—fear of communism, fear of ill-advised or hasty legislation, fear of the PRD machine, and fear of the "erratic and uncertain course" of the Administration.

Finished reading, Bosch smiled. "There are many good things here. I have written a speech for tomorrow, it is all historical, don't worry. Perhaps I can use some of this in a speech next week."

I said, "Mr. President, I do hope you take all this in the spirit in which it's offered. We want you to succeed."

His face broke and he grasped my hand hard and said, "Thank you. Thank you again," and touched my shoulder, and I his, and we turned and separated.

As always, despair as I often did of Bosch's behavior, I genuinely liked him and often was deeply touched by him.

I joined the others in a little semicircle in front of Bosch's chair, leaving an empty chair beside Bosch for Bishop Polanco. We waited for Bishop Polanco. Time passed. It was nearly eleven-thirty. Only thirty-five minutes to Mass. Nervous, I wondered whom to send for the Bishop; but he arrived. He was an impressive man, brown-skinned, straight-backed, high-browed, smiling a little as in his red and black robes he strode across the patio to Bosch, kicking over a glass on the floor and breaking it. I noticed that all rose when Polanco arrived. A few minutes ago when Bosch had joined us, only Cantolla and I had risen. Bosch would notice too.

Bosch and Bishop Polanco chatted a few minutes. Everybody else was scurrying, getting ready to leave. Carmen whispered to me that it "must" be in the papers. I told her it was too late to make tomorrow morning's *El Caribe* but I would try the others and sent Cantolla to do it.

Bishop Polanco departed. Bosch and the rest of us hurried out and got into cars and, in a strung-out motorcade, raced to the floodlit baseball stadium, unloaded, and walked under the grandstand and out onto the playing field. The floodlights were bright, the grass green, the grandstand filled. The last time I had been here was nearly two years ago when, on my mission for President Kennedy, I had attended a rally of Trujillo's Partido Dominicano. Tonight at about second base a platform had been built for the priests. Beside it stood a choir of nuns in white and a choir of children. Directly in front of them stood a machine gunner, short, squat, dark. A band was at the pitcher's mound. Policemen and soldiers were everywhere.

We sat in folding chairs close to the priests' platform. As usual, nobody knew what order to sit in; we ended up with President Bosch near the platform in the front row, then Carmen, then someone else, then Mrs. Guzmán, then I, then Foreign Minister Freites, then others. Behind us sat the Bosch Cabinet and the military.

The band played the national anthem under the stars, and we stood, then the Papal Nuncio celebrated Mass. Nobody signaled us when to rise and sit, as in the Cathedral, so we half stood, half sat, mostly at the wrong times, I fear. Then Bishop Polanco spoke.

I remembered that Bosch had told me he feared Polanco might say something that would oblige Bosch to leave. Throughout Polanco's speech, I watched Bosch's feet. What should I do if he walked out? I decided to stay until he and his companions had left, then tell the Nuncio I had been placed in an embarrassing position and ask to be excused.

At last the Bishop's speech ended—he said nothing that Bosch could consider objectionable. The Nuncio, Bishop Polanco, and other churchmen descended, shook hands with us, and departed. Then we left. Only a few in the crowd tried to shake Bosch's hand.

Off we went amid flying gravel, a racing motorcade once more, I riding with Freites and his beautiful wife Antonia. In a few blocks the motorcade came to a screeching halt; the President's car up front had run into a dead-end alley. All must turn around, and did so, amid confusion and shouting, clouds of dust and flying gravel. Off we roared, twisting and turning from street to street, sewers being built everywhere, mounds of dirt thrown up, dust clouds so thick we nearly chocked. I knew we were headed the wrong way, having got lost here myself en route to Sosua, and sure enough, soon we skidded to a stop, and this time there was scarcely room to turn around, we were in torn-up streets on the edge of town, and people peered fearfully at us from their huts, we were hemmed in by piles of gravel and sand and dirt, dust everywhere, military officers running up and down the long line of big black cars, and suddenly all the Cascos Blancos rushed up from the rear and went at a dead run forward to the President's car: They thought he was being assassinated, they ran scrambling and stumbling over the piles of gravel, now in the dark, now in blinding headlights, carrying machine guns, yelling. Freites and his PRD gunman got out. I stayed in the back seat with Antonia and told her to keep her head down in case some fool fell and his gun went off.

She said, "I've had enough." She had gotten dust under her contact lenses. She was a tall, slender young woman with blond hair and eyes aglow, and although she always seemed cheerful in public she was hard inside. She said, "Don't tell Andy"—her husband—"but have you got any Gelusil? I left mine home."

I didn't have any with me but had some at the hotel. We discussed our ulcers. She didn't want to worry her husband about hers. Everybody was getting ulcers. The gunmen and soldiers and Cascos Blancos returned, holding handkerchiefs over their faces against the dust. I thought of the retreat from Caporetto. Freites got back in the car with his gunman. Finally all the cars got turned around, and a new scramble began, more flying gravel, more clouds of dust. I told Freites if he didn't have to accompany the President, let's get out of the motorcade and go straight to the hotel and go to bed. He agreed. I thought: Any government that can't find its way home from Mass deserves to fall.

At the hotel, Antonia and I started upstairs. Freites asked where she was going. To her room, she said, and I said I was going to my room, too. He said he'd be up soon; I said I'd be down soon. She and I went to my room—I had given her the key but she hadn't wanted to go alone —and I rummaged around in my briefcase, found a bottle of Gelusil while she waited beside me, and Cantolla came to the door, stopped short, startled, and, misunderstanding the situation, said, "Oh, excuse me," and started to back out, but I told him to come in, and embarrassed, I shook the Gelusil too vigorously, and the cap flew off and white Gelusil spattered everywhere. We stood there, the lights bright, a mosquito net over the bed, paint flaking from the walls. I swore. Antonia began trying to wipe up the Gelusil, and so did I. We were laughing now, an edge of hysteria barely covered. Cantolla helped. Antonia was wearing a fashionable and expensive black dress; luckily, only a little Gelusil had hit her. I poured a glass half full of Gelusil and gave it to her and she left. I explained foolishly to Cantolla, "She has an ulcer, I was giving her some Gelusil"; then said, "Oh, the hell with it—let's go get a drink." Fran had told me for years to put the caps on bottles more tightly. It was probably the most preposterous evening of my time in the Republic.

10

I wakened refreshed: Ridiculous as last night had been, at least I had got some things said to Bosch that I wanted to say, and his going to the Mass might have helped him politically.

At 9 A.M. I went to the *Gobernación* facing the *parque*. Upstairs the big hall was packed with the Congress, diplomatic corps, and guests. I found my seat, shook hands with Senator Casasnovas, President of the Senate, and President Molina Ureña of the Chamber of Deputies and others. Senator Thelma Frías, often accused of sympathizing with Castro/ Communists, made a big point of greeting me. A man told me I had a phone call. I went to the Governor's private office. Bramble, in Santo Domingo, said that the TVA plan to develop the Yaque del Sur had been announced publicly in Washington. Bosch and I had agreed previously on no advance publicity. This would enrage him. It was precisely what we had hoped to avoid—raising false hopes, putting Bosch in the position of again "promising the moon," as his critics said. I told Bramble to cable the Department, ask for the source of the story, ask how firm the plans were, and ask whether Bosch and I could announce them immediately.

I hurried back to the hall and ran into Bosch, just arriving. I told him about the TVA leak. He had already heard about it; his face was black with anger. His wife whispered to me, "It is bad today. I have a feeling you had better stay close to him all day." I said I always would, and sat down just before he entered the hall.

All rose, outside a band played the national anthem, and a gun fired a twenty-one-gun salute, its explosions so heavy we felt the shock waves, and the Italian Ambassador raised his eyebrows and looked up to see if the chandelier might fall. Congress convened and renamed the Tavera Dam in honor of the *Restauración,* an official tripped over a microphone wire, another one upset a microphone while Governor Mainardi was introducing President Bosch, then Bosch spoke. Eloquent, carefully worked out, mostly historical, his speech drew parallels between the past and today. It declared that "the conquest of the people's liberty requires as much tenacity in the political field as in the field of battle," denounced

Trujillo as well as Heureaux and other enemies of the people, and said that if Dominicans today returned to the bloody conflicts of yesteryear they were not worthy of their heritage, declared that today the times demanded a common struggle to give the people "not only the national liberty which was won by the Trinitario and consecrated by the *Restauración*, but the profound and true liberty" that the people needed now. "In today's language that revolution means social justice, means culture for all, means health for the people, means the presence of the mass of Dominicans on the scene of the Republic as an actor of the collective drama and not as a spectator who sees it from a distance."

It was not the attack speech we had feared. Neither was it the hard-driving speech to recover momentum we had hoped for. Unfortunately, it gained Bosch little. Applause followed it, then a protocol officer led the diplomatic corps up to shake hands with the President and we left, walking down the broad stairs and across the hot street to chairs in the shady *parque* where we were to review the parade. On the way the Nuncio asked me how things were going. Not well, I said, the Christian Manifestations were a real problem, Bosch suspected the Church was back of them and last night had nearly refused to attend Mass. The Nuncio asked, "What does he want?"

I said, "I don't know, I'm tired, I won't ask you for anything more, you've already done a great deal, let's forget it."

He said, "No, while you and I are here, let's fix up him and Bishop Polanco." Walking slowly across the street, he said, "Would he settle for a picture in the paper with us, with Bishop Polanco and me?"

I said, "I don't know. We could try." We decided that after the parade the Nuncio, the Bishops, the diplomatic corps, and the President would go to Guzmán's house for a reception and we'd have pictures taken. The Nuncio would invite the Bishops and the diplomatic corps; I would get the President and arrange it with Guzmán.

The diplomatic corps and military, the President and the Cabinet, the Senators and Deputies, all the functionaries, were walking across the street, sitting down in rows of chairs in the *parque;* and now the parade began, military units marching by, flags flying, planes roaring low overhead; and amid all this I sent Cantolla for Guzmán; sent Vallimarescu to make certain the press, especially photographers, covered the reception; sent Cantolla to telephone Bramble to see if there was anything new on TVA. Every time the flag went by we had to rise suddenly and stand at attention; then sit and rapidly resume making arrangements. The other Ambassadors were looking around questioningly. The Nuncio sent word —where did Guzmán live? I sent word back—downhill from the monument, where the police were thickest. Between two flags I went to the President and told him I thought it would be a good idea for Guzmán to give a reception for him after the parade, attended by the entire diplomatic corps and all the Bishops and the Papal Nuncio—would he attend? He would be delighted. He had to make a fifteen-minute appearance in a *barrio* after the parade, but he would go from there to Guzmán's. I went back to my seat and kept working.

The sun was burning; the *Gobernación* across the street was dazzling white; the planes were deafening. Finally the parade ended. The President and his party got into their cars and roared away. The crowd broke the police lines, everyone milling about wildly. To escape being trampled, or to escape sunstroke, several diplomats made their way across the street to the *Gobernación* to await their cars; but the cars couldn't get through the crowd, and several Ambassadors asked if I knew where we were going and why, and I told them to Guzmán's house for a reception for the President, all were going. Where did he live? I told them to follow my car if they could, but if they couldn't to go toward the Trujillo statue and look for a crowd of police at a small house.

It was cool at Guzmán's house, and pleasant. Other Ambassadors began straggling in. Guzmán was there. Nothing happened. The Nuncio arrived. We stood and waited. The Nuncio suggested to me that the diplomats should be served, it had been hot at the parade and all were thirsty. I told Guzmán. He said he planned to serve champagne when the President arrived. I suggested water now. There was no water. I had forgotten.

Guzmán hurried to the kitchen to prepare Coca-Colas. We waited, waited a long time. Cokes arrived, a few. The diplomats began to grumble.

Where were the photographers? That was the whole point. I told Vallimarescu and Ruyle to telephone.

The Bishops arrived. This provided an interval—the Ambassadors and Bishops could shake hands. Then President Bosch arrived. The Cokes, just beginning to appear, were swept aside and champagne brought, but the President preferred Coke, so Coke was brought for him, champagne for the diplomats, toasts were drunk, the parade discussed; and for a few minutes it seemed like a reception starting. But it sagged; there was an air of expectancy, everybody sensed something was afoot, this was no ordinary reception; yet nothing happened.

Where were the photographers?

Vallimarescu and Ruyle said they couldn't find them by phone. I sent them and Cantolla to hunt them down in person. I kept trying to hold the diplomats while the Nuncio held the Bishops.

At last one came, one solitary photographer, and from the way he handled his equipment I judged he was an amateur. He took pictures but I feared they would be no good. I told the President and the Nuncio it wasn't enough—we needed motion pictures for television. They waited. The President talked desultorily but soon gave up. The heat was wilting everybody. I told Colonel Calderón to send gunmen to round up the photographers—they probably were at a hotel bar downtown. The gunmen left. The diplomats, mystified, began asking me what they were doing here.

By now President Bosch, the Nuncio, Bishop Polanco, and Ben Ruyle had started talking on the front porch, a most animated conversation. I drifted over. Ruyle was criticizing the Christian Manifestations bluntly and verging on criticizing the Church. I wanted him to keep it up but not get carried away. Standing behind the door, I fed him lines through Cantolla.

The still photographers arrived and immediately began taking pictures. Bishop Polanco kept backing out and being urged to come closer, to join Bosch and the Nuncio. (I do not believe his picture with Bosch ever appeared in either *El Caribe* or *Listin Diario*.) The movie photographers arrived—more pictures, this time pictures of the President with the Bishops and the diplomatic corps. The Ambassadors were feeling better. Vallimarescu arrived and handed me a message from President Kennedy congratulating President Bosch on the *Restauración*. I whispered to Bosch, suggesting I present it to him for the photographers, and he agreed, and we did it. By now, he was greatly cheered. He moved amiably through the crowd. About 1 P.M. everybody left. I asked Bosch if he wanted me that afternoon. He did, a little before three-thirty.

I went to the Ruyle's for lunch, took a thirty-minute nap at the hotel, and returned to Guzmán's at three-fifteen. Bosch was still sleeping. He wakened at three-thirty. We were due at the Instituto Superior de Agricultura, the agricultural school. Bosch and Carmen and I left immediately in his car, he saying it would help him politically if I arrived with him. On the way, small groups stood on street corners and in front of country stores and waved and yelled at him, and he called back, head and arm out of the car, "*Adios compañeros,*" and he seemed nearly in a trance. During a lull, I remarked that his six hundred thousand votes meant everything on election day and nothing in between.[1] He nodded. I did not point out that the crowds today were smaller than on an earlier trip.

At the site of the school on a dusty plain the crowd was big. This school, already begun, had been conceived by the young businessmen of Santiago, sons of the oligarchs, who had last year formed the Association for the Development of Santiago. It was being built with money provided by them, AID, and the Ford Foundation. Texas A & M was furnishing technical advice and would help train teachers. The Peace Corps

[1] Curiously, in a magazine article written since, Bosch has recalled that it was he, not I, who made this remark on this occasion.

would help. It was one of the most hopeful projects of all, proof that the *Alianza* can best help those who help themselves.

A speakers' platform had been raised on the dusty plain, and the crowd gathered round, the oligarchs up front, and Jimmy Pastoriza, son-in-law of Doña María Tavares, spoke. President Bosch, surrounded by the oligarchs, planted an oak tree to inaugurate the school, then mounted the speakers' platform. I thought he was caught by surprise, had not intended to speak. While he was being introduced I whispered an opening line to him—it was strange that under Trujillo this agricultural nation never had had an agricultural school, but now that freedom reigned it had, thanks to the work of the Santiagueros and the *Alianza*.[2] He nodded and began to speak.

Alluding to Santiago's lonely struggles against Haitian and Spaniard, Bosch praised the Santiagueros' proud traditions of independence, of fighting alone for freedom, of helping themselves and building the Republic without waiting for help from the Palace. Today Santiago was true to that heritage. He praised Jimmy Pastoriza and the other young men who had conceived the Agricultural Institute. He praised the León brothers' new cigarette factory, probably the largest Dominican business investment since Trujillo's fall. He praised the new Catholic University in Santiago and Bishop Polanco. He praised the Ford Foundation, Texas A & M, and "the Alliance for Progress, that is to say, the United States government" for their help. He praised the Peace Corps and its "spirit of service," helping not "as officials of the United States government but as young people from the United States as a country, helping us, above all, in the task of building a Dominican democracy, which is so important as an example of democracy in Latin America."

He said: "If this spirit of Santiago flowering today after one hundred years since the War of Restoration could be extended throughout the country, if it could spread from shanty to shanty and from town to town, from village to village, and from city to city, we, who have the responsibility of governing, would have no great worries. . . .

"We are sure that in this country the destinies of the people cannot change, they cannot be changed, they cannot be distorted, if the will of Santiago is opposed to it and Santiago is and will be a bulwark of democracy. . . .

"Democracy, because it makes all men free, also gives freedom to those who want to destroy it. And this can confuse the people. . . .

"Until recently the people of this country endured one of the most

---

[2] I do not mean to suggest, here or elsewhere, that I was putting words in the President's mouth or in any sense "controlling" him. I was simply doing what an aide does for a President or presidential candidate, a Senator or Governor—what I had done for President Kennedy and Adlai Stevenson many times while they were campaigning.

dreadful tyrannies of America and of the world. All dictators are alike in their methods. No matter what the ideology of a dictatorship, history shows us that from the Assyrians up to Trujillo, all dictatorships including Stalin and Hitler, do the same: They restrain freedom of thought and they put human conscience in chains, some in the name of progress and others in the name of underdevelopment.

"Since these people know what a dictatorship is, we are sure that they will not accept another at least during the present generation of Dominicans.

"There are people here who suffer from fear. I do not fear. I trust in the people, I trust in the will of these people to live freely."

As President Bosch descended from the platform, Marco Cabral embraced him and said it was the best speech he ever had heard. It was certainly one of the best Bosch ever made. Later we disseminated it as widely as possible, through tapes and transcripts. But it never got the attention it deserved—the forces moving against him overrode it.

Speaking finished, we toured the school construction, wading through dust and gravel, stopping at the dairy for *refrescos,* visiting the Peace Corps pig farm and rabbit hutches. When at 6 P.M. we arrived back at Guzmán's house, from behind a partition came the PRD song—one woman playing the piano, half a dozen singing, but, not knowing the words, singing from a scrap of paper. Bosch tried to join in.

I asked him if he needed me at tonight's *acto*—poems and prose and music on the theme of the *Restauración.* He didn't. The next day? No. Then I'd leave. He thanked me warmly—"for everything, and you know what I mean by everything." I left for the capital at 7 P.M. Ordinarily I did not travel in the country by night, but tonight, worn out, I wanted to get home. On the way, an idiot driver passed us while we were stopped behind a crowd of parked cars, pigs, dogs, and bicycle riders, and an oncoming car with blinding headlights ran off the road. We saw two bad wrecks. You nearly always did. Ambulances were flying. And always there were quiet stretches in the road, the dark, mysterious mountains to the west, the palm trees and the stars. And Bonao, where Petán once ruled below the mountains. A strange country.

Chapter Twenty-three

BETWEEN THE SWORD AND THE WALL

Never again, I think, after the tantrum and the dogfight at the *Restauración,* did I feel the same about President Bosch. One does not require that governors, or judges, or senators be great and noble. One does not even require greatness and nobility of Presidents, though one may hope for it. But surely one may expect a President to be at least adult and sensible, not childish and foolish. After the *Restauración* I was convinced, as I had said almost exactly a year before, that, like him though I did, as a President Juan Bosch simply would not do. Henceforward, I continued to act *as if* he could succeed. I continued to fight as hard for him as I had for the Consejo. But I realize now what I did not fully realize then: That it was no longer Juan Bosch I was fighting for, but the principle he stood for—the principle of representative constitutional democracy, the right of the Dominican people to elect their President.

2

Spence King, the DCM, came back from Washington on Saturday, August 17, the day after I returned from Santiago.

He reported that Ed Martin was dubious about any mediation effort, Liz's or ours, and thought Bosch ought to make his government "more competent." Otherwise what assurance was there that any new loan would not be wasted? Martin and Moscoso had just spent nine days on the Hill, testifying on the foreign aid bill before the much-feared Congressman Otto Passman's sub-committee. It was the worst season for foreign aid in years. Even Ralph Dungan of the White House would support a new loan to Bosch only if we could prove conclusively that Bosch would use it well and that nothing else would help save Bosch. King thought we might get five million dollars but no more.

Martin said the French interest in the Yaque del Sur was no longer an obstacle. AID was enthusiastic—the Yaque was the kind of developmental project it liked. A. J. Wagner, chairman of the board of TVA, and a group of TVA experts would fly to Santo Domingo on September 28 to make a preliminary examination of the Valley.

Dungan had asked King privately: Where do we go after Bosch? And: Were we sure our MAAG and attachés were not criticizing Bosch? I decided we had better do some contingency planning—planning what we would do if Bosch fell.

3

On Monday, taking Bramble with me, I went to Bosch's house, told him I had been misled when, on returning from Washington July 10, I had informed him that the TVA men would arrive immediately, and said they would arrive on September 28.

Bosch didn't like it, and I didn't blame him. Six weeks had passed since I first had promised the experts. Nothing had happened. Now he must wait six weeks more. He and I had agreed on no publicity, but the story had leaked anyway. Now, with more delay, his opponents would say this was another of his idle dreams. Anyway, what would the engineers do? I explained this would be only a "preliminary examination" of the Valley—engineering studies would come later, by TVA or some engineering firm. He said, "Studies upon studies."

He said coldly he did not want the TVA. He might use Kaiser—or even better, someone entirely new, a smaller firm.

I let him go on, nodding sympathetically, then pointed out that bringing in someone wholly new would almost surely take at least six weeks and who knew—they might be fly-by-nighters who would arrive amid fanfare, hold receptions and cocktail parties at the Hotel Embajador, fly around the Valley once, hold press conferences and make glowing predictions, then depart, never to be heard from again. TVA had worldwide prestige. The very fact that they were so cautious proved that they would raise no false hopes. If TVA did it, it would be done right. He could leave no finer monument to his Presidency than a garden in the Southwest created out of desert. Bosch seemed somewhat impressed. Sacha Volman supported me, as did Bramble, speaking quietly but with authority. Bosch said, "I will take my decision very carefully and very slowly."

After that I had to tell him the bad news about the new loan. Bosch took the news stoically.

He said he expected to make Cabinet changes in about a week. He had recalled Ambassador Héctor García-Godoy from London to help select good men. Next day at the Palace he and I announced the rice loan publicly.

4

I set to work on a long contingency paper.

The paper laid out three dangers to the Bosch government. It might simply fail—fail to satisfy the aspirations of the people, fail to govern. It might be taken over by the Castro/Communists. Most likely of all, it might be overthrown by the politico-military right—and probably would be, if the *civicos* ever convinced the military that Bosch was handing the Republic over to the Communists.

The U.S. government was taking certain risks by continuing to support the Bosch government. If he failed, he might flee, tending to discredit the entire Latin American non-Communist left and our support of it. If he lost control to the Castro/Communists, we would have to accept a second Communist government in the Caribbean or more decisively against it. If he were overthrown by the right, we would lose friends in the democratic left throughout Latin America, for many would refuse to believe we had not connived at his overthrow, and we might accelerate the chain reaction of military *golpes* throughout Latin America, perhaps jeopardizing the *Alianza* itself.

What, then, were the alternatives to continuing to support Bosch?

First, we could connive at Bosch's overthrow, working secretly with the military, which would force him out and replace him with a civilian junta that would hold elections in a year or two. Moral questions aside, this was extremely difficult and risky—and probably unnecessary; for we could—

Second, tacitly consent to his overthrow. We could, in private conversations and public acts, make known we were withdrawing our support. The scenario would be about the same as if we connived actively— military *golpe*, civilian junta, future elections. Among the military, Rib and General Luna probably would desert Bosch first; General Hungría might hang back but not long; General Viñas would move last and only when convinced he had to. General Hermida, often the center of conspiratorial talk, might emerge. General Belisario Peguero would go whichever way he saw power and money. The key was Colonel Wessin y Wessin. The military, however, would be reluctant to accept the responsibility of governing and would set up a civilian junta. Fiallo, Jimenes Grullón, and Horacio Julio Ornes probably would try to control the junta but couldn't. Donny Reid, my paper said, "might prove to be a key figure, though he would probably prefer to become President by election." Ex-President Bonnelly would be important "but probably only behind the scenes." The Castro/Communists would have no chance to enter the government; they would, if not locked up, fight in the streets. The Social Christians probably would end up supporting the junta. The PRD would be smashed by the arrest and deportation of its leaders, mainly Ángel Miolán. Later Imbert would try to take charge and might succeed, but "only if the junta were *in extremis*." This plan was "a slightly less risky but no less bankrupt policy" than actively conniving at a *golpe*.

Third, we might attempt a "behind-the-scenes takeover." We could offer Bosch money plus a guarantee of U.S. armed intervention or threat of it to keep him in power; in return he would permit us to pick his Cabinet, dictate his policies, and run his government. This alternative was impossible—Bosch was too proud, and we did not want to run the Republic. Of course, we might try to subvert, infiltrate, and surround him—that is, woo his own supporters and Ministers, use almost every means to get rid of those we could not control, put our own people close to him, and, through these people, run his government without his knowing it. This would require "a sizable clandestine apparatus capable of buying, compromising, or otherwise subverting government officials—in a few words, actually doing what we are always being accused of doing." It was extremely difficult and risky. And, again, we didn't want to do it because we didn't want to run the Republic.

Finally, we could attempt to persuade or pressure Bosch and Vice President González Tamayo to leave the Republic quietly and, in accordance with the Constitution, let Senator Casasnovas, President of the Senate, assume office as Provisional President, then within fifteen days, convene the two houses of Congress jointly as an Assembly to elect a new President, probably Casasnovas himself or the man behind him in the line of succession, President of the Chamber of Deputies Molina Ureña. This would preserve constitutionality but was almost surely impossible.

I concluded that all alternative policies were so unacceptable that they should be adopted only in dire necessity. "Dire necessity" meant an imminent danger of a Castro/Communist takeover or "clear demonstration that Bosch would fail and imminently fall or flee."

I recommended that we immediately begin planning for either a covert power takeover or an overthrow with our tacit consent.

But I emphasized that at present, our interests still lay in supporting the Bosch government and that so long as this was true, we dare not give an inch, in public or in private, in all-out support for him, either in the Dominican Republic or in Washington.

I finished this paper on August 23. But I never sent it to the Department or the White House or anywhere else. It never left my private safe. Only two other people knew it even existed—King and Shlaudeman. I did not send it because it might become known, I doubted that the Department would adopt it, and therefore it could only further undermine Washington's confidence in Bosch. I might send it later. But I never got a chance—the *golpe* actually happened almost exactly a month later, and it followed with eerie faithfulness the scenario I had foreseen. Had we adopted its policy of "overthrow with our tacit consent," we might have been better able to control events. But innocence was a better moral position.

5

At 8 A.M. next day, Saturday, August 24, President Bosch telephoned and asked if I could come to his house. Amiama and Imbert were with him. They left reluctantly. Imbert looked very serious.

The President said calmly, "We were discussing a plot to assassinate me. If it is true, they would be in great danger too."

Then he described the most fantastic plot of all.

Until now, I have mentioned frequently the dark subterranean world of Caribbean exile politics. Here it was, brought to the surface on Bosch's sunlit patio, as, from a file of papers on his lap, he selected documents and handed them to me.

The first was startling. It was on the stationary of the Soviet Embassy in Havana, bore the seal of the Soviet Union, was dated July 3, 1963, was signed by a Colonel Boris Panteleymonovich, was written in Cyrillic (the Russian language alphabet), and showed a photograph of General Viñas and other members of the Dominican high command, including Commodore Rib, probably General Hungría, probably Imbert, and a man whose face had been inked out and marked with an arrow. President Bosch said the photograph had been taken at a ceremony in June at the 27th of February Camp, the Army's main post in Santo Domingo, apparently by a Soviet agent. Nobody in the high command, he said, could identify the inked-out face marked with an arrow. The document appeared to have been sent to Prague or Moscow from the Soviet Embassy in Havana by the Soviet secret police. I asked Bosch where he had got it. Somewhat reluctantly he said, "I have an agent in Europe who sends me things every month or so."

"Then from South America," he said, and handed me more documents.

One, on stationery of the "Headquarters Pro-Recovery of Dominican Government," was dated March 28 in New York, was signed by "The New York Delegate," and was headed "Operation Olive Green." It said that in accordance with recent conversations with "our emissary, 'White Rabbit'" in "the capital city," the following arrangements had been made: Two high Dominican military officers would provide uniforms and arms to "Army captains" who would arrive at President Bosch's house ten minutes before the changing of the guard. They would take him prisoner and, if necessary, kill him on the spot. Members of "the Federation" would seize the government and name a military junta comprised of the "two high-ranking Army officers" and "The Fallen One."

The assassins would take Bosch's body to the Palace. The plotters would announce over Radio Santo Domingo, already seized, that Bosch had met with an accident. Two "chosen ones" infiltrated into the Electricidad would, with prior synchronization of watches, turn out the lights in the entire city. Martial law would be proclaimed. Two military airplanes would carry a large group of military leaders out of the country. Those "who are not on the deportation lists" would be shot "in the military camps already in our grasp." The Archbishop and Bishops would be forced at machine gun-point to speak to the people in support of the *golpe*. Several important churches would be burned, ostensibly by the PRD. If the *golpe* could not be carried out on "_____of_____"—the date was left blank—it would be postponed, but no longer than one month. "The Fallen One" would be made a member of the junta only to win the support of his followers; in a few days he would be given "his just desserts, in accordance with instructions received from the High Command." The Santiago and Barahona Air Bases would be captured similarly.

Weapons for the *coup* would be shipped in from a nearby key—deposited in three rubber balls marked with small signals to be picked up by fishing boats "at the north coast locations previously agreed upon." "Rafael Faxas"—probably Rafael Miguel Faxas Canto, a leading Castro/Communist—would lead a company of Cuban guerrillas. All codes now in the possession of the commanders in key cities should be memorized and burned. Generals Viñas, Belisario Peguero, Luna, Rivera Cuesta, and Colonels Neit Rafael Niver Seijas and Herman Despradel would be shot if they resisted. Deported immediately would be Ministers Luís E. Lembert Peguero and Humbertilio Váldez; Ángel Miolán; and the Bosch family. Deportation aircraft would depart at 11 P.M. "Large sums in dollars" would be distributed immediately "among the political leaders of the Federation" to gain support. *El Caribe* would be bombed "to silence the Press for a few days." Fires would be set along the frontier according to a coded plan. Identification cards obtained by "our Chiefs in Cuba" would be valid only if printed in Russian. Copies of this order, on yellow paper, were being sent to the movement's delegates in Nicaragua and Guatemala. Those for Mexico would be sent three days before the event.

Another document was a letter on the stationery of Ramfis Trujillo, dated in Madrid on April 8 and signed by Gilberto Sánchez Rubirosa as Ramfis' "personal secretary"; it was sent to "J. Sebastiano" in Guatemala and informed Sebastiano that Ramfis was "very interested in the matter" and would communicate with "Negro" (presumably Héctor Trujillo, brother of the dictator) to determine whether Gilberto Sánchez Rubirosa or Fernando A. Sánchez, Jr., should travel to make final arrangements. As for money, the writer supposed that "Victor" was already in contact with "the Delegate in New York," since he had left Madrid a few days ago with a Spanish passport. "Sebastiano" was to come directly to Ramfis' house in Madrid.

Another document said that in June a New York attorney wrote to Diego Bordas, saying that one "Michael Gómez"—possibly Marco Gómez, Ramfis' financial adviser whom I had met—was trying to buy, through an intermediary, ten thousand guns in New York to ship to the Republic.

Another document signed by Virgilio Álvarez Pina, a former Trujillo financial adviser now believed in New York, said he had given the New York Delegate ten thousand dollars.

A document signed by Héctor Trujillo said he had given the New York Delegate forty-three thousand dollars.

A document, written on the stationery of the Dominican Army and signed by Juan E. Pérez Guillen, the present supply officer to the Armed Forces, and formerly an aide to General Rodríguez Echavarría, was addressed "Dear Rabbit" and said he had met with Colonel Braulio Alvarez Sánchez, a notorious Trujillista now in charge of transport for the Dominican Armed Forces, and completed "all the preparations," including weapons.

Other documents were false identification cards printed in Bulgarian.

Another was a letter dated July 25 from the manager of a big hotel in San Juan, Puerto Rico, informing its owner, Benítez Rexach, that a Dominican named Zenon Castillo de Aza had arrived from Miami and wanted to see Benítez Rexach urgently. (Benítez Rexach had dealt extensively with Trujillo, and all the previous year had repeatedly pressed claims against the Consejo, insisting that as a U.S. citizen he was entitled to the Embassy's assistance). Castillo de Aza apparently did not get to see Benítez Rexach. He told the hotel manager that he was traveling in connection with a plot against Bosch, that the plotters needed a million and a half dollars, that "Cucho Álvarez" already had contributed two hundred thousand dollars, that Rodríguez Echavarría had contributed, that the *golpe's* leader was "Fran Caminero" (the naval attaché at the Dominican Embassy in Washington whom Rib had replaced the previous year as Navy commander), that Duvalier of Haiti was involved and would receive eight hundred thousand dollars, that the "operations center" would be in Haiti, that Castillo de Aza was going there immediately to await "the final contacts," that Generals Belisario Peguero and Luna and Commodore Rib were involved in the *golpe,* that Bosch would be assassinated by a young Puerto Rican named Miguel Quiñones who was a friend of Rodríguez Echavarría, that the *golpe* had "the complete approval" of the U. S. Department of State, that "Secretary of State Mac'Nara" was also "completely in agreement" and had told Caminero so at a reception in Washington, and that Castillo de Aza wanted Benítez Rexach to contribute "a substantial sum" to the cause.

Another document, written in longhand, said that a man named Julio Castillo Cortes was carrying Honduran passport No. 22773, issued at San Pedro Sula, Honduras, on December 4, 1962. It said that this was the passport and the name under which "Father Zenon Castillo de la Aza" was traveling. His U.S. address was 88-15 168th Street, Apartment 9G, Jamaica 32, New York, telephone OL 7-8604.

Some of the documents were originals, some copies, some photostats. There were more, including photostats of cash receipts and canceled checks.

I asked Bosch what he made of it.

"It is a typical plot of Trujillo," he said. He didn't fully understand it. On the surface, however, it appeared to him that General Rodríguez Echavarría, who had perpetrated the two-day *golpe* against the Consejo in January 1962, was plotting with the Trujillos, President Duvalier, and Trujillistas still on active duty in the Dominican military to assassinate Bosch and take over the government, and that one of their couriers was a man who used at least four names—Rafael Ruíz Castillo, Haza del Castillo, Julio Castillo Cortes, and Zenon Castillo de la Aza (or de Aza). Castillo de Aza was now in Central America or Haiti, Bosch said—"he is going to inform us." Who was, I asked? Castillo de Aza himself, Bosch said, implying that Castillo de Aza was playing a double game. Bosch had been told he himself would be assassinated on September 3, ten days away he now thought it might be sooner.

I asked who all these people were.

Bosch guessed that "White Rabbit" might be Johnny Abbes García, former head of the SIM. The "New York Delegate" might be Candido Tejeda, Bosch thought, describing him as the last head of the SIM. He believed "The Fallen One" was General Rodríguez Echavarría; "the capital city" was Santo Domingo. He thought Rafael Faxas Canto's name was "a red herring" in the document, intended to confuse. He said former President Balaguer knew nothing of the plot. Bosch was keeping under surveillance one courier who shuttled between New York and Santo Domingo.

Bosch seemed remarkably calm about the whole affair. I asked what he wanted me to do. He wanted to know where Rodríguez Echavarría and Ramfis Trujillo were, and to determine the reliability of his source in Prague, whether the Soviet Embassy document was authentic.

I went to the Chancellery and called in King and Shlaudeman. Bosch had selected the documents with some care; he was not giving me everything. Was the whole exercise a fake to create a diversion? Shlaudeman, with experience in Bulgaria, said the document from the Soviet Embassy in Havana looked a trifle dubious—"Havana" was misspelled, and so was "July," in Cyrillic script.

I said, "If Bosch has a penetration in Prague, he doesn't need us—
we need him."

It would have been easy to ignore the whole thing, but I didn't dare.
sent an urgent cable asking for surveillance of Rodríguez Echavarría, an
effort to find Castillo de Aza, and a checkup on Ramfis' whereabouts.
So began a nightmare investigation on three continents.

We spent the weekend studying the documents. I talked to Bosch several times, and he added more details. Zenon Castillo de Aza, he said,
was an unfrocked Catholic priest who had served Trujillo. Castillo de
Aza, Bosch said, was going to Guatemala to get a Guatemalan passport
for Rodríguez Echavarría under the fictitious name of Rafael Ruíz
Castillo. He had gone from Puerto Rico to Haiti, then to Mexico, then
to Guatemala. He had two photographs of Rodríguez Echavarría with
him for passport purposes. From Guatemala, he would go to Spain. Bosch
felt sure that José Trujillo Nicolás, a nephew of the dictator, was in Miami and was involved with the plot. More cables went flying around the
Hemisphere and across the Atlantic.

And now Colonel Cass came in with what looked like another piece of
the plot, though I now think it was only a wild story and Cass and I
wondered at the time. Castillo de Aza had turned up at the Dominican
Embassy in Washington at 2 A.M. several weeks ago, asked to see Ambassador del Rosario, and, shunted aside, had talked to the naval attaché,
Francisco Rivera Caminero. (Rivera, visiting Santo Domingo, had told
the story to Colonel Cass.) Aza had informed Rivera Caminero of the
"New York Delegate" plot. Colonel Braulio Alvares Sánchez was involved, he said. Aza was traveling on a Guatemalan passport (not Honduran, as Bosch had thought). He was carrying two pictures of Rodríguez Echavarría and said he was going to Honduras or Guatemala to
get a false passport for Rodríguez Echavarría; he asked Rivera's help
in getting a visa. Later Rivera received a letter from Castillo de Aza
on the stationery of a hotel in San Salvador but mailed in Miami on
August 19, saying he had visited Nicaragua where "Tachito" Somoza,
son of the dictator Somoza, had promised the plotters "everything," saying the Salvadoran government was equally enthusiastic but limited its
promise of help to "available means," and saying that Colonel Peralta,
who had seized power in Guatemala, had expressed "sympathy" with the
plotters' "ideals" but found it "inconvenient internationally" to get involved himself.

All this tended to confirm that a plot existed involving high Dominican
military officers and that Castillo de Aza was trying to put it together.

Our own study yielded more questions than answers. Was there one
plot or several? Had Bosch really obtained the Soviet Embassy document in Eastern Europe? We guessed that one of the recent travelers to

Cuba had given it to him. If the plot was authentic, why were such names as Viñas, Rib, and Lembert Peguero misspelled? Why would the Olive Green plotters or Castillo de Aza need ten thousand guns? (*Verde Oliva* is the official organ of the Cuban armed forces under Castro.) Why would the Trujillos want to kill Bosch rather than Imbert and Amiama? Why would Castillo de Aza disclose his plot to Bosch's own naval attaché at the Dominican Embassy in Washington? If this was really a Trujillo plot to kill Imbert and Amiama, why go to all this trouble? Why were the false identification cards printed in Bulgarian, not Russian, as stipulated? Why had Bosch given me, along with the other documents, two worthless Dominican intelligence reports on Castro/Communists? Was it possible that Bosch really was plotting the murder of Amiama and Imbert and going to these lengths to camouflage it? Was it possible that he had invented the whole affair and intended to publicize it shortly to distract attention?

I sent the documents to the Department with a request that our intelligence services try to determine their authenticity; that they check on the recent movements through U.S. immigration of the persons mentioned; that they establish a surveillance on Rodríguez Echavarría in New York and seek out Zenon Castillo de Aza there; that they establish a spot check on Ramfis Trujillo, Rhadamés Trujillo, Gilberto Sánchez Rubirosa, Fernando A. Sánchez, Jr., all in Spain or Paris, and on José Trujillo Nicolás, probably in Miami.

We would await the results and go about our business.

6

It was the last week in August. Severo Cabral, the right wing UCNer, called on an Embassy officer and warned him that he planned to attack me publicly because I was ruining the Dominican Republic by supporting Juan Bosch. I thought this might mean that, after the rapprochement between Bosch and the Church at Santiago, the Christian Manifestations were running out of steam. In the course of the conversation, Severo Cabral said, "Do you know why there are no Protestants in Spain? Because they boiled them all in oil." That characterizes rather well the extreme rightist *civico* opposition to Bosch.

Senator Javits and others arranged to ship a huge quantity of free polio vaccine to the Republic. Carmen Bosch and I went to the airport to receive it.

The CIA chief was convinced that Bosch's man, "Pupito" Sánchez, didn't want our help in setting up an anti-subversive police force. And he wondered whether Bosch himself did, though he had asked for it himself. Moreover, although our own service was growing, it did not yet approach what I had asked for in July—enough men to undertake surveillance. I asked again. The Department and CIA refused. (It will be recalled that Assistant Secretary Ed Martin had assured President Kennedy that the CIA could handle matters as well or better than the FBI, which the President had suggested. As I recall it, it was Martin who now refused my renewed request for help.)

Bosch replaced Foreign Minister Freites with García-Godoy and Minister of Justice Lembert Peguero with Julio Cuello, both good men and men whose appointment should appease the *civicos*. (But would anything?)

We received reports that a wave of strikes was imminent. Was this pure trade-union activity or an attempt to overthrow Bosch? One night the lights went out all over the city. The dark was eerie. I had planned to go to Nisibón for the weekend with Fran and the boys, but on Thursday, nervous about the way things were going, sent them on without me, promising to join them if I could.

Friday was a dreadful day. That morning's *El Caribe* announced strikes at the electric company and Haina, and said one was threatened at the telephone company. These were PRD unions. Was the PRD turning on Bosch? Were Castro/Communists taking over the unions?

Bev Cass said he had received two reports that "a military group" had sent a letter to President Bosch, demanding that he change his policy toward communism or they would overthrow him. General Hungría would tell Fritz Long nothing, but seemed tense and finally admitted that the military had been "meeting and discussing a solution to the Communist problem." We had no word on the Air Force—Richardson had just been transferred, and his replacement was too new to be effective.

A new disquieting rumor came in—that the PRD had held an important meeting the previous night.

We had three problems—the strikes, the military, and the PRD—and we could learn little about any.

I saw former President Bonnelly at five. He said fear was rising and so was pressure on Bosch; the strikes might bring matters to a head. But he said nothing about an imminent *golpe*.

King could get no solid information on what had happened at the PRD meeting the previous night but reported that Donny Reid thought the PRD itself might overthrow Bosch, saw its hand in the strikes, and was worried because the electric strike had darkened the city. Cass and Long reported the military quiet—for now.

At my request, Ángel Miolán came to the Residence. He looked calm, even well pleased with himself, as he settled into the easy chair in my study. I asked, "What's going on, Ángel?"

Miolán said, "There were small differences between the President and the party. We held meetings, and today we met with the President, and everything is straightened out. The party will become inactive for the time being but will remain alert."

He said the PRD by now had received about seventy-five hundred out of forty-two thousand government jobs. This took care of the party leaders. "The rest are *campesinos*," Miolán said.

I said, "Then the rumors are not true about a break between the PRD and the President?"

"No. Last night the rumor was that you and the Nuncio told President Bosch that I had to leave the country. I can't believe it."

I said, "It's absolutely ridiculous. I don't want you to leave. I want you to stay. That's about the last thing I'd want."

He nodded. "There were also rumors that I was offered ambassadorships to London, Caracas, everywhere."

"You don't want to be an Ambassador?"

"No."

"I always thought you had good sense; now I'm sure of it. Don't ever be an Ambassador."

He laughed, said, "I understand it's hard work."

"Then you're not leaving the country?"

"No. I'm going to a little hotel in the interior for a couple of months, retire, study."

"Where?"

"Perhaps Constanza."

"What study?"

"Economics, English," vaguely.

I asked who had met with the President. He, Casasnovas, Molina Ureña, Peña Gómez, and Majluta. He said they were counting heavily on the *Alianza* to create jobs. I told him money was much harder to get this year than last—Congress faced an election next year, AID and the Department were more cautious. Then I asked about the strikes—were they political?

Miolán said, "The Electricidad, yes. Extremist leftists. Haina, I think not."

"You said a few minutes ago that the party, though it will retire, will remain 'alert.' 'Alert' is a military word. Won't this alarm the Armed Forces?"

"No. It is political word here, too."

"What does it mean?"

"Alert to defend democracy if necessary. The *juventud* [the PRD youth] is very radical on the question of a *golpe*. If one started it would be horrendous. They would set fire to entire cities. It has been said that the military would only rule over the ashes of the country. Imagine setting fire to entire cities. This has never happened here before."

Then Miolán said, "I want your advice. How can I handle the charges that I am a Communist? Both here and in the United States. Get recommendations from people who know my political history? Get an investigation by an international body to prove it one way or other?"

I thought a bit, disturbed. It was the old question—how do you prove you are *not* something? I said slowly, "I'm not sure it's advisable to do anything. It might be better to let it die."

"But it doesn't die."

"I know. And you want to confront it. I'd like to think about it. I'll help if I can."

He thanked me and left. What Miolán said troubled me; there was simply no way he could clear his reputation, however unfair it might be.

Well, back to politics. Miolán seemed to have won a fight—Bosch had tried to dump him and the party hadn't let him. Whether Miolán used the indirect pressures of strikes was uncertain. Now, having won, Miolán was pressing to establish his reputation as a non-Communist, probably in order to revive his long-standing ambition to succeed Bosch as President.

I went to President Bosch's house and congratulated him on the Cabinet change. Bosch said he would make others—it was hard to find good men. "Today I ordered troops and the police to Haina. As soon as they heard this, they called off the strike. Also today I ordered the firing of all the agitator leaders in the Electricidad. Without severance pay. I had the electric strike declared illegal. The judge had intended to wait till Monday. I called the new Minister of Justice and told him to tell the judge to issue the order today." It was all true—Bosch, unlike the Consejo the previous year, had broken the leftist-led strikes.

Bosch asked my help in sending "from 98 to 120" men from the Armed Forces secretly to Puerto Rico for training in operating the waterworks, the telephone company, and the electric company. They would constitute an emergency unit in case Castro/Communists tried to shut down all three.

Bosch took all such anti-Communist steps in secret, so he got no credit for them among his enemies.

I asked about the trouble in the PRD. "No, no, no, no trouble," the President said. "No trouble at all." Were no meetings held? No. I was surprised; rumors had even been printed in the newspapers. He said, "They do not understand the psychology of the Dominican people. Very few people, perhaps only one, understand. I do. Having won so great a victory, I have to ask forgiveness of people. So the party will stop making politics. It will become educational. It will teach literacy."

"Is the party satisfied with this?"

"Yes."

"Who will pay the party's literacy teachers?"

"They do not need pay. They will not be all-day schools, just little schools at night. Besides," laughing, "Dominican bureaucrats only work half a day."

"That's one reason they don't get much done."

We talked about other things. Toward the end of our conversation, he said, "I did meet this morning with the PRD, with Miolán, Majluta, Molina Ureña, Peña Gómez. They will issue a communiqué tomorrow." I suppose he realized I already knew. It was midnight when I got to bed.

7

Next morning I called on Foreign Minister García-Godoy, then started out for Nisibón, on the remote and deserted northeast coast, alone in our Jeep. I had a detail map of the area and that night, planning where to fish tomorrow, discovered that Castillo de Aza owned a good deal of land there. When we went down to the sea at dawn to fish, driving along the lonely beach, we found little white flags on long sticks placed at intervals in the sand. I had never seen them before. A solitary hut stood on the long lonely beach. I asked a man in it about the flags—what were they, when had they been put up, what did they mean? He knew nothing, and though I hadn't asked, he denied owning any white cloth, and seemed afraid. The flags stuck up high above the sand, and stood out white against the green palm fronds. I wondered if they marked landing places for invaders. They faced Puerto Rico. And Castillo de Aza owned land here. So even here, in beautiful, peaceful Nisibón, the shadow of plots darkened the Republic. Back in the capital on Tuesday I sent Cass out by helicopter to look at the flags. They were gone; no trace of them remained.

King reported that General Luna was purchasing for the Dominican Air Force twelve Hawker Hunter Mark VI jet fighters and other equipment from the British at a cost of about five million dollars. Commodore Rib was purchasing several sixty-foot patrol boats made in Germany and costing about sixty thousand dollars each. Our military men said those boats were unsuitable for the open seas around the island.

Colonel Wolfe smelled graft in the Hawker Hunter deal. Luna claimed he had to do something to appease his Vampire jet pilots—they were restless because, the Vampires being obsolete, they had no jets to fly. Wolfe wasn't sure the pilots were really so dissatisfied. Wolfe said we had a T-33 jet trainer ready for delivery and would provide two more within the year. If, however, Luna bought British planes, he would have to obtain British parts and training, and this might mean that we would withdraw our entire air mission in the MAAG. Luna kept saying his pilots wanted to fight Soviet MIGs and he couldn't hold their loyalty. Wolfe thought it was our job to guard against MIGs and Luna's job to control his pilots. Wolfe said San Isidro Air Base had lapsed into the playboy's paradise it had been under Ramfis Trujillo.

The purchase of five million dollars' worth of Hawker Hunters would divert funds needed for social and economic development. While we loaned money to the Republic almost without interest, Luna proposed to buy British aircraft he didn't need at 2.3 percent interest repayable in five years. If he did it, the Navy and Army would want to make similar purchases. We heard that Molina Ureña was concerned, that Bosch opposed the Hawker Hunter purchase but was afraid to tell Luna. The Hawker Hunter purchase was building up into a major issue.

We heard that Bosch was saying privately that he intended to shift all Dominican purchases from the United States to England and that by the end of the year he would have nationalized South Puerto Rico Sugar and the Grenada (United Fruit) Company. Cass stumbled into a group of junior naval officers, one of them saying, "What are we going to do with bauxite?" presumably after Alcoa was nationalized. This all seemed the result of the rumor factory. Andrés Freites, having resigned as Foreign Minister, was leaving the country discouraged—Bosch would never succeed.

During that first week in September, we lived in an atmosphere of tense uncertainty. A New York *Herald Tribune* writer said that "the guarded hope" which had greeted Bosch's election had "turned to doubt" and Bosch "may soon be forced out of office." An article in *The Progressive* said Bosch might "become simply another victim of Latin American militarism, and of U.S. policy characterized by lack of understanding." Tad Szulc wrote in the New York *Times* that high stakes were involved—failure could strengthen Castro's claim that only violent revolution could set Latin America free.

Bosch's political opponents charged that Minister del Rosario had visited Cuba. They began centering their fire on the British Overseas deal, charging corruption. We kept hearing rumors of unrest in the Armed Forces, particularly the Air Force. Severo Cabral attacked me publicly, as he had threatened. The Dominican Senate repudiated the attack. Speakers at a Christian Manifestation in the capital launched "acrimonious attacks" against me, according to *El Caribe*. One speaker said, "If President Bosch is a Communist, what is Ambassador Martin? I don't want to accuse Ambassador Martin of being a Communist; however, Ambassador Martin does not acknowledge that the Communists are taking over the country, as neither did Ambassador Bonsal recognize it in Cuba when Fidel Castro first took over." MPD *tigres* started a riot, and the police arrested three people. It was curious—Bosch was ending with the support only of the U. S. Embassy and the Communist parties, the MPD and PSP. The PSP was having difficulty holding even the 14th of June's support for him. He was virtually isolated, getting caught between the sword and the wall. And so were we.

Bosch was lying low, had made no public speech since the *Restauración*. I felt more and more alone. None of my Dominican "friends" from last year's government came to help. The Nuncio had left for Rome. Williams of AID was touring the Republic. Al Mayne, the planner, had gone to the States for a vacation. Cass wanted to go in October. Meanwhile Bosch inaugurated a series of lectures on Dominican history. Didn't he know what was going on? I felt uneasy, uncertain, depressed.

The smashed strikes, the confrontation with the PRD, the restless military, Washington's coolness, the continuing opposition attacks on Bosch and now on me—I thought we were approaching the breakup.

8

Our intelligence services located Zenon Julio Castillo de Aza. He was in New Jersey. He said that five or six months ago he had been telephoned by Pedro José Trujillo Nicolás, a nephew of the dead dictator, and told to see General Rodríguez Echavarría. They had met in a New York restaurant, he said, and Rodríguez Echavarría had proposed a plot to overthrow Bosch and assassinate Imbert. The backers were Ramfis and Petán Trujillo. Rodríguez Echavarría had suggested that Castillo de Aza travel through Central America to get help and had given him two photographs of himself so he could get him a Central American passport. Castillo de Aza had asked for money. Rodríguez Echavarría told him to get it where he could, Ramfis would reimburse and reward him.

Then, according to Castillo de Aza, he, De Aza, had double-crossed the plotters—had by devious means informed Imbert of the plot. Imbert had instructed him to pretend to go ahead and had given him six hundred dollars. Promptly, he said, he had gone to Washington and informed Ambassador del Rosario of the plot. In July, he said, he had gone to Miami, met another nephew of the dictator, and, through his intercession, obtained a Haitian visa. Traveling on a Honduran passport, No. 22773, issued to a fictitious person, Julio Castillo Cortes, Castillo de Aza had gone to San Juan, Puerto Rico, talked to the hotel manager and an exiled Dominican Trujillista army colonel and to a man whose name he didn't know but who had been introduced to him as the Puerto Rico chief of the plot. This mystery man, according to Castillo de Aza, told him he was sending a man at once to Santo Domingo to assassinate Bosch and Imbert—a grenade in the car of each. Castillo de Aza said he had immediately warned Imbert.

Castillo de Aza had returned to Miami and been told by another Trujillo relative that all was going well. He had then traveled to San

Salvador, where he saw the family of a man who had collaborated closely with Trujillo but had found it uninterested; then to Nicaragua, where he had seen the two Somoza brothers and been rebuffed. He had returned to New York. He admitted he entered the United States illegally.

General Rodríguez Echavarría denied the whole thing. He knew Castillo de Aza—for a time they had been partners in Rodríguez Echavarría's small dress manufacturing business in New York—but they had fallen out. As for the supposed plot, Rodríguez Echavarría knew nothing about it.

I was not quite satisfied. Our agencies would continue checking.

9

Bosch told me he was going to Mexico on September 13 or 14 and was taking Luna with him. I asked about the Hawker Hunter deal. "Luna says his Vampire jet pilots have low morale and that might make trouble," Bosch said uneasily. "Maybe he is a businessman. I will talk to him on the way to Mexico." I said it was a political decision—five million dollars spent on Hawker Hunters would appease a few pilots, but five million dollars spent on public works would put several thousand ordinary people to work; I was having trouble getting money out of Washington and the Hawker Hunter deal wouldn't help any. If he bought English planes, there would be no point in having a large U.S. air mission in the MAAG. Bosch said, "That might create a political problem."

I went to see Imbert, the first visit in a long time. In his new upstairs study, virtually a bulletproof prison, I told him about the Castillo de Aza plot. He told me the Castro/Communists had decided to ignore such small blows as the smashing of the recent strikes and to strike their own blow next January. Imbert said that Luna's deal involved nothing but money —the pilots weren't pushing him at all. He had talked to Viñas and Hungría that night. They had said they must take power away from Bosch.

I asked, "You mean a *golpe?*"

"No. To run it for him, not steal it or grab it for themselves. Just run it."

So he, too, had been thinking along this line.

He reminded me of last year's summit meeting between Fiallo and Bosch and said, "I told you then you couldn't trust Dominican politicians," laughing, then again that terrible phrase: "I know my people."

I told him a military *golpe* would play into the hands of the Castro/Communists and asked if one was coming. He recalled that it had been Wessin y Wessin who had stopped Rodríguez Echavarría's two-day *coup* in 1962 at gun-point. "He is hard against communism," he said. "He is brave." I asked if Wessin was going to move. Imbert didn't know. Not now, he thought. He talked about thievery in the Armed Forces. It was as though everybody was trying to get his before the dam broke.

10

An old man, a U.S. citizen born in Puerto Rico who had lived here most of his life, came to see me. He had visited the consul and Embassy officers innumerable times. I half led him, decrepit, shabby, dignified, to a chair, and he told his story. His wife had been murdered, his own life was in danger, he was suing the Dominican government for eight hundred thousand dollars, seven men were squatting on his property and menacing him, he had filed complaints against them and they had been sentenced to jail for six months but had never served their sentences, and now he was trying to find copies of the complaints, the papers, the eternal papers, and he began fumbling in a worn envelope for the papers, and six months ago three other men had been sentenced to jail but were still at large, he needed the papers to start his lawsuit.

I tried to understand the story. The seven had been sentenced two years before—or was it longer? He was not sure. He lived in the Cibao, he kept shuttling to and fro between our Consulates in Santiago and Santo Domingo, Dominican courts and police stations, but "they" were against him, everyone was against him, he would, however, fight, forever if need be, to avenge his murdered wife and protect his property. I tried to find out who had killed his wife but could not, it seemed to have been a long time ago, or was it only 1959?

How could I help him? I found myself asking the maddening questions that bureaucrats ask—was he registered as an American citizen? "Sí señor, I bed your pardon, yes sir," he said. Who was his lawyer? He had several. I suppose he had been in and out of court for many years. What could we do? Help him, he said. But how—where to start—where seek justice—and I had so many other things—it was grotesque. I told him to see Ben Ruyle, our consul in Santiago, and told him we would give him every protection his citizenship entitled him to (again that bureaucratic language).

I telephoned Ruyle. The old man shuffled out, bowing several times. I never saw him again. Nor understood the problem, much less solved it.

11

On Tuesday, September 10, I went to see Bosch, taking Harlan Bramble. If he wanted the TVA mission to come down on September 28, he had to say so now.

He said, "I do. I don't want the World Bank to study it—it is slow, costly, I cannot wait. But the TVA must come not as the *Alianza* but as private enterprise."

I pointed out the TVA was not a private enterprise. He said, "Well, keep the *Alianza* out of it."

"All right, but what is the TVA to be?"

"Let the TVA come as TVA—nothing else—and to work," emphasizing it.

"All right, but what will we call it?"

"It will be a contribution of the United States government."

"Fine."

"Also," he said, "Moscoso can come but he can't talk about the Yaque."

I told him it'd be hard to keep Moscoso quiet but we'd transmit Bosch's views. We made plans for the mission's visit of September 28, emphasizing not receptions in the capital but work in the Valley itself.

12

Next day I talked to Williams, sent cables, began making detailed plans for the TVA mission. Colonel Cass came in and said, "Rib called me in this morning, and said, 'What is going to be the United States attitude toward a military junta?' "

I asked if he was sure Rib had said precisely that. Cass was sure— Rib seemed to take it for granted a *golpe* would take place.

When? I told the attachés to stay in town this weekend, while Bosch was in Mexico. Vallimarescu reported that ex-President Bonnelly planned to go on national radio-TV Friday night, after Bosch's departure. We had feared that for months.

Bosch's enemies, having failed to overthrow him by first attacking him under the banners of the discredited political parties, by second mounting a campaign in the U.S. and Dominican press against him, and by third launching the Christian Manifestations, were now turning to Bonnelly.

Tony Ríz, our man helping train the police, reported that a police colonel might attempt a *golpe*—he was a hothead and a close friend of Wessin y Wessin. Volman came in to talk about the Parvin Foundation's literacy program. Forty of the one hundred tapes had been produced, but so far nobody had come up with the television receivers. We received cables from Spain. The important Trujillos were there. The Department said that we could deliver a T-33 jet trainer October 1. Perhaps that would forestall the Hawker Hunter deal. Cass reported, as Imbert had, that the pilots were not pressing Luna for Hawker Hunters; it was Luna's own idea.

On Friday morning, September 13, I went to see Bosch at the Palace at 8 A.M. to tell him all this. At one forty-five, Fran and I drove out to San Isidro to see him off to Mexico, as did the diplomatic corps and the

Dominican government. At the gate of San Isidro the humps in the road installed by Trujillo still remained. We drove to a big hangar. The military high command arrived, Rib, Luna, Hungría; several Cabinet ministers, Jaar, Humbertilio Váldez, Majluta, others; Vice President González Tamayo; the other Ambassadors and their wives. Jaar and Humbertilio Váldez stood near us. We chatted briefly with Luna.

The presidential plane was waiting, a DC-4. The DC-4 is little used today except in the troubled backwaters of the world where rusty guns and obsolete aircraft ultimately find their graveyard, taking hapless dark-skinned people with them. Fran asked what kind of plane it was and said she was glad she wasn't going to Mexico in it. I said it would be all right—Luna was going with him.

At last President Bosch arrived with a motorcade of cars containing, as I recall it, his new Foreign Minister, García-Godoy, and General Viñas and their wives. The Dominicans surged forward, and Bosch and his party surged to meet them, a great welter of embracing humanity. We Ambassadors had been told we would form into a receiving line but had known better—it was always catch-as-catch-can. I hung back, wondering where the Mexican Ambassador was—after all, they were going to his country. Foreign Minister García-Godoy stood aside, one of the few Dominicans I ever knew who really looked like a distinguished diplomat, well-dressed, neat, graying, hair close-combed, small mustache clipped, always smiling an urbane little smile. His wife, usually urbane too, today was making nervous little remarks—"I do hope we take off all right," glancing at the DC-4 lonely on the runway. Bosch made his way through the press of people, his white head visible among the others, and we shook hands with him as he passed and wished him a good trip, and he continued through the crowd, then moved out of the hangar's shade and into the blazing midday sun and so to the plane. The military accompanied him to the foot of the steps. At the plane door he turned to wave to us, then disappeared inside. I had an odd moment of wondering if I ever would see him again.

Others must have wondered too. Big Commodore Rib made straight for me, and as he approached I said to Fran, "I think I'll ask him, '¿Ya, Juli?'"—"Ready, Juli?"—but didn't. He stood close beside me, took off his cap, and mopped the sweat from his brow with a handkerchief. Many times that year when I had seen Rib, short and fat and solid, I had asked him, "¿Como va las cosas?"—"how are things," and he had always replied, "Bien—hasta ahora,"—"all right, so far." It had become a sort of joke between us. Some joke! We all watched, waiting.

The pilot started the engines. The two on the left side started, then the right inboard. But the right outboard balked. Minutes passed. The plane door opened, an arm gestured, a couple of mechanics ran out to the plane carrying a stepladder and some tools, they climbed up on the

THE LITTLE CLINIC OF HIGÜEY

Higüey, the provincial capital, had no functioning public medical facilities.... Fran picked
site in Higüey where the poor would not hesitate to come—a muddy square behind the
market. Two Peace Corps poured a 15-foot by 20-foot slab of concrete. Sacha Volman
found a military tent. People in town gave lumber to make tables and chairs...."

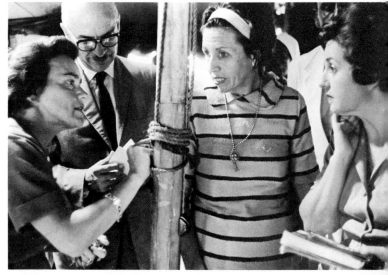

*orld Health Organiza-
on representative, Mrs.
osch's sister, and Mrs.
uan Bosch visit Fran
Martin (far left) at the
nt clinic*

"For weeks Fran worked to train the young women volunteers....They were attractive, intelligent, voluble, eager, proud of their new white uniforms made by the sewing co-op. But somehow the card-index file languished and so did the educational work. Finally it was clear...the attractive, white-clad volunteers were as illiterate as their clients. They couldn't keep a card file because they didn't know the alphabet."

Dominican volunteer treats a patient who didn't understand the mobile unit was for babies

10

In a private house of a Santo Domingo barrio

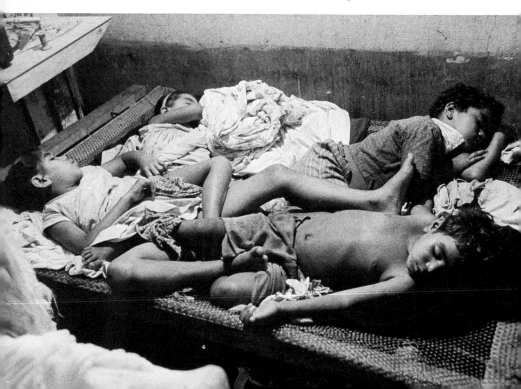

"Thirty or forty mothers came the first day. Soon, as word spread through the *campo,* over sixty were coming each day, mothers and often fathers bringing their babies on horseback or carrying them miles afoot, waiting patiently for hours. Medicine ran short, doctors didn't show up, neither did volunteers, and when it rained the clinic flooded. Once the tent blew down...."

11

"Should they try to recruit another doctor? One existed, young, ambitious, with a flourishing practice....He refused. ...Many months later, a band of guerrillas went into the hills nearby and after the fighting ceased, the army brought down four bodies to the *Fortaleza* in Higüey. Several families refused to identify the bodies as their sons'. One was the family of this young doctor...."

Dr. Pumarol inside the Little Clinic

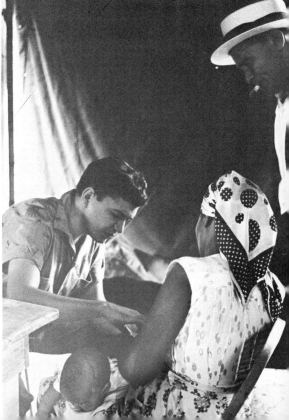

"Dignitaries came and went, inspecting, dictating reports. The people stayed, stayed the same, filthy, hungry, wretched. Who could help, who cared?...The tent Clinic was a pathetically small drop in an enormous bucket....Could we, in the Dominican Republic or in any other of the emerging nations, move fast enough? Could we recover the wasted years, the lost generations, the wasted people in time?"

ladder to work on the engine. Several of us groaned. The pilot had shut off the engine beside the mechanics but the two on the left side were running. The mechanics hammered and poked at the engine for fifteen minutes, then clambered down. The pilot tried it. No, not yet. Jaar said to me tensely, "I begged the President not to fly to Mexico in that thing. I even got prices from Pan American. I wanted a jet. Ten thousand dollars. That's all it would have cost. Ten thousand dollars. I begged him. But he said no. And look," gesturing bitterly toward the ancient DC-4. Humbertilio Váldez nodded. I realized, for the first time fully, that these two, unlike Bosch's sycophants, really cared about him.

The mechanics put the stepladder up, and tried again. This time the engine caught, and they walked away. The pilot started the engine beside it. But now one on the left side quit, its propeller slowly dying. Again the plane door opened. Jaar groaned aloud. The mechanics started out to fix it. I glanced around. Vice President González Tamayo was a short distance away. I moved closer to him. I did not want the military between me and him if anything went wrong on takeoff.

Just before the mechanics got to the plane the engine started, the prop wash blew the plane door shut, all four engines roared mightily, as mightily as they could, though I thought one was coughing, then slowly the plane began to move. I glanced at a Dominican Air Force officer I knew, and he shrugged, eyebrows raised, and I moved a little closer to the Vice President in his crumpled white suit. Now no military man was between us. The plane taxied out to the runway, stood a moment while the pilot ran up the engines, then slowly started its lumbering takeoff run. Jaar could not bear to watch; he turned his back to the runway, suffering. I was watching the plane and the military commanders. Slowly, ever so slowly, reluctantly, almost, the plane left the earth; slowly rose into the bright pale empty sky. Some left at once, but we waited until it was out of sight, and when I saw González Tamayo get in his car, Fran and I got in ours and drove out of San Isidro.

That night Bonnelly spoke, and we watched on television. It was a reasoned speech, well organized, calmly delivered, calmly defending his own regime and attacking Bosch's. It was highly critical. But it was moderate in tone, it dealt mainly with economics, and it did not once mention communism. Certainly it was not an incendiary speech.

13

On Sunday at 6:30 P.M. Bev Cass telephoned and said, "There's something going on. None of the chiefs are at home." I told him to come over, called King and told him to alert Shlaudeman and the CIA chief, called the administrative officer, Quintanilla, and asked him to get me a driver —I had given mine the weekend off.

Colonel Cass came to the Residence at 7 P.M. looking worried. He said the service commanders, except Luna, who was with Bosch, were at their offices and had sent out a call for all officers to report for duty—on Sunday night. Where was Wessin y Wessin? He didn't know. Imbert and Amiama? He didn't know.

We had first heard about it when Rivera Cuesta's wife had telephoned Fritz Long about 5:45 P.M. and said, "How are you? I haven't seen you for so long." That wasn't true—Long spent a good deal of time with Rivera and his wife. Long had said, "Fine, how are you?" She had said, "I'm in bed with a cold." He had said, "I'll come see you." (All Dominicans, assuming their phones are tapped, habitually talk like this on the phone.) He had gone, and she had said her husband had gone to the office, saying something about a *golpe* tonight. She said that "tonight was Amiama and Imbert's night."

Long and Cass had started checking. General Hungría had told Cass he was uneasy. Rib was in his office and had told Cass, "I don't know what's going on." Wessin y Wessin was not in his office at San Isidro but all his officers were there or on their way. Tony Ruíz, our police man, said Imbert's phone didn't answer. Fritz Long and Tom Fishburn, the new air attaché, were on their way to the Palace to try to talk to General Viñas' number two man. (Viñas and his wife were with Bosch.) They also would try to find Rivera Cuesta and Pagán, who earlier had been at Pagán's office but now had disappeared.

I told Cass to go first to Imbert's house, then to Rib's office, but only briefly—to hurry to San Isidro and find Wessin y Wessin. Long and Fishburn should stay with Hungría.

At seven-fifty I told King, Shlaudeman, and the CIA chief to come over. The CIA man had just received word from two independent sources that all troops were confined to barracks.

At eight o'clock Colonel Cass came back. Imbert had left his house at seven-fifteen, and so had Amiama. Rib had gone to Hungría's office at seven-fifteen. Long was there and would stay. At this moment, truckloads of sailors were pulling up at Navy headquarters and being given hand grenades. Cass said, "I have the impression, one, that the Armed Forces is gathering at Hungría's office, and, two, that they are going to stop, not start, a *coup*."

I asked, "Then who's starting it?"

He said, "I dunno."

The only commanders unaccounted for were Wessin y Wessin, Imbert, and Amiama. And dozens of colonels and lower-ranking officers. We'd try to find the missing commanders first.

Somebody remembered that Wessin y Wessin's son had been injured recently—Wessin's bodyguard had dropped his gun, and it had gone off, and the bullet had hit Wessin's son, and we had sent the boy to our military hospital in San Juan, Puerto Rico. (I always wondered what happened to the bodyguard.) Was it possible Wessin had gone to San Juan to visit his son this weekend? Cass would inquire. I told Shlaudeman to find Vice President González Tamayo and Miolán. I told King to call the Operations Center in the Department in Washington and tell them to alert Assistant Secretary Ed Martin or Undersecretary George Ball.

The phones in my study began ringing. I had three phones there, two through the Chancellery switchboard and a direct outside unlisted line, plus, in our upstairs bedroom, the hot line to Washington. I told Quintanilla to get a secretary to answer the phones. I went out to the living room to pace and think.

If we could locate Wessin y Wessin, Imbert, and Amiama, and if they weren't doing anything, then either nothing was going on or the middle-grade officers were moving. On the other hand, we ourselves must be careful not to escalate it. A suspicion crossed my mind. Rivera Cuesta's wife, who had first given us the rumor and had pinned it on Imbert and Amiama, was notoriously pro-Balaguer. Was it possible she hoped to get rid of Imbert and Amiama, thus making it safe for Balaguer to return to the Republic? This sounded, as Shlaudeman said, "pretty Balkan." But what wasn't?

Shlaudeman couldn't get Vice President González Tamayo or Miolán by phone. Cass called in—Wessin y Wessin had indeed gone to Puerto Rico earlier in the day but had come back during the afternoon. At eight-thirty I got a call from a woman in Bosch's household saying that the Air Force was "doing something" and the Army was confined to barracks. At eight-thirty Tony Ruíz came in—a high police police official said the whole affair was a false alarm.

Sacha Volman arrived. He didn't know what was going on but was sure something was. As usual, he assumed the blame lay with Amiama and Imbert. He didn't know where Miolán was but had more phone numbers for him than we. (Address-telephone books were always crucial. Nearly all phone numbers that we needed were unlisted, and the subscribers kept changing them.) Volman knew a house where González Tamayo might be. He said Molina Ureña, President of the Chamber of Deputies, had left his own home about a half hour ago, apparently in fear of being arrested, and Volman was off to try to find him. I asked him first to take Shlaudeman to González Tamayo's house. If a *golpe* really was afoot, Shlaudeman should invite González Tamayo to the Embassy Residence as my overnight guest. (Unlike Latin American countries, the United States government, as a general rule, does not officially offer the right of asylum. There was no reason, however, why I could not have a house guest.)

At eight fifty-five Cass came in. "No *golpe* tonight," he said. "It was a

Tony show." He had just come from Imbert's house. Imbert had told him the following:

Late in the afternoon, General Hungría had called Imbert, Belisario Peguero, Rib, Vice President González Tamayo, and Colonel Neit Nivar Seijas to Hungría's office. (Neit Nivar Seijas belonged to "the San Cristóbal group," high-ranking military Trujillistas who had been put on the shelf after the Generalissimo's assassination. Only in the past few weeks had I begun to hear his name.) Hungría had told them he had heard that a *golpe* was afoot and he wanted them all to know he was not behind it. He said he had first heard the rumor from Chagito Rodríguez Echavarría. This was astonishing to me—Chagito was the younger brother of General Rodríguez Echavarría, and I had had the impression that both were in New York. What was he doing here? Was this the Castillo de Aza plot?

Imbert had replied to Hungría that he had no intention of making a *golpe,* then had gone home. Cass had just come from Imbert's house. It was full of military men. Cass said, "I think he put the show on for my benefit." That is, Imbert had wanted to impress Cass with the fact that he had friends in all the services and that he was loyal to Bosch—for now. Imbert said he considered the whole thing a fake—Hungría had simply been trying to ingratiate himself with Bosch by pretending to stop a *golpe* which never, in fact, existed.

I asked where Wessin was. Cass didn't know. Had Amiama been at Imbert's? Cass hadn't seen him.

I wasn't wholly satisfied. Hungría was a big, lumbering, plain soldier. That he would invent a plot to ingratiate himself with Bosch seemed out of character. Nor was I convinced Imbert had gone to so much trouble to impress us. And we still didn't know where Wessin or Amiama were.

At nine twenty-five Tony Ruíz came in. A police official had told him that a group of officers led by Chagito Rodríquez Echavarría had gone to Vice President González Tamayo today and told him they proposed to get rid of Bosch and take over. González Tamayo had called Hungría and asked if it was true. Hungría had said no. González Tamayo then had defied the officers. They had departed.

That made even less sense than Imbert's story. Why would a group of military officers confront the acting President of the Republic, allow the brother of a discredited exile General to speak for them, demand power, permit the acting President to telephone the Army chief, then, when he defied them, meekly depart?

The CIA chief, who had left earlier to get in touch with his sources, came back at nine forty-five. He said 14th of June members might arm themselves to defend the government. On the other hand, it was possible they had started the whole rumor.

At ten, Shlaudeman came back. He had found González Tamayo.

From him and others with him, including Ministers Jaar and Domínguez Guerra, Shlaudeman had pieced together this version:

A sister—not brother—of General Rodríguez Echavarría had told someone there would be an uprising that night by the police, plus part of the Navy. Hungría, Rib, and Vice President González Tamayo had met, probably on Hungría's initiative. The Vice President had put no stock in the rumor, but Hungría had ordered all troops confined to barracks, and Rib had started handing out grenades, and that had touched off everything else. Shlaudeman had advised the Vice President to call us if anything else happened. Shlaudeman was inclined to discount the whole affair.

I was still not sure.

At 11:15 P.M. Long and Fishburn came in. They said the whole thing had started with Chagito Rodríguez Echavarría. He had told Colonel Neit Nivar Seijas that a *golpe* was afoot that night. Neit Nivar Seijas had told Hungría. Hungría had called in all the chiefs, plus Imbert, the Vice President, and Domínguez Guerra. They had decided it was an unfounded rumor and had disbanded. At about that same time, Wessin's unit commanders had been meeting separately at Wessin's headquarters in the Armed Forces Training Center at San Isidro, on whose command nobody knew. But Wessin himself had not been there—his tankers had said he was out trying to find out what was going on—and Long never had found him. Long doubted the plot had been genuine, but thought it might have been "a dry run," a rehearsal.

Cass came in at eleven-thirty. He had just left Rib. Rib was going to spend the rest of the night trying to find Wessin. He had ordered the Palace guard to keep everyone out of the Palace that night. He said about ten of his Navy officers were "on Imbert's team" and he could find none of them. Cass had told him they were at Imbert's house. Rib had said he was trying to stop a *golpe*.

Cass now was convinced that the Army and Navy had acted to defend the government against a *golpe* by Imbert. So, probably, had the Air Force. Cass said, "They are all pro-constitutional government tonight. they are against this *coup*—but only because it was Imbert's."

I asked everybody if they thought it would stay quiet the rest of the night. All did. They went home, and I went to bed. After all, it was a little difficult to overthrow a President who wasn't even in the country.

For several days, we picked up fallout from Sunday's *golpe,* or non-*golpe.*

One of Shlaudeman's sources said that Sunday afternoon Manolo Tavárez Justo had visited relatives; a car containing an army colonel had driven up, Tavárez Justo had gone out to talk to him, the car had driven away, and Tavárez Justo had come back inside, said great things were afoot, and run off.

The city was full of rumors. A woman in Bosch's entourage told Fran she was getting ready to leave—*"Conde me habla,"* that is, "Conde speaks to me," El Conde, the main street of town, the street of rumors. A rumor ran through the city that I had been assassinated; friends telephoned to see if I was all right. Soon I was warned that I would be assassinated by rightist extremists in such a way as to put the blame on the Castro/Communists, thus giving the extreme right a pretext to overthrow Bosch and win Washington's applause for saving the Republic from communism.

Wessin y Wessin told Fritz Long he had known nothing about the plot till eleven o'clock Sunday night, said Imbert would get no support from San Isidro, but said that Bosch had to do something about communism. Commodore Rib told Cass, "I hope that after this weekend the President now knows we're loyal to him and his government. But he must repay us by doing something about what we feel is endangering our country: Communism." Cass believed that pressure on communism was rising from the majors, captains, and lieutenants in all three branches.

Shlaudeman reported that Miolán had spent all Sunday night hiding, fearing arrest or murder. Once just after he had left the home of an officer of a foreign Embassy, a truckload of soldiers had arrived. I wondered if that were not the key piece of information. Had the military *golpistas,* whoever they were, been able to seize Miolán, they might have gone ahead with the *golpe.* "Miolán is convinced a *golpe* is coming," Shlaudeman said. "He says he'll be the first one killed."

I thought several theories possible: That it had been an Imbert plot blocked by Hungría and Rib (it wasn't the way Imbert would move); that it had been a rehearsal to test strength (foolish); that it had been an attempt by Hungría or Rib to advance themselves (out of character for Hungría); that it had been a devious attempt to kill Imbert and overthrow Bosch, triggered by Chagito on orders of Rodríguez Echavarría or Castillo de Aza with Trujillo backing (too devious); that it had been nothing at all, mere escalated rumor (this could not be); that it had been a troublemaking maneuver by the 14th of June; that it had been a plot by Wessin y Wessin and had failed because Imbert got into it (I doubted it). Several things bothered me—we couldn't find Wessin or Amiama till Monday; the involvement of Manolo Tavárez Justo; Miolán's near-arrest.

Like so much else, the affair remained shrouded.

14

The Department of State had an idea. It was preparing charts and flow sheets which would "program" the strategic plan for each country, thereby, it hoped, ensuring more orderly implementation of policy. It had selected the Dominican Republic, along with one other Latin American country, to test the system. It sent two or three men down to explain the system to us, and they did so at a country team meeting, enlarged to include section chiefs in the Embassy, on Monday, September 16, the day after the confused *golpe*. They used elaborate charts and flip cards to explain the system, showing, for example, under "input," such things as "AID" (money), "Personnel" (AID technicians, Peace Corps volunteers), "Influencing" (USIS press contacts, political officers' contacts). The whole thing had an air of having been borrowed from the Pentagon or IBM. Actually, it made sense. But I wasn't sure it would work here, in this lunatic asylum. I saw no flip cards on how to handle Tony Imbert, or Rib's hand grenades.[1]

I had opened the meeting by reading a telegram I had sent last week reporting Rib's question to Cass, "What is going to be" the United States position on a *coup* and the Department's tough reply, instructing me to tell Rib and anyone else of like mind that we unequivocally supported Bosch. Reading, I omitted Rib's name. I went on to say that it was the responsibility of every mission head, and of every section head, to see to it that his subordinates understood the policy of the United States government very clearly. It was not my policy, not the Embassy's policy. It was the United States government's policy. And the policy was to support Juan Bosch. Therefore, anyone who in his contacts with Dominicans or Americans in any way wavered in his support of Bosch was undermining the policy of the United States government and could expect the consequences. I said specifically that this meant that all hands must, if asked, reply without hesitation or equivocation that we supported Juan Bosch; more than that, it meant that they must not stand silent if at a cocktail party they heard Bosch criticized, by inference permitting their silence to assent. They must, in other words, each of them, and at all times, affirmatively support the Bosch government.

15

Our Embassy in London cabled that the British government declined to stop the purchase of Hawker Hunters. Colonel Wolfe worked out a program for both aircraft and coastal patrol boats which I could present to Bosch as an attractive alternative to Luna's and Rib's grandiose purchases. The difficulty was that most of Wolfe's plan hinged on Congressional approval of the foreign aid bill, still uncertain.

Dato Pagán's accursed school advertised for students in *El Caribe*.

[1] Worse things happen. I once heard a man in the U.S. government say that if he could put the same resources into Brazil that were being put into the Cuban exile movement in Miami, he could make anything of Brazil that anybody wanted. It was the new "organization man" speaking—the IBM mind. I wondered if he knew about such problems as Juan Bosch's personality.

I spent Monday writing a long dispatch summing up Bosch's first six months in office. It assayed his chances of survival: Not good. Thus far all efforts of his political enemies to overthrow him had failed. But they had two weapons left—a general strike led by businessmen similar to their successful 1961 strike against the Ramfis-Balaguer government; and a military *golpe*. A general strike probably could not overthrow Bosch unless the military joined it. The military was the key. Recent events were hardly reassuring.

Bosch needed to regain the initiative by enacting serious reform legislation—but if he did, the right probably would overthrow him. He was trapped. If Bosch survived this year he might survive four; but it would be foolish to predict he would survive tomorrow.

Our own position was worsening. Many American private citizens thought we were mistaken in supporting Bosch, so did, even, some members of our mission; increasingly the attachés reported that the Dominican military would not talk to them. We, like Bosch, were becoming isolated. In the final analysis, our ability to influence events depended on our willingness to bring the fleet to the horizon. But it was one thing to send the fleet to eject the Trujillos, quite another to stop an anti-Bosch *coup*.

I recommended we move along the lines I had described previously— quietly influence Bosch's government, proceed with the TVA, get enough AID to tide Bosch over, build politically for the future, and present an appearance of withdrawing from the scene a bit: If we got through the next few weeks, I myself might take a trip around the Caribbean.

The next night, Tuesday, September 17, Bosch was due home. I went to San Isidro to meet him, thinking he might be taken prisoner on landing. Luna's officers kept me in an anteroom alone. Bosch's plane was hours late. I waited till past midnight, then went home. He arrived at 1:20 A.M. and went home safely. I sent off my long dispatch about Bosch's prospects on September 22. By the time it reached Washington, the sword had pinned him to the wall.

Chapter Twenty-four

THE FALL OF JUAN BOSCH

A general strike was announced. It would start at 6 A.M. on Friday morning, September 20. It was called a "Christian" strike against "international communism." It was arranged by businessmen. My staff and I were working on a schedule for the TVA visit to develop the land while these "responsible," "moderate," and "Christian" businessmen were plotting to destroy their country's last chance at representative democracy.

The general strike by businessmen, not by labor, had been developed as a revolutionary technique in the Republic after the fall of Trujillo when the UCN had sprung up as a civic movement under Fiallo's leadership. It had cost twenty-eight thousand dollars a day—not all "responsible," "moderate," and "Christian" businessmen are patriotic, the big ones pay the small ones to keep their shops shut.

All that summer, as the *civicos'* opposition to Bosch continued, and as the Christian Manifestations had run their course, we had known that a general strike might be the *civicos'* ultimate weapon. They would try to shut down both Santo Domingo and Santiago. Labor unions might join. If they could keep the cities shut down for two or three days, tension would get screwed tight, and rioting might start. Troops must quell riots. Thus might they pull the military into their plot. That day—a Friday, of course—the test began.

It was ironic that the very *civicos* who had struck against Ramfis and his troops in the fall of 1961 were now, exactly two years later, rising again in exactly the same way against the elected government they had fought for and we were still fighting for.

2

I got to the office early. Junior officers reported that a quick run around town showed most stores closed. At nine-ten Ben Ruyle called from Santiago—the merchants there had hesitated a few minutes, then *El*

Gallo, a store owned by Gustavo Tavares, Doña María's son, had opened, and the rest had followed. I told Ruyle to congratulate Gustavo Tavares for me personally and to speak to Eduardo León and our other friends in Santiago.

But the capital was the key. King said all the Armed Forces chiefs were at the Palace.

At ten-fifteen, Bev Cass came to my office. Imbert and Amiama intended to hide all day—too many people were putting pressure on them. They were angry at Bosch for shutting down the radio stations and denying them to the strikers—he hadn't prevented the Castro/Communists from using them. Cass said all the Armed Forces were confined to barracks. Commodore Rib had said he had "not yet" joined the strike. Did he expect to, Cass had asked? No, Rib had said, but he didn't know what was going to happen. Cass said a naval officer had said that all the younger officers favored a *golpe* but needed leadership. We had a ship coming to port that day. Cass had heard the MPD planned to sabotage it. We warned the commander.

King said that one big store downtown had reopened: The Read hardware store on Parque Independencia, in front of which the assassins Antonio de la Maza and Juan Tomás Díaz had been murdered by the SIM.

A private source told us that the strike had been organized at a secret meeting at the home of Severo Cabral, the UCN right-winger who admired the Spaniards for heaving Protestants in boiling oil. At a meeting last night the "responsible moderate" (and "Christian") businessmen had been told that the military were in sympathy with the strike, though Viñas and Hungría had reservations. The police favored the strike. Imbert was deeply involved. The strike leaders intended to use the strike to overthrow the government and bring in a civilian junta headed by José Antonio Jimenes, a wealthy elderly cattle rancher from near Higüey. That night the responsible moderate businessmen had been forming "shock troops" and handing out money. They intended to present an ultimatum to Bosch the next day.

At 11 A.M. Conatral, the AFL-CIO labor federation formerly called Foupesa Libre, issued a communiqué: It repudiated the strike and called on its members to be alert for a *golpé.* This was the first good news. If the *civicos* could not pull the unions in, they might not pull the military in. Our job was to help Bosch prevent it. If the *civicos* lost this one, Bosch should hit them hard—arrest Severo Cabral, Bonilla Aybar, Enrique Alfau, and other strike leaders, and close down Bonilla Aybar's *Prensa Libre.*

A message came from Sacha Volman. He reported the 14th of June was saying that a "Colonel Simmons" had arrived from the United States to help bring about a *golpe.* I sent back word that this was absurd. At

THE FALL OF JUAN BOSCH 549

eleven-thirty Volman came to the Residence. He said President Bosch intended to deport "some Spaniards." I asked who. Businessmen, Volman said. It was typical of Bosch—never hit the center, always the edge. He was angry at Conatral. Why? It was supporting him. Because it was only "paying lip service" to him, Volman said, and was secretly plotting against its rival, Foupsa Cesistrado, the PRD labor federation. Bosch wanted me to get a new labor attaché, considering Fred Somerford too close to Conatral.

I told Volman he was crazy—Conatral had publicly repudiated the strike, at least in part because of Somerford's influence. As for Simmons, I told Volman how in November 1961, when Simmons was working to force the Trujillos out, Petán Trujillo had aimed his submachine gun at Simmons' stomach and pulled the bolt back; how Simmons had told him, "It's too late—the fleet is here."

"This," I told Volman bitterly, "is the Simmons your 14th of June friends are telling Bosch is now plotting against the government. Simmons is in Washington, working for the Joint Chiefs of Staff. You go tell your boyfriend so."

Some time earlier, we had scheduled a party for the Embassy staff for that afternoon, including our Dominican employees. They began arriving at noon, and with Fran as hostess, they sat around the pool under the beautiful trees, while I moved in and out between telephone calls in my study.

Manolo Tavárez Justo was going to Puerto Rico to talk with Puerto Rican independence leaders. (Extremists of that movement had tried to assassinate President Truman several years ago and had shot up the House of Representatives in Washington.) I ordered Manolo's U.S. visa canceled and ordered the news given to the press.

John Perry, retained by Justice Douglas and the Parvin Foundation to oversee production of the television literacy program, arrived. The first tapes were magnificent but the project had run into difficulties. If I could put it back on the track, we could start broadcasting in October.

King came to the Residence at four-thirty. The city was shut down tight. Even the drugstores were closed. So were the banks. Some filling stations were open, some closed. One store owner had been told to close or see his windows smashed. All day the government had been broadcasting exhortations to store owners to reopen, promising police protection. It had had no effect. Thus far there had been no trouble downtown, traffic was moving normally, but gangs of thugs could be seen on the side streets, reminiscent of the *paleros* of September 1961.

Santiago, King said, was open; the Chamber of Commerce there was meeting now to decide whether to close tomorrow. San Pedro de Macorís, Barahona, Baní, La Romana, and Puerto Plata were closed. Baní would not allow traffic to pass. The military was quiet, still in barracks. The police were behaving. No union had joined the strike.

At five-thirty, two Cabinet ministers came to my office, Antonio Guzmán and Ramón Vila Piola. They said they were under heavy pressure from certain leaders of two labor federations, CASC (the Social Christian federation) and Conatral (AFL-CIO), to pay the Haina workers a bonus amounting to twenty million dollars. (Maybe Volman had been right—it was Conatral's price for denouncing the strike.) The union leaders were demanding an answer today. The Ministers wanted us to help take the pressure off. I asked what they could offer the unions. They said an immediate one-month bonus of 4.5 million dollars, or a truce in negotiations for ten days or two weeks. They had been negotiating all morning, and had agreed at noon to a truce until 5 P.M. It was now five-thirty. They feared the unions would join the general strike. They thought the UCN was putting pressure on Conatral, and the Social Christians on CASC. They felt if the strike lasted only through this weekend, the government would survive, but if it went into next week, it might not, and union support would probably push it into next week.

They hurried away. I called in Shlaudeman and the CIA chief and sent them to talk to the Social Christians and Conatral. This might be crucial.

At five-fifty, Bev Cass called me. A delegation of military officers was on its way to see him. General Hermida was leading it. I asked what they wanted. Cass didn't know but could guess. So could I.

At 6 P.M. King brought the administrative officer, Joe Quintanilla, in. Salvador Pittaluga, a Bosch supporter and sometimes anti-American editor of a fly-by-night newspaper, La Tarde, had called Quintanilla that morning and asked if his home telephone number was 2-4518. No, it was 2-4528. Pittaluga had said, "Ah, this is a clarification very important." Quintanilla had asked what it was all about. Pittaluga had said that numerous telephone calls organizing the general strike had been traced to 2-4518. Quintanilla had said he knew nothing about it, he had nothing to do with political matters, and anyway his number was 2-4528. Now La Tarde was out; King showed it to me. It said that although Quintanilla denied it, "a source which merits complete credit" had stated "categorically" that many telephone calls both in Santo Domingo and around the country had been made from 2-4528 (Quintanilla's actual number), organizing not only today's general strike but last weekend's abortive golpe.

This was clearly a frame-up. Pittaluga had had the number wrong and had changed it after talking to Quintanilla.

Maybe this time we could nail the man close to Bosch who was making trouble between him and me.

I called the manager of the telephone company, obtained permission to examine the toll tickets, and sent John Perkey, our commercial attaché, down to the telephone company, telling him to work with one or two independent witnesses.

I sent Vallimarescu down to *La Tarde*. Three reporters on *La Tarde* told him they had tried to kill the story, since they didn't believe it, but Pittaluga had insisted on publishing it. Vallimarescu demanded to know Pittaluga's source. Pittaluga refused to divulge it. But from other things he said, Val guessed it was Minister Domínguez Guerra.

King and I began writing cables. Shlaudeman came in at six-twenty— CASC, the Social Christian labor federation, would stop pressing the government for the bonus. We could not get so categorical a guarantee from Conatral but got enough to take the pressure off. This was a major victory.

At eight-fifteen, Sacha Volman called me. He said that cars were being burned on Calle Conde and attempts were being made to sabotage the waterworks and the electric plant. I told King to send somebody to check. He did, and came to the Residence with Shlaudeman. King said General Hermida and two other officers had called on Cass and asked for the official U.S. view of the strike. "Despicable," Cass had said. They had said, "Fine, we won't ask what the position of the United States government would be toward a *golpe* because we know. So let's talk as friends, unofficially." They were always trying that. Cass had replied he couldn't talk unofficially, everything he said was official. The conversation had ended with their saying, "If you tell us to go, we'll go," meaning they'd overthrow Bosch. "If you say no, that's all right, too." Cass had their promise not to make a *golpe* that night or during the general strike. He thought Hermida wanted Viñas' job as Minister of Defense. Luna wanted the Hawker Hunters.

While we were talking, Shlaudeman had been telephoning. One car had been burned on Calle Sánchez, not Calle Conde. A young officer in Shlaudeman's section made a run through the heart of the city. All was quiet on Calle Conde, on Arzobispo Nouel, the street which paralleled it, and in the two main parks, Independencia and Colón. I sent him to check on the burned car on Calle Sánchez. Volman called about nine. He'd driven up Calle Conde, out Jorge Washington by the sea, and up Simón Bolívar, and all was quiet, people were strolling as usual.

It was dark now. We waited.

Presently Volman called again, and asked me, "Is there a Major Lobrania—" so he spelled it "—in the MAAG?"

I didn't know. King thought there was somebody with a similar name. I asked why.

Volman asked, "Was he in a meeting with Dominican officers this morning?"

I said, "Listen, Sacha. What's this all about?"

Volman said he was with the President. The President was upset. He wanted to know the answers to those questions.

King thought the MAAG was giving a party; he checked the name. I called and asked for Major Lombraña. Noise of a party, then he came on. I asked the question. He stammered, wouldn't answer, finally said, "Just a minute," and Fritz Long came on. I told him what I wanted to know, and heard him, over the party's noise, asking Lombraña (who, not recognizing my voice, hadn't wanted to talk). From 8 to 11:30 A.M. at the 16th of August Camp, Lombraña had administered a test in map reading to a class of company commanders and platoon leaders of the Juan Pablo Duarte Battalion. Finished, Lombraña had driven away, stopped briefly at MAAG headquarters behind the Palace, and reached his home a few minutes past noon. He had spent the afternoon grading the examination papers at home and after dinner had gone to the party.

As I was about to call Volman back, Tony Ruíz came in, said police headquarters was quiet, the city was quiet.

We heard the ridiculous rumor about Colonel Simmons of the Joint Chiefs indirectly from two more people—Molina Ureña, President of the Chamber of Deputies, and Colonel Calderón, President Bosch's bodyguard. I was furious. Volman's friends in the 14th of June were telling him the United States was involved in the strike, and Volman half-believed it, and suspected that "the Pentagon" was double-crossing the Department, the White House, and me. His conspiratorial contacts in the 14th of June had been useful the previous year; but now, having risen high and gaining direct access to the President, the President of the Chamber of Deputies, and the President's bodyguard, Volman was still repeating the tales of the irresponsible kids in the 14th. Misled himself, he misled the President. It was even possible that Colonel Calderón, a rather naïve man, had all unwittingly repeated the rumor to other Army officers—and they, being ready to overthrow Bosch anyway, would have been delighted to learn the United States was backing them.

A little past nine-thirty, Volman called and talked to Shlaudeman. His secretary had seen sixty policemen mounted on horses, with black automobiles between each two horses, the whole cavalcade headed for President Bosch's house. Volman was going to check on it, then come here.

The whole affair was assuming a nightmare quality. I told Shlaudeman I thought Volman had lost his mind. He arrived in a few minutes, small, wearing old pants and sport shirt and sneakers, as usual, looking unshaven and exhausted. He said he could not find the horsemen, all was quiet in the city. But, he said, the police protection of the Electricidad and the bridge was "absolutely insufficient." He suspected police sabotage.

I told him the facts about Major Lombraña, who had simply been doing his job, not, as Bosch apparently suspected, encouraging a *coup*. I had intended to tell him harshly but didn't—I felt sorry for him, and for Bosch, too. Volman was restless. I suggested he drive around town and let us know about the police protection.

John Perkey called. He had examined more than four thousand telephone toll tickets. He could find not a single long-distance call made from either 2-4518 or 2-4528, Quintanilla's number. He had been working with the telephone company's chief of security. There was no question— it was a frame-up. Vallimarescu said Salvador Pittaluga repeated the story on radio that night, and *Listin Dairio* called Vallimarescu to check the story. Val denied it, and I told him to give them the proof.

3

The city was quiet Saturday. Many stores did not open that morning. We heard the *civicos* were paying small shopkeepers a hundred dollars each to stay closed. We divined the *civicos'* intentions. Some stores were normally closed Saturday afternoon and all day Sunday. The *civicos* would try to keep them closed on Monday. Tuesday was a holiday. If the *civicos* could keep them closed until Wednesday morning, they would appear to have carried on a strike nearly a week long but would have had to pay for only two or two and a half days.

Sometime in the last few days I had heard that General Ramírez, the Senator from San Juan de la Maguana, was going on national radio-television Saturday or Sunday to speak about the development of the Río Yaque del Sur. The Department had confirmed the TVA trip for next Saturday, the 28th, on Bosch's conditions, including no advance publicity. If Ramírez now blundered in, he would wreck the plans. So I had him to lunch and persuaded him to keep quiet, promising in return that the TVA experts would visit his hometown, San Juan de la Maguana, personally.

Ramírez left at four; I was due at President Bosch's at four, and went alone, my pockets stuffed with notes. He looked rather grim and forbidding as he took me into his private study.

I took up first the Yaque del Sur. The TVA mission would arrive the following Saturday. It would study the Yaque Valley and the Azua plain. It would report to the President of the Dominican Republic, with a copy to the U.S. government. It would make a preliminary determination of whether the area could be developed in an integrated way for irrigation, flood control, hydroelectric power, soil conservation, and watershed protection. The mission would ascertain the views of President Bosch, other government officials, and local people. It would collect previous piecemeal studies. It would consider proposals for specific projects that might be started soon.[1]

Williams and I had worked out a detailed schedule. The mission would go into the field Sunday, stay there till Thursday or Friday, then return here. I would send Shlaudeman out to handle Senators, Deputies, and Governors of each province so none would monopolize the mission's time. Williams and I would stay in the Capital, keeping Moscoso busy.

President Bosch invited Moscoso, Williams, and me to breakfast at the Palace on Monday morning. I suggested he and his Cabinet Ministers have breakfast with me on Saturday morning at the Residence to prepare for the mission's arrival. He agreed, and hoped I could have a good map on hand. Bosch asked that the mission in the field examine the water wells in the sisal fields near Azua. It would. I asked if he would receive the mission at the Palace next Friday after it returned from the Valley— that was the time for any press release, not before it went to the Valley. He would—we would all have lunch at the Palace. "We will make the publicity then," he said, "you and I." He paused, put his fingertips together, looked at a corner of the room, and said, "Mr. Martin."

"Sí, Señor Presidente."

"Mr. Martin. If one small dam is finished while I am President, it will be named John B. Martin."

I was caught by surprise. I didn't know he realized how long I'd hoped to turn the dusty valley green. I blurted, "You shouldn't have said that, Mr. President. That's not fair." Then, "Besides, you don't know what else I have to tell you."

He touched my knee, and said, "Go on."

I asked if he had stopped Luna's Hawker Hunter jet deal. Not yet. All right—I was holding a T-33 jet trainer that could be delivered between October 1 and 5. As for the patrol boats, MAAG had the money now to build one $350,000 hundred-foot patrol boat at Haina; it would be finished in December 1965. If Congress appropriated more money, as expected, MAAG also intended to give the Dominicans another hun-

---

[1] The TVA mission had clearly defined objectives. It would recommend for or against the next steps—specific engineering studies and a full-scale feasibility study. Those studies would embrace, among other things, natural boundaries, rainfall, river runoff, underground water table, crop shifts, land classification and land use, population distribution, community development, mineral and forest resources, agricultural and industrial and commercial development, transportation and communications, pertinent legislation including the pending Confiscation Law and *plus valía* law and Agrarian Reform Law, agricultural extension service and agricultural credit, cooperatives, schools, hospitals, housing. They would determine how the Yaque would fit into the national goals of the entire Republic. They would develop plans, specifications, and priorities for construction of dams, irrigation and drainage systems, aqueducts, wells, power plants, roads, ports, airfields, warehouses. They would recommend legislation, possibly an autonomous Valley Authority. They would estimate costs and recommend financing arrangements.

dred-foot boat next year worth $350,000, but could instead give the Dominicans three sixty-three-foot rebuilt U. S. Navy boats by July 1964. Bosch asked if he could buy those three now for cash himself. He could. He asked whom Commodore Rib should talk to. Wolfe, I said, and gave him the specifications of the boats.

Then I asked about Sunday night's abortive *golpe*. He thought it was connected with the Castillo de Aza plot. What was he going to do about it? Nothing now, he said, because the Armed Forces were supporting him during the general strike.

I asked how he viewed the strike. He said, "It is a failure."

What was he going to do about the strike? He said without enthusiasm he would prosecute Alfau and perhaps others. I said if he had the evidence he should prosecute all the strike leaders vigorously—nobody had a right to overthrow the government.

He said, "I am going to prosecute the Spaniards."

I said impatiently, "They're not important. The important ones are the Dominican rightists. Not the Spaniards."

He nodded but said nothing, and I wondered suddenly why he was so wan and weak. Why wouldn't he fight? Did he want to be overthrown?

"When this is over, hit the extreme right and the extreme left. Hit them hard. We'll support you. We've been supporting you, we watched the *golpe* while you were gone to Mexico, I waited for you at San Isidro the night you came home, we've helped you with the labor unions, we're doing everything we can. It's cost us friends, and I've been called everything but a Communist, and there's pressure in the U.S. press. I don't care. We're going to continue to support you," and I told him I had read forcible instructions to my entire mission. "But you've got to do the job. Nobody but you can. It isn't the Spaniards. It's the Dominican right. And the Dominican left. You've got to hit them, and hard."

He nodded but still said nothing.

I said, "There are too many foolish rumors and plots. We're wasting too much time on them. You can't build a nation that way." I told him the story about Colonel Simmons. He brushed it aside. I pressed on—what about the MAAG officer, Lombraña? Bosch said, "I only wanted the information to prove to the man who brought me the story that it was silly."

"The charges that Salvador Pittaluga made against Quintanilla aren't silly. He accused Quintanilla, in print, and on a government-owned radio-TV station, on a program sponsored by a government corporation, Haina, of plotting to overthrow the Dominican government. This amounts to accusing me and the United States government of trying to overthrow your government." I told him we had checked four thousand telephone toll tickets and the story was a fake and a serious one.

President Bosch, somewhat taken aback, said, "Pittaluga must make a declaration."

"I agree—he certainly must. Furthermore, I want to know the name of Pittaluga's source. Where did he get that story? Somebody is trying to make serious trouble between you and me—and it's somebody close to you—and I'm tired of it. It's divisive, it's corrosive, it's dangerous. Another thing," and I showed him a clipping containing the ad for Dato Pagán's school.

He said, "It is not in a public school."

"Yes it is," and I showed him proof.

"I have written the Minister—did he show you his letter to Dato Pagán closing the school?"

"No."

"I thought he had," he said vaguely. "He showed someone. Fifteen days ago."

"It doesn't matter—the school's still open."

"I will call him," he said decisively, and left the room.

I waited, wondering if he was telephoning or stalling. He returned, sat down, said, "I beg your pardon," then sat waiting.

I told him about more travelers to and from Cuba. He said he would send a constitutional amendment to Congress next week to stop them. I said a law was easier. He said it would be unconstitutional. So what? I said—let the courts decide. He insisted on a constitutional amendment.

"All right. But look, Mr. President. We must not lose sight of what is really going on. Today the extreme right is making a serious effort to over-throw your government. Your only support is from the extreme left and from us. The left is trying to divide you and me. Then the 14th of June will go to municipal elections next year and win. And after that they'll win the presidential election. This is the PSP plan—they will use the 14th of June as their road to power. And it's working."

"I agree with you."

"It won't work—if you and I stick together."

"I am in accord," he said. Then, leaning back in his chair, he said, "Maybe I will go to the United States on a state visit next year."

I concealed impatience—he was talking about next year when he might not survive next week. "That would be fine, I'm sure President Kennedy would be pleased."

"In the spring," he said. "Maybe we could use as an excuse a con-ference on the *Alianza* or something."

"I'm sure we could."

I realized I'd reached a dead end. I wound up a couple of other pieces of business—Rear Admiral William E. Ferrall, Commandant of the Fifteenth Naval District, was arriving on Monday, and I recommended President Bosch receive him publicly at the Palace lest the 14th of June say that Ferrall, not Simmons, had been sent to give the "Pentagon word" to overthrow him. He agreed—5 P.M. at the Palace. I told him I'd received a memorandum from Abe Chayes on land expropriation and hoped he wouldn't move without consulting me. He wouldn't. Before leaving, I said, "Let me just tell you this—I'll do anything for you, any time. I'll see my old *tu-tum-pote* friends for you, Bonnelly, Imbert, Fiallo, anybody. Just ask. I want to help."

He nodded, and as we rose he touched my shoulder. It had been a long conversation and a serious one. We weren't playing games any longer, and we both knew it. Perhaps we both knew that little time remained.

4

On Sunday, I rested and thought. Until now I had told Fran I thought we would succeed—would save Bosch. That Sunday I told her I thought that sooner or later we would fail. "We're going to lose it unless Bosch will give us something. But he's stuck on dead center and won't or can't do a thing."

We received vague reports of trouble on the Haitian border, and early Monday morning Foreign Minister García-Godoy summoned the diplomatic corps to the Foreign Office and told us that a "delicate situation" existed between the Republic and Haiti, that trouble had broken out today near Dajabón, that automatic weapons and "cannon" fire had been heard, that "projectiles had fallen on Dominican soil," that "armed groups" had crossed the border in civilian clothes, and that "I cannot predict the outcome." So far as he knew no Dominican troops had crossed the border and nobody had been killed yet. He had informed the OAS and the UN but asked no specific action. He would advise us whether we could send observers to the frontier. The situation was of the utmost gravity and the Dominicans intended to "take all measures necessary to defend Dominican territory." We left. If only all Cabinet ministers were as able as García-Godoy! (Again—the oligarchy: His wife was a Pastoriza and he himself was a Cáceres.)

Back at the office, King and Shlaudeman said the general strike was over. Nearly all stores had opened at the usual hour this morning; the rest were open by now. I asked why. They didn't know but assumed the strike simply had collapsed, having failed to pull in either the unions or the military.

At twelve-twenty, Fritz Long came in. He had seen General Viñas. Viñas doubted that the Haitians intended to invade the Dominican Republic. There had been fighting inside Haiti near the border, and he had sent two companies to reinforce the border defense. Long was more concerned about the repercussions in the Armed Forces. Wessin y Wessin suspected Bosch would send the Armed Forces to Haiti to keep them pinned down or even destroy them.

Long said a *golpe* had almost happened Friday night or Saturday. Yesterday, Sunday, he had thought it stopped. Now he was less sure.

I asked who, specifically, he was talking about. Among the moderates, those opposed to a *golpe,* he listed Rivera Cuesta, Pagán, and the Vice Minister of the Navy. Among the *golpistas* he listed Wessin y Wessin, the Air Force pilots, General Hermida, General Montás, Belisario Peguero, and several middle-level naval officers. He did not think Hungría or his deputy were in the *golpe* crowd. But some commanders in the interior were. The *golpe* move—it was really more a slide, or slippage, than a determined and decisive move—had been slowed down by the failure of the strike, by our attachés' pressure, and by the moderate military men. Now, however, Haiti might stir things up. I asked what the *golpistas* wanted to do. Long said, "They want to deport Bosch and Dato Pagán and Corpito Pérez Cabral and Ducoudray and López Molina."

I said, "Oh, for God's sake."

It was really incredible. Grown men were seriously considering overturning the whole democratic system, won back after thirty-one years of Trujillo, for such a purpose. Long, unmoved, said, "That's what they say."

It was time to go: I had invited the Dominican high command and other military men and their wives to a lunch for Admiral Ferrall and his wife at the Residence. I made it there just as the guests arrived, perhaps fifty of them, the Dominican high command, Admiral Ferrall, and the usual U.S. military men except Cass, who had been suddenly summoned home for consultation. It was a leisurely lunch, pleasant enough. I had Mrs. Ferrall, General Viñas, and one or two others at my table. I don't remember what we talked about. During coffee and brandy, I excused myself, asked Viñas if I could have a word with him alone, and led him into my study. Everyone saw us go; I wanted to be sure of that.

I closed the doors, and we sat down, he short and solid, calm and taciturn as ever, not a wrinkle on his face, a rather round young face.

I asked, "How serious is the Haitian matter?"

He said he didn't know, he had sent some officers to observe it, he would know later in the afternoon.

"What effect will it have on the Armed Forces?"

He hesitated, sipping his coffee. "There is some inquietude," he said. "We will see tomorrow."

"What is your opinion of the situation in general?"

He shrugged a little, as he always did, sipped his coffee, then asked, "What is *your* opinion?"

I said, "I am glad you asked me. I don't like it. I want you to know that we do not consider communism the clear and present danger to the

Dominican Republic. In the long run, perhaps. Now, no. I also want you to know that we support Juan Bosch. He is the constitutional and elected President of the Republic. We support those principles."

He nodded.

I went on. "As you know, for us it would be very hard to recognize and almost impossible to assist any government that gets power by a *golpe.*"

He nodded. He had heard it before. He said, "Will you advise me if you think it is a danger?"

"Communism?"

"Yes."

"Yes, I will. It is not now. We are sure. Our intelligence services say so. We watch the Communists very carefully. One more thing I want you to know. We will not permit another Castro in the Caribbean." I said it slowly and with great emphasis.

He nodded. "That is true."

"We have heard rumors of a *golpe.* What is your position?"

Viñas said, "I am opposed. I am for the democratic system." I'd heard that before too.

"What about the others? The service commanders. Can you control them?"

"Yes."

"Luna?"

"Yes."

"Hungría?"

"Yes."

"Rib?"

"Yes."

"Wessin y Wessin?"

"Yes."

"Amiama and Imbert?"

"Yes," smiling a little, almost contemptuously.

I said, "Excellent. Then what is the problem?"

He said slowly, "If there is one, it is at San Isidro."

"That's what I thought. You can hold it?"

"Yes."

I said, "Excellent." I thanked him for this interview, said we had worked together for many months and I knew we would continue to; he thanked me, we patted each other in a half *abrazo,* and went back to the living room. Lunch, really, was over. We had broken it up.

Later in the afternoon Long reported that Wessin seemed depressed. "He feels the world is going to hell and nobody's doing anything about it. But he's sold on the idea they all have to do it together, if at all."

5

I, too, was depressed, couldn't sleep that night, and felt morose next morning, Tuesday. Fran was taking the kids to the beach and wanted me to go, I'd feel better. I said no, I'd better stay here. They left. I stayed alone in my study, doing nothing. I remember it as a rather dark day. We had indeed received hurricane warnings. As before, during the gathering storm a year ago before the elections, and the past summer, I felt the brooding sense of doom that lay over this island. It was a sickness. I felt trapped, almost immobilized. I kept trying to shake it off, trying to think my way through the situation. What could we do that we hadn't done? Should I go to see the military? I'd seen them. Wessin? It might undermine Viñas, upset the delicate balance, and arouse Bosch's worst suspicions. What about the *civicos?* The oligarchs? Whom could I see that I hadn't seen? What could I do that I hadn't done? I kept running over and over it in my mind but got nowhere, always coming back into the same trap. And in the process I realized what was wrong with me. For the first time in my adult life, I was facing the very real possibility of failure. I might fail. It was a shocking idea. President Kennedy had sent me down here to hold this place, and difficult as I had known it was from the outset, I never had really doubted that I would somehow hold it. I no longer felt that way. I might lose it, might fail him.

At 1 P.M., I was still sitting in my study, eating lunch alone, when Sacha Volman came in the front door and said, "The President is at my house, he called me and asked me to bring you there in ten minutes."

I said, "Let's go." Fran had our government car and driver. I got our own car out of the garage and told Volman to lead the way. He drove fast, more than fifty miles per hour past Trujillo's house and down Máximo Gómez to Jorge Washington and along the sea, picking up speed to eighty near the Fairgrounds, passing the scene of the assassination, then a little distance beyond slowing, signaling, turning into a gate guarded by two soldiers, telling them to let me in. We stopped in a driveway beside a swimming pool between two houses. This had been the estate of Flor de Oro, daughter of Trujillo. Volman lived here. I never had been here before.

Bosch in a dark suit was standing alone in the circular driveway, smiling. I have the impression a few soldiers were scattered in the shade. Bosch started for one house, hesitated, Volman said the other had an air conditioner, we turned around and passed the pool, Bosch halting momentarily pensive beside it. The little house had been shut up and was superheated. It was empty. Volman took us into a little bedroom, turned on an air conditioner, and brought Cokes. We took off our coats. Bosch, holding up his fingernails to examine them, said, "There is a *golpe*. Yes. They are going to kill me or overthrow me."

"When, Mr. President?"

"Today. I have sent General Viñas to say—he is going to meet with Colonel Wessin y Wessin. To try to control the situation. He told me not to sleep at home tonight. I shall, anyway."

I asked what made him so sure a *golpe* was afoot. He said that it had been scheduled for Sunday night. "One group believed I should be killed," he said, examining the end of his cigarette. "One group believed I should only be overturned. I sent for Colonel Wessin y Wessin. He did not come. He did not send a message. Yesterday I looked for him. I could not find him. Yesterday I learned there is a meeting of high military officials in the Palace, at noon. And I also learned that last night Colonel Wessin y Wessin ordered the officer in charge of the tanks at the Palace be replaced. Without telling either Colonel Calderón or me or the chief of the forces at the Palace."

I was convinced: Wessin was planning a *golpe* now.

Bosch went on. Viñas had learned of the plot on Sunday night. (So he had known when I talked to him at lunch Monday.) He had rescinded the order to change the Palace tank commander and had asked Calderón not to tell Bosch, as it would worry him. Viñas had thought he could stop the *golpe*—he trusted Wessin. "But today the thing has gotten out of control," Bosch said.

I asked what he intended to do. He said, "I am going to wait for Viñas to come. And I suppose they all will be with him. I will see them tonight. I will change the high command. If I get a chance."

Were any civilians involved? Bonnelly, he said, and Viriato Fiallo. Already there was trouble. A number of people had taken asylum in foreign embassies today because they had opposed the general strike and the *civicos* were after them. An hour ago nine people had broken into the Brazilian Embassy, beaten up a policeman on guard, and searched the Embassy, apparently looking for asylees.

I asked who else was in the *golpe*. He said Horacio Julio Ornes, Severo Cabral, Antinoe Fiallo (Viriato Fiallo's brother), Enrique Alfau. He thought Wimpy, the American supermarket operator, might be involved, "and any United States citizen is important because Dominicans think he speaks for the United States government." Amiama "might be" involved "but Imbert I don't know, he is hated, too, he could be a victim." In the military, he named, besides Wessin y Wessin, several colonels and middle-grade officers in the Air Force, the Armed Forces Training Center, and the Navy.

What about the high command? He did not think they favored the *golpe*—not Viñas, Rib, Hungría, Pagán, Rivera Cuesta, Montás Guerrero, or Hermida. He did not know where Luna stood. Who was in charge of the tanks at the Palace? Was he still loyal? Yes. The plot was, then, primarily one led by Wessin y Wessin and possibly Luna, plus colonels and middle-level officers at San Isidro? Yes, he thought so—Viñas would find out. He added that Admiral Ferrall's presence gave them a smoke screen. I asked if Haiti had triggered it. He said he had told the officers yesterday that under no circumstances would he get involved with Haiti.

I asked where things stood. He said there was a meeting going on now at San Isidro. Viñas was there. He would report back to Bosch at 4 P.M.

Bosch was very calm. He was sitting relaxed in the only chair in the little bedroom. I was on the bed. It was cool, the air conditioner had started to work. I said, "Mr. President, I think we can stop this thing." He looked interested but only mildly. I said, "I do not want to presume to give you advice you haven't asked for but it's very late. I think you're right, this time there really is a *golpe* on. I think we can stop it. But you are the one who has to do it."

He said, "How can I do it?"

"You have to beat them to it. You have to move before they do. May I tell you what I think you should do?"

"Of course," smiling.

"All right. I don't think the military really want to do this. They've been pushed into it by the *civicos*. The *civicos* have convinced them you're handing the country over to the Communists. I know it isn't true, you know it isn't true, but you've got to prove it isn't true. You can do it now, this afternoon, and stop the whole thing. Call a special session of Congress. Tell them, first, to enact something like our Smith Act. Second, tell Congress to stop travel to Cuba—pass a law making it a crime to violate passport restrictions. Third, tell them to enact a law permitting deportations."

He started to say something but I went on. "You should announce this on the radio, every hour. Congress can pass the laws today and tomorrow. Tomorrow you have to act under the laws. You have to hit both the right and the left. And hit them hard. I mean arrest them, put them in prison, and deport some of them. Deport the Communists they're always yelling about—López Molina, Ducoudray, the others—you know who they are. Deport some of the rightist strikers. And start a wholesale roundup of both the civilian right and left, and put them in jail and charge them with conspiring to overthrow the government. But let the military alone."

Again he started to say something, but again I went on. "If you will do this, and go on the radio right now, I will undertake to hold the military until tomorrow. I'll go to San Isidro myself, or send my attachés if you prefer, and stop this nonsense."

He smiled rather wanly. He said, "You do not understand. There are two problems. The politicians are conspiring," and he spoke at some length about their plots. "Then the other problem is the desire of the young officers to push themselves up," and he spoke more vaguely on this. He said, "The revolution is frustrated. I cannot make the revolution now."

"You're right but it doesn't make any difference. If you do what I said, you'll cut the ground out from under the politicians. Then the military, the high command, will support you. They don't want to govern. That's the last thing they want. But they've been talked into it by the Communist scare."

He said, "But all the laws you suggest are unconstitutional."

I said, "The hell with that. Tell Congress to pass them anyway, then act under them. Let the courts decide next winter. Our problem is today."

"The UCN would say I am acting against the Constitution."

"If you don't, the UCN will overthrow you tonight."

"Besides, I have already ordered the Constitution reformed."

Surprised, I asked what he meant. He said, "Yes. I have ordered it reformed, so nobody can sell mortgaged property, freedom of travel will be limited, and we will have something like your Smith Act."

I said, "Fine. Announce it. Today."

He shook his head. "The amendments are not ready. Luisito is drafting them."

"Luisito!" He was the Palace lawyer. I said, "Mr. President! Luisito will take a year to draft them. Let us do it. We can draft the amendments or the laws in an hour. Two hours, anyway," glancing at my watch. "It's a quarter past two o'clock now. Viñas is due back at 4 P.M. I'll go to San Isidro. I'll get one of my staff to draft the amendments. I can be back here with the amendments by four. And you can go on the radio and television and call Congress into session and announce you're sending them emergency legislation. You don't even have to wait until four—do it now. Start the radio announcing right now that you are going to make a transcendental declaration tonight."

He shook his head. "It is impossible."

"Why?"

"Because it is a holiday."

I asked what he meant. He said, as though explaining something to a child, "Today is a holiday. The Congress is not in session. They could not receive my message. They are at their homes all over the Republic."

I said, "But Mr. President! The problem is here, today, now. The hell with it's a holiday. Get your announcement on the radio now. Outline your laws and constitutional amendments. Order Congress to convene first thing tomorrow morning. Get Casasnovas and Molina Ureña to work tonight so they can have the bills ready early tomorrow. Keep the radio going, and as soon as the bills are passed, start the roundup and the deportation."

He kept shaking his head slowly, his expression calm, almost wistful. I kept hammering at him. He said, "If I do it under military pressure, I will no longer be President, the Army will be President."

He was right. "I agree—you're right. Therefore, let me go to San Isidro right now and take the military pressure off and get you a few hours to take these measures. You take them just because you want to. There will be no military confrontation. You won't even talk to a military man. I'll keep them at San Isidro."

"No, it would be under pressure anyway."

"Not as far as the people know."

But Bosch just kept shaking his head, saying he could not do it, there was nothing to be done now, it was a holiday, the bills were unconstitutional, he would wait for Viñas, perhaps they all would come with him and kill or overthrow him here. He did not seem to mind. He kept saying, "The revolution is frustrated," and "I can do nothing." I finally became convinced he simply was not going to act, he was simply not going to do anything at all.

I said, "Well, I'll do what I can. I'll send my attachés out to San Isidro, or wherever the military is, and send Shlaudeman and the others out to the *civicos,* and make it damn clear to everybody we support you."

He thought a moment, then said it was all right for us to talk to the civilians but he didn't want me to turn the attachés loose, at least not now. I should have known he wouldn't want to appear a Yankee puppet. I argued briefly, he held firm, and I finally said all right, I'd hold the attachés till he heard from Viñas.

I asked if he intended to wait here for Viñas. He did. I asked if he wanted me to wait with him, in case they all came—perhaps my presence would deter them from killing or overthrowing him. He said no, he would wait alone. I said I didn't like to leave him and asked him what he planned to do after Viñas returned at four. He said he would go home, rest a while, then go to the Armed Forces Club at the Fairgrounds, where the Dominican Armed Forces were giving a reception in honor of Admiral Ferrall. We agreed to meet there at 7 P.M. and meanwhile to keep in touch by phone. We put on our coats and went out of the bedroom and as I started for my car, Volman asked softly, "Mr. Ambassador, what did the United States do in November of 1961 when the Trujillos returned?"

I knew what he wanted. "We sent the fleet," I said.

Volman hesitated, and looked at Bosch. I looked at him, too, waiting. Bosch said nothing. Volman asked, "How long would it take them to get here now?"

I said, "I can't say precisely where they are at this moment, but ordinarily, twelve hours."

"Do you think they would send them?"

"I don't know, and I don't know if the President wants them." I waited. Bosch said nothing. I said, "We have talked several times about bringing a carrier in and taking you aboard for lunch, Mr. President."

Bosch said, "Could we do that now?"

"We might, though I don't know how much time we have—it's late."

Bosch thought a minute. Then he said, "Could you get them please?"

I said, "If you want a carrier, I'll ask for an alert on it."

"Yes, I would be very grateful."

"But I'll have to ask you this now—do you want Marines to land?"

He said, "No."

I drove back to the Chancellery fast, called the Crisis Crowd into my office, told them what was going on, asked them to think about what we could do, and wrote and sent a top-priority cable. Now, after dozens of false alarms stretching over a year and a half, now, this time, the *golpe* was for real. I relayed Bosch's request for a carrier, recommended that a carrier at least be alerted, inquired how far away one was, and outlined the course of legislative action I had proposed and he had rejected.

Volman called at four—Viñas had not yet arrived. He called again at four-thirty—Viñas still had not arrived, the President wanted "nothing done internally" and wanted to know "if the twelve hours could be reduced to four or six." I said I'd see and sent a cable. I asked the Crisis Crowd what they thought.

Shlaudeman said Bosch ought to do one of two things immediately. He could convoke Congress, declare a state of siege under Title 4, Article 114, Paragraph 7 of the Constitution, suspend Article 60 which guaranteed that no one could be imprisoned without a court order, Article 61 which guaranteed habeas corpus, and Article 73 which guaranteed the right to travel. A state of siege would not permit deportation but would permit the arbitrary arrest of both leftists and rightists. Alternatively, Bosch should immediately ask Congress to amend the Constitution as I had proposed.

I liked the state of siege idea. It was cleaner, quicker, more decisive. I asked Shlaudeman to figure out how it could be extended to permit deportations. I also asked the political section to write out a fake instruction to me from the Department that I could read to the military if a need arose during the night.

At four fifty-five Volman called: Viñas had just arrived and was talking to Bosch. I told him to call me back when they had finished.

The fake "instruction" was ready. I made it a little stronger and told my secretary to type it as an "incoming cable," making it look official. It said:

"For Ambassador:

"You are instructed as follows:

" 'I have been instructed by my government to inform you that the United States government is unequivocally opposed to any attempt by anyone to overthrow the legally constituted and democratically elected government of President Juan Bosch. The United States government recognizes and supports the present Dominican government and will continue to do so. The United States government is fully aware of the many serious problems which are creating impatience and concern in the Dominican Republic but wishes to point out that the transition from three decades of dictatorship to democracy cannot be achieved without facing difficult problems.

" 'Finally, I am instructed to inform you that the United States government would find it exceedingly difficult to recognize and virtually impossible to assist any regime which might come to power in the Dominican Republic as a result of the overthrow of President Bosch.'

"USG"

In a tight situation, it might help me bluff. I stuck it in my pocket.

We waited. Finally, at 5:50 P.M., Volman called. He said Viñas had not gone to San Isidro at all. Instead, he had sent someone else. Wessin had sent back no answer. There were no troops at San Isidro. The President wanted to "reaffirm the six-hour thing," the carrier lag time. I asked where Volman and the President were. At the President's house. Thinking that even now he and the President might be prisoners, I asked several questions that could be answered yes or no—Were he and Bosch all right? Were they in any immediate danger? Was anyone beside him? Anybody unwelcome? Volman reassured me.

I told King to cut the attachés loose. Viñas' failure to go to San Isidro personally, and Wessin's failure to reply to his message, sounded ominous. And I had no idea what Volman meant by saying there were no troops at San Isidro. Where were they? I wished I had cut the attachés loose two hours before. And I wished fervently that Cass were here, not in Washington. Long was only one man; Lieutenant Colonel Tom Fishburn, who had replaced Bill Richardson as air attaché, was too new to be very helpful. I sent a cable to Washington instructing Cass to return immediately. I told King to tell the attachés to concentrate on Wessin. I told Shlaudeman and the CIA chief to start working on the politicians. I told all to use maximum pressure. We were starting very late. I didn't know if we could hold it.

I went to the Residence, ate and dressed fast, telling Fran, home from the beach, what was going on, and we went together to the Armed Forces Club.

6

Downstairs in the big empty lobby of the Armed Forces headquarters the same handful of languid enlisted men stood around the door as always; the same small elevator rose uncertainly as always; the same faces appeared near the club door in a wobbly receiving line as always —Viñas, Rib, Hungría, their wives. The same photographers scurried around, the same Dominican officers were posing self-consciously with Admiral Ferrall, the same big U-shaped table stood on the dance floor loaded with food, the same Navy band was playing *merengues*.

But as I moved around the room I saw that two people were missing: Wessin and Luna. And their officers: I saw nobody from San Isidro, and, passing Fritz Long, confirmed it—he had not yet found Luna or Wessin. And I saw something else: In the dark corners, some half hidden behind draperies, were, as always, the machine gunners, the bodyguards. But tonight they seemed to be new ones; I saw none I recognized.

President Bosch had not arrived. It was 7:05 P.M. As I shook hands with Shlaudeman, he said, "There's something going on all right. You can smell it." I moved around, shaking hands with Dominicans I knew, keeping an eye on the door. At seven-forty Bosch still had not arrived. I found King, and said, "You'd better call his house, he was due at seven sharp." I kept moving, and spoke a few minutes to Admiral Ferrall. He knew what was up and asked how things were going. I said not well. We kept smiling. King came back: Somebody at the house said Bosch had just left to come here. By now almost everyone had stopped milling around, was standing in a semicircle, facing the door.

Bosch entered, Calderón behind him, his face powdered white; the television floodlights flared, flashbulbs popped, and Fran stepped forward with her hand out to greet Bosch, and then Bosch was moving in, shaking hands, blue eyes shining, broad smile beaming. He made his way to Admiral Ferrall and me, shook hands, posed for pictures, and I told Bosch quietly, "I think it's on. Wessin and Luna are not here, we can't find them, I'd better stay with you." He nodded. I did not tell him about the strangers with machine guns in the shadows. The band played the Dominican national anthem, and "The Star-Spangled Banner," and all stood at attention; then relaxed, the low hum of talk rose, though not so loud as usual, and side by side Bosch and I moved around the room, shaking hands with people, talking a few minutes, then moving on.

Shlaudeman was right: Despite the reassuring clink of glasses, the talk, the smiles and smoke, you could smell the tension. These affairs were always stiff, almost never fun except once last year when Bonnelly and everybody else had danced and drunk till very late; but they were never as tense as this. I told King to tell Long and Fishburn to leave. He under-stood—I wanted them to find Luna and Wessin.

At a few minutes to nine, Bosch told me, "I am going now."

I said, "I'll go with you." He nodded and, still smiling, we passed on out, I telling King on the way to see that Fran got home and to wait for me at the office. Dominicans crowded into the elevator with Bosch; I had to wait. The unknown bodyguards were there, too. The elevator came back, I went down, hurried out, saw Bosch pulling away; my driver came up fast, and we raced after Bosch to his house.

He and I sat in rocking chairs outdoors on the paved patio under the sky, with the drive-in screen luminous beyond the wall where machine gunners patrolled. Bosch said he attached no particular significance to Viñas' not having gone to San Isidro, nor to Wessin's not having replied to Viñas' message. I didn't believe it. He said, "General Viñas is coming now with some others pretty soon." I asked what for. He said, "I think they are going to tell me what they found out."

I said, "With your permission, I think I'll wait with you."

So we waited, rocking. I knew it was not a good time to talk to him. But I might not get another chance—I didn't know who would come with Viñas, nor for what purpose, and I didn't think Bosch knew either. So I told him I had asked for the carrier but it was going to be a little difficult to pretend to take him to lunch at midnight, even assuming the carrier could get here so fast. What we needed to do that night was buy some time. Only a few hours. The next day we could regroup. But that night, I said, he must act. After studying the Constitution, we thought that Bosch should immediately convoke Congress, declare a state of siege, and hit the right and left. He said, "No, I cannot do that."

Using notes Shlaudeman had given me, I cited the provisions in the Constitution he could invoke.

He just kept saying no. Nor would he say why he refused.

I reminded him he had intended to amend the Constitution anyway—what articles did he mean to change?

He listed them—Article 27, on mortgages; Articles 70 and 71 on free speech, Article 73 on freedom to travel, Article 66 on deportation, and Article 123 on presidential eligibility for re-election. We were still going over these when General Viñas came in, followed by General Hungría, Commodore Rib, and a colonel.

Bosch did a strange thing. He started to seat them here, even pulled up chairs for them; then abruptly changed his mind, said to me, "I beg your pardon," and led them away to the private office at the back of the house.

I suppose he did it because he wanted to stand alone before them, not shielded, as it were, by the U. S. Ambassador.

Waiting, I fingered the fake instruction in my pocket. Should I use it now? If Viñas, Hungría, and Rib were really on Bosch's side, it might give them a weapon to use with Wessin and Luna. On the other hand, if they were already succeeding in helping Bosch, I might offend them by intervening. I knew Bosch would not like it—it would, in his view, make him our puppet. I decided I couldn't do it in front of him, at least not in these circumstances. I'd have to use it with the military alone, or only in his presence after they had declared against him. I took my hand off it.

They stayed only about a half hour, perhaps less. They left, grave. The President sat down again with me. He said, "They are afraid it is still on. They do not know where Colonel Wessin y Wessin or General Luna are." I asked what they were going to do now. He said, "They are going to their headquarters to try to get support for me." I asked if he thought they could do it. "I don't know. They will try. I am going to the Palace to meet with all the chiefs at eleven o'clock."

That, then, would be the showdown.

I said I would wait with him for a while, and when he went to the Palace I thought it might be best if I went along. He said he would see. We were quiet, rocking. Then he got up decisively, telephoned the editor of *Listin Diario,* and said he had an announcement to make. I listened closely. He told the editor he intended to send a law to Congress tomorrow. It would deal with industrial development.

I wondered if he were really mad.

He came back and sat down and we rocked in silence.

Minister of Agriculture Guzmán and Minister of Interior and Police Domínguez Guerra were sitting in a secluded anteroom. Others came and went. President Bosch paid little heed. At about ten-thirty he said, "It is time to go."

I said, "I'd like to go with you, Mr. President."

"No, it is better that I go alone."

"My being there might deter them."

He shook his head.

I said, "If I may, I'd like to say one thing to you, Mr. President."

"Of course," smiling.

"I hope you won't do anything to provoke the military tonight."

His face grew stern. "I have to hit them first. Before they hit me."

I said, "I don't think you have much to hit them with tonight, Mr. President, if I may say so. If you are careful, we may get through tonight. Don't provoke them."

He shook his head, called, "Antonio," and Minister Guzmán said, "*¿Señor Presidente?*" and came to us. He looked small and a little afraid. I asked Bosch once more if he would not permit me to go with him. He said no. I asked him to call me at eleven-thirty and asked for his phone number at the Palace, and he agreed and gave me the number. Then he left, taking only Guzmán and Calderón. I knew why he was taking the

Minister of Agriculture: Guzmán and General Viñas were married to sisters.

I went out with them, nodding to Domínguez Guerra, stood aside while Bosch and Guzmán got into the President's car and, accompanied by the usual carloads of gunmen, roared off; then I got into my own car and drove to the Chancellery. It was about ten-forty.

7

King, Shlaudeman, and Fritz Long were in my office. Wessin's office had promised to locate him by eleven-fifteen. Nobody knew where Luna was. Long said there was a meeting going on now at Army headquarters at the 27th of February Camp, across the bridge near where the *Angelita* was moored. Viñas was there, and so were Hungría, Neit Nivar Seijas, Rivera Cuesta, Pagán, and probably others.

And then the cable we had been waiting for came in. It said that the Department could do little more to save Bosch in view of his past performance despite all my efforts to persuade him to govern effectively. The forces arrayed against him were largely of his own creation. Now he must save himself. The Department did not oppose the moves I had already recommended to him but warned me not to tie such moves to any commitment by the United States. It suggested that perhaps he also should take some "positive" steps. (I wondered how.) As for the aircraft carrier, the Department refused to intervene militarily unless a Communist takeover were threatened. A show of force that we were not prepared to back up would only be a meaningless gesture, ineffective in a situation which had gone so far.

I presumed the cable had been cleared with the White House. I showed it to King and Shlaudeman and told them that nevertheless we would do everything we could to save Bosch tonight. I went up to the Residence, telling the Marine to put any calls through to me there.

Eleven o'clock. Bosch must be meeting with the chiefs now. I waited alone in my study. Fran had gone to bed. Should I have used the "instruction" on Viñas, Hungría, and Rib at Bosch's house?

At 11:05 P.M. Shlaudeman came up. He had talked with Ramón Castillo, the minor but helpful politician. Castillo, who had been right so often, said it was certain that Bosch would be overthrown tonight. The presidential guard company had been approached; it would not resist. The tanks were ready to move. A few civilians were involved, including Severo Cabral, but by now the *golpe* had largely been taken over by the military.

Shlaudeman waited with me. At eleven-fifteen the phone rang. Shlaudeman answered. It was Volman. He had lost touch with the situation, and wanted to know what was going on.

While they were talking, Fritz Long called. He had talked to a Major Tapia, whom he thought was Wessin's tank commander. Tapia expected to see Wessin in a half hour. Wessin had left word he wanted to see Long.

I suspected Tapia or Wessin of stalling Long. I was sure the *golpe* was on. I told Shlaudeman to try to locate Vice President González Tamayo; the President of the Senate, Juan Casasnovas; and the President of the Chamber of Deputies, Molina Ureña, the constitutional successors to Bosch. He began calling.

Long called back at eleven-thirty. The commanders were neither at Army headquarters nor at the Palace. He had lost them. I told him to find them as fast as he could.

Still Bosch had not called. I waited fifteen minutes longer, then called him at the Palace number he had given me. He answered himself. He said the military had not arrived yet. He was waiting. I asked if he wanted me to go to the Palace. He said no. He promised to call me back as soon as he had met with the military.

Five minutes later Long called. An officer at Navy headquarters said all the chiefs must be at the Palace by now. Nothing definite had been decided. Nobody was at Army headquarters. Long called back at midnight. Viñas was expected home soon. Long had left word for him to call either Long or me.

I told Long to go to San Isidro. We had hesitated to do this—San Isidro was a half hour's drive away; Long was, in effect, the only attaché I had, and I disliked having him leave the city. But he had checked everywhere in the city and found nobody, so would try San Isidro. He asked what I wanted him to tell Wessin if he found him. I said, "Tell him that we do support Bosch, that we consider the right, not the left, the danger now, that in the long run we are worried about communism just as he is, that Bosch will not move against the Communists under military pressure, and that if they will take the military pressure off we will put all our pressure on to force Bosch to hit the right and the left, stop the travel to Cuba flat, close that damned school of Dato Pagán's, deport López Molina, and all the rest of it. But tell him we can't do a thing with Bosch when the military pressure is on because he's stubborn." Long said it sounded good and Wessin might accept it. He would leave at once. I told him to hurry.

Shlaudeman was still telephoning around town, trying to locate González Tamayo, Casasnovas, and Molina Ureña. King came up to the Residence. He had a duty officer in the office now and a secretary and an extra driver. We waited. I went into the living room alone to think. What else could we do, I kept asking myself, what else could we do? I went back to the study, and asked King and Shlaudeman if they thought

I should go to the Palace. They didn't. In fact, I might wreck things—we didn't know what was going on.

Why didn't Viñas call as he had promised? Why didn't Bosch?

I tried to call Bosch. The number he had given me didn't answer. I tried others, all the other numbers I had, even the ordinary Palace switchboard. None answered. I tried calling Viñas' house. No answer there either. Maybe everybody was at San Isidro. That's where Long was. Why didn't he call? Shlaudeman couldn't find any of the three Bosch successors. He couldn't find Miolán. We were stuck helpless. It had never happened before.

It was 1:40 A.M. Shlaudeman called Volman. Volman said that sometime after midnight Colonel Calderón had telephoned him from the Palace and said the meeting was going on and he would call when it was over. But where were they meeting? Where was Bosch?

More than twelve hours had passed since the first alarm. We were getting sleepy.

At 2:25 A.M. Long called. He said, "Stand down. For tonight anyway. I'm leaving the Center," that is, the Armed Forces Training Center, Wessin's headquarters. Had he talked to Wessin? He said he had. Long seemed to be with somebody and didn't want to talk freely. I asked if Wessin was going to do anything. "Not tonight at least."

"What about Luna?"

"I'm on my way to see him now. The other fellow tells me he's okay. You can stand down for tonight."

I thanked him, said all right, but asked him to call me if things turned out to be not as good as they appeared.

I told the others. It looked as if it was all over for tonight.

But it didn't make sense—a Navy officer had said earlier there was a meeting at the Palace, and Volman said Calderón had told him the same thing after midnight, but now Long had called at two-thirty from San Isidro and said Wessin and Luna were there and nothing would happen tonight.

Shlaudeman and King went home, and I went upstairs and went to bed. It was nearly 3 A.M. Fran woke up and asked if everything was all right. I told her I guessed so, for tonight at least, and went to sleep.

8

The phone rang, and, answering it, I looked at my watch. It was a little before 4 A.M. Long said he was at the Palace, the entire military establishment was there, Viñas, Hungría, Rib, Luna, Wessin, everybody. They had been meeting with Bosch, and, so far as Long could find out, still were. Bosch had demanded Wessin's resignation, the military had refused, and

Bosch had thereupon told them he would go before Congress tomorrow and resign.

I said, "Do you think I can help any if I come over?"

Long said, "Not with the military. They won't budge."

"How about Bosch?"

"I don't know. He says he'll resign."

I thought a minute. I said, "I don't think he'll resign." Long said nothing. I said, "The hell with him. Let him go."

Long said, "God bless you, sir."

I said, "No, wait a minute. On second thought, you'd better come on over so we can start sending a cable."

I lay down again for about fifteen minutes then, hearing his car in the driveway, went downstairs and let him in. He told me again what he'd said—I'd been half asleep, and he was worn out, too—and I started writing a cable.

It was getting daylight outside. While I was writing, the phone rang at 4:45 A.M. It was a woman in Bosch's household calling from Bosch's home. She said, "The President is in jail in the Palace by the aviation. He has resigned. All the Ministers have resigned."

I asked who had told her so. She said Minister Jaar had, and had asked her to tell me.

I hung up and told Long. He didn't know anything about it. It didn't make sense. I went on writing. The phone rang again. It was Ben Ruyle, from Santiago: Someone had told him Bosch had resigned and fighting was expected. I said we couldn't confirm it. At 5 A.M., Tony Ruíz, our police adviser, came in. He said Bosch was "in custody" and Belisario Peguero had started a manhunt—sent police out all over town looking for Miolán, Diego Bordas, López Molina, Volman, all the PRD, all the Communists. He said they had started at 3 A.M.

That didn't jibe at all with what Long had told me. Long shrugged, couldn't explain it. Something was wrong with the timetable. No matter— apparently Bosch had been overthrown.

I told Ruíz, "You go back to police headquarters and you tell Belisario Peguero that the civilized world will not condone killing. Just that, nothing more. Tell him I said so. Then turn around and walk out." He left.

The phone kept ringing, somebody in the PRD said, "The police are after me, I've got to go," my own people began arriving, King, Shlaudeman, the CIA chief, others, and so did Volman and one or two more of Bosch's people. Bosch had been overthrown and was in custody in the Palace. The police had missed Miolán, he was running from house to house, staying one jump ahead of them so far. The police had just missed Volman. Somebody said they had got Vice President González Tamayo. Somebody called and said a carload of policemen was driving through the city firing in the air. Mrs. Bosch called (from Puerto Rico, I learned later) and, her voice edged with hysteria, told me, "My husband is under arrest and the government has fallen." I told Shlaudeman to try to find Casasnovas and Molina Ureña, next in line of succession behind the Vice President. He tried Molina first, got him out of bed, and asked what I wanted him told. I said, "Tell him to come here, or go get him, and tell him we can't give asylum but he's my guest for breakfast." Shlaudeman left. I told King to come with me—we'd better go to the Palace.

9

Somebody went to get my driver, José, and I got dressed, and as I went out the door somebody told me Casasnovas had been arrested on his way to the Palace. So Molina Ureña was all we had—if we had him.

José, his face grave, brought the car around. I told him to drive us to the front gate of the Palace. The morning was fresh and bright. The iron gate was closed and guarded by a crowd of troops. They waved us away. I told José to go around to the back gate. Luckily a noncom there recognized me and let us in.

I wasn't sure where the back door of the Palace itself was and thought we might get shot wandering around, so told José to drive around to the main front steps. They were vast and deserted. King and I walked up them, as I had a hundred times before. This time no protocol officer came halfway down to greet us, and we walked into the lobby alone. It was absolutely deserted. The Palace was like a vast beached ocean liner.

I started down the long narrow corridor leading to the President's offices. The corridor, usually full of soldiers, was empty, too. It was a place of the dead. We turned the corner at the end and there, at the door to the President's reception room, was Colonel Calderón.

His shirt was dirty and salt lines made half-moons on it where sweat from under his arms had spread and dried. His face was neither its natural dark brown nor the powdered white he affected; it was gray, and his beard was stubbly. He looked grief-stricken. He had no machine gun. I had never seen him without one. Instead, he had a fancy little gold and pearl and nickel revolver. On him it looked like a toy. Seeing me, he said, "We are all prisoners."

I wasn't sure I had understood. "Prisoners?"

"Sí, señor."

I said, "I wish to see the President."

He squirmed, then said, "No hay"—"There is none."

I asked what he meant. He repeated it—there was no President.

I asked where Señor Bosch was. Inside, he gestured. Could I see him? No, he was sorry, he had orders not to let anyone in or out. I asked whom I needed permission from. He said from the military. I asked where they were. In their office, he said.

I'd never been to their office but thought I knew where it was. We turned around, walked back down the long corridor, and crossed the empty lobby. King wasn't sure we should go see Viñas—it might imply U.S. recognition of the *golpista* government, perhaps we had better leave. I said I didn't want to leave without seeing Bosch. For all we knew, they'd kill him, or had already killed him. And we didn't know how many others they had locked up. I said I'd make it clear I was speaking to Viñas in his capacity as Minister of Defense in the Bosch government to which I was accredited. King thought that would be all right.

We started down the opposite corridor, long and narrow like the other, but this one crowded with soldiers, all with machine guns, all talking and grinning. Some fell silent when they saw me. King asked where the Minister of Defense's office was, and they showed us, and I rapped on the door, then opened it.

The room was filled with men, all in uniform—Rib, Luna, Hermida, Imbert, a crowd jammed into a small room filled with smoke, sunlight filtering in gray, pale night lights still on, the men unshaven but all laughing and talking loudly. I knew them all, had hunted or fished or drunk or talked with them for months, and they greeted me like a long-lost brother, as though to say, "Now we have got rid of *him,* we can really be friends again."

I went through them quickly, shaking hands as little as possible, avoiding *abrazos* entirely, noticing civilians among them, asking for Viñas. He was off to one side, looking surprisingly small and unkempt, he who always looked so polished and neat. I had told King I wanted to speak only English and wanted him to translate. I said, "Mr. Minister, I want to speak with you for a minute if I may in your capacity as Minister of Defense in the Bosch government."

He said, "Of course," and led the way to a frayed red settee. I said, "I only want to ask permission to speak with President Bosch in order to obtain information about what is going on so I may report to my government."

He said, "Yes, of course."

I thanked him and waited, and he signaled to a junior officer, told him what I wanted, and King and I walked back down the long corridor and across the lobby and down the other long corridor to Calderón, and the escort spoke to him, and he opened the door, and we went into the reception room of the President's suite, the room the Consejo had always met in and which in Bosch's time had been full of hangers-on. It too was filled with men, it too was smoky and disordered, but the men were sitting, not standing, and they were silent. They were the Bosch Cabinet. Some were in shirt-sleeves. All looked up when I came in Casasnovas, del Rosario, Guzmán, others, some smiling a little, some indifferent.

I shook hands with a few and asked where the President was, and one went into his inner office for a moment, then held the door open, and I went in, the same square, high-ceilinged little office overlooking the white city and the sea beyond. Bosch was at his desk, and came half around it to shake hands, smiling, and gave us chairs. As we sat down I noticed two other men in a corner: Vice President González Tamayo and, apparently guarding him with a submachine gun, General Montás Guerrero.

I asked, "What is the situation, Mr. President?"

"We are in prison in the Palace," he said. "Yes. I, the Ministers, not all of them, not the Minister of Justice, Foreign Relations, Labor, the General says they are not arrested, but the others."

"Are you under arrest, Mr. President?"

"Yes."

"Are the others?"

"Yes. The Vice President," nodding to where González Tamayo sat beside the General with the machine gun, "I think is also under arrest. I do not know about Senator Casasnovas. The President of the House"—the Speaker, Molina Ureña—"is here I think, under arrest, no, I am not sure. But," throwing up his hands and leaning back, and smiling, "we are arrested. It is ended."

I asked who had told him he was under arrest and when—I wanted to know from him what had happened so I could report to my government.

He said that General Viñas had placed him under arrest, not in person but sending "a messenger" to tell him, at about 4:15 A.M. I asked why.

He said, "I met with twelve or fourteen high officers and I demanded the separation of Colonel Wessin y Wessin. They refused—the Armed Forces refused, they said they do not admit that. So I said in that condition I was going to resign. Because I was elected to be a President, not to take orders. They are forming a government now, Amiama and Imbert too."

I thought suddenly there might still be a chance. "Mr. President, may I suggest something?"

"Of course."

"Mr. President, it seems to me there is something very important at stake here. You, and your government, of course; but more than that, Dominican democracy and even, perhaps, democracy throughout the hemisphere. I do not think you should let democracy stand or fall on whether a tank commander is canceled or not."

He shook his head. He said, "It is impossible to preserve democracy because of the decomposition. There is no discipline in the Armed Forces."

I asked if he had resigned. He said no, under the Constitution he could resign only to Congress, sitting as an Assembly, and Congress had been "dissolved" by the "de facto government."

I said, "Mr. President, there isn't any de facto government. Not yet. There is just a disagreement between you and the Armed Forces over Wessin."

"No, there is a new government. They offered the Minister of Justice, Cuello, to stay. He refused. The Foreign Minister, García Godoy, to stay. He refused. They took the radio, everything."

I brushed this aside. "They've got the Palace and don't know what to do with it. They're all milling around, trying to figure out what to do next. Give me a chance. Let me try to put it back together again. You recede from your position on Wessin, let me go talk to them, it may not be too late yet, they don't want to run this country, they don't know how to run it," and though he tried several times to speak I kept on, pleading with him for, I think, twenty minutes or longer, arguing that he simply must not let this happen, too much was at stake. "It is your country's future that is at stake here, and more besides."

Bosch simply sat smiling and shaking his head, a little sad, wistful, but refusing. "I cannot recede—this would represent a failure of the people's faith," and "I cannot be confident one minute more in them," and "They have changed in the last few days," and "It is a matter of politics," and "Already they are broadcasting the communiqués," and finally, I thought, the truth: "It is a question of temperament. I must have all the authority or none. It is impossible."

A question of temperament.

When it is a question of temperament, indeed all the king's horses and men can't put it together again.

I tried once more. Bosch was adamant. So I gave up, getting information as fast as possible, still hoping to save something but seeing now I could not do it here, I must do it at the other end of the Palace if at all.

Bosch said the officers had come from San Isidro at 2:30 A.M. to "make a *golpe*." He had taken the offensive, demanded—he said now—not that Wessin be "canceled," that is, dismissed from the service, but only that he be sent abroad to a diplomatic post or otherwise moved out of the tank command. The officers had refused, he had held fast, they had retired to their quarters, consulted briefly, and put him under arrest. What would they do with him now? "Probably they will send me out of the country," he said calmly. Had he resisted? "Who could resist 250 men with guns?" Did he consider that he was in any danger now? No, he did not think so. Would he resign? No—he could only resign in front of the Assembly, and since it was dissolved, he could not resign. "No, I cannot resign, I expect they will come and throw me out," smiling broadly, almost as though he were enjoying it. Had he asked permission to go home? "I cannot ask them for permissions. I am in jail." He would not ask permission to resign, to go home, to do anything.

I got up and asked his permission to speak to the Vice President. He said of course. I asked the General's permission. He said of course. Everybody was saying of course this morning. I asked González Tamayo, sitting small on a gold settee in a rumpled white suit, if he was under arrest. Yes—the officer here guarding him said so, Colonel Calderón had told him. What did he intend to do? Remain calm—what else could they do? Did he intend to resign? He didn't know. To leave? He didn't know "what they are planning for me but I believe they will send me out," deport him. Did he consider himself in danger? No. Had he issued a public statement? No. Would he? No.

I shook hands with him, hesitated, then turned back toward Bosch. He was standing uncertainly by his desk, the Dominican flag behind him. Bosch said, "I am going to have some breakfast. Will you join me?"

I said, "No thank you, Mr. President. I have things to do." Then I said goodbye, and we embraced, and King shook hands with him, and we walked out of the office.

In the anteroom I asked Senator Casasnovas and Minister Guzmán the same questions, asking loudly enough so the other Cabinet Ministers could hear, and getting substantially the same answers. Ending, I asked the others if they concurred in what Casasnovas and Guzmán had said. They did. Did any think his life in danger? Silence. We left. And went, King dubiously, back to Viñas.

I knew there was no hope now for Bosch; I wanted to make one more try at saving constitutional government.

Viñas' office was crowded as before, and I asked if I could speak to him alone for a few minutes as Minister of Defense. He said of course. But he said it without enthusiasm, his eyes narrow and suspicious. I asked what, really, had happened, and why it had happened.

Viñas said, "What we want is that the country cease the turmoil it has been in and take the road of progress. The military have taken this step in a patriotic spirit." I asked what step. He said, "To take charge." Was Bosch under arrest, as he said? "No, they are in the Palace, they will be sent out of the country and be given the courteous treatment their high rank deserves—the President, the Vice President, President of the Senate, Cabinet, all of them." He wasn't sure when, today or tomorrow. I asked if he would personally guarantee their safety. Of course, he said —no one wanted to hurt them. Then he went on, "No military officer is interested in taking power."

I said, "But somebody has to take power. Who's going to run the country?"

"The military is in charge of the country," his eyes narrowing. "Soon we will designate one or several civilians to take charge."

"Who will designate them?"

"All of the Armed Forces."

I asked if Bosch's demand that Wessin leave had touched it off. He said, "That was one of the points."

I remarked that I noticed three civilians here in the room, among the military. He glanced up; they were hard to find in the crowd. I asked who they were. He said, "Some doctors we asked to come so we could get advice." I asked their names. He said he didn't know, and called a junior officer over and asked him to find out. They were, he reported, Arturo Despradel, Carlos Sánchez, and Gustavo Henriquez. The names meant nothing to me. Viñas said they were here "to exchange impressions," not to govern. He said the military had called in "all the political parties." I asked which ones. He said, "All of them—UCN, ASD, the one of General Ramírez, all of them."

I asked, "Vanguardia?"

"Yes."

"The PDC?"

He bristled, suspicious. "That's the Social Christians."

I said no, it was Mario Read Vittini's splinter off the Social Christians. Yes, Viñas said, they had been called. All had been called.

"The PRD?" I asked.

He looked surprised, and said no. Not the Social Christians either, nor the 14th of June. (These three were at that time the only three political parties that existed in the Republic, in any meaningful sense of the term.) Viñas knew little of such matters. He went on, with some force, "But these party leaders are not going to govern. We won't accept their leaders. We have called them in, but only to advise." It was the old military, the old Dominican, mistrust of politicians. Viñas then asked, "What is the view of the United States of this?"

I said, "I have no instructions. As the Ambassador I am accredited to the Bosch government. You know what we thought all along about a *golpe*. I told you yesterday at lunch, the day before yesterday it was. You've known it all along." He nodded, looking resentful. I went on, "I'd like to say a couple of things. I can't say them officially, since I can't speak officially, the government I was accredited to has apparently ceased to exist, but speaking unofficially, as a friend of the Republic." He told me to go ahead. I said, "I've known you a long time, and knowing your character, I'm confident you don't want to fight the people, or to have any killing."

He said, "*Sí, señor.*"

I said, "The Armed Forces doesn't want, can't afford, another Calle Espaillat," the place just off Conde where, on October 20, 1961, troops under Ramfis' orders had killed students on the rooftops.

He said, "*Sí, señor.* There will be none of that."

I said I was glad to hear him say it. I went on. "The Armed Forces has taken on a grave responsibility. It may face serious trouble in the days ahead. Is it united?"

"Yes."

"Can you control it? Control the others?"

"Yes."

"Can you control Wessin? Imbert? Luna? All of them?"

"Yes," looking at once resentful and worried.

"I certainly hope so. I don't like killing, you don't, the civilized world doesn't."

"That is what we want to avoid."

I then asked about the constitutional situation—would Bosch resign before the Assembly, how would power be transferred? Viñas knew little about the Constitution. This did not bother him. He said, "Under the communiqué, the Constitution is null and void."

"What communiqué?"

"Ours. We are broadcasting it now. Radio Santo Domingo is reading it."

"What does it say?"

"I don't know exactly, somebody else wrote it, but it says the Constitution is null and void, the Congress is dissolved, all the Armed Forces high command is in charge. I signed it as Chief of the Armed Forces."

I said, "If I can make a suggestion, it seems to me that you could avoid a lot of trouble by leaving the Constitution alone. A great many people think highly of the principle of constitutionality. We do, that is, the United States, and so do many Latin American nations. I don't see much advantage in not having a Constitution."

He shrugged.

I went on, "Of course, under the Constitution, since Bosch and the Vice President and Casasnovas are gone, I should think the Speaker of the House is President."

He said sharply, "Molina Ureña is not the President. The Armed Forces are in charge of everything."

"I understand that, but he could be President temporarily and make an easy transition for you. You might avoid a lot of trouble that way. There could be serious trouble, you know. I don't know what the people will do."

His jaw set. He said nothing.

I asked, "Do you expect trouble?"

Looking past me, he said, "There has been no reaction yet. We will know during the day."

"Who is in charge now?"

"I am. As the superior officer."

"But you don't want to stay in charge?"

"No. We are going to select a new civilian government today or to-morrow. Not a military government, there will be no military men in the junta."

I asked who the civilians might be and tried once more, gently, on Molina Ureña. It was useless: Molina Ureña was a leader of the hated Bosch's hated PRD.

Viñas said he didn't know who the civilians would be "but I promise you that whoever comes will not be a member of any political party and will be a person of capacity, honesty, and sincerity."

I thanked him, shook hands with him, got up and headed for the door, and the others, especially Imbert, seeing me leaving, moved again toward me, smiling, wanting to be friends; but I didn't feel like their friend that day and I didn't think my government should either, so I just kept going and opened the door myself—it stuck, I had to jerk it open—and walked out and down the corridor and through the lobby and down the steps to my car.

So ended, after seven months less two days, the Dominican Republic's first freely elected government in thirty-eight years.

10

From the Palace King and I went straight to the Residence, went upstairs, and I telephoned Ed Martin at 8:15 A.M. Unruffled, he said the Department would be sending me instructions.

Downstairs, Molina Ureña was sitting in my study, a small, thin man in a big upholstered chair, miserable. Shlaudeman was there, and Fran, and I think some others. I told Molina how sorry I was. He said we had done everything we could. I said it hadn't been very good. Molina had big brown eyes. He talked little. He was suffering, near tears. Not for himself. For the country, and what he believed in. We were very kind to him that morning. A lot of good that did.

Dr. Mendoza, the Minister of Health arrived, saying in a burst of emotion, "We have returned"—gone back to militarism—and, taking Fran in his arms, "my companion in Higüey, I am sorry." The polio inoculation program was to have been completed Saturday and Sunday; now that was gone. Mendoza had heard there was a street battle going on downtown in Parque Independencia or Parque Colón; the people had booed the police, and the police had attacked.

We checked. It wasn't true. The city was quiet.

The phones started ringing. The Colombian Embassy was filled with asylees, including Miolán. Venezuela was going to break diplomatic relations with the Republic. So might Brazil. So would Mexico—Mexico, which because of its own revolutionary history almost automatically recognized any government that takes power. (In this case, I presume,

Mexico felt itself personally affronted, since the *golpe* had come just after Bosch had visited there.)

The government television station was broadcasting live from the Palace, beaming Generals, stern Generals, haggard Generals, grinning civilians, communiqués. Between calls the others watched; I'd seen enough. Ruíz came in, said the police had rounded up about two dozen MPD and 14th of June members, and had wrecked the 14th of June headquarters. They had missed Manolo Tavárez Justo.

Shlaudeman took me aside: Molina Ureña was worried about his family, soldiers had surrounded his house. I was uncertain. There was no way he could gain power at this time. On the other hand, we didn't want him arrested and beaten up. I thought he ought to take asylum in a foreign embassy. He did. We had already gotten another Bosch man into hiding. Somebody had rescued Justice Douglas' television tapes from Sacha Volman's office; we locked them in my safe. I wrote a cable, repeating for the record what I'd told Ed Martin on the phone. I'd been up almost continuously more than twenty-four hours. I went to bed; King and Shlaudeman would keep track of things. I told them they'd better take turns, we might have a lot to do during the night, Miolán had often said the people would rise if Bosch fell, and by evening the military and police would be exhausted and might do anything.

That afternoon the Department cabled instructions. Since the government had been deposed, the Embassy should cease all formal contacts with members of the new regime, unless it followed the constitutional succession. The question of recognition would not arise until a new government had been organized.

The Embassy was flooded with phone calls. Juan Vicini wanted to know when we were going to press the military to hold the wage line at Haina. Minister Majluta's wife suspected her husband was being mistreated. Bosch's niece, Milagros, said a fight had taken place between Calderón and a drunken military officer. Bombs, probably noise bombs the police used to frighten people, were exploding all over town. The PRD was reported arming. The police were busy with their roundup. Miolán, still plotting, sent me a scheme to collaborate with a new government that would deport Communists but allow the PRD freedom to operate. It was hopeless. King told me Shlaudeman's father was dying in California. I told Shlaudeman he ought to go; he did, later. The regime announced an after-dark curfew but, thoughtfully, sent me a safe-conduct pass. That was where I came in: When I had first arrived as Ambassador, the same thing had happened.

King and Shlaudeman would keep checking around town through the evening and had arranged for a duty officer to sleep in my office. He would keep track of the hurricane that was spinning our way from south of Puerto Rico. Outside now the sky was dark, the wind was rising.

King called at 10:20 P.M. Miolán's only remaining free man was calling a general strike for tomorrow. But numerous labor organizations were on the radio supporting the new regime.

I remember little more about that day, the day Bosch fell. The date was September 25, 1963. I remember sitting around the living room, now with Fran and the boys, now with the Crisis Crowd, doing nothing, just sitting in front of the big round marble coffee table, where I'd had coffee and brandy so many times with a member of the Bosch government or the Consejo. I recalled that several nights before I had noticed an unusually large number of cars in front of Bonnelly's house. I supposed that he and other old friends from the Consejo days had been in this *golpe*. Well, I could understand. And Bosch had indeed been a poor President.

But none of that, to my mind, justified the *golpe*. For it overthrew not merely Bosch. It overthrew the principle: Constitutional government, representative democracy, the right of people to elect their own rulers. This was the point the *civicos* missed. This was the real Dominican tragedy. It always had been. Sumner Welles had known it. Welles had worked hard for Dominican democracy. So had many others. Now it was gone. All that work, all that money, all that caring for the people—now it was all swept away in a few minutes by a bunch of machine gunners in the night in the preposterous peach-colored Palace.

Yet could they really be blamed? I supposed they had thought they were doing their duty, saving the Republic from communism. Some of them, at least—Wessin y Wessin. Not Luna. Anyway, now it was gone. Once again the machine gun ruled the Palace.

It was for this then that Imbert had risked his life on the highway that night more than two years ago. It was for this that so many had died in Trujillo's prisons and torture chambers. It was for this that the people had gone to El Conde, to Parque Independencia, to Calle Espaillat, against Ramfis Trujillo's tanks.

For months we had stopped innumerable plots against Bosch. But Bosch, by what he did and failed to do, by his very election, had set in motion forces too powerful for either him or us to control finally. Blind chance had played a role too. If the Pentagon had not picked that time to call Bev Cass home, we would have had three attachés running around that night instead of, effectively, one, and we might somehow have held it. Despite all the plotting, I do not believe that when Viñas and the others left Bosch and me at Bosch's house that evening they knew precisely what would happen. Gleeful as the *civicos* and politicians were after it happened, swiftly as they had moved this morning, I do not believe that anyone knew until Bosch fell how he would fall, or by whose hand. Rather, it was as though, as I have said before, a large group of men had for a long time grappled clumsily with one another, struggling in the dark, stumbling locked in fatal embrace along the edge of an abyss, and finally fallen over. It was so senseless, so shocking, so needless.

11

Thursday. Minister Majluta's brother-in-law wanted a U.S. visa for Majluta. O.K. Mrs. Bosch was on her way here from Puerto Rico by commercial plane, accompanied by two of Muñoz Marín's political aides. Bev Cass was back. The Santo Domingo telephone operator refused to let King call the Department. Bosch was still in the Palace. There was no way to call a strike against the *golpistas*—they had seized all radio stations. Government offices were functioning. All Social Christians were on the arrest list. CIDES had been raided. The streets were quiet but tense. A crowd was booing the police in Parque Independencia. Costa Rica would suspend relations.

Ambassador Stevenson reported from the United Nations that Betancourt's Venezuelans were talking about a meeting of Foreign Ministers of the hemisphere, not to try to restore Bosch to power but to bring "moral influence" to bear on the *golpistas*, since *golpes* were bad in principle. Three elected Presidents had fallen in the last six months— in Guatemala, Ecuador, the Dominican Republic. The elected President of Honduras was in danger. The Nicaraguans and Guatemalans were inclined to say "I told you so." And Castro, of course, was delighted.

At 11:30 A.M., the regime closed the airport. Mrs. Bosch had already landed. So had the U.S. press, Vallimarescu said, and was inquiring about the coincidence of Admiral Ferrall's presence and asking to see me. I told King to prepare a summary of the messages on Admiral Ferrall's visit and told Vallimarescu I'd have a press conference at four-thirty.

The new government came on television: a *Triumvirato* (soon derided as a *"Triumviriato,"* a pun on Viriato Fiallo's name) composed of Emilio de los Santos, head of last year's Electoral Board; Ramón Tapia, Bonnelly's protégé; and our old friend with the burro train on the beach, Manuel Tavares.

Callers arrived—Mrs. Bosch, accompanied by Mrs. Majluta and Governor Muñoz' associates. Mrs. Bosch had held a press conference in Puerto Rico, and Muñoz had denounced the *golpe*. Now Mrs. Bosch, pale and tense, said the military would not let her see her husband. I thought that outrageous but couldn't do anything about it except to suggest she talk to the U.S. press. The officers and gentlemen in the Palace, I was told, shut off the lights and water in Mrs. Bosch's home and repossessed her unpaid-for furniture. She took refuge that night in the Chilean Embassy.

She kept calling Fran. The military finally relented—said she could visit her husband if she went to the Palace alone and was escorted to her husband by a General. She refused, and told Fran she wanted to be escorted by a gentleman of her choice, and have him place her hand in her husband's hand, and didn't Fran think that part of her "civil rights as a woman?" Fran said she herself would go alone and be escorted to her husband by anybody available and stay with him until they were released together. In the end, I believe, Mrs. Bosch won her point, and was escorted by a Chilean diplomat. (It is not impossible that she thought if Bosch could grasp the Chilean's hand, it would give him asylum in the Chilean Embassy.) I was told that at one point a newspaperman or radio-TV man arranged a telephone hookup so she could talk to Bosch by phone. She said to him, "What message do you have for the free world, Juan?" Quixotic melodrama? Perhaps; but indeed the fate of free men was involved. And is.

12

Thursday afternoon the hurricane was ninety miles southeast of Santo Domingo, heading for Barahona. It had behaved in a most peculiar way, changing course many times, suddenly picking up speed, suddenly standing still. (Like Bosch.) It would hit the coast at 5 or 6 A.M. Friday. We could expect tides of from eight to twelve feet at Santo Domingo. Already it was driving rain ahead of it; gusty wind-driven downpours beat on the glass windows of the study; the palms and great trees swooped in the wind, and the sky was black. No one will ever know whether the people would have gone to the streets to protest Bosch's fall if it had not rained. That night the hurricane shifted again—it would hit the coast in the East instead, on the coast near Nisibón and on the Peninsula of Samaná. Gale winds hammered the capital, seventy-five miles per hour. Curious—Trujillo had consolidated power shortly after his takeover by suspending constitutional guarantees when a hurricane flattened the capital, and, ruling, he is said to have almost superstitiously feared the hurricane season. This hurricane's velocity was a hundred miles an hour at the center, and it extended for sixty miles—small but very dangerous. Like the Republic itself.

Bosch had smuggled a communiqué out. My notes on it read: "Neither alive nor dead, in power or in the street, would it be fitting if we changed our conduct. We will always oppose ourselves against privilege, excess, and torture. We believe in the dignity and right of the Dominican people to always have democracy with liberty. In seven months we have not spilled one drop of blood, not stolen one cent. We have permitted lies, tolerated insults, because we believe that democracy should be tolerant. . . . Men may fall but principles not. We can feel that the people cannot permit that democracy fall. The people should defend democracy. Here we are, prepared to defend it."

King and Shlaudeman came in at 10:30 P.M. On my instructions, our people had been talking with various political leaders. We thought the new regime wasn't working. The Triumvirate had handed the Cabinet seats over to the political parties, but the parties were quarreling over them among themselves. The police were getting rough with prisoners. In a day or two the regime would be faced with shooting. Kids with rocks were on the rooftops of Calle Espaillat that night; the police were down below with tear gas. The regime was heading toward repression. That night the police were arresting all engineers; who knew why?

I wanted to bring down the *golpista* regime in order to enable the Dominicans to return to constitutionality and escape tyranny. The best time was now. But how? The regime's crucial error, we thought, was in handing the Cabinet over to the quarreling parties—defeated minority parties that represented little or nothing. It could not succeed on this multi-party basis.

We talked long past midnight. In the end, we agreed to get in touch with Manuel Tavares, indirectly who, we thought, had been installed to please us, and see if we could convince him that the multi-party regime was unworkable and military domination dangerous and persuade him to resign. If so, the entire Triumvirate might collapse. We also would explore the possibility of persuading several party leaders to resign from the Cabinet.

13

Friday morning King told me that Balaguer, in New York, was saying that the U.S. government was back of the *golpe*. Vallimarescu reported that all the U.S. press he had seen, including the New York *Times,* had condemned the *golpe* strongly. The U.S. newsmen here considered the regime's performance to date "shocking." Tavares had made a strong plea for U.S. recognition. The Haitian uprising had been crushed. There, too, it was all over.

By noon, King reported our approaches seemed fruitless. Messages we had sent to Tavares, the key figure, had gone unanswered. Nor were the party leaders responsive. Our people would keep trying. I decided to write a cable and, if we had made no progress by late afternoon, to send it.

The cable said that although the Triumvirs were decent men, the Cabinet posts were in the hands of quarreling, discredited politicians, including some inimical to us, and the real power remained with the military, led by Wessin but including some of the worst Trujillistas. The regime desperately wanted U.S. recognition. We had been saying for a long time that we believed in the right of peoples to choose their own rulers. Perhaps this was the time and place to prove we meant what we said. We must set our face against this *golpe*. The principle was not Bosch, nor liberalism, nor even the non-Communist left in Latin America; it was the right of people to choose their rulers. We must make it plain to the Dominican people and to the hemisphere that we favored constitutional, representative democracy, not military rule. I recommended that I be instructed to leave the Republic immediately, taking with me the AID, MAAG, USIS, and Peace Corps chiefs.

I showed the telegram to King and Shlaudeman at 4 P.M. They agreed. I sent it. We had chosen another—the last—fork in the road.

14

I was getting worried about Bosch. It was Friday night; he had been confined to the Palace since early Wednesday morning. Vallimarescu said four reporters had seen Bosch sleeping there that afternoon. I asked if they were sure he was sleeping. Vallimarescu looked shocked—apparently no one had thought he might be dead.

Donny Reid now told a CBS man that the *Mella* would leave tomorrow, taking Bosch to Europe. Increasingly, Reid seemed to be acting as spokesman for the regime. He sent word to me "as a friend" that he would become Foreign Minister.

At 11:10 A.M. on Saturday, Ed Martin called on the hot line. I could leave, taking Williams and Wolfe with me "for consultation." I didn't want to say it was for consultation; I wanted to announce we were leaving period. Reluctantly he agreed. I asked if I should bring Fran. He thought not. (She didn't want to go. Nor did the boys.) Ed Martin said, rightly I now believe, I could not take USIS or the Peace Corps with me. Ed Martin was concerned about Bosch's personal safety—the new Foreign Minister should be told that nothing could so completely destroy any possibility of recognition as any harm done Bosch.

I called Reid direct and asked him to come to the Residence. I hadn't seen him for a long time. I gave him Ed Martin's message about Bosch's safety. He said, "If anything happens to him, I'll resign."

I said, "That won't help Bosch. Or this new government of yours."

He said, "When I was in the Consejo, I could take decisions. I cannot now. But I will go to Tapia—he's at Bonnelly's house now—and Tavares and tell them."

He paused, then plunged on, leaning forward. "I want to tell you how I got in this government."

"You don't have to, Donny."

He shook his head. "No, but I mean, I want to. Yesterday at 1 P.M. they sent for me. Viñas. I saw him. Also Tavares and Tapia. Also all the party leaders. They told me I was the only one acceptable to everybody. Tavares said if I didn't accept, he would resign." (I thought: Damn! We'd missed it. Yesterday morning we should have tried to reach Donny Reid, not Tavares.) Reid went on: "There is no road back. The military took it, they can't stop now. I know this is a setback for democracy. But I have to help my country. If I don't, it might get terrible. I will not stand for killing. And they know it. It is a greater sacrifice for me than before." He trailed off, looking up at me.

I had always liked him. But now— Well, anyway. I said, "I understand, Donny. The thing now is Bosch's safety. Remember, as long as he's on a Dominican boat, or in a Dominican plane, he's your responsibility. Put him on a Pan American plane, or some other line, and get him to Puerto Rico or somewhere close."

Reid hesitated, then said, "They're afraid he'll jeopardize your recognition, he'll make manifestos."

"He'll always make manifestos. If it'll help you with the others, I can assure you that my government will take its own decision on recognition and he will not influence it. Nor will anyone else."

He left. I called King and Shlaudeman, and they came up. Plane reservations were ready: We would leave at 5:15 P.M. How did we see the situation, and what did we want our government to do?

The regime was not stable and not unified. The Triumvirate would not tolerate police brutality but probably could not control Belisario Peguero. Splits might occur in the military. The prime movers had been Wessin and Luna. Then Rib had come in. Then Amiama and Imbert. Viñas and Hungría had been last. Corruption in the military was divisive. Would Luna get his Hawker Hunters now? The Triumvirate itself was none too stable. And even Bonnelly seemed nervous and not entirely happy—I'd seen him briefly that morning about Bosch's safety, and he had told me indignantly the new regime had arrested a friend of his from Santiago and the friend's daughter, an outrage. He had warned Tapia they must be moderate—but the new Minister of Interior and Police was none other than Severo Cabral, he who had applauded the Spaniards' boiling Protestants in oil.

The real danger of repression came from Wessin, Colonel Neit Nivar Seijas, and others like him. The military didn't know how to govern, couldn't possibly face such difficult problems as a strike at Haina, so they were vulnerable. They would get little help from the quarreling politicians. It was not at all impossible that if we kept the pressure on, withheld recognition, we might bring down the regime. Our main objective ought to be restoring constitutionality. Bosch was finished. Once he and the Vice President were out of the country, the line of succession would start. Under the Bosch Constitution, Casasnovas could proclaim that the President and Vice President were "definitively absent," he himself was provisional President, and he was convoking both houses of Congress to meet within fifteen days as a National Assembly and elect a President. There was little hope we could bring that about unless the military, disgusted with the politicians, saw it as a way out. At that point, negotiations could begin over whom the Congress would elect. The military would reject Casasnovas, Molina Ureña, Miolán, or anyone else closely identified with Bosch; the PRDista Assembly would reject anyone closely identified with the Christian Manifestations, the Council the State, the UCN, or any other party. Perhaps they could find an acceptable compromise—somebody from the Bosch cabinet and also acceptable to the military, such as Guzmán or García-Godoy. Or somebody entirely outside politics, such as Marco Cabral. In any case, what mattered now was that we keep the pressure on by withholding recognition.

15

I went upstairs to pack. A *Time-Life* reporter and photographer came up. I had written a press release. It said:

"My government has ordered me, John Bartlow Martin, United States Ambassador to the Dominican Republic; Mr. Newell F. Williams, Director of the AID mission in the Dominican Republic; and Colonel David C. Wolfe, Chief of the Military Assistance and Advisory Group to the Dominican Republic, home. We are departing via Caribair at 5:15 P.M. today. We will transit Puerto Rico, departing San Juan at 10:30 P.M. tonight via Pan American Airways Flight 286 and arriving New York at 1:15 A.M." We included the times and flight numbers to ensure newspaper coverage of our withdrawal.

I finished my suitcase, and went down to pack my briefcase. King had some papers for me, including the Bosch Constitution and the 1962 Constitution, which the regime had proclaimed in effect. Wolfe and Williams arrived. Fran and the boys wanted to go to the airport with me. I thought they shouldn't. I wanted it to be a cold, official departure. I said goodbye to them, then got in the car. King got in with me, and I waved to Fran and Dan and Fred, standing in the white doorway under the portico, then we headed for the airport.

The streets seemed normal, crowded as ever in the old Upper Town, bicycles and trucks and wagons and people and *públicos* snarled all together, a man selling peeled oranges at the curb, the city smelling hot and fresh after the rains. I asked King to look after Fran and the boys. The hurricane was hovering off the north coast, still poised to strike. Yesterday mountainous seas had roared over Avenida Jorge Washington, but today as we crossed the bridge and picked up speed on the highway, the sea beside the palms was calm, sending little geysers spurting up in the coral coast as it had twenty-five years ago when first I had seen it on the old road to Boca Chica.

Photographers and reporters were at the airport, and so was Vallimarescu, and we issued the statement, handing out copies, reading it for television. Soon the plane was ready. We went aboard, and in a few minutes the plane taxied out, then ran the bright runway, climbed and leveled off, and I looked down at the green and brown earth of the Republic. September 28, Saturday—it was the day the TVA mission was to have arrived. Now that was gone, and all the work that had gone into it since our first trip to Azua and the gray people of Vicente Noble. Gone now; and so was the television literacy program, and the other dreams. So much gets washed out in a *golpe*. In five minutes, or five seconds, with a machine gun. The poor country. The poor people.

PART THREE

The Seventy-seven Days in Washington

Chapter Twenty-five

LIMITS OF AMERICAN POWER

Many times in the Dominican Republic, during or after a crisis, or when we were considering a major move, one of us would say, "I don't know how this would sound at the post-mortem." Now the post-mortem on Dominican democracy was at hand.

Our own prestige was heavily involved. In his State of the Union message in 1962, President Kennedy had singled out the Dominican Republic as a hopeful omen. I had known that Bosch's fall would set off a strong reaction in the United States. But I was not prepared for uproar.

The New York *Times* said the *coup* was "utterly deplorable," called for a meeting of OAS Foreign Ministers, and said, "Whatever Mr. Bosch's faults and weaknesses, he had been freely and fairly elected. His inauguration in February was a dawn of hope and freedom after more than three decades of bestial tyranny. Freedom has now been thrown away, as if it were a paltry gift. The ostensible reasons for the *coup* have a stale sound—the usual accusations of pro-Communism, Socialism, and mismanagement. . . . The *coup d'état* is a severe blow to democracy in Latin America and a frightening development for the democratic Caribbean powers. Naturally, Castroite Cuba will rejoice. The Alliance for Progress will be the Number One victim."

The Washington *Post* declared, "There was absolutely no warrant for a military uprising," approved our suspending relations and foreign aid, and said, "The aim of United States policy, in concert with other Latin American countries, will surely be to bring about a swift return to constitutional government."

The New York *Herald Tribune* said, "Things are looking up for the Communists in the Caribbean. And they are looking down for us." The Des Moines *Register* said, "The junta is gambling on paralyzing the U.S. from taking any action against it by proclaiming its anti-Communism, and by hiding behind the 'non-intervention' pledges of the inter-American agreements." The *Christian Science Monitor,* recalling the OAS' sanctions against Trujillo, anticipated that the nations of the Hemisphere might now take similar collective action against the present *golpistas.*

On the other hand, the Cincinnati *Enquirer,* though saying that the *coup* "bodes ill for the cause of representative government" in Latin America, pointed out that military regimes there "have frequently been considerably more realistic" than civilian governments, "which are altogether too often swayed by the kind of mobocracy at which international Communism excels. . . . It is too early to say that what happened in the Dominican Republic this week is not for the best."

Oddly, in the press I was becoming Bosch's greatest champion.

On the whole, editorial opinion seemed to have set against the *golpistas.* But what about the White House and the Congress?

2

On the same day I left the Republic, the *golpistas* had deported Bosch aboard the *Mella.* At his own request he had been accompanied by, of all people, Tony Imbert—he had called Imbert "my good friend." They were this weekend on the high seas, bound for Guadeloupe or Martinique, where the Bosches would take a plane to Puerto Rico. Why Bosch took Imbert, I do not know. Possibly he hoped to split the military, to guarantee his own life, or to take Imbert down with him. Similarly, Vice President González Tamayo had been taken to deportation at the airport, in the custody of, at his own request, his "good friend" Luís Amiama Tió.

Staying in Georgetown that Sunday with Arthur Schlesinger, I began working on a paper setting forth my views. The policy I intended to press for was the one I had outlined in my cable when I asked to be recalled: A hard line against the *golpistas,* a pullout of U.S. help, and a clear declaration that we believed in the right of people to choose their own rulers.

To my mind, however, this did not mean bringing Bosch back. How could we restore a Dominican President to the Palace whose own voters did not protest his overthrow? We could do it, of course, with armed force. But ought we? What kind of a democracy is it that can be kept in the Palace only by a foreign fleet in the harbor? By so using force to "support democracy," you destroy the thing you try to create. We had the force. But we could not use it. Force alone is not power. Force may be unlimited. But power is always narrowly limited. And the greater the power the narrower the limits, as we discovered in the ensuing weeks.

The *golpistas'* "anti-Communist" case was weak. They had arrested some five hundred people but couldn't seem to find any important Castro/Communists in or out of the Bosch government. They had captured not one top leader of the PSP, MPD, or 14th of June. And they had announced that all government workers could keep their jobs—including, presumably, all the "Communists in government" they had complained of.

The Triumvirate consisted of three decent men of fair capacity, but they were only a front for the machine gunners who seized power. They had made the fatal mistake of distributing Cabinet posts among the defeated quarrelsome parties. (Horacio Julio Ornes had taken the two fattest ministries—Public Works, and Commerce and Industry, which controlled Haina.)[1] The regime was untrustworthy—it had now announced that the PRD and even the 14th of June could operate, but when Miolán emerged from hiding the regime promptly jailed him. It was hunting Manolo Tavárez Justo.

The regime was shaky. Quarrels among the military or the parties might topple it; so might killings or public disorders. It was difficult to see how it could survive long without our recognition.

Several policy alternatives were open to us.

First, we could try to bring Bosch back.

Second, we could recognize the present regime now.

Third, we could recognize the present regime after considerable delay and much close bargaining.

Fourth, we could decide not to recognize and search actively for a way to replace the regime with one with a stronger claim to constitutional legitimacy. This could succeed if the present regime started to disintegrate and the military wanted a way out. As disintegration began, we could work with the military and the Assembly to find a presidential candidate to be elected by the Assembly, hopefully Senator Casasnovas or Speaker Molina Ureña—the constitutional heirs—or if they proved unacceptable to the military, a "nonaligned" man such as Donny Reid or Marco Cabral, or someone from the Bosch Cabinet such as Antonio Guzmán, García-Godoy, Buenaventura Sánchez, Vila Piola, de Moya.

This was what I thought we ought to attempt. And I believed the chance of success was good. For right now our prestige was higher than it

[1] The *golpista* Cabinet lined up this way:

PRD (Bosch)—58.72 percent of the popular vote in 1962; no Cabinet seats.

UCN (Fiallo)—30.08 percent of the popular vote; three Cabinet seats (Interior/ Police, Labor, Health); four counting Foreign Minister Donny Reid as UCN.

PRSC (Social Christians)—5.18 percent of the popular vote; no Cabinet seats.

PNRD ("General" Ramírez)—3.39 percent of the popular vote; two Cabinet seats (Agriculture, Public Property).

ASD (Juan Isidro Jimenes Grullón)—1.70 percent of the popular vote; two Cabinet seats (Justice, Finance).

VRD (Horacio Julio Ornes)—0.65 percent of the popular vote; two Cabinet seats (Public Works, Industry/Commerce).

PN (General Vilomar)—0.16 percent of the popular vote; no Cabinet seats.

PRDA (Nicolás Silfa)—0.12 percent of the popular vote; no Cabinet seats.

PDC (Mario Read Vittini)—no popular vote; two Cabinet seats (Presidency, Education).

PPDC (Ramón Castillo); no popular vote; one Cabinet seat (without Portfolio). General Viñas continued in Defense.

had been since we sent the fleet to throw the Trujillos out, and every Latin American government that refused to recognize the *golpista* regime strengthened our hand.

Finally, I made these notes on a piece of notepaper:

"3 dangers to JFK
"soft on communism
"something that won't work
"soft on *golpes*"

These were the things I must keep in mind.

3

On Monday, the U.S. government began the arduous, bruising process of grinding out a new policy. It was a process that contained some order, in retrospect. But at the time, besieged day after day by telephone calls, overloaded with callers, sitting in meetings, hurrying up and down stairs and elevators and endless corridors, hurrying to the Capitol, to the Senate Office Building, to the House Office Building, to the White House, I thought it resembled a process carried out in another political hurricane. And here, of course, was a whole new set of powerful forces to contend with.

In the Department, I had one of those gray-walled offices with a gray steel desk and a gray steel chair, barren as a prison cell, so indistinguishable from all the other offices that many times I blundered into the wrong office. Nearby were the Dominican desk man, Bill Sowash, and Kennedy Crockett, Acting Director of the Caribbean Area, getting bald, wearing glasses, usually noncommittal, blunt at times, a man I came to respect and like immensely during the weeks ahead. We were on the third floor of the Department.

Ed Martin and his deputy, Sterling Cottrell, were on the sixth.

I got in early that Monday morning and read the cables from Spence King, now chargé at the Embassy. The Social Christians and Peña Gómez of the PRD were urging us to withhold recognition as long as possible. Suspecting they were toying with making common cause with the 14th of June, King and Shlaudeman warned them such a common front might drive the United States to support the regime. The regime was saying privately that if it didn't get recognition early that week and therefore fell, the Republic would "go Communist" or "go Trujillo." And in this I saw a real danger—the regime would try to blackmail us into reluctant recognition by screaming, "Save us or we'll go Communist."

At 10 A.M., in his antiseptic, soundproof sixth-floor conference room, Assistant Secretary Ed Martin held a meeting—Ralph Dungan from the White House; Moscoso of the *Alianza;* Ed Martin, Cottrell, Crockett and Sowash from the Department; and my people from Santo Domingo.

Moscoso looked as if he had been kicked in the stomach. He had been deeply committed to Bosch's experiment in democracy. He said almost nothing at all, but when he did speak it was to say tensely that he wanted to pull the whole AID mission out at once.

I agreed with Moscoso, and went on to argue that we should withhold recognition, that we should watch for splits and explore alternatives, pressing for some sort of return to constitutionality. We should cable U.S. press reaction to the Embassy so it could feed it to the Dominican press.

Ed Martin, the brusque, precise man, asked what we did if the situation deteriorated; thought that only he or I should talk to the U.S. press; hoped the remaining MAAG could influence the Dominican military politically; thought we needed to define exactly which additional people we would pull out, if any. He asked for a set of papers laying out the policy alternatives. For in a few days we must recommend a course of action to the President.

That day the Dominican question exploded on Capitol Hill.

Senator Ernest Gruening (Democrat, Alaska) on the Senate floor denounced the *golpistas* as "sordid gangsters," rejected their pretext that Bosch was "soft on communism," declared that the United States "must stand firm" in defense of Dominican democracy, and said, "I [urge] that the United States send a destroyer to intercept the vessel carrying President Bosch into exile and order it to return him to the Dominican Republic," boarding it if necessary.

Senator William Proxmire (Democrat, Wisconsin) cautioned against intervening on our own initiative, without invitation.

Senator Stephen M. Young (Democrat, Ohio) proposed that we "associate ourselves" with other hemisphere nations to restore Bosch to office and reverse the *coup*. Had it been a Communist takeover instead of a "Fascist" takeover, he said, the demand that we send in our military and air power would have been overwhelming.

Senator Frank Church (Democrat, Idaho) suggested a "dramatic gesture": Rescuing Bosch off the *Mella,* putting him aboard a U.S. destroyer, and bringing him to asylum in the United States.

Gruening said that in any case to acquiesce in the Dominican *coup* was almost to invite a *coup* in Venezuela, where elections, scheduled for December, were in danger. He concluded, "I very much hope the Administration will not—as it has done in the past—first say, 'We will not recognize this power-hungry group of usurpers; we will deny them economic aid,' but then, in three or four weeks, devise a face-saving formula by which it will say, 'Well, they promise to be good boys, and they will hold another election in a few months.' . . . In that event, we might as well kiss the Alliance for Progress goodbye."

Senator Wayne Morse (Democrat, Oregon), speaking as chairman of the Latin American subcommittee of the Senate Committee on Foreign

Relations, rejected Gruening's proposal to return Bosch to the Palace by force as tantamount to an act of war but urged that we insist that Bosch be restored to office before economic aid was resumed. In addition Senator Morse urged that we impose a trade embargo except for "food and medicines," state publicly we were withholding diplomatic recognition, call for an immediate Meeting of Foreign Ministers to "condemn the *coup* formally and to consider collective measures—economic, political, and perhaps military—to bring about the restoration of the legitimate government of President Bosch." Morse, a leading critic of military aid, said we had "built up this military junta" by giving the Republic military aid.

Senator Jacob K. Javits (Republican, New York) declared, "The national interest is to say 'No' to the military junta."

A contrary view was expressed that day on the other side of the Capitol.

In the House, Congressman William C. Cramer of Florida said, "I oppose the restoration of Juan Bosch to power because it would be the height of idiocy and would risk the eventual Communist takeover of the Dominican Republic." He quoted with approval a statement by Wessin y Wessin that Bosch's actions indicated he was a Communist and Hal Hendrix' spring articles, including his attack on me.

Congressman Armistead Selden, while not applauding the *coup,* said, "Let me put it bluntly—a dictatorship is odious. But if driven to a choice I prefer a dictatorship seeking our support and friendship than a Communist dictatorship capable of furnishing missile emplacements to those who would bury us."

I had lunch at the White House with Ralph Dungan. There was, he said, no fixed Administration position. On Saturday, the prevailing opinion had tended to favor acquiescence in the *coup,* "but you're 50 percent ahead of that already."

I went over to Capitol Hill, saw Congressman John Brademas, and went to the Majority Whip's office in the Senate and talked to Senator Humphrey. Humphrey thought this was the best time and the best place to take a stand for constitutionality—to hold firm against recognition.

Late that night I called Fran in Santo Domingo. She was all right, indignant at the *golpistas,* hoping I'd come back soon. I think it was some time before she realized I was not going back.

4

Tuesday morning, on the Department's advice, I went once again to the Hill. The debate in the Senate was getting shrill. Senator Morse and Senator Frank J. Lausche of Ohio exchanged bitter recriminations on the Senate floor.

Senator Humphrey said:

"I say to the President of the United States and to the Secretary of State—men to whom I am dedicated in terms of my political loyalty and my friendship. . . . Make it crystal clear that military juntas are out, that they will not be given any help, that they will not be recognized, that they will not be tolerated. I can think of nothing that would do more to destroy the Alliance for Progress and literally to destroy the foreign aid program than to condone what is being done by these military juntas in the Western Hemisphere."

In the crowded Senate lobby, Senator Javits took me aside and asked for background information, and, sitting with him on a window ledge in the dark old ornate lobby, I told him how Bosch had fallen. He said that Senate sentiment seemed to be crystallizing against the *golpistas*. Senator Paul Douglas, my own Senator from Illinois and an old friend, came out, and we talked at length. I hurried back to the Department to have lunch with Averell Harriman, then Undersecretary of State for Political Affairs, and urge that we set our face against the *golpistas*.

Late that afternoon I talked with Ed Martin in preparation for testifying before the House and Senate Committees. Senator Morse was charging that officials of U.S. companies had conspired with the *golpistas*. Who were they? I knew of two that might have sympathized with them— Wimpy, and the Santo Domingo manager of Texaco, Duane Luther. Both had been violently anti-Bosch and close to the *civicos*. Senator Morse was charging that the *golpistas* had received training in U.S. military schools—was it true? Viñas had but I wasn't sure about the others. We would see the President on Friday.

That night I went to dinner at the Costa Rican Embassy—Gonzalo Facio was both Costa Rican Ambassador to the United States and President of the Council of the OAS—along with Senator Humphrey, Ed Martin, Ted Moscoso, Ralph Dungan, and others. Humphrey spoke of attaching amendments to the Foreign Aid Bill denying aid to *golpista* regimes.

The lines of force seemed to be setting. Most of the press seemed to believe we ought not recognize the *golpista* regime unless forced to. Sentiment in the Senate was swinging that way. The House was less clear. The President would decide.

5

On Wednesday morning I spent an hour with Bob Kennedy, telling him what had happened, then read the cables from Santo Domingo. The Embassy felt that the prospects of reversing the *coup* were diminishing. Dominicans were frightened or apathetic. The PRD had collapsed. The 14th of June was either underground or had made a deal with the regime.

Students seemed terrified. All was calm. The regime's only serious problem was our recognition—it needed us for prestige and money. Lacking our recognition, it might be forced to turn to harsh repression. The Embassy proposed that we refuse to recognize the regime until it got rid of Wessin and Luna, replaced one Triumvir with Casasnovas, and promised to hold free Congressional elections in six months.

For two hours that afternoon, I testified before the House Foreign Affairs Committee in closed session.[2]

6

When I arrived at the Department on Thursday morning, I learned that the government of Honduras had been overthrown by a military *coup* led by Colonel Osvaldo López. The classic announcement had come over the radio: "The patriotic armed forces" had overthrown President Villeda Morales "to end flagrant violations of the Constitution and obvious Communist infiltration." With this news in our ears, Ed Martin and I went over to the Capitol to appear in closed session before the Senate Foreign Relations Committee. The Senators, like the Congressmen, were courteous, interested, informed, and sympathetic.

Ed Martin originally had intended to present to the President a series of policy papers laying out the alternatives ranging from immediate recognition to a flat "no." At a meeting that afternoon with Undersecretary Harriman, we decided to present only one agreed paper to the President. If he approved, he or the Secretary would issue a statement. Following the sense of the meeting, I worked with Cottrell and Crockett late that night on the policy paper and the statement.

The policy paper set forth these objectives: Ultimately a return to constitutional representative democracy; meanwhile, effective government; the prevention of either harsh military dictatorship or Castro/Communist growth; a position strong enough to discourage other military *coups* in the hemisphere. It set forth these concessions we wanted in exchange for recognition: Free political activity for non-Communist parties; restoration of some semblance of constitutionality by the appointment of Casasnovas to head the Triumvirate; reconstitution of the Cabinet to include PRDistas; removal of Wessin and Luna; honesty and efficiency in running the former Trujillo properties; social and economic reforms in accordance with the *Alianza*. We hoped for a presidential election in one year and on a new Constitution later. King could let the regime know now that we wouldn't recognize it as things stood, for it represented a minority of the Dominican people and must somehow return to constitutional democracy. Then we would wait a week or ten days. We hoped to end the entire negotiation

[2] As the reader undoubtedly knows, it is impossible to print what is said in an executive session of a Congressional Committee.

in one month. We must, however, take care that delay did not push all opposition into Castro/Communist hands with bloodshed resulting. The Peace Corps, CARE, and CARITAS would stay; we would study the question of PL-480 food.

7

On Friday at 5 P.M., riding to the White House with Ed Martin, I said the Secretary's statement contained nothing specific about nonrecognition —it merely said we could not cooperate with the regime under the Alliance for Progress. Martin said I should have said so sooner—I'd approved the statement. This was true; I'd had second thoughts. We assembled in the Cabinet room—as I recall it, Undersecretaries Ball and Harriman, Assistant Secretary Martin, men from the CIA and the Pentagon, Dave Bell (head of AID), Moscoso, Dungan, others. (It is possible the men concerned with Honduras were present. Certainly the shadow of Honduras hung over everything we said and did henceforward.) President Kennedy came in, walking fast as ever, looking somber. He read the position paper and the statement rapidly, then looked at me and said, "I take it we don't want Bosch back."

I said, "No, Mr. President."

"Why not?"

"Because he isn't a President."

Silence; then we began discussing the paper point by point, the President asking sharp questions, crisp, informed, skeptical. When he came to the Secretary's statement, I said I wanted something in it about nonrecognition. The President didn't want to use the word. Harriman suggested "normalization of relations." The President rewrote the statement, asked what time it was, said, "We've got to get it out right now if we want to catch the bulldog" [the early editions of tomorrow morning's papers], and picked up a phone, got no answer, jiggled the receiver impatiently, and still got no answer. Dungan took the statement and hurried out to release it.

The statement, over Secretary Rusk's name, said:

"We view the recent military *coups* in the Dominican Republic and Honduras with the utmost gravity. The establishment and maintenance of representative and constitutional government is an essential element of the Alliance for Progress. Stable and effective government, responsive to the popular will, is a critical factor in the attainment of social and economic progress.

"Under existing conditions in the Dominican Republic and Honduras there is no opportunity for effective collaboration by the United States under the Alliance for Progress or for normalization of diplomatic relations. Accordingly, we have stopped all economic and military aid to these countries and have commenced an orderly reassignment of the personnel involved."

It was a tough statement, the kind I'd wanted. I believe "orderly reassignment" was Harriman's phrase. It had a nice ring.

The meeting broke up. I wished I had had an opportunity to explain to President Kennedy how Bosch had fallen, and later asked Dungan if I could. Dungan said, "If you're worried that the President has lost confidence in you, forget it—he hasn't." I was grateful, but it wasn't that. It was a guilty need to give him an accounting. I never got the chance.

8

Over the weekend press reaction in the United States mounted, augmented now by the *coup* in Honduras. For since the Alliance for Progress had begun, this was the sixth *coup* against a government that was cooperating with the Alliance, and it called into question our entire Latin American policy.

Ed Martin wrote a piece on Latin American policy for the New York *Herald Tribune* syndicate. He said, "By tradition and conviction as well as a matter of policy, the United States opposes the overthrow of constitutional and popular democratic governments anywhere," especially in Latin America. But sometimes the military overthrew dictators—*e.g.,* Perón in Argentina. Nor did the military universally support those who resisted social and political change. Some military-controlled governments were "reform" governments. "Nor can we," Martin wrote, "as a practical matter, create effective democracy by keeping a man in office through use of economic pressure or even military force when his own people are not willing to fight to defend him."

Martin concluded: "I fear there are some who will accuse me of having written an apologia for *coups*. I have not. They are to be fought with all the means we have available."

Coming at the time it did, however, Martin's piece was widely regarded precisely as he had feared—as an apologia for military *coups*. Senator Morse declared that it "undercuts and destroys the entire premise of the Alliance." The Washington *Post* said editorially, "Before the election, Mr. Kennedy said that this country should 'strengthen the cause of freedom throughout all Latin America'; that we should not allow Latin America to be 'unsure of our stand on native dictators as well as Communist dictators'; that we ought to 'make the American Revolution the chief import of Latin America.' . . . The President made some good speeches about Latin American affairs, during the campaign. Assistant Secretary Martin ought to read them."

9

In Santo Domingo, Severo Cabral was reported drafting anti-Communist "purification" decrees and passing out guns to his friends. From Puerto Rico, Bosch broadcast a call to the Dominican people to "throw yourselves into the streets to revive liberty," though making it clear he meant peaceful demonstrations, not violence. PRD leaders did not want Bosch to return. The New York *Times* reported that two thousand students, led by girls and carrying banners demanding a "return to constitutionalism," marched on the Palace and were driven back by police with tear gas, rifle butts, sabers, and night sticks. The police wounded several and arrested "scores." Dominican Navy frogmen fired machine guns. At dark, truckloads of police with San Cristóbal rifles pulled up at the University gates. The regime declared a state of siege.

In Washington, I received a report that Bosch had told somebody in Puerto Rico that he felt I had double-crossed him and intended to have me assassinated. I didn't believe it. Moscoso still wanted to pull the AID mission out rapidly. The Pentagon wanted to pull the MAAG out slowly. Cottrell, Ed Martin's deputy, negotiated with both as with foreign powers, trying to hold Moscoso back, prodding the Pentagon. OAS members urged speed in convoking a meeting of OAS Foreign Ministers to deal with military *coups*. Governor Nelson Rockefeller of New York accused President Kennedy of allowing the Alliance for Progress to fail. I went to the Hill and talked with Senator Everett Dirksen, the Republican leader and my own Senator from Illinois, then had dinner with Justice Douglas, an unhappy post-mortem. I got home to the Schlesingers in time to hear the end of a lecture by George Kennan before the Hickory Hill group.

On Tuesday, the Dominican police were looking for Senator Casasnovas and Speaker Molina Ureña to deport them, Donny Reid having accused them of agitating for a convocation of Congress.

On Wednesday, at a regular press conference, President Kennedy was asked about Ed Martin's article. He said it represented no policy reversal, Martin was "merely attempting to explain some of the problems in Latin America, why *coups* take place, and what problems they present us with." The President said flatly "we are opposed to military *coups*." Asked if he was satisfied we had done everything possible short of using force to prevent the Dominican and Honduran *coups,* President Kennedy replied:

"Yes, I am. I have looked over the conversation, the minutes, of cables and so on, and I think we did. This idea that we ought to send the United States Marines into Honduras, which, of course, we couldn't have done under the conditions, because of the time gap, I think is a very serious mistake. . . .

"So I think we did the best we could. It may be possible to always do better, but we did the best we could, and we are going to continue to do so."

That day Ed Martin and Ralph Dungan left for Argentina. They would return the next week. We all agreed that neither we nor the Dominican regime was likely to make a move. I went up to Upper Michigan for a few days' partridge hunting.

In Michigan I kept in touch with the Department by telephone. But mostly I gave myself up to the Michigan woods, beautiful now in October, the leaves on the hardwood shimmering golden against the dark spruce and balsam and pine, wet leaf-smell on the trails and logging roads, the air sharp, nights frosty, morning sun bright and thin.

I had been there two nights when on Saturday night, Bob Sayre, Crockett's deputy, telephoned and said that President Kennedy wanted me in Washington by noon tomorrow—Ambassador del Rosario had informed the Department that the Bosch Assembly had elected Juan Casasnovas President, and Casasnovas had requested U.S. recognition as President of the Dominican Republic.

10

Early next morning, Sunday, October 13, they sent the President's C-140, a small, fast new Jet Star, to the SAC Base about fifty miles from my hunting camp. We took off at eight forty-five. By eleven forty-five I was in Cottrell's office in the Department, deserted on Sunday but for him.

Cottrell was busy drafting a cable to the Embassy. He said that Casasnovas, President of the Dominican Senate, had cabled President Kennedy and Secretary Rusk that he had been elected President of the Dominican Republic at a meeting of the Assembly at San Pedro de Macorís (Casasnovas' hometown) on October 10 and 11, and he asked recognition. Bosch had cabled President Kennedy supporting this request, though saying the recognition question did not arise, since constitutional succession had not been broken.

Cottrell and Kennedy Crockett preferred to sit tight but Undersecretary George Ball said we couldn't. We met at twelve-thirty in Ball's office. Ball said the President had received an intelligence report indicating the start of armed resistance to the regime. This, coupled with Casasnovas' and Bosch's cables, had made the President decide to move.

The Embassy didn't like it—it said the Assembly had met in secret rump session, Casasnovas had, in effect, elected himself, and only a handful of people supported him. The Embassy feared his move might trigger demonstrations and serious trouble; the Triumvirate might arrest Casasnovas and Molina Ureña and head down the road toward harsh repression. The Embassy advised waiting.

Ball said we couldn't wait and asked what I thought of Casasnovas. I said that he was our best hope to restore constitutionality and we didn't want to throw him away. I said he was safe. (Others in the U.S. government disagreed, suspecting him of leftist leanings and anti-Americanism.) But could we recognize Casasnovas as President if he was in hiding and could not control the government? On the other hand, how could we accept a new proposal now made by the Triumvirate to hold elections for a constitutional Assembly within a year, then municipal elections, then a presidential election? Could we find a compromise between the two? Ball told Cottrell and me to try.

Cottrell and I ate lunch, talked, wrote drafts, finally agreed on a cable, and sent copies to President Kennedy, who was spending the weekend at Camp David, and to Secretary Rusk and Undersecretary Ball, then went at 7 P.M. to Ball's house.

He called the Secretary, who approved the cable with one change. Ball called the President, talked to him, then I talked to him. The President wanted to know about Casasnovas, and I told him. I explained my misgivings about moving now. President Kennedy said, "The danger is we could lose the best of both worlds," that is, if we passed up this opportunity we might not get another to restore constitutionality, but if we pushed too hard we might force the *golpista* regime into intransigence and harsh repression. Casasnovas had legitimacy but no power, while the Triumvirate had power but no legitimacy. President Kennedy suggested we point out to the regime that it now had an opportunity to find its way back to constitutionality and that it could take credit for having stopped communism. Thus it could save face and might accept Casasnovas.

We sent the cable. It instructed King to go to Manuel Tavares and tell him that Secretary Rusk's original statement was still in force—we would not deal with the present regime and would pull out AID and MAAG people. King should ask what plans the Triumvirate had to become constitutional. If Tavares replied with the strung-out election schedule, King should say that we would not recognize on that basis and we were studying the request of Casasnovas for recognition. He should ask for the Triumvirate's view of Casasnovas' position, saying that we assumed it meant that Bosch and his Vice President were out, the Triumvirate would step down, Casasnovas would be free to select his own Cabinet, and civilian government would be restored. If the regime agree, we would recognize immediately. Thereupon the regime could take credit for preserving civilian control and seeking constitutionality. Moreover, the regime could find justification for the *golpe* in our insistence that Casasnovas control the Castro/Communists. The Embassy should convey all this to General Viñas as well as to Tavares.

11

Next day we got the results. King saw Tavares. Tavares was astonished that we were taking Casasnovas' request for recognition seriously. He said he would have to consult his confreres but for himself thought it might cause civil war—neither the political parties nor the military would accept it.

Later King saw Viñas. Viñas flatly refused to consider the Casasnovas idea. He had no ideas of his own. If the United States refused assistance, the regime would go it alone. If this meant terror and civil war and Castro/Communist guerrilla warfare, the regime would do its best. With the United States' help, it might win; without it, it might lose.

And suddenly the regime counterattacked.

Past midnight, the Triumvirate called King in and, with Donny Reid present, read him a statement declaring that our proposal was offensive and prejudicial to the national dignity and sovereignty. Why would anyone think that those in power would surrender power to a "clandestine" group (that is, the freely elected Bosch Assembly)? The regime protested vehemently our "intervention" in internal Dominican affairs. It asked that Shlaudeman leave the country—he had been conspiring with "clandestine" groups.

King replied that he had not attempted to impose Casasnovas on the Republic but had merely asked for the Triumvirate's attitude toward Casasnovas' request for recognition. King finally persuaded them to withdraw their request that Shlaudeman leave the Republic.

But the regime went further. It complained officially to the OAS about King's "intervention."

Obviously the regime was trying to crush opposition by rallying support to the ancient battle cry of anti-Americanism and intervention, surely a curious undertaking for our old friends Manuel Tavares and Donny Reid.

The regime sent the old Foreign Minister from Consejo days, Bonilla Atiles, to Washington, and he addressed the OAS eloquently on the subject of intervention. He was always eloquent. Indeed, he had been most eloquent two years ago when the United States sent the fleet to throw out the Trujillos and he told the United Nations, "Blessed be the moment when the American fleet came to Dominican waters."

But that had been in 1961, this was 1963; Bonilla Atiles was a flexible man.

The whole affair was preposterous, and I rather favored our saying so on the floor of the OAS. Ed Martin and Ward Allen, our alternate delegate to the OAS, refused, wisely, I now think—we might have aroused sympathy for Bonilla. We confined ourselves to rejecting the re-

gime's charges of intervention and saying we had merely inquired about
the regime's intentions to return to constitutional government.

It was absurd. But it was a defeat. We had run head on into a limit
of our power.

Now the regime would be more united than ever. We had thrown
away Casasnovas and with him probably any real hope of constitutionality. The best we could get would likely be a reconstitution of the
Triumvirate, the ouster of some of the military, and elections. We had,
however, accomplished one thing: We had convinced the regime we really
meant it when we said we wouldn't recognize it. Until then, they hadn't
believed it.

12

We spent a day or two making our position clear, publicly and privately around the Hemisphere. Ed Martin returned. Worried about violence, he told me to bring my family out. President Kennedy called a
meeting.

Again all gathered in the Cabinet room. President Kennedy was stern.
Somebody tried to open the meeting by explaining the situation but the
President cut him off and said the intelligence summary he'd been given
over the weekend, indicating imminent armed resistance to the regime,
was not supported by the cables and had misled him into ordering the
Casasnovas move. Now it had backfired. The CIA men took responsibility. Moreover, President Kennedy went on, what could we accomplish if
King was "going to blow the instructions we give him"? Everyone was
silent; though King was a career officer, the Department did not defend
him; I did: "Mr. President, I don't think King blew it. He did what we
told him to. If anybody blew it, we did." He looked at me a long minute,
then asked everybody where we stood.

I said we ought to stand firm in our present position for constitutionality
and against the *golpista* regime. Only this way could we hold the young
people, where the future lay. We should abandon this course only if the
country appeared on the verge of serious violence.

A CIA man said several Dominican labor leaders wanted to launch a
general strike against the regime. I said I doubted it could succeed,
probably would result in bloodshed, and might provide a pretext for a
harsh military dictatorship. All agreed.

The President said, "They've got to give us something" (in return for
recognition).

"We need a fallback position," Ed Martin said. "We could propose a
slate of PRD people to the Triumvirate and let them choose one as
President, then hold elections in December of 1964," more than a year

away. "The parties should be free to operate. Luna should leave. We should get the Social Christians into the government."

I asked, "What about Wessin y Wessin?"

Martin said he didn't think we could get rid of him—Bosch had fallen trying to.

I said we'd better be sure Bosch would hold still—if he thought we were dumping him, he could make trouble. The President told Dungan to go to Puerto Rico and see Bosch. As we left, the President said, "I'd also like to see a paper from the Ambassador on the most we can get."

Outside, we divided up the work. I'd write the "most-we-can-get" paper and a "talking paper" for Dungan to use with Bosch. Cottrell and Crockett would write the fallback paper suggested by Ed Martin. Dungan said George Walker, the Koppers' executive who had surveyed the former Trujillo industries, was going down soon. Crockett would write a paper for him.

13

Next day the regime suddenly backed off its attack on us—said the "King intervention" incident was closed and spoke of holding Constituent Assembly elections in April or May of 1964 and a presidential election in September, said the PRD could join the provisional government. At least, so the New York *Times* reported. As things turned out, this might have been a better settlement than the one we eventually got; but at the time it seemed inadequate.

The Embassy reported rumors of a counter-*coup* by junior officers but discounted them. The Embassy said our own prestige was never higher with the opposition and the students—we had stuck to our principles. Police broke up a demonstration with tear gas and arrested fifty-one. I thought that if violence spread, one or more of the Triumvirs would surely resign. A Peace Corps boy came home, refusing to work in a country run by *golpistas.* Bonilla Aybar's newspaper, *Prensa Libre,* was denouncing King and Shlaudeman hysterically, calling Shlaudeman an agent of international communism. Several *civicos* and military men reproached our Embassy people, saying, "Don't abandon us—we need you now more than ever." Curious words from the very people who had helped perpetrate the *golpe.*

Ed Martin's Second Position proposed that the Triumvirate add one man to the Triumvirate from a slate of PRD-elected or -appointed officials; broaden the Cabinet to include PRD, Social Christians, and unaligned men, with emphasis on effectiveness; hold elections in December 1964 or sooner; and send Luna abroad.

My "most-we-can-get" paper differed from his in proposing that we make no settlement now at all, probe for a single PRD President or a non-aligned Consejo instead of his Quadrumvirate, talk secretly to a few opposition leaders and encourage demonstrations, and see what we could get.

The "talking paper" for Dungan suggested that he tell Bosch that the statements of the Secretary and the President stood still but that forces were polarizing dangerously and Bosch and we must do nothing to encourage the shedding of innocent blood in a hopeless cause.

Walker, a businessman close to Donny Reid, would explain our problems to the regime—we feared a chain reaction of Latin American military *coups*, important members of Congress were outraged, we did not seek to impose any single solution on the Dominicans but we could not risk *golpes* elsewhere and must insist that the wish of the Dominican people to elect their own rulers be respected.

Dungan left for Puerto Rico, and Walker for the Dominican Republic.

14

Fran and I had exchanged a few letters. As soon as the curfew had been lifted, she had taken the boys out to dig for Indian relics and helped Dan write a paper for school on pre-Columbian pottery. But with the hurricane looming, she had been closed into the dark, shuttered Residence, and had written about all the things that had gone wrong, what we might have done differently—"I'd shut down all these bureaucratic agencies and leave nothing in the country but Americans teaching and working. . . . A little money, a little brains, and a lot of heart." I'd told her, "I'm staying at Arthur's but rarely see him except that we usually ride to work together in the morning. You can imagine what Ed's office has been like especially since Honduras fell. Maybe you can't." Letters from the cold war.

Now Fran and the boys came home to Washington, and we moved into the house of Phil Stern, an old friend from politics and writing. They arrived on Friday, October 18, we talked the weekend through, and during the next week I worked at the Department by day and came home late and talked still later, talked Dominican politics and policy. Such was our obsession.

Fran worried about loose ends in the Republic—dismantling the Dominican art exhibit on the walls of the Residence, sending a chest of medical instruments to Mrs. Bonnelly for use at Santo Domingo's Maternity Hospital; labeling half a hundred fragments of pre-Columbian pottery she'd dug up, and starting an archaeological museum for future students of the Republic's Indian heritage. The three threads, really, running through her life there.

King had told me that after the *golpe,* people had sacked the Little Clinic of Higüey. I hadn't the heart to tell Fran. But she had already known and hadn't the heart to tell me. After I left, Fran had gone several times to Higüey, taking more than a hundred cartons of used clothing that Bev Cass had gotten from the Navy. The carpenter, Colorado Santana, and his wife proposed a rummage sale, with the proceeds going to the Community Center. The Peace Corps kids were enthusiastic. Fran was skeptical because of the political situation. The sale was a disaster. They had run out of clothes, and several hundred enraged women, quickly joined by groups of hostile young men, ransacked the building, tore out the new doors and windows and paneling, and wrecked or stole baby clinic supplies, educational materials, and vocational equipment. Santana managed to save the new ping-pong table and jukebox; Sue Feldman, the Peace Corps nurse, slipped out the back door to bank the money. But everything else—baby scales, medicines, books, tools, vitamins, crochet hooks, yard goods, soap, cabinets—everything they had built and used in all the community projects—was gone. Just so had Dominicans in inchoate rage sacked Trujillo's houses after his fall—then moved into them. Colorado Santana had said simply, "I'll never lift my hand again to help my community."

Now in Washington, Dan and Fred went sight-seeing, went to the Department a time or two, but their heart wasn't in it. Like Fran and me, they felt beaten. They had loved the Republic and wanted to go back. Dan said he'd go back tomorrow, but Fred, two years younger, asked indignantly, "What's the matter with you? Haven't you got any principles?" There was nothing for them to do, and they were missing school. After a week, with no solution in sight, Fran and the boys went home to Highland Park, weeping. There our house was leased; they stayed with friends. I stayed in Washington, working, and moved in with old friends, John Steele, head of the *Time-Life* bureau in Washington, and his wife. They lived in an old house with an attic, and I occupied it, the Ambassador in the Attic, they said.

15

After the strong man with the dagger, Lord Acton says somewhere, comes the little man with the sponge.

Where was the sponge? A month had passed since the *golpe.* All our efforts had produced nothing. My original hope for a reversal of the *golpe* was gone. So was virtually all hope for Casasnovas and constitutionality. Bosch had told Dungan firmly that the military must be defeated and constitutionality restored, and had indicated he might encourage a strike. But the police were in control; no party could stage successful strikes or demonstrations. True, our firm stand had prevented the Castro/Communists from collecting all opposition. But the situation was deadlocked. Where did we go from here?

Despite all effort, the mighty United States had been unable to save Bosch. Now we could not budge the men who overthrew him. This did not become clear all at once. Rather, little by little we retreated. Little by little we fell back from position to position. One by one we gave up our objectives, until we were left with almost nothing.

Thus our Second Position, modified from Ed Martin's draft in many meetings and drafting sessions and cabled to the Embassy for its comment on October 21, declared constitutionality unattainable, said the Triumvirate had maintained public order, the military seemed united, our frozen position might make negotiation impossible, and so perhaps we now should make our second move—try to broaden the regime to include PRDistas, Social Christians, and neutrals; get elections by December 1964; get rid of Luna.

The Embassy replied it wanted to narrow, not broaden, the Cabinet. It doubted that the Triumvirate itself could be broadened to include PRDistas—probably only Antonio Guzmán would be acceptable to the regime, and probably he would refuse. The regime opposed one-shot winner-take-all elections because it feared another "demagogue" like Bosch would sweep the country.

On October 24, a month after the *golpe,* we cabled the Second Position to the Embassy for action. This scenario abandoned entirely the idea of constitutionality and nearly abandoned the idea of getting rid of the military *golpistas.* For we felt that time was no longer on our side. We instructed King not to go first to the regime, but rather to the PRD and Social Christians—to tell them that prolonged delay might bring severe military repression; that we had nothing to insist on, hoped the Dominicans could find an answer, but we were thinking about the regime's inviting the OAS to the Republic to observe its government, about its holding elections in a year, about its reconstituting the Triumvirate to make it less *civico* dominated and the Cabinet to make it less party dominated, about getting rid of Luna and working toward the goals of the *Alianza.* If the PRD and Social Christians did not turn these ideas down flatly, King would send them to the Triumvirate indirectly.

It was a soft position. It was so soft it might succeed—but would make Secretary Rusk eat his original tough statement. (Someone had said earlier that the Secretary might have to exist largely on a diet of statements.) And even before we sent it, it had almost been "overtaken by events," as the Department phrase goes, for the Social Christians and PRDistas already had refused to enter the regime. They now made counterproposals to King. So King found himself negotiating not with the regime but with its opposition, and a divided opposition at that, surely a fruitless enterprise. And messages began coming in saying that the military was divided, Chagito Rodríguez Echavarría was in the Republic stirring up trouble on behalf of his brother Rodríguez Echavarría, and the 14th of June was preparing to go to the hills. Severo Cabral warned that further mass demonstrations in the Republic would provoke "annihilation without contemplation."

16

I thought we should stop seeking solutions through the political parties or the Triumvirate and instead deal directly with the military, which was after all the real power. Perhaps we could persuade them to get rid of the parties. Perhaps we could even pick a military man not in the inner circle and encourage him to mount a counter-*golpe*. Or perhaps they would accept a Bishop as provisional President.

And so on—we kept falling back to a Third Position, then a revised Third Position, then a Fourth Position, then a revised Fourth Position— it was all so complex we had to keep a flow sheet. Each time the grinding machinery followed the same pattern. Down on the third floor in our sterile offices Kennedy Crockett or I would get an idea, write drafts, exchange drafts, rewrite them, discuss and modify them, rewrite again, then take them up to the sixth floor and propose them to Cottrell. More redrafting, more discussion; then we would talk to Ed Martin. We would go back downstairs, rewrite the paper, take it back up, argue for it, get it cleared in principle, go back downstairs, polish it, have it typed as a cable, take it back up to Cottrell, then take it to Martin and usually Dungan and sometimes George Ball, defend it, argue for it, go over it sentence by sentence, word by word, sometimes rewrite it and rewrite it again, and finally send it to the Embassy—but for comment only. The Embassy would comment. And the whole process would start anew. Finally it would go out as a policy instruction for action. By that time parts of it would have been overtaken by events. For all this time things were happening in the Republic, and in Washington too. I felt we were becoming increasingly remote from reality. Both Dominican and American reality, sealed off in our sterile cubicles in the massive Department. How far away we had moved from the gray people at Vicente Noble!

We tried everything. Secretly I met Miolán, who looked curiously out of place in a Washington office. Secretly Crockett met with Bonilla Atiles. The regime sent emissaries and secretly we saw them. We called King home—President Kennedy wanted to gauge him personally and I took him to the White House to see the President. The Papal Nuncio sent word to me from Rome by way of the Apostolic Delegate in Washington that he was concerned about the situation, wanted to know our position, and wanted to work closely with us. We talked to journalists, Latin American diplomats, U. S. Senators and Congressmen. We kept in touch with Bosch. We sent Colonel Simmons, the former attaché who had braved Petán's machine gun, up to New York to talk to his friend Rodríguez Echavarría, then down to the Republic to talk to the Dominican military. The White House sent other unofficial emissaries. We had detailed analyses made of the regime's economic situation, including its sugar crop and quota—how much economic leverage did we have?

Day after day the machinery ground on—idea, draft, rewrite, argue; upstairs, argue; downstairs, rewrite; type as cable in quintuplicate, wait upstairs for clearance signatures, distribute copies, send; await Embassy comment; dissect comment, discuss again, rewrite as paper, argue, rewrite; type as cable in quintuplicate, wait for clearance signatures, distribute copies, send for action; await results. None. Or worse. The machinery ground on.

Nothing succeeded. Our every effort failed. The regime was unyielding. The Triumvirate by now felt its prestige committed—and felt the military's guns at its back. We were blocked at every turn. Here were limits of American power.

The Dominican regime had only to sit tight, maintain control, and wait. We on the other hand were being pushed hard to settle. Many things pushed us. We feared a collapse of the Triumvirate might bring a reversion to a military dictatorship. We feared a leftist Castro/Communist guerrilla rising. We feared that our firm stand might encourage non-Communist young people to rise and fight and die, only to have us recognize later anyway. We feared that if we continued to hold firm, then were forced to capitulate, we would have suffered a major diplomatic defeat. Moreover, other nations were pressing us—they wanted to recognize. We held them as long as we could, but Great Britain recognized after about a month, an extraordinarily long period for her. (But she did stop the sale of the Hawker Hunters.) France, West Germany, and Italy quickly recognized. Honduras and Nicaragua recognized and though these bothered us little, others would bother us much. To continue to oppose the regime looked quixotic. And we had to consider Honduras too. Several Congressmen and editorial writers began to speak out for recognition.

Worst of all, perhaps, was the pressure of the vacuum. Down there, the people were silent. Up here, Congress turned its attention to other matters. So did the U.S. press. So did the White House. The crisis in Vietnam was deepening, soon the Diem regime would fall bloodily, and our frustrations there overrode our frustrations, remarkably similar, in the Dominican Republic. History was moving. I began to feel that the United States' relations with the Dominican Republic, and I, were in danger of being left behind. No more phones rang, meetings were fewer. In crisis, as when Bosch or Trujillo fell, the Republic claimed tense attention. Between times—well, there are other things to worry about.

At a press conference on November 14, President Kennedy seemed to back off a little from constitutionality and to indicate we might settle for assurances that the regime would hold free elections within a year. Indeed that was about the position to which we had by then been reduced.

Inevitably, I suppose, the strains of policy frustration produced personal strains among us. We all had ties to each other from the past—Martin and Ball had gone to college together, Ball and I had campaigned together for Adlai Stevenson, Martin and I had worked together throughout most of my tenure, the President respected Martin but I believe had no personal relationship with him, the President had known me throughout his campaign. And so on—we all had ties but also differences. Martin was abstemious, tough-minded, unshakable, a little like a tank moving down a road; but criticism of his *Herald Tribune* article had made him edgy, and so had all the mounting problems of Latin America—and no wonder. And I was edgy too—I'd lost a government. Once during a meeting, I proposed a gambit, and Martin dismissed it out of hand; once he told me I need not come to a meeting with the President. I was offended, and sulked, staying in my third-floor office for a couple of weeks, sending papers up to his office by messenger, until a sixth-floor emissary inquired indirectly whether I was angry. It was all foolish, all inevitable.

From the ancient past came an echo: Our intelligence agencies reported that the documents on the Castillo de Aza affair were forgeries. Had Bosch known it? Probably not. Probably Castillo de Aza had simply been trying to collect money from various people. It had all been unreal. So seemed my own days now. Instead of arriving early and working till 10 P.M. or later, I came in around nine, read the paper, read the cables (fewer now), and left at six. Once more, instead of a bustling, purposeful place, the Department resembled an immaculate hospital never used—long empty corridors, rooms with empty desks, a locked ward.

It seems to me it was always cold and wet in Washington that fall. Some mornings the wind whipped and rain froze when I walked down the long hill from the Steeles' house to Connecticut Avenue and stood shivering as the rush-hour cars rolled by, waiting, taxi after taxi passing loaded, splashing dirty mud and water at the curb; then one would stop, though already crowded as a *público* and turn fast onto Rock Creek Parkway, the grass brown, the black trees bare, nothing moving in the wood, only traffic on the black asphalt; and I would pay the driver at the corner and get out and hurry into the blocky State Department, glancing up—clouds low, no planes flying today, airport closed—and step aside while clerks and typists and desk officers hurried by; go to the soft-lit automatic elevator, girls already carrying trays of paper cups of coffee, and a warning bell, silent elevator doors closing, up without feel of movement, off at the third floor with strangers, nobody I knew, and find my way down the empty corridors. I felt an exile in my own country.

Chapter Twenty-six

OVERTAKEN BY EVENTS

To get away for a few days, I went to New York the weekend of November 15, saw Adlai Stevenson and other friends, and went to the theater. Returning on Sunday, I tried to think where we stood. We were rapidly approaching, if indeed we had not already reached, a choice between two bad alternatives: Dig in for the winter or longer, simply refusing recognition; or recognize virtually on the regime's own terms.

Pressures undoubtedly would increase to recognize and get it over with. But I wanted to make one last try. Some of our difficulties had arisen because communication had broken down between us and the Dominicans. To re-establish them, I wanted to see former President Bonnelly myself. He had told King he had not taken part in the *golpe* and was not entirely happy with it. He and I had gone through a good deal together. Perhaps we could work something out.

By now we would settle for free elections in 1964 and a revision of the Cabinet to represent all the people. Perhaps if I could see Bonnelly, I could get an additional face-saver, such as the ouster of Luna. (Nobody was even talking any more about getting rid of Wessin.)

Events urged speed. We were receiving more reports that guerrilla activity was about to begin, or was actually beginning. Sporadic bombings occurred in the capital, so did minor strikes, and one night the locks on the stores in Calle Conde were filled with molten metal. The regime had invited Ambassador Goytía of Panama, head of the 1963 OAS Commission, and Peter Nehemkis, an American businessman friendly to Donny Reid and Bonilla Atiles, to go to the Republic "unofficially" to recommend a timetable for elections. The regime hoped to gain some color of legitimacy—but this would make our own negotiations more difficult. I wanted to try Bonnelly first.

2

It had not been a good year for President Kennedy, probably his worst, as many Presidents' third year seems to be the worst. He had been unable to get his civil rights bill and his tax cut bill through Congress. Congress was chopping his foreign aid bill to pieces. He had slipped from his high point in 1962, the time of the Cuban missile crisis. The Alliance for Progress "is in a state of crisis," the New York *Times* said that Sunday. Next day, Monday, November 18, President Kennedy, starting a southern and southwestern trip in Miami Beach, powerfully defended the Alliance. In words that might have been addressed directly to the Dominican Republic, he said, "Political democracy and stability is at the core of our hopes for the future. There can be no progress and stability if people do not have hope for a better life tomorrow. That faith is undermined when men seek the reins of power and ignore the restraints of constitutional procedures. They may even do so out of a sincere desire to benefit their own country. But democratic governments demand that those in opposition accept the defects of today and work toward remedying them within the machinery of peaceful change. Otherwise, in return for momentary satisfaction, we tear apart the fabric and the hope of lasting democracy."

3

A Puerto Rican source said Bordas, Miolán, and Casasnovas were trying to raise fifty thousand dollars for a general strike. A bomb exploded in the home of a rightist leader in Santo Domingo. Four "guerrillas" were arrested near San Juan de la Maguana. Political activity had collapsed—Casasnovas had been deported, leaving no rallying point. Donny Reid was anxious for reconciliation with us. Uneasiness prevailed.

On Monday I drafted my Bonnelly proposal.

Its objectives were as before—free elections in 1964, a broader interim Cabinet, and, if possible, the removal of Luna.

But I would attempt it by meeting secretly with Bonnelly about Thanksgiving, somewhere outside the Dominican Republic.

We had been sounding like a broken record. What I wanted to say was something like "Look, Mr. President, you're a constitutional lawyer. Let's go to the heart of the Dominican problem." Then I would propose to him a whole new constitutional scheme—a referendum on a "new" Constitution containing something for everyone.

Under this plan, the Triumvirate would order the Electoral Board to prepare immediately, and in secret, and preferably with OAS technical help, a new Constitution, with a thirty-day deadline. A popular referendum would be held on the new Constitution thirty days after it was drafted. If the vote was "yes" the new Constitution would be in force and we would grant recognition immediately—the referendum would be a popular mandate justifying our recognition. The Constitution would be so drawn as to encourage all parties to work for a "yes" vote. To make the PRD and Social Christians want it, it would contain a preamble committing the Republic to social justice and economic progress and political freedom, and it would provide for free elections in 1964. To quiet the regime's fear of a winner-take-all election, the Constitution would separate congressional and presidential elections. To quiet their fear of a four-year untrammeled reign of a "demagogue" or a "do-nothing" President, the Constitution would provide that at the end of his first year in office, the President must face an automatic referendum on the question, "Do you approve of the way the President is doing his job?" If the answer was "no," he must schedule a new election within thirty days and could not be a candidate himself. If the answer was "yes," he would continue two more years then face another referendum. His term would end after five years. Such a provision, I believed, would provide a constitutional alternative to the unconstitutional military *coup d'état*. It might have grounded the military lightning that struck down Bosch—if I could have told the military in September that they need not overthrow him, for the people would vote him out in referendum in February, they might have desisted. Moreover, every politician in the Republic would favor the provision, because it would give him a second chance. So the prospects for a "yes" vote on the Constitution seemed good.

To assure the PRD and Social Christians that elections would actually occur, the new Constitution would contain a firm election timetable. But neither they nor the Triumvirate wanted elections soon—neither was sure of winning. So I worked out a timetable that was rather protracted and contained enough flexibility to avoid crises if deadlines could not be met. The entire process would be completed late in 1964 or early in 1965.[1]

---

[1] It may be argued that if a President must face a popular referendum on how well he is doing his job after his first and third years in office, nothing but political chaos could result. But chaos is what we had anyway. This was an attempt to institutionalize political instability. In the past, political instability had arisen from two principal sources: The impatience of the people, and the refusal of defeated politicians to accept electoral defeat. The politicians could usually enlist the aid of the military. A rigid four-year presidential term imposed an unacceptably long presidency on irreconcilable losers and impatient people. This proposal attempted to adapt constitutionalism to Dominican conditions. It provided a constitutional alternative to the unconstitutional military *golpe*—a safety valve. It would substitute a people's veto for the military veto. It amounted to "more democracy." I also considered limiting congressional power severely so that the President's authority would match his periodic accountability to the people. That accountability to the people, not to the military, was the heart of the system. Granted, the system would make long-term planning all but impossible, would reward popular, hasty, and ir-

To succeed, this idea must appear to originate in the Republic, not in Washington, though the Dominicans must understand that if the first referendum on the new Constitution itself was "yes," we would recognize immediately. The best man to bring forth the idea, I thought, was Bonnelly.

Crockett and I drafted and redrafted the paper on Tuesday. We took it upstairs to Cottrell that night. He rather liked it and would recommend it to Ed Martin the next day.

Late in the afternoon on Wednesday, Crockett said the Honduran *golpista* regime had proposed an election plan that we probably would accept. We called Ed Martin and asked him to hurry his decision on the Bonnelly paper—we didn't want the Hondurans to beat the Dominicans. Martin thought our recognizing Honduras might help soften up the Dominicans. I thought the opposite—the Dominicans would say we were "discriminating" against them. We reached no decision on the Bonnelly plan. As the reader must know by now, the record is made on the cables, the historical record, and Department officials are loathe to sign a cable that some day might look ill-advised, too interventionist, or otherwise objectionable. Hence caution, hence delay; thus are new ideas smothered, maneuvers overtaken by events.

4

On that Wednesday, November 20, or possibly a day earlier, Ethel Kennedy, the wife of Attorney General Robert Kennedy, called to invite me to a surprise birthday party for Bob that night.

The party was big and gay and noisy. The President was not there—had left town, as I have said, for a speaking trip in the South and Southwest. But old friends from the campaign were, Kenny O'Donnell and Steve Smith, the President's brother-in-law, and while most of the guests danced the twist, we talked about the coming 1964 campaign.

I had known Bob since the 1956 political campaign, when he had ridden with us on the Stevenson campaign plane. When Bob became counsel to the Senate rackets committee, I saw him often, for I was writing a series of magazine articles on the committee's pursuit of Jimmy Hoffa, president of the Teamsters' Union. I came to know Bob well, and to like and admire him greatly, and Ethel, too. At that time, as I recall it,

---

responsible measures. But these evils existed anyway. I would expect three or four or even more years of one-year presidencies—presidents turned out of office each year by an impatient people aroused by defeated politicians. True, the people, or the military, might grow weary of so much "democracy." But on the other hand they might, with practice, learn something of responsibility—and so might their candidates.

Bob arranged for me to meet his brother, the then Senator John F. Kennedy, and we had breakfast together in New York, talking about the political prospects for 1960. He wanted to know what I thought the issues were and how he could break into the stronghold of the intellectuals that Stevenson seemed to have captured. Then he went off with a friend on a cold bright noonday to a football game, looking incredibly young and healthy. A little later, after I had finished my articles, I had dinner with him and his wife, Jacqueline, and Bob and Ethel in Washington. At about that time—by then it was early 1960—Bob Kennedy asked if I would work on speeches for his brother during the 1960 campaign, including the primaries. In other words, immediately.

I couldn't. I was for his brother. But Adlai Stevenson had not yet taken himself out of the running for the 1960 nomination, I had known Stevenson for many years in Illinois, had worked for him in two campaigns, and while I was opposed to his running a third time in 1960 and had told him so, I did not feel free to work for anybody else until he took himself out. The Kennedys understood. Almost immediately after his brother won the Democratic nomination, he asked me to go to work in the campaign, and I did, traveling with John Kennedy around the country, sometimes riding the campaign plane, sometimes going out alone ahead of it to talk to people and discover the issues and write speech drafts. Ted Sorensen and Dick Goodwin were on the campaign plane all fall.

During the stress of a campaign, whistlestopping by bus or train or plane, sometimes making a dozen speeches a day, you get to know a man well. John Kennedy was not merely as good as I had hoped; he was infinitely better. He made the big decisions himself, made them fast, and made them right—to debate Nixon on television, to speak before the Houston ministers on his Catholicism, to telephone Martin Luther King's wife while King was in jail. It was a tough and expert campaign—as people said during the convention, "Those Kennedys play with a hard ball." And as somebody else said, "They only throw you the ball once. If you drop it, that's it." The candidate wasted no time, was impatient when someone took fifteen minutes to say what could be said in a sentence. Yet he was a deeply thoughtful, deeply compassionate, deeply human man, and very funny, all qualities which seemed to flourish after he reached the White House. As I have said, he had a way of making you feel you were better than you knew. And all the while I was his Ambassador, I had him in the back of my mind. As a writer, I always had had, while writing, someone in mind who was looking over my shoulder. For many years it was Frederick Lewis Allen, my first editor at *Harper's*. As an Ambassador, whatever I did, I had in mind President Kennedy looking over my shoulder. What would *he* do, what would *he* say, what would *he* think?

Because of him, Washington seemed to me during those years more than the capital of the United States; it seemed the most exciting and interesting place on earth, and when you went back to the Caribbean, you took a little of the glow with you.

5

Thursday morning Crockett and I decided to make an all-out effort to get Ed Martin's approval of the Bonnelly plan. With Cottrell, we went in to see Martin at ten-thirty. I wanted to cable the entire plan to King. Martin balked. We finally compromised and sent a cable simply instructing King to tell Bonnelly that I wanted to meet him somewhere outside the Dominican Republic urgently and privately—we suggested several places—to discuss new ideas we had. No one must know of the meeting in advance. We hoped we could meet this weekend.

This was our Fifth Position. It almost amounted to a rout. We had been driven to it. This would be, really, our last effort. I was counting on my personal relationship with Bonnelly. I wanted Joe Fandino to go with me—he would have a good effect on Bonnelly—and, with some difficulty, arranged to break him loose temporarily from his post in Toronto.

King sent a top-priority cable from the Republic. He was dubious about my mission, and feared Bonnelly would tell Reid and Tapia about it.

Crockett and I went back up to Cottrell and Ed Martin and sent a cable overriding King, telling him to see Bonnelly immediately. By now it was 5 P.M.

We waited. A routine cable came in saying that a bomb had gone off the previous night at Viriato Fiallo's house. We waited. John Crimmins was giving a party that night for an ARA (American Republics Area) secretary who was getting married, and invited me. Schlesinger called, inviting me to a movie at the White House. I went to Crimmins' party briefly, then to the White House, taking with me an ARA girl I knew. The movie was in the projection room in the East Wing near the swimming pool. This fall I'd seen other movies here. The one I remember most vividly was a documentary made by USIA called "Four Cities in June," which had shown President Kennedy delivering his speech at the Berlin Wall, a determined young man pacing the platform in the sunlight like a young lion, and, behind him, the gray, grim emptiness of East Berlin beyond the Wall, one of the most thrilling political scenes I ever witnessed. Tonight's movie was a James Bond thriller. *From Russia with Love.* Ted Sorensen was there, as I recall it, and others on the White House staff and in the Administration. (It was a joke that *real* insiders, when invited to the White House to see a movie, asked "What's playing?") The President's chair up front was empty, a white blanket with his initials on it lying loosely over it. He was in Texas.

When the lights went up, an usher called my name. Cottrell had telephoned. King had cabled that Bonnelly's first reaction was favorable but he wanted to think it over till morning.

Walking across Lafayette Park in the cool crisp autumn night, I felt excited. Tomorrow might be decisive—if Bonnelly heard about the Honduras settlement first, he wouldn't come and might denounce the United States and me. But if I could meet him quickly, I'd get a settlement, I felt sure. Now it was a matter of hours. Across the park from the White House I stopped for a drink at the Hay-Adams Hotel, where I usually stayed when I was in Washington, then went home to the Steeles', unable to sleep, thinking of things to say to Bonnelly.

6

Friday morning, November 22, 1963. A cable came in early: Bonnelly would not meet me without consulting the Triumvirate and Donny Reid. Back up to Cottrell and Ed Martin; all right, let him consult, what could we lose? We sent the cable. And waited. Ethel Kennedy sent my topcoat—I'd left it at their house. A young Harvard student writing a paper on the Republic came to my office, and while we talked, calls kept coming in, arrangements for my trip to meet Bonnelly—there was an air of expectancy. The student left. I didn't want to go out to lunch, afraid I'd miss a cable. Eating lunch at my desk I assembled papers I'd need with Bonnelly. Finished, restless, I was pacing in the outer office where the typists worked, when Bob Sayre came in and said, at 1:50 P.M., "Mr. Ambassador, the President was shot in Dallas. They got Connally too."

I did not believe it.

I went back to my office and called John Steele. He said it was true.

I said, "He isn't dead, is he?"

"They don't know yet. He's bleeding from the head. The car drove off. He's still alive. They think."

I sat a minute. The sun was bright outside. I called Ethel Kennedy to ask if I could help her. Whoever answered said she was not taking any calls. I knew then: He must be dead. I still didn't believe it. I called Ralph Dungan to offer to help him. His secretary was trying desperately to get him at the Chilean Embassy. I offered to go get him. She'd already sent someone else.

Somebody said Ed Martin had a radio. I went up to his office and listened with the others. At two-forty the radio said the President was dead.

I left. And went downstairs and called Fran. She knew.

I must have spent the rest of the afternoon wandering around the Department. Somebody asked about Bonnelly. Who cared? Ed Martin held a staff meeting. I did not go. Word came that everybody could go home.

A high-ranking career officer asked if the Latin American Policy Committee meeting was still scheduled, and I had to explain to him twice that it was canceled.

I sat staring out the window. In the sunlight the flags went down to half-mast. It had happened in Dallas. I remembered thinking: One shithead with a squirrel rifle can change the fate of mankind. I was afraid. I knew what President Kennedy had done about the Cuban missile crisis. I did not know what someone else might have done. I was afraid. People were wandering in and out of the long corridors, the offices. Somebody remembered that Adlai Stevenson had been spat on a few weeks ago, in Dallas. Lyndon Johnson, running for Vice President in 1960, had been roughed up, and so had his wife, in Dallas. I knew Dallas myself, and hated it—money, oil, hate, money. I wandered into Crockett's office. He was holding a staff meeting, passing on Ed Martin's instruction that the desk officers prepare a list for the Secretary to give to President Johnson—President Johnson! how strange it sounded!—of what problems were most urgent, what could be delayed. I also remember he said, "The Latin Americans are talking about making the Alliance for Progress a monument to President Kennedy." I got up and almost ran from the room. It was the first time I had wept.

In my office I just sat looking out the window at the low American flag, unable to think, numb. I called Schlesinger's home. Marian, his wife, was alone, and asked me to come over in a little while. I would. The Bonnelly papers were on my desk, and, staring at them, I thought I would not go, nor would he, it was over, but something had to be done, what? Maybe King could talk to him. I started writing a telegram telling King to say to Bonnelly what I would have said. Crockett came in and we finished it, and took it upstairs and left it.

Outside, it was getting dark, raining hard. I started to walk, hunting a cab. A car pulled alongside me at a corner, Bob Sayre, who took me to Schlesinger's house. There was a note for me on the door. It said something like, "This is an upset household, forgive us if we'd rather be alone." I left the note in place and walked down the steps and down O Street in the rain and stood awhile at the corner of Wisconsin, then a cab came along, and I went home to the Steeles'.

It was still raining. We sat. I kept thinking of the President. Of talking to him one night about a speech during the 1960 campaign, it was in Chicago, almost the last night of the campaign, and he had been taking a bath while we talked; he wanted me to go on to Boston and Hyannis Port for the windup. Of how tall he was, his vigor, how he made you hope; all, now stilled. The poor people. The poor country.

I went upstairs to the attic and went to bed. Far away, sirens seemed to scream all night.

7

A telegram from Robert Kennedy wakened me early Saturday morning, saying I should go to the White House between 2 and 5:30 P.M. The Department called and said I should go between eleven and two. Later it called back and said between twelve and two. Louise Steele drove me down Connecticut Avenue to the Hay-Adams at eleven-thirty. It was rainy, dark, foggy, a cold, wet day. I waited a few minutes at the hotel, then walked across Lafayette Park in the rain to the White House main gate. Others were arriving in long black limousines, the terrible long black limousines that come to the side door in time of crisis, now to the front door in time of death. I walked up the curving driveway, alone, wet, and went inside and on red carpets to the East Room where the President's body lay in state with an honor guard. An old man and his wife were ahead of me; I waited till they passed on, then went in and stood by the flag-draped casket alone, and said I was sorry and thanked him, as once I had when Fran's mother died, and felt some vague stirring to ask God to help him and us all, then went out of the room, the honor guard changing slowly, too.

Downstairs on my way out I saw Clayton Fritchey, a friend from the 1956 campaign, now with Adlai Stevenson at the United Nations. He was waiting for the Averell Harrimans. They offered me a ride. Mrs. Harriman was crying and because I was beside her I held her hand. It was something I could do. Harriman told Fritchey to get Ted Sorensen to work on President Johnson's eulogy to President Kennedy, and asked me to work on one for Stevenson. Harriman and I got out at the Department and he asked me to go up to his office with him, lonely, too, I guess, and we went and talked a long time, mostly about the Dominican Republic and the Alliance. He wanted me to think about the Alliance for him and help him—"I should pay more attention to Latin America, I don't know what we ought to be doing, why do I have the impression that we are using it for our own purposes?" and then, "When you go back to the Dominican Republic, you should think about this too." I told him I didn't think I'd be going back. He asked sharply why not. I said it wasn't customary; he brushed that aside impatiently. I said I had no heart for it, now; he said I had to, as a matter of duty, I knew more about it than anybody else. I said I didn't know that President Johnson would want me to; and we fell to talking about the future, where our country now might head. He is a great man, tough, principled, with the highest sense of duty and purpose.

Leaving, I ran into Ed Martin and said I intended to resign that day. He said I couldn't, President Johnson had asked that no Ambassadors resign. I said I'd stay a few days then I'd like to go home for Thanksgiving, and he said of course, the time pressure was off now anyway, for the Honduran election offer had fallen short of what we had expected. The Department had set up a special office to "coordinate all activities connected with" visiting dignitaries coming to President Kennedy's funeral. Necessary, of course; hideous, too. I went down to Crimmins' office, and talked a little, and tried to write something for Stevenson about President Kennedy but I couldn't write yet, then went to Harriman's house in Georgetown, hoping that talking to Fritchey would help get me started.

We put together a draft for Stevenson, though it wasn't very good. We went downstairs and had a drink with Mrs. Harriman and George Backer, a New York Democrat who had come down to the Dominican Republic for Bosch's inauguration. But it wasn't any good, they didn't help me, and I couldn't help them, we didn't know each other well enough, so I went around to the Schlesingers' house. Marian was there looking withdrawn, and their four children, and some friends from Boston, Governor Peabody of Massachusetts and others. Schlesinger came home, looking awful; he had worked till 5 A.M., then talked to Dick Goodwin till seventhirty, then worked all day, and he was disturbed about President Johnson's first speech to Congress—some wanted it to be a tough speech arguing for a tax cut, others urged a reaffirmation of liberal principles, and they had quarreled. Another couple arrived, then "Pepe" Figueres and Ambassador Facio of Costa Rica, and we had a drink, talked in a desultory way, a little talk, long silences, staring at the dying fire.

8

Sunday was bright and cold and clear, and I slept late, and after breakfast was told of a sudden the assassin had himself been shot. So came the final nightmare. The television screen had become a mirror of madness. Our country was terribly hurt. How could we lead the world? Latin Americans changed governments by assassination; the power transfer in Russia was fearsome and bloody. But we?

Until now, I had not really thought about what had happened as a crime. Now, after the second murder, I did. As a writer, over the years I had spent much time in prisons and jails, talking to teen-age rebels who killed for no discernible reason, studying their crimes and lives, rummaging in the useless files of poor school records, warning signs from truant officers and "guidance directors" and psychologists and psychiatrists, reports of first arrests and probations, all unheeded; and I had visited the homes of their stricken parents, their teachers and wardens; and over the years too I had been around police stations and criminal courts enough to know their tawdry hangers-on, the bail bondsmen and prostitutes and bootleggers and fixers and gamblers, a sordid world. Now it had all come fearsomely together—the great President, the young punk prating of Castro, and this final horror, a strip-tease owner hanging around the dirty police station in Dallas, Texas.

Soon in Washington, already perhaps, a sordid struggle for power would begin. I wanted none of it. I was going home, as soon as I could. Already the obituaries, the recollections of others, were beginning to distort the President Kennedy I had known. Three things were getting lost —his humor; his toughness; the hard, bright clarity of his mind.

He had said funny things that were outrageous, often mocking his own earnest beliefs and serious purpose. And he had been tough, had understood power. True, he had, as everyone said, used it with grace. But he had used it fearlessly; wisely, but relentlessly even. He was a moderate and temperate man in public policy, except once on steel and near the end on civil rights; he had not aroused bitter hatred as had Roosevelt and Truman. Nonetheless, he had used his power. And in this nuclear age he had possessed the power to destroy the earth, had been put in a seat almost godlike, not a seat for man. He had not abused that power. He had striven, desperately and successfully, to forswear it—by building conventional forces to keep wars small, by leashing himself in the Cuban missile crisis. But the power he had.

9

Monday came, and the President was buried. I walked down in the brilliant sun from the Department to Constitution Avenue where Henry Bacon Drive runs off on a slant to the Lincoln Memorial and the bridge to Arlington; stood in the crowd behind a rope and watched and waited, and soon the procession came, slowly, so slowly, the terrible black and muffled drums. A Negro woman beside me held her child higher and higher so he could see, and I stepped back to make a place for her, as though she were a member of the family. In a way, she was.

So it ended. I wrote some notes to his family, his staff. There was nothing more to do. I kept asking the unanswerable: Why? Days passed, it got worse, not better. Among the tributes to the President then being published, one quoted Mrs. Kennedy as referring to the musical play, *Camelot*. In a sense, there had indeed been a magic, a Camelot, a princess-and-pumpkin air to the Kennedy years. And to all our lives. There is a certain fairy-tale quality to all political office. In an instant, it disappears, as sun burns morning fog. President Kennedy had somehow enhanced the fairy tale, increased it, lit, as he had promised, a White House glow that suffused the world. While he lived, it had not been a fairy tale. It had been real. Cervantes makes Don Quixote say, "Sancho, my friend, you may know that I was born, by Heaven's will, in this our age of iron, to revive what is known as the Golden Age." So had President Kennedy. But now it was over, our age was iron again.

10

President Johnson had announced he would address Latin American diplomats, together with U. S. State and AID officials, and United States Ambassadors to OAS countries who happened to be in town, at the White House at 3 P.M. on Tuesday. I went, the first time I had been in the White House since Saturday, in the East Room with President Kennedy's body. Scores of Latin American diplomats were milling around in a lower lobby, smiling, chattering, shaking hands, embracing. I stood aside. Did they know the world had changed? Bonilla Atiles was moving from one to another, voluble, smiling; seeing me, his face switched masks, became grave; I could not but remember his solemn mien and comic whisper at the dreadful funeral of the father of Marcio Mejía Ricart. We shook hands, spoke briefly, I drifted away, finally found Dave Bell, the AID director, a friend since the campaign of 1952, writing speeches for Stevenson in the Elks Club in Springfield; and he and I went off to one side and stood together at the edge of the room, not talking much, just standing together. Ralph Dungan joined us, quiet, too. Secretary Rusk passed by, asked if there was any sign of movement in the Republic, I said yes, we were trying to clear a cable that we hoped would give us an opening, he nodded and almost without stopping passed on, doing his work. Bell and Dungan and I stood apart and waited.

Ushers and protocol officers showed us the way up to the East Room, again the East Room. In the semicircle of small gold chairs, we Americans found space at the rear, Bell, Dungan, Schlesinger, Moscoso, others, and I, while the Latin Americans sat up front, all waiting for the President. He did not come in first. Jacqueline Kennedy did. I gasped, and so did Bell, and all stood. She was in black, she walked slowly but firmly up the aisle, and stood and turned to face us, on her face a fixed half smile, Mrs. Johnson walking behind her then standing beside her; then the new President came in, tall, serious of mien. The ladies sat, so did we, President Johnson spoke.

He reaffirmed his dedication to President Kennedy's policy in Latin America and the Alliance for Progress. Then Alberto Lleras Camargo, former President of Colombia, spoke. Then all rose, and Mrs. Kennedy and Mrs. Johnson started shaking hands with the Latin Americans, and so did the President; the two women left, and President Johnson and Secretary Rusk went to the door to shake hands with all as they departed.

I walked back to the Department. They still were tearing down some buildings near it, a towering crane swinging an iron ball at broken concrete and twisted steel. The work had been going on all fall. I remembered noticing the day the President was killed a steam shovel left standing in the excavation, its bucket half raised, as though the man who ran it had heard the news and simply shut off the engine and climbed down and gone home.

Crockett and I waited until six-thirty for Ed Martin. He rejected our cable with asperity. We had no business telling the Dominicans how to write their Constitution, he wanted to wait to find out what Goytía and Nehemkis had done, he didn't see anything important in a message from the Nuncio that now was the time to move. I tried to explain. He wouldn't listen. Crockett supported me. Martin listened but overrode him. I said I didn't know Nehemkis was even in the Republic—when I last had hear of him, I had told him not to go. Martin asked why the hell I had done that? Because Dungan had told me to, I said. (Actually, Crockett, Cottrell, Dungan, and I had all agreed he ought not go.) Martin said, angrily, "Dungan's not the boss." I gave up. Crockett tried to salvage something. In the end, they patched together an innocuous cable asking the Embassy what it thought of the Nuncio's view and what it thought the Triumvirate would propose if we asked them to propose something. It was, I thought, a stall—Martin didn't want to move till he saw which way the new President wanted to go. How could President Johnson be expected to know what ought to be done in the Dominican Republic? It was our duty to advise him, I thought, to move, not to stall and play it safe.

Because the record is written in cables, and Ed Martin did not want to put in writing a proposal to rewrite the Dominican Constitution, I had been allowed to send only half the cable on Bonnelly, so King had never known everything I wanted to say to Bonnelly. Now for a similar reason—Ed Martin didn't know President Johnson's views—we could not send a cable telling King that we were ready to settle for what we had. So King went plodding ahead trying to win concessions we had long since abandoned.

I left the meeting, left the building, and next day went home to Illinois for Thanksgiving. It was over for me, for now at least.

11

When I arrived home I found calls from Crockett and Dungan. The Dominicans had come up with an election timetable—a series of separate elections for local officials, a Constituent Assembly, Congress, and President, culminating in a presidential election on August 16, 1965. The first election would constitute a registration for subsequent ones. Dungan and Crockett wanted to know what I thought. It was Bonilla Atiles' old idea—building democracy from the grass roots, he would say; controlling the machinery of power, I would say. Probably it was the best we could get now. But we must be sure the registration provision was not a device to rig the election.

Fran had retrieved our house. Dan had lettered a sign and put it on my desk: "Ask not what your country can do for you—ask what you can do for your country." Dan had decided he wanted to become President. I talked to Fran and Dan and Fred, trying to explain why we were not going back to the Republic. Not now, anyway. Maybe some day, as private citizens. Not now. I wanted to get out of government, to think, to write, to be with them and live privately and quietly, to leave Washington for a while. I would go back briefly after Thanksgiving, see things through to recognition, resign, come home and buy some property far out in the woods in Michigan, maybe go there for Christmas vacation. But the Dominican Republic, what we had gone there to try to do for the Dominicans, for our own country, for President Kennedy—that was all over, ended. The world was a different place now.

It was hard for them, they had loved the Republic so. More, Fran thought I should stay to help the Dominicans, and the United States, and our faith in what Stevenson had stood for in 1952 and 1956 and Kennedy in 1960, for if all who so believed departed, what then? Dreams die hard. Fran was worried too about the clinic; the Bishop in Higüey had started it anew. Well, we would help to keep it going with the small private foundation here. But not go ourselves. We needed to draw together, rebuild. In our family we do not usually say a prayer or offer a toast at Thanksgiving, but I tried that year—to the memory of our President and the success of our new President and the future of our children. That weekend the young daughter of a friend of mine was murdered.

12

I went back to Washington on Monday. Nehemkis had reported on his "mission." The Dominican regime had succeeded in selling him the Bonilla Aybar line—the Dominican military had overthrown Bosch in the nick of time to save the Republic from communism.

Next day I called Dungan and asked what he was doing and he said nothing, come on over. He had moved out of his big office on the first floor to a small office on the third floor, and we talked for two hours, Schlesinger dropping in once. I told him I thought I could do no more now, but at the same time did not want to abandon President Johnson and the things we all believed in, and I asked his advice. He suggested I write a letter to the President similar to those submitted by the White House staff—"In order to assist you in the task of forming a new government, I wish to submit my resignation as Ambassador to the Dominican Republic, to be effective at your convenience," and send it, through the Secretary, to President Johnson.

That afternoon I saw a paper that was going up to the Secretary on Dominican recognition, containing all the pros and cons, carefully hedged.

I added a paragraph pointing out that since this would be President Johnson's first act in Latin America, watched closely for any sign of a policy shift, we should, to protect the President, privately and fully explain our recognition to Latin Americans, the U.S. press, and Congress.

Next day President Johnson came to the Department and, in the auditorium, addressed the senior officers, an excellent speech. Afterward he and Secretary Rusk and the half dozen or so Ambassadors who happened to be in town talked awhile in Rusk's office, Rusk introducing me to the President as "Mr. Martin, who has been in the Dominican Republic" and introducing another Ambassador as "Mr. ———, who is going to the Dominican Republic," a complete surprise to the other man and me. (He did not go.) The President spoke quietly, sitting, bending forward, kneading his big hands, speaking well of Rusk and the Department, then talking about himself, his boyhood on a poor Texas farm, now President of the United States. He told a favorite joke: After his first election, a friend had said his victory "made every ignorant son of a bitch in the precinct feel good, because if you can make it, they can." Watching him, I remembered warning him in Santo Domingo during Bosch's inauguration to get out of the dangerous crowd.

13

Two weeks ensued, a sad December, in public all serene, backstage knives flashing, private wounds slowly healing then slashed open by a word or glance. But somehow—unity. The nation, to save itself, needed to draw together, to become again if not great at least a nation, not a killer's madhouse; and slowly did. Irreparable harm had been done our country. Only unprecedented unity could save us. And did.

The Venezuelans held elections. And all the while the cables from the Embassy in Santo Domingo came and went, Dominican plots and counter-plots, American responses, a floundering, blundering sort of time, somewhat like the weeks of August and September. I thought we must recognize, but could get no one to move. The entire Dominican predicament had been overtaken by events. So were we all.

In the hills near Las Matas, where we had spent a weekend long ago with the Cabrals, troops hunted down guerrillas. The Nuncio (I learned later) tried to go to see the guerrillas and talk them out of the hills, to stop them before much blood was shed, but the military refused permission. Wessin might be moving to replace Viñas. A bomb exploded in Santiago. Balagueristas were astir. *Listin Diario* attacked the regime— "six tenacious politicians . . . have imposed their own illusions as a nightmare on their nation." The regime announced increasing guerrilla activity. The regime arrested two PRD Senators—two duly elected Senators, elected with Bosch by the people—and charged them with "usurpation of function," that is, impersonating Senators. And the occasion on which they had done the "impersonation" had been a memorial service for President Kennedy.

14

Washington was still a city full of heartbroken people. And full of people clawing and elbowing their way toward the top. It was beautiful no longer, only hard in the winter sun. The grass was brown, the trees bare. Across the river the flame burned in Arlington. Crowds went there. I thought to go but didn't. The hurt got worse, not better, and sometimes broke loose all unexpected, once while watching the Army-Navy football game on television, which President Kennedy would have attended—"Why did they have to kill him? Why?" The empty ancient question without answer.

A news report said that the Dominicans had caught a fishing boat, loaded with men and guns, headed for Cuba. No, they had captured four Castro/Communists coming *from* Cuba—Francisco Ramos Peguero, Cayetano Rodríguez, Leopoldo Grullón, Islander Selig, attempting a landing near Monte Cristi in a boat called, of all things, the *Scarlet Woman.* Was it a fake, perpetrated by the regime? Or was it the real thing, Castro's move? The men were MPD leaders.

We had accomplished all we could by withholding recognition. If civil authority weakened, we would be blamed. Nobody would benefit except the military, and later, the Castro/Communists. We should recognize before the guerrillas gained. The regime had already outlawed the 14th of June. If the PRD took to the hills, and the regime then outlawed the PRD, we would end by aligning ourselves with a military regime that was fighting the masses.

But no one would move. I was tired of the Department. Nobody would take decisions, nobody would assume responsibility. Time and again I had heard Department officers regale each other with tales of their prowess abroad. What emasculated them here? And tired too of their flip schoolboyish cant—"Ed Martin's shop" for the American Republics Area, "piece of paper" for cable.

I called Dungan and told him we must delay recognition no longer. Dungan agreed and said he'd call George Ball.

Early next morning—it was December 10, a Tuesday—Ed Martin called a meeting. He said that at George Ball's request he had drafted a paper recommending recognition of both Honduras and the Dominican Republic by next Monday at the latest. Martin told me privately that, if I agreed, he intended to recommend that the President accept my resignation before we recognized, so it would not appear I was resigning in protest over the recognition. I did agree.

A military report came in, saying that Casasnovas was collecting money in Puerto Rico, presumably to finance guerrilla activity or a general strike. This, if true, could mean disaster for the PRD and for us. The Dominican press kept saying the guerrillas had "opened a fourth front," or "a fifth front," or "a sixth front." "Front" probably meant three or four ragged men in hiding. But it sounded ominous in cables and public communiqués. Who could be sure it wasn't—Castro had started, some say, with eleven men to take Cuba.

The Nuncio saw Bonnelly privately and sent word strongly recommending we recognize now. Bonnelly was frightened. He said the military seemed unable to cope with the guerrillas. An Air Force pilot had defected. The Triumvirate was fast losing power and talking, as usual, of quitting. U.S. recognition was essential, he said. He offered to serve as intermediary between the Triumvirate and King.

Everything seemed off the track. Not only the Dominicans but the Embassy seemed not to understand what we in Washington wanted. No wonder! We were not sending any cables from Washington, just talking to each other inside the Department's walls.

Of a sudden, we recognized.

I heard about it after it had happened, first from a man in the elevator about 1 P.M. on December 12, then from a secretary who asked if I'd cleared "the recognition cable—your name was on it." Later I pieced together what had happened.

About 11 A.M. a rumor of counter-*coup* against the regime had come up from San Juan, Puerto Rico, through a U.S. military channel, had swept through the U.S. government, had reached President Johnson, and at twelve-fifteen the President had called in five Senators, George Ball, and Ed Martin and said we would recognize. By this time Sowash had telephoned King and learned that the rumor was false. No matter. And no matter either that a meeting called by George Ball for two-thirty to "consider," at long last, the recognition paper was also overtaken by events. President Johnson simply did it. I thought it a fitting ending, grotesque enough to be suitable to the Dominican situation. A Department officer, however, outdid it. He telephoned to inform me that "S/S—Secretary's Secretariat"—was sending my photograph, taken with President Johnson in Rusk's office a few days ago, to the White House for the President's autograph and requested that he draft a "suitable inscription," and he now inquired what my wishes were. I said I wouldn't presume to tell the President what to write on my picture. He said he had to have it and dutifully submitted several alternatives for my consideration, not forgetting to inquire whether it should be addressed, "Mr. Ambassador" or "Mr. Martin."

At 11 A.M. on Saturday, December 14, a cold day with freezing rain falling, Ed Martin, the Ambassador to Honduras, and I met the press in the Department and Martin announced our recognition of the governments of Honduras and the Dominican Republic. Afterward, he told me there had been no time to get my resignation approved before recognition, so we would put it off a week or ten days. (It was accepted January 14, 1964, effective February 15.) That night I heard on the radio that the President had replaced Ed Martin with Thomas C. Mann, then Ambassador to Mexico. Subsequently he gave Mann not only Martin's job but also Moscoso's and that part of Dungan's which pertained to Latin America—complete authority in the Hemisphere. Martin's last public act had been recognition of the Republic. If I were superstitious, I might think the Republic was, as we often had said while there, a graveyard. It got colder that night, and at the Steeles' there was ice on the garbage can lid.

15

I spent the week cleaning up loose ends and saying goodbye. I did not want to leave with rancor. We had suffered enough that terrible fall. I had a talk with Ed Martin, wishing him well in Argentina, where he was going as Ambassador. I saw others in the Department—Kennedy Crockett; Bill Crockett, the Deputy Undersecretary for Administration; others. One snowy night a voice from the past came over the phone: Carmen Bosch's. She was snowbound. I got a car and picked her and her son up and took them to the airport, bound to meet her husband in Connecticut for Christmas. We arranged to have him guarded.

I saw Schlesinger, Dungan, several others, all trying as I was to figure out what to do with the rest of our lives. I had lunch with Sargent Shriver. He had been asked on "Meet the Press" to sum up in a single sentence what the Peace Corps had accomplished, and I wondered how I'd have answered if asked about the Dominican Republic. I'd probably have stammered around and might have said, "We helped give the Dominican people, after thirty-one years of Trujillo, a glimpse of freedom and convinced them that we believe in it too." At least I guessed it was true. I didn't feel very sure of anything any more. I could not leave town without saying goodbye to Bob Kennedy, hardest of all. How his face had aged in the years I'd known him. Well, whose hadn't? I stayed only a minute or two, telling him I'd do anything for him, thanking him, telling him I was going home to write a book. With that odd tentative half-smile, so well known to his friends, so little to others, he murmured, "Everybody's writing a book," and "All right, thanks, John." And then, "Well, three years is better than nothing."

Afraid of the weather, afraid of the Christmas rush, and, perhaps, just plain afraid, I canceled my plane reservation to Chicago and, on December 19, took a train. Never in my life have I been so glad to leave a city. That night I could not sleep but dozed, wakened, dozed, wakened again, and once, half asleep, saw the train long past midnight pulling along beside a river, with ice growing out from the edges, and factories lit, somewhere near Pittsburgh, I suppose. I wept, and kept thinking as I had for so long, "Why, oh why, did they kill him? Why him?" Tonight along the icy river I did not like the Dominican Republic, or its people, or the United States, or its people. Perhaps some day I would again. Not now. This nation was too powerful and too evil; that one too weak and too evil. I did not feel young and eager and confident and hopeful any more. I felt old and without hope, with heart for nothing. It was all gone. And destroyed by blind malevolent chance. That was what hurt the most of all. Why? Why him? Why that way?

These were night thoughts, dark thoughts, perhaps they would pass.

In the hard bright winter morning the train crossed northern Indiana, the state where I grew up, the flat, endless plain, white houses, red barns, two pheasants standing in a snowy stubblefield, a woodlot, the neat rectangles of the earth scattered complacent. This was where I came from. I thought of the day twenty-seven years ago when, a few months out of college, I had crossed the plain, heading for the Caribbean, suffocated by the flat land, eager for the great world; and had sailed the Gulf of Mexico, Puerto Rico, Cuba, the Caribbean, and, finally Ciudad Trujillo. How strange, how long ago. At that time the flat fields of Indiana had seemed drab, dispiriting, and even the piney woods and red clay banks of Louisiana excited, while the Caribbean, deep and blue, with flying fish scattering before the prow, had seemed miraculous.

The Midwest looked so different now. The widely scattered houses, the big town lots, a cord of stovewood in a backyard, here and there a rivulet, a gully—my father and I used to hunt rabbits on cold days like this in the gullies, though he always said we'd find more in the corn and wheat stubble, and he was right but it was less fun, the gullies were shadowed. Now it all looked comforting. I needed, the nation needed, comfort. Where was I going now? I didn't know. But home. For how long? I didn't know. Not forever. I felt too deeply committed to the dream, to the Hemisphere, to the people down there, I knew last night's thoughts would pass some day, I'd write something, do something again, if not for a while.

Bill Crockett had said when I went to say goodbye that he had grown up in Kansas, and in those days in Kansas they had thought they were the greatest, the best, the right, the good, they had invented the airplane and automobile and everything, then had righteously tried to make the world safe for democracy and all those other bad nations had thrown it away, so let them go, we had our place, our own Midwest, the salt of the earth. But now, he said, they realized that none of it had been true.

Kennedy Crockett called almost when I arrived home. The Dominican military had killed Manolo Tavárez Justo in the hills near El Rubio, near Las Matas, and fourteen or fifteen others with him, and a story was going around that the guerrillas had surrendered, then been massacred, and de los Santos had resigned in protest from the Triumvirate, and Tavares and Tapia had asked Donny Reid to replace him. The parties were quarreling, the UCN threatening to leave the government, the little parties clinging to power, and the military seemed to be dividing, some for, some against the Triumvirate. I said I thought we should try to hold the Triumvirate, Wessin, and Viñas together, get the parties out, and send an Ambassador as fast as possible. Crockett agreed, and would speak to Tom Mann, now preparing to assume his duties.

Our daughter Cindy and her husband came home for Christmas from Guatemala, and my mother and aunt came from Indiana, and after Christmas all of us except my mother and aunt went up to Michigan. It was cold, twenty-five below zero, less snow than usual, only a couple of feet. The boys found an otter's track near camp, and we went rabbit hunting in a big swamp with half a dozen men, and the dogs chased a rabbit into a hollow pine log, and we rode the toboggan down a hill onto the frozen lake; and one day driving in the Jeep back in the woods with Joe Heikkinen we saw a herd of deer, dark in a swamp; and I bought 170 acres of land and most of a lake in the rough, rocky, uninhabited country north. After New Year's the others went home, but I stayed alone, snowshoeing, seeing a few people, dreaming about building a camp far out in the woods next summer, thinking about this book and about my life, at night alone in camp in front of the fire, healing. I kept warm.

PART FOUR

Seventeen Days in May—and Beyond

Chapter Twenty-seven

PRESIDENTIAL MISSION: 1965

In March of 1964, a private citizen once more, I was appointed a Fellow at the Center for Advanced Studies at Wesleyan University in Middletown, Connecticut, to write this book. I continued writing through the rest of the year and during the spring of 1965.

All during that period, I kept in touch with the Dominican situation during trips to Washington and when Dominican friends visited the U.S. At Christmastime of 1964 Fran and the boys and I went for a brief vacation to the Republic, spending most of our time at Sosua.

Juan Bosch stayed in exile in Puerto Rico, so far as I knew, writing his own book at the University of Puerto Rico. Miolán—who had broken with Bosch—and most of the other PRD leaders were in exile. So was ex-President Balaguer, in New York. So were the Trujillos, in Europe. According to the New York *Times,* a Dominican court sentenced Ramfis and three of the dictator's brothers in absentia to thirty years' imprisonment; another brother was sentenced to ten years.

Bishop Pepén took over the clinic in Higüey. Civic leaders there rebuilt the community center. The United Nations allocated funds for development of the two great Yaque rivers.

Over a period of months, all three original members of the *golpista* Triumvirate resigned. Emilio de los Santos, as noted, resigned on December 22, 1963, apparently in protest over the killing of the 14th of June guerrillas. Donny Reid replaced him and soon became "President" of the Triumvirate. Ramón Tapia resigned April 8, 1964, and was replaced by Ramón Cáceres, who, it will be recalled, had been a Cabinet member under the Consejo. Manuel Tavares resigned June 27, 1964, and was not replaced. Thereafter the "Triumvirate" consisted in only two men—Reid and Cáceres. And Cáceres became an almost silent partner. Reid ruled.

Reid in power developed the stubborn strength that seemed only latent while he was a member of the Consejo. He purged the Cabinet—

sent Severo Cabral abroad as ambassador to Israel—and in mid-1964 began replacing the entire military high command—Viñas, Luna, Rib, and Hungría—a process completed early in 1965 with the removal of Belisario Peguero. He took for himself Viñas' post as Secretary of State for Defense. All this Reid did under stress and not without personal danger. But he got away with it—or thought he had. Significantly, he did not replace Elías Wessin y Wessin, now a General.

Reid closed the military stores, which after the *golpe* were driving merchants out of business by selling cut-rate merchandise smuggled in duty free aboard Dominican Air Force planes. When we visited at Christmas, the capital streets looked cleaner and quieter than in our time, not necessarily a good sign; and at Bonao police were checking license numbers.

Reid's economic policies—but not his political policies—were remarkably like Bosch's. Reid launched an economic policy of austerity. He received a twenty-five-million-dollar standby credit from the IMF, private bank loans, and a ten-million-dollar loan from AID. AID resumed assistance for agrarian reform and agricultural production, farm-to-market road construction, education, civic action, and other programs we had launched earlier. But the economic condition of the Republic worsened, due mainly to the inefficiency of Haina and the disastrous drop in the world market price of sugar to 2.2 cents. To cut the cost of sugar production, Reid laid off thousands of sugar workers, increasing unemployment. Ordinary Dominicans saw prices rising and earning power falling. The better life they had hoped for under Juan Bosch was disappearing. Castro/Communists were returning to the Republic, as Ambassador W. Tapley Bennett, who had replaced me, had warned Reid as early as November of 1964.

The Government's own information bulletin said that "undoubtedly the Triumvirate is an unpopular government" but said it "acts in favor of the people, even if against the will of that people," a sentence with a rather ominous ring. The opposition political parties said that Reid had invaded individual liberty, banned all outdoor political rallies and some political radio broadcasts, and had arbitrarily imprisoned the guerrillas and their sympathizers. They also complained bitterly about corruption in the military. At various times the regime used troops to put down strikes. Rightist politicians complained that Reid planned to rig the elections to keep himself in power. The civicos complained that business was bad. On the whole, while Reid governed firmly, he did not appear to have reverted to severe repression. And he appeared to have regained control from the military.

The fact remained, however, that his rule was illegitimate. He ruled not by popular mandate but by fiat granted indirectly by the *golpistas*. He announced general elections for September 1965, but forbade campaigning until June. Although he carefully concealed it publicly, nearly all Dominican political figures were convinced, and as was I, that Reid himself intended to run for President—and without leaving the Palace. He had no political party. As President, he had gained little personal popularity. When I was there at Christmas, it seemed doubtful that Reid could defeat either Bosch or Balaguer in a free election. It was equally doubtful that he would permit either to return and run against him. But how meaningful would an election be without Bosch? And a private poll showed Balaguer the most popular potential candidate, no doubt because, under him and Trujillo, the masses had been untouched by Trujillo's terror, and remembered Balaguer chiefly as the President who raised wages and gave away taxis, cows, bicycles, and other things just before he departed. Could Reid, in the face of this, and despite what were undoubtedly his personal good intentions, get away with an election that was so transparently intended simply to legitimatize himself? In brief, could he successfully execute the ancient and fatal Dominican presidential maneuver, *prolongación,* or *continuísmo?*

Our own position was difficult. Since Reid descended from the *golpe* we had opposed, we could not give him all-out support. On the other hand, he was a decent man and he held the center between extreme right and left, so we could not oppose him. We tried to pursue a middle course —much sympathetic interest, some economic assistance, and political disengagement. Ambassador Bennett was a State Department career officer. A tall, red-haired Georgian, he had been in the Santo Domingo Embassy years earlier as a junior officer, when Trujillo was in power. He had friends among the oligarchy, and soon after he arrived as Ambassador, he laid flowers on the grave of Doña María's father. He liked Reid and might have wanted to support him more strongly. He tried hard to get economic assistance for the Republic. Nearly every time I saw him, Ambassador Bennett was deeply worried about the Republic's economic situation. He was indignant at military thievery, and at Belisario Peguero's amoral ambitions. But Bennett maintained the traditional ambassadorial role of staying out of internal political affairs. Indeed, he told me at Christmas 1964 that he never had talked politics with Donny Reid. It was a vastly different role from mine. But, then, the situation was vastly different.

On trips to Washington, I talked to Ralph Dungan and to people in the Department. I considered our policy correct as far as it went, but wished we were building something politically for the future. We seemed to have few ties to the young people and to the left. And where did we go politically if Reid failed? But I did not want to get involved.

2

At the Center for Advanced Studies, I was less interested in what was going on in the Republic now than in what had happened while I had been there. I needed to understand it. I did a good deal of reading and thinking, trying to make sense out of what had happened in Santo Domingo, in Washington, and in Dallas.

Once my old friend, the Papal Nuncio, Monseñor Clarizio, passed through New York, and I went to see him; he chided me gently for wasting time in writing when I should be doing. He was right, no doubt; but it was easier for him, who had his metaphysics clear, as I had not. I stayed cloistered.

On April 24, 1965, the Dominican Republic blew up in Civil War.

First reports indicated that a popular uprising against Reid had begun, led by Bosch supporters and defecting military men; that Reid had been overthrown; that Wessin y Wessin's troops were fighting the people in the streets. All week in Connecticut, I read the newspapers with increasing dismay, and when we sent the U. S. Marines, I feared that once again we were on the wrong side—*for* an unpopular regime, *against* the people. Therefore, when on Thursday Bill D. Moyers, Special Assistant to the President, and Undersecretary of State George Ball called and said that President Johnson and Secretary Rusk wanted me to go to Washington to consult with them, I went gladly, grateful for an opportunity to advise and participate.

They sent a Jet Star for me, and I arrived in Washington about 6:30 A.M. on April 30—a Friday—and went to the White House Situation Room. There I talked to Bill Bowdler, a Department man I'd first met in Santo Domingo in 1961 while on my mission for President Kennedy, and read the cables and papers. Intelligence officers and Harry Shlaudeman, by then Dominican desk man in the Department, joined us to discuss in detail the charges that Communists were leading or influencing the rebel movement.

I did not have time that morning to learn everything—I was hurrying back and forth between the Situation Room downstairs and the Cabinet Room upstairs, where President Johnson was meeting with Secretary Rusk, Secretary McNamara, Undersecretary Ball, Deputy Secretary of Defense Cyrus Vance, Admiral William Raborn of CIA, General Earle Wheeler, Chairman of the Joint Chiefs of Staff, McGeorge Bundy, Special Assistant to the President on national security affairs, and others.

But from what I was told that morning, and from what I learned later—some of it much later—this is what had happened.

3

In December of 1964 and early in 1965, Juan Bosch's PRD and the Social Christians had agreed in exile to work together to get rid of Reid and restore the 1963 Constitution. It seems likely that the Social Christians regarded this Río Piedras Pact[1] as an electoral pact—they would

---

[1] It was made at Río Piedras, Puerto Rico, where Bosch was in exile. It was not secret.

support Bosch for President and he would support their leader for Vice President, in elections. But it also seems likely that Bosch held a different view. He had consistently maintained that he was in fact still the elected President. Therefore, no new election was necessary. It seems likely that he intended a return to power and constitutionality without elections.

Soon the 14th of June and the two real Communist parties, the PSP and MPD, took it on themselves to support this movement, though the five groups were by no means always in harmony.

On February 20, 1965, in a leaflet bearing the slogan, "Sweet and Honorable it is to Die for the Fatherland," the 14th of June denounced imperialism and Reid's *"continuismo,"* called for "a front of constitutional struggle" to unite labor unions, *campesino* organizations, student groups, and professional associations, and declared, "Only thus, in a Front of National Struggle, can the country direct the popular forces with sufficient power to rout the interventionist clique and usurpers."

On the same day, February 20, the MPD, in a leaflet signed

"Liberty or Death, Central Committee,

Dominican Popular Movement

Marxist-Leninist Party"

and headed "The Struggle against the Coup is a Struggle against Yankee Imperialism" said: "Yankee imperialism and the oligarchy destroyed the democratic Constitution of 1963, murdered the guerrilla fighters [of 1963], and continue the repression of laborers, peasants, and all the workers. . . . Whatever group or political party does not fight for public liberty and for the Constitution of 1963, even through the PRD-PRSC [PRD-Social Christian] pact, serves imperialism and betrays the struggle of the people." It concluded with the slogan: "To fight against the *golpe* is to fight against the Yankees! To fight against pacification is to fight against the *golpe* and the Yankees!"

In a leaflet distributed in March, headed "PSP Popular Front, for the Return of Juan Bosch," and signed by "The Julio Antonio Mella Cell of the PSP," a cell of the true Moscow-directed Communist party of the Republic said:

"At the present moment, the struggle of the working class and all the people should be directed toward the re-establishment of democracy, to ensure the return of Juan Bosch at the head of the constitutional government.

"The return of Juan Bosch should be the result of popular struggle. . . . It should never be the result of compromise with Yankee imperialism. . . .

"Now then, the working class and all the people should know that the Bosch regime, the political liberties it will bring, will not solve the great problems of the country. It will only permit the organization of the working class in its Party to struggle on for superior objectives.

"The problems of hunger, lack of housing, water, unemployment will only be solved when the people frees itself of the imperialist yoke, and when the working class takes power, destroys the exploiting capitalistic regime, implants the dictatorship of the proletariat and builds a socialist society free of all exploitation.

"ALL THE PEOPLE TO THE STRUGGLE FOR THE RETURN OF JUAN BOSCH AND THE 1963 CONSTITUTION."

On March 9 the PSP distributed a leaflet signed by the Secretariat of its Central Committee calling for unified action by all "democratic forces" based on "the mobilization of the masses," arguing for mass unity and struggle by a broad united front, saying that "Our Party" had manifested its support for all forces which fought against despotism and the *golpista* regime and would fight with any party or group even though it might have ideological differences with some of them. Therefore, the leaflet continued:

"The PSP has considered insufficient the unitary step taken by the PRD and the Social Christians and ratifies that it ought to be completed with the incorporation of all the parties, organizations, groups, and persons who have combated the military *golpe* of the 25 of September. We repeat: The PRD-PRSC accord is an important step, but limited. The situation demands a fuller, stronger, and more active unity. All the anti-*golpista* forces ought to oppose a single front of struggle to the enemies of the people!"

The leaflet concluded:

"Let us impel the mobilization of the masses.

"All united against the *golpista* government!

"Constitution of 1963."

On the 16th of March, the PSP Central Committee itself issued a Manifesto adorned with a picture of Lenin. Declaring that popular outcry for the return of Bosch was rising throughout the Republic, the Manifesto repeated the old charges that Bosch had been overthrown by a "clerical-militarist" *golpe* under the auspices of imperialism through "Admiral [*sic*] O'Meara and other known functionaries of the North American Navy." The Manifesto rejected the "way out of the crisis through elections" and called for the "return of Juan Bosch and the restoration of the 1963 Constitution on the basis of mass actions." But the restoration of Bosch was not the final goal.

"The return of Professor Bosch to the Presidency of the Republic does not signify solution of the national problems. The political liberty and the democratic conquests which the return of the Bosch government imply as a result of popular mobilization will not liberate the working people from misery and oppression.

"The working people will get their total liberation if they unite and fight to win the power to eliminate the economic domination of North American imperialism, and to establish socialist democracy which puts in the hands of the people all the riches of the country. . . .

"The outburst of a unified action of the great popular masses that is capable of imposing the re-establishment of the government overthrown by the *golpistas* constitutes in any case only a democratic guarantee for the country, constitutes a step of indispensable advance for the fulfillment of the historic objectives of the Dominican people. . . .

[2] "[Therefore,] Bosch should be returned to power through popular action and not through compromise with the enemies of the people. The return of Bosch on the basis of mass action signifies not only the restoration of the national dignity and sovereignty of the people. It will signify above all an extremely important step toward uniting the forces which will lead the Dominican people to complete liberation.

"At present the struggle for the fulfillment of this task must be headed by the Dominican working class—the only class capable of leading the people as a whole and heading the struggle for their supreme objectives.

"Therefore, the *Partido Socialista Popular* calls on the working class and the people as a whole to launch a struggle for the return of President Bosch to the post of head of the legitimate government of the Republic on the basis of the democratic gains recorded in the 1963 Constitution.

"Fight in the streets, squares, factories, and in the countryside for the return of President Bosch as head of the constitutional government!"

After Bosch reached agreement in Puerto Rico with the Social Christians, 14th of June leaders said he had indicated he would welcome their support too. But Bosch never officially brought the 14th of June into the PRD-Social Christian pact. There is no evidence that he talked with MPD or PSP leaders, and he can hardly be blamed if they decided to support his PRD-Social Christian movement. That they did support it seems clear from the foregoing Manifestos and from their subsequent actions during the Civil War itself. In any case, as the Manifestos show, all three parties—14th of June, MPD, and PSP—came out in support of the PRD-Social Christian pact in February and March of 1965, although, as has been said, they were not in full harmony at all times, and the PSP made it explicitly clear that the return of Bosch was only a first step toward the establishment in the Dominican Republic of "socialist democracy" (and a PSP cell changed "socialist democracy" to "dictatorship of the proletariat").

On one thing all except the Social Christians were agreed: Restoration of Bosch and the 1963 Constitution without elections.

[2] The portion of the Manifesto that follows was published much later (issue of December 1965) in the *World Marxist Review,* in an article signed by "J. I. Quello" and "N. Isa Conde," presumably two Dominican PSP leaders, José Israel Cuello Hernández and Narciso Isa Conde. I have adopted the *World Marxist Review*'s translation, though it is somewhat less literal than mine of the earlier portion. The entire article appears in the Appendix.

During this period, however, something far more important was going on: A conspiracy, or rather several conspiracies, within the Dominican Armed Forces.

During my time, the far left had constantly tried to organize a united front. Frequently they had issued Manifestos proclaiming one. But their efforts had failed because of Manolo Tavárez Justo. And in any case a united front without force was an automobile without a motor. Now Manolo was gone. The military split provided the motor.

Bosch himself had during my tenure claimed to have supporters in the Armed Forces, particularly among enlisted men and lower- and middle-grade officers. Knowing that this was "an army of *campesinos*," remembering his own theoretical stratification of Dominican society, Bosch understood that the lower ranks might well resent the privileges of the higher officers and might therefore offer an opportunity to split the Armed Forces. This opportunity increased as high-ranking officers prospered through graft under Reid. Bosch alone seems to have grasped the significance of this. We did not (though Bosch had several times predicted a military split while I was the Ambassador, both publicly and in private to me). And only later, the Communists have said, did they understand it.[3]

As I have said, various conspiracies were going on. The real one, the military conspiracy launched on behalf of Bosch, the one that ultimately succeeded, may have begun as early as August or September of 1964, as its ultimate leader, Lieutenant Colonel Francisco Caamaño Deño, once indicated. The probable leaders were Colonel Rafael Tomás Fernández Domínguez and Lieutenant Colonel Miguél Ángel Hernando Ramírez. Colonel Fernández was about thirty years old, had spent most of his time in the Dominican Air Force, and was a friend of Bosch. Bosch while President had appointed him Director of the Military Academy; when Bosch fell, he was removed immediately and sent to Madrid as military attaché in October 1963, for he was known to have opposed the *golpe* and suspected of plotting an immediate counter-*golpe*. Subsequently he was sent to Santiago, Chile, as military attaché. But during the fall of 1964 and early 1965 he visited San Juan, where Bosch was exiled, and may have visited the Dominican Republic, plotting within the Armed Forces against Reid on behalf of Bosch.

Now during this period various others were plotting, each for his own advantage, including such military men as General Luna (who, though ordered abroad, never had actually left) and Colonel Neit Nivar Seijas, the notorious Trujillista, and such civilians as the former PRD leader, Nicolás Silfa. Evidence indicates that the Bosch plotters, both civilian and military, kept track of those plots. But the conspiracy that succeeded was the PRD's—civilian and military.

[3] See *World Marxist Review* article in Appendix.

How much did the U. S. Government know about all this at the time? We knew about the Manifestos but apparently attached little importance to them. We knew plots were afoot but did not have them well sorted out.

On April 11 and 12, the CIA reported that Juan Bosch's party, the PRD, was plotting with military officers to overthrow the Reid government and set up a military junta under Bosch. It was working through retired and active junior officers, mainly in the Air Force, the CIA thought. At the same time, the CIA said, Colonel Neit Nivar Seijas was plotting against Reid with noncommissioned officers in the Army. The Embassy confirmed this. High-ranking officers, including some of those who had overthrown Bosch, were also plotting to overthrow Reid. And Army Lieutenant Colonel Miguel Ángel Hernando Ramírez was plotting on behalf of the PRD.

Reid ordered Neit Nivar Seijas to leave the country immediately, together with other officers of the Trujillista "San Cristóbal group."

Subsequent U.S. reports tended to confirm, if not to clarify, serious trouble inside the military. The Embassy attachés reported that General Rivera Cuesta, now Army chief, said that one of Juan Bosch's most dedicated supporters, José Francisco Peña Gómez, had returned from exile in Puerto Rico with money to buy support for a *coup* by the Army. And only five days before actual rebellion began, the CIA reported that Army officers and enlisted men had intended to seize Reid when he visited an Army installation and, simultaneously, kidnap Wessin y Wessin. Two of the leaders in that plot were Lieutenant Colonel Pedro Augusto Alvarez Holguin and Lieutenant Colonel Hernando Ramírez. Reid isolated Alvarez Holguin. He called in Hernando Ramírez and asked what he was planning. Nothing, Hernando Ramírez said. But Hernando Ramírez a few days later emerged as a rebel leader. And so did Alvarez Holguin.[4]

The Department called Ambassador Bennett home for consultation. He left Santo Domingo on Friday, April 23, and stopped in Georgia to visit his aged parents, intending to go to Washington Sunday night.

On Saturday afternoon, April 24, William Connett, Bennett's DCM and *chargé d'affaires* in Bennett's absence, reported that a thousand people were milling around the Palace and that rebels had seized Radio Santo Domingo and proclaimed the overthrow of Reid. Later, however,

---

[4] I have adopted the term "rebels" for the forces that overthrew Reid, "loyalists" for the San Isidro military that supported him. The "rebels," of course, say they were "constitutionalists" merely reversing the 1963 *coup* against Bosch and returning to constitutionality and therefore it is they who were "loyal" to democracy, not the San Isidro *golpistas*. I have no quarrel with this interpretation, but have adopted the common terminology for clarity's sake.

Connett reported that forces loyal to Reid, including Wessin y Wessin and the Air Force and Navy, had recaptured Radio Santo Domingo, and Reid had announced over it that the *golpe* was crushed except at two Army bases. General Wessin y Wessin was named Secretary of State for Defense. Connett believed that PRDistas probably had been involved in the *golpe*.

President Johnson was informed. Ambassador Bennett, having heard the news on the radio in Georgia, hastened to Washington.

Later it transpired that Reid had sent General Rivera Cuesta, Army commander, to the 27th of February camp to cancel the commissions of four officers accused of plotting against him. The plot had not yet fully developed. Reid thought—and had told Ambassador Bennett—that the plot was scheduled for late May or early June. But leading rebels themselves have since said it was scheduled for the following Monday, April 26. Rivera Cuesta's visit triggered the plot prematurely. He called in an aide, Captain Mario Peña Taveras, and ordered him to arrest the conspirators. Instead, Captain Peña Taveras, himself one of the conspirators, arrested Rivera Cuesta and seized control of the camp. This was the beginning of the military rising. Early that afternoon, Saturday, April 24, Peña Gomez of the PRD, formerly a radio announcer, accompanied by a few civilian and military friends, went to Radio Santo Domingo, barricaded himself in a studio, declared Reid overthrown, and called on the people to go to the streets and hail the Bosch revolution. Reid's police cleared the streets. Reid himself appeared on television to announce that the *golpe* had been stopped and to deliver an ultimatum: He ordered the rebellious officers at the 27th of February camp to surrender by 5 A.M. Sunday or face attack. Washington—and the Embassy —believed the Reid government had regained control.

Sunday morning reports of the situation changed radically. Connett cabled that rebel troops were entering Santo Domingo and trying to recapture Radio Santo Domingo, crowds were rioting in the streets and demanding the return of Juan Bosch, the police and loyalist troops were doing nothing, the electricity was shut off, public order had collapsed.

Obviously, if the Reid government could not guarantee public order, American lives were in danger. President Johnson ordered a Naval task force to a position over the horizon, prepared to evacuate American citizens.

A minor PRD functionary called the Embassy and said Reid had offered to turn the government over to the PRD in the presence of a U.S. representative. The Embassy had just been in touch with Reid; he had apparently mentioned no such plan (and has since denied it). The PRD functionary represented no significant segment of the PRD. The Embassy did not respond and, while the record is not entirely clear, probably could have achieved nothing had it responded.

The situation worsened rapidly that Sunday. Reid's commanders held their troops on base to protect their own personal positions. They would not enforce Reid's ultimatum. The Air Force and Navy were wobbling. A mob was hunting Bonilla Aybar, the journalist-TV commentator who had helped overthrow Bosch; he took asylum in the Guatemalan Embassy.

The military men who had rebelled on Saturday had taken guns with them. They handed them over to ex-soldiers that night. On Sunday, and on Monday and Tuesday, they hauled several thousand guns—estimates go as high as seven thousand—into downtown Santo Domingo in Army trucks, private trucks (one of them owned by Buenaventura Johnson Pimentel of the PSP), and private cars, including one or two *públicos*. The military men began passing guns out to crowds on the streets. And the CIA reported that an eyewitness saw Castro/Communist leaders joining them in that work near Parque Independencia, using trucks loaded with guns—Felix Ducoudray and Hugo Tolentino Dipp of the PSP, Fidelio Despradel Roque and Eduardo Houellemont Roques of the 14th of June. Other Castro/Communists joined in the work—Alejandro Lajara González, Daniel Ozuña Hernández, and Máximo Bernard Vásquez of the 14th of June; Juan Ducoudray, and Gerardo Rafael Estévez Weber of the PSP. The CIA received reports that rebels were executing loyalists at two walls, one at Parque Independencia, one on Calle Espaillat, where students on rooftops had defied Ramfis' tanks in 1961. The most credible reports said that police were being shot at a *paredon*—wall—at Parque Independencia. Rebels were forcing filling station operators to fill Coca-Cola bottles with gasoline for anybody on the street; they made Molotov cocktails from them. The bloodbath was being prepared. And the key to it was this indiscriminate distribution of weapons.

In these first hours, however, the premature triggering of the rebellion seems to have taken the Castro/Communists by surprise to the extent it had taken the loyalist military men by surprise.

The PSP's leaders met early that Sunday morning and decided to try to seize control of the rebellion. They armed themselves—Narciso Isa Conde, Manuel González González, Diomedes Mercedes Batista, and Asdrúbal Domínguez, the student whom I had met long ago on Fandino's porch. They passed out arms to their followers. A band led by Nicolás Pichardo Vicioso and Antonio Isa Conde of the PSP and Eduardo Houellemont Roques of the 14th of June seized the office of *Prensa Libre,* Bonilla Aybar's newspaper.

The MPD leaders, also apparently caught by surprise, instructed their followers not to become involved—they suspected the United States had perpetrated the *golpe* to prevent elections or to provoke the leftists into rising and thus identifying themselves. As late as 8 A.M. that first Sunday, MPD leaders had not ordered their followers to join the fighting. But some of their followers accepted arms from PSP leaders and the rebel military. At first the MPD leadership was poor—Máximo López Molina was out of the country and Cayetano Rodríguez del Prado was under arrest in a hospital, to which he had been moved from La Victoria prison. On Sunday a rebel major freed Cayetano Rodríguez. From extreme leftists in the 14th of June, he obtained weapons and distributed them to the MPD rank and file. By Monday—Tuesday at the latest—the MPD was fully committed.

As for the 14th of June, it became involved early. On the first day, Saturday, the rebel officers at the 27th of February camp, planning to move troops into the city that night, sent Colonel Caamaño to reconnoiter downtown, and as he drove around looking for defensible strongpoints in the old town, Ciudad Nueva, he was accompanied by Daniel Ozuña of the 14th of June. On Sunday eyewitnesses saw 14th of June men with machine guns driving through the streets, urging the people to move toward Duarte Bridge over the Ozama River. Diomedes Mercedes Batista (PSP) was driving around the city in a car with a public address system, calling on the people to rebel. PSP men began making posters, setting up strong points, command posts, and arms caches in the downtown area, including a house at 56 Calle Espaillat, and buildings on Arzobispo Portes, a building at the corner of Arzobispo Merino and Calle Luperón, and one at the corner of El Conde and Calle Hostos.

The rebels recaptured Radio Santo Domingo on Sunday and announced that the Republic would return to constitutionality under the leadership of Juan Bosch. They captured the Palace easily and arrested Donny Reid and Ramón Cáceres. At a series of meetings in the Palace that Sunday afternoon, while crowds of armed civilians milled about inside and outside, some military men advocated establishing a military junta and holding early elections. But rebellious officers, PRDistas, and Castro/Communist leaders insisted that Molina Ureña be installed as provisional President. They prevailed. Juan Bosch, from exile in Puerto Rico, apparently had authorized Molina Ureña's installation and was preparing to return to the Dominican Republic himself. This prospect so horrified the Air Force commander, General Juan de los Santos, that he lined up solidly with General Wessin y Wessin to fight the rebels, though Wessin y Wessin has said since that de los Santos did so only at machinegun point. Later, Wessin y Wessin says, de los Santos cooperated voluntarily. So did the Navy, after its commander, Rivera Caminero, said that Wessin was determined to fight and had the force to do it. Thus the Generals, though unwilling to fight for Reid, were willing to kill their own countrymen to prevent Bosch's return. They told the rebels they would attack at once unless a military junta was installed.

In the Palace, Molina Ureña was about to be sworn in as Provisional President. But the deposed "President," Reid, was still there too. And, the CIA reported, so were the following PSP men: Diomedes Mercedes Batista, Luís Gómez Pérez, Silvano Lora Vicente, Antonio Isa Conde, Narciso Isa Conde,[5] José Israel Cuello Hernández,[5] Ariosto Sosa Valerio, Rafael Evangelista Alejo, and Miguel Angel Santamaría Demorizi. And so were Moises Blanco Genoa, Amin Abel Hasbun, Ema Tavárez Justo (a sister of Manolo), Daniel Ozuña Hernández, and Alejandro Lajara González, all of the 14th of June. Also present was Facundo Gómez, a member of Bosch's PRD who had been part owner of the *Scarlet Woman,* the vessel which had carried three armed MPD leaders, including Cayetano Rodríguez, to the Dominican Republic after the *golpe* of 1963.

Inside the Palace, confusion prevailed. Some military men who had rebelled because they were anti-Reid, or anti-Wessin, or pro-Balaguer, were leaving, having discovered the rebellion was pro-Bosch. Still, armed civilians and military men crowded the corridors, some drinking. Rebel Army men in the Palace knew the Palace might be attacked by air, for the Air Force had given them an ultimatum. Friends of the civilian rebels in the telephone company warned the MPD that the Palace was going to be bombed or strafed immediately, the MPD immediately warned one of the leading military rebels, Captain Mario Peña Taveras, and he warned the rebels in the Palace to leave immediately. Donny Reid, arrested by the rebels, had been taken to an upstairs room. But now Dominican warplanes began rocketing and machine-gunning the Palace. Reid was taken downstairs. In the confusion, he and Cáceres slipped away (with, interestingly, Colonel Caamaño's help). Molina Ureña was sworn in.

The Air Force fired on rebel strongpoints. Radio Santo Domingo, in rebel hands, kept urging the people to go into the streets.

The air attacks inflamed the people, who by now were armed. They began looting and sacking the stores and homes of Trujillistas and Reid supporters. They wrecked the headquarters of the UCN, Vanguardia, and Luís Amiama's party. Bosch said from Puerto Rico he was preparing to return and until then Molina Ureña would be the constitutional President. Connett, who had first suggested that the U.S. government not impede Bosch's return, then had suggested it do so, now recommended we stay neutral, adding that nobody seemed to want the return of Reid or Balaguer and the best hope seemed to be a military junta, already proposed by the loyalist forces. The fact is that at no time did the U.S. government prevent Bosch's return. But he did not return.

That same Sunday evening PRD leaders called at the U. S. Embassy

[5] Co-authors of the article in the *World Marxist Review.*

to ask that the Embassy persuade the Air Force to stop strafing the Palace. Embassy officers replied by asking the PRD leaders to persuade their rebel military colleagues to negotiate in good faith with the loyalists, saying that the United States feared bloodshed might create a situation favorable to a Communist takeover, and offering to facilitate talks between the two sides but refusing to support either.

Monday morning at five-thirty General de los Santos' planes began to rocket and strafe the Duarte bridge into the city, Connett reported, and General Wessin's troops, ordinarily stationed at San Isidro about nine miles east of Santo Domingo, would try to cross Duarte Bridge and enter the capital. Rebels seized the wives of Air Force pilots, Connett reported, put them on television, and announced they would put them on the bridge where they would be in the line of fire; over Radio Santo Domingo, the rebels exhorted the populace to sack the pilots' homes.

A high naval officer told our attaché that the Navy had gone over to the rebels. But stories spread that the Navy was shelling the city, trying to hit the rebels. The PSP established a strongpoint and arms depot at the corner of Arzobispo Portes and Calle Sánchez. Armed civilians were brought into commando units led by trained Communist guerrilla fighters; the "Luperón Commando" held a position at Calle Hostos and Calle Luperón. Another commando force used a strongpoint on Calle José Gabriel García Street. Other operation bases were established. Marauding bands spread through the city, some purposeful, some random. One, "Dagoberto Ricart," was led by Juan Miguel Román Díaz. Another called itself "Gatillo Alegre," trigger happy.

That Monday evening, Lee Echols, a U.S. police adviser, telephoned Colonel Caamaño, whom he knew rather well, and asked why the rebel soldiers had given guns to so many Communists. Caamaño replied, "I know we've given the Communists plenty of guns, but we had to do it to win and get rid of Reid. When we get in power, we will pick up all the guns."

Connett reported, somewhat inexplicably, that Generals Wessin and De los Santos had asked for U.S. troops and been told not to expect them —but Connett also said that there was a serious threat of a Communist takeover, and Connett thought a U.S. show of force might be needed later but not now. A little later he reported that the Embassy was advising Americans to prepare for evacuation—their lives were in danger. He said De los Santos had given him one hour to arrange a meeting with rebel leaders to avoid further bloodshed. Connett thought this all but impossible.

At 12:30 P.M., Monday, April 26, Secretary Rusk, Undersecretary Ball, Thomas C. Mann (now Undersecretary for Economic Affairs), Jack Hood Vaughn (who had replaced Mann as Assistant Secretary for

Latin America), and Ambassador Bennett went to the White House and presented the confused problem to President Johnson. The President told Bennett to return to Santo Domingo immediately and asked to be kept constantly informed.

The Embassy's Army attaché finally reached a rebel leader and urged him to meet with General de los Santos to avoid further bloodshed. The rebel leader replied he had tried to talk to the San Isidro Generals previously but they would not listen.

Broadcasting from San Isidro, the loyalist Generals declared that the rebels were controlled by "Fidelistas" and that they themselves favored a junta with free elections in September for all candidates. The rebel radio replied that the rebels would "never" confer with the "reactionary" forces of San Isidro. The Embassy, however, reported that General Rivera Cuesta had said he was at the Palace seeking agreement with the rebels and had asked the Embassy to tell De los Santos so, hoping he would not bomb for another hour. De los Santos agreed.

The State Department notified the Embassy that it had received requests that U.S. citizens in the Republic be evacuated, and instructed Connett to ask for an immediate cease-fire to permit the evacuation of citizens of any nation. Secretary Rusk met with Ellsworth Bunker, U. S. Ambassador to the OAS.

Molina Ureña appeared on rebel television as the Provisional President. He declared that victory was near and Bosch would soon arrive. Connett asked two of Molina Ureña's aides for a cease-fire to permit the safe evacuation of Americans and others by helicopter from the polo field at the Hotel Embajador, by ship from the port of Haina. The rebels agreed to cooperate fully. So did loyalist commanders. Evacuation would begin at 6 A.M. the next day, Tuesday, April 27. By then about a thousand persons had requested evacuation; the task force had moved in closer to shore.

On Tuesday the rebels continued to hand out arms to civilians, some of whom used them to settle old grudges. The 14th of June was handing out guns, including machine guns, from an arms depot on García Street. But the three Castro/Communist groups—Dato Pagán's PNR had ceased to exist by then, and he was in jail—were still not united. Some of the Castro/Communists thought the time had come for an all-out assault. Others, fearing the Dominican Air Force, disagreed. Some criticized their own leaders for permitting the evacuation of Americans and advocated the murder of all that remained. Some suspected the military rebels. But as they received more weapons, especially mortars and 50-caliber machine guns, all Castro/Communist groups fused together and fused with the military rebel leadership. By Thursday, the CIA reported, the

PSP, under the military leadership of Manuel González González, was ready to do battle with the U. S. Marines.

At evacuation time—6 A.M. Tuesday morning—with new air and naval bombardment of the rebels imminent, Navy Commodore Rivera Caminero agreed to draw a line around the Embajador Hotel to safeguard evacuees. Representatives of Molina Ureña gave Connett similar assurances. The rebel commander, Colonel Hernando Ramírez, called Connett to ask about the evacuation. He also asked if Connett knew of a rumored imminent air and naval bombardment. Connett did but said no. He was apparently primarily concerned at that moment with safe evacuation and wanted nothing to upset it. The Air Force announced over the radio at about 9 A.M. that aerial bombardment would begin. The rebels' "Foreign Minister" came to the U. S. Embassy asking—and receiving—our help in last-minute mediation. But at twelve-thirty that effort broke down—loyalist Air Force officers left a meeting with the U.S. naval attaché to begin bombing.

Meanwhile, at the Hotel Embajador evacuation point, a wild shooting affray broke out. At about 7 A.M. Bonilla Aybar, the anti-Bosch journalist-TV commentator, went to the evacuation area disguised by dark glasses and a big hat pulled down over his face. He was escorted by about eight men with revolvers, rifles, knives, and submachine guns. Not surprisingly, this made the other evacuees nervous. At eight-fifteen a group of some twenty men with rifles, submachine guns, revolvers, and knives took control of the hotel and searched the staging area. They apparently were rebels looking for Bonilla Aybar. Suddenly a shot was fired from a balcony. Immediately submachine gun fire broke out. The evacuees threw themselves on the ground and behind parked cars. When the firing stopped, the leader of the rebel gunmen told the evacuees to go inside the hotel and lie on the floor. He told Embassy officers his men intended no harm to the evacuees but neither did they intend to permit Bonilla Aybar and a colleague to escape. (Bonilla Aybar was evacuated later, a fact that Bosch taxed me with subsequently. Actually, Bonilla had escaped from the Embajador and returned to asylum in the Guatemalan Embassy and was later evacuated like any other asylee, a fact I did not know at the time I talked to Bosch and that he probably did not know either. In any case, the shooting affray at the Embajador, understandable though it was to anyone who knew how ruthlessly Bonilla Aybar had worked to overthrow Bosch, was a serious rebel mistake, for it indicated to the world that the rebels were irresponsible, law and order had broken down, and the lives of U.S. citizens and other evacuees were gravely endangered.)

Evacuation began—by early afternoon a thousand people had been evacuated.

In Washington, Uruguay's Ambassador to the OAS called on Assistant

Secretary Vaughn and suggested that the Inter-American Peace Committee be informed. Vaughn agreed. Ambassador Bunker's deputy asked the chairman of the Inter-American Peace Committee to convene the Committee urgently. He also called the Dominican Ambassador, and the dean of the Washington diplomatic corps who is also a member of the Peace Committee. Vaughn and a White House staffer discussed opening a channel to Juan Bosch and one was soon opened unofficially and indirectly.

The Department sent a cable to Santo Domingo setting forth U.S. objectives—the restoration of law and order, the protection of U.S. lives, and the prevention of a possible Communist takeover. The cable told the Embassy to get in touch with the military leaders of the contending forces and propose the establishment of a provisional government to restore law and order, stop any Communist takeover, guarantee no reprisals, and hold free elections as soon as possible.

Ambassador Bennett arrived in Santo Domingo at 12:40 P.M. that day, Tuesday, April 27, a crucial day.

At this point, planes from San Isidro were strafing and rocketing the city. Antonio Martínez Francisco, secretary general of the PRD, asked an Embassy officer to go to his house and talk by telephone to Bosch himself in Puerto Rico. Ambassador Bennett refused and sent word to Bosch that in Bennett's opinion Bosch now should demonstrate his patriotism and responsibility by calling on the rebels to put down their arms.

A little later Martínez Francisco came to see Bennett, as did several military rebels, including a key figure, Captain Mario Peña Taveras. Ambassador Bennett told all of them that the time had come to end "this senseless slaughter," that regardless of politics women and children had the right to live in peace, and that the massacre of which the PRD complained had been started by its own followers. He emphasized that the United States wanted a cease-fire so that a new provisional government could be formed, that the rebel government of Molina Ureña which now held the Palace was not governing effectively, and that extreme leftists were taking advantage of the situation. Reminding them of previous efforts to arrange postponement or avoidance of the air attack, Ambassador Bennett said this now seemed useless. Since, in Bennett's view, San Isidro now held superior military force, the rebels should capitulate and permit reconstruction to begin.

Martínez of the PRD seemed receptive, promised to try to locate his executive committee and, if necessary, overrule Molina Ureña.

Bennett next talked to General Herman Despradel, the Police Chief, and told him his first duty was to restore public order. Despradel said he was already at work and the streets "would be cleaned tonight." Bennett also reported that one thousand troops had arrived from San Cristóbal and General Wessin y Wessin and the Air Force infantry had now crossed the bridge. In Bennett's judgment, the "mop-up" should be successful though it might be "rough."

And at a little before 4 P.M. Molina Ureña, Bosch's stand-in Provisional President, came to the U. S. Embassy accompanied by fifteen or twenty political and military rebels, including Lieutenant Colonels Hernando Ramírez and Francisco Caamaño Deño. Bennett ordered their weapons picked up when they entered. Molina Ureña, Bennett reported, seemed dejected and nervous and, while others spoke bravely, Bennett thought it clear that all believed the San Isidro troops could overwhelm them. They were, in fact, at the Embassy to negotiate a settlement.

Bennett emphasized that bloodshed must end and they had started it. He said the United States had loyally supported Bosch while he was President and had made clear our disapproval of his overthrow. But, Bennett said, the present effort to restore him to power was obviously doomed and the time had come to make a fresh start. Bennett emphasized to the rebels that beyond question Communists had taken advantage of the PRD's legitimate movement, having previously been tolerated by the PRD. He also said that the rebels now had distributed arms indiscriminately to civilians and had tolerated looting and mistreatment of innocent people. Bennett expressed personal sympathy with Molina Ureña but told him he could not deny that his movement had been seriously infiltrated and influenced by Communists. Bennett cited weekend TV broadcasts by bearded men "spouting pure Castroism." Molina said these were only "details." Bennett said the United States considered them important "details." Bennett considered Molina Ureña's answers and the others' unconvincing.

The rebels asked that Ambassador Bennett dissuade Wessin from crossing the bridge and De los Santos from bombing the city. Bennett replied that the Embassy had done so four times yesterday but that each time the rebels had taken advantage of the time gained, had failed to appear at meetings the Embassy had arranged, and had insisted that the military commanders acknowledge Molina Ureña's position as Provisional President by calling on him at the Palace. Bennett asked the rebels if they considered the incident at the Hotel Embajador an example of democracy at work.

In the end, Molina Ureña asked whether Ambassador Bennett would accompany him to commence negotiations with the San Isidro forces if a churchman and the acting dean of the diplomatic corps were willing to join the negotiations. Bennett replied that he had no authority to do so. He said the United States believed an accord should be reached between Dominicans. He said the United States looked forward to early elections and hoped they could be entirely free, including, presumably, PRD participation.

As it turned out, this was a crucial meeting. Molina Ureña left. He and other PRD leaders abandoned their cause and went into asylum in the Colombian and other Embassies. So did Lieutenant Colonel Hernando Ramírez and other military rebels.

But Colonel Caamaño and still other military rebels, desperate and with no alternative, went back to the streets to fight. By now they were so deeply committed that they had no choice but to kill or be killed. Caamaño now emerged as the rebels' maximum leader in Santo Domingo.

That night heavy gunfire was continuous. Several Embassies were hit by small arms fire, including ours. Bennett sent a cable emphasizing that rebel TV broadcasts showed a "Castro flavor," that all sources agreed that Communists among the rebels were well organized and heavily armed, that the Communists were "clearly committing their full resources," and that rebel tactics had reached the "limit of human decency."

Wednesday, April 28, was the day of decision. Early that morning, Ambassador Bennett sent the MAAG chief to San Isidro. The MAAG chief found the commanders in disarray, discouraged and disorganized, declaring their troops advance into the city was stalled and the troops might not even be able to hold the Ozama River bridgehead on the city side of the river. Colonel Pedro Bartolomé Benoit of the Air Force, appointed a few hours later to head a military junta, said the loyalist troops could not protect U.S. lives, which he thought were in danger.

By noon Despradel of the police told Bennett the same thing.

Bennett reported Benoit's view to the Department by telephone and the police view by cable about 1 or 2 P.M.

He also reported that disorders continued, that armed civilians were shooting and looting, but that Radio San Isidro said General Wessin's forces were ready to resume the attack. General de los Santos urgently requested fifty walkie-talkies, and Ambassador Bennett recommended they be provided, saying that he regretted having to turn to a military solution for a political crisis, but that now, with all responsible rebels in hiding or asylum, the struggle had developed into one between Castro/Communists and the loyalists. The Department at first refused to intervene even to the extent of giving San Isidro walkie-talkies. Late that afternoon, however, on Bennett's urging, the Department acquiesced.

Bloodshed in the city was increasing. The Dominican Red Cross estimated that in the fierce fighting around Duarte Bridge on Tuesday and Wednesday, and in the air attacks there, as many as nine hundred or a thousand had died. When Red Cross officials were finally able to enter the area on May 1, they buried some 350 bodies in a common grave and cremated another eighty or ninety bodies.

At noon on Wednesday, Radio San Isidro announced the formation of the military junta, three Colonels representing the three service branches —Colonel Benoit of the Air Force; Colonel Enrique Apolinar Casado Saladin of the Army, and Captain Manuel Olgo Santana Carrasco of the Navy. The junta announced that its principal purpose was to prepare the nation for free and democratic elections. Then, Colonel Benoit, who presided, telephoned the Embassy to ask the United States to land twelve hundred Marines "to help restore peace."

In reporting the oral request to the Department in a cable received in Washington at 3:16 P.M., Ambassador Bennett said he did not believe the situation at that time justified a landing by U. S. Marines. He reported, however, that while the junta possessed preponderant military power, General Wessin had not advanced beyond his bridgehead on the west side—the city side—of the Ozama River bridge and did not appear to be very aggressive. The attachés considered the outcome still in doubt. Bennett recommended contingency planning to protect U.S. lives.

At about 3 or 3:30 P.M. Wednesday, Colonel Benoit, on behalf of the junta, formally requested in writing that the U.S. government give its "unlimited and immediate military assistance" to put down the rebellion which, the junta declared, was directed by Communists armed to "convert the country into another Cuba." Benoit said nothing about protecting American lives.

At 4:45 P.M., Secretaries Rusk and Ball went to the White House to review the Vietnam situation with the President. McGeorge Bundy, the President's special assistant, showed Ambassador Bennett's cable to the President, saying that Colonel Benoit had asked for a Marine landing but Bennett did not consider it necessary at that time. The meeting on Vietnam continued. At 5:30 P.M. the President was handed another cable from Bennett labeled "critic," the highest priority. It said that the situation had deteriorated rapidly, the police, far from being able to "mop up," could now hope for no more than to defend a few of their own key installations; the police could no longer protect evacuation and American lives were in danger; the Generals at San Isidro were dejected, several were weeping and one was hysterically urging "retreat," and Ambassador Bennett and the Embassy's Country Team unanimously believed that the time had come to land the Marines. Bennett recommended that the Marines establish control of the evacuation center at the polo field near the Hotel Embajador and take possession of the U. S. Embassy grounds.

Bennett followed this quickly with another cable saying he had just asked the aircraft carrier *Boxer* to provide helicopter evacuation from the polo field and to send a platoon of Marines to protect the Embassy. He recommended that the U.S. government give serious thought to "armed intervention which goes beyond the mere protection of Americans" and not only seek to establish order but to prevent "another Cuba" if the San Isidro forces collapsed, as seemed likely.

By 6 P.M. President Johnson had taken his decision: To land the Marines to protect American lives.

Undersecretary Mann telephoned Bennett from Washington at about 6 or 6:30 P.M. and instructed him to ask Benoit to put in writing for the record Benoit's earlier request for Marines on the ground that they were needed to protect U. S. lives which he considered were in danger.

That night Bennett asked Benoit for this written statement and cabled it to Washington after midnight. This statement, the juridical basis for the Marine landing, said that Benoit, in his previous written request, had neglected to state that in his opinion American lives were in danger and he could not protect them adequately and for that reason was requesting "temporary intervention" to restore public order.

By that time the first Marines had already landed. At about 7 P.M. some four hundred Marines went ashore and took up positions around the Hotel Embajador to safeguard evacuation. In all, about five thousand people, U.S. citizens as well as citizens of forty-five other countries, were evacuated.

Ambassador Bennett reported that, landing, Marines found the Hotel Embajador polo field already under fire. A Marine platoon went by automobile from the Hotel Embajador to guard the Embassy. The Embassy had been under sniper fire for two days. The acting dean of the diplomatic corps asked for Marines to protect other Embassies, but not enough were ashore at that time. The French government sent a transport to evacuate Frenchmen; as far as I know, it never arrived. The Dominican police had suffered terrible casualties—patrols sent downtown had been killed by heavy weapons fired from rooftops. Some policemen were taking off their uniforms and going into hiding in civilian clothes. Police, attacking a rebel strongpoint in a tank, were killed by rebel bazooka fire. By now the police were only attempting to hold Fortaleza Ozama, headquarters of the Cascos Blancos we had trained. A British vice-consul toured downtown and saw bands of armed men roaming the streets and a hospital filled with wounded lying on the floor. Looting and sacking were spreading.

President Johnson called in Congressional leaders. Then, at about 8:40 P.M., he went on national radio and television and told the American people that Americans were in danger, Dominican authorities could not safeguard them, we were evacuating them, four hundred Marines had already landed, we had "appealed repeatedly in recent days for a cease-fire" between the contending Dominican forces, and the Dominican Ambassador had informed the Council of the OAS. The President himself appealed for a cease-fire. Ambassador Bunker called the OAS to ask for a special OAS meeting the next morning.

Early Thursday morning the U. S. Task Force Commander requested clearance to land aboard his own plane at San Isidro. Ambassador Bennett feared this might be interpreted as evidence that the Marines' purpose was to support the San Isidro military, as Radio San Isidro was already implying. Furthermore, Bennett said that Donny Reid and Ramón Cáceres had asked asylum in the U. S. Embassy; Bennett, saying the rebels would surely kill them if they could, would be glad to shelter them—if the Department approved. The Department did not—while it shared Bennett's concern, it felt that to give them asylum or arrange their evacuation would undermine our position of neutrality. And of course we do not officially give asylum. (One night subsequently Reid and Cáceres did enter the U. S. Embassy unofficially but otherwise they hid in private Dominican homes.)

The Department sent another cable that morning making it clear to Ambassador Bennett that U.S. troops should not move for the time being beyond the perimeter of the evacuation areas already held, and that participation by U.S. troops in aggressive action against anybody, including leftist extremists, could only be ordered by the President. The Department did, however, accept Bennett's view that leftist extremists had seized control from legitimate PRD rebels, told Bennett to consider urgently whether he ought to use a few U.S. officers to help San Isidro develop operational plans to take the rebel stronghold downtown, and asked why San Isidro had lost its will to fight.

Ambassador Bennett replied that he had instructed the Task Force Commander that all troops were to remain at the Hotel Embajador pending further orders. Bennett appeared to believe that they would have to expand the perimeter of the evacuation area in order to protect foreign and private American homes, most of which lay in a residential area between the Hotel Embajador and the Palace. Bennett reported that the San Isidro Generals had accomplished nothing during the day. He intended to use three MAAG officers at San Isidro to help the San Isidro Generals develop operational plans. The "operation mop-up" which the San Isidro Generals had envisaged had, in short, come to nothing.

The proposal to help San Isidro develop operational plans was overtaken by events—by a decision that night to send U. S. Airborne troops to the Dominican Republic. The Department told Bennett by telephone to forget about the proposal.

At 10:30 A.M. Thursday, April 29, Ambassador Bunker reported formally to a special meeting of the OAS Council that Marines had landed to protect U.S. lives. (OAS Ambassadors had been notified informally the night before.) Mexico, Costa Rica, Colombia, Venezuela, and Chile indicated concern at our unilateral intervention. The COAS (Council of the OAS) approved a message to the Papal Nuncio in Santo Domingo asking him to arrange a cease-fire.

MISSION TO THE CIVIL WAR

…eneral Imbert, temporily to be President, and …mbassador Martin

"Since it was impossible to go into the rebel zone at night, I saw several Dominicans in the International Zone. One was Tony Imbert. In the current crisis, everybody told me, Imbert had kept apart from the San Isidro generals whom the rebels hated....I had not known Colonel Caamaño, the rebel leader...and I thought Imbert could tell me about him....Imbert thought Caamaño had lost his mind...."

Negotiations with the rebels: Martin, Héctor Aristy, Caamaño Deño, and the Nuncio

…tried to talk to Caamaño but the roar outside was deafening. He …id, *"Un momento,"* went to the doorway, and in an instant all was …iet. He was not crazy. And he had command presence, crowd pres-…ce. I told him again my purpose and emphasized the important of an …mediate cease-fire. Héctor Aristy went out and made an impas-…oned speech about me and my friendship for the Dominican people …d the cause of constitutionality....Now I was caught."

"This was hate, real and naked....We had taught them to believe in constitutional democracy, and they had rebelled against the regime that overthrew Bosch....And, finally, the rebellion had been joined by hundreds, perhaps thousands, of ordinary Dominicans who had emerged from Trujillo's tyranny and who had been told by me and others that the United States would help them get a better life...."

Rioting Dominicans surround a correspondent's car, shouting slogans and abuse

"The military rebels had looted the arsenals of huge quantities of weapons....The killing began. Blind fury and anarchy overwhelmed the city....Nobody knows how many died, probably at least two thousand. ...Marauding bands spread through the city, some purposeful, some random...."

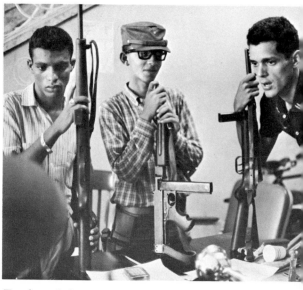

To the rebel cause came liberals, military men, adventurers—and virtual children

14

The distribution of weapons armed the populace, and set the stage for violence

"As our helicopter slanted down where Shlaudeman used to play golf, to land on the polo field behind the Hotel Embajador, we saw Marines manning foxholes and gun emplacements around the helicopter pad. Almost every night they were attacked.... Sullen smoke arose from burning buildings at the harbor. Offshore stood the U.S. fleet ... gray and low and powerful...."

A U.S. artillery emplacement near the Hotel Embajador

U.S. Marines seek a sniper along the George Washington Avenue

15

"U.S. planes were landing and taking off every two or three minutes. U.S. soldiers were setting up tents and unloading supplies. U.S. jeeps and trucks raced across the base and around the hangars. This was a troop buildup. Within a couple of days we had something like twenty-one thousand troops in Santo Domingo—nearly as many as we then had in Vietnam...."

Lieutenant General Bruce Palmer, Jr. (right) presents OAS flag to General Hugo Panasco Alvim of Brazil on May 29, 1965

"McGeorge Bundy, Special Assistant to the President; Undersecretary of State Mann; Deputy Secretary of Defense Vance; and Assistant Secretary of State Vaughn arrived in the Dominican Republic May 15 on President Johnson's instructions to try to help establish a government of national concord....Bundy and the others worked day and night, nearing exhaustion. It was an extremely difficult, not to say dangerous, negotiation...."

Harry Shlaudeman and
McGeorge Bundy

The Papal Nuncio and Ambassador Martin

Undersecretary Mann and
Ambassador Tapley Bennett

1

The State Department instructed all our Ambassadors in the Hemisphere to urge the governments they were accredited to to support convocation of a Meeting of Foreign Ministers.

Ambassador Bennett reported that "bombing" and strafing became heavy during the afternoon. The Red Cross was burying the bodies· of people where they fell. Food was needed desperately. The United States distributed tons of beans, flour, milk, and oil to the people. The Embassy came under heavy sniper fire. It reported that the Salvadoran Embassy was violated. The Ambassador asked the Navy to bring its ships nearer to shore. U. S. Marines were fired on and returned the fire. That afternoon about fifteen hundred more Marines landed.

That evening, Secretaries Rusk and McNamara and others asked Ambassador Bennett by telephone if he agreed with their view that a rebel victory would probably lead to a pro-Communist government. Bennett did, adding that the rebels might install Bosch but probably would quickly discard him. They asked if direct military action was necessary to prevent the installation of a pro-Communist government and to protect American lives. Bennett said this seemed likely because of the weakness of the San Isidro Generals. The Administration leaders in Washington told Bennett he should not hesitate to recommend whatever action he thought was needed. Bennett replied that others were more qualified than he to decide the nature and size of forces needed but "now that we are in this we must do the full job as needed."

Washington leaders said that obviously the U.S. government wished to avoid military action "as long as there is a reasonable chance orderly forces can prevail." Bennett said he hoped that additional Marine support would spur the San Isidro forces on. The Administration leaders asked about the situation in the rest of the Republic. The Ambassador thought it all right so far. The Administration leaders were considering plans to use the Marines to establish an international safety zone that would include the residential area from the Hotel Embajador to the U. S. Embassy to the sea. Ambassador Bennett, who had made a similar recommendation earlier, now said the area was inhabited mostly by well-to-do people and to safeguard them might appear to discriminate against poorer Dominicans. Asked what should be done in the next six to twelve hours, Ambassador Bennett replied that "we should commit sufficient troops to do the job here rapidly and effectively." (He did not specify what he meant by "the job.") The Administration leaders asked about the feasibility of sealing off the downtown section including the rebel stronghold in the old Spanish quarter, Ciudad Nueva, thus establishing an enforceable cease-fire, after which the OAS would be asked to negotiate a political settlement. Bennett thought this politically desirable and recommended asking the Task Force Commander whether it was militarily feasible. The Ambassador added that the U. S. Marines had just killed the fifth sniper on the edge of the Embassy grounds.

Some eighteen hundred or two thousand U.S. airborne troops, already alerted, were ordered to land at San Isidro airfield. Two Battalion Combat Teams of the 82nd Airborne Division did land at 2:30 A.M. on Friday, April 30.

The Council of the OAS met Thursday night until about 3:00 A.M. It adopted a resolution calling upon everybody in the Dominican Republic to cease fire and to cooperate in the immediate establishment of an international neutral refugee zone including the foreign embassies. It voted to inform the Security Council of the UN of its action. U. S. Marines began setting up the International Zone. It would initially reach from the Hotel Embajador to the U. S. Embassy and might be expanded to include the National Palace.

Friday morning, April 30, the Department sent Ambassador Bennett a résumé of U.S. policy. Ambassador Bennett should use his influence to induce San Isidro to cooperate with the OAS' request for a cease-fire. San Isidro should ensure that the OAS action would not result in the ascendancy of Communist groups to political power. The U.S. government was concerned lest the San Isidro junta believe that the United States intended to join it in aggressive action against rebel forces. This, the Department said, was not the case. The immediate objective of the United States was to establish the International Zone under the COAS resolution. San Isidro should cooperate. The immediate purpose of the Airborne forces at San Isidro was to secure their position there and the bridge over the Río Ozama. (This did not rule out later sealing off the rebels in the downtown area.) The Department instructed Bennett to cooperate with the Papal Nuncio, who, in accordance with the OAS request, had begun his efforts to achieve a cease-fire. (Ambassador Bennett felt misgivings, thought the Nuncio's good intentions might outrun his judgment.)

4

It was on that Friday morning, April 30, that I arrived in Washington, summoned from Connecticut by the President.

In the Cabinet Room, the Administration leaders said that the Marines were already establishing the International Zone. One element of the 82nd Airborne Division was moving from San Isidro toward the Duarte Bridge where Wessin y Wessin was still precariously holding a bridgehead on the far side, the city side, of the Río Ozama; their commander said he needed more troops to push on into the city. At that time, the Administration leaders were considering but had not yet decided to send the Airborne column into the city to seal off the rebels in Ciudad Nueva and open up a corridor to the International Zone. Since, however, the Administration leaders had not decided to open the corridor at this time, this meant that the International Zone had no link with the bridge, and the rebels controlled not only the old Spanish quarter, Ciudad Nueva, between Calle Conde and the sea, but also the central business district, and they had free access to the Palace and to the northern part of the city and suburbs and, indeed, to the exit roads leading to Santiago and the interior. Bosch would tell the rebel leader, Colonel Caamaño, to sign the Papal Nuncio's cease-fire. The Nuncio had expected to meet with both sides that morning. While we were talking, a cable came in—Fortaleza Ozama "appeared" to have fallen to the rebels. Fighting in that waterfront area was heavy. The San Isidro forces might collapse today. But should we send U.S. troops into the capital city to shoot Dominicans?

The President asked if we couldn't persuade the OAS to meet again this morning. Rusk and Ball doubted it—the OAS had met till 3 A.M. The President asked Secretary McNamara and General Wheeler what they would need to take the Republic. One or two divisions, they said. The President said he foresaw two dangers—very soon we would witness a Castro/Communist-dominated government in the Dominican Republic, or we would find ourselves in the Republic alone without any support in the Hemisphere. He didn't want either one to happen. The President told Rusk and Ball to get to work with the OAS, told McNamara and Wheeler to get ready to do whatever might have to be done, and told me to go to the Republic to help Ambassador Bennett, to open up contact with the rebels, to help the OAS and the Nuncio get a cease-fire and stop the bloodshed, and to find out what the facts were and report to the President. Cognizant of criticism that had already begun, the President said he had every intention of working for peace through the OAS or any other channel but did not intend "to sit here with my hands tied and let Castro take that island. What can we do in Vietnam if we can't clean up the Dominican Republic? I know what the editorials will say but it would be a hell of a lot worse if we sit here and don't do anything and the Communists take that country."

I said that if I was going, I'd like to go fast and, with his permission, would leave immediately. He said go ahead. It was then 10:30 A.M.

Taking Shlaudeman with me, I went to Andrews Air Force Base and left for the Dominican Republic. Shlaudeman didn't have even a toothbrush with him. I had a suitcase—I'd told Fran I'd go to Santo Domingo if asked, though no heroes would emerge from this mess.

5

I saw four dangers—a Communist takeover, a full-scale U.S. military occupation, an entrenched Dominican dictator supported by us, or a U. S. Hungary—a frontal assault on the rebel stronghold in Ciudad

Nueva, with U.S. troops slaughtering thousands of Dominicans, including innocents. (Apparently the decision to send the Airborne into San Isidro, not to another airport, had been based on a Pentagon contingency plan and its political implications were not discussed. I had asked Secretary McNamara if my own plane could land elsewhere. He'd said it was impossible.) I was still not convinced that Communists had taken control of the rebel movement and if I found they had not, I intended to say so and had been assured that I should. From the tenor of the White House meeting, I judged we had at least twenty-four hours, and possibly the weekend but no more, to find out what the facts were and influence our policy.

On the plane, Shlaudeman and I made a list of people we would try to see yet today and divided them between us—Ambassador Bennett, the CIA station chief, and Ben Ruyle and other Embassy political officers first. Then Molina Ureña and Peña Gómez of the PRD, the Papal Nuncio, Imbert, Donny Reid, Benoit, Wessin, Caamaño, and other military rebel leaders, an active leader of the 14th of June we knew, the Social Christian leaders, the British Embassy officer who had toured downtown. Tomorrow we would talk to Antonio Guzmán, Amiama, Bonnelly, Pichardo, Salvador Jorge Blanco, and Marco Cabral. (At that time we had no idea how difficult it would be to locate people and get to them in the war-wrecked Republic.)

The plane came in over the empty northern coast and in a few minutes we were over San Isidro. The air was full of U.S. military helicopters and enormous C-130s, I think they call them, the big boxcars that carry dozens of men and tons of heavy equipment. As we touched down on the runway we saw a bunch of GIs beating out a fire in dry grass near the runway where they had pitched their tents. A Dominican Air Force plane was nosed over, wrecked just off the runway. The old Dominican Mustang fighters and Vampire jets were parked on the taxi apron as usual, half dismantled, many cannibalized to make a few flyable. Those that were airworthy had rockets under their wings. U.S. planes were landing and taking off every two or three minutes. U.S. soldiers were setting up tents and unloading supplies. U. S. Jeeps and trucks raced across the base and around the hangars. This was a troop buildup. Within a couple of days we had something like twenty-one thousand troops in Santo Domingo—nearly as many as we then had in Vietnam.

Ambassador Bennett had just arrived at San Isidro by helicopter, and so had the Papal Nuncio, Monseñor Clarizio, come to talk to the military junta about a cease-fire. I joined them in the Commander's office. General Wessin was there, and other Dominican Generals I had known, and the three Colonels who made up the junta. So were a U. S. Army General and several other officers. So was a big young man in a white shirt with a homemade Red Cross emblem on his shirt-sleeve, Héctor

Conde, representing the rebels. And Fausto Caamaño, brother of the rebel leader. Colonel Benoit, head of the junta, a rather short, dark-skinned man, was speaking, his voice filled with passion—everyone wanted a cease-fire, but how could his forces accept one when hundreds of Dominican officers and men had been massacred, a dozen had been captured and shot down in cold blood by the rebels, and an officer had been beheaded and his head paraded through the rebel zone on a pole? Others spoke, their voices rising—their homes had been sacked, their friends murdered; and Héctor Conde, the big young rebel spokesman, replied vehemently—his people, too, had suffered, they had been butchered, they were hungry, and the Generals at San Isidro could dictate no peace.

This was hate, real and naked. At one point somebody suggested a cease-fire for a few hours to collect the bodies that littered the streets, and a discussion began of how to do it—with garbage trucks? Soldiers with Thompson submachine guns and San Cristóbals hurried in and out, the Generals began to move about to talk in little groups, the meeting was disintegrating; and an officer hurried in, whispered to Colonel Benoit, spoke quickly to the others, then said his forces were under heavy rebel fire; and the Generals and Colonels began leaving in haste.

We were not going to get the cease-fire.

I went to General Wessin y Wessin, stocky, swarthy, carrying a submachine gun. I had not seen him since the dawn he overthrew Juan Bosch. I reminded him of that, said he and I must forget our past differences, told him that President Johnson was deeply concerned about the senseless killing of the Dominican people, told him the President had sent me here to try to help stop it, and asked him to be the first to sign the cease-fire.

Wessin hesitated, then went with me to the Papal Nuncio and signed. So then did Benoit and the other two members of the San Isidro junta.

The cease-fire, typed on a torn-off half sheet of paper, contained only two sentences:

"1. Security of saving life is given to all persons, regardless of ideology or cause, including prisoners and asylees.

"2. An OAS commission is requested to serve as arbitration in the conflict."

It was a start.

The Nuncio went to broadcast it to the people over Radio San Isidro. I mingled with Dominicans I knew—roly-poly Rib, who used to use a gold-plated deep-sea fishing reel, now sweaty and glum; tense Commodore Rivera Caminero, who once with his wife had taken Fran and me on a weekend fishing trip; General Rivera Cuesta, who had made a voyage aboard the *Mella* with Bosch and us; others. When last I had seen most of them, it had been when they overthrew Bosch.

From them, and also from American military men I knew at the base, and in subsequent interviews, I learned that the Dominican Armed Forces had virtually disintegrated. Of the nearly thirty thousand men who had been under arms in my time, the San Isidro Generals now could command the loyalty of no more than fifteen hundred Army, nine hundred Air, and probably 150 tankers, plus part of the Navy, several thousand virtually useless soldiers scattered in garrisons around the country, and about a thousand police. The Generals themselves were demoralized. A MAAG officer, disgusted, told me they wouldn't fight. Belisario Peguero, he said, had run to San Isidro in tears. Not even Wessin would fight; he had pulled his troops back from the bridgehead across the Duarte Bridge; our Airborne manned it. Now that our troops had arrived, Wessin and the other commanders were talking belligerently once more. But I suspected they wanted us to do their fighting for them.

What had happened to their troops? Many had been killed. That very morning, when Fortaleza Ozama fell, the Cascos Blancos had run out the back door above the Río Ozama; some, I was told, had been shot, some had drowned, some had been eaten by sharks. At the very outset of the rebellion, Army crack troops had joined the rebels, including two good battalion commanders whom we had trained in the Canal Zone and an entire company of counter-insurgency troops whom we had trained in my time. We had taught them to believe in constitutional democracy, and they had rebelled against the regime that overthrew Bosch. Many other young officers and men had been sickened by the corruption of the Generals during the Reid regime—or had been jealous of it. They too had gone over to the rebels. And no doubt hundreds, perhaps thousands, uncertain of which side would win, had simply melted into the civilian population.

I was surprised at Wessin; I always had considered him strong. I can only surmise that, seeing other elements of the Armed Forces collapsing around him, confronting a well-armed determined foe almost alone, he had not wanted to risk losing his tanks and had pulled them back to protect his personal power position.

With Ambassador Bennett, Shlaudeman and I got into a helicopter to go to the U. S. Embassy, flying out over the Caribbean, keeping clear of the rebel stronghold along the waterfront. Sullen smoke rose from burning buildings at the harbor. Offshore stood the U.S. fleet, its flagship the aircraft carrier *Boxer*. I remembered how in my time its crew in whites had manned the rail as we took Bonnelly to it by helicopter for lunch, its guns of peace booming out the presidential salute; how its Marines had rebuilt the orphanage. Now the *Boxer* stood gray and low and powerful, its task force grouped around it, silent, its guns of war waiting, its Marines in battle dress. As our helicopter slanted down where Shlaudeman used to play golf, to land on the polo field behind the Hotel Embajador, we saw Marines manning foxholes and gun emplacements around the helicopter pad. Almost every night they were attacked.

As night fell, an officer in a tent with a flashlight got a car and several Marines with automatic rifles to take us to the Chancellery. The Chancellery was shuttered and heavily guarded. Unseen sentries challenged us at the driveway. Rebel snipers were across the street in an old house. Soon several sets of billowing draperies blocked the Chancellery doorway so that you passed between them, and lights did not show outside. Nights were the worst. You had to try to get everything done before dark; after that nobody was supposed to go out, though of course Shlaudeman and I had to. Inside, the Chancellery was a shambles, crowded with Embassy people and soldiers and Marines, telephone technicians and secretaries sent down from Washington to relieve those worn out. The little lobby was littered with paper cups, pop bottles, emergency telephone lines. People hurried to and fro in a blur. Tony Ruíz, our police adviser, lay sleeping on a couch in the Ambassador's secretary's office, one arm dangling.

Ambassador Bennett showed me a flysheet calling on civilian and military rebels to defeat "the criminal band of Wessin" and dictatorship. It was signed by the "Constitutional Military Command"—Lieutenant Colonel Francisco Caamaño Deño, Lieutenant Colonel Montes Arache, Lieutenant Colonel Noguera Nuñez, Lieutenant Colonel Miguel Hernando Ramírez, Major Héctor Lachapelle, Major Claudio Caamaño Grullón, Major Alejandro Deño Suero, and Major Jesús de la Rosa.

Shlaudeman and I talked to the Ambassador, found C-rations to eat and desk corners to work on, read documents, then started out separately to see people we knew.

The night was black. There were no streetlights. No houses were lit. My driver stopped at checkpoints manned by shadowy men with guns. The troops of all three sides—rebels, loyalists, United States—wore the same uniforms. Sometimes far away, sometimes close, we heared gunfire— sniper fire, machine gun fire, and heavy fire, mortars and 106 mm. recoilless rifles. We saw only one or two other cars. The driver drove fast; a moving target is harder to hit. The International Zone had been established on paper, U.S. troops patrolled its perimeter, but the Zone itself had not been cleared, and rebel snipers lay in many houses. As Ambassador, I had many times refused an armed guard. Tonight, on orders, I sat in front with two U. S. Marines in the back seat with automatic rifles. They told me, "If this car is fired on, get down flat."

Since it was impossible to go into the rebel zone at night, I saw several Dominicans in the International Zone. One was Tony Imbert. In the current crisis, everybody told me, Imbert had kept apart from the San Isidro Generals whom the rebels hated. Those generals never had accepted him anyway. They stayed out at San Isidro. Imbert alone stayed in the city. I had not known Colonel Caamaño, the rebel leader, in my time but he had been in the police, Imbert's police, and I thought Imbert could tell me about him.

While Imbert and I were talking, I received an urgent message from the Chancellery: Juan Bosch was calling me from Puerto Rico. I hurried to the Chancellery. After long delay—the telephone exchange was in rebel hands, and sometimes did not work at all—I got Bosch on the phone. He said that U. S. Marines were attacking rebel positions so that Wessin's troops could advance behind ours, it was a conspiracy. I told him that so far as I knew his information was untrue; I would inquire. I told him the San Isidro Generals had signed the cease-fire that afternoon and I was going to see to it that they honored it and I hoped he would see to it that the rebel commander, Colonel Caamaño, signed it and honored it, too. He would. The San Isidro Generals didn't believe Caamaño could control his forces. Bosch said he could. I hoped to see Caamaño the following day. Bosch gave me Caamaño's telephone numbers and told me that my arrival was the best news he had received.

I told Shlaudeman to try to get Caamaño and arrange a meeting for the next morning, then hurried back to Imbert's house. The gate was closed. No guards were visible but I knew they always hid behind the hedge and wall. I told my driver to stop and turn on the inside dome light, and made a "pssst" sound. In a minute or two, a guard appeared out of the darkness and came carefully to the car. Unfortunately he did not recognize me. I told him who I was. It was near 1 A.M. Dubiously, he went back to the sentry post to call the house. I could dimly see other guards near him. At that moment a string of shots went off behind my ear. I dived for the floor, began calling out to the guards not to shoot, it was an accident, and waited, expecting Imbert's guards to open up with their machine guns. They did not. My Marine guard said that, while trying to put his gun on safety, his finger had slipped. I kept calling to the Imbert guards. Finally they let me in. After that, I took no guard with me.

Imbert and I talked more, sitting in his dining room with a kerosene lamp. Once heavy automatic fire began, sounding as though it came from across the street, and he, who had assassinated Trujillo, told me to get to the floor, and we went crouching low to the living room.

I asked him who was leading the rebels. He said Isa Conde (though he did not specify which of the Isa Conde brothers), Fidelio Despradel, and Juan Miguel Román, all Communists, and Colonels Montes Arache and Caamaño, both military defectors. He said Montes Arache had been the leader of the frogmen and "the frogmen are hell." During my time, Caamaño had been the leader of the police at Palma Sola.[6] His

---

[6] Caamaño's detractors say that he led the massacre after General Rodríguez Reyes was killed. Caamaño himself has said that he was knocked unconscious in the melee at the outset and was not responsible for the massacre.

father had been a much-feared Trujillista. Caamaño had not been a
Bosch supporter, had not opposed Bosch's overthrow. He was an opportunist. That spring he had become involved prematurely in intrigue
against Belisario Peguero. Reid had appointed him to a foreign consulate; he had refused to go; Reid had transferred him to the Air Force
at San Isidro for reassignment. Caamaño hated Wessin and disliked Reid.
He had probably joined the rebellion for revenge. The San Isidro Generals hated Caamaño above all others, said he had committed atrocities
during the bloodbath in the first days of rebellion, and said he had been
crazed by blood. Imbert thought Caamaño had lost his mind—he had told
Imbert that he had fifty thousand troops, and Imbert considered this
ridiculous.

I asked Imbert how the whole thing started. He said on Saturday
while he was hunting in the interior, the police had told him by radio
that a *golpe* had begun. Reid's decision to run for President had caused
it. Taking back roads, Imbert had reached Santo Domingo and gone
to the Palace. According to Imbert, Donny Reid had told him that four
truckloads of PRDistas had gone to an Army camp and Army headquarters, been given guns, and had handed them out from the trucks on
street corners in downtown Santo Domingo.

Imbert told me the Army had no guns left to fight with—the rebels
took ten thousand automatic rifles and machine guns with them, plus
mortars, howitzers, and bazookas, though they had insufficient ammunition. Today, Imbert said, they had put a howitzer or a 50-caliber
machine gun on the roof of the ancient Cathedral, apparently on the
theory nobody would shoot it off for fear of damaging the Cathedral.

Imbert said the PRD had started the rebellion but lost control of it to
the Communists. Imbert said it was good we'd sent our troops but didn't
want us to send more—"we can win the day after tomorrow ourselves."
He said some rebels, fearing the Marines, were hiding their guns. "Let's
push ahead tomorrow. Your troops can go to 30 de Marzo from the
bridge to Parque Independencia. And we can go into Ciudad Nueva." He
said he had several hundred prisoners already. He said he had three
hundred counter-insurgency troops at the Palace, the only worthwhile
troops available. He said, "When we settle up this mess then is the time to
reduce the Armed Forces. To cleanse them. Now we've got the excuse."
He was disgusted with the San Isidro Generals.

I asked if the rebels could be defeated any other way than by a
frontal attack on their stronghold, Ciudad Nueva. He said, "Yes, if we
get pressure on them. Surrender and surrender arms; promise not to deport or jail them."

I asked Imbert to find out more about the rebel leadership—"you've
always had lines out to everybody, including the Communists."

He said, smiling, "Not as much any more. But I will try."

"You've been in touch with Caamaño—he told you how many troops he had. See if you can get in touch with others. The thing I want to do is to stop the killing, stop the bloodshed. That's the first thing."

Back at the Chancellery, Shlaudeman said he had talked to Colonel Caamaño by telephone. He sounded cold as ice, not crazy at all. He had instructions from Bosch to talk to me and to sign a cease-fire with the Nuncio—he would have signed it tonight but nobody could move in the rebel zone at night. He wanted me to know that he and his followers had complete confidence in me and wanted to see me early in the morning.

The Nuncio called me and said Caamaño had asked for medicines for one thousand or two thousand people—could I help? We did.

It must have been about 3 A.M. when Ambassador Bennett and I walked up to the Embassy Residence in the blackness with a Marine guard. The Residence was filled with Embassy employees; they could not safely go home after dark. They were sleeping everywhere. A girl lit a candle, and we stepped carefully over people sleeping on the porch and living room floor. The Ambassador and I slept on the floor in the study. The Residence was under sporadic rebel fire all night. In the distance we could hear the crunch of mortars. When our troops fired the 106 mm. recoilless rifles, the earth trembled.

6

In the morning, Shlaudeman and I began an elaborate charade, arranging to see Colonel Caamaño. We called him, he called us, we called the Papal Nuncio, he called us, and so on. It was difficult. Caamaño refused to leave the rebel stronghold. I would have to go to him—cross the line into the rebel zone. I wanted as much guarantee of my life as he could give. He had to get word to his troops and snipers and could not categorically guarantee safety. Shlaudeman and I met his emissary, Héctor Conde, at the Papal Nunciatura and we started out in the Nuncio's car, its hood covered with the flag of the Vatican, the Nuncio himself driving, wearing his long white robe and his red cap.

At the line of the International Zone on Avenida Independencia, I got us through the checkpoint, guarded by U. S. Marines, rolls of barbed wire, sandbags, heavy recoilless rifles, machine guns, a huge armored personnel carrier, and a tank. Beyond, we were in rebel territory.

We drove slowly, so snipers could see the Nuncio and his flag, and kept our windows rolled up, so snipers would know we did not intend to shoot.

Near Lina's Restaurant where we used to have dinner, we turned off Independencia and headed into Ciudad Nueva—narrow streets, narrow sidewalks, thick-walled Spanish colonial buildings, high-arched doorways. Long ago I had come here to see Fiallo in his house. Normally the doors and windows are open. Now they were shut tight. Normally the streets are jammed; now they were all but deserted. No cars moved. Garbage and filth littered the streets, shattered glass and broken plaster. The city looked dead.

Carefully, the Nuncio threaded his way, Héctor Conde guiding him through a circuitous prearranged route. On a narrow street we stopped and went into a small drugstore and on into a tiny room behind, tile floor, thick walls, high ceiling, and sat in straight-backed chairs; and in a moment Colonel Caamaño came in.

He was young—thirty-two—stocky, brown-skinned, wearing khakis, looking strong but a trifle uncertain. With him was a short young man, Héctor Aristy, whom I had known while Ambassador and had considered a playboy, a smooth operator in both business and politics, intelligent, ambitious, joining party after party and movement after movement. Many thought Aristy simply an opportunist. But I had noticed previously —and noticed again today—that he was astonishingly well-informed about military matters. We wondered if Aristy had received training in military tactics in a Soviet bloc country. We could find no evidence he had traveled there.

I asked Caamaño how he saw the situation. He said, "The entire city is asking for the return to the 1962 Constitution with Juan Bosch."

Aristy corrected him: It was the 1963 Constitution—Bosch's—that they wanted; not the 1962 one.

Caamaño said, "We of the command are sure that the only man who has the moral standard to save the Republic is Juan Bosch. We have close to twenty-five thousand armed citizens and he is the only man who can tell us to give up our arms. I am completely sure."

I asked about the cease-fire. He already had signed it. He would honor it. I asked if he could control all his troops.

Artisty answered for him and spoke volubly about constitutionality and Bosch.

I told Aristy I wanted Caamaño to answer. Nevertheless, as the conversation proceeded, Aristy did much of the talking for Caamaño. Caamaño said he had control of his military troops and his armed civilians. He had the radio and telephone systems.

The Nuncio suggested that both sides surrender arms. They wouldn't without Bosch's approval.

It was essential that U.S. troops not cross the line, Caamaño said. U. S. 82nd Airborne troops had crossed the bridge with Wessin's troops, and already Wessin's troops were breaking the cease-fire—about forty-five minutes before, two 106 mm. recoilless rifles had fired into the rebel zone from across the river and blown up a house. (A 106 can pierce ten inches of armor.) I told him I didn't know anything about it and said that during the first hours of a cease-fire, incidents were inevitable. He agreed, but said there better not be too many incidents. He said, "It is immediately necessary that the United States troops be sure where they are and that they stay to the line." I went over a map with him that Bennett had given me, showing the International Zone line, and he agreed to it. I also explained that we were moving the line two blocks eastward today so that the Embassy itself would not be under sniper fire. He agreed to this too. He complained that the Marines were providing advance cover beyond the line for the police, who were firing over their heads from their headquarters near the Embassy. I told him, truthfully, I didn't know anything about it. Later I learned that two Marines were indeed killed at that point, out of the Zone. Nobody had told them where the line was.

Caamaño said the two most dangerous places were the police headquarters and the bridgehead on the city side of the river. He said he had 50-caliber machine guns massed south of the bridge and they would open up if the American troops did not stop helping Wessin. He claimed that he had sent ten civilians to repair the Electricidad this morning; either U.S. or Wessin troops across the river had shot them.[7]

Ambassador Bennett had told me he'd heard the rebels planned to blow up the Electricidad that night and also attack the U. S. Embassy. I asked Caamaño about it. He gave me his personal assurance neither would happen.

He complained that several times his men had tried to cross the line to go to their homes to see their children or get clean clothes, and Marines had disarmed them and handed them over to the police, who beat them up. I told him that the only solution was to tell his men not to approach the line armed. I pressed hard on the cease-fire, and Caamaño said his forces would honor it. He would welcome OAS observers.

He brought in three of his fellow military commanders. We shook hands, other crowded in, we embraced, everyone talked at once, two or three women came in, the tiny room was aswirl with men and guns, and a chair fell over; and all said over and over, "We trust you, Mr. Martin." Outside a crowd of about two hundred had gathered, and during our conversation had set up the five-beat chant, *"Da-da-da, Juan Bo,"* that is, Juan Bosch, and had been firing shots into the air.

I tried to talk to Caamaño but the roar outside was deafening. He said, *"Un momento,"* went to the doorway, and in an instant all was quiet. He was not crazy. And he had command presence, crowd presence. I told him again my purpose and emphasized the importance of an immediate cease-fire. Héctor Aristy went out and made an impassioned speech about me and my friendship for the Dominican people and the cause of constitutionality. I had hoped to avoid being used by either side. Now I was

---

[7] Caamaño always told me he controlled the Electricidad. Our military commanders always told me we did.

caught. The Nuncio and I waited, hoping the crowd would disperse, but Aristy held it. We decided to leave as rapidly as possible. When we appeared at the doorway in the dazzling sunlight, the crowd cheered wildly; we pushed through, got into the car, but people, just ordinary people, an emaciated aged woman in a flowered dress, a toothless old man, teen-agers and children, kept thrusting their hands into the car to me to shake hands, crying out, "We trust you, Mr. Martin," and "We have faith in you," and "We want democracy." Slowly we drove away, children running after. These were the people, the poor, the Dominican people. They *did* trust me. They knew nothing of politics or international power. They were the real sufferers, hungry, penniless, disease-ridden. They would be killed if we launched an all-out military assault against Ciudad Nueva. They counted on me.

Yet at the same time, I knew the demonstration had been well-organized. And Shlaudeman noticed something else: A black-shirted young man whom he recognized as a member of the MPD, the Castro/Communist terrorist party, had yelled beside the car, "Yankees go home," and immediately a powerful hand had gripped his shoulder from behind and jerked him away out of sight. He had used the wrong script.

That same Saturday the OAS Secretary General, José A. Mora of Costa Rica, arrived. (A five-man OAS commission arrived Sunday with unusually broad powers to investigate all aspects of the situation.) Ambassador Bennett and I met with Mora and the San Isidro Generals. Mora urged the necessity of observing the cease-fire and saving lives. Colonel Benoit of the junta assured him the cease-fire would be honored, but then talked about beheadings, and Commodore Rivera Caminero began to scream about Radio Havana—Rivera's own house had been looted by the rebels—and Héctor Conde answered angrily that the people wanted Juan Bosch back, the military said *they* were the people, and a long quarrel ensued, getting nowhere. Benoit recited Dominican history starting with Ulises Heureaux and ending with Bosch, saying that the Dominican people cheer every President in office but when he falls they immediately yell, *"¡Qué bandido!"*, What a bandit.

Ambassador Bennett wanted me to sign a cable saying the cease-fire was breaking down. I refused, saying we should give it a chance. I went with Mora and the Nuncio to the Nunciatura. Héctor Aristy called me and said that near the bridge our troops had tied five Dominicans to lampposts. He said there were tanks and Jeeps across the bridge. Caamaño called and said that now the Marines had gone far beyond the bridge, indeed, to Parque Independencia, and if they didn't retire he would attack. I said I wanted to talk to him. He said he had no time to talk. Soon it would be dark. I got Héctor Aristy on the phone again, told him that Mora and the Nuncio and I wanted to see Caamaño immediately, and he finally agreed to meet us at Parque Independencia and take us to Caamaño. We got in the car. An aide of the Nuncio's came out to plead with him not to go, it was too dangerous. They discussed it. The sun was sinking beyond the far mountains. Finally time ran out—night came. The cease-fire might break down, slaughter might resume.

When I had come to the Dominican Republic in September of 1961 for President Kennedy, I had thought I was seeing a destroyed society. Now I thought it was a society in the process of utter disintegration.

Late that night I sat alone with Shlaudeman in the Ambassador's darkened office. During my tenure as Ambassador, I had time and again sent the Crisis Crowd out on rumor of trouble. I suppose they had some-times thought me overconcerned. But I thought I knew the Dominicans, and I lived night and day with the fear of a bloodbath. Now my private nightmare was being acted out before my eyes. Sitting in the half-dark, I told Shlaudeman I was nearly fifty years old and never had done a dishonorable thing until that day. He asked what I meant. I said I had accepted the friendship of the rebels and the ordinary people at their headquarters but soon they would all be slaughtered. Shlaudeman said they might not—the cease-fire I'd helped get might save thousands of lives, now we must work to avoid another Hungary. I doubted that we could. I'd heard a young Marine say, "I almost got one today," and his buddy, "I got my first one yesterday." They had been so trained. What a world.

7

Miraculously, the cease-fire was holding. We heard gunfire all night, but lighter and more sporadic than on any night before.

Shlaudeman had spent Saturday afternoon, and he and I spent Satur-day night and Sunday, studying the massive evidence assembled by our intelligence agencies and quietly talking to Dominicans we knew personally on both sides. A frightened businessman said, "Your troops saved us from communism." And a foreign diplomat shouted, "You saved our lives." A rebel leader said bitterly, "Your troops killed the revolution—we had won when they arrived." One day a stranger cried happily, "Meester Martin! ¡Aquí viene la democracia!"—that is, freely, "Here's Mr. Martin, here comes democracy!" Late one night, riding in a bucking helicopter, a man whose son was fighting alongside the rebels told me, "They have all gone crazy. All the Dominicans."

I took stock.

At the outset, the rebellion had been a long-planned military revolt led politically by Juan Bosch's PRD, aided by other politicians, in an attempt to reverse the *golpe* against Bosch of September 1963. Among the PRD leaders had been Molina Ureña and Peña Gómez, both pas-sionately dedicated to Bosch's—and our—ideals of liberty and justice.

Among the military men, some had been well-intentioned, some adventurers. The plotting of Bosch, the plotting of the military, and Reid's own ambition had converged to overthrow him.

And the rebellion had been joined too by Castro/Communists. Among these were several the reader will recognize from my time—Juan and Félix Ducoudray, the PSP leaders; Asdrúbal Domínguez and Antonio Isa Conde of the PSP; Gustavo Federico Ricart Ricart and Cayetano Rodríguez, both central committee members of the MPD; and Jaime Durán and Fidelio Despradel, both of the extremist wing of the 14th of June.[8] U.S. intelligence sources listed some seventy others, including Pedro Julio Mir Valentine, PSP central committee member and friend of Fidel Castro, frequent traveler to Cuba; and Hugo Tolentino Dipp, who had received guerrilla training in Cuba and Soviet bloc countries and become the PSP chief of a Cuba-trained guerrilla unit. During the Civil War, our intelligence agents saw many of these men at rebel headquarters or strongpoints. Independently, Shlaudeman and I were told by thoroughly trustworthy sources that they were there. Both true Communist parties—PSP and MPD—were represented, and so was the extremist

[8] Juan Ducoudray Mansfield—to give him his full name—had traveled in recent years to both Soviet Russia and Communist China, had gone as the official Dominican delegate to the worldwide Communist Party Congress in Moscow in 1960, and in 1962 had worked on broadcasts over Radio Havana aimed at the Dominican Republic. His brother, Félix Servio Ducoudray Mansfield, Jr., returned to the Dominican Republic in 1963 after having received indoctrination in the U.S.S.R., worked for the New China News Agency in Cuba, and traveled to China on a Cuban passport. Asdrúbal Ulises Domínguez Guerrero, a PSP man, in my time led the Communist-dominated student group FED (Federación de Estudiantes Dominicanos), and was, in August 1962, a delegate to the Congress of the International Union of Students in Leningrad. Antonio Emilio José Isa Conde, PSP member and onetime student leader, attended the "26th of July" celebrations in Havana in 1963, received guerrilla warfare training there and, later in 1963, received money in Prague. Gustavo Federico Ricart Ricart, a central committee member of the MPD, was in Cuba in 1962–63 and brought back about fifty thousand dollars to finance his group. Cayetano Rodríguez del Prado, MPD Central Committee member deported in May 1964, had traveled to Communist China, been photographed with Chairman Mao, written a pamphlet on Chinese revolutionary methods, returned to the Republic, and was in police custody until April 25; released, he contacted 14th of June leaders, came to be regarded as a principal Communist leader during the Civil War, was, with his thin almost emaciated physique and ascetic intellectuality, enormously popular with students, and in January of 1966 attended the Tri-Continental Congress in Havana, where he promised to convert the Dominican Republic into another Vietnam. We have met him before, when, in the fall of 1963, he landed in the Republic aboard the boat, the Scarlet Woman. Jaime Durán Hernando, of the 14th of June, had received guerrilla training in Cuba in 1964 and then gone to the U.S.S.R. with other trainees. Fidelio Despradel Roque had received guerrilla training in Cuba in 1963 and money from the Chinese Communists in Europe in 1964. Our old friend, Dato Pagán, early reported active in the rebellion, was actually in jail at the time.

wing of the 14th of June. The PSP and 14th of June seem to have been the most militant, at least at the outset, although in my time the MPD had been more violent. (Later on, the PSP officially changed its name to the Dominican Communist Party, saying, in a newspaper that sprang up during the Civil War, that everyone knew it had always been Communist in ideology and its new name was adopted because it was "scientifically exact." The MPD, vying with the PSP for Dominican Communist leadership, and demonstrating pointedly its adherence to the Peking, not the Moscow, line, sent "fraternal greetings" to the "Workers Party [Communist Party] of Albania.")

And, finally, the rebellion had been joined by hundreds, perhaps thousands, of ordinary Dominicans who had emerged from Trujillo's tyranny and who had been told by me and others that the United States would help them get a better life. They had voted for Bosch, and they had seen the cost of living rising and their hopes disappearing during the Reid regime.

That, then, was how the revolt had begun. But in a flash it had changed. The military rebels had looted the arsenals of huge quantities of weapons. Quickly they and the Castro/Communists had handed out guns on street corners to anybody, as we have seen. A twelve-year-old boy, wishing to join the excitement, tried to get a weapon in his home town; unable to do so, he walked to the capital and, on the way, met a truckload of soldiers; one of them gave him a machine gun.

The killing began. Blind fury and anarchy overwhelmed the city. Dominican troops killed Dominican troops. Dominican civilians killed each other. Dominican warplanes and naval vessels attacked the Dominican capital. Nobody knows how many died, probably at least two thousand. Colonel Caamaño told me he had lost fourteen hundred men. Hospitals and makeshift hospitals filled up. Doctors operated on patients by lamplight on hospital floors without anesthetic.

On Tuesday, thinking they were losing, the rebels asked Ambassador Bennett to help them negotiate a settlement. He refused.

Thereupon, the PRD leaders went into asylum in foreign Embassies. And Caamaño and the other military men, already so deeply committed they knew they must win or die, went back to the streets to fight. The PRD leaders gone, a political vacuum existed. Quickly the Castro/Communists filled that vacuum. They took over political leadership of the rebellion.

The senseless slaughter which ensued was just that—senseless slaughter. It was, indeed, the bloodbath that should logically have followed Trujillo's assassination nearly four years ago and that many Dominicans had told me in my time was some day inevitable. For Trujillo had held the lid down tight for thirty-one years, a whole generation, and pressures built up that could not be contained forever without blood. Or so some said.

In my time, we had maintained a precarious balance. We had been very careful to distinguish among the twenty-six parties, especially among the four Castro/Communist parties—and between those parties and Juan Bosch's non-Communist PRD.

When the military-*civico* right overthrew Bosch, the delicate political mosaic into which he had tried to fit himself collapsed. Hatreds polarized, the left-right polarization we always had feared. The powerful forces that had been unleashed by Trujillo's death wracked the Republic, and the political structure failed completely, and when rebels overthrew Reid, Civil War began.

This failure of the political structure has happened time and again in Dominican history. It has happened only once in the United States— and our own Civil War resulted. When a political structure collapses, nothing can replace it but fratricidal warfare, the most terrible of all.

What happened in the Dominican Republic was the Spanish Civil War —but without content or ideas.

The bloodbath drowned the ideals and purposes which had created the rebel force. Each man had rebelled for his own reason—Boschist idealism, revenge, plunder, Communist directive, anti-Reid, anti-corruption, sheer adventure and excitement, the highest ideals of liberalism and the meanest effort to pick a winner. In those terrible hours, all ideals vanished. The old party structure, the distinctions we had been so careful to make, were swept away, as though by a flood in a mountain valley. The rebels become welded together. By the time I arrived distinctions had become meaningless. It did not matter what party each man once had belonged to, nor what his original motive had been. All had forgotten for what they fought. All had become extremists in the true sense of the word—men of violence.

Men and women like this have nowhere to go except to the Communists. All other doors are shut. And the men and women themselves become transformed by the bloodshed and hate. People I had known in the past had changed. A woman I had known as a gentle idealistic leftist, vigorously opposed to communism, went one day to rebel headquarters to obtain supplies. A teen-ager stopped her—did she have a note from Party headquarters? No. Then she must get one. Instead, she called a rebel officer and denounced the boy to him as a "counter-revolutionary deviationist." Like others, she had become, in a word, unhinged.

It is not names of Communists, or numbers, that is important. It is the process itself—the fusion process of the bloodbath.

Out of the noble French Revolution came the Terror, paving the way for the despot Napoleon. Out of the heroic risings against the Czar came the tyrant Stalin. Out of the brave opposition to Batista came the "show trials" and the *paredón,* and the Communist dictator Castro. From Trujillo's prisons emerged heroes to make a revolution—and now their revolution was about to devour its children.

In all my time in the Dominican Republic, I had met no man whom I thought might become a Dominican Castro—until I met Caamaño. He was winning a revolution from below. He had few political advisers in Santo Domingo at that time but Communists.

It makes little difference when Castro "became a Communist." It would make little difference when Caamaño became one.

In any case, after all this blood and all this hate, I saw no chance whatsoever for a political settlement at that time.

But the obvious alternative was to my mind also unacceptable— sending our own forces against the rebels. And I detected a rising determination to do it. Some Dominican military men wanted us to. Some U.S. military men considered the present U.S. military position tactically untenable (they were probably right from a purely military viewpoint, though not from a political one.) I began to think our gravest danger lay in being provoked into a massacre. Indeed, now that the U.S. troops had landed and the Communists knew they could not win, perhaps the Communists' new objective was to provoke us into just that.

The only hope was to gain some time—to maintain a cease-fire and hope that people might come to their senses, that new openings might appear for reconciliation, that new leaders or new political constellations might arise. Dr. Mora and the OAS Commission, as well as the Papal Nuncio, would bring their prestige to bear to keep the peace.

I reported all this to President Johnson by telephone. At a press conference, I said the U. S. Marines had originally come here to protect U.S. lives but that in my opinion their purpose now was or should be to prevent a Castro/Communist takeover, because what began as a PRD revolt had in the last few days fallen under the domination of Castro/Communists and other violent extremists. It was the first time we had said so. The President said approximately the same thing at home in a national radio-television speech that same night, Sunday, May 2. On his instructions I went that night to Puerto Rico to see Juan Bosch.

8

I went secretly; we sent a message to our military at San Isidro and Puerto Rico which did not mention my name or destination. It was long past dark when I left the Embassy. A Marine walked me to the helicopter pad next door to where our military headquarters had been set up in the old Trujillo mansion, used for the Agrarian Reform Institute— and as a polling place—in my time. It was dark and raining and windy as we took off over the treetops. The helicopter was open. A soldier kept a gun aimed downward. I sat on a case of mortar shells. We flew in darkness, other helicoptors dimly visible in the rainy mist. We flew high over the rebel zone to avoid ground fire. At San Isidro we landed amidst our own planes so the San Isidro Generals would not see me and guess where I was going. While a General took a flying boxcar off the line, I ate a warmed-up can of C-rations, then took off.

I met Juan Bosch in the home of Jaime Benítez, chancellor of the University of Puerto Rico. To enter the quiet living room, to see paintings and statuary and books, was like emerging from a nightmare.

Bosch, tall, erect, was friendly to me as a person but he did not want to talk about events, because that afternoon I had told the press that in my judgment the rebellion had fallen under the domination of Castro/Communist elements. Eventually, however, he permitted me to describe the situation as I saw it—his movement had been taken over by adventurers and Castro/Communists, they were using his name, his nation had been destroyed.

He could not believe it. How could he? He was in Puerto Rico, not Santo Domingo. True, he was talking by telephone to Colonel Caamaño or other rebels several times a day. But he had no idea of what had really happened to his country. I had never thought I would see the Dominican Republic ripped to pieces as it was now. I would not have believed it either had I not seen it.

Bosch simply could not accept it. Like all of us, Bosch, perhaps more than some, has woven into his being a dreamlike structure that helps to hold his personality together. To accept as true what I told him would destroy that structure. He could not do it.

Leaning back in his chair, skin drawn tight around his mouth, he said calmly, "Yes, I agree with you. It is social war. It is kill, kill, kill," and he gestured as though sweeping a machine gun around the room. "But leaning back in his chair, "I cannot accept that it is all over for my country. Perhaps I shall go back."

"Mr. President, you'd be killed."

"Then, the only solution is a Marine occupation for many, many years." And he folded his arms.

Presently he fell to talking about the history of revolutions in other Latin American nations—Mexico, Venezuela, others—and making distinctions between "civil war" and "social war."

I told him we had no desire whatsoever to occupy his country and explained our purpose there—first to protect American lives and property, then to prevent a Castro/Communist takeover and seek peace.

He said, "Yes. Molina Ureña should be the constitutional President. On Monday was proclaimed a meeting of the Congress for Wednesday. It will vote general amnesty for everybody. Then the forces of the Commander—" Caamaño "—will take him to the Palace."

I have seldom felt more helpless. I said, "But, Mr. President, I'm afraid you don't understand." He was still thinking of the old days, when he was President, his PRD was the strongest party in the country, and his PRD-dominated Congress was meeting in the Palace of the Congress to draft the 1963 revolutionary Constitution. I tried to explain that a meaningful "meeting of the Congress" was impossible in his chaotic city, that it was extremely doubtful that Molina Ureña would accept the presidency, and I showed him on a map the whereabouts of forces and the utter physical impossibility of Caamaño's men crossing the Zone line, taking Molina Ureña out of asylum in the Colombian Embassy, and conducting him back across the Zone line into the Palace—in no-man's-land.

Bosch said calmly, "Yes. Perhaps the United States Marines will conduct him."

I said I'd like to see Molina Ureña President but thought it couldn't be done, at least not now.

Bosch criticized Ambassador Bennett bitterly for spurning Molina Ureña on that critical Tuesday. I said we had to think about the future. Molina Ureña probably wouldn't do it now, if he did he'd be under Castro/Communist domination, and he might be killed.

Bosch shrugged. "Then there is no solution."

It was past 1 A.M. Benítez suggested we talk more in the morning, after resting. I said I would if President Johnson would permit me to; he had instructed me to return to Santo Domingo that night.

From the headquarters of the U. S. Navy's Caribbean Sea Frontier, I finally got a call through to the President at about 3:30 A.M. It was the third or fourth time I'd talked to him that day. I reported on my conversation and asked if he wanted me to pursue it. He did. I asked if our installing Molina Ureña as President was a real possibility and if I should explore it. President Johnson said yes. He added, "I want Mr. Bosch to know that our purpose is to protect lives and have a progressive liberal government there and have elections. We want nothing except to stop the bloodshed and let self-determination operate."

For the first night since I left Connecticut, I slept in a bed and took a shower.

Bosch, Benítez, and I met the next morning at a friend's house to avoid the press. Benítez and I first talked alone. He proposed that Bosch himself return to the Republic to serve out his constitutional term, that the Marines remain for six months or so, that the OAS give its blessing and its help in reconstruction. I said we had no objections whatsoever but I didn't think Bosch would go and if he did he would be under Castro/Communist domination and might be killed. Moreover, his own prestige would suffer if he returned while U.S. troops were present. He would stand less chance of succeeding, in my opinion, than Molina Ureña. And

Molina's chance wasn't good, though, again, we had no objection. Nonetheless, I thought we should discuss with Bosch his own return.

Bosch said now that the Dominican Congress would meet on Wednesday and elect either Lieutenant Colonel Caamaño or Colonel Rafael Fernández Domínguez, now in Puerto Rico, President under the 1963 Bosch Constitution to serve out the remainder of Bosch's own term, until February 27, 1967. Bosch described Fernández Domínguez—who, as we have seen, had been an early pro-Bosch military conspirator—as being "like a son to me."

The 1963 Bosch Constitution would seem to prohibit a military man from being President. I did not say so.

I asked Bosch if he himself did not intend to return.

"No," putting up one hand. "I cannot. I am—how do you say it?—burned." Always in Bosch's thought there was a hard glint of reality. "I have been accused in the United States of being a Communist. There is no confidence in me. I prefer a military man."

"Would you return to advise and assist in rebuilding the country?"

"No. I cannot, if I return, I am the President. The Constitution provides for only one President."

I told him about Benítez' plan for Bosch's own return. Bosch said, "I would accept," but started laying down conditions, and the phone rang: A call for me from Washington. Abe Fortas, a close friend of President Johnson (since appointed a U. S. Supreme Court Justice), who previously had been talking to Jaime Benítez, also his friend, said Benítez had proposed his own plan for Bosch's return to Fortas; Fortas thought we ought to explore it as well as the Molina Ureña idea carefully, and suggested Bosch issue a statement now, saying he recognized the danger of a Castro/Communist takeover and the need to eliminate it, calling for an end to killing and the resumption of public services, and accepting the presence of U.S. forces for the minimum period needed to keep order.

Bosch refused. He wrote out a different statement. It said, in substance, that the pattern of 1916 was being repeated—"the U. S. Marines occupy now the sacred soil of Juan Pablo Duarte," a "fact of force exercised by a powerful country against a weak nation." Bosch's statement continued! ". . . We must face it with the only arms which we can raise—the determination to maintain without dismay the old and quiet heroism of those who must work every day in a task perhaps without glory but with meaningful and certain results so that the military occupation be soon nothing more than a recollection in the Dominican consciousness. It is the duty of the Dominican people and it is the inexorable obligation of the Constitutionalist forces to avoid above everything else that the military occupation achieve permanency and consequently avoid the establishment of a foreign military government. . . . Our country must have a legitimate government, one which can deal in the name of the people with the American military chiefs rather than the OAS. . . . All of this is achievable only through due respect to the Constitution of 1963. . . . In a week of tragic greatness, the Dominican people proved to the world a capacity to fight which is not inferior to that of any other country, not even the giants of history. Now it must achieve another type of victory. . . . We Dominicans must show before the world that we are able to govern ourselves with maturity, integrity, ability, and patriotism. To achieve this, the first thing that must be done is that not a single additional shot be heard any more. Let the weapons be silent that the voice of patriotism be heard. In venerable remembrance of those who have fallen, let us all unite in the common task of raising again the statue of the fatherland."

We tried to reconcile the two statements. It was impossible. We agreed to issue no statements at all, at least for a few days. We agreed to press all sides to observe the cease-fire.

We had talked, in all, for about eight hours. I went to the Navy base, telephoned President Johnson, and went back about dark to Santo Domingo—back to the ceaseless clatter of helicopters overhead, the dust and hustle of troops, and, day and night, gunfire.

That was the end of the first phase of my work—the fact-finding and the cease-fire.

9

The International Zone had been extended slightly to enclose safely all Embassies and to get our Embassy off the Zone line. Since the Zone was isolated from the bridge, and therefore from both the San Isidro airport and Aeropuerto Punta Caucedo, U.S. troops, with OAS approval, had opened a corridor connecting the Zone and the bridge; were patrolling it. Though called the Line of Communication, this corridor was similar to the cordon contemplated earlier, sealing off the rebels in Ciudad Nueva. However, the rebels also had scattered troops north of the corridor, and we permitted noncombatants to cross the corridor. If, as the rebels charged, our intention had been to help Wessin defeat them, we would not have permitted them to cross the corridor, we would not have given them food and medicines but would have starved them out, and, indeed, we would not have worked to get a cease-fire in the first place, since it left them in control of the central city, Radio Santo Domingo, and the telephone exchange.

The second phase of my work began late that same Monday night, May 3. Imbert called me to his house and said that various people, both military and civilian, had told him that they could support neither the rebels nor the San Isidro crowd. They had told him that the old Generals at San Isidro must leave the country, that the three-man military junta headed by Colonel Benoit must be reconstituted, that only he was strong enough to force the Generals out, and that it was his duty to do it and try to form a new government.

I asked, "Do you want to do it?"

He said, "I do it. For my country. Not for myself. Whatta hell I want to get into this mess for? I can sit here quiet."

He sure could—we were talking in his upstairs bulletproof sanctuary. And thus far he had kept out of the present mess almost entirely.

I said, "You can't have it all—these days, no one man can."

"I don't want any of it."

"We are not going to support a military dictatorship."

"I know."

"And I don't think any better of the old Generals than you do. Can you get rid of them?"

"I fix. You can be sure of that."

"What about the San Isidro junta?"

"We leave one of them in, Colonel Benoit. The others resign."

"Will they?"

"Su-u-u-re," drawing it out.

"What kind of a government is this going to be? Who'll be in it?"

"No politicians, you can be sure of that, Mr. Martin."

"Who, then?"

He began naming names. And so it began—the complex swirling dance of Dominican politics.

Like all nascent political movements, this one started from several directions. Indeed, I learned much later that it had started even before I arrived—immediately after the fall of the short-lived Molina Ureña government, Imbert had talked to the military about participating in a government. The San Isidro junta itself had wanted to broaden its base. Dominican civilians talked to Dr. Mora and to several U. S. Embassy officers.

I helped because I felt the situation demanded a third force if ever the Dominicans were to make peace. Caamaño and the rebels never could reach an understanding with Wessin and the San Isidro Generals. Moreover, the United States ought not tie itself to San Isidro, symbol of repression. But we could not simply cut our ties to it—this would leave only two forces in the field, ours and the rebels', and might result in a Hungary. Imbert could prevent the chaos from spreading to the countryside. The same man who in my time had been a threat to democracy was now a necessary bulwark against anarchy. Imbert was no Wessin—no fanatic, no member of the militarist establishment, no post-Trujillo Trujillista. He had learned something about politics in the Consejo. His world was not the narrow exclusively military world of Wessin, a professional soldier.

A decent government under him was for now the best solution. For a rapprochement between Caamaño and Imbert was not impossible.

Imbert wanted to start with himself and Colonel Benoit—two military men. To these he would add three civilians.

He wanted the civilians to be non-political—"politicians have ruined this country." He wanted men of stature, not identified with either side in the present conflict.

This was desirable—the old parties had been discredited earlier or shattered in the present holocaust—but might be impractical.

Imbert proposed names, his friends proposed names, I proposed names, and nearly everybody whose name was proposed in turn proposed other names. At various times we had a non-political slate, then a wholly political slate. Several times a slate was complete lacking one man but collapsed when no acceptable third man could be found. Naturally enough, Imbert wanted men he trusted; but some of his were unacceptable— too far right, too far left, too compromised with one party or another, wholly unacceptable to the military or the rebels, too Trujillista, too old, too unstable. People kept saying we had to have a Balaguerista. I couldn't see why, I was not impressed with his popularity poll rating. And if we were going to have politicians, I preferred them young and liberal, not aged and Trujillista. But liberals would not work with Imbert, or he would not work with them, or the military exploded, or they were hated as traitors by the rebels.

I talked to old friends—Antonio Guzmán, Dr. Jordi Brossa, Nick Pichardo, Jimmy Pastoriza, Héctor García-Godoy, many others. It was odd—since Bosch's fall, I had become identified publicly with Bosch, and I think President Johnson sent me to the Republic partly for that reason, but I had as many friends, perhaps more, on the other side or in the neutral center insofar as a center existed.

The days and nights went by in a blur. Often men came to Imbert's sanctuary, and I talked to one while he talked to another. Some came and talked and talked and talked, all philosophy, sociology, psychology, then left. Once I met two men in a house, discovered the U.S. press was across the street, ducked into a garage, and for two hours tried to persuade them to help their country, to no avail. Once when we wanted a man in Santiago, a friend of his and I got into a helicopter and flew over rebel territory in the dark, flying high to escape rebel machine gun fire, my friend trembling, and put down in San Isidro to get into a Caribou that would take us to Santiago. I had thought he was trembling because the flight frightened him. But no—he had a son in the rebel zone, he himself was hated by the San Isidro Generals, and here he was, in dread San Isidro itself. I told a U. S. Colonel to post a guard around the helicopter and let no one approach. In the dark the pilot of the waiting Caribou came to us. He said the landing field at Santiago had no lights or instruments, I knew from past experience it was enclosed by hills and a water tank, the weather there tonight was terrible, the chances now of landing were only ten in a hundred, it was impossible to cross the central mountain range and we would have to go to Higüey and all the way around the east coast, and by the time we reached Santiago the chances of landing probably would be less than ten in a hundred. My friend and I gave up and went back to Santo Domingo. Two civilians who had been waiting at Imbert's for us to bring the third from Santiago thereupon declined.

In the midst of all this, as Bosch had predicted, the rebels announced that the Congress had met and elected Caamaño President. He began appointing a Cabinet. Pressures mounted on us to make haste—San Isidro suspected we were stalling or double-crossing them. We were not. We were simply running into the old Dominican difficulties. Nobody trusted anybody. Upstanding, able, well-educated Dominicans helped quietly but refused to join a government publicly or accept responsibility.

Once Imbert called in three elderly gentlemen. I hid hastily in the next room, he sent word to me that they might serve but first wanted to see Dr. Mora. I ran out to the garage, got the license number of their car, drove to the two checkpoints they must pass to get to the hotel where Dr. Mora was, and told the troops to let the car pass. But when they saw Dr. Mora they talked for hours, then went home to draft a proposal, then in the morning delivered it to Dr. Mora and Imbert, and since it contained conditions wholly unacceptable to everybody, they backed out. Imbert said, "You see? We are finish."

I said we weren't, we would start over. And did. Once, needing to see Dr. Mora urgently, I was told he was aboard the *Boxer* at a lunch for the OAS. I got into a helicopter at the Hotel Embajador only to discover, after it had taken off and was well out to sea, that it was not going to the *Boxer* after all. Because of the deafening roar of the helicopter, an officer setting beside me and I wrote notes to each other:

I: "I am the President's envoy. I must see Dr. Mora. He is on the *Boxer* having lunch."

The officer (after passing note to crewman with earphones who passed it to pilot): "We are going to *Boxer*."

Changed course sharply. Pause. Then, the officer: "Radioed *Boxer*. Your man is not aboard *Boxer*. Is aboard LPD-1."

I: "Then let's go there."

The officer: "We are going to LPD-1 as soon as we get a vector."

I: "What's a vector?"

The officer: "Exact heading."

I: "In other words, we have to find it?"

Officer nods affirmatively.

I: "Our first mistake was in finding Hispañola."

Officer laughs. Helicopter flies on and on, changing course to and fro. Officer: "We are having a hard time finding LPD-1."

More deafening flying, now out of sight of land. Then, the officer: "LPD-1 too far at sea. No fuel. We are returning."

I: "To where we started?"

Officer: "Affirmative."

Mora landed at the hotel polo field a few minutes after I did.

Thursday night I slept an hour and a half. Friday morning three civilians accepted and were accepted.

One I met for the first time that day, Alejandro Zeller Cocco, a young hydraulic engineer who seemed to have no interest in politics but had impressed Ambassador Bennett by his technical knowledge and willingness to work.

Two I had known from long ago—Carlos Grisolía, a lawyer from Puerto Plata elected a UCN Senator when Bosch was elected, an intelligent, level-headed man who, while not nationally known, had shown considerable promise; and Julio D. Postigo, a close personal friend of Juan Bosch, the bookstore owner and publisher who long ago had given the autographing party for Bosch's new book, *David*. Today, Postigo had joined Imbert's government, a rival to Caamaño's Bosch-inspired government. If ever a man joined a government not for himself but for his country, it was Julio Postigo.

Technicalities almost wrecked the new Government of National Reconstruction, as the Imbert government was called, before it could be sworn in: Nobody could find two notaries public, let alone the Chief Justice of the Supreme Court, and, moreover, when the new government went to the Palace of the Congress at the Fairgrounds, the door was locked and nobody had a key. The functionaries were found, however, the glass door was broken, and the new five-man government was duly sworn in on May 7. In a few days it began to behave surprisingly like a government—it appointed a Foreign Minister, asked recognition, treated with the OAS, and started getting people back to work in the government-owned industries so that the nation's economy would not continue at a standstill. It was a faltering beginning. But it was a beginning. And its members were surprisingly good men—far from a military dictatorship. That night I spoke to the Peace Corps kids, some of whom were sympathetic to the rebels.

So ended the second phase of my work.

During all this time, Ambassador Bennett had been working with the OAS, other diplomats, our military, and many others, as well as keeping Washington informed. More, he had to take the heat. For the rebels were blaming him for the entire catastrophe, and during this third week mounted a radio propaganda attack on him that can only be described as vicious. In English, which was all that some U.S. journalists could pick up, the broadcasts were relatively restrained: Ambassador Bennett merely had "misled" the President. But in Spanish, he had "fooled" the White House, he was a "fiend," a "maniac," and his words were "lies, lies, lies."

Amid this, Ambassador Bennett undertook an extremely delicate operation: The removal of the San Isidro Generals.

Urged by Bennett—whom I in turn had encouraged—General Wessin y Wessin, who had become a symbol of the hated San Isidro military, wrote a letter to Ambassador Bennett, declaring that the other San Isidro Generals had to go and that, if it would help the Republic, he himself would go too. He would not, however go with the others, since he considered himself more honest and honorable.

Wessin listed those who should go. It was virtually the same list that Caamaño had given me and that Imbert had given me, except that it contained the names of General de los Santos and Commodore Rivera Caminero whom Imbert had appointed to hold the loyalty of the Dominican Armed Forces and the name of a Colonel who was a close personal friend of Imbert's. Imbert at first balked at the Colonel, then gave in. He balked at the other two flatly. And he insisted that Wessin go, too. He got rid of the rest, including Hungría, Rib, Rivera Cuesta, Belisario Peguero, Hermida, and Luna—lured them to the Haina naval base, disarmed them, put them aboard a Dominican warship, and sent them to sea.

Now it was Wessin's turn. Ambassador Bennett went to San Isidro. Wessin welshed on his offer to go.[9]

10

Meanwhile, I began the third phase of my work: Trying to find a political solution. As I had thought might happen, new groupings and new leaders had emerged—"President" Imbert and the men around him, "President" Caamaño. I began the third week trying to start talks between Caamaño and Imbert. For every war ends in negotiation. It is much better to have the negotiation before the war.

Shlaudeman and I, working separately, talked to people we knew on the rebel side, especially people in the old PRD and in the old Social Christian Party. I kept in close touch with the Papal Nuncio. I tried to

[9] Wessin has since said he did not, in his letter to Bennett, offer to leave the Republic himself immediately: "I said that when the situation returned to normal I would retire from the Army. I did not mean immediately." Curiously, in 1961, Ramfis Trujillo wrote a letter to an American official about his own military retirement or departure from the Republic that was similarly ambiguous.

open up new indirect channels to the rebel leaders. We picked up bits of evidence that the formation of the Imbert government had shaken the rebels. Defections and surrenders increased. The MPD, some of whose members detested Caamaño as a former policeman, instructed its members to enter private homes, seize money and arms and begin withdrawing from rebel commands groups. Some became convinced Caamaño would make a deal with Imbert. Inside their own stronghold, and by crossing rooftops at night and heading north, they began caching arms to fight another day.

Indeed, our intelligence reports indicated that a sharp shift in Communist tactics had occurred before the establishment of the Imbert government. After the Airborne landed on the night of April 29–30, the PSP, MPD, and 14th of June leadership had met quickly to decide how to deal with the new situation that the large U.S. troop landings created. Leading Communists also met with rebel military officers—the Ducoudrays, Antonio Isa Conde, Manuel González González, Asdrúbal Domínguez, Hugo Tolentino Dipp of the PSP, and Juan Miguel Román Díaz and Fidelio Despradel Roque of the 14th of June. On April 30— the day I arrived—the rebel radio instructed armed mobs not to fire on U.S. troops. During the next few days Radio Havana continued to exhort the rebels to fight on; on rebel requested Radio Havana to desist. On May 4, the PSP and 14th of June discussed whether their top leaders ought to withdraw from overt participation in the movement in order to save their lives and to conceal from the press Communist involvement in the rebellion. On May 5, after several meetings, the Communist leaders decided that while rank-and-file members of the three parties would fight on, the top leaders would withdraw. Some, including the Ducoudrays, went into hiding. Others went north into the *campo* with instructions to organize local resistance or guerrilla groups. Milvio Pérez Pérez of the PSP provided false identity cards.

Still there was shooting in the city—and no sign yet of a political settlement. In our work, Shlaudeman and I took targets of opportunity, political opportunity—anybody we happened to run into who might offer a possibility. Much of the work we did at night. Every night, usually long past midnight, a Marine walked me up to the Residence in the dark. At the hedge near the swimming pool a Marine would step out and you would hear a voice say "Halt" and in a moment, "Advance and be recognized," and then, "Halt" again, and then the Marine with me would give the password. I am nearly night-blind and so I memorized the number of steps in the Residence garden—the garden where my daughter had been married. Near the fence between the Residence and the former Trujillo mansion, where my small sons had built a play fortress, Marines now were encamped behind barbed wire.

Between times I talked to newspapermen, helped arrange for food and medicine for Dominicans, helped a man in the Imbert government get his wife and children out of their house in the rebel zone. One day a U.S. military band marched up the driveway in front of the Chancellery and played "The Star-Spangled Banner." I suggested it learn the Dominican anthem.

People were beginning to show themselves on the streets in the International Zone. More cars were out. An old woman was rocking on her porch. Children appeared at the fence of the Trujillo mansion, and our troops gave them candy. Beside a Marine encampment, teen-agers started a baseball game.

But a mortar shell exploded in the garden next door. A Marine was shot on the Embassy perimeter. Another nearby was killed by a sniper. Once more pressures began to mount to take the entire city. For some thought that time was working for the rebels, that they were taking advantage of the cease-fire to send revolutionaries into the northern part of the city and on into the interior, thus spreading the rebellion throughout the Republic. And certainly their radio station, powerful Radio Santo Domingo, heard all over the Republic, was promoting their cause. It repeatedly broadcast a tape-recorded speech by Juan Bosch, attacking the United States and calling on Dominicans throughout the Republic to rise. All reports indicated that the people at large were becoming increasingly sympathetic to the rebels. Imbert's government was not gaining popular support. The rebels were linking food and jobs in the people's mind with constitutionalism. Constitutionism had become the rebels' battle-cry. In the 1920s Sumner Welles had worked for constitutionalism. So had I in 1962–63. Now the rebels were using it. And it was succeeding. The rebels began holding mass meetings in the center of the city. They said little about Bosch. They talked about constitutionalism, anti-Americanism, and Caamaño.

On the morning of Tuesday, May 11, I received a message from the Papal Nuncio at 8:30 A.M. asking me to call. I did. Caamaño wanted to see me. Almost at the same time Shlaudeman received word that Caamaño was willing to talk to Imbert but wanted to see me first.

Once more from the Nunciatura, with the Nuncio in flowing robe, we crossed the Zone line on Avenida Independencia and entered the rebel zone—Héctor Conde, the Nuncio, Shlaudeman, and I. At Parque Independencia, shrine of Dominican liberty, cars were moving, a barber shop was open, rebel policemen were directing traffic, and as we drove down narrow Calle Arzobispo Nouel, past an old Spanish colonial church, we saw a garbage truck at work. Life was beginning again a little in the rebel zone, too.

We turned north a block, near where my car had been burned in 1962, then back west on Calle Conde, its stores steel-shuttered but young men walking briskly up and down. Rebel cars painted with the word *"pueblo,"* "people," drove rapidly past; press cars painted *"prensa"* passed more slowly. In front of a tall building, Edificio Copello, where a small crowd stood, we stopped and got out, and a man from long ago, Governor Mainardi of Santiago, embraced me, and strangers reached for my hand as we hurried into the office of Colonel Caamaño. (He had moved his headquarters there.)

Héctor Aristy was with him and, from time to time, the man he had appointed Foreign Minister, Jottin Cury. In an office bare except for a long table and straight chairs we sat to talk.

I said, "I would hope that our coming here will not be used for propaganda purposes."

Aristy quickly reassured me. I asked Caamaño if he agreed. He did. I said I had received his message and it seemed to me desirable that both sides—he and Imbert—begin to talk to each other.

Aristy said, "It is impossible to talk with Imbert as long as Commodore Rivera Caminero is his Secretary of Armed Forces and Wessin y Wessin and General de los Santos are at San Isidro."

I said, "There's no point arguing about that now—it's something for you to negotiate with Imbert. The question now is—where are you going to meet?"

"But there's no use talking as long as those three are there."

And Caamaño, "Imbert is not a free agent with them there."

And Aristy, "We have the people with us. They will not accept those three."

And Caamaño, "Imbert is not my enemy. He inspired me to rise against Belisario Peguero."

Others joined, all were talking at once.

Shlaudeman said, "We need to forget the past," and I picked the line up and pushed it, trying to hold them to the mechanics of how the talks could be held.

But Aristy kept saying, "Today the tanks moved and broke the cease-fire," and Caamaño said, "There is a sniper and a bazooka, North Americans, on the other side of the river, firing into the Electricidad and the post office, and they have killed twenty-two of our people."

I said, "I don't know anything about it but I'll look into it."

The Nuncio said, "Just a minute. It is a terrible thing, the loss of one life. But we cannot talk about incidents. We must talk about peace. What do you say—will you talk at the Nunciatura?"

Caamaño said, "No, I cannot go there."

I said, "Well, where can you go?—let's find a place," and touched his sleeve and said, "Let's look on the map—show me the place where you say we violated the cease-fire."

I wanted to get him alone. I took him to the far end of the table. Shlaudeman immediately began a conversation with Aristy.

Caamaño and I, standing close together alone for the first time, began looking at the map. I asked in a low voice, "Are you a free agent?"

He said, "I am a free agent."

"Can you leave here?"

He hesitated, said, "My people say that talking won't do any good as long as those three are there. If I did, I'd be out."

"That's what I'm asking you—are you a free agent? Who'd put you 'out'? Who are 'your people'?"

"I would have to consult my advisers."

"Who?"

"My *militantes*. The Cabinet. Some Senators."

Militantes, in this cloudy context, could mean either soldiers like himself who had defected or Castro/Communists. I asked, "Who are the *militantes?*"

Caamaño hesitated again, then said, "The officers," and named the military leaders who had defected with him.

I said, "Not the Communists?"

"There are no Communists."

"We know there are. What I want to know is whether you are free of them. Whether you are a free agent."

He said, looking away, speaking hesitantly, "There may be individual Communists in the Zone. But they are not in the leadership. After we get this over, we get rid of them."

I was far from sure. And I thought he was, too.

I had the names of two Italians who had turned up at Caamaño's headquarters and whom the CIA suspected were Communists sent from Europe. I asked Caamaño who they were. He said, "They are my bodyguards."

I asked why he needed Italian bodyguards when he had a city full of Dominican gunmen. He didn't answer. I said, "If you are the President, why can't you go anywhere you want to?"

He repeated that he would be finished as a popular leader if he opened talks while Wessin, Rivera Caminero, and De los Santos were in the Imbert group.

"You can't set preconditions like that to talking. Those are negotiating points. You have to talk without preconditions. Just talk."

He said, "I cannot."

"I have something to tell you. Time is running out. We have been trying to get Betancourt, Figueres, and Muñoz Marín to come here under the OAS, but they are not coming."[10]

10 After I published a brief account of the Civil War in the May 28, 1965, issue of *Life* magazine, Betancourt, Figueres, and Muñoz said they were always willing to help but the OAS had failed to "take the pertinent action," presumably to ask them to help. This may be. But what I told Caamaño at the time was what I understood to be the case.

Caamaño looked shocked. He had been counting on their support, and he realized instantly the significance of their decision. He said, "I cannot talk to Imbert on any basis except constitutionalism." And thereafter he dropped his demand about the removal of the three military men and concentrated on constitutionalism as his precondition.

After much discussion, we reached agreement that he would talk—if he talked—at any of three points: At the Obelisk on the seafront several blocks inside the rebel zone, where long ago I had stood on a balcony while Ramfis' airplane buzzed a UCN crowd; in a house on the Zone line, or in the Brazilian Embassy office just inside the rebel zone. But Caamaño repeated he would have to consult his advisers first. And he insisted on taking Aristy along. Caamaño would call the Nuncio at 3 P.M. to say whether he would talk.

I told Aristy, who had been watching us together, what Caamaño and I had agreed on. He did not seem happy. I told him about Betancourt, Figueres, and Muñoz. He looked flattened, then started talking again about preconditions. I said, "Look here. My only purpose is to get talks started between the two sides to see if they can work out a solution. I want you to know that time is running out and patience is wearing thin, both here and in the United States. You know the United States. We are losing men, our troops are getting killed. Public opinion and the Congress won't stand for it much longer. I'm not in any sense making any threats. I'm simply telling you the facts. If you want a peaceful solution, you had better start talking to the other side."

Aristy started to say something, stopped, and said, "We cannot talk except on a basis of constitutionality." He looked tense, even afraid.

I said, "We'll wait for your call at three o'clock."

We shook hands all around, and went out a side door and down to the street. This time there was no demonstration—just people, smiling, friendly, eager, in that heart-breaking, childlike way Dominicans have when they trust you. Leaving I thought: We've *got* to find a political solution or they'll all be killed.

I went to Imbert, told him I'd seen Caamaño, and asked if he would talk at the designated places. Imbert would talk at two—not at the Obelisk far inside the rebel zone. I didn't blame him. He set no preconditions.

Back at the Chancellery we waited. Two hours passed, three. It was just past 3 P.M. The Nuncio called; Shlaudeman and I hurried to him. He was with Mora. Caamaño had just called and said that the meeting was off—twenty minutes before, he said, "troops of Wessin" (who controlled no troops in the capital) had attacked the Dragon Restaurant on Avenida Independencia inside the rebel zone, using U.S. forces as cover, and had killed one rebel and wounded others. Caamaño had been extremely angry, particularly at the United States, and said he would talk to no one but the OAS Commission.

We tried to find out what had happened at the Dragon Restaurant. Caamaño's right-hand military man, Montes Arache, called and told Shlaudeman harshly that American troops across the river near the bridge were killing every unarmed civilian that showed himself on the dock and that tonight the rebels would "level" the flour mill across the river.

My suspicion grew that the rebels did not want to talk, that they were creating incidents to sabotage the talks—not Caamaño, but the Communists behind him.

On Wednesday I pulled back—the OAS Commission was there, and I wanted to let them alone to talk with both sides. The rebels seemed to be crossing the Zone line from Ciudad Nueva to the north, perhaps to seize the industries in the north part of the capital, perhaps to head for cities in the interior. Imbert's people were discouraged—the rebels were winning the political and propaganda war, they were spreading rebellion, they were taking new positions, while Imbert's own hands were tied by the OAS and cease-fire. Pressures were mounting on every side for U.S. forces to smash the rebel stronghold—take the city and get it over with. In the shuttered Chancellery an uneasiness settled down with night. We worked very late, sending cables and trying to hold the status quo. During the night gunfire seemed heavier than it had been in almost two weeks.

I slept late on Thursday and was having breakfast in the Residence when the telephone rang. It was Jottin Cury, Caamaño's "Foreign Minister." He said he was speaking for Caamaño. He said, "The North American troops have violated the cease-fire. They are at Calle Vicente Noble—" Vicente Noble! "—and Santa Barbara. Also at Calle Mella and Duarte."

I said, "Wait a minute," and tried to spread out my map, by now torn and worn-out. Cury kept talking. I told him to wait. I was trying to find the locations. He went on, "Two North American soldiers have been killed. Colonel Caamaño has given orders that if the North Americans do not return to their positions in half an hour he will open fire on all North American troops."

I said, "I want to talk to Caamaño."

"He is with the troops."

"Get him—I won't talk to anybody else."

Cury seemed to be talking to others.

Both locations were south of the bridge near the Electricidad. One appeared to be several blocks inside rebel territory.

Cury came back on. "Colonel Caamaño has mobilized all his forces.

I have talked to Dr. Bosch and he put me in charge to call you and tell you."

I said, "I want Caamaño."

More waiting; then a man speaking English: "Caamaño order forty-five minutes ago that if all U.S. troops were not back in their positions by twelve o'clock, he would attack."

It was already twelve-fifteen.

I said, "I want to talk to Caamaño."

He said, "They are shooting right now in Parque Enriquillo," still another location.

Another voice came on. "Dr. Cury says that Dr. Bosch authorized him to say that this attitude of the United States troops breaks the convention of you and Dr. Bosch."

I said, "What convention?"

"Also he fears a catastrophe."

"Listen, I want to talk to Caamaño. Right now."

More delay; then Caamaño came on. He was almost screaming. "North American troops went to Duarte and Mella and we threw them back. If that continues, we are men of honor, we are tired of talking, we will fight to the death."

I said, "Just a minute."

But he rushed on, "If they do not retire, this is the final hour."

Someone else said, "We will attack any troops outside—"

I said, "Get me Caamaño."

Caamaño came back "—the final hour. We are fighting, getting shot, we are men of honor—"

I said, "Wait a minute. The way to start talks for peace is not to issue ultimatums. I don't know what happened but I'll find out and call you back. I—"

He broke off. Someone said, "He has gone to be with his troops."

I hung up, hurried down to the office, called Lieutenant General Bruce Palmer, the U.S. commander, and asked what had happened. He said that as far as he knew, last night the rebels had fired down on our troops near the Electricidad from a tall building that could not be effectively reached with return fire. This morning our troops had moved out and stopped it. This was in accordance with their orders and with the cease-fire agreement. They had now returned to their positions. General Palmer had reiterated the standing order—fire only if fired upon, do not move out from positions unless unable to silence fire otherwise.

I called Caamaño back and told him what the General had said.

He said, "They have not gone back. They are fighting."

I said, "The General says they have gone back. He is investigating. He has repeated the standing orders."

Caamaño said, "I do not admit we broke the cease-fire."

I said, "We do not admit we broke it."

He said, "We will protest to the OAS and ask the OAS Commission to investigate."

"That's fine. We will, too."

"I propose that we send an officer and you send an officer with them."

"If you want to, ask the OAS. That's their decision."

"Your troops went all the way to Duarte and Mella."

"Not as far as I know. Let the OAS investigate it."

"We are protesting."

"All right. But listen—these incidents are inevitable. We are talking about one life or two, but we ought to be talking about saving thousands of lives. You cannot start peace talks by telling me you're going to start an all-out attack on United States troops. You've got to start talking to Imbert and quick."

He said, "We are tired of talking."

I said, "Look, Colonel. You and I understand each other. We want peace. I think somebody is inciting incidents to prevent peace. Yesterday at the Dragon Restaurant, today near the Electricidad."

"Your troops did it. And Wessin's."

"You don't understand, Colonel." I was almost pleading now. He seemed like a drowning man slowly letting go a life raft. "Somebody on your side is trying to make trouble between you and me. If we want peace, we must not let it happen."

He said, "We are men of honor. We will fight to the end. We will protest to the OAS."

"Colonel, I'm only trying to help make peace. Any time you want to talk to me, call me. I am at your disposition."

"Thank you."

We hung up. The ultimatum had dissolved into agreement to protest separately to the OAS. But I was more sure than ever that somebody on the rebel side, perhaps Caamaño himself, perhaps the Communists, did not want peace.

And we ourselves were fumbling in the dark—apparently a U. S. Jeep had indeed gone to the corner of Duarte and Mella, deep in rebel territory, for the bodies of two American soldiers were found there. About dusk yesterday our troops at the Electricidad and at two nearby roadblocks had been fired on from the tall building. They had returned the fire. The fire fight had continued into the night. Our troops, unable to stop the rebel fire, at 3:30 A.M. had advanced, taking the building, entered it, and found blood spattered over the walls of one room. They had occupied the building and set up an "observation post." As soon as higher authorities learned of this, they had ordered the "observers" back to the line. General Palmer could only guess that one Jeep had been returning from the building to the line and become lost in the maze of narrow streets in the old Spanish quarter.

I was in a back room at the Chancellery writing a cable on all this when suddenly a terrible clatter broke out—heavy firing and the roar of low-flying aircraft, right outside the shuttered window. I moved away from the window into a corner—the Chancellery is thick-walled concrete—and waited. Finally the firing died away.

Unidentified warplanes equipped with rockets had swung in low and level over the Embassy and General Palmer's headquarters next door, a shallow dive for a strafing run, and our troops had opened up, individual soldiers in the trees where my boys' fort had stood, 50-calibers at headquarters. Later we learned that Imbert's Air Force commander, General de los Santos, had sent five planes against Radio Santo Domingo in no-man's-land a few blocks north. They had leveled out for their run at it over our headquarters, and we had fired, and as they passed beyond the Zone line, rebels had fired too. The planes had hit the radio station with rockets and knocked it out. But ground fire, probably ours, had knocked down one of their planes. We protested to the OAS. So did the rebels. It was all upside down. And by next morning Radio Santo Domingo was back on the air, using another transmitter. And the United Nations Security Council voted to invite Secretary General U Thant to send a representative here. The UN came.

Imbert bulled his way ahead—he rallied a thousand transportation troops in the northwest sector of the capital, brought in six hundred fresh troops from San Cristóbal, ferried tanks by sea from San Isidro to Haina, and began a sweep eastward in the section of the city north of the corridor. In that area lay the cemetery, where rebels had been reported caching arms; most sizable industries; and *barrios* of the poor. It had been held loosely by rebel troops. Now Imbert attacked, the first offensive launched against the rebels since the early days of the rebellion. Our military men were skeptical—and no wonder, considering the record of the San Isidro Generals. But Imbert succeeded. In several days of hard fighting, he moved past the cemetery and on toward the great curve in the Río Ozama. When he reached it, he would have to turn south. That turn would bring him down to the corridor we had opened between the International Zone and the bridge. We held the corridor. At that point he would either have to stop or smash across the corridor and into Ciudad Nueva.

I proposed that when he reached the corridor which our troops patrolled we stop him—that we thus simply interpose our forces physically between his and Caamaño's and sit there—sit there, enforcing the cease-fire as best we could, until a political solution could be worked out. That is what we did. For the first time the swirling military mass became stabilized.

11

Perhaps by now the reader knows enough about my own difficulties in finding a political solution to understand why another effort also failed of immediate success.

McGeorge Bundy, Special Assistant to the President; Undersecretary of State Mann; Deputy Secretary of Defense Vance; and Assistant Secretary of State Vaughn arrived in the Dominican Republic May 15 on President Johnson's instructions to try to help establish a government of national concord. They talked to Imbert, the San Isidro military, rebel leaders. Especially they talked to Antonio Guzmán. Guzmán, as we have seen, had been Juan Bosch's Minister of Agriculture and had accompanied him to the Palace to be overthrown. He had been my first choice to enter the Imbert government; I had tried unsuccessfully for hours to persuade him to do it. Bundy and the others now undertook the task of building a government around him acceptable to all sides.

En route to Santo Domingo, Bundy and Vance had stopped in San Juan, Puerto Rico. Shlaudeman had taken Guzmán there. Bundy and Bosch had reached an agreement—Guzmán would serve out the remainder of Bosch's presidential term, the 1963 constitution would be restored, and the new Guzmán government would be purged of Communist influence.

Bundy, a youngish man of piercing intelligence, had been Dean of the Harvard Faculty of Arts and Sciences and had come to Washington to work in the White House for President Kennedy. As Special Assistant for national security affairs, he had set up a "little State Department" in the White House basement and had participated in virtually every important policy decision that President Kennedy took. After Lyndon Johnson became President, Bundy stayed on. He seldom left Washington. He was a policy man.

When the President sent him to Santo Domingo, I was instructed to desist from my efforts to bring Caamaño and Imbert together. (As Dick Goodwin of the White House staff said later, the U.S. press unfortunately saw little difference between Wessin and Imbert, though the difference was great.) The Administration now swung to a Boschist formula. I can only surmise that it was reacting to harsh U.S. press criticism. In any case, now in Santo Domingo, Bundy started the Guzmán move.

Caamaño agreed to step aside in Guzmán's favor. But Imbert, winning in the north, balked. And so did the men around Caamaño. The principal stumbling blocks were two: Precisely what measures would be taken to ensure a government free of Communist domination and, more important, precisely who would head the Armed Forces and its three service branches? Although Bundy had thought he had obtained a firm commitment from Bosch in Puerto Rico on the removal of Communist influence, Guzmán in Santo Domingo backed away from it, probably because the rebel leaders simply could not accept it. I had little or nothing to do with this negotiation.

When Bundy and the others began, Imbert summoned me to his house. With Imbert was Zeller, one of the three civilians in Imbert's government. It was dark; we talked in Imbert's upstairs sanctuary by lamplight. Zeller, a rather excitable young man, accused me of double-crossing him and Imbert—of putting them in office nine days earlier and now dumping them. He thought I had done it deliberately. I said I had not. He said I had been playing games with him. I said I had not, had acted in good faith. Now the decision had been taken to explore another avenue, other U.S. government officials had arrived to do it, up to this time no commitments had been given and no final decisions taken. I said that there was very little more I could say without being disloyal either to my friends—that is, Imbert—or to my government.

Imbert, who had sat silent on the sofa beside me, roused himself and said that next day he would denounce the United States and go it alone.

I waited a moment. Then I said, "I've already asked you to do so much that I won't ask you to do anything else—or not do anything else."

His wife walked by, an old friend of Fran's and mine. I held out my hand to her. She tossed her head and walked on. I said, "Guachi, don't do that to me." Imbert looked the other way. He seemed near tears.

We talked a little desultorily. I thought: This is the second time I have betrayed my Dominican friends. First the rebels; now Imbert. Presently I left.

By the next night Imbert had decided to resist us. He summoned the attachés to his house. His military leaders who had been fighting the rebels in the north were there. The attachés returned to the Chancellery while Bundy, Mann, Vance, Vaughn, and I were in a little room, talking by telephone to President Johnson. The President was asking each of us if we preferred Guzmán to Imbert. The naval attaché said he had feared for his life at Imbert's. When it came my turn, I told the President if forced to choose I preferred Guzmán's political coloration to Imbert's, but doubted he represented anybody or that anything would come of the effort to establish his government. Our conversation finished, I wanted to go see Imbert. The others dissuaded me—they thought I might be killed.

We talked to President Johnson several times a day. His appetite for information was insatiable. At first the only telephone we could reach him on was in the Chancellery lobby, clamorous, jammed with strangers, including journalists. Later Ambassador Bennett set up a press tent outdoors and got a hot line to the White House established in a private office.

Bundy and the others worked day and night, nearing exhaustion. It was an extremely difficult, not to say dangerous, negotiation. One night Bundy and Vance met with Caamaño and Guzmán and others, taking Shlaudeman along, in the deserted old Partido Dominicano building on the seafront. An open field of fire between the Zone line and the rebel stronghold, it was called the *Zona Muerte,* the dead zone. Nobody went there; nothing moved. While the meeting was going on, heavy firing began outside. It was agreed that two men would go to stop the fire. Shlaudeman went with a kid from the rebel side. They drove toward the U.S. roadblock where a Colonel who had helped me and now was helping Shlaudeman was waiting for them, and Shlaudeman kept sticking his head out of the car window and yelling, "Colonel, Colonel." They finally got the firing stopped on both sides.

One night Bundy and Shlaudeman went to see Guzmán, in a house near the Embassy but inside the rebel zone. I urged them not to go but they went; and they walked. The Colonel escorted them with a fire team. They reached the house safely and conducted their negotiation with sniper fire outside all the time.

Sometimes one wondered whether talking was worth the risk. The meetings seemed endless. Mornings we would assemble in the Chancellery. Bundy had a clear crisp grasp of things—the strengths and weaknesses of the people on both sides, what each wanted, what each could, and could not, give up. He would tick off his negotiating points coolly and precisely, then go off to another meeting, and another, all through the wilting day, until coolness and crispness vanished.

In the early stages of the Bundy negotiation, a rather mysterious figure arrived on the scene, a Spaniard who, to prove he was not a Communist, said he had fought with Franco throughout the Spanish Civil War and had served in the Spanish Blue Division on the Russian Front in World War II. He seemed to be trying to control Guzmán but for what purpose and on whose orders nobody seemed to know. And at the same time, Colonel Rafael Fernández Domínguez arrived. As we have seen, when I talked to Bosch in Puerto Rico, he had said he would accept either Colonel Caamaño or Colonel Fernández as Provisional President. Bundy and the others had brought him here now, sent by Bosch to tell Caamaño to withdraw in favor of Guzmán. Colonel Fernández had been in the Republic only four days when he was killed while leading a night patrol at the Palace. His men fired a few shots into the international corridor and our troops fired back. Imbert's police inside the Palace also opened fire. Fernández was caught in the crossfire and killed. So were at least four others of his 20-man patrol—Juan Miguel Román Díaz, 14th of June Central Committee member, foremost military leader of the 14th of June, trained in Cuba; Miguel López and Ramón Tavárez, members of the 14th of June; and José Jiménez Rosario, possibly a 14th of June member (his body was wrapped in a 14th of June flag for burial). One of Caamaño's two Italian friends may have been killed. Among the wounded were two MPD members.

The circumstances of this episode are still unexplained. Why would a man of Colonel Fernández Domínguez' importance he sent on an unimportant and dangerous patrol? Its only known purpose was to reach the back of the Palace where supplies and ammunition were thought to be stored.

Subsequently I heard that Fernández had been killed elsewhere and his body taken there and dumped. At that time Bundy's negotiation with Guzmán was going fairly well. Fernández' death derailed it. Just so had the incidents at the Dragon Restaurant and near the Electricidad helped derail my efforts to bring Caamaño and Imbert together. It is not impossible that Communists in the rebel camp killed Fernández, as Communists had killed allies during the Spanish Civil War.

I do not know whether my efforts to bring Caamaño and Imbert together would have succeeded. Certainly the negotiation was not going very well, and the Communists were doing their utmost to sabotage it. But a certain logic attached to it—it represented the third step in our efforts to reach a peaceful solution. First, I had established contact with the rebels. Second I had cut our ties with San Isidro and helped set up the Imbert government. The third step was to bring Imbert and Caamaño together, something neither thought impossible.

The Guzmán effort was beset with difficulties from the outset. Tactically, it was overtaken by Imbert's successful offensive in the north, when rebel morale was low and Imbert's morale was high; so it played into the rebels' hands. Imbert's attack may have wrecked the negotiation. More fundamentally, Bundy was negotiating principally with Guzmán, not with Caamaño, but had no way of knowing how much Guzmán could deliver, while Vance was negotiating with the San Isidro Generals, not with Imbert himself. I did not think Guzmán could deliver. Not even Bosch could deliver completely. As I saw the rebel structure at that time, Caamaño was the nominal leader but real control resided in three or four Communists and one or two military men. Their bridge to Caamaño was Héctor Aristy. Guzmán represented, really, nothing. Later on, however, these negotiations bore fruit.

12

I left Santo Domingo the evening of May 18 with Undersecretary Mann. (Curiously enough, Mann, who is usually considered a conservative, had worked with Bundy on the Guzmán gambit, while I, a liberal sent down to talk to the rebels, had ended by helping set up the Imbert government.) In Washington near midnight, Mann and I saw Secretary Rusk briefly, then went to bed. Next day we met with the President, the Vice President, Secretaries Rusk and McNamara, Admiral Raborn, and others for four hours. President Johnson went into the most minute details of the Dominican situation. He wanted to know everything. He kept emphasizing his slogan "Constitutionalism *Sí,* Communism *No.*" He said he did not want a Communist government nor did he want a military dictatorship. He was willing to pursue the Guzmán effort a few more days. (It soon collapsed.) He wanted more OAS action. He complained about criticism from liberals and the press.

A few days later the President, in a speech at Baylor University, said:

"Out of the Dominican crucible the twenty American nations must now forge a stronger shield against disaster. The opportunity is here now for a new thrust forward to show the world the way to true international cooperation in the cause of peace and in the struggle to win a better life for all of us. . . .

"In today's world, with the enemies of freedom talking about wars of national liberation, the old distinction between the civil war and international war has already lost much of its meaning. . . .

"When the forces of freedom move slowly, whether on political or economic or military fronts, the forces of slavery and subversion move rapidly and they move decisively. . . .

"It is clear that we need new international machinery geared to meet the fast-moving events. When hours can decide the fate of generations, the moment of decision must become the moment of action. . . ."

13

I stayed in Washington till May 28. By then the OAS, in an unprecedented action, had voted 14 to 5 to send an inter-American force to the Dominican Republic. Brazil announced it was sending 1300 troops, and a Brazilian general, Hugo Panasco Alvim, took over command of all inter-American forces, including U.S. troops. Honduras, Costa Rica, Nicaragua and Paraguay sent token forces. The inter-American forces settled down to patrol the Zone and the Corridor, interposing themselves between Imbert's troops and the rebels. As other troops arrived, ours left. (By October we had about 8500 troops there.) In all, 26 U.S. troops were killed and 155 wounded in action.

The OAS sent a three-man mission to make peace—Ambassadors Ilmar Penna Marinho of Brazil, Ramón de Clairmont Dueñas of El Salvador, and Ellsworth Bunker of the United States. For weeks and months they labored, talking to both sides, traveling throughout the Republic, trying to find a formula that the contending sides would agree to, and encountering all the difficulties we had encountered. Sporadically, fighting resumed. Former President Balaguer returned to the Republic.

The OAS mission proposed Héctor García-Godoy for provisional president, offered an "institutional act" in lieu of a constitution under which he could govern until free elections could be held, and proposed other arrangements. As we have seen, García-Godoy, a Santiaguero, had briefly been Bosch's Foreign Minister; I had tried unsuccessfully to persuade him to enter the Imbert government. For a time it appeared that neither side would accept him. But the rebel negotiating committee split, and the PRD, led by Peña Gómez with Bosch's backing, overrode the intransigent Aristy and Caamaño, perhaps because Bundy's earlier Guzmán gambit had begun the split. Similarly, Vance's negotiation with Imbert's generals probably paved the way for that side to accept a settlement. In any case, in September, after extremely difficult negotiations, both Imbert and Caamaño stepped aside and accepted García-Godoy.

He faced formidable problems—forming a broad-based Cabinet, disarming civilians, reintegrating rebel troops into the military, abolishing the Zone and opening the city, dealing with, on the one hand, Wessin y Wessin and, on the other hand, Juan Bosch. He attempted to move forward firmly and fairly but carefully. He came under attack from both right and left. He appointed Wessin y Wessin consul general in Miami, and Wessin left under OAS and U.S. duress (but in Miami announced he would not serve as consul general and protested our forcing him out). Juan Bosch returned to Santo Domingo on September 25, the second anniversary of his overthrow. The New York *Times* reported that he was "visibly shocked" by the strength of the Communists in the rebel camp. However, he denounced the United States for intervening militarily in the Republic, saying that "the next President" ought to sue the United States before the World Court in The Hague for one billion dollars in damages. (He also recommended suing Brazil, Nicaragua, and Paraguay, though Paraguay for only one million dollars since it was "a poor country.") He said he did not intend to run for President. (Most people thought he would.)

In October, Severo Cabral was killed, apparently while attempting to reclaim furniture from his apartment in the rebel zone. A few days later several people were killed in fighting between Dominican troops and civilians who refused to surrender arms. Once more young men with guns and Molotov cocktails appeared on downtown streets of the uneasy capital. Once more disturbing reports were heard of trouble in the interior, reminding us that in 1916 the Marines had been obliged to occupy the entire Republic and to disarm all Dominicans, killing some in the process.

In all, we spent about $150 million in the Dominican Republic in 1965, a tragic irony if one recalls the difficulty both Ambassador Bennett and I had in getting far less money for peaceful works.

The winter passed tensely. Once an angry soldier guarding the Palace deliberately shot a taunting seventeen-year-old demonstrator in the back, killing him, and his classmates carried his body through the streets. In December, Caamaño and his followers went to Santiago to attend a memorial service for Colonel Fernández Domínguez and were besieged by an Army patrol in the Hotel Matúm; more than a score of men were killed, and the U. S. Airborne had to rescue Caamaño and his men. Through January and February, García-Godoy maneuvered carefully to persuade the military leaders of both sides to leave the country. Caamaño left on January 22, 1966, to become military attaché in London; Rivera Caminero left February 11 to become military attaché in Washington (as he had under the Consejo). Other Caamaño military leaders, including Montes Arache and Peña Taveras, also departed. But other loyalist leaders refused to leave, including General de los Santos and Colonel Jacinto Martínez Arana, so García-Godoy gave them powerless jobs. García-Godoy worked quietly and achieved remarkable though unspectacular success.

One night Bosch's son was shot and wounded. Monseñor Clarizio, together with three Jeep-loads of U.S. troops and several U.S. newspapermen, were caught in a shooting spree and pinned down for ten minutes. Strikes began, some supported by Bosch. Bosch said various people were plotting to kill him. Imbert challenged him to a duel. The election was scheduled for June 1, 1966. The campaign began on March 1.

Former President Bonnelly was nominated for President by a new party and supported by Luís Amiama Tió. Former President Balaguer was nominated by the Partido Reformista. The Social Christians were active. The Communist PCD (formerly PSP) announced it would support Bosch if he ran, though pointing out that its ultimate objectives were not those of his PRD and it was supporting him only because its immediate aims were his—the fight against "oligarchical minorities" and "the United States intervention." Héctor Aristy launched a "24th of April Movement," announced it had as its first goal the withdrawal of the Inter-American Peace Force, praised Caamaño, and spoke enigmatically of other long-term objectives. The government legitimized the 14th of June. The Electoral Board certified a dozen parties.

During the early campaign skirmishing, bombs exploded, shooting broke out between political partisans in towns in the interior, political leaders charged terrorism, a policeman killed a student at San Juan de la Maguana, U.S. troops wounded several Dominicans near the Río Ozama bridge in the capital, a number of PRD men were beaten or shot, a Bosch bodyguard was killed, and somebody painted on the walls of the Papal Nunciatura "Long live Bosch, so that we can kill him." Through it all, Ambassador Bunker persevered with great skill and patience.

Evidently Bosch really did not want to run for President. He said so repeatedly. Once he said he would support Caamaño. Perhaps he feared assassination. On April 10, however, the PRD convention nominated Bosch for President and Antonio Guzmán for Vice President. Bosch, in his acceptance speech, compared the Dominican predicament to that of David confronting Goliath (the United States) and welcomed any support. The 14th of June announced it would support him provided he would fight for expulsion of foreign troops, re-establish the 1963 Constitution, bring back Caamaño and other rebel military leaders, and refuse to accept help from U.S. agencies, including AID, CIA, MAAG, and the Peace Corps. Bosch promptly rejected the conditions and 14th of June support. The 14th of June, which had fought for him a year earlier, attacked him bitterly.

April 24, the anniversary of the 1965 rising, which some had thought might be the occasion of trouble, passed relatively quietly; speakers at a meeting in Parque Independencia demanded that U.S. troops leave, and demonstrators burned a U.S. flag and displayed MPD, 14th of June, and PCD (formerly PSP) signs—but not the signs of Bosch's PRD.

Bonnelly and Balaguer were touring the Republic, campaigning. Bosch left his home only twice: To visit his wounded son, and to accept the PRD nomination. He campaigned from his house by radio. This circumstance, no doubt prompted by legitimate fear of assassination, established an advantageous political position for him—underdog, clandestine—and, in a campaign devoid of issues—even Balaguer, sometimes considered rightly or wrongly "the U.S. candidate," was demanding the withdrawal of foreign troops—created an issue for Bosch: His own safety. He used it as he had used the Church issue to monopolize attention in the 1962 campaign. Bosch's party platform called for the withdrawal of foreign troops but did not say when. Bosch himself had taken care several times to disassociate himself from the Castro/Communists. They themselves were badly split, and a photograph published in March in a Spanish-language magazine of Cayetano Rodríguez and Chairman Mao didn't help. (The photograph was taken, the magazine said, in July 1964.)

The OAS prepared to send observers to the election. At the end of April, most experts considered the chance of holding a clean election good—always adding that nobody in his right mind would predict what might happen in the Dominican Republic. The police seemed greatly improved. The Armed Forces, under General Enrique Pérez y Pérez, said they abjured politics. They had often said so before. Possibly this time they meant it, remembering the bloodbath they had caused by overthrowing Bosch. Most experts agreed that the dangerous period would come between the election on June 1 and the inauguration of the new President on July 1. Most thought the OAS could bring the troops home after the inauguration, perhaps even earlier, after the election. And at the end of April, most thought Bosch likely to be elected. Whether the Republic could then resume normal life was uncertain.

Everything, obviously, depended on whether the delicate political balance that had produced Bosch's election in 1962 could be restored and maintained. It would not be easy. Should it be achieved, García-Godoy and Ambassador Bunker could take immense satisfaction in their work.

Any civil war causes wounds that do not heal for years, though the winner imposes a peace of one sort or another on the loser. In this Civil War, neither side had won; we and the OAS had refused to permit either to win. After so much hate and killing, it would seem to be difficult for Dominicans to live together again in peace. Friends of the Republic could only fervently hope and work to help make it possible.

Chapter Twenty-eight

EACH MUST ACT

As I write, it is more than four years since I left Upper Michigan to go to the Dominican Republic on a fact-finding mission for President Kennedy. During those years I lived through the death throes of Trujillo's old order and the birth agony of Dominican democracy, the strangulation of that democracy and the assassination of President Kennedy, the Dominican Civil War that swept away everything we had built; and I undertook missions for two Presidents, President Kennedy and President Johnson. Four years—what can we conclude from all this?

2

Let us deal first with the Civil War of 1965.

Our policy in the Dominican Republic that spring has been severely criticized by much of the influential United States press, by Senator Fulbright and other political leaders, by students and intellectuals in the United States, and by various diplomats and government officials around the world.

Some of that criticism, I believe, sprang from vague but deep misgivings people had felt about our foreign policy since the day President Kennedy died. Those misgivings may be totally unfair to President Johnson. The fact remains that the Dominican crisis, coming as it did when we were becoming more deeply involved in Vietnam, triggered attacks on President Johnson's entire foreign policy.

Critics asked five main questions about our Dominican policy:

—Was there really danger of a Communist takeover?

—Should we have intervened militarily and unilaterally?

—Hadn't we overreacted?

—Having intervened, why didn't we espouse the rebel cause or at least maintain strict neutrality between the rebels and loyalists?

—Wasn't our policy erratic, uncertain, and contradictory? Weren't we less than candid in explaining it?

And of course: How did we get into such a mess? And how do we get out?

On the first point, I have no doubt whatsoever that there was a real danger of a Communist takeover of the Dominican Republic. I have set forth the evidence in the preceding chapter. Again I wish to emphasize that this is not primarily a question of names and numbers. It is a question of the process, of the bloodbath that fuses men and women of all ideologies into a fanatic mass and erases the fine distinctions that are possible in ordinary times.

On the second point, given the circumstances that existed at the time, in my opinion President Johnson had no choice but to send the troops. There can be no question that, with the police and military demoralized and all but defeated, with thousands of armed and embittered civilians roaming the streets, U.S. lives were endangered. Had the President not sent the troops, the rebels probably would have defeated the San Isidro troops, spread the rebellion throughout the Republic, killed some Americans and many Dominicans, and in the end established a Communist-dominated government. When I speak of "the circumstances that existed at the time," however, I mean not only a breakdown in law and order, but the fact that the rebellion had fallen under the domination of Communists, not PRDistas. And, reluctant as I am to say it, in my opinion this had happened at least in part because on the first Tuesday of the rebellion Ambassador Bennett rejected the rebels' plea to help negotiate a settlement.

It is extremely disagreeable to second-guess any Ambassador. Moreover, no Ambassador can know everything; to a considerable extent he must rely on what he is told. Ambassador Bennett had returned to Santo Domingo only a few hours before he faced his crucial decision. He thought the rebels were losing; they said so themselves. But when he rejected their overtures, the PRDistas went into hiding—and the military rebels and the Communists went back to the streets to fight; and they nearly won. The only door open to them was the Communist door; Bennett had shut our door. Had he not, everything else might have turned out differently. Having said this, I must add that it might not have— Caamaño was already so deeply committed he might have fought on anyway, the Communists were gaining ascendancy anyway, Wessin had his tanks at the bridge and was in no mood to negotiate, and Bennett's move may have made no difference. Who knows? History does not reveal its alternatives. At the least, Bennett's move was important, if only because it persuaded Molina Ureña to abandon the struggle. In any case, presented with the situation as it existed after Tuesday, President Johnson had to intervene.

Intervene unilaterally? The OAS Charter specifically prohibits unilateral intervention. Therefore, our intervention was illegal, or at least contrary to the spirit of the Charter.[1] We could have asked for an emergency meeting of the OAS, but the OAS is not noted for swift, decisive action. I do not believe we could have waited; there simply wasn't time. We could, however, have informed the OAS before we sent the troops. This would have been no less illegal. It would have made little difference to the Dominicans. It probably would have looked better, and our reputation probably would have suffered somewhat less.

On the third point, whether we "overreacted" and sent too many troops—"more than twenty thousand troops to catch fifty Communists," as critics have put it—I would point out that in such a situation a few leaders can exert great leverage on large numbers of uninformed people. The situation in the capital was chaotic and that in the interior virtually unknown. If, as the troop buildup increased, our purpose became to prevent a Communist takeover, then prudence argued for a large force. From a purely military point of view, how many is too many? I am not competent to judge but certainly would have hesitated to send only four hundred Marines to rescue several thousand civilians in the face of several thousand armed rebels. The Marines might have been thrown out. How many did we need to patrol the International Zone and other areas? I do not know, but U.S. forces had to hold a total perimeter of more than thirty miles. At the peak, on May 17, U.S. troops in Santo Domingo totaled 22,289. Putting so many troops ashore in little Santo Domingo hurt us politically and helped the Castro/Communists throughout the Hemisphere. But the Defense Department, once called upon, takes no unnecessary risks and throws in overwhelming numbers, on the ground that doing so is the best guarantee against losing many lives on both sides. This is hard to quarrel with.

On the fourth point, we did not espouse the rebel cause because it had fallen under Communist domination. As we have seen, we did everything possible to support President Bosch before he was overthrown in 1963. It would have been logical to support him in 1965 had he returned to lead the rebellion at its very outset. But although his men started the rebellion, and although Molina Ureña and other PRD leaders apparently expected him to return immediately, Bosch did not return. Why he did not has never been satisfactorily explained, even by Bosch himself in all his writings on the rebellion that I have seen.[2] He does say that he

---

[1] Lawyers argue that any nation has a right in international law to use arms to protect its citizens' lives, hence our intervention was not illegal.

[2] Bosch has written several magazine articles and given several interviews since the Civil War. He has been critical of our policy and of some of our policymakers. He has differed from me in his recollection of certain events, notably our conversations of May 2–3, 1965. Readers may find a summary of his views in *The New Leader* of June 21, 1965, and other magazines mentioned in the

twice asked us for a plane. He did not ask me. So far as I know, he did not ask any American official or unofficial representative. Nor did we, so far as I know—and I inquired at the time—interpose any obstacle to his return. He could have returned in the first days without consulting us. True, San Isidro Air Base was in Wessin's hands, and Bosch could not have landed there. But had he wanted to go, he could have landed at any of several other airports. He did not. Therefore, with Bosch in Puerto Rico, and Molina Ureña in asylum, and Communists dominating the rebels, we could hardly support them.

As for maintaining neutrality, we did a good deal of talking about it, and journalists criticized us severely for not doing it. My own view is that in the very beginning some of our people on the spot understood that they were there to fight communism, and this meant, to them, fighting alongside Wessin, although our policy never so dictated; that we stopped this and set up the Zone lines and the corridor and, after Imbert's offensive in the north, interposed our troops between the hostile Dominican forces and thus did in fact maintain neutrality, shooting only when shot at; and that we did our shooting mostly at rebels because with few exceptions only rebels shot at us. And my further view is that once we had decided we were in the Republic to stop communism, we should have stopped pretending neutrality. For it is incomprehensible to me how we could contain one side and at the same time stay neutral.

On the fifth point, I believe our policy seemed more erratic than it was. During the first few days, in a situation so chaotic and confused, it would be surprising if we had been able to lay out a policy neatly. (But in fact, on two fundamental points, our policy did set early and never changed: To protect United States lives, and to prevent a Castro/Communist takeover.) Most critics, however, complained that at various times we seemed to be collaborating first with San Isidro, then with Caamaño, then with Imbert, then with Guzmán. This can be called erratic; it can also be called exploring all possibilities. I myself was sent to the Republic to open a channel to the rebels, and did. Then on May 2 I said the rebellion had in the past few days fallen under the domination of Communists and other extremists because I believed it was true, because I thought it time we said so, and because I thought saying it might help split the rebels and thus save the non-Communist rebels. Then I helped set up the Imbert government, for the reasons I have stated. I see no policy inconsistency here either. Some reporters criticized us too because it seemed to them inconsistent that we labeled the rebels Communist-dominated then opened negotiations with them through Guz-

bibliography. He wrote his book, *Crisis de la Democracia de América en la República Dominicana,* before the Civil War. Regrettably the recent edition in English has not been brought up to date.

mán. I see no inconsistency here: A pre-condition of our proposed support for Guzmán was that his government be free of Communist influence. The reporters who criticized did not know that. They did not know because they were not told.

Reporters cannot be told everything while a negotiation is in progress, but on the whole I feel that what we did in Santo Domingo was better than what we said. Ambassador Bennett repeated to U.S. correspondents —in all good faith, I feel sure, though without checking them—atrocity stories told him by the San Isidro generals; when they turned out not to be true, the correspondents suspected him of having deliberately lied to them, and some of them never trusted him again. The President himself, again in all good faith, repeated some of the stories. Thus began the "crisis of credibility" in the Administration so much discussed for many months. A great deal of hostility toward U.S. policy and suspicion of U.S. motives that colored correspondents' stories stemmed from those early statements; journalists who think they have been lied to do not forgive. Not until Sunday, May 2, nine days after the rebellion started and five days after the first Marines landed, did we say publicly that we were there to stop communism. Previously we had maintained that we were there to protect American lives. I think we would have come out better if at the moment we sent the Marines, or certainly when we sent the Airborne, we had announced that we were sending them to protect American lives, to help restore peace, to stop the combatants from tearing their country to pieces, and to prevent a Castro/Communist takeover, calling on the OAS to help us. At the same time we should have made it clear that we had no intention of setting up or propping up a military dictatorship under Wessin or anybody else—that our purposes were to suppress anarchy and give the Dominican people a chance once more to choose their own leaders in a free and peaceful election, a chance they would never have had if the Communists had won. But, again, hindsight is easy.

Finally, how did we get into this mess? And how do we get out?

Despite all our differences, despite what I consider his shortcomings, I do not believe the *civicos* and the military were justified in 1963 when they overthrew Juan Bosch, and I believe that their *golpe* led directly to the Civil War. Bosch's voters had expected—and deserved—from him a better life. After his overthrow, the political system collapsed—his party and others were banned, the democratic left movement was destroyed, and a fatal far left-far right polarization began. It ended in Civil War.

The Civil War was also a reaction, four years delayed, to the downfall of Trujillo. During Trujillo's rule, vast changes occurred elsewhere in the world—the Great Depression, a World War, the leveling process in our own society, the breakup of nineteenth-century colonialism, and the outburst of freedom on three continents. People everywhere, long dominated by colonialists and homegrown dictators, glimpsed a better life and demanded a share of it. What Adlai Stevenson had called in the 1950s a "revolution of rising expectations" had become by the 1960s a loud—and long overdue—demand for justice at any cost. But during the generation of Trujillo's rule, nothing happened in his country—nothing at all.

When Trujillo fell, many Dominicans believed a bloodbath inevitable. It did not occur immediately, thanks largely to the U.S. fleet, the OAS, and the delicate arrangement of political power that culminated in Bosch's election.

Just as Trujillo's fall let loose all the hopes and aspirations his tyranny had repressed, Bosch's election collected and focused them. During my time, in 1962 and 1963, our objective was to guide these inchoate and unpredictable forces into political channels, achieving a precarious balance. Bosch's overthrow cut them loose again. The political structure crumbled, guerrilla activity began in December, an onset of violence that increased the polarization of left and right.

Reid made many mistakes, climaxed by his wrongheaded (though unannounced) determination to extend his term as President. But so did we make mistakes. During Reid's presidency, our Embassy kept hands off, stayed strictly out of Dominican politics. Although I was not there, I have the impression that the Embassy did not even keep closely informed of the rapidly shifting political situation. In my opinion, this was mistaken; in such a country it is essential to maintain the political structure, the peaceable political process. And our help may be needed. It is too much to blame the Civil War on a year and a half of do-nothingism by us. Nevertheless, had the Embassy not chosen to stand aside, conceivably it might have contained or deflected or at least moderated the contending forces; the circumstances that compelled President Johnson to send the troops might never have arisen. Political non-involvement in such a country is very likely to lead to military intervention—and did.

Furthermore, when Reid got into financial trouble, he turned to the International Monetary Fund. The IMF has been accused of having almost forced Reid to push deflationary measures despite some economists' views that devaluation—and therefore inflation—was necessary. At one point, even some IMF staff members favored devaluation. But the IMF never took an official position favoring devaluation (and Reid himself opposed it). Rather, the IMF urged various other stabilization measures, such as import controls to curtail the outflow of foreign exchange, and the Department agreed, and Reid took some. What resulted was austerity —and a worsening of the daily life of the ordinary Dominican. This, to my mind, is the second lesson to be learned: Sound international banking is not always good local politics. Finally, the Dominicans failed themselves. As I had known before, and as I saw again last spring—and as

Bundy and Bunker must have seen—Dominican leadership is very thin and very reluctant. Once you have skimmed off a dozen names—always the same names—you find there is nothing down below.

All the while Reid was President, the same subsurface currents that followed Trujillo's and Bosch's removal continued to erode the dike. Seen thus, the Civil War was, quite simply, the end result of a revolutionary process that had been stifled by Trujillo's secret police and directed into peaceful channels by Bosch's election. And we were drawn in, partly by what seems to me poor Embassy staff performance and reporting for some months and unwise diplomacy in the first days of the rebellion, partly by the actual circumstances that existed on Wednesday (which in turn resulted in part from poor diplomacy during the preceding days).

How do we get out? The Dominican Republic lost a whole generation under Trujillo. I fear it may have lost another during the bloodbath of 1965. The best hopes now are the OAS or successful free elections. As we have seen, "Pepe" Figueres proposed an OAS trusteeship after Trujillo fell. It is very nearly what we had in the Republic by late 1965, in fact if not in name. Perhaps it is the only solution in a country so shattered, though it is doubtful that the Dominicans would accept it or the OAS undertake it for any extended period. As for elections, by the time this book is published we shall know more about whether they can be held and the winner installed successfully. Whether he can govern remains to be seen. It would appear that only an elected President able to govern, or some kind of OAS responsibility, will enable the United States to disengage.

For a hundred years, even before we nearly annexed it, the Dominican Republic has occupied what is probably a unique place in the United States' relationships with other countries. It is a small nation, but its problems, and our responses to them, have importantly affected our broader policies. The Republic's problems produced the Roosevelt Corollary to the Monroe Doctrine; "dollar diplomacy"; OAS sanctions against a member state; OAS supervision of elections; the trend in 1962 toward democratic leftist ascendancy in Latin America and in 1963 toward military *golpes;* our intervention and our far-ranging foreign policy debate in 1965–66. OAS or no, for better or worse, the Republic will continue to occupy our own sometimes pained attention for a long time to come.

No one should be denied the right to criticize our policy there. Most criticism in the beginning in 1965 came from liberals. After the banishment of Wessin y Wessin, it came from the right. Perhaps this speaks rather well of our policy. If we did help restrain the Dominicans from destroying their society, if we did preserve their free choice, if by what at this moment seems to require little short of a miracle an effective, freely elected, representative, and constitutional government does emerge, then we can take considerable satisfaction in what we did.

No one should imagine that the rebellion of 1965 was a mere rising of the outs against the ins. No one should imagine that the rebels won—at least for a time, and in part—the people's sympathy solely because the rebels controlled the crucial radio outlet. This rebellion went very deep. It went to the roots of discontent that first Trujillo, then the OAS and we, held in check. Our troops choked off the rebellion, but the roots remain. This was the start of "the revolution from below, Communist-led" that I had foreseen if Bosch fell. We encouraged the Dominican people's yearning for a better life, and rightly. We must continue to. If we do not, someone else will.

The powerful torsion of these dangerous and revolutionary times ripped the Republic to pieces. It will never be the same again, nor will other nations around the world which have been wracked by these same storms. This is what we, the United States, must deal with, and by the very fact that our power is so great, its limits are extremely narrow. There we sat in Santo Domingo, with might enough to flatten the city. But then what? Kill thousands of innocent Dominicans to get rid of some Communists? Occupy the entire Republic, perhaps for years? Of course not.

Our role is not easy. Motives are mixed, purposes obscure, events confused. Around the world men are dying in battles they seldom understand. We cannot forget the old lady who shook my hand in the street outside rebel headquarters; nor the thousands who thought constitutionality meant bread; nor the men who said we saved them from communism; nor the MPD *tigre* who yelled "Yankees go home"; nor the woman who overnight learned the vocabulary of "counter-revolutionary deviationist"; nor the two young American soldiers lost and shot dead in a narrow street in Santo Domingo.

3

Now let us go back to the Dominican Republic before the Civil War.

Long after I had resigned, I learned why I had been appointed. As we have seen, I had thought that President Kennedy had sent me fact-finding to the Republic in September of 1961 simply because he did not have enough facts to base policy on. Later I discovered it had not been quite that simple. Few things are.

In the spring of 1961, before Trujillo was assassinated, word had somehow reached Joseph P. Kennedy, the President's father, that Trujillo was in trouble—the OAS sanctions were squeezing him—and that if he fell, Castro/Communists might take over. The President or the State Department had sent Robert D Murphy, an experienced diplomat who had ably served President Roosevelt during World War II in sometimes distasteful dealings with Admiral Darlan and others, to the Dominican Republic.[3] He had been accompanied by Igor Cassini, a Hearst gossip columnist and brother of Oleg Cassini, a dress designer. The Cassinis moved in international cafe society, "the jet set" of the gossip columns. Oleg Cassini saw President Kennedy occasionally at Palm Beach. Igor Cassini was close to Porfirio Rubirosa,[4] the Dominican "international playboy" who had been married to Trujillo's daughter, Flor de Oro, Doris Duke, Barbara Hutton, and two French actresses. Rubirosa knew members of the Kennedy family.

Igor Cassini was the link, or rather tried to become the link, between Trujillo and the Kennedys. Cassini was married to a daughter of a close friend of the President, Charles Wrightsman, of Palm Beach. Cassini had close ties to Trujillo, although he did not disclose them. In fact, he had acted as an agent of Trujillo; subsequently he was convicted of failing to register as such with the United States government. His wife—Wrightsman's daughter—committed suicide. In the spring of 1961, Igor Cassini had gone to the Republic with Robert Murphy "to introduce him," as Cassini later said. What Murphy reported I do not know.

After Trujillo was assassinated May 30, our Dominican policy was urgently discussed at several White House meetings, and Robert Murphy met in New York with Igor Cassini and Luís Mercado, then Dominican consul general in New York, soon named head of Trujillo's Partido Dominicano.

Reports of Castro/Communist activity in the Dominican Republic were alarming; reports of the new non-Communist political movements were not reassuring. Ramfis Trujillo and Balaguer were promising to "democratize" the Republic and maintain stability and a strong anti-Communist position. A considerable body of important opinion in Washington favored supporting Balaguer, with the understanding that Ramfis would leave and permit Balaguer to govern without repression. But others held that we should reject the Trujillos and Balaguer, support the new political parties, and make a fresh start in the Republic.

A decision was to be taken at a meeting with President Kennedy on August 28. At that point, two or three Dominicans, leaders of the emerging political parties, arrived in Washington and called on Attorney General Kennedy. After listening to them, he went to the White House and said he did not see how we could hope for much from such people. He and White House staff men suggested that not enough facts were known and that I should be sent down to the Republic to report. President Kennedy called me to Washington.

[3] Murphy, in his book, *Diplomat Among Warriors*, published in 1964, does not cover this Dominican episode.
[4] Rubirosa was killed driving a sports car in France in 1965.

The men I talked to in Washington—Bob Kennedy, George Ball, Steve Smith, Robert Murphy, Dick Goodwin, Arthur Schlesinger—told me simply to report the facts as I found them. I did and, as we have seen, in all innocence recommended keeping on the OAS sanctions and getting rid of the Trujillos.

Two other points should be made here. It was Attorney General Kennedy who later prosecuted Igor Cassini; and it was President Kennedy, not Igor Cassini or Porfirio Rubirosa or anyone else, who finally decided our policy.

At that time, the Dominican Trujillistas were using the Communist bogeyman to try to influence us. Just so, the *golpistas* used it against Juan Bosch two years later; and some thought San Isidro was doing it again in 1965. The conclusion is inescapable: Policy must be not rigidly doctrinaire but based on the facts as they exist at the time.

I have often wondered what would have happened had the President chosen the other fork in the road—supported the Ramfis-Balaguer regime. After all, we ended up with a military *coup* and a Marine occupation—and, unhappily, Balaguer now seems a leading presidential candidate.

Once again, however, it is not that simple. For, from the death of Trujillo to the fall of Juan Bosch, the Dominican people enjoyed 848 days of freedom. Not much, perhaps; but not little either, when one considers all Dominican history. It is difficult to believe that a Ramfis-Balaguer regime would have permitted so much. Also, from the standpoint of our own national interest, we gained much—we came down on the side of the people against the Trujillos, the very symbol of tyranny throughout the Hemisphere. None of this is unimportant.

4

By now, it is perhaps clear that throughout my time as Ambassador, we were conducting a quiet war. Some may call it "intervention." I would point out that our every effort was aimed at maintaining in office the Consejo and President Bosch, never at overthrowing them; that our every effort was aimed at maintaining constitutionalism and representative democracy; that our every effort was aimed at assisting the Dominican people to replace a dictatorship with a stable democratic government of their own choice. I reject the idea that our deeds constituted intervention and I maintain that we acted as a moderator among contending forces, as a helping hand in a difficult time. We did it because we believed we were promoting the freedom of the Dominican people. We did it because we believed that that freedom served our own interests. We had no wish to run their Republic. We wanted to create conditions in which no one else could run it—only the Dominican people.

Around the world, year after year, day after day, night after night, United States Ambassadors and their staffs conduct a ceaseless, quiet war to protect and advance the interests of the United States. It is an enormous responsibility, for one man's act—or failure to act—can alter history. The Ambassador works within certain policy guidelines hammered out in his Embassy and in Washington. Vast history swings on the hinge of foreign policy, but often that foreign policy looks far less clear to the Ambassador on the firing line than it looks to the White House or to "the seventh floor," the seventh floor of the State Department, where the Secretary and Undersecretaries and the Policy Planning Staff dwell. Despite guidelines and contingency papers, now and then the Ambassador suddenly confronts a major decision, and he must make it, for better or worse, alone.

We have more than one hundred Ambassadors. About two-thirds of them are career men, about one-third political appointees, like myself. This rough ratio has obtained since 1956, regardless of which political party was in power. I see no merit *per se* in the appointment of a career officer as Ambassador. I see no merit in the appointment of either a State Department hack or a political hack. Neither is good enough today; there are no longer any "easy" posts. A career man knows automatically much Department routine and many other things that I had to learn. On the other hand, a political appointee has certain advantages. I took risks that few career men would have taken. Why not? After all, if I failed, I could return to my previous profession; but a man who has invested twenty-five years of his life in a Foreign Service career is not likely to risk it in some doubtful adventure in a small Caribbean country. He is more likely to stand aside, let events take their course, and seek instruction from Washington. I sometimes acted first and then told Washington what I'd done. If I succeeded, I would get little public credit, for when diplomacy succeeds, all is quiet; newspapers cover crises —policy failures—not quiet successes. If I failed, I would go home. This is not a complaint. It is simply a fact known to all who serve it: Government is indifferent to persons, and sometimes even cruel.

To me, at times, the gap between Washington and Santo Domingo seemed unbridgeable, as it must have seemed at times to other Ambassadors—and to Washington. How could the cool and comfortable men on the seventh floor understand the people in the *barrios*? How could AID economists see that Bosch found it hard to ask us for money? How could President Kennedy fully understand why Bosch behaved as he did during the Haitian crisis, not to mention the *Restauración*?

On the whole I had the support of Washington. True, our support of Bosch was less enthusiastic than had been our support of the Consejo. But support him we did.

5

Nevertheless, during my time, Dominican democracy failed. Why? Again that difficult, crucial question—why?

It would be easy to single out a villain, establish a thesis, make a case.

One could, for example, say that this is what happens when someone like the late Senator McCarthy gets in the saddle. By cries of "Communists in government," Bonilla Aybar and his *civico* friends accomplished in their country what McCarthy could not accomplish in his: They destroyed the Constitution and the very system of government.

Or one could say, as the Communists might, that this is what happens when the military power, the money power, and the Church combine with imperialists.

Or one could say that the Trujillo-trained military simply took back by force the power it had temporarily relinquished.[5]

Or one could say that we, the United States, pushed the Dominicans into an election for which they were unprepared, thus ensuring disaster.

Or one could simply blame Bosch himself.

Other theses, other villains, are ready to hand. Each has plausibility. But none alone is sufficient.

To say that what killed Dominican democracy was McCarthyism is to ignore Bosch's very real failures to meet the people's needs, and our own failure to give him all-out support.

To say that the military cynically recaptured power is to ignore the very real, if misguided and primitive, fear of communism that Wessin y Wessin and others felt.

To say that the money power combined with the military power is to forget that a number of oligarchs and their friends, such as Marco Cabral

---

[5] Bosch himself has written in his book: "Although there were many other factors, the Dominican *coup* of 1963 was principally caused by corruption." He refers specifically to his opposition to Luna's plan to buy six million dollars' worth of Hawker Hunters, and says that although the "customary commission" taken by Army purchasers was 10 percent, the commission on this deal was to have been 20 percent, 1.2 million dollars. This was worth overthrowing the government for, Bosch says. He adds, however, that other factors were involved. Indeed, the conspiracy was afoot even before he took office, he says, launched by political leaders, priests, businessmen, and journalists. And the Armed Forces that perpetrated it were Trujillo's, formed during the U.S. occupation. He says he heard rumors while he was President that our military mission conspired to overthrow him, though he could not prove it—"but I am sure that if a captain of the mission had said that the government ought to be overthrown, it would have been in one hour, because that captain had more authority over the Dominican high command than the people, the Constitution, the President." The *golpe* was carried out by twenty-six generals and colonels who, he says, were moved by fear of change and lust for power and riches just as were their *civico* confederates.

and the publisher of *Listin Diario,* Carlos Alberto Ricart, opposed the *golpe.*

To blame the Church is to ignore completely the desperate efforts of the Papal Nuncio and other churchmen to avert disaster.

And to blame history is to declare that man cannot change his destiny, which may be so but cannot be proved.

The case against Bosch is strong. Put at its harshest, it reads that what he brought to his high office—and nearly all he brought—was an almost obsessive love of conspiracy learned in twenty-five years of Caribbean exile politics. It reads that during his seven months in office he accomplished nothing, that he made fatal political mistakes, that he had no idea of what "being President" means, that he was a divider, not a builder. Like Mazzini, he inflamed a generation but could not lead it. It may even be doubted that he wanted to be President. Certainly he showed a suicidal tendency to overthrow himself.

Yet such a judgment is far too harsh. It is difficult to feel anything but pity for a man who put twenty-five years of his life into preparing to free his country from tyranny only to fail after seven months. Nor can one ignore the obstacles he faced—a people almost gone blind in the Trujillo night, a right and a left determined to destroy one another and anyone in between, nobody to help him, history itself. Nor can one ignore the indisputable fact that his brief Administration may well have been the most honest in Dominican history, if not in Latin America. Finally, Juan Bosch gave the 3½ million Dominican people seven months of peace and seven months of freedom, things rare and precious in the tragic Republic. While Bosch was President, the state killed no one. While Bosch was President, almost no one was arbitrarily imprisoned. This, indeed, may be his monument.

When one indicts Juan Bosch, one must remember that his flaws, his failings, are really those of the Dominican people themselves. Sweeping generalizations about "the national character" in any country are always dangerous. But there is an inescapable parallel between Bosch's ridiculous behavior at Santiago during the *Restauración* on the one hand and, on the other, the swaggering vanity of the Air Force pilots with their dirks and scarves and worn-out airplanes; the insistence of a provincial hospital superintendent that he needs a new hospital when what he really needs is to clean up the one he has; the doctor who insists on penicillin and scorns soap and water; the boy who refuses to learn radio repair because he dreams of being an electronic engineer. Vanity, pride, posturing, rigidity, hopelessly grandiose dreams, volatility and instability, an almost childlike refusal to assume responsibility—these were flaws in Bosch's character, as they are flaws in the Dominican character; and for that matter who can say they are not flaws in us all? In any case, they hurt Bosch, and they hurt his people.

So did impatience. Ought the people who elected him to have turned on him after only three or four months? Yet it is not surprising they were impatient, so long deprived. It is painful, if not totally unfair, to indict a people who have suffered so much throughout their history. Sumner Welles, recalling the Dominicans' struggle against the Haitian invader, repeatedly spoke of their bravery. No cowards killed Trujillo, and the people showed real courage against his son's tanks and torture chambers. Again, one may think such men as Manolo Tavárez Justo bad, or foolish—and certainly he died for dubious cause, seeking a victory that could only have handed his country over to alien control—but one ought not forget what he bravely bore in Trujillo's torture chambers, nor the murder of his wife and her sisters Mirabal. One may think the people of the Güaley slum foolish and irresponsible, who voted for Bosch in December and booed him in the spring; but before condemning them, one should live in Güaley's hovels. In a very real sense, Juan Bosch accurately reflected his people's character and their shortcomings, and if he failed them, so did they fail him.

But there is a nobler side to the Dominican people, and to Bosch's PRD. Here is a letter to Fran from a PRD official who lent equipment for our Fourth of July children's party. Returning some cigarettes she had sent him as a gift, he wrote, in prose reminiscent of that of condemned Bartolomeo Vanzetti: "I shall try to explain myself a little. The men of our PRD, presently in power, those of us who feel deeply in their ideals the painful and problematical situation, did not come to Santo Domingo to follow business interests, to look for jobs or money. . . . To do business and earn money, it would not have been necessary for us to have come. We could have remained there, where we were established and things would go better for us; or in your interesting country, for example, where we also live, one works well, and earns more. We have come to this Country of ours to be at its service and to earn only the intimate and formidable satisfaction of having helped Our People. That, we think, is what you did on this occasion and for which our assistance was required. . . . You will easily understand that we have imposed on ourselves the rigorous duty of establishing standards and establishing precedents, each time a case so requires it, as also why we beg you to accept the return of your kind gift which we include herewith." A few weeks later, after the *golpe,* he was arrested for carrying a gun.

What of the case against the military? Here again the matter is muddled. One must take into account so many men, so many motives—Wessin y Wessin, restless and troubled on his cot in his ascetic cell near his tanks; the old Trujillista "San Cristóbal group" suddenly emerging from obscurity to reclaim their dreadful heritage; the ambitious young officers below, pressing those on top; and Luna counting pesos at the thought of the Hawker Hunters, while Belisario Peguero was building a mansion. And yet, and yet—what do you expect? In Chicago, a slum boy's only ladder up from the gutter is the political organization, and if, born to poverty and reared in crime, he becomes a political leader of doubtful honesty, who can be surprised? Just so, why seems it strange that a Dominican boy born in a hut in the squalid *barrio* of a provincial capital, taught to claw or beg for every penny and every rag, joins the military and rises to high place and suddenly finds himself wearing polished boots, dining in Embassies, dazzling the acquiescent beauties of the Hotel Embajador, empowered to spend millions of dollars and to make or break or even kill his fellows—why seems it strange if such a man is less than honest with the millions, or less than gracious with his power? True, one might hope that now and then ordinary decency would prevail. But dares one hope that to decency will be added political acuity? Dares one hope that such a man, schooled by Trujillo's bloody politics, observing the fate of Batista's officers, hearing our own cant about communism, seeing only black and white, left and right, politically primitive and ridden by fears, manipulated by more sophisticated politicians, unacquainted with the subtleties of the politics of the left, indifferent to the dignity of constitutionalism—does one reasonably hope that such men will not one night take the Palace with machine guns in the name of *Dios, Patria, y Libertad?* Hardly.

The case against the *civicos* is perhaps the strongest of all. And for two reasons: They had in the past suffered least, and they knew better. These were not deprived slum-dwellers, nor ignorant *campesinos,* nor provincial military men. These were business and professional men, educated, traveled. They knew better; *they knew better.* Bonnelly, a lawyer, knew what constitutionalism means. (But ought one blame him if he retaliated against Bosch's indicting him for murder?) Bonilla Aybar had observed journalism in the United States—we sent him!—and knew that freedom of the press also entails responsibility. It is hard to believe that he was anything more than a self-serving adventurer. As for the politicians, one knows that such men as Viriato Fiallo really believed Bosch was handing the country over to the Communists, and that such men as Severo Cabral were fanatics; but it is hard to believe that anything more than sheer ambition moved such men as Juan Isidro Jimenes Grullón and Horacio Julio Ornes.

Apart from those who worked actively to overthrow Bosch, other business and professional men denied Bosch their help. They knew that Dominicans of ability and experience in government were extraordinarily rare. They refused to accept responsibility; they "did not want to get involved." Yet is this surprising? Trujillo scarcely enhanced the appeal of "government service." They claimed a free man's right to stand aside, to remain a private person. Yet is it not a free man's duty to fight for freedom?

The bald fact is that the Dominican politicians and *civicos* simply refused to accept electoral defeat at Bosch's hands and so defeated him by other means. And yet, it must also be said that Bosch's every move alarmed, repelled, and disgusted them; that if they were poor losers, so was he a poor winner. It is not surprising that they practiced, as did Bosch himself, not the politics of democracy but the politics of annihilation.

The politics of annihilation, it seems to me, is one of the most pernicious afflictions of the emerging world. It is the function of politics to adjust differences, to reach accommodation where discord prevails. President Johnson's "come, let us reason together" is, in a sense, the heart of the politics of democracy, and the bipartisan Civil Rights Act of 1964 is an example of how it works. Such a system is almost unknown in the emerging nations. In the Congo, in Vietnam, in the Dominican Republic, across Africa and Southeast Asia and Latin America, all too often the lot of the loser is deportation or death, while the winner takes all. A Latin American joke says, "We have a two-party system—one party is in the Palace and the other is in jail." It is useless and wrong to hope that all nations will model their affairs on ours, but a politics of accommodation would have served both Bosch and the *civicos* well. After all, they have to live on the same island.

More was involved in Bosch's fall—Dominican society, Dominican tradition, Dominican institutions, Dominican history. A Dominican's responsibility seldom extends beyond his own tribe of cousins to the wider community—to his neighborhood, to his town, to his country. The Republic, cut in pieces by mountain ranges and rivers, was virtually without roads until the 1920s; tribal isolation was a geographical fact. Nineteenth-century political *caciques* built their power on conglomerations of families. In Trujillo's bleak prison, a man could scarcely trust anyone and was thrown back into the shelter of house and clan. So a tribal people faced a national election in today's complex world; and after the election the contending forces lapsed back into the pursuit of tribal, not national, interests.

Dominican tradition mistrusts politicians. It respects, out of fear, naked military power. It expects government to be authoritarian, unlawful, and unconstitutional. Trujillo's terrible legacy weighed heavily. You don't build confidence with suspicion, or courage with fear, or love with hate.

Nor did Dominican democracy have the support of effective free and voluntary institutions—labor unions, professional societies, cooperatives, service clubs. We in the United States seldom realize how much strength our society derives from them. They assist enormously in adjusting differences; they provide safety valves for extremism and conduits for a dialogue among men who disagree. After the fall of Bosch, the distinguished International Commission of Jurists castigated the Dominican bar, declaring that it had been basically opposed to Bosch and stood silent at the *golpe*. Fair enough. But again, in exculpation, one must remember that a Bar Association worth anything was unthinkable under Trujillo. And so was any other free institution.

Finally, the awful odds of history were against democracy. Juan Bosch was the second civilian ever to be freely elected President of the Republic. When we had Lincoln, the Dominicans had General Santana (if not the ineffable Baez). When we had Cleveland, they had General Heureaux. When we had Wilson, they had our Marines. When we had Franklin D. Roosevelt, they had Generalissimo Trujillo. Perhaps I have said enough to indicate that throughout Dominican history "successful," or lasting, governments have been short-lived. Indeed, it is almost an axiom of Dominican history that when the ruler thrives, freedom dies; and, conversely, when freedom flourishes, the ruler is quickly overthrown. To the dozen years of freedom under Espaillat and Cáceres and Vásquez, Bosch was able to add only seven months. Those who believe with Marx and Spengler that history is a straitjacket will conclude that it must be ever thus in the Republic. Those who believe, as I do, that, in Reinhold Niebuhr's phrase, man is the creator as well as the creature of history, will hope that the historical current can be reversed, even though we will disregard that current at our peril.

No attempt to determine who killed Cock Robin can ignore the outside forces which were at play. They were two: The Communists and the United States. The Communists' purpose, of course, was to destroy Dominican democracy. Our purpose was to nurture and save it.

The Communists were poorly organized, divided, and by and large ineffective if their purpose was the infiltration and subversion of the Dominican government or the takeover of Bosch's electoral revolution. But if their purpose was the overthrow of Bosch and therefore of the constitutional democratic system, they succeeded completely, for they provided the pretext which the military and *civicos* needed. This served them well; for as Communist doctrine teaches, and as events around the world have shown, communism gains adherents under authoritarian governments but loses them under democracies. Without question, no single event in a generation drew so many ordinary Dominicans to communism's banner up to that time as the *coup* of September 25, 1963. As old, withered Sánchez Cabral remarked, the real loser on September 25 was the military itself. And the real winner, in the long run, was the Communist movement. The Civil War proved him right. And our military intervention almost surely drew many more to communism.

What of the United States?

We had some successes. We helped keep the Republic out of the hands of the Castro/Communists or another Trujillo. We built some schools, some houses, some farm-to-market roads; we distributed some land, saved some forests, taught some people how to farm and how to repair diesel engines; we fed hungry people and gave school children primers. We put people to work.[6]

We helped give the Dominican people a chance to choose their President. Some have said we should not have insisted on elections in 1962. We had to. The Consejo could not have survived much longer. Moreover, how do people "get ready for democracy" except by having it? Certainly Trujillo had not prepared them, nor would party anarchy. A start had to be made. The only way to start is to let the people vote. President Kennedy once quoted a Chinese proverb, "A journey of a thousand miles must begin with a single step." We began. And the Dominican people, having tasted freedom—freedom from torture, freedom from the arbitrary power of the state, freedom to vote—will never be the same.

Nevertheless, we failed.

I should like to point out what seem to me, in retrospect, to have been my own mistakes and failures.

I should have tried to reverse the policy, set before I arrived, of spurning Manolo Tavárez Justo and others in the 14th of June. I should have spent more time with University students, difficult as they were, and with local labor leaders, scarce as they were.

At the same time, I should have cultivated more the middle class—professional and business men, the *civicos*. For I think now that we were operating in the Republic, and are still operating in many parts of the world, under a fundamental misapprehension. We believe that economic development under AID will automatically create a middle class, and that this middle class will automatically advance political freedom and progressive ideas. This is just not so. The rising middle class is far more likely to oppose reforms than promote them. In the United States, support for liberal ideas comes mainly from the richest and the poorest, not from the middle class—not from the junior managerial class in the suburbs, for example, who have escaped poverty but still have their big money to make. In the Dominican Republic, Bosch's support came from the oligarchy and the poor.

[6] Between February of 1962 and September of 1963, we had authorized 56.1 million dollars in AID money (including the twenty-two million dollars in sugar fees) and actually spent 47.8 million dollars; obligated 17.9 million dollars under PL-480 Food for Peace; obligated through the Export-Import Bank 3.4 million dollars and spent 2.6 million dollars; obligated through the Social Progress Trust Fund 6.5 million dollars. Thus our total obligations to the Republic had come to 83.9 million dollars and expenditures to 50.4 million dollars in twenty-two months. Our military assistance program had spent an additional 2.3 million dollars.

A good many U.S. citizens who resided as businessmen in the Republic opposed Bosch, and a few worked actively to overthrow him, or at least encouraged the Dominican *golpistas*. If I could not dissuade them, I should have used every legal means of stopping them from undermining the policy of the United States government.

I should not have left the Dominican military to the attachés. More particularly, from the first night I met Wessin y Wessin and recognized the visage of power, I should have made him mine.

I probably should have protested the verbal attacks on General O'Meara, Fred Somerford, and others. I should have held a tighter rein on MAAG and AID. It is really astonishing, as I look back, the list of things I never got around to—visiting more often the headquarters of MAAG, AID, USIS, the consulate, various sections of the Embassy—and innumerable other things—visiting the University, labor union headquarters, the 27th of February Camp, La Victoria, the national museum, police headquarters, courts, party headquarters, various ministries, and, for that matter, the gambling casinos and a movie or two.

Late in the game, in September, I probably should have sent in that contingency paper or gone to Washington myself, rather than let events take their course. (But I feared my departure might trigger a *golpe;* Bennett's may have, in 1965.)

I think now that on the night of September 24th, 1963 I should have gone to San Isidro or the Palace myself—or persuaded Bosch to go to bed, though that was probably impossible. It might have gained twenty-four hours. If we had survived that night, we might have survived another, and another, and somehow muddled through. Who knows?[7]

I wonder now whether by refusing so long to recognize the *golpista* regime we did not encourage the deadly process of left-right polarization —the polarization that ended in Civil War. (This is a question of timing; recognition was delayed a little by President Kennedy's death.)

Looking back at our mistakes, it seems to me that perhaps all of us—

---

[7] The timetable of that night is not yet clear, and probably never will be. At 2:30 A.M. Fritz Long told me by telephone that he was at San Isidro, had just seen Wessin y Wessin, was on his way to see Luna, and believed nothing would happen that night. A little before 4 A.M. he telephoned and said he was at the Palace, Bosch had confronted the military and demanded Wessin's replacement, the military had refused, and Bosch had declared he would resign in the morning. Other evidence indicates Bosch was actually overthrown at about 2:30 A.M., though Bosch told me it happened a little after 2:30. Our police adviser said the police started their roundup at 3 A.M. By 4:15 Bosch's household knew he had been overthrown. I cannot reconcile the discrepancy. The essential point is that had I known at 2:30 A.M. or a little later that Bosch was already a prisoner, I might have gone to the Palace immediately, before the *golpistas* issued their communiqué, and, using my fake instruction, bluffed the military into backing down, persuaded Bosch to withdraw his challenge to Wessin, or reached some other accommodation. By the time I learned Bosch was a prisoner and went to the Palace, it was too late—the communiqué was already being broadcast and the new regime proclaimed.

myself, the U.S. government, Bosch, Bonnelly, the Dominican military, Fiallo, Imbert, everyone—could have used a little more humility, a little less pride in our power, a little more recognition of its limits.

Even had we tried, the U.S. could not have elected Fiallo, stopped the Overseas deal, imposed the world sugar quota bill on the Consejo, or overthrown Duvalier. We tried but could not give Bosch the twenty-two million dollars quickly, nor stop travel to Cuba, nor close Dato Pagán's school, nor persuade Bosch to quit making speeches and get to work, nor stop the *golpe*.

The Dominicans, too—the Consejo could not stop the quarreling, self-seeking parties from trying to wreck the elections and, after the election, Bosch could not silence his irreconcilable critics.

Finally, one of our limits is the rock-bottom one: The human condition itself, human limitation. This is not necessarily to postulate a divine power; it is merely to take account of history's lesson—not only can humans err but, more important, there are limits to what their effort can accomplish. Bosch, in a real sense, overthrew himself, and so did we all—Trujillo, Bosch, the military, I. It is an idea older than Greece that all men carry within themselves the seeds of their own destruction.

All power carries a terrible burden of guilt, sometimes felt in its use, always felt in its failure; and all power has limits. Ours as Americans is limited by all sorts of things—by our own ideals of justice and liberty, by the need to concert with our allies, by our adherence to the UN and OAS, by our assertion that nations are equal, by the moral force of world opinion, by our own broad policy interests and treaty obligations, by the will of other men and nations, by the size of our own production and natural resources. Nuclear power narrows these limits to the width of a razor's edge.

All, or most, of us in the Dominican Republic in my time thought we were right: Bosch, Fiallo, Bonnelly, the Social Christians, Wessin y Wessin, Severo Cabral, I myself. At this inquest there are no heroes and no villains. Rather, there is only that group of men, locked together in a fatal embrace on the edge of the abyss. It was so silly, so unnecessary. The Nuncio used to tell me privately that it was all ridiculous, that there was nothing wrong that he and I and a couple of Boy Scouts couldn't straighten out. He was right. Yet with all our power we failed, and in a few hours it was gone. Whose fault? Everybody's, and nobody's.

6

All over Latin America, all over the world, Imberts are killing Trujillos, Manolo Tavárez Justos are dying and Caamaños rising, Bosches are being elected, oligarchs or military men or other entrenched classes are resisting. What should United States policy be?

Latin America is a bewildering place. To many of us in the United States it seems foreign, alien. Though these nations are, with Canada, our nearest neighbors, they seem stranger to us than Europe. Our ancestral roots are in Europe. We were taught from textbooks which largely ignored Latin America. Confronted with the tangle of Latin American politics, most people in the United States throw up their hands. Some laugh. And some say, "Send the fleet."

Nearly all ask, "Why can't those people govern themselves?"

It is an invidious question in itself, of course, implying that we govern ourselves better, a proposition by no means self-evident unless one ignores the corruption and crime in our own big cities, the hidden power of money and the—till recently—hidden stain of poverty, the size and condition of our prisons and mental hospitals, the assassination of our President, and the segregation of the Negro that is still the torment and the shame of the United States. (And I daresay that an outsider, observing our recent history, might draw an indictment of "the American character" at least as damaging as mine of "the Dominican character.") Moreover, the proposition is by no means self-evident unless one ignores a number of Latin American countries, such as Mexico and Costa Rica, that appear to govern themselves at least as well as we do.

Nonetheless, when people in the United States ask why Latin Americans can't govern themselves, they have some reason. For whatever happens, the basic system of government of the United States has remained the same, while that of some Latin American nations has seemed to change with bewildering rapidity and ease. They are asking why turmoil is endemic there, a question which deserves examination.

I have heard at least four explanations, none satisfactory.

One blames goegraphy: Our temperate zone is more conducive to stable government than the tropics. But this ignores the turmoil in such temperate zone countries as Argentina.

A second theory is that of race. Apart from the rather sinister implications of this theory, it is plain that turmoil has afflicted the black nation of Latin America, Haiti; the predominantly Indian nations such as Guatemala; and the predominantly white nations such as Argentina.

The third theory is that of Carlos Fuentes: That the United States system derives from the Reformation, with its emphasis on individuality and conscience, while the Latin American system is rooted in the Counter-Reformation, with its feudal authoritarianism and hostility to new ideas. This has a certain plausibility, but to accept it is to accept the larger idea that history is a straitjacket, and this I reject. The permutations and combinations of human events are infinite, some are governed by blind chance, and no Marxist or other iron hypothesis can take them all into account.

Finally, a fourth theory holds that the British came to North America to plant colonies and rear families and build, while the Spaniards and Portuguese came to Central and South America to conquer and kill, to extract and exploit. This theory, which might really be subsumed under Fuentes', also has some plausibility; but to it I raise the same objection: History is not immutable.

I know of no single thesis that will answer the question why so many Latin American nations and people have lived in turmoil so often in the past. But I think it is clear—and more important—why they are in turmoil today.

Around the earth, from the Dominican Republic to Tanzania, from Southeast Asia to Rhodesia, from Indonesia to the Congo to Brazil, the ordinary people of the world have entered history. It is not that there is going to be a revolution in this emerging world: There is one now, and has been for many years. It may be uncomfortable but it is necessary to face the fact that a considerable element in this revolution is color. We see it in the United States itself, and not merely in darkest Mississippi and Alabama but in the slums and suburbs or our northern cities. As a people, we are a white minority in a black and yellow and brown world. It has been estimated that thirty-five years from now the world will contain 6500 million people, and of these only 1342 million will live in North America, the Soviet Union, and Europe combined. China itself will contain 1750 million and the rest of Asia 2250 million. For this reason alone, if not for nobler ones, we shall have to reach an accommodation with those millions. Their revolution is worldwide. It has set the poor against the rich in each country; it has set the poor nations against the rich nations. It has set, in some countries, black and yellow and brown men against white (and Peking's present rulers may hope it soon will set the colored nations in concert against the white). All this results in part from the breakup of the old nineteenth-century empires. It is complicated by the crumbling of the postwar alliances and by technological changes that widen the already awesome gap between the industrial nations and our tropical agricultural neighbors. And it is further complicated by the inexorable pressure of population. Latin America's economy is growing at a rapid rate but so is its population—its population growth rate is the highest on earth. In some years Latin America has to run faster than it can merely to stand still.

In my view, the revolution now in progress is not only inevitable, not only at hand, but will continue throughout our lifetimes and probably through our children's. In the ordering of our public affairs as in the living of our private lives, struggle with it we must—struggle as if victory were possible. This is man's fate. These are our times. This is our world. We cannot escape it.

7

Latin America forms a land mass more than twice as big as the United States. Its present population of two hundred million will pass five hundred million only thirty-five years from now. It is by no means a hopeless swamp—its ratio of people to land is much more favorable than Asia's. Rich in natural resources, it is the principal source of many raw materials we need. It is a huge market for us. If it remains united, and if it realizes its economic potential, it can play a crucial role in our own future and the world's. But unity is in question and communism, which seems to be withering away in Western Europe, is alive in Latin America.

It is often said, "If we can't succeed in Latin America we can't succeed anywhere." But in my view, our task, if anything, is more difficult in Latin America than elsewhere, for there most heavily lies the burden of our past mistakes.

In the earliest years of our national life, in the early 1800s, when Simón Bolívar and other Latin American patriots won political freedom from Old World powers, we were the first to recognize their revolutionary governments, for we felt kin to them, having so recently won our own freedom. After the middle of the nineteenth century, however, except for a few brief interludes, as during the Good Neighbor Policy of Franklin Roosevelt, we lapsed into the exclusive pursuit of our business interests and our national security. Hence, lamentably, gunboat diplomacy and dollar diplomacy.

It was against this background that Fidel Castro came to power in Cuba in 1959. Under President Eisenhower, in 1960, we joined with the other nations of the Hemisphere in the Act of Bogotá, which, based on a proposal put forth by former President Juscelino Kubitschek of Brazil, pledged mutual effort to promote social justice and economic progress throughout the Hemisphere. President Kennedy proclaimed the Alliance for Progress, and under him and Secretary Rusk we joined in 1961 with the other nations of the Hemisphere in signing the Charter of Punta del Este, making firm our joint commitment to specific economic and social goals.[8]

[8] Even today few people realize the scope and depth of the changes the *Alianza* demands. The Charter of Punta del Este begins: "We, the American Republics, hereby proclaim our decision to unite in a common effort to bring our people accelerated economic progress and broader social justice within the framework of personal dignity and political liberty." It sets forth these objectives: A rate of economic growth in each Latin American country of not less than 2.5 percent per capita per year in order to narrow the gap between living standards there and in more developed countries; a "more equitable distribution of national income"; a "balanced diversification of national economic structures," making them less dependent upon the export of raw materials and the import of capital goods; accelerated

The Alliance for Progress, keystone of the Kennedy policy toward Latin America, was really only the concrete manifestation of President Kennedy's broader policy view—that we had wrongly allowed the Communists to evict us from the leadership of "local patriots" who proclaimed the watchwords of our own revolution, that we had been "made to appear as the defenders of the status quo" instead of the "vanguard force, pointing the way to a better, brighter, and braver order of life."

As President Kennedy himself would have been the first to concede, it is not always easy to identify the local patriots, nor to persuade them to accept our aid. Nor is it easy to make the Alliance for Progress work. In the Dominican Republic, the Consejo did enact income tax and agrarian reform laws, and we did loan the Republic money; but these halting first steps stopped abruptly at the roadblock of Bosch's politics and the *golpistas'* scheming. And the inept Dominican and ponderous U.S. bureaucracies nearly smothered the Alliance.[9]

During those two years, no fewer than six Latin American governments fell—and in every one we were attempting to work with a regime friendly to the Alliance. Apologists for the Alliance maintain that this was evidence of the Alliance's impact—it shook the oligarchs into retaliation. This may be true, but it strikes me as more a rationalization of failure

---

industrialization and increased productivity; increased agricultural productivity; agrarian reform to transform "unjust structures and systems of land tenure and use"; tax reform; fair labor standards; stimulation of private enterprise; an end to adult illiteracy, assuming by 1970 access to at least six years of primary education for each school-age child in Latin America; increased life expectancy at birth of at least five years by improving individual and public health; increased construction of low-cost housing; maintaining stable price levels; strengthening existing agreements on economic integration with a view to establishing a Latin American common market; cooperative programs to prevent the harmful effects of wide commodity price swings. The Charter declared that these programs should be carried out "in accordance with democratic principles" and that national programs should be based "on the principle of self-help." It recognized, however, that Latin America would need outside capital, both public and private—at least twenty billion dollars in the next ten years. The United States undertook to provide "a major part" of the twenty billion dollars, including more than one billion dollars in the first year (actually about eight months). The Latin American nations agreed "to devote a steadily increasing share of their own resources to economic and social development, and to make the reforms necessary to assure that all share fully in the fruits of the Alliance for Progress." The Charter set up machinery to carry out its programs, spelled out immediate and short-term action programs, and called on each country to produce a long-range national development program.
[9] Bosch, in his book, says the Alliance failed in the Dominican Republic because Dominican technicians were lacking, U.S. technical studies were expensive, the Republic lacked a stable trained bureaucracy, and AID attempted too much and thus diluted its effect. And he says the vitality and spirit of reform in the Alliance for Progress died with President Kennedy.

than evidence of success. Moreover, it seems to me that the Alliance contains an unresolvable internal contradiction: It expects that much of the outside money for Latin American development will come from private investment, yet its laudable social and economic goals promote the very instability that frightens off private investment. If implemented fully, the Alliance demands radical changes in each country's internal affairs—tax reform, agrarian reform, redistribution of income—an "intervention" odious to some Latin Americans if it results from outside pressure. Finally, the economic goals of the Alliance require a trained manpower pool which simply does not exist in Latin America—it was precisely such a manpower pool in Western Europe that made the Marshall Plan a stunning success. Without skilled manpower, money pumped into Latin America will not produce the transformation it produced in postwar Europe.

I do not, however, believe that any of this proves that the Kennedy policy was incorrect or unworkable. On the contrary, I believe that the Kennedy policy is the only one that can succeed.

We have several choices in Latin America.

We can become frankly imperialistic, promoting our political and economic interests to the exclusion of all other interests. Such a policy proclaims, as the Athenians did in their pride in power, that "the strong do what they can, and the weak submit." But Athens, seeking to extend its empire, dealt ever more harshly with friend and foe, betrayed its own democratic ideals, and in the end destroyed itself. Imperialism is incompatible with democracy. To embark upon a frankly imperialistic policy in Latin America would, I believe, involve us in collaboration with the most odious and authoritarian elements in that part of the world, earn us nothing but the implacable hatred of the great mass of the people there, cost us the allegiance of unnumbered millions in other parts of the world, betray our own revolution and our own ideals, cost us unimaginable billions in money and even no small number of lives, since we would surely be obliged to occupy several countries militarily, and, in the end, lead us to irretrievable disaster in our own backyard. Hardly anyone, I think, advocates this policy.

We can leave the Latin Americans to work out their own destinies with our sympathy but without our close collaboration and assistance. This would be to shirk our responsibilities to our neighbors, who look to us for help, would cost us the goodwill of millions, and would abandon the field to the Castro/Communists.

We can pursue the Kennedy policy. That, in my view, is the policy that will best advance our own interests and those of our Latin American friends. It flows fundamentally from the fact that Latin America is in revolution. Indeed, one might argue for the Kennedy policy on the most cynical of grounds: That the Czar might have averted the Russian Revolution if he had heeded the warning of the Winter Palace. I prefer to argue for the Kennedy policy not only on the ground of our own national interest but on the ground that it best upholds our ideals and best promotes the legitimate aspirations of the Latin American masses.

What, more specifically, does pursuing this policy mean?

Latin America is twenty nations—twenty-two if one counts Jamaica and Trinidad-Tobago—and to speak of a Latin American policy is perhaps impossible. Nevertheless, certain broad guidelines may be suggested.

In my view, we should actively join the forces at work for change in Latin America. We should align ourselves with the young, the students, the workers, the intellectuals, the labor leaders, *campesino* leaders, progressive churchmen, and others, who will lead the rising masses, for inevitably the future belongs to them, and by and large they are on the side of justice.

On my fact-finding mission to the Dominican Republic for President Kennedy in September of 1961, I talked to Manolo Tavárez Justo, Alfredo Manzano, one of the Isa Conde brothers, and Asdrúbal Domínguez, as well as to López Molina and one of the Erickson brothers. The last two were old Communists hopelessly committed to the MPD. The others, however, were young men then in the nascent 14th of June. Later at least two of them went into the PSP, the Moscow-directed Communist party. But when I first met them, all but Manzano seemed malleable, unformed young men. I think we need not have lost them by default to communism. Precisely when we lost some of them I do not know, but our own course seemed set before I arrived as Ambassador—the Department, and its senior officers on the scene, perhaps seeking stability and fearing an explosion, seemed to have maintained close ties to such "moderate" and "responsible" representatives of stability as Viriato Fiallo and Donny Reid rather than to the unpredictable student leftists. In any case, lose them we did—Moscow and Havana were busy.

The lesson is clear. When an upheaval such as Trujillo's death occurs, we must identify and help young men like those. It is not easy. An Ambassador, and even the President of the United States, is at the mercy of experts—"old Dominican hands," "old China hands," "old Cuban hands." He will disregard them at his peril. But he may heed them to his sorrow. For all too often their expertise derives from long ago and sometimes irrelevant experience, from adherence to tradition, and from caution.

In designing economic assistance programs, we should remember that the problem is not "underdeveloped nations" or "underdeveloped economies," but, rather, underdeveloped people. What the people of Latin America need is not fine public buildings, nor highways and dams alone, but better health, more food, broader opportunities, a more equitable distribution of income, and, above all, better education. I would put our heaviest emphasis on education—on conventional academic and vocational schoolroom education and on education by every shortcut available, including educational radio and television. I would hope we could undertake both sound long-range economic development projects and "political" projects, but if forced to choose between them, I would usually choose the "political" projects. They affect the people quickly and directly. A political struggle is going on in Latin America and until it is resolved sound economic development is virtually impossible anyway.

We need new political ideas. Perhaps we need an Alliance for Political Progress. I have suggested a new idea for the Dominican Constitution. Walter Lippmann has proposed that we join with South Americans in developing the vast interior wilderness of South America, an idea, perhaps derived from Kubitschek of Brazil and Belaunde Terry of Peru, that is ostensibly economic but has profound political implications. As Lippmann has pointed out, at present the South American heartland is impenetrable jungle and so the nations are little more than isolated coastal enclaves. It is as though everything between the Appalachians and the Rockies were unexplored wilderness. Opening up this last frontier might change the Hemisphere profoundly.

The attorney, Lloyd Cutler, has suggested a treaty to deal with *golpes*. Cutler has proposed that the United States and any three or more other freely elected constitutional Hemisphere governments committed to the policies of the OAS charter agree by treaty that upon the overthrow of one of them by internal or external force or other unconstitutional means, and on appeal by a ranking official of that government, the other governments would consult immediately; and if a majority so voted, all or each would take whatever military, economic, and political measures were deemed appropriate to restore constitutionality.[10]

We must support constitutionalism in Latin America. We must not align ourselves with dictators in the name of anti-Communism. We must

[10] Cutler points out that such a treaty would apply only among like-minded constitutional governments, and intervention would be only on request—and even after a majority had voted intervention, any signatory could abstain in whole or part from the intervention. Such a treaty, he argues, would prevent governments opposed to intervention under any circumstances from blocking adoption of the treaty or subsequent action under it (as they frequently do in the frustrated OAS). Such a treaty would provide a legal basis for intervention against unconstitutional *golpes* by right or left. Its mere existence might help deter *golpistas*. Many difficulties surround such an idea. Its heart is military intervention, and this almost surely means military intervention by the United States, since the United States alone has the military capability, especially of airborne and seaborne transport. If it were adopted outside the framework of the OAS, its effect on the OAS might be disastrous.

seek to strengthen elected progressive regimes. They alone offer the people an alternative to communism and rightist dictatorship. This is not to say we should try to impose our system of democracy everywhere, a course both impossible and undesirable. (Mexico gets along fine with a one-party system.) Rather, we should encourage the growth of strong, independent nations with elected democratic governments of their choice. To abstain from politics would abandon the field to Castro and to local military power. It would strengthen the right. It would abandon the center entirely. It would leave the people nowhere to turn but to communism. It did in the Dominican Republic in 1965.

The Latin American masses will not wait forever. If we offer them no political standard to which they can repair, if we merely promote economic growth, if we merely protect our own nine-billion-dollar investment, if we merely announce that we are against communism, then we shall surely throw the people into the Communist complex. As Vice President Humphrey wrote in July of 1964 when he was a Senator, "The Alliance must have a political content and an ideological substance, in addition to a strong program of economic development. It must come to symbolize the hopes and aspirations of both the elite groups and the masses of Latin American people. It must have a mystique all its own, capable of inspiring a following." The mystique is ready to hand—the mystique of the first revolution in the Hemisphere against colonialism. Perhaps the Alliance also needs a leader, a man. People rally to a banner held up by a leader, not hoisted laboriously by an institution.

We must reach the people directly through the Peace Corps, AID, and every means possible. Without being patronizing we should teach them the ways of democracy. Once when Fran described the League of Women Voters to the wives of Santiago businessmen, they seemed mildly interested and amused but wholly uncomprehending, as though she were describing some quaint social custom on a distant planet. Once when she suggested to a man that if he didn't like Bosch he put a sign on his car saying, "Don't blame me, I didn't vote for him," the man not only didn't think it funny but declared vehemently that Bosch was no good and the only thing to do was get rid of him. In 1961, disheartened by the quality of Dominican leadership, I thought we should establish a school for revolutionaries; later, observing the ineptitude of the Bosch government, I thought we should establish an institute of public affairs.[11] I still think so—leaders are scarce. For the young, alienated intellectuals, the enemy is the local military dictator and the Colossus of the North. How can we offer them a mystique? By concrete acts—AID, help for leftist political movements, and in some countries divorce from the oli-

[11] At the time of Adlai Stevenson's death, his family and several of us who were his friends decided to establish a similar institute as a memorial to him.

garchs and military. By education and propaganda—distributing USIA propaganda that is pro-democracy, not anti-Castro, sending professors and intellectuals to Latin America, printing and distributing cheap editions of good U.S. books, publishing Latin American authors in the United States, providing educational radio and television programs. By assistance to trade unions—and in Latin America today, it is virtually impossible to cling to the Gompers tradition of non-political trade unionism. By low-interest loans and technical advice to farmers. By encouraging U.S. investors to pursue enlightened policies. (Once an officer in my Embassy suggested to a La Romana official that its overseers on horseback in the cane fields stop wearing pith helmets, almost the symbol of colonialism; he was met with incomprehension.) By the Peace Corps, the best we've done so far. And, yes, by sending Louis Armstrong—he would have been cheaper than the Marines. And perhaps by a wholly new agency, or combination of agencies, that would combine certain features of the CIA and AID and Peace Corps and Sacha Volman's workers' and *campesinos'* school to train new leaders in political techniques and send political agents to do precinct work in the countryside and city slums. Thus might we turn nationalistic reform movements away from anti-Americanism and pro-Castroism. In some countries this might set us to helping to subvert the feudal order. Well, why not? The feudal order is helpful to no one but itself. It is absurd, really, to identify our democratic private enterprise system with the Latin American oligarchy, whose fortune was built on four centuries of exploitation and which has nothing whatsoever to do with private enterprise. Ambassadors who talk "private enterprise" and "GNP" bore Latin Americans and caricature ourselves. To Latin Americans, what they say is simply not relevant.

The Castro/Communists, operating on a shoestring, reach the groups that will matter in the future—young people, labor, and restless, rootless city dwellers. We, spending millions, influence existing governments but fail to reach those groups at all. We lack an articulate ideology, tend to deal with governments and not with people, use methods too sophisticated, tend to report too much and perform too little, look for immediate results and final solutions. The Castro/Communists are more effective, for they preach not stability but revolution; they need no answers, only questions; no solutions, only attacks; no programs, only slogans; and they are in no hurry. Shut off from government, they deal with the people. They stay in the streets and fields and docks. Their agents are poor, so are the people.

We have failed badly to make use of the reservoir of skills and good intentions among the people of the United States. People seem concerned —but convinced they themselves can do nothing. It seems to me there is much they can do. Any woman with nurse's training could spend her vacation in Latin America teaching nursing. In the whole of Puerto

Plata province there is but one qualified surveyor; construction workers in Sosua still break rock by building a fire on it then pouring cold water on it. Indeed, any American who can do anything—plumbing, welding, carpentry, anything—could usefully teach it there. All this might be unwieldy and might bedevil our Ambassadors inordinately; remembering delicate moments in the Republic, I shudder at the idea of a flock of well-intentioned busybodies running around loose; some Ambassadors might, in self-defense, try to smother such a program in the bureaucracy; but I feel sure a capable Embassy officer could watch do-gooders closely enough to avoid calamity. At the very least, such a program would promote our over-all policy purpose—to identify ourselves with the people of Latin America against an unjust status quo. We must make plain our purpose at every opportunity, for we need the understanding both of Latin Americans and of our own people.

Finally, we must work to strengthen the OAS. The OAS has seldom faced up to its responsibilities. And in all candor we have sometimes tried to manipulate it for our own purposes. Perhaps now is the time, and the Dominican Republic the place, for the OAS to grow up—and for us to join it wholeheartedly. This entails a certain loss of sovereignty on our part and on the part of the Latin American nations. It entails renunciation or modification of the doctrine of non-intervention.[12] True, many Latin Americans genuinely fear our intervention—and no wonder. But all too often non-intervention has become a slogan used by pontifical Latin American "elder statesmen" who have lived well in Washington for many years, making speeches at the OAS; self-serving politicians back home who raise the ancient battle cry solely for political advantage; and the Castro/Communists. Moreover, the Alliance for Progress, the OAS, and the UN imply some surrender of sovereignty.

Sumner Welles' hope for non-intervention in the Hemisphere seems now to belong with Booth Tarkington and heliotrope and the swish of the garden hose at summer dusk. He had to deal only with quarreling Dominican *caciques,* Dominican governmental inability, and U.S. and European capitalists' machinations. Today we also have to deal with the violent intervention of export communism. In today's world a more useful doctrine for the Hemisphere would seem to be one of interdependence.

Adlai Stevenson said to me the last time I saw him, "It's time now everywhere to decide whether we're going to be international and multilateral or not." The OAS Charter of 1948 did not foresee Castro and assumed that, with Hitler defeated, threats from Europe had ended. But it wasn't so, and in 1961 the OAS edged toward the Communist problem by discussing "intervention of extracontinental powers directed toward breaking American solidarity." During the Cuban missile crisis of 1962, and

12 Talleyrand once said, "Non-intervention is a political and metaphysical term and means about the same as intervention."

again during the Dominican intervention of 1965, it has assumed new responsibilities, evidence that the OAS nations, despite their outcries of "intervention," consider Castro/Communism a real danger to themselves. The OAS, however, has never taken concrete steps to set up machinery to deal with emergencies. At an Inter-American meeting in Río in November 1965, the OAS did not discuss establishing a permanent standby multilateral military force to deal with emergencies. And I must say I have misgivings about such a force—it almost surely would contain many Wessin y Wessins, might accelerate the resurgence of the Latin military, and probably would be supported most enthusiastically by such nations as Nicaragua and Paraguay and Honduras where the military is already supreme. Perhaps the OAS's best gateway to political interdependence is not through the military but through economics. The Central American common market seems to be working well. So might other regional economic groupings, though some have already failed, and the difficulties are enormous. If they could be arranged, however, they might lead to more political interdependence in the Hemisphere. In any case, the OAS can succeed only if it tries.

8

Now, the people of the United States should understand that what I advocate is not an easy policy to execute. In fact, it is the most difficult of all. It is far easier to seek stability.

Stability is tempting. It is pleasant. It is safe. It encourages foreign investment. During 1962, the year of crisis, when the Alliance first took hold and uproar commenced and I went to the Dominican Republic, foreign investors took more capital out of Latin America than they put in. They put only sixty-four million dollars into it in 1963, the year of the *coups* in Honduras and the Dominican Republic. In 1964 they invested 175 million dollars in the first nine months alone. The reasons, according to *Time,* were that Castro's influence had waned, so had fears of Communist takeovers, commodity prices rose, the United States made investment guarantees, and more governments were "moving toward stability." There can be no doubt: With stability comes fresh money. With stability are usually linked other U.S. purposes—to foster economic growth, protect the nine-billion-dollar U.S. investment in Latin America, avoid intervention in internal politics, and oppose communism.

But to seek stability means, in most of Latin America, to align ourselves with the military and the oligarchy. We could gain stability that way, for a time. But in the end, the "stable" repressive establishment will go down. And we would go down with it. Such a policy opposes history—seeks non-change in a time of revolutionary change. We cannot ride both the horses of revolution and counterrevolution. Stalin in the name of realism tried it in China in 1926 and 1927. He failed, Chiang slaughtered tens of thousands of Communists, and to this day the Soviets are paying for that betrayal. A policy of stability strikes at the heart of the Alliance for Progress. It strikes at the Peace Corps, which seeks to help people change their lives. Such a policy avoids political involvement and thus reverses the Kennedy policy of working to strengthen political democracy in Latin America. And finally, by putting all their emphasis on economic growth, the stability-seekers forget that population growth alone will defeat them.

Nevertheless, stability is attractive, revolution uncomfortable.

Some people seem to think that supporting the revolutionary Alliance is soft-hearted liberalism. It is, rather, a highly practical matter. We have no alternative, really, but to surpass the Marxists in getting rid of archaic institutions and unjust rulers and systems. If we begin by understanding that the whole political fleet in Latin America has set sail leftward, it becomes easier to separate out the various leaders whom we shall have to deal with. We must stop seeing communism as our only enemy. If by the Communist danger we mean an international conspiracy directed from Moscow or Peking or both to set up governments in Latin America bent on our ultimate destruction, it is thus far ineffective. Its best hope lies with young nationalistic revolutionaries who turn to communism if we spurn them.

Castro is an immediate danger to democratic governments in Latin America. Beyond doubt, he has tried to subvert or forcibly overthrow them. Up to now, he has failed in every case. What he has succeeded in doing—and this is really his chief weapon—is to strengthen unnaturally the military right in Latin America. Before he came to power, the old-fashioned military dictators were on the wane—Trujillo was nearly the last. Castro revived them. For the danger he posed caused many moderates to turn to the military for rescue. The military quickly seized the opportunity and did what they had wanted to do all along: Take over the government, reverse the trend toward reform, and restore the feudal status quo ante. This, not direct subversion, has been Castro's greatest success. And we have helped him unwittingly. For while we want to encourage the democratic left, our hand is stayed by fear of Castro, and we tend to turn to the military right as our friends. But they are not our friends. Nor are they the Latin American people's friends. They are friends to no one but themselves. It is sometimes said that the military in Latin America today is progressive, not repressive. In view of the military's past performance, the burden of proof is on it. We can judge it only by how much personal and political freedom it permits and to what extent its reforms benefit the people at large, not itself and the favored few.

What we must remember, and what our Latin American friends must remember, is that we are great nations, that Castro is not ten feet tall, that his means of exporting revolution are severely limited by his own problems at home and by Russia's unwillingness to be dragged into his adventures and China's limited ability to help him, that his efforts very often more nearly resemble fireworks than gunfire, that the noise he makes cannot blow down a solid democratic government that has the people's support, that we can compete with him, if we only will, for the allegiance of the young nationalists, and that our worst enemy is not Castro but fear of Castro, while the worst enemy of the Latin American people is not Castroism but hunger and want.

The most powerful force at work today in Latin America is not communism, not democracy, not militarism, but nationalism. Around the world, emerging nations are intensely nationalistic. Just as nationalism becomes anti-Russianism on the rim of the Soviet Union, so does nationalism become anti-Americanism on the rim of the United States. We shall almost surely encounter a new and more genuine and more potent kind of anti-Americanism than we have faced in the past. Nobody likes big brother.

If the people in some little country do not behave the way we wish, it is simply not possible to force them to. We must understand this. It is a limit on our power to influence history. Moreover, the struggle is often obscure. It is not easy to identify our friends, much less assist them, nor to identify our enemies, much less defeat them.

In the assassination of Trujillo and the election of Bosch and the overthrow of Bosch and the Dominican Civil War, something elemental was involved. It is very likely that whatever we do we cannot prevent such events. Probably the most we can hope to do is influence them, throwing our weight on the side of human justice and our own national security.

Our road ahead is hard. Our power has narrow limits. The odds seem against us. Can we succeed? Can we help the Latin American people make a revolution without blood and without losing their liberty, as the Cuban people have lost theirs? I am frank to say I do not know. Carlos Fuentes says not, and maintains that only blood can wash out feudalism. I do not believe it; but we have yet to prove him wrong. To this great task, in my view, despite all difficulties, we must wholeheartedly devote ourselves. We have reached an historic decision. With revolution ablaze, having already fed the fire with the Alliance, we simply cannot smother it.

9

In speech after speech, starting in the East Room four days after President Kennedy died, President Johnson has reaffirmed his support of the Alliance for Progress and the Kennedy policy.

Nevertheless, somehow during 1964 and early 1965, one missed the sense of dedicated urgency of 1961–62, when the Alliance was new. Perhaps because President Kennedy had been the symbol of the Alliance, perhaps because by 1964–65 the Alliance was no longer new, perhaps because our attention was drawn to Southeast Asia, perhaps because Castro was no longer the issue he had been, perhaps because Latin America had achieved surprising economic growth and fewer governments fell—for whatever reason, Latin Americans and North Americans alike felt that Latin America no longer claimed its share of our attention—until the Dominican Republic blew up.

During that explosion President Johnson spoke repeatedly on the Dominican crisis. Once he said:

"We seek no territory. We do not seek to impose our will on anyone. . . .

"We want for the peoples of this hemisphere only what they want for themselves: liberty, justice, dignity, a better life for all.

"More than 'a few agitators' was necessary to bring on the tragic and the cruel bloodshed in the Dominican Republic. They needed additional help and a deeper cause, and they had both.

"For the roots of the trouble are found wherever the landless and the despised, the poor and the oppressed, stand before the gates of opportunity seeking entry into a brighter land; they can get there only if we narrow the gap between the rich nations and the poor, and between the rich and the poor within each nation."

After the Dominican explosion the President sent Undersecretary Mann, Assistant Secretary Vaughn, Ambassador Harriman, and others to Latin America. On August 17, 1965, in what was probably his best-received speech to Latin Americans to date, the President declared that the United States would support to the utmost the goals of the Alliance and said the United States would support the economic integration of South America, the improvement of rural life and agriculture, an integrated hemisphere fertilizer and pesticides industry, and efforts to control commodity price swings.

10

Beyond all this, however, lay unanswered questions raised by our Dominican intervention. At that time of acute crisis, President Johnson, in a rapid-fire series of speeches, had said several things which the press thought added up to the "Johnson Doctrine"—that our goal in the Republic was to "help prevent another Communist state in this hemisphere"; that "we will defend our nation against all those who seek to destroy not only the United States but every free country of this hemisphere"; that "we don't propose to sit here in our rocking chair with our hands folded and let the Communists set up any government in the Western Hemisphere"; and that he had sent troops to the Republic to "save those people from conquest." Asking Congress for a seven-hundred-million-dollar appropriation to "persist in our effort to halt Communist aggression" in South Vietnam, he indicated that some of the money might be spent in the Dominican Republic, said the war in Vietnam "is not civil war," and declared:

"But we will not be fooled or deceived in Vietnam or any place in the world where we have a commitment. This kind of war is against the independence of nations. And we will meet it, as we have met other shifting dangers for more than a generation. . . . When freedom is in danger we must stand up to that danger. . . . There are those who ask why this responsibility should be ours. The answer is simple. There is no one else who can do the job."

Although the Administration denied that all this added up to a new "Johnson Doctrine," the press said it did. The President at the same time stressed his desire for peace, his willingness to negotiate, his collaboration with the OAS, his abhorrence of war. Taking some of his remarks out of context, as I have done above, the press constructed an interpretation of them ranging all the way from a mere affirmation of our right to defend our interests, to a declaration that the United States would intervene automatically against the threat of a Communist takeover in any Latin American country, to an even more sweeping declaration that we would deny power to any movement anywhere that President Johnson feared might fall under Communist domination. The New York *Times* thought this meant no *détente* with the Soviet bloc, military resistance to the advance of communism anywhere, an insistence that no one else can insure "the right of all people to shape their own destinies," and an assertion of U.S. omnipotence—"the unenviable, self-righteous and self-defeating position of world policeman."

The columnist Walter Lippmann thought that U.S. intervention in the Dominican Republic ought not to be justified on the ground that it was our duty to police the world but, rather, on the ground that it was our right to intervene in our "sphere of influence." Lippmann thought there was nothing wrong with a "sphere of influence" *per se.* Indeed, he said, it was an alternative to pernicious globalism and would ultimately provide the basis for a formula for coexistence between the United States and Communist China.

The foreign policy debate continued for many months, on campuses, in Congress, and in the press. The Dominican intervention had triggered it, but often it broadened to include Vietnam and more. And perhaps the most insistent note was this: Can we, should we, police the world?

Mankind seems to have a fatal urge to establish a universal state. Dostoyevsky's Grand Inquisitor says, "There have been many great nations with great histories, but the more highly they were developed the more unhappy they were, for they felt more acutely than other people the craving for worldwide union." Now with world power thrust upon us, we are in truth uneasy, seeking peace and shunning empire, but facing war and pushed toward empire.

In 1904, in his annual message to Congress, President Theodore Roosevelt said: "Chronic wrongdoing, or an impotence which results in a general loosening of the ties of civilized society . . . may force the United States, how ever reluctantly, in flagrant cases of such wrongdoing or impotence, to the exercise of an international police power." Roosevelt's "Corollary" to the Monroe Doctrine—collecting Dominican customs to service foreign debts—soon led us into military occupation of the Dominican Republic, Haiti, and Nicaragua. This police action became so burdensome to us and so offensive to all Latin America that we formally renounced it.

Must we, can we, today police the world?

We must decide. For in today's world, innumerable revolutions are inevitable, and most will contain Communist elements, and the process— the fusion process in bloody Santo Domingo—will confront us in other places. Must we oppose every one? We shall be very busy. Obviously communism is a danger to freedom—our freedom and others'. But at the same time, we confront today not one but many Communist powers, and Communist powers with conflicting aims. Can we learn to live with Communist nations? We are doing it—with Yugoslavia, for example. Where do we draw the line? In 1965 in the Dominican Republic we refused to accept a second Communist state established by revolution in the Caribbean. What would we do if one was established by revolution much farther south, in, say, San Romántico, a mythical small country several thousand miles farther south? And what would we do if somewhere in the Hemisphere one was elected?

My guess is that while it was politically impossible in the United States to accept a revolutionary Communist regime in the Dominican Republic, it might not be impossible to accept one farther away. Aside from the danger to U.S. lives, aside from the question of whether a Communist-dominated government in the Dominican Republic would truly have threatened our national security, I think we could not permit it on the simple ground that public opinion in the United States would not have tolerated a second Cuba in the Caribbean. It may be objected that this is making foreign policy on the basis of domestic politics. To my mind, in our open society, the makers of foreign policy must take into account domestic public opinion, that is, domestic politics; and if the time comes when they do not, our society will no longer be an open one.

The four American Presidents since World War II—Truman, Eisenhower, Kennedy, and Johnson—have committed us to defending freedom around the world. The American people have supported this commitment, and sacrificed much blood and money for it. The four Presidents had in mind stopping the spread of international communism. In the days when the Cold War seemed ice-locked irretrievably, the Communist danger seemed more clear, more immediately present, and above all more monolithic than it does today. The Chinese-Soviet split, the explosive emergence of one new nation after another, and the threat of thermonuclear extinction have altered the world scheme of things. And so has the shift of the Communist-non-Communist struggle from the world's heartland to its rimlands. Such crisis centers of the 1950s as Suez and Berlin have been replaced by Santo Domingo and Saigon. The two great powers shifted the scene of conflict to fill local vacuums and because it was safer. The confrontation at Berlin was more dangerous than the confrontation in the waters around Cuba because the true vital interests of both sides were engaged. Around the world, during the recent period of rimland struggle, as during the earlier period of heartland pressure, the policy of the United States has been one of containment—containing the expansion of Communist power. During the period of heartland pressure, this policy was unquestionably necessary, it was wise, and it saved the peace. But I am far less sure it is appropriate to the new period of rimland struggle. Obviously the architects of containment did not intend it to last forever.

In a revolutionary world, rigid containment seems to me to be a sterile policy, for its basic objective is to defend the status quo, and in a revolutionary time, the status quo is in the long run indefensible. The Alliance for Progress was designed to oppose, not defend, the status quo. The containment policy that created NATO to block Soviet power when the danger was clear and present in the heart of Europe may lead us now to send the troops to any out-of-the-way place where tyranny has toppled and local patriots are suspect and nothing is clear though almost everything seems present. That is, containment, if pursued to its final extension in today's fragmented international politics, threatens to lead us to policing the world.

I cannot see how policing the world is possible—we lack the strength —or essential—our national security is not necessarily threatened by every Communist regime everywhere in the world—or right—it leads to self-righteousness and might lead to imperialism.

What we ought to do today, it seems to me, is to modify, to make flexible, to adapt to a world that has changed, the policy originally called containment.

A few years ago it may have been possible to divide the world into the Good Guys and the Bad Guys (or policy-makers into hawks and doves). But a more sophisticated view is necessary now. And what might emerge from a leftist extremist success in San Romántico might bear little resemblance to Brezhnevism, or Maoism, or Titoism, or Castroism. Our pluralistic world is, or ought to be, spacious enough to accommodate great diversity.

I think we shall have to come to terms with emerging revolutions. If some of their leaders turn out to be Marxist, we may have to come to terms with them too. For basically a commitment to "defend freedom" is a commitment to defend our own interests, which we believe lie in preserving a pluralistic world permeated insofar as possible with freedom and justice. Our interests change as the world changes.

Probably the wisest thing an American statesman has said since World War II was Secretary George Marshall's observation at a time when deadlock of the Cold War seemed unbreakable. He said that if we could just hang on for twenty or thirty years without starting nuclear war, we could be sure of one thing and one thing only: The world would be a different place. It is. Probably the greatest triumph of American foreign policy is that we did hang on, and without sacrificing either freedom or world peace. If today we can once more recall those words, we shall spare ourselves much.

Great issues are at stake here. We own no empire, we want none. But we have power, the greatest on earth. And "it is not safe to let it go," as Pericles said of Athens' empire, whether or not it was right to acquire it. Circumstances thrust it on us. We cannot shed it. I think our people might wish we could (we have tried to disengage both in Vietnam and the Dominican Republic). I think they would prefer that international organizations take up the burden. But if those organizations are not ready, then our people are prepared, I think, to bear the burden.

Today, for the first time in history, an open society—ours—has achieved preponderant power in the world. We find it uncomfortable. Sometimes the alternative to limited military action is nuclear holocaust. It is not impossible that we may be living in a time when our lot will be to fight a scattered twenty-year war, or a thirty-year war, or a hundred-year war, in the rimlands. Certainly the present leaders of Communist China seem to entertain that possibility. Bleak though such a prospect is, it is less dreadful than nuclear war. Quite possibly these limited scattered wars may lead to some sort of sphere-of-influence accommodation among the United States, the Soviet Union, and Red China, though most likely not under that name and, hopefully, through international organizations. We Americans tend to think of "wartime" and "peacetime" as two wholly different things, not as parts of the same thing, the process of history. This has been our experience in the past. It has not been the experience of nations which formerly possessed preponderant power. It may not be our experience in the future.

Our danger today is that fear, or righteous self-assurance, or misguided honor, will lead us to abuse our power. A democracy is slow to anger, but once angered fights fiercely, for it quickly conceives its cause as holy, and demands unconditional surrender. We may forget that our power not only entails responsibilities but is very narrowly limited. It is limited by our national greatness and our obligations to mankind. And the fact that man is the creature as well as the creator of history has become a practical as well as a moral question in a time when we have learned how to destroy creation itself.

11

That short time in that small place—with President Kennedy alive, with Trujillo fallen, with the Alliance new and hope so high—was it only a symbol of a brief moment, a moment unique, never to be repeated? Will the old earth sink back into despond, will we have no second chance? We had so little time. Hope and faith—this is what the country lost in Dallas. It did not know it had it till it lost it. In the Republic, too, we lost—dedication and good intentions are not enough. What is? I do not know. This troubles me. For it involves the question of meaning, and someone like myself, unfortunately, is deeply troubled by absence of meaning. Writing is a search for meaning. But it yields none here. What happened in the Dominican Republic shook me badly because I failed, but shook me worse because I could not understand why. The pure politics of it, of course, is clear. But there is more—the awful incalculables. Malevolent fate? Or mere blind chance? For centuries shaken men have offered one another answers; none satisfies.

Chance led me to the Embassy. Twenty-five years ago I went to the Dominican Republic wholly by chance and, returning, met by chance a man in Florida who urged me to write the Trujillo story, and so I did and quit the newspaper and went to Chicago to become a writer. There I met Fran, and on our honeymoon we went to Upper Michigan, picking out a spot on the map at random. There we met John Voelker, then a county prosecutor. Through Voelker, I met a lawyer in Chicago, and through him another lawyer, and that one, Louis A. Kohn, introduced me to Adlai Stevenson, then Governor of Illinois. Thus I got into politics—worked in Stevenson's and Kennedy's campaigns. And so went to the Dominican Republic for President Kennedy, and later for President Johnson. In the summer of 1965, while I was up in Michigan, Adlai Stevenson died, and Fran and I went to Washington and then to Springfield for his funeral. The dream—had he awakened it? Twice defeated though he was, he set the course. He told us justice could triumph, though privately he sometimes doubted that it would. He reminded us of our best ideals but warned us of our limits. He told us the truth as he saw it. He gave us a vision of what our nation might become. This is his legacy. In Springfield I thanked him too, and said goodbye. And then went back to Michigan to finish this book.

Upper Michigan remains, the woods and the water. It is no haven, really—one day walking deep in the woods I came upon a ball of tinfoil. It had been dropped by a giant bomber from the nearby SAC base, practicing to jam Soviet radar. No escape.

Slowly the tragic sense of President Kennedy's death and Adlai Stevenson's death and America's truncated destiny passed. The world moves, one must live in it. President Johnson unified us, and so saved us, when President Kennedy died. The nightmare Civil War began in the Republic, and President Johnson asked me to go, and I did what I could. I'll leave Michigan again, for the Nuncio was right, and so was Pericles: A man who holds himself aloof from public life is not quiet but useless. Today no one really has the right to stand aside. Events may overtake us, we may know we cannot triumph, but it is necessary to behave *as if* we could, for we are as free as men can be.

Appendixes

THE PRINCIPAL DOMINICAN ACTORS

(Spanish usage places a man's patronym, or surname, before his mother's name. Thus Antonio IMBERT Barrera's father's name was IMBERT and his mother's maiden name was Barrera. In this list I have capitalized the surname and alphabetized it.)

Johnny ABBES García, former head of the SIM, Trujillo's secret police.

Enrique J. ALFAU, engineer, UCN right-winger, president of the anti-Bosch Committee for Manifestation of Christian Affirmation.

Luís AMIAMA Tió, one of two surviving assassins of Trujillo; member of Consejo de Estado 1962; Army General.

Lieutenant Colonel Manuel Ramón Montes ARACHE (variant spelling AR-RACE), military defector and rebel leader in the Civil War of 1965.

Héctor ARISTY, adviser to rebel leaders in the Civil War of 1965.

Tulio ARVELO Delgado, Castro/Communist leader (PSP).

Marino AUFFANT, merchant, business leader.

José AYBAR Castellanos, a guiding spirit of the ADI, an anti-Bosch group in 1963.

Buenaventura BAEZ, a nineteenth-century President of the Dominican Republic (and one of its worst).

Miguel Ángel BAEZ Díaz, member of the group that assassinated Trujillo. Dead.

Joaquín BALAGUER, the last of Trujillo's puppet Presidents (1960–61), today an important politician.

Luís Manuel BAQUERO, an important leader of UCN.

Colonel Pedro Bartolomé BENOIT, Air Force, member of three-man San Isidro junta in Civil War of 1965.

Octavio A. BERAS, Archbishop of Santo Domingo.

José Antonio BONILLA Atiles, Secretary of State for Foreign Affairs under the Consejo.

Rafael BONILLA Aybar, for a time editor of government-owned newspaper *La Nación* under Consejo; under Bosch, editor of new tabloid *Prensa Libre*, radio-TV commentator, guiding spirit of the anti-Bosch ADI and influential opponent of President Bosch in 1963.

Rafael F. BONNELLY, President of the Dominican Republic and of the Consejo de Estado (Council of State) that governed the Republic during 1962 and in 1963 until February 27.

Diego BORDAS, Minister of Commerce and Industry under President Bosch.

Juan BOSCH, elected President of the Dominican Republic December 20, 1962; inaugurated February 27, 1963; desposed by military *coup d'état* September 25, 1963.

Carmen Quidiello de BOSCH, wife of Juan Bosch.

Lieutenant Colonel Francisco CAAMAÑO Deño, military defector who became maximum leader of the rebels in the Civil War of 1965; "President" of the "Constitutionalist" government at that time.

José María CABRAL, leader of the Cabral family and other allied oligarchical families.

Marco A. CABRAL, Santiago lawyer and member of the important Cabral family.

Luís Manuel CÁCERES, member of the group that assassinated Trujillo. Dead.

General Ramón CÁCERES, assassin (1899) of the dictator Ulises Heureaux; President of the Republic from 1906 until 1911, when he was himself assassinated. A good President.

Ramón CÁCERES Troncoso, Secretary of State for the Presidency and, later, of Finance under the Consejo; member of post-Bosch Triumvirate.

Colonel Juan CALDERÓN, bodyguard to Presidents Bonnelly and Bosch and to President of the Triumvirate Reid.

Colonel Enrique Apolinar CASADO Saladin, Army, member of three-man San Isidro junta in Civil War of 1965.

Juan CASASNOVAS Garrido, President of the Senate in Bosch government; in October 1963 "elected" President by rump Assembly after Bosch's overthrow.

Ramón A. CASTILLO, leader of minor political party (PPDC). (Technically, he had U.S. citizenship but I am listing him here as a Dominican.)

Guido d'ALESSANDRO, a leader of the Social Christian party.

Antonio DE LA MAZA, one of two principal leaders of the group that assassinated Trujillo. (The other was Juan Tomás Díaz.) Dead.

Ernesto DE LA MAZA, brother of Antonio, killed by secret police interrogators though apparently not directly involved in Trujillo's assassination. Dead.

Octavio DE LA MAZA, brother of Antonio. In 1956, he was involved in the disappearance of Dr. Jesús de Galíndez and subsequently he was killed, probably on Trujillo's order because he knew too much about the Galíndez case, though his death was officially termed a suicide.

Enriquillo DEL ROSARIO Ceballos, Dominican Ambassador to the United States under Bosch.

Luís DEL ROSARIO Ceballos, brother of Enriquillo, Minister of Public Works under Bosch.

Emilios DE LOS SANTOS, head of the Electoral Board, 1962; President of the ruling Triumvirate after Bosch's overthrow, 1963; resigned.

General Juan DE LOS SANTOS Céspedes, Air Force Chief of Staff during the 1965 Civil War.

Fidelio DESPRADEL Roque, Castro/Communist leader (left wing of the 14th of June).

Juan Tomás DÍAZ, one of two principal leaders of the group that assassinated Trujillo. (The other was Antonio de la Maza.) Dead.

Modesto DÍAZ, cousin of Juan Tomás; member of the group that assassinated Trujillo. Dead.

Miguel Ángel BAEZ Díaz, cousin of Juan Tomás; member of the group that assassinated Trujillo. Dead. (Listed here non-alphabetically to more readily relate.)

Miguel Ángel DOMÍNGUEZ Guerra, Minister of Interior and Police under Bosch.

Asdrúbal Ulises DOMÍNGUEZ Guerrero, Castro/Communist leader (PSP), leader of a Communist-dominated student group (FED).

General Juan Pablo DUARTE, one of the three heroic fathers of the Republic who led its victorious war for independence from Haiti in 1844. Though the Trinitario included Generals Sánchez and Mella as well as Duarte, it is Duarte who is often called "the George Washington" of the Dominican Republic.

Juan DUCOUDRAY Mansfield, probably the maximum leader of the PSP (a Communist party).

Felix Servio DUCOUDRAY Mansfield, Jr., brother of Juan and also a PSP (Communist) leader.

Jaime DURÁN Hernando, a Castro/Communist leader (left wing of the 14th of June).

José ESPAILLAT Rodríguez, a Castro/Communist leader (PSP).

General Arturo Rafael ESPAILLAT, notorious Trujillo henchman, consul general in New York, Secretary of State for Security; called *La Navaja,* The Razor Blade.

Victor ESPAILLAT, Progressive young businessman, landowner, and oligarch of Santiago.

Ulises Francisco ESPAILLAT, from Santiago, elected President of the Dominican Republic in 1876, overthrown after four months in office, revered today as one of the best of all Dominican Presidents.

Salvador ESTRELLA Sadhala, member of the group that assassinated Trujillo. Dead.

Rafael Miguel FAXAS Canto, a Castro/Communist leader (PSP).

José FERNÁNDEZ Caminero, physician, member of the Consejo.

Viriato A. FIALLO, physician, civic leader, anti-Trujillo, presidential candidate of UCN in 1962.

Andrés FREITES Barrera, Dominican Ambassador to the United States under the Consejo, Foreign Minister under Bosch.

Jesús María de GALÍNDEZ, teacher at Columbia University in New York, author of an anti-Trujillo book; disappeared 1956; believed murdered by Trujillo.

Héctor GARCÍA-GODOY Cáceres, Foreign Minister under Bosch (succeeded Freites); Provisional President under Institutional Act arranged by OAS to end the Civil War of 1965.

Lieutenant Amado GARCÍA Guerrero, member of the group that assassinated Trujillo. Dead.

Antonio GARCÍA Vásquez, Attorney General under the Consejo.

Manuel GONZÁLEZ González, a Castro/Communist leader (PSP central committee member).

Segundo Armando GONZÁLEZ Tamayo, elected Vice President of the Dominican Republic with Juan Bosch December 20, 1962; deposed with him September 25, 1963.

Carlos GRISOLIA, elected UCN Senator from Puerto Plata in 1962, member of Imbert's "Government of National Reconstruction" during the Civil War of 1965.

Alejandro GRULLÓN, progressive young Santiago businessman, banker, and oligarch.

Leandro GUZMÁN, a leader, at least at the outset, of the right wing of the 14th of June.

Silvestre Antonio GUZMÁN Fernández, Minister of Agriculture in Bosch Cabinet; proposed for Provisional President during the Civil War of 1965.

General Félix HERMIDA, Jr., Army.

General Ulises HEUREAUX, President and dictator of the Dominican Republic 1882–99.

General Renato HUNGRIA Morell, Army Chief of Staff (appointed by Consejo near end of its term; served under Bosch).

Antonio IMBERT Barrera, one of the two surviving assassins of Trujillo (Luís Amiama Tió is the other); member of the Consejo; General; head of the "Government of National Reconstruction" during the Civil War of 1965.

General José María IMBERT, General in the War of Independence against Haiti, 1844.

General Segundo IMBERT, one of the dictator Heureaux's Vice Presidents (1886).

Segundo IMBERT Barrera, brother of Antonio Imbert Barrera, military officer at Puerto Plata under Trujillo, imprisoned by Trujillo and killed in prison almost immediately after Trujillo's assassination.

Antonio Emilio José ISA Conde, a Castro/Communist leader (PSP).

Narciso ISA Conde, brother of Antonio and also a Castro/Communist leader (PSP).

Abraham JAAR, Minister for the Presidency in Bosch Cabinet.

Juan Isidro JIMENES Grullón, ASD party candidate for President in 1962.

Juan Isidro JIMENES, elected President of the Dominican Republic, served 1914–16. His partisans became known as the Jimenistas. Grandfather of today's ASD leader.

Father LÁUTICO García, Jesuit priest critical of Bosch's political writings.

Colonel Luís José LEÓN Estévez, Air Force, husband of Angelita, the daughter of the dictator Trujillo; cruel playboy friend of Ramfis Trujillo, the dictator's son.

Pedro LIVIO Cedeño, member of the group that assassinated Trujillo. Dead.

Máximo LÓPEZ Molina, the maximum leader of the Castro/Communist party MPD.

General Miguel Atila LUNA Pérez, Chief of Staff, Air Force, 1962 and 1963.

General Gregorio LUPERÓN, hero of the War of Restoration (1863).

Virgilio MAINARDI Reyna, Governor of Santiago, 1962; presidential candidate of PNRD 1962, with rebels in Civil War of 1965.

Jacobo MAJLUTA, Minister of Finance in Bosch Cabinet.

Alfredo MANZANO, a Castro/Communist extremist expelled from the 14th of June.

Ramón Matías MELLA, one of the Trinitario (with Duarte and Sánchez) who led the Dominican war for independence from Haiti in 1844.

Ángel MIOLÁN, head of Juan Bosch's political party, the PRD.

José Rafael MOLINA Ureña, President of the Chamber of Deputies (Speaker of the House) during President Bosch's tenure; rebel "President" briefly during the Civil War of 1965.

Alfonso MORENO Martínez, leader and presidential candidate of the Social Christian party in 1962.

Germán ORNES, editor and publisher of *El Caribe*, the leading newspaper.

Horacio Julio ORNES, brother of Germán, maximum leader and presidential candidate in 1962 of the Vanguardia party (VRD).

Colonel Ramón PAGÁN Montás, Army.

Dato PAGÁN Perdomo, Castro/Communist leader; with Pérez Cabral, he operated the PNR. He also ran a Communist indoctrination school during the Bosch administration.

Roberto PASTORIZA, one of the group that assassinated Trujillo. Dead.

Tomás A. ("Jimmy") PASTORIZA, young progressive Santiago businessman with ties to the oligarchy.

General Belisario PEGUERO Guerrero, Chief of National Police.

José Francisco PEÑA Gómez, a young leader of the left wing of PRD in 1962, an important PRD leader of the rebels in the Civil War of 1965.

Pedro PÉREZ Cabral ("Corpito" Pérez), Castro/Communist leader; with Dato Pagán, he operated the PNR.

Monseñor Elisio PÉREZ Sánchez, member of the Consejo.

Nicolás PICHARDO, physician, First Vice President of the Consejo.

Hugo POLANCO Brito, Bishop of Santiago.

Julio D. POSTIGO, publisher, bookstore owner; member of Imbert's "Government of National Reconstruction" during the Civil War of 1965.

"General" Miguel Ángel RAMÍREZ Alcántara, member of the Caribbean Legion, elected Senator from San Juan de la Maguana in 1962 while leader of PNRD; Secretary of Agriculture in Triumvirate Cabinet after Bosch's overthrow.

Andrés RAMOS Peguero, Castro/Communist terrorist (MPD).

Donald J. REID Cabral, Second Vice President of the Consejo in 1962; Foreign Minister under Triumvirate after Bosch's overthrow; later member of Triumvirate; finally President of Triumvirate; overthrown by rebels at outset of Civil War of 1965.

Commodore Julio Alberto RIB Santamaría, Navy Chief of Staff under Consejo (he succeeded Rivera Caminero) and under Bosch.

Gustavo Federico RICART-RICART, a Castro/Communist leader (MPD).

Commodore Francisco Javier RIVERA Caminero, Navy Chief of Staff, 1962; naval attaché in Washington; again Navy Chief of Staff during Civil War of 1965; also at that time "Secretary of State for Defense" in

Imbert's "Government of National Reconstruction" and, later, in García-Godoy's provisional government.

General Marcos Anibal RIVERA Cuesta, Army Chief of Staff for a time under the Consejo, then Under Secretary of State for Armed Forces.

Cayetano RODRÍGUEZ del Prado, a Castro/Communist leader (MPD central committee member).

General Pedro Rafael RODRÍGUEZ Echavarría, Army Chief of Staff in the earliest days of the Consejo when Balaguer was its President; overthrew the Consejo in January of 1962 but two days later was himself overthrown by its supporters and subsequently exiled to New York.

"Chagito" RODRÍGUEZ Echavarría, brother of Pedro Rafael.

General José René ROMÁN Fernández, Trujillo's last Secretary of State for Armed Forces who betrayed him and joined the plot to assassinate him. Dead.

General Fernando A. SÁNCHEZ, Jr., Air Force Chief of Staff under Ramfis Trujillo.

Francisco del Rosario SÁNCHEZ, one of the Trinitario (with Duarte and Mella) who led the Dominican war for independence from Haiti in 1844.

"Pupito" SÁNCHEZ, security chief under Consejo and Bosch.

Buenaventura SÁNCHEZ Félix, right-wing PRD leader, Minister of Education in Bosch Cabinet.

Pedro SANTANA, nineteenth-century General and President.

Captain Manuel Olgo SANTANA Carrasco, Navy, member of three-man San Isidro junta during the Civil War of 1965.

Islander SELIG Delmonte, a Castro/Communist leader (MPD).

Ángel SEVERO Cabral, rightist extremist leader of UCN, Secretary of Agriculture under Consejo, a leading conspirator against Bosch in 1963, Secretary of State for Interior and Police under the Triumvirate after Bosch's overthrow. Dead.

Ramón TAPIA Espinal, Secretary of State for Presidency under Consejo; member of Triumvirate after Bosch's overthrow.

María Grieser Viuda TAVARES, *grande dame* of the Santiago oligarchy.

Manuel TAVARES Espaillat, Secretary of Finance and head of Fomento under Consejo; member of Triumvirate after Bosch's overthrow; resigned.

Gustavo TAVARES Espaillat, brother of Manuel, Santo Domingo businessman.

Gustavo A. TAVARES Grieser, son of María Tavares, Santiago businessman.

Manuel ("Manolo") TAVÁREZ Justo, Castroesque maximum leader of the 14th of June; killed in guerrilla warfare, December 1963.

Huascar TEJEDA Pimentel, member of the group that assassinated Trujillo. Dead.

Angelita TRUJILLO, daughter of the dictator, wife of Colonel Luís José León Estevéz.

Arismendi ("Petán") TRUJILLO, brother of the dictator.

Flor de Oro TRUJILLO, daughter of the dictator, married to several men including Porfirio Rubirosa.

Héctor ("Negro") Bienvenido TRUJILLO, brother of the dictator, President of the Republic.

María Martínez de TRUJILLO, third and last wife of the dictator, mother of Ramfis, Rhadamés, and Angelita.

Generalissimo Rafael Leonidas TRUJILLO y Molina, the dictator. Dead.

Rafael Leonidas TRUJILLO Martínez, Jr. ("Ramfis"), son of the dictator.

Rhadamés TRUJILLO Martínez, son of the dictator.

Humbertilio VALDEZ Sánchez, Minister without Portfolio in Bosch Cabinet.

General Horacio VÁSQUEZ, President 1924–30. His followers were called Horacistas.

Juan B. VICINI Cabral, sugar planter, landowner, rancher, and a leader of the important oligarchical Cabral family.

"General" Virgilio VILOMAR, leader of the PN.

General Victor Elby VIÑAS Román, Secretary of State for Armed Forces under Consejo, Minister of Defense under Bosch (same job, different titles).

Colonel Elías WESSIN Y WESSIN, director of Armed Forces Training Center and tank commander at San Isidro under the Consejo and Bosch; leader of the *coup d'état* against Bosch; immediately promoted to General; leader of San Isidro loyalist forces against rebels at the outbreak of the Civil War of 1965.

Alejandro ZELLER Cocco, engineer, member of Imbert's "Government of National Reconstruction" during the Civil War of 1965.

THE POLITICAL PARTIES

Of the twenty-six-odd parties which arose in the Dominican Republic after the fall of Trujillo, the following participated in the election of December 20, 1962, or figure prominently in this book:

ASD. *Alianza Social Democratica* (Democratic Social Alliance). Maximum leader and presidential candidate: Juan Isidro Jimenes Grullón. Percent of popular vote: 1.70. Orientation: indeterminate.

14th of June.   Maximum leader: Manuel "Manolo" Tavárez Justo. Presidential candidate: none. Orientation: Castro/Communist (Castroite).

MPD. *Movimiento Popular Dominicano* (Dominican Popular Movement). Maximum leader: Máximo López Molina. Presidential candidate: none. Orientation: Castro/Communist (extremist, advocating terror, by 1965 following Peking line).

PN. *Partido Nacional* (National Party). Maximum leader: "General" Virgilio Vilomar. Presidential candidate: Carbuccia. Percent of popular vote: 0.16. Orientation: rightist.

PNR. *Partido Nacional Revolucionario* (National Revolutionary Party). Maximum leaders: Dato Pagán and Pérez Cabral. Presidential candidate: none. Orientation: Castro/Communist (small intellectual elite tending toward Trotskyism).

PNRD. *Partido Nacional Revolucionario Dominicano* (Dominican National Revolutionary Party). Maximum leader: "General" Miguel Ángel Ramírez Alcántara. Presidential candidate: Virgilio Mainardi Reyna. Percent of popular vote: 3.39. Orientation: Probably right-center.

PRD. *Partido Revolucionario Dominicano* (Dominican Revolutionary Party). Maximum leader and presidential candidate: Juan Bosch (elected). Percent of popular vote: 58.72. Orientation: non-Communist left.

PRDA. *Partido Revolucionario Dominicano Autentico* (Authentic Dominican Revolutionary Party). Maximum leader: Nicolás Silfa. Presidential candidate: none (proposed Joaquín Balaguer; candidacy rejected). Orientation: indeterminate.

PRSC. *Partido Revolucionario Social Cristiano* (Social Christian Revolutionary Party). Maximum leader and presidential candidate: Alfonso Moreno. Percent of popular vote: 5.18. Orientation: Catholic non-Communist left.

PSP. *Partido Socialista Popular* (Popular Socialist Party). Maximum leader: Probably Juan Ducoudray Mansfield. Presidential candidate: none. Orientation: Castro/Communist. (This was the orthodox official Communist Party, recognized as such by the Communist Party of the U.S.S.R. In 1965, it changed its name to the PCD, *Partido Comunista Dominicano,* Dominican Communist Party.)

UCN. *Unión Civica Nacional* (National Civic Union). Maximum leader and presidential candidate: Viriato Fiallo. Percent of popular vote: 30.08. Orientation: center in 1962; moved right later.

VRD. *Vanguardia Revolucionaria Dominicana* (Dominican Revolutionary Vanguard). Maximum leader: Horacio Julio Ornes. Presidential candidate: Ornes was nominated but at the last minute merged with Bosch's PRD. Percent of popular vote: 0.65. Orientation: indeterminate.

ACKNOWLEDGMENTS

I wish to express my gratitude to the Center for Advanced Studies at Wesleyan University in Middletown, Connecticut, which appointed me a Fellow 1964–65 so that I could write this book; to President Victor Butterfield of Wesleyan, Paul Horgan, Director of the Center, and Douglass Cater, Associate Director of the Center and Special Assistant to President Johnson. I wish also to thank the secretaries at the Center who typed the manuscript in several drafts, Beatrice Burford, Barbara Satton, and Tania Senff; and Roxane Eberlein and Alton B. Smith, who typed various drafts.

I wish to express my gratitude for their editorial help to Ken Mc-Cormick, Samuel S. Vaughan, and especially Eric Larrabee, my editor on this book, all of Doubleday.

I wish to thank here the members of the Embassy staff, including my secretary, Minna Krakauer; numerous Dominican friends; the State Department; the then White House staff, especially Ralph Dungan, Richard N. Goodwin, and Arthur M. Schlesinger, Jr.; and other friends in government, including William O. Douglas, Robert F. Kennedy, Hubert Humphrey, and the late Adlai E. Stevenson, all of whom gave me their support during my term as Ambassador.

I wish to express my gratitude to the late President Kennedy and to President Johnson for their faith in me.

And I wish to express my gratitude to my wife Fran for her love of this book, our country, the Dominican people, and me.

BIBLIOGRAPHICAL NOTE

The principal source for this book is my personal notebooks and files. I intend to place them in the Kennedy Library or a University library at a later date where they will be available to scholars.

Because they are the principal source, I have decided not to print here a formal bibliography of books, periodicals, and documents I have examined while writing the book but, rather, to set forth the following remarks which may be helpful to a reader who wishes to pursue the subject further:

By far the best history in English of the Dominican Republic covering the pre-Trujillo period is *Naboth's Vineyard: The Dominican Republic 1844–1924*, by Sumner Welles (New York: Payson & Clarke Ltd., 1928; two vols.). Unfortunately, it ends with the accession of President Vásquez. Judged by our standards today, it shows traces of race prejudice. One must remember, however, that it was written at a time when the climate in the United States was far different and, further, that it is a very Dominican book—and Dominicans themselves are not free of racism. Otto Schoenrich's *Santo Domingo: A Country with a Future* was published (Macmillan) in 1918 shortly after the U. S. Marine occupation began. The same author's *The Legacy of Christopher Columbus* (Glendale, California: The Arthur H. Clark Company, 1949; two vols.) is a history of litigation involving Columbus' discoveries, will, family, and descendants. Samuel Eliot Morison and Mauricio Obregón have retraced Columbus' voyages and recently published *The Caribbean As Columbus Saw It* (Boston: Little, Brown and Company, 1964). *Intervention and Dollar Diplomacy in the Caribbean 1900–1921*, by Dana G. Munro (Princeton, N.J.: Princeton University Press, 1964) covers its subject excellently and is a thoroughly engrossing book. The U. S. Marine occupation of 1916–24 was the subject of a Congressional investigation, and its hearings have been published. (Hearings also were held by the Senate Foreign Relations Committee after the 1965 Civil War, but they were held in executive session and to date have not been published.) In Spanish, the best histories of the Republic before Trujillo are perhaps *La República Dominicana*, by Ramon Marrero Aristy (Editora del Caribe, C. por A.,

Ciudad Trujillo, 1957; two vols.), and *De Lilís a Trujillo,* by Luis F. Mejía (Caracas: Editorial Elite, 1944), covering the period from Heureaux to Trujillo.

On the Trujillo era, I know of no good book in either English or Spanish, nor of any good biography of Trujillo himself, which is a pity. Books about him are many, but they were written either by sycophants or exiled enemies. Among the sycophantic works are the official twenty-volume history, *La Era de Trujillo: 25 Años de Historia Dominicana* (Ciudad Trujillo: Impresora Dominicana, 1955); *Trujillo: The Biography of a Great Leader,* by Abelardo R. Nanita (New York: Vantage Press, 1957); and *Military Biography of Generalissimo Rafael Leonidas Trujillo Molina* . . . , by Ernesto Vega y Pagan, translated into English by Ida Espaillat (Editorial Atenas, Ciudad Trujillo, 1956). Among the exile works are Juan Bosch's *Trujillo: Causas de una tiranía sin ejemplo* (Caracas: Librería "Las Novedades," 1959); *Trujillo: Little Caesar of the Caribbean,* by Germán Ornes (New York: Thomas Nelson & Sons, 1958); and Jesús de Galíndez' *La Era de Trujillo* (Buenos Aires, 1962). (So far as I know, Galíndez' book never has been published in English, although an English translation exists in manuscript form in the Special Collections of the Columbia University Libraries, is entitled "Trujillo's Dominican Republic: A Case Study of Latin American Dictatorship," was copyrighted in 1957 by Jacques Barzun, Dean of the Graduate Faculties, and bears Publication Number 20,090 in the Doctoral Dissertation Series prepared by University Microfilms, Ann Arbor, Michigan.) Probably no work conveys so well, although unwittingly, the vulgarity of the Trujillo regime as the two-volume picture book published in honor of the dictator's ill-fated World's Fair, *Album de Oro* (Ciudad Trujillo, 1956 and 1957; two vols.). A similar grandiose effort is *Dominican Republic,* by various Dominican "collaborators," including, interestingly enough, Joaquín Balaguer and Fausto E. Caamaño, and translated into English by William J. Hamann (Volume XII of "Colección América," Editora Barranquilla, Barranquilla, Colombia, 1955). A handsome picture book with English and Spanish captions entitled *La República Dominicana* was "produced" by Francis Stopelman and printed by Nederlandsche Rotogravure Maatschappij, Leiden (n.d.).

No student of Trujillo should overlook the Generalissimo's own speeches; some are printed in English in *The Basic Policies of a Regime,* by Rafael L. Trujillo (Ciudad Trujillo: Editora del Caribe, C. por A., 1960). Nor those of his brother, President Héctor Trujillo; some are printed in Spanish in two slender volumes, *Discursos y Mensajes 1952–1957* (n.d., n.p.). The regime produced innumerable fascinating documents, such as the official *White Book of Communism in Dominican Republic,* published in English by the Ministry for Home Affairs in 1958. (The *golpistas* who overthrew President Juan Bosch published a similar work in Spanish,

Libro Blanco de las Fuerzas Armadas y de la Policía Nacional de la República Dominicana [Santo Domingo: Editora del Caribe, C. por A., 1964]). Bosch has the distinction of being denounced in both; I, alas, in but one. The official source on the Trujillo regime is, of course, the periodical *Gaceta Oficial.*

The literature on what has happened since Trujillo's death is equally extensive and far more reliable. In the Republic, *El Caribe* and *Listin Diario,* as well as other newspapers, published freely. In the United States, a great many magazine articles and news stories have been published, particularly immediately after Bosch fell and at the time of the 1965 Civil War. Of special interest are a long piece in the Washington *Post* of June 27, 1965 by Murrey Marder and various pieces in U.S. magazines, including *The New Republic, The New Leader, The Saturday Review,* and *Commentary,* by President Bosch and the journalists Tad Szulc, Norman Gall, Theodore Draper, and Richard H. Rovere. So is a piece in the Communist publication, *World Marxist Review* (December 1965); I have reprinted it here in the Appendix. *Time* and *Newsweek* have given considerable space to the Republic. *Look* has published the memoirs of Trujillo's daughter, Flor de Oro, written in collaboration with Laura Bergquist. The magazine pieces can be located in the *Reader's Guide to Periodical Literature;* the New York *Times,* of course, publishes its own *Index,* though the files of other newspapers, such as the Chicago *Tribune* and the Washington *Post,* should not be ignored. As to post-Trujillo books, they too are numerous. I have mentioned Bosch's own book, *Crisis de la Democracia de América en la República Dominicana* (Centro de Estudios y Documentación Sociales, A.C.; Mexico, D.F.; 1964). This has since been published in English as *The Unfinished Experiment: Democracy in the Dominican Republic* (New York: Frederick A. Praeger, 1965). Unfortunately, Bosch did not include the 1965 Civil War in either edition. Two men once in the Trujillo regime have published memoirs— the notorious Arturo R. Espaillat, in *Trujillo: The Last Caesar* (Chicago: Henry Regnery Company, 1963), and Teodoro Tejeda, who says he was placed in charge of the investigation of Trujillo's assassination, *Yo Investigué la Muerte de Trujillo* (Barcelona: Plaza & Janes, S.A., 1963). Neither is of great value. Several U.S. journalists have published books on the Civil War of 1965, including Dan Kurzman, *Santo Domingo: Revolt of the Damned* (New York: G. P. Putnam's Sons, 1965) and Tad Szulc, *Dominican Diary* (New York: Delacorte Press, 1965); a book by a third, Barnard Collier, has been announced for publication, as I wrote. So has *Dominican Debacle* (Viking Press), by Theodore Draper; it apparently is an expanded version of Draper's long article in the December 1965 issue of *Commentary.*

Since 1960, much Dominican history has been recorded—not to say made—in the OAS and the UN; numerous publications are available at

UN headquarters in New York and the OAS in Washington. Similarly, the U. S. Congress has conducted various investigations and published reports, available in the Library of Congress in Washington. The same may be said of the State Department and the Agency for International Development. The Brookings Institution lent its auspices to a study of the DORSA Colony at Sosua, *Refugee Settlement in the Dominican Republic* . . . (Washington: the Brookings Institutions, 1942). The International Monetary Fund and other international agencies have studied and reported on the Republic. The *Public Papers of the Presidents of the United States* (U. S. Government Printing Office) contain President Kennedy's and President Johnson's public messages, speeches, and statements on the Republic. In addition, I have used White House and State Department press releases and, for earlier years, the *Foreign Relations of the United States*.

In the Republic, a number of interesting books recalling the past were published in Spanish in 1962 and 1963, such as *Cancionero de Lilís* and *Papeles de Espaillat* (Editora del Caribe, C. por A., Santo Domingo, 1962 and 1963 respectively). During this same period, as I have indicated, Castro/Communists published newspapers, and they also edited books or booklets—Máximo López Molina of the MPD appropriated old General Luperón in an introduction to an epic poem on Luperón by Ramón Alberto Ferreras, the talented editor of *Claridad*.

In recent years authors and publishers have flooded the United States with books on Latin America. Some of the best (and some of the worst) have dealt with Cuba, particularly with the Bay of Pigs. Others have touched the Dominican Republic tangentially. But I know of no really satisfactory recent book on either the Republic or Latin America as a whole. Our literary as well as our political awareness seems only to be beginning.

ADDRESS TO THE CHAMBER OF COMMERCE OF THE AMERICAS

Although during my tenure as Ambassador I made many informal public appearances, I gave only three major policy speeches. Of these, the most important was delivered on June 19, 1963, to the Chamber of Commerce of the Americas, a group of businessmen from various Latin American nations and the United States which met for several days at the Hotel Embajador in Santo Domingo. I took the occasion to discuss broad questions of policy in the Caribbean and Latin America, drafting the speech with care and clearing it in advance with the State Department. The full text follows:

I am honored to meet with distinguished business leaders of our hemisphere —and by choosing to hold your thirteenth annual meeting in Santo Domingo, the cradle of the hemisphere and its newest birthplace of democracy, you honor with your presence and with your confidence the brave Dominican people and their elected and dedicated President, Juan Bosch.

Your deliberations will reach far beyond this lovely island. They have the capacity to help shape the future. For yours is an absolutely crucial role in hemispheric development, not only your capital but your technical knowledge and above all your flexibility, your confidence, and your constructive leadership of the revolutionary change which is the condition of our life today.

Change is everywhere. The splendored jets which brought you here glided into Aeropuerto Punta Caucedo over the heads of ragged women on burros, carrying charcoal to market; and what concerns that woman is not the European Common Market but the market on Avenida Mella, and the pennies she can take home to her children tonight. Change, wrenching change; contrast and contradiction; campesinos plowing the earth with forked sticks while the hydrogen bomb ticks away, one man orbiting the earth while below him millions starve—this is the world we live in, this is the basic fact of our life.

Whatever we do, whatever anyone does, the plain truth is that Latin America is having, and will continue to have, a revolution. Whether it will be peaceful and maintain liberty, or will be bloody and destroy freedom, is to a considerable extent in your hands.

I would not presume to lecture this audience on such technical though vitally important questions as those you have discussed this week—capital formation and capital flight, systems of housing finance, investment guarantees, and so on.

Rather, I should like, if I may, to set our discussions in a somewhat larger frame of reference.

For we must not forget that in all our deliberations, in all our common efforts, our common purpose is to make a revolution. And the questions we must confront are these: Is social revolution compatible with a business system of free enterprise? Is it compatible with peace, with democracy, with individual freedom? And are we up to the task—can we summon the wisdom, the courage, the patience, and above all the confidence we need—confidence in ourselves, confidence in the ordinary people?

Our opponents answer no.

And we would do well to heed them. A leading theoretician of the extreme left in Latin America has told us plainly what he thinks. Speaking directly to the United States, he said that we have had four centuries of uninterrupted development, of industrial revolution and liberal democracy within a capitalistic structure, while, he says, Latin America has had four centuries of continuous underdevelopment, misery, and stagnation, within a feudal structure derived from old Spain, with its tyranny, great estates, denial of rights to the masses, and barriers raised against modern ideas. Our theoretician contends that the only solution for Latin America today is to destroy its feudal structure once and for all. He tells us the Alliance for Progress is a sham and that its only real structural reform, agrarian reform, is doomed by the Latin American oligarchy. Agrarian reform, he argues, "can only be brought about by revolution, with a gun in hand." And our theoretician continues—and I quote him directly—

"Revolution? Yes, because, as Mexico and Cuba have shown, only revolution can destroy feudalism—not aspirin and good wishes.

"Revolution? Yes, because as Cuba and Mexico have shown, only armed revolution can destroy forever the armies which guard the old order . . .

"Revolution? Yes, because, as Mexico and Cuba have shown, only a revolution can bring about the structural changes necessary to modernize our countries, put stagnating natural resources to work, recoup ill-spent and estranged resources, carry through agrarian reform, create an internal market, diversify production, promote popular education and industrialization.

"Revolution! You cry out and put your hands to your heads, weeping to see the violence and the spilling of blood. Yes, because unfortunately, it has never been possible to convince the ruling classes of a feudal country that their hour has come. . . . Blood? Yes, historical delay is paid for in blood. Remember Jefferson. From Spartacus to Fidel Castro, through Protestant, English, French, United States, Mexican, and Russian revolutions, revolutions have been violent. Revolutions are not made by Mickey Mouse. They are made by hungry, courageous, angry, desperate men."

Now, it is manifestly absurd to equate the Mexican Revolution, which was indigenous and has remained so, with the Cuban revolution, which is the creature of a foreign colonial power; it is also absurd to pretend that tragic Cuba proves that violent revolution promotes economic growth.

But I think our theoretician raises a serious question which deserves an answer when he asserts that revolution can be made only with rifles and not with reason; only by bullets, never by bankers; only with blood, never with brains.

I assert, and I deeply believe, he is wrong.

I refuse to believe that the human race has learned nothing since Spartacus, that history is an iron vise, and that reason, good will, education, and a passionate devotion to freedom cannot loosen that vice-like grip on mankind.

History is not a straitjacket. The human race does learn. Change is the one certitude. The dismal factories of nineteenth-century England on which Karl Marx founded his historical postulates resemble in no way the institutions of modern capitalism in the 1960s. And our doctrinaire theoretician is as wrong in his interpretation of history today as Karl Marx was wrong when he predicted that communism was unlikely in Russia in the near future but historically inevitable in England and Germany.

The experience of my country demonstrates that a profound social and economic revolution can indeed be made by peaceful means and without destroying individual freedom. We had one. It began in the 1930s, and it is continuing yet. I belong to the generation of Americans who grew up in the Great Depression—like some of you, I daresay. I not only remember the long lines of unemployed at factory gates—I stood in them, every day at daybreak all one icy winter. I can not only recite the history of the New Deal and its great leader—I also remember that one of its reforms saved my parents' home from the mortgage holder, that one of its emergency programs put my father to work, and that I received my own first increase in pay, from $9 a week to $14.50 a week, because of the minimum-wage law. And I have not only read Franklin Roosevelt's speeches but I heard his voice coming over the old-fashioned radio in our home—"The only thing we have to fear is fear itself."

If ever a great free nation might have gone under to authoritarian revolution; if ever free men were tempted to barter freedom for bread, it was in the United States in the 1930s. But instead, unrestrained finance capitalism was thoroughly and peaceably reformed. And we erected a new structure which preserved the free enterprise system but created mechanisms for protecting the people—and business itself—against excess. Stock market regulation, social security, federal housing, bank deposit insurance, legislation guaranteeing minimum wages and maximum hours and the right to collective bargaining, agricultural credit and extension systems, rigorous income and inheritance tax reform, the Tennessee Valley Authority and the other grand river valley developments that made deserts bloom and destroyed private power monopolies—these measures were at the time viewed with alarm; yet today they are accepted as ordinary and necessary safeguards to make a free society work.

Nor is this all. Since World War II, instead of the predicted postwar bust, we have enjoyed a postwar boom. And its most striking aspect is this: Far from fullfilling Marx's gloomy prophecy that the rich always get richer and the poor poorer, under the umbrella of the new society forged in the 1930s, the poor have moved upward, the middle class has broadened enormously, and prosperity has reached so many that we can afford to become concerned not about the quantity of what we have but about its quality—the quality of the education of our children, of the medical care of our parents, of the growth patterns of our new suburban metropolis.

I am not contending all our problems are solved. Far, very far, from it. No American conscience can lie easy while any American citizen is denied his rights because of the color of skin. But I am particularly proud to stand before you today as the representative of an American President who last week told my countrymen with unmistakable clarity: "The time has come for this nation to fulfill its promises." And fulfill them we will—and with all the world watching.

Now, no doubt our theoretician would say that our recent social and economic revolution merely proves his case: We could do it peaceably precisely because we never bore the burden of feudalism.

But is this also true of Western Europe, of Italy, of France, of West Germany? Is it also true of Japan? In those countries, since World War II, under private enterprise nurtured by built-in government safeguards, led by far-sighted statesmen both in government and in private business, and assisted by the United States, other revolutions have been wrought; other feudal classes have been broken; other masses have been lifted; other peoples have been set free; and all by peaceful means.

Indeed, the most dynamic revolution afoot on earth today is not Communist imperialism but the dramatic surge of abundance and the dramatic rise of the middle class under private enterprise capitalism. This is the force which is making the advance to the future. And Soviet colonialism, with its enslavement of peoples in so-called people's democracies, with its collapsing agriculture and its consumer starvation, is marching rapidly backward to the darkness of the past.

I would agree with our theoretician that it is difficult to reconcile the nineteenth-century history of private enterprise with today's irresistible force of social progress. I think we all recognize that in the past some of us, North Americans and Latin Americans alike, in one Latin American country or another, while committing ourselves *in principle* to social change, have said, "But of course, we mustn't rock the boat *here*."

But I think we recognize now that no rational confidence in an unchanged society is possible in today's world. Confidence today requires the expectation of change and progress—of social betterment, of dramatic, sometimes explosive and confused, sometimes even frightening and dangerous change.

I remind you that the heart of the free enterprise we cherish is risk-taking. Call it venture capital, call it risk capital, call it by any name, its heart is risk.

We have not feared change and risk in the past. This is why we have progressed. We cannot fear it now if we intend to survive.

But there is more. Every one of us here, traveling through the lovely but impoverished countryside of Latin America, contemplating not only its beauties but its misery—every one of us who has left his office and walked through the *barrios* where the displaced *campesinos* dwell in squalor without job or decent home, where a single *barrio* contains a thousand unchecked cases of raging cholera and where nine human beings, a man and wife and seven children, exist in a six-by-six thatched hut with a dirt floor and a single bed—every one of us here today has seen such sights in these nations, sights that make us ashamed to be a human being. These men are our brothers; these children are our future leaders. This is how they are passing their formative years. I have seen them, you have seen them, we all have seen them. And I say to you that the revolution to which we are dedicated is not necessary because we must defeat the Communists. It is necessary because it is morally right; because these people deserve a better life; because they belong to the family of man. It is, quite simply, necessary if we really believe with the Psalmist that the Creator is mindful of man, that He "hast made him a little lower than the angels."

What, then, must we do?

Our chosen instrument in this part of the world is the Alliance for Progress.

It would be superfluous, not to say presumptuous, for me to discuss the *Alianza* at length with you gentlemen. I shall content myself with four observations.

First, it cannot be said too often that the *Alianza* is widely misunderstood as a United States giveaway program and that, as Assistant Secretary Edwin Martin has said, the United States is "strictly a junior partner" in the *Alianza*.

Second, I agree with Senator Hubert Humphrey that delays are still much too long and businessmen "quite rightly do not care to wait eighteen months" to find out whether a project qualifies for an investment guarantee; and that in the lending process in general, "the unconscionably long delays must be eliminated."

Third, at the same time, too much progress cannot be expected too fast. The *Alianza* is not a recipe for instant Utopia. In this slow, hard business of nation-building, we would all be better off if we stopped thinking in terms of target dates, deadlines, and final victory, for although on the first Wednesday after the first Monday in November every four years in the United States we know who won the election, only our children's historians, perhaps not us at all, may know whether the *Alianza* has won. (Though we may know if it loses.)

Fourth, we have learned from the experience of the *Alianza*'s first twenty-one months that Latin America is not postwar Western Europe, and the *Alianza* is not the Marshall Plan, for the conditions are different. True, we need highways, power plants, factories, ports, all the tools of economic development. But what we need just as badly is human development. I am not speaking now in the general terms of social justice. I am speaking of education, especially vocational education—specifically, of management and administrative skills, both in government and in private business, and of skilled labor. It may well be that not only capital but an equally valuable contribution which foreign private enterprise can make at this stage is the skills and habits of trained and expert work—on-the-job training, intramural schools, sometimes shared, as Mr. Morrison suggested, with outsiders. And it may well be that government's most valuable contribution can be made in education—primary and secondary education, adult education, and vocational training, particularly in public administration and agriculture, using not only traditional methods but audiovisual techniques, radio, and television. As Adlai Stevenson has said, "People are the one common denominator of progress. No improvement is possible with unimproved people. Advance is inevitable when people are liberated and educated."

I should like to discuss one final matter briefly.

I do not know but I can guess that underlying all your deliberations this week has been a sometimes spoken, sometimes unspoken, but always vital question: The question of confidence.

The statesmen of the Inter-American Social and Economic Council, who framed the Charter of Punta del Este, agreed that if the Alliance is to work, governments alone cannot do everything; fully 80 percent of the needed capital investment must come from the private sector. The question is: Will it come? Does private capital possess enough confidence to invest?

The returns are not all in yet, but the short-term results suggest that the issue is in doubt. Senator Humphrey wrote that in the first year of the *Alianza*, "Too many wealthy Latin Americans are still refusing to make large new investments. United States firms are reluctant to make large new investments." David Rockefeller has said that in the first year total investment came "hearteningly close to the target," but too much came from governments, too little from the private sector, and he added, with, I thought, considerable grace, that many Latin American capitalists "sought safer havens for their money abroad."

Almost daily we hear that a "climate of confidence" must be created. What creates confidence? And what undermines it?

The answers will vary from country to country in this hemisphere of differences. But I think we might agree on half a dozen factors of importance:

Capital, the traditionally timid million dollars, desires political stability. It dislikes upheaval and confusion, which interfere with business as usual.

Capital desires monetary stability. As Mr. Rockefeller has said, governments "cannot put local capital to work effectively in an inflation-ridden economy where the price level soars sixfold as it did between 1953 and 1961 in Brazil, 10-fold as in Chile, or 26-fold as in Bolivia."

Capital applauds fiscal responsibility—a balanced budget, an efficient public administration, a sensibly managed public debt, realistic exchange rates instead of debilitating exchange controls, a free market unhampered by artificial monopolies.

Capital wants a government strong enough not only to insist on a tax and land reform but on labor responsibility; and labor wants a government strong enough to guarantee its right to true collective bargaining.

Capital wants honesty in government, a government with a reputation as impeccable as that of Caesar's wife.

Capital wants a good market and a high rate of economic growth—but I would point out that it is mainly capital itself which must create growth and markets. Today in Latin America millions of people dwell not only in misery but entirely outside the money economy itself; and as the *Alianza* improves their lot, they will become your customers, your new and untapped market. What is good for the people and their standard of living is good for business. The rising tide lifts all the boats.

And yet, when all this has been said, I think it leaves unsaid the one thing which frightens capital, both foreign and domestic, more than anything else in Latin America today. It is something seldom talked about in public, though ceaselessly in private. It is the almost nameless dread that this country or that will "go Castro," "become another Cuba." And to this question I should like to address myself.

Let me begin by saying that everyone recognizes that Communist Cuba exists and that it is a clear and present danger to the peace, democracy, and freedom of the hemisphere; that its treacherous leader betrayed the legitimate aspirations of the revolution made by the Cuban people and handed their country and themselves over bodily to a foreign colonialism; that today Castro's Cuba is the first Soviet beachhead in the New World; that from it Castro seeks to export violence and subversion throughout the hemisphere; and that, in the succinct words of the Punta del Este confidence, Castro's Cuba is "incompatible" with the principles of the Inter-American system.

We know that, as Senator Humphrey has said, Castro is no military threat to the United States, except as an extension of Soviet military power. But we also know that he is a real threat to the other American republics—that he is training guerrillas and exporting them, sending out propaganda if not weapons; that he is seeking to infiltrate other Latin American nations and governments on every level, especially the military, the labor movement, youth groups, and certain key government ministries; and that in addition he seeks a mass following in the yearnings of the restless and long-neglected masses of *barrio* and *campo*.

But let us for a moment look beyond Cuba. Let us look beyond that tragic country to the new bastion of democracy here in the Dominican Republic, and to the great nations to the north of this island, and to the great nations to the south and west.

And let us remember these nations would confront pressing, even explosive, social and economic problems if Castro were removed tomorrow, indeed, if he had never existed. As Senator Humphrey has said, "We must keep in mind that Cuba, however important, is only a part of the total problem. . . . If the Alliance for Progress is to succeed in meeting the staggering problems of poverty, illiteracy, maldistribution of wealth, and economic stagnation in vast areas of Latin America, we must administer and support the Alliance with the same sense of urgency that presently motivates our thinking about Cuba."

I would suggest to you that it is not only Castro's arms and his guerrillas, his subversive agents and propaganda experts, which threaten our governments and endanger our progress.

I would suggest that it is, also, the fear we feel about him.

For Castro possesses the dangerous potential of strengthening the extreme right in Latin America. Men of property and of goodwill, fearing the spread of the Castro disease to their own countries, may become deflected from their forward march to progress; may be tempted to seek refuge from the storm in a rightist storm cellar instead of moving confidently ahead toward progressive reform.

Men afraid of Castro may hesitate to invest in the future of the *Alianza* and of their own countries. For the *Alianza* demands a wrenching readjustment of national wealth and power, and thus tends to encourage the very political and social unrest they might not fear without Castro but do fear with him—for who knows, they ask, whether they can trust the politics of hope when the politicians preaching hope may turn out to be Fidel's agents?

In brief, we are in danger not only of being subverted or attacked by Castro but also of being mesmerized and paralyzed by fear of him.

Why else, but for fear, would we allow the leftist extremists in some cases to take over the nationalist reform movements which are perhaps the most powerful force at large in the hemisphere today? Close to Russia's borders, as in Hungary and Rumania, nationalism is on our side; but not always in Latin

America. Yet it should be. For Soviet colonialism never permits national identity—it destroys it. But we encourage it—as President Kennedy has said, "Diversity and independence, far from being opposed to the American conception of world order, represent the very essence of our vision of the future."

Why else, but for fear, would we invent the bogeyman of the Red superman —in the face of the evidence of the wreckage of Cuba's economy, the Soviet diplomatic disaster in Guinea, and the shipment of Soviet snowplows to Burma?

Why else, but for fear, would we dissipate our energies looking under the bed for Communists when we should be looking to modern technology for the techniques of social betterment—or to the stars for inspiration?

Why else, but for fear, would responsible men sometimes mistrust and doubt the governments of the leaders of the democratic left in Latin America? For they are in fact, as anyone knows, the governments constitutionally elected by the people themselves, and responsive to the legitimate aspirations of the people. And they do in fact, as anyone knows, represent the hopes of freedom in our hemisphere today.

No, it is really asking too much to ask a developing nation to go through the industrial revolution, the revolution against colonialism, emergence from feudalism, the Great Depression, and McCarthyism in a single year, or even a single decade.

We must not slide back into an unfortunate past, when patriotic but misguided men made us afraid of shadows; when journalists well-intentioned but incompletely informed distorted our perception of reality; when friends of freedom were deceived into fostering the schemes of adventurers. We must take care today that our assessment of the Castro menace is not beclouded by unreasoning fear. We must be vigilant but sensible.

Let us never close our eyes to the very real danger of Castro/Communist subversion. But let us not permit that danger to blind us to our might or deflect us from our goal, to tie our hands or paralyze our will or mesmerize our minds.

Let us remember that, as Victor Hugo said, "No army can destroy the force of an idea whose hour has come." Our idea is a better way of life, and peace and freedom, for our peoples and our children. And its hour has come.

Gentlemen talk of confidence today; but I would remind you, as visitors to this Republic, of what really destroys confidence. It is Trujillo, and all he stood for. The knock on the door at 4 A.M., the unsuspected police informer next door or in one's own family, friends who disappear into prisons whence none return, the jackboot, the slave-labor camp, wire taps, spies, surveillance, the murder factory, all the odious trappings of the police state, and above all fear itself—*this* is what destroys confidence. Look back in this Republic two years, or thirty years. Who could even be confident he would be alive tomorrow? Look back two years or thirty, and ask what happened to people's confidence in each other, even in themselves. Trujillo destroyed it. He destroyed it by the fear he spawned. Look across the seas today to tragic Hungary and Rumania and East Germany and ask what is happening to confidence. The Soviets are destroying it. Their weapon is fear.

Confidence is not merely what bankers demand. Confidence is what blesses family life. Confidence is what makes good neighbors. Confidence makes friendship possible. Confidence is what enables men to live together. Confidence is the glue that binds civilized society together.

And fear is what corrodes and finally destroys it. Fear of Trujillo. Fear of the Kremlin. Fear of Castro.

Fear is our enemy, the irrational, intangible fear that unnerves and corrodes and destroys.

Why should we be afraid? We come from great nations. We know what needs doing and how to do it. We know that social betterment and economic progress —a better life for the ordinary man—is not merely the bar to Castro but the only acceptable road to national independence and individual human dignity. We know that to be independent, a people must be free. And to be free they must be educated. And to afford education they must have bread. We know that change is long overdue in this part of our world and that it is inevitable, and if the developing nations assume unfamiliar configurations, we should welcome them nonetheless, not force them into a Procrustean bed. We know that change is the only certitude of life. We know that risk and danger are the lot of our generation. We know that now for the first time we possess the technological knowledge to destroy the earth—or abolish poverty from its face. And what we do today will shape this choice. We know that this is the terror and the glory of being alive today. We know our decisions will decide our children's fate, even their survival. We know the human spirit can soar. We know its only chains are fear. And we can hear the echo of the past, in an hour of different peril and a moment of great decision, the echo of the voice of Franklin Roosevelt: "The only thing we have to fear is fear itself."

And on that note, which struck home because it bespoke the yearnings of millions and the greatness of one, but which prevailed because it spoke the truth, I choose to leave you, confident of your confidence in yourselves and your future. Let us put fear aside. And let us get on with our great work.

"REVOLUTIONARY STRUGGLE IN THE DOMINICAN REPUBLIC AND ITS LESSONS"

The *World Marxist Review,* published in Prague and elsewhere in seventeen languages, including Russian, Spanish, Mongolian, English, and Vietnamese, is an authoritative organ of the worldwide Communist movement. The December 1965 issue contained an article on the 1965 Dominican Civil War signed by "J. I. Quello" and "N. Isa Conde," presumably two Dominican leaders of the PSP, the Moscow-directed Partido Socialista Popular which, after the Civil War, changed its name to the PCD, Partido Comunista Dominicano. That article, carefully edited to advance Communist purposes, has since been used in the United States by both critics and advocates of our 1965 Dominican policy to buttress their cases. To quote excerpts from it to "prove" or "disprove" points in our own debate over U.S. policy is unwise, not to say misleading.

Like other articles in the *Review,* it cannot be taken at face value but should be read as a self-serving *ex post facto* document—one intended to serve Communist aims and written after the fact of Civil War, during a period when Dominican Communists were engaged in soul-searching and self-criticism. Although it is of little use in proving or disproving facts, I am reprinting it here because it is an interesting exhibit of Communist thought and may not be readily available to some readers. The article, in its entirety, follows:

On April 24, 1965, the people of the Dominican Republic rose against the dictatorship installed by the *coup* of September 1963. The rebels demanded the return to power of a government headed by President Juan Bosch, who had been duly elected in December 1963, and the restoration of the Constitution adopted during his administration. The democratic Constitutionalist movement, in which the armed masses took part, grew by leaps and bounds. Within three days the old tyrannical structure had been toppled and the army, which had been built up and controlled by the United States, defeated. Another facet was added to the new situation in the Latin American liberation movement marked by an upsurge in the struggle for national liberation and socialism with revolutionary Cuba setting the example for the peoples of the Americas. Only by direct armed intervention was U.S. imperialism able to prevent the Dominican democrats and Constitutionalists from achieving their immediate aims, to retain its grip on the Republic and temporarily to check the development of the revolution. The fact that imperialism had to take this action is, however, a sign of its weakness, of its inability to preserve its spheres of influence and prevent popular uprisings.

These events made our country and its capital, Santo Domingo, one of the key sectors of the international struggle. The Dominican uprising is new proof that October 1917 ushered in an epoch of world-wide revolutionary reconstruction and that nothing can prevent the final victory of the peoples.

1. U.S. Imperialism—Always an Aggressor

The U.S. intervention in the Dominican Republic was by no means unprecedented. The first landing of U.S. troops on Dominican territory took place as far back as 1898. In 1903 and 1904 gunboats were used to protect the investments of the American capitalists and the local rulers subservient to them. In 1905 Washington used the threat of a new intervention to impose on the Dominican Republic a treaty which placed its Customs in the hands of U.S. officials. Little by little the U.S. monopolies, ousting the Belgian, British, Dutch and French monopolies, established their undivided domination over the Republic.

In 1915 the United States insisted on the Dominican Republic "accepting" a U.S. financial adviser and a comptroller of the armed forces. In 1916 troops were again landed, and this time they remained until 1924. U.S. military government was established. It "relinquished" the reins of power on the following conditions:

1. That Customs control and supervision over finances, including payments on the foreign debt, remained in U.S. hands;

2. That an "electoral law" approved by the United States was enforced;

3. That a new "national guard" trained by U.S. officers took the place of the old national army.

By 1924 the United States had established complete economic control. It could now withdraw its troops, since the imperialists could count on the new "national guard" fully protecting their interests. The "national guard" was placed under the command of a reliable officer who had "distinguished" himself by persecuting patriots and suppressing struggles waged by the sugar refinery workers—Rafael Leonidas Trujillo.

In 1930 a *coup* took place which put Trujillo in power.

The Trujillo regime was a military tyranny of the classical type, subservient to the oligarchy (the semi-feudal latifundists and the big bourgeoisie who had betrayed the nation) and U.S. imperialism. Its distinguishing feature was that Trujillo used his political power to enrich (through state monopolies) his own economic group while coming into conflict with equally reactionary groups of the traditional oligarchy. The national economy largely fell under the absolute control of the Trujillo group which retained close ties with its sponsors, the U.S. monopolies.

This group basically set out not to promote capitalist development as such or to head the so-called national bourgeoisie, as some people hold, but to prevent the free, independent growth of national capitalism in order to build up a single giant monopoly closely linked with imperialism. This monopoly owned all the big industrial enterprises and the best land, which it seized by force of arms. Consequently, during the military occupation and the Trujillo regime a peculiar type of capitalism developed in both industry and agriculture, under which the natural trends of growth and expansion were distorted by the monopoly on which it rested. This deformed capitalist structure experienced its own specific types of crises and periods of recession and recovery.

2. Thirty-one Years of Pro-Imperialist Dictatorship

Throughout the thirty-one years of the "Trujillo era" the Dominican people carried on an unflagging clandestine struggle against the most ruthless dictatorship in Latin America. Thousands of Dominicans were arrested, tortured or killed.

Only during a very brief period was it possible to wage an open struggle against the regime. In 1945 a movement for higher wages and better living conditions spread through the U.S. monopoly-owned sugar refineries. This movement, and also the atmosphere of anti-fascist unity during the Second World War, enabled the Communist Party, founded secretly in 1942 and originally called the Popular Socialist Party, to function legally in 1946–48. But with the beginning of the cold war these legal possibilities were reduced to nil. Many members of our Party were thrown into prison, and many others fell in the struggle or were forced to emigrate. The only organised political opposition in the country was suppressed.

The years of economic upswing from 1950 to 1956 were the most stable period for the Trujillo regime. But during this period too the completely unorganised Dominican democrats who came out against the regime were viciously persecuted.

The specific features of the economic base of the regime, its policy aimed at retarding the march of history, and its naked despotism led, however, to growing conflicts between the ruling camarilla and all other classes, strata and groups of Dominican society.

The twenty-fifth anniversary of Trujillo's advent to power, into the celebration of which millions of dollars were poured, was followed by a crisis that deprived the regime of its principal domestic bulwark, the support of the pro-imperialist bourgeoisie, and prompted new influential groups to join the fight against the dictatorship. At the same time a broad democratic movement was sweeping the entire Caribbean area. This movement overthrew the regimes of Magloire in Haiti, Rojas Pinilla in Colombia, Perez Jimenez in Venezuela and Batista in Cuba, and enabled the Dominicans in exile to intensify their activities and to cement their unity. Cuba set our people an example of how to fight dictators. A large number of Dominican exiles fitted out an armed expedition which landed in the Republic on June 14, 1959. Its heroism notwithstanding, the force was destroyed, but the blood shed was not in vain. The Revolutionary June 14 Movement was organised in secret. Resistance to the regime grew in all parts of the country, finding legal expression in the Dominican Popular Movement led by a group of revolutionaries who returned in 1960.

In the meantime the Cuban revolution, rapidly passing through its national-liberation stage, entered the phase of socialist reconstruction. The dawn of socialism in Latin America gave a new powerful impulse and set the example to all peoples oppressed by imperialism, our people included.

Imperialism was now compelled to manoeuvre in the Dominican Republic in order to check the maturing of a second revolution in the Antilles. It was precisely this that was the object of the conspiracy engineered by the U.S. Embassy which led to Trujillo's downfall. The dictator was assassinated by a group of his close associates on May 30, 1961. At this period U.S. imperialism was engaged in working out forms of domination better suited to meet the requirements of the epoch of rapid growth of the national-liberation movement and to counteract the example Cuba had set for all the oppressed peoples of the Western Hemisphere. The methods used then were those devised by Kennedy and his entourage and abandoned after his assassination. (Today too these methods are taken out of moth-balls from time to time and used in combination with Johnson's hard-riding Texan methods.)

However, the assassination of Trujillo, far from stopping the maturing of the crisis, accelerated developments. All sections of the population, all classes whose interests prompted them to resist Trujillo, now openly carried on the fight. New conflicts took place and new crises developed in the overall context of the deep-going general structural crisis from which the Dominican Republic cannot extricate itself so long as it remains in the capitalist orbit.

3. Assassination of Trujillo—Catalyst of National Crisis

After Trujillo's death, leadership of the national-democratic movement was temporarily taken over by the National Civic Union (NCU). Ostensibly pursuing patriotic objectives, this organisation was controlled by bourgeois elements with close links with the U.S. Embassy. At the same time a number of prominent leaders of Juan Bosch's Dominican Revolutionary Party (DRP) returned from exile. The Revolutionary June 14 Movement (then known as the June 14 Political Group) emerged from illegality. These organisations were the main political forces in the country at the time. The Popular Socialist Party (now the Communist Party) began reorganising itself after the secret return from exile of some of its leaders. The Dominican Popular Movement (DPM), which at first functioned legally, was soon outlawed.

The mass struggles of August-November 1961 forced the remaining members of the Trujillo family to leave the country, and the eleven-day general strike of November-December 1961 shook the rule of Joaquin Balaguer, Trujillo's principal puppet during the last years of his regime. Early in 1962 U.S. imperialism, operating through the NCU, and with State Department officials openly taking a hand in the matter, installed in power the so-called State Council consisting of spokesmen of the traditional oligarchy.

During his brief administration Balaguer was compelled to confiscate the property of Trujillo's family and his accomplices who controlled 60 per cent of all investments in trade and industry. The oligarchy did not venture to lay hands on this property, though it launched a campaign against "unprofitable state companies" and to boost the virtues of private property.

Imperialism, whose policy was then shaped by the proponents of the view that the Dominican Republic should be made a "show window" of the Alliance for Progress, wanted early elections, counting on a NCU victory. Bosch's party, believing that the oligarchy could be voted out of the saddle, likewise supported the idea.

The Left forces, headed by the Revolutionary June 14 Movement which enjoyed wide popular support and adhered to clear-cut patriotic and democratic positions, refused to recognise the State Council as the legitimate government and called for its overthrow and the establishment of a national unity government based on the programme advanced by the participants in the heroic 1959 expedition. All classes, economic groups and the country's three main political forces (DRP, NCU and the Revolutionary June 14 Movement) were to be represented in this government. The Left forces called for a boycott of the elections. Our Party, which in June 1962 hesitantly urged the convocation of a democratic constituent assembly, later consistently supported the stand of the other Left groups.

The elections were held on December 20, 1962, with a great popular turnout at the polls. Although the people generally did not support the Left boycott of the elections, they voiced their democratic aspirations by voting for Juan Bosch, the most progressive candidate standing for election. Bosch put forward a programme condemning latifundism and calling for the preservation and promotion of the state sector (though without further nationalisation), as well as a return to secular education. The underlying idea of his campaign was the struggle of the poor against the rich.

Bosch polled 400,000 votes more than his chief opponent (out of a total electorate of one million).

The outcome of the elections made it impossible for imperialism and the oligarchy to lay their hands by legal means on the property left by the Trujillo family.

4. Progressive Bourgeois-Democratic Government in Office

In April 1963, during the Bosch administration, a democratic Constitution was adopted. It set forth the following basic principles:

—Labour is the foundation of national wealth.

—The latifundia, being unprofitable enterprises, are undesirable.

—Dominican land is to be sold only to Dominicans.

—Private ownership is the basis of economic development.

—It is the duty of the state to protect national wealth and not sell it to private individuals.

—The state should guarantee education on a scientific footing for all and exercise control over education.

—The workers must be guaranteed a share in the profits of enterprises.

—Private industrial and trade monopolies are prohibited.

—Democratic freedoms must be fully observed.

—The people are the basis of national sovereignty. Those who would turn national sovereignty into an object of barter with foreigners should be severely condemned.

President Bosch annulled the agreement signed by Balaguer with Esso Standard Oil on the construction of an oil refinery. His government pursued an independent foreign policy founded on respect for the right of nations to self-determination. It gradually moved towards the Mexican position and away from that of the pro-imperialist reformist government of Venezuela. A few days before the *coup d'état,* following a meeting between Bosch and Lopez Mateos, a statement was published defending the right of the peoples to choose their own governments without foreign interference.

The law fixing the maximum price of sugar brought Bosch into sharp conflict with the South Puerto Rico Sugar Co., a U.S. monopoly.

All this explains why the oligarchy and the reactionary military closely linked with the Pentagon began feverish preparations for the overthrow of the Bosch administration.

At that time two trends became apparent in the policy of the U.S. rulers. Ambassador John Martin, appointed by Kennedy, actively supported the Bosch government and advocated extending long-term loans and economic aid to it. On the other hand, General O'Meara, commander of the U.S. armed forces in the Caribbean, representing the Pentagon, openly engaged in conspiratorial activity against the constitutional regime (without official invitation he made several visits to the airforce base in San Isidoro—the stronghold of the conspirators).

Our Party was the first to expose the preparations for the *coup* several weeks before it took place, and called upon the people to take a united stand against the putschists. The other Left forces (the Revolutionary June 14 Movement and the DPM) also called for action against the *coup,* although some people in these organisations believed that the *coup* should be allowed to take place since this would make it easier to start guerrilla actions. Many people who failed to understand that popular unity against the putschists would in any event help to unite the people against the dictatorship which a successful *coup* might install, accused our Party of "Boschism."

In an address to the Dominican youth, Bosch also exposed the preparation of a *coup* and laid the blame for it on the military, the Catholic hierarchy and the U.S. sugar monopoly. He called for action to safeguard state property, against the sale of Dominican land to foreigners and against shameful concessions to foreign oil monopolies (as in the case of building the oil refinery). However, apart from this impassioned appeal, Bosch did nothing to prevent the *coup* in the three months during which it was obviously maturing. His party—DRP— did not urge the masses to bar the way to the *coup,* hoping to prevent it through negotiations with the U.S. Embassy and the top military rather than through actions of the masses whose support it enjoyed.

5. *Struggle Against the* Coup

On September 25, 1963, the reactionary military, expressing the interests of the oligarchy and the U.S. investor-monopolies, seized power with the support of the Pentagon and the CIA.[1] Bosch was banished, Parliament dissolved, and the 1963 Constitution abolished.

After the *coup* even the democrats had different, often conflicting, views concerning the methods of struggle against the putschist government—the so-called triumvirate.

The most influential group among the Left—the Revolutionary June 14 Movement—advocated guerrilla war at all costs. In so doing, they ignored the concrete conditions necessary for its development and victory at the given moment. In practice this slogan led to weakening the struggle of the masses. This was connected, in particular, with the problem of the so-called "counter-*coup*." It was feared that a military "counter-*coup*" which would reinstall Bosch in office would abolish the conditions created as a result of the reactionary putsch, conditions which some Left leaders believed to be conducive to guerrilla struggle. For some time the leaders of the Revolutionary June 14 Movement directed all their efforts towards preparing military actions and did nothing to draw the masses into the democratic struggle.

This erroneous trend manifested itself even more among the leaders and rank and file of the Dominican People's Movement, who maintained that any mobilisation of the masses and any political strike could be used for a "counter-*coup*." Even before the uprising which was being prepared by the June 14 Movement, they tried to form their own guerrilla unit. But these guerrillas were soon taken prisoner in the Cevicos Mountains.

Activity of this kind tended to isolate these parties from the masses, although many admired their heroism.

Early in November an attempt to organise a general strike ended in failure because it was not supported strongly enough by all the forces opposed to the triumvirate. At the end of November the June 14 Movement formed five guerrilla units in the mountains, but hardly a month had passed before they were defeated. Many fighters fell in the battles fought by the last guerrilla detachment, among them Manuel A. Tavarez Justo, leader of the Revolutionary June 14 Movement and a popular national figure. For a time, though not for long, the struggle slackened. Our Party, which stood for the all-round development of the mass struggle, published a critical appraisal of these events. At the same time the Party did all it could to support the revolutionaries who risked and sacrificed their lives in the heroic struggle.

As regards the Bosch party (DRP), it was under the influence of various

---

[1] In respect to the *coup*, the difference between the two tactics of U.S. imperialism in Latin America was revealed again. Kennedy and his group, who wanted to turn the Dominican Republic into a "show-window" of the Alliance for Progress, sharply denounced it (the USA recognised the new regime only after the assassination of Kennedy on November 22). On the other hand, the Pentagon, Thomas Mann and the U.S. military attachés actively supported the dictatorial regime.

tactical concepts of struggle against the *coup*. The most conservative of its leaders, for instance, cherished illusions with regard to the course of action the U.S. Embassy and State Department would take.

Their tactical differences notwithstanding, all these forces, including the Christian Socialists (who at first were extremely passive and hesitant in their opposition to the *coup*), became more united in the struggle for the reinstatement of the constitutional regime. A broad front for the restoration of democratic institutions gradually came into being, although still without a common tactical line and a clear-cut organisational structure.

The changes in the policies of the different parties were due to the changes in the political attitude of the classes and social groups of Dominican society. In its early days the *coup* was actively resisted only by the students and also the national bourgeoisie which had previously opposed Bosch's programme in the elections, but later, during his presidency, came to realise that he was defending its interests against both the parasitic oligarchy and the U.S. monopoly investors, as well as against the working class. But the support extended by the national bourgeoisie to Bosch diminished as the aims of the struggle, under the impact of developments, went beyond the range of its interests.

The most important changes took place in the political struggle of the working class. It should be noted that throughout the 30 years of the Trujillo dictatorship the Dominican proletariat was unorganised (except in 1945–47). And the labour movement had barely been organised, when, in 1961–63, it split into three main trade union centres. This was due not only to the pressure brought to bear by the U.S. Embassy and the activity of the agents of the clergy; it was above all the result of the general low level of class consciousness of the proletariat. The working class thus began the struggle against the dictatorship with its trade unions and parties divided, and lacking a party effectively representing its class interests. (That the working class did not fully support Bosch at the critical moment was also due to the temporary increase in unemployment caused by some of the economic measures of his government and to repressions against the strike movement.) But as this struggle mounted, the militancy and consciousness of the working class grew.

On May 2, 1964, a strike of public transport workers in the capital, supported by the dockers' union, rapidly acquired features of an armed uprising. Barricades were erected in the working class neighbourhoods and the police proved powerless against the people. Only after four days of heroic resistance was the strike crushed by the joint actions of the army and the police.

In the course of the struggle against the *coup* changes took place in the leadership of the movement, with the working class coming to the fore, especially after the uprising of May 2. The strike movement gained scope, drawing in all the active opposition forces. On the other hand, the national bourgeoisie, fearing the growing mass movement, increasingly adapted its positions to those of the oligarchy and imperialism, and, in particular, supported the attempts of the oligarchy to find a way out of the crisis through elections.

It should be admitted that for some time our Party, too, was under the influence of these views. By advancing, during the rule of the triumvirate, an erroneous thesis calling for an "impartial and serious government which would hold elections," our Party departed from the Marxist concept of the state and supported an idea which did not have the backing of the masses. This was a grave tactical mistake.

6. Eve of the Explosion

A stubborn internal struggle in our Party led to the defeat of the Right opportunist concept and to repudiation of the "impartial and serious government" thesis.

On March 16, 1965, the Central Committee of our Party published a Manifesto rejecting the "way out of the crisis through elections" and calling for the "return of Juan Bosch and the restoration of the 1963 Constitution on the basis of mass actions." The Manifesto helped to provide a revolutionary orientation to the mass movement, which subsequently developed into an armed uprising.

"Bosch should be returned to power through popular action," stressed the Manifesto, *"and not through compromise with the enemies of the people. The return of Bosch on the basis of mass actions signifies not only the restoration of the national dignity and sovereignty of the people. It will signify above all an extremely important step towards uniting the forces which will lead the Dominican people to complete liberation.*

"At present the struggle for the fulfilment of this task must be headed by the Dominican working class—the only class capable of leading the people as a whole and heading the struggle for their supreme objectives.

"Therefore the Popular Socialist Party calls on the working class and the people as a whole to launch a struggle for the return of President Bosch to the post of head of the legitimate government of the Republic on the basis of the democratic gains recorded in the 1963 Constitution.

"Fight in the streets, squares, factories and in the countryside for the return of President Bosch as head of the constitutional government!" concluded the Manifesto.

This document had the widest circulation of any ever put out by our Party. The entire Party understood the significance of the slogan proclaimed in the Manifesto, supported it and acted in accordance with it before and during the uprising. The Dominican People's Movement and the Revolutionary June 14 Movement came out against our position, maintaining that our slogan imparted a personal character to the struggle of the people, allowing the personality of Bosch to overshadow, as it were, the entire democratic movement. However, a little more than a month later the living dialectics of history demonstrated the rallying and mobilising force of this popular slogan. In the first days of the armed uprising the demand for the return of Bosch symbolised all the aspirations of the people. Subsequently, the masses extended their support to Caamano, insofar as he showed himself to be an ardent champion of the general democratic aims of the people. Moreover, the entire struggle acquired an anti-interventionist (essentially anti-imperialist) character in the course of the resistance to the U.S. troops.

The period of the despotic rule of the triumvirate saw events move inexorably towards an armed uprising of the people. At the end of April 1965, a revolutionary situation developed in the country. The masses no longer wanted to live in the old way, while the rulers had exhausted all possibilities of manoeuvring to preserve their power by the old methods.

The growing political character of the strikes, the rapid disintegration of the army and the universal indignation at the actions of the despotic regime paved the way to the realisation of the slogan put forward by our Party and supported by the whole people. We saw all this and were able to advance the slogan that could unite the whole people. But we failed to see that an armed uprising was inevitable. Consequently, our Party found itself unprepared for the uprising and was unable to head it, although as far as possible it took a firm and resolute part in it.

Besides, our Party adopted a sectarian attitude to the armed forces, lumping them all together as a group of "gorillas" in the service of reaction. We did not take into account the class composition of the army, whose ranks reflect the contradictions and struggles taking place in society, although as a whole it defends the interests of the reactionary state. Lenin pointed out that "the history of the Russian revolution, like the history of the Paris Commune of 1871, teaches us the incontrovertible lesson that militarism can never and under no circumstances be defeated and destroyed, except by a victorious struggle of one section of the national army against the other section." Our sectarian attitude to the army, on the contrary, prevented us from correctly assessing the changes taking place in it and isolated us from the entire process of preparation of the *coup* in the barracks. As a result constitutionalist officers and soldiers established contact primarily with the vacillating and moderate circles of the democratic movement, which were planning armed action merely as a counter-*coup*.

Although Bosch himself undoubtedly linked a military conspiracy with the struggle of the masses, the DRP leaders in Santo Domingo did not understand this and for months engaged solely in preparing a military conspiracy, doing nothing to rally the people.

In the process of preparing a counter-*coup* three main groups of conspirators emerged in the armed forces. One supported the slogan of the masses for the return of Bosch and the restoration of the Constitution; another insisted on overthrowing the regime installed by the *coup*, forming a junta of young officers and holding free elections; the third was only interested in thoroughly purging the armed forces of smugglers, hired assassins and similar elements, regardless of what government carried out the purge. But under the impact of events, as the conspiracy developed and later in the course of the armed struggle, a large part of the officers realised the need to be in the van of the armed movement which was destined to carry the constitutionalist democratic struggle to completion.

Originally, the movement was conceived only as a *coup d'état* with democratic aims which greatly enhance the role of the army as an arbiter in relation to the rest of the national institutions. In other words, even though this *coup* would have had a progressive significance, it would have led to the strengthening of an organism which, in the specific conditions of Latin America, would in the long run present a permanent threat to all other state institutions (despite the fact that in the beginning it might have consolidated them for a time).

Developments, however, took a different course.

7. The Armed Uprising Begins

Alarmed by the arrest of one of their members, the military conspirators took action earlier than originally planned. On April 24 two infantry barracks mutinied. When the news reached the capital, the entire population poured into the streets in jubilation. The members of our Party and other parties (chiefly the Left) who had opposed the triumvirate also came out. The popular struggle had begun.

From the very outset, however, it was clear that the people would not have as easy a victory as some optimists had predicted. Donald Reid Cabral, the chairman of the triumvirate, announcing the mutiny on television, said he had appointed General Wessin commander of the armed forces and member of the triumvirate, and that the rebels had been given until dawn the next day to surrender.

Through the night of April 24, however, the mass movement in the capital continued to mount; the rebel army units now had the backing of the people and entered the city in support of the popular demands. Thus, the patriotic actions of the democratic-minded armymen merged with the actions of the working people. What had started out as a military *coup* became a popular uprising, a revolution of a profoundly democratic nature.

On the morning of April 25 the city was occupied by the rebel units supported by powerful mass demonstrations. It was during the capture of the National Palace that Colonel Caamano, little known until then, distinguished himself by persuading the palace guard not to offer resistance and arresting their officers with their assistance. Shortly after midday Jose Molina Urena, chairman of the Chamber of Deputies, was proclaimed acting President pending the return of Bosch.

Continued reports of troops in the provinces coming over to the side of the rebels were broadcast over the national radio and TV. At the same time, the commander of the air base in San Isidro, under U.S. pressure, refused to adhere to the decision of the people and the rest of the army. A committee of air force officers attempted to persuade the rebel leaders to form a military junta. When this proposal was rejected, the "gorillas" subjected the National Palace and adjacent residential districts to machine gun and artillery fire from air and sea. (A tape recording of the negotiations during which the air attaché of the U. S. Embassy issued the order to open fire has been preserved.)

The bombardment of residential districts of the city continued throughout the following two days (April 26 and 27). U. S. Ambassador Bennett invited Molina Urena and members of his cabinet to the embassy and advised them to ask the U.S. government for "military protection." Molina Urena and the officers accompanying him emphatically rejected the proposal. Caamano strongly objected to this open interference by the U.S. ambassador and the use of threats and provocation. Later on, however, the group which had been invited to the embassy divided. Molina Urena, several officers and almost the entire leadership of the DRP found asylum in the embassies of Latin American countries; Caamano, Montes Arache and a number of other officers went back to the centre of the town to organise resistance.

The leaders of the uprising left the National Palace, taking with them the contents of the palace arsenal. Repairs were started on the radio and television station which had been badly damaged by shelling. The masses proceeded to set up a military organisation to offer armed resistance.

The constitutionalist military command, consisting of the officers, headed by Caamano, who had decided to offer resistance, published a statement pledging to carry on the struggle until the return of President Bosch and the restoration of the 1963 Constitution. The document, put out in the form of a leaflet, also contained advice of a military nature to the civilian population. Among other things it pointed out that the city could not be captured by air attack. This could only be done by infantry. But the resistance of the people had prevented it from entering and would continue to do so. This leaflet, which gave the masses a general orientation, finally established Caamano as the leader of the struggle. That role was assigned to him not by decision of a political party or on orders from some embassy. It was determined primarily by his actions at the head of the popular resistance. Leaders are not made by impromptu decisions, they are born and gain stature in the course of the mass struggle. Only those political, military and trade union leaders retained their positions who, in the crucible of the battle, proved worthy to hold such positions. The rest were left behind on the rubbish heap of history.

In the course of the fighting in the capital the police barracks were captured along with a considerable quantity of weapons. In the hinterland provinces army units in many places joined the movement under pressure from the masses. There, however, weapons were not distributed to the civilian population on the pretext that the armed forces would protect them from the reactionaries.

Th decisive engagement with the "gorillas" on the streets of Santo Domingo was fought on April 28. On that day, twenty-three of Wessin's tanks managed to cross the Duarte bridge, but were later destroyed or captured by the people. The Ozama fortress, the last stronghold of reaction in the capital, was taken at the same time along with a substantial quantity of arms. The people, supported by army units, thus obtained the wherewithal to continue the struggle. Control over the use of the weapons was established and sentry posts set up. So-called "comandos" were organised for the defence of the city. These were military-political bodies organised at the height of the struggle by political parties, trade unions and other popular organisations in the various districts, streets and separate buildings, and acting within their particular zone as organs of executive power. This was a new and original form of people's power. Headed by those who displayed the most organisational ability and courage in the fighting, the "comandos" represented a wide cross-section of the population, including soldiers and civilians, workers and students, intellectuals and unemployed.

With the destruction of Wessin's tanks and the capture of the Ozama fortress, the military machine of repression set up by the USA in 1924 and subsequently modernised by Trujillo was for all practical purposes abolished. The chief obstacle to the development of the revolution was thus removed and the people directed their efforts toward wiping out the last seat of putschist resistance, the San Isidro military base, where Wessin and the millionaire cutthroats in league with him were hiding to escape retribution for the bombardment of the civilian population. It was at this juncture that the U.S. marines landed.

8. Armed U. S. Intervention

The repressive machine of Dominican reaction having been smashed by the masses, U.S. imperialists hastened to replace it with their troops in an attempt to check the development of the revolution which treatened to advance beyond the democratic-constitutional demands. "A people which fights so resolutely for democracy cannot be content with simple democracy," said Juan Bosch at the time, speaking in Puerto Rico. The more far-reaching objectives of the movement emerged, needless to say, not by the will of the notorious "group of 56 or 57 Communists." They stemmed from the dialectics of the struggle of the armed masses who within the space of a few days had destroyed the hypertrophied military machine. At the same time, the development of the democratic-constitutional revolution depended (and still depends) on united mass action for immediate objectives and the gradual winning of these objectives.

The political consciousness of our people had risen to the point where they succeeded in launching an armed uprising against their *internal enemies*. They knew who these enemies were and they dealt them defeat after defeat. However, at the moment when the U.S. troops landed, our people were not prepared to offer organised resistance to their main, *external* enemy. The opinion of the fighters differed as regards the object of the U.S. intervention. Many actually believed that the Americans had landed for the purpose of protecting the people from Wessin's air attacks, or to ensure the return of Bosch. It was thanks to this initial confusion that the USA was able to begin landing troops without immediately encountering the armed resistance of our people.

Only the more politically advanced among the participants in the struggle saw at once the real object of the U.S. intervention. The Communist Party explained the situation to the masses and predicted that events would very soon reveal the true purpose of the U.S. action. That is precisely what happened. Within a few days the interventionists, who had begun by using the "gingerbread" method, handing out corn flour, Coca-Cola and ice cream, took recourse to armed force. Vigorous action on the part of the population of the capital, however, eventually halted their offensive.

At that point, however, the constitutionalist leadership was taken unawares by the proposal for a "cease fire" and the signing of an "act of reconciliation." In these negotiations the U.S. troops and the remainder of the Dominican reactionary forces, the OAS delegates and the Papal Nunico represented a bloc of world reaction poised in opposition to the progressive forces of the modern world. One might say that the lack of anti-imperialist consciousness which caused the temporary wavering of the masses at the time of the U.S.

troop landing was to a great extent reflected in the position of the military-political leadership when it agreed to the cease fire and the establishment of a "safety zone" and a U.S. cordon. The cease fire and the terms on which it was enforced at this juncture (the precise moment when the revolution was on the ascendant, and when a major offensive had been launched against the San Isidro base) only facilitated the penetration of U.S. troops and the rearming of Wessin's forces. At the same time it isolated the revolutionary movement inside the city, with the territory occupied by the constitutionalists, moreover, cut in half by the "international safety zone." The armed uprising now passed from the offensive to the defensive.

This was a serious setback for the movement. Before long, however, when events revealed the real object of the imperialist intervention, the vacillation in the leadership ended.

Around the beginning of May, when the capital, occupied by the constitutionalist forces, was surrounded by U.S. troops, when the entire Dominican people supported the struggle in Santo Domingo and the movement of international solidarity was steadily mounting, negotiations began. (It was at this time that Caamano was elected constitutional President.)

Realising that the military and political situation at this time did not augur well for their success at the negotiation table, the imperialists decided to change that situation. Around the middle of May, in violation of the cease fire, they permitted and helped Wessin's forces, newly armed by them, to attack the northern part of the capital. For over a week a bloody and unequal battle was fought in this quarter. The resistance of the defenders of the northern zone was no less heroic than that of the fighters in the southern part of the town operating later against direct attack by the U.S. forces. But here the situation was complicated by the lack of weapons, terrain affording little cover, and the absence of trenches, anti-tank barriers and well-fortified barricades. Besides, insufficient use was made of guerrilla tactics in courtyards and back alleys. Added to this was the lack of co-ordination and centralised command, which made itself increasingly felt as the ring of U.S. troops tightened around this sector, isolating it more and more from the neighbouring sector where the main leaders were and which was better supplied with arms and reserves. On May 22–23 organised resistance in the northern zone ended. Part of its defenders succeeded in joining up with the main forces of the constitutionalists, but hundreds fell in battle or were shot down in cold blood on the streets by the military.

At the end of May the negotiations were resumed. Representatives of the OAS, the United States' "ministry of the colonies," participated in the talks not as mediators but as spokesmen for imperialism, the oligarchy and the military putschists. (It is not for nothing that the constitutionalists repeatedly appealed to the United Nations to mediate between the OAS and those it represented, on the one hand, and the national-democratic movement, on the other.)

At first the constitutionalists went to the talks without any definite plan, and this gave the imperialists and their skilled diplomats certain advantages. However, a plan was finally worked out on the basis of Caamano's "five points" providing for the restoration of the 1963 Constitution, reconvening the National Congress, the participation of democratic leaders in the future government, retention by the constitutionalists of commanding posts in the army and the immediate withdrawal of foreign troops.

Early in June an agreement was concluded on this basis. Understanding was reached on the establishment of a constitutional government headed by Antonio Guzman (a landowner and member of Bosch's party who had held the post of minister of agriculture in his government and had the reputation of being a democrat). Moreover, until then Guzman had been regarded with favour by U.S. officials and by Johnson himself. But the United States government went back on the agreement following the intervention of Thomas Mann and his backers.

The imperialists resorted to diverse manoeuvres to wrest further concessions from the constitutionalists. On June 15 and 16, in an effort to secure better bargaining positions, they launched a major offensive in which U.S. troops took part openly for the first time. The people, however, put up a heroic resistance, showing that they were prepared to die fighting rather than permit the "peaceful" occupation of Free Santo Domingo by foreign troops. The imperialists had not expected the constitutionalists to hold out for more than 24 hours, but the fighting continued for 48 hours without abating. After the enemy attack had been halted at the cost of considerable losses for the constitutionalists (nearly 30 per cent of whose territory was captured) a cease fire was arranged with the help of the United Nations. The U.S. forces lost heavily in the engagement. The valiant resistance offered by the masses in these two days gave fresh impetus (though not immediately) to the international solidarity movement which had begun to wane.

It was thanks to the heroism of the fighting men and also to the lessons of the actions fought in the northern sector of the city that the constitutionalists were able to repulse the enemy in the June 15 and 16 fighting. They had strengthened their defences, dug trenches, converted ordinary jeeps armed with heavy machine guns (some taken from tanks damaged in the fighting) and protected with sheet steel into makeshift "armoured carriers," employed more mobile fire power and made extensive use of anti-tank ditches, mines and other obstacles. Guerrilla tactics too were employed with greater effect. At the same time propaganda conducted among the masses and in the "commandos" strengthened the conviction that the invaders could be driven out provided the people united their forces and waged a resolute struggle.

9. Negotiations with the Imperialists

The imperialists called off their offensive because of the armed resistance of the Dominican masses and the growing indignation of people all over the world. Immediately after the fighting of June 15 and 16, however, taking advantage of the new balance of military strength, they advanced proposals which ruled out the possibility of a government being established on the basis of the 1963 constitution and thereby rejected in effect the basic demands of the Dominican people.

After the events of June 15 and 16 it became clear to the U. S. State Department that to score a military victory and to break the resistance of the revolutionaries the constitutionalist sector of Santo Domingo would have had to be reduced to rubble and its defenders and the population generally exterminated. In view of this the offensive, undertaken in the hope of being able to occupy Santo Domingo within the space of a few hours and thereby to face the world with a *fait accompli,* was conceded to be a failure.

The imperialists realised that the total destruction of the constitutionalist sector would have only increased the hatred of the Dominicans for the invaders and their local allies, and led to the establishment of a military dictatorship and still heavier fighting in the immediate future. The political crisis would have remained as acute as ever with no prospect of stable government. Moreover, a massacre of the constitutionalists would have given new impetus to the protest movement in Latin America, in the United States itself, and throughout the world, aggravating the difficulties in which imperialism found itself as a result of the intervention. These considerations strengthened the positions of those sections of the imperialists and their Latin American servitors who advocated negotiations as a tactical move best able to perpetuate their rule in our country and throughout Latin America.

These groups realised that only by means of a compromise with the constitutionalists was it possible to achieve relatively stable government.

On their part the constitutionalists were compelled to negotiate a political settlement inasmuch as it was impossible, so long as they were completely surrounded, to win a military victory over the army of intervention such as that won in April over the San Isidro generals. As the negotiations got under way it also became clear that only complete victory of the revolution (which was made impossible by the U.S. intervention) could have restored the 1963 Constitution with all its implications. To have insisted on this demand as the only acceptable solution to the national crisis would have been tantamount, under the circumstances, to refusal to negotiate and plunging headlong into a frontal military collision with the enemy in a situation favourable to the latter.

In view of this, the constitutionalist government put forward in its talks with the Organisation of American States a counter-proposal which roughly incorporated the project advanced by the U.S. proconsuls and provided for the establishment of a provisional government and elections in nine months' time. At the same time, however, the constitutionalist proposal, reflecting the aspirations of the people who wanted to see democratic freedoms restored and the army of intervention withdrawn at the earliest possible date, called for a revision of many of the stipulations of the original OAS draft. It was underscored that the guarantee of the realisation of the popular demands was vigilance and militancy on the part of the people, and certainly not the commitments that might be undertaken by the representatives of an imperialist power notorious for its readiness to go back on its word.

Our Party was fully aware that although negotiations as a way out of the crisis were an expedient forced upon us which did not meet the democratic aspirations of the people, they nevertheless made it possible for the revolutionary forces to fall back in an organised way and escape the imperialist military encirclement with the least losses and under conditions favourable for a subsequent regrouping of forces and renewal of the revolutionary struggle in more propitious circumstances.

In other words, the enemy was able to force the rebels to go over from the offensive to positional defence. Consequently, our political demands too could not remain unchanged. From a popular armed offensive, the highest form of revolutionary struggle, the movement had to go over to negotiations and political concessions. A compromise became imperative since we could not defeat the enemy on the battlefield. The balance of forces may at times necessitate exceedingly unpleasant compromises, but this is not a reason for despair if the object of the compromise is not surrender but better political and military preparation of the masses for new battles.

"It would be a crime from the standpoint of the defence of the country to engage an immeasurably stronger and better prepared enemy in battle knowing that you do not have an army," Lenin said. "From the standpoint of the defence of the country we are obliged to sign the most onerous, the most oppressive, the most harsh and ignominious peace—not to 'capitulate' to imperialism but to learn and to prepare to fight him in a serious, proper way." It was by this counsel that our Party was guided in giving its support to the constitutionalist government at that grave and trying moment when it was necessary to abandon at the negotiation table demands for which thousands of Dominican patriots had laid down their lives.

At the same time two erroneous approaches crystallised in regard to negotiations and the practical tasks of the movement.

The Right-wing, conservative elements in the movement exaggerated from the outset the military strength of imperialism and underestimated both our ability to resist and the heroism of the Dominican people and other peoples who stood by us against the common enemy. For these elements any resistance to imperialism spelled meaningless sacrifice and defeat; they sowed pessimism and defeatism in the ranks of the fighters. "We must find a way out as soon as possible, we can no longer resist, we must accept what the Yankees propose!"— this was the cry of those with little faith in the masses and the revolution.

On the other hand, the ultra-revolutionaries, those "without a blot on their escutcheon," who would not "enter into any compromise with imperialism or the bourgeoise," took a diametrically opposite stand, demonstrating their utter lack of understanding of Marxist method. They minimised the military potential of imperialism and argued that no concession should be made to it, for this allegedly meant betraying the revolution. They tried to persuade the masses that the Constitution of 1963 could be restored and the immediate withdrawal of the interventionist troops brought about through negotiation.

The Right-wing opportunists considered imperialism omnipotent and hence pressed for abject submission to its dictates. For the ultra-Left, imperialism was weak and hence it did not have to be taken seriously; these people, reiterating the catchword "we shall remain firm," thought the negotiations could be dragged out endlessly.

The conservative position was shared by the Right-wing of the DRP and groups of the national bourgeoisie who "privately" took part in the struggle. The leadership of the Revolutionary Social Christian Party published declarations in support of the "untainted" position (i.e., the position that the 1963

Constitution afforded the only basis for negotiations) while some of its members spread defeatism in the masses. Eventually, however, this party supported the proposal of the constitutional government.

The Dominican Popular Movement adhered throughout to an ultra-Left stand, rejecting negotiations out of hand. It charged the government and those who supported its proposals with "betrayal" and "conciliation."

The Revolutionary June 14 Movement, although it did not agree with the position of the constitutionalist government, nevertheless did not wish to sow dissension in the masses. It published an ambiguous proposal suggesting that the role of mediator be transferred from the OAS to the United Nations (thereby recognising the OAS as mediator at the time), yet qualifying both organisations as "instruments of North American neocolonialism." While maintaining that the negotiations should be conducted on the basis of the 1963 Constitution, the June 14 Movement refrained from levelling charges of betrayal and conciliation at those who supported the proposals of the government. Its position was synthesised in the formula: "support for the government but no negotiations." The duality of the Movement's attitude was a reflection of the erroneous understanding of struggle for the purity of political line which prevailed in this organisation worthy of the esteem of the Dominican people, an organisation with an irreproachable revolutionary record but not always with the correct political orientation.

The negotiations lasted for more than two months, during which period there was no diminution of vigilance or resolve to fight the perfidious enemy who sought to terrorise the civilian population by keeping residential quarters under mortar fire night after night.

More was done during these months for the defence of Free Santo Domingo than on the eve of the actions of June 15–16. New fortifications were built and systematic political work conducted in the commandos to forestall the dissension threatened by the spread of Right-wing defeatist attitudes. Mass demonstrations were organised which showed that the people stood firmly behind their sons and daughters who had taken up arms in defence of national sovereignty and democracy. At the initiative and under the leadership of the Revolutionary June 14 Movement (which came to carry the greatest weight in the armed forces), a military school (April 24 Academy) was established both for the fighting men and unarmed reservists. Until then training for armed action had been given on the go, which cost the movement many unwarranted losses.

All this prepared the masses for the decisive and inevitable battles to come against the powerful enemy, battles for aims the achievement of which had been checked temporarily by the intervention. These measures strengthened the hand of the constitutionalists at the negotiating table, showing as they did their resolve to repel, at a moment's notice and at whatever cost, any armed offensive the enemy might undertake.

In the course of the prolonged discussion of proposals and counter-proposals, which the enemy deliberately dragged out in the hope of weakening the constitutionalist position, imperialism had to make concessions. Stipulations providing for the restoration of all civil liberties and prohibiting the sale or resale of state property were included in the Institutional Act by which the provisional government was to be guided. At the final phase of the negotiations, when the so-called Dominican Act of Reconciliation was deliberated, an attempt was made to open the doors to immediate political persecution and to empower to this end the "inter-American Peace Force" to confiscate all weapons in the hands of civilians. This move was foiled by the threat of a breakdown in the negotiations. The solution of this delicate problem was finally entrusted to constitutionalist officers, which made it possible to effect an organised retreat. Similarly, agreement was reached to reinstate all constitutionalist officers, including those who had been discharged from the army because of their democratic views before the uprising of April 24.

Our Party maintained that it was extremely important during the negotiations to compel the imperialist to set the exact date for the withdrawal of their troops so as to provide the movement with a basic demand around which the struggle could be continued. However, this aim was not achieved because, firstly, the negotiations followed a pattern laid down by the enemy, with priority given to the search for a candidate for president and examination of the basic issues and concretisation of the fundamental commitments left until later. Secondly, the composition of the negotiators on behalf of the movement did not adequately reflect the real sentiment of the armed masses (spokesmen of the Right occupied a disproportionately big place among them). Thirdly, the differences caused by the defeatist attitudes of some and the splitting activities of others afforded imperialism an opportunity to advance more and more demands, whereas the representatives of the movement knew that time was not on their side. There was open disagreement among the negotiators for the movement as to the time limit for the withdrawal of U.S. troops; some wanted to leave the matter to Garcia Godoy, while others insisted on the immediate signing of a document on this question. In the end the more conservative and conciliatory group got the upper hand. But at the same time the movement as a whole reserved the right to carry on the struggle for its original aims and for the withdrawal of the interventionist troops.

The provisional government was thus created as a result of U.S. intervention, a government completely without the support of the people and the national political forces (with the exception of cases when one or another positive or negative move on its part has the corresponding backing of either progressive or reactionary groups). The Garcia Godoy administration has no army apart from the interventionist troops. This is a new element in the Dominican situation.

10. The Present Political Situation and the Perspectives

After the establishment of the provisional government, consolidation of the gains of the April uprising began throughout the country. When the participants in the movement returned from the constitutionalist zone to their own districts campaigns were organised against those government employees who had been involved in the 1963 *coup* and the subsequent repressions. The workers of the state-owned Azucarera Haina company (the republic's main sugar producer, with assets running to $100 million), by means of a general strike and subsequently by direct mass action, threw out the managers appointed by the triumvirate. The same happened at all other state-owned companies. At the same time workers and office employees dismissed for patriotic activities were reinstated in their jobs.

A few days before the withdrawal of the constitutionalist armed detachments, the political forces supporting the movement began discussing the formation of a united front of struggle for the common aims which still remain to be achieved. There still are differences on this question, and especially as regards the organisational structure of the united front. The Revolutionary Social Christian Party is against any united front with the Communists "on principle" and, though favouring united action, is opposed to organisational unity. The Right wing of the DRP steers clear of any joint statements with the Communists, although it in practice accepted co-operation and united action with them. The more progressive sector of this party is not opposed to unity of all constitutionalist groups. The three Left parties are already working to build a nation-wide united front. The differences of a secondary nature among them as regards a common programme are being overcome in the course of practical actions.

We believe that the durable popular unity achieved in the recent struggle will make it possible, on the basis of the continued practical development of this struggle, to overcome the existing disagreements. The entire people is ready to fight for the withdrawal of the occupation forces and for the 1963 Constitution. The establishment on this basis of a united front which will give battle to the invaders and defeat them is today the paramount organisational task of the popular movement.

The chief obstacle to the development of the Dominican revolution is the presence of imperialist troops. Their expulsion by popular action would pave the way to immediate revolutionary changes in the economic structure of the country.

The basic form of struggle essential for defeating the enemy and establishing revolutionary government is armed struggle—not only against the reactionary segment of the army but also against the powerful imperialist aggressor.

The Communist Party is working towards the realisation of this momentous immediate task—the expulsion of the U.S. troops from our country. At the same time we proclaim as our ultimate aim the building of socialism and communism, the only social system which will abolish exploitation.

The contemporary Dominican scene is marked by a powerful upsurge of mass struggle. The forces of intervention are trying to intimidate the democrats, and clashes take place between troops and demonstrators. Popular feeling is running high. The people remain united in the fight for the original aims of the movement and against the intervention. It may be said that this unity and the heightened political consciousness of the masses are the most important result of the five months of armed struggle.

The oligarchy and its politicians, defeated and lacking mass support, are resorting to terror and are whetting the dictatorial appetites of some generals. It is not excluded that a naked military tyranny may be installed. Hence it is imperative to combine the struggle to carry further the gains won and to secure the withdrawal of foreign troops with the struggle against putschist schemes.

The terror unleashed by the Right underscores the urgency of organising self-defence groups. This task has already been tackled. It was begun even before the barricades of the constitutionalist zone were taken down and before its fighting forces returned to their respective districts throughout the country.

For the first time a powerful fight for the land is developing in the countryside. The peasants are demanding division of the latifundia which once belonged to Trujillo and later passed over to the army officers and landlords behind the *coup*. The arrest of hundreds of peasants in the La Vega area and the emergence of new contradictions among diverse groups of the military with regard to this problem paves the way to the growth of a strong guerrilla movement fighting for the peasants' demands. In the long run this movement is destined to become part of the mustering of the entire people for a new country-wide uprising.

All the manoeuvres and aggressive actions of imperialism are encountering the resistance of a people united and ready for battle under the watchword: "Yankees, get out of the Dominican Republic!"

INDEX

INDEX

Abbes García, Johnny, 51, 58, 59, 62, 66, 281, 296, 747; Bosch assassination plot, 526 ff.

Acheson, Dean, 48

Act of Bogotá, 726

Acton, Lord, 610

Adenauer, Konrad, 309

ADI (*Acción Dominicana Independiente*): Bosch, 448; leaders, 501; membership, 358, 398; rise, 403

AFL-CIO, international arm. *See* ORIT

Africa: politics, 719; revolution, 14

Agency for International Development. *See* AID

Agrarian reform, 97, 111, 114, 115, 119, 132, 151, 186, 187, 297; AID, 146 and n (*see* AID); Bosch, 352 n, 462–63; land laws, 459 (*see* Land)

Agrarian Reform Institute, 124, 186, 187, 216, 456, 457, 516–17; Communists, 211; salaries, 356

Agrarian Reform Law, 554 n

Agricultural Bank, 186, 187

Agriculture, Minister of, 367

AID (Agency for International Development), 7–8, 86, 97, 110, 120, 121, 136, 145, 146 and n, 148, 156, 157, 299, 352–53, 375, 389, 450–51, 494, 516, 517, 638; Bosch, 309, 354, 370; bureaucracy, 372; chief, 328, 601; functioning of, 145–46; Hickenlooper amendment, 355; Martin, 149, 722, plan, 471; personnel, 471; projects, 146 and n, 181, 216; record, 721 n; reforms, 137; restrictions, 370; sugar problem, 163–64; Washington, 145–46; Yaque del Sur, 520. *See* Williams, Newell

Air Force, 36, 78, 82, 116, 205, 254; Communists, 211; equipment, 95, 532–33; size, 118. *See* Armed Forces

Alba de Moya, Silvestre, 366

Albania, 764

Alcoa. *See* Aluminum Company of America

Alexander the Great, 43

Alfau, Enrique J., 498, 548, 747

Algiers, 143

Alianza, 165, 170, 186, 320, 517; spirit of, 104. *See* Alliance for Progress

Allen, Frederick Lewis, 619

Allen, Ward, 606

Alliance for Progress, 5, 13, 121, 320, 602; Bosch, 269, 358, 361, 370; Consejo, 163–64, 172; Coordinator, 137; Johnson, 626, 736; Kennedy, 65, 247, 616, 726–28, 737; status quo, 740. *See* Alianza

Aluminum Company of America (Alcoa), 105–6, 107, 301, 357, 533

Alvarez Holguin, Pedro Augusto, 645

Álvarez, Horacio, 399, 400

Álvarez Pina, Virgilio, 525

Alvares Sánchez, Braulio, 527

American Civil Liberties Union, 100

American Jewish Joint Distribution Committee, 190

American Legion, 149

American University, 475

Amiama Castillo, 486

Amiama Tió, Luís, 7, 12, 13, 53–63, 66, 87, 88, 99, 106–7, 110, 170–71, 228, 594, 701, 747; assassin, 99, 153, 203, 204, 219–20, 258; Bosch, 313, 360, 387–88, 523; characteristics, 95, 153, 154, 204–6; Consejo, 114; elections, 158, 159, 207 ff., 214; family, 151, 301;

general, 252–56, 264–66, 280; -Imbert coalition, 224 ff.; Martin, 156; military, the, 115, 119, 204–5, 484 ff., *golpe*, 541 ff.; missile crisis, 243; plots, 126, 166–67; power play, 204–5, 217–22, 224 ff., 230, 246 ff., 273–78; security, 209 ff.; supporters, 250, 251; Triumvirate, 588

Amiama Tió, Señora, 270

Amnesty, 677

Anatomy of a Murder, 474

Anderson, Sherwood, 407

Angelita, 36, 83, 153, 175, 181 and n, 182; cruise, 215–24

Annihilation, politics of, 719

Anti-Americanism, 29, 85, 98, 125 n, 127, 129, 142–43, 151, 156, 251, 407; Bosch, 326, 349, 358, 407; center, 357; Communists, 99, 131; Duvalier, 417; rebels, 687; Triumvirate, 606

Anti-Semitism, 191, 212

AP (Associated Press), 291, 495

ARA (American Republics Area), 620

Arache, Manuel Ramón Montes, 747

Arawak Indians, 19

Arévalo, Juan José, 309, 394

Argentina, 89, 128, 393, 602, 604, 632, 724; Bosch, 327; racism, 724

Aristy, Héctor, 669–71, 688, 698, 747

Arkansas Gazette, 375

Armed Forces, 80, 117–18, 141, 158, 234, 254, 360, 435, 436 n, 487, 664; Bosch, 276, 313, 322–23, 432 n, 354, 437–38, 446–47, restoration, 648; Consejo, 93, 114–15, 313; conspiracies, 82, 83, 644 ff.; Constitution, 328; control of, 252–55; counter-insurgency troops, 141, 145, 156, 664; equipment, 95, 532–33, 545 (*see* Hawker Hunter deal); generals: corruption, 664, decree, 252–56, 264–66, 273–74, 283; *golpe,* 535 (*see under* the Military); Haitian crisis, 425 ff.; headquarters, 567; high command, 323 (*see under* name); loyalty, 117; motto, 118; power, 91; purge, 114–15, 119; purpose, 117; size, 118. *See* Amiama; Imbert, power play; Civil War

Armed Forces Training Center, 484

Armstrong, Louis, 419 and n, 732

Army, 28, 29, 42–43, 205; size, 118; Trujillo, 117, 434–35; U.S., 141. *See* Armed Forces

Arvelo Delgado, Tulio, 47, 357, 365, 747

ASD (*Alianza Social Democratica*), 137, 236, 388, 754; Confiscation Law, 495; elections, 199 n, 201, 307; *golpista* Cabinet, 595 n

Ashmore, Harry, 375

Asia, 726; Southeast, 14, 719, 725, 737

Assassin, 6 n, 94, 256, 258. *See* Amiama; Imbert

Association of Industries, 400

Asylum, right of, 541

Auffant, Marino, 388, 502–3, 747; Bosch, 448, 449

Austria, 189–90

Aybar Castellanos, José, 501, 747

Aza. *See* Castillo de Aza, Zenon

Azua, 20, 21, 102–4, 105, 186

Backer, George, 624

Baez, Buenaventura, 20–21, 22–23, 345, 483, 747

Baez Díaz, Miguel Ángel, 55, 62, 747, 749

Baez family, 308

Baez, Ramón, 483

Bailey, Austin, 9, 85, 142–43, 182, 184, 261

Balaguer, Joaquin, 40, 60, 77, 136, 252, 279, 713, 747; candidacy, 263–64, 271; characteristics, 77; "democratization," 78, 712; elections, 246, 701–2; exile, 84–85, 93, 637; Martin on, 81–82; military *golpe,* 586; opposition, 70–71, 83, 87, 89; popularity, 639; President, 54, 59, 65, 75, 639; reform, 137; return, 270–71, 289, 699; successor, 83; supporters, 82–83, 224, 541; Trujillo, 77, Ramfis, 78–79 (*see* Trujillo, Ramfis); U.S., 82, 347

Balagueristas, 629, 682

Ball, George, 120, 121, 123, 299, 471, 612, 640; Bosch, 308; Casasnovas, 604–5; Haiti, 441–42; recognition issue, 630 ff., Triumvirate, 601

Ball, Maurice, 474

Ballots, 272, 275–76

Baquero, Luís Manuel, 12, 111–12, 207,

247, 280, 281, 747; Bosch, 266;
campaign, 268 ff., 284 ff.; generals'
decree, 254
Barahona, 104–5, 109, 136, 307
Barbot, Clement, 439, 442, 446
Barletta, Amadeo, 448, 449
Barrios (slums), 106, 136–37, 138, 139,
152, 268, 319, 372
Batista, Fulgencio, 74; Castro, 117,
675–76; Trujillo, 50
Bautista Vicini Burgos, Juan, 30
Baylor University, 699
Bay of Pigs, 25, 65, 123
Bazalon, David, 299
Beata (island), 106
Belaunde, Terry, 730
Belgium, 26
Bell, David, 471, 601, 626
Bell & Howell, 381
Ben Bella, 443, 446
Benítez, Jaime, 374, 677–79
Benítez, Rexach, 525 ff.
Bennett, W. Tapley, 638, 639, 645–46,
684–85, 722; Civil War, 651 ff.;
Martin on, 705
Benoit, François, 423, 424, 428, 437,
440, 445
Benoit, Pedro Bartolomé, 655, 681, 682,
747; military junta, 656, 657
Beras, Octavio A., 286, 289, 293, 294,
747
Berlin: crisis (1950s), 740; Wall, 123
Bermúdez de Batlle, Ana Idalia, 75–76
Bermúdez de Batlle, Erasmus, 76
Bermúdez family, 308, 448
Bernardino, Felix, 66
Berry, Lorenzo ("Wimpy"), 12, 85,
330, 599
Berry, Mrs. Lorenzo, 12
Betancourt, Rómulo, 51–52, 210, 224,
283, 314, 330, 338, 392, 464; as-
sassination plot, 331, 332; Bosch,
316, 343, 428, 440–41, 451; Civil
War, 689 and n, 690; Communists,
406; inaugural, 331, 339; Tru-
jillo, 51, 339, 430; U.S., 51
Bethesda Naval Hospital, 201, 206, 335
Biambi, Colonel, 437
Birth rate, 373
Blanco Genoa, Moises, 649
Blas Roca, 129, 130, 174, 356
Bloodbath, 674–76
Bobadilla, Frank, 422, 423, 433

Boca Chica, 36
Bolívar, Simón, 20, 726
Bolívar de León, Lieutenant, 182, 183
Bolivia, 428
Bonao, 39, 66, 124, 132
Bonilla Atiles, José Antonio, 7, 8, 9,
12, 13, 140–42, 240, 279, 606, 612,
626, 747; Bosch, 315, 451; elections, 202, 234–35, 238–39; Haiti,
155–56
Bonilla Atiles, Mrs. Dora, 12, 239
Bonilla Aybar, Rafael, 168, 229, 393,
501, 548, 652, 715, 747; arrest,
398–401, 455; assessment, 718;
Bosch, 494
Bonnelly, Rafael F., 4, 6, 7, 8, 12, 13,
83, 85, 87, 88, 90–93, 102, 109,
110, 114, 124, 155, 201, 248, 257,
305, 747; Ambassador to Venezuela, 89; Armed Forces, 118–19,
145, 176, 181–82, 208; assassination threat, 283; assessment, 718;
background, 345; Bosch, 316–17,
452–53, 537, 539; Castro, 92–93;
characteristics, 88–90, 115, 194,
274, 280, 369; Consejo accomplishments, 295; Cuban missile
crisis, 236, 239–43; election(s),
159, 181, 200–1, 297–98, (1966),
701–2, campaign, 208 ff., 222, 225,
230–34, 237; family, 177, 200–1,
272, 279; friends, 279; generals'
decree, 253–55; labor, 192–93;
Martin, 88–89, 306–7, 615–18,
620–21; office, transfer of, 314–
15; oligarchy, 133; power, 217;
Secretary of State of Interior and
Police, 89; State Department paper,
616–18, 620–21; sugar crisis, 164–
65, 166, 169, 170–72, 174; tactics,
90, 326; Trujillo, 89; U.S. support, 93, 194, 271; whistlestopping,
409
Bonnelly, Mrs. Rafael F., 12, 193–94,
195, 215, 609
Bonsal, Philip W., 533
Bordas, Diego, 46, 350, 353, 359, 360,
369, 456, 748; Bosch, 525 ff., Minister of Commerce and Industry,
364, 365; resignation, 402
Bosch, Barbarita (daughter), 460, 493
Bosch, Juan, 46, 56 n, 71, 112–13, 158,
159, 161, 198, 199 n, 266, 322–

23, 397, 748; administration, 343 ff., 359, 361–63, 368 ff., 374, 387, 453 ff., assessment, 716, attacks on, 402, breakup, 403–4, corruption, 402; "agitation in power," 390; ambition, 395; Armed Forces, 322–23; assassination attempt, 394–95, 523 ff.; background, 343–46; beliefs, 180 n; bodyguards, 312, 328; Cabinet, 310, 330, 336, 354–55, 359, 360, 364–68, 407, 502, 503, 520, 529, 575; campaign, 266 ff., 280–81, 293 ff., 412 (see whistlestopping); Casasnovas, 604; characteristics, 112, 179–80, 180 n, 201, 206–13, 228, 269, 288, 299, 315–16, 320, 343–46, 353, 362, 364, 371, 390–91, 421, 429, 438, 458, 461–62, 716; charges against, 213; Church, 283–90; Civil War, 666, 668, 669; communism, 347; confidant, 309–10 (see Sacha Volman); Consejo, 313–16, 324; constitutional successors, 571; coup d'etat (see military golpe); crisis of confidence, 451 ff.; criticisms, 398; deportation, 594; Duvalier, 394–95, 417, 424, 430, 441, 442, 446 (see Haitian crisis); elections, 159, 178 ff., 199–201, 249, 701–2; Europe, 309, 324, loan, 370–71 (see British Overseas contract); exile, 20, 51, 113, 200, 258, 344, 462, 603, 637, politician, 499; fall of, 547 ff., U.S. reaction, 593 ff.; family, 288, 524; Fiallo, 225, 228, 230; friends, 367, 448, 539, 594; Haitian crisis, 423 ff., 434–35; Haitian exiles, 418; handicaps, 363; hangers-on, 361–64, 369, 410; homecoming, 321 ff., speech, 324–27, 338; hundred days, 458; Imbert, 254, 310, 313, 316–17, 322–23, 326–27, 348–49, 360, 387–88, 391, 413, 594; imprisonment, 587; inauguration, 299, 314–15, 319, 327, 330–40, 449, address, 336–38; issues, 266–67, 267 n; Johnson, 339–40; Láutico García debate, 294; leftists, 357; Martin, 179–81, 320, 322–24, 348, 389, 395–96, 405, 436 n, 555–57, 666, 676–80, fight for, 475 ff., on, 329–30; masses, the, 334, 448, 450, 459, 721; Mella

cruise, 405–15; military golpe, 561 ff.; Miolán, 311, 312; mystique, 397; opportunity, 343; opposition to, 124, 316–17, 326–27, 346, 358, 360, 387, 397–98, 400, 451 ff., 497 ff., 533 ff., 537, 546; overthrow, 499, 573, 576–81, 583 ff., causes, 715 n, timetable, 722 n, U.S. position, 582, (see military golpe); party, (see PRD); planning, 308–10, 314 (see Volman, Sacha), board (see CIDES); plots, 314, 344, 354, 391, 396, 401; politics, 418, 449, 465, 556, 557, judgment, 462, philosophy, 349; power structure, 326–27; President, 15, 124, 511, desire for, 199–201, election, 297–300, 307–8; pressure on, 494 ff., 500 ff., 533 ff.; problems, 346 ff., 459, 479–80; program, 316–17, 324–25, 328–29, 331, 334, 336–38, 359, 361, 369, 394, 414, 458, 470, 487–88; promises, 513; reputation, 374; resignation, 487, 489, 573, 576–77; restoration, 640 ff., 654; return, 700, 706–7; revolution, 325, 343, 347, 353, 368–69, 413, 450, 487, 514, 563, 564; speeches, 390, 489–92, 495, 503–4; "summit" meeting, 225–29; supporters, 357, 477, 500, 721; tactics, 290–91, 296, 326, 344, 409, 429–30, 434, 446, 490, 508, 549; U.S., 269, 327, 418–19, 421, 429–30, 449, aid, 414–15, 470, 488, 504, 519–20, disaffection, 451–52, in, 298–300, 308–10, support of, 504, 545, 706; whistlestopping, 409–12; writings, 284–85, 299, 328, 344, 345, 368, 389, 436, 637, 684, 706 n–7 n. See Amiama, Imbert, military, the; PRD

Bosch, Mrs. Juan (Carmen), 276, 284, 285, 287, 288, 298, 300, 321, 322, 343, 361, 378, 396, 431, 441, 506–8, 748; Martin, 632; military golpe, 484 ff., 584–85

Bosch, Milagros (niece), 361, 406, 408, 460, 488

Bosch, Patricio (son), 298, 395–96, 701

Boschistas, 365, 366

Bowdler, Bill, 640

Boxer (aircraft carrier), 182, 193–95, 320, 332, 334, 425, 439, 444; Civil War, 664; task force, 434

Brademas, John, 335, 340, 471, 598
Bramble, Harlan, 145, 148, 151, 164, 239, 381, 310, 311, 351–52, 481, 494; Bosch, 496; sugar crisis, 165
Brazil, 699, 725, 726, 730; Dominican Republic, 581; inter-American forces, 699; President, 315
Brea, Dr. Aulio, 292
Brea, José, 483–84
British Overseas contract, 370–71, 372, 387, 452, 533
British West Indies, 34
Brossa, Dr. Jordi, 449
Brouwer, Pompilio, 224, 225, 248–51
Budget, 351, 352 n, 353, 356, 390, 450
Bulgaria, 197, 526
Bundy, McGeorge, 640, 656, 710; background, 695; Bosch, 695–96; Guzmán negotiation, 695 ff.
Bunker, Ellsworth, 651, 653, 657, 701, 710; peace mission, 699, 703
Burgués (bourgeois), 267 and n
Burke, Edmund, 346
Burt, Al, 464
Businessmen, 136, 140, 448, 500; Bosch, 359, 370; Council on International Understanding, 116; general strike, 546–48 ff.; U.S., 106, 615, 722. See Civicos
Bustamante, Alexander, 338

Caamaño, Fausto, 663
Caamaño Deño, Francisco, 644, 648, 649, 665 ff., 676, 687, 748; Bosch, 668, 669, 677; London, 701; Martin, 688–91; President, 683, 688
Caamaño Grullon, Claudio, 665
Cabo Rojo, 105, 140, 223, 301, 302, 307
Cabral, José María, 448, 449, 748; oligarchy, 133
Cabral, Manuel José, 136
Cabral, Marco, 133, 136, 140, 141, 505, 748
Cabral, Rosita, 140
Cabral family, 308
Cáceres, Luís Manuel, 62, 748
Cáceres, Mario, 138
Cáceres, Ramón, 12, 23, 26, 27, 138, 720, 748; assassination, 27
Cáceres family, 308, 557
Cáceres Troncoso, Ramón, 12, 279,

648, 649, 658, 748; Triumvirate, 637
Caesar, 43
Calderón, Juan, 328, 407, 552, 574, 748; Mella cruise, 405; military crisis, 484 ff.
Caldwell, Henry H., 488
Calié, 34 and n, 66, 91, 93; trails, 111, 114
Calventi, Arturo, 425, 441
Camelot, 625
"Caminero, Fran," 525
Compañero (companion), 267
Campbell, Anthony V. M., 212
Campesinos, 40, 88, 109, 110, 112 n, 113, 117, 132, 134, 136–37; Bosch, 308, 363; school, 113; vote, 207
Campo, 319
Canada, 330
Canal Zone, 236, 240, 242
Cantolla, Marc, 460, 504, 508–9, 511
Cape Canaveral, 182
Cap Haitien, 317, 437
Capotillo, 21
Caracas, 89, 284, 387, 406; Bosch, 113; FALN, 314
CARE, 146, 376, 377, 379, 385, 386
Caribbean, 5, 10, 16, 17, 48, 50, 210, 418; frontier, 17, Legion, 46–47; neutralism, 479; stability, 48
CARITAS, 146, 189, 379
Casado Saladin, Enrique Apolinar, 656, 748
Casals, Pablo, 460
Casasnovas Garrido, Juan, 266, 450, 574, 610, 616, 748; President of Senate, 368; President, 604–6; U.S., 607
CASC (Social Christian Labor Federation), 550, 557
Cascos Blancos, 122, 175, 193, 242, 312, 483, 664
Cass, Bev, 115, 166, 173, 175, 216, 223, 276, 303–5, 326–27, 481 ff., 504–5, 527 ff.; generals' decree, 253–54; military golpe, 539 ff.
Cassini, Igor, 712–13
Cassini, Oleg, 712
Castillo, Ramón, 198, 199 n, 201, 224, 225, 248–51, 570, 748
Castillo Cortes, Julio, 526 ff.
Castillo de Aza, Zenon, 525 ff., 532, 534–35, 614

Castro, Fidel, 5, 47, 50–51, 64, 66, 72, 74, 92, 95, 97, 193, 267, 285 n, 312, 320, 372, 478, 673, 733; Batista, 117; Bosch, 584; CIA, 451; Dominican Republic, 7, 8, 13, 50, 130, 494–95; Duvalier, 426; 14th of June, 113, 129; language, 267; missile crisis, 243; mystique, 397; "new Communists," 130, 174; power, 273, 726; revolution, 50, 129, 533; take-over, 533; U.S., 51, 66, 390, 463

Castro, Raul, 175

Castro/Communists, 20, 29, 47, 51, 69, 87, 88, 92–93, 97, 99, 106, 145, 151, 164, 174, 281, 347, 495, 496, 500, 676; Betancourt, 314; Bosch, 308, 359, 418, 419; Civil War, 673 ff.; dangers, 496, 735; effectiveness, 732, 735; election(s), 207–8, 246, 282; front (FNR), 199 n; labor, 126, 192–93; leaders, 100, 398, 647; line, 143; meaning of term, 128; missile crisis, 241; opposition, 93, 99–100; party, 199 (see PNR); split, 702

"Castroism," 654

Catholicism, 210. See Church

Catholic University (Santiago), 517

Caudillo, 33 n

Cayo Confites, 46–47, 158, 319; Bosch, 344

CBS, 291, 372, 449

Cédulas (identification cards), 16, 33, 41, 80, 203, 283; offices, 295; voting, 264

Center for the Study of Democratic Institutions, 375

Central America, 46

Centrales (sugar mills), 38

Cervantes, Miguel de, 625

Chalmers, Réne, 427, 531, 440

Chamber of Commerce of the Americas, 462, 463; Martin speech, 463 and n, 761–69

Charamicos, 190, 191

Charter of Punta del Este, 65, 487, 726–27 and n

Chayes, Abram, 472, 479

Chiang Kai-shek, 735

Chicago, 468

Chicago Daily News, 464

Chicago Tribune, 358, 455, 501

Children, 151, 376–86. See Higüey Clinic

Chile, 128, 428, 658; Bosch, 113

China. See Red China

Christian Democratic parties, 210

Christian Manifestations, 498, 500–5, 514, 528

Christian Science Monitor, 593–94

Christophe, Henri, 20, 317

Church: Bosch, 283–90, 326, 346, 430, 434, 498, 528; chaplains, 483 ff.; influence, 154; pastoral letter, 283–84, 286–87, 289; politics, 268, 283–92; power center, 448; Trujillo, 37, 52. See Papal Nuncio

Church, Frank, 597

Church World Services, 146

CIA (Central Intelligence Agency), 49, 87, 91, 92, 97, 115, 120, 121, 130, 173–74, 197, 331, 451, 528–29; Balaguer, 270–71; Bosch, 476; Civil War, 647 ff.; election(s), 206, 284; functions, 148; Haitian crisis, 442–43; Martin, 148; military golpe, 539 ff.; missile crisis, 243; Trujillo return, 281

Cibao (valley), 18, 21, 23, 24, 25–26, 284, 327; characteristics, 132; Martin, 125; oligarchy, 134

CIDES, 309, 310, 329, 457

Ciguapa, 155

Cincinnati Enquirer, 594

Ciudad Trujillo, 16, 36, 50, 65–66, 102, 344

Civic action programs, 480–81

Civicos, 360, 361–62, 500, 528, 715, 721; assessment, 718; Bosch, 448, 459, 501, 506–7, Cabinet, 367; general strike, 547 ff., 557; power center, 448

Civil liberties, 8, 316, 469; Bosch, 420

Civil War (1965), 15, 20, 492 n, 640 ff.; Armed Forces, 664; beginning, 674, 675; bloodbath, 674–76, 710; Bosch, 653, -Martin meeting, 676–80; casualties, 655, 674; causes, 708–10; cease-fire, 658 ff., 666, 668, 669, 671, 692; Communists, 654–55, 673–74; "Constitutional Military Command," 665; dangers, 661–62; inter-American forces, 699; International Zone, 660–61, 665, 670; loyalists, 645 n, 655, leaders, 701; Martin,

661 ff.; military junta, 656, 663, 701; OAS, 699 ff.; peace talks, 693, 694, mission, 699 ff.; police, 657; political solution, 685 ff.; political vacuum, 674; rebels, 645 n ff., 655, 687, 691, leaders, 655, 666, structure, 698; San Isidro generals, 665–66, 671 ff., 680–81, 685; U.S.: casualties, 699, citizens, 650, 656–58, evacuation, 646, 651, 652, 657, cost, 700, Marines, 652 ff., military: buildup, 662, 706, position, 676, policy, 653, 654, 660, 677, 678, 704 ff.

Clairmont Dueñas, Ramón de, 699

Claridad, 130–31, 167, 173

Clarizio Monseñor Emanuele, 150, 270, 283, 285–86, 292, 332, 377, 534, 612, 627, 743; Bosch, 286–87, 289–95, 503; Civil War cease-fire, 658, 660–69, 671 ff., 687; Confiscation Law, 495; Constitution, 429; Martin, 640, 723

Class(es): Bosch, 327; "issue," 266, 267 n; middle, 721; propertied, 316–17, 390, 495; structure, 112 n, 267 n, 417, 644

Cleveland, Grover, 720

Coastwatchers, 260–61

Coexistence, 357

Cold War, 129, 750; George C. Marshall, 741

Collins, LeRoy, 374, 375

Colombia, 20, 198, 306, 428, 626, 658

Colonialism, 189–90, 725; breakup, 708–9; symbol, 732

Color problem, 152–53, 190; revolutionary factor, 725

Columbia University, 48

Columbus, Bartholomew, 19, 36

Columbus, Christopher, 9–10, 19, 36, 68, 138 n; tomb, 19

Columbus, Diego, 19

Communism(ists), 7, 8, 13, 14, 29, 46, 50, 51, 95–96, 99–100, 126, 128, 129–31, 186, 412–13, 456–57, 726; activities, 72, 74, 92, 131, 211, 330, 331, 332; Bosch, 349, 357–58, 361, 387–97, 406–7, 439, 459, 465, 476; Catholicism, 210; Civil War, 641 ff.; doctrine, 128–29, 720; drift toward, 356 ff.; fear of, 510, 650; intellectuals, 99, 130; leaders, 129–

31 (*see under* name); military, the, 117, 127, 481 ff., 544; missile crisis, 236; -non-Communist struggle, 740; number, 129; objective, 131, 720; opposition to, 388; party (*see* PSP), Moscow Congress (1960), 357, 673 n; spread, 740; Trujillo, 40, 46, 48, 74, 80; U.S. political section's report, 456–58. *See* Castro/Communists; Havana; Moscow; Peking; *under* name of country

Community development, 147, 379, 382; AID, 146 n; Peace Corps, 146–47. *See* Higüey Clinic

Conatral, 483, 548–49, 550, 551

Concubinage, 316, 328

Conde, Héctor, 662–63, 668–69, 671, 687

Confidence, crisis of, 451 ff.

Confiscation Law, 495–97, 498, 554 n

Congo, 123, 719, 725

Congress of the International Union of Students, 128, 673 n

Connally, John, 621

Connett, William, 645, 649, 650, 652

Consejero, 51, 54, 55, 69, 90, 94, 257

Consejo de Estado (Council of State), 4, 6–13, 83, 84, 87, 274; accomplishments, 114, 295, 308; Bosch, 113, 289, 293 ff., 299, 309, 313–15, 353, 363, 452–53; characteristics, 85, 86, 111, 114, 308; Communists, 92–93; elections(s), 156–61, 178 ff., 192, 193, 196, 198–201, 207 ff., 233–34, 275; Emergency Law, 8, 91, 99; FENEPIA, 276; foreign policy, 295; generals' affair, 265; *golpe*, 526; labor, 193, 311; Martin plan, 92, 111; military, the, 93, 113–14, 118–19; missile crisis, 239–41, 243, 246; opposition, 93; personalities, 154; program, 97, 103, 137; split, 88; strength, 155–56; sugar crisis, 163–65, 169–73; supporters, 87–88, 160–61; terminal date, 107, 120, 156, 340; UCN, 111–12, 116; U.S., 347, aid, 145–46, 451, 470, policy, 224, 282. *See* Bonnelly, Rafael F.

Conspiracies, 715 n, 716

Constanza, 18, 50, 51, 145, 149, 282; invasion, 125 n, 155, 210; Martin, 154–55

Constitution, 24, 29, 31, 199, 295, 374, (1963), 429, 640 ff., 669; Bosch, 325, 361, 426, 428, 435, 568; defense of, 489; new, and opposition, 309, 316–17, 324, 326–28; promulgation, 426, 428, 429–30; Triumvirate, 589; Trujillo, 156

Constitutionalism, 31, 491, 492 n, 500, 580, 603, 610, 687, 690; Cutler, 730 and n; U.S., 588

"Continental fraternization," 295

Cooley, Harold, 162, 172; bill, 163, 164, 165, 168; Committee, 162–63

COPEI (Venezuelan Social Christian Party), 291

Cordillera Central, 18, 102, 140, 154, 187, 306, 375

Cortés, Hernando, 19, 103

Costa Rica, 13, 268, 283, 310, 344, 624, 658, 671; Bosch, 113; Caribbean Legion, 47; Dominican Republic, 584; government, 331, 724, Haiti, 442; Institute of Political Education, 113; inter-American forces, 699; Volman Institute, 368

Cottrell, Sterling, 596, 600 ff.

Counter-Reformation, 724

Cozumel (Mexican island), 47

Cramer, William C., 598

Crimmins, John, 85, 87, 111, 121, 164, 168, 255, 271, 289, 292, 299, 427, 471, 620; sugar crisis, 161 ff., 169–70, 173

Crises, 100, 119

Crockett, Kennedy, 471, 427 ff., 475, 634; Martin, 596; Triumvirate, 600 ff.

Crockett, William, 471

Cruzado Pena, 486

Cuba, 14, 21, 46–47, 50, 71, 72, 74, 92, 95, 99, 116, 128, 307, 330, 331, 436 n, 478, 496, 673 and n; Bosch, 113, 344, 361, 362, 465; Communists, power struggle, 130; Dominican Republic, 129, 356, 494, 496, 509–10; exiles (1960s), 47; guerrilla training, 673 and n; liberators, 345; missile crisis, 235–47, 253, 357, 616, 733–34; New China News Agency, 673 n; "old Communists," 129, 130; size, 17; Soviet Union, 116–17, 273; sugar, 161, 163; tourism, 18; 27th of February

Camp, 523; UN, 140; U.S., 332; Verde Oliva, 528. See Castro; Havana; Radio Havana

Cuello, Julio, 529

Cuello Hernández, José Israel, 643 n, 649

Cultists, 303–4

Curaçao, 21, 99

Cury, Jottin, 688, 691–92

Cutler, Lloyd, 371, 460, 461, 471, 730 and n

Czechoslovakia, 75, 128, 422, 424, 494–95

Dajabón, 306

d'Alessandro, Guido, 210–11, 213, 253–54, 391, 748

Darlan, Jean François, 711

David, 328

Day of the Three Kings, 306

DCM (Deputy Chief of Mission), 86, 92, 148, 253

DeGaulle, Charles, 274; Bosch, 309; Haitian crisis, 443, 444

Dejoie, 392, 441, 443

De la Maza, Antonio, 50, 53 ff., 61, 219, 548, 748

De la Maza, Ernesto, 59, 748

De la Maza, Octavio, 48–50, 53, 54, 748

De la Maza family, 60–61, 133

De la Rosa, Jesús, 665

De los Santos, Emilio, 584, 748; Triumvirate, 634, 637

De los Santos Céspedes, Juan, 648, 650, 701, 748

Del Rosario Ceballos, Enriquillo, 367, 471, 534, 604, 748

Del Rosario Ceballos, Luís, 366–67, 406, 408, 460, 480, 488, 500, 748

Democracy, 96, 127, 197, 227, 301, 627, 728; base, 196; Bosch: fall, 583, 593 ff., on, 517–18, 585–86; Dominican tragedy, 583; failure, reasons for, 715 ff.; free institutions, 719–20; history, 720; Kennedy, 616; in Latin America, 13, 584; meaning of, 159; military-civilian relationship, 117; politics of, 719; readiness for, 159–60; "showcase," 151; traditions, 80; Trujillo, 46

Democratic government, U.S. position on, 602
"Democratization," 65, 66, 76, 77–78, 80, 81, 712
De Moya, Manuel, 136
Deño Suero, Alejandro, 665
Deportations, 81, 91, 99–100, 125, 229, 247, 256, 257, 263, 485, 487, 524; Consejo, 347; political losers, 719; U.S., 477, 478
Deportees, U.S. controls, 347–48, 349, 350, 455 n, 456
Des Moines *Register*, 593
Despradel, Herman, 524, 653, 655, 656
Despradel Roque, Fidelio, 496, 647, 748; Civil War, 666, 673 and n
Dessalines, Jean Jacques, 19
"De-Trujilloization," 50
Díaz, Juan Tomás, 53–54, 55–56, 57, 58, 59, 60, 61, 219, 258, 548, 749
Díaz, Miguel Ángel Baez. *See* Baez Díaz, Miguel Ángel
Díaz, Modesto, 55, 62, 205, 749
Dictators, 50, 82, 89, 253, 256–57, 327, 359; Caribbean Legion, 46. *See under* name
Dictatorship, 97, 249; Bosch, 489, 518; Imbert, 273. *See* Trujillo
Diem regime, 613
Diplomacy, 125, 149–50, 236–38, 243, 575, 714; *aide mémoire*, 237–38; diplomatic corps, 150; dollar, 710, 726; gunboat, 726; *note verbale*, 237; protocol, 3–4, 5, 85, 88; U.S., 726
Diplomat Among Warriors, 712 n
Dirksen, Everett, 299, 603
Divorce, 316, 328
Doctors, 380, 381–82. *See* Health
Dollar diplomacy, 710, 726
Domínguez Guerra, Miguel Ángel, 358, 364–65, 388, 456, 551, 749; Bosch, 431
Domínguez Guerrero, Asdrúbal Ulises, 355, 647 and n, 729, 749
Dominican-Haitian problem, 416 ff.
Dominican Republic, 8–9, 17, 29, 98, 101–10, 165; affect on U.S. policies, 710; beauty, 105; culture, 19, 79; family, 11, 12, 257, 308; frontier, 306; fund for children's clinics, 377 and n; geography, 18; Haiti, 20, 77, 87, 107, 155–56, 203, frontier,

107, 108; heroes, 19, 50–51; history 18–32, 257, non-, 31–32 (*see* History); independence, 20, shrine, 419; Indians, 19, 105; language, 89, 90, 135 n, 267 and n; leaders, 22, 23, 24; life, 151–52, 406–7; problem, crux of, 139–40; protectorate, 20–22; relationships, 124; size, 17; Soviet Union, 128; Spain, 20, 21; sugar, 17, 38–39, 52; tourism, 18; U.S., 3–4, 20, 21, 26–28, 42–44, 64, 65, 75, 82–83, 87, 119, 156, 159–60, 196–97, 202, 322, 470, 480, 632, 639, 695 ff., aid, 7–8, 13, 48, 95, 97, 103, 116–17, 120, 121, 139, 142, 145–46, 281, 340, annexation, 22–23, Consulate, 98, 99, 120, deportees, 99–100, 347–48, 350, disengagement, 710, Embassy, 86, 101, 709–10, occupation, 28–31 (*see* U. S. Marines), policy, 120, 322, 741 (*see* Ambassador *under* Martin); Venezuela, 428
Dominicans, 14, 53, 79, 80, 105, 107, 108, 132, 151–54, 184, 274, 314, 379–80, 386, 417, 466, 690, 716–17; Bosch, 361, 362; Martin, 670–71; party, 282 (*see* PRD); responsibility, 716, 718, 719
DORSA, 190–92
Dos Passos, John, 407
Dostoyevsky, Fédor, 197, 739
Douglas, Paul H., 162, 299, 479, 599
Douglas, William O., 373–75, 471, 472, 549, 603
Drake, Sir Francis, 19
Duarte, Juan Pablo, 20, 21, 308, 337, 749
Dubois, Jules, 358, 455, 501
Ducoudray Mansfield, Juan, 129, 130, 174, 356–57, 358, 365, 458, 647, 673 and n, 749; Imbert, 263
Ducoudray Mansfield, Jr., Felix Servid, 130, 357, 458, 647, 673 and n, 749
Duke, Doris, 712
Dulles, John Foster, 48, 141
Dungan, Ralph, 122, 161, 164, 165, 169, 299, 471, 519–20, 596, 598, 599–602, 626, 627; Bosch, 476 ff., 608, 609, 610; recognition issue, 628–30
Durán Hernando, Jaime, 673 and n, 749
Duvalier, François (Papa Doc), 156,

307, 417, 418, 422–24, 442; assassination attempt, 422, 423; Bosch, 394–95, 417, 424, 430, 434, 436 n, 437, 441, 525 ff.; Castro, 426; Haitian crisis, 417 ff.; opposition, 87, 392, 418; "reelection," 126; *ton-ton-macoute*, 439; Trujillo, 416; tyranny, 318; UN, 438, 440; U.S., 156, 438

East Germany, 128
Echols, Lee, 650
Economic affairs, 17, 52, 102, 115–16, 139–40, 350, 450–51, 483; austerity, 352, 354, 638, 639, 709; Bosch, 346, 351–54, 454; British Overseas contract, 370–71, 372, 387, 452, 533; czar, 359 (*see* Diego Bordas); education, 373; Reid, 638
Ecuador, 253, 428; democracy, 584; military *golpe*, 481, 489
Education, 159, 186, 365, 372–75, 387, 398, 730; AID, 146 and n; television, 373, 374–75, 386, 479, 549. *See* Higüey clinic
Eisenhower, Dwight D., 52, 227, 478, 726; foreign policy, 141; Trujillo, 48
El Caribe, 34, 35, 37, 47, 84, 152, 158, 209, 211–12, 223, 262, 276, 290, 317, 398; Bosch, 495; election(s), 281, 285, 291–94, 296; military crisis, 488; publisher (*see* Germán Ornes)
Election(s), 111, 115, 131, 155, 178 ff., 192; (1924) 228; (1966) 701–2; AID, 146 n; ballots, 272, 275–76; campaign, 206–22, 233, 266 ff., 280 ff.; *campo* vote, 91; crisis, 195 ff.; Day, 297–98; Electoral Board, 157, 158, 159, 161, 192, 264, 275–76, 282, problems, 246; Electoral Law, 119, 156–57, 178, 181, 237; foreign interference, 291; four-point agreement, 225, 227–28; free, 77, 80, 87, 88, 157, 213, 224, 230, 246, 710, U.S. position, 227, 251; OAS, 111, 124, 284, 300; official vote, 307–8; press, 272, 276, 284 ff., 296; problems, 156–61, 246, 263 ff.; "readiness" for, 160; "summit" meeting, 225–29, 230, 231, 281, 300, 330; tickets, 264, 266; Triumvirate, 615, 617; Trujillo, 40;

U.S.: "intervention," 233–39, 243, policy, 224, 230, 282–83, 286, 292; whistlestopping, 189. *See* Amiama, power play, Imbert, power play
Electoral Law, 119, 156–57, 178, 181, 237
Electricity, 372–73, 383, 480, 670 and n
Elías Piña, 18, 318
El Mundo, 347
El Salvador, 428, 699
El Tiempo, 538
Emergency Law, 8, 91, 347, 349, 359, 502
Emerging nations, 719, 725
Enchanted Valley, 155, 167
Encyclopaedia Britannica, 375
Ends-means principle, 100
Engelman, Commander, 432
Enriquillo, 19, 105, 407
Era de Trujillo, La, 43, 77
Erickson Álvarez, Tomás Parmenio, 331
Espaillat, Arturo, 58, 749
Espaillat, Ulises Francisco, 23–24, 31, 177, 484, 720, 749
Espaillat, Victor, 136, 749
Espaillat Rodríguez, José, 357, 358, 365, 749
Española (the Spanish Isle), 19
Espionage, 25, 33, 35
Esquire, 16
Esso, 309, 310, 324–26; contract, 339, 350
Estero Hondo, 50, 51
Estévez Weber, Gerardo Rafael, 647
Estrella Jacobo, José, 398, 500
Estrella Sadhala, Salvador, 57, 61, 62, 749
Estrella Ureña, Rafael, 34, 43–44
Europe, 79, 128; Bosch, 309, 312, 324, 361, 362, 370; civil liberties, 8; Dominican Republic, 25, 26; Eastern, 38, foreign aid, 370, 473; Latin America, 26–27, 370; Western: communism in, 726, Marshall Plan, 728, political parties, 210
Evangelista Alejo, Rafael, 649
Exile politics, 299, 344, 523, 716
Exiles, 66, 71, 140, 258, 319; Haitian, 87; in Dominican Republic, 418; party, 71
Export-Import Bank, record, 721 n

Extremists, 127, 675
Eyewitness to History, 449

Facio, Gonzalo, 395, 426, 427 ff., 624
FALN (Venezuelan Castro Terrorist Group), 314, 331, 338
Fandino, Joe, 6, 65, 66, 71, 79, 81, 88, 90, 94, 109, 125, 136, 142, 154, 182, 215, 277, 279, 297–98, 306, 321, 444–45, 620; characteristics, 176; Cuban missile crisis, 239–40; elections, 234; "summit" meeting, 225; sugar crisis, 164; transfer, 460
Farm-to-market roads, 146 and n. *See* AID
Fascell, Congressman, 471
Faxas Canto, Rafael Miguel, 457, 524, 749
FBI (Federal Bureau of Investigation), 314
Fears, 510
FED, 355, 673 n
"Federation, The," 523 ff.
Feldman, Sue, 384–85, 610
FENEPIA (government employees union), 126, 192–93; Bosch, 457; Consejo, 276; strike, 439, 456
Fernandez Caminero, José, 6, 51, 69, 72, 92, 94, 140, 170, 193, 197, 230–31, 247, 249, 749; Cuban missile crisis, 243; elections, 158, 159, 196, 207, 237; Presidency, 106–7, 110; UCN, 111
Fernández Domínguez, Rafael, 644, 697
Ferrall, William E., 556, 558, 584
Ferreras, Ramón Alberto "Chino," 130
Feudalism, destruction of, 736
Fiallo, Viriato A., 69, 70, 87–88, 91, 111, 157, 159, 178–79, 257, 398, 749; assessment, 718; Bosch, 225, 228, 330; characteristics, 206, 207, 225, 228, 267; elections, 198, 208, 209–10, 214, 267 ff., 249, 300, 307–8; hero, 300; "summit," 225–29
Fignole, 392, 441, 443
Figueres, José "Pepe," 13, 47, 113, 624, 710; Bosch, 316; Civil War, 689 and n, 690
Figueroa Carrión, Colonel, 59
"Final solutions," 475
Finance, Minister of, 367
Fincas (farms), 38
Fishburn, Tom, 540

Florida, 19, 374
FNR, election crisis, 199 n
Folch Pérez, Juan N., 486
Fomento, 116, 124, 146 n, 359
Food, 69, 183, 189, 479–80; aid (*see* CARITAS); cost, 378, 414; rice loan, 520; scarcity, 481; U.S. aid, 504. *See* Food for Peace Law
Food for Peace Law (PL-480), 324, 389, 479, 504; record, 721 n
Force, U.S. position, 224. *See* Loeb formula
Foreign aid, 472–73. *See under* Europe; name of country
Foreign investments, 22, 311, 339, 356; Bosch, 329; private, and politics, 462; U.S., 309
Foreign Service, 176
Fortaleza Ozama, 34
Fortas, Abe, 679
Foupsa Libre, 192
"Four Cities in June," 620
Fourteenth of June (movement), 51, 52, 69, 72–73, 113, 125 n, 129, 143, 158, 174, 357, 412–13, 415, 459, 491, 754; *agrupación*, 130 n; Bosch, 397, 491, 492 n, 500, 641 ff.; campaign, 280; characteristics, 72; communism, 71, 130; elections, 199 and n, 201, 207–8, 282, 702; extremists, 673 and n; following, 130; Imbert, 262; leaders, 95; Martin on, 81; martyr, 52; PSP, 129; split, 72, 91; symbol, 175; youth, 69, 71
Fragua (student group), 357
France, 8, 37; Bosch, 484; Dominican Republic, 21, 26, 472, 519–20, 613; Haiti, 19–20; revolution, 19; Spain, 20
Franco, Francisco, 125, 697; Trujillo, 48
Franco, Luís, 505
Franco, Pericles, 129
Freedman, Max, 456
Freedom, 721; cost of, 197, 241; Johnson on, 738; Martin on, 743; postwar, 708–9; rulers' relationship, 720; U.S. commitment to, 202, 740, 741
Free institutions, 719–20
Freeman, Orville, 310
Freites Barrera, Andrés, 12, 165, 173, 174, 208, 216, 221–22, 225, 529, 533, 749; Bosch, 448; connections,

392; Foreign Minister, 360, 365, 392; Haitian crisis, 422 ff., 439; "intervention," 238–39; Kennedy, 169
Freites Barrera, Mrs. Andrés (Antonia), 12, 512–13
French Revolution, 19, 675
Frias, Thelma, 430, 456–57, 513
Fritchey, Clayton, 623
From Russia with Love, 620
Frontier, 306; "Dominicanization," 318
Fuentes, Carlos, 724–25, 736
Fulbright, J. W., 168, 172, 442
Furr, 357

García, Bienvenido, 57
García-Godoy Cáceres, Héctor, 520, 557, 589, 749; appearance, 538; Foreign Minister, 529; Provisional President, 699–700, 701, 703
García Guerrero, Amado, 56 and n, 57, 60, 219, 749
García Vásquez, Antonio, 96, 125, 205, 215, 303, 304, 305, 749
Generals' decree, 272–74, 279, 280, 283
Germán, Felix, 272
Germany, 27, 28, 36, 89, 210; Dominican Republic, 532; East, 128; Jews, 189–90, 191–92; U.S., 28
Gladstone, William E., on liberty, 30
Goldwach, Jerry, 467, 468
Golpe, 88 and n, 92, 131, 223, 404–5; Bosch assassination plot, 523 ff.; Cutler treaty idea, 730 n; military, 481, 535, 539 ff.; 1965 uprising (*see* Civil War)
Golpistas, 272; opposition, 593–94; regime, 584, 594 ff. (*see* Triumvirate)
Gómez, Facundo, 649
Gómez, Marco, 78, 79, 80, 359, 525 ff.
Gómez Pérez, Luís, 649
Gompers, Samuel, 126
González González, Manuel, 647, 652, 750
González Tamayo, Segundo Armando, 266, 340, 367–68, 541 ff., 594, 750
Good Neighbor Policy, 23, 46, 726
Goodwin, Richard, 123, 165, 397, 471, 479, 619, 695; Martin, 713; speechwriter, 492
Göring, Hermann, 37
Government, 4, 13, 24, 31, 143–44, 156, 192–93, 363, 695, 720; Assembly, free, 316, 317; Cabinet, 225, 364–

68, *golpista,* 595 and n; caretaker, 113, 116 (*see* Consejo); Chamber of Deputies, 299, 308, 368; coalition, 80, 94; Communists, 456–57; Congress, 34, 45, 495; Council of State (*see* Consejo); employees union (*see* FENEPIA); *golpista* regime, 584 ff., 594 (*see* Triumvirate); interim, 90, 91 (*see* Bonnelly); interregnum, 274; Latin American, 724 ff.; Martin on, 371; missile crisis, 242; of National Reconstruction, 680–84, 687 ff., 691 ff.; newspaper, 141; old order, 497; opposition, 69 ff., 80, 206, 225, 228; Palace, 3–5, 6, 30, 85, 87, 93, 166, 575, 577, 581, 583; people, relationship, 22; power centers, 205; power play (*see under* Amiama; Imbert); President, 7, 198, 199–200, 210, 249, 300, 314–15, 511, 588–89; provincial, 207; provisional (*see* Consejo); Provisional President (1916), 230; Senate, 308, 368; transition, 109 (*see* Consejo); Triumvirate (*see* Triumvirate); vacuum, 313. *See* Bosch; Consejo; Trujillo
Goytía, Victor, 275, 292, 615, 627
Graft, 204, 361, 370, 532, 536, 715 n
Grant, U. S., 22
Great Britain, 306; Bosch, 533; colonization, 725; Dominican Republic, 22, 25, 532–33, 545, 613; Palestine, 366; Spain, 20
Great Depression, 708
Greater Antilles, 17, 18
Greece, 723; Athens, 728
Grenada Company (United Fruit), 311–12, 396–97, 533
Grisolía, Carlos, 684, 750
Groups, 358. *See under* name
Gruening, Ernest, 597
Grullón, Alejandro, 136, 750
Grullón, Leopoldo, 630
Guadeloupe, 83, 281
Guarda de espalda, 90
Guardia National (constabulary), 28, 29, 42, 43 n
Guatemala, 47, 309, 524, 527, 634; Bosch, 327, 393–94; democracy, 584; racism, 724
Guerrilla warfare, 50, 113, 129, 141, 208, 629; training, 128
Guevara, Che, 208, 220

"Guilt by association," 89
Guzmán, Mrs. Antonio, 460, 461
Guzmán, Leandro, 52, 75
Guzmán Fernández, Silvestre Antonio, 192, 367, 460, 480, 505, 506–8, 514–16, 589, 750; U.S., 695 ff., 699, 707–8

Hache, Major, 487, 490, 491
Haciendas (estates or plantations), 38
Haina, 38–39, 41, 62, 77, 101, 211, 280, 299, 355–56, 359, 595; graft, 204; inefficiency, 638; strike, 311; sugar complex, 79, 97, 162, 204
Haiti, 20, 21, 23, 267 n, 281, 306, 317–18, 416–17, 432, 525; Bosch, 327, 394–95; Costa Rica, 442; crisis, 416 ff., 422–47; Czechoslovakia, 422, 424; Dominican Republic, 20, 31, 77, 87, 107, 108, 155–56, 203, 557–58, problem, 416 ff.; economic conditions, 317–18; exiles, 87, 314, 392, 418, 441; France, 19–20; government, 307, 441, 443; invasion route, 102; labor, 38, 259; location, 17; Poland, 422; population, 17; race, 417, 724; Soviet bloc, 439; *ton-ton-macoutes*, 425, 442; tourism, 18; Trujillo, 45; U.S., 442, 443–47, Ambassador, 125–26, Marine occupation, 30, policy, 392, 418; Venezuela, 442. *See* Duvalier
Haitian massacre, 16, 45 and n, 50, 77, 417
Harold Ober Associates, 389
Harper's, 17, 619
Harriman, Averell, 599, 600–2, 737; Bosch, 451; Martin, 623–24
Harriman, Mrs. Averell, 623, 624
Harvard University, 310, 695
Hasbun, Amin Abel, 649
Havana, 14, 21, 50, 72, 99, 128, 436 n; Radio, 66, 121, 296, 308, 686; Tri-Continental Congress, 673 n; Trujillo, 131, "26th of July" celebrations, 673 n
Hawker Hunter deal, 532–33, 535, 613, 715 n
Haya de la Torre, 71, 161
Health, 372, 373, 376, 479, 528; in *barrios*, 319; Higüey clinic, 376–86; Minister of, 365; programs, 138–39, 146; superstitions, 385

Heikkinen, Gwen, 474
Heikkinen, Joe, 474, 634
Heinl, Robert, 318
Hemba, Al, 92, 115, 131, 140, 148, 170; DCM, 10; Ecuador, 253
Hemispheric solidarity, 242
Hendrix, Hal, 454–56, 472, 510, 598
Hermida, Felix, Jr., 234, 252–53, 255, 551, 685, 750
Hernandez, Andres, 110, 147, 379
Hernando Ramírez, Miguel Ángel, 644–45, 652
Heroes, 267, 300
Herrera, Fabio, 271
Heureaux, Ulises, 26, 31, 74, 79, 203, 720, 750; assassination, 24–25, 26, 27, 132, 138, 206
Hickenlooper amendment, 355, 473
"Hickory Hill Group." *See* Kennedy, Robert F.
Higüey, 18; clinic, 376–86, 610, 637; radio station, 285, 288
Hildegarde, Señorita, 79
Hill, John, 11, 65, 82, 83, 84, 85, 86
Hispañola, 17
History, 31–32, 716, 719, 723; odds against democracy, 720; process of, 741; stability and, 734; theories of, 22, 720, 724–25. *See under* Dominican Republic
Hitler, Adolf, 46, 153, 191, 310, 518, 733; Jews, 190
Hoffa, Jimmy, 618
Holidays, 306
Honduras, 331, 584, 600, 601, 602, 734; Dominican Republic, 613; inter-American forces, 699; U.S., 632
Horacistas, 25, 26, 30
Hospitals, 380–81. *See* Health
"Hot line," 246
Houellemont Roques, Eduardo, 647
Housing, 139–40, 146 and n, 488
Huckleberry Finn, 407
Hughson, Pat, 106, 357
Hull, Cordell, 46
Humphrey, Hubert, 299, 471, 493–94, 598, 599; Alliance for Progress, 731; Bosch, 310, 335, 339, 455–56, 472; Martin, 464
Humphrey, Mrs. Hubert, 339
Hungary, 128, 672, 681
Hungría Morell, Renato, 23, 313, 323, 360, 482, 542, 638, 685, 750;

Bosch, 523 ff.; Haitian crisis, 425, 434 ff.

Hurricane season, 585

Hutton, Barbara, 712

IBM, 545 and n
Iguana, 105
Illiteracy, 269, 363, 380
Imbert, José María, 20, 203, 250, 750
Imbert, Segundo, 23, 203, 750
Imbert Barrera, Antonio, 7, 12, 13, 20, 55, 57, 60, 61, 63, 66, 87, 88, 91–2, 94–9, 106–7, 110, 193, 197, 204, 248, 274, 305, 313, 404, 481 ff., 750; Amiama coalition, 224 ff.; Armed Forces, 115–16, 119, 166, 204–5, 223, 323 (see General); assassin, 203, 219–20, 258; background, 203, 250; Betancourt, 314; Bosch, 254, 310, 313, 316–17, 322 ff., 348–49, 360, 387–88, 391, 413, 594, assassination plot, 523, 534; characteristics, 94–95, 154, 203–5, 315; Civil War, 665–68, 694; Consejo, 114; Cuban missile crisis, 240–45; democracy, 230; election(s), 158, 159, 207–14; family, 301; general, 252–56, 264–66, 280; government, 680–95, 707; Jews, 192; Martin, 218–21, 306–7; Mella cruise, 406; military golpe, 541 ff.; plots, 126, 166–67; power play, 203–5, 211, 213, 217 ff., 229–31, 246 ff., 262–63, 272–78; President, 680 ff., 691; security, 209 ff.; "summit meeting," 228; supporters, 248–51; Triumvirate, 588; Trujillo, 203 (see assassin); visa, 391
Imbert Barrera, Señora Antonio, 60, 270, 306
Imbert Barrera, Segundo, 55, 60, 203, 750
IMF (International Monetary Fund), 7, 116, 146, 352 n, 353, 450, 638, 709
India, 17
Indianapolis Times, 16
Indians, 19
Indonesia, 725
Inflation, 115–16
Insumergibles, 153, 366
Intellectuals, 13, 14; alienation, 99, 125 n, 406, 731; communism, 99,

130; 14th of June, 72; Trujillo, 40, 51
Inter-American Development Bank, 146
Inter-American Peace Committee, 653
Inter-American Peace Force, 699, 701
Inter-American Press Association, 211. See SIP
Interdependence, doctrine, 733
International Commission of Jurists, 720
International law, 706 n
International Monetary Fund. See IMF
International politics, 46
International Union of Students, 355
Ireland, 331
Isabela de Torres, 138 and n
Isa Conde, Antonio, 496, 647, 649, 666, 673 and n, 750
Isa Conde, Narciso, 496, 643 n, 647, 649, 750
Isidro, Juan, 249
Isla Beata, 307
Italy, 210, 613
Izaguirre, Alejandro, 223–29

Jaar, Abraham, 366, 369, 377, 379, 398, 406 ff., 450, 750; Bosch, 448, 539
Jackson, Jacob, 174, 276, 313, 358
Jamaica, 18, 729
Japan, 190, 356
Javits, Jacob, 335, 338–39, 479, 528, 598, 599
Jefferson, Thomas, 122
Jews, 46, 189–90, 203, 469; DORSA, 190–92
Jimenes, José Antonio, 548
Jimenes, Juan Isidro, 23, 25 n, 26, 750
Jimenes Grullón, Juan Isidro, 25 n, 46, 88, 137, 199 n, 201, 292, 388, 487, 750; assessment, 718; Bosch, 310, 370, 451: election(s), 226, 235–36; Imbert, 223
Jiménez Rosario, José, 697
Jimenistas, 25, 26, 30
Jinetes del Este, Los (Riders of the East), 66
John XXIII, Pope, 286
Johnson, Lyndon B.: Bosch, 339–40, 348, 349, 461, inauguration, 319–20, 330 ff., 340; characteristics, 335, 696; "come, let us reason together," 719; "crisis of credibility," 708; Dallas, 622; Doctrine, 737–38; Dominican Civil War, 640–46,

651, 656–57, 661, 678, 680, 698–99, 737; foreign policy, 626, 704 ff., 736–37; friends, 679; Kennedy, 623; Martin, 335–36, 340, 640, 661, 676, 678, 680, 683, on, 743; President, 622, 629, speechwriters, 492; Vice President, 5, 87, 315; Vietnam, 738
Johnson, Mrs. Lyndon B., 386, 622, 626; Bosch inauguration, 332–35, 339, 340
Johnson Pimentel, Buenaventura, 647
José (driver), 261, 287, 302
Juancito (houseboy), 254
Judiciary, 93, 97, 114, 367
Juventud. See under PRD

Kaiser, Edgar, 371, 459, 460, 461–62, 463, 471, 479
Kaiser Engineering, 462
Kennan, George, 164, 603
Kennedy, John F., 4, 14, 97, 114, 136, 166, 188, 202, 246, 248, 332, 367, 713; administration, 320, 616; Alliance for Progress, 69–70, 247, 726–27 and n; assassination, 15, 621–25, 630, 722, 743; Berlin Wall speech, 620; Bosch, 308 and n, 361, 464, 473, 477–78; Bundy, 695; campaign (1960), 619, 622; characteristics, 82, 121, 122, 124, 601, 619, 625; civil rights, 462, 469; Communists, 478, 480; Cuban missile crisis, 235–43, speech, 239, 240, 241; Dominican Republic, 5, 64, 83, policy, 82; foreign policy, 51, 120–22, 141, 711–13, 727 ff.; friends, 712; funeral, 624; grave, 630; Haitian crisis, 440, 447; inaugural address, 65; Latin America, 5, 14, 602, 626; leadership, 475; Martin, 5, 64, 83, 84, 119, 121, 122, 123, 371, 474, 477–78, 517 n, 560, 614, 619–20, 625, 633, 672, on, 742, report to, 81–82; military coups, 603–4; mystique, 478; political philosophy, 721; religion, 283; Special Forces, 141; speeches, 65, 239–41, 320, 462, 475, 593, 620; speechwriters, 5, 492; staff, 122; State of Union message, 320, 593; sugar crisis, 161 ff., tactics, 326; Triumvirate, 601–2, 605, 607–8, 613–14

Kennedy, Mrs. John F. (Jacqueline), 381, 619, 625, 626
Kennedy, Joseph P., 711
Kennedy, Robert F., 122, 123, 252, 299, 472, 618, 712; Bosch, 308, 479; "Hickory Hill Group," 478, 603; Martin, 618–19, 632, 713; Triumvirate, 599
Kennedy, Mrs. Robert F. (Ethel), 618–19, 621
Kennedy family, 712
Khrushchev, Nikita, 241, 372
Kilometer 9, 35–36, 60, 61, 210
King, Martin Luther, 619
King, Spencer, 148, 279, 298, 303 ff., 427, 449, 482, 497, 502–3, 526, 565, 627; characteristics, 253; DCM, 396; intervention charge, 606, 607, 608; recall, 612; Triumvirate, 596 ff.; Washington mission, 519–20
Kiplinger Letter, 456
Knapp, H. S., 28–29
Kohn, Louis A., 742
Koppers Company, 116
Korean War, 227
Kubitschek, Juscelino, 726, 730
Ku Klux Klan, 131

Labor, 126, 192–93, 223, 311, 732; federations, 192, 483, 550 (see under name); Minister of, 366; ORIT, 126, 192, 483; problems, 126. See Strikes; Unions
La Chapelle, Héctor, 665
La Cuarenta (The Forty), 35, 50, 51, 56 n, 59, 60, 185
La Cueva (The Cave), 344
Lago Limón, 261
La Grenada, 306
Lajara González, Alejandro, 647, 649
Lake Enriquillo, 38, 107, 108
La Nación, 141, 168, 229, 284, 286, 429, 430, 444
Land, expropriation, 459, 464, 470–73, 489; U.S. attitude, 471 ff.
La Nevera, 154
Language, 89, 90, 135 n, 267 and n
Lansing, Robert, 28
Laos, 123
La Revista, 43
La Romana, 170, 209, 211, 258–60, 407; strike, 223, 483
Las Matas, 140, 141, 238, 303, 318

La Tarde, 550–51

Latin America, 13, 35, 48, 124, 144, 719, 726; army, typical, 118; asylum, right of, 541; Castro, 463; *coups,* 602; democracy, 584; diplomats, 626; enemies, 736; Europe, 27, 370; foreign investments, 734; foreign services, 176; governments, 87, 724 ff., 727; intellectuals, 40, 99; Kennedy policy, 727, 728 ff.; military, the, 393–94, 594, 735; Monroe Doctrine, 26–27; nationalism, 14; parties, 126, 210; political traditions, 406; population, 725, 726; problem, 320; universities, 98–99; U.S., 5, 104–5, 106, 197, 246, investment in, 734, Martin on, 729 ff., policy, 390, 602, 626, 726–28, reputation, 30

Lausche, Frank, 598

Láutico García, Father, 284–85, 286, 291, 294, 498, 750; Bosch debate, 294

La Vega, 132, 142, 210, 211; Martin, 142–44; radio station, 285, 288, 290

La Victoria prison, 75, 210, 211, 399, 401–2

Law(s), 47, 486–87; Agrarian Reform, 554 n; Bosch, 459; Confiscation, 495, 497, 498, 554 n; electoral, 119, 156–57, 178, 181, 237; Emergency, 8, 91, 347, 349, 359, 502; fear of, 510; land: *plus valía,* 490, 495, 498, 554 n; organic military, 265; Trujillo, 36

Leadership, 475, 709–10, 731; mystique, 397

Lebrón, Alfredo, 268 ff.

Leftists, 359, 381–82

Lembert Piguero, Luís E., 367, 529

Lenin, Nikolai, 128, 285, 450, 642; *State and Revolution,* 285; tactics, 344, 510

Leningrad, 128, 355, 673 n

León, Eduardo, 136, 493, 548

Léon Estévez, Luís José, 39, 55, 62, 67, 750

Léon Grullón, José Antonio de, 486

Lesser Antilles, 17

Lewis, Sinclair, 407

Liberators, 345

Libertad, 9, 70, 282

Liberty, 30, 41, 98

Liborio, 303

Life, 689 n

Lilienthal, David, 137, 472

Limitation, human, 723

Limited Nuclear Test Ban Treaty, 499

Lincoln, Abraham, 159, 462, 720

Lindbergh, Charles, A., 136

Lippmann, Walter, 730, 738

Listin Diario, 45, 401, 629, 716

Literature, 248

Livio Cedeño, Pedro, 57, 58, 59, 62, 750

Liz, Ángel, 499, 500, 520

Lleras Camargo, Alberto, 626

Lobo (sugar dealer), 356

Lobraña, Major, 551–52

Lockhart, Stephen A., 306

Loeb, Jim, 122, 127, 196; formula, 122, 126

Lombardo Toledano, 71

London, U. S. Embassy, 147

Long, Luther F. "Fritz," 115, 126, 166, 252, 255, 287, 303, 304–5, 327, 540; generals' decree, 254; Haitian crisis, 426, 434; military *golpe,* 557–58, 565 ff.

Longroño, Alvaro, 3–4, 315

López, Miguel, 697

López, Osvaldo, 600

López Molina, Maximo, 40, 74, 91, 92, 95–96, 129, 244, 252, 253, 330, 331, 364, 648, 729, 750; Castro, 95; deportation, 485, 487

Lora Vicente, Silvano, 649

Los Angeles, California, 122, 144

Los Cocuyos de las Cordilleras (Fireflies of the Mountains), 39

Luna Pérez, Miguel Atila, 92, 116–17, 166, 205, 215, 254, 323, 360, 482, 532–33, 535, 638, 644, 750; Bosch plot, 524 ff.; deportation, 685; Haitian crisis, 425; Hawker Hunter deal, 537, 715 n; *Mella* cruise, 406 ff.; military *glope,* 562 ff.

Luperón, Gregorio, 23, 24, 47, 55, 158, 249, 750; Bosch, 344; "Commando," 650

Luther, Duane, 599

MAAG, 86, 116, 121, 145, 148, 149, 242, 276, 350, 452, 532, 535, 554–55, 655, 658; Bosch, 354; chief, 304; Martin, 149, 722; program,

173, 358; purpose, 145; record, 721 n

Macao, 261

McCarthy, Joseph, 100, 227, 715

Maceo, Antonio, 345

McGhee, George, 82, 120

Macho (manhood), 53

MacLeish, Archibald, 474

McNamara, Robert, 500, 640, 659

Madrid, 281

Mafia, 131

Maimón, 50, 51

Mainardi Reyna, Virgilio, 136, 137, 293, 506–8, 688, 751

Majluta, Jacobo, 367, 460, 483–84, 751

Manifest Destiny, 22

Mann, Thomas C., 632, 634, 650 ff., 695, 698, 737

Manning, Bob, 471

Manpower, skilled, 728

Manzano, Alfredo, 72, 130, 398, 494, 496, 500, 509, 729, 751

Mao Tse-tung, 129, 152, 673 n, 702

Marshall, George C., 741

Marshall Plan, 728

Martí, José Julien, 345

Martin, Cindy (daughter), 98, 182–83, 188, 634, 686; marriage, 212, 239

Martin, Dan (son), 9, 84, 85, 90, 101, 102, 104, 106, 109, 117, 123 ff., 153–55, 174, 182–84, 187, 188, 212, 215, 221, 240, 260, 261, 306, 317, 375, 460, 497, 587, 589, 609–10, 628; health, 334–35, 340, 355

Martin, Edwin, 65, 120, 121, 165, 201, 327, 426–29, 471–73, 475, 519, 627, 632; Ambassador to Argentina, 632; Bosch, 308, 309, 333, 335, 473, 581; characteristics, 614; Latin American policy, 602; Martin, 529; Triumvirate regime, 587, 596–99

Martin, Fred (son), 9, 84, 85, 90, 101, 102, 104, 106, 109, 117, 123 ff., 153–55, 174, 182–84, 187, 188, 212, 215, 221, 240, 260, 261, 302–3, 306, 317, 328, 375, 460, 497, 587, 589, 609–10, 628

Martin, John B.: aims, 87, 104, 472; Ambassador, 3–4, 7 n, 13, 15, 17, 31, 83, 85, 86, 145, 195, 440, 587, 589, 614, 714; appointment, 5, 83, 84; attacks on, 143, 533; background, 16, 633; Bosch, 345, 366,

440, 510, 519, 546, 676 ff.; chance, 742; characteristics, 4, 302, 468, 614; contingency planning, 520, 521–23, 722; Crisis Crowd, 148, 169, 174, 175, 279, 498, 672, Bosch: Cuban missile crisis, 239, election(s), 200, 209–11, 225, 237, 294, 297, fall, 583, generals' decree, 253–56, 266, Haitian crisis, 435 ff., inaugural, 330, military crisis, 485 ff., military *golpe*, 565 ff., political crisis, 498 ff.; diplomacy, 301; duties, 5–6, 147–50; Embassy, 248, 254; errors, 127, 292, 393, 492, 721–23, 742; family, 98, 258, 609–10, 637, 686; fear, 672; friends, 114, 123, 299, 307, 534, 609, 615, 618, 623, 626, 628, 634; health, 106, 109, 197, 200, 201, 292, 686; hobbies, 184, 260–62, 307, 474–75; limitations, 101; philosophy, 469–70, 475, political, 22, 371, 594, 743; presidential missions (1961), 64–83, 97, 101, 355, 640, 672, 711, 712, 729, (1965), 661 ff., 707; replacement, 475–76; resignation, 371, 628, 630, 632; responsibilities, 6, 320; retreat, 259–62, 474–75; salary, 147; social events, 167–68, 172–73, 270, 274–75, 292, 300–1, 306, 448–50, 460–62, 493; speeches, 130–31, 149, 195, 463 and n, 761–69; speechwriter, 119, 122, 510, 517 n, 619, 623–24; staff, 3, 6, 10, 86, 91–92, 115, 117, 126, 145, 192, 305, 310, 327, 435–36 and n, 456–58, 587 (*see under* name of man); tactics, 168, 448–50 (*see* Crisis Crowd); tensions, 614; trips, 16, 17, 101, 125, 131–44, 154–55, 182, 213, 258, 301–2, 306–7, 317–19, 375, 376, 496–98; on U.S. policy, 723 ff., 729 ff.; Washington, 119–22, 471 ff., 594 ff., 698–99; writings, 16–17, 202, 389, 632, 637, 640, 689 n. *See under* events, people, policies.

Martin, Mrs. John B. (Fran), 5, 9, 10, 63, 64, 84, 100, 101, 104, 106, 109, 123, 134, 142–43, 147, 154–55, 172, 174, 182–84, 188, 193–94, 215, 240, 270, 272, 274, 311, 317,

335, 375, 382–83, 448, 449, 468, 496, 587, 589; Bosch inaugural, 339; Dominican Republic, 609–10, 628; friends, 239, 307; *golpistas*, 598; health, 497–98; Higüey clinic, 376–86; hobbies, 260; marriage, 742; official functions, 150; PRD letter, 717; teaching, 731
Martínez, María, 36
Martínez Arana, Jacinto, 701
Martínez Francisco, Antonio, 653
Marx, Karl, 128, 720
Marxism, 35, 92, 256; -Leninism, 198, 284–85
Marxist revolution, 256
Masses, the, 14, 459; Bosch, 334, 448, 450, 459, 721
Mater et Magistra, 286
Matías Mella, Ramón, 337
Matos Rivera, Juan José, 331
Mayne, Alvin, 309, 329, 457, 471, 534
Mazzini, Giuseppe, 716
Medicine, voodoo, 376. *See* Health
Mejía, "Bebe," 496
Mejía Ricart, Marcio, 125 and n
Mejía Saufront, 422, 423, 424, 433
Mejía y Mejía, Bienvenido, 399, 401
Mella, 306, 307, 405–15, 418, 460–62, 594, 597
Mella, Ramón Matías, 20, 21, 751
Mellizos, 303–5
Mencken, Henry L., 407
Mendoza Moya, Samuel, 365–66, 377, 581
Mercado, Luís, 77, 712
Mercedes Batista, Diomedes, 647, 648, 649
Merengue (dance), 188, 215, 218, 221
Mestizo, 19
Mexico, 103, 128, 345, 524, 632, 658; Bosch, 537–38; Communists, 71; conquest of, 19; Dominican Republic, 581–82; government, 724, 731; Miami *News*, 454–56
Michigan, 604
Mikoyan, Anastas, 273
Military, the, 9, 14, 30, 93, 175, 176, 208, 212, 303–4, 458, 486, 532–34, 547, 553, 557, 611–12, 722, 735; assessment, 717–18; Bosch, 326–27, 346, 360, 402–4, 481 ff., 521, 523; chaplains, 483 ff., communism, 127, 544; Consejo, 114–15;

golpe, 196, 499, 537, 539 ff., 546, 558, 561 ff., 715–16, U.S. position, 559, 570, 582; leaders, 127, 701; night of the generals, 479–92; politics, 117–18; power, 109, 448; purge, 166, 176; Trujillo, 16, 33–34, 36, 87; U.S. position, 122, 599, 602. *See* Armed Forces
Military Assistance and Advisory Group. *See* MAAG
Miller, Captain, 89–90
Minow, Newton, 123, 299
Miolán, Ángel, 71, 88, 113, 126, 179, 192, 198, 207, 254, 268, 309, 343, 360, 393 n, 404–5, 456, 482, 529–32, 612, 751; Bosch, 311–12, 315–16, 326, 524; characteristics, 312, 313–14; communism, 358; election, 281; exile, 637; *golpe*, 544; Johnson, 334; labor, 311–12, 313, 484; "summit" meeting, 226
Miolán, Mrs. Ángel, 334
Mirabal sisters, 52, 72, 168, 717; trial, 178, 197
Mir Valentine, Pedro Julio, 673
Missile crisis (Cuban), 235–36
"Mr. Jackson," 16
Moca, 25, 26, 132, 135, 138–39
Molina, Julia, 36, 187
Molina Ureña, José Rafael, 328, 360, 429, 430, 450, 581, 582, 751; President, Chamber of Deputies, 368; "President," 648 ff., 677–78
Monroe Doctrine, 26–27; Roosevelt "Corollary," 710, 739
Monte Cristi, 23, 25, 311
Montes Arache, Lieutenant Colonel, 665, 666, 701
Mora, José A., 671–72, 676, 681, 683–84, 697
Morales Carríon, Arturo, 471
Moreno, Alfonso, 391
Moreno, Jorge, 175, 176
Moreno, Luís (Luisito), 460, 461
Moreno Martinez, Alfonso, 751
Morison, Samuel Eliot, 19, 138 n
Morse, Wayne, 472, 597–98, 599, 602
Moscoso, Teodoro, 121, 137, 335, 372, 471, 519, 626; Bosch, 308, 451, 473, 596–97, 599; Yaque, 473
Moscow: Party Congress (1960), 128, 357, 673 n. *See* Soviet Union
Moyers, William D., 640

MPD (*Movimiento Popular Domini-cano*), 74, 91, 92, 95, 113, 129–30, 357, 382–83, 436 n, 459, 491, 494, 673 and n, 754; Bosch restoration, 641 ff.; insurrection, 174; leadership, 364, 398, 630, 648; symbol, 175

"Munichs," 266

Muñoz Marín, Luis, 124, 296, 338, 365, 460, 584, 690; Bosch, 315–16

Murmansk, 496

Murphy, Gerald, 48, 49

Murphy, Robert D., 711–12, 712 n, 713

Mussolini, Benito, 43

Naboth's Vineyard, 22

Nagua, 187–89

Napoleon, 20, 43, 250, 675

National anthem(s), 3, 4, 19, 73–74, 175, 194, 306

National Association of Broadcasters, 374

National Association of Secondary Students, 143

National Institute for Potable Water, 489

Nationalism, 14, 156, 157, 463, 736; Bosch, 345, 347, 459

Nationalists, 129, 130

Nationalization, 533

National Planning Board, 456, 457

NATO, 473, 740

Natural rights of man, 8

Navy, 118, 166, 175, 176, 205, 223; Cuban missile crisis, 242; equipment, 532

NBC, 291

Nehemkis, Peter, 615, 627

Neiba, 21, 38, 108–9

Neit Nivar Seijas, Rafael, 524, 542 ff., 644 ff.

New Hampshire, 17

New Leader, The, 706 n

Newsweek, 291

New York City, 47, 467–68

New York *Herald Tribune*, 533, 593, 602

New York *Times*, 165, 168, 172, 291, 320, 343, 358, 430, 434, 438, 593, 608, 616, 637, 700

Ney Garrido, Colonel, 108

Nicaragua, 108, 524, 535, 584; Bosch, 327; Dominican Republic, 613; in-ter-American forces, 699; U. S. Marine occupation, 30

Niebuhr, Reinhold, 720

Night of the generals, 479–92

Nigua, 62, 249, 270

Nisibón, 259–62, 532

Nixon, Richard, 48, 619

Nobel Prize, 122

Non-intervention, doctrine, 733 and n, 734

Nouel, Monseñor, 249

Nuclear power, 723, 740

Numinen, Earl, 474

Nuremberg trials, 53

OAS, 13, 62, 65, 75, 100, 359, 615, 710, 734–35; Bosch, 309, 446; Charter, 705–6, 733; Civil War, 657 ff., 670, 671, 689 and n, 691; Consultative Organ, 236, 240; Council, 395, 658, 660; Cuban missile crisis, 236, 240–241; election(s), 111, 124, 156, 157, 158, 161, 178, 181, 196, 275, 276, 284, 292, 296; Foreign Ministers, 593; Haitian crisis, 416, 418, 423 ff.; Human Rights Commission, 156; in-ter-American forces, 699; non-intervention, 237; peace mission, 699 ff.; principles, 237; sanctions, 52, 64, 65, 67, 68, 75, 78, 80, 83, 593–94; San José meeting, 51–52; Secretary General, 671; technical assistance, 146; Trujillo, 711; U.S., 438 n, 651, 723, 733

O'Donnell, Kenneth, 478, 618

Orlich, Francisco, 331, 332, 338

Oil, 103–4

Oligarchy, 11, 14, 72, 75, 77, 140, 267, 301, 557, 715–16; Bosch, 346, 453, 721; characteristics, 133–35, 448; party, 282 (*see* UCN); rebellion against, 129; seat of, 18, 89, 132; Trujillo, 39, 40

Olson, Keith, 379, 381–84

O'Meara, Andrew P., 93, 280, 489, 722

Opa-locka, 364

Opinion, La, 43

Oppenheimer, Robert, 374

Organic Military Law, 265

Organization of American States. *See* OAS

ORIT, 126, 192, 483
Ornes, Germán, 34–35, 37, 211–12, 399, 400, 419, 420–22, 495, 751
Ornes, Horacio Julio, 46, 47, 158, 199 n, 212, 224, 237, 247, 249, 293, 294, 310, 402, 494, 595, 718, 751
Oswald, Lee Harvey, 624
Ozuña Hernandez, David, 647, 648, 649

Pacem in Terris, 286
Pagán Montás, Ramón, 254, 305, 751
Pagán Perdomo, Dato, 130, 199 n, 308, 357, 387–88, 397, 405, 407–8, 673 n, 751; Bosch, 465 (*see* school); school, 419–20, 496, 509, 545, 556
Palace, 3–5, 6, 30, 85, 87, 93, 166, 575; *golpe,* 577, 581, 583
Palestine, 366
Palma Sola, 303–5, 359
Palmer, Bruce, 692, 693–94
Panama, 93, 145, 275, 280, 312, 615
Panama Canal, 28, 407
Pan American Airways, 271–72, 310
Pan American Health Bureau, 310
Panasco Alvim, Hugh, 699
Panteleymonovich, Boris, 523
Papal Nuncio. *See* Clarizio, Monseñor
Paraguay, 327, 699
Paris, France, 79, 83, 99, 281
Parker, W. H., 122
Partido Dominicano, 40–41, 44, 76, 80, 110, 511; demise, 87; Martin on, 82; slogans, 77. *See* PNRD
Parvin, Albert, 374
Parvin Foundation, 374, 479, 549
Passman, Otto, 519
Passports, 494–96
Pastoriza, Roberto, 57, 58, 62, 751
Pastoriza, Tomás (Jimmy), 136, 137, 493, 506, 517, 751
Pastoriza family, 557
Patronage, 228, 360, 450, 502
PCD, 701–2
PDC, 595 n
Peabody, Endicott, 624
Peace Corps, 86, 110, 138, 139, 146–47, 148, 153, 301, 318, 350–51, 375, 397, 479, 516; Bosch, 349; director, 147; Higüey clinic, 376 ff.; personnel, 471
Peacekeeping, responsibilities, 438

Pedernales, 105, 106, 107
Peguero, Luís E. Lembert, 524
Peguero, Ramós, 96
Peguero Guerrero, Belisario, 92, 193, 197, 205, 242, 279, 303, 398–402, 638, 751; Bosch, 310, 360, 524; deportation, 685; military crisis, 483 ff.
Peking. *See* Red China
Peña Gómez, José Francisco, 288, 368, 645, 646, 751
Peña Taveras, Mario, 646, 649, 653, 701
Penna Marinho, Ilmar, 699
Pepén, Bishop, 376, 379, 384, 637
Peralta, Colonel, 527
Pérez Cabral, Pedro ("Corpito"), 130, 199 n, 387, 398, 407–8, 751
Pérez Guillen, Juan E., 525
Pérez Pérez, Milvio, 686
Pérez Sánchez, Elisio, 6, 85, 154, 158, 229, 751
Pérez y Pérez, Enrique, 702
Perides, 743
Perkey, John, 327, 399
Perón, Juan, 89; fall, 602
Perry, John, 549
Peru, 19, 122, 161, 730; APRA, 71; military *golpe,* 192, 193, 196–97; U.S., 192
Peynado, Francisco, 30, 31
Peynado, Jacinto B., 40, 45
Peynado, Julio, 158, 354
Philippines, 161
Pichardo, Nicolás, 6, 7, 8, 9, 12, 13, 94, 111, 163, 170–71, 333, 647, 751; characteristics, 157; Cuban missile crisis, 240; elections, 156–57, 198–201, 207, 223–34
Pichardo, Nicolás, Mrs., 12, 333
Picó, Rafael, 97, 115–16, 121, 145, 157
Pico Duarte, 18, 142, 154, 155
Pilgrims, 303–5. *See* Cultists
Pinta, 19
Pittaluga, Salvador, 550–51, 553, 555–56
Pizarro, Francisco, 19
Plots, 314, 499, 523 ff., 644
PN, *Partido Nacional* (National Party), 212, 595 n, 754
PNR, *Partido Nacional Revolucionario*

(National Revolutionary Party), 130, 199, 201, 357, 459, 754

PNRD, *Partido Nacional Revolucionario Dominicano* (Dominican National Revolutionary Party), 198, 199 n, 388, 595 n, 754

Polanco, Bishop Hugo, 495, 507, 511, 751

Poland, 422

Police, 8–9, 43 and n, 67, 93, 100, 122, 205, 211, 213, 217, 312, 483–84; Bosch, 310–11, 348–49, 391; *Cascos Blancos*, 122, 175, 193, 242, 312, 483, 664; Civil War, 653 ff.; loyalty, 94; politics, 262, 278–79; secret, 33–34, 43, 312 (*see* SIM); training, 124, 358–59

Political affairs, 346, 498 ff., 638

"Political independents," 224

Political instability, 616, 617 n

Political parties, 12, 25, 40, 71–72, 87–88, 91, 93, 157, 158, 178, 218; activities, 431; Bosch, 336, 356, 640 ff., 675; Castro/Communist, 92, 281; Christian Democratic, 210; coalition, 264, 280, 388; Confiscation Law, 495; Constitution, new, 328; discipline, 228; elections, 196 ff., 206 ff., 246, 248, 293, 701–2, problems, 263–64; extremists, 72; *golpe(ismo)*, 491, 595 and n; labor unions, 126; leaders, 74, 77; leftist drift, 356 ff.; leftists, 312; list, 754–55; Liz mediation, 499, 500, 501, 503, 509; moderates, 72; opposition, 74, 80, 81; rightists, 509–10, 556; symbols, 210; system, 458; Triumvirate, 611–12; unity, 192; vest-pocket, 199 and n, 200–1, 212. *See under* name of party

Political structure, 675, 709

Politicians, 274, 319, 326, 535; assessment, 718; characteristics, 248, 497; distrust of, 579, 719; exile, 499

Politics, 9, 27, 231, 681–82, 388; of accommodation, 719; of annihilation, 719; axiom, 273; Bosch, 349, 418, 449, 462, 465, 556, 557; characteristics, 247–48, 462; Church, 268, 283–92; emerging nations, 719; exile, 299, 344, 523, 716; function, 719, international, 46;

the military, 117–18. *See* Power politics

Ponce de León, 19

Population, 17; explosion, 373, 725; world, 725

Port-au-Prince, 307, 317

Portugal, 725

Postigo, Julio D., 328, 684, 751

Potemkin Village(s), 10, 372

Poverty, 106, 185, 203, 319, 372. *See Barrios*

Power, 14, 256–57, 346, 363, 204; absolute, 220, 256; axiom, 273; base (troops), 16; Castro, 273, 726; centers, 448; direction, 278, 279; Kennedy, 625; limits, 14, 101, 202, 723; machinery, 627; military, 36, 91, 127; nuclear, 723, 740; structure, 14, 326–27, 346; U.S., 468–69, 741–42, limits, 594 ff., 607, 613, 711, 723, 736, 742; vacuum, 487

Power politics, 256

PPDC, 198, 199 n, 595 n

Prague, 330, 331

PRD, *Partido Revolucionario Dominicano* (Dominican Revolutionary Party), 71, 81, 108, 112–13, 129, 158, 159, 189, 266, 289, 357, 358, 644 ff., 754; Bosch, 88, 112, 121, 344, 360, 450, 529–30, 531, 640 ff.; characteristics, 206; Communists, 654; dissension, 88, 91, 199 n, 360, 369; election(s), 199 n, 206–13, 225 ff., 266, 308, 701–2; *golpista* Cabinet, 595 n; *Juventud* (youth group), 384, 465, 530; labor, 126, 223, 549; leadership, 109–10, 360, 367, 368, 393 and n, 450; machine, fear of, 510; membership, 225; opposition, 192; position, 365; standards, 717

PRDA, *Partido Revolucionario Dominicano Autentico* (Authentic Dominican Revolutionary Party), 293, 595 n, 754

Prensa Libre, 494, 548, 608, 647

Press, the, 16, 34, 43, 45, 84, 167, 247–48, 326, 420–21, 438, 472, 708; Bosch, 454–55, 473, 498, 593 ff., Communist, 130–31; election(s) 272 ff.; freedom of, 400–1; government, 168; Trujillo, 35, 37; U.S.,

165, 454–56, 473, 494, 501, 586, 599, 738
Priests, 283–90
Princeton University, 374
Prío Socarrás, 113, 344
Private property, 316, 327–28, 452, 495
Progressive, The, 533
Provisional governments, 87. *See* Consejo
Proxmire, William, 597
PRSC, *Partido Revolucionario Social Cristiano* (Social Christian Revolutionary Party), 121, 128, 158, 191, 199 n, 210, 595 n, 754; Bosch, 640 ff; campaign, 272 ff.; elections, 198, 201, 207 ff., 286, 307, 701–2; labor, 223, 550; leader, 210, 391; ORIT, 126; PRD, 192
Prud'homme, Emilio, 74
PSP, *Partido Socialista Popular* (Popular Socialist Party), 129, 130, 356–57, 367–68, 459, 491, 641, 755; leadership, 358, 365, 673; Manifesto, 642–43 and n. *See* PCD
Public order, 143–44, 158, 214
Public works, 151, 394, 488; Minister of, 366–67
Puerto Plata, 13, 18, 22, 23, 25, 47, 52, 55, 91, 92, 135, 186, 190, 203, 242, 266, 308; characteristics, 137–38
Puerto Rico, 17, 18, 19, 58, 93, 149, 183, 211, 296, 344, 365, 366, 483; Bosch, 361, 362, 603, Martin meeting, 676–80; Haitian exiles, 441; independence leaders, 549; people, 124; terrorist independence movement, 212
Punta del Este Declaration, 65, 487, 726–27 and n

Quadros, Jânio, 315
Quiñones, Miguel, 525
Quintanilla, Joe, 463, 539, 550

Raborn, William, 640, 698
Race(ism), 152–53, 266, 267, 268, 417, 724, 725; Trujillo, 33, 45; U.S., 469
Radio Caribe, 178, 397
Radio Havana, 66, 121, 296, 308, 686
Radio Santo Domingo, 694

Radio stations, 285, 288, 290, 297
Ramfis-Balaguer regime, 712, 713. *See under* Balaguer; Trujillo, Martinez, Jr.
Ramírez Alcántara, Miguel Ángel, 46, 47, 198, 199 n, 224, 249, 318–19, 388–89, 751
Ramos Peguero, Andrés, 92, 751
Ramos Peguero, Francisco, 630
Raymont, Henry, 358, 440
Reader's Digest, 291
Read Vittini, Mario, 388, 389, 487
Red China, 14, 125 n, 128, 305, 357, 436 n, 673 n, 741; Castro, 736; Dominican Republic, 129, 130; MPD, 130; policy, 357, 725; population, 17
Red Cross, 655, 659
Reformation, 724
Reforms, 106–7, 111, 114, 115, 124, 138–39; Aid, 137; Balaguer, 137; Consejo, 103, 137; legislation, 546; opposition to, 721
Reid and Pellerano, 401
Reid Cabral, Donald J., 6, 8, 9, 88, 90, 92, 94, 113, 118, 151, 197, 216, 265, 273–74, 279, 358, 648, 649, 658, 751; Bosch, 316–17, 328, 359, 448, 449, 494, 501; characteristics, 141; election(s), 158, 159, 207, 233–34, 238–39; errors, 709; family, 11, 12, 13; military, 114–15, 638; oligarchy, 114, 133; opposition, 640 ff.; overthrow, 645 ff., 675; sugar crisis, 163, 165, 169, 171; Triumvirate regime, 587–88, 606, 634, "President," 637 ff., 667, 709–10
Reid Cabral, Mrs. Donald J. (Clara), 11–12, 27, 239, 449
Reid Cabral, Dr. Robert, 12, 61
Reilly, Bishop, 376
Religion, 153–54
Renovación, 285
Responsibility, concept of, 379–80
Restauración, 24, 306, 499, 500, 503, 506, 513, 514, 519, 534, 716
Restaurants, 104
Reston, James, 320
Revolution(s), 13, 26, 319, 735–36, 741; French, 19, 675; Marxist, 256; necessity of, 320; opposition, 317; Russian, 152, 450, 729; Spain,

20; techniques, 547; types, 285, 497; worldwide, 13–14, 725. *See under* Bosch

Reynoso, Teresa Oviedo de, 418, 422, 424 ff.

Reynoso Mates, Luís, 418, 422

Rhodesia, 725

Rib Santamaría, Julio Alberto, 176, 215, 306, 323, 360, 405, 482, 545, 663, 638, 685, 751; Bosch, 326–27, 402–3, 523; generals' decree, 253; *golpe*, 537, 538, 543, Haitian crisis, 425, 427

Rib Santamaría, Señora Julio Alberto, 306

Ricart, Carlos Alberto, 716

Ricart-Ricart, Gustavo Federico, 331, 673 and n, 751

Richardson, William, 91, 115, 166, 255, 330, 432, 434, 482 ff.

Río Piedras Pact, 640 and n

Rioting, 85, 87, 88, 91–92, 94, 97, 99–100, 102, 122, 140, 168, 210, 398–400, 500; advertising, 206; Communists, 124, 131; cost, 97; organized, 97–98

Río Treaty, 236, 241, 426, 427

Rivera Caminero, Francisco Javier, 166, 175, 176, 482, 486, 527, 648, 663, 751–52; Civil War, 652 ff.; Washington, 701

Rivera Cuesta, Marcos Anibal, 176, 223, 224, 225, 254, 313, 327, 405, 524, 645, 646, 663, 685, 752

Rivera Cuesta, Señora, 224, 540, 541

Rivero, Horacio, Jr., 419, 430

Robbins, Allen, 471

Rockefeller, Laurance, 310

Rockefeller, Nelson, 603

Rodríguez del Prado, Cayetano, 20, 494, 496, 630, 648, 673 and n, 702, 752

Rodríguez Echavarría, Chagito, 542, 612, 613, 752

Rodríguez Echavarría, Pedro Rafael, 82–83, 84, 89, 118, 154, 279, 369, 525, 534–35, 752; exile, 84–85, 93

Rodríguez García, Juan ("Juancito"), 47

Rodríguez Reyes, General, 234, 302–5, 666 n

Román Díaz, Juan Miguel, 666, 697

Román Fernandez, José René, 53–54,

57, 58, 59, 60, 61–62, 204, 219, 752

Roosevelt, Franklin D., 406, 463, 625, 711, 720; Good Neighbor Policy, 726; Hundred Days, 458; Latin America, 5; Trujillo, 75

Roosevelt, Theodore, 26–27; Corollary to Monroe Doctrine, 27, 28, 710, 739

Rubirosa, Porfirio, 45, 712 and n, 713

Ruíz, Tony, 485, 665

Rumors, 118, 126, 153, 192, 197, 201, 500, 544, 715 n

Rusk, Dean, 120, 141, 172, 312, 611, 626, 650, 659 ff., 726; Bosch, 308; Martin, 371, 477, 640

Russian Revolution, 152, 450, 729

Ruyle, Ben, 293, 311, 389, 505, 516, 547–48

Sabana de la Mar, 182

Salcedo, 52

Salinger, Pierre, 419

Samaná, 22, 25, 183–85, 213, 216, 218, Bay of, 132, 182–83, 261

Sánches Rubirosa, Gilberto, 524

Sánchez, Fernando A., Jr., 79, 81, 82, 83, 124, 524, 752

Sánchez, Francisco del Rosario, 20, 21, 337, 752

Sánchez, "Pupito," 205, 233, 266, 312, 458, 752

Sánchez Cabral, Eduardo, 100–1, 720

Sánchez Félix, Buenaventura, 266, 365, 480, 752

San Cristóbal, 37, 42, 56, 57, 101, 316; arsenal, 38, 50

San Isidro Air Base, 36, 50, 57, 70, 78, 82, 91, 125 n, 145, 270, 304, 481 ff.; crisis, 481 ff.; generals, 665–66, 671 ff., 685, *golpe*, 571–72

San José de Ocoa, 154

San Juan, 21

San Juan de la Marguana, 270, 318–19; uprising, 302–3

San Pedro de Macorís, 29, 266, 268; strike, 223

San Salvador, 534–35

Santamaría Demorizi, Miguel, 649

Santana, Colorado, 610

Santana, Pedro, 20, 21, 345, 720, 752

Santana Carrasco, Manuel Olgo, 656, 752

Santana family, 308

Santiago, 11, 13, 18, 20, 23, 41, 66, 75, 76, 133, 146 n, 296, 389, 505, 547–48; Agricultural Institute, 136, 146 n, 516–17; *barrios* (slums), 136–37; Bosch, 503–6, 510, 513–14, 517–18; characteristics, 136–37; elections, 308; Martin, 125, 136, 138, 140; oligarchy, 89, 497; people (Santiagueros), 493, 505–6, 517; riots, 91, 92; society, 135; spirit, 517; Trujillo, 133; U. S. Consulate, 208, (*see* Ruyle, Ben)

Santo Domingo, 3, 9–10, 11, 16, 18, 28, 36, 91, 268, 397; Archbishop, 286, 289, 293, 294, 747; Civil War (1965), 20; cost of living, 16; founding history, 19; intellectuals, 99; Radio, 694; Trujillo, 44–45; U.S., 9

Santos Céspedes, Juan de los, 486

Saona Island, 221, 409

Sarah Lawrence College, 188

Saturday Evening Post, The, 17, 389

Sayre, Bob, 604, 621

Scarlet Letter, The, 407

Schlesinger, Arthur, Jr., 64, 122, 299, 471, 624, 626, 628; Bosch, 308; Martin, 478, 594, 603, 609, 620, 622, 713

Schlesinger, Mrs. Arthur, Jr. (Marian), 622, 624

Seibo, 29

Selden, Armistead, 455 and n, 471, 472, 479, 594, 598

Selig Delmonte, Islander, 331, 496, 630, 752

"Seven Presidents," 4

Severo Cabral, Ángel, 280, 364, 528, 548, 588, 603, 612, 700, 752; assessment, 718; military crisis, 487

Seward, William H., 21

Shaw, Dave, 182, 184, 189

Shell Oil Company, 212

Shlaudeman, Harry, 10, 87, 92, 111, 115, 127, 131, 148, 158, 168, 192, 223, 303 ff., 311–12, 449, 485, 498, 661; Bosch, 179, 330, 389, 526; characteristics, 197–98; Civil War, 685 ff., communism report, 456–58; elections, 198–200, 206, 207, 229–30, 234, 235, 237, 267, 269, 282 ff.; generals' decree, 252 ff.;

Haitian crisis, 425, 442–43; military *golpe*, 539 ff., 565 ff.; State Department, 640; "summit" meeting, 225, 227; Triumvirate, 596 ff., 608

Shlaudeman, Mrs. Harry (Carol), 298, 449

"Showcase of democracy," 5

Shriver, Sargent, 147, 299, 349, 350–51, 471, 632

Silfa, Nicolás, 88, 199 n, 263, 271

Silva, Father Marcial, 484, 487, 490, 491

SIM, 41, 51, 52–53, 56 n, 58 ff., 66, 81, 89, 185, 210, 211, 548; chief, 526 (*see* Abbes, Johnny); Martin on, 82

Simmons, Ed, 82, 548–49, 552, 612–13

Sinclair, Upton, 407

Sino-Soviet split, 130, 740

SIP (Inter-American Press Association), 211, 420–21

Smester, Fernández, 354

Smith, Adam, 351

Smith, Earl E. T., 478

Smith, Stephen, 64, 618, 713

Smith Kline & French, 382

Snowden, Thomas, 29

Social Christian Party. *See* PRSC

Social Democrats, 388

Social Progress Trust Fund, 721 n

Somerford, Fred, 67–68, 126, 192, 311, 549, 722

Somoza, Anastasio, 527

Somoza, "Tachito," 527

Somoza brothers, 535

Sorensen, Theodore, 619, 620, 623

Sosa Valerio, Ariosto, 649

Sosua, 46, 186, 189, 190, 203

South America, 17, 19

Southeast Asia, 725; politics, 719; revolution, 14; U.S., 737

South Puerto Rico Sugar Company, 250, 454, 483, 533

Sovereignty, surrender of, 733

Soviet bloc, 439, 669, 673

Soviet Union, 14, 18, 72, 99, 125 n, 128, 164, 494; Bosch, 523; Castro, 736; coexistence policy, 357; Cuba, 116–17, 273, missile crisis, 235–36, 239, 243; Dominican Republic, 128, 129, 130, 273, 278, 494; foreign policy, 357; Party control, 40; satellites, 494; Test Ban Treaty,

499; Trujillo, 46, 131; U.S., 256, 436 n; West, 46

Sowash, Bill, 296, 471, 596

Spain, 33, 37, 42, 190, 319; Bosch, 327; Civil War, 408, 675, 697; colonization, 189–90, 725; Dominican Republic, 19, 21, 31, 191, 345; France, 20; Great Britain, 20 Trujillo, 48, 84

Spengler, Oswald, on history, 720

Stability, policy of, 734–35

Stalin, Joseph, 310, 450, 518, 675, 734–35

"Star-Spangled Banner, The," 4, 194

State and Revolution, 285

Steele, John, 610, 614, 621, 632

Steele, Mrs. John (Louise), 623

Stern, Phil, 609

Stevenson, Adlai E., 4, 84, 98, 196, 248, 299, 584, 622; Ambassador to UN, 440, 441; Bosch, 308; death, 742; Kennedy, 623–24; McCarthy, 100; Martin, 119, 517 n, 614, 618, 619, 733, 742–43; memorial, 731 and n; 1952 election, 227; political philosophy, 742–43; "revolution of rising expectations," 709; speechwriters, 626

Strikes, 152, 192–3, 209, 222, 223, 311, 456, 483, 529–30; Communists, 131; employees, 500; general, 93, 546, 547; leaders, 531, 548; legality, 366; Municipal employees, 214, 216–17; students, 91, 92, 249; unions, 126; U.S., 552

Strongman. See Dictators

Students, 74, 98, 99, 125, 186, 357, 721, 729; disorientation, 152; FED, 355, 673 n; 14th of June movement, 71, 72; International Union, 355; strike, 91, 92, 249; Triumvirate, 603

Succession, 588–89, 604

Suez crisis, 740

Sugar, 361; crisis, 145–77; Dominican production, 162; lobbyists (Washington), 259; quota system, 8, 161–62; strikes, 223; Trujillo, 38–39; U.S., 161 ff.; contracts, 355, 356, fees, 87, 109, interests, 353, legislation, 140, mills, 209, 258–59, quota, 120; world price, 638

Sumner, Charles, 23

Sunderland, T. E., 311–12

Switzerland, 39

Syria, 319, 406

Szulc, Tad, 165, 172, 440, 443, 456, 473, 533

Tábare Álvarez, 217, 296

Talleyrand, 733 n

Tanzania, 725

Tapia Espinal, Ramón, 90, 279, 584, 637, 752

Tatem, J. W., Jr., 258–59

Tavares, Gustavo, 135 and n

Tavares, María Grieser Viuda, 135–36, 497, 517, 548, 752

Tavares Espaillat, Gustavo, 448, 752

Tavares Espaillat, Manuel, 61, 62, 75, 123–24, 133, 637, 752

Tavares Espaillat, Señora Manuel, 74–75, 123–24

Tavares family, 308, 448

Tavares Grieser, Gustavo, 136, 497, 548, 752

Tavárez Justo, Ema, 649

Tavárez Justo, Manuel ("Manolo"), 51, 52, 71–72, 95, 126, 127, 130, 137, 167, 208, 249, 349, 357, 412–13, 431, 549, 606, 729, 752; assessment, 717; characteristics, 130; death, 634; Martin, 131

Tax reforms, 97, 111, 115, 124, 134, 192

Technical assistance, 145–46. See under name of agency

Tejeda, Candido, 526

Tejeda, Teodoro, 59 n, 60

Tejeda Pimentel, Huascar, 55–56, 57, 62, 752

Tejera, Luís, 27

Television, 398–99, 419; educational, 373, 374–75, 386, 479, 549

Terror(ism), 91, 130, 131, 357, reaction to, 25

Texaco, 599

Texas A & M, 516, 517

Thermonuclear confrontation, 240. See Cuban missile crisis

30th of May plot, 364

Three-mile limit, 432

Thurston, Raymond, 125–26, 317, 318, 392; Haitian crisis, 418, 425, 426, 438, 442

Time, 291, 734

Time-Life, 589, 610
Tokyo, 281
Tolentino Dipp, Hugo, 647, 673 n
Ton-ton-macoute, 394, 425, 439, 442
Totalitarianism, opposition to, 388
Tourism, 18, 103, 461–62
Toussaint L'Ouverture, 19, 20
Tri-Continental Congress (1966), 673 n
Trinidad Sánchez, Maria, 187
Trinidad-Tobago, 729
Trinitario, 20. *See under* Duarte, 749
Trippe, Juan, 310
Triumvirate, 584, 595 ff., 603, 615, 617,
    637–39; legitimacy, 615; recogni-
    tion, 613 (*see* U.S.); Reid, 634; U.S.
    position, 587–89, 596, 610, 615,
    630–32, 639, press, 599
Trizza, Samuel, 174, 175, 239
Troncosco de la Concha, Manuel de
    Jesús, 40
Trotsky, Leon, 450
Trotskyites, 130, 407
Trujillistas, 87, 88, 92, 93, 230, 282,
    366, 525; Bosch, 308; deportations,
    347; purge, 115
Trujillo, Angelita, 37, 39, 55, 67, 135,
    752
Trujillo, Anibal, 45
Trujillo, Arismendi (Petán), 39, 66, 82,
    87, 132, 295, 296, 394, 418, 752;
    exile, 83, 281, 287
Trujillo, Flor de Oro, 42, 45, 560, 712,
    752
Trujillo, Héctor ("Negro"), 39, 40, 45,
    78–79, 82, 281, 296, 312, 524,
    752; exile, 83; President, 57
Trujillo, María Martínez de, 753
Trujillo, Néne, 281
Trujillo, Virgilio, 45, 418, 422, 424
Trujillo family, 36, 37, 39, 49, 78–79,
    82, 83; exile, 84, 281, 327, 637;
    Haiti, 417–18, 422, 424; nepotism,
    45
Trujillo Lora, José Rafael, 418, 422, 424
Trujillo Martinez, Jr., Rafael Leonidas
    ("Ramfis") 36, 39, 48, 49, 50, 54,
    59–62, 68, 70, 74, 75, 76–79, 82,
    135, 153, 210, 270, 279, 281, 359,
    637, 753; Bosch, 524, 534; charac-
    teristics, 78, 79, 117; "democratiza-
    tion," 65, 66, 76, 77–78, 80, 81, 712;
    exile, 83; Martin on, 81–82; op-

position, 87, 546, 547; role, 79–
    80; women, 79, 152
Trujillo Martínez, Rhadamés, 39, 61, 62,
    528, 753
Trujillo Molina, Rafael Leonidas, 24,
    25, 32, 38–39, 46, 48, 93, 101,
    108, 135–36, 147, 153, 189–90,
    753; achievements, 41; aftermath,
    65–83, 90, 92, 153, 282, 708–9;
    Ambassador, 47–48; appearance,
    41–42; Army, 66, 117, 434–35,
    303–4; assassination, 5, 6 n, 12, 15,
    26, 27, 38, 39, 50, 52 ff., 205,
    219–20; background, 42–44; Bala-
    guer, 224; Betancourt, 430; Bosch,
    344, 526; Castro, 50; charac-
    teristics, 27, 37–38, 204; Church,
    37; Congress, 429; Constitution, 31;
    construction, 10, 102, 137; decline,
    48 ff.; "Dominicanization," 318; Du-
    valier, 416; elections, 40; espio-
    nage, 25, 35, 274; failures, 37–38;
    fall of, 3, 4, 14, 131, 153; Haitian
    massacre, 417; hatred of, 50; hon-
    ors, 43; legacy, 186, 346, 396, 719;
    methods, 33–36, 40–41, 46, 50, 62,
    106, 107; monuments, 43, 76, 133,
    137; nicknames, 12, 16, 42 and n;
    OAS, 593–94, 711; oligarchy, 134;
    opinions of, 16–17, 39–40, 45, 50;
    opposition to, 46–47, 48, 51, 52,
    53, 69, 74; party (*see* PD);
    Potemkin Village, 10; power, 40–
    41, 585; President, 44; private life,
    39; properties, 79, 116, 120, 354,
    459; regime, 8, 9, 17, 18, 33–66,
    308, files, 41; secret police (*see*
    SIM); slave labor, 35, 38–39, 102,
    187; successors, 77 (*see* Balaguer;
    Trujillo, Martinez, Jr.); supporters,
    36–37, 45, 74; tactics, 35, 281, 407–
    11; terror, 16, 33, 38, 40, 44, 48;
    titles, 36, 37; tyranny, 33–36, 50,
    59–60, 85; uniforms, 37; wealth,
    38–39; women, 25, 35. *See* SIM
Trujillo Nicolás, Pedro José, 527, 534
Trujillo Reynoso, Francisco, 418, 422,
    424
Truman, Harry S., 48, 549, 625
Tugwell, Rexford, 125, 374
Turba (riot). *See* Rioting
Tu-tum-potes, 266–67, 267 n, 268, 288,
    324, 325

TVA, 472, 473, 479, 547; Bosch, 536–37; mission, 553–54 and n, 590; Yaque del Sur, 513, 514, 520
Twain, Mark, 407
"24th of April Movement," 701

UCN, *Union Civica Nacional* (National Civil Union), 12, 69–70, 77, 81, 83, 87, 88, 108, 121, 157, 223, 266, 491, 755; Bonnelly, 89; Bosch, 113; characteristics, 71, 206; collapse, 358, 402, 403; Communists, 338; Confiscation Law, 495; Consejo, 95, 111–12, 116, 119; defections, 137; election(s), 160, 198, 199 n, 201, 206–8, 225, 308, 313; *golpista* Cabinet, 595 n; leaders, 87, 88, 109, 487; military, the, 93; oligarchy, 134–35, 282; ORIT, 126; PSP, 129; purpose, 70; splinter, 199 n (*see* ASD); split, 91, 88, 211. *See* Fiallo
UN, 17 n, 65, 140, 146, 310, 381, 584, 623; Charter, 438 n; Cuban missile crisis, 241; Dominican Republic, 637, 694; Haiti, 438, 440; Security Council, 241, 438, 440; Trujillo, 47; U.S., 723
Underdeveloped people, 13–14
Unemployment, 103, 104, 109, 151, 186, 389, 413–14, 450, 465, 483, 638
Unfinished Experiment: Democracy in the Dominican Republic, 56 n
Unions, 126, 131; *civicos*, 548; general strike, 550; government employees, 192–93 (*see* FENEPIA)
United Fruit Company, 190, 203, 306, 311–12, 396–97, 533
United Nations. *See* UN
United States: asylum, right of, 541, 658; Bosch, 113, 269, 308–9, 344, 347, 359, 361, 370, 389, 391, 396, 402, 415, 534, fall, 593 ff., formula, 695, in, 308–9, 310, inaugural delegation, 319, 330–35, support of, 471, 476 ff., 545; business(men), 106, 148, 258–59, 722, private foreign investments, 309, 462; Caribbean policy, 17, 86; civil rights, 469, Act (1964), 719; companies, 311–12 (*see under* name); Communist powers, 739; Congressional Record, 455, 456; Constitution, 66, 314; cultural exchange program,

363; Dominican Republic (*see under* Civil War; Dominican Republic; Triumvirate); economic assistance programs, 729–30 (*see* AID and foreign aid); embassies, 174; European aid to Latin America, 370; experts, 729; foreign aid, 145–46, 156, 187, 188, 281, 320, 352, 470, 519, record, 146 and n, 721 n (*see* AID); foreign policy, 13, 22, 23, 26–27, 30, 46, 48, 64, 65, 75, 82, 86, 87, 119, 164, 241, 390, 438 n, 559, 630–32, containment, 740–41, debate, 738–39, disengagement, 710, 741, massive retaliation, 141 (*see under* countries; names of Presidents); free institutions, 719–20; Germany, 28; government, 476, 724; Haiti, 30, 418, 434, 438, 441 ff.; imperialism, 125 n, 126, 130; intervention, 230, 606–8, 656–58, 705–6 and n; Joint Chiefs of Staff, 246; Latin America, 5, policy, 602 (*see under* Kennedy), reputation in, 30; loans, 145–46 (*see* foreign aid); Midwest, 633; military, 489; Monroe Doctrine, 26–27, 28; Negroes, 13, 469, 724, 725; Nicaragua, 30; Peru, 192; PL-480, 324, 389, 479, 504, 721 n; power, limits of, 14, 607, 613, 723; press, 358, 454–56, 494, 738; public opinion, 739; purpose, 202; race problem, 469; Smith Act, 349, 485, 487; Soviet Union, 256 (*see* Cuban missile crisis); Special Forces, 141; sugar: lobbyists, 259, quota system, 8, 161–62; Trujillo, 35, 40, 45–46, 48, 711–13; unity, 629; visas, 98, 99; White House, 120–21, 122, 164, 471, 620, 640; World War I, 28; World War II, 46. *See* special listings *under* U.S.
Universities, 125, 242, 354, 489; traditions, 98–99
University of Puerto Rico, 125, 374, 637, 677
University of Santo Domingo, 98–99, 364
UPI, 291, 358, 443, 445–46
Urbanization, 136, 138, 139
Uruguay, 66, 652–53
U. S. Army, 36, 38

U. S. Chamber of Commerce, 361
U. S. Congress, 35, 120, 121, 188;
appropriations, 472–73; Bosch, 597;
civil rights bill, 469; foreign aid,
530, bill, 473; Martin, 471, 472;
sugar bill, 162, 163, 168–69
U. S. Defense Department, 706
U. S. Fleet, 425, 664
U. S. House of Representatives, 549,
598; Cooley bill, 163; Foreign Affairs Committee, 472, 600 and n;
Subcommittee on Inter-American
Affairs, 455
USIA, 276; documentary "Four Cities
in June," 620
U. S. Immigration Service, 272
U. S. Information Service. See USIS
USIS, 85, 86, 91, 137, 148, 150, 202,
319; chief, 272; Martin, 722
U. S. Marines, 41, 194, 318; 640; Cuban
missile crisis, 239, 241, 242; Do-
minican Republic, 20, 25, 26, 27,
28–31, 42, 69, 75, 230, 303, 370,
652, 656 ff., 720; Haiti, 30; Nica-
ragua, 30
U. S. Navy, 5, 9, 18, 22, 23, 82, 87,
118, 140–41, 156, 425, 664; Carib-
bean Sea Frontier, 678
U. S. News & World Report, 393
U.S.S. Albany, 22
U.S.S. Davis, 271
U. S. Senate, 23; Cooley bill, 164;
Foreign Relations Committee, 23,
442, 472, 600; sugar crisis, 165,
168, 170, 171; Triumvirate, 597 ff.
U.S.S. Nantasket, 22
U.S.S. Newport News, 313
U.S.S. Olympia, 28
U.S.S. Roberts, 291
U. S. State Department, 7 n, 17 n, 48,
64, 65, 119, 120, 123, 243, 427;
ambassadors, 147, 149 and n, 639,
714; Balaguer, 271–72; Bonnelly
paper, 616–18, 620–21; characteristics, 198; circular, 493–94; Foreign Service, 5, 6; Haitian crisis,
438; Kennedy, 64, 621 ff.; language,
86; Martin, 292, report to, 81–82;
methodology, 611–13, 627; organization, 65, 85; "overtaken by
events," 611, 612, 618, 631; personnel, 85–86, 471, 472, 596, 607,
630; policy making, 612, implemen-

tation, 544–45; posts, classification,
147; Secretary of, 5–6; Triumvirate
position paper, 600–1, 607–9; work,
478
U. S. Supreme Court, 308
U.S.S. Yankee, 26
U. S. Treasury, 479
U Thant, 694

Vallimarescu, Serban, 272, 276, 295,
319, 431
Valdez Sánchez, Hubertilio, 390, 524,
539, 753; Higüey clinic, 377, 379;
Minister without Portfolio, 366
Vance, Cyrus, 640, 695
Vanguardia Party. See VRD
Vanzetti, Bartolomeo, 717
Vásquez, Horacio, 25–26, 27, 135, 720,
753; President, 30–31, 42–43, 250;
Trujillo, 42–43
Vásquez, Máximo Bernard, 647
Vatican, 668; Concordat, 268, 316, 328;
Dominican Republic, 150
Vaughn, Jack Hood, 650–51, 653,
695 ff., 737
Venezuela, 11, 89, 223, 227, 268, 283,
344, 366, 658; Communists, 357;
Dominican Republic, 50, 428, 431,
433, 581; elections, 597, 629;
FALN, 314, 331, 338; Haiti, 442;
political parties, 210, 291, 338
Ventura brothers, 303
Vermont, 17
Vicente Noble, 104, 110, 590, 612
Vicini Cabral, Juan B., 133, 753
Vicini family, 223, 308, 448
Vietnam, 613, 656, 662, 673n, 719;
Johnson, 738; U.S. policy, 741
Vila Piola, Ramón, 481, 550
Villa, Francisco (Pancho), 345
Villeda Morales, Ramón, 331, 338, 600
Vilomar, "General" Virgilio, 212, 224,
225, 248–52, 308, 753
Viñas Román, Victor Elby, 114, 115,
156, 166, 176, 192, 254, 305, 360,
406, 482, 606, 638, 753; Bosch,
276, 523; characteristics, 117, 265;
Haitian crisis, 427 ff.; Martin, 558–
59; military golpe, 561; Minister of
Defense, 117, 252, 255, 365
Violence, 305, 311
Visas, 120, 141, 156, 263
Voelker, John, 474, 742

Voice of America, 240, 295
Volman, Sacha, 113, 207, 321–23, 360, 375, 393, 398, 456, 481, 541, 548–49, 551–53; characteristics, 309–11; *Conatral*, 549, 550; Costa Rica Institute, 368; Higüey clinic, 376; military *golpe*, 560
Von Wald, Mr., 311–12
Voodoo(ism), 303–5, 307, 376, 385, 417
Voting, 180, 283, 294, 295, 296, 297, 300; *cédula*, 264; education for, 373
VRD, *Vanguardia Revolucionaria Dominicana* (Dominican Revolutionary Vanguard), 158, 212, 224, 231, 358, 755; Confiscation Law, 495; election(s), 199n, 293 ff., 308; *golpista* Cabinet, 595 n

Wagner, A. J., 520
Wagner, Robert F., 310
Walker, George, 116, 608, 609
Wallace, Henry, 149
Wall Street Journal, 394, 479
War: negotiation, 685; rimland, 741
Ward, Norm, 194, 216
Washington, D.C., 47, 626–27, 630. *See* United States
Washington de Peña, 393 and n
Washington *Post*, 320, 456, 494, 593, 602
Washington *World*, 456
Water, 103, 104, 108, 109, 110, 372
Welles, Sumner, 22, 25 n, 135, 195, 228, 583, 687, 717; Commissioner to Dominican Republic, 30–31; *Naboth's Vineyard*, 22; "new era," 42; non-intervention, 733
Wesleyan University, 637, 639–40
Wessin y Wessin, Elías, 114, 234, 277, 304, 354, 438 ff., 481 ff., 535–36, 540–41, 615, 638, 700, 753; Bosch, 572, 576–77, 579, 598; characteristics, 126–27, 254–55, 484–85; Civil War, 648, 653, 663, 664; communism, 715; generals, 264–65, 685 and n; Haitian crisis, 433 ff.; Martin, 722; military *golpe*, 561 ff.; Secretary of State for Defense, 646
West, the, 46
West Germany, 613
Wheeler, Earle, 640, 661
Whistlestopping, 409–12
Wilhelm, Kaiser, of Germany, 28
Williams, Newell, 145, 151, 157, 164, 169, 181, 212, 216, 281, 351–52 and n, 389, 445, 450–51, 471, 494, 534, 587, 589; agricultural loan, 473, 479; Bosch, 328–29, 345
Wilson, Woodrow, 28, 720
Windward Passage, 307
Withey, Francis ("Pancho"), 120, 208
Wolfe, David C., 145, 173, 276, 304, 358, 485, 587, 589
Women, 25, 33, 35, 74–76, 79, 135 n, 152, 154, 205; names, 135 n
World Bank. *See* IMF
World Marxist Review, 643 n, 644 n, 649 n, 770
World War I, 28, 30
World War II, 45–46, 48, 89, 210, 256, 708, 711
Wrightsman, Charles, 712

Yale University, 75, 124
Yanqui imperialism, 369, 436 n
Yaque del Norte, 14, 124, 136, 137, 200
Yaque del Sur, 104, 110, 319, 372, 451, 452, 462, 472, 479, 520, 553
Ydígoras, fall of, 393–94
Young, Stephen M., 597
Youth, 14, 74, 97, 98, 99, 188, 195, 383; disorientation, 152; 14th of June, 129; unemployment, 465. *See* Intellectuals; Students
Yugoslavia, 739
Yuma River, 187, 216

Zárate, Jesús, 306
Zeller Cocco, Alejandro, 684, 696, 753

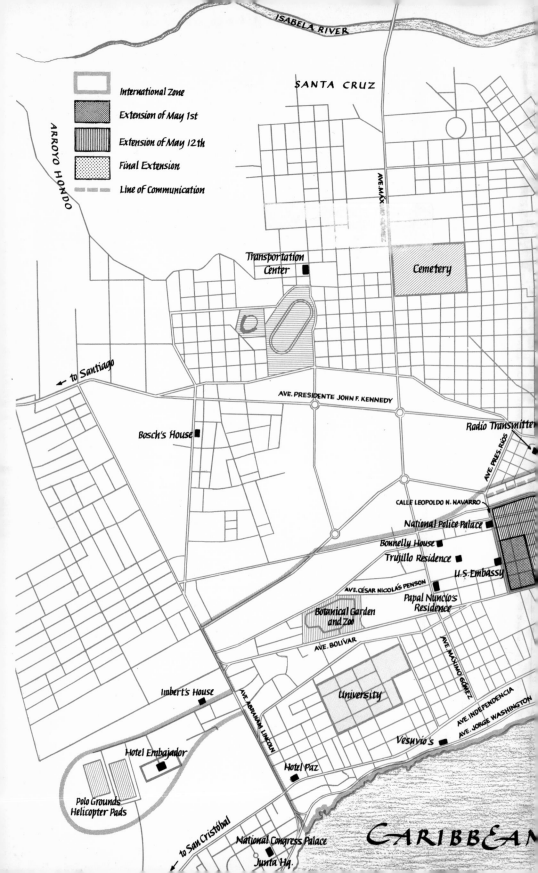

ISABELA RIVER

SANTA CRUZ

□ International Zone

▨ Extension of May 1st

▥ Extension of May 12th

⬚ Final Extension

╌╌ Line of Communication

ARROYO HONDO

AVE. MÁX.

Cemetery

Transportation Center ■

to Santiago →

AVE. PRESIDENTE JOHN F. KENNEDY

Bosch's House ■

Radio Transmitter

AVE. PRES. RÍOS

CALLE LEOPOLDO N. NAVARRO

National Police Palace ■

Bonnelly House ■

Trujillo Residence ■

U.S. Embassy

AVE. CÉSAR NICOLÁS PENSON ■

Papal Nuncio's Residence

Botanical Garden and Zoo

AVE. BOLÍVAR

AVE. MÁXIMO GÓMEZ

Imbert's House ■

AVE. ABRAHAM LINCOLN

University

AVE. INDEPENDENCIA

AVE. JORGE WASHINGTON

Vesuvio's

Hotel Embajador ■

Hotel Paz ■

Polo Grounds Helicopter Pads

to San Cristóbal →

National Congress Palace ■

Junta Hq. ■

CARIBBEAN